ENGLISH RECUSANT LITERATURE
1558–1640

Selected and Edited by
D. M. ROGERS

Volume 267

The New Testament
of Jesus Christ
1582

The New Testament of Jesus Christ 1582

The Scolar Press
1975

ISBN 0 85967 263 8

Published and printed in Great Britain by
The Scolar Press Limited, 59-61 East Parade,
Ilkley, Yorkshire and
39 Great Russell Street,
London WC1

NOTE

Reproduced (original size) from a copy in Cambridge University Library, by permission of the Syndics. Uneven inking on page 118 of this copy has rendered part of the text illegible: the marginal note in the top left-hand corner reads: 'Whereby it is euident that more is required then only faith.'

The Rhemes New Testament is named after the ancient archiepiscopal city (Reims, Rheims) in N. E. France where it was published in 1582. Fourteen years earlier, in 1568, William Allen, the future Cardinal, had opened a house of studies for Englishmen within the newly-founded University of Doway, in the Spanish Netherlands. Staffed by a group of eminent scholars who, forfeiting their posts and careers in Oxford and Cambridge, had chosen exile rather than accept the new Elizabethan state Church, Allen's Doway College was founded to prepare a cadre of trained and learned English Catholic priests for the Church in England when (as they hoped) Catholicism should be restored. By 1574 Allen had begun to send some of his priests back to England to minister to those who clung to the old faith. Such was the flow of recruits to train for the priesthood that in 1578 he opened another seminary, the English College in Rome. That same year a local upsurge of Calvinism drove the first English College from Doway. It took temporary refuge on French soil, at Rhemes, and it was there, about 16 October 1578, as the College Diary recorded, that Gregory Martin 'started an English version of the Bible'. Three years and six months later the same Diary recorded the publication of the New Testament, which for the time being was all that the chronic poverty of the exiles enabled them to print.

The need to publish this translation had distant historic origins. Because of Lollardy, the bishops prohibited unauthorized vernacular versions of any portions of the Bible to be read in England, a country where both literacy and the vernacular itself developed later and more slowly than in neighbouring countries. One important effect was that the religious upheavals of the sixteenth century found England without any accepted Catholic version of the Bible in the language of the common people. The prolongation of those upheavals for a further fifty years faced Allen in 1582 with still no Catholic alternative to set against a series of Protestant versions which, whatever their literary merits, were, in his eyes and those of his Catholic contemporaries, contaminated by deliberate and tendentious mistranslations and omissions, introduced to 'prove' the doctrines propagated by the Reformers.

In training his new priests, Allen prescribed a full course of Biblical studies, including Greek and Hebrew. But though their studies were learned, they needed also the ability to preach in English to their less educated flock at home, and to answer in public and in private the texts quoted by their opponents in support of the new doctrines. Therefore for pastoral, doctrinal and not least devotional reasons, the printing of an approved Catholic translation of the Scriptures in English, with annotations to help the reader to the true meanings of the text, had long been sorely needed.

Gregory Martin, whom Allen chose for the task, abandoned a brilliant career at Oxford when he fled in 1570 to Doway and began teaching at the English College. He was a master of Greek and Hebrew and so could have translated from the original tongues had he chosen. A deep reverence for the traditional Bible of Latin Christendom, and a belief, not altogether ill-founded, that its text was purer and better authenticated than, for example, Erasmus's Greek, probably underlay the decision to make as faithful a rendering as possible of the Vulgate, interpreted (as the title-page proclaims) in the light of the Greek. His resolve to stay close to the phrases and even where required to the vocabulary and syntax of an original which his Church had recently pronounced to be inspired and free from error, obviously determined Martin's style. To the taunts of adversaries that he translated 'of purpose to darken the sense', he had already answered in his preface that the meanings of Scripture were indeed deep and often difficult, and not, as the Reformers maintained, for every casual reader to interpret. Orthodoxy, even at the expense of easiness of expression, was his aim, but has earned him reproaches from critics more concerned with literary graces.

Martin's fine preface deserves most careful reading; it forestalls the strictures which critics have since reiterated endlessly, that he disfigures and obscures his text with untranslated words, with Latinisms and neologisms. He gives sound reasons (which modern translators ought to ponder) for choosing these rather than 'some usual English wordes that express them not'. It was Gregory Martin's misfortune, and ours too, that his version was never given a fair chance of acceptance, for in English — then as now a free, unlegislated language ready to assimilate elements of all it encounters — the only test of what *is* English is its acceptance into common speech. What prevented its acceptance was a deliberate campaign of vilification and physical suppression. From the first, Martin's translation was a proscribed book. For two centuries copies were searched for, seized and burnt; by every means this version was kept from the eyes of all but a learned few who read only to condemn it on theological grounds. How different were the fortunes of the Authorized Version. Though nowadays recognized to be in a language already partly archaic in its own day, its official backing no less than its intrinsic qualities carried it through edition after edition and into every home, to be read and re-read until its phraseology became part of the mental habits of the ordinary Englishman.

Yet the attempt to suppress Martin's translation never wholly succeeded. His version, afterwards modified, as was natural, to suit the altered vocabulary of later centuries, continued as the standard and well-loved Bible of his English co-religionists down to our own lifetime. More than that, recent scholarship has unearthed the long-concealed debt of the Authorized Version itself to the Rhemes New Testament. That debt was large-scale and almost wholly beneficial; it has been amply demonstrated and generously acknowledged. But, we may fairly comment, if words and phrases first fashioned by

Gregory Martin (and they are many) have passed into the idiom of our language because they were taken over by the translators of the Authorized Version, there are probably many others which did not deserve the oblivion which has been their lot. The present facsimile, presenting the whole text of Martin's version just as it first appeared with all its explanatory apparatus, puts before the modern reader an important book which, though far from rare, has been undeservedly neglected, and enables him to appreciate some of its true merits for himself.

References: Allison and Rogers 567; STC 2884; A. S. Herbert, *Historical Catalogue of Printed Editions of the English Bible 1525–1961* (1968), item 177.

Oxford, 1975 DAVID ROGERS

THE

NEVV TESTAMENT OF IESVS CHRIST, TRANSLATED FAITHFVLLY INTO ENGLISH,

out of the authentical Latin, according to the best corrected copies of the same, diligently conferred vvith the Greeke and other editions in diuers languages: Vvith ARGVMENTS of bookes and chapters, ANNOTATIONS, and other necessarie helpes, for the better vnderstanding of the text, and specially for the discouerie of the CORRVPTIONS of diuers late translations, and for cleering the CONTROVERSIES in religion, of these daies:

IN THE ENGLISH COLLEGE OF RHEMES.

Psal. 118.

Da mihi intellectum, & scrutabor legem tuam, & custodiam illam in toto corde meo.

That is,

Giue me vnderstanding, and I vvil searche thy lavv, and vvil keepe it vvith my vvhole hart.

S. Aug. tract. 2. in Epist. Ioan.

Omnia quæ leguntur in Scripturis sanctis, ad instructionem & salutem nostram intentè oportet audire: maximè tamen memoriæ commendanda sunt, quæ aduersus Hæreticos valent plurimum: quorum insidiæ, infirmiores quosque & negligentiores circumuenire non cessant.

That is,

Al things that are readde in holy Scriptures, vve must heare vvith great attention, to our instruction and saluation: but those things specially must be commended to memorie, vvhich make most against Heretikes: vvhose deceites cease not to circumuent and beguile al the vveaker sort and the more negligent persons.

PRINTED AT RHEMES,
by Iohn Fogny.

1582.

CVM PRIVILEGIO.

THE CENSVRE AND APPROBATION.

CVM huius versionis ac æditionis authores, nobis de fide & eruditione sint probè cogniti, aliique S. Theologiæ & linguæ Anglicanæ peritissimi viri contestati sint, nihil in hoc opere reperiri, quod non sit Catholicę Ecclesię doctrinæ, & pietati consentaneum, vel quod vllo modo potestati ac paci ciuili repugnet, sed omnia potius veram fidem, Reip. bonum, vitæque ac morum probitatem promouere: ex ipsorum fide censemus ista vtiliter excudi & publicari posse.

PETRVS REMIGIVS *Archidiaconus maior Metropolitanæ insignis Ecclesiæ Rhemensis, Iuris Canonici Doctor, Archiepiscopatus Rhemensis generalis Vicarius.*

HVBERTVS MORVS, *Rhemensis Ecclesiæ Decanus, & Ecclesiastes, & in sacratissima Theologiæ facultate Doctor.*

IOANNES LE BESGVE, *Canonicus Rhemensis, Doctor Theologus, & Cancellarius Academiæ Rhemensis.*

GVLIELMVS BALBVS, *Theologiæ professor, Collegij Rhemensis Archimagister.*

S. August. lib. 1. c. 3. de serm. Do. in monte.

Paupertate spiritus peruenitur ad Scripturarũ cognitionem: vbi oportet hominem se mitem præbere, ne peruicacibus concertationibus indocilis reddatur.

VVe come to the vnderstanding of Scriptures through pouertie of spirit: vvhere a man must shevv him self meeke-minded, lest by stubburne contentions, he become incapable and vnapt to be taught.

THE

THE PREFACE TO THE READER TREATING OF THESE THREE POINTS: OF THE TRANSLATION OF HOLY SCRIPTVRES INTO THE vulgar tongues, and namely into English: of the causes vvhy this nevv Testament is translated according to the auncient vulgar Latin text: & of the maner of translating the same.

THE holy Bible long since translated by vs into English, and the old Testament lying by vs for lacke of good meanes to publish the vvhole in such sort as a vvorke of so great charge and importance requireth: vve haue yet through Gods goodnes at length fully finished for thee (most Christian reader) all the NEVV TESTAMENT, vvhich is the principal, most profitable & comfortable peece of holy vvritte: and, as vvel for all other institution of life and doctrine, as specially for deciding the doubtes of these daies, more propre and pregnant then the other part not yet printed.

Translation of the Scriptures into the vulgar tõgues, not absolutely necessarie or profitable, but according to the time.

Vvhich translation vve doe not for all that publish, vpon erroneous opinion of necessitie, that the holy Scriptures should alvvaies be in our mother tonge, or that they ought, or vvere ordained by God, to be read indifferently of all, or could be easily vnderstood of euery one that readeth or heareth them in a knovven language: or that they vvere not often through mans malice or infirmitie, pernicious and much hurtful to many: or that vve generally and absolutely deemed it more conuenient in it self, & more agreable to Gods word and honour or edification of the faithful, to haue them turned into vulgar tonges, then to be kept & studied only in the Ecclesiastical learned languages: Not for these nor any such like causes doe vve translate this sacred booke, but vpon special consideration of the present time, state, and condition of our countrie, vnto vvhich, diuers thinges are either necessarie, or profitable and medicinable novv, that othervvise in the peace of the Church vvere neither much requisite, nor perchance vvholy tolerable.

The Churches vvisedom and moderatiõ con-

In this matter, to marke onely the vvisedom & moderatiõ of holy Church and the gouernours thereof on the one side, and the indiscrete zeale of the

cerning vulgar translation.

popular, and their factious leaders, on the other, is a high point of prudence. These later, partly of simplicitie, partly of curiositie, and specially of pride and disobedience, haue made claime in this case for the common people, vvith plausible pretences many, but good reasons none at all. The other,* to vvhom Christ hath giuen charge of our soules, the dispensing of Gods mysteries and treasures (among vvhich holy Scripture is no smale store) and the feeding his familie in season vvith foode fit for euery sort, haue neither of old nor of late, euer vvholy condemned all vulgar versions of Scripture, nor haue at any time generally forbidden the faithful to reade the same: yet they haue not by publike authoritie prescribed, commaunded, or authentically euer recommended any such interpretation to be indifferently vsed of all men.

Mat. 24, 45. 1 Cor. 4, 1.

The Scriptures in the vulgar languages of diuers nations.

The Armenians say they haue the Psalter and some other peeces translated by S. Chrysostom into their language, vvhen he vvas banished among them: and George the Patriarch, in vvriting his life, signifieth no lesse. The Slauonians affirme they haue the Scriptures in their vulgar tongue, turned by S. Hierom, and some vvould gather so much by his ovvne vvordes in his epistle to Sophronius, but the place in deede proueth it not. Vulpilas surely gaue the Scriptures to the Gothes in their ovvne tonge, and that before he vvas an Arrian. It is almost three hundred yeres, since Iames Archbishop of Genua, is said to haue translated the Bible into Italian. More then tvvo hundred yeres agoe, in the daies of Charles the fifth, the Frenche king, vvas it put forth faithfully in Frenche, the sooner to shake out of the deceiued peoples hãdes, the false heretical translations of a secte called *Vvaldenses*. In our ovvne countrie, notwithstanding the Latin tonge vvas euer (to vse Venerable Bedes vvordes) common to all the prouinces of the same for meditation or studie of Scriptures, and no vulgar translation commonly vsed or occupied of the multitude, yet they vvere extant in English euen before the troubles that Vvicleffe and his folovvers raised in our Church, as appeareth, as well by some peeces yet remaining, as by a prouincial Constitution of Thomas Arundel Archbishop of Canturburie, in a Councel holden at Oxford. vvhere straite prouision vvas made, that no heretical version set forth by Vvicleffe, or his adherentes, should be suffered, nor any other in or after his time be published or permitted to be readde, being not approued and allovved by the Diocesan before: alleaging S. Hierom for the difficultie and danger of interpreting the holy Scripture out of one tonge into an other, though by learned and Catholike men. So also it is there insinuated, that neither the Translations set forth before that Heretikes time, nor other aftervvard being approued by the lavvful Ordinaries, were euer in our countrie wholy forbidden, though they were not (to say the truth) in quiet and better times (much lesse when the people vvere prone to alteratiõ, heresie, or noueltie) either hastily admitted, or ordinarily readde of the vulgar, but vsed onely, or specially, of some deuout religious and contemplatiues persons, in reuerence, secrecie, and silence, for their spiritual comforte.

Bib. Sãct. li. 4.

Hiero. ep. 134.

Bib. Sãct. lib. 4.

Aũcient Catholike translations of the Bible into the Italian, Frenche, & English tongue.

Li. 1 hist. Angl. c. 1.

An aunciẽt prouincial cõstitution in England concerning English translations. *See Linvvod li. 5 tit. de Magistris.*

The like Catholike and vulgar translations in many coũtries, since Luthers time.

Now since Luthers reuolt also, diuers learned Catholikes, for the more speedy abolishing of a number of false and impious translations put forth by sundry sectes, and for the better preseruation or reclaime of many good soules endangered thereby, haue published the Bible in the seueral languages of almost all the principal prouinces of the Latin Church: no other bookes in the world being so pernicious as hereticall translations of the Scriptures, poisoning the people vnder colour of diuine authoritie, & not many other remedies

being

being more soueraine against the same (if it be vsed in order, discretion, and humilitie) then the true, faithful, and sincere interpretation opposed therevnto.

Vvhich causeth the holy Church not to forbid vtterly any Catholike translation, though she allow not the publishing or reading of any absolutely and without exception, or limitation: knowing by her diuine and most sincere wisedom, how, where, when, and to whom these her Maisters and Spouses giftes are to be bestowed to the most good of the faithful: and therfore neither generally permitteth that which must needes doe hurt to the vnworthy, nor absolutely condemneth that which may doe much good to the worthie. Vvherevpon, the order which many a wise man wished for before, was taken by the Deputies of the late famous Councel of Trent in this behalfe, and confirmed by supreme authoritie, that the holy Scriptures, though truely and Catholikely translated into vulgar tonges, yet may not be indifferétly readde of all men, nor of any other then such as haue expresse licence therevnto of their lawful Ordinaries, with good testimonie from their Curates or Confessors, that they be humble, discrete and deuout persons, and like to take much good, and no harme thereby. Vvhich prescript, though in these daies of ours it can not be so precisely obserued, as in other times & places, where there is more due respecte of the Churches authoritie, rule, and discipline: yet we trust all wise and godly persons will vse the matter in the meane while, with such moderation, meekenes, and subiection of hart, as the handling of so sacred a booke, the sincere senses of Gods truth therein, & the holy Canons, Councels, reason, and religion do require.

The Churches order & determinatió concerning the reading of Catholike translatiós of the Bible in vulgar tógues.

Ind. lib. prohibit. regula 4.

Vvherein, though for due preseruation of this diuine worke from abuse and prophanation, and for the better bridling of the intolerable insolencie of proude, curious, & contentious wittes, the gouernours of the Church guided by Gods Spirit, as euer before, so also vpon more experience of the maladie of this time then before, haue taken more exacte order both for the readers and translatours in these later ages, then of old: yet we must not imagin that in the primitiue Church, either euery one that vnderstoode the learned tonges wherein the Scriptures were written, or other languages into which they were translated, might without reprehension, reade, reason, dispute, turne and tosse the Scriptures: or that our forefathers suffered euery schole-maister, scholer, or Grammarian that had a litle Greeke or Latin, straight to take in hand the holy Testament: or that the translated Bibles into the vulgar tonges, were in the handes of euery husbandman, artificer, prentice, boies, girles, mistresse, maide, man: that they were sung, plaied, alleaged, of euery tinker, tauerner, rimer, minstrel: that they were for table talke, for alebenches, for boates and barges, and for euery prophane person and companie. No, in those better times men were neither so ill, nor so curious of them selues, so to abuse the blessed booke of Christ: neither was there any such easy meanes before printing was inuented, to disperse the copies into the handes of euery man, as now there is.

The holy Scriptures neuer read of al persons indifferently, at their pleasure.

They were then in Libraries, Monasteries, Colleges, Churches, in Bishops, Priests, and some other deuout principal Lay mens houses and handes: who vsed them with feare and reuerence, and specially such partes as perteined to good life and maners, not medling, but in pulpit and schooles (and that moderately to) with the hard and high mysteries and places of greater difficultie. The poore ploughman, could then in labouring the ground, sing the hymnes

Vvhere and in vvhose handes the Scriptures vvere in the primitiue Church.

 and

Hovv the laietie of those daies did read them, vvith what humilitie and religion, and enformation of life and maners.

and psalmes either in knowen or vnknowen languages, as they heard them in the holy Church, though they could neither reade nor know the sense, meaning, and mysteries of the same. Such holy persons of both sexes, to whom S. Hierom in diuers Epistles to them, commendeth the reading and meditation of holy Scriptures, were diligent to searche all the godly histories & imitable examples of chastitie, humilitie, obedience, clemencie, pouertie, penance, renoũcing the world: they noted specially the places that did breede the hatred of sinne, feare of Gods iudgement, delight in spiritual cogitations: they referred them selues in all hard places, to the iudgement of the auncient fathers and their maisters in religion, neuer presuming to contend, controule, teach or talke of their owne sense and phantasie, in deepe questions of diuinitie. Then the Virgins, did meditate vpon the places and examples of chastitie, modestie and demurenesse: the maried, on coniugal faith and continencie: the parents, how to bring vp their children in faith and feare of God: the Prince, how to rule: the subiect, how to obey: the Priest, how to teach: the people, how to learne.

The fathers sharply reprehend as an abuse, that al indifferently should reade, expound, and talke of the Scriptures.

Then the scholer taught not his maister, the sheepe controuled not the Pastor, the yong student set not the Doctor to schoole, not reproued their fathers of error & ignorance. Or if any were in those better daies (as in al times of heresie such must needes be) that had itching eares, tikling tonges and wittes, curious and contentious disputers, hearers, and talkers rather then doers of Gods word: such the Fathers did euer sharply reprehend, counting them vnworthy and vnprofitable readers of the holy Scriptures. S. Hierom in his Epistle to Paulinus, after declaration that no handy craft is so base, nor liberall science so easy, that can be had without a maister (which S. Augustine also affirmeth, *De vtilitate cred. cap. 7.*) nor that men presume in any occupation to teach that they neuer learned, *Only* (saith he) *the art of Scripture is that vvhich euery man chalengeth: this the chatting old vvife, this the doting old man, this the brabling sophister, this on euery hand, men presume to teach before they learne it.* Againe, *Some vvith poise of lofty vvordes deuise of scripture matters among vvomen: othersome (phy vpon it) learne of vvomen, vvhat to teach men, and lest that be not ynough, by facilitie of tong, or rather audacitie, teach that to others, vvhich they vnderstand neuer a vvhit them selues. to say nothing of such as be of my facultie: vvho stepping from secular learning to holy scriptures, and able to tickle the eares of the multitude vvith a smothe tale, thinke all they speake, to be the Law of God.* This he wrote then, when this maladie of arrogancie and presumption in diuine matters, vvas nothing so outragious as now it is.

Hiero. ep. 103 c. 6.

S. Gregorie Nazianzene made an oration of the moderation that vvas to be vsed in these matters: where he saith, that some in his time thought them selues to haue all the wisedom in the world, when they could once repeat tvvo or three wordes, and them ill couched together, out of Scriptures. but he there diuinely discourseth of the orders and differences of degrees: how in Christes mysticall body, some are ordeined to learne, some to teach: that all are not Apostles, all Doctors, all interpreters, all of tonges and knovvledge, not all learned in Scriptures & diuinitie: that the people went not vp to talke with God in the mountaine, but Moyses, Aaron, & Eleazar: nor they neither, but by the difference of their callings: that they that rebell against this ordinance, are guilty of the conspiracie of Corè & his cõplices: that in Scripture there is both milke for babes, and meate for men, to be dispensed, not according to euery ones greedines

In orat. de moderatio. in disputa. seruanda.

greedines of appetit or vvilfulnes, but as is most meete for eche ones necessitie and capacitie: that as it is a shame for a Bishop or Priest to be vnlearned in Gods mysteries, so for the common people it is often times profitable to saluation, not to be curious, but to folovv their Pastors in sinceritie & simplicitie: vvhereof excellently saith S. Augustine, *Fidei simplicitate & sinceritate lactati, nutriamur in Christo: & cum parui sumus, maiorum cibos non appetamus.* that is, *Being fed vvith the simplicitie and sinceritie of faith, as it vvere vvith milke, so let vs be nourished in Christ: and vvhen vve are litle ones, let vs not couet the meates of the elder sort.* Vvho * in an other place testifieth, that the vvord of God can not be preached nor certaine mysteries vttered to all men alike, but are to be deliuered according to the capacitie of the hearers: as he proueth both * by S. Paules example, vvho gaue not to euery sort strong meate, but milke to many, as being not spiritual, but carnal and not capable: and * by our lordes also, vvho spake to some plainely, and to others in parables, & affirmed that he had many things to vtter vvhich the hearers vvere not able to beare.

De agone Christ. c. 33.

De bono perseuer. c. 16.

1 Cor. 3.

Io. 16.

The Scriptures must be deliuered in measure and discretion, according to eche mans neede and capacitie.

Hovv much more may vve gather, that all thinges that be vvritten, are not for the capacitie and diet of euery of the simple readers, but that very many mysteries of holy vvritte, be very far aboue their reach, & may and ought to be (by as great reason) deliuered them in measure & meane most meete for them? vvhich in deede can hardly be done, vvhen the vvhole booke of the Bible lieth before euery man in his mother tonge, to make choise of vvhat he list. For vvhich cause the said Gregorie Nazianzen vvisheth the Christians had as good a lavv as the Hebrues of old had: vvho (as S. Hierom also vvitnesseth) tooke order among them selues that none should read the *Cantica Canticorum* nor certaine other pieces of hardest Scriptures, till they vvere thirtie yeres of age.

In orat. de modera. in disp. serua. in fine. Hiero. in procem. cõmentar. in Ezechi.

The Ievves lavv for not reading certaine bookes of holy Scripture vntil a time.

And truely there is no cause vvhy men should be more loth to be ordered and moderated in this point by Gods Church and their Pastors, then they are in the vse of holy Sacraments: for vvhich as Christ hath appointed Priestes and ministers, at vvhose handes vve must receiue them, and not be our ovvne caruers: so hath he giuen * vs doctors, prophetes, expoũders, interpreters, teachers and preachers, to take the lavv and our faith at their mouthes: because our faith and religion commeth not to vs properly or principally by reading of Scriptures, but (as the Apostle saith) by hearing of the preachers lavvfully sent: though reading in order and humilitie, much confirmeth and aduanceth the same. Therfore this holy booke of the Scriptures, is called of S. Ambrose, *Liber sacerdotalis, the booke of priestes,* at vvhose handes and disposition vve must take and vse it. *Li. 1. ad Grat.*

Eph. 4.

Ro. 10, 17.

The vvise vvil not here regard vvhat some vvilful people do mutter, that the Scriptures are made for all men, and that it is of enuie that the Priestes do keepe the holy booke from them. Vvhich suggestion commeth of the same serpent * that seduced our first parents, vvho persuaded them, that God had forbidden them that tree of knovvledge, lest they should be as cunning as him self, and like vnto the Highest. No, no, the church doth it to keepe them from blind ignorant presumption, and from that vvhich the Apostle calleth *falsi nominis scientiam knovvledge falsely so called*: and not to embarre them from the true knovvledge of Christ. She vvould haue all vvise, but *vsque ad sobrietatem, vnto sobrietie*, as the Apostle speaketh: she knovveth the Scriptures be ordained for euery state, as meates, elements, fire, vvater, candle, kniues, svvord, & the like: vvhich

Gen. 3.

1 Tim. 6, 20.

Ro. 12, 3.

The popular obiections of vvithholding the Scriptures from the people, ansvvered.

Vvhy the Church permitteth not euery one at their pleasure to reade the Scripture.

vvhich are as needful (most of them) for children as old folkes, for the simple as the vvise: but yet vvould marre all, if they vvere at the guiding of other then wise men, or vvere in the handes of euery one, for whose preseruation they be profitable. She forbiddeth not the reading of them in any language, enuieth no mans commoditie, but giueth order hovv to doe it to edification, and not destruction: hovv to doe it without casting *the holy to dogges*, or *pearles to hogges*: (See S. Chrysost. *ho.24 in Matth.* declaring these hogges & dogges to be carnal men & Heretikes, that take no good of the holy mysteries, but thereby do both hurt them selues & others:) how to doe it agreably to the soueraine sinceritie, maiestie, & depth of Mysterie conteined in the same. She vvould haue the presumptuous Heretike, notvvithstanding he alleage them neuer so fast, flying as it vvere through the whole Bible, and coting the Psalmes, Prophets, Gospels, Epistles, neuer so readily for his purpose, as Vincentius Lirinensis saith such mens fashion is: yet she vvould according to Tertullians rule, haue such mere vsurpers quite discharged of all occupying and possession of the holy Testament, which is her old and onely right and inheritance, and belongeth not to Heretikes at all, vvhom Origen calleth *Scripturarũ fures, theeues of the Scriptures.* She would haue the vnvvorthy repelled, the curious repressed, the simple measured, the learned humbled, and all sortes so to vse them or absteine from them, as is most conuenient for euery ones saluation: with this general admonition, that none can vnderstand the meaning of God in the Scriptures* except Christ open their sense, and make them partakers of his holy Spirit in the vnitie of his mystical bodie: and for the rest, she committeth it to the Pastor of euery prouince and people, according to the difference of time, place, and persons, how and in vvhat sort the reading of the Scriptures is more or lesse to be procured or permitted.

The holy Scriptures to carnal men & Heretikes, are as pearles to svvine.

Mat. 7, 6.

Li. de praescriptionibus.

Orig. in 2 ad Ro.

Luca 24.

Vvherein, the varietie of circũstances causeth them to deale diuersly: as we see by S. Chrysostoms people of Constantinople, vvho vvere so delicate, dull, vvorldly, and so much giuen to dice, cardes, specially stage-plaies or theaters (as S. Gregorie Nazianzene witnesseth) that the Scriptures & all holy lections of diuine things were lothsome vnto them: whereby their holy Bishop was forced* in many of his sermons to crie out against their extreme negligence and contempt of Gods vvord, declaring, that not onely Eremites and Religious (as they alleaged for their excuse) but secular men of all sortes might reade the Scriptures, and often haue more neede thereof in respect of them selues, then the other that liue in more puritie and contemplation: further insinuating, that though diuers thinges be high and hard therein, yet many godly histories, liues, examples, & precepts of life and doctrine be plaine: and finally, that when the Gentiles vvere so cunning and diligent to impugne their faith, it were not good for Christians to be so simple or negligent in the defense thereof. as (in truth) it is more requisite for a Catholike man in these daies vvhen our Aduersaries be industrious to empeache our beleefe, to be skilful in Scriptures, then at other times vvhen the Church had no such enemies.

S. Chrysostoms exhortations to the reading of holy Scriptures, and vvhen the people is so to be exhorted.

In vita Athanasij.

** Ho. 2 in Mat. & ho. 3 de Lazaro. et ho. 3 in 2 ad Thess. & alibi saepe.*

To this sense said S. Chrysostom diuers thinges, not as a teacher in schole, making exact and general rules to be obserued in all places & times, but as a pulpit man, agreably to that audiẽce & his peoples default: nor making it therfore (as some peruersely gather of his wordes) a thing absolutely needful for euery poore artificer to reade or studie Scriptures, nor any vvhit fauouring the presumptuous, curious, and contentious iangling and searching of Gods secretes, reproued by the foresaid fathers, much lesse approuing the excessiue pride and madnes

S. Chrysostom maketh nothĩg for the popular and licentious reading of Scriptures vsed among the Protestants novv a daies.

madnes of these daies, vvhen euery man and vvoman is become not only a reader, but a teacher, controuler, and iudge of Doctors, Church, Scriptures and all: such as either contemne or easily passe ouer all the moral partes, good examples, and precepts of life (by vvhich as vvell the simple as learned might be much edified) & only in a maner, occupie them selues in dogmatical, mystical, high, and hidden secretes of Gods counsels, as of Predestination, reprobation, election, prescience, forsaking of the Ievves, vocation of the gentiles, & other incomprehensible mysteries, *Languishing about questions* of onely faith, fiduce, nevv phrases and figures, *euer learning*, but *neuer comming to knovvledge*, reading and tossing in pride of vvitte, conceit of their ovvne cunning, and vpon presumption of I can tell vvhat spirit, such bookes specially and Epistles, as S. Peter foretold that the vnlearned and instable vvould depraue to their ovvne damnation.

Euery simple artificer among them readeth much more the deepest & hardest questiōs of holy Scripture, then the moral partes.

1. Tim. 6. 2 Tim. c. 3 2 Pet. 3.

They delight in none more then in the Epistle to the Romans, the *Cantica canticorum*, the Apocalypse, which haue in them as many mysteries as wordes. they find no difficultie in the sacred booke *clasped vvith seuē seales. they aske for no expositor * vvith the holy Eunuch. they feele no such depth of Gods science in the scriptures, as S. Augustine did, vvhen he cried out, *Mira profunditas eloquiorum tuorum, mira profunditas (Deus meus) mira profunditas: horror est intendere in eam, horror honoris, & tremor amoris.* that is, *O vvonderful profoundnes of thy vvordes: vvonderful profoundnes, my God, vvonderful profoundnes: it maketh a man quake to looke on it: to quake for reuerence, and to tremble for the loue thereof.* they regard not that vvhich the same Doctor affirmeth, that the depth and profunditie of vvisedom, not only in the vvordes of holy Scripture, but also in the matter & sense, is so vvonderful, that, liue a man neuer so long, be he of neuer so high a vvitte, neuer so studious, neuer so feruēt to attaine the knovvledge thereof, yet vvhen he endeth, he shall confesse he doth but begin. they feele not vvith S. Hierom, that the text hath a hard shel to be broken before vve come to the kirnel. they vvill not stay them selues in only reading the sacred Scriptures thirtene yeres together, vvith S. Basil & S. Gregorie Nazianzene, before they expound them, nor take the care (as they did) neuer othervvise to interpret them, then by the vniforme consent of their forefathers and tradition Apostolike.

They presuppose no difficulties, which al the learned fathers felt to be in the Scriptures.

Apoc. 5, 1. Act. 8. Confess. lib. 12. cap. 14. See ep. 3. Aug. Hiero. ep. 13. c. 4. Ruff. Ec. hist. li. 2. c. 9.

If our nevv Ministers had had this cogitation and care that these and all other vvise men haue, and euer had, our countrie had neuer fallen to this miserable state in religion, & that vnder pretence, colour, and coūtenance of Gods vvord: neither should vertue and good life haue bene so pitifully corrupted in time of such reading, toiling, tumbling and translating the booke of our life and saluation: vvhereof the more pretious the right and reuerent vse is, the more pernicious is the abuse and prophanation of the same: vvhich euery man of experience by these fevv yeres proofe, and by comparing the former daies and maners to these of ours, may easily trie.

Maners and life nothing amended, but much worse, since this licentious tossing of holy Scriptures.

Looke vvhether your men be more vertuous, your vvomen more chast, your childrē more obedient, your seruants more trustie, your maides more modest, your frendes more faithful, your laitie more iust in dealing, your Cleargy more deuout in praying: vvhether there be more religion, feare of God, faith and conscience in al states novv, then of old, vvhen there vvas not so much reading, chatting, and iangling of Gods vvord, but much more sincere dealing, doing, and keeping the same. Looke vvhether through this disorder, vvomen teach not their husbands, children their parents, yong fooles their old and vvise fathers, the scholers their maisters, the sheepe their pastor, and the People

Scriptures as profanely cited as heathen poëtes.

the Priest. Looke vvhether the most chast and sacred sentences of Gods holy vvord, be not turned of many, into mirth, mockerie, amorous ballets & detestable letters of loue and leudnes: their delicate rimes, tunes, and translations much encreasing the same.

Scriptures erroneously expounded according to euery vvicked mans priuate fansie.

This fall of good life & prophaning the diuine mysteries, euery body seeth: but the great corruption & decay of faith hereby, none see but vvise men, who onely knovv, that, vvere the Scriptures neuer so truely translated, yet Heretikes and ill men that follovv their ovvne spirit and knovv nothing, but their priuate fantasie, and not the sense of the holy Church and Doctors, must needes abuse them to their damnation: and that the curious simple and * sensual men vvhich haue no tast of the things that be of the Spirit of God, may of infinite places take occasion of pernicious errors. for though the letter or text haue no error, yet (saith S. Ambrose) the Arrian, or (as vve may novv speake) the Caluinian interpretation hath errors. *lib. 2 ad Gratianum ca. 1.* and Tertullian saith, *The sense adulterated is as perilous as the style corrupted. De Præscript.* S. Hilarie also speaketh thus: *Heresie riseth about the vnderstanding, not about the vvriting: the fault is in the sense, not in the vvord. lib. 2 de Trinit. in principio.* and S. Augustine saith, that many hold the scriptures as they doe the Sacraments, *ad speciem, & non ad salutem: to the outvvard shevv, and not to saluation. de Baptis. cont. Donat. lib. 3 ca. 19.* Finally all Sect-maisters and rauening vvolues, yea * the diuels them selues pretend Scriptures, alleage Scriptures, and vvholy shroud them selues in Scriptures, as in the vvooll and fleese of the simple sheepe. Vvhereby the vulgar, in these daies of generall disputes, can not but be in extreme danger of error, though their bookes vvere truely translated, and vvere truely in them selues Gods ovvne vvord in deede.

1 Cor. 2.

Al Heretikes pretend Scriptures.

Mat. 4.

The Scriptures haue been falsely and heretically translated into the vulgar tongues, and sundrie other vvaies sacrilegiously abused, and so giuen to the people to reade.

But the case novv is more lamentable: for the Protestants and such as S. Paul calleth *ambulantes in astutia, vvalking in deceitfulnes*, haue so abused the people and many other in the vvorld, not vnvvise, that by their false translations they haue in steede of Gods Lavv and Testament, & for Christes vvritten vvill and vvord, giuen them their ovvne vvicked vvriting and phantasies, most shamefully in all their versions Latin, English, and other tonges, corrupting both the letter and sense by false translation, adding, detracting, altering, transposing, pointing, and all other guileful meanes: specially vvhere it serueth for the aduantage of their priuate opinions. for vvhich, they are bold also, partly to disauthorise quite, partly to make doubtful, diuers vvhole bookes allovved for Canonical Scripture by the vniuersal Church of God this thousand yeres and vpward: to alter al the authentical and Ecclesiastical vvordes vsed sithence our Christianitie, into nevv prophane nouelties of speaches agreable to their doctrine: to change the titles of vvorkes, to put out the names of the authors, * to charge the very Euangelist vvith follovving vntrue translation, to adde whole sentences proper to their sect, into their psalmes in meter, * euen into the very Creede in rime. al vvhich the poore deceiued people say and sing as though they vvere Gods ovvne vvord, being in deede through such sacrilegious treacherie, made the Diuels vvord

2 Cor. 4.

* *Beza an not. in c. 1. Lu. v. 78.*

* *See the tenth article of their Creede in meter.*

Al this their dealing is noted (as occasion serueth) in the Annotations vpon this Testament: and more at large in a booke lately made purposely of that matter, called, A DISCOVERIE &c.

To say nothing of their intolerable liberty and licence to change the accustomed callings of God, Angel, men, places, & things vsed by the Apostles and all antiquitie, in Greeke, Latin, and all other languages of Christian Nations, into nevv names, sometimes falsely, and alvvaies ridiculously and for ostentation taken of the Hebrues: to frame and fine the phrases of holy Scriptures after the forme of prophane writers, sticking not, for the same to supply, adde, alter or diminish as freely as if they translated Liuie, Virgil, or Terence. Hauing

Hauing

uing no religious respect to keepe either the maiestie or sincere simplicity of that venerable style of Christes spirit, as S. Augustine speaketh, vvhich kind the holy Ghost did choose of infinite vvisedom to haue the diuine mysteries rather vttered in, then any other more delicate, much lesse in that meretricious maner of vvriting that sundrie of these new translators doe vse: of vvhich sort Caluin him selfe and his pue-fellovves so much complaine, that they professe, Satan to haue gained more by these nevv interpreters (their number, leuitie of spirit, and audacitie encreasing daily) then he did before by keeping the word from the people. And for a paterne of this mischeefe, they giue Castalion, adiuring all their churches and scholars to bevvare of his translation, as one that hath made a very sport and mockery of Gods holy vvord. so they charge him: them selues (and the Zuinglians of Zuricke, vvhose translations Luther therfore abhorred) handling the matter vvith no more fidelitie, grauitie, or sinceritie, then the other: but rather vvith much more falsification, or (to vse the Apostles vvordes) *cauponation* and *adulteration* of Gods vvord, then they. besides many vvicked gloses, prayers, confessions of faith, conteining both blasphemous errors* and plaine contradictions to them selues and among them selues, all priuileged and authorised to be ioyned to the Bible, and to be said and sung of the poore people, and to be beleeued as articles of faith and vvholy consonant to Gods vvord.

Pref. in noui Testa. Gal. 1567

Iosias Simlerus in vita Bullingeri.

2 Cor. 2, 17.

Caluin cōplaineth of the new delicat trā. slators, namely Castalion: him self & Beza being as bad or vvorse.

* See the 4 article of their Creede in meter, vvhere they professe that Christ descēded to deliuer the fathers, & afterward in their cōfessiō of thei faith, they deny *Limbus patrum.*

Vve therfore hauing compassion to see our beloued countrie men, vvith extreme danger of their soules, to vse onely such prophane translations, and erroneous mens mere phantasies, for the pure and blessed vvord of truth, much also moued thereunto by the desires of many deuout persons: haue set forth, for you (benigne readers) the nevv Testament to begin vvithal, trusting that it may giue occasion to you, after diligent perusing thereof, to lay avvay at lest such their impure versions as hitherto you haue ben forced to occupie. Hovv vvell vve haue done it, vve must not be iudges, but referre all to Gods Church and our superiors in the same. to them vve submit our selues, and this, and all other our labours, to be in part or in the vvhole, reformed, corrected, altered, or quite abolished: most humbly desiring pardon if through our ignorance, temeritie, or other humane infirmitie, vve haue any vvhere mistaken the sense of the holy Ghost. further promising, that if hereafter we espie any of our ovvne errors, or if any other, either frende of good vvil, or aduersarie for desire of reprehension, shal open vnto vs the same: vve vvil not (as Protestants doe) for defense of our estimation, or of pride and contention, by vvrangling vvordes vvilfully persist in them, but be most glad to heare of them, and in the next edition or othervvise to correct them: for it is truth that vve seeke for, and Gods honour: which being had either by good intention, or by occasion, al is vvel. This vve professe onely, that vve haue done our endeuour vvith praier, much feare and trembling, lest vve should dangerously erre in so sacred, high, and diuine a vvorke: that vve haue done it vvith all faith, diligence, and sinceritie: that vve haue vsed no partialitie for the disaduantage of our aduersaries, nor no more licence then is sufferable in translating of holy Scriptures: continually keeping our selues as neere as is possible, to our text & to the very vvordes and phrases vvhich by long vse are made venerable, though to some prophane or delicate eares they may seeme more hard or barbarous, * as the whole style of Scripture doth lightly to such at the begining: acknowledging with S. Hierom, that in other writings it is ynough to giue in trāslation sense for sense, but that in Scriptures, lest vve misse the sense, vve must keepe the very

The purpose & commoditie of setting forth this Catholike edition.

The religious care & sinceritie obserued in this translatiō.

See S. August. li. 3 confes. c. 5.

vvordes. *Ad Pammach. epiſtola* 101. *ca.* 2 *in princip.* Vve muſt, ſaith S. Auguſtine, ſpeake according to a ſet rule, leſt licence of wordes breede ſome vvicked opinion concerning the thinges conteined vnder the vvordes. *De ciuitate lib.* 10. *cap*, 12. Vvhereof our holy foreſathers and auncient Doctors had ſuch a religious care, that they vvould not change the very barbariſmes or incongruities of ſpeach vvhich by long vſe had preuailed in the old readings or recitings of ſcriptures. as, *Neque nubent neque nubentur*, in Tertullian li. 4. in Marcion. in S. Hilarie in c. 22 Mat. and in al the fathers. *Qui me confuſus fuerit, confundar & ego eum*, in S. Cyprian ep. 63 nu. 7. *Talis enim nobis decebat ſacerdos* (vvhich vvas an elder tranſlation then the vulgar Latin that novv is) in S. Ambroſe c. 3 *de fuga ſeculi.* and S. Hierom him ſelf, vvho othervviſe corrected the Latin tranſlation that vvas vſed before his time, yet keepeth religiouſly (as him ſelf profeſſeth *Præfat. in* 4 *Euang. ad Damaſum*) theſe and the like ſpeaches, *Nonne vos magis pluris eſtis illis?* and, *filius hominis non venit miniſtrari, ſed miniſtrare*: and, *Neque nubent, neque nubentur*: in his commentaries vpon theſe places. and, *Non capit Prophetam perire extra Hieruſalem*, in his commentaries *in c.* 2. *Ioël. ſub finem.* And S. Auguſtine, vvho is moſt religious in al theſe phraſes, counteth it a ſpecial pride and infirmitie in thoſe that haue a litle learning in tonges, & none in thinges, that they eaſily take offenſe of the ſimple ſpeaches or ſolecíſmes in the ſcriptures. *de doctrina Chriſt. li.* 2. *cap*, 13. See alſo the ſame holy father *li.* 3 *de doct. Chriſt. c* 5 and *tract.* 2 *in Euang. Ioan.* But of the maner of our tranſlation more anon.

The auncient fathers kept religiouſly the very barbariſmes of the vulgar Latin text.

Mat. 22. Mar. 8. Hebr. 7. Mat. 6. 20. 22. Luc. 13.

Now, though the text thus truely tranſlated, might ſufficiently, in the ſight of the learned and al indifferent men, both controule the aduerſaries corruptions, and proue that the holy Scripture vvhereof they haue made ſo great vauntes, make nothing for their nevv opinions, but vvholy for the Catholike Churches beleefe and doctrine, in all the pointes of difference betvvixt vs: yet knovving that the good and ſimple may eaſily be ſeduced by ſome fevv obſtinate perſons of perdition (vvhom vve ſee giuen ouer into a reprobat ſenſe, to whom the Goſpel, vvhich in it ſelf is the odour of life to ſaluation, is made the odour of death to damnation, ouer vvhoſe eies for ſinne & diſobedience God ſuffereth a veile or couer to lie, whiles they read the nevv Teſtamét, euen as the Apoſtle ſaith the Ievves haue til this day, in reading of the old, that as the one ſort can not finde Chriſt in the Scriptures, reade they neuer ſo much, ſo the other can not finde the Catholike Church nor her doctrine there neither) and finding by experience this ſaying of S. Auguſtine to be moſt true, *If the preiudice of any erroneous perſuaſion preoccupate the mind, vvhatſoeuer the Scripture hath to the contrarie, men take it for a figuratiue ſpeach*: for theſe cauſes, and ſomevvhat to help the faithful reader in the difficulties of diuers places, vve haue alſo ſet forth reaſonable large ANNOTATIONS, thereby to ſhevv the ſtudious reader in moſt places perteining to the controuerſies of this time, both the heretical corruptions and falſe deductions, & alſo the Apoſtolike tradition, the expoſitions of the holy fathers, the decrees of the Catholike Church and moſt auncient Coúcels: which meanes vvhoſoeuer truſteth not, for the ſenſe of holy Scriptures, but had rather folow his priuate iudgemét or the arrogát ſpirit of theſe Sectaries, he ſhal vvorthily through his owne wilfulnes be deceiued. beſeeching all men to looke vvith diligence, ſinceritie, and indifferencie, into the caſe that concerneth no leſſe then euery ones eternal ſaluation or damnation.

Of the ANNOTATIONS, vvhy they vvere made, & vvhat matter they cóteine.

2 Cor. 2. 2 Cor. 3. De doctr. Chriſt. lib. 3. cap. 10.

Vvhich if he doe, vve doubt not but he ſhal to his great contentment, find the holy Scriptures moſt clerely and inuincibly to proue the articles of Catholike

like doctrine against our aduersaries, vvhich perhaps he had thought before this diligent search, either not to be consonant to Gods vvord, or at least not conteined in the same, and finally he shal proue this saying of S. Augustine to be most true. *Multi sensus &c. Many senses of holy Scriptures lie hidden, and are knowen to some fevv of greater vnderstanding: neither are they at any time auouched more commodiously and acceptably then at such times, vvhen the care to ansvver heretikes doth force men thereunto. For then, euen they that be negligent in matters of studie and learning, shaking of sluggishnes, are stirred vp to diligent hearing, that the Aduersaries may be refelled. Againe, hovv many senses of holy Scriptures, cōcerning Christes Godhead, haue been auouched against Photinus: hovv many, of his Manhod, against Manichæus: hovv many, of the Trinitie, against Sabellius: hovv many, of the vnitie in Trinitie, against the Arrians, Eunomians, Macedonians: hovv many, of the Catholike Church dispersed through out the vvhole vvorld, and of the mixture of good and bad in the same vntil the end of the vvorld, against the Donatistes and Luciferians and other of the like errour: hovv many against al other heretikes, vvhich it vvere to long to rehearse? Of vvhich senses and expositions of holy Scripture the approued authors and auouchers, should othervvise either not be knovven at al, or not so vvel knovven, as the contradictions of proud heretikes haue made them.*

In Psal. 67. propè finem.

Heresies make Catholikes more diligent to search and finde the senses of holy Scripture for refelling of the same.

Thus he saith of such thinges as not seeming to be in holy Scriptures to the ignorant or heretikes, yet in deede be there. But in other pointes doubted of, that in deede are not decided by Scripture, he giueth vs this goodly rule to be folovved in all, as he exemplifieth in one. *Then doe vve hold* (saith he) *the veritie of the Scriptures, vvhen vve doe that vvhich novv hath seemed good to the Vniuersal Church, vvhich the authoritie of the Scriptures them selues doth cōmend: so that, forasmuch as the holy Scripture can not deceiue, vvhosoeuer is afraid to be deceiued vvith the obscuritie of questions, let him therein aske counsel of the same* CHVRCH, *vvhich the holy Scripture most certainely and euidently shevveth and pointeth vnto.* Aug. li. I. Cont. Cresc. con. c. 13.

NOVV TO GIVE thee also intelligence in particular, most gentle Reader, of such things as it behoueth thee specially to knovv concerning our Translation: Vve translate the old vulgar Latin text, not the common Greeke text, for these causes.

Many causes vvhy this nevv Testament is trāslated according to the auncient vulgar Latin text.

1. It is so auncient, that it vvas vsed in the Church of God aboue 1300 yeres agoe, as appeareth by the fathers of those times.

It is most auncient.

2. It is that (by the common receiued opinion and by al probabilitie) vvhich S. Hierom aftervvard corrected according to the Greeke, by the appointment of Damasus then Pope, as he maketh mention in his preface before the foure Euangelistes, vnto the said Damasus: and *in Catalogo in fine,* and *ep.102.*

Corrected by S. Hierom.

3. Consequently it is the same vvhich S. Augustine so commendeth and allovveth in an Epistle to S. Hierom.

Ep. 10.

Commēded by S. Augustine.

4. It is that, vvhich for the most part euer since hath been vsed in the Churches seruice, expounded in sermons, alleaged and interpreted in the Commentaries and vvritings of the auncient fathers of the Latin Church.

Vsed and expounded by the fathers.

5. The holy Councel of Trent, for these and many other important considerations, hath declared and defined this onely of al other latin translations, to be authentical, and so onely to be vsed and taken in publike lessons, disputations, preachings, and expositions, and that no man presume vpon any pretence to reiect or refuse the same.

Sess. 4.

Only authentical, by the holy Councel of Trent.

6. It is the grauest, sincerest, of greatest maiestie, least partialitie, as being vvithout al respect of controuersies and contentions, specially these of our

Most graue, least partial.

time,

time, as appeareth by those places vvhich Erasmus and others at this day translate much more to the aduantage of the Catholike cause.

Precise in folovving the Greeke.

7. It is so exact and precise according to the Greeke, both the phrase and the word, that delicate Heretikes therfore reprehend it of rudenes. And that it folovveth the Greeke far more exactly then the Protestants translations, beside infinite other places, we appeale to these. Tit. 3, 14. *Curent bonis operibus praeesse.* προΐστασθαι. Engl. bib. 1577, *to mainteine good vvorkes.* and Hebr. 10, 20. *Viam nobis initiauit*, ἐνεκαίνισεν. English Bib. *he prepared.* So in these vvordes, *Iustificationes*, *Traditiones*, *Idola &c.* In al vvhich they come not neere the Greeke, but auoid it of purpose.

Preferred by Beza him self.

8. The Aduersaries them selues, namely Beza, preferre it before al the rest. *In praefat. no. Test an.* 1556. And againe he saith, that the old Interpreter translated very religiously. *Annot. in 1. Luc. v. 1.*

Al the rest misliked of the Sectaries them selues, eche reprehending an other.

9. In the rest, there is such diuersitie and dissension, and no end of reprehending one an other, and translating euery man according to his fantasie, that * Luther said, If the vvorld should stand any long time, vve must receiue againe (which he thought absurd) the Decrees of Councels, for preseruing the vnitie of faith, because of so diuers interpretations of the Scripture. And Beza (in the place aboue mentioned) noteth the itching ambition of his felovv-translators, that had much rather disagree and dissent from the best, then seeme them selues to haue said or vvritten nothing. And Bezas translation it self, being so esteemed in our countrie, that the Geneua * English Testaments be translated according to the same, yet sometime goeth so vvide from the Greeke, and from the meaning of the holy Ghost, that them selues which protest to trāslate it, dare not folow it. For example, *Luc.* 3, 36. They haue put these wordes, *The sonne of Cainan*, which he wittingly and wilfully left out: and *Act.* 1, 14. they say, *Vvith the vvomen*, agreably to the vulgar Latin: where he saith, *Cum vxoribus, vvith their vviues.*

* *Cochla. c. 11 de Cano. Script. authoritate.*

The nevv Test. printed the yere 1580. in the title.

It is truer then the vulgar Greeke text it self.

10. It is not onely better then al other Latin trāslations, but then the Greeke text it self, in those places where they disagree.

The auncient fathers for proofe therof, and the Aduersaries them selues.

The proofe hereof is euident, because most of the auncient Heretikes were Grecians, & therfore the Scriptures in Greeke were more corrupted by them, as the auncient fathers often complaine. Tertullian noteth the Greeke text which is at this day (1 *Cor.* 15, 47) to be an old corruption of Marcion the Heretike, and the truth to be as in our vulgar latin, *Secundus homo de coelo coelestis, The second man from heauen heauenly.* So reade other * auncient fathers, and Erasmus thinketh it must needes be so, and Caluin him self folovveth it *Instit. li.* 2. *c.* 13. *parag.* 2. Againe S. Hierom noteth that the Greeke text (1 *Cor.* 7, 33) which is at this day, is not the *Apostolical veritie* or the true text of the Apostle: but that which is in the vulgar Latin, *Qui cum vxore est, solicitus est quae sunt mundi, quomodo placeat vxori, & diuisus est. He that is vvith a vvife, is careful of vvorldly things, hovv he may please his vvife, and is deuided or distracted.* The Ecclesiastical historie called the Tripartite, noteth the Greeke text that now is (1 *Io.* 4, 3) to be an old corruption of the auncient Greeke copies, by the Nestorian Heretikes, & the true reading to be as in our vulgar Latin, *Omnis spiritus qui soluit* IESVM, *ex Deo non est. Euery spirit that dissolueth* IESVS, *is not of God:* and Beza confesseth that Socrates in his Ecclesiastical historie readeth so in the Greeke, πᾶν πνεῦμα ὃ λύει τὸν Ἰησοῦν χριστὸν &c.

Li. 5 *cont. Marcionē.*

Ambros. Hierom.

Li. 1, *cont. Iouin. c.* 7.

Li. 12. *c.* 4.

Li. 7. *c.* 32.

But the proofe is more pregnant out of the Aduersaries them selues. They forsake the Greeke text as corrupted, and translate according to the vulgar Latin,

tin, namely Beza and his ſcholers the Engliſh tranſlatours of the Bible, in theſe places. Hebr. chap. 9, verſ. 1. ſaying, *The firſt couenant*, for that vvhich is in the Greeke. *The firſt tabernacle.* vvhere they put, *couenant*, not as of the text, but in an other letter, as to be vnderſtood, according to the vulgar Latin, vvhich moſt ſincerely leaueth it out altogether, ſaying, *Habuit quidem & prius iuſtificationes &c. The former alſo in deede had iuſtifications &c.* Againe, *Ro. 11, verſ. 21.* They tranſlate not according to the Greeke text, *Tempori ſeruientes, ſeruing the time,* vvhich Beza ſaith muſt needes be a corruption: but according to the vulgar Latin, *Domino ſeruientes, ſeruing our Lord.* Againe, *Apoc. 11, verſ. 2.* they tranſlate not the Greeke text, *Atrium quod intra templum eſt, the court vvhich is vvithin the teme*: but cleane contrarie, according to the vulgar Latin, vvhich Beza ſaith is the true reading, *Atrium quod eſt foris templum, the court vvhich is vvithout the temple.* Onely in this laſt place, one Engliſh Bible of the yere 1562, folovveth the errour of the Greeke. Againe, *2 Tim. 2. verſ. 14.* they adde, *but*, more then is in the Greeke, to make the ſenſe more cōmodious and eaſie, according as it is in the vulgar Latin. Againe, *Ia. 5, 12.* they leaue the Greeke, and folovv the vulgar Latin, ſaying, *leſt you fall into condemnation. I doubt* not (ſaith Beza) *but this is the true and ſincere reading, and I ſuſpect the corruption in the Greeke came thus &c.* It vvere infinite to ſet dovvne al ſuch places, vvhere the Aduerſaries (ſpecially Beza) folovv the old vulgar Latin and the Greeke copie agreable thereunto, condemning the Greeke text that novv is, of corruption.

διαθήκη / *σκηνὴ* — *καιρῷ* / *κυρίῳ* — *εἰς ὑπόκρισιν*

The Caluiniſtes them ſelues oftē forſake the Greeke as corrupt, and tranſlate according to the aūcient vulgar latin text.

Againe, Eraſmus the beſt tranſlatour of al the later, by Bezas iudgement, ſaith, that the Greeke ſometime hath ſuperfluities corruptly added to the text of holy Scripture. as *Mat. 6.* to the end of the *Pater noſter*, theſe vvordes, *Becauſe thine is the kingdom, the povver, and the glorie, for euer-more.* Vvhich he calleth, *nugas*, trifles raſhly added to our Lords praier, and reprehendeth Valla for blaming the old vulgar Latin becauſe it hath it not. likevviſe *Ro. 11, 6.* theſe vvordes in the Greeke, and not in the vulgar latin: *But if of vvorkes, it is not novv grace: othervviſe the vvorke is no more a vvorke.* and *Mar. 10, 29.* theſe vvordes, *or vviſe*, and ſuch like. Yea the Greeke text in theſe ſuperfluities condemneth it ſelf, and iuſtifieth the vulgar Latin exceedingly: as being marked through out in a number of places, that ſuch and ſuch vvordes or ſentences are ſuperfluous. in al which places our vulgar Latin hath no ſuch thing, but is agreable to the Greeke vvhich remaineth after the ſuperfluities be taken avvay. For example, that before mētioned in the end of the *Pater noſter*, hath a marke of ſuperfluitie in the Greeke text thus ''. and *Marc. 6, 11* theſe vvordes, *Amen I ſay to you, it ſhal be more tolerable for the land of Sodom and Gomorrhe in the day of iudgement, then for that citie.* and *Mat. 20, 22.* theſe vvordes, *And be baptized vvith the baptiſme that I am baptized vvith?* Vvhich is alſo ſuperfluouſly repeated againe verſ. 23. and ſuch like places exceeding many: which being noted ſuperfluous in the Greeke, and being not in the vulgar Latin, proue the Latin in thoſe places to be better, truer and more ſincere then the Greeke.

Superfluities in the Greeke, vvhich Eraſmus calleth trifling and raſh additions.

See *No. Teſt. Græc. Rob. Stephani in folio*, and *Criſpini.*

Vvhereupon vve conclude of theſe premiſſes, that it is no derogation to the vulgar Latin text, which we tranſlate, to diſagree from the Greeke text, wheras it may notwithſtanding be not onely as good, but alſo better. and this the Aduerſarie him ſelf, their greateſt and lateſt tranſlatour of the Greeke, doth auouch againſt Eraſmus in behalfe of the old vulgar Latin trāſlation, in theſe notorious vvordes. *Hovv vnvvorthely and vvithout cauſe* (ſaith he) *doth Eraſmus blame the old Interpreter as diſſenting from the Greeke? he diſſented, I graunt, from thoſe Greeke copies vvhich he had gotten: but vve haue found, not in one place, that the ſame interpretation*

Beza præfat. No. Teſt. 1556. See him alſo Anno. in 13. Act. v. 20.

The vulgar Latin tranſlation agreeth vvith the beſt Greeke copies, by Bezas ovvne iudgement.

terpretation vvhich he blameth, is grounded vpon the authoritie of other Greeke copies, & those most auncient. Yea in some number of places vve haue obserued, that the reading or the Latin text of the old Interpreter, though it agree not sometime vvith our Greeke copies yet it is much more conuenient, for that it seemeth he folovved some better and truer copie. Thus far Beza. In vvhich vvordes he vnwittingly, but most truely, iustifieth and defendeth the old vulgar Translation against him self and al other cauillers, that accuse the same, because it is not alwaies agreable to the Greeke text: Vvhereas it vvas translated out of other Greeke copies (partly extant, partly not extant at this day) either as good and as auncient, or better and more auncient, such as S. Augustine speaketh of, calling them *doctiores & diligentiores, the more learned and diligent Greeke copies*, vvherevnto the latin translations that faile in any place, must needes yeld. *Li. 2. de doct. Christ. c.* 15.

Vvhen the Fathers say, that the Latin text must yeld to the Greeke, & be corrected by it, they meane the true and vncorrupted Greeke text.

And if it were not to long to exemplifie and proue this, which would require a treatise by it self, we could shew by many and most cleere examples through out the new Testament, these sundrie meanes of iustifying the old translation.

First, if it agree with the Greeke text (as commonly it doth, and in the greatest places cõcerning the controuersies of our time, it doth most certainely) so far the Aduersaries haue not to complaine: vnles they wil complaine of the Greeke also, as they doe *Ia. 4. v.* 2. and 1 *Pet. 3. v.* 21. where the vulgar Latin foloweth exactly the Greeke text, saying, *Occiditis*: and, *Quod vos similis formæ*, &c But Beza in both places correcteth the Greeke text also as false.

The vulgar Latin Translatiõ, is many waies iustified by most auncient Greeke copies, & the Fathers.

2 If it disagree here and there from the Greeke text, it agreeth with an other Greeke copie set in the margent, whereof see examples in the foresaid Greeke Testaments of Robert Steuens and Crispin through out. namely 2 *Pet.* 1, 10. *Satagite vt per bona opera certam vestram vocationem faciatis.* διὰ τῶν ἀγαθῶν ἔργων. and Marc. 8. v. 7. *Et ipsos benedixit*, εὐλογήσας αὐτὰ.

3 If these marginal Greeke copies be thought lesse authentical then the Greeke text, the Aduersaries them selues tel vs the cõtrarie, vvho in their translations often folow the marginal copies, and forsake the Greeke text. as in the examples aboue mentioned *Ro.* 11. *Apoc.* 11. 2 *Tim.* 2. *Iac.* 5. &c. it is euident.

4 If al Erasmus Greeke copies haue not that which is in the vulgar Latin, Beza had copies which haue it, and those most auncient (as he saith) & better. And if al Bezas copies faile in this point and wil not helpe vs, Gagneie the Frenche kings preacher, and he that might commaund in al the kings libraries, he found Greeke copies that haue iust according to the vulgar Latin: & that in such place as would seeme otherwise lesse probable. as *Iac. 3. vers.* 5. *Ecce quantus ignis quam magnam siluam incendit! Behold hovv much fire vvhat a great vvood it kindleth!* A man would thinke it must be rather as in the Greeke text, *A litle fire vvhat a great vvood it kindleth!* But an approued auncient Greeke copie alleaged by Gagneie, hath as it is in the vulgar Latin. And if Gagneis copies also faile sometime, there Beza and Crispin supply Greeke copies fully agreable to the vulgar Latin. as *ep. Iudæ vers.* 5. Scientes semel *omnia*, quoniam IESVS &c. and *vers* 19. Segregant *semetipsos*. likewise 2 Ephes 1. *Quòd elegerit vos primitias*: ἀπαρχὰς in some Greeke copies. Gagn. & 2 *Cor.* 9. *Vestra æmulatio*, ὁ ὑμῶν ζῆλος. so hath one Greeke copie. Beza.

Codex veronensis. ἡλίκον πῦρ

πάντα,

ὅτι Ἰησοῦς.

ἑαυτοὺς

5 If al their copies be not sufficient, the auncient Greeke fathers had copies and expounded them agreable to our vulgar Latin. as 1 Tim. 6, 20. *Prophanas vocum nouitates.* So readeth S. Chrysostom and expoundeth it against Heretical & erroneous nouelties. Yet now we know no Greeke copie that readeth so.

καινοφωνίας

Likewise

Likewise *Io.* 10,29. *Pater meus quod mihi dedit maius omnibus est.* so readeth S. Cyril and expoundeth it *li.* 7 in *Io.c.*10. likewise 1 *Io.* 4, 3. *Omnis spiritus qui soluit* IESVM, *ex Deo non est.* so readeth S. Irenæus li.3.c.18. S. Augustine *tract.* 6. *in Io.* S. Leo *epist.* 10.c.5. beside Socrates in his Ecclesiastical historie, *li.*7.c.22. and the Tripartite *li.*12.c.4, vvho say plainely, that this was the old and the true reading of this place in the Greeke. And in what Greeke copie extant at this day is there this text *Io.*5,2. *Est autē Hierosolymis probatica piscina?* and yet S. Chrysostom, S. Cyril, and Theophylacte read so in the Greeke, and Beza saith it is the better reading. and so is the Latin text of the Romane Masse booke iustified, and eight other Latin copies, that reade so. for our vulgar Latin here, is according to the Greeke text, *Super probatica.* & Ro. 5. v. 17. *Donationis & iustitiæ.* so readeth Theodorete in Greeke. & *Lu.*2.*v.*14. Origen & S. Chrysostom reade, *Hominibus bonæ voluntatis*, and Beza liketh it better then the Greeke text that novv is.

The Greeke fathers.

ἐπὶ προβατικῇ

6. Vvhere there is no such signe or token of any auncient Greeke copie in the fathers, yet these later Interpreters tel vs, that the old Interpreter did folovv some other Greeke copie. as Marc. 7, 3. *Nisi crebro lauerint.* Erasmus thinketh that he did read in the Greeke *πυκνῆ, often*: and Beza and others commend his coniecture, yea and the English Bibles are so translated. vvhereas novv it is *πυγμῇ* vvhich signifieth the length of the arme vp to the elbovv. And vvho vvould not thinke that the Euangelist should say, The Pharisees vvash often, because othervvise they eate not, rather then thus, *Vnles they vvash vp to the elbovv, they eate not?*

7. If al such coniectures, and al the Greeke fathers help vs not, yet the Latin fathers vvith great consent vvil easily iustifie the old vulgar trāslation, vvhich for the most part they folovv and expound. as, Io. 7, 39. *Nondum erat spiritus datus.* so readeth S. Augustine *li.* 4 *de Trinit.c.*20. and li.83 *Quæst. q.* 62. and *tract.* 52 *in Ioan.* Leo *ser.* 2 *de Pentecoste.* Vvhose authoritie vvere sufficient, but in deede Didymus also a Greeke Doctor readeth so *li.* 2 *de Sp. sancto*, translated by S. Hierom, and a Greeke copie in the Vaticane, and the Syriake nevv Testament. Likevvise Io.21, 22. *Sic eum volo manere.* so reade S. Ambrose, *in Psal.* 45. & *Psal.* 118. *octonario Resh.* S. Augustine and Ven. Bede vpon S. Iohns Gospel.

The Latin fathers.

See Annot. Louan. in No. Test. and Annot. Lucæ Brugensis in biblia.

8. And lastly, if some other Latin fathers of auncient time, reade othervvise, either here or in other places, not al agreing vvith the text of our vulgar Latin, the cause is, the great diuersitie and multitude that vvas then of Latin copies, (vvhereof S. Hierom complaineth) til this one vulgar Latin grevv onely into vse. Neither doth their diuers reading make more for the Greeke, then for the vulgar Latin, differing oftentimes from both. as vvhen S. Hierom in this last place readeth, *Si sic eum volo manere, li.* 1. *adu. Iouin.* it is according to no Greeke copie novv extant. And if yet there be some doubt, that the readings of some Greeke or Latin fathers, differing from the vulgar Latin, be a checke or condemnation to the same: let Beza, that is, let the Aduersarie him self, tel vs his opinion in this case also. *Vvhosoeuer*, saith he, *shal take vpon him to correct these things* (speaking of the vulgar Latin translation) *out of the auncient fathers vvritings, either Greeke or Latin, vnles he doe it very circumspectly and aduisedly, he shal surely corrupt al rather then amend it, because it is not to be thought, that as often as they cited any place, they did alvvaies looke into the booke, or number euery vvord.* As if he should say, Vve may not by and by thinke that the vulgar Latin is faultie and to be corrected vvhen vve read othervvise in the fathers either Greeke or Latin, because they did not alvvaies exactly cite the vvordes, but folovved some

Præfat. in 4. Euang. ad Damasum.

Præfat. citata.

commo-

commodious and godly ſenſe thereof.

The fevv and ſmal faultes negligently crept into the vulgar Latin tranſlation.

Thus then vve ſee that by al meanes the old vulgar Latin tranſlation is approued good, and better then the Greeke text it ſelf, and that there is no cauſe vvhy it ſhould giue place to any other text, copies, or readings. Marie if there be any faultes euidently crept in by thoſe that heretofore wrote or copied out the Scriptures (as there be ſome) them vve graunt no leſſe, then vve vvould graunt faultes novv a daies committed by the Printer, and they are exactly noted of Catholike vvriters, namely in al Plantins Bibles ſet forth by the Diuines of Louan: and the holy Councel of Trent vvilleth that the vulgar Latin text be in ſuch pointes throughly mended, & ſo to be moſt authentical. Such faultes are theſe, *In fide*, for, *in fine*: *Praſcientiam*, for, *præſentiam*: *Suſcipiens*, for, *Suſpiciens*: and ſuch like very rare. vvhich are euident corruptions made by the copiſtes, or grovven by the ſimilitude of vvordes. Theſe being taken avvay, vvhich are no part of thoſe corruptions and differences before talked of, vve tranſlate that text vvhich is moſt ſincere, and in our opinion and as vve haue proued, incorrupt. The Aduerſaries contrarie, tranſlate that text, vvhich them ſelues confeſſe both by their vvritings and doings, to be corrupt in a number of places, & more corrupt then our vulgar Latin, as is before declared.

Seſſ. 4.

The Caluiniſts confeſſing the Greeke to be moſt corrupt, yet tranſlate that only, and hold that only for authentical Scripture.

And if vve vvould here ſtand to recite the places in the Greeke vvhich Beza pronounceth to be corrupted, vve ſhould make the Reader to vvonder, hovv they can either ſo plead othervviſe for the Greeke text, as though there vvere no other truth of the nevv Teſtament but that: or hovv they tranſlate onely that (to deface, as they thinke, the old vulgar Latin) vvhich them ſelues ſo ſhamfully diſgrace, more then the vulgar Latin, inuenting corruptions vvhere none are, nor can be, in ſuch vniuerſal conſent of al both Greeke and Latin copies. For example, Mat. 10. *The firſt Simon, Vvho is called Peter.* I thinke (ſaith Beza) this vvord πρῶτος, *firſt*, hath been added to the text of ſome that vvould eſtabliſh Peters Primacie. Againe *Luc.* 22. The Chalice, *that is ſhed for you.* It is moſt likely (ſaith he) that theſe vvordes being ſometime but a marginal note, came by corruption out of the margent into the text. Againe *Act.* 7. Figures vvhich they made, *to adore them.* It may be ſuſpected (ſaith he) that theſe vvordes, as many other, haue crept by corruption into the text out of the margent. And 1 *Cor.* 15. He thinketh the Apoſtle ſaid not νῖκος, *victorie*, as it is in al Greeke copies, but νεῖκος, *contention.* And *Act.* 13. he calleth it a manifeſt errour, that in the Greeke it is, 400 *yeres*, for, 300. And *Act.* 7. *v.* 16. he reckeneth vp a vvhole catalogue of corruptions. namely *Marc.* 12. *v.* 42. ὅ ἐστι κοδράντης, *Vvhich is a farthing*: and Act. 8. *v.* 26. αὕτη ἐστὶν ἔρημος, *This is deſert.* and *Act.* 7. *v.* 16 the name of Abraham, & ſuch like. Al vvhich he thinketh to haue been added or altered into the Greeke text by corruption.

* *In Annot. No. Teſt. an.* 1556.

They ſtanding preciſely vpon the Hebrue of the old, and Greeke text of the nevv Teſtament, muſt of force denie the one of them.

But among other places, he laboureth excedingly to proue a great corruption *Act.* 7. *v.* 14. vvhere it is ſaid (according to the *Septuaginta*, that is, the Greeke text of the old Teſtament) that Iacob vvent dovvne into Ægypt vvith 75 ſoules. And *Luc.* 3. *v.* 36. he thinketh theſe vvordes τοῦ καϊνάν, *Vvhich vvas of Cainan*, to be ſo falſe, that he leaueth them cleane out in * both his editions of the nevv Teſtament: ſaying, that he is bold ſo to doe, by the authoritie of Moyſes. Vvhereby he vvil ſignifie, that it is not in the Hebrue text of Moyſes or of the old Teſtament, and therfore it is falſe in the Greeke of the nevv Teſtament. Vvhich conſequence of theirs (for it is common among them and concerneth al Scriptures) if it vvere true, al places of the Greeke text of the nevv Teſtament, cited out of the old according to the Septuaginta, and not according

* *An. Do.* 1556 *and* 1565.

ding

ding to the Hebrue (vvhich they knovv are very many) should be false. and so by tying them selues onely to the Hebrue in the old Testamét, they are forced to forsake the Greeke of the nevv: or if they vvil mainteine the Greeke of the nevv, they must forsake sometime the Hebrue in the old. but this argument shal be forced against them els vvhere.

By this litle, the Reader may see vvhat gay patrones they are of the Greeke text, and how litle cause they haue in their owne iudgements to translate it, or vaunt of it. as in derogation of the vulgar Latin translation, & how easily we might answer them in a word, why we translate not the Greeke: forsooth because it is so infinitely corrupted, But the truth is, we do by no meanes graũt it so corrupted as they say, though in comparison we know it lesse sincere & incorrupt then the vulgar Latin, and for that cause and others before alleaged we preferre the said Latin, and haue translated it.

They say the Greeke is more corrupt then vve vvil graunt them.

If yet there remaine one thing which perhaps they wil say, when they can not answer our reasons aforesaid: to wit, that we preferre the vulgar Latin before the Greeke text, because the Greeke maketh more against vs: we protest that as for other causes we preferre the Latin, so in this respect of making for vs or against vs, we allow the Greeke as much as the Latin, yea in sundrie places more then the Latin, being assured that they haue not one, and that we haue many aduantages in the Greeke more then in the Latin, as by the Annotations of this new Testament shal euidently appeare: namely in al such places where they dare not translate the Greeke, because it is for vs & against them. as when they translate, δικαιώματα, *ordinances*, and not, *iustifications*, and that of purpose as Beza confesseth *Luc.* 1, 6. παραδόσεις, *ordinances* or *instructions*, and not *traditions*, in the better part. *2 Thess.* 2, 15. πρεσβυτέρους, *Elders*, and not *Priests*: εἴδωλα, *images* rather then *idols*. and especially when S. Luke in the Greeke so maketh for vs (the vulgar Latin being indifferent for them and vs) that Beza saith it is a corruption crept out of the margent into the text. Vvhat neede these absurd diuises and false dealings with the Greeke text, if it made for them more then for vs, yea if it made not for vs against them? But that the Greeke maketh more for vs, see 1 Cor. 7. In the Latin, *Defraude not one an other, but for a time, that you giue your selues to prayer.* in the Greeke, *to fasting and prayer. Act.* 10, 30. in the Latin Cornelius saith, *from the fourth day past vntil this houre I vvas praying in my house and behold a man &c.* in the Greeke, *I vvas fasting, and praying.* 1 Io. 5, 18. in the Latin, *Vve knovv that euery one vvhich is borne of God, sinneth not. but the generation of God preserueth him &c.* in the Greeke, *but he that is borne of God preserueth him self. Apoc.* 22, 14. in the Latin, *Blessed are they that vvash their garmẽts in the bloud of the lambe* &c. in the Greeke, *Blessed are they that doe his commaundements. Rom.* 8, 38. *Certus sum &c. I am sure that neither death nor life, nor other creature is able to separate vs from the charitie of God.* as though he vvere assured, or we might and should assure our selues of our predestination. in the Greeke, πέπεισμαι, *I am probably persuaded that neither death nor life* &c. In the Euangelists about the Sacrifice and B. Sacrament, in the Latin thus: *This is my bloud that shal be shed for you*: and in S. Paul, *This is my body vvhich shal be betraied or deliuered for you*: both being referred to the time to come and to the sacrifice on the crosse. in the Greeke, *This is my bloud vvhich is shed for you*: and, *my body vvhich is broken for you*: both being referred to that present time when Christ gaue his body and bloud at his supper, then sheading the one and breaking the other, that is sacrificing it sacramentally and mystically. Loe these and the like our aduantages in the Greeke, more then in the Latin.

We preferre not the vulgar Latin text, as making more for vs.

The Greeke text maketh for vs more then the vulgar Latin.

Luc. 22. *v.* 20.

For the real presence.

For fasting.

For free vvil.

Against only faith.

Against special assurance of saluation.

For the sacrifice of Christs body and bloud.

But

The Protestāts condemning the old vulgar translation as making for vs, cōdemne them selues.

But is the vulgar translation for al this Papistical, & therfore do we folow it? (for so some of them call it, and say it is * the worst of al other.) If it be, the Greeke (as you see) is more, and so both Greeke and Latin and consequently the holy Scripture of the new Testament is Papistical. Againe if the vulgar Latin be Papistical, Papistrie is very auncient, and the Church of God for so many hundred yeres wherein it hath vsed and allowed this translation, hath been Papistical. But wherein is it Papistical? forsooth in these phrases and speaches, *Pœnitentiam agite. Sacramentum hoc magnum est.* AVE GRATIA PLENA. *Talibus hostiis promeretur Deus.* and such like. First, doth not the Greeke say the same? see the Annotations vpon these places. Secondly, could he translate these things Papistically or partially, or rather prophetically, so long before they were in controuersie? thirdly, doth he not say for, *pœnitentiam agite*, in an other place, *pœnitemini*: and doth he not translate other mysteries, by the vvord, *Sacramentum*, as *Apoc.17, Sacramentum mulieris*: and as he translateth one vvord, *Gratia plena*, so doth he not translate the very like vvord, *plenus vlceribus*, vvhich them selues do folow also? is this also Papistrie? Vvhen he said Heb.10,29. *Quanto deteriora merebitur supplicia* &c, and they like it vvel ynough: might he not haue said according to the same Greeke word, *Vigilate vt mereamini fugere ista omnia & stare ante filium hominis.* Luc.21, 36. and, *Qui merebuntur sæculum illud & resurrectionem ex mortuis &c.* Luc.20, 35. and, *Tribulationes quas sustinetis, vt mereamini regnum Dei, pro quo et patimini.* 2 Thess.1,5. Might he not (we say) if he had partially affectated the word merite, haue vsed it in al these places, according to his and * your owne translation of the same Greeke word Hebr. 10, 29? Vvhich he doth not, but in al these places saith simply, *Vt digni habeamini*, and, *Qui digni habebuntur.* And how can it be iudged Papistical or partial, when he saith, *Talibus hostiis promeretur Deus*, Heb.13? Vvas Primasius also S. Augustines scholer, a Papist, for vsing this text, and al the rest, that haue done the like? Vvas S. Cyprian a Papist, for vsing so often this speach, *promereri Dominum iustis operibus, pœnitentia, &c*? or is there any difference, but that S. Cyprian vseth it as a deponent more latinly, the other as a passiue lesse finely? Vvas it Papistrie, to say *Senior* for *Presbyter*, *Ministrantibus* for *sacrificantibus* or *liturgiam celebrantibus*, *simulachris* for *idolis*, *fides tua te saluum fecit* sometime for *sanum fecit*? Or shal we thinke he was a Caluinist for translating thus, as they thinke he was a Papist, when any word soundeth for vs?

Against D. Sand. Rocke pag. 147. See Kemnis. in exam. Cōc. Trid. sess. 4.

Mat. 3. & 11. Eph. 5. Luc. 1. Heb. 13.

Mar. 1. κεχαριτωμένη ἡλκωμένος. Luc. 16. v. 20.

It is void of al partialitie.

No. Test. 1580.

in ep. ad Hebr.

Ep. 14 & 18.

The Papistrie thereof (as they terme it) is in the very sentences of the Holy Ghost, more then in the translatiō.

Againe, was he a Papist in these kinde of wordes onely, and was he not in whole sentences? as, *Tibi dabo claues, &c. Quicquid solueris in terra, erit solutum & in cœlis.* and, *Quorum remiseritis peccata, remittuntur eis.* and, *Tunc reddet vnicuique secundum opera sua.* and, *Nunquid poterit fides saluare eum? Ex operibus iustificatur homo & non ex fide tantùm.* and, *Nubere volunt, damnationem habentes, quia primam fidem irritam fecerunt.* and, *Mandata eius grauia non sunt.* and, *Aspexit in remunerationem.* Are al these and such like, Papistical translations, because they are most plaine for the Catholike faith which they call Papistrie? Are they not word for word as in the Greeke, and the very wordes of the holy Ghost? And if in these there be no accusatiō of Papistical partiality, vvhy in the other? Lastly, are the auncient fathers, General Councels, the Churches of al the west part, that vse al these speaches & phrases now so many hundred yeres, are they al Papistical? Be it so, and let vs in the name of God folow them, speake as they spake, translate as they translated, interprete as they interpreted, because we beleeue as they beleeued. And thus far for defense of the old vulgar Latin translation, and why we translated it before al others: Now of the maner of translating the same.

Mat. 16. Io. 20. Mat. 16. Iac. 2. 1 Tim. 5. 1 Io. 5. Heb. 11.

The maner of this translation, and what hath been obserued therein.

IN THIS OVR TRANSLATION, because we wish it to be most sincere, as becōmeth a Catholike translation, and haue endeuoured so to make it: we are very precise & religious in folowing our copie, the old vulgar approued Latin: not onely in sense, which we hope we alwaies doe, but sometime in the very wordes also and phrases, which may seeme to the vulgar Reader & to common English eares not yet acquainted therewith, rudenesse or ignorance: but to the discrete Reader that deepely weigheth and considereth the importance of sacred wordes and speaches, and how easily the voluntarie Translatour may misse the true sense of the Holy Ghost, we doubt not but our consideration and doing therein, shal seeme reasonable and necessarie: yea and that al sortes of Catholike Readers wil in short time thinke that familiar, which at the first may seeme strange, & wil esteeme it more, when they shal * otherwise be taught to vnderstand it, then if it were the common knowen English.

* *See the last Table at the end of the booke.*

Certaine vvordes not English nor as yet familiar in the English tongue.

For example, vve translate often thus, *Amen, amen, I say vnto you.* Vvhich as yet seemeth strange, but after a while it wil be as familiar, as *Amen* in the end of al praiers and Psalmes. and euen as when we end with, *Amen*, it soundeth far better then, *So be it:* so in the beginning, *Amen Amen*, must needes by vse and custom sound far better, then, *Verily verily.* Vvhich in deede doth not expresse the asseueration and assurance signified in this Hebrue word. besides that it is the solemne and vsual word of our Sauiour *to expresse a vehement asseueration, and therfore is not changed, neither in the Syriake nor Greeke, nor vulgar Latin Testament, but is preserued and vsed of the Euangelistes and Apostles them selues, euen as Christ spake it, *propter sanctiorem authoritatem*, as S. Augustine saith of this and of *Allelu-ia, for the more holy and sacred authoritie thereof, li. 2. Doct. Christ. c. 11.* And therfore do we keepe the word *Allelu-ia.* Apoc. 19. as it is both in Greeke and Latin yea and in al the English translations, though in their bookes of common praier they translate it, *Praise ye the Lord.* Againe, if *Hosanna, Raca, Belial*, and such like be yet vntranslated in the English Bibles, why may not we say, *Corbana*, and *Parasceue*: specially when they Englishing this later thus, *the preparation of the Sabboth*, put three wordes more into the text, then the Greeke word doth signifie. *Mat. 27, 62.* And others saying thus, After the day *of preparing*, make a cold translation and short of the sense: as if they should traslate, Sabboth, *the resting*. for, * *Parasceue* is as solemne a word for the Sabboth eue, as *Sabboth* is for the Iewes seuenth day. and now among Christians much more solemner, taken for Good-friday onely. These wordes then we thought it far better to keepe in the text, and to tel their signification in the margent or in a table for that purpose, then to disgrace bothe the text & them with translating them. Such are also these wordes, *The Pasche. The feast of Azymes. The bread of Proposition.* Vvhich they translate *The Passeouer, The feast of svveete bread, The shevv bread.* But if *Pentecost* Act. 2 be yet vntrāslated in their bibles, and seemeth not strange: why should not *Pasche* and *Azymes* so remaine also, being solemne feastes, as Pentecost was? or why should they English one rather then the other? specially whereas *Passeouer* at the first was as strange, as *Pasche* may seeme now, and perhaps as many now vnderstand *Pasche*, as *Passeouer.* and as for *Azymes*, when they English it, *the feast of svveete bread*, it is a false interpretatiō of the word, & nothing expresseth that which belongeth to the feast, concerning vnleauened bread. And as for their terme of *shevv bread*, it is very strange and ridiculous. Againe, if *Proselyte* be a receiued word in the English bibles *Mat. 23. Act. 2*: why may not we be bold to say, *Neophyte.* 1 Tim. 3? specially when they translating it into English, do falsely expresse the signification

See annot. Io. c. 8. v. 34. & Apoc. c. 19. v. 4

Amen.

Alleluia.

No. Test. an. 1580. Bib. an. 1577.

Parasceue.

Mar. 14. v. 42.

Pasche.

Azymes.

Bib. 1577. Mat. 26. 17.

Neophyte.

cation of the word thus, *a yong ſcholer.* Vvhereas it is a peculiar word to ſignifie them that were lately baptized, as *Catechumenus*, ſignifieth the newely inſtructed in faith not yet baptized, who is alſo a yong ſcholer rather then the other, and many that haue been old ſcholers, may be *Neophytes* by differring baptiſme. And if *Phylacteries* be allowed for Engliſh *Mat.23*, we hope that *Didragmes* alſo, *Prepuce*, *Paraclete*, and ſuch like, wil eaſily grow to be currant and familiar. And in good ſooth there is in al theſe ſuch neceſſitie, that they can not conueniently be tranſlated. as when S. Paul ſaith, *conciſio, non circumciſio*: *Phil. 3.* how can we but folow his very wordes and alluſion? And how is it poſſible to expreſſe *Euangelizo*, but as vve do, *Euangelize*? for *Euangelium* being the Goſpel, what is, *Euangelizo* or *to Euangelize*, but to ſhew the glad tydings of the Goſpel, of the time of grace, of al Chriſts benefites? Al which ſignification is loſt, by tranſlating as the Engliſh bibles do, *I bring you good tydings.* Luc. 2, 10. Therfore we ſay *Depoſitum*, 1 Tim. 6. and, He *exinanited* him ſelf, Philip. 2. and, You haue *refloriſhed*, Philip. 4. and, *to exhauſt*, Hebr. 9, 28. becauſe vve can not poſſibly attaine to expreſſe theſe vvordes fully in Engliſh, and vve thinke much better, that the reader ſtaying at the difficultie of them, ſhould take an occaſion to looke in the table folovving, or othervviſe to aſke the ful meaning of them, then by putting ſome vſual Engliſh vvordes that expreſſe them not, ſo to deceiue the reader. Sometime alſo vve doe it for an other cauſe. as vvhen vve ſay, *The aduent of our Lord*, and, *Impoſing of handes.* becauſe one is a ſolemne time, the other a ſolemne action in the Catholike Church: to ſignifie to the people, that theſe and ſuch like names come out of the very Latin text of the Scripture. So did *Penance*, *doing penance*, *Chalice*, *Prieſt*, *Deacon*, *Traditions aultar*, *hoſt*, and the like (vvhich vve exactly keepe as Catholike termes) procede euen from the very vvordes of Scripture.

Vvhy vve ſay, *our Lord*, not, *the Lord* (but in certaine caſes) ſee the Annotations 1 *Tim.6. pag.* 585.

Catholike termes proceding from the very text of Scripture.

Moreouer, we preſume not in hard places to mollifie the ſpeaches or phraſes, but religiouſly keepe them vvord for vvord, and point for point, for feare of miſsing, or reſtraining the ſenſe of the holy Ghoſt to our phantaſie. as Eph. 6. *Againſt the ſpirituals of vvickednes in the celeſtials.* and, *Vvhat to me and thee vvoman?* *Io. 2.* whereof ſee the Annotation vpon this place. and 1 Pet. 2. *As infants euen novv borne, reaſonable, milke vvithout guile deſire ye.* Vve do ſo place, *reaſonable*, of purpoſe, that it may be indifferēt both to infants going before, as in our Latin text: or to milke that folovveth after, as in other Latin copies and in the Greeke. *Io.* 3 vve tranſlate, *The ſpirit breatheth vvhere he vvil &c.* leauing it indifferent to ſignifie either the holy Ghoſt, or vvinde: vvhich the Proteſtants tranſlating, *vvinde*, take avvay the other ſenſe more common and vſual in the auncient fathers. Vve tranſlate Luc. 8, 23. *They vvere filled*, not adding of our ovvne, *vvith vvater*, to mollifie the ſentence, as the Proteſtants doe. and c. 22. *This is the chalice, the nevv Teſtament &c.* not, *This chalice is the nevv Teſtament.* likevviſe, Mar. 13. *Thoſe daies ſhal be ſuch tribulation &c.* not as the Aduerſaries, *In thoſe daies*, both our text and theirs being othervviſe. likevviſe Iac. 4, 6. *And giueth greater grace*, leauing it indifferent to the *Scripture*, or to the *holy Ghoſt*, both going before. Vvhereas the Aduerſaries to to boldly & preſumptuouſly adde, ſaying *The Scripture giueth*, taking avvay the other ſenſe, which is far more probable. likevviſe *Hebr.* 12, 21 vve tranſlate, *So terrible vvas it vvhich vvas ſeen, Moyſes ſaid &c.* neither doth Greeke or Latin permit vs to adde, *that* Moyſes ſaid, as the Proteſtants preſume to doe. So vve ſay, *Men brethren*, *A vvidovv vvoman*, *A vvoman a ſiſter*, *Iames of Alphaus*, and the like. Sometime alſo we folow of purpoſe the Scriptures phraſe. as, *The hel of fire*, according to Greeke and *Mat. 5.* Latin

Certaine hard ſpeaches and phraſes.

The Proteſtāts preſumptuous boldnes and libertie in tranſlating.

Latin. vvhich we might say perhaps, *the firy hel*, by the Hebrue phrase in such speaches, but not, *hel fire*, as commonly it is translated. Likevvise *Luc.* 4, 36. Vvhat *vvord* is this, that in povver and authoritie he cōmaundeth the vncleane spirits? as also, *Luc.* 2. Let vs passe ouer, and see the *vvord* that is done. Vvhere we might say, *thing*, by the Hebrue phrase, but there is a certaine maiestie and more signification in these speaches, and therfore both Greeke & Latin keepe them, although it is no more the Greeke or Latin phrase, then it is the English. And vvhy should vve be squamish at nevv vvordes or phrases in the Scripture, vvhich are necessarie: vvhen vve do easily admit and folovv nevv vvordes coyned in court and in courtly or other secular vvritings?

Gehenna ignis.

Vve adde the Greeke in the margent for diuers causes. Sometime vvhen the sense is hard, that the learned reader may consider of it and see if he can helpe him self better then by our translation. as Luc 11. *Nolite extolli.* μὴ μετεωρίζεσθε. and againe, *Quod superest date eleemosynam.* τὰ ἐνόντα. Sometime to take away the ambiguitie of the Latin or English. as Luc. 11. *Et domus supra domum cadet.* Vvhich we must needes English, *and house vpon house, shal fall.* by the Greeke, the sense is not, one house shal fal vpon an other. but, if one house rise vpon it self, that is, against it self, it shal perish. according as he speaketh of a kingdom deuided against it self, in the wordes before. And Act. 14. *Sacerdos Iouis qui erat.* in the Greeke, *qui*, is referred to Iupiter. Sometime to satisfie the reader, that might otherwise conceiue the translation to be false. as *Philip.* 4. v. 6. *But in euery thing by praier, &c.* ἐν παντὶ προσευχῇ, not, *in al praier*, as in the Latin it may seeme. Sometime when the Latin neither doth, nor can, reache to the signification of the Greeke word, we adde the Greeke also as more significant. *Illi soli seruies, him only shalt thou serue,* λατρεύσεις. And *Act.* 6. Nicolas a *stranger* of Antioche, προσήλυτος. and, *Ro.* 9. *The seruice,* ἡ λατρεία. and Eph. 1. to *perfite, instaurare omnia in Christo,* ἀνακεφαλαιώσασθαι. And, *Vvherein he hath gratified vs,* ἐχαρίτωσεν. & Eph. 6. *Put on the armour,* πανοπλίαν. and a number the like. Sometime, when the Greeke hath two senses, and the Latin but one, we adde the Greeke. 2. Cor. 1. *By the exhortation vvherevvith vve also are exhorted.* the Greeke signifieth also *consolation &c.* and 2 Cor. 10. *But hauing hope of your faith increasing, to be &c.* vvhere the Greeke may also signifie, *as* or *vvhen your faith increaseth.* Sometime for aduantage of the Catholike cause, when the Greeke maketh for vs more then the Latin. as, Seniores, πρεσβυτέρους. *Vt digni habeamini.* ἵνα ἀξιωθῆτε. *Qui effundetur,* τὸ ἐκχυνόμενον, *Præcepta,* παραδόσεις. & Io. 21. ποίμαινε, *Pasce & rege.* And sometime to shew the false translation of the Heretike. as when Beza saith, *Hoc poculum in meo sanguine qui.* τὸ ποτήριον ἐν τῷ αἵματί μου τὸ ἐκχυνόμενον. *Luc.* 22, &, *Quē oportet cœlo cōtineri.* ὃν δεῖ οὐρανὸν δέξασθαι, *Act.* 3. Thus we vse the Greeke diuers waies, & esteeme of it as it is worthie, & take al cōmodities thereof for the better vnderstāding of the Latin, which being a translation, can not alwaies attaine to the ful sense of the principal tonge, as vve see in al translations..

The Greeke added often in the margent for many causes.

Mat. 4.

Act. 15. *2 Thes.* 2. *1 Cor.* 11.

Item vve adde the Latin vvord sometime in the margent, vvhen either vve can not fully expresse it, (as *Act.* 8. They tooke order for Steuens funeral, *Curauerunt Stephanum.* and, Al take not this vvord, *Non omnes capiunt.*) or vvhen the reader might thin[illegible] can not be as vve translate. as, *Luc.* 8. A storme of winde descended into the [illegible]ake, and *they vvere filled, & complebantur.* and Io. 5. vvhen Iesus knevv that he had novv a long time, *quia iam multum tempus haberet.* meaning, in his infirmitie.

The Latin text sometime noted in the margent.

This precise folovving of our Latin text, in neither adding nor diminishing, is the cause why we say not in the title of bookes, in the first page, S. Matthew

In the beginning of bookes, Matthew, Paul &c. not S. Matthew. S. Paul &c.

thevv, S. Paul: because it is so neither in Greeke nor Latin. though in the toppes of the leaues folovving, where vve may be bolder, we adde, S. Matthevv & c. to satisfie the reader. Much vnlike to the Protestants our Aduersaries, vvhich make no scruple to leaue out the name of Paul in the title of the Epistle to the Hebrues, though it be in euery Greeke booke vvhich they translate. And their most authorised English Bibles leaue out (Catholike) in the title of S. Iames Epistle and the rest, vvhich vvere famously knovven in the primitiue Church by the name of *Catholicæ Epistolæ*. Euseb. hist. Eccl. li. 2 c. 22.

Bib. an. 1579. 1580. an. 1577. 1562.

An other reading in the margent.

Item vve giue the Reader in places of some importance, an other reading in the margent, specially vvhen the Greeke is agreable to the same. as Io. 4. *transiet de morte ad vitam.* Other Latin copies haue, *transiit*, and so it is in the Greeke.

The pointing sometime altered.

Vve binde not our selues to the pointes of any one copie, print, or edition of the vulgar Latin, in places of no controuersie, but folovv the pointing most agreable to the Greeke and to the fathers commentaries. As Col. 1, 10. *Ambulantes dignè Deo, per omnia placentes. Vvalking vvorthy of God, in al things pleasing.* ἀξίως τοῦ κυρίου εἰς πᾶσαν ἀρεσκείαν. *Eph.* 1, 17. Vve point thus, *Deus Domini nostri Iesu Christi, pater gloriæ.* as in the Greeke, and S. Chrysostom, & S. Hierom both in text and commentaries. Vvhich the Catholike reader specially must marke, lest he finde fault, vvhen he seeth our translation disagree in such places from the pointing of his Latin Testament.

The margent reading sometime preferred before the text.

Vve translate sometime the word that is in the Latin margent, and not that in the text, when by the Greeke or the fathers we see it is a manifest fault of the writers heretofore, that mistooke one word for an other. As, *In fine*, not, *in fide*, 1. Pet. 3. v. 8. *præsentiam*, not, *præscientiam*, 2 Pet. 1. v. 16. Heb. 13. *latuerunt*, not, *placuerunt*.

Thus we haue endeuoured by al meanes to satisfie the indifferent reader, and to helpe his vnderstanding euery way, both in the text, and by Annotations: and withal to deale most sincerely before God and man, in translating and expounding the most sacred text of the holy Testament. Fare wel good Reader, and if we profit the any whit by our poore paines let vs for Gods sake be partakers of thy deuout praiers, & together with humble and contrite hart call vpō our Sauiour Christ to cease these troubles & stormes of his derest spouse: in the meane time comforting our selues with this saying of S. Augustine: *That Heretikes, vvhen they receiue povver corporally to afflict the Church, doe exercise her patience: but vvhen they oppugne her onely by their euil doctrine or opinions, then they exercise her vvisedom.* De ciuit. Dei li. 18. ca. 51.

THE SIGNIFICATION OR MEANING OF THE NVMBERS AND MARKES vsed in this Nevv Testament.

THE numbers in the inner margent of the text,ſhevv the number of verſes in euery Chapter.

The numbers in the Arguments before euery Chapter, point to the ſame numbers of verſes in the text, treating of the ſame matter.

The numbers in the beginning of the Annotations, ſignifie, that the Annotation is vpon ſuch a verſe of the text.

The numbers in the inner margent, or els vvhere, ioyned to the citations of Scripture,if they be vvritten thus,Gen.4,16. the firſt is the chapter,the ſecond is the verſe.If thus,Gen.4.16. both are the Chapters.If thus,Gen.4,16.17.18.the firſt is the chapter,al the reſt,the verſes.If thus,Gen.4,16.5,7.it ſignifieth, chap.4.verſ.16. and chap.5.verſ.7.

† This croſſe ſignifieth the beginning of euery verſe.

" This marke in the text, ſignifieth that there is an Annotation vpon that vvord or vvordes vvhich folovv the ſaid marke.

* This ſtarre in the text,or in the Annotatiōs, ſignifieth the allegations cited ouer againſt the ſame in the margent,or ſome other thing anſvvering therevnto.

' ' This marke ſhevveth an other reading in the margent. And if there be nothing in the margent, it ſignifieth that thoſe vvordes are not in ſome copies.

:: c b Theſe notes in the text, referre the reader to the ſelf ſame in the margent.

Mt. for Matthevv.

Mr. for Marke.

⊣ This marke ſignifieth the ending of Goſpels and Epiſtles.

Their beginning is knovven by the margent, vvhere directly at the beginning of them,is ſet, *The Goſpel, or , The Epiſtle vpon ſuch a day.* And if it could not be ſo ſet directly (becauſe of other marginal notes) then b is the marke of their beginning. And if ſome fevv by ouerſight be not noted in the margent,it is ſupplied in the table of Epiſtles and Goſpels,at the end of this booke.

THE BOOKES OF THE NEVV Testament, according to the counte of the Catholike Churche.

1 The infallible authoritie and excellencie of them aboue al other writings.

S. Augustine li. 11. cont. Faustum. cap. 5.

THe excellencie of the Canonical authoritie of the old and new Testament, is distincted from the bookes of later writers: which being confirmed in the Apostles times, by the successions of Bishops, and propagations of Churches, is placed as it were in a certaine throne on high, whereunto euery faithful & godly vnderstanding must be subiect and obedient. There, if any thing moue or trouble thee as absurd, thou maiest not say, The author of this booke held not the truth: but, either the copie is faultie, or the Translatour erred, or thou vnderstandest not. But in the workes of them that wrote afterward, which are conteined in infinite bookes, but are in no case equal to that most sacred authoritie of CANONICAL SCRIPTVRES: in which soeuer of them is found euen the same truth, yet the authoritie is far vnequal.

2 The discerning of Canonical from not Canonical, and of their infallible truth, and sense, commeth vnto vs, only by the credite vve giue vnto the CATHOLIKE CHVRCHE: through vvhose cõmendation vve beleeue both the Gospel and Christ him self. Vvhereas the Sectaries measure the matter by their fantasies and opinion.

S. Augustine cont. Epist. fundamenti cap. 5.

I for my part, vvould not beleeue the Gospel, vnles the authoritie of the CATHOLIKE CHVRCH moued me. They therfore whom I obeied saying, Beleeue the Gospel: vvhy should I not beleeue them saying, Beleeue not * Manichæus? Choose vvhether thou vvilt. If thou wilt say, Beleeue the Catholikes: loe they vvarne me that I giue no credite vnto you: and therefore beleeuing them, I must needes not beleeue thee. If thou say, Beleeue not the Catholikes: it is not the right vvay, by the Gospel to driue me to the faith of Manichæus, because I beleeued

Luther, Caluin.

ued the Gospel it self by the preaching of Catholikes.

Againe li. de vtilit. credend. cap. 14.

I see that concerning Christ him self, I haue beleeued none, but the confirmed and assured opinion of peoples and nations: and that these peoples haue on euery side possessed the mysteries of the CATHOLIKE CHVRCH. Vvhy should I not therfore most diligently require, specially among them, what Christ commaunded, by vvhose authoritie I vvas moued to beleeue, that Christ did commaund some profitable thing? Vvilt thou (ô Heretike) tel me better vvhat he said? vvhom I vvould not thinke to haue been at al, or to be, if I must beleeue, because thou saiest it. Vvhat grosse madnes is this, to say, Beleeue the Catholikes, that Christ is to be beleeued: and learne of vs, vvhat he said.

Againe cont. Faustum li. 11. cap. 2.

Thou seest then in this matter what force the authoritie of the CATHOLIKE CHVRCH hath, vvhich euen from the most grounded and founded seates of the Apostles, is established vntil this day, by the line of Bishops succeding one an other, & by the consent of so many peoples. *Vvhereas* thou saiest, This is *Scripture*, or, this is such an Apostles, that is not: because this soundeth for me, and the other against me. Thou then art the rule of truth. vvhatsoeuer is against thee, is not true.

3 No heretikes haue right to the Scriptures, but are vsurpers: the Catholike Church being the true ovvner and faithful keeper of them. Heretikes abuse them, corrupt them, and vtterly seeke to abolish them, though they pretend the contrarie.

Tertullian li. De præscriptionibus, *bringeth in the* CATHOLIKE CHVRCH *speaking thus to all Heretikes.*

Vvho are you, vvhen, and from vvhence came you? vvhat doe you in my possession, that are none of mine? by vvhat right (Marcion) doest thou cut dovvne my wood? vvho gaue the licence (ô Valentine) to turne the course of my fountaines? by vvhat authoritie (Apelles) doest thou remoue my boundes? and * you the rest, vvhy do yovv sovv and feede for these companions at your pleasure? It is my possession, I possesse it of old, I haue assured origins thereof, euen from those authors vvhose the thing vvas. I am the heire of the Apostles. As they prouided by their Testament, as they comitted it to my credite, as they adiured me, so doe I hold it. You surely they disherited alvvaies and haue cast you of, as forainers, as enemies.

§ Luther, Zuinglius, Caluin.

** Their scholers & folovvers.*

Againe in the same booke.

Encountering vvith such by Scriptures, auaileth nothing, but to ouerturne a mans stomake or his braine. This heresie receiueth not certaine Scriptures: and if it do receiue some, yet by adding and taking avvay, it peruerteth the same to serue their purpose: and if it receiue any, it doth not receiue them vvholy: and if after a sort it receiue them vvholy, neuertheles by diuising diuers expositions, it turneth them cleane an other vvay &c.

4 Yet do they vaunt them selues of Scriptures excedingly, but they are neuer the more to be trusted for that.

S. Hierom aduersus Luciferianos in fine.

Let them not flatter them selues, if they seeme in their ovvne conceite to affirme that vvhich they say, out of the chapters of Scripture: vvhereas the Diuel also spake some thinges out of the Scriptures, and the Scriptures consist not in the reading, but in the vnderstanding.

Vincentius Lirinensis li. cont. prophanas hæresum Nouationes.

Here perhaps some man may aske, vvhether heretikes also vse not the testimonies of diuine Scripture. Yes in deede do they, and that vehemently. For thou shalt see them flie through euery one of the sacred bookes of the Lavv, through Moyses, the bookes of the kings, the Psalmes, the Apostles, the Gospels, the Prophets. For, vvhether among their ovvne fellowes, or strangers: vvhether priuatly, or publikely: vvhether in talke, or in their bookes: vvhether in bankets, or in the streates: they (I say) alleage nothing of their ovvne, which they endeuour not to shadow vvith the wordes of Scripture also. Read the vvorkes of Paulus Samosatenus, of Priscillian, of Eunomian, of Iouinian,* of the other plagues & pestilences: thou shalt finde an infinite heape of examples, no page in a manner omitted or voide, which is not painted and coloured with the sentences of the new or old testament. But they are so much the more to be taken heede of, & to be feared, the more secretly they lurke vnder the shadowes of Gods diuine law. For they knovv their stinkes vvould not easily please any man almost, if they were breathed out nakedly & simply them selues alone, & therfore they sprinkle them as it vvere vvith certaine pretious spices of the heauenly vvord: to the end that he vvhich would easely despise the errour of man, may not easely contemne the oracles of God. So that they doe like vnto them, vvhich vvhen they vvil prepare certaine bitter potions for children, do first anoint the brimmes of the cup vvith honie, that the vnwarie age, vvhen it shal first feele the svvetnes, may not feare the bitternes.

* Of Caluin, of Iuel, of the rest.

5 **The cause vvhy, the Scriptures being perfit, yet vve vse other Ecclesiastical vvritings and tradition.**

Vincentius Lirinensis in his golden booke before cited, aduersus prophanas hæresum Nouationes.

Here some man perhaps may aske, for asmuch as the Canon of the Scriptures is perfit, and in all pointes very sufficient in it self, vvhat neede is there, to ioyne therevnto the authoritie of the* Ecclesiastical vnderstanding? for this cause surely, for that all take not the holy Scripture in one and the same sense, because of the deepenes thereof. but the speaches thereof, some interpret one vvay, & some an other vvay, so that there may almost as many senses be picked out of it, as there be men. for, Nouatian doth expound it one vvay, and Sabellius, an other vvay, othervvise Donatus, othervvise Arius, Eunomius, Macedonius, othervvise Photinus, Apollinaris, Priscillianus, othervvise Iouinian, Pelagius, Celestius, lastly othervvise Nestorius.* And therfore very necessarie it is, because of so great vvindinges and turninges of diuers errours, that the line of Prophetical and Apostolical interpretation, be directed according to the rule of the Ecclesiastical and Catholike sense or vnderstanding.

* So he calleth the Churches sense, and the fathers interpretations of Scriptures.

* Othervvise Wicleffe, Luther, Caluin, Puritanes.

S. Basil li. de Spiritu sancto cap. 27.

Of such articles of religion as are kept and preached in the Churche, some vvere taught by the vvritten vvord, other some vve haue receiued by the tradition of the Apostles, deliuered vnto vs as it vvere from hand to hand in mysterie secretly: both vvhich be of one force to Christian religion: and this no man vvil deny that hath any litle skill of the Ecclesiastical rites or customes. for if vve goe about to reiect the customes not conteined in Scripture, as being of smal force, vve shal vnvvittingly and vnavvares mangle the GOSPEL it self in the principal partes thereof, yea rather, vve shal abridge the very preaching of the Gospel, and bring it to a bare name.

THE

THE SVMME OF THE NEW TESTAMENT.

THAT *which was the summe of the Old Testament, to wit,* Christ and his Church, *as S. Augustine saith catechizing the ignorant: the very same is the summe of the New Testament also. For (as the same S. Augustine saith againe)* In the Old Testament there is the occultation of the New: and in the New Testament there is the manifestation of the Old. *And in another place:* In the Old doth the New lye hidden, and in the New doth the Old lye open. *And therupon our Sauiour said:* I am not come to breake the Law or the Prophets, but to fulfill them. For assuredly I say vnto you, til heauen and earth passe, one iote or one title shall not passe of the Law, till all be fulfilled. *In vvhich vvordes he shevveth plainely, that the nevv Testament is nothing els but the fulfilling of the old.*

Aug. de cat. rud. cap. 3. 4.

Super Exod. q. 73.

Mat. 5.

Therfore to come to the partes: The Gospels *doe tell of Christ him selfe (of vvhom the Old Testamēt did foretell) and that euen from his coming into the vvorld, vnto his going out therof againe.* The Actes of the Apostles *doe tell of his Church beginning at Hierusalem the headcitie of the Ievves, and of the propagation therof to the Gentiles and their headcitie Rome. And* the Apocalypse *doth prophecie of it, euen to the consummation therof, which shal be in the end of the world.* The Epistles of the Apostles *do treat partly of such questions as at that time were moued, partly of good life and good order.*

The Summe of the 4 Gospels.

THE *Gospels doe tell historically the life of our Lord Iesus, shevving plainely, * that he is Christ or the king of the Ievves, vvhom vntil then, al the time of the Old Testament, they had expected: and vvithal, that they of their ovvne mere malice and blindnes (the iniquitie beginning of the Seniors, but at the length the multitude also consenting) vvould not receaue him, but euer sought his death: vvhich for the Redemption of the vvorld, he at length permitted them to compasse, they deseruing thereby most iustely to be refused of him, and so his Kingdom or Church to be taken avvay from them, and giuen to the Gentils. For the gathering of vvhich Church after him, he chooseth Tvvelue, and appointeth one of them to be the cheefe of al, vvith instructions both to them and him accordingly.*

Io. 20, 31.

The storie hereof is vvritten by foure: vvho in Ezechiel and in the Apocalypse are likened to foure liuing creatures, euery one according as his booke beginneth. S. Matthevv to a Man, because he beginneth vvith the pedegree of Christ as he is man. S. Marke to a Lion, because he beginneth vvith the preaching of S. Iohn Baptist, as it vvere the roaring of a lion in the vvildernes. S. Luke to a Calfe, because he beginneth vvith a priest of the Old Testament (to vvit, Zacharie the father of S. Iohn Baptist) vvhich Priesthood vvas to sacrifice calues to God. S. Iohn to an Egle, because he beginneth vvith the Diuinitie of Christ, flying so high as more is not possible.

Eze. 1. Apoc. 4.

The first three do report at large vvhat Christ did in Galilee, after the imprisonment of S. Iohn Baptist. Vvherefore S. Iohn the Euangelist vvriting after them all, doth omit his doinges in Galilee (saue onely one, vvhich they had not vvritten of, the vvonderful bread vvhich he told the Capharnaites he could and vvould giue, Io. 6.) and reporteth first, vvhat he did vvhiles Iohn Baptist as yet vvas preaching and baptizing: then, after Iohns imprisoning, vvhat he did in Iurie euery yere about Easter. But of his Passion all foure do vvrite at large.

Vvhere it is to be noted, that from his baptizing (vvhich is thought to haue been vpon Tvvelfthday, vvhat time he was beginning to be about 30 yere old, *Luk. 3.) vnto his passion, are numbred three monethes and three yeres, in vvhich there vvere also 4 Easters.*

The argument of S. Matthewes Gospel.

S. Matthevves Gospel may be vvell diuided into fiue partes. The first parte, as touching the Infancie of our Lord Iesus: Chap. 1 and 2.

The second, of the preparation that vvas made to his manifestation: chap. 3. and a piece of the 4.

The third, of his manifesting of him selfe by preaching and miracles, and that in Galilee: the other piece of the 4. chap. vnto the 19.

The fourth, of his comming into Iurie, tovvard his Passion: chap. 19. and 20.

The fifth, of the Holy vveeke of his Passion in Hierusalem: chap. 21 vnto the end of the booke.

Of S. Matthew vve haue Mat. 9. Mar. 2. Lu. 5: How being before a Publican, he vvas called of our Lord, and made a Disciple. Then Luk. 6. Mar. 3. Mat. 10: Hovv out of the vvhole number of the Disciples he vvas chosen to be one of the tvvelue Apostles. And out of them againe he vvas chosen (and none but he and S. Iohn) to be one of the foure Euangelistes. Among vvhich foure also, he vvas the first that vvrote, about 8 or 10 yeres after Christes Ascension.

THE

THE HOLY GOSPEL OF IESVS CHRIST ACCORDING TO MATTHEW.

THE FIRST part of this Gospel, of the Infancie of our Sauiour Christ.

CHAP. I.

*The pedegree of Iesus, to shew that he is Christ, promised to * Abraham and * Dauid. II. That he was conceiued and borne of a Virgin, as Esay prophecied of him.*

1 THE booke of the * generation of IESVS Christ, the sonne of Dauid, the sonne of Abraham.

2 †* Abraham begat Isaac, And Isaac begat Iacob. And Iacob begat Iudas and his brethren: 3 † And Iudas begat Phares and Zaram of" Thamar. * And Phares begat 4 Esron. And Esron begat Aram. † And Aram begat Aminadab. And Aminadab begat Naasson. And Naasson begat 5 Salmon. † And Salmon begat Booz of Raab. And Booz begat 6 Obed of Ruth. And Obed begat Iesse. † And Iesse begat Dauid the King.

And * Dauid the King begat Salomon of her that was the 7 vvife of Vrias. † And * Salomon begat Roboam. And Ro- 8 boam begat Abia. And Abia begat Asa. † And Asa begat Iosaphat. And Iosaphat begat Ioram. And Ioram begat Ozias. 9 † And Ozias begat Ioatham. And Ioatham begat Achaz. And 10. Achaz begat Ezechias. † And Ezechias begat Manasses. And 11 Manasses begat Amon. And Amon begat Iosias. † And Iosias begat Iechonias & his brethren * in the Transmigration of Babylon.

12 † And after the Transmigration of Babylon, * Iechonias 13 begat Salathiel. * And Salathiel begat Zorobabel. † And Zorobabel begat Abiud. And Abiud begat Eliacim. And Eliacim 14 begat Azor. † And Azor begat Sadoc. And Sadoc begat Achim. 15 And Achim begat Eliud. † And Eliud begat Eleazar. And 16 Eleazar begat Mathan. And Mathan begat Iacob. † And Iacob

This Gospel is most solemly sung in holy Church at Mattins vpō Christmas day.
As also it is the Gospel of the *Coception* and *Natiuitie* of our B. Lady: because here is declared the pedegree of her also.

begat " Ioseph the " husband of MARIE: :: of vvhom vvas borne IESVS, vvho is called CHRIST. ┤ :: *de qua*

† Therefore al the generations from Abraham vnto Dauid, 17 fourtene generations. And from Dauid to the Transmigration of Babylon, fourtene generations. And from the Transmigration of Babylon vnto CHRIST, fourtene generations.

The Gospel vpõ Christmas eue. and Vpon S. Iosephs day the 19 of Marche.

† And the generation of CHRIST vvas in this vvise. 18 When his mother MARIE vvas spoused to Ioseph, before they came together, she vvas found to be vvith childe by the Holy Ghost. † Wherevpon Ioseph, for that he vvas a iust man, 19 & vvould not * put her to open shame: vvas minded secretely to dimisse her. † But as he vvas thus thinking, behold the 20 Angel of our Lord appeared to him in sleepe saying: Ioseph sonne of Dauid, feare not to take MARIE thy vvife. for that vvhich is " borne in her, is of the Holy Ghost. † And she shal 21 bring forth a sonne: and thou shalt call his name :: IESVS. For he shal saue his people from their sinnes. ┤ † And 22 al this vvas done that it might be fulfilled vvhich our Lord spake by the Prophet saying. † *Behold " a Virgin shal be vvith childe,* 23 *and " bring forth a sonne, and they shal call his name Emmanuel,* vvhich being interpreted is, *God vvith vs.* † And Ioseph rising vp from sleepe, 24 did as the Angel of our Lord cõmaunded him, and tooke his vvife. † And he knevv her not " til she brought forth her " first- 25 borne sonne: and called his name IESVS.

Deu. 24, 1.

:: IESVS an Hebrue Word, in English SAVIOVR.

Esa. 7, 14.

ANNOTATIONS
CHAP. I.

1. Thamar.] Christ abhorred not to take flesh of some that Were il, as he chose Iudas among his Apostles: Let not vs disdaine to receaue our spiritual birth and sustenance of such as be not alWayes good.

16. Ioseph.] Ioseph marying our Lady as neere of kinne (for so Was the * law) by his pedegree sheWeth hers, and consequently Christs pedegree from Dauid. *Nu. 36.*

16. Husband.] True and perfect mariage, and continual liuing in the same, Without carnal copulation. *Aug. lib. 2. Consen. Euang. c. 1.*

20. Borne in her.] The triple good or perfection of mariage accomplished in the parents of Christ, to Wit, Issue, Fidelitie, Sacrament. *Aug. de nup. & conc. li. 1. c. 11.*

Virginitie preferred.

23. A Virgin.] Our Sauiour borne in mariage, but yet of a Virgin, Would honour both states: and Withal, teacheth vs agaynst Iouinian the old Heretike and these of our time, that virginity and the continent life are preferred before mariage that hath carnal copulation. *See S. Hierom. adu. Iouin.* and *S. Greg. Nazianz. Ser. 20. de studio in pauperes, in initio.*

23. A Virgin.] As our Ladie both a virgin and a mother, brought forth Christ the head corporally: so the Churche a virgin and a mother, bringeth forth the members of this head spiritually. *Aug. li. de Virg. ca. 2.*

Our B. Ladies perpetual virginity.

23. And bring forth.] The Heretike Iouinian is here refuted, holding that her virginity Was corrupted in bringing forth Christ. *Aug. her. 82. Li. 1 cont. Iulian. c. 2.*

25. Til

25. *Til, First-borne.*] Heluidius of old abused these wordes, *til*, and, *first-borne*, agaynst the perpetual virginity of our B. Ladie. *Hiero. cont. Helu.* Which truth though not expressed in Scripture, yet our Aduersaries also do graunt, and Heluidius for denial therof was condemned for an heretike by tradition only. *Aug. hær. 84.*

Tradition.

CHAP. II.

The Gentils come vnto Christ with their offerings, and that so openly, that the Iewes can not pretend ignorance. 3 The Iewes with Herode conspire against him. 13 He therevpon fleeth from them into Ægypt. 16 They afterward, seing their subteltie preuailed not, imagined to oppresse him by open persecution. 19 But they at length dyed, and he returneth to the land of Israel: al according to the Scriptures.

The holy feast of the *Epiphanie* called *Twelfth-day* the 6 of Ianuarie. vpon which day this is the Gospel.

Luc. 2, 7.

1 WHEN IESVS therfore vvas * borne in Bethlehem of Iuda in the dayes of Herod the King, " behold, there came Sages from the East to Hierusalem, 2 † saying, vvhere is he that is borne King of the Ievves? For vve haue seene his " starre in the East, and " are 3 come to adore him. † And Herod the King hearing this, vvas 4 troubled, & al Hierusalem vvith him. † And assembling together al the high Priestes & the Scribes of the people, he " inquired of them vvhere Christ should be borne. 5 †But they sayd to him, In Bethlehē of Iuda. For so it is vvritten by the Prophet:

Mich. 5, 2.

6 †*And thou Bethlehem the land of Iuda, art not the least among the Princes of Iuda: for out of thee shal come forth the Capitaine that shal rule my people Israel.*

7 † Then Herod secretly calling the Sages, learned diligently of 8 them the time of the starre which appeared to them: †and sending them into Bethlehem, sayd, Goe, and inquire diligently of the childe: and when you shal finde him, make reporte to me, that I also may come and adore him.

9 † Who hauing heard the king, went their way: and behold the starre which they had seen in the East, went before them, 10 vntil it came & stoode ouer, where the childe was.† And seing 11 the starre, they reioyced vvith exceding great ioy. † And entring into the house, they found the childe vvith MARIE his mother, & falling dovvne " adored him: and opening their " treasures, they offered to him *" giftes: gold, frankincense, & 12 myrrhe. † And hauing receiued an ansvver in sleepe that they should not returne to Herod, they vvent backe an other vvay into their countrey. ✠

Psa. 71, 10.

The Gospel of *Childermas* day.

13 † And after they vvere departed, behold an Angel of our Lord appeared in sleepe to Ioseph, saying: Arise, & take the childe & his mother, & flee into Ægypt: and be there vntil I shal tel the. For it vvil come to passe that Herod vvil seeke 14 the childe to destroy him. † Who arose, & tooke the childe

and his mother by night, and retyred into Ægypt: and he vvas there vntil the death of Herod: † that it might be fulfil- 15 led vvhich vvas spoken of our Lord by the Prophet, saying, "*Out of Aegypt haue I called my sonne.*

Os. 11, 2.

The Martyrdō of the holy *Innocents*, whose holy day is kept the 28 of Decembre.

† Then Herod perceauing that he vvas deluded by the Sa- 16 ges, Was exceding angrie: and sending "murdered al the men children that vvere in Bethlehem, & in al the borders therof, from tvvo yere old & vnder, according to the time vvhich he had diligently sought out of the Sages. † Then was fulfilled 17 that vvhich vvas spoken by Ieremie the Prophet saying, † *A voice in Rama vvas heard, crying out & much vvayling: Rachel bevvayling* 18 *her children, & vvould not be comforted, because they are not.* ⊣

Iere. 31, 15.

The Gospel on Twelfth eue.

† But vvhen Herod vvas dead, behold an Angel of our Lord 19 appeared in sleepe to Ioseph in Ægypt, † saying, Arise, and take 20 the childe & his mother, & goe into the land of Israel. for they are dead that sought the life of the childe. † Who arose, & 21 tooke the childe & his mother, and came into the land of Israel. † But hearing that Archelaus reigned in Ievvrie for Herod 22 his father, he feared to goe thither: and being vvarned in sleepe retyred into the quarters of Galilee. † And coming he dvvelt 23 in a citie called Nazareth: that it might be fulfilled vvhich vvas sayd by the Prophetes: That he shal be called a Nazarite.

ANNOTATIONS
CHAP. II.

1. *Behold.*] Our Lordes apparition or Epiphanie to these Sages being Gentils, their Pilgrimage to him, and in them the first homage of Gentilitie done vnto him the twelfth day after his Natiuitie: and therfore is *Twelfth day* highly celebrated in the Catholike Churche for ioy of the calling of vs Gentils. His baptisme also and first miracle are celebrated on the same day.

2. *Starre.*] Christs Natiuitie depended not vpon this starre, as the Priscillianists falsely surmised: but the starre vpon his Natiuitie, for the seruice whereof it was created. *Grego. Ho. 10.*

Pilgrimage.

2. *Come to adore.*] This coming so far of deuotion to visite and adore Christ in the place of his birth, was proprely a Pilgrimage to his person: and warranteth the faithful in the like kind of external worship done to holy persons, places, and things.

4. *Inquired of them.*] The high Priests were rightly consulted in quæstion of their law and religion, and be they neuer so il, are often forced to say the truth by priuilege of their vnction: as here and after, they did concerning the true Messias.

Adoratiō of the B. Sacrament.

11. *Adored him*] This body (*saith S. Chrysostom.*) the Sages adored in the cribbe. Let vs at the least imitate them: thou seest him not now in the cribbe, but on the altar: not a woman holding him, but the Priest present, and the Holy Ghost powred out aboundantly vpon the sacrifice. *Ho. 24. in 1. Cor. Ho. 7. in Mt. Ho. de sancto Philogonio.*

11. *Treasures.*] These treasures are as it were the first fruites of those riches and gifts, which (according to the Prophecies of Dauid and Esay) Gentilitie should offer to Christ and his Churche, and now haue offered, specially from the time of Constantine the Great. As also these three Sages, being principal men of their Countrie, represent the whole state of Princes, kings, and Emperours, that were (according to the said Prophecies) to beleeue in Christ, to humble them selues to his crosse, to foster, enriche, adorne and defend his Church. Wherevpon it is also a very conuenient and agreable tradition of antiquitie, and a receiued opinion among the faithful, * not lacking testimonies of ancient writers, and much for the honour of our Sauiour, that these three also were kings: to witte, either according to the state of those Countries, * where the Princes were

Psal. 71. Esa. 60.

Chrys. Theophyl. Cic. de Diuinat. Plin. li. 2.

The three kings.

Esther 1, 13. 14. Tob. 2. Amb. 1. Off. c.12.

were *Magi*, and * *Magi* the greatest about the Prince: or as we read in the Scriptures, of Melchisedec king of Salem, and many other kings that dwelt within a small compasse: or as * Iobes three freendes are called kings. These are commonly called the three kings of Colen, because their bodies are there, translated thither from the East Countrie: their names are said to haue been Gaspar, Melchior, Baltasar.

11. Gifts.] These Sages were three, and their gifts three, and eche one offered euerie of the three, to expresse our faith of the Trinitie. The Gold, to signifie that he was a King: the frankincense, that he was God: the myrrhe, that he was to be buried as man. *Aug. ser. 1. de Epiph.*

15. Out of Aegypt.] This place of the Prophete (and the like in the new Testament) here applied to Christ, wheras in the letter it might seeme otherwise, teacheth vs how to interprete the old Testament, and that the principal sense is of Christ and his Churche.

16. Murdered.] By this example we learne how great credite we owe to the Churche in Canonizing Saints, and celebrating their holy daies: by whose only warrant, without any word of Scripture, these holy Innocents haue been honoured for Martyrs, and their holy day kept euer since the Apostles time, although they died not voluntarily, nor al perhaps circuncised, and some the children of Pagans. *Aug. ep. 28. Orig. ho. 3. in diuersos.*

Canonizing of Saincts.

CHAP. III.

Iohn Baptist by his Eremites life, by his preaching and baptisme, calleth al vnto penance, to prepare them to Christ. 10. He preacheth to the Pharisees and Sadducees, threatening to them (vnles they truly doe penance) reprobation here and damnation hereafter: and for saluation sendeth them to Christ and his baptisme. Which being far more excellent then Iohns, yet Christ him self among those penitents vouchsafeth to come vnto Iohns baptisme. Where he hath testimonie from heauen also.

THE SEcond part of this Gospel, Of the Preparatiō that was made to the manifestation of Christ.

Mr. 1, 4. Luc. 3, 3. Es. 40, 3

1 AND in those dayes * cometh Iohn the Baptist 2 preaching in the " desert of Ievvrie, † & saying, "Doe penance: for the Kingdom of heauen is at 3 hand. † For this is he that vvas spoken of by Esay the Prophet, saying, *A voyce of one crying in the desert, prepare ye the vvay of our Lord, make straight his pathes.* 4 † And the sayd Iohn had his garment of camels heare, & a girdle of a skinne about his loynes: and his meate was locustes & vvilde honie.

5 † Then vvent forth to him Hierusalem & al Ievvrie, and 6 al the countrey about Iordan: † & vvere baptized of him in 7 Iordan, " confessing their sinnes. † And seeing many of the Pharisees & Sadducees coming to his baptisme, he sayd to them.

8 Ye vipers brood, vvho hath shevved you to flee from the vvrath to come? † Yeld therfore " fruite vvorthie of penance. 9 † And delite not to say vvithin your selues, vve haue Abraham to our father. for I tel you that God is able of these 10 stones to raise vp children to Abraham. † For novv the " axe is put to the roote of the trees. Euery tree therefore that doth :: not yeld good fruite, shal be cut dovvne, & cast into the fyre. 11 † * I in deede baptize you " in vvater vnto penance. but he that shal come after me, is stronger then I, vvhose shoes I am not vvorthie to beare, he shal baptize you in the Holy Ghost & fire

*Mr. 1, 8 Lu. 3. 16. Io. 1, 26. Act. 11, 16. 19, 4.

:: It is not only damnable, to doe il: but also, not to doe good. *Aug. Ser. 61 de temp.*

& fire. †Whose fanne is in his hand, and he shal cleane purge 12 his " floore: and he vvil gather his vvheate into the barne, but the chaffe he vvil burne vvith vnquencheable fire.

† Then cometh IESVS from Galilee to Iordan, vnto Iohn, 13 to be baptized of him. † But Iohn stayed him, saying, I ought 14 to be baptized of thee, and comest thou to me? † And IESVS 15 ansvvering, sayd to him, Suffer me for this time. for so it becommeth vs to fulfil al iustice. Then he suffered him. † And 16 IESVS being baptized, forthvvith came-out of the vvater: and loe the heauens vvere " opened to him: and he savv the Spirit of God descending as a doue, & coming vpon him. † And 17 behold a voyce from heauen saying, This is my beloued sonne, in vvhom I am vvel pleased.

ANNOTATIONS
CHAP. III.

Eremites.

1. Desert.] Of this Word *desert* (in Greeke *eremus*) commeth the name *Eremitages*, and *Eremites*, that liue a religious and austere life in deserts and solitarie places, by the example of S. Iohn Baptist, Whom the holy Doctors therfore call the Prince and as it Were the author of such profession. *S. Chrys. ho. 1 in Marcum & ho. de Io. Baptista. Hiero. ad Eustoch. de custod. virg. Isid. li. 2. c. 15 de diu off. Bernardus de excel. Io. Baptistæ.* WhereWith the Protestants are so offended that * they say, S. Chrysostom spake rashly and vntruely. And no maruel, for Whereas the Euangelist him self in this place maketh him a perfect paterne of penance and Eremitical life, for desert or Wildernes, for his rough and rude apparel, for abstayning from al delicate meates (according to our Sauiours testimonie also of him Mt. 11, 8. Luc. 7, 33) they are not ashamed to peruert all With this strange commentarie, that it Was a desert * full of toWnes and villages, his garment Was * chamlet, his meate * such as the countrey gaue and the people there vsed: to make him thereby but a common man like to the rest, in his maner of life: cleane against Scriptures, fathers, and reason.

Magdeb. Cent. 1. c. 6. pag. 711. Cent. 1. li. 1. c. 10. Cythræus in 3. cap. Mat. Bucerus ibid.

See Canis. de verb. Dei corruptelis li. 1. c. 2. 3. 4.

Penance.

2. Doe penance.) So is the Latin, Word for Word, so readeth al antiquitie, namely S. Cyprian ep. 52 often, and S. Augustine li. 13 Confes. c. 12. and it is a very vsual speache in the NeW Testament, specially in the preaching of S. Iohn Baptist, * Christ him self, and * the Apostles: to signifie perfect repentance, Which hath not onely confession and amendment, but contrition or soroW for the offense, and paineful satisfaction: such as S. Cyprian speaketh of in al the foresaid epistle. But the Aduersaries of purpose (as * namely Beza protesteth) mislike that interpretation, because it fauoureth Satisfaction for sinne, Which they cannot abide. Where if they pretend the ∷ Greeke Word, We send them to these places Mat. 11, 21. Lu. 10, 13. 1 Cor. 7, 9. Where it must needes signifie, soroWful, payneful, and satisfactorie repentance. We tel them also that * S. Basil a Greeke Doctor calleth the Niniuites repentance With fasting and hearecloth and ashes, by the same Greeke Word μετάνοιαν. And more We Wil tell them in other places.

Mt. 4, 17. Lu. 13, 3. 5. Lu. 24, 47. Act. 2, 38. 26, 20. Annot. in hunc locū. Serm. in fam. & siccit.

Μετανοεῖν. Μετάνοια.

6. Confessing their sinnes.) Iohn did prepare the Way to Christ and his Sacraments, not only by his baptisme, but by inducing the people to confession of their sinnes. Which is not to acknoWledge them selues in general to be sinners, but also to vtter euery man his sinnes.

8. Fruite Worthie.) He preacheth satisfaction by doing Worthy fruites or Workes of penance, Which are (as S. Hierom saith in 2. Ioel) fasting, praying, almes and the like.

10. The axe.) Here preachers are taught to dehort from doing euil for feare of Hel, and to exhort to doe good in hope of heauen: Which kind of preaching our Aduer. doe condemne.

Iohns baptisme and Christs.

11. In Water.] Iohns baptisme did not remitte sinnes, nor Was comparable to Christs Baptisme, as here it is playne and in manie other places. *Hiero. adu. Lucifer. Aug. de Bapt. cont. Donat. li. 5. c. 9. 10. 11.* Yet is it an article of our Adu. that thone is no better then the other. Which they say not to extol Iohns, but to derogate from Christes baptisme, so far, that they make it of no more valure or efficacie for remission of sinnes, and grace, and iustification, then Was Iohns: thereby to mainteine their manifold heresies, that Baptisme taketh not aWay sinnes, that a man is no cleaner nor iuster by the Sacrament of Baptisme then before, that it is not necessarie for children vnto saluation, but it is ynough to be borne of Christian parents, and such like erroneous positions wel knowen among the Caluinists.

12. Floore.) This floore is his Church militant here in earth, wherein are both good and bad (here signified by corne and chaffe) til the separation be made in the day of iudgement: contrarie to the doctrine of the Heretikes, that hold, the Church to consist onely of the good.

16. Opened.) To signifie that heauen was shut in the old law, til Christ by his Passion opened it, and so by his Ascension was the first that entered into it: contrarie to the doctrine of the Heretikes. *See Hebr. 9, 8. and 11, 40.*

CHAP. IIII.

Christ going into the desert to prepare him self before his Manifestation, ouercometh the Deuils tentations. 12 Beginning in Galilee, as the Prophet said he should: 18 he calleth foure Disciples: and with his preaching and miracles draweth vnto him innumerable folowers.

Mr. 1, 12 *Lu. 4, 1.* — The Gospel vpō the first Sunday in Lent.

1 THEN * IESVS was ledde of the Spirit into the " desert, to be tempted of the Deuil. 2 † And vvhen he had " fasted fourtie daies and fourtie nightes, aftervvard he vvas hungrie. 3 † And the tempter approched & sayd to him, If thou be the sonne of God, commaund that these stones be made bread. 4 † Who ansvvered & said, It is vvritten, *Not in bread alone doth man liue, but in euery word that procedeth from the mouth of God.* (*Deu. 8, 3*)

5 † Then the Deuil tooke him vp into the holy citie, and set 6 him vpon the pinnacle of the Tēple, † and sayd to him, If thou be the sonne of God, cast thy self dovvne, for " it is vvritten. *That he wil giue his Angels charge of thee, & in their hands shal they hold thee vp, lest perhaps thou knocke they foote agaynst a stone.* (*Ps. 90, 12.*) 7 † IESVS sayd to him againe, It is vvritten, *Thou shalt not tempt the Lord thy God.* (*Deu. 6, 16.*)

8 † Againe the Deuil tooke him vp into a very high mountaine: and he shevved him al the Kingdoms of the vvorld, and the 9 glorie of them, † and sayd to him, Al these vvil I giue thee, if 10 falling dovvne thou vvilt adore me. † Then IESVS sayth to him, Auant Satan: for it is vvritten, *The Lord thy God shalt thou adore, & " him onely shalt thou serue.* (*Deu. 6, 13.*) 11 † Then the Deuil left him: and behold Angels came, and ministred to him. ⁊

Mr. 1. 14 *Luc. 4, 14.* — THE THIRD part of the Gospel, of Christs manifesting him self by preaching, and that in Galilee.

12 † And * vvhen IESVS had heard that Iohn vvas deliuered 13 vp, he retyred into Galilee: † and leauing the citie Nazareth, came & dvvelt in Capharnaum a sea tovvne, in the borders of 14 Zabulon & Nephthali, † that it might be fulfilled vvhich vvas 15 sayd by Esay the Prophet. † *Land of Zabulon & land of Nephthali, the* 16 *way of the sea beyond Iordan of Galilee, of the Gentils: † the people that sate in darknesse, hath seen great light: and to them that sate in a countrey of the shadow* 17 *of death, light is risen to them.* (*Esa. 9, 1.*) † From that time IESVS began to

preach, and to say, ‖* Doe penance, for the Kingdom of heauen is at hand.

Mr. 1, 15.

The Gospel vpō S. Andrewes day.

† And IESVS * vvalking by the sea of Galilee, savv tvvo 18 brethren, Simon vvho is called Peter, & Andrevv his brother, casting a nette into the sea (for they vvere fishers) † & he sayth 19 to them, Come ye after me, and I vvil make you to be fishers of men. † But they incontinent leauing the nettes, folovved 20 him. † And going forvvard from thence, he savv * other tvvo 21 brethren, Iames of Zebedee & Iohn his brother in a shippe vvith Zebedee their father, repayring their nettes: and he called them. † And they furthvvith left their nettes & father and 22 folovved him. ⊣

Lu. 5, 1.

Mar. 1, 19. Luc. 5, 10.

† And IESVS vvent round about all Galilee, teaching in 23 their Synagogs, & preaching the Gospel of the Kingdom: and ‖ healing euery maladie and euery infirmitie in the people. † And the bruite of him vvent into al Syria, and they presented 24 to him al that vvere il at ease, diuersly taken vvith diseases and torments, and such as vvere possest, and lunatikes, and sicke of the palsey, and he cured them: † And much people folovved 25 him from Galilee and Decapolis, and Hierusalem, and from beyond Iordan.

ANNOTATIONS
CHAP. IIII.

Eremites.

1. Desert.] As Iohn the Baptist, so our Sauiour by going into the desert and there liuing in contemplation euen among brute beasts, and subiect to the assaults of the Diuel for our sinnes, geueth a warrant and example to such holy men as haue liued in wildernesse for penance and contemplation, called Eremites.

The Lent-fast.

2. Fasted fourtie daies.] Elias and Moyses (saith S. Hierom) by the fast of 40 daies were filled with the familiaritie of God, and our Lord him self in the wildernesse fasted as many, to leaue vnto vs the solemne daies of fast. (that is, Lent.) *Hiero. in c. 58 Esa.* S. Augustine also hath the very like wordes ep. 119. And generally al the ancient fathers that by occasion or of purpose speake of the Lent-fast, make it not onely an imitation of our Sauiours fast, but also an Apostolicall tradition, and of necessitie to be kept. *Contemne not Lent* (saith S. Ignatius) *for it conteineth the imitation of our Lordes conuersation.* And S. Ambrose saith plainely, that *it was not ordained by men, but consecrated by God: nor inuented by any earthly cogitation, but commaunded by the heauenly Maiestie.* And againe, that it is sinne not to fast al the Lent. S. Hieroms wordes also be most plaine: we (saith he) *fast fourtie daies, or, make one Lent in a yere, according to the tradition of the Apostles, in time conuenient.* This time most conuenient is (as S. Augustine saith ep. 119) immediatly before Easter, thereby to communicate with our Sauiours Passion: and (as other writers do adde) thereby to come the better prepared and more worthily, to the great solemnitie of Christes Resurrection: beside many other goodly reasons in the ancient fathers which for breuitie we omitte. See (good Christian Reader) 12 notable sermons of S. Leo the Great *de Quadragesima*, of Lent: namely Ser. 6 and 9. where he calleth it the Apostles ordinance by the doctrine of the Holy Ghost. See S. Ambrose from the 23 sermon forward: in S. Bernard 7 sermons, and in many other fathers the like. Last of al, note well the saying of S. Augustine, who affirmeth that by due obseruation thereof, the wicked be separated from the good, infidels from Christians, Heretikes from faithful Catholikes.

Igna. ep. 5. Ambr. de Quadrag. ser. 36. 34. Hier. ep. 54 ad Marcel. adu. Montanum.

Aug. Ser. 69. de tēp.

6. It is

6. It is written.] Heretikes alleage ſcriptures, as here the Deuil doeth, in the falſe ſenſe: the Churche vſeth them, as Chriſt doeth, in the true ſenſe, and to confute their falſehood. *Aug. cont. lit. Petil. li. 2. c. 51. to. 7.*

11. Him only ſerue.] It was not ſayd, ſayth S. Auguſtine, The Lord thy God only ſhalt thou adore, as it was ſaid, Him onely *ſhalt thou ſerue*: in Greeke, λατρεύσεις. *Aug. ſup. Gen. q. 61.* Wherevpon the Catholike Churche hath alwayes vſed this moſt true and neceſſarie diſtinction: that there is an honour dew to God only, which to giue vnto any creature, were idolatrie: and there is an honour dew to creatures alſo according to their dignitie, as to Saints, holy things, and holy places. See Euſeb. *Hiſt. Ec. li. 4. c. 14. S. Hierom. cont. Vigil. ep. 53. Aug. li. 10. Ciuit. c. 1. Li. 1. Trin. c. 6. Conc. Nic. 2. Damaſc. li. 1. de Imag. Bed. in 4. Luc.*

Latria. Dulia.

17. Doe penance.] That penance is neceſſarie alſo before baptiſme, for ſuch as be of age: as Iohns, ſo our Sauiours preaching declareth, both beginning with penance.

23. Healing euery maladie.] Chriſt (*ſaith S. Auguſtine*) by miracles gat authoritie, by authoritie found credit, by credit drew together a multitude, by a multitude obteyned antiquitie, by antiquitie fortified a Religion, which not only the moſt fond new ryſing of Heretikes vſing deceitful wiles, but neither the drowſie old errour of the very Heathen with violence ſetting agaynſt it, might in any part ſhake and caſt downe. *Aug. de vtil. cred. c. 14.*

CHAP. V.

The ſermon of Chriſt vpon the Mount: conteyning the paterne of a Chriſtian life, in theſe three chapters folowing. Wherof S. Auguſtine hath two goodly bookes to. 4.

Firſt, 3 he promiſeth rewardes, 13 and he layeth before the Apoſtles their office. 17 Secondly, he proteſteth vnto vs that we muſt keepe the commaundements, and that more exactly then the Scribes and Phariſees, whoſe iuſtice weas counted moſt perfite: but yet that it was vnſufficient, he ſheweth in the precepts of 21 Murder, 27 Aduoutrie, 31 Diuorce, 33 Swearing, 38 Reuenge, 42 Vſurie, 43 Enemies.

Luc. 6, 20.

1 AND ſeeing the multitudes, he * vvent vp into a mountaine: and vvhen he vvas ſet, his 2 Diſciples came vnto him, †and opening his mouth he taught them, ſaying.

The EIGHT Beatitudes: which are a part of the Catechiſme.

The Goſpel vpō Alholowes day, and vpon the feaſtes of many Martyrs.

3 † Bleſſed are the poore in Spirit: for theirs 4 is the Kingdom of heauen. † Bleſſed are the 5 meeke: for they ſhal poſſeſſe the land. † Bleſſed are they that 6 mourne: for they ſhal be comforted. † Bleſſed are they that hunger & thirſt after iuſtice: for they ſhal haue their fil. 7 † Bleſſed are the merciful: for they ſhal obtayne mercie. 8 † Bleſſed are the cleane of hart: for they ſhal ſee God. † Bleſſed 9 are the peace-makers: for they ſhal be called the children of 10 God. † Bleſſed are they that ſuffer perſecution ‖ for iuſtice: for 11 theirs is the Kingdom of heauen. † Bleſſed are ye vvhen they ſhal reuile you, and perſecute you, & ſpeake al that naught is 12 agaynſt you, vntruely, for my ſake: † be glad & reioyce, for your ‖ revvard is very great in heauen. ꟷ For ſo they perſecuted the Prophets, that vvere before you.

Mr. 9, 50., Luc. 14, 34.

The Goſpel on the feaſts of Doctors.

13 † You are the * ſalt of the earth. † But if the ſalt leeſe 14 his vertue, vvherevvith ſhal it be ſalted? It is good for nothing any more but to be caſt forth, and to be troden of 15 men. † You are the ‖ light of the vvorld. A citie cannot 16 be hid, ſituated on a mountaine. † Neither do men light a

* candel and put it vnder a bushel, but vpon a cādlesticke, that it may shine to al that are in the house. † So let " your light 17 shine before men: that they may see your good vvorkes, and glorifie your father vvhich is in heauen.

Mr. 4, 21
Lu. 8, 16
11, 33.

† Do not thinke that I am come to breake the Lavv or 18 the Prophets. I am not come to breake: but to fulfil. † For 19 assuredly I say vnto you, * til heauen and earth passe, one iote or one tittle shal not passe of the Lavv: til al be fulfilled. † He 20 therfore that shal * breake " one of these least commaundementes, & shal so teach men: shal be called the least in tho Kingdom of heauen. But he that shal doe and teach: he shal be called great in the Kingdom of heauen. ⁊ † For I tel you, 21 that vnles " your iustice abound more then that of the Scribes and Pharisees, you shal not enter into the Kingdom of heauē.

Luc. 16, 17.
Ia. 2, 10.

The Gospel vpō the fifth Sunday after Pentecost.

† You haue heard that it vvas sayd to them of old. * Thou 22 shalt not kil. and vvhoso killeth, shal be in danger of iudgement. † But I say to you, that vvhosoeuer is angrie vvith his 23 brother, shal be in danger of iudgment. And vvhosoeuer shal say to his brother, Raca: shal be in danger of a councel. And whosoeuer shal say, Thou foole: shal be guilty of the " hel of fyre. † If therefore thou offer thy " gift at the altar, and 24 there thou remember that thy brother hath ought agaynst the: † leaue there thy offering before the altar, and goe first 25 to be reconciled to thy brother: and then coming thou shalt offer thy gift. ⁊ † * Be at agreement vvith thy aduersarie be- 26 times vvhiles thou art in the vvay vvith him: lest perhaps the aduersarie deliuer thee to the iudge, and the iudge deliuer thee to the officer, and thou be cast into ∷ prison. † Amen I say to 27 thee, thou shalt not goe out from thence til thou repay the last farthing.

Exo. 20, 13.
Deut. 5, 17.

Luc. 12, 58.

∷ This Prison is taken of very ancient fathers, for Purgatorie: namely *S. Cypr. ep. 52. ad Anton. nu. 6.*

† You haue heard that it vvas sayd to them of old, * Thou 28 shalt not committe aduoutrie. † But I say to you, that vvho- 29 soeuer shal see a vvoman to lust after her, hath already committed aduoutrie vvith her in his hart. † And if thy right eie 30 scandalize thee, plucke it out, & cast it from thee. for it is expedient for thee that one of thy limmes perish, rather then thy vvhole body be cast into hel. † And if thy right hand scanda- 31 lize thee, cut it of, and cast it from thee: for it is expedient for thee that one of thy limmes perish, rather then that thy vvhole body goe into hel.

Exo. 20, 14.

† It vvas sayd also, * vvhosoeuer shal dimisse his vvife, let 32 him

Deu. 24, 1.
Mt. 19, 7.

33 him giue her a bil of diuorcement. † But I ſay to you, vvhoſoeuer ſhal dimiſſe his vvife, ‖ excepting the cauſe of fornication, maketh her to committe aduoutrie: And he that ſhal marie her that is dimiſſed, ‖ committeth aduoutrie.

34 † Agayne you haue heard that it vvas ſayd to them of old, * Thou ſhalt not committe periurie: but thou ſhalt performe
35 thy othes to our Lord. † But I ſay to you ‖ not to ſvveare at al: neither by heauen, becauſe it is the throne of God: † neither by the earth, becauſe it is the foote-ſtole of his feete: neither
36 by Hieruſalē, becauſe it is the citie of the great King. † Neither ſhalt thou ſvveare by thy head, becauſe thou canſt not make
37 one heare vvhite or blacke. † Let your talke be, yea, yea: no, no: and that vvhich is ouer & aboue theſe, is of euil.

Exo. 20, 7. Leu. 19, 11.

38 † You haue heard that it vvas ſayd, * An eye for an eye, and
39 a tooth for a tooth. † But I ſay to you ‖ not to reſiſt euil: but if one ſtrike thee on thy right cheeke, turne to him alſo the
40 other: † and to him that vvil contend vvith thee in iudgment,
41 and take away thy cote, let goe thy cloke alſo vnto him. † and vvhoſoeuer vvil force thee one mile, goe vvith him other
42 tvvayne. † He that aſketh of thee, giue to him: and * to him that vvould borovv of thee, turne not avvay.

Exo. 21, 24. Deu. 15, 7.

The Goſpel vpō the friday after Aſhweniday.

43 † You haue heard that it vvas ſayd, * Thou ſhalt loue thy
44 neighbour, and ∷ hate thine enemie. † But I ſay to you, loue your enemies, doe good to them that hate you: and pray for
45 them that perſecute and abuſe you: † that you may be the children of your father vvhich is in heauen, vvho maketh his ſunne to riſe vpon good & bad, and rayneth vpon iuſt &
46 ∷ vniuſt. † For if you loue them that loue you, vvhat revvard
47 ſhal you haue? do not alſo the Publicans this? † And if you ſalute your brethren only, vvhat do you more? do not alſo the
48 heathen this? † Be you perfect therfore, as alſo your heauenly father is perfect.

Leu. 19, 18.

∷ So taught the Phariſees, not the Law.

∷ We ſee then that the temporal proſperitie of perſons and countries is no ſigne of better men or truer religion.

ANNOTATIONS CHAP. V.

10. *For iuſtice.*) Heretikes and other malefactours ſometime ſuffer willingly and ſtoutly: but they are not bleſſed, becauſe they ſuffer not for iuſtice. For (ſayth S. Aug.) they can not ſuffer for iuſtice, that haue deuided the Churche. and, where ſound fayth or charitie is not, there cannot be iuſtice. *Cont. ep. Parm. li. 1. c. 9. Ep. 50. Pſal. 34. Conc. 2.* And ſo by this ſcripture are excluded al falſe Martyrs, as S. Auguſtine often declareth, and *S. Cypr. de Unit. Eccl. nu. 8.*

Falſe Martyrs.

12. *Reward.*) In Latin and Greeke the word ſignifieth very wages and hire dewe for workes, and ſo preſuppoſeth a meritorious deede.

Merces. Μισθὸς.

15. *The light.*] This light of the world, and citie on a mountayne, and candel vpon a candlesticke, signifie the Clergie, and the whole Churche, so built vpon Christ the mountayne, that it must needes be visible, and can not be hid nor vnknowen. *Aug. cont. Fulg. Donat. c. 18. Li. 16. cont. Faust. c. 17.* And therfore, the Churche being a candle not vnder a bushel, but shining to al in the house (that is) in the world, what shal I say more (sayth S. Augustine) then that they are blind which shut their eyes agaynst the candel that is set on the candlesticke? *Tract. 2. in ep. Io.*

The Church visible.

17. *Your light.*] The good life of the Clergie edifieth much, and is Gods great honour: whereas the contrarie dishonoureth him.

20. *One of these.*] Behold how necessarie it is, not only to beleeue, but to keepe al the commaundements, euen the very least.

21. *Your iustice.*] It is our iustice, when it is geuen vs of God. *Aug. in Ps. 30. Conc. 1. De Sp. & lit. c. 9.* So that Christians are truely iust, and haue in them selues inhærent iustice, by doing Gods commaundements. Without which iustice of workes no man of age can be saued. *Aug. de fid. & oper. c. 16.* Whereby we see saluation, iustice, and iustification, not to come of only fayth, or imputation of Christes iustice.

True inherent iustice.

22. *Hel of fyre.*] Here is a playne difference of sinnes, some mortal that bring to Hel, some lesse, and lesse punished, called venial.

Venial sinnes.

24. *Gift at the altar.*] Beware of coming to the holy altar or any Sacrament out of charitie. But be first reconciled to thy brother, and much more to the Catholike Churche, which is the whole brotherhod of Christian men, *Heb. 13, 1.*

32. *Excepting the cause of fornication.*] This exception is onely to shew, that for this one cause a man may put away his wife for euer: but not that he may marrie another: as it is most plaine in S. Marke and S. Luke, who leaue out this exception, saying: * *Whosoeuer dimisseth his wife and marieth an other, committeth aduoutrie.* See the Annot. Luc. 19, 9. But if both parties be in one and the same fault, then can neither of them not so much as diuorce or put away the other.

Mariage a Sacrament, and is not dissolued by diuorce.

Mr. 10, 11. Lu. 16, 18.

32. *Committeth aduoutrie.*] The knot of Mariage is a thing of so great a Sacrament, that not by separation it self of the parties it can be loosed, being not lawful neither for the one part nor the other, to marie agayne vpon diuorce. *Aug. de bo. Coniug. c. 7.*

35. *Not to sweare.*] The Anabaptists here not folowing the Churches iudgement, but the bare letter (as other Heretikes in other cases) hold that there is no othe lawful, no not before a iudge. Whereas Christ speaketh agaynst rashe and vsual swearing in common talke, when there is no cause.

39. *Not to Resist euil.*] Here also the Anabaptists gather of the letter, that it is not lawful to goe to law for our right. as Luther also vpon this place held, that Christians might not resist the Turke. Whereas by this, as by that which foloweth, patience only is signified and a wil to suffer more, rather then to reuenge. For neither did Christ nor S. Paule folow the letter by turning the other cheeke. *Io. 18. Act. 23.*

CHAP. VI.

In this second chapter of his Sermon, he controwleth the Pharisees iustice (that is, their almes, prayer, and fasting) for the scope and intention therof, which was vaine glorie. 19 Their end also was to be riche, but ours must not be so much as in necessaries.

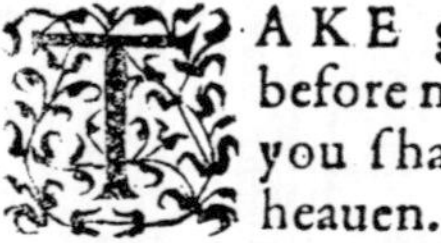

TAKE good heede that you doe not your " iustice before men, to be seen of them: otherwise reward you shall not haue with your father which is in heauen. 1

† Therfore when thou ⁖ doest an almes-deede, sound not a trompet before thee, as the hypocrites doe in the Synagogues and in the streetes, that they may be honoured of men: Amen I say to you, they haue receiued their reward. 2 † But when thou doest an almes-deede, let not thy left hand know what thy right hand doeth: 3 † that thy almes-deede may be in secrete, and thy father which seeth in secrete, wil " repay the. 4 † And

⁖ THE first worke of iustice.

5 † And vvhen ye :: pray, you shal not be as the " hypocrites, that loue to stand & pray in the Synagogs and corners of the streetes, that they may be seen of men: Amen I say to you, they
6 haue receiued their revvard. † But thou vvhen thou shalt pray, enter into thy chamber, & hauing shut the doore, pray to thy father in secrete: and thy father vvhich seeth in secrete, vvil
7 repay thee. † And vvhen you are praying, speake not much, as the heathen. For they thinke that in their " much-speaking
8 they may be heard. † Be not you therefore like to them, for your father knovveth vvhat is needeful for you, before you aske him.

:: THE SECOND worke of iustice.

Luc. 11, 2.

9 † Thus therefore shal you pray. * OVR FATHER *which art in hea-*
10 *uen, sanctified be thy name.* † *Let thy Kingdom come. Thy wil be done, as in heauen,*
11 *in earth also.* † *Giue vs to day our* :: *supersubstantial bread.* † *And forgiue vs our*
12 " *dettes, as we also forgiue our detters.* † *And* " *leade vs not into tentation. But*
13 *deliuer vs from euil. Amen.* † For " if you vvil * forgiue men their
14 offenses, your heauenly father vvil forgiue you also your
15 offenses. † But if you vvil not forgiue men, neither vvil your father forgiue you your offenses.

The PATER NOSTER.

:: In S. Luke, the Latin is, *Panem quotidianum*, *dayly bread*, the Greeke being indifferent to both, τὸν ἐπιούσιον.

Mr. 11, 25.

16 † And vvhen you :: fast, be not as the hypocrites, sad. For they disfigure their faces, that they may appeare vnto men to fast. Amen I say to you, that they haue receiued their revvard.
17 † But thou vvhen thou doest fast, anoynte thy head, and
18 vvash thy face: † that thou appeare not to men to fast, but to thy father vvhich is in secrete: and thy father vvhich seeth in secrete, vvil repay thee.

:: The third worke of iustice.

The Gospel vpō Ashwensday.

Luc. 12, 33.

19 † * Heape not vp to your selues treasures on the earth: vvhere the rust & mothe do corrupt, & vvhere theeues digge through
20 & steale. † But heape vp to your selues treasures in heauen: vvhere neither the rust nor mothe doth corrupt, and vvhere
21 theeues do not digge through nor steale. † For vvhere thy
22 treasure is, there is thy hart also. ¶ † * The candel of thy body is thine eye. If thine eye be simple, thy vvhole body shal be
23 lightsome. † But if thine eye be naught: thy vvhole body shal be darkesome. If then the light that is in thee, be darkenes: the darkenes it self hovv great shal it be?

Luc. 11, 34.

24 † No man can * serue " tvvo masters. For either he vvil hate the one, and loue the other: or he vvil sustayne the one, and contemne the other. You cannot serue God and Mammon.

Luc. 16, 13.

The Gospel on the 14 Sunday after Pentecost.

25 † Therfore I say to you, * be not " careful for your life vvhat you shal eate, neither for your body vvhat rayment you shal put on.

Luc. 12, 22.

put on. Is not the life more then the meate: and the body more then the rayment? † Behold the foules of the ayre, that 26 they sovv not, neither reape, nor gather into barnes: and your heauenly father feedeth them. Are not you much more of price then they? † And vvhich of you by caring, can adde to his 27 stature one cubite? † And for rayment vvhy are you careful? 28 Consider the lilies of the field hovv they grovv: they labour not, neither do they spinne. † But I say to you, that neither 29 Salomon in al his glorie vvas arayed as one of these. † And if 30 the grasse of the field, vvhich to day is, and to morovv is cast into the ouē, God doth so clothe: hovv much more you O ye of very smal fayth? † Be not careful therefore, saying, vvhat 31 shal vve eate, or vvhat shal vve drinke, or vvherevvith shal vve be couered? † for al these thinges the ∷ Heathen do seeke 32 after. For your father knovveth that you neede al these things. † Seeke therefore first the Kingdom of God, & the iustice of 33 him: and al these things shal be giuen you besides. ⁂† Be not 34 careful therfore for the morovv. For the morovv day shal be careful for it self. sufficient for the day is the euil thereof.

∷ They seeke temporal things only, and that not of the true God, but of their idols, or by their owne industrie.

ANNOTATIONS
CHAP. VI.

Good Workes iustifie.

1. Iustice.] Hereby it is playne that good Workes be iustice, and that man doing them doeth iustice, and is thereby iust and iustified, and not by fayth only. Al which iustice of a Christian man our Sauiour here compriseth in these three Workes, in Almes, fasting, and prayers. *Aug. li. perf. iust. c. 8.* So that to giue almes, is to doe iustice, and the Workes of mercie are iustice. *Aug. in Ps. 49, v. 5.*

Merites.

4. Repay.) This repaying and reWarding of good Workes in heauen, often mentioned here by our Sauiour, declareth that the sayd Workes are meritorious, and that We may doe them in respect of that reWard.

Hypocrisie.

5. Hypocrites.) Hypocrisie is forbidden in al these three Workes of iustice, and not the doing of them openly to the glorie of God and the profite of our neighbour and our oWne saluatiō: for Christ before (c. 5.) biddeth, saying: *Let your light so shine before men &c.* And in al such Workes S. Gregories rule is to be foloWed, *The Worke so to be in publike, that the intention remayne in secrete. Ho. 11. in Euang. c. 10.*

7. Much speaking.] Long prayer is not forbid, for Christ * him self spent Whole nights in prayer, and he sayth, * We must pray alWayes, and * the Apostle exhorteth to pray Without intermission, and the holy Church * from the beginning hath had her Canonical houres of prayer: but idle and voluntary babling, either of the heathens to their goddes, or of Heretikes, that by long Rhetorical prayers thinke to persuade God: Wheras the Collects of the Churche are most breefe and most effectual. *See S. Augustine ep. 121, c. 8, 9. 10.*

Luc. 6, 12. 18, 1. 21, 36. 1 Thes. 5, 17. Cypr. de orat. Do. in fine.

τὸν ἐπιούσιον.
The B. Sacrament.

11. Superstantial bread.) By this bread so called here according to the Latin Word and the Greeke, We aske not only al necessarie sustenance for the body, but much more al spiritual foode, namely the blessed Sacrament it self, Which is Christ the true bread that came from heauen, and the bread of life to vs that eate his bodie. *Cypr. de orat. Do. Aug. ep. 121 c. 11.* And therfore it is called here Supersubstantial, that is, the bread that passeth and excelleth al creatures. *Hiero. in 2. Tit. In 6. Mat. Amb. li. 5. de Sacr. c. 4. Aug. ser. 28. de verb. Do. sec. Mat. S. Germanus in Theoria.*

Venial sinnes.

12. Dettes.) These dettes doe signifie not only mortal sinnes, but also venial, as S. Augustine often teacheth: and therfore euery man, be he neuer so iust, yet because he can not liue Without venial sinnes, may very truly and ought to say this prayer. *Aug. cont. duas ep. Pelag. li 1. c. 14. li. 21 de Ciuit. c. 27.*

In Expos. orat. Do. Iac. 1.

13. Leade vs not.] S. Cypr. readeth, *Ne patiaris nos induci.* Suffer vs not to be led, as S. Augustine noteth *li. de bo. perseu. c. 6.* and so the holy Churche vnderstandeth it, because God (as S. Iames sayth) tempteth no man: though for our sinnes, or for our probation and crowne, he permitte vs to be tempted. Beware then of Bezaes exposition vpon this place, who (according to the Caluinists opinion) saith, that God leadeth them into tentation, into whom him self bringeth in Satan for to fill their harts: so making God the author of sinne.

God is not author of euil.

14. If you forgeue.] This poynt, of forgeuing our brother, when we aske forgiuenesse of God, our Sauiour repeateth agayne, as a thing much to be considered: and therfore commended in the parable also of the seruant that would not forgiue his felow seruant, *Mat. 18.*

Iud. 20, 26. 2. Esd. 9. Ioel. 2, 15. Ion. 3.

16. Fast.] He forbiddeth not open and publike fasts, which in the* Scriptures were commaunded and proclamed to the people of God, and the Niniuites by such fasting appeased Gods wrath: but to fast for vaine glorie and praise of men, and to be desirous by the very face and looke to be taken for a faster, that is forbidden, and that is hypocrisie.

Publike fast.

20. Treasures in heauen.] Treasures layd vp in heauen, must needes signifie, not fayth only, but plentiful almes and deedes of mercie and other good workes, which God keeping as in a booke, wil reward them accordingly: as of the contrarie the Apostle sayth, *He that soweth sparingly, shal reape sparingly. 2. Cor. 9.*

Meritorious workes.

24. Two Masters.] Two religions, God and Baal, Christ and Caluin, Masse and Communion, the Catholike Churche and Heretical Conuenticles. Let them marke this lesson of our Sauiour, that thinke they may serue al masters, al times, al religions. Agayne, these two masters doe signifie, God and the world, the fleshe and the spirit, iustice and sinne.

25. Careful.] Prudent prouision is not prohibited, but to much doubtfulnes and feare of Gods prouision for vs: to whom we ought with patience to committe the rest, when we haue done sufficiently for our part.

CHAP. VII.

In this third and last Chapter of his Sermon, because we know not mens endes, he biddeth vs beware of iudging: 6 and neuerthelesse to take open dogges (so he calleth them) as they be. 7 If these workes of iustice seeme to hard, we must pray instantly to him that giueth them. 12 In the conclusion, he giueth one short rule of al iustice. 13 and then he exhorteth with al vehemencie to the straite way both of the Catholike fayth, 21 and also of good life: because only fayth wil not suffise.

1 IVDGE "not, that you be not iudged. 2 †For *in what iudgment you iudge, you shal be iudged: and in what measure you mete, it shal be measured to you agayne. 3 †And why seest thou the mote that is in thy brothers eye: and the beame that is in thine ovvne eye thou seest not? 4 †Or how sayest thou to thy brother, Let me cast out the mote of thine eye: and behold a beame is in thine owne eye? 5 †Hypocrite, cast out first the beame out of thine owne eye, and then shalt thou see to cast out the mote out of thy brothers eye.

Luc. 6, 37. Mr. 4, 24.

6 †Giue not that which is "holy to dogges: neither cast ye your pearles before swine, lest perhaps they treade them with their feete, and turning, al to teare you.

Lu. 11, 9

7 †* Aske, and it shal be giuen you: seeke, and you shal finde, knocke, and it shal be opened to you. 8 †For "euery one that asketh, receiueth: and that seeketh, findeth: and to him

that knocketh, it ſhal be opened. † Or vvhat man is there of 9 you, vvhom if his childe ſhal aſke bread, vvil he reach him a ſtone? † Or if he ſhal aſke him fiſh, vvil he reach him a ſer- 10 pent? † If you then being naught, knovv hovv to giue good 11 giftes to your children: hovv much more vvil your father vvhich is in heauen, giue :: good things to them that aſke him?

:: These good things are grace and al ſpiritual gifts, and what ſoeuer pertayneth to the health of the ſoule.

† * Al things therfore vvhatſoeuer you vvil that men doe 12 to you doe you alſo to them. For this is the Lavv and the Prophets.

Luc. 6, 31.

* † Enter ye by the narrovv gate: becauſe brode is the gate, 13 and large is the vvay that leadeth to perdition, and many there be that enter by it. † Hovv narrovv is the gate, and ſtraite is 14 the vvay that leadeth to life: and fevv there are that finde it!

Luc. 13, 24.

The Goſpel on the 7 Sunday after Pentecoſt.

† Take ye great heede of falſe Prophets, vvhich come to 15 you in the " clothing of ſheepe, but invvardly are rauening vvolues. † " By their * fruites you ſhal knovv them. Do men 16 gather grapes of thornes, or figges of thiſtels? † Euen ſo euery 17 good tree yeldeth good fruites, and the euil tree yeldeth euil fruites. † A good tree can not yeld euil fruites, neither an euil 18 tree yeld good fruites. † Euery tree that yeldeth not good 19 fruite, ſhal be cut dovvne, and ſhal be caſt into fyre. † Ther- 20 fore by their fruites you ſhal knovv them.

Luc. 6, 44.

† Not euery one that ſayth to me, " *Lord, Lord*, ſhal enter 21 into the Kingdom of heauen: but he that doeth the vvil of my father vvhich is in heauen, he ſhal enter into the kingdom of heauen. ⊣ † Many ſhal ſay to me in that day, *Lord, Lord*, 22 haue not vve prophecied in thy name, and in thy name caſt out diuels, and in thy name vvrought many miracles? † And 23 then I vvil cõfeſſe vnto them, That I neuer knevv you. depart from me you that vvorke iniquitie. † * Euery one therfore 24 that heareth theſe my vvordes, and doeth them: ſhal be likened to a vviſe man that built his houſe vpon a rocke, † and 25 the rayne fel, and the fluddes came, & the vvindes blevve, and they beate agaynſt that houſe, and it fel not, for it vvas founded vpon a rocke. † And euery one that heareth theſe 26 my vvordes, & doeth them not, ſhal be like a fooliſh man that built his houſe vpon the ſand, † and the rayne fel, and 27 the fluddes came, and the vvindes blevve, and they beate agaynſt that houſe, and it fel, & the fall therof vvas great.

Luc. 6, 47.

† And it came to paſſe, vvhen IESVS had fully ended 28 theſe vvordes, the multitude vvere in * admiration vpon his doctrine

Mar. 1, 22. Luc. 4, 32.

29 doctrine. † For he vvas teaching them as hauing povver, and not as their Scribes and Pharisees.

ANNOTATIONS CHAP. VII.

1. Iudge not.] It is no Christian part to iudge il of mens actes which be in them selues good and may procede of good meaning, or of mans inward meanings and intentions which we can not see: of which fault they must beware that are to suspicious and giuen to deeme alwayes the worst of other men. But to say, that Iudas, or an Heretike euidently knowen to die obstinatly in heresie, is damned, and in al other playne and manifest cases to iudge, is not forbidden.

6. Holy to dogges.] No holy Sacrament and specially that of our Sauiours blessed body, must be geuen wittingly to the vnworthy, that is, to them that haue not by confession of al mortal sinnes examined and proued them selues. See the Annot. *1. Cor. 11, 27. 28, 29.*

Worthy receiuing.

8. Euery one that asketh.] Al things that we aske necessarie to saluation with humilitie, attention, continuance, and other dewe circunstances, God wil vndoubtedly graunt when it is best for vs.

15. Clothing of sheepe.] Extraordinarie apparance of zeale and holines is the sheepes cote in some Heretikes: but these of this time weare not that garment much, being men of vnsatiable sinne. This is rather their garment, common to them with al other Heretikes, to crake much of the word of the Lord, and by pretensed allegations and * sweete wordes of benediction, and specially by promise of knowledge, light and libertie of the Gospel, to seduce the simple and the sinful.

Ro. 16, 18.

Heretikes wolues in sheepeskinnes.

16. Fruites.] These are the fruites which Heretikes are knowen by, diuision from the whole Churche, diuision among them selues, taking to them selues new names and new maisters, inconstancie in doctrine, disobedience both to others and namely to spiritual officers, loue and liking of them selues, pride and intolerable vaunting of their owne knowledge aboue al the holy Doctors, corruption, falsification, and quite denying of the parts of Scriptures that specially make agaynst them, and these be common to al Heretikes lightly. Othersome are more peculiar to these of our time, as Incestuous mariages of vowed persons, Spoile of Churches, Sacrilege and profanation of al holy things, and many other special poynts of doctrine, directly tending to the corruption of good life in al states.

Heretikes knowen by their fruites.

21. Lord, Lord.] These men haue faith, otherwise they could not inuocate, *Lord, Lord: Ro. 10.* But here we see that to beleeue is not ynough, and that not only infidelitie is sinne, as Luther teacheth. Yea Catholikes also that worke true miracles in the name of our Lord, and by neuer so great fayth, yet without the workes of iustice shal not be saued. *1. Cor. 13.* Agayne, consider here who they are that haue so often in their mouth, *The Lord, the Lord*, and how litle it shal auaile them, that set so litle by good workes, and contemne Christian iustice.

Not only faith.

CHAP. VIII.

Immediatly after his Sermon (to confirme his doctrine with a miracle) he cureth a Leper. 5 But aboue him and al other Iewes, he comendeth the faith of the Centurion, who was a Gentil: and foretelleth by that occasion, the vocation of the Gentiles, and reprobation of the Iewes. 14 In Peters house he sheweth great grace. 18 In the way to the sea he speaketh with two, of folowing him: 23 and vpon the sea commaundeth the tempest: 28 and beyond the sea he manifesteth the deuils malice agaynst man, in an heard of swine.

The Gospel on the 3. Sunday after the Epiphanie.

1 AND vvhen he vvas come dovvne from the mountaine, great multitudes folovved him: 2 † And * behold a leper came and adored him saying, Lord, if thou vvilt, thou canst make me cleane. 3 † And IESVS stretching forth his hand, touched him, saying. I vvil. be thou made cleane. And 4 forthvvith, his leprosy vvas made cleane. † And IESVS sayth to

Mr. 1, 40. Lu. 5, 12.

him, See thou tel no body: but goe,* ſhevv thy ſelf to the "prieſt, & offer the "gift vvhich Moyſes commaunded for a teſtimonie to them.

Leu.14, 2.

THE GOSPEL vpon the thurſday after Aſhwenſday. And alſo in Maſſe for the ſicke.

† And * vvhen he vvas entred into Capharnaum, there 5 came to him a Centurion, beſeeching him, † & ſaying, Lord 6 my boy lieth at home ſicke of the palſey, & is ſore tormẽted. † And IESVS ſayth to him, I vvil come, & cure him. † And 7. 8 the Centurion making anſvver, ſayd, Lord "I am not vvorthie that thou ſhouldeſt enter vnder my roofe: but only ſay the vvord, and my boy ſhal be healed. † For I alſo am a man 9 ſubiect to authoritie, hauing vnder me ſouldiars: and I ſay to this, goe, and he goeth: and to an other, come, & he cõmeth: and to my ſeruant, doe this, & he doeth it. † And IESVS 10 hearing this, marueiled: and ſayd to them that folovved him, Amen I ſay to you, I haue not found ſo great faith in Iſrael. † And I ſay to you, that many ſhal come from the Eaſt and 11 Weſt, and ſhal ſitte dovvne vvith Abraham & Iſaac & Iacob in the kingdom of heauen: †but the children of the kingdom 12 ſhal be caſt out into the exteriour darkeneſſe: there ſhal be vveeping & gnaſhing of teeth. † And IESVS ſaid to the 13 Centurion, Goe: and as thou haſt beleeued, be it done to thee. And the boy vvas healed in the ſame houre. ꟻ

Lu. 7, 1.

† And * vvhen IESVS was come into Peters houſe, he ſavv 14 "his vviues mother layde, & in a fitte of a feuer: † and he tou- 15 ched her hand, and the feuer left her, and ſhe aroſe, and miniſtred to him. † And vvhen euening vvas come, they brought 16 to him many that had diuels: and he caſt out the ſpirites vvith a vvord: and al that vvere il at eaſe he cured: † that it might 17 be fulfilled vvich vvas ſpoken by Eſay the Prophete ſaying, *He tooke our infirmities, and bare our diſeaſes.*

Mr. 1, 29
Lu. 4, 38
Eſa. 53, 4.
1. Pet. 2, 24.

† And IESVS ſeeing great multitudes about him, com- 18 maunded to goe beyond the vvater. † And a * certaine Scribe 19 came, and ſayd to him, Maſter, I vvil folovv thee vvitherſoeuer thou ſhalt goe. † And IESVS ſayth to him, the foxes haue 20 holes, and the foules of the ayre neſtes: but the ſonne of man hath not vvhere to lay his head. † And * an other of his Di- 21 ſciples ſayd to him, Lord, permit me firſt to goe & burie my father. † But IESVS ſayd to him, Folovv me, and " let the dead 22 burie their dead.

Lu. 9, 57
Luc. 9, 59.

THE GOSPEL on the 4 Sunday after the *Epiphanie.*

† And * vvhen he entered into the boate, his Diſciples fo- 23 lovved him: † and loe a great tempeſt aroſe in the ſea, ſo 24 that

Mar. 4, 36.
Lu. 8, 22

25 that the boate vvas couered vvith vvaues, but he ſlept. † And they came to him, and raiſed him, ſaying, Lord, ſaue vs, vve 26 periſh. † And he ſaith to them, Why are you fearful O ye of litle faith? Then riſing vp " he commaunded the vvindes & 27 the ſea, and there enſued a great calme. † Moreouer the men marueled ſaying, What an one is this, for the vvindes and the ſea obey him? ⫞

Mr. 5, 1. Luc. 8, 26.

28 † And * vvhen he vvas come beyond the vvater into the countrey of the Geraſens, there mette him tvvo that had diuels, coming forth out of the ſepulcres, exceding fierce, ſo that 29 none could paſſe by that vvay. † And behold they cried ſaying, What is betvvene vs and thee IESV the ſonne of God? 30 art thou come hither to torment vs before the time? † And there vvas not farre frome them an heard of many ſvvine fee- 31 ding. † And the diuels beſought him ſaying, If thou caſt vs 32 out, ſend vs into the heard of ſvvine. † And he ſaid to thẽ, Goe. But they going forth vvent into the ſvvine, and behold the whole heard vvent vvith a violence headlong into the ſea: 33 and they dyed in the vvaters. † And the ſvvineheardes fled: and comming into the citie, told al, and of them that had been 34 poſſeſſed of diuels. † And behold the vvhole citie vvent out to meete IESVS, and vvhen they ſavv him, they beſought him that he vvould paſſe from their quarters.

ANNOTATIONS
CHAP. VIII.

4. Prieſt.] The Prieſts of the old law (ſaith S. Chryſoſtome) had authoritie and priuilege only to diſcerne who where healed of leproſie, and to denounce the ſame to the people: but the Prieſts of the new law haue power to purge in very deede the filth of the ſoule. Therfore whoſoeuer deſpiſeth them, is more vvorthie to be puniſhed then the rebel Dathan and his complices. *S. Chryſo. li. 3. de Sacerd.*

Prieſts forgiue ſinnes.

4. Gift.] Our Sauiour willeth him to goe and offer his gift or ſacrifice according as Moyſes preſcribed in that caſe, becauſe the other ſacrifice being the holieſt of al holies, which is his body, was not yet begonne. So ſaith *S. Aug. li. 2. q. Euang. q. 3. & Cont. Aduerſ. leg. & Proph. li. 1. c. 19. 20.*

8. Not Worthy.] *Orig. ho. 5. in diuerſ.* When thou eateſt (ſaith he) and drinkeſt the body and bloud of our Lord, he entereth vnder thy roofe. Thou alſo therfore humbling thy ſelf, ſay: Lord I am not worthy. &c. So ſaid * S. Chryſoſtom in his Maſſe. and ſo doeth the Cath. Churche vſe at this day in euery Maſſe. See S. Auguſtine *ep. 118 ad Ianu.*

** Liturg. S. Chryſ. Græc. ſub finem.*

DOMINE, non ſum dignus.

14. His Wiues mother.) Of Peter ſpecially among the reſt it is euident that he had a wife, but (as S. Hierom ſayth) after they were called to be Apoſtles, they had no more carnal companie with their wiues, as he proueth there by the very wordes of our Sauiour, * *He that hath left wife & c.* And ſo in the Latin Churche hath been alwayes vſed, that maried men may be and are daily made Prieſts, either after the death of the wife, or with her conſent to liue in perpetual continencie. And if the Greekes haue Prieſts that doe otherwiſe, S. Epiphanius a Greeke Doctor telleth them that they doe it agaynſt the ancient Canons, and * Paphnutius plainely ſignifieth the ſame in the firſt Councel of Nice. But this is moſt playne, that there was neuer either in the Greeke Church or the Latin, authentical example of any that married after holy Orders.

*Lib. 1. adu. Iou. c. 14. Mt. 19, 29. Epiph. hæ. 59. * Sozom. li. 1. c. 22. Socrat. li. 1. c. 8.*

Prieſts mariage.

22. Let the dead.) By this we ſee that not only no wordly or carnal reſpect, but no other laudable dutie

dutie toward our parents, ought to stay vs from folowing Christ, and choosing a life of greater perfection.

26. He commaunded.) The Churche (here signified by the boate or shippe) and Catholikes, are often tossed with stormes of persecution, but Christ who seemed to sleepe in the meane time, by the Churches prayers awaketh, and maketh a calme.

CHAP. IX.

The Maisters of the Iewes he confuteth both with reasons and miracles: 2 defending his remitting of sinnes, 9 his eating with sinners, 14 and his condescending to his weake Disciples until he haue made them stronger. 18 shewing also in two miracles, the order of his prouidence about the Iewes and Gentils, leauing the one when he called the other. 27 he cureth tvvo blind men, and one possessed. 35 And hauing vvith so many miracles together confuted his enemies, and yet they worse and worse, vpon pitie toward the people, he thinketh of sending true pastours vnto them.

The Gospel vpon the 18 Sunday after Pentecost.

AND entring into a boate, he passed ouer the vvater, and came into his ovvne citie. 1
† And * behold they brought to him one sicke of the palsey lying in bedde. And IESVS :: seeing their faith, said to the sicke of the palsey, Haue a good hart sonne, thy sinnes are forgiuen thee. 2 † And behold certaine of the Scribes sayd vvithin them selues, " He blasphemeth. 3 † And IESVS seeing their thoughtes, said. Wherfore thinke you euil in your hartes? 4 † " Whether is easier, to say, thy sinnes are forgiuen thee: or to say, Arise and vvalke? 5 † But that you may knovv that the " Sonne of man hath povver in earth to forgiue sinnes, (then sayd he to the sicke of the palsey,) Arise, take vp thy bedde, and goe into thy house. 6 † And he arose, and vvent into his house. 7 † And the multitudes seeing it, vvere afrayd, and " glorified God that gaue such povver " to men. 8 ⊣

(Margin: * Mr. 2, 3. Luc. 5, 18.)

(Margin: :: We see that the fayth of one helpeth to obtaine for an other.)

The Gospel vpō S. Matthewes day.

† And * vvhen IESVS passed forth from thence, he savv a man sitting in the custome-house, named Matthevv: And he sayth to him, Folovv me. And he arose vp, and folovved him. 9 † And it came to passe as he vvas sitting at meate in the house, behold many Publicans and sinners came, and sate dovvne vvith IESVS and his Disciples. 10 † And the Pharisees seeing it, sayd to his Disciples: vvhy doth your Master eate vvith Publicans & sinners? 11 † But IESVS hearing it, sayd: They that are in health, neede not a physicion, but they that are il at ease. 12 † But go your vvayes and learne vvhat it is, *I vvil mercie, &* " *not sacrifice.* For I am not come to cal the iust, but sinners. 13 ⊣

(Margin: * Mar. 2, 14. Luc. 5, 27. — Ose. 6, 6.)

† Then * came to him the Disciples of Iohn, saying, vvhy do vve and the Pharisees " fast often, but thy Disciples do not fast? 14

(Margin: * Mar. 2, 18. Lu. 5, 33.)

15 fast? † And IESVS sayd to them, Can the children of the bridegrome mourne, as long as the bridegrome is vvith them? But the dayes vvil come vvhen the bridegrome shal be ta-
16 ken avvay from them, and :: then they shal fast. † And no body putteth a peece of ravv cloth to an old garment. For he taketh avvay the peecing therof from the garment, and there
17 is made a greater rent. † Neither do they put " nevv vvine into old bottels. Othervvise the bottels breake, and the vvine runneth out, and the bottels perish. But nevv vvine they put into nevv bottels: and both are preserued together.

:: Christ signifieth that the Churche shal vse fasting daies after his Ascension. *Epiph. in Comp. fid. Cath. Aug. ep. 10.*

Mar. 5, 22. Luc. 8, 41.

18 † * As he vvas speaking this vnto them, behold a certaine Gouernour approched, and adored him, saying, Lord, my daughter is euen novv dead: but come, lay thy hand vpon
19 her, and she shal liue. † And IESVS rysing vp folovved
20 him, and his Disciples. † And behold a vvoman vvhich vvas troubled vvith an issue of bloud " tvvelue yeres, came behind
21 him, and touched the hemme of his garment. † For she sayd vvithin her self, If I shal " touch only his garment: I shal be
22 safe. † But IESVS turning and seeing her, sayd, Haue a good hart daughter, :: thy faith hath made the safe. And the vvo-
23 man became vvhole from that houre. † And vvhen IESVS vvas come into the house of the Gouernour, & savv minstrels
24 and the multitude keeping a sturre, † he sayd, Depart: for the vvenche is not dead, but sleepeth. And they laughed him to
25 skorne. † And vvhen the multitude vvas put forth, he entred
26 in, and held her hand. And the mayde arose. † And this bruite vvent forth into al that countrie.

The Gospel vpō the 23 Sunday after Pentecost.

:: Loe, her deuotion to the hemme of his garment, was not superstitiō, but a token of greater faith: so is the deuout touching of holy relikes.

27 † And as IESVS passed forth from thence, there folovved him tvvo blinde men crying and saying, Haue mercie on vs,
28 O sonne of Dauid. † And vvhen he vvas come to the house, the blinde came to him. And IESVS sayth to them, " Do you beleeue, that I can doe this vnto you? They say to him, Yea
29 Lord. † Then he touched their eyes, saying, According to your
30 faith, be it done to you. † And their eyes vvere opened, and IESVS threatened them, saying, See that no man knovv it.
31 † But they vvent forth, & bruited him in al that countrey.

Mat. 12, 22.

32 † And vvhen they vvere gone forth, * behold they brought
33 him a dumme man, possessed vvith a diuel. † And after the diuel vvas cast out, the dumme man spake, and the multitudes marueled saying, Neuer vvas the like seene in Israel.

† But

:: In like maner say the Heretikes, calling al miracles done in the Catholike Churche, the lying signes of Antichrist.

† But * the Pharisees sayd, :: In the prince of diuels he casteth 34 out diuels.

Mt. 12, 24.

† And IESVS vvent about al the cities, and tovvnes, tea- 35 ching in their synagogs, and preaching the Gospel of the kingdom, and curing euery disease, and euery infirmitie. † And seing the multitudes, he pitied them: because they vvere 36 vexed, and lay like sheepe that haue not a shepheard. † Then 37 he sayth to his Disciples, The haruest surely is great, but the vvorkemen are fevv. †" Pray therfore the Lord of the haruest, 38 that he send forth vvorkemen into his haruest.

ANNOTATIONS
CHAP. IX.

3. *He blasphemeth.*] When the Iewes heard Christ remitte sinnes, they charged him with blasphemie, as Heretikes now charge his priests of the new Testament, for that they remitte sinnes: to Whom he sayd, *Whose sinnes you shal forgeue, they are forgeuen* &c. *Io. 20.*

Men haue power to forgiue sinnes.

5. *Whether is easier.*] The faithlesse Iewes thought (as Heretikes now a daies) that to forgeue sinnes Was so proper to God, that it could not be communicated vnto man: but Christ sheweth that as to Worke miracles is otherWise proper to God only, and yet this power is communicated to men, so also to forgeue sinnes.

6. *The sonne of man in earth.*) Christ had poWer to remit sinnes, and often executed the same, not only as he Was God, but also as he Was a man, because he Was head of the Churche and our cheefe Bishop and Priest according to his manhod, in respect Whereof al poWer Was geuen him in heauen and earth. *Mat. 28, v. 18.*

8. *Glorified.*) The faythful people did glorifie God that gaue such poWer to men for to remit sinnes and to doe miracles, knoWing that that Which God committeth to men, is not to his derogation, but to his glorie. him self only being stil the principal Worker of that effect, men being only his ministers, substitutes, and Working vnder him and by his commission and authoritie.

8. *To men.*) Not only Christ as he Was man, had this poWer to forgeue sinnes, but by him and from him the Apostles, and consequently Priests. Mat. 28. *Al poWer is geuen me.* Mat. 18. *Whatsoeuer you shal loose in earth, shal be loosed in heauen.* Ioan. 20. *Whose sinnes you shal forgeue, they are forgeuen.*

External Sacrifice.

13. *Not sacrifice*) These are the Wordes of the Prophete, Who spake them euen then When sacrifices Where offered by Gods commaundement: so that it maketh not agaynst sacrifice, but he saith that sacrifice only Without mercie and charitie, and generally With mortal sinne, is not acceptable. The Iewes offered their sacrifices deWely, but in the meane time they had no pitie nor mercie on their brethren: that is it Which God misliketh.

Fasting.

14. *Fast often.*) By the often fasting of his disciples, We may easely gather that he appointed them a prescript maner of fasting: as it is certaine he taught them a forme of prayer. *Lu. 5.* and *11.*

17. *NeW Wine.*) By this neW Wine, he doth playnly here signifie fasting and the straiter kind of life: by the old bottels, them that can not aWay thereWith.

19. *TWelue yeres.*) This Woman a Gentil had her disease tWelue yeres, and the Gouerners daughter a IeWe (Which is here raysed to life) Was tWelue yeres old, *Luc. 8.* Marke then the allegorie hereof in the IeWes and Gentils. As that Woman fel sicke When the Wenche Was borne, so the Gentils Went their oWne Wayes into idolatrie, When the IeWes in Abraham beleeued. Agayne, as Christ here Went to rayse the Wenche, and by the Way the Woman Was first healed, and then the Wenche reuiued: so Christ came to the IeWes, but the Gentils beleeued first and Were saued, and in the end the IeWes shal beleeue also. *Hiero. in Mat.*

Relikes and Images.

21. *Touche only.*) Not only Christes Wordes, but his garment and touche thereof or any thing to him belonging, might doe and did miracles, force proceding from his holy person to them. Yea this Woman returning home * set vp an Image of Christ, for memorie of this benefite, and the hemme of the same Image did also miracles. This image Iulian the Apostata threWe doWne, and set vp his oWne in steede therof, Which Was immediatly destroyed by fyre from heauen. But the image of Christ broken in peeces by the heathen, the Christians afterWard gathering the peeces together, placed it in the Churche: Where it Was (as Sozomenus Writeth) vnto his time.

Euseb. li. 7 c. 14. hist.

li. 5 c. 20.

28. Do

28. Do you beleeue that I can.] We see here that to the corporal healing of these men he requireth onely this faith, that he is able. Which faith is not sufficient to iustifie them. How then doe the Heretikes by this and the like places pleade for their onely iustifying faith? *See the Annot. Mar. 5, 36.*

38. Pray therfore.) Therfore doth the Churche pray and fast in the Imber dayes, when holy Orders are geuen, that is, when workemen are prepared to be sent into the haruest. *See Act. 13, 2.*

CHAP. X.

He giueth to the Tvvelue the povver of Miracles, and so sendeth them to the lost sheepe of the Ievves, 5 vvith instructions accordingly: 10 and by occasion of the sending, foretelleth of the persecutions after his Ascension, arming them and al other against the same, 40 and also exhorting the people to harbour his seruants in such times of persecution.

Mr. 3, 13. 6, 7. Lu. 6, 13 9, 1.

1 ND hauing called his tvvelue Disciples together, * he gaue them " povver ouer vncleane spirites, that they should cast them out, and should cure al maner of disease, and al maner of infirmitie.

2 † And the names of the tvvelue Apostles be these: the " first, Simon vvho is called Peter, and Andrevv his brother, 3 † Iames of Zebedee, and Iohn his brother, Philip and Barthlemevv, Thomas and Matthevv the publican, and Iames of Alphæus, & Thaddæus, 4 † Simon Cananæus, and Iudas Iscariote, vvho also betrayed him.

5 † These tvvelue did IESVS send: commaunding them, saying, Into the vvay of the :: Gentiles goe ye not, and into 6 the cities of the Samaritans enter ye not: † but goe rather 7 to the sheepe that are perished of the house of Israel. † And going preache, saying, That the kingdom of heauē is at hand. 8 † Cure the sicke, raise the dead, cleanse the lepers, cast out 9 diuels: gratis you haue receiued, gratis giue ye. † Do not 10 " possesse gold, nor siluer, nor money in your purses: † not a skrippe for the vvay, neither two coates, neither shoes, nei- 11 ther rodde. for the vvorkeman is vvorthie of his meate. † And into vvhatsoeuer citie or tovvne you shal enter, inquire vvho 12 in it is vvorthie: and there tarie til you goe forth. † And vvhen ye enter into the house, salute it, saying, " peace be to this hou- 13 se. † And if so be that house be vvorthie, your peace shal come vpon it. but if it be not vvorthie: your peace shal returne to 14 you. † And vvhosoeuer shal not receiue you, nor heare your vvordes: going forth out of the house or the citie " shake of 15 the dust from your feete. † Amen I say to you, it shal be " more tolerable for the land of the Sodomites and Gomorrheans in the day of iudgement, then for that citie.

:: They haue here commission to preach only in Israel: the time being not yet come to call the Gentiles.

The Gospel vpõ the Commemoration of S. Paul, Iun. 30.

† Behold I ſend you as ſheepe in the middes of vvolues. 16 Be ye therfore :: vviſe as ſerpents, and ſimple as dooues. † And 17 take heede of men. For they vvil deliuer you vp in Councels, and in their ſynagogs they vvil ſcourge you. † And to Preſi- 18 dents and " to Kings ſhal you be ledde for my ſake, in teſtimonie to them and the Gentiles. † But vvhen they ſhal de- 19 liuer you vp, * take no thought hovv or vvhat to ſpeake: for " it ſhal be giuen you in that houre vvhat to ſpeake. † For it 20 is not you that ſpeake, but the ſpirit of your father that ſpeaketh in you. † * The brother alſo ſhal deliuer vp the bro- 21 ther to death, and the father the ſonne: and the children ſhal riſe vp agaynſt the parents, and ſhal vvorke their death, † and you ſhal be odious to al men for my name. but he that 22 ſhal perſeuêre vnto the end, he ſhal be ſaued. ⊣

:: Wiſedom and ſimplicitie both be neceſſarie in preachers, Biſhops and Prieſts.

Mar. 13, 11. Luc. 12, 11. Luc. 21, 16.

The Goſpel vpõ S. Athanaſius day. Maij 2.

† And vvhen they ſhal perſecute you in this citie, flee into 23 an other. Amen I ſay to you, you ſhal not finiſh al the cities of Iſrael, til the ſonne of man come.

† * The Diſciple is not aboue the maiſter, nor the ſeruant 24 aboue his lord. † It ſuffiſeth the diſciple that he be as his mai- 25 ſter: and the ſeruãt as his lord. If they haue called the goodmã of the houſe Beelzebub, " hovv much more them of his houſhold? † Therfore feare ye not them. For nothing is hid, that 26 ſhal not be reuealed: and ſecrete, that ſhal not be knovven. † That vvhich I ſpeake to you in the darke, ſpeake ye in the 27 light: and that vvhich you heare in the eare, preache ye vpon the houſe toppes. † And :: feare ye not them that kil the body, 28 and are not able to kil the ſoul: but rather feare him that can deſtroy both ſoul and body into hel. ⊣

Luc. 6, 40

:: A goodly cõfort for Chriſtians and Catholikes and al good men, in the perſecutiõs of Turke, of Heretikes, of al wicked men.

† Are not tvvo ſparovves ſold for a farthing: and not one 29 of them ſhal fall vpon the ground vvithout your father? 30 † But your very heares of the head are al numbered. † Feare 31 not therfore: better are you then many ſparovves. † * Euery 32 one therfore that ſhal " confeſſe me before men, I alſo vvil confeſſe him before my father vvhich is in heauen. † But he 33 that ſhal denie me before men, I alſo vvil denie him before my father vvhich is in heauen. † Do not ye thinke * that I 34 came to ſend peace into the earth: I came " not to ſend peace, but the ſvvord. † For I came to ſeparate * man agaynſt his 35 father, and the daughter agaynſt her mother, and the daughter in lavv agaynſt her mother in lavv. † And a mans ene- 36 mies, they of his ovvne houſhold. † He that loueth father or 37 mother

Mar. 8, 38. Luc. 9, 26. 12, 8. Luc. 12, 51. Mich. 7, 6.

The Goſpel vpõ a Martyrs day that is not a Biſhop.

mother" more then me, is not vvorthy of me: and he that loueth sonne or daughter aboue me, is not vvorthy of me. 38 † And he that taketh not his crosse, and folovveth me, is not 39 vvorthy of me. † He that hath found his life, shal lose it: and he that hath lost his life for me, shal finde it.

Luc. 10, 16.

40 † * He that receiueth you, receiueth me: and he that recei-41 ueth me, receiueth him that sent me. † He that receiueth a Prophet" in the name of a Prophet, shal receiue the revvard of a Prophet. and he that receiueth a ∷ iust man in the name 42 of a iust man, shal receiue the revvard of a iust man. † And * vvhosoeuer shal giue drinke to one of these litle ones a cuppe of cold vvater, only in the name of a disciple, amen I say to you, he shal not lose his revvard. ✝

∷ The reward for harbouring & helping any blessed iust person suffering for his iustice and conscience.

Mar. 9, 41.

ANNOTATIONS
CHAP. X.

1. Power.) Miracles were so necessarie to the confirmation of their doctrine beginning then to be preached, that not only Christ him self did miracles, but also he gaue to his Apostles power to doe them.

2. First Simon.) Peter the first, not in calling, but in preeminence, for (as S. Ambrose saith in 2 Cor. 12.) *Andrew first folowed our Sauiour before Peter: and yet the Primacie Andrew receaued not, but Peter.* Which preeminence of S. Peter aboue the other Apostles is so playnly signified in this word, *First*, by the iudgement euen of Heretikes, that Beza, notwithstanding he confesseth the consent of al copies both Latin and Greeke, yet is not ashamed to say that he suspecteth that this word was thrust into the text by some fauourer of Peters Primacie. Wherby we haue also that they care no more for the Greeke then for the Latin, when it maketh agaynst them: but at their pleasure say that al is corrupted.

Peters Primacie.

Beza in Annot. noui Test. 1556.

9. Do not possesse.) Preachers may not carefully seeke after the superfluities of this life, or any thing which may be an impediment to their function. And as for necessaries, they deserue their temporal liuing at their hands for whom they labour spiritually.

12. Peace to this house.) As Christ him self vsed these wordes or this blessing often, *Peace be to you*, so here he biddeth his Apostles say the like to the house where they come: And so hath it been alwaies a most godly vse of Bishops* to geue their blessing where they come. Which blessing must needes be of great grace and profite, when none but worthy persons (as here we read) might take good thereof: and when it is neuer lost, but returneth to the geuer, when the other partie is not worthy of it. Among other spiritual benefites it taketh away venial sinnes. *Amb. in 9. Luc.*

* *Aug. de ciuit. li. 22 c. 8. Leo Imp. i vit. S. Chrys. Socrat. li. 6 c. 14.*

Bishops blessing.

It remitteth venial sinnes.

14. Shake of the dust.) To contemne the true preachers, or not to receaue the truth preached, is a very damnable sinne.

15. More tolerable.) Hereby it is euident that there be degrees and differences of damnation in Hel fyre according to mens deserts. *Aug. li. 4 de Bapt. c. 19.*

18. Kings.) In the beginning Kings and Emperours persecuted the Churche, that by the very death and bloud of Martyrs it should grow more miraculously. afterward when the Emperours and kings were them selues become Christians, they vsed their power for the Churche, agaynst Infidels and Heretikes. *Aug. ep. 48.*

19. It shal be giuen.) This is verified euen at this present also, when many good Catholikes, that haue no great learning, by their answers confound the Aduersaries.

25. How much more.) No maruel therefore if Heretikes call Christes Vicar Antichrist, when their forefathers the faithles Iewes called Christ him self Beelzebub.

32. Confesse me.) See how Christ esteemeth the open confessing of him, that is, of his truth in the Catholike Churche. for as whē Saul persecuted the Churche, he sayd * him self was persecuted: so to confesse him, and his Churche, is al one. Cōtrariewise, see how he abhorreth them that deny him before men. Which is not only to deny any one litle article of the Catholike fayth cōmended to vs by the Churche: but also to allow or consent to heresie by any meanes, as by subscribing,

Confessing of Christ and his truth.

Act. 9.

coming to their seruice and sermons, furthering them any way agaynst Catholikes, and such like.

34. *Not peace but sword.*) Christ came to breake the peace of worldlings and sinners: as when the sonne beleueth in him, and the father doth not: the wife is a Catholike, and the husband is not. For to agree together in infidelitie, heresie, or any other sinne, is a naughty peace. This being the true meaning of Christes wordes, marke that the Heretikes interprete this to mainteine their rebellions and troubles which their new gospel breedeth. *Beza in no. Test. an. 1565.*

37. *More then.*] No earthly thing, nor duty to Parents, wife, children, countrie, or to a mans owne body and life, can be any iust excuse why a man should doe, or feyne him self to doe or beleeue any thing, agaynst Christ or the vnitie and faith of his Churche.

41. *In the name.*] Reward for hospitality, and specially for receiuing an holy person, as Prophet, Apostle, Bishop, or Priest persecuted for Christes sake. For by receiuing of him in that respect as he is such an one, he shal be partaker of his merites, and be rewarded as for such an one. Whereas on the contrarie side, he that receiueth an Heretike into his house and a false preacher, doth communicate with his wicked workes. *Ep. 2. Io.*

CHAP. XI.

Iohn the Baptist in prison also doing his diligence, sendeth some of his disciples to Christ: that as they heard, so they might also see his miracles vvith their eyes. 7 Aftervvard Christ declareth hovv vvorthy of credite Iohns testimonie vvas: 16 and inueigheth agaynst the Ievves, vvho vvith neither of their maners of life could be vvonne: 20 no nor vvith Christes infinite miracles: 25 praysing Gods vvisedom in this behalfe, 27 and calling to him self al such as feele their ovvne burdens.

1 AND it came to passe: vvhen IESVS had done cōmaunding his tvvelue Disciples, he passed from thence, to teach & preach in their cities.

The Gospel on the 2. Sunday in Aduent.

2 † * And vvhen Iohn had heard in prison the vvorkes of Christ: sending tvvo of his disciples, he said to him, 3 † "Art thou he that art to come, or looke vve for an other? 4 † And IESVS making ansvver said to them, Goe and report to Iohn vvhat you haue heard and seen. 5 † * The blinde see, the lame vvalke, the lepers are made cleane, the deafe heare, the dead rise againe, to the poore the Gospel is preached: 6 † and blessed is he that shal not be scandalized in me.

Luc. 7, 18.

Esa. 35, 5. 61, 1.

7 † And vvhen they vvent their vvay, IESVS began to say to the multitudes of Iohn, "What vvent you out" into the desert to see? a reede shaken vvith the vvinde? 8 † But vvhat vvent you out to see? a man clothed in soft garments? Behold they that are clothed in soft garments, are in Kinges houses. 9 † But vvhat vvent you out to see? a Prophet? yea I tel you and more then a Prophet. 10 † For this is he of vvhom it is vvritten, *Behold I send mine angel before thy face, vvhich shal prepare thy vvay before thee.* ⫞

Mal. 3, 1.

11 † Amen I say to you, there hath not risen among the borne of vvomen a greater then Iohn the Baptist: yet he that is the lesser

Luc.16, 16.

12 lesser in the kingdom of heauen, is greater then he. † And * from the dayes of Iohn the Baptist vntil novv, the kingdom of heauen suffereth violence, and the violent beare it 13 avvay. † For al the Prophets and the Lavv prophecied vnto 14 Iohn: † and if you vvil receiue it, he is * " Elias that is for to 15 come. † He that hath eares to heare, let him heare.

Mal.4, 5.

Luc. 7, 31.

16 † And * vvhereunto shal I esteeme this generation to be like? It is like to children sitting in the market-place: 17 vvhich crying to their companions, † say, We haue piped to you, and you haue not daunced: vve haue lamented, and 18 you haue not mourned. † For * Iohn came neither " eating 19 nor drinking: and they say, He hath a diuel. † The Sonne of man came eating and drinking, and they say, Behold a man that is a glotton and a vvinedrinker, a frende of Publicans and sinners. And vvisedom is iustified of her children.

Mt.3,4.

Luc.10, 13.

20 † Then * began he to vpbraide the cities, vvherein vvere done the most of his miracles, for that they had not done pe-21 nance. † Wo be to thee Corozain, vvo be to thee Beth-saida: for if in Tyre & Sidon had been vvrought the miracles that haue been vvrought in you, they had done " penance in heare-22 cloth and ashes long agoe. † But neuerthelesse, I say to you, it shal be more tolerable for Tyre and Sidon in the 23 day of iudgement, then for you. † And thou Capharnaum, shalt thou be exalted vp to heauen? thou shalt come dovvne euen vnto hel. for if in Sodom had been vvrought the miracles that haue been wrought in thee, perhaps it had remained 24 vnto this day. † But notvvithstanding I say to you, that it shal be more tolerable for the land of Sodom in the day of iudgement, then for thee.

Luc.10, 21.

The Gospel vpō S. Matthias day Feb.24. and vpon S. Francis day Octob. 4. and for many Martyrs.

25 † At that time IESVS ansvvered and said. * I confesse to thee O Father lord of heauen and earth, because thou hast hid these things from the vvise and prudent, and hast reuealed 26 thē to " litle ones. † Yea Father: for so hath it vvel pleased thee. 27 † Al things are deliuered me of my Father. And no man knovveth the Sonne but the Father: neither doth any knovv the Father, but the Sonne, and to vvhom it shal please the 28 Sonne to reueale. † Come ye to me al that labour, and are 29 burdened, and I vvil refresh you. † Take vp my yoke vpon you, and learne of me, because I am meeke, and humble of 30 hart: and you shal finde rest to your soules. † For my " yoke is svveete, and my burden light. ⊣

ANNOTATIONS
CHAP. XI.

3. *Art thou he.*] Iohn him ſelf doubted not, for he baptized him and gaue great teſtimonie of him before: *Io. 1.* But becauſe his diſciples knewe him not, nor eſteemed of him ſo much as of Iohn their owne Maiſter, therfore did he ſend them vnto Chriſt, that by occaſion of Chriſtes anſwer he might the better inſtruct them what he was, and ſo make them Chriſtes diſciples, preferring them to a better Maiſter.

Eremitical life.

7. *What went you out.*] High commendation of Iohns holineſſe, as wel for his faſting, rough attire, ſolitary life, and conſtancie, as for the dignitie of his function.

7. *Into the deſert.*] The faythful people in al ages reſorted of deuotion into wildernes to ſee men of ſpecial and rare holynes, Prophets, Eremites, Anchorites &c. to haue their prayers or ghoſtly counſel. *See S. Hierom de vita Hilarionis.*

Elias.

14. *Elias.*) As Elias ſhal be the meſſenger of Chriſtes later coming, ſo was Iohn his meſſenger and Præcurſor at his former coming: and therfore is he called Elias, becauſe of his like office and like ſpirit. *Luc. 1. Grego. ho. 7. in Euang.*

18. *Eating and drinking.*] The wicked quarrellers of the world miſconſtre eaſely al the actes and life of good men. If they be great faſters and auſtere liuers, they are blaſphemed and counted hypocrites: if they conuerſe with other men in ordinary maner, then they be counted diſſolute.

Penance.

21. *Penance in ſackcloth.*] By this ſackcloth and aſhes added here and in other places, wee ſee euidently that Penance is not only leauing of former ſinnes, and chaunge or amendement of life paſt, no nor bare ſorowfulnes or recounting of our offenſes already committed, but requireth puniſhement and chaſtiſemēt of our perſons by theſe and ſuch other meanes as the Scriptures do els where ſet forth. and therfore concerning the worde alſo, it is rather to be called Penance, as in our tranſlation: then (as the Aduerſaries of purpoſe auoyding the word) Repentance or Amendement of life: and that according to the very vſual ſignification of the * Greeke word in the moſt ancient Eccleſiaſtical Greeke writers: who for *Pœnitentes* (which in the Primitiue Church did publike penance) ſay, * οἱ ἐν μετανοίᾳ ὄντες, that is, *Men that are doing penance.* And concerning that part of penance which is Cōfeſſion, the Eccleſiaſtical hiſtorie calleth it by the ſame Greeke word, and the penitents comming to confeſſion, τοὺς μετανοοῦντας. *Sozom. li. 7 c. 16. Socrat. li. 5 c. 19.*

Μετάνοια.

* *Dionyſ. Eccl. hier. c. 3. in initio.*

25. *Litle ones.*) Theſe litle ones doe not ſignifie here only the vnlearned, as though Coblers and weauers and wemen and girles had this reuelation, and therfore do vnderſtand al Scriptures and are able to expound them: but here are ſignified the humble, whether they be learned or vnlearned: as when he ſayth, *Vnles you become as litle ones, you ſhal not enter into the Kingdom of heauen.* And ſo alſo the greateſt Doctors (who as they were moſt learned, ſo moſt humbled them ſelues to the iudgement of the Catholike Churche) are theſe litle ones: and Heretikes, who although vnlearned, yet vaunt their knowledge and their ſpirit of vnderſtanding aboue al ancient fathers and the whole Churche, can not be of theſe litle and humble ones.

Mt. 18, 3.

The commaundements poſſible.

30. *Yoke ſweete.*] What is this light burden and ſweete yoke, but his commaundements, of which S. Iohn ſayth 1. Ep. 5. *His commaundements are not heauy?* cleane contrary to the Aduerſaries that ſay, they are vnpoſſible to be kept.

CHAP. XII.

The blindnes of the Phariſees about the Sabboth he reproueth by Scriptures, by reaſon, and by a miracle. 14 and his death being therfore ſought by them, he meekely goeth out of the vvay, according as Eſay had prophecied of him. 22 His caſting out of deuils alſo he defendeth agaynſt them, 31 and ſetteth forth the daunger they ſtand in for their horrible blaſphemie. 38 And becauſe they aſke yet for a ſigne, he ſhevveth hovv vvorthely they ſhal be damned, 43 foretelling hovv the deuil ſhal poſſeſſe their Nation, 46 and teſtifying that although he be of their bloud, yet not they for this, but ſuch as keepe his commaundements are deere vnto him.

1 T that time * IESVS vvent through the corne on the Sabboth: and his Diſciples being hungrie, began to plucke the eares, and to eate. 2 † And the Phariſees ſeeing them, ſaid to him. Loe, thy Diſciples doe that vvhich is not lavvful

Mr. 2, 23. Lu. 6, 1.

3 ful for them to doe on the Sabboth-dayes. † But he ſayd to them, Haue you not read vvhat * Dauid did vvhen he vvas
4 an hungred, and they that vvere vvith him: † hovv he entred into the houſe of God, and did eate the loaues of propoſition, vvhich it vvas not lavvful for him to eate, nor for them
5 that vvere vvith him, * but for prieſtes only? † Or haue ye not read in the * Lavv, that on Sabboth-dayes the prieſtes in the temple do breake the Sabboth, and are vvithout
6 blame? † but I tel you that there is here a greater then the tẽple.
7 † And if you did knovv vvhat it is, *I wil mercie, and not* :: *ſacrifice*:
8 you vvould neuer haue condemned the innocentes. † For the Sonne of man is lord of the Sabboth alſo.

1. Re. 21, 4. — Leu. 24, 9. — Nu. 28, 9 — Oſe. 6, 6.

:: See the annotatiõ chap. 9, 13.

9 † And vvhen he had paſſed from thence, he came into their
10 ſynagogue. † And * behold there vvas a man vvhich had a vvithered hand, and they aſked him ſaying, Whether is it lavvful
11 to cure on the Sabboths? that they might accuſe him. † But he ſayd to them, what man ſhal there be of you, that ſhal haue one ſheepe: and if the ſame fall into a ditche on the Sabboths,
12 vvil he not take hold and lift it vp? † Hovv much better is a man more then a ſheepe? therfore it is lavvful on the Sab-
13 boths to doe a good deede. † Then he ſayth to the man, Stretch forth thy hand. and he ſtretched it forth, and it vvas reſtored to health euen as the other.

Mr. 3, 1, Lu. 6, 6.

14 † And the Phariſees going forth made a cõſultation agaynſt
15 him, hovv they might deſtroy him. † But IESVS knovving it, retired from thence: and many folovved him, and he cured
16 them all. † and he charged them that they ſhould not diſ-
17 cloſe him. † That it might be fulfilled vvhich vvas ſpoken by
18 Eſay the Prophete, ſaying. † *Behold my ſeruant vvhom I haue choſen, my beloued in vvhom my ſoul hath vvel liked. I vvil put my ſpirit vpon him, and*
19 *iudgement to the Gentiles ſhal he ſhew. † He ſhal not contend, nor crie out, neither*
20 *ſhal any man heare in the ſtreetes his voyce. † The reede bruiſed he ſhal not breake, and ſmoking flaxe he ſhal not extinguiſh: til he caſt forth iudgement vnto*
21 *victorie. † And in his name the Gentiles ſhal hope.*

Eſ. 42, 1

22 † Then * vvas offered to him one poſſeſſed vvith a deuil, blinde and dumme: and he cured him, ſo that he ſpake & ſaw.
23 † And al the multitudes vvere amaſed, and ſayd, Whether this
24 be the Sonne of Dauid? † But the Phariſees hearing it, ſayd. This felovv caſteth not out diuels but ″ in Beelzebub the Prin-
25 ce of the diuels. † And IESVS knovving their cogitations, ſaid to them.

Luc. 11, 14. — Mar. 3, 22

Euery kingdom :: deuided againſt it ſelf ſhal be made deſo

:: Therfore the

kingdom of Heretikes can not possibly stand, because it is alwayes ful of diuisiō and dissension.

desolate:and euery citie or house deuided agaynst it self, shal not stand. † And if Satan cast out Satan, he is deuided 26 against him self: hovv then shal his kingdom stand? † And 27 if I in Beelzebub cast out deuils: your children in vvhom do they cast out? Therfore they shal be your iudges. † But if I in 28 the Spirit of God do cast out deuils, then is the kingdom of God come vpon you. † Or hovv can a man enter into the 29 house of the strong, and rifle his vessel, vnles he first binde the strong? and then he vvil rifle his house. † He that is " not vvith 30 me, is agaynst me: and he that " gathereth not vvith me, scattereth. † Therfore I say to you, euery sinne and blasphemie 31 shal be forgiuen men, but " the blasphemie of the Spirit shal not be forgiuen. † And vvhosoeuer shal speake a 32 vvord agaynst the Sonne of man, it shal be forgiuen him: but he that shal speake against the Holy Ghost, it shal not be forgiuen him neither in this vvorld, nor " in the vvorld to come. † Either ∴ make the tree good, and his fruite 33 good: or make the tree euil, and his fruite euil. for of the fruite the tree is knowē. † You vipers broodes, hovv can you speake 34 good things, vvhereas you are euil? for of the aboundance of the hart the mouth speaketh. † A good man out of a good 35 treasure bringeth forth good things: and an euil man out of an euil treasure bringeth forth euil things. † But I say vnto 36 you, that euery " idle vvord that men shal speake, they shal render an account for it in the day of iudgement. † For of thy 37 wordes thou shalt be iustified, and of thy vvordes thou shalt be condemned.

∴ It is a mans owne free wil and election, to be a good tree or an il tree: to bring forth good fruites or bad. S. Augustine vpon this place. *li.2 c.4 de actis cum Felic. Manichæo.*

THE GOSPEL vpon vvenesday the first Weeke of Lent.

† Then ansvvered him certaine of the Scribes and Pharisees, saying, Maister, vve vvould see a signe from thee. 38 † who ansvvered, and said to them, 39

The vvicked and aduouterous generation seeketh a signe: and a signe shal not be giuen it, but the signe of Ionas the Prophet. † For as * Ionas vvas in the vvhales belly three 40 dayes and three nightes: so shal the Sonne of man be in the hart of the earth three dayes and three nightes. † The men 41 of Niniuee shal rise in the iudgemēt vvith this generatiō, and shal condemne it: because * they did penance at the preaching of Ionas. And behold more then Ionas here. † The * Queene 42 of the South shal rise in the iudgement vvith this generation, and shal condemne it: because she came from the endes of the earth to heare the vvisedom of Salomō, and behold more then

Ion. 2, 2.

Ion. 3, 5.

3. Reg. 10, 1.

Luc. 11, 24.

43 then Salomon here. † And * vvhen an vncleane ſpirit ſhal goe out of a man, he vvalketh through dry places, ſeeking 44 reſt, and findeth not. † Then he ſaith, I vvil returne into my houſe vvhence I came out. And coming he findeth it va- 45 cant, ſvvept vvith beſoms, and trimmed. † Then goeth he, and taketh vvith him ſeuen other ſpirites more vvicked then him ſelf, and they enter in and dvvel there: and * the laſt of that man be made vvorſe then the firſt. So ſhal it be alſo to this vvicked generation.

2. Pet. 2, 20.

Mar. 3, 31. Luc. 8. 20.

The Goſpel vpõ the day of the Seuen Brethren &c. Iulij 10.

46 † As he vvas yet ſpeaking to the multitudes, * behold his mother and his brethren ſtoode vvithout, ſeeking to ſpeake 47 to him. † And one ſaid vnto him, Behold thy mother and 48 thy brethren ſtand without, ſeeking thee. † But he anſvvering him that told him, ſaid, "Who is my mother, and vvho are 49 my brethren? † And ſtretching forth his hand vpon his Diſci- 50 ples, he ſaid, Behold my mother and my brethren. † For vvhoſoeuer ſhal doe the vvil of my father, that is in heauen: he is my brother, and ſiſter, and mother. ⸸

ANNOTATIONS
CHAP. XII.

24. In Beelzebub.] The like blaſphemie agaynſt the Holy Ghoſt is, to attribute the miracles done by Saincts either dead or aliue, to the Diuel.

30. Not with me.] They that are indifferent to al religions, commonly and fitly called Neuters, ioyning them ſelues to neither part, let them marke theſe wordes wel, and they ſhal ſee, that Chriſt accoumpted al them to be agaynſt him and his Church, that are not plainely and flatly with him and it.

Neuters in religion.

30. Gathereth not with me.] He ſpeaketh not only of his owne perſon, but of al to whom he hath committed the gouernement of his Church, and ſpecially of the cheefe Paſtours ſucceding Peter in the gouernement of the whole. As S. Hierom writing to Damaſus Pope of Rome, applieth theſe words vnto him, ſaying of al Heretikes, *He that gathereth not with thee, ſcattereth: that is to ſay, He that is not with Chriſt, is with Antichriſt.*

Ep. 58.

31. The blaſphemie of the Spirit.] He meaneth not that there is any ſinne ſo great, which God wil not forgiue, or whereof a man may not repẽt in this life, as ſome Heretikes at this day affirme: but that ſome heinous ſinnes (as namely this blaſphemie of the Iewes againſt the euident workes of the Holy Ghoſt, and likewiſe Archeheretikes who wilfully reſiſt the knowẽ truth and workes of the Holy Ghoſt in Gods Church) are hardly forgeuen, and ſeldom haue ſuch men grace to repent. Otherwiſe among al the ſinnes agaynſt the Holy Ghoſt (which are commonly reckened ſixe) one only ſhal neuer be forgiuen, that is, dying without repentance wilfully, called Final impenitence. Which ſinne he committeth that dieth with contempt of the Sacrament of Penance, obſtinatly refuſing abſolution, by the Churches miniſterie: as S. Auguſtine plainely declareth in theſe wordes. *Whoſoeuer he be that beleueth not mans ſinnes to be remitted in Gods Church, and therfore deſpiſeth the bountifulnes of God in ſo mighty a worke, if he in that obſtinat minde continue til his liues end, he is guilty of ſinne againſt the Holy Ghoſt*, in which Holy Ghoſt Chriſt remitteth ſinnes. *Enchir. 83. Ep. 50 in fine.*

Final impenitence.

Remiſſion of ſinnes in the Church.

32. Sonne of man.] The Iewes in their wordes ſinned againſt the ſonne of man, when they reprehended thoſe things which he did as a man, to witte, calling him therfore, a glutton, a great drinker of wine, a freend of the Publicans, and taking offenſe becauſe he kept company with ſinners, brake the Sabboth, and ſuch like: and this ſinne might more eaſely be forgiuen them, becauſe they iudged of him as they would haue done of any other man: but they ſinned and blasphemed against the Holy Ghost (called here the finger of God whereby he wrought miracles) when of malice they attributed the euident workes of God in casting out diuels, to the diuel him self: and this sinne shal not be remitted, because it shal hardly be remitted, as we see by the plague of their posteritie vntil this day.

32. *Nor in the World to come.*] S. Augustine and other Holy Doctors gather herevpon, that some sinnes may be remitted in the next life, and consequently prooue Purgatorie thereby. *De Ciuit. Dei li. 21 c. 13. D. Gregor, Dial. li. 4 c. 39.*

Purgatorie.

36. *Idle word.*] If of euery idle word we must make accoumpt before God in iudgement, and yet shal not for euery such word be damned euerlastingly: then there must needes be some temporal punishment in the next life.

48. *Who is my mother.*] The dutiful affection toward our parents and kinsfolke is not blamed, but the inordinate loue of them to the hinderance of our seruice and duty toward God. Vpon this place some old Heretikes denied Christ to haue any mother. *Aug. li. de Fid. & Symb. c. 4.* Neither euer was there any heresie so absurd, but it would seeme to haue Scripture for it.

Al Heresies alleage Scriptures.

CHAP. XIII.

Speaking in parables (as the Scripture foretold of him, and as meete vvas for the reprobate Ievves:) he shevveth by the parable of the Sovver, that in the labours of his Church, three partes of foure do perishe through the fault of the hearers. 24 and yet, by the parable of good seede and cockle (as also of the Nette) that his seruants must not for al that, neuer vvhile the vvorld lasteth, make any Schisme or Separation. 31 And by parables of the litle mustardseede and leauen, that notvvithstanding the three parts perishing, and ouersovving of cockles, yet that fourth part of the good seede shal spreade ouer al the vvorld. 44 And vvithal, vvhat a treasure, and pearle it is. 53 After al vvhich, yet his ovvne countrie vvil not honour him.

THE same day IESVS going out of the house, sate by the sea side. † And * great multitudes vvere gathered together vnto him, in so much that he vvent vp into a boate & sate: and al the multitude stoode in the shore, † and he spake to them many things in parables, saying, 1 2 3

Mr. 4, 1. Lu. 8, 4.

Behold the sovver vvent forth to sovv. † And vvhiles he sovveth, some fell by the vvay side, and the foules of the aire did come and eate it. † Othersome also fell vpon rockie places, vvhere they had not much earth: and they shot vp incontinent, because they had not deepenes of earth, † and after the sunne vvas vp, they parched: and because they had not roote, they vvithered. † And other fell among thornes: and the thornes grevve and choked them. † And othersome fell vpon good ground: and they yelded fruite, the " one an hundredfold, the other threescore, and an other thirtie. † He that hath eares to heare, let him heare. 4 5 6 7 8 9

† And his Disciples came and said to him. Why speakest thou to them in parables? † Who ansvvered and said vnto them, Because " to you it is giuen to knovv the mysteries of the kingdom of heauen: but to them it is not giuen. † For he 10 11 12

he that hath, to him ſhal be giuen, and he ſhal abound: but he that hath not, from him ſhal be taken avvay that alſo vvhich he hath. 13 † Therfore in parables I ſpeake to them: becauſe ſeeing they ſee not, and :: hearing they heare not, neither do they vnderſtand: 14 † and the prophecie of Eſay is fulfilled in them, vvhich ſaith, *With hearing ſhal you heare, and you ſhal not vnderſtand: and ſeeing ſhal you ſee, and you ſhal not ſee.* 15 † *For the hart of this people is vvaxed groſſe, and vvith their eares they haue heauily heard, and their eies " they haue ſhut: leſt at any time they may ſee with their eies, and heare with their eares, and vnderſtand vvith their hart and be conuerted, and I may heale them.* 16 † But bleſſed are your eyes becauſe they doe ſee, and your eares becauſe they doe heare. 17 † For amen I ſay to you, that * many Prophets and iuſt men haue deſired to ſee the things that you ſee, and haue not ſeen them: and to heare the things that you heare, and haue not heard them. 18 † Heare you therfore the parable of the ſovver.

:: When Gods word is preached, they properly haue eares to heare, that haue hartes to obey: and they hearing do not heare, which heare by ſenſe of their body, and obey not by conſent of their hartes. *Aug. de dono perſeu. c. 14.*

Luc. 10, 23.

19 † Euery one that heareth the vvord of the kingdom and vnderſtandeth not, there cometh the vvicked one, and catcheth avvay that vvhich vvas ſovven in his hart: this is he that vvas ſovven by the vvay ſide. 20 † And he that vvas ſovven vpon rockie places: this is he that heareth the vvord, and incõtinent receiueth it vvith ioy, 21 † yet hath he not roote in him ſelf, but is for a time: and vvhen there falleth tribulation and perſecution for the vvord, he is by and by ſcandalized. 22 † And he that vvas ſovven among thornes, this is he that heareth the vvord, and the carefulnes of this vvorld and the deceitfulnes of riches choketh vp the vvord, and he becometh fruitles. 23 † But he that vvas ſovven vpon good ground: this is he that heareth the vvord, and vnderſtandeth, and bringeth fruite, and yeldeth ſome an hundred-fold, and other threeſcore, and an other thirtie.

24 † An other parable he propoſed to them, ſaying, The kingdom of heauen is reſembled to a man that ſovved good ſeede in his field. 25 † But vvhen men vvere a ſleepe, his enemy came and ouerſovved cockle among the vvheate, and vvent his vvay. 26 † And vvhen the blade vvas ſhot vp, and had brought forth fruite, then appeared alſo the cockle. 27 † And the ſeruants of the goodman of the houſe comming ſaid to him, Sir, didſt thou not ſovv good ſeede in thy field? Whence then hath it cockle? 28 † And he ſaid to them, The enemy man hath done this. And the ſeruants ſaid to him, Wilt thou vve goe and gather it vp? 29 † And he ſaid, No: " leſt perhaps

The Goſpel vpõ the 5 Sunday after the Epiphanie.

gathering vp the cockle, you may roote vp the vvheate also together vvith it. † Suffer both to grovv vntil the haruest, and in the time of haruest I vvil say to the reapers, Gather vp first the cockle, and binde it into bundels to burne, but the vvheate gather ye into my barne. ꟷ 30

The Gospel vpõ the 6 Sunday after the Epiphanie.

† An other parable he proposed vnto them, saying, * The kingdom of heauen is like to a mustard-seede, vvhich a man tooke and sovved in his field. † Which is the "least surely of al seedes: but vvhen it is grovven, it is greater then al herbes, and is made a tree, so that the foules of the aire come, and dvvel in the branches thereof. † An other parable he spake to them, The kingdom of heauen is like to leauen, vvhich a vvoman tooke and hid in three measures of meale, vntil the vvhole vvas leauened. 31 32 33

Mar. 4, 30. Luc. 13, 18.

† Al these things IESVS spake in parables to the multitudes, and vvithout parables he did not speake to them: † that it might be fulfilled vvhich vvas spoken by the Prophet saying, *I wil open my mouth in parables, I wil vtter things hidden from the foundation of the vvorld.* ꟷ 34 35

Psa. 77, 2.

† Then hauing dimissed the multitudes, he came into the house, and his Disciples came vnto him, saying, Expound vs the parable of the cockle of the field. † Who made ansvver and said to them, He that soweth the good seede, is the Sonne of man. † And the field, is the vvorld. And the good seede: these are the childrẽ of the kingdom. And the cockle: are the children of the vvicked one. † And the enemie that sovved them, is ∷ the deuil. But the haruest, is the ende of the vvorld. And the reapers, are the Angels. † Euen as cockle therfore is gathered vp, and burnt vvith fire: so shal it be in the ende of the vvorld. † The Sonne of man shal send his Angels, and they shal gather out of his kingdom al scandals, and them that vvorke iniquitie: † and shal cast them into the furnace of fire, There shal be vveeping and gnashing of teeth. † Then shal the iust shine as the sunne, in the kingdom of their father. He that hath eares to heare, let him heare. 36 37 38 39 40 41 42 43

∷ Not God then, but the Diuel is the author of all euil.

The Gospel for Virgins & other holy Women.

† The kingdom of heauen is like a treasure hidden in a field. vvich a man hauing found, did hide it, and for ioy thereof goeth, and selleth al that he hath, and byeth that field. † Againe the kingdom of heauen is like to a marchant man, seeking good pearles. † And hauing found one precious pearle, he vvent his vvay, and sold al that he had, and 44 45 46

bought

bought it.

47 † Againe the kingdom of heauen is like to a nette caſt into the ſea, and gathering together of al kind of fiſhes.

48 † Which, vvhen it vvas filled, dravving it forth, and ſitting by the ſhore, they choſe out the :: good into veſſels, but the bad they did caſt out.

:: Here alſo are ſignified good and bad in the Church.

49 † So ſhal it be in the conſummation of the vvorld. The Angels ſhal goe forth, and ſhal ſeparate the euil from among the iuſt,

50 † and ſhal caſt them into the furnace of fire. there ſhal be vveeping and gnaſhing of teeth.

51 † Haue ye vnderſtoode al theſe things? They ſay to him, Yea.

52 † He ſaid vnto them, Therfore euery Scribe inſtructed in the kingdom of heauen, is like to a man that is an houſholder, vvhich bringeth forth out of his treaſure nevv things and old. ⊣

53 † And it came to paſſe: vvhen IESVS had ended theſe parables, he paſſed from thence.

54 † And * coming into his ovvne countrie, he taught them in their ſynagogues, ſo that they marueled, and ſaid, Hovv came this fellovv by this vviſedom and vertues?

Mr. 6, 1. Luc. 4, 16.

55 † Is not this the " carpenters ſonne? Is not his mother called MARIE, and his brethren, Iames and Ioſeph, and Simon and Iude:

56 † and his ſiſters, are they not al vvith vs? Whence therefore hath he al theſe things?

57 † And they vvere ſcandalized in him. But IESVS ſaid to them, There is not a Prophet vvithout honour but in his ovvne countrie, and in his ovvne houſe.

58 † And he vvrought not many miracles there becauſe of their incredulity.

ANNOTATIONS
CHAP. XIII.

8. One an hundred.] This difference of fruites is the difference of merites in this life, and rewardes for them in the next life, according to the diuerſities of ſtates, or other differences. of ſtates, as that the hundred fold agreeth to virgins profeſſed, threeſcore fold to religious widowes, thirtiefold to the maried. *Aug. li. de S. Virginit. c. 44 & ſeq.* Which truth the old Heretike Iouinian denied (as ours doe at this day) affirming that there is no difference of merites or rewardes. *Hiero. li. 2 adu. Iouia. Ambroſ. ep. 82. Aug. hær. 82.*

Difference of merites and rewardes.

11. To you is giuen.] To the Apoſtles and ſuch as haue the guiding and teaching of others, deeper knowledge of Gods word and myſteries is giuen, then to the common people. As alſo to Chriſtians generally, that which was not giuen to the obſtinate Iewes.

15. They haue ſhut.) In ſaying that they ſhut their owne eies, which S. Paul alſo repeateth *Act. 28*: he teacheth vs the true vnderſtanding of al other places, where it might ſeeme by the bare wordes that God is the very author and worker of this induration, and blindnes, and of other ſinnes: * Which was an old condemned blaſphemie, and is now the Hereſie of * Caluin: whereas our Sauiour here teacheth vs, that they ſhut their owne eies, and are the cauſe of their owne ſinne and damnation, God not doing, but permitting it, and ſuffering them to fall further becauſe of their former ſinnes, as S. Paul declareth of the reprobate Gentiles. *Ro. 1.*

God is not the author of euil.

Iren. apud Euſeb. li. 5 c. 19. Calu. li. 1 Inſtit. c. 4.

25. Ouerſowed.) Firſt by Chriſt and his Apoſtles was planted the truth, and falſhod came afterward, and was ouerſowen by the enemy the Diuel, and not by Chriſt, who is not the author of euil. *Tertul. de præscript.*

29. Lest you plucke vp also.] The good must tolerate the euil, when it is so strong that it can not be redressed without danger and disturbance of the whole Church, and committe the matter to Gods iudgement in the later day. Otherwise where il men (be they Heretikes or other malefactors) may be punished or suppressed without disturbance and hazard of the good, they may and ought by publike authority either Spiritual or temporal to be chastised or executed.

Good and euil in the Church.

30. Suffer both to grow.] The good and bad (wee see here) are mingled together in the Churche. Which maketh against certaine Heretikes and Schismatikes, which seuered them selues of old from the rest of the whole world, vnder pretence that them selues only were pure, and al others both Priests and people sinners: and against some Heretikes of this time also, which say that euil men are not of, or in the Churche.

32. The least of al seedes.] The Church of Christ had a smal beginning, but afterward became the most glorious and knowen common welth in earth: the greatest powers and the most wise of the world putting them selues into the same.

55. Carpenters sonne.] Herevpon Iulian the Apostata and his flatterer Libanius tooke their scoffe against our Sauiour, saying (at his going against the Persians) to the Christians, What doeth the Carpenters sonne now? and threatening that after his returne the Carpenters sonne should not be able to saue them from his furie. Wherevnto a godly man answered by the Spirit of Prophecie, *He whom Iulian calleth the Carpenters sonne, is making a wodden coffin for him against his death.* And in deede not long after there came newes that in that bataile he dyed miserably. *Sozo. li. 6 c. 2. Theodo. li. 3 c. 18.* The very like scoffe vse Heretikes that call the body of Christ in the B. Sacrament, bakers bread. It seemeth in deede to the senses to be so, as Christ seemed to be Iosephs natural sonne, but faith telleth vs the contrarie as wel in the one as in the other.

CHAP. XIIII.

Hearing the vnvvorthy decollation of Iohn Baptist by Herode, 13 he betaketh him to his vsual solitarines in the desert, and there feedeth 5000 vvith fiue loaues. 23 And then after the night spent in the mountaine in prayer, he vvalketh vpon the sea (signifying the vvide vvorld) 28 yea and Peter also: vvherevpon they adore him as the sonne of God. 35 And vvith the very touche of his garments hemme he healeth innumerable.

T that time * Herod the Tetrach heard the fame of IESVS: † and said to his seruants, This is Iohn the Baptist: he is risen from the dead, and therfore vertues vvorke in him. † For Herod apprehended Iohn and bound him, and put him into prison because of Herodias, his 'brothers' vvife. † For Iohn said vnto him, It is not lavvful for thee to haue her. † And vvilling to put him to death, he feared the people: because they esteemed him as a Prophet. † But on Herods birth-day, the daughter of Herodias daunced before them: and pleased Herod. † Wherevpon he promised with an othe, to giue her vvhatsoeuer she vvould aske of him. † But she being instructed before of her mother saith, Giue me here in a dish the head of Iohn the Baptist. † And the king vvas stroken sad: yet because of his ∷ othe and for them that sate vvith him at table, he commaunded it to be giuen. † And he sent, and beheaded Iohn in the prison. † And his head vvas brought in a dish: and

1 2 3 4 5 6 7 8 9 10 11

Mar. 6, 14. Lu. 9, 7. 3, 19.

brother Philips

A wicked and rash othe, and more wickedly fulfilled: because an vnlawfull othe bindeth no mā.

and it vvas giuen to the damſel, and ſhe brought it to her mo-
12 ther. † And his Diſciples came and tooke the body, and ″ buried it: ∷ and came and told IESVS.

∷ S. Iohns diſciples at this time had wel learned their duety toward Chriſt.

Mr.6,31 Lu.9,10 Io. 6,2.

13 † Which vvhen IESVS had heard, * he ″ retired from thence by boate, into a deſert place apart, and the multitudes hauing heard of it, folovved him on foote out of the cities.
14 † And he coming forth ſavv a great multitude, and pitied
15 them, and cured their diſeaſed. † And vvhen it vvas euening, his Diſciples came vnto him, ſaying, It is a deſert place, and the houre is novv paſt: dimiſſe the multitudes that going in-
16 to the tovvnes, they may bye them ſelues victuals. † But IESVS ſaid to them, They haue no neede to goe: giue ye them
17 to eate. † They anſvvered him. We haue not here, but fiue
18 loaues, and tvvo fiſhes. † Who ſaid to them, Bring them hi-
19 ther to me. † And vvhen he had commaunded the multitude to ſitte dovvne vpon the graſſe, he tooke the fiue loaues and the tvvo fiſhes, and looking vp vnto heauen he bleſſed and brake, and gaue the loaues to his Diſciples, and ″ the Diſciples
20 to the multitudes. † And they did al eate, and had their fil. And they tooke the leauings, twelue ful baſkettes of the frag-
21 ments. † And the number of them that did eate vvas, fiue thouſand men, beſide vvomen and children.

The Goſpel vpon the Octaue of S. Peter and S. Paul. Iulij 6.

22 † And forth vvith IESVS commaunded his Diſciples to goe vp into the boate, and to goe before him ouer the vvater,
23 til he dimiſſed the multitudes. † And hauing dimiſſed the multitude, he * aſcended into a mountaine alone to praye. And

Mr. 6, 46. Io.6,16.

24 vvhen it vvas euening, he vvas there alone. † But the boate in the middes of the ſea vvas toſſed vvith vvaues. for the vvinde
25 vvas contrarie. † And in the fourth vvatch of the night, he
26 came vnto them vvalking vpon the ſea. † And ſeeing him vpon the ″ ſea vvalking, they vvere troubled ſaying, That
27 it is a ghoſt. and for feare they cried out. † And immediatly IESVS ſpake vnto them, ſaying, Haue confidence: it is I, feare
28 ye not. † And Peter making anſvver ſaid, Lord if it be thou,
29 bid me come to thee vpon the vvaters. † And he ſaid, Come. And Peter deſcending out of the boate, ″ vvalked vpon the
30 vvater to come to IESVS. † But ſeeing the vvinde rough, he vvas afraid: and vvhen he began to be drovvned, he cried
31 out ſaying, Lord, ſaue me. † And incontinent ∷ IESVS ſtretching forth his hand tooke hold of him, and ſaid vnto him,
32 O thou of litle faith, vvhy didſt thou doubt? † And vvhen they

∷ Notwithſtāding the infirmities of them that gouerne

they vvere gone vp into the boate, the vvinde ceased. † And 33 they that vvere in the boate, came and adored him, saying, In deede thou art the sonne of God. ⊣

the Churche, yet Christ sustaineth them, and holdeth them vp. yea and by them, whatsoeuer they are, he vpholdeth and preserueth his Church.

† And hauing passed the vvater, they came into the coun- 34 trie of Genesar. † And vvhen the men of that place vnder- 35 stoode of him, they sent into al that countrie, and brought vnto him al that vvere il at ease: † and they besought him 36 that they might touche but the ∷ hemme of his garment, and vvhosoeuer did touche, vvere made hole.

∷ See before, chap. 9, 20.

ANNOTATIONS

CHAP. XIIII.

3. Because of Herodias.) It is to ordinary in Princes to put them to death that freely tel them such faultes: women, whom they fansie, specially inciting them to such mischeefe.

12. Buried it. An example of duty toward the dead bodies of the faithful. Wherein see the difference of Catholike Christian men and of al infidels, be they Pagans, Apostataes, or Heretikes. For whereas the Christians had layd the body of this blessed Prophete and Martyr * in Samaria with the Relikes of Elias and Abdias, by vertue wherof wõderful miracles were wrought in that place: in Iulian the Apostataes time, when men might doe al mischeefe freely against Christian religion, the Pagans opened the tombe of S. Iohn Baptist, burnt his bones, scattered the ashes about the fields: but certaine religious Monkes coming thither a pilgrimage at the same time, aduentured their life and saued as much of the holy Relikes as they could, and brought them to their Abbot Philip a man of God: who esteeming them to great a treasure for him and his, to keepe for their priuate deuotion, sent them to Athanasius the B. of Alexandria, and he with al reuerence layd them in such a place (as it were by the Spirit of Prophecie) where afterward by occasion of them was built a goodly chappel. *Theod. li. 3 c. 6. Ruff. li. 2 c. 28. 27.* Marke here that the Heretikes of our time doe as those Pagans, to the bodies and Relikes of al blessed Saints that they can destroy: and Catholikes contrariwise haue the religious deuotion of those old Christians, as appeareth by the honour done now to his head at Amiens in France.

Hiero. in Epitaph. Paulæ. c. 6.

Sacrilege against holy Relikes.

13. Retired.) Christ much esteemed Iohn, and withdrewe him self aside, to giue example of moderate mourning for the departed, and to shew the horrour of that execrable murder. as in the Primitiue Churche many good men seing the miserable state of the world in the time of persecution, and the sinnes that abounded withal: tooke an occasion to forsake those tumults, and to giue them selues to contemplation: and for that purpose retired into the deserts of Ægypt and els where, to doe penance for their owne sinnes and the sinnes of the world. Wherevpon partly rose that infinite number of Monkes and Eremites, of whom the fathers and Ecclesiastical histories make mention. *Hiero. to. 2 in vit. Pauli Eremitæ. Sozo. li. 1 c. 12. 13.*

Eremites.

19. The Disciples to the multitudes.) A figure of the ministerie of the Apostles, who as they here had the distribution and ordering of these miraculous loaues, so had they also to bestow and dispense al the foode of our soules in ministering of the vvord and Sacraments, neither may lay men chalenge the same.

26. Walking.) When not only Christ, but by his power Peter also walketh vpon the vvaters, it is euident that he can dispose of his owne body aboue nature and contrary to the natural conditions thereof, as to goe through a doore. *Io. 20.* to be in the compasse of a litle bread. *Epiphan. in Anchorato.*

29. Walked.] Peter (saith S. Bernard) walking vpon the waters, as Christ did, declared him self the only Vicar of Christ, which should be ruler not ouer one people, but ouer al. For many waters, are many peoples. *Bernard. li. 2 de consid. c. 8.* See the place, how he deduceth from Peter the like authoritie and iurisdiction to his successor the Bishop of Rome.

Peters Primacie.

CHAP. XV.

The Phariſees of Hieruſalem comming ſo farre to carpe him, he chargeth vvith a tradition contrarie to Gods commaundement. 10 And to the people he yeldeth the reaſon of that vvhich they reproued: 15 and againe to his Diſciples, ſhevving the ground of the Phariſaical vvaſhing (to vvitte, that meates othervviſe defile the ſoule) to be falſe. 21 then he goeth aſide to hide him ſelf among the Gentils: vvhere, in a vvoman he findeth ſuch faith, that he is faine, leſt the Gentils ſhould before the time extort the vvhole bread, as ſhe had a crumme, to returne to the Ievves. 34 vvhere (al contrarie to thoſe Phariſees) the common people ſeeke vvonderfully vnto him. and he after he hath cured their diſeaſed, feedeth 4000 of them vvith ſeuen loaues.

Mr. 7, 1.

The Goſpel vpō Wenſday the 3. Weeke in Lent.

1 THEN came to him from Hieruſalem 2 Scribes and Phariſees, ſaying, †Why do thy Diſciples tranſgreſſe the tradition of the Auncientes? For they waſh not their hãds when they eate bread. 3 †But he anſvvering ſaid to them: Why do you alſo tranſgreſſe the cõmaundement of God for your tra- 4 dition? For God ſaid, †*Honour father and mother.* and, *He that ſhal curſe* 5 *father or mother, dying let him dye.* †But you ſay, Whoſoeuer ſhal ſay to father or mother, The gift vvhatſoeuer procedeth from me, 6 ſhal profite the: †and ſhal not honour his father or his mother: and you haue made fruſtrate the cõmaundement of God 7 for your ovvne tradition. †Hypocrites, vvel hath Eſay Pro- 8 phecied of you, ſaying, †*This people honoureth me vvith their" lippes:* 9 *but their hart is farre from me.* †*And in vaine do they vvorſhippe me, teaching doctrines and " commaundements of men.*

Exo. 20, 12. Leu. 20, 9.

Eſa. 29, 13.

10 †And hauing called together the multitudes vnto him, he 11 ſaid to them, Heare ye and vnderſtand. †" Not that vvhich entreth into the mouth, defileth a man: but that vvhich pro- 12 cedeth out of the mouth, that defileth a man. †Then came his Diſciples, and ſaid to him, Doeſt thou knovv that the Pha- 13 riſees, vvhen they heard this vvord, vvere ſcandalized? †But he anſvvering ſayd: All planting vvhich my heauenly father 14 hath not planted, ſhal be rooted vp. †Let them alone: blinde they are, guides of the blinde. And if the blinde be guide to 15 the blinde, both fall into the ditch. †And Peter anſvvering 16 ſayd to him, Expound vs this parable. †But he ſayd, Are you 17 alſo as yet vvithout vnderſtanding? †Do you not vnderſtand, that al that entreth into the mouth, goeth into the 18 belly, and is caſt forth into the priuy? †But the things that proceede out of the mouth, come forth from the hart, and 19 thoſe things " defile a man. †For from the hart come forth euil cogitations, murders, aduoutries, fornications, thefts, 20 falſe teſtimonies, blaſphemies. †Theſe are the things that de-

file a man. but to eate vvith vnvvashen hands, doeth not defile a man. ⊣

The Gospel vpō Thursday the fifth Weeke in Lent.

21 † And IESVS vvent forth from thence and retired into 22 the quarters of Tyre and Sidon. † And behold * a vvoman of Chanaan came forth out of those coastes, and crying out, sayd to him, Haue mercie vpon me, O lord the Sonne of 23 Dauid: my daughter is sore vexed of a Deuil. † Who ansvvered her not a vvord. And his Disciples came and besought him 24 saying, Dimisse her: because she crieth out after vs: † And he ansvvering said: I vvas not sent but to the sheepe that are 25 lost of the house of Israel. † But she came and adored him, 26 saying, Lord, help me. † Who ansvvering, said: It is not good to take the bread of the Children, and to cast it to the dog-27 ges. † But she said, Yea lord: for the vvhelpes also eate of the 28 crummes that fal from the table of their maisters. † Then IESVS ansvvering said to her, O vvoman, ∷ great is thy faith: be it done to thee as thou vvilt: and her daughter vvas made hole from that houre. ⊣

Mr. 7, 25.

∷ It were a straunge case that Christ should commend in this woman a sole faith without good workes, that is to say, a dead faith such as could not worke by loue, and which S. James doubted not to call the faith not of Christians but of Diuels. *Aug. de Fid. & Op. c.* 16.

29 † And vvhen IESVS vvas passed from thence, he came beside the sea of Galilee: and ascending into the mountaine, 30 sate there. † And there came to him great multitudes, hauing vvith them dumme persons, blinde, lame, feeble, and many others: and they cast them dovvne at his feete, and he cured 31 them: † so that the multitudes marueled seeing the dumme speake, the lame vvalke, the blinde see: and they magnified the 32 God of Israel. † And * IESVS called together his Disciples, and said: I pitie the multitude: because three dayes novv they continue vvith me, and haue not vvhat to eate: and dimisse 33 them fasting I vvil not, lest they fainte in the vvay. † And the disciples say vnto him: vvhence then may vve gette so 34 many loaues in the desert as to fil so great a multitude? † And IESVS sayd to them, Hovv many loaues haue you? but they 35 sayd, Seuen, & a fevv litle fishes. † And he commaunded the 36 multitude to sit dovvne vpon the ground. † And taking the seuen loaues & the fishes, and geuing thankes, he brake, & gaue to his disciples, and ∷ the disciples gaue to the people. 37 † And they did al eate, and had their fill. And that vvhich vvas 38 left of the fragments they tooke vp, seuen baskets ful. † And there vvere that did eate, foure thousand men, beside children 39 & vvomen. † And hauing dimissed the multitude, he vvent vp into a boate, and came into the coastes of Magedan.

Mr. 8, 1.

∷ Here we see againe that the people must not be their owne caruers, nor receiue the Sacraments or other spiritual sustenance immediatly of Christ, or at their owne hād, but of their spiritual gouerners.

ANNOTATIONS
CHAP. XV.

8. *With their lippes.*] This is to be vnderstood properly of ſuch as haue euer God in their mouth, the Word of our Lord, the Scriptures, the Goſpel, but in their hart and al their life be in deede Godles. It may be applied alſo to ſuch as ſay their prayers Without attention or eleuation of mind to God, Whether he vnderſtand the prayers or no, that ſaith them. For many a poore Chriſtian man that vnderſtandeth not the Wordes he ſpeaketh, hath his hart neerer heauen, more feruor and deuotion, more edification to him ſelf, more profite in ſpirit (as the Apoſtle ſpeaketh) and leſſe diſtractions, then not only al Heretikes Which haue no true feeling of ſuch things, but then many learned Catholikes. And therfore it is not to be vnderſtood of praying in vnknoWen tonges, as Heretikes ſometime expound it, farre Wide from the circunſtance of the place and Chriſtes intention, ſpeaking of the hypocritical IeWes.

1. Cor. 14.

9. *Commaundements of men.*] Such only are here called traditions, doctrines, or commaundements of men, Which be either repugnant to Gods laWes, as this of defrauding their parents vnder pretenſe of religion: or Which at the leſt be friuolous, vnprofitable, and impertinent to pietie or true Worſhipe, as that other ſort of ſo often Waſhing hands and veſſels Without regard of inWard puritie of hart and mind. Let no man therfore be abuſed With the Proteſtants peruerſe application of this place againſt the holy laWes, canons, and precepts of the Church and our ſpiritual Gouernours, concerning faſtes, feſtiuities, and other rules of diſcipline and due order in life and in the ſeruice of God. For ſuch are not repugnant but conſonant to Gods Word and al pietie, and our Lord is truely honoured, Worſhiped, and ſerued both by the making and alſo by the obſeruing of them. * S. Paul gaue commaundements both by his epiſtles and by Word of mouth, euen in ſuch matters Wherein Chriſt had preſcribed nothing at al, and he chargeth the faithful to obſerue the ſame. * The Apoſtles and Prieſts at Hieruſalem made laWes, and the Chriſtians Were bound to obey them. *a* The keeping of Sunday in ſteede of the Sabboth is the tradition of the Apoſtles, and dare the Heretikes deny the due obſeruation therof to be an acceptable Worſhipe of God? *b* They preſcribed the Feſtes of Eaſter, and Whitſontide and other Solemnities of Chriſt and his Saincts, Which the Proteſtants them ſelues obſerue. *c* They appointed the Lent and Imber faſtes and other, as Wel to chaſtiſe the concupiſcence of man, as to ſerue and pleaſe God thereby, as is plaine in the faſting of* Anna, Tobie, Iudith, Eſther, Who ſerued and pleaſed God thereby. Therfore neither theſe nor other ſuch Apoſtolike Ordinances, nor any precepts of the holy Church or of our laWful Paſtors are implied in theſe Phariſaical traditions here reprehended, nor to be compted or called the doctrines and commaundements of men, becauſe they are not made by mere humane power, but by Chriſtes Warrant and authoritie, and by ſuch as he hath placed to rule his Church, of Whom he ſaith, * *He that heareth you, heareth me: he that deſpiſeth you, deſpiſeth me.* They are made by the Holy Ghoſt, ioyning With our Paſtors in the regiment of the faithful, they are made by our Mother the Church, Which Whoſoeuer obeieth not, * We are Warned to take him as an Heathen. But on the other ſide, al laWes, doctrines, ſeruice and iniunctions of Heretikes, hoW ſoeuer pretended to be conſonant to the Scriptures, be commaundements of men: becauſe both the things by them preſcribed are impious, and the Authors haue neither ſending nor commiſſion from God.

The difference betWene the IeWiſh traditions here reprehended, and the Churches Apoſtolical traditions.

2. Theſ. 2, 15.
1. Cor. 11.
**Act. 15.*
a Aug. Ser. de tẽp. 251. See 1. Cor. 16, 2.
b Epiph. hær. 75
c Hiero. ep. 54 ad Marcel. cõt. Mont.
**Luc. 2, 37 Tob. 12. Iudith c. 8 Eſth. 4.*
Luc. 10, 16
**Mat. 18, 17.*

11. *Not that Which entereth.*] The Catholikes doe not abſtaine from certaine meates, for that they eſteeme any meate vncleane either by creation or by Iudaical obſeruation: but they abſtaine for chaſtiſment of their concupiſcences. *Aug. li. de mor. Ec. Cath. c. 33.*

Difference of meates.

18. *Defile a man*] It is ſinne only Which properly defileth man, and meates of them ſelfe or of their oWne nature doe not defile: but ſo farre as by accident they make a man to ſinne, as the diſobedience of Gods commaundement or of our Superiours Who forbid ſome meates for certaine times and cauſes, is a ſinne. As the apple Which our firſt parents did eate of, though of it ſelf it did not defile them, yet being eaten againſt the precept, it did defile. So neither fleſh nor fiſh of it ſelf doth defile, but the breach of the Churches precept defileth.

Gen. 3.

Catholike abſtinence.

CHAP. XVI.

The obſtinate Phariſees and Sadducees, as though his foreſaid miracles Were not ſufficient to proue him to be Chriſt, require to ſee ſome one from heauen. 5 Whereupon forſaking them, he Warneth his diſciples to beWare of the leauen of their doctrine: 13 and Peter (the time noW approching for him to goe into IeWrie to his Paſſion) for confeſſing him to be Chriſt, he maketh the Rocke of his Churche, geuing fulnes of Eccleſiaſtical poWer accordingly. 21 And after, he ſo rebuketh him for diſſuading his Croſſe and Paſſion, that he alſo affirmeth the like ſuffering in euery one to be neceſſarie to ſaluation.

ND there came to him the Phariſees and Sadducees tempting: and they demaunded him to ſhevv them a ſigne from heauen. † But he anſvvered & ſaid to them, When it is euening, you ſay, It vvil be faire-vvether, for the elemẽt is redde. † And in the morning, This day there vvil be a tẽpeſt, for the element doth glovve and lovvre. The face therfore of the element you haue ſkil to diſcerne: and the ſignes of times can you not? † The * naughtie and aduouterous generation ſeeketh for a ſigne: and there ſhal not a ſigne be giuen it, but the ſigne of Ionas the Prophet. And he left them and vvent avvay.

1 2 3 4

Mar. 8, 12. Luc. 12, 54.

Mat. 12, 39.

† And * vvhen his diſciples vvere come ouer the vvater, they forgot to take bread. † Who ſaid to them, Looke vvel and bevvare of the leauen of the Phariſees & Sadducees. † But they thought vvithin them ſelues ſaying, Becauſe vve tooke not bread. † And IESVS knovving it, ſaid, Why do you thinke vvithin your ſelues O ye of litle faith, for that you haue not bread? † Do you not yet vnderſtand, neither do you remember * the fiue loaues among fiue thouſand men, and how many baſkets you tooke vp? † neither the *ſeuen loaues, among foure thouſand men, and hovv many maundes you tooke vp? † Why do you not vnderſtand that I ſaid not of bread to you, Bevvare of the leauen of the Phariſees & Sadducees? † Then they vnderſtoode that he ſaid not they ſhould bevvare of the leauen of bread, but of the doctrine of the Phariſees and Sadducees.

5 6 7 8 9 10 11 12

Mar. 8, 14. Lu. 12, 1.

Mat. 14, 17. 15, 34.

The Goſpel vpõ SS. Peter and Paules day Iun. 29. *And in Cathedra Petri Romæ, Ian. 18. & Antiochiæ Febr. 22. And Petri ad vincula Aug. 1.* And on the day of the creation and coronation of the Pope, and on the Anniuerſarie thereof.

† And * IESVS came into the quarters of Cæſarea Philippi: and he aſked his diſciples, ſaying, " Whom ſay men that the Sonne of man is? † But " they ſaid, Some Iohn the Baptiſt, & otherſome Elias, and others Hieremie, or one of the Prophets. † IESVS ſaith to them, But vvhom do you ſay that I am? † Simon Peter anſvvered & ſaid, *Thou art Chriſt the ſonne of the liuing God.* † And IESVS anſvvering, ſaid to him, " Bleſſed art thou Simon bar-Iona: becauſe fleſh & bloud hath not reuealed it to thee, but my father vvhich is in heauen. † And " I ſay to thee, *That " thou art* * :: Peter: *and " vpon this "* Rocke *vvil I " build my Church, and the " gates of hel ſhal not preuaile againſt it. † And I * vvil giue " to thee the " keies of the kingdom of heauen. And " vvhatſoeuer thou ſhalt binde vpon earth, it ſhal be bound alſo in the heauens: and vvhatſoeuer thou ſhalt looſe in earth, it ſhall be looſed alſo in the heauens.* ⊣

13 14 15 16 17 18 19

Mar. 8, 27. Luc. 9, 18.

Io. 1, 42. Io. 21, 15.

:: That is, a Rocke.

† Then he commaunded his diſciples that they ſhould tel

20

no

no body that he vvas IESVS CHRIST.

21 † From that time IESVS began to shevv his disciples, that he must goe to Hierusalem, & suffer many things of the Ancients & Scribes & cheefe-Priestes, and be killed, and the 22 third day rise againe. † And Peter taking him vnto him, began to rebuke him, saying, Lord, be it farre from thee, this shal not 23 be vnto thee. † Who turning said to Peter, Goe after me ∷ Satan, thou art a scandal vnto me: because thou sauourest not the things that are of God, but the things that are of men.

∷ This word in Hebrew signifieth an aduersarie, as 3 Reg. 5, 4. and so it is taken here.

24 † Then IESVS said to his disciples, If any man wil come after me, let him denie him self, and take vp his crosse, and follow 25 me. † For he that will saue his life, shal lose it. and he that shal 26 lose his life for me, shal finde it. † For what doth it profite a man, if he gaine the vvhole vvorld, and sustaine the damage of his soule? Or vvhat permutation shal a man giue for his 27 soule? † For the Sonne of man shal come in the glorie of his father vvith his Angels: and then vvil he render to euery man according to his " vvorkes. ꟻ

THE GOSPEL for a Martyr that is a bishop.

28 † Amen I say to you, * there be some of them that stand here, that shal not taste death, til they see the Sonne of man comming in his kingdom.

Mar. 9, 1. Luc. 9, 27.

ANNOTATIONS
CHAP. XVI.

OF PETERS PRIMACIE.

13. *Whom say men.*] Christ intending here to take order for the founding, regiment, and stabilitie of his Church after his decease, and to name the person to whom he meant to geue the general charge thereof, would before by interrogatories draw out (and namely out of that one whom he thought to make the cheefe) the professiō of that high and principal Article, That he was the sonne of the liuing God. Which being the ground of the Churches faith, was a necessarie qualitie and condition in him that was to be made Head of the same Church, and the perpetual keeper of the said faith and al other points thereon depending.

14. *But they said.*] When Christ asked the peoples opinion of him, the Apostles al indifferently made answer: but when he demaunded what them selues thought of him, then loe Peter the mouth and head of the whole felowship answered for al. *Chrys. ho. 55. in Mat.*

17. *Blessed art thou.*] Though some other (as Nathanael *Io. 1, 49*) seeme to haue before beleued and professed the same thing for which Peter is here counted blessed, yet it may be plainely gathered by this place, and so S. Hilarie and others thinke, that none before this did further vtter of him, then that he was the sonne of God by adoption as other Saincts be, though more excellent then other be. For it was of congruitie and Christes special appointment, that he vpon whom he intended to found his new Church, and whose faith he would make infallible, should haue the preeminence of this first profession of Christes natural diuinitie, or, that he was by nature the very sonne of God, a thing so farre aboue the capacitie of nature, reason, flesh and bloud, and so repugnant to Peters sense and sight of Christes humanitie, flesh, and infirmities, that for the beleefe and publike profession thereof he is counted blessed, as Abraham was for his faith: and hath great promises for him self and his posteritie, as the said Patriarche had for him and his seede. According as S. Basil saith, Because he excelled in faith, he receiued the building of the Church committed to him.

Hilar. can. 6 in Mat. & li. 6. de Trinit. Chrys. ho. 55 in Mat.

Basil. li. 2 adu. Eunom.

18. *And I say to thee.*] Our Lord recompenseth Peter for his confession, geuing him a great reward, in that vpon him he builded his Church. *Theophilactus* vpon this place.

PETER.

18. Thou art Peter.] Christ (in the first of Iohn v. 42) foretold and appointed that this man then named Simon, should afterward be called *Cephas*, or *Petrus*, that is to say, a *Rocke*, not then vttering the cause, but now expressing the same, *videlicet* (as S. Cyril writeth) *For that vpon him as vpon a firme rocke his Church should be builded.* Wherevnto S. Hilarie agreing saith, *O happie foundation of the Church in the imposing of thy new name. &c.* And yet Christ here doth not so much call him by the name Peter or Rocke, as he doth affirme him to be a rocke: signifying by that Metaphore, both that he was designed for the foundation and ground worke of his house, which is the Church: and also that he should be of inuincible force, firmitie, durablenes, and stabilitie, to sustaine al the windes, waues, and stormes that might fall or beate against the same. And the Aduersaries obiecting against this, that Christ only is the Rocke or foundation, wrangle against the very expresse Scriptures and Christes owne wordes, geuing both the name and the thing to this Apostle. And the simple may learne by S. Basils wordes, how the case standeth. *Though* (saith he) *Peter be a rocke, yet he is not a rocke as Christ is. For Christ is the true vnmoueable rocke of him self, Peter is vnmoueable by Christ the rocke. For Iesus doth communicate and impart his dignities, not voyding him self of them, but holding them to him self, bestoweth them also vpon others. He is the light, and yet, 2 You are the light: he is the Priest, and yet he 3 maketh Priests: he is the rocke, and he made a rocke.*

Cyril. li. 2 c. 12 Com. in Io.
Hilar. in hunc locū.
Basil. li. de pœnit.
2 Mt. 5, 14.
3 Luc. 22, 19.

18. And vpon this rocke.] Vpon that which he said Peter was, wil he build his Church: and therfore by most euident sequele he foundeth his Church vpon Peter. And the Aduersaries wrangling against this, do against their owne conscience and knowledge: specially seing they know and confesse that in Christes wordes speaking in the Syriake tonge, there was no difference at al betwene *Petrus* and *Petra*: yea and that the Greeke wordes also though differing in termination, yet signifie one thing, to wit, *a rocke*, or *stone*, as them selues also translate it. *Io. 1, 42.* So that they which professe to follow the Hebrew or Syriake and the Greeke, and to translate immediatly out of them into Latin or English, should if they had dealt sincerely, haue thus turned Christes wordes, *Thou art a rocke, and vpon this rocke*: or, *Thou art Peter, and vpon this peter wil I build my Church*: For so Christ spake by their owne confession without any difference. Which doth expresly stoppe them of al their vaine euasions, that *Petrus* the former word is referred to the Apostle: and *petra* the later word, either to Christ only, or to Peters faith only: neither the said original tonges bearing it, nor the sequele of the wordes, *vpon this*, suffering any relation in the world but to that which was spoken of in the same sentence next before: neither the wordes folowing which are directly addressed to Peters person, nor Christes intention by any meanes admitting it, which was not to make him self or to promisse him self to be the head or foundation of the Church. For his father gaue him that dignitie, and he tooke not that honour to him self, nor sent him self, nor tooke the keies of heauen of him self, but al of his father. He had his cōmission the very houre of his incarnation: And though S. Augustine sometimes referre the word (*Petra*) to Christ in this sentence (which no doubt he did because the terminations in Latin are diuers, and because he examined not the nature of the original wordes which Christ spake, nor of the Greeke, and therfore the Aduersaries which otherwise flee to the tongs, should not in this case alleage him) yet he neuer denieth but Peter also is the Rocke and head of the Church, saying that him self expounded it of Peter * in many places, and alleageth also S. Ambrose for the same in his hymne which the Church singeth. And so do we alleage the holy Councel of Chalcedon, *Act. 3 pag. 118.* Tertullian, *de præscript.* Origen, *Ho. 5 in Exo.* S. Cyprian, *De vnit. Ec.* S. Hilarie, *Can. 16 in mat.* S. Ambrose, *Ser. 47. 68. li. 6 in c. 9. Luca.* S. Hierom, *Li. 1 in Iouin. & in c. 2 Esa. & in c. 16 Hier.* S. Epiphanius, *In Anchor.* S. Chrysostom, *Ho. 55 in Mat.* S. Cyril, *Li. 2 c. 12. com. in Io.* S. Leo, *Ep. 89.* S. Gregorie, *Li. 4 ep. 32 ind. 13.* * and others: euery one of them saying expresly that the Church was founded and builded vpon Peter. For though sometimes they say the Church to be builded on Peters faith, yet they meane not (as our Aduersaries do vnlearnedly take them) that it should be builded vpon faith either separated from the man, or in any other man: but vpon faith as in him who here confessed that faith.

Thou art *Cephah*, and vpon this *Cephah*.

πέτρος / πέτρα.] rocke.

Aug. li. 1 retr. c. 21.
in Ps. 69. de verb. Do. sec. Io. ser. 49. ser. 15. 16. 26. 29 de Sanctis. Annot. in Iob c. 30.
** Theodor. li. 5 hær. Fabul. c. de pœnit.*

18. Rocke.] The Aduersaries hearing also the Fathers sometimes say, that Peter had these promises and prerogatiues, as bearing the person of al the Apostles or of the whole Church, deny absurdly that him self in person had these prerogatiues. As though Peter had been the proctor only of the Church or of the Apostles, confessing the faith and receiuing these things in other mens names. Where the holy Doctors meane only, that these prerogatiues were not geuen to him for his owne vse, but for the good of the whole Church, and to be imparted to euery vocation according to the measure of their callings: and that these great priuileges geuen to Peter should not decay or die with his person, but be perpetual in the Church in his successors. Therfore S. Hierom to Damasus taketh this Rocke not to be Peters person only, but his successors and his Chaire. *I* (saith he) *folowing no cheefe or principal but Christ, ioyne my self to the communion of Peters chaire, vpon that rocke I know the Church was built.* And of that same Apostolike Chaire S. August. saith, *That same is the Rocke which the proud gates of Hel do not ouercome.* And S. Leo, *Our Lord would the Sacrament or mysterie of this gift so to pertaine vnto the office of al the Apostles, that he placed it principally in blessed S. Peter the cheefe of al the Apostles, that from him as from a certaine head he might poure out his giftes, as it were through the whole body: that he might vnderstand him self to be an aliene from the diuine mysterie that should presume to reuolt from the soliditie or stedfastnes of Peter.*

Hiero. ep. 7, to. 2.
Psal. cont. part. Donat. to. 7.
Leo ep. 89.

18. Build

18. Build my Church.] The Church or houſe of Chriſt was only promiſed here to be builded vpon him (which was fulfilled. *Io.21,15.*) the foundation ſtone and other pillers or matter being yet in preparing, and Chriſt him ſelf being not only the ſupereminent foundation but alſo the founder of the ſame: which is an other more excellent qualitie then was in Peter, for which he calleth it *my Church*: meaning ſpecially the Church of the new Teſtament. Which was not perfectly formed and finiſhed, and diſtincted from the Synagogue til Whitſunday, though Chriſt gaue Peter and the reſt their commiſsions actually before his Aſcenſion.

18. Gates of hel.] Becauſe the Church is reſembled to a houſe or a citie, the aduerſarie powers alſo be likened to a contrarie houſe or towne, the gates wherof, that is to ſay, the fortitude or impugnations ſhal neuer preuaile againſt the citie of Chriſt. And ſo by this promis we are aſſured that no hereſies nor other wicked attempts can preuaile againſt the Church builded vpon Peter, which the Fathers call Peters ſee and the Romane Church. *Count* (ſaith S. Auguſtine) *the Prieſts from the very See of Peter, and in that order of fathers conſider vvho to vvhom hath ſucceded. that ſame is the rocke vvhich the proud gates of Hel do not ouercome.* And in an other place, *that is it which hath obtained the toppe of authoritie, Heretikes in vaine barking round about it.*

Pſal. cont. part. Donati.
De vtil. cred. c. 17.

19. To thee.] In ſaying, *to thee vvil I geue*, it is plaine that as he gaue the keies to him, ſo he builded the Church vpon him. So ſaith S. Cyprian, *To Peter firſt of al, vpon vvhom our Lord built the Church, and from vvhom he inſtituted and ſhevved the beginning of vnitie, did he geue this povver, that that ſhould be looſed in the heauens, vvhich he had looſed in earth.* Wherby appeareth the vaine cauil of our Aduerſaries, which ſay the Church was built vpon Peters Confeſsion only, cōmon to him and the reſt, and not vpon his perſon, more then vpon the reſt.

Cyp. epiſt. 73.
Greg. li. 4. ep. 32. ind. 13.

19. The keies.) That is, The authoritie or Chaire of doctrine, knowledge, iudgement and diſcretion betwene true and falſe doctrine: the height of gouernement, the power of making lawes, of calling Councels, of the principal voice in them, of confirming them, of making Canons and holeſom decrees, of abrogating the contrarie, of ordaining Biſhopes and Paſtors or depoſing and ſuſpending them, finally the povver to diſpenſe the goods of the Church both ſpiritual and temporal. Which ſignification of preeminent power and authoritie by the vvord *keies* the Scripture expreſſeth in many places: namely ſpeaking of Chriſt, *I haue the keies of death and Hel, that is, the rule.* And againe, *I vvil geue the key of the houſe of Dauid vpon his ſhoulder.* Moreouer it ſignifieth that men can not come into heauen but by him, the keies ſignifiing alſo authoritie to open and ſhut, as it is ſaid *Apoc. 3.* of Chriſt, *Who hath the key of Dauid, he ſhutteth and no man openeth.* By which wordes we gather that Peters authoritie is maruelous, to whom the keies, that is, the power to open and ſhut heauen, is geuen. And therfore by the name of keies is geuen that ſupereminent power which is called in compariſon of the power graunted to other Apoſtles, Biſhops aud Paſtors, *plenitudo poteſtatis*, fulnes of power. *Bernard. lib. 2. de conſiderat. c. 8.*

The dignities of the keies.

Apoc. 1.
Eſa. 22, 22

19. Whatſoeuer thou ſhal bind.) Al kind of diſcipline and puniſhment of offenders, either ſpiritual (which directly is here meant) or corporal ſo farre as it tendeth to the execution of the ſpiritual charge, is compriſed vnder the word, bind. Of which ſort be Excommunications, Anathematiſmes, Suſpenſions, degradations, and other cenſures and penalties or penances enioyned either in the Sacrament of Confeſsion or in the exterior Courtes of the Church, for puniſhment both of other crimes, and ſpecially of hereſie and rebellion againſt the Church and the cheefe paſtors therof.

19. Looſe.) To looſe, is as the cauſe and the offenders caſe requireth, to looſe them of any the former bandes, and to reſtore them to the Churches Sacraments and Communion of the faithful and execution of their function, to pardon alſo either al or part of the penances enioyned, or what debtes ſo euer man oweth to God or the Church for the ſatisfaction of his ſinnes forgeuen. Which kind of releaſing or looſing is called *Indulgence*: finally this *whatſoeuer*, excepteth nothing that is puniſhable or pardonable by Chriſt in earth, for he hath committed his power to Peter. And ſo the validitie of Peters ſentence in binding or looſing whatſoeuer, ſhal by Chriſtes promis be ratified in heauen. *Leo Ser. de Transfig. & Ser. 2. in anniuerſ. aſſumpt. ad Pontif. Hilar. can. 16. in Matth. Epiph. in Anchorato prope initium.* If now any temporal power can ſhew their warrant out of ſcripture for ſuch ſoueraine power, as is here geuen to Peter and conſequently to his ſucceſſors, by theſe wordes, *whatſoeuer thou ſhal binde*, and by the very keies, wherby greateſt ſoueraintie is ſignified in Gods Church as in his familie and houſhold, and therfore principally attributed and geuen to Chriſt * who in the ſcripture is ſaid to haue the key of Dauid, but here cōmunicated alſo vnto Peter, as the name of Rocke: if I ſay any temporal poteſtate can ſhew authoritie for the like ſoueraintie, let them chalenge hardly to be head not only of one particular, but of the whole vniuerſal Church.

Eſa. 22.
Apoc. 3.

27. Workes.) He ſaith not, to geue euery man according to his mercie (or their faith) but according to their workes. *Auguſt. de verb. Apoſt. Ser. 35.* And againe, How ſhould our Sauiour reward euery one according to their workes, if there were no free wil? *Auguſt. lib. 2. cap. 4. 5. 8. de act. cum Fœlic. Manich.*

Good workes.
Free wil.

CHAP.

CHAP. XVII.

As he promiſed, he giueth them a ſight of the glorie, vnto which Suffering doth bring: 9 and then againe doth inculcate his Paſſion. 14 A deuil alſo he caſteth out which his Diſciples could not for their incredulitie and lacke of praying and faſting. 22 being yet in Galilee, he reuealeth more about his Paſſion. 24 and the tribute that the Collectors exacted for al, he payeth for him ſelf and Peter: declaring yet withal his freedom both by Word and miracle.

The TRANSFIGVRATION of our Lord, celebrated in the Church the 6. of Aug.
The Goſpel of the ſaid feaſt, & of the 2. Sunday in Lent: and on the Saterday before.

ND after ſix dayes IESVS taketh vnto him Peter and Iames and Iohn his brother, and bringeth them into a high mountaine apart: † And he vvas "transfigured before them. And his face did ſhine as the ſunne: & his garments became vvhite as ſnovv. † And behold there "appeared to them Moyſes and Elias talking vvith him. † And Peter anſvvering, ſaid to IESVS, Lord, it is good for vs to be here: if thou vvilt, let vs make here three tabernacles, one for thee, and one for Moyſes, and one for Elias. † And as he vvas yet ſpeaking, behold a bright cloude ouerſhadovved them. And loe a voice out of the cloude, ſaying, This is my vvelbeloued ſonne, in vvhom I am vvel pleaſed: heare ye him. † And the diſciples hearing it, fel vpon their face, and vvere ſore afraid. † And IESVS came and touched them: and he ſaid to them, Ariſe, and feare not. † And they lifting vp their eyes, ſavv no body, but only IESVS. † And as they deſcended from the "mount, IESVS commaunded them, ſaying, Tel the viſion to no body, til the Sonne of man be riſen from the dead. ⊣ (1–9)

(Mr. 9, 2. Luc. 9, 28. 2. Pet. 1, 17.)

† And his Diſciples aſked him, ſaying, What ſay the Scribes then, that * Elias muſt come firſt? † But he anſvvering, ſaid to them, "Elias in deede ſhal come, and reſtore al things. † And I ſay to you, that Elias is already come, and they did not knovv him, but vvrought on him vvhatſoeuer they vvould. So alſo the Sonne of man ſhal ſuffer of them. † Then the Diſciples vnderſtoode, that of Iohn the Baptiſt he had ſpoken to them. (10–13)

(Mal. 4, 5.)

† And * vvhen he vvas come vnto the multitude, there came to him a man falling dovvne vpon his knees before him, † ſaying, Lord haue mercie vpon my ſonne, for he is lunatike, and ſore vexed: for he falleth often into the fire, and often into the vvater. † and I offered him to thy Diſciples: and they could not cure him. † IESVS anſvvered and ſaid, O faithles and peruerſe generation, hovv long ſhal I be vvith (14–17)

(Mar. 9, 14. Luc. 9, 37.)

you

you? Hovv long shal I suffer you? bring him hither to me. 18 † And IESVS rebuked him, and the deuil vvent out of him, and the ladde vvas cured from that houre. 19 † Then came the Disciples to IESVS secretely, and said, "Why could not vve cast him out? 20 † IESVS said to them, because of your incredulity. for, amen I say to you, if you haue "faith as a mustard seede, you shal say to this mountaine, Remoue from hence thither: and it shal remoue, and nothing shal be impossible to you. 21 † But this kinde is not cast out but by "prayer and fasting.

Mr. 9, 31. Luc. 9, 44.

† And * vvhen they conuersed in Galilee, IESVS said to 22 them, The Sonne of man is to be betraied into the hands of men: † and they shal kil him, and the third day he shal rise 23 againe. And they vvere stroken sadde excedingly.

24 † And vvhen they vvere come to Capharnaum, there came they that receiued the didrachmes, vnto Peter, and said 25 to him, Your maister doth he not pay the :: didrachmes? † He saith, Yes. And vvhen he vvas entered into the house, IESVS preuented him, saying, What is thy opinion Simon? The kings of the earth of vvhom receiue they tribute or cense? 26 of their children, or of strangers? † And he said, Of strangers. 27 IESVS said to him, Then the "children are free. † But that vve may not scandalize them, goe thy vvaies to the sea, and cast a hooke: and that fish vvhich shal first come vp, take: and vvhen thou hast opened his mouth, thou shalt find a :: stater: take that, and giue it them for "me and thee.

:: These didrachmes were peeces of money which they payed for tribute.

:: This stater was a double didrachme, and therfore was payed for two.

ANNOTATIONS
CHAP. XVII.

2. *Transfigured.*] Marke in this Transfiguration many maruelous points. as, that he made not only his owne body, which then was mortal, but also the bodies of Moyses and Elias, the one dead, the other to die, for the time as it were immortal: therby to represent the state and glorie of his body and his Saincts in heauen. By which maruelous transfiguring of his body, you may the lesse maruel that he can exhibite his body vnder the forme of bread and vvine or otherewise as he list.

Christ can exhibite his body vnder what forme he list.

3. *Appeared Moyses.*] By this that Moyses personally appeared and was present with Christ, it is plaine that the Saincts departed may in person be present at the affaires of the liuing. *August. de cura pro mort. c. 15. 16.* For euen as Angels els where, so here the Saincts also serued our Sauiour: and therfore as Angels both in the old Testament and the new, were present often at the affaires of men, so may Saincts.

Saincts after their death deale with and for the liuing.

9. *Mount.*] This mount (commonly esteemed and named of the ancient fathers Thabor) S. Peter calleth *the holy Mount* because of this wonderful vision, like as in the old Testament where God appeared to Moyses in the bush and els where to others, he calleth the place of such Apparitions, *holy ground.* Wherby it is euident that by such Apparitions, places are sanctified, and therevpon groweth a religion and deuotion in the faithful toward such places, and namely to this Mount Thabor (called in S. Hierom *Itabirium Ep. 17.*) there was great Pilgrimage in the Primitiue Church, as vnto al those places which our Sauiour had sanctified with his presence and miracles,

2. Pet. 1, 18. Exo. 3, 5.

Holy places.

Deuotion and Pilgrimage to the same.

The holy land. and therfore to the whole land of promis, for that cause called the holy land. *See S. Hiero. in Epitap. Paula. & ep. 17. & 18 ad Marcellam.*

Elias. *11. Elias shal come.*] He distinguisheth here plainly betwene Elias in person, who is yet to come before the iudgement: and betwene Elias in name, to wit, Iohn the Baptist, who is come already in the spirit and vertue of Elias. So that it is not Iohn Baptist only nor principally of whom Malachie prophecieth (as our Aduersaries say) but Elias also him self in person. *Luc. 1, 17. Mal. 4, 5.*

True miracles onely in the Cath. Church. *19. Why could not we.*] No maruel if the Exorcists of the Catholike Church which haue power to cast out diuels, yet doe it not alwaies when they wil, and many times with much a doe: wheras the Apostles hauing receiued this power * before ouer vncleane spirites, yet here cānot cast thē out. But as for hæretikes, they can neuer doe it, nor any other true miracle, to confirme their false faith. *Mt. 10.*

20. Faith as mustard seed.) This is the Catholike faith, by which only al miracles are wrought: yet not of euery one that hath the Catholike faith, but of such as haue a great and forcible faith and withal the gift of miracles. These are able as here wee see by Christes warrant not only to doe other wonderful miracles here signified by this one, but also this very same, that is, to moue mountaines in deede, as S. Paul also presupposeth, and S. Hierom affirmeth, and Ecclesiastical histories namely telleth of Gregorius Neocæsariensis, that he moued a mountaine to make roome for the foundation of a Church, called therfore and for other his wonderful miracles, Thaumaturgus. And yet faithlesse Heretikes laugh at al such things aud beleue them not. *1. Cor. 13. Hiero. in vita S. Hilarionis. Niceph. li. 6. c. 17. Greg. Niss. de vit. Gregorij.*

Gregorius Thaumaturgus.

Prayer and Fasting. *21. Prayer aud fasting.*) The force of fasting and praying: whereby also we may see that the holy Churche in Exorcismes doeth according to the Scriptures, when shee vseth beside the name of IESVS, many prayers and much fasting to driue out Deuils. because these also are here required beside faith.

26. The Children free.) Though Christ to auoid scandal, payed tribute, yet in deede he sheweth that both him self ought to be free from such payments (as being the kings sonne, aswel by his eternal birth of God the Father, as temporal of Dauid) and also his Apostles, as being of his familie, and in them their successors the whole Clergie, who are called in Scripture the lotte and portion of our Lord. Which exemption and priuilege being grounded vpon the very law of nature it self, and therfore practised euen among the Heathen (*Gen. 42, 27.*) good Christian Princes haue confirmed and ratified by their lawes in the honour of Christ, whose ministers they are, and as it were the kings sonnes. as S. Hierom declareth playnly in these wordes, *We for his honour pay not tributes, and as the Kings sonnes, are free from such payments. Hiero.* vpon this place.

The priuileges and exemptions of the Clergie.

Peters præeminence. *27. Me and thee.*] A great mysterie in that he payed not only for him self, but for Peter bearing the Person of the Churche, and in whom as the cheefe, the rest were conteyned. *Aug. q. ex no. Test. q. 75. to. 4.*

CHAP. XVIII.

To his Disciples he preacheth against ambition the mother of Schisme: 7 foretelling both the author vvhosoeuer he be, and also his folovvers, of their vvo to come. 10 and shevving on the contrary side, hovv precious Christian soules are to their Angels, to the Sonne of man, and to his Father. 15 charging vs therfore to forgiue our brethren, vvhen also vve haue iust cause against them, be it neuer so often, and to labour their saluation by al meanes possible.

The Gospel on Michelmas day Septemb. 29. And vpon his Apparition Maij 8.

T that houre the Disciples came to IESVS, 1 saying. " Who, thinkest thou, is the greater in the kingdom of heauen? † And IESVS 2 calling vnto him a litle childe, set him in the middes of them, † and said, Amen I say 3 to you, vnles you be conuerted, and become as litle children, you shal not enter into the kingdom of heauen. † Whosoeuer therfore shal humble him self as this 4 :: litle childe, he is the greater in the kingdom of heauē. † And 5 he that shal receiue one such litle childe in my name, receiueth me. † And * he that shal scandalize one of these litle 6 ones

Mr. 9, 34. Luc. 9, 46.

:: Humility, innocencie, simplicity, cōmended to vs in the state and person of a childe.

Mr. 9, 42. Lu. 17, 2

ones that beleeue in me, it is expedient for him that a milstone be hanged about his necke, and that he be drovvned in the depth of the sea.

7 † Vvo be to the vvorld for scandals. for it is necessary that scandals do come: but neuerthelesse vvo to that man

Mt. 5, 30 Mar. 9, 43.

8 by vvhom the scandall commeth. † And * if thy " hand, or thy foote scandalize thee: cut it of, and cast it from thee. It is good for thee to goe in to life maimed or lame, rather then hauing tvvo hands or tvvo feete to be cast

9 into euerlasting fire. † And if thine eye scandalize thee, plucke him out, and cast him from thee: It is good for thee hauing one eye to enter into life, rather then hauing tvvo

10 eyes to be cast into the hel of fire. † See that you despise not one of these litle ones: for I say to you that " their Angels, in heauen alvvaies do see the face of my father vvhich is in hea-

Luc. 19, 10. Lu. 15, 4

11 uen. † For * the Sonne of man is come to saue that vvhich

12 vvas perished. † * Hovv thinke you? If a man haue an hundred sheepe, and one of them shal goe astray: doth he not leaue ninetie nine in the mountaines, and goeth to seeke

13 that Which is straied? † And if it chaunce that he finde it: amen I say to you, that he reioyceth more fore that, then for the ni-

14 netie nine that vvent not astray. † Euen so it is not the vvil of your father, vvhich is in heauen, that one perish of these litle ones.

Luc. 17, 3.

15 † But * if thy brother shal offend against thee, goe, and rebuke him betvvene thee and him alone. If he shal heare thee,

16 thou shalt gaine thy brother. † And if he vvil not heare thee, ioyne vvith thee besides, one or tvvo: that in the mouth of

Deu. 19, 15.

17 * tvvo or three vvitnesses euery vvord may stand. † And if he vvil not heare them, :: tel the Church. *And if he vvil not heare*

18 *the Church, let him be to thee as " the heathen and the Publican.* † Amen I say to you, whatsoeuer you " shal binde vpon earth, shal be bound also in heauen: and vvhatsoeuer you " shal loose vpon earth,

19 shal be loosed also in heauen. † Againe I say to you, that if tvvo of you shal :: consent vpon earth, concerning euery thing vvhatsoeuer they shal aske, it shal be done to them

20 of my father vvhich is in heauen. † For vvhere there be tvvo or three gathered in my name, there am I " in the middes of them.

Lu. 17, 4

21 † Then came Peter vnto him and said, * Lord, how often shal my brother offend against me, and I forgiue him? vntil

The Gospel vpő Tuesday the 3 Weeke in Lent.

:: That is (as S. Chrysostom here expoundeth it) tell the Prelates and cheefe Pastours of the Church: for they haue iurisdiction to binde and loose such offenders, by the Wordes folowing v. 18.

:: Al ioyning together in the vnity of Christes Churche in Councels and Synods, or publike prayers, is of more force then of any particular man.

 seuen

ſeuentimes? † IESVS ſaid to him, I ſay not to thee* vntil ſeuen 22 times: but vntil " ſeuentie times ſeuen times. ⁋

Luc. 17, 4.

The Goſpel vpõ the 21 Sunday after Pentecoſt.

† Therfore is 23 the kingdom of heauen likened to a man being a king, that vvould make an account vvith his ſeruants. † And vvhen 24 he began to make the account, there vvas one preſented vnto him that ovved him ten thouſand talents. † And hauing not 25 vvhence to repay it, his lord commaunded that he ſhould be ſold, and his vvife and children, and all that he had, and it to be repayed. † But that ſeruant falling dovvne, beſought him, 26 ſaying, Haue patience tovvard me, and I vvil repay thee all. † And the lord of that ſeruant moued vvith pitie, dimiſſed 27 him, and the dette he forgaue him. † And vvhen that ſeruant 28 vvas gone forth, he found one of his felovv-ſeruants that did ovve him an hundred pence: and laying hands vpon him thratled him, ſaying, Repay that thou ovveſt. † And his felovv 29 ſeruant falling dovvne, beſought him, ſaying, Haue patience tovvard me, and I vvil repay the all. † And he vvould not: but 30 vvent his vvay, and caſt him into priſon, til he repayed the dette. † And his felovv-ſeruants ſeeing vvhat vvas done, vvere 31 very ſorie, and they came, and told their lord al that vvas done. † Then his lord called him: and he ſaid vnto him, Thou 32 vngratious ſeruant, I forgaue thee al the dette becauſe thou beſoughteſt me: oughteſt not thou therfore alſo to haue mercie vpon thy felovv-ſeruant, euen as I had mercie vpon thee? † And his lord being angrie deliuered him to the tor- 33 menters, vntil he repayed al the dette. † So alſo ſhal my hea- 34 uenly father doe to you, if you forgiue not euery one his bro ther from your hartes. ⁋

ANNOTATIONS
CHAP. XVIII.

1. Who is the greater.] The occaſion of this queſtion and of their contention for Superioritie among the reſt of their infirmities vvhich they had before the comming of the Holy Ghoſt, vvas (as certaine holy Doctors vvrite) vpon emulation tovvard Peter, vvhom only they ſavv preferred before the reſt in the payment of the tribute, by theſe vvordes of our Sauiour, Geue it them for me and thee. *Chryſ. ho. 59. Hiero. in Mat.* Vpon this place. *C. 17, v. 27*

7. Scandals.] The ſimple be moſt annoyed by taking ſcandal of their preachers, Prieſts, and elders il life: and great damnation is to the guides of the people vvhether they be temporal or ſpiritual, but ſpecially to the ſpiritual, if by their il example and ſlaunderous life the people be ſcãdalized.

8. Hand, foote, eye.] By theſe partes of the body ſo neceſſarie and profitable for a man, is ſignified, that vvhatſoeuer is neereſt and deereſt to vs, vvife, children, freendes, riches, al are to be contemned and forſaken for to ſaue our ſoule.

10. Their Angels.] A great dignitie and a maruelous benefite that euery one hath from his

Natiuitie

Natiuitie an Angel for his custodie and Patronage against the wicked before the face of God. *Hiero. vpon this place.* And the thing is so plaine, that Caluin dare not deny it, and yet he wil needes doubt of it, *lib. 1. Inst. c. 14. sect. 7.*

Protection of Angels.

17. *Not heare the Church.*] Not only Heretikes, but any other obstinate offender that wil not be iudged nor ruled by the Church, may be excommunicated, and so made as an Heathen or Publican was to the Iewes, by the discipline of the same, casting him out of the felowship of Catholikes. Which Excommunication is a greater punishement then if he were executed by sword, fire, and wild beastes. *Aug. cont. Adu. leg. li. 1. c. 17.* And againe he saith, Man is more sharply and pitefully bound by the Churches Keies, then with any yron or adamantine manicles or fetters in the world. *August. ibidem.*

Disobedience to the Church.

Excommunication.

17. *Heathen.*] Heretikes therfore because they wil not heare the Church, be no better nor no otherwise to be esteemed of Catholikes, then heathen men and Publicans were esteemed among the Iewes.

Mat. c. 16, 19.

18. *You shal binde.*] As before he gaue this power of binding and loosing ouer the whole, first of al and principally to Peter, vpon whom he builded his Church: so here not only to Peter, and in him to his successors, but also to the other Apostles, and in them to their successors, euery one in their charge. *Hieron. lib. 1. c. 14. aduers. Iouin. and Epist. ad Heliod. Cyprian. de Vnit. Eccl. nu. 3.*

Power to binde and loose.

Li. 1. de pœnit. c. 2.

18. *Shal loose.*] Our Lord geueth no lesse right and authoritie to the Churche to loose, then to binde, as S. Ambrose writeth against the Nouatians, who confessed that the Priests had power to binde, but not to loose.

20. *In the middes of them.*) Not al assemblies may chalenge the presence of Christ, but only such as be gathered together in the vnity of the Church. and therfore no conuenticles of Heretikes directly gathering against the Churche, are warranted by this place. *Cypr. de vnit. Eccles. nu. 7. 8.*

Catholike Assemblies.

22. *Seuentie times seuen.*) There must be no end of forgeuing them that be penitent, either in the Sacrament by absolution, or one man an other their offenses.

CHAP. XIX.

THE fourth part of this Gospel, Christs comming into Iurie toward his Passion.

He ansvvereth the tempting Pharisees, that the case of a man vvith his vvife shalbe (as in the first institution it vvas) vtterly indissoluble, though for one cause he may be diuorced. 10 And thereupon to his Disciples he highly commendeth Single life for heauen. 13 He vvil haue children come vnto him. 16 He shevveth vvhat is to be done to enter into life euerlasting: 20 What also, for a rich man to be perfect: 27 As also vvhat passing revvard they shal haue vvhich follovv that his counsel of perfection: 29 yea though it be but in some one peece.

Mr. 10, 1.

1 AND it came to passe, vvhen IESVS had ended these vvordes, he departed from Galilee, & came into the coastes of Ievvrie beyond Iordã, 2 †and great multitudes folovved him: and he cured them there.

The Gospel for Mariage. And for S. Agatha Febr. 5.

3 † And there came to him the Pharisees tempting him, and saying, Is it lavvful for a man to dimisse his vvife, for euery 4 cause? † Who ansvvering, said to them, Haue ye not read, that he which did "make" from the beginning, *made them male and femal?*

make man

Gen. 1, 27.

Gen. 2, 24.

5 And he said. †*For this cause, man shal leaue father and mother, and shal cleaue* 6 *to his vvife: and they tvvo shal be in one flesh.* † Therfore novv they are not tvvo, but one flesh. That therfore vvhich God hath 7 ioyned together, let " not man separate. ✠ † They say to him, Why then * did Moyses commaund to giue a bil of diuorce, 8 and to dimisse her? †He saith to them, Because Moyses for the hardnes of your hart permitted you to dimisse your vviues:

Deut. 24, 1.

but from the beginning it vvas not so. † And I say to you, that 9 * Whosoeuer shal dimisse his vvife, " but for fornication, and shal mary an other, doth committe aduoutrie: and he that shal mary her that is dimissed, committeth aduoutrie. † His 10 disciples say vnto him, If the case of a man vvith his vvife be so, it is not expedient to mary. † Who said to them, " Not al 11 :: take this vvord, but they to vvhom it is giuen. † For there 12 are eunuches which vvere borne so frō their mothers vvombe: and there are eunuches vvhich were made by men: and there are eunuches, vvhich haue " gelded them selues for the kingdom of heauen." He that can take, let him take. ¶

Mt. 5, 32. Mr. 10, 11. Luc. 16, 18. 1. Cor. 7, 11.

:: χωρoῦσι. capiunt.

† Then * were litle children presented to him, that he 13 should " impose hands vpon them & pray. And the disciples rebuked them. † But IESVS said to them, Suffer the litle 14 children, and stay them not from comming vnto me: for the kingdom of heauen is for such. † And when he had imposed 15 hands vpon them, he departed from thence.

Mr. 10, 13. Luc. 18, 15.

† And * behold one came and said to him, Good Maister, 16 vvhat good shal I doe that I may haue life euerlasting? † Who said to him, What askest thou me of good? One is 17 good, God. But :: if thou vvilt enter into life, keepe the commaundements. † He saith to him, Which? And IESVS said, 18 *Thou shalt not murder, Thou shalt not committe aduoutrie, Thou shalt not steale, Thou shalt not beare false vvitnes,* † *Honour thy father and thy mother,* * *Thou* 19 *shalt loue thy neighbour as thy self.* † The yong man saith to him, 20 Al these haue I kept from my youth: vvhat is yet vvanting vnto me? † IESVS said to him, " If thou vvilt be perfect, goe, 21 sel the things that thou hast, & giue to the poore, and thou shalt haue treasure in heauen: and come, " folovv me. † And 22 vvhen the yong man had heard this vvord, he vvent avvay sad: for he had many possessions. † And IESVS said to his 23 disciples, † Amen I say to you, that a rich man shal hardely enter into the kingdom of heauen. † And againe I say to you, 24 it is easier for a camel to passe through the eye of a nedle, :: then for a rich man to enter into the kingdom of heauen. † And vvhen they had heard this, the disciples marueled very 25 much, saying, Who then can be saued? † And IESVS behol- 26 ding, said to them. With men this is impossible: but vvith God " al things are possible. † Then Peter ansvvering, said to 27 him, Behold vve haue " left al things, & haue folovved thee: " vvhat therfore shal vve haue? † And IESVS said to them, 28 Amen

Mr. 10, 17. Luc. 18, 18.

Exo. 20, 13. * Leu. 19, 18.

:: I see not (saith S. Augustine) why Christ should say, If thou wilt haue life euerlasting, keepe the commaundements: if without obseruing of thé, by only faith one might be saued. *Aug. de Fid. & op. c. 15.*

:: S. Marke expoundeth it thus, riche men trusting in their riches. *ca. 10, 24.*

The Gospel vpō the Conuersion of S. Paul Ian.

Amen I say to you, that you vvhich haue folovved me, in the regeneration, when the Sonne of man shal sitte in the seate of his maiestie, you " also shal sitte vpon tvvelue seates, iudging the tvvelue tribes of Israel. 29 † And euery one that hath left house, or brethren, or sisters, or father, or mother, or ∵ vvife, or children, or landes for my names sake: shal receiue an hundred fold, and shal possesse life euerlasting. 30 ┤ † And * many shal be first, that are last: and last, that are first.

25. And in a votiue Masse of SS. Peter and Paul, and for holy Abbotes.

∵ Hereof is gathered that the Apostles amóg other things left their Wiues also to folow Christ. *Hiero. li. 1. aduers. Iouin.*

Mr. 10, 31. Lu. 13, 30.

ANNOTATIONS
CHAP. XIX.

6. Not man separate.] This inseparability betWixt man and Wife riseth of that, that Wedlocke is a Sacrament. *Aug. li. 2. de pec. origine c. 34. to. 7. De nupt. & concupis. li. 1. c. 10.*

9. But for fornication.) For aduoutrie one may dimisse an other, *Mat. 5.* But neither party can marry againe for any cause during life. *Aug. li. 11. de adult. coniug. c. 21. 22. 24.* for the Which vnlaWful act of marrying agayne, Fabiola that noble matrone of Rome albeit shee Was the innocent part, did publike penance, as S. Hierom Writeth in her high commendation therefore. And in S. Paul *Ro. 7.* it is plaine that shee Which is With an other man, her husband yet liuing, shal be called an aduouteresse: contrary to the doctrine of our Aduersaries.

Mariage after diuorce vnlaWful.

In Epitaph. Fabiola.

11. Not al take.) Whosoeuer haue not this gift geuen them, it is either for that they Wil not haue it, or for that they fulfil not that Which they Wil: and they that haue this gift or attayne to this Word, haue it of God and their oWne free Wil. *Aug. li. de grat. & lib. arbit. c. 4.* So that it is euident no man is excluded from this gift, but (as Origen here saith) it is geuen to al that aske for it: contrarie to our Aduersaries that say it is impossible, and that for excuse of breaking their voWes, Wickedly say, they haue not the gift.

Orig. tract. 7. in Mat.

12. Gelded them selues.) They geld them selues for the kingdom of heauen Which voW chastity. *Aug. de virginitate c. 24.* Which proueth those kind of voWes to be both laWful, and also more meritorious, and more sure to obtaine life euerlasting, then the state of Wedlocke. contrarie to our Adu. in al respectes.

VoW of chastitie.

14. He that can.) It is not said of the Precepts, keepe them Who can, for they be necessarie vnder paine of damnation to be kept: but of Counsels only (as of virginity, abstaining from flesh and Wine, and of geuing al a mans goods aWay to the poore) it is said, He that can attaine to it, let him doe it: Which is counsel only, not a commaundement. Contrary to our Adu. that say, there are no Counsels, but only precepts.

Counsels not Precepts.

Aug. ser. 6. de temp.

13. Impose.) They kneW the valour of Christes blessing, and therfore brought their children to him: as good Christian people haue at al times brought their children to Bishops to haue their blessing. See Annotation before *Chap. 10, 12.* And of Religious mens blessing see Ruffin. *li. 2. c. 8. hist.* S. Hierom *in Epitaph. Paulæ c. 7. & in vit. Hilarionis. Theodoret. in historia sanctorũ Patrum num. 8.*

Bishops and Religious mens blessing.

21. If thou Wilt be perfect.] Loe, he maketh a plaine difference betWene keeping the commaundements, Which is necessary for euery man: and being perfect, Which he counseleth only to them that Wil. And this is the state of greate perfection Which Religious men doe professe, according to Christes counsel here, leauing al things and foloWing him.

The Religious state of perfection.

21. FoloW me.] Thus to foloW Christ is to be Without Wife and care of children, to lacke propriety, and to liue in common, and this hath great reWard in heauen aboue other states of life: Which, S. Augustine saith, the Apostles foloWed, and him self, and that he exhorted others to it as much as lay in him. *Aug. ep. 89. in fine, & in ps. 103 Conc. 3. post med.*

26. Al things possible.] This of the camel through a nedels eye, being possible to God, although he neither hath done it, nor by like Wil doe it: maketh against the blasphemous infidelity of our Aduersaries that say, God can do no more then he hath done or Wil doe. We see also that God can bring a camel through a nedels eye, and therfore his body through a doore, and out of the sepulchre shut, and out of his mother a virgin, and generally aboue nature and contrary to nature do With his body as he list.

27. Left al.) This perfection of leauing al things the Apostles voWed. *Aug. li. 17. de Ciu. Dei c. 4.*

27. What shal We haue.) They leaue al things in respect of reWard, and Christ doeth Wel alloW it in them by his ansWer.

VoW of pouertie in respect of reWard.

28. You also shal sitte.) Note that not only Christ, Who is the principal and proper iudge of the liuing and the dead, but With him the Apostles and al perfect Saints shal iudge: and yet that doeth nothing derogate to his prerogatiue, by Whom and vnder Whom they hold this and al other dignities in this life and the next.

Aug. in ps. 121.

CHAP.

CHAP. XX.

To shevv hovv through Gods grace the Iewes shalbe ouerrunne of the Gentils, although they beginne after, he bringeth a parable of men working soner and later in the vineyard, but the later revvarded in the end euen as the first. 17 He reuealeth more to his Disciples touching his passion: 20 Bidding the ambitious tvvo suiters to thinke rather of suffering with him: 24 And teaching vs (in the rest of his Disciples) not to be greeued at our Ecclesiastical Superiors, considering they are (as he was him self) to toile for our Saluation. 29 Then going out of Iericho, he geueth sight vnto tvvo blind.

The Gospel vpon the Sunday of Septuagesime.

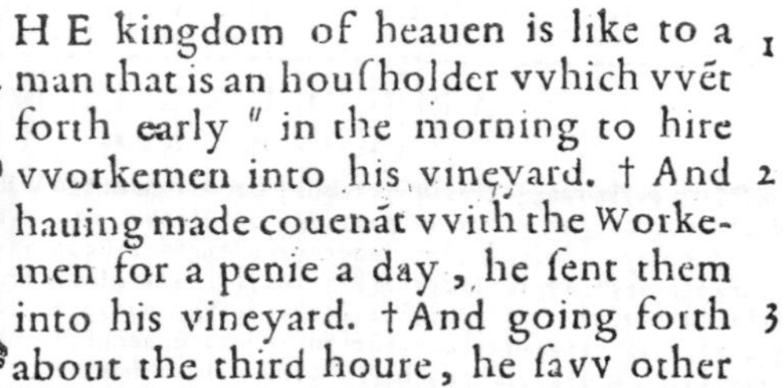

HE kingdom of heauen is like to a man that is an housholder vvhich vvẽt forth early " in the morning to hire vvorkemen into his vineyard. 1 † And hauing made couenãt vvith the workemen for a penie a day, he sent them into his vineyard. 2 † And going forth about the third houre, he savv other standing in the market place idle, 3 † and he said to them, Goe you also into the vineyard: and that vvhich shal be iust, I vvil giue you. 4 † And they vvent their vvay. And againe he vvent forth about the sixt & the ninth houre: and did likevvise. 5 † But about the eleuenth houre he vvent forth and found other standing, & he saith to them, What stand you here al the day idle? 6 † They say to him, Because no man hath hired vs. He saith to them, Goe you also into the vineyard. 7

† And vvhen euening vvas come, the lord of the vineyard saith to his bailife, Call the vvorkemen, and pay them their hire, beginning from the last euen to the first. 8 † Therfore vvhen they vvere come that came about the eleuenth houre, they receiued euery one " a penie. 9 † But vvhen the first also came, they thought that they should receiue more: and they also receiued euery one a penie. 10 † And receiuing it they ∷ murmured against the good man of the house, 11 † saying, These last haue continued one houre: and thou hast made them equal to vs that haue borne the burden of the day and the heates. 12 † But he ansvvering said to one of them, Frende, I doe the no vvrong: didst thou not couenant vvith me for a penie? 13 † Take that is thine, and goe: I vvil also giue to this last euen as to thee also. 14 † Or, is it not lavvful for me to do that I vvil? 15 is thine eye naught, because I am good? † So shal the last, be first: and the first, last. For many be called, but " fevv elect. 16 ⊣

∷ The Iewes are noted for enuying the vocation of the Gentiles, and their reward equal with thẽ selues.

The Gospel in a votiue Masse of the holy Crosse

† * And IESVS going vp to Hierusalem, tooke the tvvelue disciples secretly, and said to them, 17 † Behold vve goe vp to 18 Hierusa-

Mr. 10, 32. Luc. 18, 31.

Hierusalem, and the Sonne of man shal be deliuered to the cheefe priestes and to the Scribes, and they shal condemne 19 him to death, † and shal deliuer him to the Gentiles to be mocked, & scourged, & crucified, and the third day he shal rise againe. ⊣

Mr. 10, 35.

20 † * Then came to him the mother of the sonnes of Zebedee vvith her sonnes, adoring and desiring some thing of 21 him. † Who said to her, What vvilt thou? She saith to him, Say that these my tvvo sonnes may sitte, one at thy right hād, 22 and one at thy left hand in thy kingdom. † And IESVS ansvvering, said, You knovv not vvhat you desire. Can you drinke of the cuppe that I shal drinke of? They say to him, 23 We can. † He saith to them, My cuppe in deede you shal drinke of: but to sitte at my right hand and left, is not mine to giue to you: but "to vvhom it is prepared of my father. ⊣

The Gospel vpon S. Iames day *Iul. 25*, And *S. Iohns ante portam Latinam May 6.*

Mr. 10, 41. Lu. 22, 25.

24 † And the ten hearing it, vvere displeased at the tvvo bre-25 thren. † And IESVS called them vnto him, and said, * You knovv that the princes of the gentiles ∴ ouerrule them: and 26 they that are the greater, exercise povver against them. † It shal not be so among you. but vvhosoeuer vvil be the grea-27 ter among you, let him be your minister: † and he that vvil 28 be first among you, shal be your seruant. † Euen as the" Sonne of man is not come to be ministred vnto, but to minister, and to giue his life a redemption for many. ⊣

∴ Superiority is not here forbidden among Christians, neither Ecclesiastical nor temporal: but heathenish tyranny is forbidden, and humility commended.

Mr. 10, 46.

29 † And * vvhen they vvent out from Iericho, a great multi-30 tude folovved him. † And behold tvvo blinde men sitting by the vvay side, heard that IESVS passed by, and they cried 31 out saying, Lord, haue mercie vpon vs, sonne of Dauid. † And the multitude rebuked them that they should hold their peace. But they cried out the more, saying, Lord, haue mercie 32 vpon vs, sonne of Dauid. † And IESVS stoode, and called 33 them, and said, Vvhat vvil ye that I doe to you? † They say 34 to him, Lord, that our eies may be opened. † And IESVS hauing compassion on them, touched their eies. And immediatly they savv, and folovved him.

ANNOTATIONS
CHAP. XX.

1. In the morning.] God called some in the morning, that is, in the beginning of the World, as Abel, Enoch, Noë, and other the iust and faithful of the first age: at the third houre, Abraham, Isaac, and Iacob, and the rest of their age: at the 6 houre of the day, Moyses, Aaron, and the rest: at the 9 houre, the Prophetes: at the eleuenth, that is, at the later end of the World, the Christian

Nations. *Aug. de verb. Domini ser. 59.* breifly, this calling at diuerse houres signifieth the calling of the Iewes from time to time in the first ages of the world, and of the Gentils in the later age thereof. It signifieth also that God calleth coũtries to the faith, some soner, some later: and particular men to be his seruants, some yonger, some elder, of diuerse ages.

Diuersitie of glorie in heauen.

9. Peny.] The peny promised to al, was life euerlasting, which is common to al that shal be saued: but in the same life there be degrees of glorie, as * betwixt starre and starre in the element. *Aug. li. de virginit. c. 26.*

1. Cor. 15.

16. Few elect.] Those are elect which despised not their caller, but folowed and beleued him: for men beleue not but of their owne free will. *Aug. li. 1 ad Simplic. q. 2.*

23. To whom it is prepared.] The kingdom of heauen is prepared for them that are worthy of it and deserue it by their wel doing, as in holy Scripture it is very often, That *God wil repay euery man according to his workes.* and, *Come ye blessed, possesse the kingdom prepared for you.* Why? *because I was hungrie, and you gaue me meate: thirstie, and you gaue me drinke: &c.* Therfore doeth Christ say here, *It is not mine to giue.* because he is iust and wil not giue it to euery man without respect of their deserts: yea nor alike to euery one, but diuersly according to greater or lesser merits. as here S. Chryso. maketh it plaine, when our Sauiour telleth them, that although they suffer martyrdom for his sake, yet he hath not to giue them the two cheefe places. *See S. Hiero. Vpon this place, and li. 2 adu. Iouin. c. 15.* This also is a lesson for them that haue to bestow Ecclesiastical benefices, that they haue no carnal respect to kinred &c. but to the worthines of the persons.

Mt. 16, 27
Ro. 2. 6.
Mt. 25, 34

Difference of merites and reward.

Chrys. ho. 66 in Mt.

28. As the sonne of man.] Christ him self as he was the Sonne of man, was their and our Superiour, and * Lord and Maister, notwithstanding his humility: and therfore it is pride and haultinesse which is forbidden, and not Superiority or Lordship, as some Heretikes would haue it.

Io. 13, 13.

CHAP. XXI.

THE FIFTH part, of the Holy weeke of his Passiõ in Hierusalem.

Being now come to the place of his Passion, he entereth with humility and triumph together: 12 Sheweth his zeale for the house of God ioyned with great maruels. 15 And to the Rulers he boldly defendeth the acclamations of the children. 18 He curseth also that fruitles leafie tree: 23 auoucheth his power by the witnes of Iohn: 28 and foretelleth his in two parables their reprobation (with the Gentils vocation) for their wicked deserts, 42 and consequently their irreparable damnation that shal ensue therof.

The Gospel on Palme Sunday before the benedictiõ of the Palmes.

PALME SVNDAY.

ND vvhen they drevv nigh to Hierusalem, and vvere come to Beth-phagee vnto Mount-oliuet, then IESVS sent tvvo disciples, 2 † saying to them, Goe ye into the tovvne that is against you, and immediatly " you shal finde an asse tied and a colt vvith her: loose them & bring them to me: 3 † and if any man shal say ought vnto you, say ye, that our Lord hath neede of them: and forthvvith he vvil let them goe. 4 † And this vvas done that it might be fulfilled vvhich vvas spoken by the Prophet, saying, 5 † *Say ye to the daughter of Sion, Behold thy king commeth to thee, meeke, & sitting vpon an asse and a colt the fole of her that is vsed to the yoke.* 6 † And the disciples going, did as IESVS commaunded them. 7 † And they brought " the asse and the colt: and laide their garments vpon them, and made him to sit thereon. 8 † And a very great multitude spred their " garments in the vvay: and others did cut boughes from the trees, and stravved them in the vvay: 9 † and the multitudes

Mr. 11, 1.
Lu. 19, 20.
Io. 12, 15

Esa. 62, 11.
Zach. 9, 9.

Ps. 117, 26.

tudes that vvent before and that folovved, cried, saying, "*Hosanna to the sonne of Dauid: blessed is he that commeth in the name of our Lord.* ⊣ *Hosanna in the highest.*

10 † And vvhen he vvas entred Hierusalem, the vvhole citie 11 vvas moued, saying, Who is this? † And the people said, This 12 is IESVS the Prophet, of Nazareth in Galilee. † And * IESVS entred into the temple of God, and cast out al that :: sold and bought in the temple, and the tables of the bankers, and 13 the chaires of them that sold pigeons he ouerthrevve: † and he saith to them, It is vvritten, *My house shal be called the " house of prayer: but you haue made it a denne of theeues.* 14 † And there came to him the blinde, and the lame in the temple: and he healed them. 15 † And the cheefe priestes & Scribes seeing the maruelous things that he did, and the children crying in the temple, & saying, 16 *Hosanna to the sonne of Dauid*: they had indignatiō, † and said to him, Hearest thou vvhat these say? And IESVS said to them, Very vvel. haue you neuer read, *That out of the " mouth of infants and* 17 *sucklings thou hast perfited praise?* † And leauing them, he vvent forth out of the citie into Bethania, and remained there. ⊣

The Gospel vpō Tuesday the first vveeke in Lent.

Mr. 11, 15. Lu. 19, 45.

:: How much the abuse of Churches by merchandising, walking, or other profane occupying of them, displeaseth God, here we may see.

Esa. 56, 7. Ier. 7, 11

Ps. 8, 3.

MVNDAY.

18 † And in the morning returning into the citie, he vvas an 19 hungred. † * And seeing a certaine :: figtree by the vvay side, he came to it: and found nothing on it but leaues only, and he saith to it, Neuer grovv there fruite of thee for euer. 20 And incontinent the figtree vvas vvithered. † And the disciples seeing it, marueled saying, Hovv is it vvithered incon- 21 tinent? † And IESVS ansvvering said to them, Amen I say to you, * if you shal haue faith, and stagger not, not only that of the figtree shal you doe, but and if you shal say to this mountaine, Take vp and throvv thy self into the sea, it shal 22 be done. † And al things vvhatsoeuer you shal aske in prayer "beleeuing, you shal receiue.

Mr. 11, 13.

:: The Ievves hauing the vvordes of the lavv, and not the deedes, vvere the figtree ful of leaues, and void of fruite. *Aug. de verb. Do. Serm. 44.*

Mt. 17, 20.

TVESDAY.

23 † And vvhen he vvas come into the temple, there came to him as he vvas teaching, the cheefe Priests and auncients of the people, saying, * "In vvhat povver doest thou these things? 24 and vvho hath giuen thee this povver? † IESVS ansvvering said to them, I also vvil aske you one vvord: vvhich if you shal tell me, I also vvil tel you in vvhat povver I doe these 25 things. † The Baptisme of Iohn vvhence vvas it? from heauen, or from men? But they thought vvithin them selues, saying, 26 † If vve shal say from heauen, he vvil say to vs, vvhy then did you not beleeue him? but if vve shal say from men: vve feare 27 the multitude. for al hold Iohn as a Prophet. † And ansvvering

Mr. 11, 28. Lu. 20, 2

to IESVS they said, We knovv not. He also said to them, Neither do I tel you in vvhat povver I doe these things.

† But vvhat is your opinion? A certaine man had tvvo sonnes: and comming to " the first, he said, Sonne, goe vvorke to day in my vineyard. † And he ansvvering, said, I vvil not. But aftervvard moued vvith repentance he vvent. † And comming to the other, he said likevvise. And he ansvvering, said, I goe Lord, and he vvent not. † Which of the tvvo did the fathers vvil? They say to him, The first. IESVS saith to them, Amē I say to you, that the Publicans and vvhoores goe before you into the kingdom of God. † For Iohn came to you in the vvay of iustice: and you did not beleeue him. but the publicans and vvhoores did beleeue him: but you seeing it, neither haue ye had repentance aftervvard, to beleeue him. 28 29 30 31 32

The Gospel vpon friday the second Weeke in Lent.

† An other parable heare ye: A man there vvas an housholder vvho * planted a vineyard, and made a hedge round about it, and digged in it a presse, and builded a tovvre, and let it out to husbandmen: and vvent forth into a strange countrie. † And vvhen the time of fruites drevve nigh, he sent his seruants to the husbandmen, to receiue the fruites thereof. † And the husbandmen apprehending his seruants, one they beat, an other they killed, and an other they stoned. † Againe he sent other seruants moe then the former: and they did to them likevvise. † And last of al he sent to them his sonne, saying, They vvil reuerence my sonne. † But the husbandmen seeing the sonne, said vvithin them selues, This is the heire, come, let vs kil him, and vve shal haue his inheritaunce. † And apprehending him they cast him forth out of the vineyard, and killed him. † When therfore the lord of the vineyard shal come, vvhat vvil he doe to those husbandmen? † They say to him, The naughtie men he vvil bring to naught: and his vineyard he vvil let out to other husbandmen, that shal render him the fruite in their seasons. 33 34 35 36 37 38 39 40 41

Es. 5, 1. Mr. 12, 1 Lu. 20, 9.

† IESVS saith to them, Haue you neuer read in the Scriptures, *The stone which the builders reiected, the same is made into the head of the corner? By our lord was this done, and it is maruelous in our eyes.* † Therfore I say to you, that the kingdom of God shal be taken avvay from you, and shal be giuen to a nation yelding the fruites thereof. † And * he that falleth vpon this stone, shal be broken: and on vvhom it falleth, it shal al to bruise him. † And vvhen the cheefe Priestes and Pharisees had heard his parables, they knevve that he spake of them. † And seeking 42 43 44 45 46

Ps. 117, 22. Es. 8, 14

to

to lay hands vpon him, they feared the multitudes: because they held him as a Prophet. ⊣

ANNOTATIONS
CHAP. XXI.

2. *You shal finde.*] Christ by diuine power both knewe where these beasts were, being absent, and commaunded them for his vse, being an other mans, and sodenly made the colt fitte to be ridden on, neuer broken before.

7. *The asse and the colt.*] This asse vnder yoke signifieth the Iewes vnder the Law and vnder God their Lord, as it were his old and ancient people: the yong colt now first ridden on by Christ, signifieth the Gentiles, wilde hitherto and not broken, now to be called to the faith and to receiue our Sauiours yoke. And therfore the three last Euangelists writing specially to the Gentils, make mention of the colt only.

Hiero. in Mat. Aug. li. 12 cot. Faust. c. 42.

8. *Garments in the way.*] These offices of honour done to our Sauiour extraordinarily, were very acceptable: and for a memory hereof the holy Church maketh a solemne Procession euery yere vpon this day, specially in our Countrie when it was Catholike, with the B. Sacrament reuerently caried, as it were Christ vpon the asse, and strawing of rushes and floures, bearing of Palmes, setting vp boughes, spredding and hanging vp the richest clothes, the quire and queristers singing as here the children and the people. al done in a very goodly ceremonie to the honour of Christ and the memorie of his triumphe vpon this day. The like seruice and the like duties done to him in al other solemne Processions of the B. Sacrament, and otherwise, be vndoubtedly no lesse grateful.

Procession on Palme-sunday with the B. Sacrament.

Al deuout offices in that kinde, exceding grateful.

9. *Hosanna.*] These very wordes of ioyful crie and triumphant voice of gratulation to our Sauiour, holy Church vseth alwaies in the Preface of the Masse, as it were the voice of the Priest and al the people (who then specially are attent and deuout) immediatly before the Consecration and Eleuation, as it were expecting, and reioycing at his comming.

HOSANNA.

13. *House of prayer.*] Note here that he calleth external sacrifice (out of the Prophete Esay) prayer. For he speaketh of the Temple, which was builded properly and principally for sacrifice.

16. *Mouth of infants.*) Yong childrens prayers proceding from the instinct of Gods spirit, be acceptable: aud so the voices of the like, or of other simple folke now in the Church, though them selues vnderstand not particularly what they say, be maruelous grateful to Christ.

Prayers not vnderstood of the partie, are acceptable.

22. *Beleeuing.*] In respect of our owne vnworthinesse, and of the thing not alwaies expedient for vs, we may wel doubt when we pray, whether we shal obtaine or no: but on Gods part we must beleeue, that is, we must haue no diffidence or mistrust either of his power or of his wil, if we be worthy, and the thing expedient. And therfore S. Marke hath thus, *Haue ye faith of God.*

Marc. 11, 22.

23. *In what power?*] The Heretikes presumptuously thinke them selues in this point like to Christ, because they are asked, in what power they come, and who sent them: but when they haue answered this question as fully as Christ did here by that which he insinuateth of Iohns testimonie for his authority, they shalbe heard, and til then they shal be stil taken for those of whom God speaketh by the Prophete, *They ranne, and I sent them not.*

Hæretikes runne, not sent.

Ier. 23.

28. *The first.*) The first sonne here is the people of the Gentils, because Gentility was before there was a peculiar and chosen people of the Iewes. and therfore the Iewes here as the later, are signified by the other sonne.

CHAP. XXII.

Yet by one other parable he foreshewth the most deserued reprobation of the earthly and persecuting Iewes, and the gratious vocation of the Gentils in their place. 15 Then he defeateth the snare of the Pharisees and Herodians about paying tribute to Cæsar. 23 He answereth also the inuention of the Sadducees against the Resurrection: 34 and a question that the Pharisees aske to pose him: turning and posing them againe, because they imagined that Christ should be no more then a man: 46 and so he putteth al the busy Sectes to silence.

weeke.

The Gospel vpō the 19 Sunday after Pentecost.

ND IESVS ansvvering, spake againe in parables to them, saying: † The kingdom of heauen is likened to a man being a king, vvhich made a " mariage to his sonne. † And he sent his " seruants to call them that vvere inuited to the mariage: and they vvould not come. † Againe he sent other seruants, saying, Tel them that vvere inuited, Behold I haue prepared my dinner: my beeues and fatlings are killed, and al things are ready: come ye to the mariage. † But they neglected: and vvent their vvaies, " one to his farme, and an other to his merchandise: † and the rest laid hands vpon his seruants, and spitefully intreating them, murdered them. † But vvhen the king had heard of it, he vvas vvroth, and sending his hostes, destroied those murderers, and burnt their citie. † Then he saith to his seruants, The mariage in deede is ready: but they that vvere inuited, vvere not vvorthie. † Goe ye therfore into the high vvayes: and vvhosoeuer you shal finde, call to the mariage. † And his seruants going forth into the vvayes, gathered together al that they found, ∷ bad and good: and the mariage vvas filled vvith ghestes. † And the king vvent in to see the ghestes: and he savv there " a man not attired in a vvedding garment. † And he saith to him, Frende, hovv camest thou in hither not hauing a vvedding garment? But he vvas dumme. † Then the king said to the vvaiters, Binde his hands and feete, and cast him into the vtter darkenes: there shal be vveeping & gnashing of teeth. † For many be called, but fevv elect. ꟷ 1–14

∷ Not only good men be within the church, but also euil mē. against the Heretikes of these daies.

† * Then the Pharisees departing, consulted among them selues for to entrappe him in his talke. † And they send to him their disciples vvith the Herodians, saying, Maister, vve knovv that thou art a true speaker, and teachest the vvay of God in truth, neither carest thou for any man. for thou doest not respect the person of men: † tel vs therfore vvhat is thy opinion, is it lavvful to giue tribute to Cæsar, or not? † But IESVS knovving their naughtines, said, What do you tempt me Hypocrites? † Shevv me the tribute coine. And they offred him a penie. † And IESVS saith to them, Whose is this image and superscription? † They say to him, Cæsars. Then he saith to them, Render therfore the things that are Cæsars, " to Cæsar: and the things that are Gods, to God. † And hearing it they marueled, and leauing him vvent their vvaies. 15–22

Mr. 12, 13. Lu. 20, 20.

† * That day there came to him the Sadducees, that say there 23

* Mr. 12, 19. Lu. 20, 27.

Act. 23, 6. *Deu. 25, 5.*

24 there is no resurrection: and asked him, † saying, Maister, Moyses said, *If a man die not hauing a childe, that his brother marie his wife,* 25 *and raise vp seede to his brother.* † And there vvere vvith vs seuen brethren: and the first hauing maried a vvife, died: and not 26 hauing issue, left his vvife to his brother. † In like maner the 27 second and the third euen to the seuenth. † And last of al the 28 vvoman died also. † In the resurrection therfore vvhose vvife 29 of the seuen shal she be? for they al had her. † And IESVS answering, said to them, You do erre, not knowing the Scrip-30 tures, nor the povver of God. † For in the resurrection neither shal they marie nor be maried: but are" as the Angels of 31 God in heauen. † And concerning the resurrectiō of the dead, haue you not read that vvich vvas spoken of God saying to

Exo. 3, 6.

32 you, † *I am the God of Abraham, and the God of Isaac, and the God of* 33 *Iacob?* He is not God" of the dead, but of the liuing. † And the multitudes hearing it, marueled at his doctrine.

Mar. 12, 28.

The Gospel vpō the 17 Sunday after Pentecost.

34 † * But the Pharisees hearing that he had put the Sadducees 35 to silence, came together: † and one of them a doctor of 36 lavv asked of him, tempting him, † Maister, vvhich is the great

Deut. 6, 5.

37 commaundement in the lavv? † IESVS said to him, *Thou shalt loue the lord thy God from thy whole hart, and with thy whole soul, and with* 38 *thy whole minde.* † This is the greatest and the first commaunde-

Leu. 19, 18.

39 ment. † And the second is like to this, *Thou shalt loue thy neigh-*40 *bour as thy self.* † " On these tvvo commaundements dependeth the vvhole Lavv and the Prophets.

Mr. 12, 35. *Lu. 20, 41.*

41 † And * the Pharisees being assembled, IESVS asked them 42 † saying, What is your opinion of Christ? Whose sonne is he? 43 They say to him, Dauids. † He saith to them, Hovv then 44 doth Dauid in spirit cal him Lord, saying, † *The Lord said to my Lord,*

Ps. 109. 1.

45 *sitte on my right hand, vntil I put thine enemies the foote stole of thy feete?* † If 46 Dauid therfore call him Lord, hovv is he his sonne? † And no man could ansvver him a vvord: neither durst any man from that day aske him any more. ⊣

ANNOTATIONS
CHAP. XXII.

2\. *Mariage.*) Then did God the Father make this mariage, when by the mysterie of the Incarnation he ioyned to his sonne our Lord, the holy Church for his spouse. *Greg. hom. 38.*

3\. *Seruants.*) The first seruants here sent to inuite, were the Prophets: the second, were the Apostles: and al that afterward conuerted countries, or that haue and doe reconcile men to the Church.

Worldly excuses against reconciliation.

5\. *One to his farme.*) Such as refuse to be reconciled to Christes Church, alleage often vaine impediments and worldly excuses, which at the day of iudgement wil not serue them.

11. *A man not attyred.*] It profiteth not much to be within the Church and to be a Catholike, except a man be of good life, for such an one shal be damned, because with faith he hath not good workes: as is euident by the example of this man, who was within, and at the feast as the rest, but lacked the garment of charitie and good workes. And by this man are represented al the bad that are called. and therfore they also are in the Church, as this man was at the feast: but because he was called, and yet none of the elect, it is euident that the Church doth not consist of the elect only, contrarie to our Aduersaries.

The Church cõsisteth of good and bad.

21. *To Cæsar.*) Temporal duties and payments exacted by worldly Princes must be payed, so that God be not defrauded of his more soueraine dutie. And therfore Princes haue to take heede, how they exact: and others, how they geue to Cæsar, that is, to their Prince, the things that are dewe to God, that is, to his Ecclesiastical ministers. Wherevpon S. Athanasius reciteth these goodly wordes out of an epistle of the ancient and famous Cõfessor Hosius Cordubensis to Cõstantius the Arian Emperour: Cease I beseche thee, and remember that thou art mortal, feare the day of iudgement, intermedle not with Ecclesiastical matters, neither doe thou commaund vs in this kinde, but rather learne them of vs. to thee God hath committed the Empire, to vs he hath cõmitted the things that belong to the Church: and as he that with malicious eies carpeth thine Empire, gainesayeth the ordinance of God: so doe thou also beware, lest in drawing vnto thee Ecclesiastical matters, thou be made guilty of a great crime. It is written, Geue ye the things that are Cæsars, to Cæsar: and the things that are Gods, to God. Therfore neither is it lawful for vs in earth to hold the Empire, neither hast thou (O Emperour) power ouer incense and sacred things. *Athan. Ep. ad Solit. vitã agentes.* And S. Ambrose to Valentinian the Emperour (who by the il counsel of his mother Iustina an Arian, required of S. Ambrose to haue one Church in Millan deputed to the Arian Heretikes) saith: We pay that which is Cæsars, to Cæsar: and that which is Gods, to God. Tribute is Cæsars, it is not denied: the Church is Gods, it may not verely be yelded to Cæsar: because the Temple of God can not be Cæsars right. Which no man can deny but it is spoken with the honour of the Emperour. for what is more honorable then that the Emperour be said to be the sonne of the Church? For a good Emperour is within the Church, not aboue the Church. *Ambr. lib. 5. Epist. Orat. de Basil. trad.*

Neither must temporal Princes exact, nor their Subiects giue vnto them, Ecclesiastical iurisdiction.

30. *As Angels.*) As Christ proueth here, that in heauen they neither marry nor are married, because there they shal be as Angels: by the very same reason, is proued, that Saints may heare our prayers and helpe vs, be they neere or farre of, because the Angels do so, and in euery moment are present vvhere they list, and neede not to be neere vs, when they heare or helpe vs.

The Saints heare our prayers.

30. *As Angels.*) Not to marry nor be married, is to be like to Angels: therfore is the state of Religious men and women and Priests, for not marrying, worthely called of the Fathers, an Angelical life. *Cyp. lib. 2. de discipl. & hab. Virg. sub finem.*

Religious single life, Angelical.

32. *Of the dead.*) S. Hierom by this place disproueth the Heretike Vigilantius, and in him these of our time, which to diminish the honour of Saincts, call them of purpose, dead men.

40. *On these two.*) Hereby it is euident that al dependeth not vpon faith only, but much more vpon charitie (though faith be the first) which is the loue of God and of our neighbour, which is the summe of al the law and the Prophetes: because he that hath this double charitie expressed here by these two principal commaundemẽts, fulfilleth and accomplisheth al that is commaunded in the Law and the Prophetes.

Not onely faith.

CHAP. XXIII.

The Scribes and Pharisees after al this, continuing stil incorrigible, although he wil haue the doctrine of their Chaire obeied, yet against their workes (and namely their ambition) he openly inueigheth, crying to them eight Woes for their eightfold hypocrisie and blindnes: 34 and so concluding with the most worthy reprobation of that persecuting generation and their mother-citie Ierusalem with her Temple.

The Gospel vpõ Tuesday the second weeke in Lent.

1 THEN IESVS spake to the multitudes and to his disciples, 2 †saying, Vpon "the chaire of Moyses haue sitten the Scribes and the Pharisees. 3 † Al things therfore "vvhatsoeuer they shal say to you, obserue ye and doe ye: but according to their vvorkes doe ye not, for they say and doe not. 4 † For * they binde heauy burdens & importable: and put them vpon mens shoulders: but

Luc. 11, 46. Act. 15, 10.

but vvith a finger of their ovvne they vvil not moue them.
5 † But they doe al their vvorkes, for to be seen of men. for they make brode their :: phylacteries, and enlarge their * fringes.
6 † And they "loue the first places at suppers, and * the first chai-
7 res in the Synagogs, † and salutations in the market-place, and
8 to be called of men, Rabbi. † But be not you called Rabbi.
9 for "one is your maister, and al you are brethren. † And call none father to your self vpon earth: for one is your father,
10 he that is in heauen. † Neither * be ye called "maisters: for one
11 is your maister, Christ. † He that is the greater of you, shal
12 be your seruiteur. † And he that exalteth him self, shal be humbled: and he that humbleth him self, shal be exalted. ꟷ

Deu.22, 12. Nu. 15, 38. Mr. 12, 38.

Ia. 3, 1.

:: These phylacteries were peeces of parchement, wherein they wrote the ten cōmaundements, and folded it, and caried it on their forehead before their eies, imagining grosly and superstitiously, that so they fulfilled that which is said Deu. 6, *They shal be immoueable before thine eies.* Hiero. in 23 Mat.

13 † But vvo to you "Scribes & Pharisees, hypocrites: because you shut the kingdom of heauen before men. For your selues do not enter in: & those that are going in, you suffer not to enter.

14 † Wo to you Scribes and Pharisees, hypocrites: because you * deuoure vvidovves houses, "praying long prayers. for this you shal receiue the greater iudgement.

Lu. 20, 47.

15 † Wo to you Scribes and Pharisees, hypocrites: because you goe round about the sea and the land, to make one proselyte: and vvhen he is made, you make him the childe of hel "double more then your selues.

16 † Wo to you blinde guides, that say, Whosoeuer shal svveare by the temple, it is nothing: but he that shal svveare
17 by the gold of the temple, is bound. † Ye foolish and blinde, for vvhether is greater, the gold, or the temple that sancti-
18 fieth the gold? † And vvhosoeuer shal svveare by the altar, it is nothing: but vvhosoeuer shal svveare by the gift that is
19 vpon it, is bound. † Ye blinde, for vvhether is greater, the
20 gift, or the altar that "sanctifieth the gift? † He therfore that svveareth by the altar, svveareth by it and by al things that
21 are vpon it: † and vvhosoeuer shal svveare by the temple,
22 svveareth by it and "by him that dvvelleth in it: † and he that svveareth by heauen, svveareth by the throne of God & by him that sitteth thereon.

23 † Wo to you Scribes and Pharisees, hypocrites: because you tithe mint, and anise, and cummin, and haue left the vveightier things of the lavv, iudgemēt, and mercie, and faith. these things you ought to haue done, & not to haue omit-
24 ted those. † Blinde guides, that straine a gnat, and svvallovv a camel.

† Wo to you Scribes and Phariſees, hypocrites: becauſe 25 you make cleane that on the outſide of the cuppe and diſh: but vvithin you are ful of rapine and vncleannes. † Thou 26 blinde Phariſee, firſt make cleane the inſide of the cuppe and the diſh, that the outſide may become cleane.

they are ful

† Wo to you Scribes and Phariſees, hypocrites: becauſe you 27 are like to vvhited ſepulchres, vvhich outvvardly appeare vnto mē beautiful, but vvithin are ful of dead mens bones, and al filthines. † So you alſo outvvardly in deede appeare to men 28 iuſt: but invvardly you are ful of hypocriſie and iniquitie.

† Wo to you Scribes and Phariſees, ye hypocrites: be- 29 cauſe you build the Prophets ſepulchres, and garniſh the moniments of iuſt men, † and ſay: If vve had been in 30 our fathers dayes, vve had not been their felovves in the bloud of the Prophets. † Therefore you are a teſtimonie to 31 your ovvne ſelues, that you are the ſonnes of them that killed the Prophets. † And fil you vp the meaſure of your fathers. 32 † You ſerpents, vipers broodes, hovv vvil you flee from the 33 iudgement of hel? ¶ † Therfore behold I ſend vnto you Pro- 34 phets and vviſe men and ſcribes, and of them you ſhal kil & crucifie, and of them you ſhal ſcourge in your Synagogs, and perſecute from citie into citie: † that vpon you may come al 35 the iuſt bloud that vvas ſhed vpon the earth, from the bloud of * Abel the iuſt euē vnto the bloud of * Zacharias the ſonne of Barachias, vvhom you murdered betvvene the temple and the altar. † Amen I ſay to you, al theſe things ſhal come vpon 36 this generation. † * Hieruſalem, Hieruſalem, vvhich killeſt the 37 Prophets, and ſtoneſt them that vvere ſent to thee, hovv often vvould I gather together thy children as the henne doth gather together her chickens vnder her vvinges, and thou :: vvouldeſt not? † Behold, your houſe ſhal be left de- 38 ſert to you. † For I ſay to you, you ſhal not ſee me from hence 39 forth til you ſay, Bleſſed is he that commeth in the name of our Lord. ⊣

The Goſpel vpō S. Steuens day Decemb. 26.

:: Free Wil.

Gen. 4, 8
2. *Par.* 24, 22.
Luc. 13, 34.

ANNOTATIONS
CHAP. XXIII.

The See of Rome preſerued in truth.

2. *Chaire of Moyſes.*] God preſerueth the truth of Chriſtian religion in the Apoſtolike See of Rome, Which is in the new law anſwerable to the chaire of Moyſes, notWithſtāding the Biſhops of the ſame Were neuer ſo Wicked of life: yea though ſome traitour as il as Iudas Were Biſhop thereof, it ſhould not be preiudicial to the Church and innocent Chriſtians, for Whom our Lord prouiding ſaid, Doe that Which they ſay, but doe not as they doe. *Auguſt. Epiſt.* 165.

8. What

Cōtra lit. Petil. li. 2. c. 51.

3. Whatsoeuer they shal say.] Why (saith S. Augustin) *doest thou call the Apostolike Chaire the chaire of pestilence? If for the men, Why? Did our Lord Iesus Christ for the Pharisees, any vvrong to thee Chaire vvherein they sate? Did he not commend that chaire of Moyses, and preseruing the honour of the chaire, reproue them? For he saith: They sitte vpon the Chaire of Moyses, that vvhich they say, doe ye. These things if you did vvel consider, you vvould not for the men vvhom you defame, blaspheme the See Apostolike, vvherevvith you doe not communicate.* And againe he saith: *Neither for the Pharisees (to vvhom you compare vs not of vvisdom but of malice) did our Lord commaund the Chaire of Moyses to be forsaken, in vvhich chaire verely he figured his ovvne. for he vvarneth the people to doe that vvhich they say, and not to doe that vvhich they doe, and that the holinesse of the Chaire be in no case forsaken, nor the vnity of the flocke deuided, for the naughty Pastours.*

The dignitie of the See of Rome, notwithstanding some euil Bishops thereof.

Cōtra lit. Petil. li. 2. c. 61.

6. Loue the first places.) He condemneth not dew places of Superiority geuen or taken of men according to their degrees, but ambitious seeking for the same, and their prowde hart and wicked intention, which he saw within them, and therfore might boldly reprehend them.

8. One is your maister.) In the Catholike Church there is one Maister, Christ our Lord, and vnder him one Vicar, with whom al Catholike Doctors and teachers are one, because they teach al one thing. but in Arch-heretikes it is not so, where euery one of them is a diuerse maister, and teacheth contrarie to the other, and wil be called Rabbi and Maister, euery one of their owne Disciples: Arius a Rabbi among the Arians, Luther among the Lutherans, and among the Caluinists Caluin.

Many maisters are many Archheretikes.

10. Maisters.) Wiclefe and the like Heretikes of this time doe herevpon condemne degrees of Schole and titles of Doctors and Maisters: where they might as wel reproue S. Paul for calling him self *Doctor and Maister of the Gentiles*: and for saying * that there should be alwayes *Doctors* in the Church. and whereas they bring the other words folowing, against Religious men who are called fathers: as wel might they by this place take away the name of carnal fathers, and blame S. Paule for calling him self the only spiritual father of the Corinthians. but in deede nothing is here forbidden but the contentious diuision and partiality of such as make them selues Ringleaders of Schismes and Sectes, as Donatus, Arius, Luther, Caluin.

1. Tim. 2. 2. Tim. 1. * Eph. 4. 1. Cor. 4, 15

Doctors, Masters, and spiritual fathers.

13. Scribes and Pharisees.] In al these reprehensions it is much to be noted, that our Sauiour for the honour of Priesthod neuer reprehendeth Priests by that name. *Cypr. ep. 65.* Whereas our Heretikes vse this name of purpose in reproche and despite.

The honour of Priesthod.

14. Praying long prayers.) They are not reprehended here for the things them selues, which for the most part are good, as, long prayer, making Proselytes, garnishing the Prophetes sepulchres, &c. but for their wicked purpose and intention, as before is said of fasting, prayers, almes, *Mat. 6.*

The intention.

15. Double more.) They that teach that it is ynough to haue only faith, doe make such Christians, as the Iewes did Proselytes, children of Hel far more then before. *August. lib. de fide & oper. cap. 26.*

Not only faith.

19. Sanctifieth.) Note that donaries and gifts bestowed vpon Churches and altars, be sanctified by dedication to God, and by touching the altar and other holy things: as now specially the vessels of the sacrifice and Sacrament of Christes body and bloud, by touching the same, and the altar it self wherevpon it is consecrated. Whereof Theophylacte writeth thus vpon this place: *In the old lavv Christ permitteth not the gift to be greater then the altar, but vvith vs, the altar is sanctified by the gift: for the hostes by the diuine grace are turned into our Lords body, and therfore is the altar also sanctified by them.*

Theophyl. Mat. 23.

The altar is sanctified by our Lords body therevpon.

21. By him that dwelleth therein.) By this we see that swearing by creatures, as by the Gospel, by Saincts, is al referred to the honour of God, whose Gospel it is, whose Saincts they are.

28. Appeare to men.) Christ might boldly reprehend them so often aud so vehemently for hypocrisie, because he knew their harts and intentions: but we that can not see within men, may not presume to call mens external good doings, hypocrisie: but iudge of men as we see and know.

29. Garnish.) Christ blameth not the Iewes for adorning the sepulchres of the Prophetes, but entwyteth them of their malice toward him, and of that which by his diuine knowledge he foresaw, that they would accomplish the wickednes of their fathers in sheding his bloud, as their fathers did the bloud of the Prophetes. *Hilar.*

CHAP. XXIIII.

To his Disciples (by occasion of Hierusalem and the Temples destruction) he foretelleth, 4 vvhat things shalbe before the consummation of the vvorld, as specially, 14 the Churches ful preaching vnto al nations: 15 then, vvhat shalbe in the very consummation, to vvit, Antichrist vvith his passing great persecution and seduction, but for a short time: 29 then incontinent, the Day of iudgement to our great comfort in those miseries vnder Antichrist. 35 As for the moment, to vs it perteineth not to knovv it, 37 but rather euery man to vvatch, that vve be not vnprouided vvhen he commeth to ech one particularly by death.

ND IESVS being gone out of the temple, 1 vvent. And his disciples came to shevv him the buildings of the tẽple. † And he ansvvering said to thẽ, 2 Do you see al these things? Amen I say to you, there shal " not be left here a stone vpon a stone that shal not be destroied. (Mr. 13, 1; Lu. 21, 5)

(The Gospel for a votiue Masse in time of Warre. and for many Martyrs.)

† And vvhen he vvas sitting vpon Mount-oliuet, the disciples 3 came to him secretly, saying: Tel vs, vvhen shal these things be? and vvhat shal be " the signe of thy comming, and of the consummation of the vvorld? † And IESVS ansvvering, 4 said to them, Bevvare that no man " seduce you: 5 † for many shal come in my name saying, " I am Christ: and they shal seduce many. † For you shal heare of vvarres, & bruites 6 of vvarres. See that ye be not troubled. for these things must be done: but the end is not yet. † for nation shal rise against 7 nation, and kingdom against kingdom: and there shal be pestilences, and famines, and earth-quakes in places, † and 8 al these things are the beginnings of sorovves. ⊣ † Then * shal 9 they deliuer you into tribulation, and shál kil you: and you shal be odious to al nations for my names sake. † And then 10 many shal be scandalized: and they shal deliuer vp one an other: and they shal hate one an other. † And many :: false- 11 prophets shal rise: and shal seduce many. † And because 12 " iniquitie shal abound: the charitie of many shal vvaxe cold. † But he that shal perseuêre to the end, he shal be saued. ⊣ 13 † And this Gospel of the kingdom " shal be preached in the 14 vvhole vvorld, for a testimonie to al nations, and then shal come the consummation.

(TVESDAY night.)

(Mat. 10, 17.)

(:: There were in the people false Prophetes, as among you also shal be lying Maisters, which shal bring in Sectes of perdition. 2. Pet. 2.)

(The Gospel vpõ the last Sunday after Pentecost.)

† Therfore vvhen you shal see " *the abomination of desolation,* 15 vvhich vvas spoken of by Daniel the Prophet, standing in the holy place (he that readeth, let him vnderstand) † then 16 they that are in Ievvrie, let them flee to the mountaines: † and he that is on the house-toppe, let him not come dovvne 17 (Dan. 9, 27.)

18 to take any thing out of his house: † and he that is in the field, 19 let him not goe backe to take his coate. † And vvo to thẽ that 20 are vvith childe, and that giue sucke in those dayes. † But pray 21 that your flight be not in the vvinter or on the Sabboth. † For there shal be then great tribulation, such as hath not been from the beginning of the vvorld vntil novv, neither shal 22 be. † And vnles those daies had been shortened, no flesh should be saued: but for the elect the daies" shal be shorte- 23 ned. † Then if any man shal say vnto you, Loe ∷ here is 24 Christ, or there: do not beleeue him. † For there shal rise false-Christes and false-Prophets, and shal shevv" great signes and vvonders, so that the elect also (if it be possible) may 25 be induced into errour. † Loe I haue foretold you. † If therfore 26 they shal say vnto you, Behold he is in the desert: goe ye not 27 out: behold" in the closets, beleeue it not. † For as lightening cōmeth out of the east, and appeareth euen into the vvest, so 28 shal also the aduent of the sonne of man be. † Wheresoeuer the body is, thither shal the egles also be gathered together.

∷ Whosoeuer draweth Christ or his Church from the Communion and felowship of al Nations Christened, to one corner, towne, or Countrie, beleeue him not. *Aug. de vnit. Ec. c. 1.*

29 † And "immediatly after the tribulation of those dayes * the sonne shal be darkened, and the moone shal not giue her light, and the starres shal fal from heauen, and the powers 30 of heauen shal be moued: † and then shal appeare ∷ the signe of the Sonne of man in heauen: and then shal al tribes of the earth bevvaile: and they shal see the Sonne of man comming in the cloudes of heauen vvith much povver and maiestie. 31 † And he shal send his Angels vvith a trumpet, and a great voyce: and they shal gather together his elect from the foure vvindes, from the furthest partes of heauen euen to the endes 32 thereof. † And of the figtree learne a parable: When novv the bough thereof is tender, and the leaues come forth, you 33 knovv that sommer is nigh. † So you also, vvhen you shal see these things, knovv ye that it is nigh euen at the doores. 34 † Amen I say to you, that this generation shal not passe, til al 35 these things be done. † Heauen and earth shal passe, but my vvordes shal not passe. ⊣

Ezech. 32, 7. Ioel 3, 15 Dan. 7, 15.

∷ This signe of the Sonne of man, is the holy Crosse, which thẽ shal appeare to the Iewes to their confusion. *Chrys. in Mat. ho. 77.* It shal be no lesse confusion to Heretikes that can not abide the signe thereof.

36 † But of that day and houre no body knovveth, neither 37 the Angels of heauen, but the Father alone. † And as * in the dayes of Noe, so shal also the comming of the Sonne of man 38 be. † For as they vvere in the dayes before the floud, eating and drinking, marying and giuing to mariage, euen vnto that 39 day in vvhich Noe entred into the arke, † and knevve not til

Gen. 7, 5.

the floud came, and tooke them al: so also shal the cōming of the Sonne of man be. †Then two shal be in the field: one shal be taken, and one shal be left. 40 †tvvo vvomen grinding in the mill: one shal be taken, and one shal be left. 41 †Watch therfore because you knovv not vvhat houre your Lord vvil come. 42 †But this knovv ye, that* if the good man of the house did knovv vvhat houre the theefe vvould come, he vvould surely vvatch, and vvould not suffer his house to be broken vp. 43 †Therfore be you also ready, because at vvhat houre you knovv not, the Sonne of man vvil come. 44

The Gospel for a Cōfessor that is a Bishop. And for S. Clement martyr, Nouemb. 23.

1. Thes. 5, 1.

†Who, thinkest thou, is a faithful and vvise seruant, vvhom his lord hath appointed ouer his familie, to giue them meate in season? 45 †Blessed is that seruant, vvhom vvhen his lord cōmeth, he shal finde so doing. 46 †Amen I say to you, that ouer al his goods shal he appoint him. 47 ✠ †But if that naughtie seruant shal say in his hart, My lord is long a comming: 48 †and shal beginne to strike his felovv-seruants, and eateth, and drinketh vvith drunkards: 49 †the lord of that seruant shal come in a day that he hopeth not, and an houre that he knovveth not, 50 †and shal deuide him, and appoint his portion vvith the hypocrites: there shal be vveeping and gnashing of teeth. 51

ANNOTATIONS
CHAP. XXIIII.

2. *Not left.*] This was fulfilled 40 yeres after Christes Ascension by Vespasian the Emperour and his sonne Titus. *Euseb. li. 3. c. 6 & seq. ex Iosepho.* Vpon which wordes, *There shal not be left &c,* which threaten the destruction of the Iewes Temple: and those wordes, *Vpon this Rocke I wil build my Church,* which promise the building of the Catholike Church of al nations: S. Chrysostome making a long comparison of these two prophecies of Christ, saith thus: Thou seest in both, his great and vnspeakable power, in that that he increased and built vp them that worshipped him, and those that stumbled at him, he abased, destroyed, and plucked them vp by the roote. Doest thou see how whatsoeuer he hath built, no man shal destroy: and whatsoeuer he hath destroyed, no man shal build? He builded the Church, and no man shal be able to destroy it: he destroyed the Temple, and no man is able to build it, and that in so long time. For they haue endeuoured both to destroy that, and could not: and they haue attempted to build vp this, and they could not doe that neither. &c.

The Church cā neuer faile.

Mt. 16. Li. adu. Gentes & Christus sit Deus, prope finē.

3. *The signe.*] Our Maister knowing that it was not profitable nor seemly for them to know these secretes, gaue them by way of Prophecie, warning of diuerse miseries, signes, and tokens, that should fall, some further of, and some neerer the later day: by which the faithful might alwayes prepare them selues, but neuer be certaine of the houre, day, moneth, nor yere, when it should fall. *Aug. Ep. 80.*

4. *Seduce.*] The first and principal warning, needful for the faithful from Christes Ascension to the very end of the world, is, that they be not deceaued by Heretikes, which vnder the titles of true teachers and the name of Christ and his Gospel, wil seduce many.

Heretikes seduce vnder faire titles.

5. *I am Christ.*] Not only such as haue named them selues Christ, as Simon, Menander, and such like: but al Arch-heretikes be Christes to their folowers, Luther to the Lutherans, Caluin to the Caluinists: because they beleeue them, rather then Christ speaking in his Church.

12. Iniquity

12. Iniquity abound.] When Heresie and false teachers reigne in the world, namely toward the later day, wicked life aboundeth, and charity decayeth.

14. Shal be preached.] The Gospel hath been preached of late yeres, and now is, by holy Religious men of diuers Orders, in sundry great Countries which neuer heard the Gospel before, as it is thought.

The Gospel now preached to Infidels.

15. Abomination of desolation.] This abomination of desolation foretold, was first partly fulfilled in diuerse prophanations of the Temple of Hierusalem, when the sacrifice and seruice of God was taken away. but specially it shal be fulfilled by Antichrist and his Precursors, when they shal abolishe the holy Masse, which is the Sacrifice of Christes body and bloud, and the only soueraine worship dewe to God in his Church: as S. Hyppolytus writeth in these wordes: The Churches shal lament with great lamentation, because there shal neither oblation be made, nor incense, nor worship grateful to God. But the sacred houses of Churches shal be like to cottages, and the pretious body and bloud of Christ shal not be extant (openly in Churches) in those dayes, the Liturgie (or Masse) shal be extinguished, the Psalmodie shal cease, the reciting of the Scriptures shal not be heard. *Hippol. de Antichristo.* By which it is plaine that the Heretikes of these daies be the special fore-runners of Antichrist.

The abomination of desolation.

The abolishing of the holy sacrifice of the Masse by Antichrist and his ministers.

22. Shal be shortened.] The reigne of Antichrist shal be short, that is, three yeres and a halfe. *Dan. 7. Apoc. 11.* Therfore the Heretikes are blasphemous and ridiculous, that say, Christes Vicar is Antichrist, who hath sitten these 1500 yeres.

Antichrist.

24. Great signes.] These signes and miracles shal be to the outward appearance only, for S. Paule calleth them* lying signes, to seduce them only that shal perish. Wherby we see that if Heretikes could worke feyned and forged miracles, yet we ought not to beleeue them, much lesse when they can not so much as seeme to doe any.

2. Thes. 2.

26. In closets.] Christ hauing made the Churches authority bright and clere to the whole world, warneth the faithful to take heede of Heretikes and Schismatikes, which haue their conuenticles aside in certaine odde places and obscure corners, alluring curious persons vnto them. *Aug. li. 1. q. Euang. q. 38.* For as for the comming together of Catholikes to serue God in secrete places, that is a necessarie thing in time of persecution, and was vsed of Christians for three hundred yeres together after Christ, * and the Apostles also and disciples came so together in Hierusalem for feare of the Iewes. And Catholikes doe the same at this day in our countrie, not drawing religion into corners from the society of the Catholike Church, but practising secretely the same faith, that in al Christendom shineth and appeareth most gloriously.

Act. 1, 12.

The secrete conuenticles of Heretikes.

Catholike Christians secretely assembling in time of persecution.

29. Immediatly.] If the later day shal immediatly folow the persecution of Antichrist, which is to endure but three yeres and a halfe, as is aforesaid: then is it mere blasphemie to say, Gods Vicar is Antichrist, and that (by their owne limitation) these thousand yeres almost.

Antichrist.

CHAP. XXV.

Continuing his Sermon, he bringeth two parables, of ten Virgins, and of Talents, to shew how it shalbe in Domesday with the Faithful that prepare, and that prepare not them selues. 31 Then also without parables he sheweth that such Faithful as doe workes of mercy, shal haue for them life euerlasting: and such as doe not, euerlasting damnation.

1 THEN shal the kingdom of heauen be like to ten" virgins: vvhich taking their" lampes vvent forth to meete the bridegrome and the bride. 2 † And fiue of them vvere foolish, and fiue vvise. 3 † but the fiue foolish, hauing taken their lampes, did not take" oile vvith them: 4 † but the vvise did take oile in their vessels vvith the lampes. 5 † And the bridegrome tarying long, they slumbered all and slept. 6 † And at midnight there vvas a clamour made, Behold the bridegrome commeth, goe ye

The Gospel for holy Virgins.

ye forth to meete him. † Then arose al those virgins: and 7 they trimmed their lampes. † And the foolish said to the 8 vvise, Giue vs of :: your oile: because our lampes are going out. † The vvise ansvvered, saying, Lest peraduenture there 9 suffise not for vs and you, goe rather to them that sel: and bie for your selues. † And vvhiles they vvent to bie, the bride- 10 grome vvas come: and they that vvere ready, entred vvith him to the mariage, and the gate vvas shut. † But last of al come 11 also the other virgins, saying: Lord, Lord, open to vs. † But 12 he ansvvering said, Amen I say to you, I knovv you not. † Watch ye therfore, because you knovv not the day nor the 13 houre. ⊣

:: If we be not in the fauour of God, and haue not our owne merites, we shal not be holpen by other mens deserts at the day of iudgement.

The Gospel for a Cõfessor that is a Bishop.

† For * euen as a man going into a strange countrie, cal- 14 led his seruants, and deliuered them his goods. † And to 15 one he gaue fiue talents, and to an other tvvo, and to an other one, to euery one according to his propre facultie: and immediatly he tooke his iourney. † And he that had recei- 16 ued the fiue talents, vvent his vvay, and occupied vvith the same, and gained other fiue. † Likevvise also he that had re- 17 ceiued the tvvo, gained other tvvo. † But he that had recei- 18 ued the one, going his vvay digged into the earth, and hid his lords money. † But after much time the lord of those ser- 19 uants commeth, and made a count vvith them. † And there 20 came he that had receiued the fiue talents, and offred other fiue talents, saying, Lord fiue talents thou didst deliuer me, behold :: I haue gained other fiue besides. † His lord said 21 vnto him: Wel fare thee good and faithful seruant, because thou hast been faithful ouer a fevv things, I vvil place thee ouer many things: enter into the ioy of thy lord. † And there 22 came also he that had receiued the tvvo talents, and said, Lord tvvo talents thou didst deliuer me: behold I haue gai- ned other tvvo. † His lord said to him, Wel fare thee good and 23 faithful seruant: because thou hast been faithful ouer a fevv things, I vvil place thee ouer many things, enter into the ioy of thy lord. ⊣ † And he also that had receiued the one talent, 24 came forth, and said, Lord, I knovv that thou art a hard man, thou reapest vvhere thou didst not sovv: and gatherest vvhere thou stravvedst not: † and being afraid I vvent, and hid 25 thy talent in the earth: behold loe here thou hast that vvhich thine is. † And his lord ansvvering, said to him: :: Naughtie 26 and sloughtful seruant, thou didst knovv that I reape vvhere I sovv

Luc. 19, 12.

:: Free will with Gods grace doth merite.

:: A terrible example for al such as do not employ the very least gift of God, to his glorie.

27 I sovv not, & gather vvhere I stravved not: † thou oughtest therfore to haue committed my money to the bankers, and comming I might haue receiued mine ovvne ″vvith vsurie.
28 † Take ye avvay therfore the talent from him, and giue it him
29 that hath ten talents. † For to * euery one that hath shal be giuen, and he shal abound: but from him that hath not, that also vvhich ″he seemeth to haue, shal be taken avvay from him.
30 † And the vnprofitable seruant cast ye out into the vtter darknesse. There shal be vveeping and gnashing of teeth.

Mr. 13, 12. Lu. 8, 18

31 † And vvhen the sonne of man shal come in his maiestie, and al the Angels vvith him, then shal he sitte vpon the seate
32 of his maiestie: † and al nations shal be gathered together before him, and he shal ″separate them one from an other, as
33 the pastor separateth the sheepe from the goates: † and shal set the sheepe at his right hand, but the goates at his left.
34 † Then shal the king say to them that shal be at his right hand, Come ye blessed of my father, possesse you the kingdom ∷ prepared for you from the foundation of the vvorld.
35 † for I vvas an hungred, and ″you gaue me to eate: I vvas a
36 thirst, and you gaue me to drinke. † I vvas a stranger, and you tooke me in: naked, and you couered me: sicke, and you visi-
37 ted me. I vvas in prison, and you came to me. † Then shal the iust ansvver him, saying: Lord, vvhen did vve see thee an hun-
38 gred, and fed thee: a thirst, and gaue thee drinke? † and vvhen did vve see thee a stranger, and tooke thee in? or na-
39 ked, and couered thee? † or vvhen did vve see thee sicke or
40 in prison: and came to thee? † And the king ansvvering, shall say to them, Amen I say to you, as long as you did it to one
41 of these my least brethren, you did it to me. † Then he shal say to them also that shal be at his left hand, ″Get ye avvay from me you cursed into fire euerlasting, vvhich vvas prepa-
42 red for the Deuil and his angels. † for I vvas an hungred, and you ″gaue me not to eate: I vvas a thirst, and you gaue me
43 not to drinke. † I Was a stranger, and you tooke me not in: naked, and you couered me not: sicke, and in prison, and you
44 did not visite me. † Then they also shall ansvver him, saying, Lord, vvhen did vve see thee an hungred, or a thirst, or a stranger, or naked, or sicke, or in prison: and did not minister to
45 thee? † Then he shal ansvver them, saying, Amen I say to you, as long as you did it not to one of these lesser, neither did
46 you it to me. † And these shal goe into punishment euerlasting: but the iust, into life euerlasting. ✠

The Gospel vpō munday the first weeke of Lent.

∷ This kingdō then is prepared for those onely that do good Workes: as Christ also signifieth els Where, saying that it is not in his poWer to giue it otherWise. *See the annot. c. 20, 23.*

ANNOTATIONS
CHAP. XXV.

Good workes necessarie.

1. Virgins.] These virgins fiue wise, and fiue foolish, signifie that in the Church militant there be good and bad: which bad shal be shut out at the later day, although they haue lampes (that is faith) as the other, because their lampes are out, that is, their faith is dead without charity and good workes to lighten them *Greg. ho. 12.*

1. Lampes.] These lampes lighted, be good workes, namely of mercy, and the laudable conuersation which shineth before men. *Aug. ep. 120, c. 33.*

Right intétion.

3. Oyle.) This oyle is the right inward intention directing our workes to Gods glorie, and not to the praise of our selues in the sight of men *Aug. ep. 120, c. 33.*

27. With vsurie) Vsurie is here taken for the lawful gaine that a man getteth by wel employing his goods. When God geueth vs any talent or talents, he looketh for vsurie, that is, for spiritual increase of the same by our diligence and industrie.

We must vse Gods gifts.

29. That which he seemeth to haue.] He is said to haue Gods gifts, that vseth them, and to such an one God wil increase his giftes. He that vseth them not, seemeth to haue, rather then hath them, and from him God wil withdraw that which before he gaue.

Good and bad in the Church.

32. Separate.) Lo here is the separation, for in the Church militant they liued both together. As for Heretikes, they went out of the Church before, and separated them selues, and therfore are not to be separated here, as being iudged already.

Heauen is the reward of good workes, and Hel of the contrarie.

34. Come ye, 41 get ye away.) It is no incongruity that God should say, Goe into euerlasting fire, to them that by their free wil haue repelled his mercie: and to the other, Come ye blessed of my father, take the kingdom prepared for them, that by their free wil haue receiued faith, and confessed their sinnes and done penance. *Aug. li. 2 act. cum Fel. Manich. c. 8.*

35. You gaue me.) Hereby we see how much almes-deedes and al workes of mercy preuaile towardes life euerlasting, and to blot out former sinnes. *Aug. in Ps. 49.*

42. Gaue me not.) He chargeth them not here that they beleeued not, but that they did not good workes. For such did beleeue, but they cared not for good workes, as though by dead faith they might haue come to heauen. *Aug. de fid. & op. c. 15. & ad Dulcit. q. 2. to. 4.*

CHAP. XXVI.

To the Councel of the Iewes, Iudas by occasion of Marie Magdalens ointmét, doth sell him for litle. 17 After the Paschal lambe, 26 he giueth them that bread of life (promised Io. 6,) in a mystical Sacrifice or Separation of his Body and Bloud. 31 And that night he is after his prayer 47 taken of the Iewes men, Iudas being their captaine: and forsaken of the other eleuen for feare: 57 is falsely accused, and impiously condemned of the Iewes Councel, 67 and shamefully abused of them: 69 and thrise denied of Peter: Al, euen as the Scriptures and him self had often foretold

The Passion according to S. Matthew in these two Chapters, is the gospel at Masse vpon Palme Sunday.

TENEBRE Wenesday.

Mr. 14, 1 Lu. 22, 1

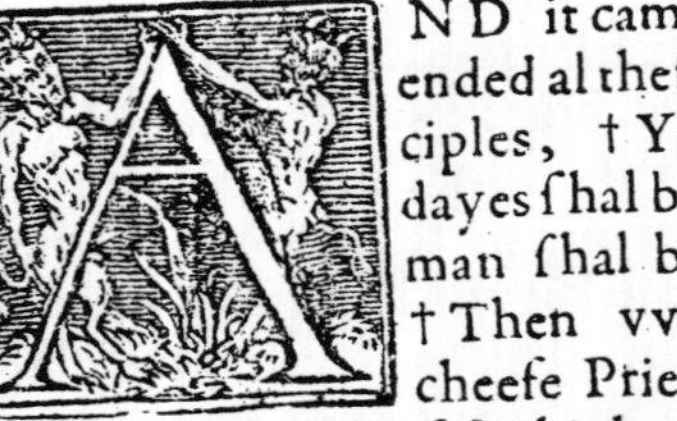

ND it came to passe, vvhen IESVS had ended al these vvordes, he said to his Disciples, 2 † You knovv that after tvvo dayes shal be Pasche, and the Sonne of man shal be deliuered to be crucified. 3 † Then vvere gathered together the cheefe Priestes and auncients of the people into the court of the high priest, vvho vvas called Caiphas: 4 † and they consulted hovv they might by some vvile apprehend IESVS, and kil him. 5 † But they said, Not on the festiual day, lest perhaps there might be a tumult among the people.

† And

Mr. 14, 3. Io. 12, 3.

6 † And * vvhen IESVS vvas in Bethania in the houſe of 7 Simon the Leper, † there came to him a vvoman hauing an alabaſter-boxe of pretious ointment, and povvred it out 8 vpon his head as he ſate at the table. † And the Diſciples 9 ſeeing it, had indignation ſaying, Whereto is "this vvaſt? † for this might haue been ſold for much, and giuen to the poore. 10 † And IESVS knovving it, ſaid to them: Why do you moleſt this vvoman? for ſhe hath vvrought a "good vvorke 11 vpon me. † For the poore you haue alvvayes vvith you: but 12 me "you haue not alvvayes. † For ſhe in povvring this oint- 13 ment vpon my body: hath done it to burie me. † Amen I ſay to you, vvhereſoeuer this Goſpel ſhal be preached in the vvhole vvorld, that alſo vvhich ſhe hath done, ∷ ſhal be re- 14 ported for a memorie of her. † * Then vvent one of the Tvvelue, vvhich vvas called Iudas Iſcarioth, to the cheefe Prieſtes, 15 † and ſaid to them, What vvil you giue me, and I vvil deliuer him vnto you? But they appointed vnto him thirtie peeces 16 of ſiluer. † And from thenceforth he ſought opportunitie to betray him.

∷ Hereby we learne that the good workes of Sainctes are to be recorded and ſet forth to their honour in the Church after their death. Whereof riſe their holy daies and Cōmemorations.

Mr. 14, 10. Lu. 22, 3

MAVNDY thurſday.

Mr. 14, 12. Lu. 22, 7

17 † And * the firſt day of the Azymes the Diſciples came to IESVS, ſaying, Where vvilt thou that vve prepare for thee to 18 eate the Paſche? † But IESVS ſaid, Goe ye into the citie to a certaine man: and ſay to him, The Maiſter ſaith, My time is at hand, vvith thee do I make the Paſche vvith my Diſciples. 19 † And the Diſciples did as IESVS appointed them, and they 20 prepared the Paſche. † But vvhen it vvas euen, he ſate downe 21 vvith his "tvvelue Diſciples. † And vvhile they vvere eating, he ſaid: Amen I ſay to you, that one of you ſhal betray me. 22 † And they being very ſad, began euery one to ſay, Is it 23 I Lord? † But he anſvvering ſaid, * He that dippeth his hand 24 vvith me in the diſh, he ſhal betray me. † The Sonne of man in deede goeth as it is vvritten of him: but vvo be to that man, by vvhom the Sonne of man ſhal be betrayed. It vvere 25 good for him, if that man had not been borne. † And Iudas that betrayed him, anſvvering ſaid, Is it I Rabbi? He ſaith to him, Thou haſt ſaid.

Pſ. 40, 10.

1. Cor. 11, 24.

26 † And * vvhiles they vvere at ſupper, IESVS "tooke bread, and "bleſſed, and brake: and he gaue to his Diſciples, and ſaid, 27 Take ye, and eate: "THIS IS" MY BODY. † And taking the chalice, "he gaue thankes: and gaue to them, ſaying: 28 Drinke ∷ ye al of this. † For THIS IS" MY BLOVD OF

∷ See the margent note Mar. 14, 23.

THE NEVV TESTAMENT, VVHICH SHAL BE SHED FOR MANY VNTO REMISSION OF SINNES. † And I say to you, I vvil not drinke from henceforth 29 of this " fruite of the vine, vntil that day vvhen I shal drinke it vvith you nevv in the kingdom of my father. † And an 30 hymne being said, they vvent forth vnto Mount-oliuet.

THVRSDAY night.

† Then IESVS saith to them, Al you shal be scandalized 31 in me, in this night. For it is vvritten, *I vvil strike the Pastor, and the sheepe of the flocke shal be dispersed.* † But after I shal be risen 32 againe, I vvil goe before you into Galilee. † And Peter an- 33 svvering, said to him, Although al shal be scandalized in thee, I vvil neuer be scandalized. † IESVS said to him, Amen I say 34 to thee, that in this night before the cocke crovv, thou shalt denie me thrise. † * Peter saith to him, Yea though I should die 35 vvith thee, I vvil not denie thee. Likevvise also said al the Disciples.

The NOCTVRNE of Mattins in the Churches Seruice, ansvvereth to this night part of our Sauiours Passion. and so consequently the other Canonical houres to the rest.

Zach. 13, 7.

Io. 13, 38

† Then IESVS commeth vvith them into a village called 36 Gethsémani: and he said to his Disciples, Sitte you here til I goe yonder, and pray. † And taking to him Peter and the tvvo 37 sonnes of Zebedee, he began to vvaxe sorovvful and to be sad. † Then he saith to them: My soul is sorovvful euen 38 vnto death: stay here, and vvatch vvith me. † And being 39 gone forvvard a litle, he fel vpon his face, praying, and saying, My Father, if it be possible, let this chalice passe from me. neuerthelesse " not as I vvil, but as thou. † And he commeth to 40 his Disciples, and findeth them sleeping, and he saith to Peter, Euen so? Could you not vvatch one houre vvith me? † " Watch 41 ye, and pray that ye enter not into tentation. The spirit in deede is prompt, but the flesh vveake. † Againe the second 42 time he vvent, and prayed, saying, My Father, if this chalice may not passe, but I must drinke it, thy vvil be done. † And he 43 commeth againe, and findeth them sleeping: for their eyes vvere become heauy. † And leauing them, he vvent againe: 44 and he prayed the third time, saying the self same vvord. † Then he commeth to his Disciples, and saith to them, 45 Sleepe ye novv and take rest: behold the houre approcheth, and the Sonne of man shal be betrayed into the hands of sinners. † Rise, let vs goe: behold he approcheth that shal be- 46 tray me.

† * As he yet spake, behold Iudas one of the Tvvelue came, 47 and vvith him a great multitude vvith svvordes and clubbes, sent from the cheefe Priestes, and the auncients of the people.

Io. 18, 3.

48 † And he that betrayed him, gaue them a signe, saying, Whom-
49 soeuer I shal kisse, that is he, hold him. † And forthvvith cōming to IESVS, he said, Haile Rabbi. And he kissed him.
50 † And IESVS said to him, Freend, vvhereto art thou come?
Then they drevve neere, and laid hands on IESVS, and held
51 him. † And behold one of them that vvere vvith IESVS,
stretching forth his hand, drevve out his svvord: and striking
52 the seruant of the high Priest, cut of his eare. † Then IESVS
saith to him, Returne thy sword into his place: for al that take
53 the svvord, shal perish vvith the svvord. † Thinkest thou
that I cannot aske my Father: and he vvil giue me presently
54 more then tvvelue legions of Angels? † Hovv then shal the
55 scriptures be fulfilled, that so it must be done? † In that houre
IESVS said to the multitudes: You are come out as it vvere
to a theefe vvith svvordes and clubbes to apprehēd me: I sate
daily vvith you teaching in the temple: and you laid no hands
56 on me. † And al this vvas done, that the scriptures of the Prophets might be fulfilled. Thē the disciples al leauing him, fled.
57 † But they taking hold of IESVS, led him to Caiphas
the high Priest, vvhere the Scribes and auncients vvere assem-
58 bled. † And Peter folovved him a farre of, euen to the court
of the high Priest. And going in he sate vvith the seruants, that
59 he might see the end. † And the cheefe Priestes and the vvhole
Councel sought false vvitnes against IESVS, that they might
60 put him to death: † and they found not, vvhereas many false
vvitnesses had come in. And last of al there came tvvo false
61 vvitnesses: † and they said, * This man said, I am able to destroy the temple of God, and after three dayes to reedifie it.

Io. 2, 19.

62 † And the high Priest rising vp, said to him: Ansvverest thou
nothing to the things vvhich these do testifie against thee?
63 † But IESVS held his peace. And the high Priest said to him:
I adiure thee by the liuing God, that thou tel vs if thou be
64 Christ the sonne of God. † IESVS saith to him, Thou hast
said. neuertheles I say to you, hereafter you shal see * the
Sonne of man sitting on the right hand of the povver of
65 God, and comming in the cloudes of heauen. † Then the
high Priest rent his garments, saying, He hath blasphemed, vvhat neede vve vvitnesses any further? behold, novv
66 you haue heard the blasphemie, † hovv thinke you? But
67 they ansvvering said, He is guilty of death. † Then did they
spit on his face, and buffeted him, and other smote his

Dan. 7, 13.

face vvith the palmes of their hands, † saying, Prophecie vnto 68 vs O Christ: vvho is he that strooke thee?

† But Peter sate vvithout in the court: and there came to 69 him one " vvenche, saying: Thou also vvast vvith IESVS the Galilean. † But he denied before them all, saying, I vvot not 70 vvhat thou sayest. † And as he vvent out of the gate, an other 71 vvenche savv him, and she saith to them that vvere there, And this felovv also vvas vvith IESVS the Nazarite. † And 72 againe he denied vvith an othe, That I knovv not the man. † And after a litle they came that stoode by, and said to Peter, 73 Surely thou also art of them: for euen thy speache doth bevvray thee. † Then he began " to curse and to svveare that 74 he knevve not the man. And incontinent the cocke crevve. † And Peter remembred the vvord of IESVS vvhich he had 75 said, Before the cocke crovv, thou shalt deny me thrise. And going forth, " he vvept bitterly.

To this time the LAVDES do answer in the Churches Seruice.

ANNOTATIONS
CHAP. XXVI.

Cost vpo Churches, altars, &c.

8. This Wast.] Cost bestowed vpon Christes body then aliue, being to the same not necessary, seemed to the disciples lost and fruitles: so the like bestowed vpon the same body in the Sacrament, vpon altars, or Churches, seemeth to the simple lost, or lesse meritorious, then if the same were bestowed vpon the poore.

Releese of the poore.

10. Good Worke.] Cost bestowed for religion, deuotion, and signification, is a meritorious worke, and often more meritorious then to geue to the poore, though both be very good, and in some case the poore are to be preferred: yea * in certaine cases of necessity, the Church wil breake the very cosecrated vessels and iewels of siluer and gold, aud bestow them in workes of mercy. But we may remember very wel, and our fathers knew it much better, that the poore were then best releeued, when most was bestowed vpon the Church.

Ambros. li. 2 Off. c. 28.

Christ alwaies with vs in the B. Sacrament.

11. Haue not.) We haue him not in visible maner as he conuersed on the earth with his disciples, needing releefe like other poore men: but we haue him after an other sort in the B. Sacrament, and yet haue him truly and really the self same body. Therfore he saith, they should not haue him, because they should not so haue him, but after an other maner. as when he said *Luc. 24* as though he were not then with them, *When I was with you.*

A wonderful mysterie in the institution of the B. Sacrament.

20. Twelue.) It must needes be a great mysterie that he was to worke in the institution of the new Sacrifice by the maruelous transmutatio of bread and wine into his body and bloud. Whereas he admitted none (although many present in the citie) but the twelue Apostles, vvhich were already taught to beleue it without contradiction *Io. 6*, and were to haue the administration and consecration thereof by the Order of Priesthod, which also was there geuen the to that purpose. Whereas at the eating of the Paschal lambe al the familie was wont to be present.

The holy Eucharist is both a Sacrifice and a Sacrament.

26. He tooke bread.) Here at once is instituted, for the continuance of the external office of Christes eternal Priesthod according to the order of Melchisedec, both a Sacrifice and a Sacrament, though the Scriptures geue neither of these names to this action: and our Aduersaries without al reason or religion accept in a sort the one, and vtterly deny the other. A Sacrifice, in that it is ordeined to continew the memory of Christes death and oblation vpon the Crosse, and the application of the general vertue thereof to our particular necessities, by cosecrating the seueral elemets, not into Christes whole person as it was borne of the virgin or now is in heauen, but the bread into his body apart, as betrayed, broken, and geuen for vs: the wine into his bloud apart, as shed out of his body for remission of sinnes and dedication of the new Testament, which be conditions of his person as he was in sacrifice and oblation. In which mystical and vnspeakable maner, he would haue the Church to offer and sacrifice him daily, and he in mysterie and Sacrament dyeth, though now not only in heauen, but also in the Sacramēt, he be in deede *per Concomitantiam* (as the Church calleth it, that is, by sequele of al his partes to ech other) whole, aliue, and immortal. Which point because our Aduersaries vnderstand not, *not knowing the Scriptures nor the power of God*, they blaspheme, and abuse the people to their damnation. It is also a Sacrament, in that it is ordeined to be receiued into our bodies and to feede the same to resurrection and immortality, and to geue grace and saluation to our soules, if we worthely receiue it.

Mat. 22, 29.

26. *Blessed.*) Our Aduersaries for the two wordes that are in Greeke and Latin, *benedixit*, and, *gratias egit*, *he blessed*, *he gaue thankes*, vse only the later, of purpose to signifie that Christ blessed not nor consecrated the bread and the wine, and so by that blessing wrought any effect vpon them, but gaue thankes only to his father, as we doe in saying grace. But the truth is that the word εὐλογεῖν, signifieth properly to blesse, and is referred to the thing that is blessed, as *Luc. 9* of the fishes, εὐλόγησεν αὐτοὺς, *benedixit eis*, *he blessed them*, and thereby wrought in them that wonderful multiplication. So the blessing of God is alwayes effectual: and therfore here also he blessed the bread, and by that blessing, with the wordes folowing, made it his body. *Ambros. li. de his qui initi. myst. c. 9. Aug. ep. 59 ad Paulinum.* Now whereas taking the cuppe it is said, *he gaue thankes*. We say that it is al one with blessing, and that he blessed the cuppe, as before the bread: as it is euident by these wordes of S. Paul, *Calix cui benedicimus*, the cuppe which we blesse: and therfore he calleth it, *Calicem benedictionis*, the cuppe of blessing, vsing the same Greeke word that is spoken of the bread. But why is it then said here, he gaue thankes? because we translate the wordes faithfully as in the Greeke and the Latin, and because the sense is al one, as we are taught by S. Paul before alleaged, and by the fathers, which cal this geuing of thankes ouer the cuppe or ouer the bread, the blessing therof. S. Iustin. *in fin. 2. Apol. Panem Eucharistisatum:* S. Irenee *li. 4. c. 34. Panem in quo gratiæ actæ sunt.* S. Cyprian *de cœn. do. Calix solenni benedictione sacratus.* that is, *The bread blessed by geuing thankes vpon it, The cuppe consecrated by solemne blessing.*

The blessing of Christ referred to the creatures and working an effect in thē.

Consecration.

1. Cor. 10.

τὸν ἄρτον εὐχαριστηθέντα.

26. *This is.*) *The bread and the wine be turned into the body and bloud of Christ by the same omnipotent power by which the world was made, and the Word was incarnate in the wombe of the virgin. Damasc. li. 4 c. 14. Cypr. de Cœn. Domini. Amb. li. de myst. init. c. 9.*

Transsubstantiation.

26. *My body.*) *He said not, This bread is a figure of my body: or, This wine is a figure of my bloud: but, This is my body, and, This is my bloud. Damasc. li. 4 c. 14. Theophyl. in hunc locum. Conc. 2. Nic. act. 6, to. 4 eiusdem actionis in fine.* When some fathers cal it a figure or signe, they meane the outward formes of bread and wine.

No figuratiue but a real presence.

28. *Bloud of the new Testament.*) As the old Testament was dedicated with bloud in these wordes, *This is the bloud of the Testament &c. Heb. 9.* so here is the institution of the new Testament in Christes bloud, by these wordes, *This is the bloud of the new Testament &c.* Which is here mystically shed, and not only afterward vpon the Crosse: for the Greeke is the present tense in al the Euangelistes, and S. Paul: and likewise speaking of the body *1 Cor. 11.* it is in the Greeke the present tense, and *Luc. 22.* and in the Latin here. And the Heretikes them selues so put it in their translations.

ἐκχυνόμενον. κλώμενον. διδόμενον.

29. *Fruite of the vine.*) S. Luke putteth these wordes before he come to the consecration, whereby it seemeth that he speaketh of the wine of the Paschal lambe, and therfore nameth it, the fruite of the vine. but if he speake of the wine which was now his bloud, he nameth it notwithstā-ding wine, as S. Paule nameth the other bread, for three causes: first because it was so before: as Eue is called Adams bone, and, *Aarons rod deuoured their roddes:* whereas they were not now roddes, but serpents. And, *He tasted the water turned into wine:* whereas it was now wine and not water: and such like. secondly, because it keepeth the formes of bread and wine, and things are called as they appeare: as when Raphael is called a yong man *Tob. 5.* and, *Three men appeared to Abraham Gen. 18.* whereas they were three Angels. thirdly, because Christ in this Sacrament is very true and principal bread and wine, feeding and refreshing vs in body and soule to euerlasting life.

The elements after consecratiō called bread and wine.

Gen. 2. Exo. 7. Io. 2.

39. *Not as I wil.*) A perfect example of obedience and submitting our self and our willes to Gods will and ordinance in al aduersity: and that we should desire nothing temporal, but vnder the condition of his holy pleasure and appointment.

41. *Watch and pray.*) Hereof came Vigils and Nocturnes, that is, watching and praying in the night, commonly vsed in the Primitiue Church of al Christians, as is plaine by S. Cyprian and * S. Hierom: but afterward and vntil this day, specially of Religious persons.

De orat. Do. nu. 15.

Vigils and Nocturnes.

69. *Wench.*) S. Gregorie declaring the difference of the Apostles before the receiuing of the Holy Ghost and after, saith thus: *Euen this very Pastor of the Church him self, at whose most sacred body we sitte, how weake he was, the wenche can tell you: but how strong he was after, his answer to the high Priest declareth, Act. 5, 29: We must obey God rather then men. Greg. ho. 20 in Euang.*

* Adu. Vigilant. ep. 53.

The vertue of the holy Ghost.

74. *To curse.*) A goodly example and warning to mans infirmity, and to take heede of presumption, and to hang only vpon God in tentations.

Mans infirmitie

75. *Wept bitterly.*) S. Ambrose in his Hymne that the Church vseth at Laudes, speaking of this, saith, *Hoc ipsa Petra ecclesiæ canente, culpam diluit.* When the Cocke crewe, the Rocke of the Church him self washed away his fault. *S. August. 1 Retract. c. 21.*

Peters teares and repentance.

CHAP. XXVII.

CHAP. XXVII.

The cheefe of the Ievves accuse him to Pilate the Gentil (his betrayer, and the Iudge, and the Iudges Wife, testifying in the meane time manifodly his innocencie:) 20 and persuade the common people also not only to preferre the murderer Barabbas, but also to crie, CRVCIFIGE: (Al, to the reprobation of their vvhole nation, and nothing but fulfilling the Scriptures.) 27 After many illusions, 31 he is crucified by the Gentils. 38 Which the Ievves seeing, do triumph as if they had novv the victorie. 45 But euen then by many vvonderful vvorkes he declareth his might, to their confusion 57 Finally being buried, they to make al sure, set souldiars to keepe his sepulcher.

PRIME or Hora prima in the Churches Seruice.

GOOD FRIday.

AND vvhen morning vvas come, al the cheefe Priestes and auncients of the people consulted together against IESVS, that they might put him to death. 1 † And they brought him bound and deliuered him to Ponce Pilate the President. 2

Mr. 15,1 Lu. 23,1. Io. 18, 28.

† Then Iudas that betrayed him, seeing that he vvas condemned, " repenting him, returned the thirtie siluer peeces to the cheefe Priestes and auncients, 3 † saying, I haue sinned, betraying iust bloud. But they said, what is that to vs? looke thou to it. 4 † And casting dovvne the siluer peeces in the temple, he departed: and vvent and " hanged him self vvith an halter. 5 † And the cheefe Priestes hauing taken the siluer peeces, said, It is not lavvful to cast them into the ∴ Córbana: because it is the price of bloud. 6 † And after they had consulted together, they bought vvith them the potters field, to be a burying place for strangers. 7 † For this cause that field vvas called *Hacéldama*, that is, *the field of bloud*, euen to this present day. 8 † Then vvas fulfilled that vvhich vvas spoken by Ieremie the Prophet, saying, *And they tooke the thirtie peeces of siluer, the price of the priced, vvhom they did price of the children of Israel:* 9 † *and they gaue them into the potters field, as our Lord did appoint to me.* 10

∴ This Corbana Was a place about the Temple, Which receiued the peoples gifts or offerings. See Mar. 12, v. 42.

Zach. 11, 12.

† And IESVS stoode before the President, and the President asked him, saying, Art thou the King of the Ievves? IESVS saith to him, Thou sayest. 11 † And vvhen he vvas accused of the cheefe Priestes and auncients, he ansvvered nothing. 12 † Then Pilate saith to him, Doest thou not heare hovv many testimonies they alleage against thee? 13 † And he ansvvered him not to any vvord: so that the President did maruel excedingly. 14

HORA TERTIA in the Churches Seruice.

† And vpon the solemne day the President had accustomed to release vnto the people one prisoner vvhom they 15 vvould

16 vvould. †And he had then a notorious prisoner, that vvas cal-
17 led Barabbas. † They therfore being gathered together, Pilate said: Whom vvil you that I release to you, Barabbas, or
18 IESVS that is called Christ? † For he knevve that for enuie
19 they had deliuered him. † And as he vvas sitting in place of iudgment, his vvife sent vnto him, saying: Haue thou nothing to doe vvith that iust man. for I haue suffred many things
20 this day in my sleepe for him. † But the cheefe Priestes and auncients persuaded the people, that they should aske Ba-
21 rabbas, and make IESVS avvay. † And the President ansvvering, said to them: Whether vvil you of the tvvo to be relea-
22 sed vnto you? But they said, Barabbas. † Pilate saith to them, What shal I doe then vvith IESVS that is called Christ? They
23 say al, Let him be crucified. † The President said to them, Why vvhat euil hath he done? But they cried the more, saying, Let
24 him be crucified. † And Pilate seeing that he nothing preuailed, but rather tumult vvas tovvard: taking vvater he vvashed his hands before the people, saying, I am "innocent of
25 the bloud of this iust man: looke you to it. † And the vvhole people ansvvering, said, His bloud be vpon vs, and vpon our
26 children. † Then he released to them Barabbas, and hauing scourged IESVS, deliuered him vnto them for to be crucified.

27 † Then the Presidents souldiars taking IESVS into the
28 Palace, gathered together vnto him the vvhole band: † *and
29 stripping him, put a scarlet cloke about him, † and platting a crovvne of thornes, put it vpon his head, and a reede in his right hand. And bovving the knee before him, they mocked
30 him, saying, Haile King of the Ievves. † And spitting vpon
31 him, they tooke the reede, and smote his head. † And after they had mocked him, they tooke of the cloke from him, and put on him his ovvne garments, and led him avvay to cruci-
32 fie him. † And in going they found a man of Cyréne, named
33 Simon: him they forced to take vp his crosse. † And they came into the place that is called Golgotha, vvhich is, the
34 place of Caluarie. † And they gaue him vvine to drinke mingled vvith gall. And vvhen he had tasted, he vvould not drinke.

35 † And after they had crucified him, they deuided his garments, casting lottes: that it might be fulfilled vvhich vvas spoken by the Prophet, saying: *They deuided my garments among them*

Marginal notes: Io. 19, 2. — Psal. 21, 19 — HORA SEXTA in the Churches Seruice.

them: and vpon my vesture they did cast lottes. † And they sate and vvatched him. † And they put ouer his head his cause vvritten, THIS IS IESVS THE KING OF THE IEWES. † Then vvere crucified vvith him tvvo theeues: one on the right hand, and one on the left. † And they that passed by, blasphemed him, vvagging their heades, † and saying, Vah, thou that destroyest the temple of God, and in three daies doest reedifie it: saue thine ovvne self: " if thou be the sonne of God, come dovvne from the Crosse. † In like maner also the cheefe Priestes With the Scribes and auncients mocking, said: † He saued other: him self he can not saue: if he be the King of Israel, let him novv come dovvne from the Crosse, and vve vvil beleeue him. † * He trusted in God: let him novv deliuer him if he vvill: for he said, That I am the sonne of God. † And the selfsame thing the theeues also that vvere crucified vvith him, reproched him vvithal. 36 37 38 39 40 41 42 43 44

Ps. 21, 9. Sap. 2, 18.

† And from the sixt houre, there vvas darkenesse made vpon the vvhole earth, vntil the ninthe houre. † And about the ninthe houre IESVS cried vvith a mighty voice, saying, *Eli, Eli, lamma-sabacthani?* that is, *My God, my God,* " *vvhy hast thou forsaken me?* † And certaine that stoode there and heard, said, He calleth Elias. † And incontinent one of them running, tooke a sponge, & filled it vvith vinegre: and put it on a reede, and gaue him to drinke. † And other said, Let be, let vs see vvhether Elias come to deliuer him. † And IESVS againe crying vvith a mighty voice, yelded vp the ghost. † And behold the vele of the temple vvas rent in tvvo peeces, from the toppe euen to the botome. and the earth did quake, and the rockes vvere rent, † and the graues vvere opened: and many bodies of the saincts that had slept, rose. † And they going forth out of the graues after his resurrection, came into the holy citie: and appeared to many. † And the Centurion and they that vvere vvith him vvatching IESVS, hauing seen the earth-quake and the things that vvere done, vvere sore afraid, saying, In deede this vvas the sonne of God. 45 46 47 48 49 50 51 52 53 54

HORA NONA in the Churches Seruice.

† And there vvere there many vvomen a farre of, vvhich had folovved IESVS from Galilee, ministring vnto him: † among vvhom vvas Marie Magdalene, and Marie the mother of Iames and Ioseph, and the mother of the sonnes of Zebedee. † And vvhen it vvas euening, there came a certaine rich 55 56 57

HORA VESPERARVM, or, Euensong.

HOLY weeke.

rich man of Arimathæa, named Ioseph, vvho also him self was
58 disciple to IESVS. † He vvent to Pilate, and asked the body
of IESVS. Then Pilate commaunded that the body should
59 be deliuered. † And Ioseph taking the body, " vvrapt it in
60 cleane sindon, † and laid it in his ovvne nevve monument,
vvhich he had hevved out in a rocke. And he rolled a great
stone to the doore of the monument, and vvent his vvay.
61 † And there was there Marie Magdalene, and the other Marie,
sitting ouer against the sepulchre.

HORA COMPLETORII, or, Complin.

62 † And the next day, vvhich is after the Parasceue, the cheefe
63 Priestes and the Pharisees came together to Pilate, † saying,
Sir, vve haue remembred, that that seducer said yet liuing,
64 After three dayes I vvil rise againe. † Commaund therfore
the sepulchre to be kept vntil the third day: lest perhaps his
Disciples come, and steale him, and say to the people, He is
risen from the dead: and the last errour shal be vvorse then
65 the first. † Pilate said to them, You haue a gard: goe, gard it
66 as you knovv. † And they departing, made the sepulchre
sure: sealing vp the stone, vvith vvatchmen.

SATVRDAY called Sabbatum sanctum.

ANNOTATIONS
CHAP. XXVII.

3. Repenting him.] Note how spedily the plague of God falleth after sinne, and specially men must note what torment of conscience, and desperation often foloweth the sheading of innocent bloud.

Horrour of conscience.

5. Hung him self.] If he had rightly repented, notwithstanding his horrible treason, he might haue obteyned mercy: but by hanging him self he tooke away al meanes of mercy and saluation, because he died finally impenitent.

Desperation.

24. Innocent of his bloud.] Though Pilate was much more innocent then the Iewes, and would haue been free from the murder of our Sauiour, seeking al the meanes that he could (without offending the people and the Emperours lawes) to dimisse him: Yet he is damned for being the minister of the peoples wicked wil against his owne conscience. euen as al Officers be, and specially the Iudges and Iuries which execute lawes of temporal Princes against Catholike men: for al such be guilty of innocent bloud, and be nothing excused by that they execute other mens will according to the lawes, which be vniust. For they should rather suffer death them selues, then put an innocent man to death.

They that execute lawes against their cōscience, are like to Pilate.

40. If thou be the Sonne.] Maruel not, when thou hearest our Sauiour in the B. Sacrament mocked at, or seest him abused of wicked men, that he straight reuengeth not such blasphemies: or that he sheweth not him self there visibly and to the senses, when faithles Heretikes wil say, Let me see him, tast him, &c. for he suffered here the like on the Crosse, when he might at his will haue come downe with as much ease as he rose when he was dead.

Christ derided in the B. Sacrament, euen as vpō the Crosse.

46. Why hast thou forsaken me?] Beware here of the detestable blasphemie of Caluin and the Caluinists, who thinking not the bodily death of Christ sufficient, say, that he was also here so forsaken and abandoned of his Father, that he sustained in soule and conscience the very feares and torments of the damned. And to take away the Article of his descending into Hel after his death, (which was with triumph and not in paine,) they say that his descending was nothing els, but that his soule suffered the very paines of Hel vpon the Crosse. Whereas in deede by these wordes out of the Psalme, our Sauiour wil signifie no more but that his paines (being now so long on the Crosse and ready to die) were very great, and therfore according to the infirmity of his humane nature, for very anguish (as before in the garden when he was but toward his Passion) he saith he

Catechis. Calu. & Instit. li. 2 16.

Caluins blasphemie.

weeke.

was forsaken, for two causes, first because it was the wil of God not to deliuer him, but that he should die: secondly, because his diuine nature did so represse it self for the time, that he felt no comfort thereof at al, but was left to die in extreme paines as a mere man.

Reuerent vsing of our L. Body.

59. Wrapped.] This honour and duty done to Christes body being dead, was maruelous grateful and meritorious. And this wrapping of it in cleane sindon may signifie by S. Hierom, that the Body of our Lord is to be wrapped not in gold, pretious stones, and silke, but in pure linnen. And so in the whole Church it is obserued by * S. Siluesters constitution, that the Corporal whereupon our Lordes body lieth on the altar, must be pure and plaine linnen.

Corporals.

S. Hiero. in hunc locum.

** to. 1, Cōcil.*

CHAP. XXVIII.

He riseth againe the third day, and (the blind most obstinate Iewes by bribery working to their owne reprobation) he appeareth to his Disciples in Galilee (as both before his Passion he foretold them Mat. 26, and now after his Resurrection, first the Angel, then also him self appointed by the women) 18 and sendeth them to al Nations, to build his Church among ehe Gentils.

The Gospel for the night Masse of Christes Resurrection, which is now vsed to be said on Easter eue in the morning.

EASTER day.

ND in the euening of the Sabboth vvhich 1 davvneth on the first of the Sabboth, came Marie Magdalene, and the other Marie " to see the sepulchre. † And behold there vvas 2 made a great earth-quake. For an Angel of our Lord descẽded from heauen: and comming, rolled backe the stone, and sate vpon it: † and his 3 countenance vvas as lightening: and his garment as snovv. † And for feare of him, the vvatchmen vvere frighted, and be- 4 came as dead. † And the Angel ansvvering said to the vvo- 5 men, Feare not you. for I knovv that you seeke IESVS that vvas crucified. † he is not here: for he is risen, * as he said. 6 come, and see the place vvhere our Lord vvas laid. † And 7 going quickly, tel ye his Disciples that he is risen: and behold he goeth before you into Galilee. there you shal see him. loe I haue fortold you.

Mr. 16, 1.
Luc. 24, 1.
Io, 20, 1.

Mt. 29, 32.

† And they vvent forth quickly out of the monument 8 vvith feare and great ioy, running to tel his Disciples. † And 9 behold IESVS mette them, saying, Al haile. But they came neere and tooke hold of his feete, and adored him. † Then 10 IESVS said to them, Feare not. goe, tel my brethren that they goe into Galilee, there they shal see me.

† Who vvhen they vvere departed, behold certaine of the 11 vvatchmen came into the citie, and told the cheefe Priestes al things that had been done. † And being assembled toge- 12 ther vvith the auncients, taking counsel, they gaue a greate summe of money to the souldiars, † saying, Say you, That his 13 Disciples came by night, and stole him avvay vvhen vve vvere a sleepe. † And if the President shal heare of this, vve 14 vvil

HOLY weeke.

15 vvil persuade him, and make you secure. † But they taking the money, did as they vvere taught. And this vvord vvas bruited abrode among the Ievves, euen vnto this day.

16 † And the eleuen Disciples vvent into Galilee, vnto the 17 mount vvhere IESVS had appointed them. † And seeing 18 him they adored, but some doubted. † And IESVS comming neere spake vnto them, saying. Al povver is giuen to me in 19 heauen and in earth. † "going therfore teach ye al nations: BAPTIZING THEM IN THE NAME OF THE FATHER AND OF THE SONNE AND OF THE HOLY 20 GHOST, † teaching them to obserue al things vvhatsoeuer I haue commaunded you, and behold I am vvith you "al daies, euen to the consummation of the vvorld. ꟻ

The Gospel vpō Friday in Easter weeke.

The Gospel in the feast of the B. Trinitie.

ANNOTATIONS
CHAP. XXVIII.

1. To see the Sepulcher.] The deuout Women came to visite our Sauiours sepulcher, and for their deuotion first deserued to know the Resurrection, and to see him risen. The honour of the Which Sepulcher and the Pilgrimage thereunto in the Primitiue Church, S. Hierom declareth in these wordes, *The Iewes sometime honoured Sancta Sanctorum, because there Were the Cherubs, and the Propitiatorie, and the Arke of the Testament, Manna, Aarons rodde, and the golden altar. Doth not the Sepulcher of our Lord seeme vnto thee more honorable? Which as often as We enter into, so often doe We see our Sauiour lie in the sindon: and staying there a While, We see the Angel againe sitte at his feete, and at his head the napkin Wrapped together. The glorie of Whose Sepulcher, We knoW Was long prophecied before Ioseph heWed it out, by Esay saying, And his rest shal be honour: to Witte, because the place of our Lordes burial should be honoured of al men.* And at this present, notWithstanding the Turkes dominion, yet doe the Religious Christian Catholike men by Gods mighty prouidence keepe the holy Sepulcher, Which is Within a goodly Church, and Christians come out of al the World in Pilgrimage to it.

In Ep. 17 Paulæ & Eustoch. ad Marcel. to. 1.

Esa. 11.

The holy Sepulcher, and Pilgrimage therevnto.

The Catholike Church to be gathered of al Nations,

19. Going then.] Commission to baptize and preache to al Nations geuen to the Apostles, and grounded vpon Christes soueraine authority, to Whom Was geuen al poWer in heauen and in earth.

20. With you al daies.] Here Christ doth promise his concurrence With his Apostles and their successors, as Wel in preaching as ministring the Sacraments, and his protection of the Church neuer to cease til the Worlds end: contrary to our Aduersaries, saying that the Church hath failed many hundred yeres til Luther and Caluin.

And Christs continual protection of the same Church.

THE ARGVMENT OF S. MARKES GOSPEL.

S. Markes Gospel may be vvel diuided into foure partes.

The first part, of the preparation that was made to the manifestation of Christ: chap. 1. in the beginning.

The Second, of his manifesting him selfe by Preaching and Miracles, and that in Galilee: the residue of the 1. chap. vnto the 10. chap.

The third, of his comming into Iurie, tovvards his Passion: chap. 10.

The fourth, of the Holy vveeke of his Passion in Hierusalem: chap. 11. to the end of the booke.

Of S. Marke and his conuersation with the tvvo Apostles S. Paul and S. Barnabee, vve haue at large Act. 12 and 15. somevvhat also Col. 4. and 2. Tim. 4. and to Philémon. Moreouer of his familiaritie vvith the Prince of the Apostles S. Peter, vve haue 1 Pet. 5. For so it pleased our Lord, that onely tvvo of the Euangelistes should be of his tvvelue Apostles, to vvit, S. Matthew and S. Iohn. The other tvvo, S. Marke and S. Luke, he gaue vnto vs of the Disciples of his two most principal and most glorious Apostles S. Peter and S. Paul. Whose Gospels therefore were of Antiquitie counted as the Gospels of S. Peter and S. Paul them selues. Marke the disciple and interpreter of Peter (*saith S. Hierom*) according to that which he heard of Peters mouth, wrote at Rome a briefe Gospel at the request of the Brethren (*about 10 or 12 yeres after our Lordes Ascension.*) Which when Peter had heard, he approued it, and with his authoritie did publish it to the Church to be read, as Clemens *Alexandrinus* writeth li. 6. hypotypos.

In Catal. Script. Ecclesiast.

In the same place S. Hierom addeth, hovv he vvent into Ægypt to preach, and vvas the first Bishop of the cheefe Citie there, named Alexandria: and hovv Philo Iudæus at the same time seeing and admiring the life and conuersation of the Christians there vnder S. Marke, vvho vvere Monkes, vvrote a booke thereof, vvhich is extant to this day. And not onely S. Hierom (in Marco, & in Philone) but also Eusebius Hist. li. 2. ca. 15. 16. 17. Epiphanius Secta 29 Nazaræorum, li. 1. to. 2. Cassianus de Instit. Cænobiorum li. 2. c. 5. Sozomenus li. 1. c. 12. Nicephorus li. 2 c. 15. and diuerse others, do make mention of the said Monkes out of the same Author. Finally, He died (*saith S. Hierom*) the 8 yere of Nero, and was buried at Alexandria, Anianus succeding in his place. *But from Alexandria he vvas * translated to Venice, Anno Dom. 830.*

Philo de Supplicibus.

In Catalogo.

* Naucler. generat. 28.

It is also to be noted, that in respect of S. Peter, vvho sent S. Marke his scholer to Alexandria, and made him the first Bishop there, this See vvas esteemed next in dignitie to the See of Rome, and the Bishop thereof vvas accounted the cheefe Metropolitane or Patriarch of the East, and that by the first Councel of Nice. Whereof see S. Leo ep. 53. S. Gregorie li. 5 ep. 60. & li. 6. ep. 37.

THE

THE HOLY GOSPEL OF IESVS CHRIST ACCORDING TO MARKE.

CHAP. I.

THE FIRST part of this Gospel: of the preparatiõ to christs manifestation.

Iohn (the Eremite of vvhom the Prophets) preaching penance, and liuing him self accordingly, baptizeth the people to prepare them to Christ, 7 telling them, that it is not his, but Christs Baptisme, in vvhich they shal receiue the Holy Ghost. 9 IESVS there is manifested from heauen: 12 and by and by he also goeth into the vvildernesse. 14 Beginning in Galilee, 16 after that he hath called foure Disciples, 21 he preacheth first in Capharnaum, confirming his doctrine vvith beneficial Miracles, to the great admiration of al: 35 then also (but first retiring into the vvildernes) in al the rest of Galilee, vvith like miracles.

1 THE beginning of the Gospel of IESVS 2 CHRIST the sonne of God. † As it is vvritten in Esay the Prophet, (*Behold I send mine Angel before thy face, vvho shal prepare thy vvay before thee,*) 3 † *A voice of one crying in the desert, Prepare ye the vvay of our Lord, make straight his pathes.* 4 † * Iohn vvas in the desert baptizing, and preaching the baptisme of penance :: vnto remission of sinnes. 5 † And there vvent forth to him al the countrie of Ievvrie, and al they of Hierusalem: and vvere baptized of him in the 6 riuer of Iordan, " confessing " their sinnes. † And Iohn vvas " clothed vvith camels heare, and a girdle of a skinne about 7 his loines: and he did eate locustes and vvild honie. † And he preached, saying, There commeth a stronger then I after me: vvhose latchet of his shoes I am not vvorthie stouping 8 dovvne to vnloose. † I haue baptized you " vvith vvater: but he shal baptize you vvith the holy Ghost.

9 † And it came to passe: in those daies came IESVS from Nazareth of Galilee: and vvas " baptized of Iohn in Iordan. 10 † And forthvvith comming vp out of the vvater, he savv the heauens opened, and " the Spirit as a doue descending, and re-11 maining on him. † And a voice vvas made from heauen, Thou art my beloued sonne, in thee I am vvel pleased.

12 † And forthvvith * the Spirit droue him out into " the de-

Mal. 3, 1. Esa. 40, 3. the prophets. Mt. 3, 1. Lu. 3, 4. Io. 1, 15.

:: Iohns baptisme put them in hope only of remissiõ of sinnes as a preparatiue to Christes Sacrament by which sinnes were in deede to be remitted. *Aug. li. 5 de bapt. c. 10*

Mt. 4, 1. Lu. 4, 1.

ſert. † And he vvas in the deſert fourtie daies, and fourtie 13 nightes: and vvas tempted of Satan. and he vvas vvith beaſtes, and the Angels miniſtred to him.

THE SECOND part of this Goſpel: of Chriſts manifeſtation.

† And * after that Iohn vvas deliuered vp, IESVS 14 came into Galilee, preaching the Goſpel of the kingdom of God, † and ſaying, That the time is fulfilled, and the kingdom 15 of God is at hand: ∷ be penitent, and beleeue the Goſpel.

Mat. 4, 12. Luc. 4, 14.

∷ He doth not preach beleeve or faith only, but penance alſo.

† * And paſsing by the ſea of Galilee, he ſavv Simon and 16 Andrevv his brother, caſting nettes into the ſea (for they vvere fiſhers) † and IESVS ſaid to them, Come after me, and 17 I vvil make you to become fiſhers of men. † And imme- 18 diatly leauing their nettes, they folovved him. † And being 19 gone thence a litle further, he ſavv Iames of Zebedee, and Iohn his brother, and them repairing their nettes in the ſhippe: † and forthvvith he called them. And leauing their 20 father Zebedee in the ſhippe vvith his hired men, they folovved him.

Mat. 4, 18. Lu. 5, 2.

† And * they enter into Capharnaum, and he forthvvith 21 vpon the Sabboths going into the Synagogue, taught them. † And they vvere aſtonied at his doctrine. for he vvas tea- 22 ching them as hauing povver, and not as the Scribes. † And 23 * there vvas in their Synagogue a man in an vncleane ſpirit: and he cried out, † ſaying, What to vs and to thee IESVS of 24 Nazareth? art thou come to deſtroy vs? I knovv vvho thou art, the Saint of God. † And IESVS threatened him, ſaying, 25 Hold thy peace, and goe out of the man. † And the vncleane 26 ſpirit tearing him, and crying out vvith a great voice, vvent out of him. † And they marueled al, in ſo much that they que- 27 ſtioned among them ſelues, ſaying, What thing is this? vvhat is this nevv doctrine? for vvith povver he commaundeth the vncleane ſpirits alſo, and they obey him. † And the bruite 28 of him vvent forth incontinent into al the countrie of Galilee.

Mat. 4, 13. Lu. 4, 31. Luc. 4, 32.

† And immediatly * going forth out of the Synagogue, 29 they came into the houſe of Simon and Andrevv, vvith Iames and Iohn. † And Simons vviues mother lay in a fit of 30 a feuer: and forthvvith they tel him of her. † And comming 31 neere he lifted her vp taking her by the hand: and incōtinent the ague left her, and ſhe miniſtred vnto them. † And vvhen 32 it vvas euening after ſunne ſet, they brought to him al that vvere il at eaſe and that had deuils. † And al the citie vvas 33

Mat. 8, 14. Luc. 4, 42.

gathered

34 gathered together at the doore. † And he cured many that vvere vexed vvith diuerse diseases: and he cast out many deuils, and he suffred not them to speake that they knevv him.

35 † And rising very early, and going forth he vvent into 36 "a desert place: and there he prayed. † And Simon sought 37 after him, and they that vvere vvith him. † And vvhen they had found him, they said to him, That al seeke for thee. 38 † And he saith to them, Let vs goe into the next tovvnes and cities, that I may preach there also: for to this purpose am I come.

39 † And he vvas preaching in their Synagogs, and in al Ga-40 lilee: and casting out deuils. † And a * leper commeth to him beseeching him: and kneeling dovvne saith to him, If thou 41 vvilt, thou canst make me cleane. † And IESVS hauing compassion on him, stretched forth his hand: and touching him, 42 he saith vnto him, I vvil, be thou made cleane. † And vvhen he had spoken, immediatly the leprosie departed from him, 43 and he vvas made cleane. † And he threatened him, and 44 forthvvith cast him forth. † and he saith to him, See thou tel no body: but goe, shevv thy self :: to the high priest, and offer for thy cleansing the things that * Moyses commaun-45 ded, for a testimonie to them. † But he being gone forth, began to publish, and to blase abrode the vvord: so that novv he could not openly goe into the citie, but vvas abrode in desert places, and they came together vnto him from al sides.

Mt.8, 2. Lu.5, 12

Leu.14, 3.

:: Our Sauiour euen When he healed the leper by extraordinarie miraculous power, would not yet breake order, but sent the partie to the Priest.

ANNOTATIONS CHAP. I.

5. Confessing their sinnes.] A certaine confession of sinnes there Was euen in that penance Which Iohn preached, and Which Was made before men Were baptized. Whereby it is cleere that Iohn made a preparation to the Sacrament of Penance Which afterWard Was instituted by Christ, as Wel as he did by baptizing prepare the Way to Christs baptisme. — Confession.

5. Their sinnes.] He doth not say that they confessed them selues to be sinners, Which may be done by a general confession: but that they confessed their sinnes, Which is a particular confession. — Particular confession.

6. Clothed.] The Holy Ghost thought it Worthy of speciall reporting how straitly this Prophete liued, and how he abstained from delicate meates and apparel. *See Mat. c. 3.* — Iohns example of penance.

8. With Water.] Iohn With Water only, Christ With the Holy Ghost, not only, as the Heretikes hold, that say Water is not necessary, but With Water and the Holy Ghost, as it is plaine Io. 3. *vnles a man be borne againe of Water and the Holy Ghost, he shal not enter into the kingdom of heauen.* — Baptisme in Water. *Calu. 4. inst.c.16.*

9. Baptized of Iohn.] The humility of Christ not disdaining his seruants baptisme. Which is an example for al faithful not to disdaine Christs Sacraments of any Priest be he neuer so simple, being by the Catholike Church lawfully called. *Aug. li. 5 de bapt. c. 9.*

10. The Spirit.] Expresse mention of the B. Trinitie. the Father speaketh from heauen, the — The B. Trinitie.

Holy Ghost appeareth in the likenesse of a doue, the Sonne also is recommended vnto vs. *Ambros. li. 1 de Sacram. c. 5.*

Christs example of penance.

12. *Desert.*] Christ doing penance by long fasting, solitarinesse, and conuersing with wilde beastes, gaue example and instruction to the Church for Lent fast, and to holy Eremites of retiring them selues to the wildernesse and prayer.

Solitarie contemplation.

35. *Desert place.*] Christ vsed very often to retire into solitary places, no doubt for our example, to teach vs that such places are best for prayer and contemplation, and that we should often retire our selues from worldly matters to solitary meditation of heauenly things.

CHAP. II.

Against the Scribes and Pharisees he defendeth first his povver to remitte sinnes in earth, 13 and his eating vvith sinners (as being the Physicion of soules, signified in those his miraculous cures vpon bodies): 18 then also he defendeth his Disciples, not hauing as yet any fastes by him prescribed vnto them, and plucking eares of corne vpon the Sabboth: signifying vvithal that he vvil change their ceremonies.

AND againe he entred into Capharnaum 1 after some daies, and it vvas heard that he vvas in the house, † and many came 2 together, so that there vvas no place no not at the doore, and he spake to them the vvord. † And they came to him brin- 3 ging one sicke of the palsey, vvho vvas caried of foure. † And vvhen they could not offer him vnto 4 him for the multitude, they " vncouered the roofe vvhere he vvas: and opening it they did let dovvne the couche vvherein the sicke of the palsey lay. † And vvhen IESVS had seen 5 :: their faith, he saith to the " sicke of the palsey, Sonne, " thy sinnes are forgiuen thee. † And there vvere certaine of the 6 Scribes sitting there and thinking in their hartes, † Why doth 7 he speake so? he blasphemeth. * Who can forgiue sinnes but only God? † Which by and by IESVS knovving in his spi- 8 rit, that they so thought vvithin them selues, saith to them, Why thinke you these things in your hartes? † Whether is 9 easier, to say to the sicke of the palsey, Thy sinnes are forgiuen thee: or to say, Arise, take vp thy couche, and vvalke? † But that you may knovv that " the Sonne of man hath 10 povver " in earth to forgiue sinnes (he saith to the sicke of the palsey) † I say to thee, Arise, take vp thy couche, and goe in- 11 to thy house. † And forthvvith he arose: and taking vp his 12 couche, vvent his vvay in the sight of al, so that al marueled, and glorified God, saying, That vve neuer savv the like.

Mt. 9, 1. Lu. 5, 18

:: Our Lord is moued to be merciful to sinners by other mens faith and desires, and not only by the parties owne meanes alvvay.

Iob. 14, 4. Esa. 43, 25.

† And he vvent forth againe to the sea: and al the multi- 13 tude came to him, and he taught them. † And vvhen he 14 passed

Mt. 9,9. Lu. 5,27

passed by, * he savv Leui of Alphæus sitting at the custome place: and he saith to him, Folovv me. And rising vp he fo-
15 lovved him. † And it came to passe, as he sate at meate in his house, many Publicans and sinners did sit dovvne together vvith IESVS and his Disciples. for they vvere many, vvho
16 also folovved him. † And the Scribes and the Pharisees seeing that he did eate vvith Publicans and Sinners, said to his Disciples, Why doth your Maister eate and drinke vvith Publi-
17 cans and sinners? † IESVS hearing this, saith to them, The vvhole haue not neede of a Physicion, but they that are il at ease. for I came not to call the iust, but sinners.

Mt. 9,13 Lu. 5,32

18 † And * the disciples of Iohn and the Pharisees did vse to fast: and they come, and say to him, Why do the disciples of Iohn and of the Pharisees fast: but thy disciples do not
19 fast? † And IESVS said to them, Why, can the children of the mariage fast, as long as the bridegrome is vvith them? So long time as they haue the bridegrome vvith them, they can
20 not fast. † But the daies vvil come vvhen the bridegrome shal be taken avvay from them: and then they shal :: fast in
21 those daies. † No body sovveth a peece of ravv cloth to an old garment: othervvise he taketh avvay the nevv peecing
22 from the old, and there is made a greater rent. † And no body putteth nevv vvine into old bottels: othervvise the vvine bursteth the bottels, and the vvine vvil be shed, and the bottels vvil be lost. but nevv vvine must be put into nevv bottels.

:: He foretelleth that fasting shal be vsed in his Church, no lesse then in the old law or in the time of Iohn the Baptist. *See Mat. 6, 9, 15.*

Mt. 12,1 Lu. 6,1.

23 † And * it came to passe againe vvhen he vvalked through the corne on the Sabboths, and his Disciples began to goe
24 forvvard and to plucke the eares. † And the Pharisees said to him, Behold, vvhy do they on the Sabboths that vvhich
25 is not lavvful? † And he said to them, Did you neuer read vvhat Dauid did, vvhen he vvas" in necessitie, and him self
26 vvas an hungred and they that vvere vvith him? † hovv * he entred into the house of God vnder Abiathar the high Priest, and did eate the loaues of Proposition, vvhich it vvas not lavvful to eate * but for the Priests, and did giue vnto them
27 vvhich vvere vvith him? † And he said to them, The Sabboth vvas made for man, and not man for the Sabboth.
28 † Therfore the sonne of man is :: Lord of the Sabboth also.

1 Re. 21, 6.

Leu. 24, 9.

:: The maker of the law may abrogate or dispense whē and where for iust cause it seemeth good to him.

ANNOTATIONS
CHAP. II

4. Uncouered.) Such diligence ought to be vsed to bring sinners to Christ in his Sacraments, as was vsed to procure this man and others, by Christ, the health of their bodies.

5. Sicke of the palsey.) Such as this man was in body by dissolution of his limmes, such also was he in soule by the noisome desires of the world occupying his hart, and withdrawing him from al good workes. *Aug. de Pastor. c. 6 to. 9.*

The Sacramēts to be called for in sicknes.

5. Thy sinnes.) Hereby it appeareth that Christ healed this sicke man first in his soule, before he tooke away his bodily infirmity: which may be an instruction for al men in bodily disease, first to call for the Sacraments, which be medicines of the soule. As hereby also may be gathered that many diseases come for sinne, and therfore can not be healed til the sinnes be remitted.

Mā hath power to remit sinnes.

10. The Sonne of man.) As Christ proueth vnto them, that him self as man, and not as God only, hath power to remitte sinnes, by that in al their sightes he was able to doe miracles and make the sickman sodenly arise: so the Apostles hauing power graunted them to doe miracles, though they be not God, may in like maner haue authority from God to remitte sinnes, not as God, but as Gods ministers.

Christ remitteth sinnes by the Priests ministerie.

10. In earth.) This power that the Sonne of man hath to remitte sinnes in earth, was neuer taken from him, but dureth still in his Sacraments, and ministers, by whom he remitteth sinnes in the Church, and not in heauen only. For concerning sinne, there is one court of conscience in earth, and an other in heauen: and the iudgement in heauen foloweth and approueth this on earth: as is plaine by the wordes of our Sauiour to Peter first, and then to al the Apostles, *Whatsoeuer you shal bind vpon earth, shal be bound in heauen: Whatsoeuer you shal loose vpon earth, shal be loosed in heauen*: Wherevpon S. Hierom saith, *That Priests hauing the keies of the kingdom of heauen, iudge after a sort before the day of iudgement.* And S. Chrysost. li. 3 de Sacerd. paul. post princip. *more at large.*

Mt. 16, 19.
Mt. 18, 18.
ad Heliod. ep. 1.

25. In necessity.) In necessity many things be done without sinne, which els might not be done: and so * the very chalices and consecrated iewels and vessels of the Church in cases of necessity are by lawful authority turned to profane vses: which otherwise to alienate to a mans priuate commoditie is sacrilege.

Amb. li. 2 off. c. 28.

CHAP. III.

The blind Pharisees seeking his death for doing good vpon the Sabboths, he meekely goeth out of the vvay: vvhere the people that flocke vnto him, and his Miracles, are innumerable. 13 Yea to his Tvvelue also (hauing neede of moe vvorkmen) he geueth povver to vvorke Miracles. 20 He so occupieth him self for soules, that his kinne thinke him madde. 22 The Scribes of Hierusalem come so farre, and yet haue nothing but absurdly to blaspeme his casting out of Diuels, to their ovvne damnation. 31 That the Ievves should not (after their maner) thinke it ynough, that he is of their bloud, he telleth that such rather are deere to him, as keepe Gods commaundements.

Mt. 12, 9
Lu. 6, 6.

1 AND he entred againe into the Synagogue, and there vvas a man there that had a vvithered hand. 2 † And they vvatched him vvhether he vvould cure on the Sabboths: that they might accuse him. 3 † And he saith to the man that had the vvithered hand, Rise vp into the middes. 4 † And he saith to them, Is it lavvful on the Sabboths to doe vvel or il? to saue a soule, or to destroy? but they held their peace. 5 † And looking round about vpon them vvith anger, being sorovvful for the blindenes of their hart, he saith to the man, Stretch forth thy hand. And he stretched it forth: and his hand vvas restored vnto him.

And

6 † And the Phariſees going forth, immediatly made a conſultation vvith the Herodians againſt him hovv they might
7 deſtroy him. † But IESVS vvith his Diſciples retired to the ſea: and a great multitude from Galilee and Ievvrie folovved
8 him, † and from Hieruſalem, and from Idumæa, and beyond Iordan. And they about Tyre and Sidon, a great multitude,
9 hearing the things vvhich he did, came to him. † And he ſpake to his Diſciples that a boate might attend on him be-
10 cauſe of the multitude, leſt they ſhould throng him. † for he healed many, ſo that there preaſed in vpon him for ∷ to
11 touch him, as many as had hurtes. † And the vncleane ſpirites, vvhen they ſavv him, fel dovvne vnto him: and they
12 cryed ſaying, † "Thou art the ſonne of God. And he vehemently charged them that they ſhould not diſcloſe him.

∷ The only touching of Chriſts holy perſon, or any part of his clothes, or whatſoeuer belonged to him, did heale al diſeaſes.

Mt. 5, 1. 10, 1. Lu. 6, 12 9, 1.

13 † And * aſcending into a mountaine, he called vnto him
14 vvhom he vvould him ſelf: and they came to him. † And he made that "tvvelue ſhould be vvith him, and that he
15 might ſend them to preach. † And he gaue them povver to
16 cure infirmities, and to caſt out diuels. † And he gaue to
17 Simon the name "Peter. † and Iames of Zebedee, and Iohn the brother of Iames: and he called their names, *Boanerges,*
18 vvhich is, *the ſonnes of thunder.* † and Andrevv and Philippe, and Bartlemevv and Matthevv, and Thomas and Iames of
19 Alphæus, and Thaddæus and Simon Cananæus, † and Iudas Iſcariote, vvho alſo betrayed him.

20 † And they come to a houſe: and the multitude reſorteth together againe, ſo that they could not ſo much as eate bread.
21 † And vvhen his had heard of it, they vvent forth to lay hands on him. for they ſaid, That he vvas become ∷ mad.
22 † And the Scribes vvhich vvere come dovvne from Hieruſalem, ſaid, * That he hath Beelzebub: and that in the prince
23 of deuils he caſteth out deuils. † And after he had called them together, he ſaid to them in parables, Hovv can Satan caſt out
24 Satan? † And if a "kingdom be deuided againſt it ſelf, that
25 kingdom can not ſtand. † And if a houſe be deuided againſt
26 it ſelf, that houſe can not ſtand. † And if Satan be riſen againſt him ſelf, he is deuided, and can not ſtand, but hath an end.
27 † No body can rifle the veſſel of the ſtrong, being entred into his houſe, vnles he firſt binde the ſtrong, and then ſhal he
28 rifle his houſe. † Amen I ſay to you, that al ſinnes ſhal be forgiuen the ſonnes of men, and the blaſphemies wherevvith

∷ See here the conceite of worldly frédes, who thinke the Zeale of Religion, madnes: and therfore count them madde, that are Zelous in Gods cauſe and for the Catholike faith: and the more Zelous, the more mad.

Mat. 12, 24. Luc. 11, 15.

they shal blaspheme. † But he that shal blaspheme against 29 the Holy Ghost, he hath not forgiuenesse for euer, but shal be guilty of an " eternal sinne. † Because they said, He hath an 30 vncleane spirit.

† And * there come his mother and brethren: and stan- 31 ding vvithout they sent vnto him calling him, † and the 32 multitude sate about him: and they say to him, Behold thy mother and thy brethren vvithout seeke thee. † And ansvve- 33 ring them, he said, " Who is my mother and my brethren? † And looking about vpon them vvhich sate round about 34 him, he saith, Behold my mother and my brethren. † For 35 vvhosoeuer shal doe the vvil of God, he is my brother and my sister and mother.

Mt. 12, 46. Lu. 8, 19

ANNOTATIONS
CHAP. III.

13. Thou art the Sonne.) The confession of the truth is not grateful to God, proceding from euery person. The diuel acknowledging our Sauiour to be the sonne of God, was bidden hold his peace: Peters confession of the same was highly allowed and rewarded. *Aug. tract. 10 in ep. Ioan. Ser. 30. 31. de verb. Apostoli.* Therfore neither Heretikes sermons must be heard, no not though they preach the truth. So is it of their prayer and seruice, which being neuer so good in it self, is not acceptable to God out of their mouthes, yea it is no better then the howling of wolues. *Hiero. in 7 Osee.*

Sermons, Seruice, and praier of Heretikes.

14. Twelue.) This number of twelue Apostles is mystical and of great importance (as appeareth * by the choosing of Mathias into Iudas place to make vp againe this number) prefigured in the 12 Patriarkes, *Gen. 49.* the 12 Princes of the children of Israel, *Num. 1.* the 12 fountaines found in Elim, *Exod. 15.* the 12 pretious stones in the Rational of Aaron, *Exod. 39.* the 12 Spies sent by Moyses, *Num. 13.* the 12 stones taken out of Iordan whereof the Altar was made, *Iosu. 4.* the 12 loues of Proposition, *Leuit. 24.* &c. *Anselm. in Mt. c. 10.* And these are the 12 foundations of heauenly Hierusalem. *Apoc. 21.*

The number of Twelue, mystical.

Act. 1.

16. Peter.) Peter in numbering the Twelue is alwaies the first, and his name is so giuen him for signification of his calling to be the * Rocke or Foundation of the Church vnder Christ: as here also the name BOANERGES is giuen to other two Apostles for signification, and so names els where in the old Testament and in the new.

Peters preeminence,

Mt. 16.

24. Kingdom against kingdom.) As this is true in al Kingdoms and Common-weales where Ciuil dissension reigneth, so is it specially verified in heresies and Heretikes, which haue alwaies diuisions among them selues as the plague of God, for diuiding them selues and others from the Church.

Dissension of Heretikes.

Greg. li. 7 ep. 3.

29. Eternal sinne.) That which is here called eternal, is (as S. Matthew expresseth it) that which shal neither be remitted in this life, nor in the life to come. Where we learne by S. Marke, that there are also sinnes not eternal: and by S. Matthew, that they are such, as shal be forgiuen either here, or in the life to come.

Venial sinnes forgiuen after death.

Mt. 12, 32.

33. Who is my mother?) Neither is it here said, that he had no mother, as some vpon these wordes falsly gather: nor ingratitude to our parents is taught vs by this answer: but we be hereby admonished to preferre the spiritual mother of the Faithful, which is the Church Catholike, and our brethren in her, and their spiritual good, aboue our carnal parents or kinne. For so our Maister being occupied here about heauenly things, accounted al them his mother and brethren, which did the will of his Father. in which number our Lady his mother was also included, for she did his fathers will. *Aug. ep. 38.* Yea and aboue al others, because she had so much grace giuen her that she neuer sinned not so much as venially in al her life. *Aug. de nat. & grat c. 36.*

Spiritual kinred and busines preferred before carnal and worldly.

The B. Virgin without sinne.

CHAP. IIII.

CHA. IIII.

The parables (in vvhich he ſpeaketh to the Ievves, becauſe they vvere reprobate) he expoundeth to his Diſciples, ſhevving that in his ſovving, three parts of foure ſhal periſh, through the fault of the hearers. 21 and that his ſeruants muſt confeſſe their faith, 24 and vſe their gifts (contrary to thoſe ſtony and thorny hearers.) 26 and that his Church (notvvithſtanding the looſing of thoſe three partes of the ſeede) ſhalbe brought by his prouidence to the harueſt, that is, to the end of the vvorld: 30 grovving ouer al in time, though in the beginning it be as the litle muſtard ſeede, 35 and though ſuch tempeſts of perſecution in the ſea of this vvorld doe riſe againſt it.

Mt.13,1. Lu.8,4.

1 AND againe he began to teach at the ſea ſide: and a great multitude vvas gathered together vnto him, ſo that he vvent vp into a boate, and ſate in the ſea, and al the multitude about the ſea vvas vpon the land: 2 † and he taught them in parables many things, and 3 ſaid to them in his doctrine, † Heare ye:

4 Behold, the ſovver vvent forth to ſovv. † And vvhiles he ſovveth, ſome fel by the vvay ſide, and the foules of the aire 5 came, and did eate it. † And otherſome fel vpon rocky places vvhere it had not much earth: and it ſhot vp immediatly, be-6 cauſe it had not deepnes of earth: † and vvhen the ſunne was riſen, it parched, and becauſe it had not roote, it vvithered. 7 † And ſome fel among thornes: and the thornes grewe vp, and 8 choked it, and it yelded not fruite. † And ſome fel vpon good ground: and it yelded fruite that grewe vp and increaſed, and it brought forth, one thirtie, one ſixtie, and one an hundred.

9 † And he ſaid, He that hath eares to heare, let him heare.

10 † And vvhen he vvas alone, the Tvvelue that vvere vvith 11 him, aſked him the parable. † And he ſaid to them, To you it is giuen to knovv the myſterie of the kingdom of God: but to ∷ them that are vvithout, al things are done in parables: 12 † that * ſeeing they may ſee, and not ſee: and hearing they may heare, and not vnderſtand: ″ leſt at any time they ſhould 13 be conuerted and their ſinnes be forgiuen them. † And he ſaith to them, Do you not knovv this parable? and hovv ſhal 14 you knovv al parables? † He that ſovveth: ſovveth the vvord. 15 † And they by the vvay ſide, are theſe: vvhere the vvord is ſovven, and vvhen they ſhal haue heard, immediatly commeth Satan, and taketh avvay the vvord that vvas ſovven in 16 their hartes. † And thy likevviſe that are ſovven vpon the rocky places, are theſe: vvho vvhen they heare the vvord, 17 immediatly vvith ioy receiue it: † and they haue not roote in

Eſa.6,9

∷ Such as be out of the Church, though they heare and read neuer ſo much, they cannot vnderſtand. Bed. in 4 Marc.

in them selues, but are temporal: aftervvard vvhen tribulation is risen and persecution for the vvord, forthvvith they are scandalized. † And other there be that are sovven among 18 thornes: these are they that heare the vvord, † and the cares 19 of the vvorld and the deceitfulnes of riches, and concupiscences about other things entring in choke the vvord, and it is made fruiteles. † And these are they that vvere sovven vpon 20 the good ground, vvhich heare the vvord and receiue it, and yeld fruite one thirtie, one sixtie, and one an hundred.

† And he said to them, * Commeth a candel to be put 21 :: vnder a bushel, or vnder a bed? and not to be put vpon the candlesticke? † For there is nothing hid, vvhich shal not 22 be made manifest: neither vvas any thing made secret, but that it shal come to light. † If any man haue eares to heare, 23 let him heare.

Lu. 8,16

:: Christ came not to teach his doctrine in corners and hucker mucker, as Heretikes doe, but to lighten the Whole World thereWith.

† And he said to them, See vvhat you heare. * In vvhat 24 measure you mete, it shal be measured to you againe, and more shal be giuen `to you'. † For he that hath, to him shal be 25 giuen: and he that hath not, that also vvhich he hath, shal be taken avvay from him.

Lu. 8,18

to you that heare.

† And he said, So is the kingdom of God, as if a man cast 26 seede into the earth, † "and sleepe, and rise vp night and day, 27 and the seede spring, and grovve vp vvhiles he knovveth not. † For the earth of it self bringeth forth fruite, first the 28 blade, then the eare, aftervvard the ful corne in the eare. † And 29 vvhen the fruite hath brought out it self, immediatly he putteth in the sickle, because haruest is come.

† * And he said, To vvhat shal vve liken the kingdom of 30 God? or to vvhat parable shal vve compare it? † As a "mustard 31 seede: vvhich vvhen it is sovven in the earth, is lesse then al the seedes that are in the earth: † and vvhen it is sovven, it 32 riseth vp, and becommeth greater then al herbes, and maketh great boughes, so that the "birdes of the aire may dvvel vnder the shadovv thereof.

Mat. 13, 31.
Luc. 13, 19.

† And vvith many such parables he spake to them the 33 vvord, according as they vvere able to heare: † and vvithout 34 parable he did not speake vnto them. but apart, he explicated al things to his Disciples.

† And he saith to them in that day, vvhen euening vvas 35 come, * Let vs passe ouer to the other side. † And dimising the 36 multitude, they take him so as he vvas in the boate: and there vvere

Mt. 8,23
Lu. 8,22

37 vvere other boates vvith him. † And there arose a great storme of vvinde, and the vvaues bette into the boate, so that
38 the boate vvas filled. † And he vvas in the hinder part of the boate sleeping vpon a pillovv: and they raise him, and say to him, Maister, doth it not pertaine to thee that vve perish?
39 † And rising vp he threatened the vvinde, and said to the sea, Peace, be stil. And the vvinde ceased: and there vvas made a
40 great calme. † And he said to them, Why are you feareful? neither yet haue you faith? And they feared vvith great feare: and they said one to an other, Who is this (thinkest thou) that both vvinde and sea obey him?

ANNOTATIONS
CHAP. IIII.

12. *Lest they should be conuerted.*] These speaches here and els where, we must not so vnderstand as though he spake in parables of purpose and to this end, that the hearers might not vnderstād, lest they should be conuerted: which were as much to say as that he would not haue them vnderstand, nor be conuerted: but we must learne the true sense of this very place in S. Matthew and in the Actes, where our Sauiour and S. Paul speake thus, *They haue heard heauily, and haue shut their eies, lest perhaps they may see, and vnderstand, and be conuerted, and I heale them.* Whereby it is euident, that the speaking in parables was not the cause (for many beside the Apostles heard and vnderstood) but them selues would not heare, and vnderstand, and be conuerted: and so were the cause of their owne wilful and obstinate infidelity. And therfore also he spake in parables, because they were not worthy to vnderstand, as the other to whom he expounded them.

Mt. 13. Act. 28.

God is not author of sinne, but mans owne will.

27. *And sleepe.*] The Church, and Christs doctrine, (sleepe we, wake we) increaseth by the great prouidence of God. only the preachers must sow, and plant, and water, and* God wil giue the increase, nourishing the seede in mens harts. And therfore we may not giue ouer, or be impatient and solicitous, if we haue not alwaies good successe: but doing our duty, commit the rest to God.

1. Cor. 3.

31. *Mustard seed.*] If the Church and Truth had more and more decaied and been obscured after the Apostles time vnto ours, as the Heretikes hold: then had it been great in the beginning, and smal afterward: where this Parable saith contrary, that it was a mustard seed first, and afterward a great tree. *vide Chrys. to. 5 contra Gentiles in vita S. Babylæ Mart.*

The Church visibly increasing.

32. *The birdes.*] Of al sectes or doctrine, Christs religion at the beginning was the smallest, and most contemptible: but the successe thereof farre passed al mans doctrine: in so much that afterward al the wisest and greatest of the world made their residence and rest therein.

Christian religion wonderfully spreading.

CHAP. V.

To the Gerasens (and in them to al men) Christ manifesteth how the Diuel of his malice would vse them, if he would permitte: 17 and yet they like not their Sauiours presence. 21 A woman Gentil, that began her sicknesse when the Iewes daughter began her life (signifying Abrahams time) he cureth by the way as he was comming to heale the Iewes: And euen then the Iewes do die, but yet them also he wil reuiue, as here the Iewes daughter.

N AND

ND they came beyond the ſtraite of the ſea into the countrie of the Geraſens. † And as he vvent out of the boate, immediatly there mette him out of the ſepulchres a man in an vncleane ſpirit, † that had his dvvelling in the ſepulchres. and neither vvith chaines " could any man novv binde him: † for being often bound vvith fetters and chaines, he had burſt the chaines, and broken the fetters. and no body could tame him. † and he vvas alvvaies day and night in the ſepulchres and in the mountaines, crying and cutting him ſelf vvith ſtones. † And ſeeing IESVS a farre of, he ranne and adored him: † and crying vvith a great voice, ſaid, What to me and thee IESVS the ſonne of God moſt high? I adiure thee by God that thou torment me not. † For he ſaid vnto him, Goe out of the man thou vncleane ſpirit. † And he aſked him, What is thy name? And he ſaith to him, My name is Legion: becauſe vve are many. † And he beſought him much, that he vvould not expel him out of the countrie. † And there vvas there about the mountaine a great heard of ſvvine, feeding. † And the ſpirits beſought him, ſaying, Send vs ⁘ into the ſvvine, that vve may enter into them. † And IESVS immediatly graunted vnto them. And the vncleane ſpirits going out, entred into the ſvvine: and the heard vvith great violence vvas caried headlong into the ſea, about tvvo thouſand, and vvere ſtifled in the ſea. † And they that fed them, fled, and caried nevves into the citie and into the fields. And they vvent forth to ſee vvhat vvas done: † and they come to IESVS, and they ſee him that vvas vexed of the deuil, ſitting, clothed, and vvel in his vvittes: and they vvere afraid. † And they that had ſeen it, told them, in vvhat maner he had been dealt vvithal that had the diuel: and of the ſvvine. † And they began to deſire him, that he vvould depart from their coaſtes. † And vvhen he vvent vp into the boate, he that h.d been vexed of the diuel, began to beſeeche him that he might be vvith him, † and he admitted him not, but ſaith to him, Goe into thy houſe to thine, and tel them hovv great things the Lord hath done for thee, and hath had mercie vpon thee. † And he vvent his vvay, and began to publiſh in Decapolis hovv great things IESVS had done to him: and al marueled.

Verse numbers in margin: 1, 2, 3, 4, 5, 6, 7, 8, 9, 10, 11, 12, 13, 14, 15, 16, 17, 18, 19, 20

Mat. 8, 28. *Luc.* 8, 26.

⁘ It is not vvith out myſterie that the diuels deſired, and Chriſt ſuffered them to enter into the ſvvine, ſignifying that filthy liuers be meete dvvelling places for diuels. *Aug. tract. 6 in ep. Io.*

† And

Mat. 9, 18. Luc. 8, 42.

21 †* And vvhen IESVS had paſſed in boate againe ouer the ſtraite, a great multitude aſſembled together vnto him, and he 22 vvas about the ſea. † And there commeth one of the Archſynagogs, named Iaîrus: and ſeeing him, he falleth dovvne at 23 his feete, † and beſought him much, ſaying, That my daughter is at the point of death, come, impoſe thy hands vpon her, 24 that ſhe may be ſafe and liue. † And he vvent vvith him, and a great multitude folovved him, and they thronged him.

Archſynagogue, cheefe gouerner of a Synagogue.

25 † And a vvoman vvhich vvas in an iſſue of bloud tvvelue 26 yeres, † and had ſuffred many things of many Phyſicions, and had beſtovved al that ſhe had, neither vvas any thing 27 the better, but vvas rather vvorſe: † vvhen ſhe had heard of IESVS, ſhe came in the preaſſe behind him, and touched his 28 garment. † for ſhe ſaid, That "if I ſhal touche but his gar-29 ment, I ſhal be ſafe. † And forthvvith the fountaine of her bloud vvas dried: and ſhe felt in her body that ſhe vvas hea-30 led of the maladie. † And immediatly IESVS knovving in him ſelf "the vertue that had proceeded from him, turning to 31 the multitude, ſaid, Who hath touched my garments? † And his Diſciples ſaid to him, Thou ſeeſt the multitude thronging 32 thee, and ſayeſt thou, Who hath touched me? † And he loo-33 ked about to ſee her that had done this. † But the vvoman fearing and trembling, knovving vvhat vvas done in her: came and fel dovvne before him, and told him al the truth. 34 † And he ſaid to her, Daughter, thy faith hath made thee ſafe, goe in peace, and be vvhole of thy maladie.

35 † As he vvas yet ſpeaking, they come \`to' the Archſynagogue, ſaying, That thy daughter is dead: vvhy doeſt thou 36 trouble the Maiſter any further? † But IESVS hauing heard the vvord that vvas ſpoken, ſaith to the Archſynagogue, 37 Feare not: "only beleeue. † And he admitted not any man to folovv him, but Peter and Iames and Iohn the brother of Ia-38 mes. † And they come to the Archſynagogs houſe, and he 39 ſeeth a tumult, and folke vveeping and vvailing much. † And going in, he ſaith to them: Why make you this a doe and 40 vveepe? the vvenche is not dead, but ∴ ſleepeth. † And they derided him. But he hauing put forth al, taketh the father and the mother of the vvenche, and them that vvere vvith him, 41 and they goe in vvhere the vvenche vvas lying. † And holding the vvenches hand, he ſaith to her, *Talithacumi*, vvhich 42 is being interpreted, "*wenche* (I ſay to thee) *ariſe*. † and forth-

\`from

∴ To Chriſt, that can more eaſily raiſe a dead man then we can doe one that is but a ſleepe, death is but ſleepe. *Aug. de verb. Do. Ser. 44.*

with the wéche rose vp, and walked. and she vvas twelue yeres old: and they vvere astonied vvith great astonishment. † And 43 he commaunded them earnestly that no body should knovv it: and he bad that some thing should be giuen her to eate.

ANNOTATIONS
CHAP. V.

Profane and natural men.

3. Could bind him.] We see here that mad men which haue extraordinary strength, are many times possessed of the diuel: as there is also a deafe and a dumme diuel, and vncleane spirits, which worke these effects in men, possessing their bodies. Al which things infidels and carnal men folowing only nature and reason, attribute to natural causes: and the lesse faith a man hath, the lesse he beleeueth that the diuel worketh such things.

The touche of Relikes.

28. If I shal touch.] So the good Catholike saith, If I might but touche one of his Apostles, yea one of his Apostles napkins, yea but the shade of one of his Saincts, I should be better for it. *Act. 5.* and *19. See S. Chrys. to. 5 cont. Gent. in principio. in vit. Babyla.* Yea S. Basil saith, He that toucheth the bone of a martyr, receiueth in some degree holinesse of the grace or vertue that is therein. *Basil. in ps. 115.*

30. Vertue,] Vertue to heale this womans maladie, proceeded from Christ, though she touched but his coate: so when the Saincts by their Relikes or garments do miracles, the grace and force thereof commeth from our Sauiour, they being but the meanes or instruments of the same.

Scripture fondly applied to proue onely faith.

36. Only beleeue.] It is our common speache, when we require one thing specially, though other things also be as necessarie, and more necessarie. As the Physicion to his patient, *Only haue a good hart*: when he must also keepe a diet, and take potions, things more requisite. So Christ in this great infidelity of the Iewes, required only that they would beleeue he was able to doe such a cure, such a miracle, and then he did it: otherwise it foloweth in the next Chapter, *He could not do miracles there because of their incredulity.* *V. 5.* Againe, for this faith he gaue them here and in al like places health of body, which they desired. and therfore he saith not, Thy faith hath iustified thee: but, hath made the safe or whole. Againe this was the fathers faith, which could not iustifie the daughter. Whereby it is most euident, that this Scripture, and the like, are folishely abused of the Heretikes to proue that only faith iustifieth.

By three dead, are signified three kind of sinners.

41. Wenche arise.] Christs miracles, besides that they be wonders and waies to shew his power, be also significatiue: as these which he corporally raised from death, put vs in minde of his raising our soules from sinne. *Aug. de verb. Do. ser. 44.* The Scripture maketh special mention only of three raised by our Sauiour. of which three, this wench is one, within the house: an other, the widowes sonne in Naim, now caried out toward the graue: the third, Lazarus hauing been in the graue foure daies, and therfore stinking. Which diuersity of dead bodies, signifie diuersity of dead soules, some more desperate then other, some past al mans hope, and yet by the grace of Christ to be reuiued and reclaimed.

CHAP. VI.

In his owne countrey (signifying the reprobate Iewes) he is contemned, and therfore worketh litle in respect. 6 His Apostles preache euery where and worke miracles, so that King Herode (who shamefully killed Iohn Baptist) and others are striken with great admiration. 30 After Iohns death he goeth into the Desert, where great concurse being vnto him, he feedeth 5000 with fiue loaues. 46 And after he hath praied long in the mountaine, he walketh vpon the sea. 53 And with the very touche of his garments hemme he healeth innumerable.

AND going out from thence, he vvent 1 into his countrie: and his Disciples folovved him. † and vvhen the Sabboth 2 vvas come, he began to teach in the Synagogue: and many hearing him vvere in admiration at his doctrine, saying, How came this felovv by al these things? and

Mt. 13, 54. Lu. 4, 16

and vvhat vvisedom is this that is giuen to him, and such vertues as are vvrought by his hands? 3 † Is not this "the Carpenter, the sonne of MARIE, the brother of Iames and Ioseph and Iude and Simon? why, are not also his sisters here vvith vs? 4 And they "vvere scandalized in him. † And IESVS said to them, That there is not a Prophet vvithout honour, but in his ovvne countrie, and in his ovvne house, and in his ovvne kinred. 5 † and "he could not doe any miracle there, but only cured a fevv that vvere sicke, imposing his hands 6 † and he marueled because of their incredulity, and he vvent about the tovvnes in circuite teaching.

Mt.10,1 Lu. 9,1.

7 † * And he called the Tvvelue: and began to send them tvvo 8 and tvvo, and gaue them povver ouer vncleane spirits. † And he commaunded them that they should take nothing for the vvay, but a rod only: not skrippe, not bread, nor money in 9 their purse, † but shod vvith sandals, and that they should 10 not put on "tvvo coates. † And he said to them, Whithersoeuer you shal enter into an house, there tarie til you depart 11 thence. † and vvhosoeuer shal not receiue you, nor heare you: going forth from thence shake of the dust from your 12 feete for a testimonie to them. † And going forth they prea-13 ched that they should doe penance: † and they cast out many diuels, and * anointed "vvith :: oile many sicke, and healed them.

Ia.5,14.

:: A preparatiue to the Sacramēt of extreme vnction. Iac. 5.

Mt.14,1 Lu.9,7.

14 † And * king Herod heard (for his name vvas made manifest) and he said, That Iohn the Baptist is risen againe from 15 the dead, and therfore vertues vvorke in him. † And others said, That it is Elias. But others said, That it is a Prophet, as 16 one of the Prophets. † Which Herod hearing, said, Iohn vvhom I beheaded, he is risen againe from the dead.

The Gospel vpō the decollation of S. Iohn Baptist Aug. 29.

17 † For the said Herod sent and apprehended Iohn, and bound him in prison for Herodias the vvife of :: Philippe 18 his brother, because he had maried her. † For Iohn said to Herod, * It is not lavvful for thee to haue thy brothers vvife. 19 † And Herodias lay in vvaite for him: and vvas desirous to 20 kil him, and could not. † For Herod feared Iohn, knovving him to be a iust and holy man: and he kept him, and by hea-21 ring him did many things: and he heard him gladly. † And vvhen a conuenient day vvas fallen, Herod made the supper of his birth-day to the Princes and the Tribunes and the 22 cheefe of Galilee. † And vvhen the daughter of the same He-

Leu. 18, 16. 20, 21.

:: He might and should by Moyses law haue maried his brothers wife, if he had been dead without issue: but this Philip was yet aliue, and had also this daughter that daunced.

rodias came in, and had daunced, and pleased Herod, and them that sate vvith him at the table: the King said to the damsel, Aske of me vvhat thou vvilt, and I vvil giue it thee. †and 23 he svvare to her, That vvhatsoeuer thou shalt aske I vvil giue thee, though the halfe of my kingdom. †Who vvhen 24 she vvas gone forth, said to her mother, What shal I aske? But she said, The head of Iohn the Baptist. †And vvhen she 25 vvas gone in by and by vvith hast to the King, she asketh saying, I vvil that forthvvith thou giue me in a platter the head of Iohn the Baptist. †And the King vvas stroken sad. 26 Because of his othe and for them that sate together at table he vvould not displease her: †but sending the hangman, 27 commaunded that his head should be brought in a platter. † And he beheaded him in the prison, and brought his 28 head in a platter: and gaue it to the damsel, and the damsel gaue it to her mother. †Which his disciples hearing came, 29 and tooke his body: and they put it in a monument. ✠

†And * the Apostles gathering together vnto Iesus, 30 made relation to him of al things that they had done and taught. †And he said to them, Come apart into the desert 31 place, and rest a litle. For there vvere that came and vvent, many: and they had not so much as space to eate. †And 32 * going vp into the boate, they vvent into a desert place apart. †And they savv them going avvay, and many knevv: 33 and they ranne flocking thither on foote from al cities, and preuented them.

Lu. 9, 10

Mt. 14, 13.

†And going forth, IESVS savv a great multitude: and 34 he had compassion on them, because they vvere as sheepe not hauing a shepheard, and he began to teach them many things. †And * vvhen the day vvas novv farre spent, his Di- 35 sciples came to him, saying, This is a desert place, and the houre is novv past: †dimisse them, that going out into the 36 next villages and tovvnes, they may bie them selues meates to eate. †And he ansvvering said, Giue ye them to eate. And 37 they said to him, Let vs goe and bie bread for tvvo hundred pence: and vve vvil giue them to eate. †And he saith to 38 them, Hovv many loaues haue you? goe and see. And vvhen they knevv, they say, Fiue, and tvvo fishes. †And he com- 39 maunded them that they should make al sit dovvne, by companies vpon the greene grasse. †And they sate dovvne in 40 rankes by hundreds and fifties. †And vvhen he had taken 41 the fiue loaues, and the tvvo fishes: looking vp vnto heauen, he

Mt. 14, 15. Lu. 9, 12. Io. 6, 5.

he blessed, and brake the loaues, and gaue to his Disciples to
42 set before them: and the tvvo fishes he deuided to al. † And
43 al did eate, and had their fill. † And they tooke vp the leauings, tvvelue ful baskets of fragments: and of the fishes.
44 † And they that did eate, vvere fiue thousand men. † And
45 immediatly he compelled his Disciples to goe vp into the boate, that they might goe before him beyond the straite to Bethsaida: vvhiles him self did dimisse the people.

Mt. 14, 23. Io. 6, 16.

The Gospel on Saterday after Ashwenesday.

46 † And * vvhen he had dimissed them, he vvent into the
47 mountaine to pray. † And vvhen it vvas late, the boate vvas
48 in the middes of the sea, and him self alone on the land. † And seeing them labouring in rovving (for the vvinde vvas against them) and about the fourth vvatch of the night he commeth to them vvalking vpon the sea: and he vvould haue passed by
49 them. † But they seeing him vvalking vpon the sea, thought it
50 vvas a ghost, and cried out. † For al savv him, and vvere troubled. And immediatly he talked vvith them, and said to them,
51 Haue confidence, it is I, feare ye not. † And he vvent vp to them into the shippe, and the vvinde ceased: and they vvere
52 farre more astonied vvithin them selues: † for they vnderstoode not concerning the loaues: for their hart vvas blinded.

Mt. 14, 34.

53 † And * vvhen they had passed ouer, they came into the
54 land of Genezareth, and set to the shore. † And vvhen they vvere gone out of the boate, incontinent they knevv him:
55 † and running through that vvhole countrie, they began to carie about in couches those that vvere il at ease, vvhere they
56 heard he vvas. † And vvhithersoeuer he entred into tovvnes or into villages or cities, they laid the sicke in the streates, and besought him that they might touche but the hemme of his garment: and as many as touched him, vvere made vvhole. ⊣

ANNOTATIONS
CHAP. VI.

3. *The carpenter.*) As his countrie-folkes seeing him not only to be a poore man, but also knowing (as they thought) his vvhole parentage to be but vulgar, not reaching to his Godhead and diuine generation, did take offence or scandal of him: so doe the Heretikes take like offence at his person in the B. Sacrament, saying, Why, this is not God: for it is bread made of corne by such a baker, of the same moulde that such a lofe is: not marking that it was not made Christ by baking, but by Conseeration, and the vertue of Christs vvordes.

3. *They*

3. They were scandalized.] This scandal rose partly of enuy of his equals by birth, who reputing them selues as good as he, tooke skorne to be taught of him. Wherevpon Christ saith, *A Prophet is not without honour but in his owne countrie*: signifying (as it is plaine in Luke) the malice and enuy of the Iewes his countrie men in refusing him (*Io. 1.*) and that the Gentils would more esteeme of him. *Chrys. ho. 49, in Mt. Lu. 4, 25.*

5. He could not.] It is said that he could not worke miracles there, not meaning that he was not able, but that on their part there wanted apt disposition to receiue them. And therfore he would not of cōgruity worke there, vvhere their incredulity vvas so great, that it vvould not haue profited them. And for this cause he saith* els where to them that wil see and enioy his miracles, *Only beleeue.* *Marc. 5, 36.*

8. Not two coates.] He forbiddeth superfluites, and to careful prouision of bodily things, when they are about Gods seruice in gaining soules. And for the contrariety that seemeth here and in S. Matthew, vnderstand that there he forbiddeth them to carie rod or staffe to defend them selues, here he permitteth a vvalking rod or staffe to leane and stay vpon: there he forbiddeth shoes to couer al the foote, such as we vveare: here he permitteth sandals, that is such as had soles only, which the poore commonly vvare in Ievvry, and novv some religious men. See S. Augustins opinion *li. 2 c. 30 de consensu Euang. to. 4.* *Mt. 10.*

13. With oile.] In the wordes of the commission oile is not mentioned, and yet it is certaine by this their vsing of oile, that either Christ did then appoint them to vse it, or they might take it vp of them selues, by vertue of the general commission.

13. With Oile). By this it is cleere that not only the Apostles or other may haue power to worke miracles, by their only word and inuocation of Christs name, but also by application of creatures: which creatures also haue a miraculous medicinal vertue to heale diseases.

CHAP. VII.

The masters of Hierusalem comming so farre to carpe him 6 he chargeth with traditions, partly friuolous, 9 partly also contrarie to Gods commaundements. 14 And to the people he yeldeth the reason of that which they carped, 17 and againe to his disciples, shewing the ground of the Iewish washing (to witte, that meates otherwise defile the soule) to be false. 24 But by and by among the Gentils, in a vvoman he findeth vvonderful faith, vpon her therfore he bestovveth the crumme that she asked, 32 returning (because the time of the Gentils vvas not yet come) to the Ievves vvith the loafe. 32 Where he shevveth his compassion tovvardes mankind so deafe and dumme, 36 and of the people is highly magnified.

ND there assemble together vnto him the Pharisees and certaine of the Scribes, comming from Hierusalem. 1 *Mt. 15, 1.*
† And vvhen they had seen certaine of his disciples eate bread vvith " common hands, that is, not vvashed, they blamed them. 2
† For the Pharisees and al the Ievves, vnles they often vvash their hands, eate not, holding the tradition of the Auncients: 3
† and from the market, vnles they be vvashed, they eate not: and many other things there be that vvere deliuered vnto them to obserue, the vvashings of cuppes and cruses, and of brasen vessels & beddes. 4
† And the Pharisees and Scribes asked him, Why do not thy disciples vvalke according to the tradition of the Auncients, but they eate bread vvith common hands? 5
† But he ansvvering, said to them, Wel did Esay Prophecie of you hypocrites, as it is vvritten, *This people honoureth me :: with their lippes, but their hart is farre from me.* 6 *Esa. 29, 13.*
† *and in vaine doe they worship me, teaching doctrines " precepts of men.* 7

:: They that say well or teache and preache well, or haue Christ and his word in their mouth, and liue naughtily, be touched in this place.

† For

8 † For leauing the commaundement of God, you hold the traditions of men, the vvaſhings of cruſes and cuppes: & many 9 other things you doe like to theſe. † And he ſaid to thē, Wel do you fruſtrate the precept of God, that you may obſerue your 10 ovvne tradition. † For Moyſes ſaid, *Honour thy father & thy mother.* 11 and, *He that ſhal curſe father or mother, dying let him dye.* † But you ſay, If a man ſay to father or mother, *Corban* (vvhich is a gift) vvhat-12 ſoeuer proceedeth from me, ſhal profit thee: † and further 13 you ſuffer him not to doe ought for his father or mother, † defeating the vvord of God for your ovvne tradition vvhich you haue giuen forth. and many other things of this ſort you doe.

Exo. 20, 12. Leu. 20, 9.

14 † And calling againe the multitude vnto him, he ſaid to 15 them, Heare me al you, and vnderſtand. † "Nothing is vvithout a man entring into him, that can defile him. but the things that proceede from a man thoſe are they that make a 16 man ∷ cōmon. † If any man haue eares to heare, let him heare. 17 † And vvhen he vvas entred into the houſe from the multi-18 tude, his Diſciples aſked him the parable. † And he ſaith to them, So are you alſo vnſkilful? Vnderſtand you not that euery thing from vvithout, entring into a man, can not make 19 him common: † becauſe it entreth not into his hart, but goeth into the belly, and is caſt out into the priuy, purging 20 al the meates? † But he ſaid that the things vvhich come 21 forth from a man, they make a man common. † For from vvithin out of the hart of men proceede euil cogitations, ad-22 uouteries, fornications, murders, † theftes, auarices, vvickedneſſe, guile, impudicities, an euil eye, blaſphemie, pride, fo-23 liſhnes. † Al theſe euils proceede from vvithin, and make a man common.

∷ See the firſt annotation vpō this chapter.

24 † And *riſing from thence he vvent into the coaſtes of Tyre and Sidon: and entring into a houſe, he vvould that no man 25 ſhould knovv, and he could not be hid. † For a vvoman immediatly as ſhe heard of him, vvhoſe daughter had an vn-26 cleane ſpirit, entred in, and fel dovvne at his feete. † For the vvoman vvas a Gentile, a Syrophænician borne. And ſhe beſought him that he vvould caſt forth the diuel out of her 27 daughter. † Who ſaid to her, Suffer firſt the children to be filled. for it is not good to take the childrens bread, and caſt 28 it to the dogges. † But ſhe anſvvered, and ſaid to him, Yea lord. for the vvhelpes alſo eate vnder the table of the crum-

Mt. 15, 21.

mes of the children. † And he ſaid to her, For this ſaying goe thy vvay, the deuil is gone out of thy daughter. † And when ſhe vvas departed into her houſe, ſhe found the maid lying vpon the bed, and the deuil gone out. 29 30

The Goſpel vpõ the 11 Sunday after Pentecoſt.

† And againe going out of the coaſtes ˋof Tyre, he came by Sidon' to the ſea of Galilee through the middes of the coaſtes of Decapolis. † And they bring to him one deafe and dumme: and they beſought him that he vvould impoſe his hand vpon him. † And taking him from the multitude apart, he put his fingers into his eares: and ″ ſpitting, touched his tongue. † and looking vp vnto heauen, he groned, and ſaid to him, ″ *Ephphetha*, vvhich is, *Be thou opened.* † And immediatly his eares vvere opened, and the ſtring of his tongue vvas looſed, and he ſpake right. † And he commaunded them not to tel any body. But hovv much he commaunded them, ſo much the more a great deale did they publiſh it, † and ſo much the more did they vvonder, ſaying, He hath done al things vvel: he hath made both the deafe to heare, and the dumme to ſpeake. ┤ 31 32 33 34 35 36 37

ˋ*of Tyre and Sidon, he came*

ANNOTATIONS
CHAP. VII.

2. Common.] Common and vncleane is al one. For the Iewes were commaunded by the Law to eate certaine kindes of meates only, and not al indifferently: and becauſe theſe were ſeparated from other meates, and as it were ſanctified to their vſe, they called the other common and profane: and becauſe the Law calleth thoſe cleane and theſe vncleane, thereof it is, that vncleane and common is al one. as in this Chapter often, and *Act. 10.*

Commaundements of men.

7. Precepts of men.] Mens ordinances which be repugnant to Gods commaundements, be here condemned: as al obſeruations not edifying nor profitable to the fulfilling of Gods commaundements, be vaine and ſuperfluous: as many obſeruations of the Phariſees were then, and the like traditions of Heretikes be now. for howſoeuer they bragge of Scriptures, al their maner of adminiſtration and miniſterie is their owne tradition and inuention without al Scripture and warrant of Gods word. But the traditions of the Apoſtles and Ancients, and al the precepts of holy Church we are commaunded to keepe, as things not preſcribed by man, but by the Holy Ghoſt. *Act. 15, 28. 41. 2 Theſſal. 2, 15.*

Traditions.

Dutie to parẽts.

11. Gift.] To giue to the Church or Altar is not forbidden, but the forſaking of a mans parents in their neceſſitie, pretending or excuſing the matter vpon his giuing that which ſhould relieue them, to God or to the Altar, that is impious and vnnatural. And theſe Phariſees teaching children ſo to neglect their duties to their parents, did wickedly.

Abſtinẽce from certaine meates.

15. Nothing entering into a man.] As theſe wordes of our Sauiour do not import, that the Iewes then might haue eaten of thoſe meates which God forbade them: no more doe they now, that we Chriſtians may eate of meates which the Church forbiddeth vs. And yet both then and now al meates are cleane, and nothing entering into a man, defileth a man. For neither they then, nor we now abſteine, for that any meates are of their nature abominable, or defile the eaters, but they for ſignification, we for obedience and chaſtiſement of our bodies.

Chriſts ſpittle worketh miracles.

33. Spitting.) Not only by Chriſts vvord and vvil, but alſo by ceremonie and by application of external creatures vvhich be holy, miracles are vvrought. as by Chriſts ſpittle, vvhich vvas not part of his perſon, being a ſuperfluity of his body, but yet moſt holy. *Theophyl. in 7 Marci.*

34. Ephphetha

34 *Ephphetha.*) The Church doth most godly imitate and vse these very vvordes and ceremonies of our Sauiour in the Exorcismes before Baptisme, to the healing of their soules that are to be baptized, as Christ here healed the bodily infirmitie and the disease of the soule together. *Ambros. li. 1 de Sacram. c 1.*

Exorcismes and other ceremonies in Baptisme.

CHAP. VIII.

Of compassion he feedeth the people, 4000 vvith seuen loaues. 10 After al vvhich miracles as though they vvere yet vnsufficient to proue him to be Christ, the obstinate Pharisees do require some miracle from heauen. 13 Wherevpon forsaking them, he vvarneth his Disciples to bevvare of the leauen of their doctrine, neither to feare vvant of necessaries. 22 He healeth a blind man by degrees and vvith ceremonies. 27 Peter confesseth him (though men al this vvhile had not learned so farre) to be Christ. 31 and by and by he reuealeth to them his passion, 32 rebuking also Peter for dissuading it, 34 and shevving that it is a thing vvherein al that vvil be saued (namely in time of persecution) must folovv him.

Mt. 15, 32.

1 IN those daies againe vvhen there vvas a great multitude, and had not what to eate: calling his Disciples together, he saith to 2 them, † I haue compassion vpon the multitude: because loe ∴ three daies they now endure vvith me, neither haue vvhat to 3 eate. † and if I dimisse them fasting into their home, they vvil faint in the vvay: for some of them 4 came farre of. † And his Disciples ansvvered him, Whence may a man fil them here vvith bread in the vvildernes? 5 † And he asked them, Hovv many loaues haue ye? Who said, 6 Seuen. † And he commaunded the multitude to sit dovvne vpon the ground. And taking the seuen loaues, giuing thankes he brake, and " gaue to his Disciples for to set before them, 7 and they did set them before the multitude. † And they had a fevv litle fishes: and " he blessed them, and commaunded 8 them to be set before them. † And they did eate and vvere filled. and they tooke vp that vvhich vvas left of the fragments, seuen maundes. 9 † And they that had eaten vvere about foure thousand: and he dimissed them.

The Gospel vpõ the 6 Sunday after Pentecost.

∴ Great feruour and deuotion in the good people, and exceding force in our Maisters preaching, that made thẽ abide fasting so long to heare his diuine sermons.

Mt. 15, 39. 16, 1.

10 † And * immediatly going vp into the boate vvith his 11 Disciples, he came into the quarters of Dalmanûtha. † And the Pharisees vvent forth, and began to question vvith him, 12 asking of him a signe from heauen, tempting him. † And groning in spirit, he saith, Why doth this generation aske a signe? Amen I say to you, If a signe shal be giuen to this ge-13 neration. † And leauing them, he vvent vp againe into the boate, and passed beyond the straite.

† And they forgot to take bread: and they had but one 14 loafe vvith them in the boate. † And he commaunded them, 15 saying, Looke vvel and bevvare of the leauen of the Pharisees, and the leauen of Herod. † And they reasoned among 16 them selues saying, Because vve haue not bread. † Which 17 IESVS knovving, saith to them, Why doe you reason, because you haue not bread? do you not yet knovv nor vnderstand? yet haue ye your hart blinded? † hauing eies see 18 you not? and hauing eares heare you not? Neither do you remember? † When * I brake fiue loaues among fiue thousand: 19 and hovv many baskets ful of fragmẽts tooke you vp? They say to him, Tvvelue. † * When also seuen loaues among foure 20 thousand, hovv many maundes of fragments tooke you vp? And they say to him, Seuen. † And he said to them, Hovv do 21 you not yet vnderstand?

Mar. 6, 38.

Mr. 8, 5.

† And they come to Bethsaida: and they bring to him one 22 blinde, and desired him that he vvould :: touche him. † And 23 taking the hand of the blinde, he led him forth out of the tovvne: and spitting into his eies, imposing his hands, he asked him if he savv any thing. † And looking vp, he said, I see 24 men as it vvere trees, vvalking. † After that againe he imposed 25 his hands vpon his eies, and be began to see, and vvas restored, so that he savv al things clerely. † And he sent him in- 26 to his house, saying, Goe into thy house: and if thou enter in to the tovvne, tel no body.

:: Our Sauiour vsed to worke much by touching: that we may learne not to cõtemne the corporal and external application of holy things, nor to chalẽge by the spirit and faith only, as Heretikes doe.

† And * IESVS vvent forth and his Disciples into the 27 tovvnes of Cæsarêa-Philippi: and in the vvay he asked his Disciples, saying to them, Whom do men say that I am? † Who ansvvered him, saying, Iohn the Baptist, some Elias, & 28 other some as it vvere one of the Prophets. † Then he saith 29 to them, But vvhom do you say that I am? Peter ansvvering said to him, Thou art Christ. † And he threatened them that 30 they should not tel any man of him.

Mt. 16, 13.
Lu. 9, 18

† And he began to teache them, that the Sonne of man 31 must suffer many things, and be reiected of the Auncients and of the high Priestes and the Scribes, and be killed: and after three daies rise againe. † And he spake the vvord open- 32 ly. And Peter taking him, began to rebuke him. † Who tur- 33 ning, and seeing his Disciples, threatened Peter, saying, Goe behind me Satan, because thou sauourest not the things that are of God, but that are of men. † And calling the multitude 34 together

together vvith his Disciples, he said to them, If any man vvil folovv me, let him deny him self, and take vp his crosse, and folovv me. 35 † For he that vvil saue his life, shal lose it: and he that shal lose his life "for me and the Gospel, shal saue it. 36 † For vvhat shal it profit a man, if he " gaine the vvhole 37 vvorld, and suffer damage of his soule? † Or vvhat permuta-38 tion shal a man giue for his soule? † For he that shal be ashamed of me, and of my vvordes in this aduouterous and sinful generation, the Sonne of man also vvil be ashamed of him, vvhen he shal come in the glorie of his father vvith the holy Angels.

ANNOTATIONS
CHAP. VIII.

6. *Gaue to his disciples.*] He serueth the people not immediatly him self, but by the Apostles ministerie: to teach vs that we must receiue Christes Sacraments and doctrine, not at our owne hand, but of his Priests and our Pastours.

7. *Blessed them.*] So is it in some ancient Greeke copies, agreable to our Latin, and in S. Luke (Luc. 9, 16.) expresly in the common Greeke text, that he blessed the fiue loaues and the two fishes: which must be alwaies marked against the Heretikes, which denie this blessing to pertaine to the creatures, but feine it alwaies to be referred to God for thanks giuing. For if it were so, he would haue said grace but once for that whole refection: but he did seuerally blesse both the bread first, and afterward the fishes also, multiplying them by his said blessing (as* he did mankind and other creatures in the beginning by blessing them) (Gen. 1, 22, 28.) and so working effectually some change or alteration in the very creatures them selues.

εὐλογήσας αὐτὰ.

Blessing of creatures vvorketh an effect in thé.

35. *For me and the Gospel.*] By the Gospel is signified, not only the foure Euangelistes, but al Scriptures, and whatsoeuer Christ said that is not in Scripture: for he saith in this very place, *He that shal be ashamed of my wordes, the Sonne of man wil be ashamed of him &c.* Neither his owne wordes only, but whatsoeuer the Apostles taught in word or writing: for our Sauiour saith (Luc. 9.), *He that despiseth you, despiseth me.* For defence of any of al these and of euery Article of the Catholike faith, we ought to die, and this is to lose our life for Christ and his Gospel.

What is to suffer for the Gospel.

36. *Gaine the whole world.*] Let such note this, that for feare or flattery of the world cōdescend to obey the vniust lawes of men touching religion, against their owne consciences: and be content for the rest of a few daies of this life, and for sauing their temporal goods, to lose their soule and the ioyes of heauen.

Doing against our owne conscience.

CHAP. IX.

The more to confirme them, he giueth them in his Transfiguration a sight of his glorie, whereunto Suffering doth bring, 9 and then againe doth inculcate his Passion. 14 A Diuel also he casteth out, which his Disciples (vpon whom therfore the peruerse Scribes triumphed in his absence) could not, for lacke of fasting and praying. 30 Being yet in Galilee, he reuealeth more about his Passion. 33 And (because in the way to Capharnaum they contended for the Primacie (he teacheth them that humility is the way to Primacie before God: 38 bidding them also, not to prohibit such as be not against them: nor to giue scandal to any one of the faithful. and on the other side, the faithful to auoid them by whom they may be scandalized and fall, be they neuer so neere vnto them.

ND he ſaid to them, Amen I ſay to you, that there be ſome of them that ſtand here, vvhich ſhal not taſt of death, vntil they ſee the kingdom of God comming in povver. † :: And after ſix daies IESVS taketh Peter and Iames and Iohn: and bringeth them alone into a high mountaine apart, and vvas transfigured before them. † And his garments vvere made gliſtering and vvhite excedingly as ſnovv, the like vvhereof a fuller cannot make vvhite vpon the earth. † And there appeared to them :: Elias vvith Moyſes: and they vvere talking vvith IESVS. † And Peter anſvvering, ſaid to IESVS, Rabbi, it is good for vs to be here: and let vs make three tabernacles, one for thee, and one for Moyſes, and one for Elias. † For he knevv not vvhat he ſaid: for they vvere frighted vvith feare: † and there vvas a cloude ouerſhadovving them, and a voice came out of the cloude, ſaying, This is my Sonne moſt deere: heare ye him. † And immediatly looking about, they ſavv no man any more but IESVS only vvith them. † And as they deſcẽded from the mountaine, he commaunded them that they ſhould not tel any man vvhat things they had ſeen: but vvhen the Sonne of man ſhal be riſen againe from the dead. † And they kept in the vvord vvith them ſelues: queſtioning together vvhat that ſhould be, *when he ſhal be riſen from the dead.*

1 2 3 4 5 6 7 8 9 10

Mt. 16, 27. 17, 1 Lu. 9, 27

:: See the Annotations vpon the 17 of S. Matthew.

:: The law and the Prophets ioyne with Chriſt and his Goſpel: the one ſignified by Moyſes, the other by Elias. By whoſe apparitions here we alſo learne that ſometime there may be perſonal entercourſe betwixt the liuing & the dead, though not ordinarily.

† And they aſked him, ſaying, What ſay the Phariſees then and the Scribes, that * Elias muſt come firſt? † Who anſvvering ſaid to them, Elias vvhen he commeth firſt, ſhal reſtore al things: and ˋ hovv' it is vvritten of the Sonne of man, that he ſhal ſuffer many things and be contemned. † But I ſay to you that "Elias alſo is come (and they haue done to him vvhatſoeuer they vvould) as it is vvritten of him.

11 12 13

Mal. 4, 5

as

† And * cõming to his Diſciples, he ſavv a great multitude about them, and the Scribes queſtioning vvith them. † And forthvvith al the people ſeeing IESVS, vvas aſtonied, and much afraid: and running to him, ſaluted him. † And he aſked them, What do you queſtion of among you? † And one of the multitude anſvvering, ſaid, Maiſter, I haue brought my ſonne to thee, hauing a dumme ſpirit, † Who, vvhereſoeuer he taketh him, daſheth him, and he fometh, and gnaſheth vvith the teeth, and vvithereth: and I ſpake to thy Diſciples to caſt him out, and they could not. † Who anſvvering them, ſaid,

14 15 16 17 18 19

Mt. 17, 14. Lu. 9, 37

The Goſpel vpõ Weneſday in the Imber Weeke of September.

said, O incredulous generation, hovv long shal I be vvith you? hovv long shal I suffer you? bring him vnto me. 20 † And they brought him. And vvhen he had seen him, immediatly the spirit troubled him: and being throvven vpon the 21 ground, he tumbled foming. † And he asked his father, Hovv long time is it since this hath chaunced vnto him? But he said, 22 From his infancie: † and often times hath he cast him into fire and into vvaters, to destroy him. but if thou canst any 23 thing, helpe vs, hauing compassion on vs. † And Iesus said to him, If thou canst beleeue, al things are possible to him that 24 beleeueth. † And incontinent the father of the boy crying out, vvith teares said, I do beleeue Lord: helpe my increduli-25 ty. † And vvhen IESVS savv the people running together, he threatened the vncleane spirit, saying to him, Deafe and dumme spirit, I commaunde thee, goe out of him, and enter 26 not any more into him. † And crying out, and greatly tearing him, he vvent out of him, and he became as dead, so that 27 many said, That he is dead. † But IESVS holding his hand, 28 lifted him vp: and he rose. † And vvhen he vvas entred into the house, his Disciples secretely asked him, Why could not 29 vve cast him out? † And he said to them, This kinde can goe out by nothing, but ∴ by prayer and fasting. ⫞

∴ Note the great force of prayer, and fasting.

Mt. 17, 22. Lu. 9, 21

30 † And * departing thence they passed by Galilee, neither 31 vvould he that any man should knovv. † And he taught his Disciples, and said to them, That the Sonne of man shal be betrayed into the hands of men, and they shal kil him, and 32 being killed the third day he shal rise againe. † But they knevv not the vvord: and they vvere afraid to aske him.

Mt. 18, 1 Lu. 9, 46.

33 † And * they came to Capharnaum. Vvho, vvhen he vvas in the house, asked them, What did you treate of in the vvay? 34 † But they held their peace. for in the vvay they had disputed among them selues, vvhich of them should be the greater. 35 † And sitting dovvne, he called the Tvvelue, and saith to them, If any man vvil be first, he shal be last of al, and the mi-36 nister of al. † And taking a childe, he set him in the middes of them. Vvhom vvhen he had embraced, he said to them, 37 † Vvhosoeuer shal receiue one of such children in my name, receiueth me. and vvhosoeuer shal receiue me, receiueth not me, but him that sent me.

Lu. 9, 49.

38 † * Iohn ansvvered him, saying, Maister vve savv one casting out deuils ″ in thy name, vvho folovveth not vs, and vve

prohi-

prohibited him. † But IESVS said, Do not prohibit him. 39 for there is no man that doth a miracle in my name, and can soone speake il of me. † for he that is not against you, is for 40 you. † For vvhosoeuer shal giue you to drinke a cuppe of 41 vvater in my name, because you are Christs: amen I say to you, he shal not lose his :: revvard. † And vvhosoeuer 42 shal :: scandalize one of these litle ones beleeuing in me: it is good for him rather if a milstone vvere put about his necke, and he vvere cast into the sea. † And if thy hand scandalize 43 thee, cut it of. it is good for thee to enter into life, maimed, then hauing tvvo hands to goe into hel, into the fire vnquencheable, † vvhere their vvorme dieth not, and the fire quen- 44 cheth not. † And if thy foote scandalize thee, choppe it of. 45 it is good for thee to enter into life euerlasting, lame, rather then hauing tvvo feete, to be cast into the hel of vnquencheable fire, † vvhere their vvorme dieth not, and the fire 46 quencheth not. † And if thine eye scandalize thee, cast it 47 out. it is good for thee vvith one eye to enter intō the kingdom of God, rather then hauing tvvo eies, to be cast into the hel of fire, † vvhere their vvorme dieth not, and the fire 48 quencheth not. † For euery one shal be salted vvith fire: and 49 ★ euery victime shal be salted vvith salt. † Salt is good. but if 50 the salt shal be vnseasoned: vvhervvith vvil you season it? Haue salt in you, and haue peace among you.

:: Revvard for almes deedes, whereby it is euident they be meritorious.

:: To giue scandal by our life to the weake in faith, is a great sinne, specially in Priests, Preachers, and Princes.

★ Leu. 2, 13

ANNOTATIONS
CHAP. IX.

Elias. Moyses.

4. *Elias with Moyses.*) Moyses representeth the persons of al the Saincts that shal be departed this life when Christ commeth in his Maiestie to iudgement: And Elias (who was then liuing) figureth the holy men that shal then be found aliue when he commeth in glorie. Who both shal then begin to reigne with Christ in glorie. *Beda in 9. Marc.*

Elias and Iohn Baptist Eremites.

13. *Elias also is come.*) Elias was Zelous for Gods Law, a great reprehender of sinne, and an Eremite, and shal be the Precursor of Christ in his second Aduent: So was Iohn before his first Aduent, a Zelatour, a Corrector, an Eremite, and his Precursor. *Theod. in caten. Thomas super hunc locum.* See S. Hierom in the life of Paul the eremite, that both Elias and Iohn Baptist vvere counted principal professours of that life.

The name of IESVS worketh miracles.

38. *In thy name.*) Miracles are vvrought sometime by the name of IESVS, whatsoeuer the men be, when it is for the proofe of a truth or for the glorie of God. In so much that Iulian the Apostata him selfe did driue away diuels with the signe of the Crosse: as *S. Gregorie Nazianzene* writeth *orat. 1 in Iulian. Theodoret. li. 3 c. 3 hist.* And so also Heretikes may doe miracles among the Heathen, to prooue any article of the Christian faith: but they neuer did nor euer shal vvorke any miracle to prooue any of their erroneous opinions. as, to prooue that Christ is not really in the B. Sacrament.

CHAP. X.

He answereth the tempting Pharisees (and againe his disciples afterward) that the case of a man with his wife shalbe (as in the first institution) vtterly indissoluble. 13 He blesseth children. 17 He sheweth what is to be done to get life euerlasting. 21 What also for a rich man, to be perfect: 28 as also what passing reward they shal haue that doe so, in time of persecution. 32 He reuealeth more to his Disciples touching his Passion: 35 bidding the two ambitious suiters to thinke rather of suffering with him: 41 and teaching vs in the rest of his Disciples, not to be greeued at our Ecclesiastical Superiours, considering they are (as he was him self) to toile for our saluation. 46 Then going out of Iericho, he giueth sight to a blinde man.

THE THIRD part of this Gospel, Christes cōming into Iewrie toward his Passion.

Mt. 19, 1

1 AND rising vp thence, he commeth into the coastes of Ievvrie beyond Iordan: and the multitudes assemble againe vnto him. and as he vvas accustomed, againe he 2 taught them. † And the Pharisees comming neere, asked him, Is it lavvful for a 3 man to dimisse his vvife? tempting him. † But he ansvvering, 4 said to them, Vvhat did Moyses commaund you? † Who said, * Moyses " permitted to vvrite a bil of diuorce, and to dimisse 5 her. † To vvhom IESVS ansvvering, said, For the hardnes 6 of your hart he vvrote you this precept. † but from the beginning of the creation * God made them male and femal. 7 † For this cause, * man shal leaue his father and mother: and 8 shal cleaue to his vvife, † and they tvvo shal be in one 9 flesh. therfore novv they are not tvvo, but one flesh. † That therfore vvhich God hath ioyned together, ∴ let not man separate.

Deut. 24, 1.

Gen. 1, 27.

Gen. 2, 24.

∴ The obligation betwixt man and wife is so great, that during life it can not be broken.

10 † And * in the house againe his Disciples asked him of 11 the same thing. † And he saith to them, Whosoeuer dimisseth his vvife and " marrieth an other: committeth aduoutrie vpon 12 her. † And if the vvife dimisse her husband, and mary an other, she committeth aduoutrie.

Mt. 19, 9

Mt. 5, 32

Lu. 16, 18.

1. Cor. 7, 11.

13 † And * they offered to him yong children, that he might touche them. And the Disciples threatened those that offered 14 them. † Whom vvhen IESVS savv, he tooke it il, and said to them, Suffer the litle children to come vnto me, and prohi-15 bit them not. for the kingdom of God is for such. † Amen I say to you: Whosoeuer receiueth not the kingdom of God 16 as a litle childe, shal not enter into it. † And embracing them, and imposing hands vpon them, he ∴ blessed them.

Mt. 19, 13.

Lu. 18, 15.

∴ Our Sauiour gaue the children his blessing.

17 † And vvhen he vvas gone forth in the vvay, a certaine man running forth and kneeling before him asked him,

* Good Maister, vvhat ſhal I doe that I may receiue life euerlaſting? † And IESVS ſaid to him, Why calleſt thou me good? 18 " None is good but one, God. † Thou knovveſt the ∵ commaundements, * *Commit not aduoutrie, Kil not, Steale not, Beare not falſe vvitneſſe, doe no fraude, Honour thy father and mother.* † But he anſvvering, ſaid to him, Maiſter al theſe things I haue obſerued from my youth. † And IESVS beholding him, loued him, and 21 ſaid to him, One thing is vvanting vnto thee: ∵ goe, ſel vvhatſoeuer thou haſt, and giue to the poore, and thou ſhalt haue treaſure in heauen: and come, folovv me. † Who being ſtroken ſad at the vvord, vvent avvay ſorovvful. for he had many poſſeſsions. † And IESVS looking about, ſaith to his Diſciples, Hovv hardly ſhal they that haue money, enter into the kingdom of God! † And the Diſciples vvere aſtonied at his 24 vvordes. But IESVS againe anſvvering, ſaith to them, Children, hovv hard is it for them that truſt in money, to enter into the kingdom of God! † It is eaſier for a camel to 25 paſſe through a nedels eie, then for " a rich man to enter into the kingdom of God. † Vvho marueled more, ſaying to them 26 ſelues, And vvho can be ſaued? † And IESVS beholding 27 them, ſaith, Vvith men it is impoſsibile: but not vvith God. for al things are poſsible vvith God. † And Peter began to 28 ſay vnto him, Behold, vve haue left al things, and haue folovved thee. † IESVS anſvvering, ſaid, ∵ Amen I ſay to 29 you, there is no man vvhich hath left houſe, or brethren, or ſiſters, or father, or mother, or children, or landes for me and for the Goſpel: † that ſhal not receiue " an hundred times ſo 30 much novv in this time: houſes, and brethren, and ſiſters, and mothers, and children, and landes, vvith perſecutions: and in the vvorld to come life euerlaſting. † But * many that are firſt, 31 ſhal be laſt: and the laſt, firſt.

† And they vvere in the vvay going vp to Hieruſalem: and 32 IESVS vvent before them, and they vvere aſtonied: and folovving vvere afraid. And * taking againe the Tvvelue, he began to tel them the things that ſhould befal him. † That, be- 33 hold vve goe vp to Hieruſalem, and the Sonne of man ſhal be betrayed to the cheefe Prieſtes, and to the Scribes and Auncients, and they ſhal condemne him to death, and ſhal deliuer him to the Gentiles, † and they ſhal mocke him, and 34 ſpit on him, and ſcourge him, and kil him, and the third day he ſhal riſe againe.

∵ Note that the keeping of Gods cōmaundements procureth life euerlaſting.

∵ This is counſel of perfectiō (not a precept) which the Religious profeſſing and keeping voluntary pouertie, doe folow.

∵ Exceding happie be they that can forſake their temporal things for religion.

Mt. 19, 16. *Lu.* 18, 18. *Exo.* 20, 13.

Mt. 19, 30. *Lu.* 13, 30.

Mt. 20, 17. *Lu.* 18, 31.

† And

Mt. 20, 20.

35 † And * there come to him Iames and Iohn the ſonnes of Zebedee, ſaying, Maiſter, vve vvil that vvhat thing ſoeuer
36 vve ſhal aſke, thou doe it to vs. † But he ſaid to them, What
37 vvil you that I doe to you? † And they ſaid, Graunt to vs, that vve may ſit, one on thy right hand, and the other on thy
38 left hand, in thy glorie. † And IESVS ſaid to them, You vvotte not vvhat you aſke. can you drinke the cuppe that I drinke: or be baptized vvith the baptiſme vvhervvith I am baptized?
39 † But they ſaid to him, Vve can. And IESVS ſaid to them, The cuppe in deede vvhich I drinke, you ſhal drinke: and vvith the baptiſme vvhervvith I am baptized, ſhal you be bapti-
40 zed: † but to ſit on my right hand or on my left, is not mine
41 to giue vnto you, but to vvhom it is prepared. † And the ten hearing, began to be diſpleaſed at Iames and Iohn.

Mt. 20, 25. Lu. 22, 25.

42 † And IESVS calling them, ſaith to them, * You knovv that they vvhich ſeeme to rule ouer the gentiles, ouerrule them:
43 and their Princes haue povver ouer them. † But it is not ſo in you. but vvhoſoeuer vvil be greater, ſhal be your miniſter:
44 † and vvhoſoeuer vvil be firſt among you, ſhal be the ſer-
45 uant of al. † For the Sonne of man alſo is not come to be miniſtred vnto, but to miniſter, and to giue his life a redemption for many.

Mt. 20, 29. Lu. 18, 35.

46 † And * they come to Iericho: and vvhen he departed from Iericho, and his Diſciples, and a very great multitude, the ſonne of Timæus, Bar-timæus the blinde man, ſate by the way
47 ſide begging. † Vvho vvhen he had heard, that it is IESVS of Nazareth: he began to crie, and to ſay, IESVS, ſonne of Da-
48 uid, haue mercie vpon me. † And many threatened him, to hold his peace. but he cried much more, Sonne of Dauid,
49 haue mercie vpon me. And IESVS ſtanding ſtil commaunded him to be called. And they call the blinde man, ſaying to
50 him, Be of better comfort, ariſe, he calleth thee. † Vvho caſting
51 of his garment leapt vp, and came to him. † And IESVS anſvvering, ſaid to him, Vvhat vvilt thou that I doe vnto thee? And the blinde man ſaid to him, Rabbôni, that I may
52 ſee. † And IESVS ſaid to him, Goe thy vvaies, thy faith hath made the ſafe. And forthvvith he ſavv, and folovved him in the vvay.

ANNOTATIONS
CHAP. X.

Toleration and permission of euil.

4. *Permitted.*) Some things are permitted, though not approued or allowed, to auoid greater inconueniences. No man may doe euil for any cause, but he may permit other mens euils for diuerse causes: as God him self doeth, who can doe no euil. So doth the Prince and Common-wealth permit lesser euils to eschew greater, and so may the Holy Church much more (as S. Augustine saith she doeth) being placed among much chaffe and much cockle, tolerate many things: and yet whatsoeuer is against faith and good life, she neither approueth, nor dissembleth with silence, nor committeth.

Aug. ep. 119 c. 19.

Mariage after diuorce vnlawful.

11. *And marrieth an other.*) That which S. Matthew vttered more obscurely, and is mistaken of some, as though he meant that for fornication a man might put away his wife and marry an other, is here by this Euangelist (as also by S. Luke) put out of doubt, generally auouching, that whosoeuer putteth away his wife and marrieth an other, committeth aduoutrie. *Aug. li. 1 de adult. coniug. c. 11 & sequentibus.*

Lu. 16, 18.

18. *None is good.*) None is entirely, substantially, and of him self good, but God: though by participation of Gods goodnes, men are truely also called good.

25. *A riche man.*) He is here called a rich man that hath his confidence (as here is expressed) in his treasure, and had rather forsake his faith and duty to God, then lose them. as al they which liue in Schisme or Heresie to saue their goods.

Their reward in this life that forsake ought for Gods sake.

30. *An hundred times so much.*) Sometime God doth so blesse men also in worldly benefites that haue forsaken al for him, as S. Gregorie, S. Augustine, and S. Paulinus: but the principal meaning is, * that he wil giue to such men in this life aboundance of grace and spiritual comfort and contentatiō and ioy of cōscience (as they feele which haue experience) the which spiritual giftes excede the temporal commodities more then an hundred fold. in so much that he that hath fully forsaken but smal things for religion, would not forsake religion to haue al the world.

Hiero. in 19 Mat.

CHAP. XI.

THE fourth part of this Gospel, the Holy weeke of his Passion in Hierusalem.

Being novv come to the place of his Passion, he entreth with triumph as their Christ. 12 He curseth that fruitlesse leafie tree. 15 He sheweth his Zeale for the house of God: for which the Rulers seeke his destruction. 24 He exhorteth his Disciples to stedfastnes of faith, and to forgiue their enemies. 27 He auoucheth his power by the witnes of Iohn who was a man sent of God.

PALME-Sunday.

Mt. 21, 1
Lu. 19, 20.
Io. 12, 15

AND vvhen they came nigh vnto Hierusalem 1 and Bethania to Mount-oliuet, he sendeth tvvo of his Disciples, † and saith to them, Goe in- 2 to the tovvne that is against you, and immediatly entring in thither, you shal finde a colt tied, vpon vvhich no man yet hath sitten: loose him, and bring him. † And if any man shal say to you, Vvhat doe you? 3 say that he is needeful for our Lord: and incontinent he vvil send him hither. † And going their vvaies, they found the colt 4 tied before the gate vvithout in the meeting of tvvo vvaies: and they loose him. † And certaine of them that stoode there, 5 said to them, Vvhat doe you loosing the colt? † Vvho 6 said to them as IESVS had commaunded them: and they did let him goe vvith them. † And they brought the colt to 7 IESVS: and they lay their garments vpon him, and he sate vpon him. † And ∷ many spred their garments in the vvay: 8 and

∷ Al these voluntary dueties were grateful to our Sauiour, and so be the like done to him in the B. Sacrament.

and others did cut boughes from the trees, and strawed
9 them in the way. † And they that went before and they
that folowed, cried saying, *Hosanna, blessed is he that commeth in the* (Ps. 117, 26.)
10 *name of our Lord.* † *blessed is the kingdom of our father Dauid that commeth,*
11 *Hosanna in the highest.* † And he entred Hierusalem into the temple: and hauing vewed al things round about, when now
the euening houre was come, he went forth into Bethania
with the Twelue.

MVNDAY.

12 † And the next day when they departed from Bethania,
13 he was an hungred. † And * when he had seen a farre of a (Mt. 21, 19.)
figtree hauing leaues, he came if happily he could finde any
thing on it. And when he was come to it, he found nothing
14 but leaues. for it was not the time for figges. † And answering he said to it, Now no man eate fruite of the any more
15 for euer. And his Disciples heard it. † And they come to Hierusalem.

And * when he was entred into the temple, he began (Mt. 21, 12. Lu. 19, 45.)
to cast out them that sold and bought in the temple, and the
tables of the bankers, and the chaires of them that sold pi-
16 geons he ouerthrew. † and he suffred not that any man
17 should carie a" vessel through the temple: † and he taught,
saying to them, Is it not written, *That my house shal be called the house* (Esa. 56, 7.)
18 *of prayer to al nations? But you haue made it" a denne of theeues.* † Which (Ier. 7, 11)
when the cheefe Priestes and the Scribes had heard, they
sought how they might destroy him. for they were afraid
of him, because the whole multitude was in admiration
19 vpon his doctrine. † And when euening was come, he
went forth out of the citie.

TVESDAY.

20 † And * when they passed by in the morning, they saw (Mt. 21, 20.)
21 the figtree withered from the rootes. † And Peter remembring,
said to him, Rabbi, behold the figtree that thou didst curse,
22 is withered. † [b] And IESVS answering saith to them, Haue
23 :: faith of God. † Amen I say to you, that whosoeuer shal
say to this mountaine, Be taken vp and be cast into the
sea, and shal not stagger in his hart, but beleeue that whatsoeuer he saith, shal be done: it shal be done vnto him.
24 † Therfore I say to you, al things whatsoeuer you aske,
praying, beleeue that you shal receiue, and they shal come
25 vnto you. ¶ † And when you shal stand to pray, forgiue if
you haue ought against any man: that also your father which
26 is in heauen, may forgiue you your sinnes. † :: If so be that

b The Gospel for S. Gregorius Thaumaturgus Nouemb. 17. And in a Votiue Masse for any necessitie.

:: Faith of God is to beleeue that he is able, and that he wil doe it if it be expedient, and no impediment on our part.

:: God neuer forgiueth sinnes to him that pardoneth not his enemies fro his hart. Whereby it is euident that ...re is requi... ...hen only ...

you vvil not forgiue, neither vvil your father that is in heauen, forgiue you your sinnes. † And they come againe to Hierusalem. 27

And * vvhen he vvalked in the temple, there come to him the cheefe Priestes and the Scribes and the Auncients, † and they say to him, In vvhat povver doest thou these things? and vvho hath giuen thee this povver, that thou shouldest doe these things? † And IESVS ansvvering said to them, I also vvil aske you one vvord, and ansvver you me: and I vvil tel you in vvhat povver I doe these things. † The baptisme of Iohn vvas it from heauen, or from men? ansvver me. † But they thought vvith them selues, saying, If vve say, From heauen: he vvil say, Vvhy then did you not beleeue him? † If vve say, From men, they feared the people. for al accounted Iohn that he vvas in deede a Prophet. † And they ansvvering say to IESVS, Vve knovv not. And IESVS ansvvering saith to them, Neither do I tel you in vvhat povver I doe these things. 28 29 30 31 32 33

Mt. 21, 23. Lu. 20, 2.

ANNOTATIONS
CHAP. XI.

Profaning of Gods Church.

16. Vessel through the temple.] He could not abide to see the Temple of God profaned, no nor suffred those things to be done in it, which otherwise were not vnlawful but honest, if they had been done in dewe place. How much lesse can he abide the profaning of Churches now with Heretical seruice and preaching of heresie and blasphemie?

17. Denne of theeues.] If the Temple was then a denne of theeues, because of profane and secular merchandise: how much more now, when the house appointed for the Holy Sacrifice and Sacrament of the Bodie of Christ, is made a denne for the Ministers of Caluins bread?

CHAP. XII.

He foretelleth to the Iewes in a parable their reprobation most worthy, and the vocation of the Church of the Gentils in their place, 10 him self being the headstone thereof. 13 He defeateth the snare of the Pharisees and Herodians, about paying tribute to Cæsar: 18 answereth also the inuention of the Sadducees against the Resurrection: 28 also the opposition of a Scribe. 35 And so hauing put al the busie sectes to silence, he turneth and poseth them on the other side, because they imagined Christ should be no more but a man. 38 Bidding the people to beware of the Scribes, being ambitious and hypocrites. 41 He commendeth the poore Widovv for her two mites, aboue al.

:: This man, is God the Father. This vineyard, is (as Esay saith 5, 1.) the house of Israel. The seruants sent, are Moyses and the Prophets, whō the Iewes did diuersely afflict and persecute.

ND he began to speake to them in parables, :: A man planted a vineyard and made a hedge about it, and digged a trough, and built a tovvre, and let it out to husbandmen: and vvent forth into a strange countrie. † And he sent to the husbandmen in season a seruant, to receiue of 1 2

Es. 5, 1. Mt. 21, 33. Lu. 20, 9.

3 of the husbandmen, of the fruite of the vineyard. † Vvho ap-
4 prehending him, bette him: and sent him avvay emptie. † And againe he sent to them an other seruant: and him they vvoun-
5 ded in the head, and vsed him reprochefully. † And againe he sent an other, and him they killed: and many other, beating
6 certaine, and killing others. † Therfore hauing yet one :: sonne most deere: him also he sent vnto them last saying,
7 That they vvill reuerence my sonne. † But the husbandmen said one to an other, This is the heier: come, let vs kill him:
8 and the inheritance shal be ours. † And apprehending him,
9 they killed him, and cast him forth out of the vineyard. † What therfore vvil the lord of the vineyard doe? :: He vvil come and destroy the husbandmen: and vvil giue the vineyard to
10 others. † Neither haue you read this scripture, *The :: stone vvhich*
11 *the builders reiected, the same is made the head of the corner:* † *By our Lord vvas this*
12 *done, and it is maruelous in our eies?* † And they sought to lay hands on him, and they feared the multitude. for they knevv that he spake this parable to them. And leauing him they vvent their vvay.

:: His Sonne is CHRIST our Sauiour, vvho the Ievves crucified out of the citie of Ierusalem, as it vvere casting him out of the vineyard.

:: The Ievves and their guides to vvhom the vineyard vvas set, destroied: and Gods vineyard giuen to the Apostles and their Successors in the Gentils.

:: CHRIST is become the corner stone of the Synagogue and the Church in vvhich the faithful both of the Ievves and Gentils are conteined.

Ps. 117, 22.

13 † * And they send to him certaine of the Pharisees and of the Herodians: that they should entrappe him in his vvord.
14 † Vvho comming, say to him, Maister, vve knovv that thou art a true speaker, and carest not for any man: for thou doest not looke vpon the person of men, but teachest the vvay of God in truth. is it lavvful to giue tribute to Cæsar: or shal
15 vve not giue it? † Vvho knovving their subteltie, said to them, Vvhy tempt you me? bring me a penie that I may see
16 it. † But they brought it him. And he saith to them, Vvhose is
17 this image, and inscription? They say to him, Cæsars. † And IESVS ansvvering, said to them, Render therfore the things that are Cæsars, to Cæsar: and that are Gods, "to God. And they marueled at him.

Mt. 22, 15. Lu. 26, 20.

18 † And * there came to him the Saducees that say there is
19 no resurrection: and they asked him saying, Maister, † * Moyses vvrote vnto vs, that if any mans brother die, and leaue his vvife, and leaue no children, "his brother shal take his vvife
20 and raise vp seede to his brother. † There vvere therfore seuen brethren: and the first tooke a vvife, and died leauing no issue.
21 † And the second tooke her, and died: and neither this left is-
22 sue. And the third in like maner. † And the seuen tooke her in like sort: and did not leaue issue. Last of al the vvoman also died

Mt. 22, 23. Lu. 20, 27. Act. 23, 6. Deu. 25, 5.

died. † In the resurrection therfore vvhen they shal rise 23 againe, vvhose vvife shal she be of these? for the seuen had her to vvife. † And IESVS ansvvering, said to them, Do ye 24 not therfore erre", not knovving the scriptures, nor" the povver of God? † For vvhen they shal rise againe from the 25 dead, they shal neither marrie, nor be married, but are as the Angels in heauen. † And as concerning the dead, that they 26 do rise againe, haue you not read in the booke of Moyses, hovv in the bush God spake to him, saying, *I am the God of Abraham, and the God of Isaac, and the God of Iacob?* † He is not the God of 27 the dead, but of the liuing. You therfore are much deceiued.

Exo. 3,6

† And *there came one of the Scribes that had heard them 28 questioning, and seeing that he had wel answered them, asked him vvhich vvas the first cõmaundement of al. † And IESVS 29 ansvvered him, That the first commaundement of al is, *Heare Israel: the Lord thy God, is one God.* † *And thou shalt loue the Lord thy* 30 *God from thy vvhole hart, and vvith thy vvhole soul, and vvith thy vvhole minde, and vvith thy vvhole povver.* This is the first commaundement. † And the second is like to it, *Thou shalt loue they neighbour as thy self.* 31 An other commaundement greater then these there is not. † And the Scribe said to him, Vvel Maister, thou hast said in 32 truth, that there is one God, and there is none other besides him. † And that he be loued from the vvhole hart, and vvith 33 the vvhole vnderstanding, and vvith the vvhole soule, and vvith the vvhole strength: and ∷ to loue his neighbour as him self is a greater thing then al holocaustes and sacrifices. † And IESVS seeing that he had ansvvered vvisely, said to 34 him, Thou art not farre from the kingdom of God. And no man novv durst aske him.

Mt. 22, 34.

Deu. 6,5

Leu. 19, 18.

∷ This excellencie of Charitie teacheth vs that faith only is not sufficiẽt.

† And* IESVS ansvvering, said, teaching in the temple, 35 Hovv do the Scribes say, that Christ is the sonne of Dauid? † For Dauid him self saith in the holy Ghost: *Our Lord said to* 36 *my Lord, sit on my right hand, vntil I put thine enemies the foote-stoole of thy feete.* † Dauid therfore him self calleth him Lord, and vvhence is 37 he his sonne? And a great multitude heard him gladly.

Mt. 22, 41. Lu. 20, 41. Ps. 109, 1.

† And he said to them in his doctrine, * Take heede of the 38 Scribes that vvil vvalke in long robes, and be saluted in the market-place, † and sit in the first chaires in the Synagogs, 39 and loue the highest places at suppers: † vvhich deuoure 40 vvidovves houses vnder the pretence of long prayer: these

shal

ſhal receiue larger iudgement.

Lu.21,2.

41 ✝* And IESVS ſitting ouer againſt the treaſurie, beheld hovv the multitude did caſt money into the treaſurie, and
42 many rich men did caſt in much. ✝ And vvhen there came a certaine poore vvidovv, ſhe caſt in tvvo mites, vvhich
43 is a farthing. ✝ And calling his Diſciples together, he ſaith to them, Amen I ſay to you, that this poore vvidovv hath
44 caſt in ∷ more then al that haue caſt into the treaſurie. ✝ For al they of their aboundance haue caſt in: but ſhe, of her penurie hath caſt in al that ſhe had, her vvhole liuing.

∷ God doth accept almes that are correſpondent to euery mans abilitie: and the more able, the more muſt a mā giue.

ANNOTATIONS
CHAP. XII.

17. To God.] Theſe men were very circumſpect and wary to doe al duties to Cæſar, but of their dutie to God they had no regard. So Heretikes, to flatter temporal Princes, and by them to vphold their Hereſies, doe not only inculcate mens dutie to the Prince, diſſembling that which is dewe to God: but alſo giue to the Prince more then dew, and take from God his right and dutie. But Chriſt allowing Cæſar his right, warneth them alſo of their dutie toward God. And that is it which Catholikes inculcate, Obey God, doe as he commaundeth, Serue him firſt, and then the Prince.

God firſt to be ſerued, and then the Prince.

19. His brother ſhal take.) Marke wel here, that the Law which ſaith, Thou ſhalt not marry thy brothers wife, is not ſuch as admitteth no diſpenſation, as though this mariage were againſt nature. For here the ſame Law ſaith, that in ſome caſe, the brother not only might, but then was bound to marry his brothers wife.

Leu. 18,16. Deu. 25,5.

Marying the brothers wife.

24. Not knovving the Scriptures.) Who would haue thought that by this place of Scripture alleaged by Chriſt, the Reſurrection were proued? and yet we ſee that Chriſt doth hereby deduce it, and chargeth theſe great Doctors and Maiſters (which arrogated to them ſelues the knowledge of Scriptures) that it is their ignorance, that they knew not ſo to deduce it. No maruel then if the Holy Doctors and Catholike Church make the like deductions ſometime and proofes, where the Heretike doth not or wil not ſee ſo much, therfore no doubt, becauſe he knoweth not the Scriptures, whereof he boaſteth ſo much, nor the ſenſe of the Holy Ghoſt in them. For example, when of that place, *It ſhal not be forgiuen in this vvorld nor in the vvorld to come,* ancient fathers deduce, that there are ſinnes remitted after this life in Purgatorie. See *Mat. 12, 32.*

Many truthes deduced out of ſcripture, which Heretikes ſee not.

24. The power of God.) Euen ſo doe Heretikes erre two waies: becauſe they know not the Scriptures, which they interprete contrarie to the ſenſe of the whole Church and of al the ancient fathers: and becauſe they know not the power of God, that as he is able to raiſe the ſelfe ſame bodies againe, ſo he can make his body preſent in many places: but being altogether faithleſſe and not beleeuing his power, they diſpute of al ſuch matters only by reaſon and their owne imaginations.

Heretikes ignorant and without faith.

CHAP. XIII.

To his Diſciples (by occaſion of Hieruſalem and the Temples deſtruction) he foretelleth, 5 vvhat things ſhalbe before the conſummation of the vvorld, as ſpecially the Churches ful preaching vnto al nations. 14 Then, vvhat ſhalbe in the very conſummation, to vvit, Antichriſt vvith his paſsing great perſecution and ſeduction, but for a ſhort time. 24 then incontinent the day of Iudgement. 28 to our great comfort in thoſe miſeries vnder Antichriſt. 32 As for the moment, to vs it perteineth not to knovv it. 33 but rather euery man to vvatch, that vve be not vnprouided vvhen he commeth to ech one particularly by death.

See the Annotations vpon S. Matthew c. 24.

Mt. 24, 1
Lu. 21, 5.

AND vvhen he vvent out of the temple, one of 1 his Disciples saith to him, Maister, behold what maner of stones, and vvhat kinde of buildings. † And IESVS ansvvering, said to him, Seest 2 thou al these great buildings? There shal not be left a stone vpon a stone, that shal not be destroied.

† And vvhen he sate in Mount-oliuet against the temple, 3 Peter and Iames and Iohn and Andrevv asked him apart, † Tel vs, " vvhen shal these things be? and vvhat shal be the 4 signe vvhen al these things shal begin to be consummate? † And IESVS ansvvering began to say to them, See, 5 that no man seduce you. † for many shal come in my name 6 saying that " I am he: and they shal seduce many. † And vvhen 7 you shal heare of vvarres and bruites of vvarres, feare not. for these things must be, but the end is not yet. † For nation 8 shal rise against nation and kingdom against kingdom, and there shal be earthquakes in places, and famines. These things are the beginning of sorovves. † But looke to your selues. 9 For they shal deliuer you vp in Councels, and in Synagogs shal you be beaten, and you shal stand before Presidents and Kings for my sake, for a testimonie vnto them. † And into al 10 nations first the Gospel must be preached. † And vvhen they 11 shal leade you and deliuer you, be not careful before hand vvhat you shal speake: but that vvhich shal be giuen you in that houre, that speake ye. For it is not you that speake, but the holy Ghost. † And brother shal deliuer brother 12 vnto death, and the father his sonne: and the children shal arise against the parents, and shal vvorke their death. † And 13 you shal be odious to al men for my name. But he that shal endure vnto the end, he shal be saued.

TVESDAY night.

Great vvarres tovvard the later end.

Much persecutiō of the faithful and Catholike men in the later end.

Great treacherie and many false brethren at the same time.

Constancie and perseuerāce necessarie in time of persecution.

† And vvhen you shal see " *the abomination of desolation*, stan- 14 ding vvhere it ought not (he that readeth, let him vnderstand) then they that are in Ievvrie, let them flee vnto the mountaines: † and he that is on the house-toppe, let him not goe 15 dovvne into the house, nor enter in to take any thing out of his house: † and he that shal be in the field, let him not re- 16 turne backe to take his garment. † And vvo to them that are 17 vvith childe and that giue sucke in those daies. † But pray 18 that the things chaunce not in the vvinter. † For those daies 19 shal be such tribulations as vvere not from the beginning of the creation that God created vntil novv, neither shal be.

Dan. 9, 27.
2. Thess. 2, 4.

20 be. † And vnles the Lord had ſhortened the daies, no fleſh ſhould be ſaued: but for the elect vvhich he hath elected, he
21 hath :: ſhortened the daies. † And then if any man ſhal ſay
22 vnto you, Loe, here is Chriſt: loe, there: do not beleeue. † For there ſhal riſe vp falſe-Chriſts and falſe-Prophets, and they ſhal ſhevv " ſignes and vvonders, to ſeduce (if it be poſsible)
23 the elect alſo. † You therfore take heede: behold I haue foretold you al things.
24 † But in thoſe daies after that tribulation * the ſunne ſhal be
25 darkened, and the moone ſhal not giue her light, † and the ſtarres of heauen ſhal be falling dovvne, and the povvers
26 that are in heauen, ſhal be moued. † And then they ſhal ſee the * Sonne of man comming in the cloudes, vvith much
27 povver and glorie. † And then ſhal he ſend his Angels, and ſhal gather together his elect from the foure vvindes, from the vttermoſt part of the earth to the vttermoſt part of hea-
28 uen. † And of the figtree learne ye a parable. Vvhen novv the bough thereof is tender, and the leaues come forth, you
29 knovv that ſommer is very nigh. † ſo you alſo vvhen you ſhal ſee theſe things come to paſſe, knovv ye that it is very
30 nigh, at the doores. † Amen I ſay to you, that this generation
31 ſhal not paſſe, vntil al theſe things be done. † Heauen and earth ſhal paſſe, but my vvordes ſhal not paſſe.
32 † But of that day or houre no man knovveth, neither the
33 Angels in heauen, nor the :: Sonne, but the Father. † Take heede, vvatch, and pray. for you knovv not vvhen the time
34 is. † Euen as a man vvho being gone into a ſtrange countrie, left his houſe: and gaue his ſeruants authoritie * ouer ech
35 vvorke, and commaunded the porter to vvatch. † Vvatch ye therfore (for you knovv not vvhen the lord of the houſe commeth: at euen, or at midnight, or at the cocke crovving,
36 or in the morning) † leſt comming vpon a ſoden, he finde
37 you ſleeping. † And that vvhich I ſay to you, I ſay to al, Vvatch. ✠

Ez. 31, 7 *Ioel. 3, 15*

Dan. 7, 13.

:: Antichriſts reigne ſhalbe three yeres and a halfe. *Dan. 7. Apoc. 13.*

:: Not as though him ſelf knew not, as the Heretikes Agnoïtę held: but becauſe he knew it not for to teach it others, as being not expedient. *Ambr. de fide li. 5 c. 8.*

The Goſpel for a Cōfeſſor that is a Biſhop, And on the Anniuerſarie of the creation of a Biſhop.

ANNOTATIONS
CHAP. XIII.

4. When ſhal theſe things be?] The miſeries which did fall before the deſtruction of the Temple and citie of Hieruſalem, were a reſemblance of the extreme calamitie that ſhal befall before the later day at the time of Antichriſt: Wherevpon Chriſt ſpeaketh indifferently of both.

6. I am he.] As before the deſtruction of Hieruſalem, diuerſe Seducers aroſe, and called them ſelues Chriſtes, promiſing the people deliuerance from the feares and dangers they were in of

Arch heretikes be Falſe-Chriſts and Falſe-Prophets.

forraine souldiars: so shal there come many towards the end of the World, and make them selues Christes and Authors of Sectes, and shal gaine many Disciples: as in plaine wordes foloweth in this chapter v. 22. *There shal rise vp False-Christs and False-Prophets &c.*

Caluinisme tendeth to the abomination of desolation.

14. The abomination of desolation.] No heresie doth so properly and purposely tend to this abomination of desolation * which by Antichrist shal be atchieued, as this Caluinisme: which taketh away with other Sacraments and external worship of God, the very sacrifice of Christes Body and bloud. Which being taken away (as S. Cyprian saith) no religion can remaine.

Hyppolyt. li. de Antichristo. Cypr. de Cœn. Do. nu. 2.

22. Signes and Wonders.] False-Christes and False-Prophets be seducers, who in the later day by the power of the diuel shal seeme to worke wonders, and yet men must not beleeue them. Much lesse these, which for their false faith can not shew so much as one false miracle.

CHAP. XIIII.

THE PASSION according to S. Marke in these two chapters, is the Gospel at Masse vpon Tuesday in the Holy Weeke.

Iudas by occasion of Marie Magdalens ointment, doth sel him to the Councel of the Ievves 12 After the Paschal lambe he giueth them the bread of life (Io. 6.) in a mystical sacrifice or separation of his bodie and bloud. 27 and that night, is after his prayer, 43 taken of thee Ievves men, Iudas being their Captaine: is forsaken of the other eleuen for feare: 53 is falsly accused, and impiously condemned of the Ievves Councel, 65 and shamefully abused of them: 66 and thrise denied of Peter. Al euen as the Scriptures and him self had often foretold.

TENEBRE Wenesday.

1 AND the Pasche vvas and the Azymes after tvvo daies: and the cheefe Priests and the Scribes sought hovv they might by some vvile lay hands on him, and kil him. *Mt. 26, 1* *Lu. 22, 1* 2 † For they said, Not on the festiual day, lest there might be a tumult of the people.

3 † And * vvhen he vvas at Bethania in the house of Simon the Leper, and sate at meate, there came a vvoman hauing an alabaster-boxe of ointment, of pretious spike-narde: and breaking the alabaster-boxe, she povvred it out vpon his head. *Mat. 26, 6. Ioan. 12, 3.* 4 † But there vvere certaine that had indignation vvithin them selues, and said, Vvhereto is " this vvast of the ointment made? 5 † For this ointment might haue been sold for more then three hundred pence, and giuen to the poore. And they murmured against her. 6 † But IESVS said, " Let her alone, vvhy do you molest her? she hath vvrought a good vvorke vpon me. 7 † for the poore you haue alvvaies vvith you: and vvhen you vvil, you may doe them good: but ∷ me you haue not alvvaies. 8 † That vvhich she had, she hath done: she hath preuented to anoint my body to the burial. 9 † Amen I say to you, Vvheresoeuer this Gospel shal be preached in the vvhole vvorld, that also vvhich she hath done, shal be told for a memorie of her.

∷ We haue not Christ here needing our almes, as when he cōuersed vpon the earth. *See Mat. 26, 11.*

10 † And * Iudas Iscariote one of the Tvvelue vvent his vvay to the cheefe Priests, for to betray him to them. *Mat. 26, 17. Lu. 22, 7* 11 † Vvho hearing

HOLY weeke.

ring it, vvere glad: and they promised him that they vvould giue him money. And he sought hovv he might betray him conueniently.

Mt. 26, 17. Lu. 22, 7

MAVNDY Thursday.

12 † And * the first day of the Azymes vvhen they sacrificed the Pasche, the Disciples say to him, Vvither vvilt thou that 13 vve goe, and prepare for thee to eate the Pasche? † And he sendeth tvvo of his Disciples, and saith to them, Goe ye into the citie: and there shal meete you a man carying a pitcher 14 of vvater, folovv him: † and vvhithersoeuer he entreth, say to the maister of the house, that the Maister saith, Vvhere is my refectorie, vvhere I may eate the Pasche vvith my Disci-15 ples? † And he vvil shevv you a great chamber, adorned: and 16 there prepare for vs. † And his Disciples vvent their vvaies, and came into the citie: and they found as he had told them,

Io. 13, 21

17 and they prepared the Pasche. † And * vvhen euen vvas 18 come, he commeth vvith the Tvvelue. † And vvhen they vvere sitting at the table and eating, IESVS said, Amen I say to you, that one of you shal betray me, he that eateth vvith 19 me. † But they began to be sad, and to say to him seuerally, 20 Is it I? † Vvho said to them, One of the Tvvelue, he that dip-21 peth vvith me his hand in the dish. † and the Sonne of man in deede goeth, * as it is vvritten of him, but vvo to that man by vvhom the Sonne of man shal be betrayed. it vvere good 22 for him, if that man had not been borne. † And * vvhiles they vvere eating, IESVS tooke " bread: and blessing brake, and gaue to them, and said, Take, THIS IS " MY BODY. 23 † And taking the " chalice, giuing thankes he gaue to them. 24 and they ∷ al dranke of it. † And he said to them, THIS IS " MY BLOVD OF THE NEVV TESTAMENT, THAT 25 SHAL BE SHED FOR MANY. † Amen I say to you, that novv I vvil not drinke of the fruite ∷ of the vine vntil that day vvhen I shal drinke it nevv in the kingdom of God. 26 † And an hymne being said, they vvent forth into Mount-oliuet.

Ps. 40, 10.

Mt. 26, 26. Luc. 21, 19. 1. Cor. 11, 24.

∷ Al dranke, to wit, al the twelue, for moe were not present. Whereby is euident that the vvordes in S. Mat. (26, 27) *Drinke ye al of this*, were spoken to al the Apostles onely, which here are said that they al did drinke. And so it is no general cōmaundement to al men.

∷ See Annot. in Mat. c. 26, 29.

THVRSDAY night.

27 † And IESVS saith to them, You shal al be scandalized in me in this night: for it is vvritten, *I vvil strike the Pastor, and the* 28 *sheepe shal be dispersed.* † But after that I shal be risen againe, 29 I vvil goe before you into Galilee. † And Peter said to him, 30 Although al shal be scandalized: yet not I. † And IESVS saith to him, Amen I say to thee, that thou this day in this night, before the cocke crovv tvvise, shalt thrise deny me.

Zach. 13, 7.

† But he ſpake more vehemently, Although I ſhould die 31 together vvith thee, I vvil not denie thee. And in like maner alſo ſaid they al.

† And they come into a farme-place called Gethſemani. 32 And he ſaith to his Diſciples, Sit you here, vntil I pray. † And he taketh Peter and Iames and Iohn vvith him: and he 33 began to feare and to be heauy. † And he ſaith to them, My 34 ſoul is ſorovvful euen vnto death: ſtay here, and vvatch. † And vvhen he vvas gone forvvard a litle, he fel flat vpon 35 the ground: and he prayed that if it might be, the houre might paſſe from him: † and he ſaid, Abba, Father, al things are poſ- 36 ſible to thee, transferre this chalice from me. but not that vvhich I vvil, but that vvhich thou. † And he commeth, and 37 findeth them ſleeping. And he ſaith to Peter, Simon, ſleepeſt thou? couldſt thou not vvatch one houre? † Vvatch ye, and 38 pray that you enter not into tentation. The ſpirit in deede is prompt, but the fleſh infirme. † And going avvay againe, he 39 prayed, ſaying the ſelf ſame vvord. † And returning, againe 40 he found them a ſleepe (for their eies vvere heauy) and they vviſt not vvhat they ſhould anſvver him. † And he com- 41 meth the third time, and ſaith to them, Sleepe ye novv, and take reſt, it ſuffiſeth, the houre is come: behold the Sonne of man ſhal be betraied into the hands of ſinners. † Ariſe, let vs 42 goe. behold, he that ſhal betray me, is at hand.

† And * as he vvas yet ſpeaking, commeth Iudas Iſcariote 43 one of the Tvvelue, and vvith him a great multitude vvith ſvvordes and clubbes, from the cheefe Prieſtes and the Scri- bes and the Auncients. † And the betrayer of him had giuen 44 them a ſigne, ſaying, Vvhomſoeuer I ſhal kiſſe, it is he, lay hold on him, and leade him vvarily. † And vvhen he vvas 45 come, immediatly going to him, he ſaith, Rabbi, and he kiſ- ſed him. † But they laid hands vpon him: and held him. † And 46 one certaine man of the ſtãders about, dravving out a ſvvord, 47 ſmote the ſeruant of the cheefe prieſt, and cut of his eare. † And 48 IESVS anſvvering, ſaid to them, As to a theefe are you come out vvith ſvvordes and clubbes to apprehend me? † I vvas 49 daily vvith you in the temple teaching, and you did not lay hands on me. But, that the Scriptures may be fulfilled. † Then 50 his diſciples leauing him, al fled. † And a certaine yong man fo- 51 lowed him clothed vvith ſindon vpõ the bare: & they tooke him. † But he caſting of the ſindon, fled from them naked. 52

Mt. 26, 47. Luc. 22, 47. Io. 18, 3.

53 † And they brought IESVS to the cheefe Priest: and al the Priests and the Scribes and the Auncients assembled to-
54 gether. † And Peter folovved him a farre of euen in vnto the court of the high Priest: and he sate vvith the seruants at the
55 fire, and vvarmed him self. † And the cheefe Priests and al the councel sought testimonie against IESVS, that they might
56 put him to death, neither found they. † For many spake false Witnes against him: and the testimonies vvere not cõuenient.
57 † And certaine rising vp, bare false vvitnes against him, saying,
58 † That vve heard him say, * I vvil dissolue this temple made vvith hand, and in three daies vvil I build an other not made
59 vvith hand. † And their testimonie vvas not conuenient.
60 † And the high Priest rising vp into the middes, asked IESVS, saying, Ansvverest thou nothing to these things that are ob-
61 iected to thee of these? † But he held his peace and ansvvered nothing. Againe the high Priest asked him, and said to
62 him, Art thou Christ the sonne of the blessed God? † And IESVS saith to him, I am. And you shal see the * Sonne of man sitting on the right hand of povver, and comming vvith
63 the cloudes of heauen. † And the high Priest renting his gar-
64 ments, saith, Vvhat neede vve vvitnesses any further? † You haue heard blasphemie. hovv thinke you? Vvho al ∷ con-
65 demned him to be guilty of death. † And certaine began to spit vpon him, and to couer his face, and to beate him vvith buffets, and to say vnto him, Prophecie: and the seruants gaue him blovves.

66 † And vvhen Peter vvas in the court beneath, there com-
67 meth one of the ∷ vvoman-seruants of the high Priest. † And vvhen she had seen Peter vvarming him self, beholding him
68 she saith, And thou vvast vvith IESVS of Nazareth. † But he denied, saying, Neither knovv I, neither vvot I vvhat thou saiest. And he vvent forth before the court: and the
69 cocke crevve. † And againe a vvench seeing him, began to say
70 to the standers about, That this fellovv is of them. † But he denied againe. And after a vvhile againe they that stoode by, said to Peter, Verily thou art of them: for thou art also a Ga-
71 lilæan. † But he " began to curse and to svveare, That I knovv
72 not this man vvhom you speake of. † And immediatly the cocke crevv againe. And Peter remembred the vvord that IESVS had said vnto him, Before the cocke crovv tvvise, thou shalt thrise deny me. And he began to vveepe.

ANNOT.

Marginal notes:

Io. 2, 19. (v. 58)

Dan. 7, 13. (v. 62)

∷ Here we may see that they were worthily reprobated and forsaken, according to our Sauiours predictió by the parable (Mar. 12) *The kingdom of God shal be také from you &c.*

∷ He feareth not afterward Rome the Lady of the world, that in the house of Caiphas was afraid of the high Priestes wench. *Leo in Natiu. Pet. & Pau. ser. 1.*

ANNOTATIONS
CHAP. XIIII.

Cost religiously bestowed vpon Christ and his Church.

4. *This wast.*] Religious offices done to Christ for signification, deuotion, or honour sake, both then in his life, and novv in the Holy Sacrament, be of some (vnder pretence of better bestowing such things vpon the poore) condemned vniustly.

6. *Let her alone.*] Christ answereth for the deuout woman, and for defence of her fact, as we must answer against the ignorant and il men, vvhen they blame good men for giuing their goods to the Church.

The real presence by Consecration.

22. *Bread.*] *This is bread before the Sacramental wordes, but the Consecration once done, of bread is made the flesh of Christ.* Ambros. li. 4 c. 4 de Sacramentis.

Very bloud vnder the forme of wine.

23. *Chalice.*] Wine and water is put into the Chalice, but is made bloud by Consecration of the heauenly word: though to auoid the lothsomnesse which would be in the sight of bloud, thou receiuest that which hath the likenes and resemblance thereof. *Ambr. ibidem.*

Faith necessarie in the B. Sacrament.

23. 24. *My bodie, My bloud.*] *Whosoeuer beleeueth it not to be true that is said, he falleth from grace and saluation.* Epiph. in Ancorato. *Let vs euer giue credite to God, and neuer resist him, though the thing that he saith, seeme neuer so absurd in our imagination, or farre passe al our sense and vnderstanding. For his wordes can not beguile vs, but our sense may easely be deceiued. Seeing therfore that he said, This is my body, let vs neuer doubt of the matter.* Chrysost ho. 83. in Mat. sub finem.

Peter.

71. *He began to curse.*] In this one Apostle, Peter, the first and cheefe in the order of Apostles, in whom the Church was figured, both sortes were to be signified, to wit, the strong and the weake, because without both the Church is not. *Aug. ser. 13 de verb. Do.* Againe, Our Sauiour would shew by the example of the cheefe Apostle, that no man ought to presume of him self, when neither S. Peter could auoid the danger of mutability. *Aug. tract. 66 in Euang. Io. Leo Ser. 9. de Pass. Do.*

CHAP. XV.

The cheefe of the Ievves accuse him to Pilate the Gentil. 6 And (he seeking to deliuer him) they persuade the common people (vvho hitherto vvere alvvaies ready to defend him) not only to preferre the murderer Barabbas, but also to crie Crucifige *(to the reprobation of the vvhole nation.) 16 After many illusions, 20 he is crucified by the Gentils. 29 Vvhich the Ievves seing, do triumph as if they had novv the victorie. 33 But euen then by many vvonderful vvorkes he declareth his might, 42 and finally is buried honorably.*

GOOD FRIDAY.

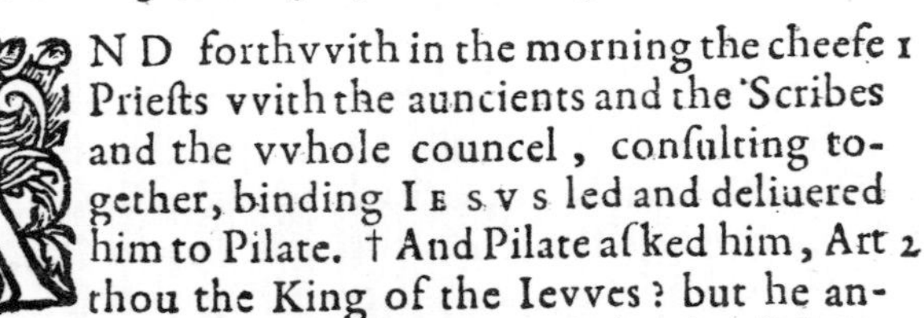

AND forthvvith in the morning the cheefe 1 Priests vvith the auncients and the Scribes and the vvhole councel, consulting together, binding IESVS led and deliuered him to Pilate. † And Pilate asked him, Art 2 thou the King of the Ievves? but he ansvvering, said to him, Thou saiest. † And the cheefe Priests 3 accused him in many things. † And Pilate againe asked 4 him, saying, Ansvverest thou nothing? see in hovv many things they accuse thee. † But IESVS answered nothing more: 5 so that Pilate marueled.

Mt.27,1 Lu.23,1. Io.18,28

† And vpon the festiual day he vvas vvont to release vnto 6 them one of the prisoners vvhomsoeuer they had demaunded. † And there vvas one called Barabbas, vvhich vvas put 7 in prison vvith seditious persons, vvho in a sedition had committed murder. † And when the multitude vvas come vp, they 8 began

began to require according as alvvaies he did vnto them. 9 † And Pilate ansvvered them, and said, Vvil you that I release 10 to you the King of the Ievves? † For he knevv that the cheefe 11 Priests for enuy had deliuered him. † But the ″cheefe Priests moued the people, that he should release Barabbas rather to 12 them. † And Pilate againe ansvvering, said to them, Vvhat 13 vvil you then that I doe to the King of the Ievves? † But they 14 againe cried, Crucifie him. † And Pilate said to them, Vvhy, vvhat euil hath he done? But they cried the more, Crucifie 15 him. † And Pilate vvilling ″to satisfie the people, released to them Barabbas, and deliuered IESVS, hauing vvhipped him, for to be crucified.

Io. 19, 2.

16 † And * the souldiars led him into the court of the Palace, 17 and they call together the vvhole band: † and they clothe him in purple, and platting a crovvne of thornes, they put 18 it vpon him. † And they began to salute him, Haile King of 19 the Ievves. † And they smote his head vvith a reede: and they did spit on him. and bovving the knees, they adored 20 him. † And after they had mocked him, they stripped him of the purple, and put on him his ovvne garments, and they leade 21 him forth to crucifie him. † And they forced a certaine man that passed by, Simon a Cyrenêan comming from the countrie, the father of Alexander and Rufus, to take vp his crosse. 22 † And they bring him into the place Golgotha, vvhich being 23 interpreted is, *The place of Caluarie.* † And they gaue him to drinke vvine mingled vvith myrrhe: and he tooke it not.

24 † And crucifying him, they deuided his garments, casting 25 lottes vpon them, vvho should take vvhich. † And it vvas 26 the third houre, and they crucified him. † And the title of his 27 cause vvas superscribed, KING OF THE IEWES. † And vvith him they crucifie tvvo theeues: one on the right hand, 28 and an other on his left. † And the Scripture vvas fulfilled 29 that saith, *And vvith the vvicked he vvas reputed.* † And they that passed by, blasphemed him, vvagging their heades, and saying, Vah, ‵he that destroieth′ the temple, and in three daies ‵buil-30 deth′ it: † ∴ saue thy self, comming dovvne from the crosse. 31 † In like maner also the cheefe Priests mocking, said vvith the Scribes one to an other, He saued others, him self he can 32 not saue. † Let Christ the king of Israel come dovvne novv from the crosse: that vve may see and beleeue. And they that vvere crucified vvith him, railed at him.

Esa. 53, 12.

‵thou that destroiest ‵buildest

∴ So Heretikes say of the B. Sacrament, If it be Christ, let him saue him self from al iniuries.

† And vvhen it vvas the ſixt houre, there vvas made darke- 33
nes vpon the vvhole earth vntil the ninthe houre. † And 34
at the ninthe houre IESVS cried out vvith a mightie voice,
ſaying, *Eloi, Eloi, lamma-ſabacthani?* Which is being interpreted, *Pſ.21, 1.*
My God, my God, vvhy haſt thou ∴ *forſaken me?* † And certaine of the 35
ſtanders about hearing, ſaid, Behold, he calleth Elias. † And 36
one running and filling a ſpunge vvith vinegre, and putting it
about a reede, gaue him drinke, ſaying, Let be: let vs ſee if Elias
come to take him dovvne. † And IESVS putting forth a 37
mightie voice, gaue vp the ghoſt. † And the vele of the temple 38
vvas rent in tvvo, from the toppe to the bottome. † And the 39
Centurion that ſtoode ouer againſt him, ſeeing that ſo crying
he had giuen vp the ghoſt, ſaid, In deede this man vvas the
ſonne of God.

∴ See (Mat. c. 27, 46) the blaſphemous expoſition of Caluin and his folovvers, and take heede thereof.

† And there vvere alſo vvomen looking on a farre of: 40
among vvhom vvas Marie Magdalene, and Marie the mother
of Iames the leſſe and of Ioſeph, and Salóme: † and vvhen he 41
vvas in Galilee, they folovved him, and miniſtred to him, and
many other vvomen that came vp together vvith him to
Hieruſalem. † And vvhen euening vvas come (becauſe it 42
vvas the Paraſceue, vvhich is the Sabboth-eue) † came Io- 43
ſeph of Arimathæa a noble Senatour, vvho him ſelf alſo vvas
expecting the kingdom of God: and he vvent in boldly to
Pilate, and aſked the body of IESVS. † But Pilate marueled 44
if he vvere novv dead. And ſending for the Centurion, aſked
him if he vvere novv dead. † And vvhen he vnderſtoode by 45
the Centurion, he gaue the body to Ioſeph. † And Ioſeph 46
" bying ſindon, and taking him dovvne, vvrapped him in
the ſindon, and laid him in a monument, that vvas hevved
out of a rocke. And he rolled a ſtone to the doore of the
monument. † And Marie Magdalene and Marie of Ioſeph 47
beheld vvhere he vvas laid.

ANNOTATIONS
CHAP. XV.

The Prieſts of the old Teſtament.

11. *Cheefe Prieſts.*] Heretikes abuſe the ignorant people with theſe naughtie Prieſts of the old Teſtament, to make that name odious, and to diſcredite the Prieſts of Chriſt in the new Teſtament. But for theſe Prieſts, thou maiſt not maruel that they are ſo buſy againſt Chriſt, * partly becauſe they were ſuch as were intruded by the ſecular power of the Roman Emperour, and from yere to yere by bribery and frendſhip, not by ſucceſſion according to the Law of Moyſes: partly becauſe the time was now come when the old Prieſthod of Aaron ſhould ceaſe, and the new begin according to the order of Melchiſedec: and, for theſe cauſes God ſuffered their former priueleges of wiſedom and iudgemēt and diſcretion to decay in theſe later vſurpers, and that according to the

* *Euſeb. Ec. Hiſt. li. 1 c. 6. ex Ioſepho.*

Ezech. 7, 26. Io. 16, 13. Luc. 22 and 10.

the Prophet saying, *The Law shal perish from the Priest and counsel from the Ancients.* But the Priesthod of the new Testament is to continew vnto the end of the world, and hath (as being the principal part of the Church) the assistāce of the Holy Ghost for euer promised, to teach it al truth: and for Peter the cheefe Priest thereof vnder Christ, our Sauiour praied, That his faith should not faile: and to the rest he said, *He that heareth you, heareth me.*

The Priesthod of the new Testament.

15. To satisfie the people.] Pilate should haue suffered death, rather then by other mens prouocation or commaundement haue executed an innocent: as a Christian iudge should rather suffer al extremitie, then giue sentence of death against a Catholike man for his faith.

Executīg lawes against innocents.

46. Bying sindon.] This dutie done to Christes body after his departure, was exceding meritorious, and is therfore by holy write so often commended for an example to faithful men, to vse al honour and deuotion towards the bodies of Saincts and holy persons.

Religious duty tovvard the bodies of Christ and his Saincts.

CHAP. XVI.

The third day, to three vvomen at his Sepulcher, an Angel telleth that he is risen, and vvil (as he promised Mar. 14, 28.) shevv him self in Galilee. 9 The same day he appeareth to Marie Magdalene, aftervvard to tvvo Disciples: yet the Eleuen vvil not beleeue it, until to them also he appeareth. 14 To vvhom hauing giuen commission into al nations, vvith povver also of Miracles, he ascendeth, and they plant his Church euery vvhere.

Mt. 28, 1 Lu. 24, 1 Io. 20, 1.

The Gospel vpō Easter day.

1 AND vvhen the Sabboth vvas past, Marie Magdalene and Marie of Iames, and Salôme " bought spices, that comming they might anoint IESVS. 2 † And very early the first of the Sabboths, they come to the monument: the sunne being novv risen. 3 † And they said one to an other, Vvho shal roll vs backe the stone from the doore of the monument? 4 † And looking, they savv the stone rolled backe. for it vvas very great. 5 † And entring into the monument, they savv a yong man sitting on the right hand, couered vvith a vvhite robe: and they vvere astonied. 6 † Vvho saith to them, Be not dismaied: you seeke IESVS of Nazareth, that vvas crucified: he is risen, he is not here, behold the place vvhere they laid him. 7 † But goe, tel his Disciples and :: Peter that he goeth before you into Galilee: there you shal see him, * as he told you. ⊣ 8 † But they going forth, fled from the monument. for trembling and feare had inuaded them: and they said nothing to any body. for they vvere afraid.

EASTER DAY.

Mr. 14, 28.

:: Peter is named in special (as often els vvhere) for prerogatiue.

9 † And he rising early the first of the Sabboth, * appeared first to Marie Magdalene, * out of vvhom he had cast seuen 10 deuils. † She vvent and told them that had been vvith him, 11 that vvere mourning and vveeping. † And they hearing that he vvas aliue and had been seen of her, did not beleeue.

Io. 20, 16. Luc. 8, 2.

Lu. 24, 13.

12 † And * after this he appeared in an " other shape to tvvo

of them vvalking, as they vvere going into the countrie. † and they going told the rest: neither them did they beleeue. 13

The Gospel vpõ the Ascension day.

† Last * he appeared to those eleuen as they sate at the 14 table: and he exprobrated their incredulity and hardnes of hart, because they did not beleeue them that had seen him risen againe. † And he said to them, * Going into the vvhole 15 vvorld preach the Gospel to al creatures. † He that " beleeueth 16 and is baptized, shal be saued: but he that beleeueth not, shal be condemned. † And them that beleeue " these 17 signes shal folow: In my name shal they cast out deuils, They shal speake vvith nevv tonges, † Serpents shal they take 18 avvay, And if they drinke any deadly thing, it shal not hurt them, They shal impose hands vpon the sicke: and they shal be vvhole.

Lu. 24, 36. Io. 20, 19. Mt. 28, 19.

The Ascension.

† And so our Lord IESVS after he spake vnto them, * vvas 19 assumpted into heauen, and sate on the right hand of God. † But they going forth preached euery vvhere: our Lord wor- 20 king vvithal, and confirming the vvord vvith signes that folovved. ⊣

Lu. 25, 51.

ANNOTATIONS
CHAP. XVI.

The vvomens deuotion tovvard Christs body novv dead.

1. *Bought spices.*] As she did bestow and consume a costly ointment vpon his body being yet aliue (c. 14, 3,) Christ him self defending and highly commending the fact against Iudas and other who accounted it to be superfluous and better to be bestowed otherwise: So not without great deuotion and merite, she and these other women seeke to anoint his body dead (though Heretikes or other simple persons may pretend such things to be better bestowed vpon the poore) and therfore, * she first before al other, * and they next, saw him after his Resurrection.

Mr. 16, 9. Mt. 28, 5.

Christs body vnder diuers formes.

12. *In an other shape.*] Christ though he haue but one corporal shape, natural to his person, yet by his omnipotencie he may be in whatsoeuer forme, and appeare in the likenesse of any other man or creature, as he list. Therfore let no man thinke it strange, that he may be vnder the forme of bread in the B. Sacrament.

Not onely faith.

16. *He that beleeueth.*] Note wel, that whereas this Euangelist mentioneth only faith and baptisme, as though to beleeue and to be baptized were ynough, S. Matthew addeth these wordes also of our Sauiour, *teaching them to obserue al things whatsoeuer I haue commaunded you*, Which conteineth al good workes and the whole iustice of a Christian man.

Mt. 28, 20.

The gift of miracles.

17. *These signes shal folow.*] It is not meant, that al Christians or true beleeuers should doe miracles: but that some for the proofe of the faith of al, should haue that gift. The which is the grace or gift of the whole Church, executed by certaine for the edification and profite of the whole.

THE

THE ARGVMENT OF S. LVKES GOSPEL.

S. *Lukes Gospel may be diuided into fiue partes.*

The first part is, of the Infancie *both of the precursor, and of Christ him selfe: chap.* 1 *and* 2.

The second, of the Preparation *that vvas made to the manifestation of Christ: chap.* 3 *and a piece of the* 4.

The third, of Christes manifesting him selfe, by preaching and miracles, specially in Galilee: the other piece of the 4 *chap. vnto the middes of the* 17.

The fourth of his comming into Iurie tovvards his Pasion: the other piece of the 17 *chap. vnto the middes of the* 19.

The fifth, of the Holy weeke *of his Pasion in Hierusalem: the other part of the* 19 *chap. vnto the end of the booke.*

S. *Luke vvas* sectator (*saith S. Hierome*) that is, a disciple of the Apostle Paul, and a companion of al his peregrination. *And the same vve see in the Actes of the Apostles: Vvhere, from the* 16 *chap. S. Luke putteth him selfe in the traine of S. Paul, vvriting thus in the storie.* Forthwith we sought to goe into Macedonia. *and in like maner, in the first person, commonly through the rest of that booke. Of him and his Gospel, S. Hierom vnderstandeth thus saying of S. Paul:* Vve haue sent with him the brother, vvhose praise is in the Gospel through al Churches. *where also he addeth:* Some suppose, so often as Paul in his Epistles saith, *According to my Gospel*, that he meaneth of Lukes booke. *And againe:* Luke learned the Gospel not onely of the Apostle Paul, who had not been with our Lord in flesh, but of the other Apostles: which him selfe also in the beginning of his booke declareth, saying, As they deliuered to vs who them selues from the beginning saw, and were ministers of the word. *It foloweth in S. Hierome:* Therfore he wrote the Gospel, as he had heard. but the Actes of the Apostles he compiled as he had seen. *S. Paul vvriteth of him by name to the Colossians:* Luke the Physicion saluteth you. *and to Timothee:* Luke alone is with me. *Finally of his end thus doth S. Hierome vvrite:* He liued fourescore and foure yeres, hauing no wife. He is buried at Constantinople: to vvhich citie his bones vvith the Relikes of Andrew the Apostle were translated out of Achaia the twentith yere of ˋ Constantinus. *And of the same Translation also in another place against Vigilantius the Heretike:* It grieueth him that the Relikes of the Martyrs are couered with pretious couerings, and that they are not either tied in cloutes or throwen to the dunghil. why, are we then* sacrilegious, when we enter the Churches of the Apostles? Was ˋ Constantinus' the Emperour sacrilegious, who translated to Constantinople the holy Relikes of Andrew, Luke, and Timothee: at which the Diuels rore, and the inhabiters of Vigilantius confesse that they feele their presence?

His sacred body is novv at Padua in Italie, Vvither it vvas againe translated from Constantinople.

Hier. in Catalago.

2. Cor. 8, 18.

Luk. 1, 2.

Col. 4, 14.

2. Tim. 4, 21.

Hiero. in Catalogo.

Constantius.

Hier. con. Vigil, 2.

Constantius

The Heretike so counted the Catholikes for their honouring of Saincts and Relikes.

THE HOLY GOSPEL OF IESVS CHRIST ACCORDING TO LVKE.

CHAP. I.

THE FIRST part: of the Infacie both of the Precursor, and of CHRIST him self.

The Annunciation and Conception, first of the Precursor: 26 and sixe moneths after, of Christ also him self. 39 The Visitation of our Ladie, vvhere both the mothers do Prophecie. 57 The Natiuitie and Circuncision of the Precursor, vvhere his father doth prophecie. 80 The Precursor is from a childe an Eremite.

BECAVSE many haue gone about 1 to compile a narration of the things that haue been accomplished among vs: † according as they haue deliuered 2 vnto vs, vvho from the beginning them selues savv and vvere ministers of the vvord: † it seemed good also 3 vnto me ″hauing diligently atteined to al things from the beginning, to vvrite to thee in order, good * Theophilus, † that thou maist 4 knovv the veritie of those vvordes vvhereof thou hast been instructed.

Act. 1, 1.

The Gospel vpō the eue of S. Iohn Baptist.

† There vvas in the daies of Herod the king of Ievvrie, a 5 certaine Priest named Zacharie, of the * course of Abia: and his vvife of the daughters of Aaron, and her name Elizabeth. † And they vvere both ″ iust before God, vvalking ″ in al the 6 commaundements ″ and iustifications of our Lord vvithout blame, † and they had no sonne: for that Elizabeth vvas bar- 7 ren, and both vvere vvel striken in their daies. † And it came 8 to passe: vvhen he executed the priestly function in the order of his course before God, † according to the custome of 9 the Priestly function, he vvent forth by lot * to offer incense, entring into the temple of our Lord: † and * al the 10 multitude of the people vvas ∷ praying vvithout at the houre of the incense. † And there appeared to him an Angel of our 11 Lord,

1 Par. 24, 10.

Exo. 3, 17.

Leu. 16, 16.

∷ We see here that the Priest did his dutie vvithin, the people in the meane time

Lord, standing on the right hand of the altar of incense. 12 † And Zacharie vvas troubled, seeing him: and feare fel vpon 13 him. † But the Angel said to him, Feare not Zacharie, for thy praier is heard: and thy vvife Elizabeth shal beare thee a 14 sonne, and thou shalt cal his name Iohn: † and thou shalt haue" ioy and exultation, and many shal reioyce in his nati- 15 uitie. † for he shal be great before our Lord: ∷ and vvine and sicer he shal not drinke: and he shal be replenished vvith 16 the Holy Ghost euen from his mothers vvombe. † and he shal * conuert many of the children of Israel to the Lord their 17 God. † and he shal goe before him * in the spirit and vertue of Elias: that he may conuert the hartes of the fathers vnto the children, and the incredulous to the vvisedom of the iust, 18 to prepare vnto the Lord a perfect people. ⊣ † And Zacharie said to the Angel, Vvhereby shal I knovv this? for I am old: 19 and my vvife is vvel striken in her daies. † And the Angel ansvvering said to him, I am Gabriel that assist before God: and am sent to speake to thee, and to euangelize these things 20 to thee. † And behold, ∷ thou shalt be dumme, and shalt not be able to speake vntil the day vvherein these things shal be done: for-because thou hast not beleeued my vvor- 21 des, vvhich shal be fulfilled in their time. † And the people vvas expecting Zacharie: and they marueled that he made 22 tariance in the temple. † And comming forth he could not speake to them, and they knevv that he had seen a vision in the temple. And he made signes to them, and remained 23 dumme. † And it came to passe, after the daies of his office 24 vvere expired," he departed into his house. † And after these daies Elizabeth his vvife conceiued: and hid her self fiue mo- 25 neths, saying, † For thus hath our Lord done to me in the daies vvherein he had respect to take avvay my reproche among men.

26 †[b] And in the sixt moneth, the Angel Gabriel vvas sent of 27 God into a citie of Galilee, called Nazareth, † * to a virgin despoused to a man vvhose name vvas Ioseph, of the house of 28 Dauid: and the virgins name vvas MARIE. † And the Angel being entred in, said vnto her, "HAILE" *ful of grace, our Lord* 29 *is vvith thee: blessed art thou among vvomen.* † Vvho hauing heard, vvas troubled at his saying, and thought vvhat maner of salutation this should be. † And the Angel said to her, Feare not 31 MARIE, for thou hast found grace vvith God. † * Behold thou

Mal. 4, 6. Mt. 11, 14.

Mt. 1, 18

Esa. 7, 14.

praying vvithout: and that the Priests functions did profite thé, though they neither heard nor saw his doings.

∷ This abstinence foretold and prescribed by the Angel, shevveth that it is a worthy thing, and an acte of religion in S. Iohn, as it was in the Nazarites.

∷ Zacharie punished for doubting of the Angels word.

b The Gospel vpó the Annunciation of our Lady, March 25. And on the Wenesday of Imber weeke in Aduét. And for a Votiue Masse of our Lady in Aduent.

The beginning of the AVE MARIE. See the rest v. 42.

thou ſhalt conceiue in thy vvombe, and ſhalt beare a ſonne: and thou ſhalt call his name IESVS. † he ſhal be great, and 32 ſhal be called the ſonne of the moſt High, and our Lord God ſhal giue him the ſeate of Dauid his father: † * and he ſhal 33 reigne in the houſe of Iacob for euer, and of his kingdom there ſhal be no end. † And MARIE ſaid to the Angel, :: 34 Hovv ſhal this be done? " becauſe I knovv not man? † And 35 the Angel anſvvering, ſaid to her, The Holy Ghoſt ſhal come vpon thee, and the povver of the moſt High ſhal ouerſhadovv thee. And therfore alſo that vvhich of thee ſhal be borne Holy, ſhal be called the ſonne of God. † And behold 36 " Eliſabeth thy coſin, ſhe alſo hath conceiued a ſonne in her old age: and this moneth, is the ſixt to her that is called barren: † becauſe there ſhal not be impoſſible vvith God any 37 vvord. † And MARIE ſaid, :: BEHOLD *the handmaid of our Lord,* 38 *be it done to me according to thy word.* ⁋ And the Angel departed from her.

Dan. 7, 14, 27.

:: She doubted not of the thing as Zacharie, but enquired of the meanes.

:: At this very moment when the B. Virgin gaue conſent, ſhe conceiued him perfect God and perfect man.

† And MARIE riſing vp in thoſe daies, vvent vnto the hil 39 countrie vvith ſpeede, into a citie of Iuda. † and ſhe entred 40 into the houſe of Zacharie, and ſaluted Eliſabeth. † And it 41 came to paſſe: as Eliſabeth heard the ſalutation of MARIE, the :: infant did leape in her vvombe. and Eliſabeth vvas repleniſhed vvith the Holy Ghoſt: † and ſhe cried out vvith a 42 loude voice, and ſaid, " BLESSED *art thou among vvomen, and bleſſed is the fruite of thy vvombe.* † And vvhence is this to me, that the " mo- 43 ther of my Lord doth come to me? † For behold as the voice 44 of thy ſalutation ſounded in mine eares, the infant in my vvombe did leape for ioy. † And bleſſed is ſhe that beleeued, 45 becauſe thoſe things ſhal be accompliſhed that vvere ſpokē to her by our Lord. † And MARIE ſaid, 46

The Goſpel vpō the Viſitatiō of our Lady, Iul. 2. And vpon the Imber friday in Aduent.

:: Iohn the Baptiſt being yet in his mothers wombe, reioyced and acknowledged the preſence of Chriſt and his mother.

MY SOVLE doth magnifie our Lord.
† *And my ſpirit hath reioyced in God my Sauiour.* ⁋ 47
† *Becauſe he hath regarded the humilitie of his handmaid: for behold from* 48 *hence forth* :: *al generations* " *ſhal call me bleſſed.*
† *Becauſe he that is mightie hath done great things to me, and holy is his name.* 49
† *And his mercie from generation vnto generations, to them that feare him.* 50
† *He hath ſhevved might in his arme: he hath diſperſed the proude in the con-* 51 *ceit of their hart.*
† *He hath depoſed the mightie from their ſeate, and hath exalted the humble.* 52
† *The hungrie he hath filled vvith good things: and the riche he hath ſent* 53 *avvay emptie.*
† *He hath receiued Iſrael his childe, being mindeful of his mercie,* 54
† *As he ſpake to our fathers, to Abraham and his ſeede for euer.* 55

MAGNIFICAT at Euenſong.

:: Haue the Proteſtants had alwaies generations to fulfil this prophecie? or do they call her bleſſed, that derogate what they can from her graces, bleſſings, and al her honour?

† And

56 † And MARIE taried vvith her about three moneths: and she returned into her house.

57 † And Elisabeths ful time vvas come to be deliuered: and she bare a sonne. 58 † And her neighbours and kinsfolke heard that our Lord did magnifie his mercie vvith her, and they did congratulate her. 59 † And it came to passe: on the eight day they came to circuncise the childe, and they called him by his fathers name, Zacharie. 60 † And his mother ansvvering, said, Not so, but he shal be called Iohn. 61 † And they said to her, That there is none in thy kinred that is called by this name. 62 † And they made signes to his father, vvhat he vvould haue him called. 63 † And demaunding a vvriting table, he vvrote, saying, " * Iohn is his name. And they al marueled. 64 † And forthvvith his mouth vvas opened, and his tonge, and he spake blessing God. 65 † And feare came vpon al their neighbours: and al these things vvere bruited ouer al the hil-countrie of Ievvrie: 66 † and all that had heard, laid them vp in their hart, saying, What an one, trovv ye, shal this childe be? For the hand of our Lord vvas vvith him. 67 † And Zacharie his father vvas replenished vvith the Holy Ghost: and he prophecied, saying,

The Gospel vpō the Natiuitie of S. Iohn Baptist Iun. 24. called Midsōmer day.

Lu. 1, 13.

68 † BLESSED BE OVR LORD *God of Israel: because he hath visited and vvrought the redemption of his people:*

BENEDICTVS at Laudes.

69 † *And hath erected the horne of saluation to vs, in the house of Dauid his seruant.*

70 † *As he spake by the mouth of his holy Prophets, that are from the beginning.*

71 † *Saluation from our enemies, and from the hand of al that hate vs:*

72 † *To vvorke mercie vvith our fathers: and to remember his holy testament,*

73 † * *The othe vvhich he svvare to Abraham our father,* 74 † *that he vvould giue to vs,*

That vvithout feare being deliuered from the hand of our enemies, vve may serue him.

Gen. 22, 6.

75 † *In holines and " iustice before him, al our daies.*

76 † *And thou childe, shalt be called the Prophet of the Highest: for * thou shalt goe before the face of our Lord to prepare his vvaies.*

Mal. 3, 1.

77 † *To giue knovvledge of saluation to his people, vnto remission of their sinnes,*

78 † *Through the bovvels of the mercie of our God, in vvhich " the * Orient, from on high, hath visited vs,*

Zac. 3, 9. 6, 12. Mal. 4, 2.

79 † *To illuminate them that sit in darkenes, and in the shadovv of death: to direct our feete into the vvay of peace.*

80 † And the childe grew, and vvas strengthened in spirit, and vvas ∵ in the deserts vntil the day of his manifestatiō to Israel.

∵ Marke that he was a voluntarie Eremite, and chose to be solitarie from a childe, til he was to preach to the people. in so much that antiquitie counted him the first Eremite. *Hiero. in vit. Pauli.*

S ANNOT.

ANNOTATIONS
CHAP. I.

Sacred Writers and holy Coũcels.

3. *Hauing diligently atteined.*] Hereby vve ſee that, though the Holy Ghoſt ruled the penne of holy vvriters that they might not erre, yet did they vſe humane meanes to ſearch out and find the truth of the things they Wrote of. Euen ſo doe Councels, and the Preſident of them, Gods vicar, diſcuſſe and examine al cauſes by humane meanes, the aſſiſtance of the Holy Ghoſt concurring and directing them into al truth, according to Chriſtes promiſe *Io. 16, 13*: as in the very firſt Councel of the Apoſtles them ſelues at Hieruſalem is manifeſt *Act. 15, 7* and *28*. Againe here vve haue a familiar preface of the Author as to his frende, or to euery godly Reader (ſignified by Theophilus) cõcerning the cauſe and purpoſe and maner of his vvriting, and yet the very ſame is confeſſed Scripture, vvith the vvhole booke folovving. Maruel not then if the Author of the ſecond booke of the Machabees * vſe the like humane ſpeaches both at the beginning and in the later end, neither do thou therfore reiect the booke for no Scripture, as our Heretikes doe: or not thinke him a ſacred vvriter.

The ſecond booke of the Machabees.

2 Mach. 2. & 15.

6. *Iuſt before God.*] Againſt the Heretikes of this time, here it is euident that holy men be iuſt, not only by the eſtimation of men, but in deede and before God.

True iuſtification by obſeruing the commaundements.

6. *In al the commaundements.*] Three things to be noted directly againſt the Heretikes of our time. firſt, that good men doe keepe al Gods commaundements: Which (they ſay) are impoſſible to be kept. Againe, that men be iuſtified not by only imputation of Chriſtes iuſtice, nor by faith alone, but by Walking in the commaundements. Againe, that the keeping and doing of the commaundements is properly our iuſtification.

Corrupt tranſlation of Heretikes.

Δικαιώματα.

6. *Iuſtifications.*] This Word is ſo vſual in the Scriptures (namely in the *Pſal. 118*) to ſignifie the commaundements of God, becauſe the keeping of them is iuſtification, and the Greeke is alwaies ſo fully correſpõdent to the ſame, that the Heretikes in this place (otherWiſe pretending to eſteeme much of the Greeke) bluſh not to ſay, that they auoid this Word of purpoſe againſt the iuſtification of the Papiſts. And therfore one vſeth Tullies Word forſooth, in Latin *conſtituta*: and his ſcholers in their Engliſh Bibles ſay, *Ordinances.*

Beza *in Annot. no. Teſt. 1556.*

14. *Ioy and exultation.*) This Was fulfilled, not only When he Was borne, but noW alſo through the Whole Church for euer, in ioyful celebrating of his Natiuitie.

The continẽcie of prieſts.

23. *He departed.*) In the old LaW (ſaith S. Hierom) they that offered hoſtes for the people, Were not only not in their houſes, but Were purified for the time, being ſeparated from their Wiues, and they dranke neither Wine nor any ſtrong drinke, Which are Wont to prouoke concupiſcence. Much more the Prieſts of the neW LaW that muſt alWaies offer ſacrifices, muſt alWaies be free from matrimonie. *Li. 1 c. 19. adu. Iouin.* and *ep. 50 c. 3.* See S. Ambroſe *in 1 Tim. 3.* And therfore if there Were any religion in Caluins Communion, they Would at the leaſt giue as much reuerence in this point, as they in the old LaW did to their ſacrifices, and to the loaues of propoſition. *1 Reg. 21.*

Often ſaying of the AVE MARIE.

28. *Haileful of grace.*) Holy Church and al true Chriſtian men doe much and often vſe theſe Wordes brought from heauen by the Archangel, as Wel to the honour of Chriſt and our B. Ladie, as alſo for that they Were the Wordes of the firſt glad tidings of Chriſts Incarnation and our Saluation by the ſame, and be the very abridgement and ſumme of the Whole Goſpel. In ſo much that the Greeke Church vſed it daily in the Maſſe.

Liturg. S. Iacobi & Chryſ.

Corrupt tranſlation of Heretikes.

κεχαριτωμένη.

ἐχαρίτωσε.

ἡλκωμένος.

28. *Ful of grace.*) Note the excellent prerogatiues of our B. Lady, and abhorre thoſe Heretikes Which make her no better then other vulgar Women, and therfore to take from her fulnes of grace, they ſay here, *Haile freely beloued*, contrarie to al ſignifications of the Greeke Word, Which is at the leſt, *endued With grace*, as S. Paul vſeth it Epheſ. 1. by S. Chryſoſtoms interpretation: or rather, *ful of grace*, as both * Greeke and Latin fathers haue alWaies here vnderſtood it, and the Latines alſo read it, namely S. Ambroſe thus, *Wel is ſhe only called ful of grace, vvho only obteined the grace, vvhich no other vvoman deſerued, to be repleniſhed With the author of grace.* And if they did as Wel knoW the nature of theſe kind of Greeke Wordes, as they Would ſeeme very ſkilful, they might eaſily obſerue that they ſignifie fulnes, as When them ſelues tranſlate the like Word (*Luc. 16, 20*) ful of ſores. Beza, *vlceroſus.*

S. Athan. de S. Dip. S. Ephrem in orat. de laud. B. virg. Ambro. in 1 Luc. li. 2. Hier. ep. 140 in exp. Pſ. 44.

Our B. Lady voWed virginitie.

34. *I knoW not man.*) Theſe Wordes declare (ſaith S. Auguſtine) that ſhe had noW voWed virginitie to God. For otherWiſe neither Would ſhe ſay, *HoW ſhal this be done?* nor haue added, *becauſe I knoW not man.* Yea if ſhe had ſaid only the firſt Wordes, HoW ſhal this be done? it is euident that ſhe Would not haue aſked ſuch a queſtion, hovv a vvoman ſhould beare a ſonne promiſed her, if ſhe had married meaning to haue carnal copulation. *c. 4 de virgin.* As if he ſhould ſay, If ſhe might haue knovven a man and ſo haue had a childe, ſhe vvould neuer haue aſked, HoW ſhal this be done? but becauſe that ordinarie Way vvas excluded by her voW of virginitie, therfore ſhe aſketh, HoW? And in aſking, HoW? ſhe plainly declareth that ſhe might not haue a childe by knoWing man, becauſe of her voW. See S. Grego. Nyſſene *de ſancta Chriſti Natiuitate.*

36. *Elisabeth thy Cosin.*) By this that Elisabeth and our Lady were cosins, the one of the tribe of Leui, the other of Iuda, is gathered that Christ came of both tribes, Iuda and Leui, of the kings and the priests: him self both a king and a priest, and the Anointed (to vvit) by grace spiritually, as they vvere vvith oile materially and corporally. *August. 2 de Consens. Euang. c. 1.*

Christ came of both tribes, Iuda and Leui.

42. *Blessed art thou.*) At the very hearing of our Ladies voice, the infant and she vvere replenished vvith the Holy Ghost, and she sang praises not only to Christ, but for his sake to our B. Lady, calling her blessed and her fruite blessed, as the Church doeth also by her vvordes and example in the AVE MARIE.

The blessed virgin MARIE.

43. *Mother of my Lord.*) Elizabeth being an exceding iust and blessed vvoman, yet the vvorthines of Gods mother doth so far excel her and al other vvomen, as the great light the litle starres. *Hiero. Præf. in Sophon.*

Her excellécie.

48. *Shal call me blessed.*) This Prophecie is fulfilled, when the Church keepeth her Festiual daies, and when the faithful in al generations say the AVE MARIE, and other holy Antems of our Lady. And therfore the Caluinistes are not among those generations which call our Lady blessed.

Her honour in al the world.

63. *Iohn is his name.*) Wee see that names are of signification and importance, God him self changing or giuing names in both Testaments: as, Abraham, Israel, Peter, and the principal of al others, IESVS: and here IOHN, vvhich signifieth, Gods grace or mercie, or, God vvil haue mercie. For he vvas the Precursor and Prophet of the mercie and grace that ensued by CHRIST IESVS. Note also that as then in Circuncision, so novv in Baptisme (vvhich ansvvereth therevnto) names are giuen. And as vve see here and in al the old Testament, great respect was had of names: so we must beware of strange, profane, and secular names (now a daies to common) and rather according to the * Catechisme of the holy Councel of Trent, take names of Sainctes and holy men, that may put vs in minde of their vertues.

Mysterie and signification in names.

What names to be giué in Baptisme.

c. de bapt. in fine.

75. *Iustice before him.*) Here also we see that we may haue true iustice, not only in the sight of men, or by the imputation of God, but in deede before him and in his sight: and that the comming of Christ vvas to giue men such iustice.

True iustice, not imputatiue.

78. *The orient.*) Maruel not if Heretikes controule the old authentical translation, as though it differed fró the greeke: vvhereas here they make much a doe to cótroule not only al the greeke interpreters of the old testament, but also S. Luke him self, for the vvord ἀνατολὴ, as differing from the Hebrevv.

The Heretikes controule both Greeke and Latin text.

Beza.

CHAP. II.

The Natiuitie of Christ, 8 and manifestation thereof to the Shepheards by an Angel, and by them to others. 21 His Circuncision. 22 His Presentation, together with Simeons (as also Annes) attestation and prophecying of his Passion, of the Iewes reprobation, and of the Gentils illumination. 41 His annual ascending to Hierusalem with his parents, to whom he was subiect, and his fulnes of wisedom shewed among the Doctors at twelue yeres of his age.

The Gospel at the first Masse vpon christmas day.

1 AND it came to passe, in those daies there came forth an edict from Cæsar Augustus, that the vvhole vvorld should be enrolled. 2 † This first enrolling vvas made by the President of Syria Cyrinus. 3 † And al vvent to be enrolled, euery one into his ovvne citie. 4 † And Ioseph also vvent vp from Galilee out of the citie of Nazareth into Ievvrie, to the citie of Dauid that is called Beth-lehem: for-because he vvas of the house and familie of Dauid, 5 † to be enrolled vvith MARIE his despoused vvife that vvas vvith childe. 6 † And it came to passe, vvhen they vvere there, her daies vvere fully come that she should be deliuered. 7 † And she brought forth her first begotten sonne,

In the yere, fró the creation of the vvorld 5199: fró Noës floud, 2957: from the Natiuitie of Abraham, 2015: from Moyses and the cóming forth of the people of Israel out of Ægypt, 1510: fró Dauid

and svvadled him in clothes, and laid him dovvne in a manger: because there vvas not place for them in the inne.

† And there vvere in the same countrie shepheards vvatching, and keeping the night vvatches ouer their flocke. 8 † And behold, an Angel of our Lord stood beside them, and 9 the brightnes of God did shine round about them, and they feared vvith a great feare. † And the Angel said to them, Fea- 10 re not: for behold I euangelize to you great ioy, that shal be to al the people: † because this day is borne to you a SAVIOVR vvhich is Christ our Lord, in the citie of Dauid. † And 11 12 this shal be a signe to you, You shal finde the infant svvadled in clothes: and laid in a manger. † And sodenly there 13 vvas vvith the Angel a multitude of the heauenly armie, praising God, and saying, † *Glorie in the highest to God: and in earth peace to* 14 *men of good vvil.* ⊣ † [b] And it came to passe: after the Angels de- 15 parted from them into heauen, the shepheards spake one to an other: Let vs goe ouer to Bethlehem, and let vs see this vvord that is done, vvhich our Lord hath shevved to vs. † And they came vvith speede: and they found MARIE and 16 Ioseph, and the infant laid in the manger. † And seeing it, 17 they vnderstood of the vvord that had been spoken to them concerning this childe. † And al that heard, did maruel: and 18 concerning those things that vvere reported to them by the shepheards. † But MARIE "kept al these vvordes, confer- 19 ring them in her hart. † And the shepheards returned, glori- 20 fying and praysing God in al things that they had heard, and seen, as it vvas said to them. ⊣

† [c] And * after eight daies vvere expired, that the childe 21 should be circuncised: his name vvas called IESVS, vvhich vvas * called by the Angel, before that he vvas conceiued in the vvombe. ⊣

† [d] And after the daies vvere fully ended of her purification 22 * according to the lavv of Moyses, they caried him into Hierusalem, to present him to our Lord († as it is vvritten in the 23 lavv of our Lord, *That euery male opening the matrice, shal be called holy to the Lord.*) † and to giue a sacrifice * according as it is vvrit- 24 ten in the lavv of our Lord, a paire of turtles, or tvvo yong pigeons. † And behold, there vvas a man in Hierusalem, na- 25 med Simeon, and this man vvas iust and religious, expecting the consolation of Israel: and the Holy Ghost vvas in him. † And he had receiued an ansvver of the Holy Ghost, that he 26 should

anointed king, 1032: from the first Olympias, 800: from the building of Rome, 752: hebdomada 63, according to the prophecie of Daniel (c. 9), that is, in the yere 440 or thereabout: in the sixt age of the vvorld, vvhen there vvas vniuersal peace in al the vvorld: the eternal God and sonne of the eternal Father, meaning to consecrate and sactifie the vvorld vvith his most blessed cōming, being cōceiued of the Holy Ghost, nine moneths after his conception, IESVS CHRIST the sonne of God is borne in Bethlehem of Iuda, in the yere of Cæsar Augustus 42. *Vsuard. in martyrol. Decēb. 25, according to the cōmon ancient supputation.*

b The Gospel at the secōd masse vpō Christmas day. And for a Votiue of our Lady frō christmas to Candlemas.

c The Gospel vpon the Circuncisiō of our Lord Ian. 1.

d The Gospel vpon the Purification of our Lady or Candlemas day.

GLORIA IN EXCELSIS at Masse.

Gen. 17, 12.

Lu. 1, 31.

Leu. 12, 6.

Exo. 13, 2.

Nu. 8, 16

Leu. 12, 8.

ſhould not ſee death vnles he ſavv firſt the :: CHRIST of our
27 Lord. † And he came in ſpirit into the temple. And vvhen his parents brought in the childe IESVS, to doe according to
28 the cuſtome of the Lavv for him: † he alſo tooke him into his armes, and bleſſed God, and ſaid,

:: See Ioh. 1, 20 and 41.

29 † NOW THOV *doeſt dimiſſe thy ſeruant O Lord, according to thy vvord in peace.*

30 † *Becauſe mine eies haue ſeen, thy* SALVATION,

31 † *Vvhich thou haſt prepared before the face of al peoples:*

32 † *A light to the reuelation of the Gentils, and the glorie of thy people Iſrael.* ⊣

NVNC DIMITTIS at Complin.

33 † And his father and mother vvere marueling vpon thoſe
34 things vvhich vvere ſpoken concerning him. † And Simeon bleſſed them, and ſaid to MARIE his mother, Behold this is ſet " vnto the ruine, and vnto the reſurrection of many in
35 Iſrael, and for a ſigne vvhich ſhal be contradicted, † and :: thine ovvne ſoule ſhal a ſvvord pearce, that out of many
36 hartes cogitations may be reuealed. † And there vvas Anne a prophetiſſe, the daughter of Phanuel, of the tribe of Aſer: ſhe vvas farre ſtriken in daies, and had liued vvith her huſ-
37 band ſeuen yeres from her virginitie. † And ſhe vvas " a vvidovv vntil eightie and foure yeres: vvho departed not from the temple, " by faſtings and praiers :: ſeruing night and
38 day. † And ſhe at the ſame houre ſodenly comming in, confeſſed to our Lord: and ſpake of him to al that expected the
39 redemption of Iſrael. † And after they had vvholy done al things according to the lavv of our Lord, they returned into Galilee, into their citie Nazareth.

:: Simeon prophecied not only of Chriſt but of our B. Lady, of al her ſorowes: Wherein ſhe was alwaies partaker with our Sauiour, from his flight into Ægypt euen to his death.

:: λατρεύουσα.

40 † And the childe grevv, and vvaxed ˋ ſtrong ˊ: ful of vviſe-
41 dom, and the grace of God vvas in him. † And his parents vvent euery yere vnto Hieruſalem, * at the ſolemne day of
42 Paſche. † And vvhen he vvas tvvelue yeres old, they going vp into Hieruſalem according to the cuſtome of the feſtiual
43 day, † and hauing ended the daies, vvhen they returned, the childe IESVS remained in Hieruſalem: and his parents knevv
44 it not. † And thinking that he vvas in the companie, they came a daies iourney, and ſought him among their kinſfolke
45 and acquaintance. † And not finding him, they returned into
46 Hieruſalem, ſeeking him. † And it came to paſſe, after three daies they found him in the temple ſitting in the middes of
47 the Doctors, hearing them, and aſking them. † And al vvere aſtonied that heard him, vpon his vviſedom and anſvvers.

ſtrong in ſpirit:

Exo. 23, 15. 34, 17. Deu. 16, 1.

The goſpel vpō the firſt Sunday after the Epiphanie.

48 † And seeing him, they vvondered. And his mother said to him, Sonne, vvhy hast thou so done to vs? behold thy father and I sorovving did seeke thee. 49 † And he said to them, Vvhat is it that you sought me? did you not knovv, that I must be about those things, vvhich are my fathers? 50 † And they vnderstood not the vvord that he spake vnto them. 51 † And he vvent dovvne vvith them, and came to Nazareth: and vvas "subiect to them. And his mother kept al these vvordes in her hart. 52 † And IESVS proceeded in vvisedom and age, and grace vvith God and men. ⊣

ANNOTATIONS
CHAP. II.

Free vvil.

14. *Men of good wil.*] The birth of Christ giueth not peace of minde or saluation but to such as be of good will, because he worketh not our good against our willes, but our willes concurring. *Aug. quæst. ad Simplic. li. 1. q. 2. to. 4.*

Our B. Lady ful of deepe contemplations.

19. *Kept al.*] Our Lady though litle be spoken of her concerning such matters in the Scriptures, because she was a woman, and not admitted to teach or dispute in publike of high mysteries: yet she knew al these mysteries, and wisely noted and contemplated of al those things that were done and said about Christ, from the first houre of his Conception til the end of his life and his Ascension.

Mens ruine and damnation is of them selues.

34. *To the ruine.*) Therfore to the ruine of some, because they would not beleeue in him, and so vvere the cause of their owne ruine, as he is els where called, *A stumbling stone*, because many would stumble at him and so fall by their owne fault. other some he raised by his grace from sinne to iustice, and so he was the resurrection of many. The Apostle vseth the like speache, saying: *We are to some the odour of life, vnto life: to others, the odour of death, vnto death.* Not that their preaching was to cause death, but because they that would not beleeue their preaching, wilfully incurred deadly sinne and damnation.

1 Pet. 2, 8.

2 Cor. 2, 16

Holy vvidowhod.

38. *A vvidow.*) Marke that widowhod is here mentioned to the commendation thereof euen in the old Testament also, and the fruite and as it were the profession thereof is here commended, to vvitte, fasting, praying, being continually in the Temple, euen as S. Paul more at large for the state of the new Testament speaketh of widowhod and virginitie, as being professions more apt and commodious for the seruice of God.

1 Cor. 7.

Fasting an act of religion.

37. *By fastings and praiers seruing.*) Seruing, in the Greeke is λατρεύουσα, that is, doing diuine worship vnto God, as by praier, so also by fasting. so that fasting is λατρεία, that is, an act of religion whereby we doe worship God, as we doe by praier, and not vsed only to subdew our flesh, much lesse (as Heretikes would haue it) as a matter of pollicie.

Dutiful obedience to parents.

51. *Subiect to them.*) Al children may learne hereby, that great ought to be their subiection and obedience to their Parents, when Christ him self, being God, would be subiect to his parents being but his creatures.

CHAP. III.

THE SECOND part: The preparation that vvas made to the manifestation of CHRIST.

Iohn, to prepare al to Christ (as Esay had prophecied of him) baptizeth them to penance, 7 insinuating their reprobation, and the Gentils vocation, 10 teaching also and exhorting ech sort to doe their dutie. 15 That him self is not Christ, he sheweth by the difference of their tvvo baptismes: 17 and saith that Christ vvil also iudge his baptized. 19 Iohns imprisonment. 21 Christ being him self also baptized of Iohn, hath testimonie from heauen, 23 as he vvhose generation reduceth vs againe to God.

And

1 AND in the fifteenth yere of the empire of Tiberius Cæsar, Pontius Pilate being Gouernour of Ievvrie, and Herod being Tetrarch of Galilee, and Philip his brother Tetrarch of Ituréa and the countrie Trachonîtis, and Lysanias Tetrarch of Abilîna, 2 † vnder the high Priests Annas and Caiphas: the vvord of our Lord vvas made vpon Iohn the sonne of Zacharie, in the desert. 3 † And * he came into al the countrie of Iordan, preaching the baptisme of :: penance vnto remission of sinnes: as it is vvritten in the booke of the sayings of Esay the Prophet: 4 † *A voice of one crying in the desert: prepare the vvay of our Lord, make straight his pathes.* 5 † *Euery valley shal be filled: and euery mountaine and hil shal be made lovv, and crooked things shal become straight: and rough vvaies, plaine:* 6 † *and al flesh shal see the* SALVATION *of God.*

The Gospel vpō Imber Saturday in Aduent. And on the 4 Sunday in Aduent.

Mt. 3,1. Mr. 1,1.

:: Penance prepareth the way to Christ.

Esa. 40, 3.

Mt. 3,7.

7 † He said therfore to the multitudes that vvent forth to be baptized of him, * Ye vipers broodes, vvho hath shevved you to flee from the vvrath to come? 8 † Yeld therfore :: fruites vvorthie of penance. and doe ye not begin to say, Vve haue Abraham to our father. For I tel you, that God is able of these stones to raise vp children to Abraham. 9 † And novv the axe is put to the roote of the trees. :: Euery tree therfore that yeldeth not good fruite, `shal be' cut dovvne, and cast into fire. 10 † And the multitudes asked him, saying, Vvhat shal vve doe then? 11 † And he ansvvering, said vnto them: :: He that hath tvvo coates, let him giue to him that hath not: and he that hath meate, let him doe likevvise. 12 † And the Publicans also came to be baptized, and said to him, Maister, vvhat shal vve doe? 13 † But he said to them, Doe nothing more then that vvhich is appointed you. 14 † And the souldiars also asked him, saying, Vvhat shal vve also doe? And he said to them, Vexe not neither calumniate any man: and be content vvith your stipends.

:: Fruites of penance be workes satisfactorie.

:: A man vvithout good workes is vnfruitful, and shal be cast into euerlasting fire.

:: Almes counseled or enioyned for sinnes and to auoid damnation.

15 † And :: the people imagining, and al men thinking in their harts of Iohn, lest perhaps he vvere Christ: 16 † Iohn ansvvered, saying vnto al, * I in deede baptize you vvith vvater: :: but there `shal come' a mightier then I, vvhose latchet of his shoes I am not vvorthie to vnloose, he shal baptize you in the Holy Ghost and fire. 17 † vvhose fanne is in his hand, and he vvil purge his floore: and vvil gather the vvheate into his barne, but the chaffe he vvil burne vvith vnquencheable fire. 18 † Many other things also exhorting did he euangelize to the people.

:: Iohn was so holy that many might by errour easily thinke he was Christ.

Mt. 3,11. Mr. 1,8. `cometh Io. 1,26. Act. 1,5. 11,16. 19,4.

:: How say then the Heretikes that the Baptisme of Christ is of no greater vertue then Iohns?

people.

† * And Herod the Tetrarch, vvhen he vvas rebuked of 19 him for Herodias his `brothers' vvife, and for al the euils vvhich Herod did: †" he added this alſo aboue al, and ſhut 20 vp Iohn into priſon.

Mt.14,3 Mar.6,17.

`brother Philips

† *And it came to paſſe vvhen al the people vvas baptized, 21 IESVS alſo being baptized and praying, heauen vvas opened: † and the Holy Ghoſt deſcended in corporal ſhape as a doue 22 vpon him: and a voice from heauen vvas made: Thou art my beloued ſonne, in thee I am vvel pleaſed. † And IESVS him ſelf 23 was beginning to be about thirtie yeres old: as it was thought, the ſonne of Ioſeph, vvho vvas" of Heli, † vvho vvas of Mat- 24 that, vvho vvas of Leui, vvho vvas of Melchi, vvho vvas of Ianné, vvho vvas of Ioſeph, † vvho vvas of Matthathias, vvho 25 vvas of Amos, vvho vvas of Naum, vvho vvas of Heſli, vvho vvas of Naggé, † vvho vvas of Mahath, vvho vvas of Mat- 26 thathias, vvho vvas of Semei, vvho vvas of Ioſeph, vvho vvas of Iuda, † vvho vvas of Iohanna, vvho vvas of Reſa, vvho 27 vvas of Zorobabel, vvho vvas of Salathiel, vvho vvas of Neri, † vvho vvas of Melchi, vvho vvas of Addi, vvho 28 vvas of Coſam, vvho vvas of Elmadan, vvho vvas of Her, † vvho vvas of Ieſus, vvho vvas of Eliézer, vvho vvas 29 of Iorim, vvho vvas of Matthat, vvho vvas of Le-ui, † vvho vvas of Simeon, vvho vvas of Iudas, vvho 30 vvas of Ioſeph, vvho vvas of Iona, vvho vvas of Elia-cim, † vvho vvas of Melcha, vvho vvas of Menna, vvho 31 vvas of Matthatha, vvho vvas of Nathan, vvho vvas of Da-uid, † * vvho vvas of Ieſſe, vvho vvas of Obed, vvho vvas 32 of Booz, vvho vvas of Salmon, vvho vvas of Naaſſon, † vvho vvas of Aminadab, vvho vvas of Aram, vvho vvas 33 of Eſron, vvho vvas of Phares, vvho vvas of Iudas, † vvho 34 vvas of Iacob, vvho vvas of Iſaac, vvho vvas of Abraham, vvho vvas of Tharé, vvho vvas of Nachor, † vvho vvas 35 of Sarug, vvho vvas of Ragau, vvho vvas of Phaleg, vvho vvas of Heber, vvho vvas of Salé, † :: vvho vvas of Cai- 36 nan, vvho vvas of Arphaxad, vvho vvas of Sem, vvho vvas of Noë, vvho vvas of Lamech, † vvho vvas of Mathuſalé, 37 vvho vvas of Henoch, vvho vvas of Iared, vvho vvas of Malaleel, vvho vvas of Cainan, † vvho vvas of Henos, 38 vvho vvas of Seth, vvho vvas of Adam, vvho vvas of God.

Mt 3,13. Mr.1,9. Io.1,32.

:: Beza boldly wipeth out of this Goſpel, theſe wordes, *vvho vvas of Cainan:* though al the Greeke copies both of the old Teſtament & of the new, haue the wordes with ful cōſent. Whereby vve learne the intolerable ſaucines of the Caluiniſts, and their cōtempt of holy Scripture, that dare ſo deale with the very Goſpel it ſelf.

ANNOT.

ANNOTATIONS
CHAP. III.

20. He added this aboue al.] The fault of Princes and other great men, that can not only not abide to heare their faults, but alſo puniſh by death or empriſonment ſuch as reprehend them for the ſame (ſpecially if they warne them, as Prophets and Prieſts doe, from God) is exceding great.

23. Of Heli.] Vvhereas in S. Matthevv, Iacob is father to Ioſeph, and here Heli, the caſe vvas thus. Mathan (named in S. Matthevv) of his vvife called Eſcha begat Iacob: and after his death, Melchi (named here in S. Luke) of the ſame vvoman begat Heli: ſo that Iacob and Heli vvere brethren of one mother. This Heli therfore marrying and dying vvithout iſſue: Iacob his brother, according to the Lavv married his vvife, and begat Ioſeph, and ſo raiſed vp ſeede to his brother Heli. Whereby it came to paſſe, that Iacob was the natural father of Ioſeph, which as (S. Matthew ſaith) begat him: and Heli was his legal father according to the Law, as S. Luke ſignifieth. *Euſeb. li. 1 Ec. Hiſt. c. 7 Hiero. in c. 1 Mat. Aug. li. 2 c. 2. 3 de conſ. Euang.*

The reconciliation of Matthew and Luke in our Sauiours petigree.

CHAP. IIII.

Christ going into the Deſert to prepare him ſelf before his manifeſtation, ouercommeth the tentations of the Diuel. 14 then beginning glorioufly in Galilee, 16 he ſheweth to them of Nazareth his commiſſion out of Eſay the Prophet, 23 inſinuating by occaſion the Ievves his countriemens reprobation. 31 In Capharnaum his doctrine is admired, 33 ſpecially for his miracle in the Synagogue. 38. from vvhich, going to Peters houſe, he ſhevveth there much more povver. 42 Then retiring into the vvilderneſſe, he preacheth aftervvard to the other cities of Galilee.

Mt. 4, 1. Mr. 1, 12

1 AND IESVS ful of the Holy Ghoſt, returned from Iordan, and vvas driuen in the ſpirit into the deſert, 2 † :: fourtie daies, and vvas tempted of the deuil. And he did eate nothing in thoſe daies: and vvhen they vvere ended, he vvas an hungred. 3 † And the Deuil ſaid to him, If thou be the 4 ſonne of God, ſay to this ſtone that it be made bread. † And IESVS made anſvver vnto him, It is vvritten, *That not in bread* 5 *alone ſhal man liue, but in euery vvord of God.* † And the Deuil brought him into an high mountaine, and ſhevved him al the king- 6 doms of the vvhole vvorld in a moment of time: † and he ſaid to him, To thee vvil I giue this vvhole povver, and the glorie of them: for to me they are deliuered, and to :: vvhom I 7 vvil, I doe giue them. † Thou therfore if thou vvilt adore 8 before me, they ſhal al be thine. † And IESVS anſvvering ſaid to him, It is vvritten, :: *Thou ſhalt adore the Lord thy God, and him* 9 *only ſhalt thou* ᶜ*ſerue.* † And he brought him into Hieruſalem, and ſet him vpon the pinnacle of the temple: and he ſaid to him, If thou be the ſonne of God, caſt thy ſelf from hence 10 dovvnevvard. † For :: it is vvritten, that *He hath giuen his Angels*

Deuter. 8, 3.

Deu. 6, 13. 10, 20. c λατρεύσεις. Pſal. 90, 11.

:: The Chuches faſt of 40 daies (called Lét) cometh of this, & is an Apoſtolical Tradition. *Clem. Conſtit. Apoſt. li. 5 c. 13. Hier. ep. ad Marcel. adu erro. Mõtani. Leo ſer. 6 et 9 de Quadrageſ.*

:: See the Annot. in S. Mathew c. 4, 11.

:: If the Diuel him ſelf alleage Scripture againſt Chriſt, no maruel that Heretikes do ſo againſt Chriſts Church.

T *charge*

charge of thee, that they preſerue thee: † *and that in their hands they ſhal* 11 *beare thee vp, leſt perhaps thou knocke thy foote againſt a ſtone.* † And 12 IESVS anſvvering ſaid to him, It is ſaid, *Thou ſhalt not tempt the Lord thy God.* † And al the tentation being ended, the Deuil " depar- 13 ted from him vntil a time.

†* And IESVS returned in the force of the ſpirit into Ga- 14 lilee, and the fame vvent forth through the vvhole countrie of him. † And he taught in their ſynagogs, and vvas mag- 15 nified of al.

†* And he came to Nazareth vvhere he vvas brought vp: 16 and he entred ∷ according to his cuſtom on the Sabboth day into the ſynagogue: and he roſe vp to reade. † And the 17 booke of Eſay the Prophet vvas deliuered vnto him. And as he vnfolded the booke, he found the place vvhere it vvas vvritten, † *The Spirit of the Lord vpon me, for vvhich he anointed me, to euan-* 18 *gelize vnto the poore he ſent me, to heale the contrite of hart,* † *to preach to the cap-* 19 *tiues remiſſion, and ſight to the blinde, to dimiſſe the bruiſed vnto remiſſiō, to preach the acceptable yere of the Lord, and the day of retribution.* † And vvhen 20 he had folded the booke, he rendred it to the miniſter, and ſate dovvne. And thē eies of al in the ſynagogue vvere bent vpon him. † And he began to ſay vnto them: That this day 21 is fulfilled this ſcripture in your eares. † And al gaue teſtimo- 22 nie to him: and they ∷ marueled in the vvordes of grace that proceded from his mouth, and they ſaid, Is not this Io- ſephs ſonne? † And he ſaid to them, Certes you vvil ſay to 23 me this ſimilitude, *Phyſicion, cure they ſelf:* as great things as vve haue heard " done in Capharnaum, doe alſo here in thy coun- trie. † And he ſaid, Amen I ſay to you, that no Prophet is ac- 24 cepted in his ovvne countrie. † In truth I ſay to you, * there 25 vvere many vvidovves in the daies of Elias in Iſrael, vvhen the heauen vvas ſhut three yeres and ſix moneths, vvhen there vvas a great famine made in the vvhole earth: † and to 26 none of them vvas Elias ſent, but into Sarepta of Sidon, to a vvidovv vvoman. †* And there vvere many lepers in Iſrael 27 vnder Eliſæus the Prophet: and none of them vvas made cleane but Naamā the Syrian. † And al in the ſynagogue vvere 28 filled vvith anger, hearing theſe things. † And they roſe, and 29 caſt him out of the citie: and they brought him to the edge of the hil, vvherevpon their citie vvas built, that they might throvv him dovvne headlong. † But he " paſſing through the 30 middes of them, vvent his vvay. Ħ

†* And

THE third part: of Chriſtes manifeſting him ſelf by preachīg and miracles, ſpecially in Galilee

∷ Our Sauiour vſed to preach in their Synagogues.

∷ He had a maruelous grace, and an extraordinarie force in mouing the harts of his hearers.

The Goſpel vpon Munday in the 3 vveeke of Lent.

Deut. 6, 16.

Mt. 4, 12. *Mr.* 1, 14

Mt. 13, 54. *Mr.* 6, 1. *Io.* 4, 43

Eſa. 61, 1

3 *reg.* 17, 9.

4 *reg.* 5, 14.

Mat. 4, 13. 7, 18. Mr. 1, 21

31 † * And he vvent dovvne into Capharnaum a citie of Galilee: and there he taught them on the Sabboths. 32 † And they vvere astonied at his doctrine: because his talke vvas in povver. 33 † And in the synagogue there vvas a man hauing an vncleane Diuel, and he cried out vvith a loud voice, 34 † saying, Let be, vvhat to vs and thee IESVS of Nazareth? art thou come to destroy vs? I know thee vvho thou art, *the* SAINCT *of God*. 35 † And IESVS rebuked him, saying, Hold thy peace, & goe out of him. And vvhen the Deuil had throvven him into the middes, he vvent out of him, and hurted him nothing. 36 † And there came feare vpon al, and they talked together one vvith an other, saying, Vvhat vvord is this, that in povver and vertue he commaundeth the vncleane spirits, and they goe out? 37 † And the fame of him vvas published into euery place of the countrie.

Mat. 8, 14. Mr. 1, 30

The Gospel vpon Thursday in the 3 vveeke of Lent. And vpon Saturday in Vvhitson-vveeke.

38 † And IESVS rising vp out of the synagogue, entred into Simons house. * And" Simons vviues mother vvas holden vvith a great feuer: and they besought him for her. 39 † And standing ouer her, he commaunded the feuer, and it left her. And incontinent rising, she ministred to them. 40 † And vvhen the sunne vvas dovvne, al that had diseased of sundrie maladies, brought them to him. But he imposing hands vpon euery one, cured them. 41 † And Deuils vvent out from many, crying and saying, That thou art the sonne of God. And rebuking them he suffred them not to speake, that they knevv he vvas Christ.

42 † And vvhen it vvas day, going forth he vvent into a desert place: and the multitudes sought him, and came euen vnto him: and they held him that he should not depart from them. 43 † To vvhom he said, That to other cities also must I euangelize the kingdom of God: because therfore I vvas sent. 44 † And he vvas preaching in the synagogs of Galilee. ✠

ANNOTATIONS
CHAP. IIII.

The diuels tentations.

13. *Departed vntil a time.*) No maruel if the diuel be often or alvvaies busie vvith Chistian men, seeing after he Was plainely ouercome by Christ, yet did he not giue him ouer altogether, but for a time.

Miracles at one place and not at an other.

23. *Done in Capharnaum.*) God maketh choise of persons and places Where he Worketh miracles or doeth benefites, though he might doe the same els Where if it liked his Wisedom. So doth he in doing miracles by Saincts, not in al places, nor toWards al persons, but as it pleaseth him. *Aug. ep. 137.*

Christs body conteined in place aboue nature.

30. Passing through the middes of them.) Either by making him self inuisible, or also more wonderfully, penetrating the multitude and passing through them, as he did through the doore, his body either being without space of place, or with other bodies in one place. By al which and the like his doings mentioned in the Gospel, it is euident that he can alter and order his body as he list, aboue the natural conditions of a body.

The Apostles left their vviues.

38. Simons Wiues mother.) It is euident that Peter had a wife, but after his calling to be an Apostle, he leaft her, as S. Hierom writeth in many places *ep. 34 & 2 ad Iulianum. Li. 1 adu. Iouin.* See the Annot. *Matth. 9, 29.*

CHAP. V.

Hauing taught the people out of Peters ship, 4 he shevveth in a miraculous taking of fishes, hovv he vvil make him the fisher of men. 12 He cureth a leper by touching him, and sendeth him to the Priest in vvitnesse that he is not against Moyses. 15 The people flocking vnto him, he retireth into the vvildernesse. 17 To the Pharisees in a solemne assembly he proueth by a miracle his povver to remit sinnes in earth. 27 He defendeth his eating vvith sinners, as being the Physicion of soules, 33 and his not prescribing as yet of any fastes to his Disciples.

The Gospel vpō the 4 Sunday after Pentecost.

1 AND it came to passe, vvhen the multitudes pressed vpon him to heare the vvord of God, and him self stoode beside the lake of Genesareth. 2 †* And he savv tvvo shippes standing by the lake: and the fishers vvere gone dovvne, and vvashed their nettes. 3 † And he going vp into " one ship that vvas Simons, desired him to bring it backe a litle from the land. And sitting, he taught the multitudes out of the ship.

Mt. 4, 18. Mar. 1, 16.

4 † And as he ceased to speake, he said to Simon, Launche forth into the deepe, and let loose your nettes to make a draught. 5 † And Simon ansvvering, said to him, Maister, labouring al the night, vve haue taken nothing: but in thy vvord I vvil let loose the nette. 6 † And vvhen they had done this, they inclosed " a very great multitude of fishes, and their nette vvas broken. 7 † And they " beckened to their fellovves that vvere in the other ship, that they should come and help them. And they came and filled both shippes, so that they did sinke. 8 † Vvhich vvhen Simon Peter did see, he fel dovvne at IESVS knees, saying, Goe forth from me, because I am a sinful man, O Lord. 9 † For he vvas vvholy astonished and al that vvere vvith him, at the draught of fishes vvhich they had taken. 10 † In like maner also Iames and Iohn the sonnes of Zebedee, vvho vvere Simons fellovves. And IESVS said to Simon, Feare not: from this time novv, " thou shalt be taking men. 11 † And hauing brought their shippes to land, leauing al things they folovved him. ⁋

Mt. 8, 2. Mar. 1, 40.

12 †* And it came to passe, vvhen he vvas in one of the cities

ties, and behold a man ful of leprosie, and seeing IESVS, and falling on his face, besought him saying, Lord, if thou vvilt, 13 thou canst make me cleane. † And stretching forth the hand, he touched him, saying, I vvil. be thou made cleane. And im- 14 mediatly the leprosie departed from him. † And he commaunded him that he should tel no body, but, Goe, ∵ shevv thy self to the Priest, and offer for thy cleansing * as Moyses commaunded, for a testimonie to them.

Leu. 14, 2.

∵ See S. Mat. Annot. c. 8, 4.

15 † But the bruite of him vvent abrode the more. and great multitudes came together to heare, and to be cured of their 16 infirmities. † And he retired into the desert, and praied.

Mt. 9, 2. Mr. 2, 3.

The Gospel vpõ Friday in whitsonvveeke.

17 † * And it came to passe one day, and he sate teaching. And there vvere Pharisees sitting and Doctors of Lavv that vvere come out of euery tovvne of Galilee and Ievvrie and Hierusalem: and the vertue of our Lord vvas to heale them. 18 † And behold men carying in a bed a man that had the palsey: and they sought to bring him in, and to lay him before him. 19 † And not finding on vvhich side they might bring him in for the multitude, they " vvent vp vpon the roofe, and through the tiles let him dovvne vvith the bed into the middes, be- 20 fore IESVS. † " Vvhose faith vvhen he savv, he said, Man, thy 21 sinnes are forgiuen thee. † And the Scribes and Pharisees began to thinke, saying, Who is this that speaketh blasphemies? 22 Who can forgiue sinnes, but only God? † And vvhen IESVS knevve their cogitations, ansvvering he said to them, Vvhat 23 doe you thinke in your hartes? † Vvhich is easier to say, Thy 24 sinnes are forgiuen thee: or to say, Arise, and vvalke? † but that you may knovv that " the sonne of man hath povver in earth to forgiue sinnes (he said to the sicke of the palsey) I say to thee, Arise, take vp thy bed, and goe into thy house. 25 † And forthvvith rising vp before them, he tooke that vvhere- 26 in he lay: and he vvent into his house, magnifying God. † And al vvere astonied: and they magnified God. And they vvere replenished vvith feare, saying, That vve haue seen maruelous things to day. ⁋

Mt. 9, 9. Mr. 2, 14

The Gospel vpõ S. Matthevves eue Septẽb. 20.

27 † * And after these things he vvent forth, and savv a Publican called Leui, sitting at the Custome-house, and he said to him, 28 Folovv me. † And " leauing al things, he rose and folovved 29 him. † and Leui made him a great feast in his house: and there vvas a great multitude of Publicans, and of others that vvere 30 sitting at the table vvith them. † And their Pharisees and Scri-

:: Christ came not to call those, who presume of their owne iustice, and that cóupt them selues to haue no neede of Christ.

:: See S. Mat. Annot. c. 9, 14.

bes murmured, saying to his disciples, Why doe you eate and drinke vvith Publicans and sinners? † And IESVS ansvvering said to them, 31 They that are vvhole, neede not the Physicion: but they that are il at ease. † :: I came not to call the 32 iust, but sinners to penance. ⊣

† But they said to him,* Vvhy doe the disciples of Iohn :: fast 33 often, and make obsecrations, and of the Pharisees in like maner: but thine doe eate and drinke? † To vvhom he said, Why, 34 can you make the children of the bridegrome fast vvhiles the bridegrome is vvith them? † But the daies vvil come: and 35 vvhen the bridegrome shal be taken avvay from them, then they shal fast in those daies. † And he said a similitude also 36 vnto them, That no man putteth a peece from a nevv garment into an old garment: othervvise both he breaketh the nevv, and the peece from the nevv agreeth not vvith the old. † And no bodie putteth nevv vvine into old bottels: other- 37 vvise the nevv vvine vvil breake the bottels, and it self vvil be shed, and the bottels vvil be lost. † But nevv vvine is to 38 be put into nevv bottels: and both are preserued together. † And no man drinking old, vvil nevv by and by. for he saith, 39 The old is better.

Mat. 9, 14. Mar. 2, 18. Lu. 5, 33.

ANNOTATIONS
CHAP. V.

Peters ship.

5. One ship Simons.) It is purposely expressed that there were two shippes, and that one of them was Peters, and that Christ went into that one, and sate downe in it, and that sitting he taught out of that ship: no doubt to signifie the Church resembled by Peters ship, and that in it is the chaire of Christ, and only true preaching.

Peters fishing.

6. A great multitude of fishes.) Likewise by this significatiue miracle wrought about Peters fishing, is euidently forshewed vvhat wonderful successe Peter should haue in conuerting men to Christ, both Ievves and Gentiles. as vvhen at one draught, that is to say, * at one Sermon he drewe into his ship, which is Christes Church, a great number of men, as he did now fishes: and so continually by him self and his Successors vnto the worlds end.

Act. 2, 41. 4, 4.

Peters coadiutors.

7. Beckened to their fellowes.) Peter had so much worke that he called for helpe and ioyned vnto him the other ship, representing to vs his Copartiners in the preaching of the Gospel, and the coniunction of the Synagogue and the people of Gentilitie vnto Peters ship, that is, to the Church of Christ. *Ambro. li. 4. in Luc. c. vlt.*

Peters preeminence in fishing for mēs soules.

10. Thou shalt be taking men.) That al this aforesaid did properly meane Peters trauailes to come, in the cōuersion of the world to Christ, and his prerogatiue before al men therein, it is euident by Christs special promis made to him seuerally and apart in this place, that he should be made the taker of men. though to other he giueth also, as to Peters cooperátors and coadiutors, the like office. *Mat. 4, 19.*

Zeale of soules.

19. Went vp vpon the roofe.) A strange diligence in procuring corporal health of and by Christ: and an example for vs of the like or greater, to obteine saluation of him either for our selues or our frendes, and to seeke to his Church and Sacraments with what extraordinarie paine soeuer.

The intercessiō of others.

20. Whose faith.) Great is God (saith S. Ambrose) and pardoneth one sort through the merites of others. therfore if thou doubt to obtaine forgiuenesse of thy great offenses, ioyne vnto thy self intercessors, vse the Churches helpe, which may pray for thee and obtaine for thee that which our Lord might denie to thy self. *Amb. li. 5 in Luc.*

In catena S. Thoma. 24. *The sonne of man in earth.*) By which act (* saith S. Cyril) it is cleere that the Sonne of man hath power in earth to remit sinnes: which he said both for him self and vs. For he, as God being made man and Lord of the Law, forgiueth sinnes. And we also haue obtained by him that wonderful grace. for it is said to his Disciples, *Whose sinnes you shal remit, they are remitted to them.* (*Io. 20, 23.*) And how should not he be able to remit sinnes, Who gaue others power to doe the same? — Priests do remit sinnes.

Hiero. in Mat. 9. 28. *Leauing al folowed him.*) The * profane Iulian charged Matthevv of to much lightnes, to leaue al and folovv a stranger, at one vvord. but in deede hereby is seen the maruelous efficacie of Christes vvord and internal vvorking, that in a moment can alter the hart of a man, and cause him nothing to esteeme the things most deere vnto him. Which he did not onely then in presence, but also daily doth in the Church. For so S. Antonie, S. Francis, and others, by hearing only the vvord of our Sauiour read in the Church, forsooke al and folowed him. (*Athan. in vit. S. Antonij. August. cōfess. li. 8 c. 12. Bonau. in vit. S. Frācisci.*) — Forsaking al, and folovving Christ.

CHAP. VI.

For reprouing by Scripture and miracle (as also by reason) the Pharisees blindnes about the obseruation of the Sabboth. 11 they seeke his death. 12 Hauing in the mountaine prayed al night, he chooseth tvvelue Apostles. 17 and after many miracles vpon the diseased. 20 he maketh a sermon to his Disciples before the people: proposing heauen to such as vvil suffer for him, 24 and vvo to such as vvil not. 27 Yet vvithal exhorting to doe good euen to our enemies also. 39 and that the Maisters must first mend them selues. 46 finally, to doe good vvorkes, because only faith vvil not suffice.

Mt. 12, 1. Mr. 2, 23.

1 AND it came to passe on the :: Sabboth second-first, vvhen he passed through the corne, his Disciples did plucke the eares, and did eate rubbing them vvith their hands. 2 † And certaine of the Pharisees said to them, Vvhy doe you that vvhich is not lavvful on the Sabboths? 3 † And IESVS ansvvering them, said, " Neither this haue you read vvhich Dauid did, vvhen him self vvas an hungred and they that vvere vvith him: 4 † * hovv he entred into the house of God, and tooke the loaues of Proposition, and did eate, and gaue to them that vvere vvith him, vvhich it is not lavvful to eate * but only for Priests? 5 † And he said to them, That the sonne of man is Lord of the Sabboth also.

(*1. Re. 21, 4. Leu. 24, 9.*)

:: S. Hierom (ep. 2 ad Nepotian.) vvriteth of him self, that being at Cōstantinople, he asked his maister Gregorie NAZIANZENE, the famous Doctor, then Bishop there, what Sabboth this vvas. Who by his answer declared that it was very hard to tel, neither is it yet knowen to the best learned. Yet the Protestants are wont to say, Al is very easie.

6 † And it came to passe on an other Sabboth also, that he entred into the synagogue, and taught. * And there vvas a man, and his right hand vvas vvithered. 7 † And the Scribes and Pharisees vvatched if he vvould cure on the Sabboth: that they might finde hovv to accuse him. 8 † But he knevv their cogitations: and he said to the man that had the vvithered hand, Arise, and stand forth into the middes. And rising he stoode. 9 † And IESVS said to them, I aske you, if it be lavvful on the Sabboths to doe vvel or il: to " saue a soule or to destroy? 10 † And looking about vpon them al, he said to the

(*Mt. 12, 10. Mr. 3, 1.*)

man

man, Stretch forth thy hand. And he ſtretched it forth: and his hand vvas reſtored. † And they vvere repleniſhed vvith 11 madnes: and they communed one vvith an other vvhat they might doe to IESVS.

The Goſpel vpō S. Bartlemevves day.

† And it came to paſſe in thoſe daies, he vvent forth into 12 the mountaine to pray, and he paſſed" the vvhole night in the prayer of God. † * And vvhen day vvas come, he called 13 his Diſciples: and he choſe tvvelue of them (" vvhom alſo he named *Apoſtles*) † " Simon vvhom he ſurnamed Peter, and An- 14 drevv his brother, Iames and Iohn, Philippe and Bartholo- mevv, † Matthevv and Thomas, Iames of Alphæus and Si- 15 mon that is called Zelótes, † and Iude of Iames, and Iudas 16 Iſcariote vvhich vvas the traitour. † And deſcending vvith 17 them he ſtoode in a plaine place, and the multitude of his Diſ- ciples, and a very great companie of people from al Ievvrie and Hieruſalem: and the ſea coaſt both of Tyre and Sidon, † vvhich vvere come to heare him, and to be healed of their 18 maladies. And they that vvere vexed of vncleane ſpirits, vvere cured. † And al the multitude ſought to touch him, becauſe 19 vertue vvent forth from him, and healed al. ⊣ † And he lif- 20 ting vp his eies vpon his Diſciples, ſaid,

Mt. 10, 1. Mr. 3, 13. 6, 7. Lu. 9, 1.

The Goſpel vpō Alholoweseue. And for many Martyrs.

* Bleſſed are ye poore: for yours is the kingdom of God. † Bleſſed are you that novv are an hungred: becauſe you ſhal 21 be filled. Bleſſed are you that novv doe vveepe: becauſe you ſhal laugh. † Bleſſed ſhal you be vvhen men ſhal hate you, 22 and vvhen they ſhal ſeparate you, and vpbraide you, and abandon your name as euil, for the ſonne of mans ſake. † " Be glad in that day and reioyce: for behold, your revvard 23 is much in heauen. ⊣ for according to theſe things did their fathers to the Prophets. † But vvo to you that are riche, be- 24 cauſe you haue your conſolation. † Vvo to you that are fil- 25 led: becauſe you ſhal be hungrie. Vvo to you that novv doe laugh: becauſe you ſhal mourne and vveepe. † Vvo, vvhen 26 al men" ſhal bleſſe you. for according to theſe things did their fathers to the falſe-Prophets.

Mt. 5, 2. 6, 7.

† But to you I ſay that doe heare, Loue your enemies, doe 27 good to them that hate you. † Bleſſe them that curſe you, 28 and pray for them that calumniate you. † And he that ſtri- 29 keth thee on the cheeke, offer alſo the other. And from him that taketh avvay from thee thy robe, prohibit not thy coate alſo. † And ∷ to euery one that aſketh thee, giue: and of him 30 that

∷ That is, to euery one iuſtly aſking. For that vvhich is vniuſtly aſked, may be iuſtly denied. *Aug. li. 1. c. 40. de Serm. Do. in monte.*

that taketh avvay the things that are thine, aſke not againe.
31 † And according as you vvil that men doe to you, doe you
32 alſo to them in like maner. † And if you loue them that loue you, vvhat thanke is to you? for ſinners alſo loue thoſe that
33 loue them. † And if ye doe good to them that doe you good:
34 vvhat thanke is to you? for ſinners alſo doe this. † And if ye lend to them of vvhom ye hope to receiue: vvhat thanke is to you? for ſinners alſo lend vnto ſinners, for to receiue as much.
35 † But loue ye your enemies: doe good and "lend, hoping for nothing thereby, and your revvard ſhal be much, and you ſhal be the ſonnes of the Higheſt, becauſe him ſelf is beneficial
36 vpō the vnkinde and the euil. † Be ye therfore merciful as alſo
37 your father is merciful. † Iudge not, & you ſhal not be iudged. condemne not, & you ſhal not be cōdemned. forgiue, and you
38 ſhal be forgiuen. † Giue, and there ſhal be giuen to you. good meaſure & preſſed dovvne and ſhaken together and running ouer ſhal they giue into your boſome. For vvith the ſame meaſure that you do meate, it ſhal be meaſured to you againe.

The Goſpel vpon the firſt Sunday after Pentecoſt.

39 † And he ſaid to them a ſimilitude alſo: Can the blinde
40 leade the blinde? doe not both fal into the ditch? † The diſciple is not aboue his maiſter: but euery one ſhal be perfect, if
41 he be as his maiſter. † And vvhy ſeeſt thou the mote in thy brothers eie: but the beame that is in thine ovvne eie thou
42 conſidereſt not? † Or hovv canſt thou ſay to thy brother, Brother, let me caſt out the mote out of thine eie: thy ſelf not ſeeing the beame in thine ovvne eie? Hypocrite, caſt firſt the beame out of thine ovvne eie: and then ſhalt thou ſee clerely to take forth the mote out of thy brothers eie. ⊣

43 † For there is no good tree that yeldeth euil fruites: nor
44 euil tree, that yeldeth good fruite. † For euery tree is knovven by his fruite. For neither doe they gather figges of thornes:
45 neither of a buſh doe they gather the grape. † The good man of the good treaſure of his hart bringeth forth good: and the euil man of the il treaſure bringeth forth euil. for of the aboūdance of the hart the mouth ſpeaketh.
46 † And vvhy cal you me, Lord, Lord: and doe not the
47 things vvhich I ſay? † Euery one that commeth to me, and heareth my vvords, and doeth them: I vvil ſhevv you to
48 vvhom he is like. † He is like to a man ∷ building a houſe, that digged deepe, and laid the foundation vpon a rocke. And vvhen an inundation roſe, the riuer bette againſt that

∷ He buildeth right & ſurely, that hath both faith and good vvorkes: he buildeth on ſand, that truſteth to his faith or reading or knovvledge of the ſcripture, and doth not vvorke or liue accordingly.

house, and it could not moue it: for it vvas founded vpon a rocke. † But he that heareth, and doeth not: is like to a man 49 building his house vpon the earth vvithout a foundation: against the vvhich the riuer did beate: and incontinent it fell, and the ruine of that house vvas great.

ANNOTATIONS
CHAP. VI.

Heretikes vnderstãd not the Scriptures.

3. *Neither this haue you read?*] The Scribes and phariseеs boasted most of their knovvledge of the Scriptures: but our Sauiour often shevveth their great ignorance. Euen so the Heretikes that novv a daies vaunt most of the Scriptures and of their vnderstanding of them, may soone be proued to vnderstand litle or nothing.

9. *Saue a soule.*] Hereby it seemeth that Christ (as at other times lightly alvvaies) did not only heale this man in body, but of some correspondent disease in his soule.

The Churches praiers at the times of giuing holy Orders.

12. *The vvholenight.*) Our Sauiour instantly prayed, alone in the mount vvithout doore, al night long, as a preparation to the designement of his Apostles the day after: to giue example to the Church of praying instantly vvhen priests are to be ordered, and a lesson to vs al vvhat vve should doe for our ovvne necessities, vvhen Christ did so for other mens.

The name and dignitie of Apostles.

13. *Vvhom he named Apostles.*.] Here it is to be noted against our Aduersaries that deceitfully measure to the simple the vvhole nature and qualitie of certaine sacred functions, by the primitiue signification and compasse of the names or vvordes vvhereby they be called. vvith vvhom as a Priest is but an elder, and a Bishop, a vvatchman or Superintendent, so an Apostle is nothing but a Legate or Messenger, and therfore (as they argue) * can make no Lawes nor prescribe or teach any thing not expressed in his *mandatum*. Know therfore against such deceiuers, that such things are not to be ruled by the vulgar signification of the Word or calling, but by vse and application of the holy Writers, and in this point by Christs ovvne expresse imposition. And so this vvord, *Apostle*, is a calling of Office, gouernement, authoritie, and most high dignitie giuen by our Maister, specially to the College of the Tvvelue: Whom he endued aboue that vvhich the vulgar etymologie of their name requireth, vvith povver to bind and loose, to punish and pardõ, to teach and rule his Church. Out of vvhich roome and dignitie, vvhich is called in the Psalme and in the actes, a Bishoprike, vvhen Iudas fel, Mathias vvas chosen to supply it, and vvas numbered among the rest, vvho vvere as founders or foundations of our religion, as the Apostle termeth them, Therfore to that college this name agreeth by special imposition and prerogatiue, though aftervvard it vvas by vse of the Scriptures extended to S. Paul and S. Barnabas, and sometimes to the Apostles successors: as also (by the like vse of Scriptures) to the first conuerters of countreis to the faith, or their coadiutors in that function. In vvhich sense S. Paul chalengeth to be the Corinthians Apostle, and nameth Epaphroditus the Philippians Apostle: as vve call S. Gregorie & his Disciple S. Augustin, our Apostles of England. In al vvhich taking, it euer signifieth dignitie, regiment, Paternitie, Principalitie, and Primacie in the Church of God: according to S. Paul 1. Cor. 12, *He hath placed in his Church, first in deede Apostles &c.* Whereby vve may see that S. Peters dignitie vvas a vvonderful eminent Prerogatiue and Soueraintie, When he vvas the head not only of other Christian men, but the head of al Apostles, yea euen of the College of the Tvvelue. And if our Aduersaries list to haue learned any profitable lesson by the vvord Apostle, more profitably and truely they might haue gathered, that Christ called these his principal officers, *Apostles*, or *Sent* (him self also specially and aboue al other being *Missus*, that is, *Sent*, and called also Apostle in the Scriptures) to vvarne vs by the nature of the vvord, that none are true Apostles, Pastors, or Preachers, that are not specially sent and called, or that can not shevv by vvhom they be sent. and that al Heretikes therfore be rather Apostates then Apostles, for that they be not sent, nor duely called, nor chosen to preach,

Calu. Inst. li. 4. c. 8.
Ps. 108, 8.
Act. 1, 20.
Eph. 2, 20.
Act. 14.
1 Cor. 12.
Eph. 4, 11.
1 Cor. 9, 2.
Phil. 2, 25.
Luc. 4, 18.
Hebr. 3, 1.

Peters preeminence.

14. *Simon.*) Peter in the numbering of the Apostles, alvvaies first named and preferred before Andrevv his elder brother and senior by calling, See *Annotat. Mt. 10, 2.*

Al persecution for Christ, is a blessing.

23. *Be glad.*) The common miseries that fall to the true preachers and other Catholike men for Christs sake, as pouertie, famin, mourning, and persecutions, be in deede the greatest blessings that can be, and are meritorious of the revvard of heauen. Contrarievvise, al the felicities of this vvorld vvithout Christ, are in deede nothing but vvo, and the enterance to euerlasting miserie.

The vanitie of Heretical preachers.

26. *Shal blesse you.*) This vvo pertaineth to the Heretikes of our daies, that delight to haue the peoples praises and blessings and shoutes, preaching pleasant things of purpose to their itching eares

eares: as did the Falſe-Prophets, vvhen they vvere magnified and commended therfore of the carnal Ievves.

35 Lend, hoping nothing.) In that vve may here ſeeme to be moued to lend to thoſe vvhom vve thinke not able nor like euer to repay againe, it muſt be holden for a counſel rather then a commaundement, except the caſe of neceſſitie. but it may be taken rather for a precept, vvherein vſurie, that is to ſay, the expectation not of the money lent, but of vantage for lone, is forbidden: as by other places of Scripture it is condemned, and is a thing againſt the Lavv of nature and nations. And greate ſhame and pitie it is, that it ſhould be ſo much vſed or ſuffered among Chriſtians, or ſo couered and cloked vnder the habite of other contractes, as it is.

Againſt vſurie.

CHAP. VII.

He teſtifieth, the faith of the Centurion vvho vvas a Gentil, to be greater then he found among al the Ievves, and cureth his ſeruant abſent. 11 the vvidovves ſonne he reuiueth and reſtoreth to her, and is renovvmed therevpon. 18 To Iohns meſſengers he anſvvereth vvith miracles, leauing to Iohn to preach thereby vnto them that he is Chriſt. 24 And aftervvard he declareth hovv vvorthy credit vvas Iohns teſtimonie, 29 inueighing againſt the Phariſees, 31 vvho vvith neither of their maners of liuing could be vvonne. 36 ſhevving alſo vnto them by occaſion of Marie Magdalen, hovv he is a frende to ſinners, not to maintaine them in ſinne, but to forgiue them their ſinnes vpon their faith and penance.

Mt. 8,5.

1 AND vvhen he had fully ſaid al his vvords into the eares of the people, he entred into Capharnaum. 2 † And the ſeruant of a certaine Centurion being ſicke, vvas readie to die: vvho vvas deere vnto him. 3 † And when he had heard of IESVS, he ſent vnto him the Auncients of the Ievves, deſiring him to come and heale his ſeruant. 4 † But they being come to IESVS, beſought him earneſtly, ſaying to him, That he is vvorthie that thou ſhouldeſt doe this for him. 5 † for he loueth our nation: and he hath″ built a ſynagogue for vs. 6 † And IESVS vvent vvith them. And vvhen he vvas novv not farre from the houſe, the Centurion ſent his frends vnto him, ſaying, Lord, trouble not thy ſelf. for ∴ *I am not vvorthie that thou ſhouldeſt enter vnder my roofe.* 7 † for the vvhich cauſe neither did I thinke my ſelf vvorthie to come to thee: but ſay the vvord, and my ſeruant ſhal be made whole. 8 † for I alſo am a man ſubiect to authoritie, hauing vnder me ſouldiars: and I ſay to this, goe, and he goeth: and to an other, come, and he commeth: and to my ſeruant, doe this, and he doeth it. 9 † Vvhich IESVS hearing, marueiled: and turning to the multitudes that folovved him he ſaid, Amen I ſay to you, neither in Iſrael haue I found ſo great faith. 10 † And they that vvere ſent, being returned home, found the ſeruant that had been ſicke, vvhole.

∴ See the Annotations vpon S. Matth. c. 8, 8.

The Gospel vpō the 15 Sunday after Pentecost. And vpō Thursday in the 4 vveeke of Lent. And for S. Monica S. Augustins mother Maij. 4.

† And it came to passe, aftervvard he vvent into a citie 11 that is called Naim: and there vvent vvith him his Disciples and a very great multitude. † And vvhen he came nigh to 12 the gate of the citie, behold a dead man vvas caried forth, the only sonne of his mother: and she, vvas a vvidovv: and a great multitude of the citie vvith her. † Vvhom vvhen our 13 Lord had seen, being moued vvith mercie vpon her, he said to her, Vveepe not. † And he came neere and touched the 14 coffin. And they that caried it, stood stil: and he said, Yong man, I say to thee, Arise. † And he that vvas dead, sate vp, and 15 beganne to speake. And he gaue him to his mother. † And 16 feare tooke them al: and they magnified God, saying, That a great Prophet is risen among vs: and, That God hath visited his people. † And this saying vvent forth into al Ievvrie of 17 him, and into al the countrie about.

† And Iohns disciples shevved him of al these things. 18 † * And Iohn called tvvo of his disciples, and sent them to 19 IESVS, saying, Art thou he that art to come: or expect vve an other? † And vvhen the men vvere come vnto him, they 20 said, Iohn the Baptist hath sent vs to thee, saying, Art thou he that art to come: or expect vve an other? † (And the self same 21 houre, he cured many of maladies, and hurtes, and euil spirits: and to many blinde he [c] gaue sight.) † And ansvvering, he said 22 to them, Goe and report to Iohn vvhat you haue heard and seen: * That the blinde see, the lame vvalke, the lepers are made cleane, the deafe heare, the dead rise againe, † ∴ the poore 23 are euangelized: and blessed is he vvhosoeuer shal not be scandalized in me.

Mt. 11, 2

[c] ἐχαρίσατο

Esa. 35, 5. 61, 1.

∴ *Pauperes euangelizantur*, that is, to the poore the Gospel is preached, and they receiue it.

† * And vvhen Iohns messengers vvere departed, he be- 24 gan to say of Iohn to the multitudes, Vvhat vvent you out into the desert to see? a reede moued vvith the vvinde? † But 25 vvhat vvent you forth to see? a man clothed in ∴ soft garments? behold they that are in costly apparel and delicacies, are in the house of kings. † But vvhat vvent you out for to 26 see? a Prophet? Certes I say to you, and more then a Prophet. † this is he of vvhom it is vvritten, *Behold I send mine Angel before* 27 *thy face, vvhich shal prepare thy vvay before thee.* † For I say to you, 28 A greater Prophet among the children of vvomen then Iohn the Baptist, there is no man. but he that is the lesser in the kingdom of God, is greater then he. † And al the people 29 hearing and the Publicans, iustified God, being baptized vvith Iohns

Mt. 11, 7

∴ Marke this vvel concerning Iohns apparel and diet. See the Annotations vpon S. Matth. c. 3, 4.

Mal. 3, 1

30 Iohns baptisme. † But the Pharisees and the lavvyers :: despised the counsel of God against them selues, being not bap-
31 tized of him. † And our Lord said, Vvherevnto then shal I liken the men of this generation, and vvherevnto are they
32 like? † They are like to children sitting in the market-place, and speaking one to an other, and saying, Vve haue piped to you, and you haue not daunced: vve haue lamented, and you
33 haue not vvept. † For Iohn the Baptist came * neither eating
34 bread nor drinking vvine: and you say, He hath a deuil. † The sonne of man came eating and drinking: and you say, Behold a man that is a gurmander and a drinker of vvine, a frende of
35 Publicans and sinners. † And vvisedom is iustified of al her children.

Mt. 3, 4.

:: As they that contẽned Iohns baptisme, despised Gods counsel and wisedõ: so much more they that make no accoumpt of the Sacraments of the Church, despise Gods counsel and ordinance touching their saluation, to their owne damnation.

36 † And one of the Pharisees desired him to eate vvith him. And being entred into the house of the Pharisee, he sate
37 downe to meate. † And behold a vvoman that was in the citie, a sinner, as she knevv that he vvas set dovvne in the Pharisees
38 house, she brought an alabaster boxe of ointment: † and standing behind beside his feete, she began to :: vvater his feete vvith teares, & vviped them vvith the heares of her head, and
39 kissed his feete, & anointed them with the ointmẽt. † And the Pharisee that had bid him, seeing it, spake vvithin him self, saying, This man if he vvere a Prophet, vvould knovv certes vvho and vvhat maner of vvomã she is vvhich toucheth him,
40 that she is a sinner. † And IESVS answering said to him, Simon,
41 I haue somevvhat to say vnto thee. but he said, Maister, say. † A certaine creditour had tvvo debters: one did ovve fiue hũdred
42 pence, and the other fiftie. † They hauing not vvherevvith to pay, he forgaue both. Vvhether therfore doth loue him
43 more? † Simon ansvvering said, I suppose that he to vvhom he forgaue more. But he said to him, Thou hast iudged rightly.
44 † And turning to the vvoman, he said vnto Simon, Doest thou see this vvoman? I entred ″ into thy house, vvater to my feete thou didst not giue: but she vvith teares hath vvatered
45 my feete, and vvith her heares hath vviped them. † Kisse thou gauest me not: but she since I came in, hath not ceased
46 to kisse my feete. † Vvith oile thou didst not anoint my
47 head: but she vvith ointment hath anointed my feete. † For the vvhich I say to thee, Many sinnes are forgiuen her, because she hath :: loued much. But to vvhom lesse is forgiuen,
48 he loueth lesse. † And he said to her, Thy sinnes are forgi-

The Gospel vpõ S. Marie Magdalens day Iul. 22. And vpon Thursday in Passion weeke. And vpõ Imber Friday in Sept.

:: A perfect paterne of true penance in this vvoman, vvho sought of Christ vvith opẽ teares & other strange vvorkes of satisfaction and deuotion, remission of her sinnes.

:: Not only faith (as you may perceiue) but loue or charitie obtaineth remission of sinnes.

uen thee. † And they that sate together at the table, began to 49 say vvithin them selues, ∴ Vvho is this that also forgiueth sinnes? † And he said to the vvoman, "Thy faith hath made 50 the safe, goe in peace. ✠

∴ As the Pharisees did alwaies carpe Christ for remissiō of sinnes in earth, so the Heretikes reprehend his Church that remitteth sinnes by his authoritie.

ANNOTATIONS CHAP. VII.

Building of Churches, Monasteries, &c.

5. Built a Synagogue.) As at that time to found a Synagogue, vvas acceptable to God, and procured the praiers of the faithful people for vvhose vse it vvas made: so novv much more in the nevv Testament, to build a Church, Monasterie, College, or any like vvorke for the honour and seruice of God, is grateful to him and procureth the praiers of the good people for vvhose vse such things be founded.

Exteriour signes of more then common deuotion.

44. Into thy house.] An exceding approbation of the extraordinary vvorkes and signes of external deuotion, vvhich seeme to carnal men (though othervvise faithful) to be often superfluous or not acceptable. This Simon vvas perhaps of a good vvil, and therfore (as diuers others did els vvhere) inuited Christ to his house, not of curiositie or captiousnes, as some other did: but of affectiō, as it may seeme by Christs familiar talke vvith him. Not vvithstanding his duties tovvardes him vvere but ordinary. but the anointing, vvashing, kissing, vviping of his feete in such sort as the vvoman did, vvere further signes of more then vulgar loue: such as is in deuout men or vvomen that goe on pilgrimage and kisse deuoutly the holy memories of Christ and his Saincts. Vvhich is no more but an exteriour expressing of their affection, and that they loue much, as euery vulgar christian man doth not.

Iustification attributed not to faith onely.

50. Thy faith.] The remission of her sinnes being attributed before to charitie, is novv also said to come of her faith. Vvhereby you may knovv that it commonly procedeth of both, and of hope also, though but one named. Because vvhen there be diuers causes concurring to one effect, the scriptures commonly name but one, and that especially vvhich is most proper to the purpose and time, not excluding the other. And therfore his vvorking miracles vpon any person, is attributed to the faith of them on vvhom or at vvhose desire they be done. Because he vvrought his miracles to induce al men to beleeue in him, and therfore specially required faith at their hands, and namely before other things, vvhether they did beleeue that he vvas able to doe that vvhich they asked at his hands: vvithout vvhich it had ben rather a mockrie and tentation of him, then a true desire of benefite at his hands.

CHAP. VIII.

Going ouer al Galilee With his traine, 4 he preacheth to the IeWes in parables because of their reprobation: 9 but to his Disciples manifestly: because he Wil not for the IeWes incredulity haue his comming frustrate: 19 signifying also that We are his kinne (though We be Gentils) and not his carnal brethren the IeWes. 22 To Whom also (signified by the Gerasens) after the tempest in his sleepe (that is, in his death) and caulme in his resurrection, he commeth: but they preferring their temporals before his presence, he leaueth them againe. 41 LikeWise comming to cure the IeWes (Who Were borne When the Gentils sickened, about Abrahams time) he is preuented With the faith of the Gentils, and then the IeWes die. but them also in the end he Wil restore.

AND it came to passe afterward, and he made 1 his iourney by cities and tovvnes preaching and euangelizing the kingdom of God: and the Tvvelue vvith him, † and 2 some vvomen that had been cured of vvicked spirits and infirmities, * Marie vvhich is called Magdalene, out of vvhom seuen deuils vvere gone forth.

Mr. 16, 9.

c *aliæ multæ*

3 forth, † and Ioane the vvife of Chuſa Herods procurator, and Suſan, and [c] many others that " did miniſter vnto him of their ſubſtance.

Mt.13,1. *Mr.4,1.*

The Goſpel vpō the Sunday of Sexageſme.

4 †And * vvhen a very great multitude aſſembled, and haſtened out of the cities vnto him, he ſaid by a ſimilitude. 5 † The ſovver vvent forth to ſovv his ſeede. and vvhiles he ſovveth, ſome fel by the vvay ſide, and vvas troden vpon, and the 6 foules of the aire did eate it. † And other ſome fel vpon the rocke: and being ſhot vp, it vvithered, becauſe it had not 7 moiſture. † And otherſome fel among thornes, and the thor-8 nes grovving vp vvithal, choked it. † And other ſome fel vpō good ground: and being ſhot vp, yelded fruite an hundred fold. Saying theſe things he cried, He that hath eares to heare, let him heare.

9 †And his diſciples aſked him vvhat this parable vvas. † To 10 vvhom he ſaid, To you it is giuen to knovv the myſterie of the kingdō of God, but to the reſt in parables, :: that * ſeeing 11 they may not ſee, and hearing may not vnderſtand. † And the 12 parable is this: The ſeede, is the vvord of God. † And they beſides the vvay: are thoſe that heare, then the deuil cōmeth, and taketh the vvord out of their hart, leſt beleeuing they be 13 ſaued. † For they vpon the rocke: ſuch as vvhen they heare, vvith ioy receiue the vvord: and theſe haue no rootes: becauſe :: for a time they beleeue, and in time of tentation they 14 reuolt. † And that vvhich fel into thornes, are they that haue heard, and going their vvaies, are choked vvith cares and 15 riches and pleaſures of this life, and render not fruite. † And that vpon good ground: are they vvhich in a good and very good hart, hearing the vvord, doe reteine it, and yeld fruite in patience. ⊣

Eſ. 6,9.

:: See the Annotations vpon S. Matthevv. c. 13, 14.

:: Againſt the Heretikes that ſay, faith once had can not be loſt, and that he vvhich novv hath not faith, neuer had.

16 † And no man lighting a candel doth couer it vvith a veſſel, or put it vnder a bed: but ſetteth it vpō a cādelſticke, that they 17 that enter in, may ſee the light. † For there is not any thing ſecrete, that ſhal not be made manifeſt: nor hid, that ſhal not be 18 knowen, & come abrode. † See therfore how you heare. For he that hath, to him ſhal be giuen: and vvhoſoeuer hath not, that alſo vvhich he thinketh he hath, ſhal be taken avvay frō him.

19 † And * his mother and brethren came vnto him: and they 20 could not come at him for the multitude. † And it vvas told him, Thy mother and " thy brethren ſtand vvithout, deſirous 21 to ſee thee. † Who anſvvering ſaid to them, My :: mother and my

:: He did not here diſdainfully ſpeake of his mother, but teacheth that

my brethren, are they that heare the vvord of God and doe it.

22 †* And it came to passe one day: and he vvent vp into a boate, and his disciples, and he said to them, Let vs strike ouer the lake. And they launched forth. 23 † And vvhen they vvere sailing, he slept: and there fel a storme of vvinde into the lake, and they [c] vvere filled, and vvere in danger. 24 † And :: they came and raised him, saying, Maister, vve perish. But he rising, rebuked the vvinde and the tempest of vvater: and it ceased, and there vvas made a calme. 25 † And he said to them, Vvhere is your faith? Who fearing, marueiled one to an other, saying, Vvho is this (trovv ye) that he commaundeth both the vvindes and the sea, and they obey him? 26 † * And they sailed to the countrie of the Gerasens vvhich is ouer against Galilee.

27 † And vvhen he vvas come forth to the land, there mette him a certaine man that had a deuil novv a very long time, and he did vveare no clothes, neither did he tarie in house, but in the monumēts. 28 † And as he savv IESVS, he fel dovvne before him: and crying out vvith a great voice, he said, Vvhat is to me and thee IESVS sonne of God most high? I beseech thee doe not torment me. 29 † For he commaunded the vncleane spirit to goe forth out of the man. For many times he caught him, and he vvas bound vvith chaines, and kept vvith fetters: and breaking the bondes vvas driuen of the deuil into the deserts. 30 † And IESVS asked him saying, Vvhat is thy name? But he said, Legion. because many deuils vvere entred into him. 31 † And they besought him that he vvould not commaund them to goe into the depth. 32 † And there vvas there a heard of many svvine feeding on the mountaine: and they desired him, that he vvould permit them to enter into them. And he permitted them. 33 † The deuils therfore vvent forth out of the man, and entred into the svvine: and the heard vvith violence vvent headlong into the lake, and vvas stifled. 34 † Which vvhen the svvineheards savv done, they fled: and told into the citie and into the tovvnes. 35 † And they vvent forth to see that vvhich vvas done: and they came to IESVS, and found the man, out of vvhō the deuils vvere gone forth, sitting at his feete, clothed, and vvel in his vvittes, and they vvere afraid. 36 † And they also that had seen, told them hovv he had been made whole from the legion. 37 † And al the multitude of the countrie of the Gerasens besought him to depart from them:

Marginal notes:

our spiritual kinred is to be preferred before carnal cognation. *Hilar. in 12 Mat.*

:: See the Annotations vpon S. Matthevv c. 8, 24.

Mt. 8, 23. Mar. 4, 36.

[c] *complebantur.*

Mt. 8, 28. Mr. 5, 1.

them: for they vvere taken vvith great feare. And he going vp into the boate, returned. 38 † And the man out of vvhom the deuils vvere departed, deſired him that he might be vvith him. But IESVS dimiſſed him, ſaying, 39 † Returne into thy houſe, and tel hovv great things God hath done to thee. And he vvent through the vvhole citie, preaching hovv great things IESVS had done to him.

40 † And it came to paſſe: vvhen IESVS vvas returned, the multitude receiued him. and al vvere expecting him. 41 † And ⋆ behold there came a man vvhoſe name vvas Iaîrus, and he vvas Prince of the Synagogue: and he fel at the feete of IESVS, deſiring him that he vvould enter into his houſe, 42 † becauſe he had an only daughter almoſt tvvelue yeres old, and ſhe vvas a dying. And it chaunced, vvhiles he vvent, he vvas thronged of the multitudes.

Mt. 9, 18. Mar. 5, 22.

43 † And there vvas :: a certaine vvoman in a fluxe of bloud from tvvelue yeres paſt, vvhich had beſtovved al her ſubſtãce vpon Phyſicions, neither could ſhe be cured of any: 44 † ſhe came behind him, and touched the hemme of his garment: and forthvvith the fluxe of her bloud ſtinted, 45 † And IESVS ſaid, Vvho is it that touched me? And al denying, :: Peter ſaid, and they that vvere vvith him, Maiſter, the multitudes throng and preſſe thee, and doeſt thou ſay, Vvho touched me? 46 † And IESVS ſaid, Some bodie hath touched me. for I knovv that there is vertue proceded from me. 47 † And the vvoman ſeeing, that ſhe vvas not hid, came trembling, and fel dovvne before his feete: and for vvhat cauſe ſhe had touched him, ſhe ſhevved before al the people: and hovv forthvvith ſhe vvas made vvhole. 48 † But he ſaid to her, Daughter, thy faith hath made the ſafe, goe thy vvay in peace.

:: See the Annotations vpon S. Matthevv c. 9, 19.

:: It is an euidẽt ſigne of prerogatiue, that Peter only is named ſo often as cheefe of the company. Mar. 1, 36. Act. 5, 29. Luc. 9, 32. Mar. 16, 7. 1 Cor. 15, 5.

49 † As he vvas yet ſpeaking, there cõmeth one to the Prince of the ſynagogue, ſaying to him, That thy daughter is dead, trouble him not. 50 † And IESVS hearing this vvord, anſvvered the father of the maide, Feare not: :: beleeue only, and ſhe ſhal be ſafe. 51 † And vvhen he vvas come to the houſe, he permitted not any man to enter in vvith him, but Peter, and Iames, and Iohn, and the father and mother of the maide. 52 † And al vvept, and mourned for her. But he ſaid, Vveepe not, the maide is not dead, but ſleepeth. 53 † And they derided him, knovving that ſhe vvas dead. 54 † But he holding her hand cried ſaying, Maide ariſe. 55 † And ″ her ſpirit returned, and ſhe roſe

:: See the Annotations vpon S. Marke c. 5, 36.

incontinent. And he bade them giue her to eate. † And her 56 parentes vvere astonied, vvhom he commaunded to tel no man that vvhich vvas done.

ANNOTATIONS
CHAP. VIII.

Holy vvomen that folovved Christ.

3. That did minister.] It vvas the custome of the Ievves that vvomen of their substance did minister meate and drinke and cloth to their teachers, going about vvith them. vvhich because it might haue been scandalous among the gentiles, S. Paul maketh mention that he vsed it not. And they ministred to our Lord of their substance for this cause, that he vvhose spiritual benefites they reaped, might reape their carnal things. *1 Cor. 9, 5. 12.*

The brethren of Christ.

20. Thy brethern.) These brethern of our Lord, vvere not the sonnes of the B. Virgin MARIE the mother of God, as Heluidius vvickedly taught: neither are they to be thought (as some others say) the sonnes of Ioseph by an other vvife: for (as S. Hierom vvriteth) not only our Lady vvas a virgin, but by reason of her, Ioseph also: that our Sauiour might be borne of a virginal matrimonie. But they are called his brethren (according to the vsual speach of the Scriptures) because they vvere his cosins, either the sonnes of Iosephs brother, or (as the more receiued opinion is) the sonnes of our Ladies sister called Marie of Iames, vvhich Iames therfore is also called the brother of our Lord. *Hiero. cōt. Heluid. c. 9. Ibidē c. 8.*

A third place after this life.

55. Her spirit returned.) This returning of the soules againe into the bodies of them vvhom CHRIST and his Apostles raised from death (specially Lazarus vvho had been dead foure daies) doth euidently proue a third place against our aduersaries, that say, euery one goeth straight to Heauen or to Hel. for it can not be thought that they vvere called from the one or the other, and therfore from some third place.

CHAP. IX.

His tvvelue also novv preaching euery vvhere and vvorking miracles, 6 Herod and al do vvonder much. 10 After vvhich, he taketh them and goeth into the vvildernesse: vvhere he cureth and teacheth, feeding 5000 vvith fiue loaues. 18 Peter confessing him to be Christ, 21 he on the other side foretelleth his Passion, and that al must in time of persecution folovv him therein. 27 Vvherevnto to encourage vs the more, 27 he giueth in his Transfiguration a sight of the glorie, vvhich is the revvard of suffering. 37 The next day he casteth out a diuel vvhich his Disciples could not. 43 Vvhom amiddes these vvonders he forevvarneth againe of his scandalous Passion. 49 And to cure their ambition, he telleth them, that the most humble he esteemeth most: 49 bidding them also, not to prohibit any that is not against them. 51 Yea and tovvard such as be against them Schismatically, to shevv mildnes for al that. 57 Of folovving him, three examples.

The Gospel vpō Thursday in Whitsōvveeke.

AND calling together the tvvelue Apostles, he 1 gaue them ∷ vertue and povver ouer al deuils, and to cure maladies. † And he sent them to 2 preach the kingdom of God: and to heale the sicke. † And he said to them, Take nothing 3 for the vvay, neither rod, nor skrippe, nor bread, nor money, neither haue tvvo coates. † And into vvhatsoeuer house you 4 enter, tarie there, and thence doe not depart. † And vvhosoeuer shal not receiue you, going forth out of that citie, shake

Mt. 10, 1 Mr. 3, 13 6, 8.

∷ To cōmaund Diuels and diseases either of body or soule, is by nature proper to God onely: but by Gods gift, men also may haue the same. euen so to forgiue sinnes.

ſhake of the duſt alſo of your feete :: for a teſtimonie vpon them. 6 †And going forth they vvent a circuite from tovvne to tovvne euangelizing and curing euery vvhere. ¶

Mt. 14, 1. Mar. 6, 14.

7 †And *Herod the Tetrarch heard al things that vvere done by him: and he ſtaggered becauſe it vvas ſaid of ſome, 8 That Iohn vvas riſen from the dead. † but of other ſome, That Elias hath appeared: and of others, that a Prophet one 9 of the old ones vvas riſen. †And Herod ſaid, Iohn I haue beheaded: but vvho is this of vvhom I heare ſuch things? And he ſought for to ſee him.

Mt. 14, 13. Mar. 6, 31. Io. 6, 5.

10 †And *the Apoſtles being returned, reported to him vvhatſoeuer they did: and taking them he retired apart into 11 a deſert place, vvhich belongeth to Beth-ſaida. †Which the multitudes vnderſtāding, folovved him: & he receiued them, and ſpake to them of the kingdom of God, and them that had 12 neede of cure he healed. †And the day began to dravv tovvards an end. And the Tvvelue comming neere, ſaid to him, Dimiſſe the multitudes, that going into tovvnes and villages here about, they may haue lodging, and finde meates: becauſe 13 here vve are in a deſert place. †And he ſaid to them, Giue you them to eate. But they ſaid, We haue no more but fiue loaues and tvvo fiſhes: vnles perhaps vve ſhould goe and bie meates 14 for al this multitude. †And there vvere men almoſt fiue thouſand. And he ſaid to his diſciples, Make them ſit dovvne by 15 companies fiftie and fiftie. †And ſo they did. And they made 16 al ſit dovvne. †And taking the fiue loaues and the tvvo fiſhes, he looked vp vnto heauen, and [c] :: bleſſed them: and he brake, and diſtributed to his diſciples, for to ſet before the multi-17 tudes. †And :: they did al eate, and had their fill. And there vvas taken vp that vvhich remained to them, tvvelue baſkets of fragments.

c εὐλόγησεν αὐτοὺς:

Mt. 16, 13. Mar. 8, 27.

18 †*And it came to paſſe: vvhen he vvas alone praying, his diſciples alſo vvere vvith him: and he aſked them ſaying, 19 Vvhom doe the multitudes ſay that I am? †But they anſvvered, and ſaid, Iohn the Baptiſt: and ſome, Elias: but ſome, that 20 one of the Prophets before time, is riſen. †And he ſaid to thē, But vvhom ſay ye that I am? Simon Peter anſvvering, ſaid, 21 The CHRIST of God. †But he rebukīg them, cōmaunded that 22 they ſhould tell this to no man, †ſaying, That the ſonne of man muſt ſuffer many things, and be reiected of the Auncients and cheefe Prieſts and Scribes, and be killed, and the

:: A great fault to reiect the true preachers, or not to admit them into houſe for needful harbour and ſuſtenance.

:: Here you ſee that he bleſſed the things, and not only gaue thanks to God. See Annot. Marci. c. 8, 7.

:: The miraculous prouidēce of God toward ſuch as folow Chriſt into deſerts, priſons, baniſhment, or whitherſoeuer.

third day riſe againe.

† And he ſaid to al, If any man vvil come after me, let him 23 denie him ſelf, and take vp his croſſe daily, and folovv me. † For he that vvil ſaue his life, ſhal loſe it: for he that ſhal loſe 24 his life for my ſake, ſhal ſaue it. † for vvhat profit hath a man 25 if he gaine the vvhole vvorld, and loſe him ſelf, and caſt avvay him ſelf? † For he that ſhal be aſhamed of me and of 26 my vvordes, him the Sonne of man ſhal be aſhamed of, vvhen he ſhal come in his maieſtie, and his fathers, and of the holy Angels. † And I ſay to you aſſuredly, There be ſome 27 ſtanding here that ſhal not taſt death, " til they ſee the kingdom of God.

The TRANSFIGVRATION.

† * And it came to paſſe after theſe vvordes almoſt eight 28 daies, and he tooke Peter and Iames and Iohn, and vvent into a mountaine to pray. † And vvhiles he prayed, the ſhape of 29 his countenance vvas altered: and his raiment vvhite and gliſtering. † And behold tvvo men talked vvith him. And 30 they vvere Moyſes and Elias, † appearing in maieſtie. And 31 they told his deceaſe that he ſhould accompliſh in Hieruſalem. † But Peter and they that vvere vvith him, vvere hea- 32 uie vvith ſleepe. And avvaking, they ſavv his maieſtie, and the tvvo men that ſtoode vvith him. † And it came to paſſe, 33 vvhen they departed from him, Peter ſaid to IESVS, Maiſter, it is good for vs to be here: and let vs make three tabernacles, one for thee, and one for Moyſes, and one for Elias: not knovving vvhat he ſaid. † And as he ſpake theſe things, 34 there came a cloud, and ouerſhadovved them: and they feared, vvhen they entered into the cloude. † * And a voice vvas 35 made out of the cloude, ſaying, This is my beloued ſonne, heare him. † And vvhiles the voice vvas made, IESVS vvas 36 found alone. And they held their peace, and told no man in thoſe daies any of theſe things vvhich they had ſeen.

Mt. 17, 1
Mr. 9, 1.

2. Pet. 1, 17.

† * And it came to paſſe the day folovving, vvhen they 37 came dovvne from the mountaine, there mette him a great multitude. † And behold a man of the multitude cried out, 38 ſaying, Maiſter, I beſeeche thee, looke vpō my ſonne becauſe he is mine only one. † and loe, the ſpirit taketh him, and he 39 ſodenly crieth, and he daſheth him, and teareth him that he fometh, and vvith much a doe departeth renting him. † And 40 I deſired thy diſciples to caſt him out, and they could not. † And IESVS anſvvering ſaid, ⁖ O faithles and peruerſe 41 genera

Mt. 17, 14.
Mar. 9, 17.

⁖ Incredulitie hindereth the effect of Exorciſmes, and

generation, hovv long ſhal I be vvith you and ſuffer you? 42 bring hither thy ſonne. †And vvhen he came to him, the deuil daſhed, and tore him. And IESVS rebuked the vncleane 43 ſpirit, and healed the lad: and rendred him to his father. †And al vvere aſtonied at the might of God: and al merueiling at 44 al things that he did, he ſaid to his diſciples, †Lay you in your hartes theſe vvordes, for it ſhal come to paſſe that the Sonne 45 of man ſhal be deliuered into the hands of men. †But they did not knovv this vvord, and it vvas couered before them, that they perceiued it not. And they vvere afraid to aſke him of this vvord.

other miraculous power giuen to the Church.

Mt. 18,1 Mar. 9, 34.

46 †* And there entred :: a cogitation into them, vvhich of 47 them ſhould be greater. †But IESVS ſeeing the cogitations of 48 their hart, tooke a childe and ſet him by him, †and ſaid to them, Whoſoeuer receiueth this childe in my name, receiueth me: and vvhoſoeuer receiueth me, receiueth him that ſent me. For he that is the leſſer among you al, he is the greater.

:: Deſire of preeminence is an humane infirmitie oftẽ euen among the good. Againſt which, Chriſt teacheth humility, but forbiddeth not Superiority.

Mar. 9, 38.

49 †* And Iohn anſvvering ſaid, Maiſter, vve ſavv a certaine man caſting out deuils in thy name, and vve prohibited him, 50 becauſe he folovveth not vvith vs. †And IESVS ſaid to him, :: Prohibit not. for he that is not againſt you, is for you.

:: There be ſome that folow not Chriſt preciſely in life and doctrine, of whom we may make our aduãtage to the propagation of Chriſtes honour and religion, whẽ they doe any thing for the aduãcemẽt thereof, of what intention ſoeuer they doe it. Philip. 1, 15.

51 †And it came to paſſe, vvhiles the daies of his aſſumption vvere accõpliſhing, and he fixed his face to goe into Hieruſa-52 lem. †And he ſent meſſengers before his face: and going they 53 entred into a citie of the Samaritans to prepare for him. †And they receiued him not, becauſe his "face vvas to goe to Hie-54 ruſalem. †And vvhen his diſciples Iames and Iohn had ſeen it, they ſaid, Lord vvilt thou vve ſay that fire come dovvne 55 from heauen and conſume ˋthemˊ? †And turning, "he rebuked them, ſaying, You knovv not of vvhat ſpirit you are. 56 †The ſonne of man came not to deſtroy ſoules, but to ſaue. And they vvent into an other tovvne.

them as Elias alſo did?

Mt. 8, 19.

57 †And it came to paſſe as they vvalked in the vvay, a certaine man ſaid to him, * I vvil folovv thee vvhitherſoeuer 58 thou goeſt. †IESVS ſaid to him, :: The foxes haue holes, and the foules of the aire neſtes: but the ſonne of man hath 59 not vvhere to repoſe his head. †But he ſaid to an other, Folovv me. And he ſaid, Lord, permit me firſt to goe, and to 60 burie my father. †And IESVS ſaid to him, Let the dead burie their dead: but goe thou, ſet forth the kingdom of God. 61 †And an other ſaid, I vvil folovv thee Lord, but permit me

:: This man would haue folowed him for temporal commodities, and therfore was not ſuffered.

first to take my leaue of them that are at home. † IESVS said 62 to him, " No man putting his hand to the plough, and looking backe, is apt for the kingdom of God.

ANNOTATIONS
CHAP. IX.

The Transfiguration.

27. *Til they see.*) To the Apostles, that had to preach the kingdom of God and to suffer so much miserie for the same in this vvorld, he vvil shevv his glorie, and giue them a tast of his owne ioyful state and of his Saincts in heauen, calling thither Moyses and Elias, that the Lavv and Prophets might be vvitnesses of the same. See the annotation vpon S. Matthevv c. 17, 2.

Schismatikes.

53. *Face to goe to Hierusalem.*) The Samaritans vvere Schismatikes from the Ievves, and had a Schismatical temple in mount Garizim, of purpose to dravv men thither from Gods temple in Hierusalem, vvhere only vvas the true and as it vvere the Catholike seruice and Sacrifice vnto God. Therfore they did not gladly receiue our Sauiour, because they perceiued he vvas going to Hierusalem.

Io. 4, 9. 3 Re. 12, 27. Tob. 1.

Desire of reuenge.

55. *He rebuked them.*) Not iustice nor al rigorous punishment of sinners is here forbidden, nor Elias fact repreheded, nor the Church or Christian Princes blamed for putting Heretikes to death: but that none of these should be done for desire of our particular reuenge, or vvithout discretion, & regard of their amendement, and example to others. Therfore S. Peter vsed his povver vpon Ananias and Sapphira, vvhen he strooke them both dovvne to death for defrauding the Church.

The Churches seueritie.

Act. 5.

Looking backe.

62. *No man looking backe.*) It is a dangerous temptation for a man that hath lost or left his goods for Christ, to looke much backe at them, and to remember vvith delight the pleasures and eases of this vvorld. for it breedeth in him discontentment of the troubles and crosses that are incident to the state of such as fully folovv Christ. In vvhich case a man should euer looke forvvard tovvards heauen, and neuer backevvard to the vvorld.

CHAP. X.

He sendeth yet 72 moe to preach to the Iewes, With power also of miracles, 13 crying Wo to the cities impenitent. 17 At their returne he agniseth the great power he gaue them, but yet teacheth them not to be proud thereof, 21 and praiseth God for his grace, 23 his Church also for her happy state. 25. To one of the Scribes he sheweth, that the loue of God and of his neighbour wil bring him to life euerlasting, 29 teaching him by the parable of the Samaritane, to take euery one for his neighbour that needeth his charitie. 38 To Martha he sheweth that Maries Contemplatiue life is the better.

The Gospel vpō S. Markes day and S. Lukes.

:: As the twelue Apostles did represent the higher degree of the clergie, called Bishops: so these Seuentie tvvo beare the figure of the inferiour clergie, called Priests. Beda.

AND after this our Lord designed also other 1 :: seuentie tvvo: and he sent them tvvo and tvvo before his face into euery citie and place vvhither him self vvould come. † And he said to them, The haruest truely is 2 much: but the vvorkemen fevv. Desire therfore the lord of the haruest, that he send vvorkemen into his haruest. † Goe: behold I send you as lambes among vvol- 3 ues. † Carie not purse nor skrip, nor shoes: and salute no 4 body by the vvay. † Into vvhatsoeuer house you enter, 5 first say, Peace to this house. † and if the sonne of peace be 6 there

there, your peace ſhal reſt vpon him: but if not, it ſhal re-
7 turne to you. † And in the ſame houſe tarie you, eating and drinking ſuch things as they haue. * For the vvorkeman is vvorthie of his hire. Remoue not from houſe to houſe.
8 † And into vvhat citie ſoeuer you enter, and they receiue you,
9 eate ſuch things as are ſet before you: † and cure the ſicke that are in it, and ſay to them, The kingdom of God is come nigh vpon you. ⊣

1. Tim. 5, 18.

10 † And into vvhatſoeuer citie you enter, and they receiue
11 you not, going forth into the ſtreates thereof, ſay, † The duſt alſo of your citie that cleaueth to vs, vve doe vvipe of againſt you. yet this knovv ye that the kingdom of God is at hand.
12 † I ſay to you, it ſhal be :: more tolerable for Sodom in that
13 day, then for that citie. † Vvo to thee Corozáim, vvo to thee Beth-ſaida: for if in Tyre and Sidon had been vvrought the miracles that haue beene vvrought in you, they had done pe-
14 nance ſitting :: in ſacke cloth and aſhes long agoe. † But it ſhal be more tolerable for Tyre and Sidon in the iudgement, then
15 for you. † And thou Capharnaum that art exalted vnto heauẽ:
16 thou ſhalt be thruſt dovvne euen vnto hel. † :: He that heareth you, heareth me: and he that deſpiſeth you, deſpiſeth me. And he that deſpiſeth me, deſpiſeth him that ſent me.

:: Differences of paines and damnation in Hel according to the differences of demerites. Aug. li. 5. c. 5. cont. Iulian.

:: True penance not onely to lead a new life, but to puniſh the body by ſuch things as here be recorded, for the il life paſt.

:: It is al one to deſpiſe Chriſt, and to deſpiſe his Prieſts and Miniſters in the the Catholike Church: to refuſe his doctrine, & theirs.

17 † And the Seuentie-tvvo returned vvith ioy, ſaying, Lord,
18 the Deuils alſo are ſubiect to vs in thy name. † And he ſaid
19 to them, I ſavv Satan as a lightening fal from heauen. † † Behold, I haue giuen you povver to treade vpon ſerpents, and ſcorpions, and vpon al the povver of the enemie, and nothing
20 ſhal hurt you. † But yet reioyce not in this, that the ſpirits are ſubiect vnto you: but reioyce in this, that your names are vvritten in heauen. ⊣

21 † In that very houre he reioyced in ſpirit, and ſaid, I confeſſe to thee O Father, Lord of heauen and earth, becauſe thou haſt hid theſe things from the vviſe and prudent, and haſt reuealed them " to litle ones. Yea Father, for ſo hath it vvel
22 pleaſed thee. † Al things are deliuered to me of my father. And no man knovveth vvho the Sonne is, but the Father: and vvho the Father is, but the Sonne, and to vvhom the
23 Sonne vvil reueale. † And turning to his Diſciples, he ſaid,
24 Bleſſed are the eies that ſee the things that you ſee. † For I ſay to you, that many Prophets and Kings deſired to ſee the things that you ſee, and ſavv them not: and to heare the things

The Goſpel vpõ the 12 Sunday after Pẽtecoſt.

things that you heare, and heard them not.

25 † And behold a certaine lavvyer stoode vp, tempting him and saying, Maister, by doing of vvhat thing shal I possesse life euerlasting? 26 † But he said to him, In the lavv vvhat is vvritten? hovv readest thou? 27 † He ansvvering said, *Thou shalt loue the Lord thy God vvith thy vvhole hart, and vvith thy vvhole soule, and vvith al thy strength, and vvith al thy minde: and thy neighbour as thy self.* 28 † And he said to him, Thou hast ansvvered right, "this doe and thou shalt liue. 29 † But he desirous to iustifie him self, said to IESVS, And vvho is my neighbour? 30 † And IESVS taking it, said, A certaine man vvent dovvne from Hierusalem into Iericho, and fel among theeues, vvho also spoiled him, and giuing him vvoundes vvent avvay leauing him "halfe-dead. 31 † And it chaunced that a certaine Priest vvent dovvne the same vvay: and seeing him, passed by. 32 † In like maner also a Leuite, vvhen he vvas neere the place, and savv him, passed by. 33 † But a certaine Samaritane going his iourney, came neere him: and seeing him, vvas moued vvith mercie. 34 † And going vnto him, bound his vvoundes, povvring in oile and vvine: and setting him vpon his ovvne beast, brought him into an inne, and tooke care of him. 35 † And the next day he tooke forth tvvo pence, and gaue to the host, and said, Haue care of him: and vvhatsoeuer thou shalt :: supererogate, I at my returne vvil repay thee. 36 † Vvhich of these three in thy opinion vvas neighbour to him that fel among theeues? 37 † But he said, He that did mercie vpon him. And IESVS said to him, Goe, and doe thou in like maner. ⊣

38 † b And it came to passe as they vvent, and he entred into a certaine tovvne: and a certaine vvoman named Martha, receiued him into her house, 39 † and she had a sister called Marie. vvho sitting also at our Lords feete, heard his vvord. 40 † But Martha vvas busie about much seruice. vvho stoode and said, Lord, hast thou no care that my sister hath left me alone to serue? speake to her therfore, that she help me. 41 † And our Lord ansvvering said to her, Martha, Martha, thou art careful, and art troubled about very many things. 42 † But one thing is necessarie. "Marie hath chosen the best part vvhich shal not be taken avvay from her. ⊣

Deu. 6, 5

Leu. 19, 18.

:: S. Augustin saith that the Apostle (1. Cor. 9.) according to this place did supererogate, that is, did more then he needed or was bound to doe, when he might haue required al duties for preaching the Gospel, but would not. *li. de op. Monach. c. 5.* Whereof it cōmeth, that the workes which we doe more then precept, be called workes of Supererogation: & whereby it is also euident against the Protestāts, that there be such workes. *See Optatus li. 6 cont. Parmen.* how aptly he applyeth this parable to S. Paules counsel of virginitie (*1 Cor. 7*) as to a worke of supererogation.

b The Gospel vpon the Assumptiō of our Lady *Aug. 15.*

:: *Supererogaueris*, προσδαπανήσῃς,

ANNOT.

ANNOTATIONS
CHAP. X.

21. To litle ones) By this place euery vulgar artificer may not presume that God hath reuealed al truth to him, and therfore refuse to be taught of the learned. for Christ did not aftervvard endevv fishers and vulgar men nor any other vvith the gifts of vvisdom and tonges, vvithout their industrie, study, and teaching. though at the beginning, of great prouidence he did it, that it might be cleere to the vvorld, that al Nations vvere conuerted to him, not by persuasion of cunning Orators or subtil Disputers, but by the plaine force of his grace and truth, vvhich S. Augustine counteth greater then al other miracles. Further we are taught by this place, that the poore humble obedient children of the Church knovv by their faith the high mysteries of Christes Diuinity, and his presence in the B. Sacrament, and such like: rather then Arius, Caluin, and other like proud Scribes and Pharisees.

The humble vnlearned Catholike knovveth Christ better then the proud learned *Heretike.*

28. This doe.) Not by faith only, but by keeping Gods commaundements we obtaine life euerlasting: not onely by beleeuing, but by doing. The heretikes say that it is impossible to keepe this commaundement of louing God with al our hart. But the Scriptures giue vs examples of diuers that haue kept and fulfilled it, as far as is requisite in this life. *3. reg. 14, 8. 2. Par. 15, 15. Ps. 118, 10. Eccli. 47, 9, 10. 4 Reg. 20, 3. 5. Luc. 1, 5.* And if it vvere impossible to keepe it, and yet by Christ proposed for the meane to obtaine life euerlasting, he had mocked this Lavvyer and others, and not taught them.

The commaundements possible to be kept.

Conc. Arausi. 2 cap. 25. to. 1. Conc. Coc. Trid. Sess. 6. c. 1.

30. Halfe dead.) Here is signified man vvounded very sore in his vnderstanding and free-wil, and al other povvers of soule and body, by the sinne of Adam: but yet that neither vnderstanding, nor free-vvil, nor the rest, vvere extinguished in man or taken avvay. The Priest and Leuite, signifie the Lavv of Moyses: this Samaritane, is Christ the Priest of the nevve Testament: the oile and vvine, his Sacraments: the host, the priests his ministers. Vvhereby is signified, that the Lavv could not recouer the spiritual life of mankind from the death of sinne, that is, iustifie man: but Christ onely, vvho by his passion and the grace and vertue thereof ministred in and by his Sacraments, iustifieth, and increaseth the iustice of man, healing and abling free-vvil to doe al good vvorkes.

The parable of the vvounded man, explicated.

42. Marie the best part.) Tvvo notable exãples, one of the life Actiue, in Martha: the other of the life Cõtẽplatiue, in Marie: representing vnto vs, that in holy Church there should be alvvaies some to serue God in both these seueral sorts. The life cõtẽplatiue is here preferred before the actiue. the Religious of both sexes are of that more excellent state. and therfore our Protestants haue wholy abandoned them out of their common wealth, which the true Church neuer wanted. But to say truth, they haue neither Martha nor Marie. our Lord geue them grace to see their miserie. If ours were not answerable to their profession, or were degenerated, why haue they no new ones? if our Churches Votaries vowed vnlawful things, Chastitie, Pouertie, Obedience, Pilgrimage: what other Votaries or lawful vowes haue they? For, to offer voluntarily by vow (besides the keeping of Gods commaundements, whereunto we are bound by precept and promise in our Baptisme) our soules, bodies, goods, or any other acceptable thing to God, is an acte of souerain worship belonging to God onely: and there was neuer true religion without such vowes and Votaries. If there be none in their whole Church that professe contemplation, or that vow any thing at al to God voluntarily, neither in their bodies nor in their goods: God and the world knovv they haue no Church nor religion at al.

The Contemplatiue or Religious life, better then the Actiue and secular.

Vovves and votaries.

CHAP. XI.

He teacheth a forme of prayer, 5 and exhorteth to pray instantly, 11 assuring that so God wil giue vs good things. 14 The Iewes blaspheming his casting out of Diuels, and asking for a miracle from heauen, 17 he defendeth his doing: 22 foretelling also the Diuels expulsion by him out of the world (that is, the vocation of the Gentils) 24 and his reentrie into their nation, 27 with their reprobation though he be of their flesh, 29 and also their final most worthy damnation. 37 Againe, to the Pharisees and Scribes he crieth wo, as authors of the said reprobation now at hand.

Y AND

ND it came to passe, vvhen he vvas in a 1 certaine place, praying, as he ceased, one of his Disciples said to him, Lord teach vs to pray, as Iohn also taught his Disciples. † And he said to them, * Vvhen you pray, 2 say, FATHER, *sanctified be thy name. Thy kingdom come,† Our daily bread giue vs this day,† and forgiue vs* 3 *our sinnes, for because our selues also doe forgiue euery one that is in debt to vs.* 4 *And lead vs not into temptation.* † And he said to them, Vvhich of 5 you shal haue a frende, and shal goe to him at midnight, and shal say to him, Frende, lend me three loaues, † because a frende 6 of mine is come out of his way to me, and I haue not what to set before him: † & he from vvithin ansvvering saith, Trouble 7 me not, novv the doore is shut, and my children are vvith me in bed: I can not rise and giue thee. † And if he shal perse- 8 uêre knocking, I say to you, although he vvil not rise and giue him because he is his frende, yet for his importunitie he vvil rise, and giue him as many as he needeth. † * And I say 9 to you, Aske, and it shal be giuen you: seeke, and you shal finde: knocke, and it shal be opened to you. † For euery one 10 that asketh, receiueth: and he that seeketh, findeth: and to him that knocketh, it shal be opened. † And vvhich of you 11 if he aske his father bread, vvil he giue him a stone? or a fish, vvil he for a fish giue him a serpent? † Or if he aske an egge, 12 vvil he reach him a scorpion? † If you then being naught, 13 knovv hovv to giue good giftes to your children, hovv much more vvil your father from heauen giue the good spi- rit to them that aske him? ˧

Mt. 6,9.

The Gospel in *Maioribus litanijs* on S. Markes day, and in the Rogation daies. And in a votiue Masse against the Pagans.

The Gospel in a votiue Masse for sinnes.

Mt. 7,7.

† * And he vvas casting out a deuil, and that vvas dumme. 14 And vvhen he had cast out the deuil, the dumme spake: and the multitudes marueiled. † * And certaine of them said, In 15 Beel-zebub the prince of Deuils he casteth out Deuils. † And 16 other tempting, asked of him a signe from heauen. † But he 17 seeing their cogitations, said to them, Euery kingdom deui- ded against it self, shal be made desolate, and [c] house vpon house, shal fall. † And if Satan also be deuided against him 18 self, hovv shal his kingdom stand? because you say that in Beel-zebub I doe cast out Deuils. † And if I in Beel-zebub 19 cast out Deuils: your children, in vvhom doe they cast out? therfore they shal be your iudges. † But if I in the ∷ finger of 20 God

Mt. 12, 22.

Mr. 3,22

The Gospel vpõ the 3 Sunday in Lent.

[c] οἶκος ἐπὶ οἶκον

∷ This finger, is the spirit of God, Mt. 12,28.

God doe cast out Deuils: surely the kingdom of God is come
21 vpon you. †Vvhen the strong armed keepeth his court:
22 those things are in peace that he possesseth. †But if a stronger then he, come vpon him and ouercome him: he vvil take avvay his vvhole armour vvherein he trusted, and vvil dis-
23 tribute his spoiles. †He that is not vvith me, is against me:
24 and he that gathereth not vvith me, scattereth. †Vvhen the vncleane spirit shal depart out of a man, he vvandereth through places vvithout vvater, seeking rest. And not finding, he saith, I vvil returne into my house vvhence I de-
25 parted. †And vvhen he is come, he findeth it svvept vvith a
26 besome, and trimmed. †Then he goeth and taketh seuen other spirits vvorse then him self, and entring in they dvvel there. And the [c] last of that man be made vvorse then the first.

27 †[b] And it came to passe: vvhen he said these things, a certaine vvoman lifting vp her voice out of the multitude said to him, "Blessed is the vvombe that bare thee, and the pappes
28 that thou didst sucke. †But he said, :: Yea rather, blessed are they that heare the vvord of God, and keepe it. ⊣

29 †And the multitudes running together, he began to say, *This generation, is a vvicked generation: it asketh a signe, and a signe shal not be giuen it but "the signe of Ionas the
30 Prophet. †*For as Ionas vvas a signe to the Niniuites: so
31 shal the Sonne of man also be to this generation. †*The Queene of the South shal rise in the iudgement vvith the men of this generation, and shal condemne them: because she came from the endes of the earth to heare the vvisedom
32 of Salomon. and behold, more then Salomon here. †The men of Niniuee shal rise in the iudgement vvith this generation, and shal condemne it, *because they :: did penance at the preaching of Ionas. and behold, more then Ionas here.

33 †*No man lighteth a candel, and putteth it in secrete, neither vnder a bushel: but vpon a candlesticke, that they
34 that goe in may see the light. †*The candel of thy body, is thine eie. If thine eie be simple, thy vvhole body shal be lightsome: but if it be naught, thy body also shal be darke-
35 some. †See therfore that the light vvhich is in thee, be not
36 darkenesse. †If then thy vvhole body be lightsome, hauing no part of darkenesse: it shal be lightsome vvholy, and as a

Y ij bright

Marginal notes (left):

c *nouissima fiunt*

Mt. 12, 29.

Ion. 2, 2.

3 Reg. 10, 1.

Ion. 3, 5.

Mt. 5, 15

Mar. 4, 21.

Mt. 6, 22.

Marginal notes (right):

b The Gospel vpon Assumption eue, and in a Votiue of our Lady betwene Candlemas and Easter, and betwene Pẽtecost and Aduent.

:: The said mother of God, in that also was blessed that she was the temporal meanes & minister of the Incarnatiõ, but much more blessed, in that she continued the perpetual keeper of his word. *Beda. Aug. tract. 19. in Ioan.*

:: μετενόησαν. Marke that the great penance of the Niniuites (Ionæ 3) is here expressed by this Greeke vvord. *See Annot. Mat. 3, 2.*

The Gospel for a Confessor that is Bishop.

bright candel it ſhal lighten thee. ⊣

37 † And vvhen he vvas ſpeaking, a certaine Phariſee deſired him that he vvould dine vvith him. and he going in ſate dovvne to eate. 38 † And the Phariſee began to thinke vvithin him ſelf and to ſay, Vvhy he vvas not vvaſhed before dinner. 39 † And our Lord ſaid to him, * Novv you Phariſees doe make cleane that on the out ſide of the cuppe and of the platter: but that of yours vvhich is vvithin, is ful of rapine and iniquitie. 40 † Fooles, did not he that made that on the outſide, make that alſo that is on the inſide? 41 † But yet [c] that that remaineth, "giue almes, & behold al things are cleane vnto you. 42 † But vvo to you Phariſees, becauſe you tithe minte and revve and euery herbe: and paſſe ouer iudgement and the charitie of God. but theſe things you ought to haue done, and not to omit thoſe. 43 † Vvo to you Phariſees, becauſe you loue the firſt chaires in the ſynagogs, and ſalutations in the market-place. 44 † Vvo to you, becauſe you are as monuments that appeare not, and men vvalking ouer, are not vvare.

45 † And one of the Lavvyers anſvvering ſaith to him, Maiſter, in ſaying theſe things, thou ſpeakeſt to our reproche alſo. 46 † But he ſaid, "Vvo to you Lavvyers alſo: becauſe you lode men vvith burdens which they can not beare, and your ſelues touch not the packes vvith one of your fingers. 47 † Wo to you that ∴ build the monumēts of the Prophets: and your fathers did kil them. 48 † Surely you doe teſtifie that you conſent to the vvorkes of your fathers: becauſe they in deede did kil them, and you build their ſepulchres. 49 † For this cauſe the vviſedō alſo of God ſaid, I vvil ſend to them Prophets and Apoſtles, and of them they vvil kil and perſecute. 50 † that the bloud of al the Prophets that vvas ſhed from the making of the vvorld, may be required of this generation, 51 † * from the bloud of Abel vnto the * bloud of Zacharie that vvas ſlaine betvvene the altar and the temple. Yea I ſay to you, it ſhal be required of this generation. ⊣ 52 † Vvo to you Lavvyers, becauſe you haue taken avvay the key of knovvledge: your ſelues haue not entred, and thoſe that did enter you haue prohibited. 53 † And vvhen he ſaid theſe things to them, the Phariſees and the Lavvyers began vehemently to vrge him, and to ſtoppe his mouth about many things, 54 † lying in waite for him, & ſeeking to catch ſomething of his mouth, that they might accuſe him.

Mt. 23, 25.

c *Quod ſupereſt,* τὰ ἐνόντα,

The Goſpel for many Martyrs.

∴ Not the building of the Prophets monuments is condemned, but their imitation of their fathers that ſlevv the Prophets. *Ambroſ.*

Gen. 4, 8

2. Par. 24, 22.

ANNOT

ANNOTATIONS
CHAP. XI.

Beda vpon this place.

27. *Bleſſed is the vvombe.*) Let vs alſo (ſaith Venerable Bede) lift vp our voice vvith the Catholike Church, of vvhich this vvoman vvas a figure: let vs lift vp our hartes among the people, and ſay to our Sauiour, Bleſſed be the vvombe that bare thee, and the pappes vvhich thou didſt ſucke. for bleſſed in deede is the mother vvhich bare the King that ruleth heauen and earth for euer. — *Our B. Lady.*

29. *The ſigne of Ionas.*) Of al miracles, his Reſurrection, after he had been according to his body, in the graue, according to his ſoule, in Hel three daies, vvas the greateſt, and moſt conuinceth the incredulous Ievves: and therfore a greater or more euident then that, he ſaith he vvil not giue them. — *The ſigne of Ionas.*

Eccli. 3, 33. Dan. 4, 24. Tob. 4, 12, 11. 9. Mat. 25. 35, 42.

41. *Giue almes.*) The great force of almes is here and in diuers places of holy vvrite ſignified. In one place, they extinguiſh ſinne: in an other, they redeeme ſinnes: in an other, they deliuer from death: in an other, to them giuen or omitted, our iudgement to heauen or hel is attributed: and here they make cleane and ſatisfie for the Ievves former offenſes. for (as S. Auguſtine ſaith c. 70 Enchiridij) almes deedes profite not a man that hath a vvill to continevv in his ſinnes, but they are to be done for a propitiation to God of former offenſes. Novv hovv vvel the Proteſtants like this doctrine ſo euidently ſet forth in Scripture, let the indifferent iudge, and hovv vvel it agreeth vvith their onely faith. — *The force of almes.*

46. *Wo to you Lavvyers.*) Theſe vvere Doctors of Moyſes Lavv, othervviſe called Scribes. Shal vve therfore crie out againſt al Lavvyers novv, or ought the name of Lavvyer be odious vvith vs, becauſe of theſe naughty Lavvyers among the Ievves? much leſſe ought the name of Prieſts to be odious (as Heretikes would haue it) becauſe of the Ievves Prieſts that vvere ſo buſy againſt our Sauiour. — *The Lavvyers and Prieſts of the old Teſtament.*

CHAP. XII.

He prepareth his Diſciples againſt perſecutions to come vpon them at their publiſhing of his doctrine. 13 With deuiding the brethrens inheritance he wil not medle, but exhorteth them againſt auarice, 22 and his Diſciples (by this occaſion) againſt ſolicitude ſo much as of neceſſaries, 32 yea counſeling them to geue al in almes, 35 and to be ready at a knocke: 41 namely admoniſhing Peter and other Prelats to ſee to their charge: 49 and al, not to looke but for perſecution. 54 The Iewes he reprehendeth for that they wil not ſee this time of grace, 58 Whereas it is ſo horrible to die without reconciliation.

1 AND when great multitudes ſtoode about him, ſo that they trode one an other, he began to ſay to his Diſciples, Take good heede of the leauen of the Phariſees, vvhich is hypocriſie.

Mt. 10, 26. Mar. 4, 22.

2 † * For nothing is hid, that ſhal not be reuealed: nor ſecrete, that ſhal not be knovven. 3 † For the things that you haue ſaid in darkneſſe, ſhal be ſaid in the light: and that vvhich you haue ſpoken into the eare in the chambers, ſhal be preached in the houſe-toppes. 4 † And I ſay to you my frendes, Be not afraid of them that kil the body, and after this haue no more to doe. 5 † But I vvil ſhevv you vvhom ye ſhal feare: :: feare him vvho after he hath killed, hath povver to caſt into hel. yea I ſay to you, feare him. 6 † Are not fiue ſparovves ſold for tvvo farthings: and one of them is not forgotten before God? 7 † Yea the heares alſo of your head are al

:: The feare of Hel alſo is profitable: contrarie to the proteſtāts, teaching ſecuritie of ſaluation, and that feare of Hel maketh men hypocrites.

al numbered. Feare not therfore: you are more vvorth then many ſparovves. † * And I ſay to you, " Euery one that confeſſeth me before men, the Sonne of man alſo vvil confeſſe him before the Angels of God. † But he that denieth me before men, ſhal be denied before the Angels of God. † * And :: euery one that ſpeaketh a vvord againſt the ſonne of man, it ſhal be forgiuen him: but he that ſhal blaſpheme againſt the holy Ghoſt, to him it ſhal not be forgiuen. † * And vvhen they ſhal bring you in to the ſynagogs and to magiſtrates and poteſtates, be not careful in vvhat maner, and vvhat you ſhal anſvver, or vvhat you ſhal ſay. † For the holy Ghoſt ſhal teach you in the very houre vvhat you muſt ſay.

8, 9, 10, 11, 12

Mt. 10, 32. Mar. 8, 38.

Mt. 12, 33. Mr. 3, 28

Mt. 10, 19. Mar. 13, 11.

:: See Annot. Mt. 12, 32.

† And one of the multitude ſaid to him, Maiſter, ſpeake to my brother that he deuide the inheritaunce vvith me. † But he ſaid to him, Man, " vvho hath appointed me iudge or deuider ouer you? † And he ſaid to them, See and bevvare of al auarice: for not in any mans aboundance doth his life conſiſt, of thoſe things vvhich he poſſeſſeth. † And he ſpake a ſimilitude to them, ſaying, A certaine riche mās field yelded plentie of fruites. † and he thought vvithin him ſelf, ſaying, :: Vvhat ſhal I doe, becauſe I haue not vvhither to gather my fruites? † And he ſaid, This vvil I doe, I vvil deſtroy my barnes, and vvil make greater: and thither vvil I gather al things that are grovven to me, and my goods, † and I vvil ſay to my ſoule, Soule, thou haſt much goods laid vp for many yeres, take thy reſt, eate, drinke, make good cheere. † But God ſaid to him, :: Thou foole, this night they require thy ſoule of thee: and the things that thou haſt prouided, vvhoſe ſhal they be? † So is he that laieth vp treaſure to him ſelf, and is not " riche to God vvard.

13, 14, 15, 16, 17, 18, 19, 20, 21

:: Giue it to the poore, that ſhouldſt thou do, ſaith S. Baſil.

:: A goodly warning for al riche men.

† And he ſaid to his Diſciples, * Therfore I ſay to you, :: Be not careful for your life, vvhat you ſhal eate: nor for your body, vvhat you ſhal doe on. † The life is more then the meate, and the body is more then the raiment. † Conſider the rauens, for they ſovv not, neither doe they reape, vvhich neither haue ſtorehouſe nor barne, and God feedeth them. Hovv much more are you of greater price then they? † And vvhich of you by caring can adde to his ſtature one cubite? † If then you be not able to doe ſo much as the leaſt thing, for the reſt vvhy are you careful? † Conſider the lilies hovv they

22, 23, 24, 25, 26, 27

Mt. 6, 25

:: He forbiddeth not cōpetent prouidēce, but to much carefulnes. See Annot. vpon S. Matth. c. 6, 25.

they grovv: they labour not, neither doe they ſpinne. But I ſay to you, Neither Salomon in al his glorie vvas araied as one of theſe. † 28 And if the graſſe that to day is in the field, and to morovv is caſt into the ouen, God ſo clotheth: hovv much more you O ye of litle faith! † 29 And you, doe not ſeeke vvhat you ſhal eate, or vvhat you ſhal drinke: and [c] be not lifted vp on high. † 30 For al theſe things the nations of the vvorld doe ſeeke. but your father knovveth that you haue neede of theſe things. † 31 But ſeeke firſt the kingdom of God, and al theſe things ſhal be giuen you beſides. † 32 [b] Feare not ∷ litle flocke, for it hath pleaſed your father to giue you a kingdom. † 33 Sel the things that you poſſeſſe, and giue almes. * Make to you purſes that vveare not, treaſure that vvaſteth not, in heauen: vvhither the theefe approcheth not, neither doth the mothe corrupt. † 34 For ″ vvhere your treaſure is, there vvil your hart be alſo. ⊣ † 35 [b] Let your ∷ loynes be girded, and candles burning in your handes, † 36 and you like to men expecting their lord, vvhen he ſhal returne from the mariage: that vvhen he doth come and knocke, forthvvith they may open vnto him. † 37 Bleſſed are thoſe ſeruants, vvhom vvhen the Lord commeth, he ſhal finde vvatching. Amen I ſay to you, that he vvil gird him ſelf, and make them ſit dovvne, and paſſing vvil miniſter vnto them. † 38 And if he come in the ſecond vvatch, and if in the third vvatch he come, and ſo finde, bleſſed are thoſe ſeruants. † 39 * And this knovv ye, that if the houſholder did knovv vvhat houre the theefe vvould come, he vvould vvatch verely, and vvould not ſuffer his houſe to be broken vp. † 40 Be you alſo ready: for at vvhat houre you thinke not, the Sonne of man vvil come. ⊣

† 41 And Peter ſaid to him, Lord, doeſt thou ſpeake this parable to vs, or likevviſe to al? † 42 And our Lord ſaid, Vvho (thinkeſt thou) is a faithful ſtevvard and vviſe, vvhom the lord appointeth ouer his familie, to giue them in ſeaſon their meaſure of vvheate? † 43 Bleſſed is that ſeruant, vvhom vvhen the lord commeth, he ſhal finde ſo doing. † 44 Verely I ſay to you, that ouer al things vvhich he poſſeſſeth, he ſhal appoint him. † 45 But if that ſeruant ſay in his hart, My lord is long a comming: and ſhal begin to ſtrike the ſeruants and handmaides, and eate and drinke, and be drunke: † 46 the lord of that ſeruant ſhal come in a day that he hopeth not, and at an houre that he knovveth not, and ſhal deuide him, and ſhal

c μὴ μετεωρίζεσθε.

Mt. 6, 20.

Mt. 24, 43.

b The goſpel for S. Paulinus Iun. 22. And for a Cõfeſſor that is not a Biſhop.

∷ It was litle at the begĩning, & is ſtil in cõpariſon of al the reprobate: but in it ſelf very great, as in the parable of the great tree that grew of the litle muſtard ſeed. Mt. 13.

b The Goſpel for a Cõfeſſor that is not a Biſhop.

∷ To girde our loines, is to keepe chaſtitie and cõtinencie. Gregor. ho. 13.

ſhal appoint his portion vvith the infidels. 47 And that ſeruant that knevv the vvil of his lord, and prepared not him ſelf, and did not according to his vvil: ſhal be beaten vvith many ſtripes. † 48 But he that knevv not, and did things vvorthie of ſtripes: ſhal be beaten vvith fevv. And euery one to vvhom much vvas giuen, much ſhal be required of him: and to vvhom they committed much, more vvil they demaund of him. † 49 I came to caſt fire on the earth: and vvhat vvil I, but that it be kindled? † 50 But I haue to be baptized with a baptiſme: and hovv am I ſtraitened vntil it be diſpatched? † 51 * Thinke you that I came to giue ∷ peace on the earth? No, I tel you, but ſeparation. † 52 For there ſhal be from this time, fiue in one houſe deuided: three againſt tvvo, and tvvo againſt three. † 53 There ſhal be deuided, the father againſt the ſonne, and the ſonne againſt his father, the mother againſt the daughter, and the daughter againſt the mother, the mother in lavv againſt her daughter in lavv, and the daughter in lavv againſt her mother in lavv.

∷ He meaneth the naughtie peace that is betvvene vvorldlings & ſinners, the agreement that is in infidelity, in Hereſie, or in any other vvickednes. he came to breake this peace. See Annot. Matth. c. 10, 34.

Mt. 10, 34.

† 54 * And he ſaid alſo to the multitudes, When you ſee a cloude riſing from the vveſt, by and by you ſay, A ſhoure commeth, and ſo it commeth to paſſe: † 55 and vvhen the ſouth vvinde blovving, you ſay, That there vvil be heate: and it commeth to paſſe. † 56 Hypocrites, the face of the heauen and of the earth you haue ſkil to diſcerne: but this time hovv doe you not diſcerne? † 57 And vvhy of your ſelues alſo iudge you not that vvhich is iuſt? † 58 * And ∷ vvhen thou goeſt vvith thy aduerſarie to the Prince, in the vvay endeuour to be deliuered from him: leſt perhaps he dravv thee to the iudge, and the iudge deliuer thee to the exactour, and the exactour caſt thee into priſon. † 59 I ſay to thee, thou ſhalt not goe out thence, vntil thou pay the very laſt mite.

Mt. 16, 2

∷ See Annot. Mt. 5, 25.

Mt. 5, 25

ANNOTATIONS
CHAP. XII.

Open confeſſiō of our faith.

8. *Euery one that confeſſeth.*] A Catholike man is bound to confeſſe his faith, being called to accoumpt or examined by Iew, Heathen, or Heretike, concerning the ſame. Neither is it ynough to keepe Chriſt in his hart, but he muſt alſo acknowledge him in his wordes and deedes. And to deny Chriſt, or any article of the Catholike faith, for ſhame or feare of any worldly creature, hath no leſſe puniſhment, then to be denied, refuſed, and forſaken by Chriſt at the houre of his death before al his Angels: Which is an other maner of preſence and Conſiſtorie, then any Court or Seſſion that men can be called to for their faith, in this world.

11. Be

11. Be not careful.] That the poore vnlearned Catholike ſhould not be diſcouraged, or make his excuſe that he is a ſimple man, not able to anſvver cunning Heretikes, nor to giue a reaſon of his beleefe, and therfore muſt ſuffer or ſay any thing rather then come before them: our Maiſter giueth them comfort, promiſing that the Holy Ghoſt ſhal euer put into their hartes at the time of their appearance, that vvhich ſhal be ſufficient for the purpoſe. not that euery one vvhich is conuented before the Aduerſaries of faith, ſhould alvvaies be endued vvith extraordinary knovvledge to diſpute and confute, as the Apoſtles and others in the primitiue Church vvere: but that God vvil euer giue to the ſimple that truſteth in him, ſufficient courage and vvordes to confeſſe his beleefe. For ſuch an one called before the Commiſſioners, ſaith ynough and defendeth him ſelf ſufficiently, vvhen he anſvvereth that he is a Catholike man, & that he vvil liue and die in that faith vvhich the Catholike Church throughout al Chriſtian countries hath and doth teach, and that this Church can giue them a reaſon of al the things vvhich they demaund of him. &c.

The holy Ghoſt teacheth euery vnlearned Catholike to giue ſufficiēt reaſon of his faith.

14. Who hath appointed?] Chriſt refuſed to medle in this temporal matter, partly becauſe the demaund proceded of couetouſnes and il intention, partly to giue an example to Clergie men, that they ſhould not be vvithdravven by ſecular affaires and controuerſies from their principal function of praying, preaching, and ſpiritual regiment: but not vvholy to forbid them al actions pertaining to vvorldly buſines, ſpecially vvhere and vvhen the honour of God, the increaſe of religion, the peace of the people, and the ſpiritual benefite of the parties doe require. In vvhich caſes S. Auguſtin (as Poſſidonius vvriteth) vvas occupied often vvhole daies in ending vvorldly controuerſies, and ſo he vvriteth of him ſelf alſo, not doubting but to haue revvard therfore in heauen.

The dealing of Clergie men in vvorldly affaires.

In vita c. 19.
Li. de op. Monach. c. 29.

21. Riche to God vvard.] He is riche tovvards God, that by his goods beſtovved vpon the poore, hath ſtore of merits, and many almeſmens praiers procuring mercie for him at the day of his death and iudgement, vvhich is here therfore called treaſure laid vp in heauen, vvhere the barnes be large ynough. The neceſſitie of vvhich almes is by Chriſt him ſelf here ſhevved to be ſo great, and ſo acceptable to God, that rather then they ſhould lacke the fruite thereof, they ſhould ſel al they haue and giue to the poore.

Meritorious vvorkes.

34. Where your treaſure is.] If the riche man vvithdravven by his vvorldly treaſure, can not ſet his hart vpon heauen, let him ſend his mony thither before him, by giuing it in almes vpon ſuch as vvil pray for him, and his hart vvil folovv his purſe thither.

Almes.

CHAP. XIII.

He threateneth the Ievves to be ſone forſaken vnles they doe penance, 10 and confoundeth them for maligning him for his miraculous good doing on the Sabboths. 18 but his kingdom (the Church) as contemptible as it ſeemeth to them novv in the beginning, ſhal ſpread ouer al the World, 20 and conuert al, 23 and vvhat an hartſore it ſhal be to them at the laſt day, to ſee them ſelues excluded from the glorie of this kingdom, and the Gentils admitted in their place. 31 foretelling that it is not Galilee that he feareth, but that obſtinate and reprobate Hieruſalem vvil nedes murder him, as alſo his meſſengers afore and after him.

1 AND there vvere certaine preſent at that very time telling him of the Galilæans, vvhoſe bloud Pilate mingled vvith their ſacrifices. 2 †And he anſvvering ſaid to them, Thinke you that" theſe Galilęans vvere ſinners more then al the Galilæans that they 3 ſuffred ſuch things? † No, I ſay to you: but vnles you ∷ haue 4 penance, you ſhal al likevviſe periſh. †As thoſe eightene vpō vvhom the toure fel in Silóe, and ſlevv them: thinke you that they alſo vvere detters aboue al the men that dvvel in 5 Hieruſalem? †No, I ſay to you: but if you haue not penance, you ſhal al likevviſe periſh.

∷ *Niſi pœnitentiam habueritis,*

∷ Or as it is vttered in other places, *do penāce,* μετανοῆτε. the vvhich in the nevv Teſtament ſignifieth perfect repentance. See Annotatiōs Mat. 3, 2. 11, 21.

The Gospel on the Imber Saturday in Sept.

:: The figtree vvith only leaues & no fruite, is the Iewes synagogue, & euery other people or persō which hath faith and faire wordes, and no good workes.

6 † And he said this similitude, A certaine man had :: a figtree planted in his vineyard, and he came seeking for fruite on it, and found not. 7 † And he said to the dresser of the vineyard, Loe it is three yeres since I come seeking for fruite vpon this figtree: and I finde not. Cut it dovvne therfore: vvhereto doth it also occupie the ground? 8 † But he ansvvering saith to him, Lord, let it alone this yere also, vntil I digge about it, and dung it. 9 † and if happily it yeld fruite: but if not, hereafter thou shalt cut it dovvne.

10 † And he vvas teaching in their synagogue on the Sabboths. 11 † And behold a vvoman that had a spirit of infirmitie eightene yeres: and she vvas crooked neither could she looke vpvvard at al. 12 † Whom vvhen IESVS savv, he called her vnto him, and said to her, Woman, thou art deliuered from thy infirmitie. 13 † And he imposed hands vpon her, and forthvvith she vvas made straight and glorified God. 14 † And the Archsynagogue ansvvering (because he had indignation that IESVS had cured on the Sabboth) said to the multitude, Sixe daies there are vvherein you ought to vvorke. in them therfore come, and be cured: and not in the Sabboth day. 15 † And our Lord ansvvering to him, said, Hypocrite, doth not euery one of you vpon the Sabboth loose his oxe or his asse from the manger, and leadeth them to vvater? 16 † But" this daughter of Abraham vvhom Satan hath bound, loe, these eightene yeres, ought not she to be loosed from this bond on the Sabboth day? 17 † And vvhen he said these things, al his aduersaries vvere ashamed: and al the people reioyced in al things that vvere gloriously done of him. ⊣

18 † He said therfore, * Vvherevnto is the kingdom of God like, and vvherevnto shal I esteeme it like? 19 † It is like to a :: mustard seede, vvhich a man tooke and cast into his garden, and it grevv: and became a great tree, and the foules of the aire rested in the boughes thereof. 20 † And againe he said, * Like to vvhat shal I esteeme the kingdom of God? 21 † It is like to leauen, vvhich a vvoman tooke and hid in three measures of meale, til the vvhole vvas leauened. 22 † And he vvent by cities and tovvnes teaching, and making his iourney vnto Hierusalem.

Mr. 13, 31.
Mr. 4, 30.

:: See Annota. Math. 13, 31.

Mt. 13, 33.

23 † And a certaine man said to him, Lord, be they fevv that are saued? 24 * But he said to them, † :: Striue to enter" by the narrovv gate: because many, I say to you," shal seeke to enter, and

:: Christians in their liues must seeke the strait way, but in religion the ancient common way.

Mt. 7, 13

25 and ſhal not be able. † But vvhen the good man of the houſe ſhal enter in, and ſhut the doore, and you ſhal begin to ſtand vvithout, and knocke at the doore, ſaying, Lord open to vs: and he anſvvering ſhal ſay to you, I knovv you not vvhence 26 you are: † then you ſhal begin to ſay, Vve did" eate before 27 thee and drinke, and in our ſtreates didſt thou teach. † And he ſhal ſay to you, I knovv you not vvhence you are, depart 28 from me al ye vvorkers of iniquitie. † There ſhal be vveeping and gnaſhing of teeth: vvhen you ſhal ſee Abraham and Iſaac and Iacob, and al the Prophets in the kingdom of God, 29 and you to be thruſt out. † And there ſhal come from the Eaſt and the Vveſt and the North and the South: and ſhal ſit 30 dovvne in the kingdom of God. † And behold, they are :: laſt that ſhal be firſt, and they be firſt that ſhal be laſt.

:: The Gentils comming into Gods fauour later, are preferred before the Iewes which were firſt.

31 † The ſame day there came certaine of the Phariſees, ſaying to him, Depart and get the hence, becauſe Herod vvil kil thee. 32 † And he ſaid to them, Goe, and tel that foxe, Behold I caſt out deuils, and perfite cures this day and to morovv, and the third 33 day I am conſummate. † But yet I muſt vvalke this day and to morovv and the day folovving, becauſe it [c] cannot be that a 34 Prophet periſh out of Hieruſalem. †* Hieruſalem, Hieruſalem vvhich killeſt the Prophets, and ſtoneſt them that are ſent to thee, hovv often vvould I gather thy childrē as the bird doth her brood vnder her vvings, and :: thou vvouldeſt not? 35 † Behold your houſe ſhal be left deſert to you. And I ſay to you, that you ſhal not ſee me til it come vvhen you ſhal ſay, Bleſſed is he that commeth in the name of our Lord.

[c] *Non capit* ἐνδέχεται. *Mt. 23, 37.*

:: The Iewes loſt their preeminence, by their owne free will, & not by Gods cauſing: who ceaſed not to call and crie vpon them, and they would not heare. Whereby free will is plainly proued.

ANNOTATIONS
CHAP. XIII.

2. *Theſe Galilæans.*) It is Gods mercie that he ſtraight puniſheth not al offenders, but ſome fevv for a vvarning to all: as that for Schiſme he ſtriketh not al ſuch as haue forſaken the Church and the lavvful Prieſts, as he did Coré and his complices: that for ſpoile of Churches he reuengeth not al, as he did Heliodorus: and al that vow and reuoke their gifts to God, as Ananias and Saphîra. Some few therfore for their iuſt deſerts, be ſo handled for example, to prouoke al others guilty of the ſame crimes to doe penance. Which if they doe not in this life, they ſhal all aſſuredly periſh in the next world. *Optatus li. 1 cont. Parmen. ſub finem.*

Nu. 16. 2 Mach. 3. Act. 5.

Some puniſhed for example.

16. *This daughter.*) We may ſee that many diſeaſes which ſeeme natural, doe procede of the Diuel by Gods permiſſion, either for ſinne, or for probation: and both thoſe kindes Chriſt ſpecially cured, for that no natural medicines could cure them, and ſpecially becauſe he came to diſſolue the workes of Satan both in body and ſoul.

Diſeaſes not natural.

24. *By the narrovv,*) Our Lord is not contrarie to him ſelf in that he anſvvereth, the gate to be ſtraite, and fevv to be ſaued, whereas els vvhere he ſaid, that many ſhould come from the Eaſt and Vveſt &c. and ioy with Abraham in the kingdom of heauen. Mt. 8, 11. For though they be few in

respect of the vvicked of al sortes, yet they be many in them selues and in the societie of Angels. the vvheate cornes are scarse seen at the threshing, vvhen they are medled with the chaffe: but vvhen the il are remoued, the vvhole barne of heauen shal be filled. *So saith S. Aug. Ser. 32 de verb. Do.*

Penance.

24. Shal seeke.) Many vvould be saued and looke to be saued, but can not, because they vvil not take paines to enter in at so straite a passage, that is to say, to fast much, pray often, doe great penance for their sinnes, liue in holy Churches discipline, abstaine from the pleasures of this World, and suffer persecution and losse of their goods and liues for Christes sake.

Schisme.

26. Eate before thee.) It is not ynough to feede vvith Christ in his Sacraments, or to heare his vvord in the Church, to chalēge heauen thereby, vnlesse vve liue in vnitie of the Catholike Church. So S. Augustine applieth this against the Donatistes, that had the very same seruice and Sacraments which the Catholike Church had, but yet seuered them selues from other Christian countries by Schisme. *Cont. lit. Petil. li. 2 c. 55.*

CHAP. XIIII.

By occasion of dining With a Pharisee, 2 after that he hath againe confounded them for maligning him for his miraculous good doing on the Sabboth, 7 he teacheth them humilitie, seing their ambition, 12 and in their Workes to seeke retribution not of men in this Worlde, but of God in the World to come: 16 foretelling also that the IeWes for their Worldly excuses shal not tast of the Supper, but the Gentils in their place. 25 Yea that so far must men be from al Worldlines, that they must earnestly bethinke them before they enter into his Church, and be ready to forgoe all: 34 specially considering they must be the salt of others also.

The Gospel vpō the 16 Sūday after Pentecost.

ND it came to passe vvhen IESVS entred into the house of a certaine Prince of the Pharisees vpon the Sabboth to eate bread, and they vvatched him. 1 † And behold there vvas a certaine man before him that had the dropsie. 2 † And IESVS ansvvering, spake to the Lavvyers and Pharisees, saying, Is it Lavvful to cure on the Sabboth? 3 † But they held their peace. but he taking him, healed him, and sent him avvay. 4 † And ansvvering them he said, Vvhich of you shal haue an asse or an oxe fallen into a pit: and vvil not incontinent dravv him out on the Sabboth day? 5 † And they could not ansvver him to these things. 6

† And he spake to them also that vvere inuited a parable, marking hovv they chose the first seats at the table, saying to them, 7 † When thou art inuited to a mariage, sit not dovvne in the first place, lest perhaps a more honorable then thou be inuited of him: 8 † and he that bade thee and him, come and say to thee, Giue this man place: and then thou begin vvith shame to take the last place. 9 † But vvhen thou art bidden, goe, sit dovvne in the lovvest place: that vvhen he that inuited thee, commeth, he may say to thee, Frende, sit vp higher: then shalt thou haue glorie before them that sit at table vvith thee. 10 † because euery one that exalteth him self, shal be humbled: and he that humbleth him self, shal be exalted. 11 ⊣

And

12 † And he said to him also that had inuited him, Vvhen thou makest a dinner or a supper, call not thy frendes, nor thy brethrē, nor kinsmen, nor thy neighbours that are riche: lest perhaps they also inuite thee againe, and recompense be made 13 to thee. † But vvhen thou makest a feast, cal the poore, feeble, 14 lame, and blinde, † and thou shalt be blessed, because they haue not to recōpense thee: for :: recompense shal be made 15 thee in the resurrection of the iust. † Vvhen one of them that sate at the table vvith him, had heard these things, he said to him, Blessed is he that shal eate bread in the kingdom of God.

:: Reward for charitable dedes, and that they may be done for reward. against our Aduersaries.

16 † But he said to him, A certaine man made a great supper, 17 and called many. † And he sent his seruant at the houre of supper to say to the inuited, That they should come, be- 18 cause novv al things are ready. † And they began al at once to make excuse. The first said to him, :: I haue bought a farme, and I must needes goe forth and see it, I pray thee hold me ex- 19 cused. † And an other said, I haue bought fiue yoke of oxen, 20 and I goe to proue them, I pray thee, hold me excused. † And an other said, I haue maried a vvife, and therfore I can not 21 come. † And the seruant returning told these things to his lord. Then the maister of the house being angrie, said to his seruant, Goe forth quickly into the streates and lanes of the citie, and the poore and feeble and blinde and lame bring in 22 hither. † And the seruant said, Lord, it is done as thou didst 23 commaunde, and yet there is place. † And the lord said to the seruant, Goe forth into the waies and hedges: and ″ com- 24 pel them to enter, that my house may be filled. † But I say to you, that none of those men that vvere called, shal tast my supper. ⁋

The Gospel vpō the 2 Sunday after Pentecost.

:: Worldlines, wealth, and voluptuousnes, are the things that specially hinder men from God.

25 † And great multitudes vvent vvith him: and turning, he 26 said to them, † * If any man come to me and hateth not his :: father and mother, and vvife and children, and brethren and sisters, yea and his ovvne life besides: he can not be my 27 disciple. † And he that doth not beare his crosse and come 28 after me: cannot be my disciple. † For, vvhich of you minding to build a toure, doth not first sit dovvne and recken the charges that are necessarie, vvhether he haue to finish it: 29 † lest, after that he hath laid the foundation, and is not able 30 to finish it, al that see it, begin to mocke him, † saying, That 31 this man began to build, and he could not finish it? † Or

Mt. 10, 37.

The Gospel for a Martyr that is a Bishop. And for S. Basil Iun. 14.

:: No creature so deere vnto vs, vvhich vve must not hate or forsake, if it hinder vs, and in that respect that it hindereth vs from Christ, or his Church, & our Saluation.

vvhat king about to goe to make vvarre against an other king, doth not first sit dovvne and thinke vvhether he be able vvith ten thousands to meete him that vvith tvventie thousands commeth against him? † Othervvise vvhiles he 32 is yet farre of, sending a legacie he asketh those things that belong to peace. † So therfore euery one of you that doth 33 not ∷ renounce al that he possesseth, cannot be my disciple. ꟻ

∷ He that is a right Christian man, must make his account that if he be put to it (as he often may be in times of persecution) he must renoũce al that euer he hath, rather then forsake the Catholike faith.

† * Salt is good. But if the salt leese his vertue, vvherevvith 34 shal it be seasoned? † It is profitable neither for the ground, 35 nor for the dunghil, but it shal be cast forth. He that hath eares to heare, let him heare. ꟻ

Mt. 5, 13. Mar. 9, 50.

ANNOTATIONS CHAP. XIIII.

Free-vvil.

23. Compel them.) The vehement persuasion that God vseth both externally by force of his vvord and miracles, and internally by his grace, to bring vs vnto him, is called compelling: not that he forceth any to come to him against their owne willes, but that he can alter and mollifie an hard hart, and make him vvilling that before vvould not. S. Augustine also referreth this compelling to the penal lawes which Catholike Princes do iustly vse against Heretikes and Schismatikes, prouing that they who are by their former professiõ in Baptisme subiect to the Catholike Church, and are departed from the same after Sectes, may and ought to be compelled into the vnitie and societie of the vniuersal Church againe. and therfore in this sense, by the two former partes of the parable, the Ievves first, and secondly the Gentils, that neuer beleeued before in Christ, vvere inuited by faire svveete meanes onely: but by the third, such are inuited as the Church of God hath power ouer, because they promised in baptisme, and therfore are to be reuoked not onely by gentle meanes, but by iust punishment also.

Heretikes may by penal lawes be cõpelled to the Catholike faith.

ep. 50 paulo post principe. & ep. 204. & li. 1 cont. ep. Gaudent. c. 25.

CHAP. XV.

By occasion of the Pharisees murmuring at him for receiuing penitent sinners, he sheweth what ioy shalbe in heauen for the conuersion of one sinner, 11 and for the yonger sonne, which is the Gentils: 25 the elder (to wit the Iewes) in the meane time disdaining thereat, and refusing to come into his Church.

The Gospel vpõ the 3. Sunday after Pentecost.

AND there approched Publicans and 1 sinners vnto him for to heare him. † And 2 the Pharisees and the Scribes murmured saying, That this man receiueth sinners, and eateth vvith them. † And he 3 spake to them this parable, saying, † * Vvhat ∷ man of you hauing an hun- 4 dred sheepe: and if he hath lost one of them, doth he not leaue the ninetie nine in the desert, and goeth after that vvhich vvas lost vntil he finde it? † And vvhen he hath found 5 it,

∷ This man, is our Sauiour Christ: whose care & trauaile in searching & reducing sinners to repentãce, al spiritual men specially should folow.

Mat. 18, 12.

6 it, laieth it vpon his ſhoulders reioycing: † and comming home calleth together his frendes and neighbours, ſaying to them, Reioyce vvith me, becauſe I haue found my ſheepe that
7 vvas loſt? † I ſay to you, that euen ſo there ſhal be ioy in heauen vpon one ſinner that doth penance, "then vpon nine-
8 tie nine iuſt that neede not penance. † Or vvhat ∴ vvoman hauing ten grotes: if ſhe leeſe one grote, doth ſhe not light a candle, and ſvveepe the houſe, and ſeeke diligently, vntil ſhe
9 finde? † And vvhen ſhe hath found, calleth together her frendes and neighbours, ſaying, Reioyce vvith me, becauſe
10 I haue found the grote vvhich I had loſt? † So, I ſay to you, there ſhal be ioy" before the Angels of God vpon one ſinner that doth penance. ⊣

∴ This vvoman is the catholike Church, vvho alſo cōtinually ſeeketh her loſt children.

11 † And he ſaid, A certaine man had tvvo ſonnes: † and the
12 yonger of them ſaid to his father, Father, giue me the portion of ſubſtance that belongeth to me. And he deuided vnto
13 them the ſubſtance. † And not many daies after the yonger ſonne gathering al his things together vvent from home into a farre countrie: and there he vvaſted his ſubſtance, liuing
14 riotouſly. † And after he had ſpent al, there fel a ſore famine
15 in that countrie, and he began to be in neede. † And he vvent, and cleaued to one of the citizens of that countrie. And he
16 ſent him into his farme to feede ſvvine. † And he vvould faine haue filled his bellie of the huſkes that the ſvvine did
17 eate: and no bodie gaue vnto him. † And returning to him ſelf he ſaid, Hovv many of my fathers hirelings haue aboun-
18 dance of bread: and I here periſh for famine? † I vvil ariſe, and vvil goe to my father, and ſay to him, Father, I haue ſin-
19 ned againſt heauen and before thee: † I am not novv vvorthie to be called thy ſonne: make me as one of thy hirelings.
20 † And riſing vp he came to his father. And ∴ vvhen he vvas yet farre of, his father ſavv him, and vvas moued vvith mercie,
21 and running to him fel vpon his necke, and kiſſed him. † And his ſonne ſaid to him, Father, I haue ſinned againſt heauen & before thee, I am not novv vvorthie to be called thy ſonne.
22 † And the father ſaid to his ſeruants, Quickely bring forth the firſt ſtole, and doe it on him, and put a ring vpō his hand,
23 and ſhoes vpon his feete: † and bring" the fatted calfe, and kil
24 it, and let vs eate, and make merie: † becauſe this my ſonne vvas dead, and is reuiued: vvas loſt, and is found. And they
25 began to make merie. † But his elder ſonne vvas in the field. and

The Goſpel vpō Saturday in the 2 weeke of Lent.

The prodigal ſonne, is a parable, both of the Gentils conuerſion, & alſo of euery diſſolute ſinner penitētly returning to God.

∴ Gods wonderful and tender mercie toward penitent ſinners.

and vvhen he came and drevv nigh to the house, he heard musicke and dauncing: † and he called one of the seruants, 26 and asked vvhat these thinges should be. † And he said to 27 him, Thy brother is come, and thy father hath killed the fatted calfe, because he hath receiued him safe. † But he had 28 indignation, and vvould not goe in. His father therfore going forth began to desire him. † But he ansvvering said to his 29 father, Behold, so many yeres doe I serue thee, and I neuer transgressed thy commaundement, and thou didst neuer giue me a kidde to make merie vvith my frendes: † but after that 30 thy sonne, this that hath deuoured his substance vvith vvhoores, is come, thou hast killed for him the fatted calfe. † But he 31 said to him, Sonne, thou art alvvaies vvith me, and al my things are thine. † But it behoued vs to make merie and be 32 glad, because this thy brother vvas dead, and is reuiued, vvas lost, and is found. ⊣

ANNOTATIONS
CHAP. XV.

Ioy in heauen for euery penitent.

7. Then vpon ninety nine iust.) Neither God, nor the Saincts in heauen, nor men in earth do for al that esteeme more of penitent sinners, then they do of them that continevv iust and godly: though by the soden motion and present affection of ioy that man taketh and expresseth in such alteration and nevv fallen good, it be here signified that the conuersion of euery sinner is exceding acceptable to God, and giueth his Saincts nevv cause of ioy and thankes giuing to God in an other kinde then for the continuance of the iust.

The Angels and Saincts knovv our hartes.

10. Before the Angels.) The Angels and other celestial spirits in heauen, do reioyce at euery sinners conuersion: they know then and haue care of vs, yea our hartes and inward repentance be open to them: how then can they not heare our prayers? And betwixt Angels and the blessed soules of Saincts there is no difference in this case, the one being as highly exalted as the other and as neere God, in whom and by whom onely they see and know our affaires, as the other. *Mt. 22, 30*

The B. Sacramēt and Sacrifice of the Altar.

23. The fatted calfe.) This feasting and festiuitie (saith S. Augustine *li. 2, qu. Euang. c. 33 to. 4.*) are novv celebrated throughout the vvhole vvorld the Church being dilated and spred: for, that calfe in the body and bloud of our Lord is both offered to the Father, and also feedeth the vvhole house. And as the calfe signifieth the B. Sacrament of the body and bloud of Christ, so the first stole may signifie our innocencie restored in baptisme, and the rest, other graces and giftes giuen vs in the other Sacraments.

CHAP. XVI.

He teacheth the riche to procure heauen vvith their riches. 14 And being therfore derided of the couetous Pharisees (vvho savv temporal riches promised in the letter of the Lavv) he shevveth that novv is come the preaching of the kingdom of God, hovvbeit the Lavv for al that in no iote shal be frustrat. 19 foretelling them also, that the couetous Ievves shal be denied of their father Abraham, vvhen poore Lazarus (the penitent Gentil) shal rest in his bosome.

AND

c οἰκονόμον

c οἰκονομίας

The Gospel vpō the 8 Sūday after Pentecost.

1 AND he ſaid alſo to his Diſciples, There vvas a cartaine riche man that had a c bailife: & he vvas il reported of vnto him, as he that had vvaſted 2 his goods. † And he called him, and ſaid to him, Vvhat heare I this of thee? render account of thy c bailiſhip: for novv thou canſt no more be bailife. 3 † And the bailife ſaid vvithin him ſelf, Vvhat ſhal I doe, becauſe my lord taketh avvay from me the bailiſhip? digge I 4 am not able, to begge I am aſhamed. † I knovv vvhat I vvil doe, that vvhen I ſhal be remoued from the bailiſhip, they 5 may receiue me into their houſes. † Therfore calling together euery one of his lords detters, he ſaid to the firſt, Hovv 6 much doeſt thou ovve my lord? † But he ſaith, An hundred pipes of oile. And he ſaid to him, Take thy bil: and ſit 7 dovvne, quickly vvrite fiftie. † After that he ſaid to an other, But thou, hovv much doeſt thou ovve? Vvho ſaid, An hundreth quarters of vvheat. He ſaid to him, Take 8 thy bil, and vvrite eightie. † And "the lord praiſed the bailife of iniquitie, becauſe he had done vviſely: for the children of this vvorld, are vviſer then the children of light in their ge-9 neration. † And I ſay to you, Make vnto you frendes of the ∴ mammon of iniquitie: that vvhen you faile, "they may re-10 ceiue you into the eternal tabernacles. ⊣ † He that is faithful in the leſt, is faithful in the greater alſo: and he that is vniuſt 11 in litle, is vniuſt in the greater alſo. † If then you haue not been faithful in the vniuſt mammon: vvith that vvhich is the 12 true vvho may credit you? † And if you haue not been faithful in other mens: that vvhich is yours, vvho vvil giue you? 13 † * No ſeruant can ſerue tvvo maiſters, for either he ſhal hate the one, and loue the other: or cleaue to one, and contemne the other. You can not ſerue God and mammon.

∴ Mãmon (ſaith S. Hierom q. 6. ad Algaſ.) in the Syriake tongue ſignifieth riches. *Mammon of iniquitie,* becauſe they are often il gotten, or il beſtowed, or occaſion of euil, or at the leaſt worldly & falſe & not the true heauēly riches.

Mat. 6, 24.

14 † And the Phariſees vvhich vvere couetous, heard al theſe 15 things: and they derided him. † And he ſaid to them, You are they that iuſtifie your ſelues before men, but god knovveth your hartes, becauſe that vvhich is high to men, is abomina-16 tion before God. † * The lavv and the prophets, vnto Iohn. from that time the kingdom of God is euangelized, and euery 17 one doth force tovvard it. • † * And it is eaſier for heauen and 18 earth to paſſe, then one tittle of the lavv to fall. † * Euery one that dimiſſeth his vvife, "and marieth an other, committeth aduoutrie: and he that marieth her that is dimiſſed from her

Mat. 11, 12.
Mat. 5, 18.
Mat. 5, 31, 19, 9. Mar. 10, 11. 1. Cor. 7, 11.

husband, committeth aduoutrie.

The Gospel vpõ Thursday in the 2 Weeke of Lẽt.

† There vvas a certaine riche man, & he vvas clothed vvith 19 purple and silke: and he fared euery day magnifically. † And 20 there vvas a certaine begger called Lazarus, that lay at his gate, ful of sores: † desiring to be filled of the crommes, that 21 fel from the riche mans table, but the dogges also came, and licked his sores. † And it came to passe that the begger died, 22 and vvas caried" of the Angels into" Abrahams bosome. And the riche man also died: and he vvas buried in hel. † And lif- 23 ting vp his eies, vvhen he vvas in torments, he savv Abraham a farre of, :: and Lazarus in his bosome: † and he crying said, 24 Father Abraham, haue mercie on me, and send Lazarus that he may dippe the tippe of his finger into vvater, for to coole my tongue, because I am tormented in this flame. † And Abra- 25 ham said to him, Sonne, remember that thou didst receiue :: good things in thy life time, and Lazarus likevvise euil: but novv he is comforted, and thou art tormented. † And beside 26 al these things, betvvene vs and you there is fixed" a great c chaos: that they vvhich vvil passe from hence to you, may not, neither goe from thence hither. † And he said, Then, fa- 27 ther, I beseeche thee that thou vvouldest send him vnto my fathers house, for I haue fiue brethren, † for to testifie vnto 28 them," lest they also come into this place of torments. † And 29 Abraham said to him, :: They haue Moyses and the Pro- phets: let them heare them. † But he said, No, father Abraham, 30 but if some man shal goe from the dead to them, they vvil doe penance. † And he said to him, If they heare not Moy- 31 ses and the Prophets, neither if one shal rise againe from the dead, vvil they beleeue. ⊣

:: Lazarus in Abrahams bosome, and rest: but both in hel, and not in the kingdom of heauen before Christ. *Hiero. ep. 3. Epitaph. Nepot.*

:: To be in continual pleasures, ease, wealth, peace, and prosperity in this world, is perilous, & a signe of paines in the next. *S. Hiero.*

:: Abrahã had knowledge of things in earth which were not in his time. as that they had Moyses and the Prophets bookes which he neuer saw. *August. de cura pro mor. c. 14.*

c *χάσμα a horrible distance.*

ANNOTATIONS
CHAP. XVI.

Good vvorkes.

8. The lord praised.) This mans deceiuing his maister is not praised, nor vve vvarrãted by his fact to gaine vniustly for to haue vvherevvith to giue almes: but his prudence, in that he prouided so substancially for him selfe vvhilest his maisters goods vvere in his handes, is commended, not for a vertue, but for a vvordly pollicie: and proposed as an example of the careful prouision that rich men (vvho are Gods stewards in earth) should make for their soules; against they be put out of their bailiship and be called to account, vvhich is the day of their death: and for a condemnation of faithful mens folly and negligence, that being assured they shal out of their offices, and vvell knovving they might gaine saluation by their money, haue so litle regard thereof.

Almes meritorious.

9. They may receiue.) A great comfort to al great almes-men, and a vvonderful force and vertue in almes, vvhich beside the merite of the vvorke of mercie, vvhich (as in other places of Scripture is said) purgeth sinne and gaineth heauen, pocureth also not onely the praiers of their beadsmen *Tob. 12, 9.* *Mat. 25,*

in earth

in earth, but their patronage in heauen also. Whereby also the praiers of Saincts for the liuing, and namely for them to whom they vvere beholding in their life, are proued. Yea and that they be in such fauour with God, that they may and doe receiue their frendes vvhich vvere once their benefactors, into their mansions in heauen, no lesse then the farmers vvhom the il stevvard pleasured, might receiue their freend into their earthly houses. Which also insinuateth to vs, that almes bestovved specially vpon holy men, vvho by their merites and praiers are great in Gods grace, may much more helpe vs then our charitable deedes done vpon vulgar men in necessitie, though that be of exceding great merite also. See al this in these Doctors folovving. *Hiero. qu. 6. ad Algas. to. 3. Ambros. in Luc. August. ser. 35 de verb. Do. c 1. Gregor. moral. li. 21 c. 14. Augu. li. 2 q. Euang. qu. 38. Chrys. ho. 33 ad po. Antioch. to. 5.*

The Saincts do pray for vs.

18. And marrieth.) The good of Mariage through out al nations and men, is in issue and fidelitie of chastitie, but among the people of God it consisteth also in holines of Sacrament: Whereby it commeth to passe that it is a heinous crime to marry againe, though there be a diuorce made, so long as the parties liue. *Aug. de bono coniug. c. 24 to. 6.* See the Annotations vpon Marke 10, 11.

Mariage after diuorce vnlavvfull.

22. Of the Angels.) Angels carie good mens soules to heauen novv, as they did then his to Abrahams bosome. See the revvard of pouerty, affliction, and patience: and on the contrarie, the end and revvard of vvealth ioyned with vnmercifulnes. Note also here, that at the day of euery mans death there is a particular iudgement, and therfore the soule sleepeth not nor hangeth in suspense til the general iudgement.

Vnmerciful riche men.

22. Abrahams Bosome.) The Bosome of Abraham is the resting place of al them that died in perfect state of grace before Christes time, heauē before being shut from men. It is called in Zacharie, *a lake vvithout vvater*, and sometimes *a prison*, but most commonly of the Diuines *Limbus patrum*, for that it is thought to haue been the higher part or brimme of Hel, the places of punishment being far lovver then the same, vvhich therfore be called *Infernum inferius.* * *the lovver hel.* Where this mansion of the fathers stood, or whether it be any part of Hel, S. Augustine doubteth: but that there was such a place, he nor no Catholike man euer doubted: as al the fathers make it most certaine, that our Sauiour descending to Hel, went thither specially, and deliuered the said fathers out of that mansion. Iren. *li. 4 c. 39.* Euseb. *Demonst. Euang. li. 10 c. 8 sub finē.* Nazian. *orat. 2 de Pasch.* Chrysost. *to. 5 in demonst. Quod Christus sit Deus paulo post initium.* Epiph. *li. in heres. 46 Tatiani.* Ambros *de myst. Pasch. c. 4.* Hiero. *in 9 Zacharie.* August. *ep. 99 & li. 20 de Ciuit. c. 15.* Paulinus *in Panegyrico Celsi.* Cyrillus *in Io. li. 12 c. 36 ad illud,* Inclinato capite. Gregor. *li. 6 ep. 179.* vvhich treth and place though of al the ancient vvriters confessed and proued by this and other Scriptures: yet the Aduersaries deny it (as they do Purgatorie) most impudently.

Zach. 9, 11. Esa. 42, 7. * Aug. in Ps. 85. Ep. 99.

Abrahams bosome. Limbus patrū.

Christ descēded into Hel, and deliuered the fathers.

26, A great chaos.) A great distance betvvixt Abrahams bosome and the inferiour hel. Some iudge Purgatorie to be placed there, from vvhence (no doubt) Christ also deliuered some at his descending to hel. for, these in Abrahams bosome vvere not in paines: and S. Augustine saith the Scriptures be plaine that he tooke some out of the places of punishment, and yet none out of the hel of the damned. What other place then can that be but Purgatorie?

Aug. ep. 99.

Purgatorie.

28. Lest they also.) If the damned had care of their frendes aliue how & for what cause soeuer, much more haue the Saincts and saued persons. And if those in hel haue meanes to expresse their cogitations and desires, and to be vnderstood of Abraham so far distant both by place and condition, much rather may the liuing pray to the Saincts and be heard of them: betvvixt earth (that is to say) the Church militant and heauen, being continual passage of soules, and * Angels ascending and descending by Iacobs ladder. Men must not for al that be curious to searche how the soules of the deceased expresse their mindes, and be heard one of an other, and so fall to blasphemie, as Caluin doth, asking whether their eares be so long to heare so far of, and wickedly measuring al things by mortal mens corporal grosse maner of vttering conceits one to an other. Which was not here done by this damned nor by Abraham, with corporal instruments of tongue, teeth, and eares: though for the better expressing of the damneds case, Christ vouchsaued to vtter it in termes agreeing to our capacitie.

Gen. 32. Calu. li. 3 instit. c. 22 sect. 24.

Saincts do heare our praiers and haue care of vs.

Caluins blasphemie.

CHAP. XVII.

So damnable it is to be author of a Schisme, 3 that we must rather forgiue be it neuer so often. 5 We must be feruent in faith, 7 and humble withal, knowing that we are bound to God, and not he to vs. 11 The nine Iewes are vngrateful after that he hath cured their leprosie: but the one Samaritane (the one Catholike Church of the Gentils) far otherwise. 20 The Pharisees asking, when cōmeth this kingdom of God (of whose approching they had now heard so much) he teacheth that God must reigne within vs: 22 and warneth vs after his Passion neuer to goe out of his Catholike Church for any new secrete cōming of Christ that Heretikes shal pretend, but onely to expect his second cōming in glorie, 26 preparing our selues vnto it, because it shal come vpon many vnprouided, 31 specially through the persecution of Antichrist a litle before it.

:: Not of mere necessitie, for then it were no fault: but præsupposing the great wickednes of men, it is impossible but there shal be scandals & therfore it foloweth, *Vvo to him by whom they come.*

AND he said to his Disciples, It is :: impossible that scandale should not come: but vvo to him by vvhom they come. 1 † It is more profitable for him, if a mil-stone be put about his necke, and he be cast into the sea, then that he scādalize one of these litle ones. 2 † Looke vvel to your selues, 3 * If thy brother sinne against thee, rebuke him: and if he doe penance, forgiue him. † And if he sinne against thee seuen times in a day, and seuen times in a day be conuerted vnto thee, saying, It repenteth me, forgiue him. 4

Mt.18,7 *Mar. 9, 42.* *Mt.18, 21.*

† And the Apostles said to our Lord, Increase faith in vs. 5 † And our lord said, * If you had faith like to a mustard seede, 6 you might say to this mulberie tree, be thou rooted vp, and be transplanted into the sea: and it vvould obey you. † And 7 vvhich of you hauing a seruant plovving or keeping cattle, that vvil say to him returning out of the field, Passe quickly, sit dovvne: † and saith not to him, Make ready supper, and 8 gird thy self, and serue me vvhiles I eate and drinke, and aftervvard thou shalt eate and drinke? † Doth he giue that ser- 9 uant thankes, for doing the things vvhich he commaunded him? † I trovv not. So you also, vvhen you shal haue done 10 al things that are commaunded you, say, Vve are " vnprofitable seruants: vve haue done that vvhich vve ought to doe.

Mat.17, 20.

THE fourth part of this Gospel, The cōming of Christ into Iewrie, towardes his Passion.

The Gospel vpō the 13 Sūday after Pentecost.

† And it came to passe, as he vvent vnto Hierusalem, he 11 passed through the middes of Samaria and Galilee. † And 12 vvhen he entred into a certaine tovvne, there mette him ten men that vvere lepers, vvho stoode a farre of: † and they lif- 13 ted vp their voice, saying, IESVS maister, haue mercie on vs. † Vvhom as he savv, he said, Goe, * shevv your selues " to the 14 Priests. And it came to passe," as they vvent, they vvere made cleane. † And one of them as he savv that he vvas made 15 cleane: vvent backe vvith a loud voice magnifying God, † and he fel on his face before his feete, giuing thankes: and 16 this vvas a Samaritane. † And IESVS ansvvering said, Vvere 17 not ten made cleane? and vvhere are the nine? † There vvas 18 not found that returned, and gaue glorie to God, but this stranger. † And he said to him, Arise, goe thy vvaies: 19 because :: thy faith hath made thee safe. ⊣

Leu.14, 2.

:: And yet we see here it vvas not only faith, but also his thankfulnes & returnig to giue glorie to God.

† And being asked of the Pharisees, Vvhen commeth the 20 kingdom of God? he ansvvered them and said, The kingdom of God

21 of God commeth not vvith obseruation: † neither shal they say, Loe here, or loe there. for loe :: the kingdom of God is vvithin you.

22 † And he said to his Disciples, The daies vvil come vvhen you shal desire to see one day of the Sonne of man: and you

23 shal not see. † * And they vvil say to you, Loe here and loe

24 there. :: Goe not, neither doe ye folovv after. † For euen as the lightening that lighteneth from vnder heauen, vnto

25 those partes that are vnder heauen, shineth: so shal the

26 Sonne of man be in his day. † But first he must suffer many things and be reiected of this generation. † And as it came to passe in the * daies of Noé, so shal it be also in

27 the daies of the Sonne of man. † They did eate and drinke, they did marie vviues and vvere giuen to mariage euen vntil the day that Noé entred into the arke: and the floud came,

28 and destroyed them al. † Likevvise as it came to passe in the * daies of Lot: They did eate and drinke, bought and sould,

29 planted, and builded: † and in the day that Lot vvent out from Sodome, it rained fire and brimstone from heauen, and

30 destroyed them all: † according to these things it shal be

31 in the day that the Sonne of man shal be reuealed. † In that houre he that shal be in the house-toppe, and his vessel in the house, let him not goe dovvne to take them vp: and he that

32 is in the field, in like maner let him not returne backe. † Be

33 mindeful of * Lots vvife. † Vvhosoeuer seeketh to saue his life, shal lose it: and vvhosoeuer doth lose the same, shal

34 quicken it. † I say to you, in that night there shal be tvvo in one bed: the one shal be taken, and the other shal be left:

35 † tvvo vvomen shal be grinding together: the one shal be taken, and the other shal be left: tvvo in the field: the one

36 shal be taken, and the other shal be left. † They ansvvering

37 say to him, Vvhere Lord? † Vvho said to them, Vvheresoeuer the body shal be, thither vvil the eagles also be gathered together.

Mt. 24, 23. Mar. 13, 21.

Gen. 7, 5

Gen. 19, 24.

Gen. 19, 26.

:: Vvhiles they aske and looke for a temporal kingdō in pompe and glorie, loe their king & Messias was now amōg thē. Whose spiritual kingdō is vvithin al the faithful that haue dominiō ouer sinne.

:: No man must runne out of the Church after Schismatikes to heare them preach Christ in corners, Christs doctrine being open in al the world. See annot. *Mt. 24, 23.*

ANNOTATIONS
CHAP. XVII.

10. *Vnprofitable seruants.*) If our Sauiour had said that the keeping of Gods cōmaundements had bene vnprofitable and not auailable to our selues, then might the Protestants haue truely argued thereby that our vvorkes deserue not heauen or any revvard at Gods hand: but so he said not, but that our seruice is to God vnprofitable, who calleth for it as duety, and not as a thing needeful or

How we are vnprofitable & profitable seruants.

or profitable to him self. And though here our Maister teach vs so humbly to conceiue of our ovvne doings tovvard him, yet him self els vvher calleth not his seruants vnprofitable vvhen they haue done their labour, but speaketh thus, *Good and faithful seruant, because thou vvast faithful in a litle, I vvil place thee ouer much: enter into the ioy of thy Lord.* Yea of such as serue him in the grace of the nevv Testament, he affirmeth that he vvil not novv *name them seruants but frendes*, yea and take them for his ovvne children, and as his frendes and sonnes he counteth of vs and our vvorkes tovvards heauen, though vve in humilitie and truth must confesse alvvaies that vve be to him vnprofitable seruants. Yea and S. Paul saith plainly, that by cleansing our selues from sinful vvorkes, vve shal be profitable vessels to our lord. *2 Timot. 2, 21.*

Mt. 25, 21. Io. 15, 14.

Confession to the Priest.

14. To the priests.) This leprosie signifieth sinne, vvhich though God may and can heale vvithout any mans meanes, yet he doth it not ordinarily but by the Priests ministerie: therfore let no man despise Gods ordinance nor say that it is ynough to confesse to God though he neuer come at the priest. *li. de visit. infirm. apud August.*

14. As they vvent.) A man may sometimes be so contrite and penitent, that his sinne is forgiuen before he come to the Priest, but then also he must notvvithstanding goe to the Priest, as these lepers did: specially vvhereas vve are neuer sure hovv contrite vve are, and because there is no true contrition, but vvith desire also of the Sacrament in time and place.

CHAP. XVIII.

The Church is taught to commit the reuenge of her persecutions to God, and to pray incessantly, for he no doubt (though in the persecution of Antichrist fevv vvil so thinke) vvil at length come. 9 We must also pray vvith humility, because vve knovv not vvith the Pharisee if vve be iust, but vve knovv vvith the Publicane that vve be sinners. 15 He vvil haue children to be brought to him, and al to be as children. 18 What is to be done to get life euerlasting. 22 What also, to get perfection, 28 and vvhat revvard they shal haue that leaue al, yea or any part, for his sake. 31 he foretelleth of his Passion most particularly, 35 and entring into Iericho, cureth one blinde man.

∴ Vve should pray alvvaies by faith, hope, and charitie, and by vvorking the thinges that be acceptable to God: though special times of vocal praiers in the Canonical houres be assigned for the sturring of vs vp to God through external signes of deuotion.

AND he spake also a parable to them that it 1 behoueth ∴ alwaies to pray, & not to be weary, † saying, There was a certaine iudge in a certaine 2 citie, vvhich feared not God, and of man made no accoumpt. † And there vvas a certaine vvi- 3 dow in that citie: and she came to him, saying, Reuenge me of mine aduersarie. † And he vvould not of a long time. but 4 aftervvard he said vvithin him self, Although I feare not God, nor make accoumpt of man: † yet because this vvidovv 5 is importune vpon me, I vvil reuenge her, lest at the last she come and defame me. † And our Lord said, Heare vvhat the 6 iudge of iniquitie sayeth. † And vvil not God reuenge his 7 elect that crie to him day and night: and vvil he haue patience in them? † I say to you that he vvil quickly reuenge 8 them. But yet the Sonne of man comming, " shal he finde trovv you, faith in the earth?

The Gospel vpõ the 10 Sunday after Pentecost.

† And he said also to certaine that trusted in them selues 9 as iust, and despised others, this parable: † Tvvo men vvent 10 vp into the Temple to pray: the one a Pharisee, and the other a Publicane. † The Pharisee standing, praied thus vvith 11 him

him ſelf: God, I giue thee thankes that I am not as the reſt of men, extorcioners, vniuſt, aduouterers, as alſo this Publicane. 12 † :: I faſt tvviſe in a vveeke: I giue tithes of al that I poſſeſſe. 13 † And the Publicane ſtanding a farre of vvould not ſo much as lift vp his eies tovvard heauen: but he :: knocked his breaſt, 14 ſaying, God be merciful to me a ſinner. † I ſay to you, this man vvent dovvne into his houſe iuſtified more then he: becauſe euery one that exalteth him ſelf, ſhal be humbled: and he that humbleth him ſelf, ſhal be exalted. ⊣

:: To take pride of faſting, tithing, or any good worke, is naught: though the workes thẽ ſelues be very good.

:: So doe the prieſts and people at the holy Altar knocke their breaſts, & ſay with the hũble Publicane, *Deus propitius.* *Auguſt. pſ. 31 conc. 3.*

Mt. 19, 13. Mr. 10, 13.

15 † ✶ And they brought vnto him infants alſo, that he might touche them. Vvhich thing vvhen the Diſciples ſavv, they 16 rebuked them. † But IESVS calling them together, ſaid, Suffer children to come vnto me, and forbid them not, for the 17 kingdom of heauen is for ſuch. † Amen I ſay to you, Vvhoſoeuer receiueth not the kingdom of God :: as a childe, ſhal not enter into it.

:: In matters of faith & religion we muſt be as humble & obedient to the Catholike Church as yong childrẽ to their parents.

Mt. 19, 16. Mr. 10, 17.

Exo. 20, 13.

18 † ✶ And a certaine Prince aſked him, ſaying, Good maiſter, 19 by doing vvhat, ſhal I poſſeſſe euerlaſting life? † And IESVS ſaid to him, Vvhy doeſt thou call me good? None is good 20 but only God. † Thou knovveſt :: the commaundements: *Thou ſhalt not kil, Thou ſhalt not commit aduoutrie, Thou ſhalt not beare falſe* 21 *vvitnes, Thou ſhalt not ſteale, Honour thy father and mother.* † Vvho ſaid, 22 Al theſe things haue I kept from my youth. † Vvhich IESVS hearing, ſaid to him, Yet one thing thou lackeſt: :: Sel al that euer thou haſt, and giue to the poore, and thou ſhalt haue 23 treaſure in heauen: and come, folovv me. † He hearing theſe 24 things, vvas ſtroken ſad: becauſe he vvas very riche. † And IESVS ſeeing him ſtroken ſad, ſaid, Hovv hardly ſhal they 25 that haue money, enter into the kingdom of God? † For it is eaſier for a camel to paſſe through the eie of a nedle, then for 26 a riche man to enter into the kingdom of God. † And they 27 that heard, ſaid, And vvho can be ſaued? † He ſaid to them, The things that are impoſſible vvith men, are poſſible vvith 28 God. † And Peter ſaid, Loe, vve haue left al things, and 29 haue folovved thee. † Vvho ſaid to them, Amen I ſay to you, There is no man that hath leaft houſe, or parents, or brethren, or :: vvife, or children for the kingdom of God, 30 † and ſhal not receiue much more in this time, and in the vvorld to come :: life euerlaſting.

:: Not faith only but alſo keeping the cõmaundements purchaſe life euerlaſting. See annot. Mat. 19, 16.

:: This is not a commaundmẽt or precept, but counſel: vvhich the religious do folow. See Annot. Mat. 19.

:: The Apoſtles among other things left their wiues alſo, as S. Hierom noteth out of this place. *li. 1 adu. Iouin.*

:: Life euerlaſtĩg the reward for leauing or loſing willingly our goods for Chriſts ſake.

Mt. 20, 17. Mr. 10, 31.

31 † ✶ And IESVS tooke the Tvvelue, and ſaid to them, Behold vve goe vp to Hieruſalem, and al things ſhal be con-

The Goſpel vpõ the Sunday of Quinquageſme.

summate vvhich vvere vvritten by the Prophets of the sonne of man. † For he shal be deliuered to the Gentiles, and shal be 32 mocked, and scourged, and spit vpon:. † and after they haue 33 scourged him, they vvil kil him, and the third day he shal rise againe. † And they vnderstoode none of these things, 34 and this vvord vvas hid from them, and they vnderstoode not the things that vvere said.

† And it came to passe, vvhen he drevv nigh to Iericho, a 35 certaine blinde man sate by the vvay, begging. † And vvhen 36 he heard the multitude passing by, he asked what this should be. † And they told him that IESVS of Nazareth passed by. 37 † And he cried saying, IESVS sonne of Dauid, haue mer- 38 cie vpon me. † And they that vvent before, rebuked him, 39 that he should hold his peace. But he cried much more, Sonne of Dauid haue mercie vpon me. † And IESVS stan- 40 ding, commaunded him to be brought vnto him. And vvhen he vvas come neere, he asked him, † saying, Vvhat vvilt 41 thou that I doe to thee? but he said, Lord, that I may see. † And IESVS said to him, Do thou see, thy faith hath made 42 thee vvhole. † And forthvvith he savv, and folovved him, ma- 43 gnifying God. And al the people as they savv it, gaue praise to God. ✠

ANNOTATIONS
CHAP. XVIII.

The Church erreth not in faith.

8. *Shal he finde faith?*) The Luciferians and Donatists vsed this place to excuse their fall from the Church, as our Aduersaries novv doe, saying that it vvas decaied in faith, vvhen they forsooke it. To vvhom vve ansWer as S. Hierom and S. Augustin ansWered them, that Christ saith not that there should be no faith leaft in earth: but by this maner of speache insinuateth, that at the later day in the great persecution of Antichrist faith should be more rare, and the faithful among so many Wicked not so notorious: specially that perfect faith containing deuotion, trust, and affection toWard God, Which our Maister so praised in certaine vpon Whom he Wrought miracles, and by force vvhereof mountaines might be moued, vvhich is rare euen vvhen the Church florisheth most.

Hier. cont. Lucif. c. 6. Aug. de vnit. Ec. c. 15. & de verb. Do. Ser. 16.

CHAP. XIX.

In Iericho he lodgeth in the house of Zachaeus a Publicane, and against the murmuring IeWes openeth the reasons of his so doing. 11 He shevveth, that the last day should not be yet, 15 and What then in the iudgement he vvil doe both to vs of his Church as vvel good as bad, 27 and also to the reprobate Ievves. 29 Being novv come to the place of his Passion, he entreth (vveeping and foretelling the destruction of blinde Hierusalem) vvith triumph as their Christ 45 He shevveth his zeale for the house of God, and teacheth therein euery day. 47 The rulers Would destroy him, but for feare of the people.

AND

1 AND entring in, he vvalked through Ieri-
2 cho. † And behold a man named Zachæus: and this vvas a Prince of the Publicans, and he riche.
3 † And he sought to see IESVS vvhat he vvas, and he could not for the multitude, because he vvas litle of stature.
4 † And running before, he ″ vvent vp into a sycomore tree that he might see him: because he vvas to passe by it.
5 † And vvhen he vvas come to the place, IESVS looking vp, savv him, and said to him, Zachæus, come dovvne in hast:
6 because this day I must abide in thy house. † And he in hast
7 came dovvne, and receiued him reioycing. † And vvhen al savv it, they murmured, saying that he turned in, to a man that
8 vvas a sinner. † But Zachæus standing, said to our Lord, Behold the halfe of my goods, Lord, I giue to the poore: and if I haue defrauded any man of any thing, ″ I restore fourefold.
9 † IESVS said to him, That this day saluation is made to this
10 house: because that he also is the sonne of Abraham. † * For the Sonne of man is come to seeke and to saue that vvhich vvas lost. ⫞

The Gospel vpō the Dedication of a Church.

Zachæus.

Mt, 18, 12.

11 † They hearing these things, he added and spake a parable, for that he was nigh to Hierusalem, and because they thought that forthvvith the kingdom of God should be manifested.
12 † He said therfore, * A certaine noble man vvent into a farre
13 countrie to take to him self a kingdom, and to returne. † And calling his ten seruants, he gaue them ten poundes, and said to
14 them, Occupie til I come. † And his citizens hated him: and they sent a legacie after him, saying, Vve vvil not haue this
15 man reigne ouer vs. † And it came to passe after he returned, hauing receiued his kingdom: and he commaunded his seruants to be called, to vvhom he gaue the money: that he might knovv how much euery mā had gained by occupying.
16 † And the first came, saying, Lord, thy pound hath gotten ten
17 poundes. † And he said to him, Vvel fare thee good seruant, because thou hast been faithful in a litle, thou shalt haue
18 povver ouer ∴ ten cities. † And the second came, saying, Lord,
19 thy pound hath made fiue poundes. † And he said to him,
20 And be thou ouer fiue cities. † And an other came, saying, Lord, loe here thy pound, vvhich I haue had laid vp in a nap-
21 kin. † For I feared thee, because thou art an austere man: thou takest vp that thou didst not set dovvne, and thou reapest

Mt. 25, 14.

The Gospel for a confessor that is not a Bishop, and namely for S. LeWis the king of France, August. 25.

∴ Marke here against the aduersaries, that the reWards of these tWo good seruants be diuers & vnæqual, according to the diuersitie or inequality of their gaines, that is, their merites. and yet one receiueth the peny (Mt. 20, 9) as Wel as the other, that is, heauen or life euerlasting.

that vvhich thou didst not sovv. † He saith to him, By thine 22 ovvne mouth I iudge thee, naughtie seruant. Thou didst knovv that I am an austere man, taking vp that I set not dovvne, and reaping that vvhich I sovved not: † and vvhy 23 didst thou not giue my money to the banke, and I comming might certes vvith vsurie haue exacted it? † And he said to 24 them that stoode by, Take the pound avvay from him, and giue it to him that hath the ten poundes. † And they said to 25 him, Lord, he hath ten poundes. † But I say to you, that to 26 euery one that hath shal be giuen: and from him that hath not, that also vvhich he hath shal be taken from him. ꟷ

See annotatiōs Matth. 27, 29, &c.

† But as for those mine enemies that vvould not haue me 27 reigne ouer them, bring them hither: and kil them before me.

THE fifth part of the Gospel, Of the Holy weeke of his Passion in Hierusalem.

PALME SVNDAY.

† And hauing said these things, he vvent before ascending 28 to Hierusalem. † And it came to passe * vvhen he vvas come 29 nigh to Bethphagé and Bethania vnto the mount called Oliuet, he sent tvvo of his Disciples, † saying, Goe into the 30 tovvne vvhich is ouer against, into the vvhich as you enter, you shal finde the colt of an asse tied, on vvhich no man euer hath sitten: loose him, and bring him. † And if any man aske 31 you, Vvhy loose you him? You shal say thus to him, because our Lord needeth his seruice. † And they that vvere sent, 32 vvent their vvaies, and found as he said to them, the colt standing. † And vvhen they loosed the colt, the ovvners there- 33 of said to them, Vvhy loose you the colt? † But they said, 34 because our Lord hath neede of him. † And they brought 35 him to IESVS. And casting their garments vpon the colt, they set IESVS therevpon. † And as he vvent, they spred 36 their garments vnderneath in the vvay. † And vvhen he ap- 37 proched novv to the descent of mount-Oliuet, al the multitudes of ˋ them that descended', began vvith ioy to praise God vvith a loude voice, for al the miracles that they had seen, † saying, Blessed is he that commeth king in the 38 name of our Lord, peace in heauen, and glorie on high. † And 39 certaine Pharisees of the multitudes said to him, Maister, rebuke thy disciples. † To vvhom he said, I say to you, That if 40 these hold their peace, the stones shal crie. † And as he drevv 41 neere, seeing the citie, he vvept vpon it, saying, † Because if 42 thou also hadst knovven, and that in this thy day, the things that pertaine to thy peace: but novv they are hid from thine eies

Mt. 21, 1
Mr. 11, 1
Io. 12, 15

his disciples,

43 eies. † For ∷ the daies ſhal come vpon thee: and thy enemies ſhal compaſſe thee vvith a trenche, and incloſe thee 44 about, and ſtraiten thee on euery ſide, † and beate thee flat to the ground, and thy children that are in thee. and they ſhal not leaue in thee a ſtone vpon a ſtone: becauſe thou haſt not knovven the time of thy viſitation.

∷ This was fulfilled 40 yeres after the death of Chriſt by Titus & Veſpaſianus, vvhen beſides incredible miſeries of famine and other diſtreſſes, there periſhed eleuē hundred thouſand, and were taken captiues 97000, the ſiege begining in the very ſame feaſt & greateſt ſolēnitie of Eaſter when they put Chriſt to death. *Euſeb. li. 3 hiſt. c. 6. 7. 8. Ioſeph. li. 7 c. 17.*

Mt. 21, 12. Mr. 11, 15. MVNDAY

45 †* And entring into the temple, he began to caſt out the 46 ſellers therein and the biers, † ſaying to them, It is vvritten, *That my houſe is the houſe of praier.* But you haue *made it a denne of theeues.* 47 † And he vvas teaching daily in the temple. And the cheeſe Prieſts and the Scribes and the Princes of the people ſought 48 to deſtroy him: † and they found not vvhat to doe to him. For al the people vvas ſuſpenſe, hearing him.

Eſ. 56, 7 Ier. 7, 11

ANNOTATIONS CHAP. XIX

4. Went vp.) Not onely invvard deuotion of faith and charitie tovvards Chriſt, but external offices of ſeeing, folovving, touching, receiuing, harbouring him, are recommended to vs in this example: euen ſo our manifold exteriour deuotion tovvards his Sacraments, Sainčts, and ſeruants, be grateful: ſpecially the endeuour of good people not onely to be preſent at Maſſe or in the Church, but to be neere the B. Sacrament, and to ſee it vvith al reuerence and deuotion according to the order of the Church, much more to receiue it into the houſe of their body.

External deuotion.

8. I reſtore foureſold.) That vvhich vve giue of our ovvne, is almes and ſatisfaction for our ſinnes: but that vvhich vve reſtore of il gotten goods by Extortion, Vſurie, Simonie, Bribrie, Theft, or othervviſe, that is called here Reſtoring. And it is of duty and not of free almes, and muſt be rendred not to vvhom vve liſt, but to the parties annoyed if it be poſſible, othervviſe it muſt be beſtovved vpon the poore, or other good vſes, according to the aduiſe of our ſuperiour & ſuch as haue charge of our ſoules. But that he yelded foureſold, that vvas more then he vvas bound, but very ſatisfactorie for his former ſinnes alſo. And herevvith vve may note, that it is not the giuing of a peny, grote, or crovvne, of a riche mans ſuperfluitie, that is ſo much recōmended to ſinners for redeeming their faultes: but this large beſtovving vpon Chriſt, to ſell al and giue it in almes, to giue the moytie of our goodes, to render foure times ſo much, for that vvhich is vvrongfully gotten, that extinguiſheth ſinnes. The poore vvidovves braſſe peny vvas very grateful, becauſe it vvas al or much of that ſhe had: but the riche mans pound of his ſuperfluitie, though it be good, yet is nothing ſo grateful.

Reſtitution.

Satisfaction.

Lu. 21, 2.

CHAP. XX.

To the Ievves he auoucheth his povver by the vvitnes of Iohn vvho vvas a man ſent of God. 9 and foretelleth in a parable their reprobation moſt vvorthy (vvith the vocation of the Gentils in their place) 17 and conſequently their irreparable damnation that ſhal enſue thereof. 20 He defeateth their ſnare about paying tribute to Caeſar: 27 he anſvvereth alſo the inuention of the Sadduces againſt the Reſurrection. 40 And ſo hauing put them al to ſilence, 41 he turneth and poſeth them, becauſe they imagined that Chriſt ſhould be no more but a man: 45 bidding al to bevvare of the Scribes (authors of the Ievves ſchiſme from him) being ambitious and hypocrites.

TVESDAY.

Mr. 21, 23. Mr. 11, 27,

ND it came to passe: in one of the daies 1 vvhen he vvas teaching the people in the temple and euangelizing, the cheefe Priests and the Scribes vvith the auncients assembled, † and spake saying to him, 2 :: Tel vs, in vvhat povver doest thou these things? or, vvho is he that hath giuen the this povver? † And IESVS ansvvering, said to them, 3 I also vvil aske you one vvord. Ansvver me, † The baptisme 4 of Iohn was it from heauē, or of men? † But they thought with- 5 in them selues, saying, That if vve say, From heauen: he vvil say, Vvhy then did you not beleeue him? † But if vve say, Of 6 men: the vvhole people vvil stone vs: for they are certaine that Iohn is a Prophet. † And they ansvvered that they 7 knevv not vvhence it vvas. † And IESVS said to them, 8 Neither doe I tel you in vvhat povver I doe these things.

:: See Annot. Marc. c. 21, 23.

† And he began to say to the people this parable, * A cer- 9 taine :: man planted a vineyard, & let it out to husbandmen: and he vvas from home a long time. † And in time he sent 10 to the husbandmen a seruant, that they should giue him of the fruit of the vineyard. Vvho beating him, sent him avvay emptie. † And againe he sent an other seruant. But they bea- 11 ting him also and reprochfully abusing him, sent him avvay emptie. † And againe he sent the third: vvho vvounding 12 him also, cast him out. † And the lord of the vineyard said, 13 Vvhat shal I doe? I vvil send my beloued sonne: perhaps vvhen they shal see him, they vvil reuerence him. † Vvhom 14 vvhen the husbandmen savv, they thought vvithin them selues, saying, This is the heire, let vs kil him, that the heritage may be ours. † And casting him forth out of the vineyard, 15 they killed him. Vvhat therfore vvil the Lord of the vineyard doe to them? † He vvil come, and vvil destroy these husband- 16 men, and vvil giue the vineyard to others. Vvhich they hearing, said to him, God forbid † But he beholding them 17 said, Vvhat is this then that is vvritten, *The stone vvhich the builders reiected, the same is become into the head of the corner*? † Euery one that 18 falleth vpon this stone, shal be quashed: and vpon vvhom it shal fall, it shal breake him to pouder. † And the cheefe 19 Priests and Scribes sought to lay handes vpon him that houre: and they feared the people. for they knevv that he spake this similitude to them.

Esa. 5, 1. Mt. 21, 33. Mr. 12, 1.

:: See the marginal annotations Marc. 12.

Ps. 117, 22.

† * And

Mt. 22, 15. Mr. 12, 13.

20 †* And watching, they sent spies which should feine them selues iust: that they might take him in his talke, and deliuer 21 him to the principaltie and povver of the Præsident. † And they asked him, saying, Maister, vve knovv that thou speakest and teachest rightly: and thou doest not accept person, but 22 teachest the vvay of God in truth. † Is it lavvful for vs to 23 giue tribute to Cæsar, or no? † But considering their guile, 24 he said to them, Vvhy tempt you me? † Shevv me a penie. Vvhose image hath it and inscription? They ansvvering said, 25 Cæsars. † And he said to them, Render therfore the things that are Cæsars, :: to Cæsar: and the things that are Gods, to 26 God. † And they could not reprehend his vvord before the people: and marueiling at his ansvver, they held their peace.

:: So duties must be done to Princes, that our duety to God be not neglected. See Annot. Mat. c. 22, 15.

Mt. 22, 23. Mr. 12, 18.

Deu, 25, 5.

27 †* And there came certaine of the Sadducees, vvhich de- 28 nie that there is a resurrection, and they asked him, † saying, Maister, Moyses gaue vs in vvriting, * If a mans brother die hauing a vvife, and he haue no children, that his brother take 29 her to vvife, and raise vp seede to his brother. † There vvere therfore seuen brethren: and the first tooke a vvife, and died 30 vvithout children. † And the next tooke her, and he died 31 vvithout children. † And the third tooke her. In like maner 32 also al the seuen, and they left no seed, and died. † Last of al 33 the vvoman died also. † In the resurrection therfore, vvhose vvife shal she be of them? sithens the seuen had her to vvife. 34 † And IESVS said to them, The children of this vvorld 35 marrie, and are giuen in mariage: † but they that ″ shal be :: counted vvorthie of that vvorld and the resurrection from 36 the dead, neither marrie, nor take vviues, † neither can they die any more, for they are ″ equal to Angels: and they are the sonnes of God, seeing they are the sonnes of the resurrectiõ. 37 † But that the dead rise againe, Moyses also shevved, beside the bush, as he calleth the Lord, *The God of Abraham, and the God of* 38 *Isaac, and the God of Iacob.* † For God is not of the dead, but of the 39 liuing. for al liue to him. † And certaine of the Scribes ansvve- 40 ring, said to him, Maister, thou hast said vvel. † And further they durst not aske him any thing.

:: The greeke οἱ καταξιωθέντες importeth also this much, *They that are made vvorthie*, to wit, by the grace of God, and so they are in deede worthie. as also in the next chapter verse *36.* & *2. Thess. 1, 5.*

Exo. 3, 6.

Mt. 22, 44. Mr. 12, 36.

Ps. 109, 1.

41 † But he said to them, * Hovv say they that Christ is the 42 sonne of Dauid? † and Dauid him self saith in the booke of 43 psalmes, *The Lord said to my Lord, Sit on my right hand,* † *til I put thine ene-* 44 *mies, the footestoole of thy feete?* † Dauid then calleth him Lord: and hovv is he his sonne?

45 † And al the people hearing him, he said to his Disciples, 46 †* Bevvare of the Scribes, that vvil vvalke in robes, and loue salutations in the market-place, and the first chaires in the synagogs, and the cheefe roomes in feastes. 47 † vvhich deuoure vvidovves houses: feining long praier. These shal receiue greater damnation.

Mt. 23, 6. Mr. 12, 38.

ANNOTATIONS
CHAP. XX.

To be worthie of heauē, or to deserue & merite it.

35. *Shal be counted vvorthie.*) This truth and speach that good men be vvorthy of heauen, is according to the Scriptures, and signifieth that mans vvorkes done by Christs grace do condignely or vvorthely deserue eternal ioy. as Sap. 3. *God proued them, and found them vvorthy of him self.* and Mat. 10. *He that loueth his father more then me, is not vvorthy of me.* and Colos. 1, *That you may vvalke vvorthy of God.* and most plainly Apoc. 3. *They shal vvalke vvith me in vvhite, because they are vvorthy.* as of Christ (c. 1) *Thou art vvorthy o Lord to receiue glorie &c.* And that, to be counted vvorthie, and to be vvorthie, is here al one, it is plaine, by the Greeke vvord, vvhich S. Paul vseth so, as the aduersaries ovvne English Testaments do testifie, reading thus Hebre. 10. *Of hovv much sorer punishment shal he be vvorthie, vvhich &c.* & it must needes so signifie, because men for sinnes are not only counted, but are in deede vvorthie of punishment, as them selues do graunt. They do greatly therfore forget them selues, and are ignorant in the Scriptures, and knovv not the force nor the valure of the grace of God, which doth not onely make our labours grateful to God, but worthie of the reward which he hath prouided for such as loue him. See the Annot. 2 Thess. 1, 5.

καταξιωθῆναι. ἀξιωθῆναι.

The new Testamēt an. 1580.

The dignitie of Saincts.

36. *Equal to Angels.*) Saincts of our kinde, now in their soules, and after their resurrection in body and soule together, shal be in al things equal to Angels: and for degree of blisse, many Saincts of greater merite shal be aboue diuers Angels: as S. Iohn Baptist, the Apostles, and others, and our B. Lady aboue al the orders of holy spirits in dignitie and blisse. and no maruel, our nature by Christ being so highly exalted aboue al Angels.

CHAP. XXI.

He commendeth the poore vvidovv for her tvvo mites, aboue al. 5 Hauing said that the Temple shal be quite destroied, 7 he foretelleth first many things that shal goe before, 20 then a signe also vvhen it is neere, after vvhich shal come the destruction it self in most horrible maner, vvithout hope of restitution, vntil al Nations of the Gentils be gathered into his Church in the very end of the vvorld. 25 And then vvhat signes shal come of the last day, terrible to the vvorld, 28 but comfortable to vs of his Church, 34 so that vve be alvvaies vvatchful.

1 AND beholding, he savv them that did cast their giftes into the treasurie, riche persons. 2 † And he savv also a certaine poore vvidovv casting tvvo brasse mites. 3 † And he said, Verely I say to you, that this poore vvidovv hath cast more then al. 4 † For al these of their aboundance haue cast into the giftes of God: but she ″ of her penurie, hath cast in al her liuing that she had.

Mr. 12, 14.

5 † And certaine saying of the temple that it vvas adorned vvith

Mt. 24, 1. Mar. 13, 1.

TVESDAY night.

6 vvith goodly ſtones and donaries, he ſaid, † Theſe things vvhich you ſee, * the daies vvil come vvherein ∷ there ſhal not be left a ſtone vpon a ſtone that ſhal not be deſtroied. 7 † And they aſked him, ſaying, Maiſter, vvhen ſhal theſe things be: and vvhat ſhal be the ſigne vvhen they ſhal begin to 8 come to paſſe? † Vvho ſaid, See you be not ſeduced. for ∷ many vvil come in my name, ſaying that I am he: and the time 9 is at hand, goe not therfore after them. † [b] And vvhen you ſhal heare of vvarres and ſeditions, be not terrified: theſe things muſt firſt come to paſſe, but the end is not yet by and 10 by. † Then he ſaid to them, Nation ſhal riſe againſt na- 11 tion, and kingdom againſt kingdom. † And there ſhal be great earth-quakes in places, and peſtilences and famines, and 12 terrours from heauen, and there ſhal be great ſignes. † But before al theſe things they vvil ∷ lay their hands vpon you: and perſecute you deliuering you into ſynagogs and priſons, dravving you to kings and preſidents for my name. 13 † and it ſhal happen vnto you for teſtimonie. † Lay vp 14 this therfore in your hartes, not to premeditate hovv you ſhal 15 anſvver. † For I vvil giue you mouth and vviſedom, vvhich al your aduerſaries ſhal not be able to reſiſt and gaineſay. 16 † And you ſhal be deliuered vp of your parents and brethren, and kinſemen & frendes: and they vvil put to death of 17 you. † And you ſhal be odious to al men for my name: 18 † and a heare of your head ſhal not periſh. † In your patience 19 you ſhal poſſeſſe your ſoules. ⊣

20 † And vvhen you ſhal ſee Hieruſalem compaſſed about vvith an armie: then knovv that the deſolation thereof is at 21 hand. † then they that are in Ievvrie, let them flee to the mountaines: and they in the middes thereof, let them depart: 22 and they in the countries, let them not enter into it. † for theſe are the daies of vengeance, that al things may be ful- 23 filled that are vvritten. † But vvo to them that are vvith childe and that giue ſucke in thoſe daies. for there ſhal be great af- 24 fliction vpon the land, and vvrath on this people. † And they ſhal fall by the edge of the ſvvord: and ſhal be led captiue into al nations. and Hieruſalem ſhal be troden of the Gentiles: til the times of nations be fulfilled.

Eze. 32, 7. Ioel. 3, 15.

25 † * And there ſhal be ſignes in the ſunne and the moone and the ſtarres: and vpon earth diſtreſſe of nations, for the 26 confuſion of the ſound of ſea and vvaues, † men vvithering

∷ This vvas fulfilled 40 yeres after the death of Chriſt, the 19 of Auguſt, being the very moneth and day vvhere in the Babylonians burnt it: from the firſt building thereof by Salomõ 1130 yeres, from the reedifying thereof vnder Cyrus, 639 yeres. *Ioſep. de bel. Iud. li. 7 cap. 10.*

∷ Many falſe-prophets & Heretikes. See An. Mt. 24. Mr. 13.

b The Goſpel for many Martyrs.

∷ Great perſecutiõ of Catholike men.

The Goſpel vpõ the 1 Sunday in Aduent.

ring

ring for feare and expectation, vvhat ſhal come vpon the vvhole vvorld. for the povvers of heauē ſhal be moued: † and 27 then they ſhal ſee the Sonne of man comming in a cloude vvith great povver and maieſtie. † But vvhen theſe things 28 begin to come to paſſe, looke vp and lift vp your heades: becauſe your redemption is at hand. † And he ſpake to them 29 a ſimilitude. See the figtree and al trees: † Vvhen they novv 30 budde forth fruite out of them ſelues, you knovv that ſummer is nigh. † So you alſo vvhen you ſhal ſee theſe things 31 come to paſſe, knovv that the kingdom of God is nigh. † Amen I ſay to you, that this generation ſhal not paſſe, til al 32 be done. † Heauen and earth ſhal paſſe: but my vvordes ſhal 33 not paſſe. ⊣

† And looke vvel to your ſelues, leſt perhaps your hartes 34 be ouercharged vvith ſurfetting and drunkēneſſe and cares of this life: and that day come vpon you ſodenly. † For as a 35 ſnare ſhal it come vpon al that ſit vpon the face of al the earth. † Vvatch therfore, praying at al times, that you may 36 be [c] accounted vvorthie to eſcape al theſe things that are to come, and to ſtand before the Sonne of man.

† And the daies he vvas teaching in the temple: but the 37 nightes going forth, he abode in the ∷ mount that is called Oliuet. † And al the people in the morning vvent vnto him 38 in the temple to heare him.

∷ Solitarineſſe or eremitage (as S. Gregorie Nazian. ſaith) is a goodly thing. this doth the mount Carmel of Elias teach, Iohns deſert, & that mount vnto which IESVS often retired, & was quietly alone with him ſelf. *Ser. 26 de amore pauperum.*

c ἵνα κατ-αξιωθῆτε See Annot. c. 20, 35.

ANNOTATIONS
CHAP. XXI.

4. Of her penurie.) To offer or giue almes of our ſuperfluites, is not ſo acceptable nor meritorious, as to beſtow ſome of that which is of our neceſſarie prouiſion, and which we may hardly ſpare from our ſelues: for, that procedeth of greater zeale, vvil, and intention, which be more reſpected of God then the ſubſtance of the gift.

CHAP. XXII.

Iudas doth ſell him to the Ievves. 7 After the old Paſchal, 19 he giueth to his diſciples the bread of life in a myſtical ſacrifice of his body and bloud, for an euerlaſting comemoration of his Paſsion. 21 He couertly admoniſheth the traitour. 24 Againſt their ambitious contention he ſhevveth them that the maioritie of any among them in this vvorld is for their ſeruice, as his ovvne alſo vvas: 28 and hovv he vvil exalt them al in the vvorld to come: 31 foretelling Peter the ſingular priuilege of his faith neuer failing, 33 and his three negations: 35 and hovv they ſhal al now be put to their ſhifies. 39 And that night, after his praier with ſvveating of bloud, 42 he is taken of the Ievves men, Iudas being their captaine: yet ſhevving them both by miracle and vvord, that they could doe nothing vnto him but by his ovvne permiſsion. 54 Then in the cheefe Prieſtes houſe he is thriſe denied of Peter, 63 ſhamefully abuſed of his keepers, 66 and in the morning impiouſly condemned of their Councel, for confeſsing him ſelf to be the Sonne of God.

AND

HOLY weeke.

The PASSION according to S. Luke in these two chapters, is the Gospel at Masse vpon Tenebre Wenesday.

Mt. 26,1 Mr. 14,1

1 AND the festiual day of the Azymes approched, vvhich is called Pasche: 2 † and the cheefe Priests and the Scribes sought hovv they might kil him: but they feared the people. 3 † And Satan entred into Iudas that vvas surnamed Iscariote, one of the Tvvelue. 4 † And he vvent, and talked vvith the cheefe Priests and the Magistrates, hovv he might betray him to them. 5 † And they vvere glad, and bargained 6 to giue him money. † And he promised. And he sought opportunitie to betray him apart from the multitudes.

TENEBRE Wenesday.

Mt. 26, 17. Mr. 14, 12.

7 †* And the day of the Azymes came, vvherein it vvas ne-8 cessarie that the Pasche should be killed. † And he sent Peter and Iohn, saying, Goe and prepare vs the Pasche, that vve 9 may eate. † But they said, Vvhere vvilt thou that vve pre-10 pare it? † And he said to them, Behold, as you enter into the citie, there shal meete you a man carying a pitcher of vvater: 11 folovv him into the house into vvhich he entreth, † and you shal say to the good manof the house, The Maister saith to thee, Vvhere is the inne vvhere I may eate the Pasche 12 vvith my Disciples? † And he vvil shevv you a great refec-13 torie adorned: and there prepare. † And they going, found as he said to them, and prepared the Pasche.

MAVNDY Thursday.

14 † And vvhen the houre vvas come, he sate dovvne, and 15 the tvvelue Apostles vvith him. † And he said to them, "Vvith desire I haue desired to eate this Pasche vvith you be-16 fore I suffer. † For I say to you, that from this time I vvil 17 not eate it, til it be fulfilled in the kingdom of God. † And "taking the chalice he gaue thankes, and said, Take and deuide 18 among you, † for I say to you, That I vvil not drinke of the generation of the vine, til the kingdom of God doe come.

Mt. 26, 26. Mr. 14, 22. 1. Cor. 11, 24.

19 †* And taking bread, he gaue thankes, and brake: and gaue to them, saying, "THIS IS MY BODY "VVHICH IS GIVEN FOR YOV. "Doe this "for a commemoration 20 of me. † In like maner the chalice also, after he had supped, saying, ∴ THIS IS THE CHALICE "THE NEVV TESTAMENT IN MY BLOVD, "VVHICH SHAL BE SHED FOR YOV.

∴ The Greeke is here so plaine, that there Was very bloud in the chalice, shed for vs, that Beza saith it is a corruption in the greeke. See the Annota. vpon this place.

Mt. 26, 21. Mr. 14, 20. Io. 13, 18

21 †* But yet behold, the hand of him that betraieth me, is 22 vvith me on the table. † And the Sonne of man in deede

goeth according to that vvhich is determined: but yet vvo to that man by vvhom he ſhal be betrayed. † And they began 23 to queſtion among them ſelues, vvhich of them it ſhould be that ſhould doe this.

†* And there fel alſo a cōtention betvvene them, vvhich 24 of them ſeemed to be greater. † And he ſaid to them, The 25 kinges of the Gentiles ouerrule them: and they that haue povver vpon them, are called beneficial. † But you not ſo: 26 but he that is the greater among you, let him become as the yonger: & he that is the leader, as the waiter. †For which is grea- 27 ter, he that ſitteth at the table, or he that miniſtreth? is not he that ſitteth? but I am in the middes of you, as he that miniſtreth: †& you are they that haue remained vvith me in my tētations. 28 †And I diſpoſe to you, as my father diſpoſed to me, a kingdō: 29 † that you may eate & drinke vpon my table in my kingdom, 30 & may ſit ::vpon thrones, iudging the tvvelue tribes of Iſrael.

Mt. 20, 25. Mr. 10, 42.

† And our Lord ſaid," Simon, Simon, behold Satan hath 31 required to haue you for to ſift as vvheate: † BVT I 32 HAVE PRAIED FOR THEE, that thy faith faile not: and thou once conuerted, confirme thy brethren. † Vvho 33 ſaid to him, Lord, vvith thee I am readie to goe both into priſon and vnto death. † And he ſaid, * I ſay to thee, Peter, the 34 cocke ſhal not crovv to day, til thou denie thriſe that thou knovveſt me. † And he ſaid to them, Vvhen I ſent you 35 * vvithout purſe and ſkrippe and ſhoes, did you lacke any thing? But they ſaid, Nothing. † He ſaid therfore vnto them, 36 But novv he that hath a purſe, let him take it, likevviſe alſo a ſkrippe: and he that hath not, let him ſel his coate, and bie a ſvvord. † For I ſay to you, that yet this that is vvritten, muſt 37 be fulfilled in me, *And vvith the vvicked vvas he reputed.* For thoſe things that are concerning me, haue an end. † But they ſaid, 38 Lord, Loe tvvo ſvvordes here. But he ſaid to them, It is ynough. †* And going forth he vvent according to his cu- 39 ſtome into mount-Oliuet. And his Diſciples alſo folovved him. † And vvhen he vvas come to the place, he ſaid to 40 them, Pray, leſt ye enter into tentation. † And he vvas pul- 41 led avvay from them a ſtones caſt: and kneeling he praied, † ſaying, Father, if thou vvilt, transferre this chalice from me. 42 But yet not my vvil, but thine be done. † And there appeared 43 to him an Angel from heauen, ſtrengthening him. And being in an agonie, he praied the longer. † And his ſvveat became 44 as

:: Straight after the former louing checke & admonition, he promiſeth to them al that haue bene partakers with him of his miſeries in this life, greater preeminence in heauen, then any Potentate can haue in this world, & therfore that they neede not be careful of dignitie or Supremacie.

Mt. 26, 34. Mr. 14, 30.

Mt. 10, 9. Lu. 10, 4.

Eſ. 53, 12

Mt. 26, 36. Mr. 14, 32. Io. 18, 1.

THVRSDAY night.

45 as droppes of bloud trikling dovvne vpon the earth. † And vvhen he vvas risen vp from praier, and vvas come to his
46 Disciples, he found them sleeping for pensifenes. † And he said to them, Vvhy sleepe you? arise, pray, lest you enter into tentation.

47 † As he vvas yet speaking, behold a multitude: and he that vvas called Iudas, one of the Tvvelue, vvent before them, and
48 approched to IESVS, for to kisse him. † And IESVS said to him, Iudas with a kisse doest thou betray the sonne of man?
49 † And they that vvere about him, seeing vvhat vvould be,
50 said to him, Lord, Shal vve strike vvith the svvord? † And one of them smote the seruant of the high Priest: and cut of
51 his right eare. † But IESVS ansvvering, said, Suffer ye thus farre. And vvhen he had touched his eare, he healed him.
52 † And IESVS said to them that vvere come vnto him, the cheefe Priests, and magistrates of the temple, and auncients, As it vvere to a theefe are you come forth vvith svvordes and
53 clubbes? † Vvhen I vvas daily vvith you in the temple, you did not lay handes vpon me, but this is your houre, and the povver of darkenesse.

54 † And apprehending him, they led him to the high Priests
55 house: but Peter folovved a farre of. † And a fire being kindled in the middes of the court, & they sitting about it, Peter
56 vvas in the middes of them. † Vvhom vvhen a certaine vvenche savv sitting at the light, and had beheld him, she
57 said, This fellovv also vvas vvith him. † But he denied him,
58 saying, Vvoman, I knovv him not. † And after a vvhile an other man seeing him, said, And thou art of them. But Peter
59 said, O man I am not. † And after the space as it vvere of one houre, a certaine other man affirmed, saying, Verely this
60 fellovv also vvas vvith him. for he is also a Galilæan. † And Peter said, Man I knovv not vvhat thou sayest. And inconti-
61 nent as he vvas yet speaking, the cocke crevv. † And our Lord turning looked on Peter. And Peter remembred the vvord of our Lord, as he had said, That before the cocke
62 crovv, thou shalt thrise denie me. † And Peter going forth a doores, vvept bitterly.

63 † And the men that held him, mocked him, beating him.
64 † And they did blindefold him, and smote his face. And they asked him saying, Prophecie, vvho is it that smote thee?
65 † And blaspheming many other things they said against him.

† And vvhen it vvas day, there assembled the auncients of 66 the people and cheefe Priests and Scribes, and they brought him into their councel, saying, † If thou be Christ tel vs. And 67 he said to them, If I tel you, you vvil not beleeue me: † if also 68 I aske, you vvil not ansvver me, nor dimisse me. † But from 69 hence forth the Sonne of man shal be sitting on the right hand of the povver of God. † And they al said, Art thou 70 then the sonne of God? Vvho said, You say that I am. † But they said, Vvhat neede vve testimonie any further? For 71 our selues haue heard of his ovvne mouth.

ANNOTATIONS
CHAP. XXII.

The old Paschal ceaseth and a new is instituted.

15. With desire I haue desired.] This great desire he had to eate this Paschal lambe, was not for it self, vvhich he had celebrated many yeres before: but because he meant immediatly after the Paschal of the Law vvas sacrificed & eaten, to institute the other new Paschal in the oblation and eating of his owne body, by vvhich the old Paschal should end and be fulfilled, and in which the old Testament and Law ceasing, the Kingdom of God (which is the state of the new Testament and of his Church) should begin. For, the very passage from the old Law to the new was in this one supper.

Two cuppes or chalices at Christes last supper.

17. Taking the chalice.] This chalice according to the very euidence of the text it self also, is not the second part of the Holy Sacrament, but that solemne cuppe of vvine vvhich belonged as a libament to the offering and eating of the Paschal lambe. Which being a figure specially of the holy Chalice, vvas there drunken by our Sauiour, and giuen to the Apostles also, with declaration that it should be the last cuppe of the Law, not to be drunken any more, til it should be drunken new in the kingdom of God, that is to say, in the celebration of the B. Sacrament of his bloud of the new Testament. And by this place it seemeth very like that the wordes in S. Matthew, *I wil not drinke of the fruite of the vine &c,* were pertaining to this cuppe of the old Law, and not to the Holy Sacrament, though they be there by repetition or recapitulation spoken after the holy Chalice. (Mt. 26, 29)

The real presence.

19. This is my body.] *Although sense tel thee it is bread, yet it is the body, according to his vvordes. let faith confirme thee, iudge not by sense. after the vvordes of our Lord let no doubt rise in thy minde.* Cyril. mystag. 4. *Of the veritie of flesh and bloud there is left no place to doubt: by the profession of our Lord him self and by our faith it is flesh and bloud in deede. Is not this truth? To them be it vntrue, which deny* IESVS CHRIST *to be true God.* Hilar li. 8 de Trinit.

Christ sacrificed his body and bloud in Sacrament at his supper.

19. Which is giuen.] As the former wordes make and proue his body present, so these wordes plainely signifie, that it is present, as giuen, offered or sacrificed for vs: and being vttered in the* present tence, it signifieth not onely that it should aftervvard be giuen or offered on the Crosse, but that it vvas then also in the Sacrament giuen and offered for vs. Whereby it is inuincebly proued that his Body is present as an host or Sacrifice: and that the making or consecrating thereof must needes be Sacrificing. And therfore the holy Fathers in this sense call it a Sacrifice. *Nissen. orat. 1 de resur. Leo ser. 7 et 8 de Pas. Hesychius li. 2 in Leuit. c. 8. Grego. ho. 37 in Euang. et Dial. li. 4, c. 59. Cyrillus Hieros. mystag. 5. Dionys. Eccl. hier. c. 3. Ignat. ep. 5. ad Smyrn. Iustinus dial. cum Tryph. circ. med. Iren. li. 4, c. 32 et 34. Tertul. de cult. fæm. et ad vxor. li. 2. Cypr. ep. ad Cæcil. et de Cæn. Do. Euseb. Demonst. euang. li. 1 c. 10 Nazian. orat. 1 cont. Iulianũ. Chrysst. ho. 83 in 26 Mat. et li. 6 de Sacerd. Ambros. li. 4 de Sacram. c. 6. et li. 1 Offic. c. 48. Hiero. in ep. ad Hedib. q 2. et ad Euagr. ep. 126 to. 3. August. in psal. 33 conc. 1. et alibi sæpe. Græci omnes in 9 Hebr. et Primasius. Conc. Nic. 1. can. 14. Ephes. ad Nestor. Constantinop. 6 can. 32. Nicen. 2 act. 6 to. 3. Lateran. Constant. Flor. Trid.*

*quod datur τὸ διδόμενον

The Sacrifice of the Altar.

Cyril. Alex. anathem. 11.

The Apostles are made Priestes, & the Sacrament of holy Orders instituted.

19. Doe this) In these vvordes the holy Sacrament of Order is instituted, because povver and cõmission to doe the principal act and vvorke of Priesthod, is giuen to the Apostles: that is, to doe that vvhich Christ then did concerning his body: Which was, to make and offer his body as a sacrifice for vs and for all that haue neede of Sacrifice, and to giue it to be eaten as Christes body sacrificed, to al faithful. For as the Paschal lambe was first sacrificed, and then eaten: so vvas his body: and thus to doe he here giueth commission and authoritie to the Apostles, and to al Priests which be be their successors in this matter. *Dionys. eal. Hierar. c. 3. Iren. li. 4, c. 32. Cypr. ep. ad Cacil. Chrys. ho. 17 in ep. ad Hebr. Ambros. in Ps. 38. & in c. 10 ad Hebr.*

19. For a commemoration.] This Sacrifice and Sacrament is to be done perpetually in the Church for the commemoration of Christ, specially of his Passion: that is to say, that it may be a liuely representation, exemplar, and forme of his Sacrifice vpon the crosse. Of vvhich one oblatiō on the crosse, not onely al other sacrifices of the Lavv vvere figures, but this also: though this in a more nigh, high, mystical, and maruelous sort then any other. for in them Christs death vvas signified as by resemblance and similitudes of external creatures and bodies of brute beasts. but in this of the neW Testament, his body visibly sacrificed on the crosse, in and by the self same body sacrificed and immolated in Sacramēt and vnder the shapes of bread and vvine, is most neerely & perfectly resembled: and therfore this is most properly cōmemoratiue, as most neerely expressing the very condition, nature, efficacie, sort, and substance of that on the crosse. For Which the holy fathers call it the very self same sacrifice (though in other maner) Which Was done on the crosse, as it is the self same thing, that is offered in the Sacrament, and on the crosse. Whereby you may see the peruersitie of the Protestants or their ignorance, that thinke it therfore not to be Christs body, because it is a memorie of his body or a figure of his body vpon the crosse: nor to be a true sacrifice, because it is a commemoratiue sacrifice. for as the thing that more liuely, neerely, and truely resembleth or representeth, is a better figure then that Which shadoWeth it a far of: so this his body in the Sacramēt, is more perfectly a figure of Christs body & sacrifice, then any other. Christ him self the Sonne of God is a figure and character of his fathers person, being yet of the self same substance. and Christs body transfigured on the holy Mount, Was a figure and resemblance of his person glorified in heauen. euen so is his body in the Sacrament to a faithful man that knovveth by his beleefe grounded on Christs oWne vvord, that in the one forme is his body, in the other his bloud, the most perfect representatiō of his death that can be. As for the sacrifice, it is no lesse a true Sacrifice, because it is commemoratiue of Christs Passion: then those of the old Testament vvere the lesse true, because they vvere prefiguratiue. for that is the condition annexed to al Sacrifice of euery Lavv, to represent Christs Passion.

Ambr. in 10. Hebr. Chrys. ho. 17 in ep. ad Hebr.

A cōmemoratiue sacrifice is a true sacrifice, no lesse then the prefiguratiue sacrifices Were true sacrifices.

To be a figure of a thing, and yet the thing it self, repugneth not.

20. The nevv Testament in my bloud.] Moyses tooke the bloud of the first sacrifice that vvas made after the geuing of the Lavv *Exod. 24.* and vvith bloud confirmed the couenant and compact betvvixt God and his people, and so dedicated the *old Testament*, vvhich vvithout bloud (saith S. Paul) vvas not dedicated. Moyses put that bloud also into a stādìng peece, and sprinkled al the people &c. vvith the same, & said these formal vvordes, *This is the bloud of the couenant* &c. or (as it is read in S. Paul) *of the Testament vvhich God hath deliuered vnto you.* Vnto al vvhich, Christ in this action about the second part of this his sacrifice, in euery of the Euangelists most cleerely alludeth, expressing that the *neW Testament* is begonne and dedicated in his bloud in the Chalice, no lesse then the old vvas dedicated, begonne, and ratified in that bloud of calues conteined in the goblet of Moyses. vvith vvhich his ovvne bloud he sprinkled invvardly his Apostles as the first fruits of the neW Testament, imitating the Wordes of Moyses, and saying, *This is the Chalice the neW Testameut &c*: Which the other Euangelists spake more plainly, *This is my bloud of the neW Testament.* By al Which it is most certaine, that Christes bloud in the Chalice, is the bloud of Sacrifice, and that in this sacrifice of the altar consisteth the external religion and proper seruice of the neW Testamēt, no lesse then the soueraine Worship of God in the old LaW did cōsist in the sacrifices of the same. For though Christes sacrifice on the Crosse and his bloud shed for vs there, be the general price, redemption, and satisfaction for vs all, and is the last and perfectest sealing or confirmation of the neW laW and Testament: yet the seruice and Sacrifice Which the people of the neW Testament might resort vnto, could not be that violent action of the Crosse, but this on the Altar, Which by Christes oWne appointment is and shal be the eternal office of the neW Testament, and the continual application of al the benefites of his Passion vnto vs.

Hebr. 9. vers. 20.

Both testamēts dedicated in bloud.

The external religion of the neW Testament principally in the sacrifice of the altar.

20. Which shal be shed.) It is much to be obserued that the relatiue, *Vvhich*, in these vvordes is not gouerned or ruled (as some vvould perhaps thinke) of the novvne *bloud*, but of the vvord *chalice*. Which is most plaine by the Greeke. Which taketh aWay al cauillations and shifts from the Protestants, both against the real presence and the true Sacrificing. For it sheWeth euidently, that the bloud as the contents of the chalice, or as in the chalice, is shed for vs (for so the Greeke readeth in the present tense) and not onely as vpon the crosse. And therfore as it foloWeth thereof inuincibly, that it is no bare figure, but his bloud in deede, so it ensueth necessarily, that it is a Sacrifice, and propitiatorie, because the chalice (that is the Bloud contained in the same) is shed for our sinnes. For al that knoW the maner of the Scriptures speaches, knoW also that this, *Bloud to be shed for sinne*, is to be sacrificed for propitiation or for pardon of sinnes. And this text proueth al this so plainely, that * Beza turneth him self roundly vpon the Holy Euangelist, charging him With Solœcisme or false Greeke, or els that the Wordes (Which yet he cōfesseth to be in al copies Greeke and Latin) are thrust into the text out of some other place: vvhich he rather standeth vpon then that S. Luke should speake incongruously in so plaine a matter. And therfore he saith plainely that it can not be truely said neither of the chalice it self nor of the contents thereof: vvhich is in deede to giue the lie to the blessed Euangelist, or to deny this to be Scripture. So cleere is the Scripture

calix qui the chalice Which τὸ ποτήριον τὸ ἐκχυνόμενον

The chalice shed for vs, must needes signifie, the bloud therein, not vvine, and the same sacrificed.

** Annot. no. Test. 1556.*

Beza condemneth the Gospel it self of falshood and impossibilitie.

ture

ture for vs, so miserable flights and shifts is falshod put vnto, God be thanked.

Ambition.

24. *Contention.*] The Apostles perceiuing Christs departure from them and his kingdom to be neere, as infirme men and not yet endewed with the spirit of God, began to haue emulation and cogitations of Superioritie one ouer an other: Which our Maister represseth in them by exhortation to humility and by his owne example, that being their Lord, yet so lately serued them: not forbidding Maioritie or Superioritie in them, but pride, tyranny, and contempt of their inferiours.

Peters faith shal neuer faile.

31. *Simon Simon.*] Lastly to put them out of doubt, he calleth Peter twise by name, and telling him the Diuels desire to sifte and trie them al to the vttermost (as he did that night) saith that he hath specially prayed for him, to this end that his faith should neuer faile, and that he being once conuerted, should after that for euer confirme, establish or vphold the rest in their faith. Which is to say, that Peter is that man whom he would make Superiour ouer them and the whole Church. Whereby we may learne that it was thought fit in the prouidence of God, that he who should be the head of the Church, should haue a special priuilege by Christes praier and promes, neuer to faile in faith. and that none other either Apostle, Bishop, or priest may chalenge any such singular or special prerogatiue either of his Office or person, otherwise then ioyning in faith with Peter and by holding of him. The danger (saith S. Leo) was common to al the Apostles, but our Lord tooke special care of Peter, that the state of al the rest might be more sure, if the head were inuincible: God so dispensing the aide of his grace, that the assurance and strength which Christ gaue to Peter, might redound by Peter to the rest of the Apostles. S. Augustine also: Christ praying for Peter, prayed for the rest, because in the Pastor and Prelate the people is corrected or commended. And S. Ambrose writeth, that Peter after his tentation was made Pastor of the Church, because it was said to him, *Thou being conuerted, confirme thy brethren.* Neither was this the priuilege of S. Peters person, but of his Office, that he should not faile in faith but euer confirme al other in their faith. For the Church, for whose sake that priuilege was thought necessarie in Peter the Head thereof, was to be preserued no lesse afterward, then in the Apostles time. Whervpon al the Fathers apply this priuilege of not failing and of confirming other in faith, to the Romane Church and Peters successors in the same. To which (saith S. Cyprian) infidelity or false faith can not come. And S. Bernard saith writing to Innocentius Pope, against Abailardus the Heretike, We must referre to your Apostleship al the scandals and perils which may fall, in matter of faith specially. For there the defects of faith must be holpen, where faith can not faile. For to what other See was it euer said, *I haue prayed for thee Peter, that thy faith do not faile?* So say the Fathers. not meaning that none of Peters seate can erre in person, vnderstanding, priuate doctrine or writings, but that they can not nor shal not euer iudicially conclude or giue definitiue sentence for falshod or heresie against the Catholike faith, in their Consistories, Courts, Councels, decrees, deliberations or consultations kept for decision and determination of such controuersies, doubts, or questions of faith as shalbe proposed vnto them: because Christes prayer and promes protecteth them therein for confirmation of their brethren. And no maruel that our Maister would haue his vicars Consistorie & Seate infallible, seeing euen in the old Law the high Priestod and Chaire of Moyses wanted not great priuilege in this case, though nothing like the Churches and Peters prerogatiue. But in both, any man of sense may see the difference betwene the person, and the Office, as wel in doctrine as life. Liberius in persecution might yeld, Marcellinus for feare might commit Idolatrie, Honorius might fall to Heresie, and more then al this, some Iudas might creepe into the Office: and yet al this without preiudice of the Office and Seate, *in which* (saith S. Augustine) *our Lord hath set the doctrine of truth*. Caiphas by priuilege of his Office prophecied right of Christ, but according to his owne knowlege and faith, knew not Christ. The Euangelists and other penners of holy Write, for the execution of that function had the assistance of God, and so far could not possibly erre: but that Luke, Marke, Salomon or the rest might not erre in other their priuate writings, that we say not. It was not the personal wisedom, vertue, learning, or faith of Christs Vicars, that made S. Bernard seeke to Innocentius the third: S. Augustine and the Bishops of Afrike to Innocentius the first, and to Celestinus, *ep. 90. 92. 95:* S. Chrysostome to the said Innocentius: S. Basil to the Pope in his time *ep. 52:* S. Hierom to Damasus *ep 57. 58. to. 2.* but it was the prerogatiue of their Office and higher degree of Vnction, and Christs ordinance, that would haue al Apostles and Pastors in the world, for their confirmation in faith and Ecclesiastical regiment, depend on Peter. The lacke of knowledge and humble acceptation of which Gods prouidence, that is, that one is not honoured and obeyed of al the brotherhod, is the cause of al Schismes and Heresies, saith S. Cyprian. A point of such importance, that al the Twelue being in Apostleship like, Christ would yet for the better keeping of vnity and truth, haue one to be head of them al, that a head being once appointed, occasion of Schisme might be taken away, saith S. Hierom. *li. 1 adu. Iouinian. c. 14.*

The Romane faith of Peters successors can not faile.

Popes may erre personally, not iudicially or definitiuely.

The learned fathers sought to the B. of Rome for resolution of doubtes.

Serm. 3. Assump. ad Pontif. *Li. q. Noui. Test. q. 75. to. 4.* *Cypr. ep. 55. nu. 6.* *Bernard. ep. 190.* *Deut. 17.* *Aug. ep. 166. in fine.* *Bernardus ep. 190.* *Chrys. ep. 1 & 2.* *Cypr. ep. 55. nu. 2*

CHAP.

CHAP. XXIII.

The Ievves accuse him to Pilate the Gentil: 4 Who seeking earnestly to deliuer him, specially after that Herod sent him backe, 17 they not onely preferre the murderer Barabbas, but also crie, CRVCIFIGE. *26 In the vvay to Caluarie he foretelleth the vvomen that lamented vpon him, the horrible destruction of their Hierusalem. 32 vpon the crosse he is betvvene tvvo theeues, 35 scorned of the Ievves, 36 of the souldiars, 39 and of one of the theeues, 40 but euen there confessed of the other theefe, 44 and after his death (because of the great miracles concurring) also of the Centurion, 48 yea and of the vvhole multitude: 50 and finally he is buried honorably.*

Mt. 27, 1, 11. Mr. 15, 1 Io. 18, 27.

GOOD FRIDAY.

1 AND all the multitude of them rising vp, led him to Pilate. 2 † And they began to accuse him, saying, Vve haue found this man subuerting our nation, & prohibiting to giue tributes to Cæsar, and saying that he is Christ the king. 3 † And Pilate asked him, saying, Art thou the king of the Ievves? But he ansvvering said, Thou sayest. 4 † And Pilate said to the cheefe Priests and multitudes, I finde no cause in this man. 5 †But they vvere more earnest, saying, He stirreth the people teaching through out al Ievvrie, beginning from Galilee euen hither. 6 † But Pilate hearing Galilee, asked if the man vvere of Galilee. 7 † And vvhen he vnderstoode that he vvas of Herods iurisdiction, he sent him backe to Herod, vvho vvas also him self at Hierusalem in those daies.

8 † And Herod seeing IESVS, vvas very glad, for he vvas desirous of a long time to see him, for because he heard many things of him: and he hoped to see some signe vvrought by him. 9 † And he asked him in many vvordes. But he ansvvered him nothing. 10 † And there stoode the cheefe Priests and the Scribes constantly accusing him. 11 † And Herod vvith his armie set him at naught: and he mocked him, putting on him a vvhite garment, and sent him backe to Pilate. 12 † And Herod and Pilate vvere made frendes that day. for before they vvere enemies one to an other.

13 † And Pilate calling together the cheefe Priests and magistrates, and the people, 14 † said to them, You haue presented vnto me this man, as auerting the people, and behold I examining him before you, haue found no cause in this man of those things vvherein you accuse him. 15 † No, nor Herod neither. for I sent you to him, and behold, nothing vvorthie of death is done to him. 16 † I vvil chasten him therfore and dimisse him.

† And

† And he of neceſſitie had to releaſe vnto them vpon the 17 feaſt day, one. † But the vvhole multitude together cried out, 18 ſaying, Diſpatch him, and releaſe vs Barabbas. † vvho vvas 19 for a certaine ſedition made in the citie and murder, caſt into priſon. † And Pilate againe ſpake to them, deſirous to releaſe 20 IESVS. † But they cried againe, ſaying, Crucifie, crucifie him. 21 † And he the third time ſaid to them, Vvhy, vvhat euil hath 22 this man done? I finde no cauſe of death in him. I vvil correct him therfore and let him goe. † But they vvere inſtant vvith 23 loude voices requiring that he might be crucified. And their voices preuailed. † And Pilate adiudged their petition 24 to be done. † And he releaſed vnto them him that for mur- 25 der and ſedition had been caſt into priſon, vvhom they de-maunded: but IESVS he deliuered to their pleaſure.

† And vvhen they led him, they tooke one Simon of 26 Cyréne comming from the countrie: and they laid the croſſe vpon him to carie after IESVS. † And there folovved 27 him a great multitude of people, and of vvomen vvhich bevvailed and lamented him. † But IESVS turning to 28 them, ſaid, Daughters of Hieruſalem, vveepe not vpon me, but vveepe vpon your ſelues, and vpon your children. † For 29 behold the daies ſhal come, vvherein they vvil ſay, Bleſſed are the barren, and the vvombes that haue not borne, and the pappes that haue not giuen ſucke. † *Then ſhal they begin to ſay* 30 *to the mountaines, Fal vpon vs: and to the hilles, Couer vs.* † For if in the 31 greene wood they doe theſe things, in the drie vvhat ſhal be done?

Oſ.10,8.

† And there vvere led alſo other tvvo malefactours vvith 32 him, to be executed. † And after they came to the place 33 vvhich is called Caluarie, there they crucified him: and the theeues, one on the right hand, and the other on the left. † And IESVS ſaid, Father, forgiue them, for they knovv 34 not vvhat they doe. But they deuiding his garments, did caſt lottes.

† And the people ſtoode expecting', and the princes 35 vvith them derided him, ſaying, Others he hath ſaued, let him ſaue him ſelf, if this be Chriſt, the elect of God. † And 36 the ſouldiars alſo mocked him comming to him, and offering him vinegre, † ſaying, If thou be the king of the Ievves, 37 ſaue thy ſelf. † And there vvas alſo a ſuperſcription vvritten 38 ouer him in Greeke, and Latine, and Hebrevv letters: THIS

behol-ding,

IS

39 IS THE KING OF THE IEVVES. † And one of those theeues that vvere hanged, blasphemed him, saying, If thou 40 be Christ, saue thy self, and vs. † But the other ansvvering, rebuked him, saying, Neither doest thou feare God, vvhere as 41 thou art in the same damnation? † And vve in deede iustly, for vve receiue vvorthie of our doings: but this man hath 42 done no euil. † And he said to IESVS, Lord, remember me 43 vvhen thou shalt come into thy kingdom. † And IESVS said to him, Amen I say to thee: this day thou shalt be vvith me " in paradise.

44 † And it vvas almost the sixt houre: and there vvas made darkenesse vpon the vvhole earth vntil the ninthe houre. 45 † And the ∴ sunne vvas darkened: and the veile of the temple 46 vvas rent in the middes. † And IESVS crying vvith a loude voice, said, *Father, into thy handes I commend my spirit.* And saying this, he gaue vp the ghost.

Ps. 30, 6.

∴ This eclipse vvas seene and vvondred at as a thing aboue nature, of Dionisius Areopagita at Thebes, vvhẽ he vvas yet a Pagan. *Dionys. ep. ad Polycarp. et ep. ad Apollophanẽ.*

47 † And the Centurion seeing that vvhich vvas done, glori- 48 fied God, saying, In deede this man vvas iust. † And al the multitude of them that vvere present together at that sight, and savv the things that vvere done, returned knocking their 49 breasts. † And al his acquaintance stoode a far of: and the vvomen that had folovved him from Galilee, seeing these things.

Mt. 27, 57. Mr. 15, 43. Io. 19, 38

50 † * And behold a man named Ioseph, vvhich vvas a se- 51 natour, a good man and a iust, † he had not consented to their counseil and doings, of Arimathæa a citie of Ievvrie, 52 vvho also him self expected the kingdom of God. † This 53 man came to Pilate, and asked the body of IESVS. † And taking it dovvne, vvrapped it in sindon, and laid him in a monument hevved of stone, " vvherein neuer yet any man had 54 been laid. † And it vvas the day of Parasceue, and the Sab- 55 both drevv neere. † And the women that vvere come with him from Galilee, folovving after, " savv the monument, and hovv 56 his body vvas laid. † And returning they prepared spices and ointments: and on the Sabboth they rested according to the commaundement.

ANNOTATIONS
CHAP. XXIII

34. *Forgiue them.*) A perfecte example of charitie in our Sauiour praying for his crucifiers, vvhich the first martyr S. Steuen did folovv, *Act.* 7: and the praiers of both vvere heard: Christs praier taking effecte in the Centurion and others, Steuens in Paul.

The good theefe.

43. In Paradise.) Thou maist not herevpon differre thy conuersion or amendment, presuming of grace at the last houre of thy life, nor looke to haue saluation by faith and confession of Christ vvithout good workes, nor to goe straight to heauen vvithout satisfaction, penance, or punishment for thy former sinnes and life il spent, nor chalenge securitie and certaine knowledge of thy saluation. for this good theeues case is not common, but a rare example of mercie and prerogatiue. but for the first point, learne only not to despaire, though thou hast been il to the last moment of thy life. for the second, that faith, hope, and charitie, repentance, and good vvil be sufficient, and good vvorkes not required, vvhere for vvant of time and opportunitie they cannot be had. for the third, that Christ gaue to this happy man for his zelous confession of him and reprehending his fellovv, not only remission of his sinnes, but also by extraordinarie grace, a pardon of al penance and satisfaction due either in this life or the next for the same. euen as the holy Church by his example and commission giueth pardons also to some of her zelous children, of al punishment due for their offenses, and such goe straight to heauen. lastly, that euery one hath not a reuelation of his saluation as this man had, and therfore can not be so sure as he was.

Pardon of due penance and satisfaction.

53. Wherein neuer.) As in the wombe of MARIE none was conceiued before nor after him, so in this monument none was laid before nor after him: which prerogatiue (no doubt) was of Gods prouidence, this Ioseph no lesse abstaining afterward to be buried in it, then the other Ioseph from copulation with the mother of our Lord. *S. Augustine.*

Visiting the Sepulcher, or Sepulcres.

55. Saw the monument.) These good vvomen of great deuotion obserued the Sepulcher for the honour of the holy body. Vvherevpon the deuotion of faithful folke vvatching and visiting on Good-Friday and Easter eue the Sepulcher made in euery Church for memorie of our Lords burial, is exceding good and godly, specially the B. Sacrament for more signification sake being present in the same Sepulcher.

CHAP. XXIIII.

Deuout vvomen not finding his body in the Sepulcher, 4 Angels tel them that he is risen according to his ovvne prediction: 9 yet the Apostles vvil not beleeue it. 12 but neither Peter findeth his body there. 13 He vvalketh vvith tvvo Disciples, declaring al this vnto them out of the Scriptures, and is knovven of them by breaking of bread. 36 The same day he appeareth to the Eleuen and others being together, is felt of them, and eateth vvith them. finally teaching them out of the Scriptures not onely of his Passion and Resurrection, 47 but also of his Catholike Church, 49 he promiseth the Holy Ghost to confirme them, 50 and so ascendeth into heauen.

EASTER DAY.

:: That is, first after the Sabboth, which is (saith S. Hiero. q.4 ad Hedib.) *dies Dominica*, our Lords day, vvherein he arose. for the weeke is deuided into the Sabboth, & the 1.2.3.4.5.6 of the Sabboth. & the Apostle (*1 Cor. 16, 2*) cōmaunded a collection of money to be made on the first of the *Sab-*

Mt. 28, 1
Mr. 16, 1
Io. 20, 1.

1 AND in the :: first of the Sabboth very early they came to the monument, carying the spices vvhich they had prepared. 2 † And they found the stone rolled backe from the monument. 3 † And going in, they found not the body of our Lord IESVS. 4 † And it came to passe: as they vvere astonied in their minde at this, behold tvvo men stoode beside them in glistering appareil. 5 † And vvhen they feared and cast dovvne their countenance tovvard the ground, they said vnto them, Vvhy seeke you the liuing vvith the dead? 6 † he is not here, but is risen. remember hovv he spake to you, vvhen he yet vvas in Galilee, 7 † saying, * That the Sonne of man must be deliuered into the handes of sinners and be crucified, and the third day rise againe. 8 † And they remembred his vvordes. 9 † And going backe

Lu. 9, 22

backe from the monument, they told al these things to those eleuen, and to al the rest. 10 † And it vvas Marie Magdalene, and Ioane, and Marie of Iames, and the rest that vvere vvith them, vvhich said these things to the Apostles. 11 † And these vvordes seemed before them as dotage, and they did not beleeue them.

both. Whereby we learne, both the keeping of Sunday, & the Churches count of daies by the 2.3.4 of the Sabboth, to be Apostolical. Which S. Syluester after Ward named, 2. 3. 4 feriam &c. *Breuiar. Roman. Decemb. 31*

Io. 20, 3.

12 † But * Peter rising vp ranne to the monument: and stouping dovvne he savv the linnen clothes lying alone, and went avvay marueiling with him self at that which was done.

Mr. 16, 12.

The Gospel vpō Munday in Easter Weeke.

13 † * And behold, tvvo of them vvent the same day into a tovvne vvhich vvas the space of sixtie furlonges from Hierusalem, named Emmaüs. 14 † And they talked betvvixt them selues of al those things that had chaunced. 15 † And it came to passe: vvhile they talked and reasoned vvith them selues, IESVS also him self approching vvent vvith them. 16 † but their eies vvere held that they might not knovv him. 17 † And he said to them, Vvhat are these communications that you conferre one vvith an other vvalking, and are sad? 18 † And one vvhose name vvas Cleophas, ansvvering, said to him, Art thou only a stranger in Hierusalem, and hast not knovven the things that haue been done in it, these daies? 19 † To vvhom he said, Vvhat things? And they said, concerning IESVS of Nazareth, vvho vvas a man a Prophet, mightie in vvorke and vvorde before God and al the people. 20 † And hovv our cheefe Priestes and Princes deliuered him into condemnation of death, and crucified him. 21 † but vve hoped that it vvas he that should redeeme Israel: and novv besides al this, to day is the third day since these things vvere done. 22 † But certaine vvomen also of ours, made vs afraid: vvho before it vvas light, vvere at the monument, 23 † and not finding his body, came, saying that they savv a vision also of Angels, vvho say that he is aliue. 24 † And certaine men of ours vvent to the monument: and they found it so as the vvomen said, but him they found not. 25 † And he said to them, O folish, and slovv of hart to beleeue, in al things vvhich the Prophets haue spoken. 26 † Ought not Christ to haue suffred these things, and so to enter into his glorie? 27 † And beginning from Moyses and al the Prophets, he did interpret to them in al the scriptures the things that vvere concerning him. 28 † And they drevv nigh to the tovvne vvhither they vvent: and he made semblaunce to goe further. 29 † And they forced

him, ſaying, Tarie vvith vs, becauſe it is tovvard night, and the day is novv farre ſpent. And he vvent in vvith them. † And it came to paſſe, vvhiles he ſate at the table vvith them, 30 he " tooke bread, and bleſſed and brake, and did reach to them. † And their eies vvere opened, and they knevv him: and he 31 vaniſhed out of their ſight. † And they ſaid one to the other, 32 Vvas not our hart burning in vs, vvhiles he ſpake in the vvay, and opened vnto vs the ſcriptures? † And riſing vp the ſame 33 houre they vvent backe into Hieruſalem: and they found the eleuen gathered together, and thoſe that vvere vvith them, † ſaying, That our Lord is riſen in deede, and hath appeared 34 to Simon. † And they told the things that vvere done in the 35 vvay: and hovv they knevv him in the breaking of bread. ⊣

The Goſpel vpõ Tueſday in Eaſter Weeke.

† * And vvhiles they ſpeake theſe things, IESVS ſtoode 36 in the middes of them, and he ſaith to them, Peace be to you: it is I. feare not. † But they being troubled and frighted, 37 imagined that they ſavv a ſpirit. † And he ſaid to them, Vvhy 38 are you troubled, and cogitations ariſe into your harts? † See 39 my handes, and feete, that it is I my ſelf. handle, and ſee: for a ſpirit hath not fleſh and bones, as you ſee me to haue. † And 40 vvhen he had ſaid this, he ſhevved them his handes and feete. † But they yet not beleeuing and marueiling for ioy, he ſaid, 41 Haue you here any thing to be eaten? † But they offred him 42 a peece of fiſh broiled, and a honie combe. † And vvhen he 43 had eaten before them, taking the remaines he gaue to them.

Mr. 16, 14. Io. 20, 19.

∴ As he ſhal be Anathema (ſaith S. Aug.) which preacheth that Chriſt neither ſuffered nor roſe againe, becauſe we learne by the Goſpel, *That it behoued Chriſt to ſuffer and to riſe againe the third day*: ſo he ſhal alſo be Anathema, whoſoeuer preacheth the Church to be els where thẽ in the cõmunion of al natiõs: becauſe by the ſelf ſame Goſpel We learne in the Wordes next folowing, *and penãce to be preached in his name & remiſſiõ of ſinnes through out al nations. Auguſt. ep. 48.*

† And he ſaid to them, Theſe are the vvordes vvhich I 44 ſpake to you, vvhen I vvas yet vvith you, that al things muſt needes be fulfilled, vvhich are vvritten in the lavv of Moyſes, and the Prophets, and the Pſalmes, of me. † Then he opened 45 their vnderſtanding, that they might vnderſtand the Scriptures. † and he ſaid to them, That ſo it is vvritten, and ſo it 46 behoued Chriſt to ſuffer, and to riſe againe from the dead the third day: † ∴ and " penance to be preached in his name 47 and remiſſion of ſinnes vnto al nations, ⊣ beginning from Hieruſalem. † And you are vvitneſſes of theſe things. † * And 48 I ſend the promes of my Father vpon you: but you, tarie in 49 the citie, til you be endued vvith povver from high.

Act. 1, 8. 2, 1.

ASCENSION DAY.

† And he brought them forth abrode into Bethánia: and 50 lifting vp his handes he bleſſed them. † * And it came to 51 paſſe, vvhiles he " bleſſed them, he departed from them, and

Mr. 16, 19. Act. 1, 9.

vvas

52 vvas caried into heauen. † And they adoring vvent backe 53 into Hierusalem vvith great ioy: † and they vvere alvvaies in the temple praising and blessing God.

ANNOTATIONS
CHAP. XXIIII.

30. Tooke bread.) The Fathers in diuers places take this to be meant of the B. Sacrament. *Author operis imperf. ho. 17.* S. Augustine *li. 39 de consensu Euang. c. 25 & ser. 140 de temp. & ep. 59 ad Paulinum q. 8.* Paulinus him self in the next epistle before that, among S. Augustines. Venerable Bede also vpon this place. Theophylacte vpon this place. And that it should be meant of the holy Sacrament, the forme of solemne taking the bread into his handes, blessing it, breaking it, and reaching it to his disciples (exceding proper to the consecration, and common to none other vulgar benediction, nor any where vsed but in Christs miraculous multiplying the loaues) and the singular effecte in notifying Christ vnto them, do proue. And if it be the Sacrament (as it is most probable) then is it an euident example and vvarrant of ministration in one kinde.

The B. Sacrament in one kinde.

46. Penance to be preached.) He shevved vnto them out of the Scriptures, not onely the things that were now accomplished in him self, but also that were yet to come about his Church: as, where it should begin, to vvit, at Hierusalem: and hovv farre it should goe, to vvit, to al nations: that he might not suffer vs (saith S. Augustine) to erre neither in the bridegrome nor in the bride. For this maketh manifestly against al Heretikes and Schismatikes, that set vp nevv churches in particular countries, dravving the people from the foresaid onely true Church, vvhich from Hierusalem so grovveth *ouer al nations, til the end of the vvorld come.

The Catholike or vniuersal Church.

De vnit. Ec. c. 10.

* *Mt. 24, 14.*

50. Blessed them.) Christ our high priest,* prefigured specially therein by Melchisedec, often gaue his blessing to his: somtimes by vvordes, as, *Peace be to you:* somtimes by imposing his handes: and now here by lifting vp his hands ouer his Disciples as it vvere for his farewel. In vvhat forme, the Scripture doth not expresse, but very like it is that in forme of the crosse, as Iacob the Patriarch blessed his nephewes for signification of Christs benediction. for now the crosse began to be glorious among the faithful, and the Apostles (as it is most certaine * by the fathers vvhich call it an ancient tradition) vsed that signe for an external note of benediction. Yea S. Augustine saith (*in Ps. 30 Conc. 3*) that Christ him self not without cause would haue his signe to be fixed in our foreheads as in the seate of shamefastnes, that a Christian man should not be ashamed of the reproche of Christ. and what forme can a Christian man vse rather to blesse him self or others, then that which was dedicated in Christs death, and is a conuenient memorial of the same? Howsoeuer it be, that the Bishops and Priests of Gods Church blesse with an external signe, no man can reprehend, being warranted by Christs owne example and action.

Christ blessed diuers waies.

Blessing with the signe of the crosse.

* *Heb. 7, 6. Io. 20, 21. 26. Marc. 10, 16. Gen. 48, 14.*

* *Tertul. de coron. milit. nu. 3 Basil. de Sp. sanct. c. 27.*

THE ARGVMENT OF S. IOHNS GOSPEL.

S. *Iohns Gospel may be diuided into foure partes.*

The first part is, of the actes of Christ before his solemne manifestation of himselfe, vvhile Iohn Baptist vvas yet baptizing: Chap. 1. 2. 3. 4.

The second, of his Actes in Iurie (hauing novv begonne his solemne manifestation in Galilee, Mat. 4,12*) the second Easter or Pasche of his preaching: Chap.* 5. *For of the first pasche, we had in the first part, chap.* 2, 13: And the pasche of* the Iewes was at hand. *And that feast vvhereof vve haue in this second part, chap.* 5,1: After this there was a festiual day of* the Iewes, *is thought of good Authors, to be the feast of Pasche.*

Iren. li. 2. c. 39.

* This speach very common in this Gospel, as appeareth by the places here marked, declareth that he writeth to the Gentils.

The third part is, of his Actes in Galilee, and in Iurie, about the third Pasche, and after it: cap. 6, *to the* 12. *For so vve haue chap.* 6, 4: And Pasche the festiual day of* the Iewes was at hand.

The fourth part is of the fourth pasche (vvhich vve haue in the end of the chap. 11, 55: And the pasche of* the Iewes was at hand) *that is to say, of the Holy vveeke of his Paßion in Hierusalem: chap.* 12. *vnto the end of the booke.*

By vvhich diuision it is manifest, that the intent of this Euangelist vvriting after the other three, vvas, to omit the Actes of Christ in Galilee, because the other three had vvritten them at large: and to reporte his Actes done in Iurie, vvhich they had omitted.

And this he doth, because Iurie vvith Hierusalem and the Temple, beeing the principal parte of the Countrey, there abode the principal of the Ievves, both for authoritie, and also for learning in the lavv or knovvledge of the Scriptures. and therfore that vvas the place, vvhere our Lord IESVS *finding in the Head it selfe and in the leaders of the rest, such vvilful obstinacie and desperate resistance, as the Prophets had foretold, did by this occasion, much more plainely then in Galilee, both say and proue, at sundry times, euen euery yere of his preaching, him selfe to be the* CHRIST *that had bene so lõg promised vnto them, & expected of them: & the same* CHRIST *to be not onely a man, as they imagined, but also the natural, consubstantial, & coëternal Sonne of God the Father, vvho novv had sent him. Therfore these vvere the vvordes and deedes that serued best the purpose of this Euangelist, being, to shevv the glorie & excellencie of this person* IESVS: *that thereby the Gẽtils might see, hovv vvorthily Hierusalem & the Ievves vvere reprobated, vvho had refused yea & crucified such an one: and hovv vvel & to their ovvne saluation themselues might doe, to receiue him and to beleeue in him. For this to haue bene his purpose, him selfe declareth in the end, saying:* These are written, that you may beleeue that IESVS is CHRIST the Sonne of God: and that beleeuing, you may haue life in his name.

Io. 20, 31.

And herevpon it is, that S. Hierome vvriteth thus in his life: Iohn the Apostle, [a] whom IESVS loued very much, the [b] sonne of Zebedee, [b] the brother of Iames the Apostle [c] whom Herod after our Lords Passion

Hier. in Catal.
a Io. 21, 20.
b Mat. 4, 21.
c Act. 12, 2.

sion beheaded, last of al wrote the Gospel, at the request of the Bishops of Asia, against Cerinthus, and other Heretikes, and specially against the assertion of the Ebionites then rising, who say that Christ was not before MARIE. Wherevpon also he was compelled to vtter his Diuine Natiuitie. *Of his three Epistles, and of his Apocalypse, shal be said in their ovvne places.*

It folovveth in S. Hierome, that In the Second persecution vnder Domitian, fourtene yeres after the persecution of Nero he was exiled into the ile Patmos. But after that Domitian was slaine, and his actes for his passing crueltie repealed by the Senate: vnder Nerua the Emperour he returned to Ephesus, and there continuing vnto the time of Traiane the Emperour, he founded and gouerned al the Churches of Asia. and worne with old age, he died the threescore and eighteth yere after the Passion of our Lord, and was buried besides the same citie.

Whose excellencie the same holy Doctor thus breifly describeth. li. 1. Aduers. Iouinianum.

IOHN the Apostle, one of our Lords Disciples, vvho vvas the yongest among the Apostles, and vvhom the faith of Christ found a virgin, remained a virgin, and therefore is [a] *more loued of our Lord, and* [a] *lieth vpon the breast of* IESVS*: and that vvhich Peter durst not aske,* [a] *he desireth him to aske: and after the resurrection, vvhen Marie Magdalen had reported that our Lord vvas risen againe, both of them ranne to the Sepulchre,* [b] *but he came thither first: and vvhen they vvere in the ship and fished in the lake of Genezareth,* IESVS *stood on the shore, neither did the Apostles knovv vvhom they savv:* [c] *onely the virgin knovveth the virgin, and saith to Peter,* It is our Lord. *This Iohn vvas both an Apostle, and Euangelist, and Prophet: an Apostle, because he vvrote to the Churches as a Maister: an Euangelist, because he compiled a booke of the Gospel, vvhich (except Matthew) none other of the tvvelue Apostles did: a Prophet, for he savv in the ile Patmos, where he was banished by Domitian the Emperour for the testimonie of our Lord, the Apocalypse, conteining infinite mysteries of things to come. Tertullian also reporteth, that at Rome being cast into a barrel of hote boiling oile, he came forth more pure and fresher or liuelier, then he vvent in. Yea and his Gospel it self much differeth from the rest. Matthevv beginneth to vvrite as of a man: Marke of the prophecie of Malachie and Esay: Luke of the Priesthod of Zacharie: the first hath the face of a man, because of the genealogie: the second the face of a lion, for the voice of one crying in the desert: the third the face of a calfe, because of the Priesthod. But Iohn as an Eagle flieth to the things on high, & mounteth to the Father him self, saying:* In the beginning was the VVORD, and the VVORD was with God, and God was the VVORD. *Thus far S. Herome.*

a Io. 13, 23. 24. & c. 21, 20.

b Io. 20, 4.

c Io. 21, 7.

Vpon this Gospel there are the famous commentaries of S. Augustine called Tractatus in Euang. Ioan. to. 9. *and tvvelue bookes of S. Cyrils commentaries.*

THE HOLY GOSPEL OF IESVS CHRIST ACCORDING TO IOHN.

CHAP. I.

The 1 parte: THE ACTES of Christ before his manifestation, whiles Iohn Baptist was yet baptizing.

The preface of the Euangelist, commending Christ (as being God the Sonne incarnate) to the Gentils, and setting out the blindnes of the Ievves in not receiuing him. 19 Then, the testimonies of Iohn Baptist, first to the solemne legacie of the Ievves: 29 secondly, vvhen he savv IESVS come to him: 35 thirdly, to his ovvne Disciples also, putting them ouer from him self to IESVS. Vvho made it plainer to them that he is Christ, 40 and so began he also to haue Disciples.

The Gospel at the third Masse vpõ Christmas day. And euery day at the end of Masse.

IN THE beginning " vvas the WORD, 1 and the WORD vvas " vvith God, and " God vvas the WORD. † This vvas in 2 the beginning vvith God. † Al things 3 vvere made " by him: and vvithout him vvas made ˋnothing. That vvhich vvas made', † in him vvas life, and the life vvas 4 the light of men: † and the light shineth in darkenesse, and 5 the darkenesse did not comprehend it. † There vvas a man 6 sent from God, vvhose name vvas Iohn. † This man came 7 for testimonie: to giue testimonie of the light, that al might beleeue through him. † He vvas not the light, but to giue 8 testimonie of the light. † It vvas the true light, vvhich ligh- 9 teneth euery man that commeth into this vvorld. † He vvas 10 in the vvorld, and the vvorld vvas made by him, and the vvorld knevv him not. † He came into his ovvne, and his 11 ovvne receiued him not. † But as many as receiued him, " he 12 gaue them povver to be made the sonnes of God, to those that beleeue in his name. † Vvho, not of bloud, nor of the 13 vvil of flesh, nor of the vvil of man, but of God are borne.

nothing that vvas made.

ET VERBVM CARO FACTVM EST.

† AND " THE VVORD VVAS MADE FLESH, 14 and dvvelt in vs (and vve savv the glorie of him, glorie as it vvere of the only-begotten of the Father) ful of grace and veritie.

15 veritie. ┤ † Iohn giueth teſtimonie of him, and crieth ſaying, This vvas he of vvhom I ſpake, He that ſhal come after me,
16 :: is made before me: becauſe he vvas before me. † And of
17 his fulnes al vve haue receiued, and grace for grace. † For the lavv vvas giuen by Moyſes, grace and veritie vvas made
18 by IESVS Chriſt. † God "no man hath ſeen at any time: the only-begotten Sonne vvhich is in the boſome of the father, he hath declared.

:: He is preferred & made of more dignitie and excellencie then I, becauſe he vvas before me & al things, eternal God.

19 † And this is Iohns teſtimonie, vvhen the Ievves ſent from Hieruſalem Prieſts and Leuites to him, that they ſhould aſke
20 him, Vvho art thou? † And he confeſſed, and did not denie:
21 and he confeſſed, That I am not CHRIST. † And they aſked him, Vvhat then? Art thou * Elias? And he ſaid, I am
22 not. Art thou :: * the Prophet? And he anſvvered, No. † They ſaid therefore vnto him, Vvho art thou, that vve may giue an anſvver to them that ſent vs? vvhat ſaieſt thou of thy ſelf?
23 † He ſaid, *I am the voyce of one crying in the deſert, make ſtraight the vvay of*
24 *our Lord*, as Eſaie the Prophet ſaid. † And they that vvere ſent,
25 vvere of the Phariſees. † And they aſked him, and ſaid to him, Vvhy then doeſt thou baptize, if thou be not Chriſt, nor
26 Elias, nor the Prophet? † Iohn anſvvered them, ſaying, * :: I baptize in vvater: but there hath ſtood in the middes of you
27 vvhom you knovv not. † The ſame is he that ſhal come after me, that is made before me: vvhoſe latchet of his ſhoe I am
28 not worthie to vnlooſe. † Theſe things were done in Bethania beyond Iordan, vvhere Iohn vvas baptizing. ┤

The Goſpel vpō the 3 Sunday in Aduent.

Mal. 4, 5

Deu. 18, 15.

:: By like the Ievves ignorātly vnderſtood not the place in Deuteronomie, of Chriſt, and therfore they aſke alſo whether he be the Prophet there ſpoken of. See alſo c. 7, 40.

Eſa. 40, 3.

Mt. 3, 11. *Mr.* 1, 8. *Lu.* 3, 16

:: He doth oftē here ſignifie the great difference of his baptiſme & of Chriſts, as of his perſon & Chriſts. See Annot. Mat. 3.

29 † The next day Iohn ſavv IESVS cōming to him, and he ſaith, *Behold the lambe of God, behold him that taketh avvay the* '*ſinne*'
30 *of the vvorld.* † This is he of vvhom I ſaid, After me there commeth a man, vvhich is made before me: becauſe he vvas
31 before me. † And I knevv him not, but that he may be ma-
32 nifeſted in Iſrael, therefore came I baptizing in vvater. † And Iohn gaue teſtimonie, ſaying, That I ſavv "the Spirit deſcending as a doue from heauen, and he remained vpon him.
33 † And I knevv him not: but he that ſent me to baptize in vvater, he ſaid to me, He vpō vvhom thou ſhalt ſee the Spirit deſcending and remaining vpon him, he it is that baptizeth in
34 the holy Ghoſt. † And I ſavv: and I gaue teſtimonie that this is the ſonne of God. ┤

The Goſpel on the octaue of the Epiphanie.

ſinnes

AGNVS DEI at Maſſe.

35 † The next day againe Iohn ſtoode, and tvvo of his diſ-
36 ciples. † And beholding IESVS vvalking, he ſaith, Behold

The Goſpel vpō S. Andrews eue.

the lambe of God. † And the tvvo Disciples heard him 37 speaking, and they folovved IESVS. † And IESVS turning, 38 and seeing them folovving him, saith to them, Vvhat seeke you? Vvho said to him, Rabbi (vvhich is called by interpretation, Maister) vvhere dvvellest thou? † He saith to them, 39 Come and see. They came, and savv where he abode and they taried vvith him that day: and it vvas about the tenth houre. † And Andrevv the brother of Simon Peter vvas one of the 40 tvvo that had heard of Iohn, and folovved him. † He findeth 41 first his brother Simon, and saith to him, Vve haue found :: MESSIAS, vvhich is being interpreted, CHRIST. † And he brought him to IESVS. And IESVS " looking 42 vpon him, said, Thou art Simon the sonne of Iona: thou shalt be called :: *Cephas*, vvhich is interpreted, *Peter*. † On 43 the morovv he vvould goe forth into Galilee, and he findeth Philippe. And IESVS saith to him, Folovv me. † And Phi- 44 lippe vvas of Bethsaida, the citie of Andrevv and Peter. † Philippe findeth Nathanael, and saith to him, Him vvhom 45 Moyses in the lavv, and the Prophets vvrote of: vve haue found IESVS the sonne of Ioseph, of Nazareth. † And Na- 46 thanael said to him, From Nazareth can there be any good? Philippe saith to him, Come and see. † IESVS savv Natha- 47 nael comming to him, and he saith of him, Behold an Israelite in very deede, in vvhom there is no guile. † Nathanael 48 saith to him, Hovv knovvest thou me? IESVS ansvvered and said to him, Before that Philippe did cal thee, vvhen thou wast vnder the figtree, I saw thee. † Nathanael ansvvered him, 49 and saith, Rabbi, thou art the sonne of God, thou art the king of Israel. † IESVS ansvvered, and said to him, Because I said 50 vnto thee, I savv thee vnder the figtree, thou beleeuest: greater then these things shalt thou see. † And he saith to him, 51 Amen Amen I say to you, You shal see the heauen opened, and the * Angels of God ascending and descending, vpon the Sonne of man. ⊣

:: Messias in Hebrue, in Greeke Christ, ĩ English Anointed, to witte, With the spiritual oile of grace aboue his brethren. *Ps.* 44.

:: Cephas in Syriake, & Peter in Greeke, in English, Rocke. See Mat. 16, 18.

The Gospel in a votiue Masse of the holy Angels.

Gen. 28, 12.

ANNOTATIONS
CHAP. I.

How God the Sonne is called the VVORD.

1. *Was the Word,*] The second Person in Trinitie which is the natural, onely, and eternal Sonne of God the Father, is called the WORD: not as the holy Scriptures or speaches of the Prophets and Apostles (vvritten and spoken by Gods commaundement for the vttering of his diuine wil towards man) be called his word, but in a more diuine, eminent, and ineffable sort, to expresse vnto

vs

vs in a sort, by a terme agreable to our capacitie, that the Sonne of God so is, and so from euerlasting is borne of God the Father, as our prime concept (which is our internal and mental word) is and issueth out of our intelligence & minde. This WORD then, Sonne, or second Person in the holy Trinitie, was and had his being then already, when other creatures (of what sort so euer) had but their beginning, and therfore can not be a creature, as many Heretikes before the writing of this Gospel thought, and as the Arrians after taught. And this first sentence of the Gospel not onely the faithful, but the Platonikes did so admire (as S. Augustine writeth) that they wished it to be written in gold.

August. de Ciu. Dei li. 10, c. 29.

The Platonikes.

1. With God.) Because a man might say, If the WORD were before any thing was created, where or how could he be? the Euangelist preuenting that carnal concept, saith first, that he was with God, whose being dependeth not vpon time, place, space, or any other creatures, al which were made by him. secondly, he giueth vs to vnderstand, that the WORD hath his proper subsistence or personalitie distincte frō God the Father, wherby Sabellius the old Heretike is refuted. thirdly, here is insinuated the order of these two persons, one towardes the other, to wit, that the Sonne is with and of the Father, and not the Father of the Sonne. Fourthly, you may confute here the blasphemie of Caluin, holding the second Person to be God, not as of God the Father, but as of him self. And yet such are the bookes that our youth now read commonly in England, and that by commaundement.

The WORD coeternal with the Father, distinct in person, and of the Father.

Calu. inst. li. 1 c. 13. sect. 23 & 25.

1. God was the Word.] Lest any man vpon the premisses, which set forth the relation and distinction of the second Person from the first, might thinke that the Father onely were God, the Euangelist expresly teacheth, the WORD to be God. for though the wordes seeme to lie otherwise (because we haue of purpose so owed the elegancie which the Euangelist him self obserued in placing them so, and therfore they stand so both in Greeke and Latin) yet in deede the construction is thus, *The WORD was God*, and (as in his first Epistle the same Apostle writeth) *true God*: lest any might say (as the Arians did) that he was God in deede, but not truely and naturally, but by common adoption or calling, as good men in the Church be called the sonnes of God. What wonderful wrangling and tergiuersation the Arians vsed to auoid the euidence of this place, we see in S. Augustine *li. 3 de Doct. Christ. c. 2.* euen such as the Protestants do, to auoid the like wordes, *Thus is my body*, concerning the B. Sacrament.

The WORD true God by nature.

1 Io. c. 5, 20.

The Protestants are like the wrāgling Ariās.

3. By him.] Againe, by this he signifieth the eternitie, diuinitie, omnipotencie, and equalitie of the WORD or Sonne, with God the Father, because by him al things were created. al things he saith, both visible of this world: and inuisible, as Angels and al spiritual creatures. Wherevpon it is euident also, that him self is no creature, being the creator of al: neither is sinne of his creation, being a defecte of a thing, rather then a thing it self, and therfore neither of nor by him.

The WORD not a creature but the creator.

12. He gaue them power.] Free wil to receiue or acknowledge Christ, & power giuen to men, if they wil, to be made by Christ the sonnes of God: but not forced or drawen therevnto by any necessitie.

Free-wil.

14. The Word made flesh.] This is the high and diuine testimonie of Christs incarnation and that he vouchsaued to become man. for the acknowledging of which inexplicable benefite and giuing humble thankes for the same, al Christian people in the world by tradition of the Fathers prostrate them selues or kneele downe, when they heare it sung or said at the holy Masse, either in this Gospel: or in the Crede by these wordes, ET HOMO FACTVS EST.

Humble kneeling at the solemne wordes of Christs incarnation.

18. No man hath seen.] Neuer man in this mortalitie saw God in the very shape and natural forme of the diuine essence, but men see him onely in the shape of visible creatures, in or by which it pleaseth him to shew him self vnto many diuersly in this world: but neuer in such sort as when he shewed him self in the person of the Sonne of God, being made truely man and conuersing with men.

How mortal men see God.

32. The Spirit.] Here is an euident testimonie of the third Person in Trinitie, which is the Holy Ghost: so that in this one Chapter we finde expresly against al Heretikes, Iewes, & Pagans, set furth the truth of the Churches doctrine concerning the whole Trinitie.

The B. Trinitie.

42. Looking vpon him.] This beholding of Simon, insinuateth Christs designement and preferring of him to be the cheefe Apostle, the Rocke of the Church, and his Vicar. and therfore vpon that Diuine prouidence and intention he accordingly changeth his name, calling him for Simon, *Cephas*, which is a Syriake word, as much to say as, Rocke or Stone. And S. Paul commonly calleth him by this name Cephas, whereas other both Greekes and Latines call him altogether by the Greeke word, *Peter*, which signifieth the self same thing. whereof S. Cyril saith, that our Sauiour by foretelling that his name should no more now be *Simon*, but *Peter*, did by the word it self aptly signifie, that on him, as on a rocke and stone most firme, he would build his Church.

Cephas. Petrus.

Li. 2 c. 12 in Ioan.

Peter by his new name designed to be the Rocke of the Chnrch.

CHAP. II.

At the request of his mother he vvorketh his first miracle, turning vvater into vvine at a mariage in Galilee, although the time of his manifestation be not yet come. 12 Then in Hierusalem at Pasche, being but one, and yet obscure, he throweth out of the Temple most miraculously al the marchantes. 18 And being yet of the blind Ievves asked a signe, he signifieth so long before, that they should kill him, but he vvil rise againe the third day. 23 Vvhich also presently they vvould doe, but that he knovving their falses hartes (though many beleeue in him) vvil not tarie among them.

The Gospel vpō the 2 Sunday after the Epiphanie.

ND the third day there vvas a mariage 1 made in Cana of Galilee: and the mother of IESVS vvas there. † And "IESVS 2 also vvas called, and his Disciples to the mariage. † And the vvine failing, the mo- 3 ther of IESVS saith to him, "They haue no vvine. † And IESVS saith to her, 4 Vvhat is to me and thee vvoman? my houre commeth not yet. † His mother saith to the ministers, "Vvhatsoeuer 5 he shal say to you, doe ye. † And there were set there sixe vva- 6 ter-pottes of stone, according to the purificatiō of the Ievves, holding euery one tvvo or three measures. † IESVS saith 7 to them, Fil the vvater-pottes vvith vvater. And they filled them vp to the toppe. † And IESVS saith to them, Dravv 8 novv, and carie to the cheefe stevvard. And they caried it. † And after the cheefe stevvard tasted the ∴ vvater made 9 vvine, and knevv not vvhence it vvas, but the ministers knew that had dravvne the vvater: the cheefe stevvard calleth the bridegrome, † and saith to him, Euery man first setteth the 10 good vvine: and vvhen they haue vvel drunke, then that vvhich is vvorse. But thou hast kept the good vvine vntil novv. † This beginning of miracles did IESVS in Cana of 11 Galilee: and he manifested his glorie, and his Disciples beleeued in him. ⊣

∴ He that seeth Water turned in to Wine, nedeth not dispute or doubt hovv Christ changed bread into his body.

† After this he vvent dovvne to Capharnaum him self 12 and his mother, and his brethren, and his disciples: and there they remained not many daies. † And the Pasche of the 13 Ievves vvas at hand, and IESVS vvent vp to Hierusalem: † and he found in the temple them that sold oxen and 14 sheepe and doues, and the bankers sitting. † And vvhen he 15 had made as it vvere a vvhippe of litle coardes, he "cast them al out of the temple, the sheepe also and the oxen, and the money of the bankers he powred out, and the tables he ouerthrevv. † And to them that sold doues, he said, Take avvay 16

The Gospel vpō Munday in the fourth vveeke of Lent.

these things hence, and make not the house of my father, a
17 house of marchandise. † And his Disciples remembred that
18 it is vvritten, *The zeale of thy house hath eaten me.* † The Ievves therfore
ansvvered and said to him, Vvhat signe doest thou shevv vs,
19 that thou doest these things? † IESVS ansvvered and said to
them, * Dissolue this temple, and in three daies I vvil raise it.
20 † The Ievves therfore said, In fourtie and sixe yeres vvas this
21 temple built, and vvilt thou raise it in three daies? † But he
22 spake of the temple of his body. † Therfore vvhen he vvas
risen againe from the dead, his Disciples remembred, that he
said this, and they beleeued the scripture and the vvord that
23 IESVS did say. † And vvhen he vvas at Hierusalem in the
Pasche, vpon the festiual day, many beleeued in his name,
24 seeing his signes vvhich he did. † But "IESVS did not com-
25 mit him self vnto them, for that he knevv al, † and because
it vvas not needeful for him that any should giue testimonie
of man: for he knevv vvhat vvas in man. ⊣

Ps. 68, 10.

Mt. 26, 61. 27, 40.

ANNOTATIONS
CHAP. II.

2. *IESVS also vvas called.*) By his vouchsauing to come with his to the Mariage, he approueth the custome of the Faithful in meeting at honest festes and recreations for maintenance of loue, peace, and amitie among them selues: he reproueth the heresie of Tatian, Marcion, and such like condemning wedlocke: lastly (as S. Cyril saith) he sanctifieth and blesseth the Mariage of the Faithful in the new Testament, making it a new creature in him, and discharging it of the manifold maledictions and disorders wherein it was before. By which benediction the often diuorces, remariages, and pluralities of wiues, and the womens seruile subiection and imparitie in that case, be redressed and reduced to the primitiue institution, and so Christian mariage made a Sacrament. See S. *Aug. de nupt. & concup. li. 1 c. 10 & 21. li. 1 de adult. coniug. c. 8.*

Cyril. in 2 Io. c. 22.

Christ with his presence honoureth and approueth Mariage.

3. *They haue no vvine.*) Our Lady many vvaies vnderstood that now the time approched of manifesting him self to the world by miracles and preaching, and nothing doubted but that he would now begin at her request. Whereby we learne that Christ ordinarily giueth not his graces, but humbly asked and requested therevnto, and that his mothers intercession is more then vulgarly effectual, and that he denieth her nothing.

Our Ladies intercession.

4. *What is to me and thee?*) Because this speach is subiect to diuers senses, we keepe the wordes of our text, lest by turning it into any English phrase, we might straiten the holy Ghosts intention to some certaine sense either not-intended, or not onely intended, and so take avvay the choise and indifferencie from the reader, vvhereof (in holy Scripture specially) al Translatours must bevvare. Christ then may meane here, What is that, Woman, to me & thee being but strãgers, that they want wine? as some interpret it. or (which is the more proper vse of that kinde of speach in holy write) what haue I to doe with thee? that is, why should I haue respect to thy desire in this case? In matters touching my charge & the cõmission of my father for preaching, working miracles, and other graces, I must not be tied to flesh and bloud. Which vvas not a reprehẽsion of our Lady, or significatiõ that he vvould not heare her in this or other things pertaining to Gods glorie or the good of men, for the euent shevveth the contrarie. but it vvas a lesson to the companie that heard it, and namely to his Disciples, that respect of kinred should not dravv them to doe any thing against reason, or be the principal motion vvhy they doe their dueties, but Gods glorie.

Translatours of holy Scriptures.

5. *Whatsoeuer he shal say.*) By this you see, our Lady by her diuine prudence and entiere familiaritie and acquaintance with al his maner of speaches, knew it was no checke to her, but a doctrine to others: and that she had no repulse, though he seemed to say his time was not yet come to

Our lady doubteth not but Christ vvil grãt her petition.

to worke miracles: not doubting but he would begin a litle before his ordinary time for her sake, as S. Cyril thinketh he did: and therfore she admonisheth the waiters to marke wel, & to execute whatsoeuer Christ should bid them doe. *li. 2 in Io. c. 23.*

Profaners of Gods Church are to be punished in soul & body by the Spiritual power.

15. Cast them out.) By this chastising corporally the defilers and abusers of the Temple, he doth not onely shew his power, that being but one poore man he could by force execute his pleasure vpon so many sturdy fellowes: but also his soueraine authoritie ouer al offenders, and that not vpon their soules onely, as by excommunication and spiritual penalties, but so far as is requisite for the execution of spiritual iurisdiction, vpon their bodies and goods also. That the Spiritualtie may learne, how far and in what cases, for iust zeale of Christs Church, they may vse and exercise both spiritually and temporally their forces and faculties against offenders, specially against the prophaners of Gods Church, according to the Apostles allusion 1 Cor. 3. *If any defile the Temple of God, him vvil God destroy.*

The B. Sacrament is not to be giuen to nouices or yonglings in faith.

24. IESVS committed not him self.) S. Augustine applieth this their first faith and beleefe in Christ, sodenly raised vpon the admiration of his wonders, but yet not fully formed or established in them, vnto the faith of Nouices or Catechumens in the Church: and Christs not committing his Person to them as yet, to the Churches like warinesse and wisedom, in not opening nor giuing to them our Lord in the B. Sacramēt, because al were not to be trusted with that high point without ful trial of their faith. *Tract. in Io. 11.*

CHAP. III.

He teacheth Nicodemus, that to come to the kingdom of God, Baptisme is necessarie, as being our Regeneration. 10. Vvhich point Nicodemus as then not vnderstāding, 11 he shevveth that they must beleeue him, and vvhat good cause there is for them so to doe. 23. After this he also baptizeth, and Iohn likevvise at the same time. 25. Wherevpon a question being moued, Whether Baptisme is better, 25 Iohn ansvvereth it by saying, that he is so far inferiour to Christ, as a mere man to God most high.

The Gospel vpō Holy Roode day, Maij 3.

AND there vvas a man of the Pharisees, named Nicodemus, a prince of the Ievves. 1 † This man came to IESVS by night, and said to him, Rabbi, vve knovv that thou art come from God a maister, for no man can doe these signes vvhich thou doest, vnles God be vvith him. 2 † IESVS ansvvered, and said to him, Amen, Amen I say to thee, Vnles a man be borne againe, he can not see the kingdom of God. 3 † Nicodemus said to him, Hovv can a man be borne, vvhen he is old? can he enter into his mothers vvombe againe and be borne? 4 † IESVS ansvvered, Amen, Amen I say to thee, Vnles a man be " borne againe of vvater and the Spirit, he can not enter into the kingdom of God. 5 † That vvhich is borne of the flesh, is flesh: & that vvhich is borne of the spirit, is spirit. 6 † Marueil not, that I said to thee, You must be borne againe. 7 † The spirit breatheth vvhere ∷ he vvil: and thou hearest his voice, but thou knovvest not vvhence he commeth and vvhither he goeth: so is euery one that is borne of the Spirit. 8 † Nicodemus ansvvered, & said to him, Hovv can these things be done? 9 † IESVS ansvvered, and said to him, Thou art a 10 maister

∷ We folow rather S. August. & those ancient fathers, which most cōmoly vnderstand this place of the holy Ghost, & not of the Winde: although both senses be good.

maiſter in Iſrael, and art thou ignorant of theſe things? 11 † Amen, Amen I ſay to thee, that vve ſpeake that vvhich vve knovv, and that vvhich vve haue ſeen vve teſtifie, and our teſtimonie you receiue not. 12 † If I haue ſpoken to you earthly things, and you beleeue not: hovv if I ſhal ſpeake to you heauenly things, vvil you beleeue? 13 † And no man hath aſcended into heauen, but he that deſcended from heauen, the Sonne of man vvhich is in heauen. 14 † And as * Moyſes exalted the ſerpent in the deſert, ſo muſt the Sonne of man be exalted: 15 † that euery one vvhich beleeueth in him, periſh not, but may haue life euerlaſting. 16 † For ſo God loued the vvorld, that he gaue his only-begotten ſonne: that euery one that beleeueth in him, periſh not, but may haue life euerlaſting. ⊣ 17 † For God ſent not his ſonne into the vvorld, to iudge the vvorld, but that the vvorld may be ſaued by him. 18 † He that beleeueth in him, is not iudged. but he that doeth not beleeue, [n] is already iudged: becauſe he hath not beleeued in the name of the only-begotten ſonne of God. 19 † And this is the iudgment: becauſe the light is come into the vvorld, and men haue loued the darkeneſſe rather then the light: for their vvorkes vvere euil. 20 † For euery one that doeth il, hateth the light, and commeth not to the light, that his vvorkes may not be controuled. 21 † But he that doeth veritie, commeth to the light, that his vvorkes may be made manifeſt, becauſe they vvere done in God. ⊣

Nu. 21, 9

The Goſpel vpō Munday in the Whitſon weeke.

22 † After theſe things IESVS came and his Diſciples into the countrie of Ievvrie: and there he abode vvith them, and baptized. 23 † And Iohn alſo vvas baptizing in Ænon beſide Salim: becauſe there vvas much vvater there, and they came, and vvere baptized. 24 † For Iohn vvas not yet caſt into priſon. 25 † And there roſe a queſtion of Iohns diſciples vvith the Ievves concerning purification. 26 † And they came to Iohn, and ſaid to him, Rabbi, he that vvas vvith thee beyond Iordan, to vvhom * thou didſt giue teſtimonie, behold he baptizeth, and al come to him. 27 † Iohn anſvvered and ſaid, A man can not receiue any thing, vnleſſe it be giuen him from heauen. 28 † Your ſelues doe beare me vvitneſſe, * that I ſaid, I am not CHRIST: but that I am ſent before him. 29 † He that hath the bride, is the bridegrome: but the frende of the bridegrome that ſtandeth and heareth him, reioyceth vvith ioy for the voice of the bridegrome. This my ioy therfore is filled

Io. 1, 19.

Io. 1, 20.

led. † He muſt increaſe, and I diminiſhe. † "He that cõmeth 30 from aboue, is aboue al. He that is of the earth, of the earth 31 he is, and of the earth he ſpeaketh. He that commeth from heauen, is aboue al. † And vvhat he hath ſeen and heard, 32 that he teſtifieth: and his teſtimonie no man receiueth. † He 33 that hath receiued his teſtimonie, hath ſigned that God is true. † For he vvhom God hath ſent, ſpeaketh the vvordes of 34 God. for God doth not giue the ſpirit by meaſure. † The Fa- 35 ther loueth the Sonne: & he hath giuen al things in his hand. † He that beleeueth in the Sonne, hath life euerlaſting: but he 36 that is incredulous to the Sonne, ſhal not ſee life, but the vvrath of God remaineth vpon him.

ANNOTATIONS
CHAP. III.

Baptiſme in water neceſſarie to ſaluation.

5. *Borne againe of Water.*] As no man can enter into this world nor haue his life and being in the ſame, except he be borne of his carnal parents: no more can a mã enter into the life & ſtate of grace which is in Chriſt, or attaine to life euerlaſting, vnles he be borne and baptized of water and the Holy Ghoſt. Whereby we ſee firſt, this Sacrament to be called our regeneration or ſecond birth, in reſpect of our natural and carnal which was before. Secondly, that this Sacrament conſiſteth of an external element of water, and internal vertue of the Holy Spirit: Wherein it excelleth Iohns Baptiſme, which had the external element, but not the ſpiritual grace. thirdly, that no man can enter into the kingdom of God, nor into the fellowſhip of Holy Church, without it. Whereby the * Pelagians, and Caluiniſts be condemned, that promiſſe life euerlaſting to yong children that die without Baptiſme, and al other that thinke onely faith to ſerue, or the external element of water ſuperfluous or not neceſſarie: our Sauiours wordes being plaine and general. Though in this caſe, God which hath not bound his grace, in reſpect of his owne freedom, to any Sacrament, may and doth accept them as baptized, which either are martyred before they could be baptized, or els depart this life with vow and deſire to haue that Sacrament, but by ſome remedileſſe neceſſitie could not obtaine it. Laſtly, it is proued that this Sacrament giueth grace *ex opere operato*, that is, of the worke it ſelf (which al Proteſtants denie) becauſe it ſo breedeth our ſpiritual life in God, as our carnal birth giueth the life of the world.

Baptiſme in two caſes not neceſſarie, but othervviſe ſupplied.

* *Auguſt. hæreſ. 88.*

Euery infidel, and namely heretikes, are iudged already.

18. *Is iudged already.*] He that beleeueth in Chriſt with faith which worketh by charitie (as the Apoſtle ſpeaketh) ſhal not be condemned at the later day nor at the houre of his death. but the Infidel, be he Iew, Pagan, or Heretike, is already (if he die in his incredulitie) by his owne profeſſion and ſentence condemned, and ſhal not come to iudgement either particular or general, to be diſcuſſed according to his workes of mercie done or omitted. In which ſenſe S. Paul ſaith that the obſtinate Heretike is condemned by his owne iudgement, preuenting in him ſelf, of his owne free wil, the ſentence both of Chriſt and of the Church.

Gal. 5, 6.
Tit. 3, 11.

The excellencie of Chriſts povver and graces.

31. *He that commeth from aboue.*] As though he ſhould ſay, No maruel that men reſort to Chriſt ſo faſt and make leſſe account of me. for, his baptiſme and his preaching and his perſon are al from heauen immediatly. He bringeth al from the very boſome, mouth, and ſubſtance of God his Father. Whatſoeuer is in me, is but a litle drop of his grace. His ſpirit and graces are aboue al meaſures or mens gifts, euen according to his Manhod: and al power temporal and ſpiritual, the kingdom and the Prieſthod, and al ſoueraintie in heauen and earth are beſtowed vpon him as he is man alſo.

CHAP. IIII.

Leauing Ievvrie because of the Pharisees, in the vvay to Galilee he talketh vvith a Samaritane vvoman, telling her that he vvil giue vvater of euerlasting life, 16 shevving him self to knovv mens secretes, 19 preferring the Ievves religion before the Samaritanes, but ours (the Christian Catholike religion) before them both, 25 and vttering vnto her that he is Christ. 28 vvhich by her testimonie and his preaching very many Samaritanes do beleeue: he in the meane time fore telling his Disciples, of the haruest he vvil send them in to. 45 The Galilæans also receiue him, vvhere againe he vvorketh his second miracle.

1 WHEN IESVS therfore vnderstoode that the Pharisees heard that IESVS maketh mo Disciples, 2 and baptizeth, thē Iohn, † (hovvbeit ∷ IESVS did not baptize, but his Disciples) † 3 he left Ievvrie, and vvent againe into Galilee. † 4 and he had of necessitie to passe through Samaria. † 5 He commeth therfore into a citie of Samaria vvhich is called Sichar: * beside the maner that Iacob gaue to Ioseph his sonne. † 6 And there vvas there the fountaine of Iacob. IESVS therfore vvearied of his iourney, sate so vpon the fountaine. It vvas about the sixt houre.

Gen. 48, 22.

∷ He did not baptize ordinarily. yet that he baptized his Apostles, S. Aug. thinketh it very probable, *ep. 108.*

The Gospel vpō Friday in the 3 Weeke in Lent.

7 † There commeth ∷ a vvoman of Samaria to dravv vvater, IESVS saith to her, Giue me to drinke. † 8 For his Disciples vvere gone into the citie, to bie meates. † 9 Therfore that Samaritane vvoman saith to him, Hovv doest thou being a Ievve, aske of me to drinke, vvhich am a Samaritane vvomā? For the Ievves ∷ do not communicate vvith the Samaritanes. 10 † IESVS ansvvered, and said to her, If thou didst knovv the gift of God, and vvho he is that saith vnto thee, Giue me to drinke: thou perhaps vvouldest haue asked of him, and he vvould haue giuen thee [c] liuing vvater. † 11 The vvoman saith to him, Sir, neither hast thou vvherein to dravv, and the vvel is deepe: vvhence hast thou the liuing vvater? † 12 art thou greater then our father Iacob, vvho gaue vs the vvel, and him self dranke of it, and his children, and his cattel? † 13 IESVS ansvvered, and said to her, Euery one that drinketh of this vvater, shal thirst againe: but he that shal drinke of the vvater 14 that I vvil giue him, shal not thirst for euer, † but the vvater that I vvil giue him, shal become in him a fountaine of vvater springing vp vnto life euerlasting. † 15 The vvoman saith to him, Lord giue me this vvater, that I may not thirst, nor come hither to dravv.

∷ This woman is a figure of the Church, not yet iustified, but now to be iustified. *Aug. tract. 15 in Ioan.*

∷ There were many other causes why the faithful Iewes could not abide the Samaritans, but their precise abstaining from their companie & cōuersation, was their Schismatical Temple and seruice in mount Garizim.

c He speaketh of his baptizing in the Holy Ghost. See Io. c. 7, 39.

16 † IESVS saith to her, Goe, call thy husband, and come 17 hither. † The vvoman ansvvered and said, I haue no husband

band. IESVS ſaith to her, Thou haſt ſaid vvel, that I haue no huſband. † For thou haſt had fiue huſbands: and he 18 vvhom thou novv haſt, is not thy huſband. this thou haſt ſaid truely.

† The vvoman ſaith to him, Lord, I perceiue that thou art 19 a Prophet. † "Our fathers adored in this mountaine, and you 20 ſay, * that at Hieruſalem is the place vvhere men muſt adore. † IESVS ſaith to her, Vvoman beleeue me, that the houre 21 ſhal come, vvhen you ſhal neither in this mountaine, nor in Hieruſalem adore the Father. † * You adore that you knovv 22 not: vve adore that vve knovv, for ſaluation is of the Ievves. † But the houre commeth, and novv it is, vvhen the true 23 adorers ſhal adore the Father " in ſpirit and veritie. for the Father alſo ſeeketh ſuch, to adore him. † God is a ſpirit, and 24 they that adore him, muſt adore in ſpirit and veritie. † The 25 vvoman ſaith to him, I knovv that MESSIAS commeth, (vvhich is called CHRIST): therfore vvhen he commeth, he vvil ſhevv vs al things. † IESVS ſaith to her, I am he, that 26 ſpeake vvith thee.

Deu. 12, 6. Pſ. 121 13.

4 Reg. 17, 28, 36.

† And incontinent his Diſciples came: and they marueiled 27 that he talked vvith a vvoman. No man for al that ſaid, Vvhat ſeekeſt thou, or vvhy talkeſt thou vvith her?

† The vvoman therfore left her vvater-pot: and ſhe vvent 28 into the citie, and ſaith to thoſe men, † Come, and ſee a man 29 that hath told me al things vvhatſoeuer I haue done. Is not he CHRIST? † They vvent forth therfore out of the citie, 30 and came to him.

† In the meane time the Diſciples deſired him, ſaying, 31 Rabbi eate. † But he ſaid to them, I haue meate to eate 32 vvhich you knovv not. † The Diſciples therfore ſaid one to 33 an other, Hath any man brought him for to eate? † IESVS ſaith 34 to them, My meate is to doe the vvil of him that ſent me, to perfit his vvorke. † Doe not you ſay that yet there are foure 35 moneths, and harueſt commeth? Behold I ſay to you, lift vp your eies, and ſee the countries, that they are vvhite already to harueſt. † And he that reapeth, receiueth hire, 36 and gathereth fruite vnto life euerlaſting: that both he that ſovveth, and he that reapeth, may reioyce together. † For 37 in this is the ſaying true: that it is one man that ſovveth, and it is an other that reapeth. † I haue ſent you to reape that 38 vvhich you laboured not: others haue laboured, and you

haue

haue entred into their labours.

39 † And of that citie many beleeued in him of the Samaritans, for the vvord of the :: vvoman giuing testimonie, that 40 he told me al things vvhatsoeuer I haue done. † Therfore vvhen the Samaritans vvere come to him, they desired him that he vvould tarie there. And he taried there tvvo daies. 41 † And many moe beleeued for his ovvne vvord. † And 42 they said to the vvoman, That novv not for thy saying doe vve beleeue: for our selues haue heard, and doe knovv that this is the Sauiour of the vvorld in deede. ꟻ

:: This womā mystically beīg the Church, it is here signified, that they which at the first beleeue because the Church teacheth so, afterward be much confirmed, finding it in the Scripture also, and by other instructions.

43 † And after the tvvo daies he departed thence: and vvent 44 into Galilee. † For IESVS him self gaue testimonie that a 45 Prophet hath not honour in his ovvne countrie. † Therfore *vvhen he vvas come into Galilee, the Galilæans receiued him, vvhereas they had seen al things that he had done at Hierusalem in the festiual day: for them selues also came to the festiual day.

Mt. 4, 12 Mr. 1, 14 Luc. 4, 14.

46 † He came againe therfore into Cana of Galilee, *Vvhere he made vvater vvine. And there vvas a certaine lord vvhose 47 sonne vvas sicke at Capharnáum. † He hauing heard that IESVS came from Ievvrie into Galilee, vvent to him, and desired him that he vvould come dovvne & heale his sonne. 48 for he began to die. † IESVS therfore said to him, Vn-49 lesse you see signes and vvonders, you beleeue not. † The lord saith to him, Lord, come dovvne before that my sonne 50 die. † IESVS saith to him, Goe, thy sonne liueth. The man 51 beleeued the vvord that IESVS said to him, and vvent. † And as he vvas novv going dovvne, his seruants mette him: and 52 they brought vvord, saying, That his sonne liued. † He asked therfore of them the houre, vvherein he vvas amended. And they said to him, That yesterday at the seuenth houre the feuer 53 left him. † The father therfore knevv that it vvas in the same houre vvherein IESVS said to him, Thy sonne liueth. and 54 him self beleeued and his vvhole house. ꟻ † This againe the * second signe did IESVS, vvhen he vvas come from Ievvrie into Galilee.

Io. 2, 9.

The Gospel vpō the 20 Sunday after Pentecost.

Io. 2, 11.

ANNOTATIONS
CHAP. IIII,

20. *Our Fathers adored.*] By adoration is meant doing of sacrifice. for other offices of Religion might be done in any place. The Samaritanes to defend their adoring in Garizim, pretended their Worshiping there to be more ancient then the Iewes in Hierusalem, referring it to Iacob

The Schismatical tēple contendeth against the true Tēple.

Iacob: Whereas in deede that Patriarch adoring there before the Temple vvas appointed, or the Lavv giuen, made nothing for their Schisme: Which vvas begone by Manasses a fugitiue Priest, onely to hold his vnlavvful Wife thereby, and to obtaine Superioritie, in Schisme: vvhich he could not doe in the vnitie of his brethren: long after the Temple of Hierusalem, from vvhich the reuolt vvas made. Therfore Christ giueth sentence for the Ievves and the Temple of Hierusalem, affirming that they had a good ground thereof, but the Samaritanes none at al.

Ioseph. li. antiq. 11. c. 8.

Iosephus also recordeth hovv the Samaritanes demaunded of Alexander the Great, the like priuileges and immunities as he had graunted to the high Priest and Temple of Hierusalem, pretending their Temple to be as great and as vvorthy, and them selues to be Ievves as the other, and to vvorship the same God. but their Schismatical hypocrisie vvas easely spied and dimissed vvith nothing. An other time the Ievves and Samaritanes (as the same vvriter testifieth) made a great sturre in Alexandria about the truth and antiquitie of the Schismatical temple and seruice in Garizim and the other true Temple of Salomon: in so much that the matter vvas put to arbitrement by Ptolomæus the kings commaundement, onely to trie Whether of the tWo Was first. And the Schismatikes (as their custome is) *per saltum* can make their Church or seruice as old as they list, referring it to the Patriarches, as our Schismatikes do noW to Christ and the Apostles. But When the trial Was made, onely they of Hierusalem did inuincibly proue by continual succession of their Priests, and by the iust note of the time When the Schismatikes Went out from them, that theirs Was the lavvful, and the other the false temple and false adoration. and so it Was iudged, and the Samaritanes put to silence. AfterWard the said Schismatikes (Which is lightly the end of al Schismes) reuolted quite from the IeWes religion, and dedicated their temple in Garizim to Iupiter Olympius, as Caluins supper and his bread and Wine is like at length to come to the sacrifice of Ceres and Bacchus.

The true Temple preuaileth.

Ioseph. li. 13. antiq. c. 6.

The true Temple is proued by continual succession.

23. *In Spirit and veritie.*) Our Sauiour foretelleth her that the end & ceasing of their sacrifice & adoration in both the Temples should shortly be, and euen then vvas begone to be fulfilled: instructing her in three things concerning that point. first, that the true Sacrifice should be tied no more to that one place or nation, but that true adoration should be through out al Nations according to the Prophecie of Malachie. Secondly, that the grosse and carnal adoration by the flesh and bloud of beastes and other external terrene creatures, not hauing in them grace, spirit, and life, should be taken avvay, & an other sacrifice succeede, Which should be in it self inuisible, celestial, diuine, ful of life, Spirit, and grace. and thirdly, that this adoration and sacrifice should be the veritie it self, vvhereof al the former sacrifices and hostes Were but shadovves and figures. and he calleth that here spirit and truth, vvhich in the first Chapter is called grace and truth. Al vvhich is no more but a prophecie and description of the Sacrifice of the faithful Gentils in the body and bloud of Christ: not that it is not by external meanes giuen to vs (for othervvise vve being men consisting of flesh and bloud could not be capable thereof) but that it is spirit and life in it self, being the flesh of the VVORD of God. And if a man enlarge the vvord of Adoratiõ, (vvhich here as is said, signifieth properly the Worship of God by sacrifice) to al the Sacraments of the new LaW, they al likeWise be spirit and grace, the Holy Ghost Working inuisibly and internally vpon our soules by euery one of them. Wherevpõ our Baptisme, is Water & the Holy Ghost: our Penance, the Word of absolution and the Holy Ghost: our Confirmatiõ, oile & the Holy Ghost by imposition of handes: finally, al the adoration of the Catholike Church, is properly spiritual, though certaine external creatures for our natures, state and necessitie, be ioyned therevnto. Take heede therfore thou gather not of Christs Wordes, that Christian men should haue no vse of external office toWards God: for that Would take aWay al sacrifice, Sacraments, praiers, Churches, and societie of men in his Seruice.

Christian adoratiõ throughout al natiõs in euery place, in spirit & veritie: that is, in the Sacraments and seruice of the new law, ful of spirit & grace: in the veritie of things before prefigured, specially the true sacrifice of Christs body and bloud.

Mal. 1, 11.

Io. 1, 17.

The 2 part: THE ACTES of Christ in Iewrie (hauing already begonne his solemne Manifestation in Galilee Mt. 4, 12) the second Pasche of his preaching.

CHAP. V.

Curing a bedred man at the pond of miracle, because he doth it on the Sabboth, the blind Ievves do persecute him, 7 and againe because he saith that God is his natural father. 19 He therevpon continueth saying, the Fathers operation and his to be in euery thing al one, and that he shal do greater things then these miraculous cures, to vvit, 21 quicken the dead in soule by sinne, as being appointed Iudge of al, 28 yea and quicken the dead in bodies also. incõtinent iudging al vprightly. 31 And that these are not bragges of his ovvne, but his vvitnesses to be, 33 Iohn Baptist, 36 his ovvne miraculous vvorkes, 37 his fathers voice at his baptisme, 39 the Scriptures also, namely of Moyses.

AFTER

1 AFTER these things there vvas a festiual day of the Ievves, and IESVS vvent vp to Hierusalem. 2 † And there is at Hierusalem' vpon' ∷ Probatica a" pond vvhich in hebrevv is surnamed ' Bethsaida', hauing fiue porches. 3 †In these lay a great multitude of sicke persons, of blinde, lame, vvithered, expecting the stirring of the vvater. 4 † And an Angel of our Lord descended at a certaine time into the pond: and the vvater vvas stirred. And he that had gone dovvne first into the pond after the stirring of the vvater, vvas made vvhole of vvhatsoeuer infirmitie he vvas holden. 5 † And there vvas a certaine man there that had been eight and thirtie yeres in his infirmitie. 6 † Him vvhen IESVS had seen lying, & knevv that[c] he had novv a long time, he saith to him, Vvilt thou be made vvhole? 7 † The sicke man ansvvered him, Lord, I haue no man, vvhen the vvater is troubled, to put me into the pond. For vvhiles I come, an other goeth dovvne before me. 8 † IESVS saith to him, Arise, take vp thy bed, and vvalke. 9 † And forthvvith he vvas made vvhole: and he tooke vp his bed, and vvalked. And it vvas the Sabboth that day. 10 † The Ievves therfore said to him that vvas healed, It is the Sabboth, thou maist not take vp thy bed. 11 † He ansvvered them, He that made me vvhole, he said to me, Take vp thy bed, and vvalke. 12 † They asked him therfore, Vvhat is that man that said to thee, Take vp thy bed, and vvalke? 13 † But he that vvas made vvhole, knevv not vvho it vvas. For IESVS shronke aside from the multitude standing in the place. 14 † Aftervvard IESVS findeth him in the temple, and said to him, Behold thou art made vvhole: " sinne nomore, lest some vvorse thing chaunce to thee. 15 † That man vvent his vvay, and told the Ievves that it vvas IESVS that made him vvhole. 16 ⊣ † Therevpon the Ievves persecuted IESVS, because he did these things on the Sabboth.

17 † But IESVS ansvvered them, My father vvorketh vntil novv: and I doe vvorke. 18 † Therevpõ therefore the Ievves sought the more to kil him: because he did not only breake the Sabboth, but also he said God was his father, making him self æqual to God. 19 † IESVS therfore ansvvered, and said to them, Amen, amen I say to you, The Sonne can not doe any thing of him self, but that vvhich he seeth the Father doing.

' *Bethesda,*

[c] *multũ tempus haberet,*

The Gospel vpõ friday in the first vveeke of Lent.

∷ By our latin text and the Greeke, this miraculous pond vvas in or vpon *Probatica*, that is, a place vvhere the sheepe to be sacrificed, vvere kept. But by other latin copies, S. Hierom, and some Greeke fathers, *Probatica* is the very põd it self: so called, because the sheepe of sacrifice vvere there vvashed.

For vvhat things ſoeuer he doeth, theſe the Sonne alſo doeth in like maner. † For the Father loueth the Sonne, and ſhevveth him al things that him ſelf doeth, and greater vvorkes then theſe vvil he ſhevv him, that you may marueil. † For as the Father doth raiſe the dead and quickeneth: ſo the Sonne alſo quickeneth vvhom he vvil. † For neither doth the Father iudge any man: but al iudgement he hath giuen to the Sonne, † that al may honour the Sonne, as they doe honour the Father. He that honoureth not the Sonne, doth not honour the Father, vvho ſent him. † Amen, amen I ſay to you, that he vvhich heareth my vvord, and beleeueth him that ſent me, hath life euerlaſting. and he commeth not into iudgement, but ˋſhal paſſe' from death into life.

is paſſed

The Goſpel vpõ Alſoules day.

† Amen, amen I ſay to you, that the houre commeth, and novv it is, vvhen the dead ſhal heare the voice of the Sonne of God, and they that haue heard, ſhal liue. † For as the Father hath life in him ſelf: ſo he hath giuen to the Sonne alſo to haue life in him ſelf: † and he hath giuẽ him povver to doe iudgement alſo, becauſe he is the Sonne of man. † Marueil not at this, becauſe the houre commeth vvherein al that are in the graues, ſhal heare his voice, † and they that haue ∴ done good things, ſhal come forth into the reſurrection of life: but they that haue done euil, into the reſurrection of iudgement. ⊣ † I can not of my ſelf doe any thing. As I heare, ſo I iudge: and my iudgement is iuſt. becauſe I ſeeke not my vvil, but the vvil of him that ſent me. † If I giue teſtimonie of my ſelf, my teſtimonie is not true. † There is an other that giueth teſtimonie of me: and I knovv that the teſtimonie is true vvhich he giueth of me.

∴ Not faith only, but good and il deedes ſhal be counted, and accordingly revvarded at the day of iudgement.

† * You ſent to Iohn: and he gaue teſtimonie to the truth. † But ʺI receiue not teſtimonie of man: but I ſay theſe things that you may be ſaued. † He vvas the lampe burning and ſhining. And you vvould for a time reioyce in his light. † But I haue a greater teſtimonie then Iohn. For the vvorkes vvhich the Father hath giuen me to perfit them: the very vvorkes them ſelues vvhich I doe, giue teſtimonie of me, that the Father hath ſent me. † And the Father that ſent me, him ſelf hath * giuen teſtimonie of me. neither haue you heard his voice at any time, nor ſeen his ſhape, † and his vvord you haue not remaining in you: becauſe vvhom he hath ſent, him you beleeue not. † ʺSearch the ∴ ſcriptures, for you thinke

Io. 1,19.

Mt. 3,17.

∴ Catholikes ſearche the ſcriptures, and finde there, Peters & his ſucceſſors Primacie, the real preſence, the Prieſts povver to forgiue ſinnes, iuſtification by faith & good vvorkes, Virginitie preferred before matrimonie, breach of the vovv of cõtinencie damnable, voluntarie pouertie, Penãce, almes, and good deedes meritorious, diuers revvardes ĩ heauẽ accordĩg to diuers merites, & ſuch like.

thinke in them to haue life euerlasting: and the same are they
40 that giue testimonie of me: † and you vvil not come to me
41 that you may haue life. † Glorie of men I receiue not. † But
42 I haue knovven you, that the loue of God you haue not in
43 you. † I am come in the name of my Father, and you receiue me not: if :: an other shal come in his ovvne name, him you
44 vvil receiue. † Hovv can you beleeue, that receiue glorie one of an other: and the glorie vvhich is of God only, you seeke
45 not? † Thinke not that I vvil accuse you to the Father. there
46 is that accuseth you, Moyses, in vvhom you trust. † For if you did beleeue Moyses: you vvould perhaps beleeue me
47 also. for of me he hath vvritten. † And if you doe not beleeue his vvritings: hovv vvil you beleeue my vvordes?

:: He meaneth specially Antichrist. How thē can the Pope be he, seing the Iewes receiue him not?

ANNOTATIONS
CHAP. V.

2. A pond.) This is as great a wonder and worke as was in the old Law, yet neuer recorded in the Scripture before: the conditions and circumstances of the same much to be distinctly weighed against the Miscreants of this time for many causes. First, that God without derogation to his honour, yea to the great cōmendation of it, doth giue vertue of miracles and cure to water or other creatures. Secondly, that he giueth such vertues to these creatures specially which be by vse and occupying in sacred functions or otherwise, as it were sanctified: for this pond was it wherein the carcasses of sheepe (therfore called Probatica) & other beasts to be sacrificed, were first washed, to which being alwaies red (as S. Hierom saith) with the bloud of hostes, this force was giuen, for the commendation of the sacrifices of the Law there offered. How much more may we acknowledge such workes of God miraculously done in or about the Sacrifice or Sacraments of the new Testament, which faithlesse men wholy reiect and condemne for fables, because they know not the Scriptures nor the power of God. Thirdly, that this operation was giuen at one time more then an other, & rather on great festiual daies then other vulgar times (for this vvas the feast of Pasche or of Pentecost) as daies more sanctified, and vvhen the people made greater concourse: which shevveth that vve should not vvonder to see great miracles done at the Memories and feastes of Martyrs or other great Festiuities, more then at other places and times. Fourthly, that the Angels or some special Saincts are Presidents or Patrones of such places of miracle, and workers also vnder God of the effects that there extraordinarily be done. Which ought to make Christians lesse doubt, that the force of diuers waters in the world is still attributed by our forefathers and good stories to the prayers and presence of Saincts, which profane incredulous men referre onely to nature, vntruely pretending that God is more glorified by the workes of nature, which be of his ordinarie prouidence, then by the graces of Miracle giuen to his Saincts or Angels by his extraordinarie prouidence. Fifthly, that miracles be not wrought on men by their faith onely and as wel by their presence in spirit as in body, or vpon the parties desire or deuotion onely, according to the Heretikes pretext that God is a like present by his power and grace to euery man and place: and therfore that men neede not to go from their owne houses or countries to seeke holines or health at the places of Christs or his saincts birth, death, memories: for none could haue benefite of this water but he that could touch it, and be in it corporally, and at that iust time when the water was in motion by the Angel. Yea sixtly, we may consider that in such cases to make the matter more maruelous, rare, and more earnestly to be sought for, and to signifie to vs that God hath al such extraordinary operations in his owne wil and commaundement, without al rules of our reasons and questioning thereon, none could be healed but that person who first could get into the pond after the Angel came and stirred the same. Seuenthly, that these graces of corporal cures giuen to this water, * prefigure the like force of the Sacrament of Baptisme for the cure of soules, though we neede not seeke the correspondence thereof to the figure in euery point.

Lastly, Christ by his power of excellencie and prerogatiue could and did heale this poore man that

Hiero. de locis Hebr. post med.

Hiero. con. Lucifer. c. 3 to. 2.

1 Vertue of miracles giuen to creatures.

2 The same giuē specially to sanctified creatures.

3 Miracles done at on time more thē at an other, specially ī greater solemnities.

4 Angels and Sainctes patrones & workers in places of miracles.

5 Miracles in certaine places, & wrought vpō thē that corporally visite the same. See S. Augustine ep. 137.

6 Al reasonig in these matters must yeld to Gods pleasure.

7 This water is a figure of Baptisme.

8 Christ extraordinarily healeth and saueth vvithout creatures.

that could get no body to help him into the Water, because he earnestly and long desired the remedie by God appointed, but Was excluded by necessitie: as our Lord saueth al such as die Without Baptisme, if they in their owne persons earnestly intended, desired, and sought for the same.

Sinne the cause of sicknes and infirmities.

14. Sinne no more.) We may gather hereby that this mans long infirmitie Was for punishment of his sinnes, and that men often attribute their sicknes to other natural defects, and seeke for remedies of the World in vaine, When the sinne for Which it Was sent, remaineth, or is not repented of: and therfore that in al infirmities men should first turne to God & goe to their Ghostly father, and then call for the Wordly Phisicions afterWard.

34. I receiue not.) Our Maister meaneth that mans testimonie is not necessarie to him, nor that the truth of his Diuinitie dependeth on Worldly Witnesses or mens commendations: though to vs such testimonies be agreable and necessarie. and so for our instruction he vouchsaued to take the testimonies of Iohn the Baptist and Moyses and the Prophets: and departing out of this World, to send forth al his Apostles, and in them al Bishops and LaWful Pastors, to be his Witnesses from Hierusalem to the ends of the World.

Neither Ievves nor Heretikes finde the truth, because they searche not the Scriptures deepely, but read superficially.

39. Searche the Scriptures.) He reprehendeth the IeWes, that reading daily the Scriptures and acknoWledging that in them they should finde life and saluation, they yet looked ouer them so superficially that they could not finde therein him to be CHRIST their King, Lord, life, and Sauiour. For the special maisters & Scribes of the Ievves then, Were like vnto our Heretikes novv, vvho be euer talking and turning and shuffling the Scriptures, but are of al men most ignorant in the deepe knovvledge thereof. And therfore our Maister referreth them not to the reading onely or learning them Without booke, or hauing the sentences thereof gloriously painted or vvritten in thier Temple, houses, or coates: but to the deepe searche of the meaning and mysteries of the Scriptures, vvhich are not so easily to be seen in the letter.

CHAP. VI.

The 3 part. HIS ACTES in Galilee, & in Iewrie, about the third Pasche and after.

Hauing vvith fiue loaues fed fiue thousand 16 (vvalking also the night after vpon the sea) 22 on the morovv the people there vpon resorting vnto him, 27 he preacheth vnto them of the Bread vvhich he vvil giue: telling them that he is come from heauen, and therfore able to giue such bread as cā quicken the World, euen his ovvne flesh: and that al his Elect shal beleeue as much. 60 Many notvvithstanding do murmur at this doctrine, yea and become apostataes, thoug he tel them that they shal see by his Ascension into heauen, that he is descended from heauen. but the Tvvelue sticke vnto him, beleeuing that he is God omnipotent, as he said. Among vvhom also (that no man be scandalized) he signifieth that he foreknovveth vvhich vvil become a traitor: as among the foresaid, vvhich vvould become apostataes.

The Gospel vpō Midlent Sūday.

AFTER these things IESVS vvent beyond 1 the sea of Galilee, vvhich is of Tiberias: † and a great multitude folovved him, be- 2 cause they savv the signes vvhich he did vpon those that vvere sicke. † IESVS ther- 3 fore went vp into the mountaine, and there he sate vvith his Disciples. † And the Pasche vvas at hand, 4 the festiual day of the Ievves. † Vvhen IESVS therfore had 5 lifted vp his eies, and savv that a very great multitude commeth to him, he saith to Philippe, Vvhence shal vve bie bread: that these may eate? † And this he said, tempting him. 6 for him self knevv vvhat he vvould doe? † Philippe ansvve- 7 red him, Tvvo hundred penie vvorth of bread is not sufficient for them, that euery man may take a litle peece. † One 8 of his Disciples, Andrevv the brother of Simon Peter, saith to

Mt. 14, 13. Mar. 6, 32. Lu. 9, 10

9 to him, † There is a boy here that hath fiue barley loaues, &
10 tvvo fishes: but vvhat are these among so many? † IESVS therfore saith, Make the men to sit dovvne. And there vvas much grasse in the place. The men therfore sate dovvne, in
11 number about fiue thousand. † IESVS therfore tooke the loaues: and vvhen he had giuen thankes, he distributed to them that sate. in like maner also of the fishes as much as they
12 vvould. † And after they vvere filled, he said to his Disciples, Gather the fragments that are remaining, lest they be
13 lost. † They gathered therfore, and filled tvvelue baskets vvith fragments of the fiue barley loaues, vvhich remained to
14 them that had eaten. † Those men therfore vvhen they had seen vvhat a signe IESVS had done, said, That this is the
15 Prophet in deede that is to come into the vvorld. † IESVS therfore vvhen he knevv that they vvould come to take him, and make him king, * he fled againe into the mountaine him self alone. ⊣

Mt. 14, 23. Mr. 6,46.

16 † And vvhen euen vvas come, his Disciples vvent dovvne
17 to the sea. † And vvhen they vvere gone vp into the shippe, they came beyond the sea into Capharnáum. and novv it vvas
18 darke, and IESVS vvas not come vnto them † And the sea
19 arose, by reason of a great vvinde that blevv. † Vvhen they had rovved therfore about fiue and tvventie or thirtie furlonges, they see IESVS vvalking vpon the sea, and to
20 dravv nigh to the shippe, and they feared. † But he saith to
21 them, It is I, feare not. † They vvould therfore haue taken him into the shippe: and forthvvith the shippe vvas at the land to vvhich they vvent.

22 † The next day, the multitude that stoode beyond the sea, savv that there vvas no other boate there but one, and that IESVS had not entred into the boate vvith his Disciples,
23 but that his Disciples only vvere departed: † but other boates came in frō Tiberias beside the place vvhere they had eatē
24 the bread, our Lord ∷ giuing thankes. † Vvhen therfore the multitude savv that IESVS vvas not there, nor his Disciples, they vvent vp into the boates, & came to Capharnaū seeking
25 IESVS. † And vvhē they had found him beyond the sea, they
26 said to him, Rabbi, vvhē camest thou hither? † IESVS ansvvered them, and said, Amen, amen I say to you, you seeke me not because you haue seene signes, but because you did eate
27 of the loaues, and vvere filled. † ″ Vvorke not the meate that

∷ These Wordes do plainly import, that the giuing thankes was an effectual blessing of the bread and working the multiplication thereof.

Gg perisheth

perisheth, but that endureth vnto life euerlasting, vvhich the Sonne of man vvil giue you. For him the Father, God, hath signed. † They said therfore vnto him, Vvhat shal vve doe that vve may vvorke the vvorkes of God? † IESVS ansvvered, and said to them, This is the vvorke of God, that you beleeue in him vvhom he hath sent. † They said therfore to him, Vvhat signe therfore doest thou, that vve may see, and may beleeue thee? vvhat vvorkest thou? 28 29 30

† Our * fathers did eate Manna in the desert, as it is vvritten, *Bread from heauen he gaue them to eate.* † IESVS therfore said to them, ∴ Amen, amen I say to you, Moyses gaue you not the bread from heauen, but my Father giueth you " the true bread from heauen. † For the bread of God it is that descendeth from heauen, and giueth life to the vvorld. † They said therfore vnto him, Lord, giue vs alvvaies this bread. † And IESVS said to them, I am the bread of life, he that commeth to me, shal not hunger: and he that beleeueth in me, shal neuer thirst. † But I said to you that both you haue seen me and you beleeue not. † Al that the Father giueth me, shal come to me: and him that commeth to me I vvil not cast forth. † Because I descended from heauen, not to doe mine ovvne vvil, but the vvil of him that sent me. † For this is the vvil of him that sent me, the Father: that al that he hath giuē me I leese not thereof, but raise it in the last day. † And this is the vvil of my father that sent me: that euery one that seeth the Sonne, and beleeueth in him, haue life euerlasting, and I vvil raise him in the last day. ✠ 31 32 33 34 35 36 37 38 39 40

Exo. 16, 4. 14. Ps. 77, 24.

∴ Why we keepe the hebrue word, *Amen*, & translate it not, See the Annot. *c. 8. vers. 34.*

The Gospel in the Añiuersarie of the dead.

† The Ievves therfore murmured at him, because he had said, I am the bread vvhich descended from heauen: † and they said, Is not this IESVS the sonne of Ioseph, vvhose father and mother vve knovv? Hovv then saith he, That I descended from heauen? † IESVS therfore ansvvered and said to them, Murmure not one to an other: † no man can come to me, vnles the Father that sent me, " dravv him: and I vvil raise him vp in the last day. † It is vvritten in the Prophets, *And al shal be docible of God.* Euery one that hath heard of the Father, and hath learned, commeth to me. † Not that any man hath seen the Father, but he vvhich is of God: this hath seen the Father. † Amen, amen I say to you, he that beleeueth in me, hath life euerlasting. † I am the bread of life. † Your fathers did eate " Manna in the desert: and they died. 41 42 43 44 45 46 47 48 49

The Gospel vpō Imber vvenesday in vvhitsonvveeke.

Esa. 54, 13.

† This

50 † This is the bread that descendeth from heauen: that if any
51 man eate of it, he die not. † I am the liuing bread, that came dovvne from heauen. If any man eate of this bread, he shal liue for euer: and * the bread vvhich I vvil giue, is my flesh for the life of the vvorld. ⊣

The Gospel in a daily Masse for the dead.

Mt. 26, 26. Mr. 14, 22. Lu. 22, 19. 1. Cor. 11, 24.

52 † The Ievves therfore stroue among them selues, saying,
53 "Hovv can this man giue vs his flesh to eate? † IESVS therfore said to them, Amen, amen I say to you, "Vnles you eate the flesh of the Sonne of man, "and drinke his bloud, "you
54 shal not haue life in you. † He that eateth my flesh, and drinketh my bloud, hath life euerlasting: and "I vvil raise him
55 vp in the last day. ⊣ † For my flesh, is "meate in deede: and
56 my bloud is drinke in deede. † He that eateth my flesh, and
57 drinketh my bloud, abideth in me, and I in him. † As the liuing father hath sent me, and I liue by the father: and he that
58 eateth me, the same also shal liue by me. † This is the bread that came dovvne from heauen. Not as your fathers did eate Manna, and died. " He that eateth this bread, shal liue for e-
59 uer. ⊣ † These things he said teaching in the Synagogue, in Capharnáum.

The Gospel vpõ CORPVS CHRISTI day.

60 † Many therfore of his Disciples hearing it, said, This
61 saying is hard, and vvho can heare it? † But IESVS knovving vvith him self that his Disciples murmured at this, he said to
62 them, Doth this scandalize you? † "If then you shal see * the
63 Sonne of man ascend vvhere he vvas before? † It is the spirit that quickeneth, "the flesh profiteth nothing. The vvor-
64 des that I haue spoken to you, be spirit and life. † But there be certaine of you "that beleeue not. For IESVS knevv from the beginning vvho they vvere that did not beleeue, and
65 vvho he vvas that vvould betray him. † And he said, Therfore did I say to you, that no man can come to me, vnles it
66 be giuen him of my Father. † After this many of his Disciples "vvent backe: and novv they vvalked not vvith him.

Io. 3, 13.

67 † IESVS therfore said to the Tvvelue, Vvhat, vvil you
68 also depart? † Simon "Peter therfore ansvvered him, Lord, to vvhom shal vve goe? thou hast the vvordes of eternal life.
69 † And vve beleeue and haue knovven that thou art Christ
70 the sonne of God. † IESVS ansvvered them, Haue not I cho-
71 sen you the Tvvelue: & of you one is a deuil? † And he meant Iudas Iscariot, Simons sonne: for this same vvas to betray him, vvhereas he vvas one of the Tvvelue.

ANNOTATIONS
CHAP. VI.

27. *Worke not the meate.*] By their greedy seeking after him for meate of the body, he taketh occasion to dravv them to the desire of a more excellent foode which he had to giue them, and so by litle to open vnto them the great meate and mysterie of the B. Sacrament: which (as he proueth) doth not onely far passe their ordinarie bread or his marueļous multiplied loaues, but Manna it self, which they thought came from heauen, and so much wondered at it.

Why Christ is called bread: & beleeuing, eating.

32. *The true bread.*] Though the person of Christ incarnate, euen out of the Sacrament also, be meant vnder the Metaphores of bread and drinke from heauen: and our beleefe in him, be signified by eating and feeding: yet the causes why they should be recommended vnto vs in such termes, were, that he was to be eaten and drunken in deed in the formes of bread and wine: for the which cause his body on the crosse is called * his bread: & his bloud shed on the crosse, * the bloud of the grape: no doubt because the same body and bloud were in Holy Sacrament to be eaten and drunken. In vvhich speaches, either of Christs person generally, or peculiarly of the same as in the B. Sacrament, *the true bread* is not taken proprely and specially for that substance which is of corne, and called vvith vs bread: but generally for food or meate, and therfore it hath ioyned vvith it lightly a terme signifying a more excellent sort of sustenance: as, the true bread, the bread of heauen, the bread of life, Supersubstantial bread. in which sort the holy Sacrament which is Christs body, is both here, and in S. Luke and S. Paul also, often called bread, euen after consecration: not onely for that it was made of bread, but because it is bread more truely, and by more excellent property and calling, then that vvhich ordinarily is named bread.

Ierem. 11, 19. Gen. 49, 11.

What signifieth, The true bread.

The B. Sacrament called bread.

Lu. 24, 35. Act. 2, 42. 20, 7. 1 Cor. 10.

God draweth vs vvith our free wil.

44. *Dravv him*] The Father dravveth vs and teacheth vs to come to his Sonne, and to beleeue these high and hard mysteries of his incarnation and of feeding vs vvith his ovvne substance in the Sacrament: not cōpelling or violenty forcing any against their will or without any respect of their consent, as Heretikes pretend: but by the svveete internal motions and persuasions of his grace and spirit he wholy maketh vs of our owne vvill and liking to consent to the same.

Aug. cont. duas Ep. Pelag. li. 1 c. 19. & Ser. 2 de verb. Ap. c. 2.

The manifold preeminēces of the B. Sacramēt aboue Manna.

49. *Manna, and died.*] The Heretikes holding the fathers of the old Testament to haue eaten of the same meate, and to haue had as good Sacraments as vve, be here refuted: Christ putting a plaine difference in the very substaunce thereof, and in the graces and effects much more at large. Manna vvas onely a figure of the B. Sacrament, though a very excellent figure thereof for many causes. It came in a sort from heauen, our Sacrament more: it vvas made by God miraculously, our Sacrament more: it vvas to be eaten for the time of their peregrination, our Sacrament more: it vvas to euery man vvhat he liked best, our Sacrament more: a litle thereof serued and sufficed as vvel as much, our Sacrament more: it vvas reserued for such daies as it could not be gathered, and our Sacramēt much more: it vvas kept for a memorial in the arke of the Testament, our Sacrament much more: the discontented and incredulous murmured and gainsaid it, at our Sacrament much more: it sustained their bodies in the desert, our Sacrament both body and soule much more.

In the B. Sacrament, *Hovv*, is a Iewish word.

52. *Hovv can this man?*] *It came not to their minde that nothing vvas impossible to God, that vvickedly said, Hovv can this man giue vs his flesh? but vve may make great profite of their sinne, beleeuing the Mysteries, and taking a lesson, neuer to say or once thinke, Hovv? for it is a Ievvish vvord and vvorthy al punishment.* so saith *S. Cyril. li. 4 c. 13 in Io.* Neuertheles if one asked onely for desire to learne in humility, as our Lady did touching her hauing a childe in her virginitie, then he must take the Angels answer to her, That it is of the Holy Ghost. so saith S. Damascene *li. 4. c. 14.*

The real presence.

53. *vnles you eate.*) *Christ cōmending the Sacrament of the faithful vnto vs, said, Except you eate &c. you can not haue life in you. So the life saith of life, and to him that thinketh the life to be a lier, this meate shal be death & not life to him.* August. *Ser. 2 de verb. Ap. c. 1.* And S. Leo thus, *Because our Lord saith, Except you eate &c. let vs so communicate that vve nothing doubt of the truth of Christes body and bloud: for that is receiued vvith mouth, vvhich is beleeued in hart: and they ansvver Amen in vaine, that dispute against that vvhich they receiue.*

Ser. 6 de ieiun. 7. mens.

Receiuing in both kindes not necessarie.

53. *And drinke.*) This the Protestants alleage for the necessitie of receiuing in both kindes: but in respect of them selues (who lightly hold al this chapter to pertaine nothing to the Sacramental receiuing, but to spiritual feeding on Christ by faith onely) it can make nothing for one kinde or other. And in respect of vs Catholikes, who beleeue Christs whole person both humanitie and Diuinitie, both flesh and bloud to be in either forme, and to be vvholy receiued no lesse in the first, then in the second or in both, this place commaundeth nothing for both the kindes.

The Sacramental receiuing of Christs body, not alwaies necessarie to saluation.

53. *You shal not haue life.*) Though the Catholikes teach these wordes to be spoken of the Sacrament, yet they meane not (no more then our Sauiour here doth) to exclude al from saluation, that receiue not actually and Sacramentally vnder one or both kindes. For then children that die after they be baptized and neuer receiued Sacramentally, should perish: which to hold, were heretical. Neither did S. Augustine meane, applying these wordes to infants also, that they could not be saued without receiuing sacramentally, as not onely the Heretikes, but Erasmus did vnlearnedly

Li. 1 de pec. merit. c. 20

nedly mistake him: but his sense is that they were by the right of their Baptisme ioyned to Christs body Mystical, and thereby spiritually partakers of the other Sacrament also of Christs body and bloud. As al Catholike men that be in prison, ioyning with the Church of God in hart and desire to receiue and be partakers with the Church of this Sacrament, and those specially that deuoutly heare Masse and adore in presence the body and bloud of Christ, ioyning in hart with the Priest, al these receiue life and fruite of the Sacrament, though at euery time they receiue not sacramentally in one or both kindes. And although in the Primitiue Church the holy Sacrament in the second kind were often giuen euen to infants to sanctifie them, yet (as the holy Councel hath declared) it was neuer ministred vnto them with opinion that they could not be saued without it. and therfore the Heretikes do vntruely charge the Church and the Fathers with that errour.

The true meaning of S. Augustins vvordes touching infants receiuing of the B. Sacrament.

Côc. Trid. Sess. 21 c. 4.

54. I vvil raise him.) *As the Sonne liueth by the Father, euen so do vve liue by his flesh*, saith S. Hilarie. *li. 8. de Trin.* And S. Cyril againe thus, *Though by nature of our flesh vve be corruptible, yet by participation of life vve are reformed to the propertie of life. For not onely our soules vvere to be lifted vp by the holy Ghost to life euerlasting, but this rude grosse terrestrial body of ours is to be reduced to immortalitie, by touching, tasting, and eating this agreable food of Christes body. And vvhen Christ saith, I vvil raise him vp, he meaneth that this body vvhich he eateth, shal raise him. Our flesh* (saith Tertullian) *eateth the body and bloud of Christ, that the soule may also be fatted. therfore they shal both haue one revvard at the Resurrection.* And S. Irenæus, *Hovv do they affirme that our bodies be not capable of life euerlasting, vvhich is nourished by the body and bloud of our Lord? Either let them change their opinion, or els cease to offer the Eucharist.* S. Gregorie Nyssene also saith, *That liuely body entering into our body, changeth it and maketh it like and immortal.*

Cyril. li. 4 c. 14, 15.

Tertul. de resur. car. nu. 7.

Li 4, c. 34.

Nyss. in orat. catech. magna.

The effects of the B. Sacramēt both in our body and soule.

55. Meate in deede.) Manna, was not the true meate: nor the water of the rocke, the drinke in deede: for they did but driue avvay death or famine for a time and for this life. *But the holy Body of Christ is the true food nourishing to life euerlasting, and his bloud the true drinke that driueth death avvay vtterly, for they be not the body and bloud of a mere man, but of him that being ioyned to life is made life: and therfore are vve the body and members of Christ, because by this benediction of the mysterie vve receiue the sonne of God him self.* So saith S. Cyril li. 4 c. 16 in Io.

The B. Sacrament is the true Manna & vvater of the rocke.

58. He that eateth this bread.) By this place the holy Councel proueth that for the grace and effect of the Sacrament, which is the life of the soule, there is no difference whether a man receiue both kindes or one. because our Sauiour vvho before attributed life to the eating and drinking of his body and bloud, doth here also affirme the same effect, vvhich is life euerlasting, to come of eating onely vnder one forme. Therfore the Heretikes be seditious calumniators that would make the people beleeue, the Catholike Church and Priests to haue defrauded them of the grace and benefite of one of the kindes in the Sacrament. Nay, it is they that haue defrauded the world, by taking away both the real substance of Christ, and the grace from one kinde and both kindes, and from al other Sacraments. The Church doth onely (by the wisedom of Gods Spirit and by instruction of Christ and his Apostles, according to time and place, for Gods most honour, the reuerence of the Sacrament, and the peoples most profite thereby) dispose of the maner and order, how the Priest, how the people shal receiue, and al other particular pointes, *Which him self* (saith S. Augustine) *did not take order for, that he might cōmit that to the Apostles, by vvhom he vvas to dispose his Churches affaires.* though both he and the Apostles and the Fathers of the primitiue Church left vs example of receiuing vnder one kind. Christ *at Emmaus*, The Apostles *Act. 2, 42.* The primitiue Church in giuing the bloud onely to children, *Cypr. li. de lapsis, nu. 10.* in reseruing most commonly the body onely, *Tertul. li. 2 ad vxo. nu. 4. Cypr. li. de lapsis, nu. 10.* in houseling the sicke therewith, *Euseb. Ec. hist. li. 6 c. 36.* in the holy Eremites also that receiued and reserued it commonly and not the bloud, in the wildernes, *Basil. ep. ad Cæsariam Patritiam.* and in diuers other cases which were to long to rehearse.

Côc. Trid. Sess. 21 c. 1.

Ep. 118 c. 6 ad Ianuarium.

Lu. 24, 35.

The vvhole grace and effect thereof in one kinde, and therfore the people not defrauded.

Receiuīg in one or both kindes, idifferēt, according to the holy Churches appointment.

Authoritie of Scriptures and the Primitiue Church for receiuing in one kinde.

Whereby the Church being warranted and in the ruling of such things fully taught by Gods spirit, as wel for the reprouing of certaine heresies, that Christ God and man vvas not vvhole and al in euery part of the Sacrament, as specially for that the Christian people being novv enlarged, and the communicants often so many at once, that neither so much vvine could be conueniently consecrated, nor vvithout manifold accidents of sheading or abusing be receiued (vvhereof the Protestants haue no regard, because it is but common vvine vvhich they occupie, but the Church knovving it to be Christs ovvne bloud, must haue al dreadful regard) therfore I say she hath decreed and for some hundreth yeres put in vse, that the Priest saying Masse, should alvvaies both consecrate and also receiue both kindes, because he must expresse liuely the Passion of Christ, and the separation of his bloud from his body in the same, and for to imitate the vvhole action and institution as vvel in sacrificing as receiuing, as to vvhom properly it vvas said, *Do this*, for that vvas spoken onely to such as haue povver thereby to offer and consecrate. But the Lay men, and the Clergie also vvhen they do not execute or say Masse them selues, should receiue in one kinde, being thereby no lesse partakers of Christs vvhole person and grace, then if they receiued both. For (as S. Paul saith) *He that eateth the hostes, is partaker of the altar.* He that eateth, saith he: for though there vvere drink-offerings or libaments ioyned lightly to euery sacrifice, yet it vvas ynough to eate onely of one kinde, for to be partaker of the vvhole.

The causes of the Churches practise & ordināce cōcerning one kinde.

The Priests that say Masse, must receiue both kindes.

Lu. 22, 19. 1 Cor. 11.

1 Cor. 10, 18.

62. If

Christ insinuateth that faithles mé shal not beleeue his presence in the B. Sacrament, because he is ascéded.

62. If you shal see.) Our Sauiour seemeth to insinuate, that such as beleeue not his Wordes touching the holy Sacrament, and thinke it impossible for him to giue his Body to be eaten in so many places at once, being yet in earth, should be much more scandalized and tempted after they saw or knew him to be ascended into heauen. Vvhich is proued true in the Capharnaites of this time, whose principal reason against Christs presence in the Sacrament is, that he is ascended into heauen: yea, who are so bold as to expound this same sentence for them selues thus, It is not this body or flesh which I wil giue you, for that I wil carie with me to heauen. Whereby if they meant onely that the condition and qualities of his body in heauen should be other then in the Sacrament, it were tolerable: for S. Augustine speaketh sometime in that sense. but to deny the substance of the body to be the same, that is wicked.

The Capharnaites grosse vnderstanding of Christs flesh to be giuen or eaten. And, hovv his flesh doth profit, and not profit.

63. The flesh profiteth nothing.) If this speach were spoken in the sense of the Sacramentaries, it would take away Christs Incarnation, manhod, and death, no lesse then his corporal presence in the Sacrament. for if his flesh were not profitable, al these things were vaine. Therfore CHRIST denieth not his owne flesh to be profitable, but that their grosse and carnal conceiuing of his wordes, of his flesh, and of the maner of eating the same, was vnprofitable. Which is plaine by the sentence folowing, where he warneth them, that his wordes be spirit and life, of high Mystical meaning, and not vulgarly and grosly to be taken, as they tooke them. And it is the vse of the Scripture to call mans natural sense, reason, and carnal resisting or not reaching supernatural truthes, flesh or bloud. as, *Flesh and bloud reuealed not this to thee &c. Mat. 16.*

This carnalitie then of theirs, stood in two points specially: first, that they imagined that he would kill him self, and cut & mãgel his flesh into partes, & so giue it them raw or rost to be eaten among them. Which could not be meant, saith S. Augustine: for that had conteined an heinous and barbarous facte, and therfore they might and should haue bene assured, that he would commaund no such thing: but some other sweete sense to be of his hard, mystical, or figuratiue wordes, and to be fulfilled in a Sacrament, mysterie, and a maruelous diuine sort, otherwise then they could comprehend. Secondly, they did erre touching his flesh, in that they tooke it to be the flesh of a mere man, and of a dead man also, when it should come to be eaten: of which kind of flesh Christ here pronoũceth, that it profiteth nothing. Wherevpon S. Cyril saith, *This body is not of Peter or Paul or any other like, but of Christ* IESVS *Who is the life it self: and therfore this Body giueth life, the very fulnes of the Diuinitie dvvelling in it.* And the holy Councel of Ephesus in the 11 Anathematisme expounded also by the said S. Cyril: *The Eucharist is not the body of any common person (for the flesh of a common man could not quicken) but of the* VVORD *it self. But the Heretike Nestorius dissolueth the vertue of this Mysterie, holding mans flesh onely to be in the Eucharist.* Thus there. And S. Ignatius cited of Theodorete, and many other Fathers haue the like. Whereby we may see that it commeth of the Diuinitie and Spirit (without which Christs flesh can not be) that this Sacrament giueth life.

August. de Doct. Chr. li. 3 c. 13.

Christs flesh giueth life because it is the flesh of God & man.

Li. 4 c. 11 in Io.

Ignatius apud Theodor. dial. 3.

Iudas the cheefe of them that beleeue not the real presence.

64. That beleeue not.) It is lacke of faith, you seee here, that causeth men to spurne against this high truth of the Sacrament: as also it may be learned here, that it is the great and merciful gift of God that Catholike men do against their senses and carnal reasons, beleeue and submit them selues to the humble acknowledging of this Mysterie: lastly, that it may wel * by Christs insinuation of Iudas, be gathered, that he specially spurned against our Maisters speaches of the holy Sacrament.

** vers. 64.*

Heretikes beleeue not the real presence, because they see bread and wine: as the Iewes beleeued not his Godhead because of the shape of a poore man.

66. Went backe.) It can be no maruel to vs now that so many reuolt from the Church, by offense or scandal vniustly taken at Christs body and bloud in the Sacrament: seeing many of his Disciples that savv his vvonderful life, doctrine, and miracles, forsooke Christ him self, vpon the speach & promes of the same Sacramẽt. for the mysterie of it is so supernatural and diuine in it self, and withal so low & base for our sakes, by the shew of the formes of these terrene elements vnder which it is, and we eate it: that the vnfaithful and infirme do so stumble at Christ in the Sacrament, as the Iewes and Gentils did at Christ in his humanitie. For, the causes of contradictions of the Incarnation and Transsubstantion be like. And it may be verily deemed, that whosoeuer now can not beleeue the Sacrament to be Christ, because it is vnder the formes of bread and wine, and is eaten and drunken, would not then haue beleued that Christ had bene God, because he was in shape of man, and crucified. To conclude, it was not a figure nor a mysterie of bare bread and wine, nor any Metaphorical or Allegorical speach, that could make such a troupe of his Disciples reuolt at once. When he said he was a doore, a vine, a way, a Pastor, and such like (vnto which kinde of speaches the Protestants ridiculously resemble the wordes of the holy Sacrament) who was so mad to mistake him, or to forsake him for the same? For the Apostles at the least would haue plucked them by the sleeues, and said, Goe not away my maisters, he speaketh parables. The cause therfore was their incredulitie, and the height of the Mysterie, for that they neither knew the meanes how it might be present, nor would beleeue that he was able to giue his flesh to be eaten in many places. And euen such is the vnbeleefe of the Heretikes about this matter at this day.

The disciples reuoltĩg at Christs wordes, proue that he spake not metaphorically, as at other times.

As Iudas of al vnbeleeuing heretikes, so Peter beareth the per-

68. Peter ansvvered.) Peter answereth for the Twelue, not knowing that Iudas in hart was already naught, and beleeued not Christs former wordes touching the B. Sacrament, but was to reuolt afterward as wel as the other. * Wherein Peter beareth the person of the Church and al Catholike men, that for no difficulty of his word, nor for any reuolt (be it neuer so general) of

** Cypr. ep. 55. nu. 3.*

Schisma-

Schismatikes, Heretikes, or Apostataes, either for this Sacrament or any other Article, wil euer forsake Christ. And when company draweth vs to reuolt, let vs say thus: Lord, whither or to whom shal we goe, when we haue forsaken thee? to Caluin, Luther, or such: and forsake thee and thy Church with the vnfaithful multitude? No, thou hast the wordes of life, and we beleeue thee, and thy Church wil not nor can not beguile vs. *Thou hast* (saith S. Augustine) *life euerlasting in the ministration of thy body and bloud.* and a litle after, *Thou art life euerlasting it self, and thou giuest not in thy flesh and bloud but that vvhich thy self art.*

son of al beleeuing Catholikes: namely in the B. Sacrament.

Tract. 27 in Euang. Io.

CHAP. VII.

The Iewes (of Hierusalem) seeking his death, he walketh in Galilee: where he signifieth to his brethren, that not in this feast Scenopégia, but in an other (to wit, Pasche folovving) the Ievves should kil him: that is, not vvhen they vvould, but vvhen he vvil. 10 In so much that at this feast he teacheth openly in the Temple, and conuerteth many, 14 both in the middle day 37 and the last day thereof, vvithout any hurt, though also the Rulers send to apprehend him.

The Gospel vpō Tuesday in Passion weeke.

1 AFTER these things IESVS vvalked 'into Galilee', for he vvould not vvalke 'into Ievvrie': because the Ievves sought to kil him. 2 † And the festiual day of the Ievves, * :: Scenopégia, 3 vvas at hand. † And his brethrē said to him, Passe from hence, and goe into Ievvrie: that thy Disciples also may 4 see thy vvorkes vvhich thou doest. † For no man doeth any thing in secrete, and seeketh him self to be in publike. If thou 5 doe these things, manifest thy self to the vvorld. † For nei- 6 ther did his brethren beleeue in him. † IESVS therfore saith to them, My time is not yet come: but your time is alvvaies 7 readie. † The vvorld can not hate you. but me it hateth: because I giue testimonie of it, that the vvorkes thereof are euil. 8 † Goe you vp to this festiual day: 'I goe not vp' to this festiual day: because my time is not yet accomplished.

9 † When he had said these things, him self taried in Ga- 10 lilee. † But after his brethren vvere gone vp, then he also vvent vp to the festiual day, not openly, but as it vvere in 11 secrete. † The Ievves therfore sought him in the festiual 12 day, and said, Vvhere is he? † And there vvas much murmuring in the multitude of him. For certaine said, That he is good. And others said, No, but he seduceth the multi- 13 tudes. † Yet no man spake openly of him for feare of the Ievves. ⊣

in Galilee, in Iurie: Leu. 23, 34.

I vvil not yet goe vp.

:: *Scenopégia* (*Leu. 23* σκηνῶν ἑορτὴ) is the *feast of Tabernacles*, which the Iewes kept frō the 7 octob. for eight daies together, by Gods commaundement, for a memorie that their fathers dwelt by Gods protectiō fourtie yeres in tabernacles or tentes, and not in houses, comming out of Aegypt. *See Leuit. 23, 34.*

The Gospel vpō Tuesday in the 4 weeke of Lent.

14 † And vvhen the festiuitie vvas novv halfe done, IESVS 15 vvent vp into the tēple, and taught. † And the Ievves marueiled.

ueiled, saying, Hovv doth this man knovv letters, vvhereas he hath not learned? † IESVS ansvvered them, and said, My 16 doctrine is not mine, but his that sent me. † If any man 17 :: vvil doe the vvil of him, he shal vnderstand of the doctrine vvhether it be of God, or I speake of my self. † :: He that 18 speaketh of him self, seeketh his ovvne glorie. But he that seeketh the glorie of him that sent him, he is true, and iniustice in him there is not. † Did not Moyses giue you the lavv, 19 and none of you doeth the lavv? † * Vvhy seeke you to kil 20 me? The multitude ansvvered, and said, :: Thou hast a deuil, vvho seeketh to kil thee? † IESVS ansvvered, and said to 21 them, One vvorke I haue done: and you doe al marueil. † Therfore * Moyses gaue you circuncision: not that it is 22 of Moyses, but * of the fathers, and in the Sabboth you circuncise a man. † If a man receiue circuncision in the Sabboth, 23 that the lavv of Moyses be not broken: are you angrie at me because I haue healed a man vvholy in the Sabboth? † Iudge 24 not according to the face, but iudge iust iudgement.

:: The vvay to come to knovv the truth, is to liue vvel.

:: It is spoken of Antichrist specially, and it is true in al Heretikes. *August. tract. 29. in Euang. Io.*

:: No maruel, vvhen these speake thus to Christ him self, if Heretikes call his vicar Antichrist.

Io. 5, 18.

Leu. 12, 3.

Gen. 17, 10.

† Certaine therfore of Hierusalem said, Is not this he 25 vvhom they seeke to kil? † And behold, he speaketh openly, 26 and they say nothing to him. Haue the Princes knovven in deede that this is CHRIST? † But this man vve knovv vvhēce 27 he is. But vvhen CHRIST cōmeth, no man knovveth vvhence he is. † IESVS therfore cried in the temple teaching, and 28 saying, Both me you doe knovv, and vvhence I am you knovv. And of my self I am not come, but he is true that sent me, vvhom you knovv not. † I knovv him, because I am of 29 him, and he sent me. † They sought therfore to apprehend 30 him: and no man laide handes vpon him, because his houre vvas not yet come. † But of the multitude many beleeued 31 in him, ⊣ and said, CHRIST vvhen he cōmeth, shal he doe more signes then these vvhich this man doeth? † The Pha- 32 risees heard the multitude murmuring these things touching him: and the ` Princes' and Pharisees sent ministers to apprehend him. † IESVS therfore said to them, Yet a litle time 33 I am vvith you: and I goe to him that sent me. † * You seeke 34 me, and shal not finde: and vvhere I am, you can not come. † The Ievves therfore said among them selues, Vvhither vvil 35 this man goe, that vve shal not finde him? Vvil he goe into the dispersion of the Gētiles, and teach the Gentiles? † Vvhat 36 is this saying that he hath said, You shal seeke me, and shal not

The Gospel vpō Mūday in Passion vveeke.

cheefe Priests

Io. 13, 33.

not finde: And vvhere I am, you can not come.

Leu. 23, 36.

37 † And in the last, the * great day of the festiuitie IESVS stoode, and cried, saying, If any man thirst, let him come to 38 me, and drinke. † He that beleeueth in me, as the scripture 39 saith, *Out of his belly shal flovv riuers of liuing vvater.* † (And this he said * of the Spirit that they should receiue vvhich beleeued in him. ⁜ :: for as yet the Spirit vvas not giuen: because IESVS vvas not yet glorified.)

Ioel. 2, 28. * Act. 2, 1.

:: This was fulfilled on Whitsunday Act. 2, & afterward alwaies by imposition of hands in the Sacrament of Confirmation: visibly in the primitiue Church, and inuisibly to the end of the world.

40 † Of that multitude therfore, vvhen they had heard these 41 wordes of his, some said, This is the Prophet in deede. † others said, This is CHRIST. But certaine said, Vvhy, doth 42 CHRIST come from Galilee? † Doth not the * scripture say, that of the seede of Dauid, and from Bethlehem the tovvne 43 vvhere Dauid vvas, CHRIST doth come? † Therfore there 44 arose dissension in the multitude for him. † And certaine of them vvould haue apprehẽded him: but no man laid handes 45 vpon him. † The ministers therfore came to the cheefe priests and the Pharisees. And they said to them, Vvhy haue 46 you not brought him? † The ministers ansvvered, Neuer 47 did there man so speake, as this man. † The Pharisees ther- 48 fore ansvvered them, Vvhy, are you also seduced? † Hath 49 any of the Princes beleeued in him, or of the Pharisees? † but 50 this multitude that knovveth not the lavv, are accursed. † Nicodemus said to them, :: he * that came to him by night, vvho 51 vvas one of them, † Doth our lavv iudge a man, vnles it first 52 heare him, and knovv vvhat he doeth? † They ansvvered, and said to him, Vvhy, art thou also a Galilęan? Search, and see 53 that from Galilee a Prophet riseth not. † And euery man returned to his house.

Ps. 131, 11. Mich. 5, 2.

Io. 3, 2.

:: Christ hath some good alwaies euen amõg the vvicked, which secretly serue him and by vvise delaies auert the execution of vniust lawes against him and his people, as Nicodem⁹ and Gamaliel.

CHAP. VIII.

Againe in the Temple (absoluing an aduoutresse after his merciful maner, and yet vvithal declaring against his enemies that he is not a fauourer of sinne, no more then Moyses) 12 he teacheth openly, and is not for al that apprehended, telling them both of his Godhead, 21 and of their reprobation, 28 of his exaltation also by their Crucifying of him. 31 exhorting the beleeuers to perseuere: 33 and shevving them that seeke his death, that they are neither free, 39 nor of Abraham, 41 nor of God, 44 but of the Diuel. 45 but that him selfe is of God, 52 and greater and auncienter then Abraham. 59 For the vvhich they goe about to stone him, but in vaine.

The Gospel vpō Saturday the 3 Weeke of Lent.

AND IESVS vvent into the Mount-oliuet: † and early in the morning againe he came into the temple, and the people came to him, and sitting he taught them. 1 2

† And the Scribes and Pharisees bring a vvoman taken in aduoutrie: and they did set her in the middes, † and said to him, Maister, this vvoman vvas euen novv taken in aduoutrie. † And * in the lavv Moyses commaunded vs to stone such. What saiest thou therfore? † And this they said tempting him: that they might accuse him. But IESVS bovving him self dovvne, vvith his finger vvrote in the earth. † Vvhen they therfore continued asking him: he lifted vp him self, and said to them, :: He that is vvithout sinne of you, let him first throvv the stone at her. † And againe bovving him self, he vvrote in the earth. † And they hearing, vvent out one by one, beginning at the seniours: and IESVS alone remained, and the vvoman standing in the middes. † And IESVS lifting vp him self, said to her, Vvoman, vvhere are they that accused thee? hath no man condemned thee? † Vvho said, No man, Lord. And IESVS said, :: Neither vvil I condemne thee. Goe, and novv sinne no more. ꟼ 3 4 5 6 7 8 9 10 11

Leu. 20, 10.

:: We can not conueniently reprehend or cōdemne other mens faults, if our selues be guilty of the same or other greater. *Cyril in Io.* See *Annot. Mt. 7, 1.*

:: S. Augustine by this example of our Maister prooueth that Clergie men specially should be giuen much to mercie: and that they ought oftē, as the cause and time require, to get pardō of the secular Magistrates for offenders that be penitēt. *Ep. 54.*

b The Gospel vpon Saturday the 4 Weeke in Lent.

† b Againe therfore IESVS spake to them, saying, I am the light of the vvorld. he that folovveth me, vvalketh not in darkenesse: but shal haue the light of life. † The Pharisees therfore said to him, Thou giuest testimonie of thy self: thy testimonie is not true. † IESVS ansvvered, and said to them, Although I doe giue testimonie of my self, my testimonie is true: because I knovv vvhence I came, & vvhither I goe: but you knovv not vvhēce I come, or whither I goe. † You iudge according to the flesh: I doe not iudge any man. † And if I doe iudge, my iudgement is true: because I am not alone, but I and he that sent me, the Father. † And in your lavv it is vvritten, that * the testimonie of tvvo men is true. † I am he that giue testimonie of my self: and he that sent me, the Father, giueth testimonie of me. † They said therfore to him, Vvhere is thy father? IESVS ansvvered, Neither me doe you knovv, nor my Father. If you did knovv me: perhaps you might knovv my Father also. † These vvordes IESVS spake in the Treasurie, teaching in the temple: and no man apprehended him, because his houre vvas not yet come. ꟼ 12 13 14 15 16 17 18 19 20

Deu. 17, 6. 19, 15.

† Againe

21 † Againe therfore IESVS ſaid to them, I goe, and you ſhal ſeeke me, and ſhal die in your ſinne. Vvhither I goe, you
22 can not come. † The Ievves therfore ſaid, Vvhy, vvil he kil him ſelf, becauſe he ſaith, Vvhither I goe, you can not come?
23 † And he ſaid to them, You are from beneath, I am from
24 aboue. you are of this vvorld, I am not of this vvorld. † Therfore I ſaid to you that you ſhal die in your ſinnes. for if you
25 beleeue not that I am he, you ſhal die in your ſinne. † They ſaid therfore to him, Vvho art thou? IESVS ſaid to them,
26 :: The beginning vvho alſo ſpeake to you. † Many things I haue to ſpeake and iudge of you. but he that ſent me, is true: and vvhat I haue heard of him, theſe things I ſpeake in the
27 vvorld. † And they knevv not that he ſaid to them that his
28 father vvas God. † IESVS therfore ſaid to them, Vvhen you ſhal haue exalted the ſonne of man, then you ſhal knovv that I am he, and of my ſelf I doe nothing, but as the Father
29 hath taught me, theſe things I ſpeake: † and he that ſent me, is vvith me: and he hath not left me alone, becauſe the things
30 that pleaſe him I doe alvvaies. ⁋ † Vvhen he ſpake theſe things, many beleeued in him.

31 † IESVS therfore ſaid to them that beleeued him, the Ievves: If you :: abide in my vvorde, you ſhal be my diſ-
32 ciples in deede. † And you ſhal knovv the truth, and the
33 truth ſhal make you free. † They anſvvered him, Vve are the ſeed of Abraham, and vve neuer ſerued any man: hovv ſaieſt
34 thou, You ſhal be free? † IESVS anſvvered them, Amen, amen I ſay to you, that * euery one vvhich cōmitteth ſinne,
35 is the ſeruant of ſinne. † and the ſeruant abideth not in the
36 houſe for euer: the ſonne abideth for euer. † If therfore the
37 ſonne make you free, you ſhal be :: free in deede. † I knovv that you are the children of Abraham: but you ſeeke to kil
38 me, becauſe my vvorde taketh not in you. † I ſpeake that vvhich I haue ſeen vvith my father: and you doe the things
39 that you haue ſeen vvith your father. † They anſvvered, and ſaid to him, Our father is Abraham. IESVS ſaith to them, If you be the children of Abraham, :: doe the vvorkes of Abra-
40 ham. † But novv, you ſeeke to kil me, a man that haue ſpoken the truth to you, vvhich I haue heard of God. this did not
41 Abraham. † You doe the vvorkes of your father. They ſaid therfore to him, Vve vvere not borne of fornication. vve
42 haue one father, God. † IESVS therfore ſaid to them, If

Hh ij God

The Goſpel vpō Munday in the 2 Weeke of Lēt.

:: So read S. Cyril, S. Ambroſe, & S. Auguſtine: expounding it of Chriſtes perſon, that he is the beginning or cauſe of al creatures.

:: Onely faith is not ſufficient Without perſeuērance or abiding in the keeping of his cōmaundements.

Ro. 6, 16
2 Pet. 2, 19.

:: Man Was neuer Without free Wil: but hauīg the grace of Chriſt, his Wil is truely made free (as S. Auguſtine ſaith) from ſeruitude of ſinne alſo. *tract. 41 in Euang. Io.*

:: Not onely faith but good Workes alſo make men the childrē of Abraham. according as S. Iames alſo ſpeaketh of Abrahams Workes c. 2.

God vvere your father: verely you vvould loue me. for from God I proceded, and came: for I came not of my self, but he sent me: † Vvhy doe you not knovv my speach? Because you [43] can not heare my vvord. † You are of your father the Diuel, [44] and the desires of your father you vvil doe. he vvas a ∷ mankiller from the beginning, and he stoode not in the veritie: because veritie is not in him. vvhen he speaketh a lie, he speaketh of his owne, because he is a lyer, and the father thereof. † But because I say the veritie, you beleeue me not. [45] † Vvhich of you" shal argue me of sinne? If I say the veritie: [46] vvhy doe you not beleeue me? † He that is of God, heareth [47] the vvordes of God. Therfore you heare not, because you are not of God. † The Ievves therfore ansvvered, and said to [48] him, Doe not we say vvel that thou art a Samaritane, and hast a diuil? † IESVS ansvvered, ∷ I haue no deuil: but I doe ho- [49] nour my Father, and you haue dishonoured me. † but I seeke [50] not mine ovvne glorie. there is that seeketh and iudgeth.

† Amen, amen I say to you, If any man keepe my vvord, he [51] shal not see death for euer. † The Ievves therfore said, Novv [52] vve haue knovven that thou hast a deuil. Abraham is dead, and the Prophets: and thou saiest, If any man keepe my vvord, he shal not tast death for euer. † Vvhy, art thou [53] greater then our father Abraham, vvho is dead? and the Prophets are dead. Vvhom doest thou make thy self? † IESVS [54] ansvvered, If I doe glorifie my self, my glorie is nothing. it is my father that glorifieth me, vvhom you say that he is your God. † And you haue not knovven him, but I knovv him. [55] And if I shal say that I knovv him not: I shal be like to you, a lyer. But I doe knovv him, and doe keepe his vvord. † Abra- [56] ham your father reioyced that he might see my day: and he savv, and vvas glad. † The Ievves therfore said to him, Thou [57] hast not yet fiftie yeres, and hast thou seen Abraham? † IESVS [58] said to them, Amen, amen I say to you, before that Abraham vvas made, I am. † They tooke stones therfore to cast at him. [59] but IESVS hid him self, and vvent out of the temple. ⫞

∷ S. Augustine compareth Heretikes in their spiritual murder by driuīg Christian men out of the Church, to the Diuel that droue our parents out of Paradise. *Cont. lit. Petil. li. 2, c. 13.*

The Gospel vpō PASSION Sunday.

∷ He denieth not that he is a Samaritane, because he is our keeper or protector, as the word signifieth, and because he is in deede that merciful Samaritane in the parable of the vvounded man Luc. 10, 33. *Aug. tract. 43 in Ioan.*

ANNOTATIONS CHAP. VIII.

Why *Amen, amen*, is not translated.

34. *Amen, amen.] What is it (saith S. Augustine vpon this place) vvhen our Lord saith,* Amen, amen? *He doth much cōmend and vrge the thing that he so vttereth, doubling it. It is a certaine othe of his, if a man may so say. for* Amē *in Hebrue signifieth* verum, a truth. *Yet is it not translated, Whereas it might haue been said,* verum, verū *dico vobis. but neither the* * *Greeke interpreter durst doe it, nor the Latin. the Hebrue Word hath remained stil, that so it might be the more esteemed. Tract. 41 in Ioan. By vvhich vvordes and the like* * *recorded in other places of this nevv Testament, the Reader may see great reason, vvhy vve also say,* Amen, amen, *and durst not translate it and such like vvordes into our English tongue.*

* Ἀμὴν, ἀμὴν.

*See the preface, & Annot. in *Apocal. c. 19. 4.*

CHAP.

CHAP. IX.

To shevv that by his Baptisme (being the Sacrament of illumination or faith) he vvil take avvay the blindnes of the vvorld, he giueth vvith strange ceremonies sight to one borne blinde. 8 By vvhich vvonderful miracle (the attestation of the partie him self and of his parents concurring) first the neighbours, then also the Pharisees them selues are plainely confounded. Yet so obstinate they are, that because it vvas the Sabboth vvhen he vvrought it, they inferre that he is not of God: yea and throvv out of their Synagogue the partie for confessing him. 35 But our Lord receiueth him: 39 and foretelleth by this occasion, the excecation of the Ievves (because of their vvilful obstinacie) and illumination of the Gentils vvho confesse their ovvne blindnes.

1 AND IESVS passing by, savv a man blinde from his natiuitie: 2 † and his disciples asked him, Rabbi, vvho hath sinned, this man, or his parents, that he should be borne blinde? 3 † IESVS ansvvered, ∴ Neither hath this man sinned, nor his parents: but that the vvorkes of God may be manifested in him. 4 † I must vvorke the vvorkes of him that sent me, vvhiles it is day. 5 The night commeth, ∴ vvhen no man can vvorke. 6 † As long as I am in the vvorld, I am the light of the vvorld. † Vvhen he had said these things, he spit on the ground, and "made clay˙ of the spettle, and spred the clay vpō his eies, 7 † and said to him, Goe, [c] vvash in the poole of Siloé, vvhich is interpreted, *Sent*. He vvent therfore, and vvashed: and he came seeing.

8 † Therfore the neighbours, and they vvhich had seen him before, that he vvas a begger, said, Is not this he that sate, 9 and begged? Others said, That this is he. † But others, No, 10 not so, but he is like him. But he said, That I am he. 11 † They said therfore to him, Hovv vvere thine eies opened? † He ansvvered, That man that is called IESVS, made clay: and anointed mine eies, and said to me, Goe to the poole of Siloé, and wash. 12 And I vvent, and vvashed, and savv. † And they said to him, 13 Vvhere is he? He saith, I knovv not. † They bring him that 14 had been blinde, to the Pharisees. † And it vvas the Sabboth vvhen IESVS made the clay, and opened his eies.

15 † Againe therfore the Pharisees asked him, hovv he savv. But he said to them, He put clay vpō mine eies, & I vvashed: 16 and I see. † Certaine therfore of the Pharisees said, This man is not of God, that keepeth not the Sabboth. But others said, Hovv can a man that is a sinner doe these signes? And there

Hh iij vvas

The Gospel vpō Wenesday in the 4 weeke of Lent.

∴ Though many infirmities fall for sinne, yet not al. some cōming for probation, and some sent that God by the cure thereof may be glorified.

∴ The time of working, and meriting, is in this life: after death we can deserue no more by our deedes, but must onely receiue good or il, according to the difference of workes here.

c This was a figure of Baptisme, to which al men borne in sinne and blindnes are sent for health & sight. *Ambr. li. 3 c. 2 de Sacramentis.*

vvas a ſchiſme among them. † They ſay therfore to the 17 blinde againe, Thou, vvhat ſaieſt thou of him that opened thine eies? And he ſaid, That he is a Prophet. † The Ievves 18 therfore did not beleeue of him, that he had been blinde and ſavv: vntil they called the parents of him that ſavv, † and 19 aſked them, ſaying, Is this your ſonne, vvhom you ſay that he vvas borne blinde? hovv then doeth he novv ſee? † His 20 parents anſvvered them, and ſaid, Vve knovv that this is our ſonne, and that he vvas borne blinde: † but hovv he 21 novv ſeeth, vve knovv not, or vvho hath opened his eies, vve knovv not, aſke him ſelf: he is of age, let him ſelf ſpeake of him ſelf. † Theſe things his parents ſaid, becauſe they fea- 22 red the Ievves. for the Ievves had novv conſpired, that if any mã ſhould cõfeſſe him to be CHRIST, he ſhould be put out of the Synagogue. † Therfore did his parents ſay, That he is 23 of age, aſke him ſelf. † They therfore againe called the man 24 that had been blinde, and ſaid to him, ∷ Giue glorie to God. vve knovv that this man is a ſinner. † He therfore ſaid to 25 them, Whether he be a ſinner, I know not: one thing I know, that vvhereas I vvas blinde, novv I ſee. † They ſaid therfore 26 to him, Vvhat did he to thee? hovv did he open thine eies? † He 27 anſvvered them, I haue novv told you, and you haue heard: vvhy vvil you heare it againe? vvil you alſo become his diſci- ples? † They reuiled him therfore, & ſaid, Be thou his diſciple: 28 but we are the diſciples of Moyſes. † We know that to Moyſes 29 God did ſpeake: but this man vve knovv not vvhence he is. † The man anſvvered and ſaid to them, For in this it is mar- 30 ueilous that you knovv not vvhence he is, and he hath ope- ned mine eies. † and vve knovv that ſinners God doth not 31 heare. but if a man be a ſeruer of God, and doe the vvil of him, him he heareth. † From the beginning of the vvorld it hath 32 not been heard that any man hath opened the eies of one borne blinde. † Vnles this man vvere of God, he could not 33 doe any thing. † They anſvvered, and ſaid to him, Thou 34 vvaſt vvholy borne in ſinnes, and doeſt thou teach vs? And they did caſt him forth.

∷ So ſay the Heretikes whẽ they derogat frõ miracles done by Saincts or their Relikes, phariſaically pretending the glorie of God. As though it were not Gods glorie, whẽ his Saincts do it by his power and vertue: yea his greater glorie, that doeth ſuch things by his ſer uants, & by the meaneſt things belonging to them, as Peters ſhadow *Act. 5.* & Paules napkin *Act. 9.*

† IESVS heard that they caſt him forth: and vvhen he 35 had found him, he ſaid to him, Doeſt thou beleeue in the ſon- ne of God? † He anſvvered, and ſaid, Vvho is he Lord, that 36 I may beleeue in him? † And IESVS ſaid to him, Both thou 37 haſt ſeen him: and he that talketh vvith thee, he it is. † But he 38 ſaid,

said, I beleeue Lord. And falling dovvne he adored him. ✠
39 † And IESVS said to him, For iudgement came I into this vvorld: :: that they that see not, may see: and they that see, 40 may become blinde. † And certaine of the Pharisees that vvere vvith him, heard: and they said to him, Vvhy, are vve 41 also blinde? † IESVS said to them, If you vvere blinde, you should not haue sinne. but novv you say, That vve see. Your sinne remaineth.

:: By this we see that this miracle was not onely maruelous and beneficial to the blinde, but also significatiue of taking away spiritual blindnesse.

ANNOTATIONS CHAP. IX.

6. Made clay.] Christ that could haue cured this man by his onely wil or word, yet vsed certaine creatures as his instruments in working, and diuers circumstances and ceremonies, clay, water, anoynting, washing, &c. No maruel then that he and his Church vse such diuersities of Sacraments and ceremonies external in curing our soules.

External ceremonies.

22. Put out of the Synagogue.) The Heretikes vntruely translate here (& v. 35.) *Excommunicate*: to make the simple conceaue the Churches Excōmunication to be no other, or no better, or no more rightly vsed against them, then this casting out of the Synagogue of such as confessed our Sauiour. They might as wel haue translated for Synagogue, Church: for the Old Testament, the new: for Law, grace: for flesh, spirit: for Moyses, Christ. For no lesse difference is there betwene, casting out of the Synagogue, and, Excommunication. Besides that, not euery one which was not of the Iewes Synagogue, was therfore out of the communion of the Faithful, many true beleeuers being in other partes of the world not subiect to the Iewes Synagogue, Law, nor Sacraments. And therfore it was not al one to be out of the Synagogue, and to be excommunicated. as now, whosoeuer is out of the Churches communion, either by his owne wil, or for his iust deserts thrust out of it by the spiritual Magistrate, he is quite abandoned out of al the societie of Saincts in heauen and earth, so long as he so continueth.

Heretical trāslation.

Casting out of the Synagogue.

The Churches Excōmunicatiō. See in the Annot. Mat. 18, 17.

As for the cause of thrusting this poore man and such other out of the Synagogue, and excommunicating Heretikes, there is as great oddes as betwixt heauen and hel: he being vsed so for folowing Christ and his Church, these for forsaking Christ and his Church. Some more agreement there is betwene that corrupt sentence of the Iewes against the folowers of Christ, and the pretended excommunication executed against Catholike men by our Heretikes. although in truth there is no great resemblance. For, the Iewes though they abused their power sometimes, yet had they authoritie in deed by Gods law so to punish contemners of their Law, & therfore it was feared and respected euen of good men. But the excommunication vsed by heretikes against Catholikes or any offenders, is not to be respected at al, being no more but a ridiculous vsurpation of the Churches right and fashion of the same. for, out of their Synagogues al faithful men ought to flee, and not tarie to be thrust out: according to the warning giuen against Coré and Dathan. *Be ye separated from their tabernacles, lest you be vvrapped in their sinnes.*

The Heretikes ridiculous Excommunicatiō.

Num. 16.

CHAP. X.

He continueth his talke to the Pharisees, shevving that they and al other that wil not enter in by him, are wolues: and that they which heare them, are not the true sheepe. 11 But that him self is the good Pastor, and therfore to saue the sheepe from these wolues, he wil yeld his life, which othervvise no might of theirs could take from him: foretelling also his Resurrection, and vocation of the Gentils. 22 Againe an other time, he telleth these Iewes openly, that they are not of his sheepe, and that no might of theirs shal take from him his true sheepe, because he is God, euen as his Father is God. 31 Which by his miracles and by Scripture he sheweth to be no blasphemie: and they in vaine seeking to stone and to apprehend him, 40 he goeth out to the place where Iohn Baptist had giuen open witnes of him.

The Gospel vpō Tuesday in Whitsonweeke.

∷ The theefe, is the Heretike specially, & any other that vnlawfully breake in vpō the sheepe to kil & destroy them by false doctrine and otherwise.

∷ That is the fashion of Iewrie & other countries, signifying that the shepheard or Pastor must teach the sheepe, and not they him.

AMEN, amen I say to you, he that entreth 1 not by the doore into the folde of the sheepe, but climeth vp an other vvay: he is ∷ a theefe and a robber. † But he that 2 entreth by the doore, is the Pastor of the sheepe. † To this mā the porter openeth: 3 & the sheepe heare his voice: and he calleth his ovvne sheepe by name, and leadeth them forth. † And 4 vvhen he hath let forth his ovvne sheepe, he ∷ goeth before them: and the sheepe folovv him, because they knovv his voice. † But a stranger they folovv not, but flee from him: 5 because they knovv not the voice of strangers. † This pro- 6 uerbe IESVS said to them. But they knevv not vvhat he spake to them.

† IESVS therfore said to them againe, Amen, amen I say to 7 you, that I am the doore of the sheepe. † And hovv many so- 8 euer haue come, are theeues and robbers: but the sheepe heard them not. † I am the doore. By me if any enter, he shal 9 be saued: and he shal goe in and shal goe out, and shal finde pastures. † The theefe commeth not but to steale and kil and 10 destroy. I came that they may haue life, and may haue more aboundantly. ⊣ † I am the good Pastor. * The "good Pa- 11 stor giueth his life for his sheepe. † But the hireling and he 12 that is not the Pastor, vvhose ovvne the sheepe are not, seeth the vvoulfe comming, and leaueth the sheepe, and fleeth: and the vvoulfe raueneth, and disperseth the sheepe. † And the 13 hireling " fleeth because he is a hireling: and he hath no care of the sheepe. † I am the good Pastor: and I knovv mi- 14 ne, and mine knovv me. † As the Father knovveth me, and 15 I knovv the Father: and ∷ I yeld my life for my sheepe. † And 16 c other sheepe I haue that are not of this folde: them also I must bring, and they shal heare my voice, and there shal be made * one folde and one Pastor. ⊣ † Therfore the Father 17 loueth me: because I yeld my life, that I may take it againe. † No man taketh it avvay from me: but * I yeld it of my self. 18 and I haue povver to yeld it: and I haue povver to take it againe. This commaundement I receiued of my father.

† A dissension rose againe among the Ievves for these 19 vvordes. † And many of them said, He hath a deuil and is 20 mad: vvhy heare you him? † Others said, These are not the 21 vvordes of one that hath a deuil. can a deuil open the eies of

The Gospel vpō the 2 Sunday after Easter, and for S. Thomas of Canterburie, *Decemb. 29.*

∷ Christes death was so necessarie for the flocke, that when he might haue escaped, he voluntarily offered him self to death for his flocke.

c He meaneth the Church of the Gentils.

Esa. 40, 11. *Ezec.* 34, 23.

Ezec. 37, 24.

Esa. 53, 7

of blinde men?

1 Mach. 4,56.59

22 †* And " the Dedication vvas in Hierusalem: and it vvas 23 vvinter. † And IESVS vvalked in the temple, in Salomons 24 porche. † The Ievves therfore compassed him round about, and said to him, Hovv long doest thou hold our soule in suspẽse? if thou be CHRIST, tel vs openly. 25 † IESVS answered them, I speake to you: and you beleeue not. the vvorkes that I doe in the name of my Father, they giue testimonie of me. 26 † but you doe not beleeue, because you are not of my sheepe. 27 † My sheepe heare my voice: and I knovv them, and they 28 folovv me. † And I giue them life euerlasting: and they shal not perish for euer, and no man shal plucke them out of my 29 hand. † My father, " that vvhich he hath giuen me, is greater then al: and no man can plucke them out of the hand of my 30 father. † I and the Father are [c] one.

The Gospel vpõ Wenesday in Passion Weeke.

An other reading is, *My father that hath giuen me, &c.*

[c] *vnum.*

31 † The Ievves tooke vp stones, to stone him. † IESVS 32 ansvvered them, Many good vvorkes I haue shevved you from my father, for vvhich of those vvorkes doe you stone 33 me? † The Ievves ansvvered him, For a good vvorke vve stone the not, but for blasphemie, and because thou being a 34 man, makest thy self God. † IESVS ansvvered them, Is it 35 not vvritten in your lavv, that *I said, you are goddes?* † If he called them goddes, to vvhom the vvord of God vvas made, and 36 the scripture can not be broken: † vvhom the Father hath sanctified and sent into the vvorld, say you, That thou blas-37 phemest, because I said I am the sonne of God? † If I doe 38 not the vvorkes of my father, beleeue me not. † But if I doe, and if you vvil not beleeue me, beleeue the vvorkes: that you may knovv and beleeue that the Father is in me, and I in the 39 Father. ⊣ † They sought therfore to apprehend him: and he vvent forth out of their handes.

Ps. 81,6.

40 † And he vvent againe beyond Iordan into that place 41 vvhere Iohn vvas baptizing first: and he taried there. † and many came to him. and they said, That Iohn in deede did no signe. But al things vvhatsoeuer Iohn said of this man, vvere 42 true. † And many beleeued in him.

ANNOTATIONS
CHAP. X.

1. Climeth an other vvay.) Whosoeuer taketh vpon him to preach without lawful sending, to minister Sacraments, and is not Canonically ordered of a true Catholike Bishop, to be a Curate of soules, Person, Bishop, or what other spiritual Pastor so euer, and commeth not in by lawful election and holy Churches ordinance to that dignity, but breaketh in against order by force or fauour of men, and by humane lawes, he is a theefe and a murderer. So came in Arius, Caluin, Luther, and al Heretikes: and al that succede them in roome and doctrine. And generally euery one that descendeth not by Lawful succession in the knowen ordinarie line of Catholike Bishops and Pastors that haue been in al Countries since their conuersion. And according to this rule *S. Irenæus li. 3 c. 3* trieth the true shepheards from the theeues and Heretikes. So doe *Tertul. de Præscr. nu. 11. S. Cypr. de unit. Ec. nu. 7. S. August. ep. 165. & cont. ep. Manich. c. 4.* and *Lirinensis.*

Arch-heretikes specially, are the theeues that clime in an other way, not by the doore.

11. Good Pastor.) The good Pastor, is he whose special care is not of his owne aduantage, but of the safty of the flocke. The hireling, is he that respecteth not the profite and good of the flocke, but his owne lucre. The Woulfe, is the Heretike, or any persecutor of the Church, which is Christs flocke.

13. Fleeth.) Euery Bishop and Pastor is bound to abide with his flocke in times of danger and persecution euen to death, except him self be personally sought for, rather then the flocke, or the flocke it self forsake him. for in such cases the Pastor may flee, as the Apostles did, and S. Athanasius, and others. *S. Athan. Apol. de sua fuga. August. ep. 180.*

Whē the Pastor must tarie, or may flee.

22. The dedication.) This is the feast of Dedication instituted by Iudas Machabæus *li. 1 Mach. c. 4.* Christ vouchsafed to honour and keepe that feast instituted by him: & our Heretikes vouchsafe not to pray and sacrifice for the dead, *vsed and approued by him. The Dedication also of Christian Churches is warranted thereby, with the annual memories thereof. And it proueth that such things may be instituted without any expresse commaundement in Scripture.

Iudas Machabæus. Dedication of Churches.

* 2 Macha. 12.

29. That vvhich he gaue me.) Thus read also diuers of the Fathers, namely *S. Hilar. Trin. li. 7 post medium. S. Ambr. de Sp. S. li. 3. c. 18. S. August. in Io. tract. 48. S. Cyril. li. 7 in Io. c. 10.* and vse it to proue that Christ had his essence and nature of the Father. And therfore some Heretikes of our time wickedly accuse the Councel of Laterane for falsifying this place and applying it to the same purpose. Which they lesse can abide, for that it is against Caluins Autotheisme, holding that Christ tooke his person of the Father, but not his substance. *See the 2 Annot. in 1 Io. v. 1.*

Christs essence & diuine nature of the Father.

Caluins autotheisme.

CHAP. XI.

He cōmeth once againe into Ievvrie boldly (the time that he vvould be killed of them, being not yet come) and raiseth Lazarus foure daies buried. 47. At vvhich miracle the blind malice of the rulers so increaseth, that in Councel they conclude to make him avvay. hovvbeit the high Priest prophecieth vnavvares, of the saluation of the vvorld by his death. 54 He there vpon goeth againe out of the vvay.

The Gospel vpō Friday in the 4 weeke of Lent.

AND there vvas a certaine sicke man, Lazarus of Bethánia, of the tovvne of Marie and Martha her sister. († And Marie vvas she * that anointed our Lord vvith ointemēt, and vviped his feete vvith her heare: vvhose brother Lazarus vvas sicke.) † His sisters therfore sent to him saying, Lord, behold, he vvhom thou louest, is sicke. † And IESVS hearing, said to them, This sicknesse is not to death, but for the glorie of God: that the sonne of God may be glorified by it. † And IESVS loued Martha, and her sister Marie, and Lazarus. † As he heard therfore that he vvas sicke, then he taried in the same place tvvo daies: † then after this he saith to his Disciples, Let vs goe into Ievvrie againe. † The Disciples say to him, Rabbi, novv the Ievves sought to stone thee: and goest

1 2 3 4 5 6 7 8

* Lu. 7, 37 Mat. 26, 7. Mar. 14, 3. Io. 12, 3.

9 goest thou thither againe? † IESVS ansvvered, Are there not tvvelue houres of the day? If a man vvalke in the day, he 10 stumbleth not: because he seeth the light of this vvorld: † but if he walke in the night, he stumbleth, because the light is not 11 in him. † These things he said: and after this he saith to them, Lazarus our frende sleepeth: but I goe that I may raise 12 him from sleepe. † His Disciples therfore said, Lord, if he 13 sleepe, he shal be safe. † but IESVS spake of his death: & they 14 thought that he spake [c] of the sleeping of sleepe. † Then ther- 15 fore IESVS said to them plainely, Lazarus is dead: † and I am glad for your sake, that you may beleeue, because I vvas not 16 there. but let vs goe to him. † Thomas therfore, vvho is called Didymus, said to his condisciples, Let vs also goe, to die vvith him.

c de dormitione somni.

17 † IESVS therfore came, and found him novv hauing 18 been foure daies in the graue. († And Bethánia vvas nigh 19 to Hierusalem about fiftene furlonges.) † And many of the Ievves vvere come to Martha and Marie, to comfort them 20 concerning theire brother. † Martha therfore vvhen she heard that IESVS vvas come, vvent to meete him: but Marie 21 sat at home. † Martha therfore said to IESVS, Lord if thou 22 hadst been here, my brother had not died. † but novv also I knovv that vvhat things soeuer thou shalt aske of God, 23 God vvil giue thee. † IESVS saith to her, Thy brother shal 24 rise againe. † Martha saith to him, I knovv that he shal rise 25 againe in the resurrection, in the last day. † IESVS said to her, I am the resurrection and the life: he that beleeueth in 26 me, although he be dead, shal liue. † and euery one that liueth, and beleeueth in me, shal not die for euer, Beleeuest 27 thou this? † She saith to him, Yea Lord, I haue beleeued that thou art CHRIST the sonne of God that art come into this vvorld. ⊣

The Gospel in a Masse for the dead vpon the day of the burial or deposition.

28 † And vvhen she had said these things, she vvent, and called Marie her sister secretely, saying, The maister is come, 29 & calleth thee. † She, vvhẽ she heard, riseth quickely, & com- 30 meth to him. † For IESVS was not yet come into the towne: but he vvas yet in that place vvhere Martha had mette 31 him. † The Ievves therfore that vvere vvith her in the house and did comfort her, vvhen they savv Marie that she rose quickly and vvent forth, folovved her, saying, That she 32 goeth to the graue, to vveepe there. † Marie therfore vvhen

ſhe vvas come vvhere IESVS vvas, ſeeing him, fel at his feete, and ſaith to him, Lord, if thou hadſt been here, my brother had not died. † IESVS therfore vvhen he ſavv her vveeping, 33 and the Ievves that vvere come vvith her, vveeping, he groned in ſpirit, and troubled him ſelf, † and ſaid, Vvhere haue 34 you laid him? They ſay to him, Lord, come and ſee. † And 35 IESVS vvept. † The Ievves therfore ſaid, Behold hovv he 36 loued him. † But certaine of them ſaid, Could not he that 37 * opened the eies of the blinde man, make that this man ſhould not die? † IESVS therfore againe groning in him 38 ſelf, commeth to the graue. and it vvas a caue: and a ſtone vvas laid ouer it. † IESVS ſaith, Take avvay the ſtone. Mar- 39 tha the ſiſter of him that vvas dead, ſaith to him, Lord, novv he ſtinketh, for he is novv of foure daies. † IESVS ſaith 40 to her, Did not I ſay to thee, that if thou beleeue, thou ſhalt ſee the glorie of God? † They tooke therfore the ſtone 41 avvay. And IESVS lifting his eies vpvvard, ſaid, Father, I giue thee thankes that thou haſt heard me. † and I did knovv 42 that thou doeſt alvvaies heare me, but for the people that ſtandeth about, haue I ſaid it, that they may beleeue that thou haſt ſent me. † Vvhen he had ſaid theſe things, he cried 43 vvith a loude voice, Lazarus, come forth. † And forthvvith 44 he came forth that had been dead, bound feete and handes vvith vvinding bandes, and his face vvas tied vvith a napkin. IESVS ſaid to them, :: Looſe him, and let him goe.

Io. 9, 6.

:: S. Cyril *li. 7 c. vlt. in Io.* and S. Auguſt. *Tract. 49 in Io.* apply this to the Apoſtles and Prieſts authoritie of abſoluing ſinners: affirming Chriſt to reuiue none frō ſinne, but in the Church and by the Prieſts miniſterie.

† Many therfore of the Ievves that vvere come to Marie 45 and Martha, and had ſeen the things that IESVS did, beleeued in him. ⊣ † And certaine of them vvent to the Phariſees, and 46 told them the things that IESVS did. † The cheefe prieſts 47 therfore and the phariſees gathered a councel, and ſaid, Vvhat doe vve, for this man doeth many ſignes. † If vve let him 48 alone ſo, al vvil beleeue in him: and the Romanes vvil come, and :: take avvay our place and nation. † But one of them na- 49 med Caiphas, being the high prieſt of that yere, ſaid to them, You knovv nothing, † neither doe you cōſider that it is expe- 50 dient for vs that one man die for the people, and the vvhole natiō periſh not. † And this he ſaid not of him ſelf: but " being 51 the high prieſt of that yere, he prophecied that IESVS ſhould die for the nation: † and not only for the nation, but to ga- 52 ther into one the children of God that vvere diſperſed. † From that day therfore they deuiſed to kil him. † IESVS 53 therfore 54

The Goſpel vpō friday in Paſſion vveeke.

:: Al men, but ſpecially Natiōs muſt take heede, that vvhiles to ſaue their temporal ſtate, they forſake God: they loſe not both as the Iewes did. *Aug. tract. 49 in Io.*

therfore vvalked no more openly among the Ievves, but he vvent into the countrie beside the desert vnto a citie that is called Ephrem, and there he abode vvith his Disciples. ꟷ

55 . † And the Pasche of the Ievves vvas at hand: and many of the countrie vvent vp to Hierusalem before the Pasche to

56 sanctifie them selues. † They sought IESVS therfore: and they communed one vvith an other, standing in the temple, Vvhat thinke you, in that he is not come to the festiual day? And the cheefe Priests & Pharisees had giuen cõmaundemẽt, that if any man should knovv vvhere he vvas, he should tel, that they might apprehend him.

ANNOTATIONS
CHAP. XI.

51. Being the high Priest.] Maruel not that Christ preserueth his truth in the Church as wel by the vnworthy as the worthy Prelates thereof: the giftes of the Holy Ghost folowing their Order and office, as we see here in Caiphas, and not their merites or person. And if this man being many waies wicked, and in part an vsurper, and the Law and Priesthod being to decline and to giue place to Christs new ordinance, had yet some assistance of God for vtterance of truth which him self meant not, nor knew not: how much more may we be assured, that Christ wil not leaue Peters Seate, *whose faith he promised should neuer faile, though the persons which occupie the same, were as il as the blasphemous and malitious mouthes of Heretikes do affirme?

The priuilege of the office & order, though in a wicked person.

Lu. 22, 32.

CHAP. XII.

The Rulers dealing as if he hid him self, 1 he cometh to Bethania. 3 Where by occasion of Iudas the theefe murmuring at Marie Magdalens costly deuotion, he foretelleth his death. 12 From thence, though they did novv intend to kil Lazarus also, he rideth openly into Hierusalem, the people (because he had raised Lazarus) confessing with their acclamations that he is Christ. 20 Where certaine Gentils desiring to see him, 23 he foretelleth the conuersion of the vvhole vvorld from the Diuel to him, to be novv instant, as the effect of his death vpon the Crosse. 28 The Father also ansvvering from heauen to his prayer made to that purpose, 37 yet after al this, the Ievves continevv incredulous as Esay prophecied of them: 42 though many beleeued, but vvere ashamed to confesse him. 44 Wherevpon he shevveth that it is glorious before God, and saluation to them selues, to beleeue in him, and confesse him: and damnable, to despise him.

The 4 part. THE 4 Pasche, & holy weeke of his Passion in Hierusalem.

Mt. 26, 6. Mar. 14, 3. PALME SVNDAY eue.

The Gospel vpõ Munday in Holy weeke.

1 IESVS therfore sixe daies before the Pasche came to Bethánia, vvhere Lazarus vvas, that had been dead, vvhom IESVS

2 raised. † And they made him a supper there: and Martha ministred, but Lazarus vvas one of them that sate at the table

3 vvith him. † :: Marie therfore tooke a povvnd of ointement of right spikenard, pretious, and

:: Of this womans extraordinarie offices of deuotion, & how acceptable they were to Christ, see the *Annot. Mt. 26.*

anointed the feete of IESVS, and vviped his feete vvith her heare: and the house vvas filled of the odour of the ointmēt. 4 † One therfore of his disciples, Iudas Iscariote, he that vvas to betray him, said, 5 † a Vvhy vvas not this ointment sold for three-hundred pence, and giuen to the poore? 6 † And he said this, not because he cared for the poore: but because he vvas a theefe, and hauing the purse, caried the things that vvere put in. 7 † IESVS therfore said, Let her alone that she may keepe it for the day of my :: burial. 8 † For the poore you haue alvvaies vvith you: but :: me you shal not haue alvvaies. 9 † A great multitude therfore of the Ievves knevv that he vvas there: and they came, not for IESVS only, but that they might see Lazarus, vvhom he raised from the dead. ⊣ 10 † But the cheefe Priests deuised for to kil Lazarus also: 11 † because many for him of the Ievves vvent avvay, and beleeued in IESVS.

:: The deuout offices of balming and anointing the dead bodies of the faithful are here also allowed.

:: Not in visible and mortal cōdition, to receiue almes of you or such like offices for supply of my necessities.

The Gospel vpō Saturday in Passion weeke.

PALME SVNDAY.

12 † And on the morovv a great multitude that vvas come to the festiual day, vvhen they had heard that IESVS commeth to Hierusalem: 13 † they tooke the * boughes of palmes, and vvent forth to meete him, and cried, *Hosanna, blessed is he that commeth in the name of our Lord, the king of Israel.* 14 † And IESVS foūd a yong asse, and sate vpon it, as it is vvritten, 15 † *Feare not daughter of Sion: behold, thy king commeth sitting vpon an asses colt.* 16 † These things his disciples did not knovv at the first: but vvhen IESVS vvas glorified, then they remembred that these things had been vvritten of him, and these things they did to him. 17 † The multitude therfore gaue testimonie, vvhich vvas vvith him vvhē he called Lazarus out of the graue, and raised him from the dead. 18 † For therfore also the multitude came to meete him, because they heard that he had done this signe. 19 † The Pharisees therfore said among them selues, Doe you see that vve preuaile nothing? behold, the vvhole vvorld is gone after him.

*Mt. 21, 7. Mr. 11, 7. Lu. 19, 35.

Ps. 117, 26.

Zach. 9, 9.

20 † And there vvere certaine Gentiles of them that :: came vp to adore in the festiual day. 21 † These therfore came to Philippe vvho vvas of Bethsaida of Galilee, and desired him, saying, Sir, vve are desirous to see IESVS. 22 † Philippe commeth, and telleth Andrevv. Againe Andrevv & Philippe told IESVS. 23 † But IESVS ansvvered them, saying, The houre is come, that the Sonne of man shal be glorified. 24 † b Amen, amen I say to you, vnles the graine of vvheate falling into the ground, die:

:: We may see there is a great differēce where a man pray or adore, at home or i the Church & holy places: when the Gentils also came of deuotion a pilgrimage to the Temple in Hierusalem.

b The Gospel for S. Ignatius *Febr. 1.* And for a martyr that is no Bishop, as namely S. Laurence *Aug. 10.*

die: it self remaineth alone. but if it die, it bringeth much
25 fruite. † He that loueth his life, shal lose it: and he that hateth his life in this vvorld, doth keepe it to life euerlasting.
26 † If any man minister to me, let him folovv me: and vvhere I am, there also shal my minister be. If any man minister to
27 me, my father vvil honour him. ⊣ † Novv my soule is troubled. And vvhat shal I say? Father, saue me from this houre.
28 But therfore came I into this houre. † Father, glorifie thy name. A voice therfore came from heauen, Both I haue glo-
29 rified it, and againe I vvil glorifie it. † The multitude therfore that stoode and had heard, said that it thundered. Others
30 said, An Angel spake to him. † IESVS ansvvered, and said,
31 This voice came not for me, but for your sake. † Novv is the iudgemēt of the vvorld: novv the Prince of this vvorld
32 shal be cast forth. † And I, *if I be exalted from the earth,
33 vvil dravv al things to my self. († and this he said, signi-
34 fying vvhat death he should die.) † The multitude ansvvered him, Vve haue heard out of the lavv, that CHRIST abideth for euer: and hovv saiest thou, The Sonne of man
35 must be exalted? Vvho is this Sonne of man? † IESVS therfore said to them, Yet a litle vvhile, the light is among you. Vvalke vvhiles you haue the light, that the darkenesse ouertake you not. And he that vvalketh in darkenesse, knovveth
36 not vvhither he goeth. † Vvhiles you haue the light, beleeue in the light, that you may be the children of light. ⊣ These things IESVS spake and he vvent avvay, and hid him self from them. ⊣

The Gospel vpō Holy roode day *Septemb. 14.* in latin, *Exaltatio S. Crucis.*

Io. 3, 14.

37 † And vvhereas he had done so many signes before them,
38 they beleeued not in him: † that the saying of Esay the Prophet might be fulfilled, vvhich he said, *Lord, vvho hath beleeued the*
39 *hearing of vs? and the arme of our Lord to vvhom hath it bene reuealed?* † Ther-
40 fore they ∷could not beleeue, because Esay said againe, † *He hath blinded their eies, and indurated their hart: that they may not see vvith their eies, nor vnderstand vvith their hart, and be conuerted, and I heale them.*
41 † These things said Esaie, vvhen he savv his glorie, and spake
42 of him. † But yet of the Princes also many beleeued in him: but ∷ for the Pharisees they did not confesse, that they might
43 not be cast out of the Synagogue. † for they loued the glorie of men more, then the glorie of God.

Es. 53, 1.

Esa. 6, 9. Mt. 13, 14. Mr. 4, 12. Lu. 8, 10. Act. 28, 27.

∷ If any man aske (saith S. Augustine) why they could not beleeue: I answer roūdly, because they would not. *Tract. 53. in Io.* See the meanīg of this speach Annot *Mat. 13, 15. Mar. 4, 12.*

∷ This is the case of many principal men in such countries where heresie hath the vpperhand, who know and beleeue the Catholike faith: but

44 † But IESVS cried, and said, He that beleeueth in me, doth
45 not beleeue in me, but in him that sent me. † And he that seeth

seeth me, seeth him that sent me. † I a light am come into this 46 vvorld: that euery one vvhich beleeueth in me, may not remaine in the darkenesse. † And if any man heare my vvordes, 47 and keepe them not: I doe not iudge him. for I came not to iudge the vvorld, but to saue the vvorld. † He that despiseth 48 me, & receiueth not my vvordes, hath that iudgeth him. the vvord that I haue spoken, that shal iudge him in the last day. † Because of my self I haue not spoken, but the Father that 49 sent me, he gaue me commaundement vvhat I should say, and vvhat I should speake. † And I knovv that his com- 50 maundement is life euerlasting. The things therfore that I speake: as the Father said to me, so doe I speake.

but making choise rather to keepe mans fauour thē Gods, they dare not confesse the same. Such may pray that God and the World agree together: for els it is seen whose part they wil take.

ANNOTATIONS
CHAP. XII.

Church ornaments.

5. Why vvas.) So wicked, couetous, and sacrilegious persons reprehend good men for bestowing their goods vpon Church ornaments &c. vnder pretence of better bestowing them on the poore. such prouide for the poore as Iudas did.

Toleration of the euil.

6. A theefe.) Iudas did not then first perish when he sould our Lord, for he was a theefe before: and being lost he yet folowed Christ, not in hart, but in body onely. Which our Maister tolerated, to giue vs a lesson to tolerate the il, rather then deuide the body. *Aug. tract. 50 in Io.*

CHAP. XIII.

At his last supper, to giue his farevvel, and that in most vvonderful louing maner, 4 he vvasheth his Disciples feete, 6 beginning vvith Peter, 8 (shevving hovv necessarie it is for vs to be vvashed by him in Baptisme, and needful also after Baptisme) 12 and by this example teaching them al humilitie one tovvard an other. 21 Then he foretelleth, that (notvvithstanding his exceding loue tovvard them) one euen of them vvil betray him, meaning Iudas, 22 as to Iohn he secretly shevveth. After whose going out, he reioyceth and saith that euen now the houre is come, 34 commendeth vnto them to loue together, as a nevv commaundement, 36 and foretelleth Peter vvho presumed to much of his ovvne strength, that euen this night he vvil deny him thrise.

The Gospel vpō Maūdy thursday at Masse, and at the Washing of feete.

MAVNDY THVRSDAY.

Mt. 26, 1. Mr. 14, 1. Luc. 22, 1.

ND before the festiual day of Pasche, 1 IESVS knovving that his houre was come that he should passe out of this vvorld to his Father: vvhereas he had loued his that vvere in the vvorld, vnto the end he loued them. † And vvhen ∷ supper vvas 2 done, vvhereas the deuil novv had put into the hart of Iudas Iscariote the sonne of Simon, to betray him: † knovving 3 that the Father gaue him al things into his handes, and that he came from God, and goeth to God: † he riseth from sup- 4 per

∷ By supper, he meaneth the eating of the Paschal lambe. for, the institution of the B. Sacrament was after this.

per, and laieth aside his garments, and hauing taken a
5 tovvel, girded him self. † After that, he put vvater into a bason, and " began to vvash the feete of the disciples, and to vvipe them vvith the tovvel vvherevvith he vvas girded.
6 † He commeth therfore to Simon Peter. And Peter saith to
7 him, Lord, doest thou vvash my feete? † IESVS ansvvered and said to him, That vvhich I doe, thou knovvest not
8 novv, hereafter thou shalt knovv. † Peter saith to him, Thou shalt not vvash my feete for euer. IESVS ansvvered him, If I vvash thee not, thou shalt not haue part vvith
9 me. † Simon Peter saith to him, Lord, not only my feete,
10 but also handes, and head. † IESVS saith to him, He that is vvashed, nedeeth not but " to vvash his feete, but is cleane
11 vvholy. And you are cleane, but not al. † For he knevv vvho he vvas that vvould betray him. therfore he said, You are not cleane al.

12 † Therfore, after he had vvashed their feete, and taken his garments, being set dovvne, againe he said to them, Knovv
13 you vvhat I haue done to you? † You cal me, Maister, and
14 Lord: and you say vvel, for I am so. † If then I haue vvashed your feete, Lord and Maister, you also ought to vvash one
15 an others feete. † For I haue giuen you an example, that as
16 I haue done to you, so you doe also. ⊣ † Amen, amen I say to you, a seruant is not greater then his lord, neither is an apostle
17 greater then he that sent him. † If you knovv these things,
18 you shal be blessed if you doe them. † I speake not of you al: I knovv vvhom I haue chosen. But that the scripture may be fulfilled, *He that eateth bread vvith me, shal lift vp his heele against me.* (Ps. 40, 10.)
19 † From this time I tel you, before it come to passe: that vvhen
20 it shal come to passe, you may beleeue, that I am he. † Amen, amen, I say to you, he that receiueth any that I send, receiueth me: & he that receiueth me, receiueth him that sent me.

21 † VVhen IESVS had said these things, he vvas troubled in spirit: and he protested, and said: * Amen, amen I say to
22 you: that one of you shal betray me. † The disciples therfore looked one vpon an other, doubting of whom he spake. (Mat. 26, 18. Mar. 14, 16. Luc. 22, 21.)
23 † There vvas therfore one of his disciples leaning in the bo-
24 some of IESVS, he vvhom IESVS loued. † Therfore Simon Peter beckeneth to him, and said to him, Who is it of vvhom
25 he speaketh? † He therfore leaning vpon the breast of IESVS,
26 saith to him, Lord, vvho is he? † IESVS ansvvered: He it is

to vvhom I ſhal reach the dipped bread. And vvhen he had dipped the bread, he gaue it to Iudas Iſcariote Simons ſonne. † And after the morſel, then Satan entred into him. 27 And IESVS ſaith to him, That vvhich thou doeſt, doe it quickely. † But no man knevv of thoſe that ſate at table to vvhat 28 purpoſe he ſaid this vnto him. † For certaine thought, becauſe 29 Iudas had the :: purſe, that IESVS had ſaid to him, Bie thoſe things vvhich are needeful for vs to the feſtiual day: or that he ſhould giue ſome thing to the poore. † He therfore ha- 30 uing receiued the morſel, incontinent vvent forth. And it vvas night.

:: Chriſt had ſome prouiſion before hand giuen him by the Collections of the faithful, which was vſed both in his owne neceſſities, & beſtowed vpon the poore.

† Vvhen he therfore vvas gone forth, IESVS ſaid, Novv 31 the Sonne of man is glorified, and God is glorified in him. † If 32 God be glorified in him, God alſo vvil glorifie him in him ſelf, and incōtinent vvil he glorifie him. † Litle children, yet a 33 litle vvhile I am vvith you. You ſhal ſeeke me, & * as I ſaid to the Ievves, Vvhither I goe, you can not come: to you alſo I ſay novv. † * A" nevv cōmaundemēt I giue to you, That you 34 loue one an other: as I haue loued you, that you alſo loue one an other. † In this al men ſhal knovv that you are my 35 diſciples, if you haue loue one to an other. † Simon Peter 36 ſaith to him, Lord, vvhither goeſt thou? IESVS anſvvered, vvhither I goe, thou canſt not novv folovv me, but hereafter thou ſhalt folovv. † Peter ſaith to him, Vvhy can not I fo- 37 lovv thee novv? * I vvil yeld my life for thee. † IESVS an- 38 ſvvered him, Thy life vvilt thou yeld for me? Amen, amen I ſay to thee, the cocke ſhal not crovv, vntil thou denie me thriſe.

Io. 7, 34.

1 Io. 3, 23.

Mt. 26, 35. Mr. 14, 29. Lu. 22, 33.

ANNOTATIONS
CHAP. XIII.

Puritie required to the receiuing of the B. Sacrament.

5. Began to vvaſh.) This lotion vvas not onely of curteſy, ſuch as the Iewes vſed tovvard their ghests, nor onely for example of humilitie: but for myſterie and ſignification of the great puritie that is required before vve come to receiue the holy Sacrament, vvhich ſtraight after this vvaſhing vvas to be inſtituted and giuen to the Apoſtles. *Ambr. li. 3 de Sacra. c. 1 Bernard. de cœna Domini Serm. 1.*

Venial ſinnes taken avvay by ſacred ceremonies.

10. To vvaſh his feete.) The foulnes of the feete, vvhen al the reſt is cleane, ſignifieth the earthly affections and relikes of former ſinnes remitted: vvhich are to be cleanſed by deuout actes of charitie & humilitie, as *S. Ambroſe li. 3 de Sacr. c. 1.* and *S. Auguſtine ep. 108. & tract. 56 in Io.* do note. And becauſe this vvas onely a ceremonie, & yet had ſuch force, both now and aftervvard vſed of the Apoſtles, that it purged ſmaller offenſes and filthines of the ſoule, as *S. Ambroſe* and *S. Bernard* gather, it may not ſeeme ſtrange that holy vvater and ſuch ceremonies may remit venial ſinnes.

Ambr. & Bern. locis citatis.

14. You alſo ought.) Our Maiſter neuer ſpake plainer, nor ſeemed to commaund more preciſely, either of Baptiſme or the Euchariſt or any other Sacrament: and yet by the Churches iudgement

directed

directed by the Holy Ghost, we know this to be no Sacrament nor necessarie ceremonie, and the other to be. And why do they beleeue the Church in this, and do not credit her affirming the chalice not to be necessarie for the communicants?

wecke.

The Church defineth which are Sacraments and which not &c.

34. *A nevv commaundement.*) The commaundement of mutual loue was giuen before, but manifoldly misconstrued, and abridged by the Iewes to freends onely, to this life onely, for earthly respects onely: but Christ reneweth it and enlargeth it after the forme of his owne loue toward vs, and giueth grace to fulfil it.

CHAP. XIIII.

They being sad, because he said that he must goe from them, he comforteth them many waies, as, putting them in hope to folovv him vnto the same place, so that they keepe his commaundements. Where he telleth them, that him self is the vvay thither according to his Humanitie, and also the end according to his Diuinitie, no lesse then his Father, because he is consubstantial. 15 promising also to send vnto them (that is, to his Church) the Holy Ghost to be after his departure with them for euer. 28 And saying that it is his promotion (according to his Humanitie) to goe to the Father, for whose obediēce this his death shalbe, & not for any guilt of his owne.

The Gospel vpō SS. Philip and Iacobs day *Maij. 1.*

1 LET not your hart be troubled. You beleeue in God, beleeue in me also. 2 † In my fathers house there be ∷ many mansions. If not, I vvould haue told you, Because I goe to prepare you a place. 3 † And if I goe, and prepare you a place: I come againe and vvil take you to my self, that vvhere I am, you also may be. 4 † And vvhither I goe you knovv, and the vvay you knovv.

∷ These mansiōs signifie differences of glorie in heauen. *Hiero. li. 2. adu. Iouin.*

5 † Thomas saith to him, Lord, vve knovv not vvhither thou goest: and hovv can vve knovv the vvay? 6 † IESVS saith to him, I am the vvay, and the veritie, and the life. no man commeth to the Father, but by me. 7 † If you had knovven me, my father also certes you had knovven: and from hence forth you ` shal knovv him, and you haue seen him.

` doe knovv

8 † Philippe saith to him, Lord shevv vs the Father, and it sufficeth vs. 9 † IESVS saith to him, So long time I am vvith you: & haue you not knovvē me? Philippe, he that seeth me, seeth the Father also. Hovv saiest thou, Shevv vs the father? 10 † Doest thou not beleeue that I am in the Father, & the Father in me? The vvordes that I speake to you, of my self I speake not. But my father that abideth in me, he doeth the vvorkes. 11 † Beleeue you not, that I am in the Father and the Father in me? Othervvise for the vvorkes them selues beleeue. 12 † Amen, amen I say to you, he that beleeueth in me, the vvorkes that I doe, he also shal doe, and " greater then these shal he doe, 13 † because I goe to the Father, and vvhatsoeuer you shal aske in my

 name,

name, that wil I doe: ⊣ that the Father may be glorified in the Sonne. † 14 If you aske me any thing in my name, that vvil I doe. † 15 If you :: loue me, keepe my commaundements. † 16 And I vvil aske the father, and he vvil giue you an other c Paraclete, that he may abide vvith you" for euer, † 17 "the Spirit of truth, vvhom the vvorld can not receiue, because it seeth him not, neither knovveth him. but you ` knovv' him: because he shal abide vvith you, and shal be in you. † 18 I vvil not leaue you orphanes: I vvil come to you. † 19 Yet a litle vvhile: and the vvorld seeth me no more. But you see me: because I liue, and you shal liue. ⊣ † 20 In that day you shal knovv that I am in my father, and you in me, and I in you. † 21 He that hath my commaundements, and keepeth them: he it is that loueth me. And he that loueth me, shal be loued of my father: and I vvil loue him, and vvil manifest my self to him. ⊣

The Gospel in a votiue Masse for the election of the Pope, & vpon Whitsun eue.

:: It is then possible both to loue Christ, and to keepe his cōmaundements.

c *Paraclete* by interpretation is either a comforter, or an aduocate: and therfore to trāslate it by any one of them only, is pҁaps to abridge the sense of this place.

` shal knovv

† 22 Iudas saith to him, not that Iscariote, Lord, vvhat is done, that thou vvilt manifest thy self to vs, and not to the vvorld? † 23 IESVS ansvvered, and said to him, If any loue me, he vvil keepe my vvord, and my father vvil loue him, and vve vvil come to him, and vvil make abode vvith him. † 24 He that loueth me not, keepeth not my vvordes. And the vvord vvhich you haue heard, is not mine: but his that sent me, the Fathers. † 25 These things haue I spoken to you abiding vvith you. † 26 But the Paraclete the holy Ghost, vvhom the Father vvil send in my name, he shal ::teach you al things, & suggest vnto you al things vvhatsoeuer I shal say to you. † 27 Peace I leaue to you, my peace I giue to you. not as the vvorld giueth, doe I giue to you. Let not your hart be troubled, nor feare. † 28 You haue heard that I said to you, I goe and I come to you. If you loued me, you vvould be glad verily, that I goe to the Father: because the" Father is greater then I. † 29 And novv I haue told you before it come to passe: that vvhen it shal come to passe, you may beleeue. † 30 Novv I vvil not speake many things vvith you. for the prince of this vvorld commeth, and in me he hath not any thing. † 31 But that the vvorld may knovv that I loue the Father: and as the Father hath giuen me commaundement, so doe I: ⊣ Arise, let vs goe hence.

The Gospel vpō Whitsunday. And in a Votiue Masse of the holy Ghost.

:: See the Annot. vpō the 16 Chap. vs. 12 & 13.

ANNOT.

ANNOTATIONS
CHAP. XIIII.

li. de Babyla mart. 10. 5.

** Act. 5, 15 19, 12.*

** See Annot. Mat. 17, 20.*

We may and must easely beleeue the miracles ot Saincts & of their relikes, whẽ Christ him self foretelleth they shal doe such wonderful things.

12. *Greater then these.*) S. Chrysostom in a Whole booke against the Pagans proueth that this Was fulfilled not onely in Peters shadow, and Pauls garments, Which as We read in the * Actes, healed infirmities: but also by the Relikes and monuments of Saincts, namely of S. Babylas, of Whom he there treateth: thereby inferring that Christ is God, Who could and did performe these Wonderful Wordes, by the very ashes of his seruants. The Protestants cleane contrarie, as patrones of the Pagans infidelitie, as though our Sauiour had promised these & the like miraculous Workes in vaine, either not meaning or not able to fulfil thẽ, so do they discredite al the approued histories of the Church concerning miracles Wrought by Saincts, namely that S. *Gregorie Thaumaturgus* *remoued a mountaine, the miracles of *S. Paul* the eremite and *S. Hilarion* Written by *S. Hierom*, the miracles of *S. Martin* Written by *Seuerus Sulpitius*, the miracles testified by *S. Augustine de Ciuit. Dei*, the miracles approued by *S. Gregorie* in his Dialoges, the miracles reported by *S. Bede* in his Ecclesiastical storie and liues of Saincts: and al other miracles neuer so faithfully recorded in Ecclesiastical Writers. In al Which things aboue their reach of reason and nature, they are as litle persuaded and haue no more faith then had the Pagans, against Whom *S. Chrysostom* in the foresaid booke, and *S. Augustine de Ciu. Dei li. 22 c. 8*, and other Fathers heretofore haue Written. No man therfore needeth to maruel that the very Image of our Lady, & the like, doe miracles, euen as Peters shadow did: nor Wonder, if such things seeme stranger and greater then those Which Christ him self did: Whereas our Sauiour to put vs out of doubt, saith expresly, that his Saincts shal doe greater things then him self did.

The Heretikes as faithles ĩ this point, as the old Pagans.

16. *For euer.*) If the Holy Ghost had been promised onely to the Apostles, their successors and the Church after them could not haue chalenged it. but it vvas promised them for euer. Whereby We may learne, both that the priuileges and promisses made to the Apostles Were not personal, but pertaining to their offices perpetually: and also that the Church and Pastors in al ages had and haue the same Holy Ghost to gouerne them, that the Apostles and primitiue Church had.

The HOLY GHOST is promised to the CHVRCH for euer.

17. *The spirit of truth.*) They had many particular giftes and graces of the Holy Ghost before, and many vertues by the same, as al holy men haue at al times: but the Holy Ghost here promised to the Apostles and their successors for euer, is to this vse specially promised, to direct them in al truth and veritie: and is contrarie to the spirit of errour, heresie, and falshod. And therfore the Church can not fall to Apostasie or Heresie, or to nothing, as the Aduersaries say.

The Spirit of truth shal assist the CHVRCH alvvaies.

28. *Father greater then I.*) There is no place of Scripture that seemeth any thing so much to make for the Sacramentaries, as this and other in outWard shew of Wordes seemed to make for the Arians, Who denied the equalitie of the Sonne With the Father. Which Wordes yet in deede rightly vnderstood after the Churches sense, make nothing for their false secte, but only signifie that Christ according to his Manhod Was inferior in deede, and that according to his Diuinitie he came of the Father. And if the Heresie or disease of this time Were Arianisme, We should stand vpon these places and the like against the Arians, as We now do vpon others against the Protestants, Whose secte is the disease and bane of this time.

The Arians alleage as plaine Scriptures as the Protestãts.

CHAP. XV.

He exhorteth them to abide in him (that is, his Church, being the true vine, and not the Synagogue of the Ievves any more) 9 and in his loue, louing one an other, and keeping his commaundements: 13 shevving hovv much he accounteth of them, by this that he dieth for them, 15 and reuealeth vnto them the secretes of heauen, 17 and appointeth their fruite to be perpetual: 18 confirming them also against the persecutions and hatred of the obstinate Ievves.

 I AM

weeke.
The Gospel for one Martyr.
:: Christ hath some branches in his body mystical that be fruitles. therfore il liuers also may be members of Christ & the Church.
:: Man may cōtinually increase in iustice and sanctification, so long as he liueth.
:: S. Augustine expoundeth it of the Sacramētal word of Baptisme, and not as Heretikes do, of preaching onely. *Tract. 80. in Io.*
:: If a Schismatike pray neuer so much, he is not heard, because he remayneth not in the body of Christ.

I AM the true vine: and my father is the husband-man. † Euery :: branche in me, not bearing fruite, he vvil take it avvay: and euery one that beareth fruite, he vvil purge it, :: that it may bring more fruite. † Novv you are cleane for the :: word vvhich I haue spoken to you. † Abide in me: and I in you. As the branche can not beare fruite of it self, " vnles it abide in the vine: so you neither, " vnles you abide in me. † I am the vine: you the branches. he that abideth in me, and I in him, the same beareth much fruite: for vvithout me you can doe nothing. † If any abide not in me: he shal be cast forth as the branche, and shal vvither, and they shal gather him vp, and cast him into the fire, and he burneth. † If you :: abide in me, and my vvordes abide in you: you shal aske vvhat thing soeuer you vvil, and it shal be done to you. ⊣ † In this my father is glorified: that you bring very much fruite, and become my Disciples. † As my father hath loued me, I also haue loued you. Abide in my loue. † If you " keepe my precepts, you shal abide in my loue: as I also haue kept my fathers precepts, and doe abide in his loue. † These things I haue spoken to you, that my ioy may be in you, and your ioy may be filled. † * This is my precept, that you loue one an other, as I haue loued you. † Greater loue then this no man hath, that a man yeld his life for his frendes. † You are my frendes, if you doe the things that I commaund you. † Novv I cal you not seruants: for the seruant knovveth not vvhat his lord doeth. But you I haue called frendes: because al things vvhatsoeuer I heard of my father, I haue notified vnto you. † You chose not me, but I chose you: and haue appointed you: that you goe, & bring fruite: and your fruite abide: that vvhatsoeuer you aske the father in my name, he may giue it you. ⊣ † These things I commaund you, that you loue one an other.

The Gospel vpō S. Barnabees day, and on the eue of an Apostle.

Io. 13, 34.

The Gospel vpō SS. Simon and Iudes day.

† If the vvorld hate you: knovv ye that it hath hated me before you. † If you had been of the vvorld, the vvorld vvould loue his ovvne. but because you are not of the world, but I haue chosen you out of the vvorld, therfore the vvorld hateth you. † Remembre my vvord that I said to you, * The seruant is not greater then his maister. If they haue persecuted me, you also vvil they persecute. if they haue kept my vvord, :: yours also vvil they keepe. † But al these things they vvil

:: He foreshevveth that many wil not obey the Churches wordes. & no maruel, because they cōtemned Christes ovvne precepts.

Io. 13, 16 Mt. 10, 24. Lu. 6, 40.

doe

doe to you for my name ſake: becauſe they knovv not him
22 that ſent me. † If I had not come, and ſpoken to them, they
ſhould not haue ſinne: but novv they haue no excuſe of their
23 ſinne. † He that hateth me, hateth my Father alſo. † "If I had
24 not done amōg them vvorkes that no other man hath done,
they ſhould not haue ſinne: but novv both they haue
25 ſeen, and they doe hate both me and my Father. † But that
the vvord may be fulfilled, vvhich is vvritten in their lavv:
26 *That they hated me gratis.* ꟷ † But vvhen the Paraclete commeth
"vvhom I * vvil ſend you from the Father, the Spirit of truth,
vvhich procedeth from the Father, he ſhal giue teſtimonie
27 of me: † and" you ſhal giue teſtimonie, becauſe you are
vvith me from the beginning.

Pſ. 24, 19.
Act. 2, 1.

The Goſpel vpō Sunday after the Aſcenſion. and in a Votiue of the B. Trinitie.

ANNOTATIONS
CHAP. XV.

4. Vnles you abide.] Theſe conditional ſpeaches, *If you remaine in the vine, If you keepe my commaundements*, and ſuch like, giue vs to wit that we be not ſure to perſiſt or perſeuēre, nor to be ſaued, but vnder conditions to be fulfilled by vs. *Aug. de corrept. & gra. c. 13.*

No man ſure of perſeuērance.

4. Vnles it abide.) Whoſoeuer by Hereſie or Schiſme or for any other cauſe is cut of or ſeparated from the Church, he can do no meritorious worke to Saluation.

10. Keepe my precepts.] This careful and often admonition of keeping his commaundements, proueth that a Chriſtian mans life is not onely or principally in faith, but in good workes.

Not onely faith.

24. If I had.) If the Iewes had not ſinned by refuſing Chriſt, in caſe he had not done greater miracles then any other: then were it a great folly of Catholikes to beleeue Luthers or Caluins new opinions without any miracles at all.

26. Whom I vvil ſend.) The Holy Ghoſt is ſent by the Sonne, therfore he procedeth from him alſo, as from the Father: though the late Schiſmatical Greekes thinke otherwiſe.

27. You ſhal giue.) He vouchſafeth to ioyne together the teſtimonie of the Holy Ghoſt, and of the Apoſtles: that we may ſee the teſtimonie of truth ioyntly to conſiſt in the Holy Ghoſt and in the Prelats of the Church.

CHAP. XVI.

The cauſe vvhy he foretelleth them their perſecution by the Ievves, is, that they be not aftervvard ſcandalized thereat. 6 Though they thinke this heauie nevves, it is for their vantage that he departeth, becauſe of the great benefites that they ſhal receiue by the comming then of the Holy Ghoſt, vvho ſhal alſo be his vvitnes againſt his enemies. 16 Although in this vvorld they ſhal ſo be perſecuted, yet to his heauenly Father they and their praiers made in his name, ſhal be moſt acceptable. and at length the childe (that is, Chriſt in al his members) being borne, their ioy ſhal be ſuch as no perſecutor can take from them. 31 Hovvbeit at this inſtant of his apprehenſion, they vvil al forſake him.

Theſe

:: The Heretikes translate, *Excommunicate you.* See what corruption this is, and the reason thereof, *Annot. c. 9, 22.*

HESE things haue I spoken to you, 1 that you be not scandalized. † Out of 2 the synagogs they vvil :: cast you: but the houre commeth, that euery one vvhich killeth you, shal thinke that he doeth seruice to God. † and these 3 things they vvil doe to you: because they haue not knovven the Father, nor me. † But these things I haue spoken to you: that vvhen the 4 houre shal come, you may remember them, that I told you. ꟗ † But I told you not these things from the beginning, be- 5 cause I vvas vvith you. And novv I goe to him that sent me, and none of you asketh me: Vvhither goest thou? † But be- 6 cause I haue spoken these things to you, sorovv hath filled your hart. †But I tel you the truth. it is expedient for you that 7 I goe. For if I goe not, the Paraclete shal not come to you: but if I goe, I vvil send him to you. † And vvhen he is come, 8 he shal argue the vvorld of sinne, and of iustice, and of iudgement. † of sinne: because they beleeue not in me. † but of 9 iustice: because I goe to the Father: and novv you shal not 10 see me. † and of iudgement: because the prince of this vvorld 11 is novv iudged. † "Yet many things I haue to say to you: 12 but you can not beare them novv. † But vvhen he," the Spi- 13 rit of truth, commeth, :: he shal teach you al truth. for he shal not speake of him self: but vvhat things soeuer he shal heare, he shal speake: and the things that are to come he shal shevv you. † He shal glorifie me: because he shal receiue of mine, 14 and shal shevv to you. ꟗ † Al things vvhatsoeuer the Fa- 15 ther hath, be mine. Therfore I said, that he shal receiue of mine, and shal shevv to you. † A litle vvhile, and novv you 16 shal not see me: and againe a litle vvhile, and you shal see me: because I goe to the Father.

The Gospel vpō the 4 Sunday after Easter.

:: If he shal teach al truth, & that for euer (as before c. 14, 16:) how is it possible, that the Church can erre, or hath erred at any time or in any point?

The Gospel vpō the 3 Sunday after Easter.

† Some therfore of his disciples said one to an other, Vvhat 17 is this that he saith to vs: A litle vvhile, and you shal not see me: and againe a litle vvhile, and you shal see me, and, because I goe to the Father? † They said therfore, Vvhat is 18 this that he saith, A litle vvhile? vve knovv not vvhat he speaketh. † And IESVS knevv, that they vvould aske him: 19 and he said to them, Of this you doe question among your selues, because I said to you, A litle vvhile, and you shal not see me: and againe a litle vvhile, and you shal see me. † Amen, 20

amen I ſay to you, that you ſhal vveepe, and lament, but the vvorld ſhal reioyce: and you ſhal be made ſorovvful, but 21 your ſorovv ſhal be turned into ioy. † A vvoman vvhen ſhe trauaileth, hath ſorovv, becauſe her houre is come: but vvhen ſhe hath brought forth the childe, novv ſhe remembreth not the anguiſh for ioy, that a man is borne into the 22 vvorld. † And you therfore, novv in deede you haue ſorow, but I vvil ſee you againe, and your hart ſhal reioyce: and 23 your ioy no man ſhal take from you. ⊣ † And in that day me you ſhal not aſke any thing. Amen, amen I ſay to you, if you aſke the Father any thing ∴ in my name, he vvil giue it 24 you. † Vntil novv you haue not aſked any thing in my name. 25 Aſke and you ſhal receiue: that your ioy may be ful. † Theſe things in prouerbes I haue ſpoken to you. The houre commeth vvhen in prouerbes I vvil no more ſpeake to you, but 26 plainely of the Father I vvil ſhew you. † In that day you ſhal aſke in my name: and I ſay not to you, that I vvil aſke the Fa-27 ther for you. † For the Father him ſelf loueth you, becauſe you haue loued me, and haue beleeued that I came forth 28 from God. † I came forth from the Father, and came into the vvorld: againe I leaue the vvorld, and I goe to the Father.

The Goſpel for many Martyrs.

The Goſpel vpõ the 5 Sunday after Eaſter.

∴ Vpon this the Church cõcludeth al her praiers, *Per Chriſtũ Dominum noſtrũ*, euen thoſe alſo that be made to Saĩcts.

29 † His diſciples ſay to him, Behold novv thou ſpeakeſt 30 plainely, and ſaieſt no prouerbe. † novv vve knovv that thou knovveſt al things, and thou needeſt not that any man aſke thee. in this vve beleeue that thou cameſt forth from 31 God. ⊣ † IESVS anſvvered them, Novv do you beleeue? 32 † * Behold the houre commeth, and it is novv come, that you ſhal be ſcattered euery man into his ovvne, and me you ſhal leaue alone: and I am not alone, becauſe the Father is 33 vvith me. † Theſe things I haue ſpoken to you, that in me you may haue peace. In the vvorld you ſhal haue diſtreſſe: but haue confidence, I haue ouercome the vvorld.

Mt. 27, 31. Mr. 14,27.

ANNOTATIONS
CHAP. XVI.

12. *Yet many things.*) This place conuinceth that the Apoſtles and the faithful be taught many things, Which Chriſt omitted to teach them for their Weaknes: and that it Was the prouidence of God that Chriſt in preſence ſhould not teach and order al things, that We might be no leſſe aſſured of the things that the Church teacheth by the Holy Ghoſt, then of the things that him ſelf deliuered.

Chriſt left many things to be taught by the Church.

The Spirit of truth.

13 The Spirit of truth.) Euer note that the Holy Ghost in that he is promised to the Church, is called the Spirit of truth. Which Holy Spirit for many other causes is giuen to diuers priuate men and to al good men, to sanctification: but to teach al truth and preserue in truth and from error, he is promised and performed onely to the Church and the cheefe Gouerner and general Councels thereof.

CHAP. XVII.

After his Sermon of farevvel, he prayeth to his Father, that seing he hath novv finished his vvorke, he vvil giue him his appointed glorie, for the conuersion of al nations, 6 and preserue his Apostles, and his Church after them in vnitie and veritie (that is, from Schisme and Heresie:) 24 finally also glorifie them vvith him in heauen.

The Gospel vpō Ascension eue.

:: The Father glorifieth the Sonne by raising him from death, exalting him vp to his right hand, making al creatures to bow downe at his Name, and geuing him al power and iudgement. The Sonne againe glorifieth the Father, by making his honour, which onely in a maner was in Iewrie before, now knowen to al Nations.

1 THESE things spake IESVS: and lifting vp his eies into heauen, he said, Father, the houre is come, :: glorifie thy sonne, that thy sonne may glorifie thee. 2 † As thou hast giuē him povver ouer al flesh that al vvhich thou hast giuen him, to them he may giue life euerlasting. 3 † And this is " life euerlasting that they knovv thee, the only true God, and vvhom thou hast sent IESVS CHRIST. 4 † I haue glorified thee vpon the earth: I haue consummated the vvorke vvhich thou gauest me to doe: 5 † and novv glorifie thou me O Father vvith thy self, vvith the glorie vvhich I had before the vvorld vvas, vvith thee. 6 † I haue manifested thy name to the men vvhom thou gauest me out of the vvorld. Thine they vvere, and to me thou gauest them: and they haue kept thy vvord. 7 † Novv they haue knovven that al things vvhich thou gauest me, are from thee: 8 † because the vvordes vvhich thou gauest me, I haue giuen them: and they haue receiued, and knovven in very deede that I came forth from thee, and haue beleeued that thou didst send me. 9 † For them doe I pray: Not for the vvorld doe I pray, but for them vvhom thou hast giuen me: 10 † because they be thine: and al my things be thine, and thine be mine: and I am glorified in them. And novv I am not in the vvorld, and these are in the vvorld, and I come to thee. ✠

The Gospel in a Votiue Masse against Schisme.

:: His petition is specially to keepe the Apostles and his Church in vnitie and from Schismes.

11 † Holy father, :: keepe them in thy name, vvhom thou hast giuen me: that they may be one, as also vve. 12 † Vvhen I vvas vvith them, I kept them in thy name. Those * vvhom thou gauest me, haue I kept: and none of them perished, but the sonne of perdition, that the * scripture may be fulfilled. 13 † And novv I come to thee: and these things I speake in the world, that they may haue my ioy filled in them selues.

Io. 18, 9.

Ps. 40, 10. 108, 8.

† I

14 † I haue giuen them thy vvord, and the vvorld hath hated them, becauſe they are not of the vvorld: as I alſo am not of
15 the vvorld. † I pray not that thou take them avvay out of
16 the vvorld, but that thou preſerue them from euil. † Of the
17 vvorld they are not: as I alſo am not of the vvorld. † ″ San-
18 ctifie them in truth. Thy vvord is truth. † As thou didſt ſend me into the vvorld, I alſo haue ſent them into the vvorld.
19 † And for thē I doe ∷ ſanctifie my ſelf: that they alſo may be
20 ſanctified in truth. † And not for them only doe I pray, ″but
21 for thē alſo that by their vvord ſhal beleeue in me: † that they al may be one, as thou (Father) in me, and I in thee, that they alſo in vs may be one: that the vvorld may beleeue that thou
22 haſt ſent me. † And the glorie that thou haſt giuen me, haue I giuen to them: that they may be one, as vve alſo are one.
23 † I in them, and thou in me: that they may be conſummate in one: ⊣ and the vvorld may knovv that thou haſt ſent me,
24 and haſt loued them, as me alſo thou haſt loued. † Father, vvhom thou haſt giuen me, I vvil, that vvhere I am, they alſo may be vvith me: that they maye ſee my glorie vvhich thou haſt giuen me, becauſe thou haſt loued me before the
25 creation of the vvorld. † Iuſt Father, the vvorld hath not knovven thee. but I haue knovven thee: and theſe haue
26 knovven, that thou didſt ſend me. † And I haue notified thy name to them, and vvil notifie it: that the loue vvhervvith thou haſt loued me may be in them, and I in them.

∷ To ſanctifie him ſelf, is to ſacrifice him ſelf, by dedicating his holy body and bloud to his Father, both vpon the Croſſe, and in the holy Sacramēt.

ANNOTATIONS
CHAP, XVII.

3. *Life euerlaſting.*) Both the life of glorie in heauen, and of grace here in the Church, conſiſteth in the knowledge of God: that, in perfect viſion: this, in faith working by charitie. for, knowledge of God without keeping his commaundements, is not true knowledge, that is to ſay, it is an vnprofitable knowledge. *1 Io. 2.*

True knovvledge of God.

17. *Sanctifie them.*) Chriſt prayeth that the Apoſtles, their ſucceſſors, & al that ſhal be of their beleefe, may be ſanctified in truth. Which is as much to ſay, as to deſire that the Church may euer haue the Spirit of truth, and be free from errour. Which praier of Chriſt had not been heard, if the Church might erre.

The Church can not erre.

20. *But for them.*) He expreſſeth (and it is a great comfort) that he praieth not onely for the Apoſtles, but for the whole Church after them, that is, for al beleeuers. And al this profound and diuine praier is reſembled in the holy Canon of the Maſſe before the conſecration, as here it was made before his viſible Sacrifice on the croſſe.

The Canon of the Maſſe.

CHAP. XVIII.

Being gone to the place that Iudas the Traitor did knovv, 4 he offereth him self to the band of his enemies, shevveth his Diuine might in ouerthrovving them al vvith a vvord, and in sauing his Apostles from them also vvith a vvord: 10 rebuketh Peter that vvould defend him from them: 12 and so being apprehended, is brought bound to Annas and Caiphas, vvhere he is striken by a seruant, and thrise denied of Peter. 28 Againe in the morning he is by them brought to Pilate. 29 Who demaunding their accusation, vvhereas they vvould oppresse him vvith their authoritie, 33 and examining the point of his kingdom, pronounceth him innocent: yet they crie rather to haue a theeues life saued.

THVRSDAY night. The PASSION according to S. John in these two Chapters, is the Gospel at Masse vpon Good friday. So the PASSION is read in holy weeke foure times, according to the foure Euangelistes, as S. Augustine appointed also in his Church at *Hippo. Ser. 144. de tempore.*

WHEN IESVS had said these things, he vvent 1 forth vvith his disciples beyond the Torrent-Cedron, vvhere vvas a garden, into the vvhich he entred and his Disciples. † And Iudas also, that 2 betraied him, knevv the place: because IESVS had often resorted thither together vvith his Disciples. †* Iudas therfore 3 hauing receiued the band of men, and of the cheefe Priests and the Pharisees, ministers, commeth thither vvith lanternes and torches and vveapons. † IESVS therfore knovving al 4 things that should come vpon him, vvent forth, and said to them, Vvhom seeke ye? † they ansvvered him, IESVS of 5 Nazareth. IESVS saith to them, I am he. And Iudas also that betraied him, stoode vvith them. † As sone therfore as he 6 said to them, I am he: they vvent backvvard, and fel to the ground. † Againe therfore he asked them, Vvhom seeke ye? 7 And they said, IESVS of Nazareth. † IESVS ansvvered, I 8 haue told you, that I am he. if therfore you seeke me, let these goe their vvaies. † That the vvord might be fulfilled 9 vvhich he said, * That of them vvhom thou hast giuen me, I haue not lost any. † Simon Peter therfore hauing a svvord, 10 drevve it out: and smote the seruant of the high priest: & cut of his right eare. And the name of the seruant vvas Malchus. † IESVS therfore said to Peter, Put vp thy svvord into the 11 scabbard. The chalice vvhich my father hath giuen me, shal not I drinke it? † The band therfore and the Tribune & the 12 ministers of the Ievves apprehended IESVS, and bound him: † and they brought him to Annas first, for he vvas father in 13 lavv to Caiphas, vvho vvas the high priest of that yere. † And 14 * Caiphas vvas he that had giuen the counsel to the Ievves, That it is expedient that one man die for the people.

† * And Simon Peter folovved IESVS, and an other dis- 15 ciple. And that Disciple vvas knovven to the high priest, and vvent

Mt. 26, 36. Mr. 14. 32. Lu. 22, 39.

Mt. 26, 47. Mr. 14, 43. Luc. 22, 47.

Io. 17, 12

Io. 11, 49.

Mt. 26, 58. Mr, 14, 54. Lu. 22, 54.

16 vvent in vvith IESVS into the court of the high prieſt. † but Peter ſtoode at the doore vvithout. The other diſciple therfore that vvas knovven to the high Prieſt, vvent forth, and 17 ſpake to the portreſſe, and brought in Peter. † The vvench therfore that vvas portreſſe, ſaith to Peter, Art not thou alſo 18 of this mans diſciples? He ſaith to her, ∷ I am not. † And the ſeruants and miniſters ſtoode at a fire of coles, becauſe it vvas cold, and vvarmed them ſelues. And vvith them vvas Peter alſo ſtanding, and vvarming him ſelf.

∷ It is al one for a man to deny Chriſt, and, that he is a diſciple of Chriſt, or a Catholike, or a Chriſtian man, vvhen he is demaunded. *Aug. tract. 113 in Io.* for ſo Peter here denieth Chriſt, in denying him ſelf to be his Diſciple.

19 † The high prieſt therfore aſked IESVS of his diſciples, 20 and of his doctrine. † IESVS anſvvered him, I haue openly ſpokē to the vvorld: I haue alvvaies taught in the ſynagogue, and in the temple vvhither al the Ievves reſort together: 21 and in ſecrete I haue ſpoken nothing. † Vvhy aſkeſt thou me? aſke them that haue heard vvhat I haue ſpoken vnto 22 them: behold they knovv vvhat things I haue ſaid. † Vvhen he had ſaid theſe things, one of the miniſters ſtādi̇ng by, gaue IESVS a blovv, ſaying, Anſvvereſt thou the high prieſt ſo? 23 † IESVS anſvvered him, If I haue ſpoken il, giue teſtimonie of euil: but if vvel, vvhy ſtrikeſt thou me?

24 † And Annas ſent him bound to Caiphas the high prieſt. 25 † And Simon Peter vvas ſtanding, and vvarming him ſelf. They ſaid therfore to him, Art not thou alſo of his diſciples? 26 He denied and ſaid: I am not. † One of the ſeruants of the high prieſt ſaith to him, his coſin vvhoſe eare Peter did cut 27 of, Did not I ſee thee in the garden vvith him? † Againe therfore Peter denied: and forthvvith the cocke crevve.

GOOD FRIDAY.

Mt. 27, 1 Mr. 15, 1 Lu. 23, 1

28 † * They therfore bring IESVS from Caiphas into the Palace. And it vvas morning: and they vvent not in into the Palace, that they might not be contaminated, but that they 29 might eate the Paſche. † Pilate therfore vvent forth to them vvithout, and ſaid, Vvhat accuſation bring you againſt this 30 man? † They anſvvered and ſaid to him, If he vvere not a malefactour, vve vvould not haue deliuered him vp to thee. 31 † Pilate therfore ſaid to them, Take him you, and according to your lavv iudge him. The Ievves therfore ſaid to him, It is 32 not lavvful for vs to kil any man. † * That the vvord of IESVS might be fulfilled vvhich he ſaid, ſignifying vvhat death he ſhould die.

Io. 12, 33 Mt. 20, 19.

Mt. 27, 11. Mr. 15, 2. Lu. 23, 4.

33 † * Pilate therfore vvent into the Palace againe, and called IESVS, and ſaid to him, Art thou the king of the Ievves?

† IESVS ansvvered, Saiest thou this of thy self, or haue 34 others told it thee of me? † Pilate answered, Vvhy, am I a Iewe? 35 :: Thy nation, and the cheefe priests haue deliuered thee vp to me: vvhat hast thou done? † IESVS ansvvered, My king- 36 dom is not of this vvorld. if my kingdō vvere of this vvorld, my ministers verily vvould striue that I should not be deliuered to the Ievves. but novv my kingdom is not from hēce. † Pilate therfore said to him, Art thou a king then? IESVS 37 ansvvered, Thou saiest, that I am a king. For this vvas I borne, and for this came I into the vvorld: that I should giue testimonie to the truth. Euery one that is of the truth, heareth my voice. † Pilate saith to him, Vvhat is truth? 38

:: It pleased god, that Christ who was to dy both for the Iewes & the Gétiles, should be betraied of the one, and put to death by the other.

And vvhen he had said this, he vvent forth againe to the Ievves, and saith to them, I finde no cause in him. †* But 39 you haue a custome that I should release one to you in the Pasche: vvil you therfore that I release vnto you the king of the Ievves? † They al therfore cried againe, saying, Not him 40 but Barabbas. And Barabbas vvas a theefe.

Mt. 27, 15. Mr. 15, 6. Lu 23, 17.

CHAP. XIX.

The Ievves are not satisfied vvith his scourging and irrision. 8 Pilate hearing them say that he made him self the Sonne of God, is more afraid. 12 Yet, they vrging him vvith his loialty tovvard Cæsar, and professing that them selues vvil no king but Cæsar, he yeldeth vnto them. 17 And so Christ carying his ovvne Crosse, is crucified betvvene tvvo theeues, 19 Pilate vvriting notoriously the onely cause of his death to be, for that he is their king or Christ. 23 His garments be so vsed, euen as the Scriptures foretold. 25 He hath special care of his mother to the end. 28 He signifieth al that vvas vvritten of his Passion, to be fulfilled, and so yeldeth vp his ghost. 31 Then by the Ievves meanes also other Scriptures about his legges and side, are fulfilled. 38 And finally, he is honorably buried.

HEN therfore Pilate tooke IESVS, and 1 scourged him. † And the souldiars plat- 2 ting a crovvne of thornes, put it vpon his head: and they put about him a purple garment. † And they came to him, and 3 said, Haile king of the Ievves, and they gaue him blovves. † Pilate vvent forth 4 againe, and saith to them, Behold I bring him forth vnto you, that you may knovv that I finde no cause in him. † IESVS 5 therfore vvent forth carying the crovvne of thornes, and the purple vestiment. And he saith to them, Loe the man. † Vvhen 6 the cheefe priests therfore and the ministers had seen him, they

Mt. 27, 27. Mr. 15, 16.

they cried, ſaying, Crucifie, crucifie him. Pilate ſaith to them, Take him you, and crucifie him. for I finde no cauſe in him.

7 † The Ievves anſvvered him, Vve haue a Law: and according to the Law he ought to die, becauſe he hath made him ſelf the ſonne of God.

8 † Vvhẽ Pilate therfore had heard this ſaying, he feared more.

9 † And he entred into the Palace againe: and he ſaith to IESVS, Vvhence art thou? But IESVS gaue him no anſvver. 10 † Pilate therfore ſaith to him, Speakeſt thou not to me? knovveſt thou not that I haue povver to crucifie thee, and I haue povver to releaſe thee? 11 † IESVS anſvvered, Thou ſhouldeſt not haue any povver againſt me, vnles it vvere giuen thee from aboue. Therfore he that hath betraied me to thee, hath the greater ſinne.

12 † From thence forth Pilate ſought to releaſe him. But the Ievves cried, ſaying, If thou releaſe this man, thou art not Cæſars frend. euery one that maketh him ſelf a king, ſpeaketh againſt Cæſar. 13 † But Pilate vvhen he had heard theſe vvordes, brought forth IESVS: and he ſate in the iudgemẽt ſeate, in the place that is called Lithóſtrotos, and in Hebrevv Gábbatha. 14 † And it vvas the Paraſceue of Paſche, about the :: ſixt houre, and he ſaith to the Ievves, Loe your king. 15 † But they cried, Avvay, avvay vvith him, crucifie him. Pilate ſaith to them, Shal I crucifie your king? The cheefe prieſts anſvvered, Vve haue no king, but Cæſar. 16 † Then therfore he deliuered him vnto them for to be crucified.

:: He meaneth midday, counting from ſunne riſing. for ſo doth the Scripture count the houres of the day. *Mat. 20. Mar. 15. Luc. 23. Io. 4. Act. 3 & 10.*

17 And they tooke IESVS, and led him forth. † * And bearing his ovvne" croſſe he vvent forth into that vvhich is called the place of Caluarie, in Hebrevv Gólgotha. 18 † vvhere they crucified him, and vvith him two others, on the one ſide and on the other, and in the middes IESVS. 19 † And Pilate vvrote a title alſo: and he put it vpon the croſſe. And it vvas vvritten, IESVS OF NAZARETH THE KING OF THE IEVVES. 20 † This title therfore many of the Ievves did reade: becauſe the place vvhere IESVS vvas crucified, vvas nigh to the citie: and it vvas vvritten in :: Hebrevv, in Greeke, and in Latin. 21 † The cheefe prieſts therfore of the Ievves ſaid to Pilate, Vvrite not, *The king of the Ievves*: but that he ſaid, I am king of the Ievves. 22 † Pilate anſvvered, That vvhich I haue vvritten, I haue vvritten.

Mt. 27, 33. Mr. 15, 20. Lu. 23, 33.

:: Theſe three tongues being for other cauſes moſt famous before in al the world, are now alſo dedicated to God in the triumphãs title of the Croſſe of Chriſt, and in them the holy Scriptures are more conueniently written, taught, & preſerued.

23 † The * ſouldiars therfore vvhen they had crucified him,

Mt. 27. 35. Mr. 15, 24. Luc. 23, 34.

:: This coate without seame is a figure of the vnitie of the Church. *Cypr. de vnit. Ec.* And Euthymius and other write that our Lady made it.

The Gospel in a votiue Masse of our B. Lady betweene Easter & Whitsuntide.

::The great loue faith, courage, compassion, and sorovves', that our Lady had: who forsooke not the Crosse and her sonne, when so many were fled from him, and his cheefe Apostles denied him.

b The Gospel in a votiue Masse of the Passion.

him, tooke his garments (and they made foure partes, to euery souldiar a part) & his coate. And his :: coate vvas vvithout seame, vvrought from the toppe through out. † They said 24 therfore one to an other, Let vs not cut it, but let vs cast lottes for it vvhose it shal be. That the scripture might be fulfilled saying, *They haue parted my garments among them: and vpon my vesture they haue cast lottes.* And the souldiars did these things.

Ps. 21, 19.

† And there stoode beside the crosse of IESVS, :: his mo- 25 ther, and his mothers sister, Marie of Cléophas, and Marie Magdalene. † Vvhen IESVS therfore had seen his mother 26 and the disciple standing vvhom he loued, he saith " to his mother: Vvoman, behold thy sonne. † After that, he saith 27 " to the disciple, Behold thy mother. And from that houre the disciple tooke her to his ovvne. ꟷ

b † Aftervvard IESVS knovving that al things vvere novv 28 consummate, that the * scripture might be fulfilled, he saith, I thirst. † A vessel therfore stoode there ful of vinegre. And 29 they putting a sponge ful of vinegre about hyssope, offered it to his mouth. † IESVS therfore vvhen he had taken the 30 vinegre, said, It is cõsummate. And bovving his head, he gaue vp the ghost.

Psa. 68, 22.

† The Ievves therfore (because it vvas the Parasceue) 31 that the bodies might not remaine vpon the crosse on the Sabboth (for that vvas a greate Sabboth day) they desired Pilate that their legges might be broken, and they might be taken avvay. † The souldiars therfore came: and of the first 32 in deede they brake the legges, and of the other that vvas crucified vvith him. † But after they vvere come to IESVS, vvhen 33 they savv that he vvas dead, they did not breake his legges, † but one of the souldiars vvith a speare opened his side, and 34 incontinent there came forth " bloud and vvater. † And he 35 that savv it, hath giuen testimonie: and his testimonie is true. ꟷ And he knovveth that he saith true, that you also may beleeue. † For these things vvere done that the scrip- 36 ture might be fulfilled, *You shal not breake a bone of him.* † And againe 37 an other scripture saith, *They shal looke on him vvhom they pearsed.*

Exo. 12, 46.
Zac. 12, 10.

† And after these things * Ioseph of Arimathæa (because 38 he vvas a disciple of IESVS, but secrete for feare of the Iewes) desired Pilate that he might take avvay the body of IESVS. And Pilate permitted. He came therfore, and tooke avvay the body of IESVS. † * Nicodemus also came, he that at the 39 first

*Mt. 27, 57. Mr. 15, 42. Lu. 23, 50.
Io. 3, 1. 7, 50.

first came to IESVS by night, bringing a mixture of myrrhe
40 and aloés, about an hundred poundes. † They tooke therfore the body of IESVS, and bound it in linnen clothes vvith
41 the spices, as the maner is vvith the Ievves to burie. † And there vvas in the place vvhere he vvas crucified, a garden: and in the garden a nevv monument, vvherein no man yet had
42 been laide. † There therfore because of the Parasceue of the Ievves, they laid IESVS, because the monument vvas hard by.

ANNOTATIONS
CHAP. XIX.

15. His owne crosse.] This crosse, for that it was the instrument of our redemption, and as it were the altar of the supreme sacrifice, highly sanctified by the touching, bearing, and oblation of the sacred body and bloud of our Lord, is truely called the HOLY CROSSE: and hath been endued vvith vertue of miracles, both the whole and euery litle peece thereof. For the which causes, and specially for the most neere memorial of Christes Passion, it hath been visited in Pilgrimages, honoured by festiual daies and otherwise, reserued & reuerenced of the ancient fathers, with al deuotion: as contrariwise it hath been abused of Pagans, Apostataes, and Heretikes, seeking in vaine to deface and destroy it. See S. Cyril *li. 6 cont. Iulian.* S. Hierom *ep. 17. S. Paulinus ep. 11. Ruffinus li. 1. c. 7. & 8. Euagr. histo. li. 4 c. 25.* S. Leo *ep. 72. and Ser. 8 de Passione. Paulus Diac. li. 18.*

The HOLY CROSSE.

26. To his mother.) The maruelous respect that Christ had to his mother, vouchsauing to speake to her, and to take order for her euen from the crosse in the middes of his infinite anguishes and mysteries a working for mankind.

By this you see why in Catholike Churches MARIE and Iohn stand by the Roode.

27. To the Disciple.) A great honour to Iohn and charge, to haue that blessed iewel in keeping: and an vnspeakable comfort, that from that day forward the one was to the other mother and sonne. *virginem virgini commendauit*, saith S. Hierom. *He commended the virgin to a virgin.*

li. 1. adu. Iouinian.

34. Bloud and vvater.) This pearsing of Christs side, though on the souldiars part it was done blindly and insolently, yet by Gods ordinance it conteined great mysteries, and was prefigured by Moyses striking the rocke with his rodde: as this streame of bloud and water drawen miraculously out of his dead body, running in the Sacraments of the Church after the people of God, was signified by the water of the same rocke folowing the Israelites in the desert. *Out of this side* (saith S. Augustine) *issued the Sacraments. Hence* (saith S. Chrysostom) *the great mysteries haue their beginning.* Who vvarneth vs, that vvhen vve come to drinke of the holy chalice, vve should so approche, as though vve drevv the bloud out of Christes side. And both bloud and vvater apart did flovv forth, to shevv vs the fountaine of the tvvo principal Sacraments, and their seueral matters, Baptisme and the Eucharist, springing to life euerlasting in the Church. The fathers also say that the Church vvho is Christs spouse and his coadiutrice in applying the bloud and vvater to the benefite of the Faithful, was here formed, bulded, and taken out of this holy side of Christ sleeping on the Crosse, as * Eue was of Adams side, when he was cast a sleepe in Paradise.

Exo. 17. Num. 20. Tract. 9 in Ioan. Hom. 84 in Ioan.

The Sacraments issued out of Christs side, and thence haue their vertue.

The CHVRCH builded of Christs side, as Eue of Adams.

Gen. 2, 21.

CHAP. XX.

Vpon Easter day his body is missed in the Sepulcher, first by M. Magdalene, 3 secondly by Peter also and Iohn, the vvinding clothes yet remayning. 11 Then to M. Magdalene, after she had seen tvvo Angels, IESVS *also him self appeareth. 18 She hauing told to the Disciples, he appeareth to them also the same day, and sendeth them as him self vvas sent, giuing them the Holy Ghost to remitte and to reteine sinnes. 26 Againe vpon lovv Sunday he appeareth to them, letting Thomas see, that he might beleeue, and commending such as not seeing yet do beleeue. 30 The effect of this booke.*

The Gospel vpō Saturday in Easter weeke.

:: That is, the first day of the weeke, as some interprete it, taking Sabboth (as sometime it is) for a weeke. This is our Sunday, called *Dies Dominica*, because of our Lords resurrection. See the *marg. annot. Luc. 24, 1.*

EASTER DAY. *Mt. 28,1* *Mr. 16,1* *Lu, 24,1*

AND the :: first of the Sabboth, Marie Magdalene commeth early, vvhen it vvas yet darke, vnto the monument: and she savv the stone taken avvay from the monumēt. † She ranne therfore and cōmeth to Simon Peter, and to the other disciple vvhom IESVS loued, and saith to them, They haue taken our Lord out of the monument, and vve knovv not vvhere they haue laid him. 1 2

† Peter therfore vvent forth and that other disciple, and they came to the monument. † And both ranne together, and that other disciple did out-runne Peter, and came first to the monument. † And vvhen he had stouped dovvne, he savv the linnen clothes lying: but yet he vvent not in. † Simon Peter therfore cōmeth, folovving him, and vvent in to the monument, and savv the linnē clothes lying, † and the napkin that had been vpon his head, not lying vvith the linnen clothes, but apart, vvrapped vp into one place. † Then therfore vvent in that other disciple also vvhich came first to the monument: and he savv, and beleeued. † For as yet they knevv not the scripture, that he should rise againe from the dead. ⊣ † The disciples therfore departed againe to them selues. 3 4 5 6 7 8 9 10

Luc. 24, 12.

b The Gospel vpō Thursday in Easter weeke.

:: The Sepulchres of Martyrs (saith *S. Hierom ep. 17.*) we do honour euery where, & putting their holy ashes to our eies, if we may, we touch it also with our mouth: and be there some that thinke the monumēt wherein our Lord was laid, is to be neglected: where the Diuel and his Angels, as often as they are cast out of the possessed before the said monument, tremble and roare as if they stoode before the iudgement seate of Christ?

Mt. 28, 1 *Mr. 16, 5* *Luc. 24, 4.*

† b But * Marie stoode at the :: monument vvithout, vveeping. Therfore as she vvas vveeping, she stouped dovvne, & looked into the monument: † and she savv tvvo Angels in vvhite, sitting, one at the head, and one at the feete, vvhere the body of IESVS had been laid. † They say to her, Vvomā, vvhy vveepest thou? She saith to them, Because they haue taken avvay my Lord, and I knovv not vvhere they haue put him. † Vvhen she had said thus, she turned backvvard, and savv IESVS standing: and she knevv not that it is IESVS. † IESVS saith to her, Vvomā, vvhy vveepest thou? vvhom seekest thou? She thinking that it vvas the gardiner, saith to him, Sir, if thou hast caried him avvay, tel me vvhere thou hast laid him: & I vvil take him avvay. † IESVS saith to her, Marie. She turning saith to him, Rabbóni (vvhich is to say, Maister.) † IESVS saith to her, Do not touche me, for I am not yet ascended to my Father: but goe to my brethren, and say to them, I ascend to my Father and your Father, my God and your God. † Marie Magdalene commeth and telleth the 11 12 13 14 15 16 17 18

the disciples, That I haue seen our Lord, and thus he said vnto me. ⊣

Mr. 16, 14. Lu. 24,36. 1.Cor.15, 5.

19 † Therfore vvhen it vvas * late that day, the first of the Sabboths, and " the doores vvere shut, vvhere the disciples vvere gathered together for feare of the Ievves, IESVS came and stoode in the middes, and saith to them, Peace be to you. 20 † And vvhen he had said this, he shevved them his handes and side. The disciples therfore vvere glad vvhen they savv 21 our Lord. † He said therfore to them againe, :: Peace be to 22 you." As my Father hath sent me, I also doe send you. † Vvhen he had said this, " he breathed vpon them: and he saith to 23 them, Receiue ye the Holy Ghost: † " VVHOSE SINNES YOV SHAL FORGIVE, THEY ARE FORGIVEN THEM: AND VVHOSE YOV SHAL RETEINE, 24 THEY ARE RETEINED. † But Thomas one of the Tvvelue, vvho is called Didymus, vvas not vvith them vvhē 25 IESVS came. † The other disciples therfore said to him, Vve haue seen our Lord. But he said to them, Vnles I see in his handes the print of the nailes, and put my finger into the place of the nailes, and put my hand into his side: I vvil not beleeue.

The Gospel vpō Dominica in albis or Lovv Sunday.

:: Though he gaue them his peace hard before, yet novv entering to a nevv diuine action, to prepare their hartes to grace and attention, he blesseth them againe.

The Gospel vpō S. Thomas the Apostles day, Decemb. 21.

26 † And after eight daies, againe his disciples vvere vvithin: and Thomas vvith them. IESVS commeth :: the doores being shut, and stoode in the middes, and said, Peace be to 27 you. † Then he saith to Thomas, Put in thy finger hither, and see my handes, and bring hither thy hand, and put it into 28 my side: & be not incredulous but faithful. † Thomas an-29 svvered, & said to him, My Lord, & my God. † IESVS saith to him, Because thou hast seen me, Thomas, thou hast beleeued: :: blessed are they that haue not seen & haue beleeued. ⊣

LOVV SVNDAY.

:: See the annotation on the 19 verse of this Chapter.

Io. 21,25

30 † * Many other signes also did IESVS in the sight of his 31 disciples, vvhich are not vvrittē in this booke. † And these are vvritten, that you may beleeue that IESVS is CHRIST the sonne of God: and that beleeuing, you may haue life in his name. ⊣

:: They are more happy that beleeue without sensible argumēt or sight, then such as be induced by sense or reason to beleeue.

ANNOTATIONS
CHAP. XX.

19. The doores vvere shut.) Such Heretikes as deny Christs body to be or that it can be in the B. Sacrament, for that it is in heauen, and can not be in two places at once, nor without the natural

The being of Christs body in the B Sacramét without space or quãtitie correspondét there vnto, is proued by other examples í Scripture.

maner of the quantitie, space or place agreable to the condition of his humanitie, be inuincibly refuted by Christs entering into the Disciples, the doores shut: and by that that his true natural body, whole and perfect in al his limmes, length, bredth, and thicknes, distincte and diuers from the substance and corpulence of the wood, was in the same proper place that the wood was in, and passed through the same: as he also came out of his mothers wombe, the clausure not sturred: and passed through the stone, out of his Sepulcher. By al which the Heretikes being plainely reproued, and conuinced of infidelitie, they boldly deny the plaine Scriptures, or so fondly shift them selues from the euidéce thereof, that their impudencie is specially to be marked in this point.

Heretical shifts to auoid plaine Scripture.

Some say, that he came in at the window: some, that the doore opened of it self to let him in: some, that to come in, the doores being shut, signifieth no more, but that he came in late in the euening, at what time men vse to shut their doores: and such other flightes to defend falshod, against expresse Scriptures, and against the Apostles testimonie, who therfore tooke him to be a Spirit, because they saw him stand sodenly in the middes of them, al the house being close shut. And the Fathers al confesse that he went in, the doores being shut. See S. Ambrose *li. 10 in Lucam c. 24.* S. Augustine *ep. 3 ad Volusian. & li. 22 de ciuit. c. 8*, & S. Cyril, *in Io. li. 12, c. 53.* & S. Hiero. *li. 1 cont. Iouinianum c. 21.* We know it is the natural course od Gods ordinance, that euery body should haue but one and his owne proper place fitted to the lineaments, quantitie, termes and limites of the same: without which naturally the bodies were no where, and consequently not at al, as S. Augustine saith *ad Dardanum.* but that God supernaturally and miraculously can not by his omnipotencie dispose otherwise of his owne body, then the natural forme or quantitie or qualitie thereof require, that is great incredulitie. seing we must beleeue that he can doe so with any other body of mere men or other creatures, the Scripture being plaine that he can make a camel passe through a nedles eie, continuing in his natural figure and quantitie stil: and S. Augustine telleth of a woman whose ring fel from her girdle, both being fast and whole: and Rupertus of a Religious man, whose girdle fast buckled fel downe before him from his body. *De off. Eccl.*

Christ can dispose of his owne body & others aboue nature.

August. ep. 57.

Mat. 19.

Aug. li. 22 c. 8 de ciu. Dei.

Vbiquetaries or Brentiani.

Therfore it is to much vnfaithfulnes, by rules of place to embarre Christ of his wil or wisedom to be in the Sacrament how him self list, and on as many altars or places as he liketh. We detest for al that, the wicked heresie of certaine Protestants, holding quite contrarie to the Zuinglians, that Christ according to his Humanitie is in euery place where the Diuinitie is: which is both against faith, and the common rules of nature and diuinitie.

Christ sheweth his commission & so giueth the Apostles power to remit sinnes.

21. *As my Father.*) As when he gaue them commission to preach and baptize through the world, he made mention of his owne power therein: so here before he institute the Sacrament of Penance, and giue them authoritie to remitte sinnes, lest the wicked should aske afterward, by what right they do such great functions, he sheweth his Fathers commission giuen to him self, and then in plaine termes most amply imparteth the same to his Apostles: that whosoeuer deny the Apostles & their successors, the Priests of Gods Church, to haue right to remitte sinnes, should deny consequently Christ as man to haue authoritie to doe the same.

The holy Ghost is here purposely giuen to the Apostles, to remit sinnes.

22. *He breathed.*) He giueth the Holy Ghost in and by an external signe, to his Apostles, not visibly and to al such purposes as afterward at whitsuntide, but for the grace of the Sacrament of Orders, as S. Augustine saith, and that none make doubt of the Priests right in remission of sinnes, seing the Holy Ghost is purposly giuen them to doe this same. In which case if any be yet cótentious, he must deny the Holy Ghost to be God, and not to haue power to remitte sinnes. *It is not absurd* (saith S. Cyril) *that they forgiue sinnes, vvhich haue the Holy Ghost. For vvhen they remitte or reteine, the Holy Ghost remitteth or reteineth in them, and that they doe tvvo vvaies, first in Baptisme, and then in Penance.* As S. Ambrose also (*li. 1 c. 7 de pœnitentia*) refelling the Nouatians (a Sect of old Heretikes which pretending Gods glorie as our new Sectaries do, denied that Priests could remitte sinnes in the Sacrament of Penance) asketh, vvhy it should be more dishonour to God, or more impossible or inconuenient for men, to forgiue sinnes by Penance then by Baptisme, seing it is the Holy Ghost that doeth it, by the Priests office and ministerie in both.

Augu. q. no. Test. q. 93 Cót. ep. Parmen. li. 2, c. 11.

Cyril. li. 12 c. 56 in Io.

The Sacrament of PENANCE instituted.

23. *Whose sinnes.*) Power to offer Sacrifice, which is the principal function and acte of Priesthod, was giuen them at the institution of the B. Sacrament: the second and next special facultie of Priesthod, consisting in remitting sinnes, is here bestowed on them. And withal the holy Sacrament of Penance implying Contrition, Confession, and Satisfaction in the Penitent, and absolution on the Priests part, is instituted. for in that, that expresse power and commission is giuen to Priests to remitte or reteine al sinnes: and in that, that Christ promiseth, Whose sinnes soeuer they forgiue, they be of God forgiuen also: and vvhose sinnes they reteine, they be reteined before God: it folovveth necessarily, that vve be bound to submit our selues to their iudgment for release of our sinnes. For, this vvonderful povver vvere giuen them in vaine, if none vvere bound to seeke for absolution at their handes. Neither can any rightly seeke for absolution of them, vnles they confesse particularly at least al their mortal offences, vvhether they be cómitted in minde, hart, vvil and * cogitation onely, or in vvord, and vvorke. for, Gods priests being in this Sacrament of Penance cóstituted in Christs steede as iudges in causes of our conscience, can not rightly rule our cases vvithout ful and exacte cognition and knovvledge of al our sinnes, and the necessarie circunstances and * differences of the same. Which can not othervvise be had of them being mortal men, then

Men are bound to confesse, al their mortal sinnes, and that in particular.

* *Cypr. de laps. nu. 11.*

* *Hiero. in 16 Mat.*

then by our simple, sincere, and distincte vtterance to them of our sinnes, vvith humble contrite hart, ready to take and to doe penance according to theire iniunction. For that authoritie to reteine sinnes, consisteth specially in enioyning satisfaction and penitential vvorkes of praying, fasting, almes, and such like. Al vvhich Gods ordinance whosoeuer condemneth or contemneth, as Heretikes doe, or neglecteth, as some carelesse Catholikes may perhaps doe: let them be assured they can not be saued. Neither must any such Christian man pretend or looke to haue his sinnes after Baptisme, remitted by God onely, without this Sacrament: (which was the old Heresie of the Nouatians *Ambr. li. 1 de pænit. c. 2. Socrat. li. 7 Ec. hist. c. 25*) more then any may hope to be saued or haue his original or other sinnes before Baptisme, forgiuen by God without the same Sacramēt. Let no man deceiue him self, this is the *second table or borde after shipvvracke*, as S. Hierom calleth it. Whosoeuer take not hold of it, shal perish without al doubt, because they contemne Gods counsel and order for their saluation. And therfore S. Augustine (ep. 180) ioyning both together, saith it is a pitiful case, when by the absence of Gods Priests, men depart this life, *aut non regenerati, aut ligati*. that is, *either not regenerated* by Baptisme, *or fast bound*, and not absolued by the Sacrament of penance and reconciliation: because they shal be excluded from eternal life, and *destruction folovveth them*. And S. Victor (*li. 2 de persecut. Vandalica*) telleth the miserable lamētation of the people, when their Priests were banished by the Arian Heretikes. *Who* (say they) *shal baptize these infants?* Who *shal minister penāce vnto vs, & loose vs from the bandes of sinnes &c?* And therfore S. Cyprian very often (namely ep. 54) calleth it great cruelty, & such as Priests shal answer for at the later day, to suffer any man that is pœnitent of his sinnes, to depart this life without this reconciliation and absolution: *because* (saith he) *the Lavvmaker him self* (Christ) *hath graunted, that things bound in earth, should also be bound in heauen: and that those things might there be loosed, vvhich vvere loosed before here in the Church.* And it is a world to see, how the Heretikes wrastle with this so plaine a commission of remitting sinnes, referring it to preaching, to denouncing Gods threates vpon sinners, and to we can not tel what els. though to our English Protestants this authoritie seemeth so cleere, that in their order of visiting the sicke, their Ministers acknowledge & chalenge the same, vsing a formal absolution according to the Churches order, after the special cōfession of the partie. But to conclude the matter, let euery one that list to see the true meaning of Christs wordes, and the Priests great power and dignitie giuen them by the same wordes and other, marke wel these wordes of S. Chrysostome. For, saith he, *they that dvvel on the earth, and conuerse in it, to them is commission giuen to dispense those things that are in heauen. to them is it giuen to haue the povver vvhich God vvould not to be giuen neither to Angels nor Archangels. for, neither to them vvas it said, Whatsoeuer you shal binde in earth, shal be bound in heauen: and vvhatsoeuer you shal loose in earth, shal be loosed in heauen. The earthly Princes in deede haue also povver to binde, but the bodies onely: but that bond of Priests vvhich I speake of, toucheth the very soule it self and reacheth euen to the heauens: in so much that vvhatsoeuer the Priests shal doe beneath, the self same God doth ratifie aboue, and the sentence of the seruants the Lord doth confirme. for in deede vvhat els is this, then that the povver of al heauenly things is graunted them of God? Whose sinnes so euer, saith he, you shal reteine, they are reteined. What povver (I beseche you) can be greater then this one? The Father gaue al povver to the Sonne: but I see the same povver altogether deliuered by the Sonne vnto them.* And as this concerneth the Priests high authoritie to absolue, so therevpon concerning confession also to be made vnto them, the ancient Fathers speake in this sort. S. Cyprian *de Lapsis nu. 11.* They (saith he) *that haue greater faith and feare of God, though they did not fall in persecution, yet because they did onely thinke it in their minde, this very cogitation they confesse to Gods Priests sorovvfully and plainely, opening their conscience, vttering and discharging the burden of their minde, and seeking holesome medicine for their vvoundes though but smal and litle.* And a litle after, *Let euery one (my brethren) I beseeche you, confesse his sinne, vvhiles he is yet aliue, vvhiles his confession may be admitted, vvhiles satisfaction and remission made by the Priests is acceptable before God.* S. Cyril (or as some thinke, Origen) *li. 2 in Leuit.* calleth it a great part of penance, when a man is ashamed, and yet openeth his sinnes to our Lords Priest. See also *Tertul. li. de Pœnit. S. Hiero. in c. 10 Ecclesiastæ. S. Basil. in Regulis breu. quæst. 229.* Who compare sinners that refuse to confesse, to them that haue some disease in their secrete partes, and are ashamed to shew it to the Physicion or Surgeon, that might cure it. Where they must needes meane secrete confession to be made to them that may absolue. And S. Leo ep. 80 most plainely (as before S. Cyril) expresly nameth Priests. *That confession is sufficient vvhich is made first to God, then to the Priest also.* And againe, *It is sufficient that the guiltines of mens consciences be vttered to the Priests onely by the secrecie of confession.* S. Hierome in 16 Mat. saith, that Priests loose or binde, *audita peccatorum varietate, hauing heard the varietie and differences of sinnes.* S. Paulinus writeth of S. Ambrose, *that as often as any confessed his sinnes vnto him for to receiue penance, he so vvept for compassion, that thereby he caused the penitent to weepe also.* He addeth moreouer, that this holy Doctor was so secrete in this case, that no man knew the sinnes confessed, but God and him self. And S. Augustine ho. 49 de 50 homilijs to. 10. saith thus, *Doe penance such as is done in the Church, Let no man say, I doe it secretly, I doe it to God. in vaine then vvas it said,* Whatsoeuer you shal loose in earth, shal be loosed in heauen. See S. Ambrose *de pænitentia* through out. S. Cyprian *de Lapsis*, the booke *de vera & falsa pœnit.* in S. Augustine. beside al antiquitie which is ful of these speaches concerning absolution, and confession.

Hiero. ad Demetriadem. c. 6, to. 1. | *Mat. 18.* | *See the cōmunion booke.* | *Li. 3 de Sacerd.* | *In vita D. Ambr. prope finē.* | *Mat. 18.*

To reteine sinnes. | The necessitie of this Sacrament. | The Heretikes wrastling agaīst plaine Scriptnre. | The English Ministers heare confessions, and absolue. | Priests power to forgiue sinnes, is aboue the power of Angels or worldly Princes. | Confession to Priests. | Secrete or auricular Confession.

CHAP. XXI.

Appearing againe in Galilee, Where Peter Was fiſhing With his felloWes: and cauſing them after they had al night taken none, to catch a great multitude, Which Peter draWeth to land, Where he alſo dineth them: 15 He (expreſsing What this fiſhing ſignified) maketh Peter his Vicar, committing vnto him the feeding of his lambes and ſheepe: 18 and reuealeth vnto him, that he alſo ſhal be crucified, to the glorie of God, 20 admoniſhing him to minde that, rather then to be curious about Iohns death.

The Goſpel on Wenſeday in Eaſter Weeke.

1 AFTER IESVS manifeſted him ſelf againe at the ſea of Tibérias. And he manifeſted thus: 2 † There vvere together Simon Peter and Thomas vvho is called Didymus, and Nathanael vvhich vvas of Cana in Galilee, and the ſonnes of Zebedee, and tvvo others of his diſciples. 3 † Simon Peter ſaith to them, I goe to fiſh. They ſay to him, Vve alſo come vvith thee. And they vvent forth and got vp into the boate: and that night they tooke nothing. 4 † But vvhen morning vvas novv come, IESVS ſtoode on the ſhore: yet the diſciples knevv not that it vvas IESVS. 5 † IESVS therfore ſaith to them, Childrẽ, haue you any meate? They anſvvered him, No. 6 † He ſaith to them, Caſt the nette on the right ſide of the boate: and you ſhal finde. They therfore did caſt it: and novv they vvere not able to dravv it for the multitude of fiſhes. 7 † That diſciple therfore vvhom IESVS loued, ſaith to Peter, It is our Lord.:: Simon Peter vvhẽ he had heard that it is our Lord: girded his coate vnto him (for he vvas naked) and caſt him ſelf into the ſea. 8 † But the other diſciples came in the boate (for they vvere not farre from the land, but as it vvere tvvo hundred cubits) dravving the nette of fiſhes. 9 † Therfore after they came dovvne to land, they ſavv hote coles lying, and fiſh laid thereon, and bread. 10 † IESVS ſaith to them, Bring hither of the fiſhes that you tooke novv. 11 † Simõ Peter vvent vp, and drevv the nette to the land, ful of great fiſhes, an hundred fiftie three. And although they vvere ſo many, the nette vvas not broken. 12 † IESVS ſaith to them, Come, dine. And none of ˋthem that ſate at meateˊ, durſt aſke him, Vvho art thou? knovving that it is our Lord. 13 † And IESVS commeth and taketh the bread and giueth them, and the fiſh in like maner. 14 † This novv the :: third time IESVS vvas manifeſted to his diſciples, after he vvas riſen from the dead. ⁜

15 † Therfore vvhen they had dined, IESVS ſaith to Simon Peter

:: See in S. Auguſtine *tract. 122 in Io.* the great myſterie hereof concerning the CHVRCH, and in S. Gregorie *hom. 24 in Euang.* and S. Bernard *li. 2 c. 8 de conſid.* Peters PRIMACIE here miſtically ſignified.

:: Not the third apparition, but the third day of his apparitions. for he appeared in the very day of his Reſurrectiõ oftẽ, againe vpon Low Sunday, then this third time, And S. Marke ſaying, *laſt he appeared, 6.16, 14.* meaneth his laſt apparition the firſt day.

the diſciples.

Peter, Simon of Iohn, louest thou me more then these? He saith to him, Yea Lord: thou knovvest that I loue thee. he saith to him, FEEDE MY LAMBES. 16 † He saith to him againe, Simon of Iohn, louest thou me? he saith to him, Yea Lord, thou knovvest that I loue thee. He saith to him, [c]FEEDE MY LAMBES. 17 † He saith to him the third time, Simō of Iohn, louest thou me? Peter vvas stroken sad, because he said vnto him the third time, Louest thou me? And he said to him, Lord, thou knovvest al things: thou knovvest that I loue thee. He saith to him, [a]FEEDE MY SHEEPE. 18 † Amē, amen I say to thee, vvhen thou vvast yonger, thou didst girde thy self, and didst vvalke vvhere thou vvouldest. but vvhen thou shalt be old, thou shalt stretch forth thy handes, and " an other shal girde thee, and leade thee vvhither thou vvilt not. 19 † And this he said, signifying by vvhat death he should glorifie God. ⊣ [b]And vvhen he had said this, he saith to him, Folovv me. 20 † Peter turning, savv that disciple vvhom IESVS loued, folovving, * vvho also leaned at the supper vpon his breast, and said, Lord vvho is he that shal betray thee? 21 † Him therfore vvhen Peter had seen, he saith to IESVS, Lord, and this man vvhat? 22 † IESVS saith to him, [c]So I vvil haue him to remaine til I come, vvhat to thee? folovv thou me. 23 † This saying therfore vvent abrode among the brethren, that that disciple dieth not. And IESVS did not say to him, he dieth not: but, So I vvil haue him to remaine til I come, vvhat to thee? 24 † This is that disciple vvhich giueth testimonie of these things, and hath vvritten these things: and vve knovv that his testimonie is true. ⊣

25 † But there are * many ∷ other things also vvhich IESVS did: vvhich if they vvere vvritten in particular, neither the vvorld it self I thinke vvere able to conteine those bookes that should be vvritten.

Marginal notes: The Gospel on the eue of SS. Peter and Paul. — [c] ποίμαινε feede & rule — Io. 13, 23 — Io. 20, 30. — [b] The Gospel vpō S. Iohn the Euangelists day in Christmas *Decembris 27.* — [c] So readeth S. Ambrose *in Ps. 45. & ser. 20 in Ps. 118.* S. Aug. *tract. 124 in Io.* & most ancient copies and seruice bookes extant in Latine. other reade, *If I vvil*: other, *If so I vvil* &c. — ∷ Hovv fevv things are vvritten of Christs actes & doctrine in cōparison of that vvhich he did and spake? and yet the Heretikes vvil needes haue al in Scripture, trusting not the Apostles ovvne preaching, or report of any thing that our Maister did or said, if it be not vvritten.

ANNOTATIONS CHAP. XXI.

17. *Feede my sheepe.*] As it vvas promised him *Mat. 16,* that the Church should be builded vpō him, and that the keies of heauen should be giuen to him: so here it is performed, & he is actually made the general Pastor and Gouerner of al Christs sheepe. For though the other ten (as Matthias and Paul also afterward) vvere Apostles, Bishops, Priests, and had authoritie to binde and loose, to remitte and reteine, to preach, baptize, and such like, as vvel as he: Yet in these things and al other gouernement, Christ vvould haue him to be their head, and they to depend of him as head of their College, and consequently of the vvhole flocke of Christ: no Apostle nor no Prince in earth

Marginal note: Peter is here made the general Pastor, and the Church is builded vpon him.

(if

(if he acknowledge him self to be a sheepe of Christ) exempted from his charge. And that Christ maketh a difference betwixt Peter and the rest, and giueth him some greater preeminence and regiment then the rest, it is plaine by that he is asked whether he loue our Lord more then the other Apostles do: Where, for equal charge no difference of loue had bene required. *To Peter* (saith S. Cyprian) *our Lord after his Resurrection said, Feede my sheepe, and builded his Church vpon him alone, and to him he giueth the charge of feeding his sheepe. For although after his Resurrection he gaue his povver alike to al, saying, As my Father sent me, so I send you, take the Holy Ghost, if you remitte to any their sinnes, they shal be remitted &c. Yet to manifest vnitie, he cōstituted one Chaire, & so disposed by his authoritie that vnitie should haue origine of one. The rest of the Apostles vvere that Peter vvas, in equal fellovvship of honour and povver, but the beginning cōmeth of vnitie: the Primacie is giuen to Peter, that the Church of Christ may be shewed to be one, & one Chaire.* S. Chrysostome also saith thus: *Why did our Lord shede his bloud? truely to redeeme those sheepe, the cure of vvhich he committed both to Peter and also to his Successors.* And a litle after, *Christ vvould haue Peter indued vvith such authoritie, and to be far aboue al his other Apostles: for he saith: Peter, dost thou loue me more then al these do? Wherevpon our Maister might haue inferred, If thou loue me Peter, vse much fasting, sleepe on the hard floure, vvatch much, be patrone to the oppressed, father to the orphans, and husband to the vvidovves: but omitting al these things, he saith, Feed my sheepe. For, al the foresaid vertues certes may be done easily of many subiects, not onely men but vvomen: but vvhen it commeth to the gouernement of the Church and committing the charge of so many soules, al vvoman kind must needes vvholy giue place to the burden and greatnes thereof, and a great number of men also.* So writeth he.

The Protestāts otherwise denying this preeminence of Peter, yet to vphold their Arch bishops, do auouch & proue it against the Puritanes.

Cypr. de unit. Ec.

Li. 2 de Sacerd.

Peters successors succede hī in vniuersal authoritie.

And because the Protestants would make the vnlearned thinke, that S. Gregorie deemed the Popes Supremacie to be wholy vnlawful and Antichristian, for that he condemneth Iohn of Constantinople for vsurping the name of vniuersal Bishop, resembling his insolence therein to the pride of Antichrist: note wel the wordes of this holy father in the very same place and Epistle against the B. of Constantinople, by which you shal easily see that to deny him to be vniuersal Bishop, is not to deny Peter or the Pope to be head of the Church, or supreme Gouerner of the same, as our Aduersaries fraudulently pretend. *It is plaine to al men*, saith he, *that euer read the Gospel, that by our Lordes mouth the charge of the vvhole Church vvas commmitted to S. Peter Prince of the Apostles. for to him it vvas said, Feed my sheepe: for him vvas the prayer made that his faith should not faile: to him vvere the keies of heauen giuen and authoritie to binde and loose: to him the cure of the Church and principality vvas deliuered: and yet he vvas not called the vniuersal Apostle. This title in deed vvas offered for the honour of S. Peter Prince of the Apostles, to the Pope of Rome by the holy Councel of Chalcedon: but none of that See did euer vse it or consent to take it.* Thus much S. Gregorie.* Who though he both practised iurisdictiō through out al Christendom, as other of that See haue euer done, and also acknowledged the Principality and Soueraintie to be in Peter and his Successors: yet would he not for iust causes vse that title subiect to vanitie & misconstructiō. But both he & al the Popes since haue rather called them selues, *Seruos seruorum Dei*, the Seruants of Gods seruants. Though the word, *vniuersal Bishop*, in that sense wherein the holy Councel of Chalcedon offered it to the See of Rome, was true and lawful. For that Councel would not haue giuen any Antichristian or vniust title to any man. Onely in the B. of Constantinople and other, which in no sense had any right to it, and who vsurped it in a very false and tyrannical meaning, it was insolent, vniust, and Antichristian. See also the Epistles of S. Leo the Great concerning his practise of vniuersal iurisdiction, though he refused the title of vniuersal Bishop. And S. Bernard (that you may better perceiue that the general charge of Christs sheepe was not onely giuen to Peters person, but also to his successors the Popes of Rome, as S. Chrysostom also before alleaged doth testifie) writeth thus to Eugenius, Thou art he to whom the keies of heauen are deliuered, & to whom the sheepe are cōmitted. there be other Porters of heauē, & other Pastors of flockes: but thou hast inherited in more glorious & differēt sort. For they haue euery one their particular flocke, but to thee al vniuersally, as one flocke to one mā, are credited: being not onely the Pastor of the sheepe, but the one Pastor of al the Pastors them selues. but thou wilt aske me how I proue that? euen by our Lordes word. for to whom of al, I say not onely Bishops, but Apostles, were the sheepe so absolutely and without limitation cōmitted? *If thou loue me Peter, feede my sheepe.* He saith not, the people of this kingdom or that citie, but, *my sheepe*, without al distinction. So S. Bernard. And herevnto may be added that the second, *feede*, is in greeke a word that signifieth withal to gouerne and rule, as *Ps. 2. Mich. 5. Mat. 2. Apoc. 2.* and therfore it is spoken of Dauid also and other temporal Gouerners (as the Hebrew word answering therevnto) in the * Scriptures very often, and the Greeke in profane writers also.

S. Gregorie though he misliked the title of *Vniuersal Bishop*, yet is most plaine both in his writings & doings for the Popes Supremacie. as also S. Leo the great.

Grego. li. 4, ep. 76.

See li. 1. ep. 72. 75, li. 2 ep. 37. 45. li. 4 ep. 93 li. 7 ep. 63.

The title of vniuersal Bishop refused, but vniuersal iurisdiction alwaies acknowledged and practised.

Bernard. li. 2, c. 8. de cōsider.

The Pope is Pastor of al Pastors.

ποίμαινε

** 2 Reg. c. 5. Ps. 77.*

18. *An other shal gird thee.*] He Prophecieth of Peters Martyrdom, and of the kinde of death which he should suffer, that was, crucifying. Which * the Heretikes fearing that it were a steppe to proue he was martyred in Rome, deny: whereas the Fathers and ancient writers are as plaine in this, as that he was at Rome. *Origen apud Euseb. li. 3 c. 1. Euseb. li. 2 c. 24. Hist. Ec. Tertul. de praescript. nu. 14. Aug. tract. 123 in Ioan. Chrysost. Beda in hunc locum.*

Beza in hunc locū.

Peter crucified at Rome.

THE

THE SVMME, AND THE ORDER OF THE EVANGELICAL HISTORIE:

gathered breifly out of al foure, euen vnto Christs Ascension.

* * *

Mt.	Mr.	Lu.	Io.		
			1	THE preface mouing the Reader to receiue CHRIST, being the æternal VVORD of God, the life and the light.	THE I PART, conteining the Infancie of Christ and the time that he liued obscurely.
		1		The Angel telleth Zacharie of the conception of Iohn Baptist, Christs Precursor: and Elizabeth conceiueth him.	
		1		The same Angel doing his message to the B. Virgin, CHRIST is incarnate in her wombe.	
		1		Our B. Ladie visiteth Elizabeth: and Iohn Baptist is borne, and circuncised.	
1				The Angel telleth Ioseph that his vvife is vvith childe by the Holy Ghost.	
1		3		The genealogie of Christ.	
		2		The birth of Christ in Bethlehem, and his circuncision.	
2				The Sages come from the East, and adore Christ.	
		2		Christ is presented in the Temple: vvhere Simeon and Anna prophecie of him.	
2				Ioseph vvith the childe and his mother, fleeth into Ægypt: and returneth to Nazareth.	
		2		Iesus being sought of his parents, is found in the Temple among the Doctors.	
3	1	3		Iohn the Baptist preacheth and baptizeth, preparing al to receiue Christ: and among other, Christ is baptized of him.	The 2 part, conteining the time of the preparatiō toward his manifestation.
4	1	4		Christ fasteth fourtie daies, and is tempted in the vvildernesse.	
			1	Iohn giueth testimonie of Christ to the legates of the Ievves, to the people, and to his ovvne disciples.	
			2	Christ vvorketh his first miracle, turning vvater into vvine at a mariage.	
			2	In the feast of Pasche he casteth out the biers and sellers in the Temple, insinuating to the Iewes his death and resurrectiō.	THE I. PASCHE.
			3	He teacheth Nicodemus by night: and baptizeth in Iurie by the ministerie of his disciples. vvhereupon a question is moued to Iohn about their tvvo baptismes.	

Mt.	Mr.	Lu.	Io.	
14	6	3		Iohn Baptist is put into prison for reprehending Herods incestuous aduoutrie.
4			4	After Iohns emprisonment, Christ returning into Galilee by Samaria, talketh vvith the Samaritane vvoman.
			4	He healeth a lordes sonne of an ague.
4	1	4		He preacheth in Galilee, and vvaxeth very famous.
4	1	5		He calleth foure disciples out of the boate, and they folovv him.
	1	4		He healeth one possessed of a diuel, in the Synagogue.
8	1	4		He cureth Simon Peters mother in lavv, & many sicke persons.
8		9		He refuseth three that offer to folovv him.
8	4	8		He appeaseth the tempest on the sea.
8	5	8		He healeth tvvo possessed of diuels in the countrie of the Gerasens, and permitteth the diuels to enter into svvine.
9	2	5		He healeth the sicke of the palsey, being let dovvne through the tiles.
				He calleth Matthevv from the custome house, and disputeth vvith Iohns disciples and the Pharisees of fasting.
9	5	8		He raiseth the Archisynagogs daughter, and cureth her that had a fluxe of bloud.
9				He healeth tvvo blinde, and one possessed.
			5	He healeth him on the Sabboth day that lay at the Probatica and had been diseased 38 yeres.
12	3	6		He confuteth the Pharisees being offended that his disciples bruised the eares of corne on the Sabboth.
12				He refelleth the Pharisees being offended because he cured the vvithered hand on the Sabboth.
5.6. 7	3	6		He chooseth the 12 Apostles: and maketh that diuine sermon called *Sermo Domini in monte, the Sermon of our Lord in the mount*, conteining the paterne of a Christian mans life.
8	1	5		He cureth a leper.
8		7		He healeth the Centurions seruant.
		7		He raiseth the vvidovves sonne at Naim.
11		7	9	Iohn sendeth out of prison his disciples vnto Christ.
		7		He forgiueth M. Magdalens sinnes, preferring her much before the Pharisee that despised her.
12	3	11		He healeth him that had a deafe and dumme deuil, and refuteth the blaspheming Pharisees.
12	3	11. 8		He preferreth the obseruers of Gods vvord before carnal mother and brethren.
13	4	8		The parable of the sovver.
13	4			The parables of the cockle, of the seede grovving vvhen men sleepe, of the mustard seede, and of the leauen.
13				The parables of the treasure hid in the field, of the pretious stone, and of the nette.
13	6	4		Teaching in Nazareth, he condemneth it of incredulitie.
9.10	6	8.		He sendeth the tvvelue Apostles to preache.
14	6	9		Iohn is beheaded, and the fame of Iesus commeth to Herods eares.
14	6	9	6	He feedeth 5000 men vvith fiue loaues.

The 3 part, from the time that he began (*Mat.* 4, 12 & 17.) to manifest him self, by preaching and miracles.

THE 2 PASCHE.

He

Mt.	Mr.	Lu.	Io.		
14	6		6	He vvalketh vpon the ſea, and ſo maketh Peter alſo to doe.	
			6	He reaſoneth of Manna, and of the true bread from heauen.	THE 3 PASCHE.
15	7			He reprehendeth the Phariſees for cauilling at his diſciples becauſe they did eate vvith vnvvaſhed handes.	
				He healeth the daughter of the vvoman of Canaan.	
	7			He cureth a man that vvas deafe and dumme.	
15	8			He feedeth 4000 vvith ſeuen loaues.	
16	8			He reiecteth the Phariſees that aſked a ſigne, and biddeth his diſciples bevvare of their leauen.	
	8			He healeth a blinde man in Bethſaida.	
16	8	9		The time that he vvil paſſe out of this vvorld, novv dravving nigh, he maketh Peter, for confeſſing him to be Chriſt, the Rocke vpon vvhich he vvil build his Church, promiſing to giue him the keies of heauen, and vvithal foretelleth, that he muſt ſuffer in Hieruſalem, and that al muſt be ready to ſuffer vvith him.	*The 4 part,* from the time that he began (*Mat.16, 21*) to foretel to his Diſciples, that he muſt goe & ſuffer in Hieruſalem.
17		9		The Transfiguration.	
				He caſteth out the diuel vvhich his diſciples could not caſt out, commending vnto them faſting and praier.	
17	9			He paieth the didrachmes for him and Peter, after that Peter had found a ſtater in the fiſhes mouth.	
18	9	9		His diſciples contending for Superioritie, he teacheth humilitie.	
18	9			He threateneth the ſcandalizers of litle ones.	
18				He teacheth vs to forgiue our brother ſinning againſt vs.	
19	10	9	7	Leauing Galilee he goeth into Iurie, and the Samaritanes vvil not receiue him.	*The 5 part,* of his going into Ievvrie toward his Paſſion.
		17		In that iourney he healeth the ten lepers.	
			7	He teacheth in the Temple in the feaſt of Scenopégia, that is, of Tabernacles.	
			8	He abſolueth the vvoman taken in aduoutrie, teacheth in the Temple, and goeth out of their handes that vvould haue ſtoned him.	
			9	He reſtoreth ſight to him that vvas borne blinde.	
			10	He reaſoneth of the true Paſtor and his ſheepe.	
		10		He ſendeth the 70 diſciples, and they returne. The parable of the Samaritane and the vvounded man. Martha entertaineth Ieſus.	
		11		He teacheth the maner and force of praier, and reprehendeth the prepoſterous cleanneſſe of the Phariſees.	
		12		He teacheth not to feare them that kil the body onely, to caſt avvay the care of riches by the parable of him that thought his barnes to litle, and that the faithful ſeruant vvil alwaies expect the comming of his lord and maiſter.	
		13		He threateneth them, vnles they doe penance, ſhewing Gods patience by the fruitles figtree that vvas ſuffered to ſtand one yere more. He healeth the crooked vvoman, teacheth the vvay to heauen to be narrovv.	
		14		He healeth him that had a dropſie, on the Sabboth: and teacheth them to renounce al things in compariſon of him.	

Mt.	Mr.	Lu.	Io.		
			10	In the feast of Dedication he goeth out of their handes that vvould haue stoned him.	
		15		The parables of the lost sheepe, of the grote, and of the prodigal sonne.	
		16		The parable of the vniust bailife.	
19	10	16		Of the indissolubilitie of matrimonie.	
		16		The riche glutton and Lazarus.	
		17		Vvo to scandalizers. The force of faith euen to the mouing of trees vvith a vvord.	
		18		Of the Pharisee and the Publicane that vvent to pray.	
19	10	16		He imposeth or laieth his handes vpon litle children, and exhorteth a yong riche man to forsake al and become perfect.	
20				The parable of the vvorkemen hired into the vineyard.	
			11	He raiseth Lazarus, and the Iewes cōsult hovv to destroy him.	
20	10	19		He foretelleth his death, and denieth the request of Zebedees tvvo sonnes, asking the tvvo cheefe places about him.	
		18		He healeth a blinde man before his entring into Iericho.	
		19		Zachæus the Publicane entertaineth Christ. The parable of the ten poundes deliuered to ten seruants.	
20		10		He healeth tvvo blinde men as he goeth out of Iericho.	
26	14	12		At a supper in Bethánia, Marie povvred ointment vpon him.	
21	11	19	12	Riding vpon an asse he entreth gloriously into Hierusalem.	PALME sunday.
21			12	He healeth the lame and the blinde, and Gentiles desire to see him.	*The 6 part,* conteining the holy Weeke of his Passion in Hierusalem.
21	11	19		He curseth the figtree, and casteth the biers and sellers out of the Temple.	
21	11	19 20		To his enemies the Ievves, he auoucheth his povver by Iohns Baptisme vvhich vvas of God, and foretelleth their reprobation, vvith the Gentils vocation in their place, by parables: as the parable of the tvvo sonnes, the one promising to doe, the other doing his fathers commaundement.	
21	12	20		The parable of the vineyard let out to husbandmen that killed both the seruants and the sonne sent to require fruite.	
22				The parable of the king that made a mariage for his sonne, inuiting ghests to the feast, and they vvould not come.	
22	12	20		He ansvvereth their question of paying tribute to Cæsar, and the Sadducees question of the Resurrection.	
22	12			He ansvvereth the Pharisees question, of the greatest commaundement.	
22	12	20		He putteth them to silence vvith this question concerning CHRIST, hovv he could be Dauids sonne.	
23	12	20		He biddeth them doe as the Scribes teach, but not as they doe.	
[illegible]	12	21		He extolleth and preferreth the poore vvidovves offering.	
24	13	21		He foretelleth to some of his Disciples, the destruction of the Temple and of Hierusalem: and by that occasion, vvhat things shalbe before the consummation of the vvorld, and Antichrist in the consummation, and then incontinent Domesday, vvarning vs to prepare our selues against his comming.	TVESDAY night.
25				By the parable of the ten Virgins, & the parable of the talents,	

he

Mt.	Mr.	Lu.	Io.		
				he shevveth, hovv it shal be at Domesday vvith the Faithful that prepare, and that prepare not them selues: and vvithout parables, that they vvhich doe not good vvorkes, shal be damned.	
26	14	22		Iudas bargaineth vvith the Ievves to betray him. and tvvo of his disciples prepare the Paschal lambe.	TENEBRE vvenesday.
			13	At the supper he vvasheth his Apostles feete.	MAVNDY thursday.
26	14	22		He instituteth the Sacrifice of his body and bloud in the B. Sacrament.	
26	14	22	13	He foretelleth that one of the Tvvelue shal betray him (appeasing their contention for the superioritie) and that they shal al deny him.	*The 4 Pasche.*
			14	His sermon after supper.	
			17	His prayer to his father.	Al THVRSDAY night & GOOD FRIDAY.
26 27	14 15	22 23	18 19	The storie of his Passion and burial, from thursday at night, til the next day at euentide.	
28	16	24	20	He riseth the third day,	EASTER DAY.
	16		20	appeareth first to Marie Magdalene.	
28				Then to the other vvomen.	
		24		Then to Peter. ver. 34. then to the tvvo disciples going into Emmaus. ver. 15.	
	16	24	20	Then to the disciples gathered together in a house at Hierusalem, vvhen he entred the doores being shut, and gaue them povver to remit and reteine sinnes.	
			20	Then, vpon Lovv-Sunday, to the disciples likevvise gathered together, and Thomas among them.	LOVV SVNday.
			21	Then, at the sea of Tiberias, to Peter & the rest that were fishing. vvhere he committeth his sheepe to Peter.	
28	16			Then, to the disciples vpon a mount in Galilee: giuing them commission to preache and baptize through out the vvhole vvorld.	
		24		Then in Bethánia, vvhere he promiseth to send the holy Ghost (bidding them tarie in the meane time in Hierusalem)	ASCENSION day.
	16	24		and so blessing them, Ascendeth into heauen.	

THE ARGVMENT OF THE ACTES OF THE APOSTLES.

HE Gospel hauing shevved, hovv the Ievves most impiously reiected Christ (as also Moyses and the Prophets had foretold of them:) and therefore deserued to be reiected themselues also of him: novv folovveth this booke of the Actes of the Apostles (* *vvritten by S. Luke in Rome the fourth yere of Nero, An. Dom. 61) and shevveth, hovv notvvithstanding their desertes, Christ of his mercy (as the Prophets also had foretold of him) offered him selfe vnto that vnvvorthy people, yea after that they had Crucified him, sending vnto them his tvvelue Apostles to moue them to penance, and so by* Baptisme *to make them of his Church: and vvhiles al the Tvvelue vvere so occupied about the Ievves: hovv of a persecuting Ievve he made an extraordinarie Apostle (vvho vvas S. Paul) and to auoide the scãdal of the Ievves (to vvhom onely him selfe likevvise for the same cause had preached) sent him, and not any of his* Twelue *by and by, who were his knovven Apostles, vnto the Gentiles, vvho neuer afore had heard of Christ, and vvere vvorshippers of many Gods, to moue them also (for, that likevvise the* Prophets *had foretold) to faith and penance, and so by* Baptisme *to make them of his Church: and hovv the incredulous* Ievves *euery vvhere resisted the same Apostle and his preaching to the Gentiles, persecuting him and seeking his death, and neuer ceasing vntil he fel into the handes of the Gentils: that so (as not onely he euery vvhere, but also the Prophets afore him, and Christ had foretold) the Gospel might be taken avvay from them, and giuen to the Gentiles: euen from* Hierusalem *(vvhose reprobation also by name had been often foretold) the headcitie of the* Iewes, *vvhere it began, translated to Rome the headcitie of the Gentiles. Al this vvil be euident by the partes of the booke: vvhich may be these sixe.*

* Hier. in Catal.

Act. 13, 46. 18, 6. 19, 9. 28, 28. Mat. 21, 23. Esa. 1. Luc. 13, 33.

First, hovv Christ Ascending in the sight of his Disciples, promised vnto them the Holy ghost, fortelling that of him they should receiue strength, and so begin his Church in Hierusalem: and from thence dilate it into al that Countrie, that is into al Iurie: yea and into Samaria also, yea into al Nations of the Gentiles, be they neuer so far of. You shal receiue (*saith he*) the vertue of the Holy ghost cõming vpon you: and you shal be witnesses vnto me in Hierusalem, & in al Iurie, and Samaria, and euen to the vtmost of the earth. *Chap. 1.*

Secondly, the beginning of the Church in Hierusalem, accordingly. Chap. 2.

Thirdly, the propagation of it consequently into al Iurie, and also to Samaria. Chap. 8.

Fourthly, the propagation of it to the Gentiles also. Chap. 10.

Fifthly, the taking of it avvay from the obstinate Ievves, and geuing of it to the Gentiles,

Gentiles, by the ministerie of S. Paul and S. Barnabee. Chap. 13.

Sixthly, of taking it avvay from Hierusalem it selfe, the headcitie of the Ievves, and sending it (as it vvere) to Rome the headcitie of the Gentiles, and that, in their persecuting of Paul so far, **that he appealed to Cæsar and so deliuering him after a sort vnto the Romanes: as they had* * *before deliuered to them also Christ him selfe. vvhereas S. Peters first cōming thither, vvas vpon an other occasion, as shalbe said anone. Of vvhich Romanes and Gentiles therfore, the same S. Paul being novv come to Rome (the last Chap. of the Actes) foretelleth the obstinat Ievves there, saying:* Et ipsi audient. *You vvil not heare, but,* they vvil heare. *that so the prediction of Christ aboue rehearsed might be fulfilled:* And euen to the vtmost of the earth. *And there doth S. Luke end the booke, not caring to tel so much as the fulfilling of that vvhich our Lord had foretold (Act. 27, 24) to S. Paul,* Thou must appeare before Cæsar. *because his purpose vvas no more but to shevv the nevv Hierusalem of the Christians, vvhere Christ vvould place the cheefe seate of his Church, as also in deede the Fathers and al other Catholikes haue in al ages looked thither, vvhen they vvere in any great doubt: no lesse then the Ievves to Hierusalem, as they vvere appointed in the old Testament. Deut. 17, 8.*

Act. 25, 11.
Luc. 23, 1.
Act. 28, 28.

And so this Booke doth shevv the true Church, as plainely, as the Gospel doth shevv the true Christ, vnto al that do not vvilfully shut their ovvne eies. to vvit, this to be the true Church, vvhich beginning visibly at Hierusalem, vvas taken from the Ievves, and translated to the Gentils (and namely to Rome) continuing visibly, and visibly to continue hereafter also, Vntil the fulnes of the Gentiles shal be come in: *that then also* Al Israël may be saued. *and then is come the end of the vvorld. For so did Christ most plainely foretel vs:* This Gospel of the Kingdom shalbe preached in the vvhole world, for a testimonie to al Nations. and then shal come the consummation. *For the conuersion of vvhich Nations and accomplishing the fulnes of al Gentiles, the foresaid Church Catholike, being mindful of her office,* to be Christes witnes euen to the vtmost of the earth, *doth at this present (as alvvaies) send preachers to conuert and make them also Christians: vvhereas the protestants and* * *al other Heretikes do nothing els but subuert such as before vvere Christians.*

Rom. 11, 25.
Mat. 24, 14.
Tertul. de præsc.

And this being the Summe and scope of this Booke, thus to giue vs historically a iust sight of the fulfilling of the Prophets & Christes prediction about the Church: it is not to be marueiled at, vvhy it telleth not of S. Peters cōming to Rome: considering that his first cōming thither, vvas not, as S. Paules vvas, by the Ievves deliuerie of him, working so to their ovvne reprobatiō, but vpō another occasion, to vvit, to confound Simon Magus. Eus. Hist. li. 2. c. 12. 13. *For vvho also seeth not, that it maketh no mention of his preaching to any Gentiles at al, those fevv onely Act. 10 excepted, vvho vvere the first, and therefore (lest the Gentiles should seeme lesse cared for of God, then the Ievves) Peter being the Head of al, vvas elected of God, to incorporate them into the church, as before he had done the Ievves.* God *(saith he)* among vs chose, that by my mouth the Gentiles should heare the vvord of the Gospel, and beleeue. *and S. Iames thereupon:* Simon hath told how God first visited to take of the Gentiles a people to his name. *But othervvise (I say) here is no mention of Peters preaching to any Gentiles: no nor of the other eleuen Apostles. Vvil any man therfore inferre, that neither Peter, nor the other Eleuen preached to any Nation or citie of the Gentiles? No. the meaning of the Holy ghost vvas not to vvrite al the Actes of al the Apostles, no nor the preaching of Peter and his, to the Gentiles, but onely to the Ievves: thereby to set out vnto the vvorld, the great mercy of Christ tovvard those vnvvorthy*

Act. 15, 7.
Act. 15, 14.

Ievves

Ievves,and consequently their most vvorthy reprobation for cōtemning such grace and mercy. as also on the other side to shevv, hovv readily the Gentiles in so many Nations, vvere conuerted by one Apostle onely, vvho From Hierusalem euen to Illyricum replenished the Gospel of Christ. *And this parting of the vvorke so made by S. Peter vvith the rest, doth S. Paul himselfe touche:* That vve vnto the Gentiles, and they vnto the Circuncision. *Neuerthelesse before his cōming to Rome, not onely vvas the Church come to Rome (as it is euident Act. the last chap.) there plāted by S. Peter and others (as likevvise by S. Peter it vvas planted in the first Gentils, before that S. Paul began the taking of it avvay from the multitude of the Ievves, and the translating of it to the multitude of the Gentils) but also so notable vvas the same Church of Rome, that S. Paul vvriting his Epistle to the Romanes, before he came thither, saith:* Your faith is renovvmed in the vvhole vvorld. *and therefore they vvith the rest of the Gentiles, be that Nation vvhereof Christ told the Ievves, saying:* The Kingdom of God shal be taken avvay from you, & shal be giuē to a Nation yelding the fruites thereof.

Rom. 15, 19.
Gal. 2, 9.
Rom. 1, 8.
Mat. 21, 43.

As before vve noted the Gospels, as they are read both at Mattins and Masse, through out the yere, in their conuenient time and place: so the bookes folovving (as also the bookes of the old Testament) are read in the said Seruice of the Church, for Epistles and Lessons, in their time & place, as hereafter shal be noted in euery of them. *See the very same order and custome of the primitiue Church, in S. Ambrose ep. 33. S. Augustine Serm. de Tempore 139, 140, 141, 144. S. Leo Ser. 2 & 4 de Quadrag. & Ser. 13 & 19 de Paß. Domini. S. Gregorie in his 40 homilies vpon the Gospels.*

THE

The CHVRCH readeth this booke at Mattins from Low Sũday vnto the 3 Sunday after Easter: euen as in S. Augustines time. See serm. 83 & 93 de Diuersis. to. 10.

THE ACTES OF THE APOSTLES.

The 1. part. The expectatiõ of the Holy Ghost betwene the Ascensiõ of Christ, and the beginning of the Church.

CHAP. I.

Christ novv ready to ascend, biddeth the Apostles to expect the Holy Ghost vvhich he had promised, foretelling vvhere (being strengthened by him) they should begin his Church, and hovv far they should cary it. 9 After his Ascension they are vvarned by tvvo Angels to set their mindes vpon his second comming. 14 In the daies of their expectation, 15 Peter beginneth to execute his vicarship, giuing instruction and order, by vvhich Mathias is elected Apostle in the place of Iudas.

The Epistle at Masse vpon Ascension day.

1 THE * first treatise I made of ∷ al things, O Theophilus, vvhich IESVS began 2 to doe and to teache, † vntil the day vvherein" giuing commaundement by the holy Ghost to the Apostles vvhõm 3 he chose, he vvas assumpted: † to vvhõ he shevved also him self aliue after his passion in many arguments, for fourtie daies appearing to them, & speaking of the kingdom of God. 4 † And eating vvith them, * he commaunded them, that they should not depart from Hierusalem, but should expect the promisse of the Father, vvhich you * haue heard (saith he) by 5 my mouth: † for Iohn in deede baptized vvith ∷ vvater, but * you shal be ∷ baptized vvith the holy Ghost after these 6 fevv daies. † They therfore that vvere assembled, asked him, saying, Lord, whether at this time vvilt thou restore the king-7 dom to Israel? † but he said to them, " It is not for you to knovv times or moments, vvhich the Father hath put in his 8 ovvne povver: † but you shal receiue the * vertue of the holy Ghost comming vpon you, and you shal be vvitnesses vnto me in Hierusalem, and in al Ievvrie, and Samaria, and 9 euen to the vtmost of the earth. † And * vvhen he had said these things, in their sight he vvas eleuated: and a cloud recei-10 ued him out of their sight. † And vvhen they beheld him going into heauen, behold tvvo men stoode beside them in 11 vvhite garments, † vvho also said, Ye men of Galilee, vvhy

Lu. 1, 3.

Lu. 24, 49.

Io. 14, 26.

Lu. 3, 16.

Lu. 24, 49. Act. 2, 1.

Mar. 16, 19. Lu. 24, 51.

∷ Not al particularly, (for the other Euangelists write diuers thinges not touched by him) but al the principal and most necessarie things.

∷ Iohns Baptisme gaue not the Holy Ghost.

∷ The aboundãt powring of the Holy Ghost vpon them on Whitsunday, he calleth baptisme.

:: This visible companie was the true Churche of Christ, which he left, & commaũded to keepe together til the cõming of the Holy Ghost, by hĩ to be further informed & furnished to gaine al natiõs to the same Societie.

stand you looking into heauen? This IESVS vvhich is "assumpted from you into heauen, shal so come as you haue seen him going into heauen. ⁜

† Then they returned to Hierusalem from the mount that 12 is called Oliuet, vvhich is by Hierusalem, distant a Sabboths iourney. † And vvhen they vvere entred in, they vvent vp 13 into an vpper chamber, vvhere abode :: Peter & Iohn, Iames and Andrevv, Philippe and Thomas, Bartholomevv and Mathevv, Iames of Alphæus and Simon Zelótes, and Iude of Iames. † Al these vvere perseuéring vvith one minde in 14 praier vvith the :: vvomen and "MARIE the mother of IESVS, and his brethren.

:: The Heretikes, some in the text, other in the margẽt, traslate, *Wiues*, to wit, of the Apostles, most impudently, knowĩg in their cõsciences that he meaneth the Maries & other holy women that folowed Christ. as *Lu.* 8, 2. 24, 10. See Beza & the Engl. Bible 1579.

a The Epistle vpõ S. Mathias day *Febr.* 24.

† a In those daies "Peter rising vp in the middes of the bre- 15 thren, said: (and the multitude of persons together, vvas almost an hundred and tvventie) † You men, brethren, 16 the * scripture must be fulfilled vvhich the holy Ghost spake before by the mouth of Dauid concerning Iudas, vvho vvas the * captaine of them that apprehended IESVS: † vvho 17 vvas numbred among vs and obteined the lot of this ministerie. † And he in deede hath possessed a * field of the revvard 18 of iniquitie, and being hanged he burst in the middes, and al his bovvels gushed out. † And it vvas made notorious to 19 al the inhabitants of Hierusalem: so that the same field vvas called in their tonge, *Hacel-dema*, that is to say, the field of bloud. † For it [illegible] vvritten in the booke of Psalmes. *Be their habitation* 20 *made desert, and be there none to dvvel in it. And his Bishoprike let an other take.* † Therfore, of these men that haue assembled vvith vs, 21 al the time that our Lord IESVS vvent in and vvent out among vs, † beginning from the baptisme of Iohn vntil the 22 day vvherein he vvas assumpted from vs, :: there must one of these be made a vvitnes vvith vs of his resurrection.

Ps. 40, 9 *Io.* 13, 18

Luc. 22, 47. *Io.* 18, 3.

Mt. 27, 5. 7.

Psa. 68, 26.

Ps. 108, 8.

:: No smal mysterie, that the number of the twelue Apostles must needes be made vp againe.

† And they appointed tvvo, Ioseph, vvho vvas called 23 Bársabas, vvho vvas surnamed Iustus: and Mathias. † And 24 praying they said, Thou Lord that knovvest the harts of al men, shevv of these tvvo, one, vvhom thou hast chosen, † to 25 take the place of this ministerie and Apostleship, from the vvhich Iudas hath preuaricated that he might goe to his ovvne place. † And they gaue them "lottes, and the lot fel 26 vpon Mathias, and he vvas numbered vvith the eleuen Apostles. ⁜

ANNOT.

ANNOTATIONS
CHAP. I.

2. *Giuing commaundement.*] He meaneth the power giuen them to preach, to baptize, to remit sinnes, and generally the whole commission and charge of gouernement of the Church after him and in his name, steede, and right. the which Regiment was giuen them together with the Holy Ghost to assist them therein for euer.

7. *It is not for you.*] It is not for vs, nor needful for the Church, to know the times & moment of the world, the comming of Antichrist, and such other Gods secretes. This is ynough in that case, to be assured that Christs faith shal be preached, and the Church spred through out al Nations, the Holy Ghost concurring continually with the Apostles and their Successors for the same.

The times and moments of things to come pertaine not to vs.

11. *Assumpted from you.*] By this visible Ascending of Christ to heauen and like returne from thence to iudgement, the Heretikes do incredulously argue, him not to be in the Sacrament. But let the faithful rather giue eare to S. Chrysostome saying thus: *O miracle, he that sitteth vvith the Father in heauen aboue, at the very same time is handled of men beneath. Christ ascending to heauen, both hath his flesh vvith him, and left it vvith vs beneath. Elias being taken vp, left to his Disciple his cloke only: but the Sonne of man ascending left his ovvne flesh to vs. Li. 3 de Sacerd. Ho. 2 ad po. Ant. in fine. Ho. de diuit. & paup. in fine.*

Christ is ascended, and yet really in the B. Sacrament.

14. MARIE *the mother of* IESVS.] This is the last mention that is made in holy Scripture, of our B. Lady. for though she were ful of al diuine wisedom, and opened (no doubt) vnto the Euangelistes and other writers of holy Scriptures, diuerse of Christs actions, speaches, and mysteries, whereof she had both experimental and reuealed knowledge: Yet for that she was a woman, and the humblest creature liuing, and the paterne of al order and obedience, it pleased not God that there should be any further note of her life, doings, or death, in the Scriptures. She liued the rest of her time with the Christians (as here she is peculiarly named and noted among them) and specially with S. Iohn the Apostle,* to whom our Lord recommended her. Who prouided for her al necessaries, her spouse Ioseph (as it may be thought) being deceased before. The common opinion is that she liued 63 yeres in al. At the time of her death, (as S. Denys first, & after him S. Damascene *de dormit. Deipara.* writeth,) al the Apostles then dispersed into diuers nations to preache the Gospel, were miraculously brought together (sauing S. Thomas who came the third day after) to Hierusalem, to honour her diuine departure and funeral, as the said S. Denys witnesseth. Who saith that him self, S. Timothee, and S. Hierotheus were present: testifying also of his owne hearing, that both before here death and after for three daies, not onely the Apostles and other holy men present, but the Angels also and Powers of heauen did sing most melodious Hymnes. They buried her sacred body in Gethsémani. but for S. Thomas sake, who desired to see and to reuerence it, they opened the sepulcher the third day, and finding it void of the holy body, but excedingly fragrant, they returned, assuredly deeming that her body was assumpted into heauen. as the Church of God holdeth, being most agreable to the singular priuilege of the mother of God, and therfore celebrateth most solemnely the day of her Assumption. And that is consonant not onely to the said S. Denys, and S. Damascene, but to holy Athanasius also, who auoucheth the same, *Serm. in Euang. de Deipara.* of which Assumption of her body, S. Bernard also wrote fiue notable sermons extant in his workes.

Our B. LADY.

Her life.

Io. 19, 26. 27.

Dionys. ep. ad Timotheum.

Her death.

Her ASSVMPTION.

But neither these holy fathers, nor the Churches tradition and testimonie, do beare any sway now a daies with the Protestants, that haue abolished this her greatest feast of her Assumption. Who of reason should at the least celebrate it as the day of her death, as they doe of other Saincts. For though they beleeue not that her body is assumpted, yet they wil not (we trow) deny that she is dead, and her soule in glorie: neither can they aske scriptures for that, no more then they require for the deathes of Peter, Paul, Iohn, and other, vvhich be not mentioned in scriptures & yet are stil celebrated by the Protestants. But concerning the B. Virgin MARIE, they haue blotted out also both her Natiuitie, and her Conception: so as it may be thought the Diuel beareth a special malice to this woman whose seede brake his head. For as for the other two daies of her Purification & Annunciation, they be not proper to our Lady, but the one to Christs Conception, the other to his Presentation. so that she by this meanes shal haue no festiuitie at al.

The Protestãts haue no feast of her at al, as they haue of other Saincts.

But contrariwise, to consider how the auncient Church and fathers esteemed, spake, and wrote of this excellent vessel of grace, may make vs detest these mens impietie, that can not abide the praises of her *whom al generations should call blessed, and that esteeme her honours a derogatiō to her sonne. Some of their speaches we wil set downe, that al men may see, that we neither praise her, nor pray to her, more amply then they did. S. Athanasius in the place alleaged, after he had declared how al the Angelical spirits and euery order of them honoured and praised her with the AVE, wherewith S. Gabriel saluted her: We also, saith he, of al degrees vpon the earth

*Lu. 1, 48.

How the Primitiue Church & auncient fathers honoured our B. Lady.

S. Athanasius.

S. Ephrem.

extol thee with loude voice, saying, *Aue gratia plena* &c. *Haile ful of grace, our Lord is vvith thee pray for vs ô Maistresse, and Lady, and Queene, and mother of God.* Most holy and auncient Ephrem, also in a special oration made in praise of our Lady, saith thus in diuerse places thereof, *Intemerata Deipara* &c. *Mother of God vndefiled, Queene of al, the hope of them that despaire, my lady most glorious, higher then the heauenly spirits, more honorable then the Cherubins, holier then the Seraphins, and vvithout comparison more glorious thē the supernal hostes, the hope of the fathers, the glorie of the Prophets, the praise of the Apostles.* And a litle after. *Virgo ante partum, in partu, & post partum. by thee vve are reconciled to Christ my God, thy sonne: thou art the helper of sinners, thou the hauen for them that are tossed vvith stormes, the solace of the vvorld, the deliuerer of the emprisoned, the helpe of orphans, the redemption of captiues.* And afterward, *Vouchsafe me thy seruant to praise thee. Haile lady* MARIE *ful of grace, haile Virgin most blessed among vvomen.* And much more in that sense which were to long to repeate.

S. Cyril.

S. Cyril hath the like wonderful speaches of her honour, *hom. 6. contra Nestorium. Praise and glorie be to thee ô holy Trinitie: to thee also be praise, holy mother of God. for thou art the pretious pearle of the vvorld, thou the candel of vnquencheable light, the crovvne of Virginitie, the scepter of the Catholike faith. By thee the Trinitie is glorified and adored in al the vvorld: by thee heauen reioyceth, Angels and Archangels are glad, diuels are put to flight, and man is called againe to heauen, and euery creature that vvas held vvith the errour of Idols, is turned to the knowledge of the truth: by thee Churches are fouded through the World: thee being their helper, the Gentiles come to penance.* and much more which we omit. Likewise the Greeke

The Greeke Liturgies of S. Iames, S. Basil, S. Chrysostom.

Liturgies or Masses of S. Iames, S. Basil, and S. Chrysostom, make most honorable mention of our B. Lady, praying vnto her, saluting her with the Angelical hymne, *Aue Maria*, and vsing these speaches, *Most holy, vndefiled, blessed aboue al, our Queene, our Lady, the mother of God,* MARIE, *a virgin for euer, the sacred arke of Christs Incarnation, broder then the heauens that didst beare thy creatour, holy mother, of vnspeakable light, vve magnifie thee vvith Angelical hymnes. al things passe vnderstanding, al things are glorious in thee ô mother of God. by thee the mysterie before vnknovven to the Angels, is made manifest and reuealed to them on the earth. thou art more honorable then the Cherubins, and more glorious then the Seraphins. to thee, O ful of grace, al creatures, both men and Angels doe gratulate and reioyce: glorie be to thee, which art a sanctified temple, a spiritual paradise, the glorie of virgins, of vvhom God tooke flesh and made thy vvombe to be his throne.* &c.

S. Augustine.

And S. Augustine *Serm. 18 de Sanctis to. 10:* or (as some thinke) S. Fulgentius: *O blessed* MARIE, *Who can be able vvorthily to praise or thanke thee, receiue our praiers, obtaine vs our requestes, for thou art the* * *special hope of sinners, by thee vve hope for pardon of our sinnes, & in thee, ô most blessed, is the expectation of our revvardes.* And then folow these wordes now vsed in the Churches seruice: *Sancta Maria succurre miseris, iuua pusillanimes, refoue flebiles, ora pro populo, interueni pro clero, intercede pro deuoto fœmineo sexu. Sentiant omnes tuum iuuamen, quicunque celebrant tuam commemorationem. Pray thou continually for the people of God, vvhich didst deserue to beare the redeemer of the vvorld, Who liueth and reigneth for euer.* S. Damascene also *ser.* de dormitione Deiparæ. *Let vs crie vvith Gabriel, Aue gratia plena, Haile ful of grace, Haile sea of ioy that can not be emptied, haile the* * *onely ease of greefes, haile holy virgin, by vvhom death vvas expelled, and life brought in.* See S. Irenæus li. 3 c. 33. and li. 5 circa medium, & S. Augustine *de fide & Symbolo. & de agone Christiano.* Where they declare how both the sexes concurre to our saluation, the man and the woman, Christ and our Lady, as Adam and Eue both were the cause of our fall. though Adam far more then his wife, and so Christ far more excellently and in an other sort then our Lady: Who (though his mother) yet is but his creature and handmaid, him self being truely both God and man. In al which places alleaged & * many other like to these, if it please the reader to see and read, and make his owne eies witnesses, he shal perceiue that there is much more said of her, and to her, then we haue here recited, and that the very same or the like speaches and termes were vsed then, that the Church vseth now, in the honour and inuocation of the B. Virgin: to the confusion of al those that wilfully wil not vnderstand in what sense al such speaches are applied vnto her. to wit, either because of her praier and intercession for vs, whereby she is our hope, our refuge, our aduocate &c. or because she brought forth the author of our redemption and saluation, whereby she is the mother of mercie, and grace, and life, and whatsoeuer goodnes we receiue by Christ.

Sancta MARIA succurre miseris, &c.

S. Damascene.

S. Irenæus.

As Adam and Eue, so Christ & our Lady.

The meaning of the titles and termes giuen to our B. Lady.

* *unica spes*

* *unicum leuamen*

See S. Greg. Nazian. in fi. Trag. Christus patiens.

Peter beginneth to practise his Primacie.

15. Peter rising vp.) Peter in the meane time practised his Superioritie in the cōpanie or Church, publishing an election to be made of one to supply Iudas roome. Which Peter did not vpon commaundement of Christ written, but by suggestion of Gods Spirit, and by vnderstanding the Scriptures of the old Testament to that purpose: the sense whereof Christ had opened to the Apostles before his departure, though in more ful maner afterward at the sending of the Holy Ghost. And this acte of Peter in prescribing to the Apostles and the rest, this election, and the maner thereof, is so euident for his Supremacie, that * the Aduersaries confesse here that he was, *Antistes*, the cheefe and Bishop of this whole College and companie.

Beza in no. Test. Græcolan. 1565.

Casting of lottes.

26. Lottes.] When the euent or fall of the lot is not expected of Diuels, nor of the starres, nor of any force of fortune, but looked and praied for to be directed by God and his holy Saincts: then may lottes be vsed lawfully. And sometimes to discerne betwixt two things mere indifferent, they be necessarie, as S. Augustine teacheth *ep. 180 ad Honoratum.*

CHAP. II.

The Holy Ghost comming to the Faithful vpon vvhitsunday, 5 Ievves in Hierusalem of al Nations do vvonder to heare them speake al tongues. 14 And Peter to the deriders declareth, that it is not drunkennes, but the Holy Ghost vvhich Ioel did prophecie of, vvhich IESVS (Whom they crucified) being noW risen againe and ascended (as he sheWeth also out of the Scriptures) hath poWred out from heauen, cōcluding therfore that he is CHRIST, and they most horrible murderers. 37 Whereat they being compuncte, and submitting them selues, he telleth them that they must be baptized, and then they also shal receiue the same Holy Ghost, as being promised to al the baptized. 41 And so 3000 are baptized that very day. 42 Whose godly exercises are here reported, and also their liuing in state of perfection. The Apostles Worke many miracles, and God daily increaseth the number of the Church.

The 2 part. THE comming of the Holy Ghost and beginning of the Church in Hierusalem.

The Epistle vpō Whitsunday.

1 AND vvhen the daies of " Pentecost vvere accomplished, they vvere al together in 2 one place: † and sodenly there vvas made a sound from heauen, as of a vehemēt vvinde cōming, & it filled the whole house vvhere they vvere sitting. 3 † And there appeared to them parted tonges as it were * of fire, and it sate vpon euery one of them: 4 † and they vvere " al replenished vvith the * HOLY GHOST, and they began to speake vvith diuerse tonges, according as the HOLY GHOST gaue them to speake.

Act. 1,4
Mt. 3,11.
Io. 7,39.

5 † And there vvere dvvelling at Hierusalē Ievves, deuout 6 men of euery nation that is vnder heauen. † And vvhen this voice vvas made, the multitude came together, and vvas astonied in minde, because euery man heard them speake in his 7 ovvne tongue. † And they vvere al amased, and marueled 8 saying, Are not, lo, al these that speake, Galilęans, † and hovv \` haue vve heard' eche man our ovvne tongue vvherein 9 vve vvere borne? † Parthians, and Medians, and Elamites, and that inhabite Mesopotámia, Ievvrie, and Cappadocia, Pontus, 10 and Asia, † Phrygia, and Pamphilia, Ægypt and the partes of 11 Lybia that is about Cyrénee, and strangers of Rome, † Ievves also, and Proselytes, Cretensians, and Arabians: Vve \` haue heard' them speake in our ovvne tonges the great vvorkes 12 of God. ⊣ † And they vvere al astonied, and marueled, saying 13 one to an other, Vvhat meaneth this? † But others deriding said, That these are ful of nevv vvine.

do vve heare.
do heare

a The lesson before the Epistle on Imber Wenesday in Whitsonweeke.

14 † a But :: Peter standing vvith the Eleuen, lifted vp his voice, and spake to them, Ye men, Ievves, and al you that dvvel in Hierusalem, be this knovven to you, and vvith your 15 eares receiue my vvordes. † For these are not drunke, as you

:: Peter the head of the rest and now newly replenished with al knowledge and fortitude, maketh the first Sermon.

ſuppoſe, vvhereas it is the third houre of the day: † But this is it that vvas ſaid by the Prophet Ioël, † *And it ſhal be, in the laſt daies (ſaith our Lord) of my Spirit I vvil povvre out vpon al fleſh: and your ſonnes and your daughters ſhal prophecie, and your yong men ſhal ſee viſions, and your auncients ſhal dreame dreames.* † *And vpon my ſeruants truely, and vpon my handmaides vvil I povvre out in thoſe daies, of my Spirit, and they ſhal prophecie:* † *and I vvil giue vvonders in the heauen aboue, and ſignes in the earth beneath, bloud, and fire, and vapour of ſmoke.* † *The ſunne ſhal be turned into darkenes, and the moone into bloud, before the great and manifeſt day of our Lord doth come:* † *And it ſhal be, euery one vvhoſoeuer calleth vpon the name of our Lord, ſhal be ſaued.* ⸥ 16 17 18 19 20 21

Ioël. 2, 28.

† Ye men of Iſraël heare theſe vvordes, IESVS of Nazareth a man approued of God among you, by miracles and vvonders and ſignes vvhich God did by him in the middes of you, as you knovv: † this ſame, "by the determinate counſel and preſcience of God being deliuered, you by the handes of vvicked men haue crucified and ſlaine. † vvhom God hath raiſed vp" looſing the ſorovves of hel, according as it vvas impoſſible that he ſhould be holden of it. † For Dauid ſaith concerning him, *I foreſavv the Lord in my ſight alvvaies: becauſe he is at my right hand that I be not moued.* † *For this, my hart hath been glad and my tongue hath reioyced: moreouer my fleſh alſo ſhal reſt in hope.* † *Becauſe thou vvilt not leaue "my ſoul ∵ in hel, nor giue thy Holy one to ſee ∵ corruption.* † *Thou haſt made knovven to me the vvaies of life: thou ſhalt make me ful of ioyfulnes vvith thy face.* † Ye men, brethren, let me boldly ſpeake to you of the Patriarch Dauid: that * he died, and vvas buried: and his ſepulchre is vvith vs vntil this preſent day. † Vvhereas therfore he vvas a Prophet, and knevv that by an othe *God had ſvvorne to him that of the fruite of his loynes there ſhould ſit vpon his ſeate:* † forſeeing he ſpake of the reſurrection of Chriſt, for neither vvas he left in hel, neither did his fleſh ſee corruption. † This IESVS hath God raiſed againe, vvhereof al vve are vvitneſſes. 22 23 24 25 26 27 28 29 30 31 32

∵ Who but an infidel (ſaith S. Auguſtine) wil deny Chriſt to haue deſcended to Hel? *ep. 99.*

∵ As his ſoul ſuffered no paines in Hel, ſo neither did his body take any corruptiō in the graue:

Pſ. 15, 8.

3. Reg. 2, 10.

Pſ. 131, 11.

† Being exalted therfore by the right hand of God, and hauing receiued of his father the promiſſe of the holy Ghoſt, he hath povvred out ˋ this vvhom' you ſee and heare. † For Dauid aſcended not into heauen: but he ſaith, *Our Lord hath ſaid to my Lord, ſit on my right hand,* † *vntil I make thine enemies the footeſtoole of thy feete.* † Therfore let al the houſe of Iſraël know moſt certainly that God hath made him both Lord, and CHRIST, this IESVS, vvhom you haue crucified. 33 34 35 36

this gift vvhich

Pſ. 109, 1.

Contrition.

† And hearing theſe things, they were compuncte in hart, and ſaid to Peter and to the reſt of the Apoſtles, Vvhat ſhal 37

38 vve doe men, brethren? † But Peter said to them, ∴ Doe penance, and be euery one of you baptized in the name of IESVS CHRIST for remission of your sinnes: and you
39 shal receiue the gift of the holy Ghost. † For to you is the promisse, and to your children, and to al that are farre of,
40 vvhomsoeuer the Lord our God shal call. † Vvith very many other vvordes also did he testifie, and exhorted them, saying,
41 Saue your selues from this peruerse generation. † They therfore that receiued his vvord, vvere baptized: and there vvere added in that day about ∴ three thousand soules.
42 † And they vvere perseuéring in the doctrine of the Apostles, and in the communication of [c] the breaking of
43 bread, and praiers. † And feare came vpon euery soul: many vvonders also and signes vvere done by the Apostles in Hie-
44 rusalem, and there vvas great feare in al. † Al they also that
45 beleeued, vvere together, *and had ‖ al things cōmon. † Their possessions and substance they sold, and deuided them to al,
46 according as euery one had neede. † Daily also continuing vvith one accord in the temple, and breaking bread from house to house, they tooke their meate vvith ioy and sim-
47 plicitie of hart: † praising God, and hauing grace vvith al the people. And our Lord ‖ increased them that should be saued, da[i]ly together.

Act. 4, 32.

∴ Not onely amendment of life, but penāce also required before Baptisme, in such as be of age, though not in that sort as aftervvard in the Sacramēt of penance. *Aug. de fid. et oper. c. 11. et ep. 108.*

∴ Three thousand Were conuerted at this first sermon, & they Were put to the other visible companie and Church.

c This Was the B. Sacrament, Which the Apostles daily ministred to the Christians at least in one kinde. *See chap. 20, 7.*

ANNOTATIONS
CHAP. II.

1. The daies of Pentecost.) As Christ our Pasche, for correspondence to the figure, Was offered at the Iewes great feast of Pasche, so fifty daies after (in Greeke, Pentecost) for accomplishing the like figure of the LaW-giuing in Mount Sinai, he sent downe the Holy Gh[ost] iust on the day of their Pentecost. Which Was alwaies on Sunday, as appeareth *Leuit. 23, 15.* Both Which daies the Church keepeth yerely for memorie of Christs death and Resurrection, and the sending doWne of the Holy Ghost: as they did the like for record of their deliuerie out of Ægypt, and their LaWgiuing aforesaid. the said Feastes With vs conteining, besides the remembrance of benefites past, great Sacraments also of the life to come. *Aug. ep. 119, C. 16.*

The feastes of Pasche & Pentecost.

4. Al replenished.) Though the Apostles and the rest Were baptized before, and had thereby receiued the grace of the Holy Ghost to sanctification and remission of sinnes, as for diuers other purposes also: Yet as Christ * promised them they should be further indued With strength and vertue from aboue, so here he fulfilleth his promes, visibly powring downe the Holy Ghost vpon al the companie and vpon euery one of them, thereby replenishing the Apostles specially With al truth, Wisedom, and knoWledge necessarie for the gouernement of the Church, and giuing both to them and to al other present, the grace and effect of the Sacrament of Confirmation, accomplishing, corroborating, and strengthening them in their faith and the confession of the same. And lastly for a visible token of Gods Spirit, he endued them al With the gift of diuers strange tonges: al (I say) there present, as Wel our Ladie, as other holy Women and brethren, besides the Apostles. though * the Heretikes fondly argue, for the desire they haue to dishonour Christs mother, that neither she nor they Were there present, nor had the gift of tongues, contrarie to the plaine text that saith, *They vvere al together,* to Wit, al the 120 mentioned before c. 1, 15.

Lu. 24, 49

The sending of the Holy Ghost on Whitsunday and the effectes thereof.

Our B. Ladie.

Beza Annot. in hoc cap. v. 1.

23. Deliuered

Gods determination that Christ should die, excuseth not the Iewes.

23. *By the determinate counsel of God deliuered.*) God deliuered him, and he deliuered him self, for loue and intention of our saluation, and so the acte was holy and Gods owne determination. But the Iewes and others which betraied and crucified him, did it of malice and wicked purpose, and their facte was damnable, and not of Gods counsel or causing: though he tolerated it, for that he could and did turne their abominable facte to the good of our saluatio. Therfore abhorre those new Manichees of our time, both Lutherans and Caluinists, that make God the author and cause of Iudas betraying of Christ, no lesse then of Paules conuersion. beside the false translation of Beza, saying for Gods prescience or foreknowledge (in the Greeke, πρόγνωσις) *Gods prouidence.*

Beza.

24. *Loosing the sorovves.*) Christ was not in paines him self, but loosed other men of those dolours of Hel, wherewith it was impossible him self should be touched. *See* * *S. Augustine.*

* Li. 12 c. 13 de Gen. ad lit.

Corrupt translation against the Article of Christs descending into Hel.

27. *My soul in Hel,*) Where al the Faithful, according to the Creede, euer haue beleeued, that Christ according to his soul, went downe to Hel, to deliuer the Patriarches and al iust men there holden in bondage til his death, and the Apostle here citing the Prophets wordes, most euidently expresseth the same, distinguishing his soule in Hel, from his body in the graue: Yet the Caluinists to defend against Gods expresse wordes, the blasphemie of their Maister, that Christ suffered the paines of Hel, and that no where but vpon the Crosse, and that otherwise he descended not into Hel, most falsely and flatly here corrupt the text, by turning and wresting both the Hebrew and Greeke wordes from their most proper and vsual significations of, *Soule*, and *Hel*, into *body*, and *graue*: saying for, *my soule in Hel*, thus, *my body*, * *life*, *person*, yea (as Beza in his new Testament an. 1556) *my carcas* in the *graue*. and this later they corrupt almost through out the Bible for that purpose. But for refelling of both corruptions, it shal be sufficient in this place: first, that al Hebrues & Greekes, and al that vnderstand these tonges, know that the foresaid Hebrue & Greeke wordes are as proper, peculiar, and vsual to signifie, *soul* and *Hel*, as *anima* and *infernus* in Latin, yea as *soul* and *Hel* in English do properly signifie the soule of man, and Hel that is opposite to heauen: and that they are as vnproprely vsed to signifie body and graue, as to say in English, soul for body, or Hel for graue. Secondly, it doth so mislike the Heretikes them selues, that Castaleo one of their fine Translatours refelleth it, and to make it the more sure, he for, *in inferno*, translateth, *in Orco*. that is, *in Hel.* Thirdly, Beza him self partly recanteth in his later edition, and confesseth that, *Carcas*, was no fit word for the body of Christ, and therfore, *I haue* (saith he) *changed it, but I reteine and keepe the same sense stil.* meaning that he hath now translated it, *soule*, but that he meaneth thereby as before, Christs dead body. fourthly, * he saith plainely, that translating thus, *Thou shalt not leaue my carcas in the graue*, he did it of purpose against *Limbus Patrum*, Purgatorie, and Christs descending into Hel, which he calleth foul errours, and marueleth, *that most of the ancient fathers vvere in that errour*: namely of Christs descending into Hel, and deliuering the old fathers. Vvhat neede we more? He opposeth him self both against plaine Scriptures and al auncient fathers, peruerting the one, and contemning the other, to ouerthrow that truth which is an Article of our *Crede*. Whereby it is euidently false which some of them say for their defense, that none of them did euer of purpose translate falsely. See the Annotation vpon *1 Pet. 3. v. 19.*

אֶת נַפְשׁ ψυχὴν
שְׁאוֹל ᾅδου

* Eng. Bible. 1579

* No. Test. an. 1556. annot. in 2 Act. v. 27 & 24. & in 1 Pet. 3, 19.

Liuing in common.

44. *Al things common.*) This liuing in common is not a rule or a precept to al Christian men, as the Anabaptistes falsely pretend: but a life of perfection and counsel, folowed of our Religious in the Catholike Church. *See S. Aug. in Ps. 132 in principio. & ep. 109.*

The increase & perpetuitie of the VISIBLE CHVRCH.

47. *Increased.*) Moe and moe were added to the Church (as the Greeke more plainely expresseth) that we may see the visible propagation & increase of the same. from which time a diligent man may deduce the very same visible Societie of men ioyned in Christ, through the whole booke, and afterward by the Ecclesiastical storie, downe til our daies, against the pretensed inuisible Church of the Heretikes.

Προσετίθεντο τῇ ἐκκλησίᾳ.

CHAP. III.

A miracle, and a Sermon of Peters to the people, shevving that IESVS *is Christ, and exhorting them to faith in him and penance for their sinnes, and so they shal haue by him (in Baptisme) the Benediction which was promised to Abraham.*

The Epistle vpõ SS. Peter and Paules eue. Iun 28.

:: This maketh for distinction of Canonical houres and diuersitie of appointed times to pray in. *See Annot. c. 10, 9.*

ND Peter and Iohn vvent vp into the temple, at the :: ninthe houre of praier. † And a certaine man that vvas lame from his mothers vvombe, vvas caried: vvhom they laid euery day at the gate of the temple, that is called Specious, that he might aske almes of them that vvent into the temple.

1 2

3 temple. † He, vvhen he had seen Peter and Iohn about to
4 enter into the temple, asked to receiue an almes. † But Peter
5 vvith Iohn looking vpon him, said, Looke vpon vs. † But he
looked earnestly vpon them, hoping that he should receiue
6 some thing of them. † But Peter said, Siluer and gold I haue
not, but " that vvhich I haue, the same I giue to thee: In the
name of IESVS CHRIST of Nazareth arise, and vvalke.
7 † And taking his right hand, he lifted him vp, and forthvvith
8 his feete and soles vvere made strong. † And springing he
stoode, and vvalked: and vvent in vvith them into the tem-
9 ple vvalking, and leaping, and praising God. † And al the
10 people savv him vvalking and praising God. † And they
knevv him, that, it vvas he vvhich sate for almes at the Specious gate of the temple: and they vvere excedingly astonied
11 and agast at that that had chaũced to him. † And as he held
Peter and Iohn, al the people ranne to them vnto the porche
vvhich is called Salomons, vvondering.

12 † But Peter seing them, made ansvver to the people, Ye
men of Israël, vvhy maruel you at this, or vvhy looke you
vpon vs, as though " by our povver or holines vve haue made
13 this man to vvalke? † The God of Abraham, and the God
of Isaac, and the God of Iacob, the God of our fathers hath
glorified his sonne IESVS, vvhom you in deede deliuered
and denied before the face of Pilate, he iudging him to be re-
14 leased. † But you denied the holy and the iust one,* and as-
15 ked a mankiller to be giuen vnto you. † but the authour
of life you killed, vvhom God hath raised from the dead,
16 of vvhich vve are vvitnesses. † And in the :: faith of his name,
this man vvhom you see and knovv, his name hath strengthened: & the faith vvhich is by him, hath giuen this perfect
health in the sight of al you.

17 † And novv (brethren) I knovv that you did it through
18 ignorãce, as also your princes. † But God vvho foreshevved
by the mouth of al the prophets, that his CHRIST should
19 suffer, hath so fulfilled it. † Be Penitent therfore & conuert,
20 that your sinnes may be put out. ꟻ † that, vvhen the times
shal come of refreshing by the sight of our Lord, and he
shal send him that hath been preached vnto you IESVS
21 CHRIST, † c vvhom :: heauen truely must receiue vntil the
times of the restitution of al things, vvhich God spake by the
mouth of his holy prophets from the beginnĩg of the world.

Pp † Moyses

Luc. 23, 18.

ὃν δεῖ οὐρανὸν μὲν δέξασθαι

The Epistle vpõ Wenesday in Easter weeke.

:: This faith was not the faith of the lame man (for he looked onely for almes) nor a special faith of the Apostles owne saluatiõ: but the whole beleefe of Christian Religion.

:: Some Heretikes fouly corrupt this place, thus, *Who must be conteined in heauen*, of purpose (as they protest) to hold Christ in heauẽ, from the B. Sacramẽt. *Beza.* As though his presẽce there, drew him out of heauen. Neither cã they pretend the Greeke, which is word for word as in the vulgar latin, and as we translate.

† Moyses in deede said, *That a prophet shal the Lord your God raise vp to you of your brethren, as my self: him you shal heare according to al things vvhatsoeuer he shal speake to you.* 22 † *And it shal be, euery soule that shal not heare that prophet, shal be destroied out of the people.* 23 † And al the Prophets from Samuël and aftervvard that haue spoken, told of these daies. 24 † You are the children of the Prophets and of the testament vvhich God made to our fathers, saying to Abraham, *And in thy seede shal al the families of the earth be blessed.* 25 † To you first God raising vp his sonne, hath sent him blessing you: that euery one should conuert him self from his naughtines. 26

Deu. 18, 15.

Gen. 22, 18. 26, 4

ANNOTATIONS CHAP. III.

Saincts doe miracles and the like, but by the povver of God.

6. *That vvhich I haue.*] This povver of vvorking miracles vvas in Peter, and Peter properly did giue this man his health, though he receiued that force and vertue of God, and in & by him executed the same. Therfore he saith, *That vvhich I haue, I giue to thee.* and the Heretikes are ridiculous that note here, *a miracle done by Christ by the handes of the Apostles*, to make the simple beleeue that they had no more to doe then a dead instrument in the vvorkemans hand.

12. *By our povver.*] When the Apostles remit sinnes, or doe any other miracles, they doe it not by any humane, proper, or natural povver in them selues: but of supernatural force giuen them from aboue, to proue that the faith of Christ is true, and that he is God vvhom the Ievves crucified, in vvhose name and faith they vvorke, and not in their ovvne.

CHAP. IIII.

The Rulers of the Ievves oppose them selues and imprison Peter and Iohn. 4 But yet thousands of the people are conuerted: 5 and to the Rulers also, Peter boldly auoucheth by the forsaid miracle, that IESUS *is Christ, telling them of their heinous fault out of the Psalmes, and that vvithout him they can not be saued. 13 They though confounded vvith the miracle, yet procede in their obstinacie, forbidding them to speake any more of* IESUS, *adding also threates. 23 Wherevpon the Church fleeth to praier, vvherein they comfort them selues vvith the omnipotencie of God, and prediction of Dauid, and aske for the gift of boldnes and miracles against those threates. 31 And God shevveth miraculously that he hath heard their praier. 32 The vvhole Churches vnitie and communitie of life. 36 Of Barnabas by name.*

AND vvhen they vvere speaking to the people, the Priests and magistrates of the temple and the Sadducees came vpon them, 1 † being greeued that they taught the people, and shevved in IESUS the resurrection from the dead: 2 † and they laid handes vpon them, and put them into vvard, vntil the morovv, for it vvas novv euening. 3 † And ∴ many of them that had heard the vvord, beleeued: and the number of the men vvas made fiue thousand. 4

∴ Here againe vve see the proceding and increase of the Church visibly.

† And

5 † And it came to passe on the morovv, that their princes, and Auncients, and Scribes vvere gathered into Hierusalem. 6 † and Annas the high priest, and Caiphas and Iohn, and Alexander, and as many as vvere of the priests stocke. 7 † And setting them in the middes, they asked: In vvhat povver or in vvhat name haue you done this? 8 † Then Peter replenished vvith the holy Ghost, said to them, Ye princes of the people & Auncients: 9 † If vve this day be examined for a good deede vpon an impotent man, in vvhat he hath been made whole, 10 † be it knovven to al you and to al the people of Israël, that in the name of IESVS CHRIST of Nazareth, vvhom you did crucifie, vvhom God hath raised from the dead, in this same this man standeth before you vvhole. 11 † This is *the stone that vvas reiected of you the builders: vvhich is made into the head of the corner.* 12 † and there is not saluation in any other. for neither is there any other name vnder heauen giuen to men, vvherein vve must be saued. 13 † And seeing Peters constancie and Iohns, vnderstanding that they vvere men vnlettered, and of the vulgar sort, they marueled, and they knew them that they had been vvith IESVS: 14 † seeing the man also that had been cured, standing vvith them, they could say nothing to the contrarie. 15 † But they commaunded them to goe aside forth 16 out of the councel: and they conferred together, † saying, Vvhat shal vve doe to these men? for a notorious signe in deede hath been done by them, to al the inhabitants of Hierusalem: it is manifest, and vve can not denie it. 17 † But that it be no further spred abrode among the people, let vs threaten them, that they speake no more in this name to any man. 18 † And calling them, they charged them that they should 19 not speake at al, nor teache in the name of IESVS. † But Peter and Iohn ansvvering, said to them, :: If it be iust in the 20 sight of God, to heare you rather then God, iudge ye. † for vve can not but speake the things vvhich vve haue seen and 21 heard. † But they threatening, dimissed them: not finding hovv they might punish them, for the people, because all glorified that vvhich had been done, in that vvhich vvas 22 chaunced. † For the man vvas more then fourtie yeres old in vvhom that signe of health had been vvrought.

23 † And being dimissed they came to theirs, and shevved al that the cheefe priests and Auncients had said to them. 24 † Vvho hauing heard it, with one accord lifted vp their voice

Psa. 117, 22.

The name of IESVS. See Annot. Philip. 2, 10.

The Apostles constancie, learning and wisdom after the coming of the Holy Ghost, being but idiotes, that is, simple vnlettered men and timorous before.

:: Their constancie and courage after their confirmation, being so weake before. And if any Magistrate commaund against God, that is to say, forbid Catholike Christian men to preach or serue God, this same must be their answer, though they be whipped and killed for their labour. See c. 5. v. 29.

to God, and said, Lord, thou that didst make heauen & earth, the sea, and al things that are in them, † vvho in the holy 25 Ghost by the mouth of our father Dauid thy seruāt hast said, *Vvhy did the Gentiles rage, and the people meditate vaine thinges: † the kings 26 of the earth stand vp, and the princes assemble together against our* Lord, *and against his* CHRIST? † For there assembled in deede in this citie 27 against thy holy childe IESVS vvhom thou hast anointed, Herod, and Pontius Pilate, vvith the Gentiles and the people of Israël, † to doe vvhat :: thy hand & thy counsel decreed 28 to be done. † And novv Lord looke vpon their threatenings, 29 and giue vnto thy seruants vvith al confidence to speake thy vvorde, † in that, that thou extend thy hand to cures and 30 signes and vvonders to be done by the name of thy holy sonne IESVS. † And vvhen they had praied, the place vvas 31 moued vvherein they vvere gathered: and they vvere al replenished vvith the holy Ghost, and they spake the vvord of God vvith confidence.

Ps. 2, 1.

:: Christes death, as needeful for mans redemption, was of Gods determination: but as of the malice of the Iewes, it was not his act otherwise then by permission.

† And the multitude of beleeuers had one hart and 32 one soule: neither did any one say that ought vvas his ovvne of those things vvhich he possessed, but al things vvere common vnto them. † And vvith great povver did 33 the Apostles giue testimonie of the resurrection of IESVS CHRIST our Lord: and great grace vvas in al them. † For 34 neither vvas there any one needie among them. For as many as vvere ovvners of landes or houses, :: sold and brought the prices of those things vvhich they sold, † and laid it before 35 the feete of the Apostles. And to euery one vvas deuided according as euery one hade neede. † And Ioseph vvho 36 vvas surnamed of the Apostles Barnabas (vvhich is by interpretation, the sonne of consolation) a Leuite, a Cyprian borne, † vvhereas he had a peece of land, sold it, and brought 37 the price, and laid it " before the feete of the Apostles.

Act. 2, 44.

:: Note the ardent charitie and cōtempt of worldly things in the first Christians: who did not onely giue great almes, but sold al their lands to bestow on the Apostles and the rest that were in necessitie, according to Christes coūsel. *Mt. 16, 21.* Note also the great honour & credit giuen to the Apostles, in that the Christian men put al the goods & possessions they had, to their disposition.

ANNOTATIONS
CHAP. IIII.

Reuerence to holy persons.

37. *Before the feete.*) He, as the rest, did not onely giue his goods as in vulgar almes, but in al humble and reuerent maner as things dedicated to God, he laid them downe at the Apostles holy feete, as S. Luke alwaies expresseth, and gaue them not into their handes. The Sunamite fel downe and embraced Elisæus feete. Many that asked benefites of Christ (as the woman sicke of the bloudy fluxe) fel downe at his feete. and Marie kissed his feete. Such are signes of due reuerence done both to Christ and to other sacred persons, either Prophetes, Apostles, Popes, or others representing his person in earth. See in S. Hierom of Epiphanius Bishop in Cypres, how the people of Hierusalem *of al sortes flocked together vnto him, offering their children* (to take his blessing) *kissing his feete, plucking the hemmes of his garment, so that he could not moue for the throng.* Ep. 61 c. 4 cont. erro. Io. Hierosol.

4. Reg. 4, 37. Luc. 8, 47. Lu. 7, 38.

Kissing their feete.

CHAP.

CHAP. V.

Ananias and his vvife Saphira, for their sacrilege, at Peters Word fall doWne dead, to the great terrour of the rest. 12 By the Apostles miracles, not onely the number, but also their faith so increaseth, that they seeke in the streates to the very shadoW of Peter, the toWnes also about bringing their diseased to Hierusalem. 17 The Rulers againe oppose them selues, but in vaine. 19 For out of prison an Angel deliuereth them, bidding them preach openly to al: 27 and in their Councel Peter is nothing afraid of their bigge Werdes: 34 Yea Gamaliel being one of them selues casteth a doubt among them, lest the matter be of God, and therfore impossible to be dissolued. 40 Finally, the Apostles being scourged by them, count it an honour, and cease no day from preaching.

1 BVT a certaine man named Ananias, vvith Saphîra his vvife sold a peece 2 of land, † and " defrauded of the price of the land, his vvife being priuie thereto: and bringing a certaine portion, laide it at the feete of the Apo-3 stles. † And " Peter said, Ananias, vvhy hath Satan tempted thy hart, that thou shouldest lie to the holy 4 Ghost, and defraude of the price of the land? † Remaining, did it not remaine to thee: and being sold, vvas it not " in thy povver? Vvhy hast thou put this thing in thy hart? Thou 5 hast not lied " to men, but to God. † And Ananias hearing these vvordes, fel dovvne, and gaue vp the ghost. And there 6 came great feare vpon al that heard it. † And yong men rising vp, remoued him, and bearing him forth buried him. 7 † And it vvas the space as it vvere of three houres, and his 8 vvife, not knovving vvhat vvas chaunced, came in. † And Peter ansvvered her, Tel me vvoman, vvhether did you sel 9 the land for so much? But she said, Yea, for so much. † And Peter vnto her, Vvhy haue you agreed together to tempt the Spirit of our Lord? Behold, their feete that haue buried thy husband, at the doore, and they shal beare thee forth. 10 † Forthvvith she fel before his feete, and gaue vp the ghost. And the yong men going in, found her dead: and caried 11 her forth, and buried her by her husband. † And there fel great :: feare in the vvhole Church, and vpon al that heard these things.

:: Herevpon rose great reuerence, aWe, and feare of the vulgar Christians toWard the holy Apostles, for an example to al Christian people hoW to behaue thẽ selues toWard their Bishops and Priests.

The Epistle vpõ Imber Wenesday in Whitsonweeke. And Within the octaue, & in a votiue of SS. Peter and Paul.

12 † And by the handes of the Apostles vvere many signes and vvonders done among the people. And they vvere al 13 vvith one accord in Salomons porche. † But of the rest

none durst ioyne them selues vnto them: but the people magnified them. † And the multitude of men and vvomen 14 that beleeued in our Lord, vvas more increased: † so that 15 they did bring forth the sicke into the streates, and laid them in beddes and couches, that vvhen Peter came, "his shadovv at the least might ouershadovv any of them, and they all might be deliuered from their infirmities. † And there ranne 16 together vnto Hierusalem the multitude also of the cities adioyning, bringing sicke persons and such as vvere vexed of vncleane spirits: vvho vvere al cured. ¶

Peters shadow.

† And the high priest rising vp, and al that vvere vvith 17 him, vvhich is the heresie of the Sadduces, vvere replenished vvith zeale: † laid hands vpon the Apostles, and put them 18 in the common prison. † But an Angel of our Lord by night 19 opening the gates of the prison, & leading them forth, said, † Goe: and standing speake in the temple to the people al 20 the vvordes of this life. † Vvho hauing heard this, early in the 21 morning entred into the temple, and taught. And the high priest comming, and they that vvere vvith him, called together the Councel & al the auncients of the children of Israël: and they sent to the prison that they might be brought. † But 22 vvhen the ministers vvere come, and opening the prison, found them not: returning they told, † saying, The prison 23 truely vve found shut vvith al diligence, and the keepers standing before the gates: but opening it, vve found no man vvithin. † And as soone as the Magistrate of the temple and 24 the cheefe priests heard these vvordes, they vvere in doubt of them, vvhat vvould befall. † And there came a certaine man 25 and told them, That the men, loe, vvhich you did put in prison, are in the temple standing, and teaching the people. † Then vvent the Magistrate vvith the ministers, and 26 brought them vvithout force, for they feared the people lest they should be stoned. † And vvhen they had brought 27 them, they sat them in the Councel. And the high priest asked them, † saying, * Commaunding vve commaunded 28 you that you should not teach in this name: and behold you haue filled Hierusalem vvith your doctrine, and you vvil bring vpon vs the bloud of this man. † But Peter ansvvering 29 and the Apostles, said, God must be obeied, rather then men. † The God of our Fathers hath raised vp IESVS, vvhom 30 you did kil, hanging him vpon a tree. † This Prince and 31 Sauiour

An Angel leadeth them out of prison.

Act. 4, 18.

Sauiour God hath exalted vvith his right hand, to giue re-
32 pentance to Israël, and remission of sinnes. † and vve are vvitnesses of these vvordes, and the holy Ghost, vvhom God
33 hath giuen to al that obey him. † Vvhen they had heard these things, it cut them to the hart, and they consulted to kil them.

34 † But one in the Councel rising vp, a Pharisee named Gamaliel, a doctor of lavv honorable to al the people, commaunded the men to be put forth a vvhile.
35 † and he said to them, Ye men of Israël, take heede to your selues touching
36 these men vvhat you meane to doe. † For before these daies there rose Theódas, saying he vvas some body, to vvhom consented a numbre of men about foure hundred, vvho vvas slaine: and al that beleeued him, vvere dispersed, and
37 brought to nothing. † After this fellovv there rose Iudas of Galilee in the daies of the Enrolling, and drevv avvay the people after him, and he perished: and as many as euer con-
38 sented to him, vvere dispersed. † And novv therfore I say to you, depart from these men and let them alone: for if this
39 counsel or vvorke be of men, it vvil be dissolued: † but if it be ∷ of God, you are not able to dissolue them, lest perhaps you be found to resist God also. And they consented to him.
40 † And calling in the Apostles, after they had scourged them, they charged them that they should not speake in the name
41 of IESVS, and dimissed them. † And they vvent from the sight of the councel reioycing, because they vvere accoun-
42 ted vvorthy to suffer reproche for the name of IESVS. † And euery day they ceased not in the temple and from house to house to teach and euangelize Christ IESVS.

Theudas

∷ Time, and the euident successe of Christes Church and religion, proue it to be of God: no violence of the Iewes, no persecution of the Heathen Princes, no endeuour of domestical Aduersaries, heretikes, Schismatikes, or il liuers, preuailing against it. as on the other side, many attempts haue been made by Arius Macedonius, Nestorius, Luther, & the like, who thought them selues some body: but after they had plaied their partes a while, their memory is buried, or liueth only in malediction & infamie, & their scholers come to naught Therfore let no Cath. man be scandalized that this heresie holdeth vp for a time. For the Arians & some others florished much longer then these, and were better supported by Princes and learning, & yet had an end.

ANNOTATIONS
CHAP. V.

Aug. ser. 9 in append. de diuersis tom. 10.

2. *Defrauded.*) In that (saith S. Augustine) he withdrew any part of that which he promised, he was guilty at once, both of sacrilege, and of fraude. of sacrilege, because he robbed God of that which was his by promes: of fraude, in that he withheld of the whole gift, a peece. Let now the Heretikes come, and say it was for lying or hypocrisie onely that this facte was condemned: because they be loth to haue sacrilege counted any such sinne, who haue taught men not onely to take away from God some peece of that or al that them selues gaue, but plainly to spoile & apply to them selues al that other men gaue.

Sacrilege.

3. *Peter said.*) S. Peter (as you see here) without mans relation knew this fraude and the cogitations of Ananias, and as head of the College and of the whole Church against which this robbery was committed, executed this heauy sentence of Excommunication both against him, and his wife consenting to the Sacrilege. for it was excommunication by S. Augustines iudgement, (*li. 3 cont. ep. Parm. c. 1 to. 7*) and had this corporal miraculous death ioyned withal, as the Excommunication

Excommunication ioyned with corporal paines.

munication that S. Paul gaue out against the incestuous and others, had the corporal vexation of Satan incident vnto it. 1 Cor. 5.

4. *In thy povver.*) *If it displeased God* (saith S. Augustine) *to vvithdravv of the money vvhich they had vovved to God, hovv is he angry vvhen chastitie is vovved and is not performed? for to such may be said that vvhich S. Peter said of the money: Thy virginitie remaining did it not remaine to thee, and before thou didst vovv, vvas it not in thine ovvne povver? for, Whosoeuer haue vowed such things and haue not paied them, let them not thinke to be condemned to corporal deaths, but to euerlasting fire. August. Ser. 10. de diuersis.* And S. Gregorie to the same purpose writeth thus, *Ananias had vovved money to God, vvhich aftervvard ouercome vvith diuelish persuasion he vvithdrevv: but vvith vvhat death he vvas punished, thou knovvest. If then he vvere vvorthy of that death, Who tooke avvay the money that he had giuen to God, consider vvhat great peril in Gods iudgement thou shalt be vvorthy of, vvhich hast vvithdravven, not money, but thy self from almighty God, to vvhom thou hadst vovved thy self vnder the habite or vveede of a Monke.*

Vow of Chastitie, & the breache thereof.

Greg. li. 1. ep. 33.

4. *Not to men, but.*) To take from the Church or from the Gouernours thereof, things dedicated to their vse and the seruice of God, or to lie vnto Gods Ministers, is so iudged of before God, as if the lie were made, and the fraude done to the Holy Ghost him self, who is the Churches President and Protector.

15. *His shadovv.*) Specially they sought to Peter the cheefe of al, who not onely by touching, as the other, but by his very shadow cured al diseases. Where vpon S. Augustine saith, If then the shadow of his body could helpe, how much more now the fulnes of power? And if thé a certaine litle vvind of him passing by did profite them that humbly asked, how much more the grace of him now being permanent & remaining? *Ser. 29 de Sanctis*, speaking of the miracles done by the Saincts now reigning in heauen.

Peters shadow & intercession.

CHAP. VI.

By occasion of a murmur in the Church (vvhose number novv is so grovven that it cannot be numbred) Seuen of them being ordered by the Apostles in the holy order of Deacons: 8 one of them, Steuen, Worketh great miracles: and is by such as he confounded in disputation, falsely accused in the Councel, of blasphemie against the Temple and rites thereof.

AND in those daies the numbre of disciples increasing, there arose a " murmuring of the Greekes against the Hebrues, for that their vvidovves vvere despised in the daily ministerie. 1 † And the Tvvelue calling together the multitude of the disciples, said, It is not reason, that vve leaue the vvord of God, and serue tables. 2 † Consider therfore brethren, " seuen men of you of good testimonie, ful of the holy Ghost and vvisedom, vvhom vve may appoint ouer this busines. 3 † But vve vvil be instant in praier and the ministerie of the vvord. 4 † And the saying vvas liked before al the multitude. 5 And they chose Steuen a man ful of faith and of the holy Ghost, and Philippe, and Próchorus, and Nicánor, and Timon, and Pármenas, and Nicolas a c stranger of Antioche. † These they did set in the presence of the Apostles: 6 and praying they imposed handes vpon them. † And the 7 vvord of God increased, and the number of the disciples vvas multiplied in Hierusalem excedingly: a great multitude also

The election of the 7 first Deacons.

c προσήλυτον

alſo of the :: prieſts obeied the faith.

8 † [b] And Steuen ful of grace and fortitude did great vvonders & ſignes among the people. † 9 And there aroſe certaine of that vvhich is called the Synagogue of the Libertines, and of the Cyrenians, and of the Alexandrians, and of them that vvere of Cilicia and Aſia, diſputing vvith Steuen: † 10 and they could not reſiſt the vviſedom and the Spirit that ſpake. † 11 Then they ſuborned men, to ſay they had heard him ſpeake vvordes of blaſphemie againſt Moyſes and God. † 12 They therfore ſtirred vp the people, and the Auncients, and the Scribes: and running together they tooke him, and brought him into the Councel, † 13 and they ſet falſe vvitneſſes that ſaid, This man ceaſeth not to ſpeake vvordes againſt the holy place and the Lavv. † 14 for vve haue heard him ſay, that this ſame IESVS of Nazareth ſhal deſtroy this place, and ſhal change the traditions, vvhich Moyſes deliuered vnto vs. 15 † And al that ſate in the Councel beholding him, ſavv his face as it vvere :: the face of an Angel.

:: Now alſo the Prieſts and they of greater knowledge & eſtimation began to beleeue.

b The Epiſtle vpon S. Steuens day in Chriſtmas.

:: Such is the face of al conſtant & cheereful; Martyrs, to their perſecutors and iudges.

ANNOTATIONS CHAP. VI.

1. Murmuring.] It commeth of humane infirmitie, that in euery Societie of men (be it neuer ſo holy) there is ſome cauſe giuen or taken by the weake, of murmur and difference, which muſt euer be prouided for and ſtaied in the beginning, leſt it grow to further ſchiſme or ſedition. And to al ſuch defects, the more the Church increaſeth in number and diuerſitie of men and Prouinces, the more it is ſubiect. In al which things the ſpiritual Magiſtrates, by the Apoſtles example and authoritie, muſt take order, as time and occaſion ſhal require.

Murmuring & emulation.

3. Seuen men.] We may not thinke that theſe Seuen (here made Deacons) were onely choſen to ſerue profane tables or diſpoſe of the Churches mere temporalles, though by that occaſion only they may ſeeme to ſome now elected, no expreſſe mention being made of any other function. for, diuers circumſtances of this ſame place giue euidence, and ſo doth al antiquitie, that their Office ſtood not principally about profane things, but about the holy Altar. The perſons to be elected, muſt be ful of the Holy Ghoſt and wiſedom, they muſt after publike praier be ordered and conſecrated by the Apoſtles impoſition of hands, as Biſhops and Prieſts were afterward ordered. *ep. ad Tim*: Where S. Paul alſo requireth in a maner the ſame conditions in them as in Biſhops. Al which would not haue beene preſcribed for any ſecular ſtewardſhip. Yea ſtraight vpon their Ordering here (no doubt by commiſſion of the Apoſtles, which they had not before their election) they preached, baptized, diſputed, and as it may appeare by the wordes ſpoken of S. Steuen, that he was ful of grace and fortitude, they receiued great increaſe of grace by their Deaconſhip.

The 7 Deacons

1 Tim. 3. & 4.

Act. 6, 8.

But S. Ignatius *ep. 2 ad Tral.* can beſt witnes of their Office and the Apoſtles maner and meaning in ſuch things, who writeth thus: *It behoueth alſo to pleaſe by al meanes the Deacons, vvhich are for the miniſterie of* IESVS CHRIST. *For they are not ſeruiteurs of meate and drinke, but miniſters of the Church of God. For vvhat are Deacons but imitatours or folovvers of Chriſt, miniſtring to the Biſhop, as Chriſt to his Father, & vvorking vnto him a cleane and immaculate worke, euen as S. Steuen to S. Iames &c.* S. Polycarpe hath the like in his epiſtle ad Philippenſes. And S. Denys writeth that their Office was about the Altar, and putting the holy bread and chalice vpon the ſame. S. Clement alſo (*Apoſt. Conſt. li. 2 c. 61.*) that their Office among other things, is to aſſiſt the Biſhops, and read the Goſpel in the Seruice &c. S. Cyprian in diuers places (*ep. 65. & ep. 49 ad Cornel.*) calleth Deacons, the Churches and the Apoſtles Miniſters, and their Office, *adminiſtrationem ſacram*, an holy adminiſtration. S. Hierom affirmeth, *in caput 7 Michea.* and *in epiſto. 85 ad Euagrium tom. 2*, where he

The office of Deacons.

Li. Eccl. Hier. c. 3 part. 2.

he checketh some of them for preferring them selues before Priests, and putteth them in remembrance of their first calling, that they be as the Leuites were in respect of the Priests of the old Law. finally by S. Ambrose *li. 1 Offic. c. 41* and Prudentius *in Hymno de S. Laurent.* speaking of S. Laurence the Deacon, we may see their Office was most holy. See S. Augustine also of the dignitie of Deacons *ep. 148 ad Valerium. Conc. Carthag. 4. can. 37. 38. 39. 41.*

CHAP. VII.

Steuen being permitted to answer, beginning at Abraham, shevveth that God was with their fathers both in other places, and also long before the Temple. 48 and that after it vvas built, it could not be (as they grosly imagined) a house for God to dwel in. 51 then he inueigheth against their stifneckednes, and telleth them boldly of their traiterous murdering of Christ, as their fathers had done his Prophets afore him. 54 Whereat they being vvood, he seeth heauen open, and IESVS there in his Diuine Maiestie. 57 Whereat they become more mad, so that they stone him to death (Saul consenting) he commending his soul to IESVS, and humbly praying for them.

AND the cheefe priest said, Are these things so? 1 † Vvho said, Ye men, brethren and fathers, heare. 2 The God of glorie appeared to our father Abraham vvhen he vvas in Mesopotamia, before that he abode in Charan, † and said to him, *Goe forth out of thy countrie, and out of thy kinred, and come into a land that I shal shevv thee.* 3 † Then vvent he forth out of the land of the Chaldees, and dvvelt in Charan. And from thence, after his father vvas dead, he translated him into this land, vvherein you doe novv dvvel. 4 † And he gaue him no inheritance in it, no not the pase of a foote: and he promised to giue it him in possession, and to his seede after him, vvhen as he had no childe. 5 † And God spake to him, *That his seede shal be a seiourner in a strange countrie, and they shal subdue them to seruitude, and shal euil intreate them foure-hundred yeres:* 6 † *and the nation vvhich they shal serue, vvil I iudge*, said God. *and after these things they shal goe forth, and shal serue me in this place.* 7

† And he * gaue him the testament of circumcision, and so he * begat Isaac, and circumcised him the eight day: and * Isaac, Iacob: and * Iacob, the tvvelue Patriarches. 8 † And the Patriarches through emulatiō, * sold Ioseph into Ægypt. and God vvas vvith him: 9 † and deliuered him out of al his tribulations. and he * gaue him grace and vvisedom in the sight of Pharao the king of Ægypt, and he appointed him Gouernour ouer Ægypt and ouer al his house. 10 † And there came famin vpon al Ægypt and Chanaan, and great tribulation: and our fathers found no victuals. 11 † But vvhen * Iacob had heard that there vvas corne in Ægypt: he sent our 12

Gen. 12, 1.

Gen. 15, 13.

ϰαϰώσουσι

Gen. 17.

Gen. 21.

Gen. 25.

Gen. 29. 30. 35.

Gen. 37.

Gen. 41.

Gen. 42.

fa-

Gen. 45. 13 fathers first: † and at the * secōd time Ioseph vvas knovven of his brethren, and his kinred vvas made knovven vnto 14 Pharao. † And Ioseph sending, called thither Iacob his father and al his kinred in seuentie fiue soules. † And * Iacob 16 descended into Ægypt: and * he died, and our fathers. † And they vvere :: translated into Sichem, and vvere * laid in the sepulchre that Abraham * bought for a price of siluer of the sonnes of Hemor the sonne of Sichem.

Gen. 46. Gen. 49. Gen. 50. Gen. 23. Ios. 24.

:: Translation of Saincts bodies agreable to nature & Scripture. And the desire to be buried in one place more then an other (which the holy Patriarches also had *Gen. 49, 29. 50, 24. Hebr. 11, 22*) hath sometime great causes. *Aug. de Cur. pro mort. c. 1. & vlt.*

17 † And vvhen the time drevv neere of the promisse vvhich God had promised to Abraham, the people * increased and 18 vvas multiplied in Ægypt, † vntil an other king arose in 19 Ægypt, that knevv not Ioseph. † This same circumuenting our stocke, afflicted our fathers: that they should expose 20 their children, to the end they might not be kept aliue. † The same time vvas * Moyses borne, and he vvas acceptable to God, who was nourished three moneths in his fathers house 21 † And vvhen he vvas exposed, Pharaos daughter tooke him 22 vp, and nourished him for her ovvne sonne. † And Moyses vvas instructed in al the vvisedom of the Ægyptians: and he 23 vvas mightie in his vvordes and vvorkes. † And * vvhen he vvas fully of the age of fourtie yeres, it came to his minde 24 to visite his brethren the children of Israël. † And vvhen he had seen one suffer vvrong, he defended him: and striking the Ægyptian, he reuenged his quarel that susteined the 25 vvrong. † And he thought that his brethren did vnderstand that God by his hand vvould saue them: but they vnder-26 stoode it not. † And the day folovving * he appeared to them being at strife: and he reconciled them vnto peace, saying, Men, ye are brethren, vvherfore hurt you one an 27 other? † But he that did the iniurie to his neighbour, repelled him, saying, *Vvho hath appointed thee prince and iudge ouer vs?* 28 † *Vvhat, vvilt thou kil me, as thou didst yesterday kil the Ægyptian?* † And 29 Moyses fled vpon this vvord: and he became a seiourner in 30 the land of Mádian, vvhere he begat tvvo sonnes, † And after fourtie yeres vvere expired, there * appeared to him in the desert of mount Sina an Angel in the fire of 31 the flame of a bush. † And Moyses seeing it, marueled at the vision. And as he vvent neere to vevve it, the voice 32 of our Lord vvas made to him, † *I am the God of thy fathers, the God of Abraham, the God of Isaac, and the God of Iacob.* And Moyses 33 being made to tremble, durst not vevve it. † And our Lord

Exo. 1, 7. Exo. 2, 2. Exo. 2, 11 Exo. 2, 13. Exo. 3, 2.

ſaid to him, *Looſe of the ſhoe of thy feete: for the place vvherein thou ſtandeſt, is ⁿ holy ground.* † *Seeing I haue ſeen the affliction of my people vvhich is in Ægypt, and I haue heard their groning, and am deſcended to deliuer them. And novv come, and I vvil ſend thee into Ægypt.* 34

† This Moyſes, vvhom they denied, ſaying, *Vvho hath appointed the prince and Captaine?* him God ſent prince & ∷ redeemer, vvith the hand of the Angel that appeared to him in the buſh. † He ★ brought them forth doing vvonders and ſignes in the land of Ægypt, and in the redde ſea, and in the ★ deſert fourtie yeres. † This is that Moyſes vvhich ſaid to the children of Iſraël, *A prophet vvil God raiſe vp to you of your ovvne brethren as my ſelf: him you ſhal heare.* † This is he that ★ vvas in the aſſemblie in the vvilderneſſe, vvith the Angel that ſpake to him in Mount-Sina, and vvith our fathers: vvho receiued the vvordes of life to giue vnto vs. † To vvhom our fathers vvould not be obedient: but they repelled him, and in their hartes turned avvay into Aegypt, † ſaying to Aaron: *Make vs goddes that may goe before vs. for this Moyſes that brought vs out of the land of Aegypt, vve knovv not vvhat is befallen to him.* † And they made a calfe in thoſe daies, and offered ſacrifice to the Idol, and reioyced in the vvorkes of their ovvne handes. † And God turned, and ∷ deliuered them vp ᶜ to ſerue the hoſt of heauen, as it is vvritten in the booke of the Prophets: *Did you offer victims and hoſtes vnto me fourtie yeres in the deſert, O houſe of Iſraël?* † *And you tooke vnto you the tabernacle of Moloch, and the ſtarre of your God Rempham, figures vvhich you made, to adore them. And I vvil tranſlate you beyond Babylon.* 35 36 37 38 39 40 41 42 43

∷ Chriſt is our Redeemer, and yet Moyſes is here called redeemer. ſo Chriſt is our Mediator and Aduocate, and yet we may haue Saincts our inferior mediators and aduocates alſo. *See Annot. 1 Io. 2, 1.*

∷ For a iuſt puniſhment of their former offenſes God gaue them vp to worke what wickednes they would them ſelues, as it is ſaid of the Gentils *Rom. 1.*

Exo. 7. 8. 9. 10. 11. 12, 37 *Exo. 16.* *Deu. 18.* *Exo. 19, 3. 19.* *Exo. 32, 1.* ᶜ λατρεύειν. *Amos. 5, 25.*

† The tabernacle of teſtimonie vvas among our fathers in the deſert, as God ordained ſpeaking to Moyſes, *that he ſhould make it according to the forme vvhich he had ſeen.* † Vvhich our fathers ★ vvith ᶜ Ieſus receiuing, brought it in alſo into the poſſeſſion of the Gentiles, vvhich God expelled from the face of our fathers, till in the daies of Dauid, † Vvho found grace before God, and ★ deſired that he might finde a tabernacle for the God of Iacob. † And ★ Salomon built him a houſe. † But the Higheſt dvvelleth ⁿ not in houſes ★ made by hand, as the prophet ſaith: † *Heauen is my ſeate: and the earth the foote-ſtole of my feete. Vvhat houſe vvil you build me, ſaith our Lord? or vvhat place is there of my reſting?* † *Hath not my hand made al theſe things?* 44 45 46 47 48 49 50

ᶜ This is Ioſuè, ſo called in Greeke in type of our Sauiour.

Exo. 25. 40. *Ioſ. 3, 14.* *Pſ. 131, 5* *1. Par. 17* *Act. 17, 25.* *Eſa. 66, 1.*

† You ſtiffe-necked and of vncircumciſed hartes and eares, you alvvaies reſiſt the holy Ghoſt: as your fathers, your ſelues alſo. † Vvhich of the prophets did not your fathers perſecute 51 52

cute? And they slevve them that foretold of the comming of the Iust one, of vvhom novv † you haue been betraiers and murderers: vvho receiued the Lavv by the disposition of Angels, and haue not kept it.

54 † And hearing these things they vvere cut in their hartes, and they gnashed vvith their teeth at him. 55 † But he being ful of the holy Ghost, looking stedfastly vnto heauen, c savv the glorie of God, and IESVS standing on the right hand of God. 56 † And he said, Behold I see the heauens opened, and the Sonne of man standing on the right hand of God. 57 † And they crying out vvith a loude voice, stopped their eares, & vvith one accord ranne violently vpon him. 58 † And casting him forth vvithout the citie, they " stoned him: and the vvitnesses laid of their garments * beside the feete of a yong man that vvas called Saul. 59 † And they stoned Steuen inuocating, and saying: Lord IESVS, receiue my spirit. 60 † And falling on his knees, he cried vvith a loude voice, saying: :: Lord, lay not this sinne vnto them. And vvhen he had said this, he fel a sleepe. And Saul vvas consenting to his death.

Act. 22, 20.

c The comfort of al Martyrs.

:: Eusebius Emissenus saith, whé he praieth for his persecutors, he promiseth to his worshippers his manifest intercessió & suffrages. Tho. S. Steph. & S. Augustine, *Si Stephanus sic nō orasset, Ecclesia Paulū nō haberet.* Serm 1 de S. Stephano.

ANNOTATIONS
CHAP. VII.

33. *Holy ground.*) If that apparition of God him self or an Angel, could make the place and ground holy, and to be vsed of Moyses With al signes of reuerence and feare: how much more the corporal birth, abode, and wonders of the Sonne of God in Iewrie, and his personal presence in the B. Sacrament, may make that countrie and al Christian Churches & altars holy? And it is the greatest blindnes that can be, to thinke it superstition to reuerence any things or places in respect of Gods presence or Wonderous operation in the same. *See S. Hierom. ep. 17. 18. 27. of the holy land.*

The holy land.

Holy places.

48. *Not in houses.*) The vulgar Heretikes alleage this place against the corporal being of Christ in the B. Sacrament & in Churches: by Which reason they might haue driuen him out of al houses, Churches, and corporal places, When he vvas visible in earth. But it is meant of the Diuinitie only, & spoken to correct the carnal Ievves: Who thought God either so to be conteined, compassed, and limited to their Temple, that he could be no vvhere els, or at least that he vvould not heare or receiue mens praiers and sacrifices in the Churches of the Gentiles, or els vvhere, out of the said Temple. And so as it maketh nothing for the Sacramentaries, no more doth it serue for such as esteeme Churches and places of publike praier no more conuenient nor more holy then any other profane houses or chambers. For though his person or vertue be not limited to any place, yet it pleaseth him condescending to our necessitie and profite, to vvorke his vvonders and to be vvorshipped of vs in holy places rather then profane.

God is not conteined in place, yet he vvil be vvorshipped in one place more thé in an other.

58. *They stoned him.*) Read a maruelous narration in S. Augustine of one stone, that hitting the Martyr on the elbovv, rebounded backe to a faithful man that stood neere. Who keeping and carying it vvith him, vvas by reuelation vvarned to leaue it at Ancóna in Italie: vvherevpon a Church or Memorie of S. Steuen vvas there erected, and many miracles done after the said Martyrs body vvas found out, and not before. *Aug. to. 10 ser. 38 de diuersis in edit. Paris.*

Relikes.

CHAP. VIII.

The 3. part. THE propagation of the Church from Hierusalem into al Iewrie and to Samaria.

So farre is persecution from preuailing against the Church, that by it the Church groweth from Hierusalem into al Ievvrie and Samaria. 5 The second of the Deacons, Philip, conuerteth vvith his miracles the citie it self of Samaria, and baptizeth them, euen Simon Magus also him self among the rest. 14 But the Apostles Peter and Iohn are the Ministers to giue them the Holy Ghost. 18 Which ministerie Simon Magus vvould bie of them. 26 The same Philip being sent of an Angel to a great man of Æthiopia, Who came a Pilgrimage to Hierusalem, first catechizeth him: 36 and then (he professing his faith and desiring Baptisme) doth also baptize him.

AND the same day there vvas made a great persecution in the Church, vvhich vvas at Hierusalem, and al vvere dispersed through the countries of Ievvrie and Samaria, sauing the Apostles. 1 † And " deuout men [c] tooke order for Steuens funeral, and made great mourning vpon him. 2 † But Saul * vvasted the Church: entring in from house to house, and dravving men and vvomen, deliuered them into prison. 3

[c] *curauerunt* συνεκόμισαν

Act. 22, 4.

† They therfore that vvere dispersed, passed through, :: euangelizing the vvord. 4

:: This persecution wrought much good, being an occasion that the dispersed preached Christ in diuers Coũtries where they came.

The Epistle vpõ Thursday in Whitsunweeke.

† And Philippe descending into the citie of Samaria, preached CHRIST vnto them. 5 † And the multitudes vvere attent to those things vvhich vvere said of Philippe, vvith one accord hearing, and seing the signes that he did. 6 † For many of them that had vncleane spirits, crying vvith a loud voice, vvent out. And many sicke of the palsey and lame vvere cured. 7 † There vvas made therfore great ioy in that citie. ⊣ 8 † And a certaine man named Simon, vvho before had been in that citie a Magician, seducing the nation of Samaria, saying him self to be some great one: 9 † vnto vvhom al harkened from the least to the greatest, saying, This man is the povver of God, that is called great. 10 † And they vvere attent vpon him, because a long time he had bewitched them vvith his magical practises. 11 † But vvhen they had beleeued Philippe euangelizing of the kingdom of God, and of the name of IESVS CHRIST, they vvere baptized, men and vvomen. 12 † Then Simon also him self beleeued: and being baptized, he cleaued to Philippe. Seing also signes and very great miracles to be done, he vvas astonied vvith admiration. 13

† And

14 † And vvhen the Apostles vvho vvere in Hierusalem, had heard that Samaria had receiued the vvord of God: they "sent 15 vnto them :: Peter & Iohn. † Vvho vvhen they vvere come, praied for them, that they might receiue the holy Ghost. 16 † For he vvas not yet come vpon any of them, but they vvere 17 only baptized in the name of our Lord IESVS. † Then did "they impose their handes vpon them, and they "receiued the 18 holy Ghost. ⊣ † And vvhen Simon had seen that by the imposition of the hand of the Apostles, the holy Ghost 19 vvas giuen, he" offered them money, † saying, Giue me also this povver, that on vvhomsoeuer I impose my handes, he 20 may receiue the holy Ghost. † But Peter said to him, Thy money be vvith thee vnto perdition: because thou hast thought that the gift of God is purchased vvith money. 21 † Thou hast no part, nor lot in this vvord. For thy hart is not 22 right before God. † " Doe penance therfore from this thy vvickednesse: and pray to God," if perhaps this cogitation 23 of thy hart may be remitted thee. † For I see thou art in the 24 gall of bitternes and the obligation of iniquitie. † And Simon ansvvering said," Pray you for me to our Lord, that nothing come vpon me of these things vvhich you haue said. 25 † And they in deede hauing testified and spoken the vvord of our Lord, returned to Hierusalem, and euangelized to many countries of the Samaritans.

26 † [b] And an Angel of our Lord spake to Philippe, saying: Arise, and goe tovvard the South, to the vvay that goeth 27 dovvne from Hierusalem into Gaza:" this is desert. † And rising he vvent. And behold, a man of Æthiopia, an eunuch, of great authoritie vnder Candace the Queene of the Æthiopians, vvho vvas ouer al her treasures, vvas come to Hieru-28 salem :: to adore: † and he vvas returning and sitting vpon 29 his chariot, and reading Esay the prophet. † And the Spirit said to Philippe, Goe neere, and ioyne thy self to this same 30 chariot. † And Philippe running therevnto, heard him reading Esay the prophet, and he said: Trovvest thou that thou vn-31 derstādest the things vvhich thou readest? † Vvho said, And :: hovv can I, vnlesse some man shevv me? & he desired Phi-32 lippe that he vvould come vp and sit vvith him. † And the place of the scripture vvhich he did reade, vvas this: *As a sheepe to slaughter vvas he led: and as a lambe before his shearer, vvithout voice, so* 33 *did he not open his mouth.* † *In humilitie his iudgement vvas taken avvay.*

His

The Epistle vpō Tuesday in Whitsūweeke. And in a votiue of the Holy Ghost.

:: *Sæpe sibi sociū Petrus facit esse Ioannem: Ecclesiæ quia virgo placet.* Arator apud Bedam in Act.

μετανόη-σον ἀπὸ

See Apocal. 9, 21.

b The Epistle vpon Thursday in Easter weeke.

:: Note that this Æthiopian came to Hierusalem to adore, that is, on Pilgrimage. Where by we may learne that it is an acceptable acte of religion to go from home to places of greater deuotiō & sanctificatiō.

:: The Scriptures are so writtē that they can not be vnderstood without an interpreter, as easy as our Protestants make them. See S. Hierom *Ep. ad Paulinū de omnibus diuina historia libris*, set in the beginning of latin bibles.

Es. 53, 7.

His generation vvho shal declare, for from the earth shal his life be taken?
† And the eunuch ansvvering Philip, said, I beseeche thee, of 34 vvhom doth the Prophet speake this? of him self, or of some other? † And Philip opening his mouth, and beginning 35 from this scripture, euangelized vnto him IESVS. † And as 36 they vvent by the vvay, they came to a certaine vvater: and the eunuch said, Lo vvater, `vvho' doth let me to be baptized? † And Philip said, If thou beleeue vvith al thy hart, 37 thou maiest. And he ansvvering said, I beleeue that IESVS CHRIST is the sonne of God. † And he commaunded 38 the chariot to stay: and both vvent dovvne into the vvater, Philip and the Eunuch, and "he baptized him. † And when 39 they vvere come vp out of the vvater, the Spirit of our Lord tooke avvay Philip, and the eunuch savv him no more. And he vvent on his vvay reioycing. † But Philip vvas 40 found in Azótus, & passing through, he euangelized to al the cities, til he came to Cæsaréa. ⊣

vvhat

ANNOTATIONS
CHAP. VIII.

S. Steuens relikes.

2. *Deuout men.*] As here great deuotion vvas vsed in burying his body, so aftervvard at the Inuention & Translation thereof. And the miracles vvrought by the same, and at euery litle memorie of the same, vvere infinite: as S. Augustine vvitnesseth. *li.22 de Ciuit. Dei c.8. & Sermon. de S. Steph. to. 10.*

That Peter Was sent, is no reason against his Primacie.

14. *Sent Peter.*] Some Protestants vse this place to proue S. Peter not to be head of the Apostles, because he and S. Iohn Were sent by the Tvvelue. by vvhich reason they might as vvel conclude that he vvas not equal to the rest. for commonly the Maister sendeth the man, and the Superior the inferior, vvhen the vvord of Sending is exactly vsed. But it is not alvvaies so taken in the Scriptures, for then could not the Sonne be sent by the Father, nor the Holy Ghost from the Father and the Sonne: nor othervvise in cōmon vse of the vvorld, seing the inferior or equal may intreate his frend or Superior to doe his busines for him. and specially a body Politike or a Corporation may by election or othervvise choose their Head and send him. so may the Citizens send their Maior to the Prince or Parliament, though he be the head of the citie, because he may be more fitte to doe their busines. also the Superior or equal may be sent by his ovvne consent or desire. Lastly, the College of the Apostles comprising Peter vvith the rest (as euery such Body implieth both the head and the members) vvas greater then Peter their head alone. as the Prince and Parliament is greater then the Prince alone. And so Peter might be sent as by authoritie of the vvhole College, notvvithstanding he vvere the head of the same.

The Sacrament of Confirmation, ministred by Bishops onely.

17. *Did they impose.*] *If this Philip had beene an Apostle* (saith S. Bede) *he might haue imposed his handes, that they might haue receiued the Holy Ghost. but this none can doe sauing Bishops. For though Priests may baptize, and anoint the Baptized also vvith Chrisme consecrated by a Bishop: yet he can not signe his forehead vvith the same holy oile, because that belongeth only to Bishops, vvhen they giue the holy Ghost to the Baptized.* So saith he touching the Sacrament of Confirmation in 8 Act. This imposition therfore of hands together vvith the praiers here specified (vvhich no doubt vvere the very same that the Church yet vseth to that purpose) vvas the ministration of the Sacrament of Confirmation. Whereof S. Cyprian saith thus, They that in Samaria vvere baptized of Philip, because they had lavvful and Ecclesiastical Baptisme, ought not to be baptized any more: but only that vvhich vvanted, vvas done by Peter and Iohn, to vvit, that by praier made for them and imposition of handes, the Holy Ghost might be povvred vpon them. Vvhich novv also is done vvith vs, that they vvhich in the Church are baptized, be by the Rulers of the Church offered, and by our praier and imposition of hand receiue the Holy Ghost, and be signed vvith our Lordes seale. So *S.* Cyprian.

ep. 73. nu. 3 ad Iubaianum.

But

But the Heretikes obiect that yet here is no mention of oile. To vvhom vve say, that many things vvere done and said in the administration of this and other Sacraments, and al instituted by Christ him self and deliuered to the Church by the Apostles, vvhich are not particularly vvritten by the Euangelists or any other in the Scripture, among vvhich this is euident by al antiquitie and most general practise of the Church, to be one.

Ec. Hier. c. 2 & 4.

S. Denys saith, The Priests did present the baptized to the Bishop, that he might signe them *diuino & deifico vnguento*, vvith the diuine and deifical ointment. And againe, *Aduentum S. Spiritus consummans inunctio largitur*, the inunction consummating giueth the comming of the Holy Ghost. Tertullian *de resur. carn. nu. 7 & li. 1 adu. Marcio.* speaketh of this Cōfirmation by Chrisme thus: *The flesh is anointed, that the soul may be consecrated: the flesh is signed, that the soul may be fensed: the flesh by imposition of hand is shadovved, that the soul by the Spirit may be illuminated.* S. Cyprian likevvise, *ep. 70. nu. 2. He must also be anointed, that is baptized, vvith the oile sanctified on the Altar.* And ep. 72 (see also ep. 73. nu. 3) he expresly calleth it a Sacrament, ioyning it vvith Baptisme. as Melchiades doth (*ep. ad omnes Hispaniæ Episcopos nu. 2. to 1 Conc.*) shevving the difference betvvixt it and Baptisme. S. Augustine also, *cont. lit. Petil. li. 2, c. 104. The Sacrament of Chrisme in the kind of visible seales is sacred and holy, euen as Baptisme it self.* Vve omit S. Cyril *mystag. 3.* S. Ambrose *li. 3 de Sacram. c. 2. & de ijs qui mysterijs initiantur c. 7.* S. Leo ep. 88, the aūcient Councels also of Laodicea, can. 48. Carthage 3 can. 39. and Arausicanum 4 can. 1. and others. And S. Clement (*Apost. Const. li. 7, c. 44*) reporteth certaine cōstitutions of the Apostles touching the same.* S. Denys referreth the maner of consecration of the same Chrisme to the Apostles instruction. S. Basil *li. de Sp. sancto c. 27* calleth it a tradition of the Apostles. And the most aūcient Martyr S. Fabian *ep. 2 ad omnes Orientales Episcopos in initio, to. 1 Conc.* saith plainely that Christ him self did so instruct the Apostles at the time of the institution of the B. Sacramēt of the Altar. And so doth the Author of the booke *de vnctione Chrismatis apud D. Cyprianum nu. 1.* telling the excellent effects and graces of this Sacrament, and vvhy this kinde of oile and balsme vvas taken of the old Lavv, & vsed in the Sacraments of the nevv Testament. Vvhich thing the Heretikes can vvith lesse cause obiect against the Church, seeing they confesse * that Christ and his Apostles tooke the ceremonie of imposition of hands in this and other Sacraments, from the Ievves maner of consecrating their hostes deputed to sacrifice.

Chrisme in Cōfirmation.

* *Ec. Hier. c. 4.*

* *Beza in Act. c. 6. v. 6.*

To conclude, neuer none denied or contemned this Sacrament of Confirmation and holy Chrisme, but knovven Heretikes. S. Cornelius that B. Martyr so much praised of S. Cyprian, *ep. ad Fabium apud Euseb. li. 6 c. 35* affirmeth, that Nouatus fel to Heresie, for that he had not receiued the Holy Ghost by the consignation of a Bishop. Vvhom al the Nouatians did folovv, neuer vsing that holy Chrisme, as Theodorete vvriteth, *li. 3 Fabul. Hær.* And Optatus *li. 2 cont Parm.* vvriteth that it vvas the special barbarous sacrilege of the Donatists, to conculcate the holy oile. But al this is nothing to the sauage disorder of Caluinists in this point.

Old heresies against confirmation and Chrisme.

* *kemnit. in exam. conc. Trid. de Confir-*

17. And they receiued the Holy Ghost.] The Protestants charge the Catholikes,* that by approuing and commending so much the Sacrament of Confirmation, and by attributing to it specially the gift of the Holy Ghost, they diminish the force of Baptisme, chalenging also boldly the aūcient Fathers for the same. As though any Catholike or Doctor euer said more then the expresse vvordes of Scripture here and els vvhere plainely giue them vvarrant for. If they diminish the vertue of Baptisme, then did Christ so, appointing his Apostles and al the Faithful euen after their Baptisme to expecte the Holy Ghost & vertue from aboue. then did the Apostles iniurie to Baptisme, in that they imposed hands on the baptized, and gaue them the Holy Ghost. And this is the Heretikes blindnes in this case, that they can not, or vvil not see that the Holy Ghost is giuen in Baptisme to remission of sinnes, life, and sanctification: & in Confirmation, for force, strength, and corroboration to fight against al our spiritual enemies, and to stand constantly in confession of our faith, euen to death, in times of persecution either of the Heathen or of Heretikes, vvith great increase of grace. And let the good Reader note here our Aduersaries great peruersity and corruption of the plaine sense of the Scriptures in this point: some of them affirming the Holy Ghost here to be no other but the gift of vvisedom in the Apostles and a fevv moe to the gouernement of the Church, vvhen it is plaine that not only the Gouerners but al that vvere baptized, receiued this grace, both men and vvomen. Some, that it vvas no internal grace, but only the gift of diuers languages: Vvhich is very false, the gift of Tongues being but a sequele and an accident to the grace, and an external token of the invvard gift of the Holy Ghost, and our Sauiour calleth it vertue from aboue. Some say, that vvhatsoeuer it vvas, it vvas but a miraculous thing, and dured no longer then the gift of the Tongues ioyned therevnto: by vvhich euasion they deny also the Sacrament of Extreme Vnction, and the force of Excommunication, because the corporal punishments vvhich vvere annexed often times in the Primitiue Church vnto it, ceaseth. and so may they take avvay (as they meane to do) al Christs faith or religion, because it hath not the like operation of miracles as in the beginning. But S. Augustine toucheth this point fully. *Is there any man* (saith he) *of so peruerse an hart, to deny these Children on vvhom vve novv imposed hands, to haue receiued the Holy Ghost, because they speake not vvith Tongues? &c.* Lastly, some of them make no more of Confirmation or the Apostles facte, but as of a doctrine, instruction, or exhortation to continevv in the faith receiued. Vvherevpon they

The effectes of Baptisme and Confirmation differ.

Hæretical shiftes and euasiōs against manifest Scriptures, and against this Sacrament of Confirmation.

Tractat. 6 in ep. Io.

* See Conc. Trid. Sess. 7 can. 1 de Confirmat.

they haue turned this holy Sacrament * into a Catechisme. * There are also that put the baptized cōming to yeres of discretiō, to their ovvne choise vvhether they vvil cōtinevv Christiās or no. To such diuelish and diuers inuentions they fall, that vvill not obey Gods Churche nor the expresse Scriptures, vvhich tel vs of praier, of imposition of hands, of the Holy Ghost, of grace and vertue from aboue, and not of instruction, vvhich might and may be done as vvel before Baptisme, & by others, as by Apostles and Bishops, to vvhom only this Holy function pertaineth, in so much that in our Countrie it is called *Bishoping*.

* Conc. Trid. sess. 7 can. 14 de Bapt.

Bishoping.

18. Offered money.] This vvicked sorcerer Simon is noted by S. Irenæus li. 1 c. 20. and others, to haue been the first Heretike, & father of al Heretikes to come, in the Church of God. He taught, only faith in him, vvithout good life and vvorkes, to be ynough to saluation. he gaue the onset to purchase vvith his money a spiritual function, that is to be made a Bishop. for, to haue povver to giue the Holy Ghost by imposition of hādes, is to be a Bishop: as to bye the povver to remitte sinnes or to consecrate Christs body, is to bye to be a Priest, or to bye Priesthod: and to bye the authoritie to minister Sacraments, to preach or to haue cure of soules, is to bye a benefice. and likevvise in al other spiritual things, vvhereof either to make sale or purchase for money or money vvorth, is a great horrible sinne called Simonie: and in such as thinke it lavvful (as here Simon iudged it) it is named *Simoniacal Heresie*, of this detestable man vvho first attempted to bie a spiritual function or office. *D. Greg. apud Ioan. Diac. in vit. li. 3, c. 2. 3. 4. 5.*

Simonie.

22. Doe penance.] S. Augustine (ep. 108) vnderstanding this of the penance done in the Primitiue Church for heinous offenses, doth teach vs to translate this and the like places (2 Cor. 12, 21. Apoc. 9, 21) as vve doe, and as it is in the vulgar Latin, and consequently that the Greeke μετανοεῖν doth signifie so much. Yea vvhen he addeth, that very good men doe daily penance for venial sinnes by fasting, praier, and almes, he vvarranteth this phrase and translation through out the nevv Testament, specially him self also reading so as it is in the vulgar Latin, and as vve translate.

Penance.

22. If perhaps.] You may see, great penance is here required for remission of sinne, & that men must stand in feare and dread lest they be not vvorthy to be heard or to obteine mercie. Vvhereby al men that bye or sel any spiritual functions, dignities, offices, or liuings, may specially be vvarned that the sinne is exceding great.

24. Pray you for me.] As this Sorcerer had more knovvledge of the true religion then the Protestants haue, vvho see not that the Apostles and Bishops can giue the Holy Ghost in this Sacrament or other, vvhich he plainely perceiued and confessed, so surely he vvas more religious then they, that being so sharply checked by the Apostle, yet blasphemed not as they do vvhen they be blamed by the Gouerners of the Church, but desired the Apostles to pray for him.

Simon Magus more religious then the Protestants.

27. This is desert.] Intolerable boldnes of some Protestants, here also (as in other places) against al copies both Greeke and Latin, to surmise corruption or falshod of the text, saying it can not be so: Vvhich is to accuse the holy Euangelist, and to blaspheme the Holy Ghost him self. See Beza, vvho is often very saucie vvith S. Luke.

Beza.

Annot. no. Test. 1556.

38. He baptized him.] When the Heretikes of this time finde mention made in Scripture of any Sacrament ministred by the Apostles or other in the Primitiue Church, they imagine no more vvas done then there is expresly told, nor scarsly beleeue so much. As if imposition of hands in the Sacrament of Confirmation be onely expressed, they thinke there vvas no chrisme nor other vvorke or vvord vsed. So they thinke no more ceremonie vvas vsed in the baptizing of this noble man, then here is mentioned. Vvherevpon S. Augustine hath these memorable vvordes, *In that that he saith, Philip baptized him, he vvould haue it vnderstood that al things vvere done, vvhich though in the Scriptures for breuitie sake they are not mentioned, yet by order of tradition vve knovv vvere to be done.*

The ceremonies of Sacraments done, though not mentioned.

De fid. & op. c. 9.

CHAP. IX.

Saul not content to persecute so cruelly in Hierusalem, 3 is in the vvay to Damascus told by our Lord IESVS *of his vaine attempt, and miraculously conuerted to be an Apostle: and after great penance, restored to his sight by Ananias, and baptized. 20 And presently he dealeth mightily against the Ievves, prouing* IESVS *to be Christ, to their great admiration. 23 But such is their obstinacie, that they lay al Damascus to kil him, 26 From thence he goeth to Hierusalem, and there ioyneth vvith the Apostles, and againe by the obstinate Ievves his death is sought 31 The Church being novv grovven ouer al Ievvrie, Galilee, and Samaria, Peter visiteth al: and in his visitation, 33 healing a lame man, 36 and raising a dead vvoman, conuerteth very many.*

AND

Act. 22, 4 *Gal.* 1, 13.

The Epistle vpō the Conuersion of S. Paul Ian. 25.

1 AND Saul as yet breathing forth threatenings and slaughter against the disciples of our Lord, 2 came to the high priest, † and asked letters of him vnto Damascus to the synagogs, that if he had found any men and vvomen of this 3 vvay, he might bring them bound vnto Hierusalem. † And as he vvent on his iourney, it chaunced that he drevv nigh to Damascus: and * sodenly a light from heauen shined round 4 about him. † And falling on the ground, he heard a voice 5 saying to him, ∴ Saul, Saul vvhy persecutest thou me? † Vvho said, Vvho art thou Lord? And he, I am IESVS vvhom thou doest persecute. it is hard for thee to kicke against the pricke. 6 † And trembling and being astonied he said, Lord, vvhat 7 vvilt thou haue me to doe? † And our Lord to him, Arise, and goe into the citie, and it shal be told thee vvhat thou must doe. But the men that vvent in companie vvith him, 8 stood amased, hearing the voice, but seeing no man. † And Saul rose vp from the ground, and his eies being opened, he savv nothing. And they dravving him by the hādes, brought 9 him into Damascus. † And he vvas three daies not seeing, and he did neither eate nor drinke.

1. Cor. 15, 8.

∴ The heretikes that conclude CHRIST so in heauen that he cā be no where els til the day of Iudgement, shal hardly resolue a mā that would know where CHRIST was when he appeared here in the way, and spake these words to Saul.

10 † And there vvas a certaine disciple at Damascus, named Ananias: and our Lord said to him in a vision, Ananias. But 11 he said, Loe, here I am Lord. † And our Lord to him, Arise, & goe into the streate that is called Straight: and seeke in the house of Iudas, one named Saul of Tarsus. for behold he 12 prayeth. († And he savv a man named Ananias, comming in and imposing handes vpon him for to receiue his sight.) 13 † But Ananias ansvvered, Lord, I haue heard by many of this man, hovv much euil he hath done to thy saincts in Hieru-14 salem: † and here he hath authoritie from the cheefe priests 15 to binde al that inuocate thy name. † And our Lord said to him, Goe, for a vessel of election is this man vnto me, to carie my name before the Gentiles, and kinges, and the chil-16 dren of Israël. † For I vvil shevv him hovv great things he must suffer for my name.

17 † And Ananias vvent, and entred into the house: and imposing handes vpon him, he said, Brother Saul, our Lord IESVS hath sent me, he that appeared to thee in the vvay that thou camest: that thou maiest see and be filled vvith 18 the holy Ghost. † And forthvvith there fel from his eies as it

vvere ſcales,and he receiued ſight. and riſing he vvas ∷ baptized. † And vvhen he had taken meate, he vvas ſtrengthened. 19

∷ Paul alſo him ſelf, though with the diuine and heauenly voice proſtrated and inſtructed, yet was ſent to a man to receiue the Sacraments, & to be ioyned to the Church. *Auguſt. de doct. Chr. lib. 1. in proœm.*

And he vvas vvith the diſciples that vvere at Damaſcus, for certaine daies. † And incontinent entring into the ſynagogs, he preached IESVS, that this is the ſonne of God. 20 † And al that heard, vvere aſtonied, and ſaid, Is not this he 21 that expugned in Hieruſalem thoſe that inuocated this name: and came hither to this purpoſe that he might bring them bound to the cheefe prieſts? † But Saul vvaxed mightie much 22 more, and confounded the Ievves that dvvelt at Damaſcus, affirming that this is CHRIST. ⊣ † And vvhen many daies 23 vvere paſſed, the Ievves conſulted that they might kil him. † But their conſpiracie came to Sauls knovvledge. And *they 24 kept the gates alſo day and night, that they might kil him. † But the diſciples taking him in the night, conueied him 25 avvay by the vvall, letting him dovvne in a baſket.

2 Cor. 11, 32.

† And vvhen he vvas come into Hieruſalem, he aſſaied to 26 ioyne him ſelf to the diſciples, & al feared him, not beleeuing that he vvas a diſciple. † But Barnabas tooke him & brought 27 him to the Apoſtles, and told them hovv in the vvay he had ſeen our Lord, and that he ſpake vnto him, and hovv in Damaſcus he dealt confidently in the name of IESVS. † And 28 he vvas vvith them going in and going out in Hieruſalem, and dealing confidently in the name of our Lord. † He ſpake 29 alſo to the Gentiles, and diſputed vvith the Greekes: but they ſought to kil him. † Vvhich vvhen the brethren had knovven, they brought him dovvne to Cæſaréa, and ſent him 30 avvay to Tarſus.

† The ∷ CHVRCH truely through al Ievvrie & Galilee 31 and Samaria had peace, & vvas edified, vvalking in the feare of our Lord, and vvas repleniſhed vvith the conſolation of the holy Ghoſt.

The Church viſibly procedeth ſtill vvith much comfort & manifold increaſe euen by perſecution.

† And it came to paſſe, that Peter as he paſſed through 32 al, came to the ſaincts that dvvelt at Lydda. † and he found 33 there a certaine man named Æneas, lying in his bed from eight yeres before, vvho had the palſey. † And Peter ſaid 34 to him, Æneas, our Lord IESVS CHRIST ˋhealeˊ thee: ariſe, and make thy bed. And incontinent he aroſe. † And al that 35 dvvelt at Lydda and Sarόna, ſavv him: vvho conuerted to our Lord.

ˋ healeth

† And

36 † And in Ioppé there vvas a certaine disciple named Tabitha, vvhich by interpretation is called Dorcas. This vvomā vvas ful of ∷ good vvorkes and almes-deedes vvhich she 37 did. † And it came to passe in those daies, that she vvas sicke and died. Vvhom vvhen they had vvashed, they laid her in 38 an vpper chamber. † And vvhereas Lydda vvas nigh to Ioppé, the disciples hearing that Peter vvas in it, they sent tvvo men vnto him, desiring him, Be not loth to come so 39 farre as to vs. † And Peter rising vp came vvith them. And vvhen he vvas come, they brought him into the vpper chamber: and al the vvidovves stoode about him vveeping, ∷ and shevving him the coates and garments vvhich Dorcas made 40 them. † And al being put forth, Peter falling on his knees praied, and turning to the body he said: Tabitha, arise. And 41 she opened her eies: and seeing Peter, she sate vp. † And giuing her his hand, he lifted her vp. And vvhen he had called 42 the saincts and the vvidovves, he presented her aliue. † And it vvas made knovven through out al Ioppé: and many be-43 leeued in our Lord. † And it came to passe that he abode many daies in Ioppé, vvith one Simon a tanner.

∷ Behold good vvorkes and almes-deedes, & the force thereof reaching euen to the next life.

∷ The praiers of our Almes folke & beadsmen may do vs great good euē after our departure. For if they procured her temporal life, much more may they helpe vs to Gods mercie and to release of punishment in Purgatorie.

CHAP. X.

Because the Ievves so much abhorred the Gentils, for the better vvarrant of their Christening, an Angel appeareth to Cornelius the deuout Italian. 9 and a vision is shevved to Peter him self (the cheefe and Pastor of al) 19 and the Spirit speaketh to him, 34 yea and as he is Catechizing them about IESVS, *44 the holy Ghost commeth visibly vpon them: and therfore not fearing any longer the offense of the Ievves, he commaundeth to baptize them.*

The 4 part. THE propagation of the Church to the Gentils also.

1 AND there vvas a certaine man in Cæsaréa, named Cornelius, Centurion of that 2 vvhich is called the Italian band, † religious, & fearing God vvith al his house, "doing many almes-deedes to the people. 3 And alvvaies praying to God, † he savv in a vision manifestly, about the ninthe houre of the day, an Angel of God comming in vnto 4 him, and saying to him, Cornelius. † But he beholding him, taken vvith feare, said, Vvho art thou Lord? And he said to him, Thy praiers and thy almes-deedes are ascended into 5 remembrance in the sight of God. † And novv send men

vnto Ioppé, and call hither one Simon that is ſurnamed Peter. † he lodgeth vvith one Simon a tanner, vvhoſe houſe 6 is by the ſea ſide. he vvil tel thee vvhat thou muſt doe. † And 7 vvhen the Angel vvas departed that ſpake to him, he called tvvo of his houſhold, and a ſouldiar that feared our Lord, of them that vvere vnder him. † To vvhom vvhen he had told 8 all, he ſent them vnto Ioppé.

† And the next day vvhiles they vvere going on their 9 iourney, and dravving nigh to the citie, Peter vvent vp into the higher partes, " to pray about the ſixt houre. † And being 10 hungrie, he vvas deſirous to take ſomevvhat. And as they vvere preparing, there fel vpon him an exceſſe of minde: † and 11 he ſavv the heauen opened, and a certaine veſſel deſcending, as it vvere a great linen ſheete vvith foure corners let dovvne from heauen to the earth, † vvherein vvere al foure-footed 12 beaſtes, and that creepe on the earth, and foules of the aire. † And there came a voice to him, Ariſe Peter: kil, and eate. 13 † But Peter ſaid, God forbid, Lord: for I did neuer eate any 14 common and vncleane thing. † And :: a voice came to him 15 againe the ſecond time, That vvhich God hath purified, doe not thou cal common. † And this vvas done thriſe. and 16 forthvvith the veſſel was taken vp againe into heauen. † And 17 vvhiles Peter doubted vvithin him ſelf, vvhat the viſion ſhould be that he had ſeen, behold the men that vvere ſent from Cornelius, inquiring for Simons houſe, ſtood at the gate. † And vvhen they had called, they aſked, if Simon that 18 is ſurnamed Peter, vvere lodged there. † And as Peter vvas 19 thinking of the viſion, the Spirit ſaid to him, Behold three men doe ſeeke thee. † Ariſe therfore, and get thee dovvne, 20 and goe vvith them, doubting nothing: for I haue ſent them. † And Peter going dovvne to the men, ſaid, Behold, I am he 21 vvhom you ſeeke: vvhat is the cauſe, for the vvhich you are come? † Vvho ſaid, Cornelius the Centurion, a iuſt man & 22 that feareth God, and hauing teſtimonie of al the nation of the Ievves, receiued an anſvver of an holy Angel to ſend for thee into his houſe, and to heare vvordes of thee. † Ther- 23 fore bringing them in, he lodged them.

:: Here God firſt vttered to Peter that the time was come to preach alſo to the Gentiles, and to cōuerſe with them for their ſaluation, no leſſe then with the Iewes, with ful freedō to eate al meates without reſpecte of the prohibition of certaine, made in the old Law.

† And the day folovving he aroſe and vvent vvith them: and certaine of the brethren of Ioppé accompanied him. † And on the morow he entred into Cæſaréa. And Cornelius 24 expected them, hauing called together his kinne, and ſpecial frendes.

25 frendes. † And it came to passe, Vvhen Peter vvas come in, Cornelius came to meete him, and falling at his feete "adored.
26 † But Peter lifted him vp saying, Arise, my self also am a man.
27 † And talking vvith him, he vvent in, and findeth many that
28 vvere assembled, † and he said to them, You knovv hovv abominable it is for a man that is a Ievve, to ioyne, or to approche vnto a stranger: but God hath shevved to me, to call
29 no man cōmon or vncleane. † For the vvhich cause, making no doubt, I came vvhen I vvas sent for. I demaund therfore,
30 for vvhat cause you haue sent for me? † And Cornelius said, Foure daies since, vntil this houre, I vvas [c] praying the ninthe houre in my house, and behold ∴ a man stoode before me
31 in vvhite apparel, † and said: Cornelius, thy praier is heard, and thy almes-deedes are in memorie in the sight of God.
32 † Send therfore to Ioppé, and call hither Simon that is surnamed Peter: he lodgeth in the house of Simon a tanner by
33 the sea side. † Immediatly therfore I sent to thee: and thou hast done vvel in comming. Novv therfore al vve are present in thy sight, to heare al things vvhatsoeuer are commaunded thee of the Lord.

34 † And Peter opening his mouth, said, In very deede I per-
35 ceiue that God is not an accepter of persons. † but in euery nation, he that feareth him, and [c] vvorketh iustice, is accepta-
36 ble to him. † The word did God send to the children of Israël, preaching peace by IESVS CHRIST (this is Lord of al.)
37 † [b] You knovv the vvord that hath been made through al Ievvrie, for* beginning frō Galilee, after the baptisme vvhich
38 Iohn preached. † IESVS of Nazareth hovv God anointed him vvith the holy Ghost and vvith povver, vvho vvent through out doing good and healing al that vvere oppressed
39 of the Deuil, because God vvas vvith him. † And vve are vvitnesses of al things that he did in the countrie of the Ievves and in Hierusalem, vvhom they killed hanging him
40 vpon a tree. † Him God raised vp the third day and " gaue
41 him to be made manifest, † not to al the people, but to vs, vvho did eate and drinke vvith him after he rose againe
42 from the dead. † And he commaunded vs to preach to the people, and to testifie that it is he that of God vvas appointed
43 iudge of the liuing and of the dead. † To him al the prophets giue testimonie, that al receiue remission of sinnes by his name, vvhich beleeue in him. ┘

† As

In the Greeke, fasting & praying.

Mat. 4, 12.

c At the time of praier specially God sendeth men comfortable visitations.

∴ Note these apparitions and visions to S. Peter, Cornelius, and others, in the Scriptures very oftē, against the incredulity of our Heretikes, that wil beleeue neither vision nor miracle, not expressed in Scripture: these being beleeued of Christian men euē before they were written.

c Not such as beleeue only, but such as feare God and worke iustice, are acceptable to him.

b The Epistle vpō Munday in Easter weeke.

The Epistle vpō Munday in vvhitsōvveeke.

† As Peter vvas yet ſpeaking theſe vvordes, the holy 44 Ghoſt fel vpon al that heard the vvord. † And the faithful 45 of the Circumciſion that came with Peter, vvere aſtonied, for that the grace of the holy Ghoſt vvas poured out vpon the Gentiles alſo. † For they heard them ſpeaking with tonges, 46 and magnifying God. Then Peter anſvvered, † Can any man 47 forbid vvater, that theſe ſhould not be " baptized vvhich haue receiued the holy Ghoſt as vvel as vve? † And he com- 48 maũded them to be baptized in the name of our Lord IESVS CHRIST. ⁋ Then they deſired him that he vvould tarie vvith them certaine daies.

ANNOTATIONS
CHAP. X.

Good vvorkes before faith, are preparatiues to the ſame, not properly meritorious.

2. *Doing many almes deedes.*] *He knevv God creator of al, but that his omnipotent Sonne vvas incarnate, he knevv not: and in that faith he made praiers and gaue almes vvhich pleaſed God. and by vvel doing he deſerued to knovv God perfectly, to beleeue the myſterie of the Incarnation, and to come to the Sacrament of Baptiſme.* So ſaith Venerable Bede out of S. Gregorie. (Bed. in hũc locum.) And S. Auguſtine thus, *li. 1 de Bapt. c. 8. Becauſe vvhatſoeuer goodnes he had in praiers and almes, the ſame could not profite him vnles he vvere by the band of Chriſtian Societie and peace, incorporated to the Church, he is bidden to ſend vnto Peter, that by him he may learne Chriſt, by him he may be baptized, &c.* Vvhereby it appeareth that ſuch vvorkes as are done before iuſtification, though they ſuffiſe not to ſaluation, yet be acceptable preparatiues to the grace of iuſtification, and ſuch as moue God to mercie, as it might appeare alſo by Gods like prouident mercifulnes * to the Eunuche. (Act. 8.) though al ſuch vvorkes preparatiue come of grace alſo: othervviſe they could neuer deſerue at Gods hand of congruity or any othervviſe tovvard iuſtification.

The Canonical houres.

9. *To pray about the ſixt houre.*] The houre is ſpecified, for that there vvere certaine appointed times of praier vſed in the Lavv, vvhich deuout perſons, according to the publike ſeruice in the Temple, obſerued alſo priuately: and vvhich the Apoſtles and holy Church aftervvard both kept and increaſed. Vvhereof thus vvriteth S. Cyprian very notably. (De Orat. Dom. nu. 15.) *In celebrating their praiers, vve finde that the three children With Daniel obſerued the third, ſixt, and ninthe houre, as in Sacrament* (or myſterie) *of the holy Trinitie. &c.* And a litle after, *Which ſpaces of houres the vvorſhippers of God ſpiritually* (or myſtically) *determining long ſince, obſerued ſet times to pray: and aftervvard the thing became maniſeſt, that it vvas for Sacrament* (or myſterie) *that the iuſt ſo praied. For at the third houre the holy Ghoſt deſcended vpon the Apoſtles, fulfilling the grace of our Lords promis.* (Act. 2.) *and at the ſixt houre Peter going vp to the higher roome of the houſe, vvas both by voice and ſigne from God inſtructed, that al Nations ſhould be admitted to the grace of ſaluation, vvhereas of cleanſing the Gentiles he doubted before.* (Act. 10.) *and our Lord being crucified at the ſixt houre, at the ninthe vvaſhed avvay our ſinnes vvith his bloud.* (Luc. 23.) *But to vs (deerly beloued) beſide the ſeaſons obſerued of old, both the times and ſacraments of praying be increaſed. for vve muſt pray in the morning early, that the Reſurrection of our Lord may be celebrated by morning praier: as of old the holy Ghoſt deſigned in the Pſalme, ſaying, In the morning early vvil I ſtand vp to thee, early in the morning vvilt thou heare my voice.* (Pſal. 5.) Tovvard the euening *alſo vvhen the ſunne departeth, and the day endeth, vve muſt of neceſſitie pray againe.*

Mattins.

Euenſong.

S. Hierom alſo vvriting of Daniels praying *three times in a day*, ſaith: (Dan. 6.) *There are three times, vvherein vve muſt bovv our knees to God. The third, the ſixt, and the ninthe houre the Eccleſiaſtical tradition doth vvel vnderſtand. Moreouer at the third houre the Holy Ghoſt deſcended vpon the Apoſtles. at the ſixt, Peter vvent vp into a higher chamber to pray: at the ninthe, * Peter and Iohn vvent to the Temple.* (Act. 3.) Againe vvriting to Euſtochium a virgin and Nonne ep. 22 c. 16. *Though the Apoſtle bid vs pray alvvaies, and to holy perſons their very ſleepe is praier: yet vve muſt haue diſtinct houres of praier, that if perhaps vve be othervviſe occupied, the very time may admoniſh vs of our office or duety. The third, ſixt, ninthe houre, morning early, and the euening, no man can be ignorant of.* And to Demetrias ep. 8 c. 8. that in the Pſalmes and praier ſhe muſt keepe *alvvaies the third, ſixt, ninthe houre, euening, midnight, and morning.* He hath the like ep. 7 c. 5. And (ep. 27 c. 10.) he telleth hovv Paula the holy Abbeſſe

vvith

vvith her religious Nonnes *sang the Psalter in order, in the morning, at the third, sixt, ninthe houre, euening, midnight.* by midnight meaning the time of Mattins (therfore called *Nocturnes* agreably to *S.* Cyprian de Orat. Do. num. 15) and by *the morning,* the first houre called *Prime*: al correspondent to the times and houres of Christs Passion, as in S. Matthevv is noted c 26. 27. By al vvhich vve see, hovv agreable the vse of the Churches seruice is euen at this time to the Scriptures and primitiue Church: and hovv vvicked the Puritan-Caluinistes be, that count al such order and set seasons of praier, superstition: and lastly, hovv insufficient and vnlike the nevv pretended Church-seruice of England is to the primitiue vse, vvhich hath no such houres of night or day, sauing a litle imitation of the old Mattins and Euensong, and that in Schisme and Heresie, and therfore not onely vnprofitable, but also damnable.

25. Adored.] S. Chrysostom *ho. 21 in Act.* thinketh Peter refused this adoration of humilitie only, because euery falling dovvne to the ground for vvorship sake, is not Diuine vvorship or dew only to God, * the vvord of adoration and prostration being commonly vsed in the Scriptures tovvard men. But *S.* Hierom *adu. Vigil. c. 2 to. 2.* rather thinketh that Cornelius by error of Gentility, and of Peters person, did go about to adore him vvith Diuine honour, and therfore vvas lifted vp by the Apostle, adding that he vvas but a man.

*προσκυνεῖν.

Adoration of creatures.

40. Gaue him.] Christ did not vtter his Resurrection and other mysteries to al at once, and immediatly to the vulgar: but to a fevv chosen men that should be the gouernours of the rest. instructing vs thereby to take our faith and al necessarie things of saluation, at the hands of our Superiors.

47. Baptized, vvhich haue receiued.] Such may be the grace of God sometimes tovvard men, and their charitie and contrition so great, that they may haue remission, iustification, and sanctification before the external Sacrament of Baptisme, Confirmation, or Penance be receiued. as vve see in this example, vvhere at Peters preaching they al receiue the Holy Ghost before any Sacrament. but in the same vve learne one necessarie lesson, that such notvvithstanding must needes receiue the Sacraments appointed by Christ, vvhich vvhosoeuer contemneth, can neuer be iustified. *Aug. super Leuit. q. 84 to. 4.*

They that are iustified before, must not omit the Sacraments.

CHAP. XI.

The Christian Ievves reprehend the foresaid fact of Peter in baptizing the Gentils 4 But he alleaging his foresaid vvarrants, and shevving plainly that it vvas of God, 18 they like good Catholikes do yeld. 19 By the foresaid persecution, the Church is yet further dilated, not only into al Ievvrie, Galilee, and Samaria, but also into other Countries: specially in Antiochia Syria the increase among the Greekes, is notable, first by the foresaid dispersed, 22 then by Barnabas, thirdly by him and Saul together: so that there beginneth the name of Christians: 27 vvith perfite vnity betvvene them and the Church that vvas before them at Hierusalem.

1 AND the Apostles and brethren that vvere in Ievvrie, heard that the Gentiles also receiued the vvord of God. 2 † And vvhen Peter vvas come vp to Hierusalem, they that vvere of the Circumcision reasoned 3 against him, saying, † Vvhy didst thou enter in to men vncircumcised, and didst eate vvith them? 4 † But Peter began and declared to them the order, saying: 5 † * I vvas in the citie of Ioppé praying, & I savv in an excesse of minde a vision, a certaine vessel descending as it vvere a great sheete vvith foure corners let dovvne from heauen, and it came euen 6 vnto me. † Into vvhich I looking cõsidered, and savv foure footed beastes of the earth, and cattel, and such as creepe, and

Act. 10, 9.

Sf foules

foules of the aire. † And I heard allo a voice ſaying to me, 7 Ariſe Peter, kil and eate. † And I ſaid, Not ſo Lord: for 8 common or vncleane thing neuer entred into my mouth. † And a voice anſvvered the ſecond time from heauen: That 9 vvhich God hath made cleane, doe not thou call common. † And this vvas done thriſe: and al vvere taken vp againe 10 into heauen. † And behold, three men immediatly vvere 11 come to the houſe vvherein I vvas, ſent to me from Cæſaréa. † And the ſpirit ſaid to me, that I ſhould goe vvith them, 12 doubting nothing. And there came vvith me theſe ſixe brethren alſo: and vve vvent in to the mans houſe. † And he 13 told vs, hovv he had ſeen an Angel in his houſe, ſtanding and ſaying to him, Send to Ioppé, and cal hither Simon, that is ſurnamed Peter, † vvho ſhal ſpeake to thee vvordes vvherein 14 thou ſhalt be ſaued and al thy houſe. † And vvhen I 15 had begonne to ſpeake, the holy Ghoſt fel vpon them, as vpō vs alſo in the beginning. † And I remembred the vvord of 16 our Lord, according as he ſaid, *Iohn in deede baptized vvith vvater, but you ſhal be baptized vvith the holy Ghoſt.* † If therfore God hath 17 giuen them the ſame grace, as to vs alſo that beleeued in our Lord IESVS CHRIST: vvho vvas I that might prohibite God? † Hauing heard theſe things, they ∴ held their peace: 18 and glorified God, ſaying, God then to the Gentiles alſo hath giuen repentance vnto life.

Act. 1,5.

∴ Good Chriſtians heare and obey gladly ſuch truthes as be opened vnto them from God by their cheefe Paſtors, by viſion, reuelation, or otherwiſe.

† * And they truely that had been diſperſed by the tribulation 19 that vvas made vnder Steuen, vvalked through out vnto Phœnîce and Cypres & Antioche, ſpeaking the vvord to none, but to the Ievves only. † But certaine of them vvere 20 men of Cypres and Cyréne, vvho vvhen they vvere entred into Antioche, ſpake to the Greekes, preaching our Lord IESVS. † And the hand of our Lord vvas vvith them: and 21 a great number of beleeuers vvas conuerted to our Lord. † And the report came to the eares of the Church that vvas 22 at Hieruſalem, touching theſe things: and they ſent * Barnabas as farre as Antioche. † Vvho vvhen he vvas come, and 23 ſavv the grace of God, reioyced: and he exhorted al vvith purpoſe of hart to continevv in our Lord: † becauſe he 24 vvas a good man, and ful of the holy Ghoſt and faith. And a great″ multitude vvas added to our Lord. † And he vvent 25 forth to * Tarſus, to ſeeke Saul: † vvhom vvhen he had 26 found, he brought him to Antioche. And they cōuerſed there in

Act. 8,1.

The Epiſtle vpō S. Barnabees day *Iun. 11.*

Act. 4, 36.

Act. 9, 30.

in the church a vvhole yere: and they taught a great multitude, so that the disciples vvere at Antioche first named "CHRISTIANS.

The name of CHRISTIANS.

27 † And in these daies there came Prophets from Hierusalem to Antioche, † and one of them rising, named Agabus,
28 did by the Spirit signifie a great famine that should be in the
29 vvhole vvorld, vvhich fel vnder Claudius. † And the disciples according as eche man had, purposed euery one to send,
30 for to serue the brethren that dvvelt in Ievvrie: † vvhich also they did, sending to the auncients by the handes of Barnabas and Saul.

ANNOTATIONS
CHAP. XI.

24. *Multitude added.*) As before (c. 10) a fevv, so novv great numbers of Gentiles are adioyned also to the visible Church, consisting before only of the Ievves. Vvhich Church hath beene euer since Christs Ascension, notoriously seen and knovven: their preaching open, their Sacraments visible, their discipline visible, their Heades and Gouernours visible, the prouision for their maintenance visible, the persecution visible, their dispersion visible: the Heretikes that vvent out from them, visible: the ioyning either of men or Nations vnto them, visible: their peace and rest after persecutions, visible: their Gouernours in prison, visible: the Church praieth for them visibly, their Councels visible, their gifts and graces visible, their name (Christians) knovven to al the vvorld. of the Protestants inuisible Church vve heare not one vvord.

The Church visible.

26. *Christians.*) This name, *Christian*, ought to be common to al the Faithful, and other nevv names of Schismatikes and Sectaries must be abhorred. *If thou heare* (saith S. Hierom) *any vvhere, such as be said to be of Christ, not to haue their names of our Lord* IESVS CHRIST, *but to be called after some other certaine name, as Marcionites, Valentinians,* (as novv also the Lutherans, Caluinists, Protestants) *knovv thou that they belong not to the Church of Christ, but to the Synagogue of Antichrist.* Lactantius also (li. 7 Diuin. instit. c. 30) saith thus, *When Phrygians, or Nouatians, or Valentinians, or Marcionites, or Anthropomorphites, or Arrians, or any other be named, they cease to be Christians, vvho hauing lost the name of Christ, haue done on the names of men.* Neither can our nevv Sectaries discharge them selues, for that they take not to them selues these names, but are forced to beare them as giuen by their Aduersaries. For, so vvere the names of Arians and the rest of old, imposed by others, and not chosen commonly of them selues: Vvhich notvvithstanding vvere callings that proued them to be Heretikes. And as for the name of Protestants, our men hold them vvel content therevvith. But concerning the Heretikes turning of the argument against the peculiar callings of our Religious, as Dominicās, Franciscans, Iesuites, Thomists, or such like, it is nothing, except they could proue that the orders & persons so named, vvere of diuers faithes & Sectes, or differed in any necessarie point of religion, or vvere not al of one Christian name and Communion: and it is as ridiculous as if it vvere obiected, that some be Ciceronians, some Plinians, some good Augustine men, some Hieronymians, some Oxford mē, some Cambrige men, & (vvhich is most like) some * Rechabites, some * Nazareites.

Hierony. cont. Lucif c. 7. in fine.

Names of Sectaries and Heretikes.

Protestants.

Diuers religious orders are not diuers sectes.

Ierem. 35. Num. 6.

Neither doth their obiection, that vve be called Papistes, helpe or excuse them in their nevv names, for, besides that it is by them scornfully inuented (as the name Homousians vvas of the Arians) this name is not of any one man B. of Rome or els vvhere, knovven to be the author of any schisme or sect, as their callings be: but it is of a vvhole state and order of gouernours, and that of the cheefe Gouernours, to vvhom vve are bound to cleaue in religion and to obey in al things. So to be a Papist, is to be a Christian man, a childe of the Church, and subiect to Christs Vicar. And therfore against such impudent Sectaries as compare the faithful for folovving the Pope, to the diuersitie of Heretikes bearing the names of nevv Maisters, let vs euer haue in readines this saying of S. Hierom to Pope Damasus, *Vitalis I knovv not, Meletius I refuse, I knovv not Paulinus. Whosoeuer gathereth not vvith thee, scattereth: that is to say, Whosoeuer is not Christs, is Antichrists.* And againe, *If any man ioyne vvith Peters Chaire, he is mine.*

Papistes, Catholikes, and true Christians, al one.

to. 2. ep. 57 & ep. 58 ad Damas.

Not to be With the Pope, is to be With Antichrist.

The name of CHRISTIANS.

Vve must here further obserue that this name, Christian, giuen to al beleeuers and to the vvhole Church, vvas specially taken to distinguish them from the Ievves and Heathens vvhich beleeued not at al in Christ, and the same novv seuereth and maketh knovven al Christian men from Turkes and others that hold not of Christ at al. But vvhen Heretikes began to rise from among the Christians, vvho professed Christs name and sundry Articles of faith as true beleeuers doe, the name *Christian* vvas to common to seuer the Heretikes from true faithful men: and therevpon the Apostles by the holy Ghost imposed this name *Catholike* vpon the Beleeuers vvhich in al points vvere obedient to the Churches doctrine. *When heresies vvere risen* (saith S. Pacianus ep. ad Symphorianum) *& endeuoured by diuers names to teare the doue of God and Queene, and to rent her in peeces, the Apostolical people required their surname, vvhereby the incorrupt people might be distinguished. &c.* and so those that before vvere called Christians, are novv surnamed also Catholikes. *Christian is my name,* saith he, *Catholike my surname.* And this vvord, Catholike, is the proper note vvhereby the holy Apostles in their Crede taught vs to discerne the true Church from the false heretical congregation of vvhat sort soeuer. And not only the meanĩg of the vvord, vvhich signifieth vniuersalitie of times, places, and persons, but the very name and vvord it self, by Gods prouidence, alvvaies and only appropriated to the true beleeuers, and (though sometimes at the beginning of Sectes chalenged) yet neuer obtained by Heretikes, giueth so plaine a marke and euidence, that S. Augustine said, *In the lappe of the Church the very name of Catholike keepeth me.* cont. ep. fund. c. 4. And againe tract. 32 in Io. *vve receiue the Holy Ghost if vve loue the Church, if vve be ioyned together by charitie, if vve reioyce in the Catholike name and faith.* And againe de ver. rel. c. 7. to. 1. *We must hold the communion of that Church vvhich is named Catholike, not only of her ovvne, but also of al her enemies. for, vvil they nil they, the Heretikes also and Schismatikes them selues, vvhen they speake not vvith their ovvne fellovves but vvith strangers, call the Catholike Church nothing els but the Catholike Church: for they could not be understood vnles they discerne it by this name vvherevvith she is called of al the vvorld.* The Heretikes vvhen they see them selues preuented of this name *Catholike*, then they plainely reiect it and deride the name, as the Donatistes did, calling it an *humane forgerie or fiction*, vvhich S. Augustine calleth vvordes of blasphemie, *li. 1 c. 33 cont. Gaudent.* and some Heretikes of this time call them scornefully catholikes, and cacolikes. An other calleth it, *the most vaine terme Catholike. Beza in praef. no. Test. an. 1565.* An other calleth the Catholike religion, *a Catholike Apostasie or defection, Humfrey in vit. Iuel. pag. 213.* Yea and some haue taken the vvord out of the Crede,* putting *Christian* for it. But against these good fellovves let vs folovv that vvhich S. Augustine (*de vtil. cred. c. 8. to. 6.*) giueth as a rule to direct a mã the right and sure vvay from the diuersitie & doubtfulnes of al error, saying, *If after these troubles of minde thou seeme to thy self sufficiently tossed and vexed, & vvilt haue an end of these molestations, folovv the vvay of* Catholike *discipline, vvhich from Christ him self by the Apostles hath proceded euen vnto vs, and shal procede from hence to the posteritie.* See the Annotation *1 Tim. 3, c. 15.*

The name of CATHOLIKES.

CREDO ECCLESIAM CATHOLICAM.

The Protestãts deride the name CATHOLIKE.

* In the Catechismes of the Lutherans.

CHAP. XII.

Herod the first king that persecuted the Church, hauing at Hierusalem (vvhen Barnabas and Saul vvere there vvith the collation of the Antiochians) killed Iames the Apostle, 3 and to please the Ievves imprisoned Peter vvith the minde to kil him also, but frustrate by an Angel sent of God at the continual praiers of the Church made for her cheefe Pastor, 19 being puffed vp vvith such pride that at Caesaréa he refuseth not to be honoured as God: 23 is miraculously striken of Gods Angel. 24 And so after the persecutors death, the Churches preaching prospereth excedingly.

The Epistle vpõ SS. Peter and Paules day *Iun. 29.*

ND at the same time Herod the king set his hãdes, to afflicte certaine of the Church. † And he killed Iames the brother of Iohn vvith the svvord. † And seing that it pleased the Ievves, he added to apprehend Peter also. And it vvas the daies of the Azymes. † Vvhom vvhen he had apprehended, he cast into prison, deliuering him to ∷ foure quaterniõs of souldiars to be kept, meaning after the Pasche to bring him forth to the people. † And Peter in deede vvas kept in prison. But ″ praier vvas made of the Church vvithout intermission

1 2 3 4 5

∷ As Peters person vvas more notorious then others, & therfore better garded then other, for feare he should escape: so Gods prouidence in preseruing & deliuering him for the longer gouernment of his Church, is very maruelous.

6 mission vnto God for him. † And vvhen Herod vvould haue brought him forth, the same night Peter vvas sleeping betvvene tvvo souldiars, bound vvith" tvvo chaines: and the
7 keepers before the doore kept the prison. † And behold an Angel of our Lord stoode in presence: and light shined in the house: and striking Peters side, he raised him, saying,
8 Arise quickely. And the chaines fel from his handes. † And the Angel said to him, Gird thee, and put on thy shoes. And he did so. And he said to him, Put thy garment about thee, &
9 folovv me. † And going forth he folovved him, & he knew not that it vvas true vvhich vvas done by the Angel: but he
10 thought that he savv a vision. † And passing through the first & the second vvatch, they came to the yron gate that leadeth to the citie, vvhich of it self opened to them. And going out, they vvent forvvard one streate: and incontinent the
11 Angel departed from him. † And Peter returning to him self, said: Novv I knovv in very deede that our Lord hath sent his Angel, and deliuered me out of Herods hand, & from al the expectation of the people of the Ievves. ⫞

12 † And considering, he came to the :: house of Marie the mother of Iohn, vvho vvas surnamed Marke, vvhere many
13 vvere gathered and praying. † And vvhen he knocked at the doore of the gate, there came forth a vvenche to see, na-
14 med Rhodè. † And as she knew Peters voice, for ioy she opened not the gate, but running in she told that Peter stoode
15 before the gate. † But they said to her, Thou art mad. But she
16 affirmed that it vvas so. But they said, It is" his Angel. † And Peter cōtinued knocking. And vvhē they had opened, they
17 savv him, & vvere astonied. † And beckening vvith his hand to them, that they should hold their peace, he told hovv our Lord had brought him out of prison, and he said, " Tel these things to Iames & to the brethren. And going forth he vvent
18 :: into an other place. † And when day vvas come, there vvas no litle a doe betvvene the souldiars, vvhat vvas become of
19 Peter. † And Herod, vvhen he had sought him, and had not found, making inquisitiō of the keepers, cōmaūded them to be led avvay: & going dovvne frō Ievvrie into Cæsaréa, there
20 he abode. † And he vvas angrie vvith the Tyrians and the Sidonians. But they vvith one accord came to him, and persuading Blastus that vvas cheefe of the kings chamber, they desired peace, for that their countries vvere nourished by him.

:: It is much for the praise of these good Christians that the assemble to Gods seruice & praier was kept in their houses in the time of persecution, & that the Apostle came thither straight out of prison, as his first refuge. as now Christian people doe much to their cōmendatiō, in places where Heresie doth reigne.

:: Though God had so miraculously deliuered him, yet he would not tēpt God by tarying among his persecutors, but accordīg to Christes cōmaundement fled for a time.

† And vpon a day appointed, Herod being araied vvith [21] kingly attire, sate in the iudgement seate, and made an oration to them. † And the people made acclamation, The voices of [22] a God, & not of a man. † And forthvvith an Angel of our [23] Lord ∴ strooke him, because he had not giuen the honour to God: and being consumed of vvormes, he gaue vp the ghost. † But the vvord of our Lord increased and multiplied. † And [24] Barnabas and Saul returned from Hierusalem, hauing accom- [25] plished their * ministerie, taking vvith them Iohn that vvas surnamed Marke.

∴ Princes that take delite in the flattery and praises of the people, so much that they forget them selues to be mē, & to giue the honour to God, may be warned by this example.

Act. 11, 29.

ANNOTATIONS
CHAP. XII.

5. *Praier vvas made.*] The Church praied incessantly for her cheefe Pastor, and was heard of God: and al Christian people are vvarned thereby to pray for their Bishopes and Pastors in prison.

S. Peters chaines.

6. *Tvvo chaines.*] These chaines are famous for miracles, and vvere brought from Hierusalem to Rome by Eudoxia the Emperesse, vvife to Theodosius the yonger, vvhere they vvere matched & placed vvith an other chaine that the same Apostle vvas tied with by Nero, & a Church foūded therevpon, named *Petri ad vincula*, Vvhere they are religiously kept and reuerenced vntil this day, and there is a Feast in the vvhole Church for the same, the first of August, vvhich vve call, *Lammas day*.

Patronage of Angels.

15. *His Angel*] *If proper Angels* (saith S. Chrysostom) *be deputed by our Lord to such as haue only charge of their ovvne life, (as one of the iust said,* * *The Angel vvhich hath deliuered me from my youth vpvvard) much more are supernal Spirits at hand to helpe them vnto vvhom the charge and burden of the vvorld is committed.* Chrys. in laud. Pauli. ho. 7. to. 3.

Gen. 48, 16

Publike praier for S. Peter the head.

17. *Tel Iames.*] He vvilleth them to shevv this to S. Iames Bishop of Hierusalem and to the Christians, that they might see the effect of their praiers for him, & giue God thankes. for S. Iames no doubt published cōmon praier for S. Peter.

CHAP. XIII.

The 5 part. THE taking of the Gospel avvay from the obstinate Iewes, and geuing of it to the Gentils, by the ministerie of Paul and Barnabas.

The preachers of the Church of Antioche preparing thē selues, the Holy Ghost out of them al, chooseth Saul and Barnabas. 3 They being first consecrated Bishops, 4 goe their appointed circuite ouer al the land of Cypres, the Proconsul vvhereof is also conuerted, seing the miraculous excecation of a Ievv by Paul. 13 Thence, into Pamphilia: 14 and Pisidia, vvhere in Antioche Paul preacheth to the Ievves, shevving that IESVS *is Christ, 38 and that in him is saluation, and not in their Lavv of Moyses: 40 vvarning them to bevvare of the reprobation foretold by the Prophets. 44 But the next Sabboth, they blasphe-ming, he in plaine termes forsaketh them, and turneth to the Gentiles. Whereat the Gentils be as glad on the contrarie side. 50 Finally the Ievves raising persecution, they forsake them, pronouncing them to be obstinate contemners.*

AND

1 AND there vvere in the Church vvhich vvas at Antioche, Prophets and Doctors, among vvhom vvas Barnabas, & Simon that vvas called Niger, and Lucius of Cyréne, and Manahen vvho vvas the foſter-brother of Herod the Tetrarch, and Saul.

2 † And [c] as they vvere ″ miniſtring to our Lord, and faſting, the holy Ghoſt ſaid: ″ Separate me Saul and Barnabas vnto the vvorke, vvhereto I haue taken them.

[c] λειτουργούντων αὐτῶν

3 † Then they ″ faſting and praying, and ″ impoſing hands vpō them, dimiſſed them.

4 † And they being ″ ſent of the holy Ghoſt, vvent to Seleucia, and thence ſailed to Cypres. 5 † And vvhen they vvere come to Salamîna, they preached the vvord of God in the ſynagogs of the Ievves. And they had Iohn alſo in their miniſterie. 6 † And vvhen they had vvalked through out the vvhole iland as farre as Paphos, they found a certaine man that vvas a magician, a falſe-prophete, a Ievv, vvhoſe name vvas ` Bar-ieſu', 7 † vvho vvas vvith the Proconſul Sergius Paulus a vviſe man. He ſending for Barnabas & Saul, deſired to heare the vvord of God. 8 † But Elymas the magician (for ſo is his name interpreted) reſiſted them, ſeeking to auert the Proconſul from the faith. 9 † But Saul, othervviſe Paul, 10 repleniſhed vvith the holy Ghoſt, looking vpon him, † ſaid: O ful of al guile, and al deceit, ſonne of the deuil, enemie of al iuſtice, thou ceaſeſt not to ſubuert the right vvaies of our 11 Lord. † And novv behold the hand of our Lord vpon thee, and thou ſhalt be blind, not ſeing the ſunne vntil a time. And forthvvith there fel dimneſſe and darkeneſſe vpon him, and going about he ſought ſome body that vvould giue him his 12 hand. † Then the Proconſul, vvhen he had ſeen that vvhich vvas done, beleeued, marueling at the doctrine of our Lord.

` Barieu

13 † And vvhen Paul and they that vvere vvith him had ſailed from Paphos, they came to Pergè in Pamphylia. And Iohn 14 departing from them, returned to Hieruſalem. † But they paſſing through Pergè, came to Antioche in Piſidia: and entring into the ſynagogue on the day of the Sabboths, they 15 ſate dovvne. † And after the leſſon of the Lavv and the Prophets, the princes of the Synagogue ſent to them, ſaying, Men brethren, if there be among you any ſermon of exhortation to the people, ſpeake.

And

† And Paul rising vp, and vvith his hand beckening for 16 silence, said, Ye men of Israël, and you that feare God, harken: † The God of the people of Israël chose our fathers, and ex- 17 alted the people vvhen they vvere seiourners in the land of Ægypt, and in a mightie arme brought them out thereof, † and for the space of fourtie yeres tolerated their maners in 18 the desert. † And destroying seuen nations in the land of 19 Chanaan, by lot he deuided their land among them, † as it 20 vvere after foure hundred and fiftie yeres: and after these things he gaue Iudges, vntil Samuël the prophet. † And 21 thenceforth they desired a king: and he gaue them * Saul the sonne of Cis, a man of the tribe of Beniamin, fourtie yeres. † and remouing him, he raised them vp * Dauid to be king: 22 to vvhom giuing testimonie, he said, *I haue found Dauid the sonne of Iesse, a man according to my hart, vvho shall doe al my vvilles.*

Exod. *Iosue.* *Iud.* *1, Reg. 8.* *1. Reg. 16* *Ps. 88, 21*

† Of his seede God according to his * promisse hath 23 brought forth to Israël a Sauiour IESVS, † Iohn * prea- 24 ching before the face of his comming, baptisme of penance to al the people of Israël. † And vvhen Iohn fulfilled his 25 course, he said, Vvhom doe * you thinke me to be? I am not he, but behold there commeth after me, vvhose shoes of his feete I am not vvorthie to vnloose.

Psa. 131, 11. *Lu. 3, 3.* *Lu. 3, 15.*

The Epistle vpõ Tuesday in Easter vveeke.

† Men brethren, children of the stocke of Abraham, & 26 they among you that feare God, to you the vvord of this saluation vvas sent. † For they that inhabited Hierusalem, and 27 the princes thereof, not knovving him, nor the voices of the prophets that are read euery Sabboth, iudging haue fulfilled them, † and finding no cause of death in him, * desired of Pi- 28 late, that they might kil him. † And vvhen they had cõsum- 29 mated al things that vvere vvrittẽ of him, taking him dovvne from the tree, they put him in a monument. † But God 30 raised him vp from the dead the third day: † vvho vvas 31 * seen for many daies of them that came vp together vvith him from Galilee into Hierusalem, vvho vntil this present are his vvitnesses to the people. † And vve preach vnto you 32 that promisse vvhich vvas made to our fathers: † that God 33 hath fulfilled this same 'to our children', raising vp IESVS, as in the second Psalme also it is vvritten: *My sonne art thou, this day haue I begotten thee.* † And that he raised him vp from the dead, 34 not to returne novv any more into corruption, thus he said, *That I vvil giue you the holy things of Dauid faithful.* † And ther- 35 fore

Lu. 23, 1 *Act. 1, 3.* *' to vs their children,* *Ps. 2, 7.* *Esa. 55, 3.*

Ps.15,10 fore in an other place also he saith, *Thou shalt not giue thy holy one* 36 *to see corruption.* † For Dauid in his generation vvhen he had serued, according to the vvil of God slept: and he vvas laid 37 to his fathers & savv corruption. † But he vvhom God hath raised vp, savv no corruption.

38 † Be it knovven therfore to you, men brethren, that through him, forgiuenesse of sinnes is preached to you, from al the things from the vvhich you could not be iusti- 39 fied by the lavv of Moyses. † In him euery one that 40 beleeueth, is iustified. † Take heede therfore lest that come Abac.1,5 41 vpon you vvhich is spoken in the prophets, † *See ye cõtemners, and vvonder, and perish: because I vvorke a vvorke in your daies, a vvorke vvhich you vvil not beleeue, if any man shal tel it you.*

42 † And they going forth, [c] they desired them that the Sabboth folovving they would speake vnto them these wordes. 43 † And vvhen the synagogue vvas dimissed, many of the Iewes, and of the [c] strangers seruing God, folovved Paul & Barnabas: vvho speaking exhorted them to continue in the 44 grace of God. † But the next Sabboth the vvhole citie al- 45 most assembled to heare the vvord of God. † And the Ievves seing the multitudes, vvere replenished vvith enuy, & contradicted those things vvhich vvere said of Paul, blasphe- 46 ming. † Then Paul and Barnabas constantly said, To you it behoued vs first to speake the vvord of God: but because :: you repell it, and iudge your selues vnvvorthie of eternal 47 life: behold vve turne to the Gentils. † For so our Lord Es.46,6 commaunded vs: *I haue put thee to be the light of the Gentils: that* 48 *thou maiest be saluation vnto the vtmost of the earth.* † And the Gentils hearing it, vvere glad, and glorified the vvord of our Lord: and there beleeued as many as vvere preordinate to 49 life euerlasting. † And the vvord of our Lord vvas spred 50 through out the vvhole countrie. † But the Ievves stirred vp religious and honest vvomen, and the cheese of the citie, 51 and raised persecution against Paul and Barnabas: and they Lu.9,5. did cast them forth out of their coastes. † But they *shaking of the dust of their feete against them, came to Icónium. 52 † The disciples also vvere replenished vvith ioy and vvith the holy Ghost.

c the Gētiles desired
c deuout proselytes,

:: The Ievves of their ovvne free vvil repelling the truth, are vnvvorthy of Christ and vvorthily forsaken: and the Gentils though they beleeued specially by Gods grace and preordination, yet they beleeue also by their ovvne free vvil, vvhich standeth vvel vvith Gods prouidence.

Tt ANNOT.

ANNOTATIONS
CHAP. XIII.

The Apostles liturgie or Masse.

2. *As they vvere ministring.*] If vve should, as our Aduersaries do, boldly turne vvhat text vve list, and flee from one language to an other for the aduantage of our cause, vve might haue translated for *ministring*, *sacrificing*. for so *the Greeke doth signifie, and so Erasmus translated. yea vve might haue translated, *Saying Masse*, for so they did: and the Greeke Fathers hereof had their name, Liturgie, vvhich Erasmus translateth *Masse*, saying, *Missa Chrysostomi.* But vve keepe our text, as the translators of the Scriptures should do most religiously.

λειτουργούντων αὐτῶν

Paul & Barnabas are consecrated by men.

2. *Separate me.*] Though Paul vvere taught by God him self and specially designed by Christ to be an Apostle, and here chosen by the Holy Ghost together vvith Barnabas, yet they vvere to be ordered, consecrated, and admitted by men. Vvhich vvholy condemneth al these nevv rebellious disordered spirites, that chalenge and vsurpe the office of preaching and other sacred actions from heauen, vvithout the Churches admission.

Gal. 1.

Imber daies.

Præscript times of fasts.

3. *Fasting.*] Hereof the Church of God vseth and prescribeth publike fastes at the foure solẽne times of giuing holy Orders (vvhich are our *Imber daies*) as a necessarie preparatiue to so great a vvorke. as S. * Leo declareth by this place, naming it also an Apostolical tradition. See. *S. Leo Ser. 9 de ieiunio 7 mensis, & Calixtus ep. 1. to. 1 Conc. Conc. Magunt. c. 34. 35. to 3.* And this fasting vvas not fasting from sinne, nor moral or Christian temperance, as the Protestants ridiculously affirme, for such fasting they vvere bound euer to keepe: but it vvas abstinence for a time from al meates or from some certaine kindes of meates, vvhich vvas ioyned vvith praier and sacrifice, and done specially at such seasons as the Church prescribed, of al together (as in Lent, the Imber daies, Friday, Saturday) and not vvhen euery man list, as Aërius and such Heretikes did hold.. *S. August. hær. 53.*

**Leo ep. 81 c. 1.*
Epipha. in compend.
Leo ser. 3 et 4 de ieiu 7 mensis.

Imposition of handes.
Holy orders.

3. *Imposing hands.*] Because al blessings and consecrations vvere done in the Apostles time by the external ceremonie of imposition of hands, diuers Sacraments vvere named of the same, specially Confirmation, as is noted before, and holy Ordering or consecrating Bishops, Priests, and Deacons, and Subdeacons, as vve see here and els vvhere. In vvhich though there vvere many holy vvordes and ceremonies and a very solemne action: yet vvhatsoeuer is done in those Sacraments, is altogether called *Imposition of hands*: as vvhatsoeuer vvas done in the vvhole diuine mysterie of the B. * Sacrament, is named *fraction of bread.* for the Apostles (as S. Denys *Eccl. hier. c. 1 in fine* vvriteth) purposely kept close in their open speaches and vvritings vvhich might come to the hands or eares of Infidels, the sacred vvordes and actions of the Sacraments. And S. Ambrose saith, *in 1 Tim. c. 4. The imposition of the hand is mystical vvordes vvherevvith the elected is conformed and made apt to his function, receiuing authoritie (his conscience bearing vvitnes) that he may be bold in our Lordes steed to offer sacrifice to God.* And S. Hierom, *The imposition of hand is the Ordering of Clerkes, Which is done by praier of the voice, and imposition of the hand.* And this is in some inferior orders also, but Paul and Barnabas vvere ordered to a higher function then inferior Priests, euen to be Bishops through out al Nations.

**Act. 2, 42*

Hiero. in c. 58 Esa.

Spiritual officers of our soules.

4. *Sent of the Holy Ghost.*] Vvhosoeuer be sent by the Church, are sent of the Holy Ghost, though in such an extraordinarie sort it be not done. Vvhereby vve see hovv far the Officers of our soules in the Church do passe the temporal Magistrates, vvho though they be of Gods ordinance, yet not of the Holy Ghosts special calling.

CHAP. XIIII.

Next in Iconium they preach, vvhere many being conuerted of both sortes, the obstinate Ievves raise persecution. 6 Then in the tovvnes of Lycaonia, vvhere the Heathen first seing that Paul had healed one borne lame, are hardly persuaded but they are Gods. 18 but aftervvard, by the instigation of the malitious Ievves, they stone Paul, leauing him for dead. 20 And so hauing done their circuite, they returne the same vvay confirmiug the Christians, and making Priests for euery Church. 25 And being come home to Antioche in Syria, they report al to the Church there.

AND

1 AND it came to passe at Iconium that they entred together into the synagogue of the Ievves, and so spake, that a very great multitude of Ievves and of the Greekes did beleeue. 2 † But the Ievves that vvere incredulous, stirred vp and incensed the hartes of the Gentils to anger against the brethren. 3 † A long time therfore they abode, dealing confidently in our Lord, vvho gaue testimonie to the vvord of his grace, graunting signes and vvonders to be done by their handes. 4 † And the multitude of the citie vvas deuided: and certaine of them in deede vvere vvith the Ievves, but 5 certaine vvith the Apostles. † And vvhen the Gentils and the Ievves vvith their princes had made an assault, to 6 vse them contumeliously, and to stone them, † vnderstanding it, they fled to the cities of Lycaónia, Lystra and Derbé, and the vvhole countrie about, and there they vvere euangelizing.

7 † And a certaine man at Lystra impotent of his feete sate there, lame from his mothers vvombe, that neuer had vval-8 ked. † This same heard Paul speaking. Vvho looking vpon 9 him, and seeing that he had faith for to be saued, † he said vvith a loud voice, Stand vp right on thy feete. And he lea-10 ped & vvalked. † And the multitudes vvhen they had seen vvhat Paul had done, lifted vp their voice in the lycaónian tongue, saying, Gods made like to men, are descended 11 to vs. † And they called Barnabas, Iupiter: but Paul, Mer-12 curie, because he vvas the cheefe speaker. † The Priest also of [c] Iupiter that vvas before the citie, bringing oxen & garlands before the gates, vvould vvith the people " sacrifice. 13 † Vvhich thing vvhen the Apostles Barnabas & Paul heard, renting their coates, they leaped forth into the multitudes, 14 crying † and saying, Ye men, vvhy doe you these things? Vve also are mortal, men like vnto you, preaching to you for to conuert from these vaine things, to the liuing God that made the heauen, and the earth, and the sea, and al things that are in 15 them: † vvho in the generations past suffred al the Gentils 16 to goe their ovvne vvaies. † Hovvbeit he left not him self :: vvithout testimonie, being beneficial from heauen, giuing raines, and fruiteful seasons, filling our hartes vvith foode & 17 gladnes. † And speaking these things, they scarse appeased

c Διὸς τοῦ ὄντος

:: The Heathen might by the daily benefites of God haue knovven him at the least to haue beene their Creatour and only Lord, though the mysterie of our Redemption vvere not opened to them.

the multitudes from ſacrificing to them. † But there came 18 in certaine Ievves from Antioche and Icónium: and perſvvading the multitudes, and * ſtoning Paul, they drevv him out of the citie, thinking him to be dead. † But the diſciples compaſſing him round about, he riſing vp, entred into the citie, 19 and the next day he vvent forth vvith Barnabas vnto Derbè.

2. Cor. 11, 25.

† And vvhen they had euangelized to that citie, and had 20 taught many, they returned to Lyſtra and Icónium, and to Antioche: † confirming the hartes of the diſciples, and ex- 21 horting them to continue in the faith, and that by many tribulations vve muſt enter into the kingdom of God. † And 22 vvhen ∷ they ″ had ordained to them ″ Prieſts in euery Church, and had praied vvith faſtings, they commended them to our Lord in vvhom they beleeued. † And paſſing through Piſi- 23 dia, they came into Pamphylia, † and ſpeaking the vvord 24 of our Lord in Pergé, they vvent dovvne into Attalia: † and 25 from thēce they ſailed to Antioche, * vvhence they had been deliuered to the grace of God vnto the vvorke vvhich they accompliſhed. † And vvhen they vvere come, and had aſ- 26 ſembled the Church, they reported vvhat great things God had done vvith them, & that he had opened a doore of faith to the Gentils. † And they abode no litle time vvith the 27 diſciples.

∷ Vve ſee by this, firſt that SS. Paul & Barnabas vvere Biſhops, hauing here authoritie to giue holy Orders: ſecondly, that there vvas euen then a difference betvvixt Biſhops and Prieſts, though the name in the primitiue Church vvas often vſed indifferently: laſtly, that alvvaies faſting & praying vvere preparatiues to the giuing of holy Orders.

Act. 13, 2.

ANNOTATIONS
CHAP. XIIII.

Latria.

13. They vvould ſacrifice,) This loe is the diuine vvorſhip, conſiſting in external ſacrifice, and in acknovvledging the parties vvorſhipped to be gods: vvhich * may be done to no man nor creature, and therfore the Apoſtles refuſe it vvith al poſſible diligence, and al the Angels and Sainctes in heauen refuſe that adoration by ſacrifice. The Catholike Church ſuffereth no Prieſt nor other ſo to vvorſhip any Sainct in heauen or earth. She hath but one external Sacrifice, vvhich *is* in the holy Maſſe, of Chriſts body and bloud: that ſhe offereth to God alone, and *neither to Peter nor to Paul* (ſaith S. Auguſtine) *though the Prieſt that ſacrificeth, ſtandeth ouer their bodies, and offereth in their memories.* But other kindes of honours and duties, inferior vvithout al compariſon (hovv great ſo euer they be) to this, vve do, as the Scriptures and Nature teache vs, to al Superiors in heauen and earth, according to the degrees of grace, honour, and bleſſednes that God hath called them vnto, from our B. Ladie Chriſts ovvne mother, to the leſt ſeruant he hath in the vvorld. for vvhich the Heretikes vvould neuer accuſe Chriſtian people of Idolatrie, if they had either grace, learning, faith, or natural affection.

Aug. li. 10. de Ciu. Dei c. 1.

Dulia.

Aug. li. 8. de Ciu. c. 27.

22. Had ordained.) The Heretikes, to make the vvorld beleeue that al Prieſts ought to be choſen by the voices of the people, and that they neede no other Ordering or Conſecration by Biſhops, preſſing the profane vſe of the * Greeke vvord more then the very natural ſignification requireth and Eccleſiaſtical vſe beareth, tranſlate thus, *Ordained by election.* Vvhereas in deede this vvord in Scripture ſignifieth, Ordering by impoſition of hands, as is plaine by other vvordes equiualent, *Act. 6, 13. 1 Tim. 4. 5. 2 Tim. 1.* Vvhere the Ordering of Deacons, Prieſts, and others is called * Impoſition of hands: not of the people, but of the Apoſtles. And this to be the Eccleſiaſtical vſe of

Heretical tranſlation againſt holy orders.

χειροτονήσαντες

ἐπίθεσις τῶν χειρῶν.

Hiero. in 61. Esa. of the vvord, appeareth by S. Hierom saying (as is before alleaged) that χειροτονία *is the Ordering of Clerkes or Clergie men by praier of voice and imposition of hand.*

22. Priests.) Euen so here also, as before, fleing from the proper, apt, knovven, vvord & vvhich is most precisely correspondent to the very Greeke in our tongue and al nations, they translate for *Priest*, Elder, that is, for a calling of Office, a vvord of age: for a terme of art and by consent of al the Church and Apostolike authoritie and Fathers, appropriated to holy Order, a vulgar, common, and profane terme: Vvith as litle grace as if they should transiate *Pontificem*, a bridgemaker, the *Maior* of London, the Bigger of London. And thus you see vvithin three vvordes compasse they flee guilefully from the Latin to the Greeke, and againe guilefully from the Greeke to the vulgar English. Such corruption of Scriptures their hatred of Priesthod driueth them vnto. If they had translated it so vvhen the Scriptures vvere first vvritten, (at vvhich time the vvord vvas but nevvly receiued into the special and Ecclesiastical signification, and vvhen it vvas yet taken sometimes in common profane sort, as *1 Tim. 5.* or there only vvhere our aűcient Latin version turneth *Presbyter* into *Senior*, because the vvord vvas not yet vvholy and only appropriated to holy Orders, as aftervvard by vse of many hundred yeres it vvas and is) their dealing might haue had some colour of honestie and plainesse, vvhich novv can not be but of plaine falshod and corruption, and that of further purpose then the simple can see. Vvhich is to take avvay the office of Sacrificing and other functions of Priests, proper in the nevv Testamét to such as the Apostles often, and the posteritie in maner altogether call Priests, *Presbyteros*. Vvhich vvord doth so certainely imply the authoritie of sacrificing, that it is by vse made also the onely English of *Sacerdos*, the Aduersaries them selues as vvel as vve, so translating it in al the old and nevv Testament: though they can not be ignorant that *Priest* commeth of *Presbyter*, and not of *Sacerdos*: and that antiquitie for no other cause applied the signification of *Presbyter* to *Sacerdos*, but to shevv that *Presbyter* is in the nevv Lavv, that vvhich *Sacerdos* vvas in the old: the Apostles abstaining from this and other like old names at the first, and rather vsing the vvordes, Bishops, Pastors, and Priests, because they might be distinguished from the Gouernours and sacrificers of Aarons order, vvho as yet in the Apostles time did their old functions stil in the Temple. And this to be true, and that to be a Priest, is to be a man appointed to sacrifice, the Heretikes them selues calling *Sacerdos* alvvaies a Priest, must needes be driuen to confesse. Although their folly is therein notorious, to apply vvillingly the vvord *Priest* to *Sacerdos*, and to take it from *Presbyter* vvhereof it is properly deriued, not only in English, but in other languages both french and Italian. Vvhich is to take avvay the name that the Apostles and fathers gaue to the Priests of the Church, & to giue it vvholy & onely to the order of Aaron, vvhich neuer had it before our Priesthod began. Neuer did there Heretikes stand so much vpon doubtful deriuations and descant of vvordes as these Protestants do, and yet neuer men behaued them selues more fondly in the same: as vvhosoeuer marketh the distinction of their Elders, Ministers, Deacõns, and such like, shal perceiue.

Heretical trãslation against Priesthod.

If *Sacerdos*. be a Priest, much more *Presbyter*.

Presbyter.
Priest.
Prebstre.
Preti.

CHAP. XV.

Some of those Ievves also that vvere Christians, do fall, and are authors of the Heresie of Iudaizing. 2 They referre the matter to Councel: 7 Wherein after great disputation, Peter striking the stroke, 12 and other confirming his sentence vvith miracles, 13 and vvith Scriptures: 22 the Apostles and Priests do vvrite and cõmaund in the name of the Holy Ghost vvhat is to be done. 30 And the faithful thereby are straightvvaies quieted in minde. 36 After vvhich, Paul and Barnabas thinking to goe againe their aboue said circuite together, are by occasion of Marke parted, to the greater increase of the Church.

1 AND certaine comming dovvne from Ievvrie, taught the brethren: That * vnles you be circumcised according to the maner of Moyses, you can not be saued. 2 † No litle sedition therfore being risen to Paul and Barnabas against them, they "appointed that Paul and Barnabas should goe vp, & certaine others of ᵇthe rest', to the Apostles and ᶜpriests vnto Hierusalem, vpon this question.

Gal. 5, 2.

ᵇ them,
ᶜ πρεσβυτέρους

† They therfore being brought on their vvay by the 3 Church, passed through Phœnîce and Samaria, reporting the conuersion of the Gentiles: and they made great ioy to al the brethren.

† And vvhen they vvere come to Hierusalem, they vvere 4 receiued of the Church and of the Apostles and[c] Auncients, declaring vvhatsoeuer God had done vvith them. † And 5 there arose certaine of the heresie of the Pharisees that beleeued, saying, That they must be circumcised, commaunded also to keepe the lavv of Moyses. † And the" Apostles and 6 Auncients " assembled to consider of this vvord.

† And vvhen there vvas made a [b] great disputation, "Peter 7 rising vp said to them, Men brethren, you knovv that* of old daies God among vs" chose, that by my mouth the Gentiles should heare the vvord of the Gospel, and beleeue. † And 8 God vvhich knovveth the hartes, gaue testimonie, * giuing vnto them the holy Ghost as vvel as to vs, † and hath put no 9 difference betvvene vs and them, :: by faith purifying their hartes. † Novv therfore vvhy tempt you God, to put a yoke 10 vpon the neckes of the disciples, vvhich neither our fathers nor vve haue been able to beare? † but by the grace of our 11 Lord IESVS CHRIST vve beleeue to be saued, in like maner as they also.

† And al the multitude held their peace: and they heard 12 Barnabas and Paul telling vvhat great signes and vvonders God had done among the Gentiles by them.

† And after they held their peace, " Iames ansvvered, 13 saying, Men brethren, heare me. † Simon hath told hovv 14 God first visited to take of the Gentiles a people to his name. † And to this accord the vvordes of the prophets, as it is 15 vvritten: † *After these things I vvil returne, and vvil reedifie the ta-* 16 *bernacle of Dauid, vvhich vvas fallen, and the ruines thereof I vvil reedifie, and set it vp: † that the residue of men may seeke after the Lord, and al na-* 17 *tions vpon vvhom my name is inuocated, saith the Lord that doeth these things.* † To our Lord vvas his ovvne vvorke knovven from the 18 beginning of the vvorld. † For the vvhich cause "I iudge, 19 that they vvhich of the Gentiles are conuerted to God, are not to be disquieted, † but to vvrite vnto them that they 20 refraine them selues from the contaminations of Idols, and " fornication, and strangled things, and bloud. † For Moyses 21 of old times hath in euery citie them that preach him in the synagogs, vvhere he is read euery Sabboth.

c Auncients here, & often in this chapter, are the same that Priestes vers. 2 as S. Hierom taketh it also *1 Pet. 5.* & the greeke approueth, being alvvaies one, πρεσβύτεροι, Priests. *Hiero. in 1 ad Tit. et 4 ad Galat.*

b See the Annot. vers. 28 toward the ende.

:: By that faith which worketh by charitie. for a dead faith can not purifie the hart of man. See chap. 16, 31.

c πρεσβυτέρων

Act. 10, 20.

Act. 10, 45.

Amos. 9, 11.

22 † Then it pleased the Apostles and Auncients vvith the vvhole Church, to chose men out of them, & to send to Antioche vvith Paul and Barnabas, Iudas, vvho vvas surnamed 23 Barsabas, & Silas, cheefe men among the brethren, † c vvriting by their handes.

c Other latin copies and the greeke read thus *Writing by their handes an epistle conteining these things.*

The Apostles and Auncients, the brethren, to the brethren of the Gentiles that are at Antioche and in Syria and Cilicia, 24 greeting. † Because vve haue heard that certaine " going forth from vs, haue troubled you vvith vvordes, subuerting 25 your soules, to vvhom vve gaue no commaundement: † It hath pleased vs being gathered in one, to chose out men and to send them vnto you vvith our deerest Barnabas and Paul, 26 † men that haue giuen their liues for the name of our Lord 27 IESVS CHRIST: † Vve haue sent therfore Iudas & Silas, vvho them selues also vvil in vvordes report vnto you the 28 same things. † For it hath seemed good " to the holy Ghost & to vs, to lay no further burden vpon you then these necessarie 29 things: † that you absteine from the things immolated to Idols, and bloud, and that vvhich is strangled, and fornication, from the vvhich things keeping your selues, you shal doe vvell. Fare ye vvel.

30 † They therfore being dimissed vvent dovvne to Antioche: 31 and gathering the multitude, deliuered the epistle. † Vvhich vvhen they had read, they " reioyced vpon the consola- 32 tion: † but Iudas and Silas, them Selues also being prophets, vvith many vvordes comforted the brethren, and confirmed 33 them. † And hauing spent some time there, they vvere vvith peace dimissed of the brethren vnto them that 34 had sent them. † But it seemed good vnto Silas to remaine 35 there: and Iudas departed alone: † and Paul and Barnabas taried at Antioche, teaching and euangelizing vvith many others the vvord of our Lord.

36 † And after certaine daies, Paul said to Barnabas, Let vs returne and :: visite our brethren in al cities vvherein vve * haue 37 preached the vvord of our Lord, hovv they doe. † And Barnabas vvould haue taken vvith them Iohn also that vvas sur- 38 named Marke. † But Paul desired that he (as vvho * had departed from them out of Pamphylia, and had not gone vvith 39 them to the vvorke) might not be receiued. † And there rose a " dissention, so that they departed one from an other, & 40 that Barnabas in deede taking Marke sailed to Cypres. † But Paul

Act. 13, 14.

Act. 13, 13.

:: Hereof our Catholike Bishops tooke vp the necessarie vse of often visiting their flockes & cures cōmitted to their charge, for confirmatiō in faith & vertue, & reformatiō of maners both of clergie & laitie.

Paul chosing Silas departed, being deliuered of the brethren to the grace of God.

† And he vvalked through Syria and Cilicia, confirming 41 the Churches: ∷ commaunding them to keepe the præcepts of the Apostles and the Auncients.

∷ Not only the things cõmaunded by Christes expresse vvord, or vvritten in the Scriptures (as our Heretikes hold) but vvhatsoeuer the Apostles and Rulers of the Church commaund, is to be kept & obeied. See these wordes repeated againe c.16, 4. & that in the greeke, lest any man cauil, because here the greeke hath them not.

ANNOTATIONS
CHAP. XV.

The Way to end dissension in religion, is to cõmit it to a Coũcel.

1. *Appointed*] Vve learne by this example, vvhat is to be done vvhen any controuersie ariseth in religion betvvene the teachers or other Christian people. Vve see it is not ynough to contend by allegations of Scriptures or other proofes seeming to make for either part: for so of contentious part taking there should be no end, but the more vvriting, vvrestling, striuing there vvere, euery one for his ovvne fansie, cloking it vvith the title of Gods vvord and Scripture, the more Schismes, Sectes, and diuisions vvould fall: as vve see specially in the restles Heresies of our time. Vvhose fautors admitting no iudges, stand to no trial of mortal men, to no tribunal of Pope, Councels, Bishops, Synodes, but eche man to his ovvne phantastical spirit, his ovvne sense of Scriptures, and his ovvne vvilful obdurate rebellion against Gods Church and his Superiors in the same. But here vve see S. Paul and Barnabas, men that vvere Apostles and ful of the Spirit of God, and the other parties, though neuer so much partial to the ceremonies of their Lavv by their former long vse and education therein, yet not to stand stifly to their ovvne opinion on either side, but to condescend to referre the vvhole controuersie and the determination thereof to the Apostles, Priests or Auncients of Hierusalem, that is to say, to commit the matter to be tried by the heads and Bishops and their determination in Councel. This is Gods holy and vvise prouidence among other iudgements in his Church, to keepe the Christian people in truth and vnitie, and to condemne sectes and false teachers and troublers of the Church. By vvhich iudgements and order, vvhosoeuer vvil not or dare not be tried in al their doctrine and doings, they shevv them selues to mistrust their ovvne cause, and to flee from the light, and ordinance of God. Vvithout vvhich order of appeasing al differences in faith and constructions of the Scriptures, the Church had beene more defectual and insufficient, then any Commonvvealth or Societie of men in the vvorld: none of vvhich euer vvanteth good meanes to decide al discordes and dissension arising among the subiects & citizens of the same.

Of vvhat persons a Councel consisteth.

6. *Apostles and Auncients.*] The Heresies of our Protestants vvhich vvould haue al men to giue voice, or to be present in Councels, and of others that vvould haue none but the holy or elect to be admitted, are refuted by this example, vvhere vve see none but Apostles & Priests or Aũcients assembled to dispute of the matter, though many deuout people vvere in the citie the same time. Neither did euer any other in the Auncient Councels of the Church assemble to debate and define the matter, but such, though many other for other causes be euer present. Secular men or vvomen, be their gifts neuer so great, can not be iudges in causes of faith and religion. *If any thing*, saith God *be hard and doubtful, thou shalt come to the Priests of the Leuitical stocke, and thou shalt folovv their sentence.* Againe, *The lippes of the Priest shal keepe knovvledge, and the Lavv thou shalt require of his mouth.* Againe, *Aske the Lavv of the Priest.* Much more must vve referre al to our Bishops and Pastors, vvhom God hath placed in the regiment of the Church vvith much larger priuilege, then euer he did the old Priests ouer the Synagogue. to vvhom it is said, *He that despiseth you, despiseth me.* And it is to be noted that the Bishops so gathered in Councel, represent the vvhole Church, haue the authoritie of the vvhole Church, and the Spirit of God to protect them from error, as the vvhole Church: SS. Paul and Barnabas come hither for the definition of the vvhole Church. *The sentence of a plenarie or general Councel* (saith S. Augustine) *is the consent of the vvhole Church.* And so it must needes be in the Church, because the Magistrates, Senate, Councel or deputies of al commonvvealthes, represent the vvhole body: and to haue it othervvise (as the Churches Rebels vvish) vvere to bring al to hel and horrour, and them selues to be perpetually, by the seditious and popular persons, vpholden against Lavv, reason, and religion, in their vvickednes.

Deut. 17. Mal. 2, 7. Agga. 2, 12. Luc. 10, 16. li. 1. c. 18. de bapt.

A general Coũcel representeth the vvhole Church.

The first Councel at Hierusalem.

6. *Assembled.*] A Councel vvas called to discusse the matter. vvhich Councel vvas the more easily gathered, because the Christian Bishops and countries vvere not yet so many, but that the principal Gouernours of the Church being not far dispersed, and as many learned men as vvere necessarie, might be in Hierusalem, or easily called thither. And it vvas not a Prouincial Councel or Synode only, but a general Councel, consisting of the cheefe Apostles and Bishops that then vvere, though

though the number vvas nothing so great as aftervvard vsed to assemble, vvhen the Church vvas spred into al nations.

7. *Peter rising vp.*] S. Peter as the head of the Church speaketh first, as his Successors haue euer had, not only in their personal presence, but in their absence by their legates and substitutes, the cheefe voice in al Councels general, none euer receiued into authoritie and credite in the Church vvithout their Confirmation. And therfore the Councels of the Arians and of other Heretikes, vvere they neuer so great, vvanting the Popes assent, assistance, or Confirmation, did shamfully erre, as Ariminense for the Arians, and Ephesinum secundum for the Nestorians, and such like condemned Assemblies.

Peter head of the Councel, & his successors after him.

7. *Chose that by my mouth.*] Though Paul vvere called and appointed specially to be the Apostle of the Gentils, yet that vvas S. Peters special priuilege by Gods ovvne choise, that the first Gentils should be called by his mouth, and that he first should vtter to the Church that truth of the admission of the Gentils him self, for that he vvas Christes Vicar, being notvvithstanding (as his Maister vvas) *Minister Circuncisionis*, that is, Apostle of the Ievves, Christ deferring al preeminence vnto him in that point also.

Ro. 15, 8. Gal. 2, 7.

Peters preeminence both tovvard Ievves & Gentiles.

13. *Iames.*] S. Iames because he vvas an Apostle and also Bishop of Hierusalem, gaue his sentence next. for the speache interposed of SS. Paul and Barnabas, vvas but for their better information in the decision of the matter, and for confirmation of S. Peters sentence, though they being Apostles, and Bishops, had voices in the Councel also: as many mo had, though their sentences be not heare reported. And vvhere S. Iames in his speach saith, *I iudge*, it is not meant that he gaue the principal definitiue sentence: for he (as al the rest) folovved and allovved the sentẽce of S. Peter, as it is plaine in the text, the vvhole assembly for reuerence of his person and approbation of his sentence, holding their peace. *Al the multitude* (saith S. Hierom) *held their peace, and into his sentence Iames the Apostle & al the Priests did passe together.* For though S. Iames did particularise certaine points incident to the question debated, as of eating strangled meates &c. yet the proper controuersie for vvhich the Councel assembled, vvas, Vvhether the Gentils conuerted vvere bound to obserue the Lavv of Moyses. and it vvas concluded, that they vvere not bound, nor ought not to be charged vvith Moyses Lavv or the Sacraments and ceremonies of the same. this is the substance and principal purpose of this Councels decree, vvhich doth binde for euer: and *Peter* (saith S. Hierom in the same place) vvas *Prince or author of this decree.* the matter of fornication and Idolothytes being but incident to the question or resolution, and the forbidding of eating strangled and bloud, but a temporal prohibition, vvhich by the consent of the Church or othervvise aftervvard vvas abrogated, the Church of God hauing the true sense of difference of times, places, & persons, vvhen and hovv far such things are to be obserued, and vvhen not. And in such things as these, and in other like vvhich according to circunstances require alteration, it is, that S. Augustine saith, li. 2 de bapt. c. 3. to. 7. *The former general or plenarie Councels may be amended by the later.*

S. Iames and the rest folovv S. Peters sentence.

Hiero. to. 2. ep. 89 ad August. c. 2.

The principal question.

Incident questions.

Hovv later coũcels alter the former.

20. *Fornication.*] Fornication and contamination vvith Idols, are of them selues mortal sinnes, and therfore can neuer be lavvful: yet because the Gentiles by custome vvere prone to both, and of fornication made very smal account, it pleased the Holy Ghost to forbid both specially. Concerning the other points of absteining from bloud and stiffled meates, they vvere things of their ovvne nature indifferent, in vvhich for a time the Ievves vvere to be borne vvithal, and the Gentils to be a litle exercised to obedience. By vvhich vve may see the great authoritie of Gods Church and Councels, vvhich may commaund for euer, or for a time, such things as be fitte for the state of times and nations, vvithout any expresse Scriptures at al, and so by commaundement make things necessarie that vvere before indifferent.

The Churches authoritie in making Decrees.

24. *Going forth from vs.*] A proper discription or note of Heretikes, Schismatikes, and seditious teachers, to go out from their spiritual Pastors and Gouernours, and to teach vvithout their commission and approbation, to disquiet the Catholike people vvith multitude of vvordes and svveete speaches, and finally to ouerthrovv their soules.

Going out, a marke of heretikes.

28. *To the Holy Ghost and to vs.*] By this first vve note, that it is not such a fault as the Heretikes vvould make it in the sight of the simple, or any incongruitie at al, to ioyne God and his creatures, as the principal cause and the secondarie, in one speache, and to attribute that to both, vvhich though diuersely, yet procedeth of both. *God and you*, say good people commonly: *God and our Ladie, Christ and S. Iohn: We confesse to God and to Peter and Paul.* as, * *God and his Angel, To our Lord and Gedeon, The svvord of our Lord and of Gedeon, Our Lord and Moyses, Christ and his Angels. Our Lord and al Saincts.* ep. ad Philem. *S. Paul and our Lord.* 1 Thes. 1, 6. Al these speaches being partly Scriptures, partly like vnto the Scriptures speaches, are vvarrãted also by this Councel, vvhich saith boldly, & hath giuen the forme thereof to al other Councels lavvfully called and confirmed, to say the like, *It hath pleased the Holy Ghost and vs.* S. Cyprian *ep. 54. nu. 2.* reporting the like of a Synode holden in Afrike, saith, *It hath pleased vs by the suggestion of the Holy Ghost.*

God & our Ladie, and the like speaches.

*Gen. 48, 15. 16. Iud. 7, 18. 20. Exod. 14, 31. 1. Tim. 5, 21.

VISVM EST *Sp. sancto & nobis.*

Secondly vve note, that the holy Councels lavvfully kept for determination or cleering of doubtes, or condemning of errors and Heresies, or appeasing of Schismes and troubles, or reformation of life, and such like important matters, haue euer the assistance of Gods Spirit, and therfore

The holy ghost assistant in al lawful coūcels, to the vvorlds end, and that by Christs promisse.

can not erre in their sentences and determinations concerning the same, because the Holy Ghost can not erre, from vvhom (as you see here) ioyntly vvith the Councel the resolution procedeth.

Thirdly vve learne, that in the holy Councels specially (though othervvise and in other Tribunals of the Church it be also verified) Christes promes is fulfilled,* that the Holy Ghost should suggest them and teach them al truth, and that not in the Apostles time only, but to the vvorldes end. for so long shal Councels, the Church, and her Pastors haue this priuilege of Gods assistance, as there be either doubtes to resolue, or Heretikes to condemne, or truthes to be opened, or euil men to be reformed, or Schismes to be appeased. for vvhich cause S. Gregorie *li. 1 ep. 24 sub fin.* reuerenceth the foure general Councels (Nicen. Constantinop. Ephes. Chalced.) as the foure bookes of the holy Gospel, alluding to the number: and of the fifth also he saith that he doth reuerence it alike: and so vvould he haue done moe, if they had beene before his time, vvho saith of them thus, *Whiles they are concluded and made by vniuersal consent, him self doth he destroy, and not them, vvhosoeuer presumeth either to loose Whom they binde, or to binde vvhom they loose.*

Io. 16, 13.

S. Gregories reuerence of General Councels.

The Protestāts fond distinctiō betvvene the 4 first & the later Councels.

S. Gregorie therfore reuerencing al fiue alike, it may be marueled vvhence the Heretikes haue their fond difference betvvixt those foure first and other later: attributing much to them, and nothing to the rest. Vvhereas in deede the later can erre no more then the first foure, being holden and approued as they vvere, and hauing the Holy Ghost as they had. But in those first also vvhen a man findeth any thing against their Heresies (as there be diuers things) then they say plainely that they also may erre, and that the Holy Ghost is not tied to mens voices, nor to the number of sentences: Vvhich is directly to reproue this first Councel also of the Apostles, and Christes promes of the Holy Ghosts assistance to teach al truth. Yea that you may knovv and abhorre these Heretikes throughly, heare ye vvhat a principal Sect-Maister vvith his blasphemous mouth or penne vttereth, saying, that *In the very best times such vvas partly the ambition of Bishops, partly their folishnes and ignorance, that the very blind may easily perceiue, Satan verily to haue beene president of their assemblies.* Good Lord deliuer the people and the vvorld from such blasphemous tongues and bookes, and giue men grace to attend to the holy Scriptures and Doctors, that they may see hovv much, not only S. Augustine and other fathers attribute to al general Councels specially, (to vvhich they referre them selues in al doubtes among them selues and in al their controuersies vvith Heretikes:) but to vvhich euen S. Paul him self (so specially taught by God) and others also yelded them selues. Notorious is the saying of S. Augustine concerning S. Cyprian, Vvho being a blessed Catholike Bishop and Martyr, yet erred about the rebaptizing of such as vvere Christened by Heretikes. *If he had liued* (saith S. Augustine li. 2 de bapt c. 4,) *to haue seen the determination of a plenarie Councel, vvhich he savv not in his life time, he vvould for his great humilitie and charitie straight vvay haue yelded, and preferred the general Councel before his ovvne iudgement and his fellovv Bishops in a Prouincial Councel only.* Vvhereby also vve learne, that Prouincial Councels may erre, though many times they do not, and being conformable to the general Councels, or confirmed and allovved by them or the See Apostolike, their resolutions be infallible as the others are.

Bezas blasphemie against the first general Councels.

Beza in praf. Test. No. an. 1565.

Vvhat the Fathers attribute to Councels, & namely S. Augustine.

Prouincial Councels.

Notvvithstanding the Holy Ghosts assistance, yet humane meanes must be vsed to search the truth.

If any here aske, vvhat neede so much disputing, study, and trauail in Councels to find out and determine the truth, if the Holy Ghost infallibly guide them? Vve ansvver that such is the ordinarie prouidence of God in this case, to assist them vvhen they doe their endeuour, and vse all humane meanes of industrie, and not els. And so (though somvvhat othervvise) God assisted the Euangelistes and other vvriters of the holy Scriptures, that they could not erre in penning the same, but yet they did and ought to vse al possible humane diligence to knovv and learne out the histories and truth of matters, as is plaine in the beginning of S. Lukes Gospel: els the Holy Ghost vvould not haue assisted them. Euen so in this Councel of the Apostles, though they had the holy Ghost assistant, yet the text saith, *cum magna conquisitio fieret*, Vvhen there vvas great disputation, search and examination of the case, then Peter spake &c. If againe it be demaunded, vvhat neede is there to expect the Councels determination, if the Popes or See Apostolikes iudgement be infallible and haue the assistance of God also, as the Catholikes affirme? Vve ansvver, that for the Catholike and peaceable obedient children of the Church it is a comfort to haue such various meanes of determination, trial, and declaration of the truth, and that it is necessarie for the recouery of Heretikes, and for the contentation of the vveake, vvho not alvvaies giuing ouer to one mans determination, yet vvil either yeld to the iudgement of al the learned men and Bishops of al Nations, or els remaine desperate and condemned before God and man for euer. And as I said before, this assistance of the Holy Ghost promised to Peters See, presupposeth humane meanes of searching out the truth, vvhich the Pope alvvaies hath vsed, & vvil, & must vse in matters of great importance, by calling Councels, euen as here you see SS. Peter and Paul them selues and al the Apostles, though indued vvith the Holy Ghost, yet thought it notvvithstanding necessarie for further trial & cleering of truth and maintenance of vnitie, to keepe a Councel.

Lu. 1, 3.

Though the See Apostolike it self haue the same assistance, yet councels be also necessarie for many causes.

Lastly it is to be noted, that as Christ and the Holy Ghost be present by his promes, to al such assemblies as gather in the obedience & vnitie of the Church, vvith ful minde to obey vvhatsoeuer shal be determined, vvhereby the assembled though of diuers iudgements before, do most peaceably yeld to truth, and agree in one vniforme determination of the same: so al such as gather out of the Church, vvithout humilitie or intention to yeld one to an other, or to any Superior, man or Councel, or vvhat els so euer, but chalenge to them selues learning, spirit, and vve can not tel vvhat: such, hovv many meetings so euer they make, being destitute of the Holy Ghost the author of truth and concord, are further of and further out, then euer before: as God hath shevved by the successe of al Heretical Colloquies, Synodes, and Assemblies in Germanie, France, Poole, and other places in our daies. Read a notable place in S. Cyprian, that the promes of Christ, that he vvould be in the middes of tvvo or three gathered in his name, pertaineth not to them that assemble out of the Church.

de vnit. Ec. nu. 7.

Heretical or Schismatical assembles.

31. Reioyced vpon the consolation.] Straight vpon the intelligence of the Councels determination, not only the Gentils, but euen the Maisters of the former troubles and dissension, vvere at rest, & al tooke great comfort that the controuersie vvas so ended. And so should al Christian men do, vvhen they see the sectes of our time condemned by the like authoritie and most graue iudgement of the holy Councel of Trent. Against vvhich the Heretikes of our time make the like friuolous exceptions and false cauillations, as did the old Heretikes heretofore against those Councels that specially condemned their errors. The Pope and Bishopes (say they) are a partie, and they ought not to be our iudges: they are partial and come vvith preiudicate mindes to condemne vs, and vve accuse them al of Idolatrie and other crimes, and vve vvil be tried by Gods vvord only, and vve vvil expound it according to an other rule, that is to say, as vve list. So say they against this Councel, and the like said the Arians against the first Nicene Councel, and al such like against those Councels namely that condemned their heresies. And so say al theeues against their correctors and punishers, and vvould both say and do more against temporal tribunals, Iudges, Iustices, and Iuries, if they had as much licence and libertie in those matters, as men haue novv in religion.

Al good Christians rest vpon the determinatiō of a general Councel.

Al Heretikes make exceptiōs against the coūcels that condemne them.

37. Dissension.] Such occasions of differences fall out euen among the perfect men often, vvithout any great offence. And this their departing fell out to the great increase of Christians. And therfore it is very ridiculously applied to excuse the disagreing of the Heretikes among them selues in the principal pointes of religion, namely the Sacrament.

CHAP. XVI.

Paul hauing for his part visited the Churches of Syria, Cilicia, and Lycaonia, deliuering vnto them vvithal to keepe the Decrees of the Councel: 6 beginneth a nevv iourney, ouer Phrygia, Galatia, Mysia: 8 Yea into Europe also he passeth, admonished by a vision, and commeth into Macedonia, 12 and there he beginneth the Church of the Philippians, vvorking miracles, and suffering persecution.

1 AND he came to Derbé and Lystra. And behold, there vvas a certaine disciple there named Timothee, the sonne of ˋa vvidovv' vvoman that beleeued, of a father a Gentile. 2 † To this man the brethren that vvere in Lystra and Iconium, gaue a good testimonie. 3 † Him Paul vvould haue to goe forth vvith him: and taking him he circumcised him because of the Ievves that vvere in those places. For they al knevv that his father vvas a Gentile.

Ievv

4 † And vvhen they passed through the cities, they deliuered vnto them to keepe the ∵ decrees that vvere decreed of 5 the Apostles and Auncients which were at Hierusalem. † And the Churches vvere confirmed in faith, and did abound in number daily.

∵ Here againe they take order that the decrees and articles of faith agreed vpon in the Councel of Ierusalē, should be executed & obserued. vvhereby vve see both the great authoritie of Councels, & the diligence that al Prelates ought to haue to see the decrees & Canons of the Coūcels put in executiō.

6 † And passing through Phrygia and the countrie of Galatia, they vvere :: forbidden by the holy Ghost to preach the vvord in Asia. 7 † And vvhen they vvere come into Mysia, they attempted to goe into Bithynia: and the Spirit of IESVS permitted them not.

8 † And vvhen they had passed through Mysia, they vvent dovvne to Troas: 9 † and a vision by night vvas shevved to Paul: There vvas a certaine man of Macedónia standing and beseeching him, and saying, passe into Macedónia, and helpe vs. 10 † And as soone as he had seen the vision, forthvvith vve sought to goe into Macedónia, being assured that God had called vs to euãgelize to them. 11 † And sailing from Troas, vve came vvith a straight course to Samothrácia, and the day folovving to Neapolis: 12 † and from thence to Philippi, vvhich is the first citie of the part of Macedonia, a :: *colónia.* And vve were in this citie certaine daies, abiding. 13 † And vpon the day of the Sabboths, vve vvent forth vvithout the gate beside a riuer, vvhere it seemed that there vvas praier: & sitting vve spake to the vvomen that vvere assembled. 14 † And a certaine vvoman named Lydia, a seller of purple of the citie of the Thyatirians, one that vvorshipped God, did heare: vvhose hart our Lord opened to attend to those things vvhich vvere said of Paul. 15 † And vvhen she vvas baptized, and her house, she besought vs, saying: If you haue iudged me to be faithful to our Lord, enter in vnto my house, and tarie. And she constrained vs. 16 † And it came to passe as vve vvent to praier, a certaine vvenche hauing a Pythónical spirit, mette vs, that brought great gaine to her maisters by diuíning. 17 † This same folovving Paul and vs, cried saying, :: These men are the seruants of the high God, vvhich preach vnto you the vvay of saluation. 18 † And this she did many daies. And Paul being sorie, and turning, said to the spirit, I cõmaund thee in the name of IESVS CHRIST to goe out from her. And he vvent out the same houre. 19 † But her maisters seeing that the hope of their gaine vvas gone, apprehending Paul and Silas, brought them into the market place to the Princes: 20 † and presenting them to the magistrates, they said, These men trouble our citie, being Ievves: 21 † and they preach a fashion vvhich it is not lavvful for vs to receiue, nor doe, being Romanes. 22 † And the people ranne against them: and the magistrates tearing their coates, commaunded them

:: This people had not the Gospel denied vnto them altogether, but for a time: because (as Venerable Bede thinketh) God foresavv they vvould not beleeue, & so should haue been more greuously damned.

:: *Colonia*, is such a citie where the most inhabitants are strangers, sent thither from other great cities & States, namely from the Romanes.

:: Either the Diuel vvas compelled by the vertue of Paules presence to say truth, or els (as such do often times) he spake truth novv, that they might the more trust him, and he better beguile them at other times.

23 them to be beaten vvith roddes. † And vvhen they had laid *many stripes vpon them, they did cast them into prison, commaunding the keeper that he should keepe them dili-

2.Cor.11.

24 gently. † Vvho vvhen he had receiued such commaundement, cast them into the inner prison, and made their feete
25 fast in the stockes. † And at mid-night, Paul and Silas praying, did praise God. And they that vvere in prison, heard
26 them. † But sodenly there vvas made a great earthquake, so that the foundations of the prison vvere shaken. And forthvvith al the doores vvere opened: and the bands of al vvere
27 loosed. † And the keeper of the prison vvaked out of his sleepe, and seeing the doores of the prison opened, dravving out his svvord, vvould haue killed him self, supposing that
28 the prisoners had been fled. † But Paul cried vvith a loud voice, saying, Doe thy self no harme, for vve are al here.
29 † And calling for light, he vvent in, and trembling fel dovvne
30 to Paul and Silas at their feete: † and bringing them forth,
31 he said, Maisters, vvhat must I doe that I may be saued? † But they said, :: Beleeue in our Lord IESVS: and thou shalt be sa-
32 ued and thy house. † And they preached the vvord of our
33 Lord to him vvith al that vvere in his house. † And he taking them in the same houre of the night, [c] vvashed their vvoundes: and him self vvas baptized and al his house in-
34 continent. † And vvhen he had brought them into his ovvne house, he laid the table for them, and reioyced vvith al
35 his house, beleeuing God. † And vvhē day vvas come, the ma-
36 gistrates sent the sergeants, saying, Let those men goe. † And the keeper of the prison told these vvordes to Paul, That the magistrates haue sent that you should be let goe. novv ther-
37 fore departing, goe ye in peace. † But Paul said to them: Being vvhipped openly, vncōdemned, men that are Romanes, they haue cast vs into prison: & novv do they send vs out secretly?
38 Not so, but let them come, & let vs out them selues. † And the sergeants reported these wordes to the magistrates. And they
39 vvere afraid hearing that they vvere Romanes: † and comming they besought them, & bringing them forth they desi-
40 red them to depart out of the citie. † And going out of the prison, they entred in vnto Lydia: and hauing seen the brethren, they comforted them, and departed.

:: It is no other faith that saueth but that vvhich vvorketh by Charitie. *Aug. Enchirid. c. 67.*

c Happie Gailers that doe mercie tovvard their godly prisoners, and receiue againe by them such spiritual benefites.

CHAP. XVII.

Hovv in other parts of Macedonia he planted the Church, and namely at Thessalonica, 5 vvhere the obstinate Ievves are so malicious, that they pursue him also into Berœa. 14 From vvhence being conducted into Greece, he preacheth at Athens both to the Ievves and Gentiles, disputing vvith the Philosophers, 19 and in Areopagus, persuading them from their Idols vnto one God and IESVS CHRIST *raised from the dead.*

AND vvhen they had vvalked through Amphipolis and Apollonia, they came to Thessalonica, vvhere there vvas a synagogue of the Ievves. † And Paul according to his custome entred in vnto them, & three Sabboths he discoursed to them out of the Scriptures, † declaring and insinuating that it behoued CHRIST to suffer and to rise againe from the dead: and that this is IESVS CHRIST, vvhom I preach to you. † And certaine of them beleeued, and vvere ioyned to Paul and Silas, and of the Gentiles that serued God a great multitude, and noble vvomen not a fevv. † But the Ievves :: enuying, & taking vnto them of the rascal sort certaine naughtie men, and making a tumult, stirred the citie: and besetting Iasons house, sought to bring them forth vnto the people. † And not finding them, they drevv Iason and certaine brethren to the princes of the citie, crying, That these are they that stirre vp the vvorld, and are come hither, † vvhom Iason hath receiued, and al these doe against the decrees of Cæsar, saying that there is an other king, IESVS. † And they moued the people, and the princes of the citie hearing these things. † And taking a satisfaction of Iason and of the rest, they dimissed them. † But the brethren forthvvith by night sent avvay Paul and Silas vnto Berœa.
1 2 3 4 5 6 7 8 9 10

:: *Zelantes.* This is the zeale of Heretikes, and a liuely paterne of their dealing at this day against Catholike Priests and preachers and the good *Iasons* that receiue them.

Vvho vvhen they vvere come, entred into the synagogue of the Ievves. † (And these were more noble then they that are at Thessalonica, vvho receiued the vvord vvith al greedines, daily "searching the scriptures, if these things vvere so. † And many surely of them beleeued, and of honest vvomen Gentiles, and men not a fevv.) † And vvhen the Ievves in Thessalonica vnderstood, that at Berœa also the vvord of God vvas preached by Paul, they came thither also, mouing and troubling the multitude. † And then immediatly the brethren
11 12 13 14

brethren sent avvay Paul, to goe vnto the sea: but Silas and Timothee remained there. 15 † And they that conducted Paul, brought him as farre as Athens, and receiuing commaundement of him to Silas and Timothee, that they should come to him very speedily, they departed.

16 † And vvhen Paul expected them at Athens, his spirit vvas incensed vvithin him, seeing the citie giuen to Idolatrie. 17 † He disputed therfore in the synagogue vvith the Ievves, & them that serued God, and in the market-place, euery day vvith them that vvere there. 18 † And certaine Philosophers of the Epicures and the Stoikes disputed vvith him, and certaine said, Vvhat is it that this [b] vvord-sovver vvould say? But others, He seemeth to be a preacher of nevv [c] gods. because he preached to them IESVS and the resurrection. 19 † And apprehẽding him, they led him to Areopagus, saying, May vve knovv vvhat this new doctrine is that thou speakest of? 20 † for thou bringest in certaine nevv things to our eares. Vve vvil knovv therfore vvhat these things may meane. 21 († And al the Athenians, and the strangers seiourning there, emploied them selues to nothing els but either to speake, or to heare some nevves.) 22 † But Paul standing in the middes of Areopagus, said:

Ye men of Athens, in al things I perceiue you as it vvere superstitious. 23 † For passing by and seeing your [c] Idols, I found an altar also vvherevpon vvas vvritten, *To the vnknovven God.* That therfore vvhich you vvorshippe, not knovving it, the same do I preach to you. 24 † The God that made the vvorld and al things that are in it, he being Lord of heauen & earth, dvvelleth ∷ not in * temples made vvith hand, 25 † neither is he serued vvith mens hands, needing any thing, vvhereas him self giueth life vnto al, and breathing, and al things: 26 † and he made of one al mãkinde, to inhabite vpon the vvhole face of the earth, assigning set times, and the limits of their habitation, 27 † for to seeke God, if happily they may feele or finde him, although he be not farre from euery one of vs. 28 † For in him vve liue and moue and be, as certaine also of your ovvne poëtes said, *For of his kinde also vve are.* 29 † Being therfore of Gods kinde, vve may not suppose, " the Diuinitie to be like vnto gold or siluer, or stone, the grauing of art and deuise of man. 30 † And the times truely of this ignorance vvhereas God dispised, novv he denounceth vnto men that al euery vvhere

b σπερμολόγος
c *dæmoniorum.*

c τὰ σεβάσματα

Act. 7, 48.

Aratus.

The Epistle for S. Dionysius Areopagita. Octob. 9.

c The Aduersaries (in the nevv Test. 1580) trãslate, *your deuotions*, most corruptly against the nature of the Greeke vvord (2 *Thess.* 2, [illegible]) and most vvickedly, against the laudable deuotion of good Christians, calling the Pagãs idolatrie and superstitiõ, their deuotions.

∷ God is not concluded in Temples, nor needeth them for his necessitie of dvvelling, or other vses of indigence. See Annot. c. 7. Act. v. 48.

vvhere doe penance, † for that he hath appointed a day 31 wherein he vvil iudge the world in equitie, by a man vvhom he hath appointed, giuing al men faith, raysing him vp from the dead.

† And vvhen they had heard the resurrection of the dead, 32 certaine in deede mocked, but certaine said, Vve vvil heare thee againe concerning this point. † So Paul vvent forth out 33 of the middes of them. † But certaine men ioyning vnto him, 34 did beleeue: among vvhom vvas also "Dionysius Areopagîta, and a vvoman named Dámaris, and others vvith them. ⊣

Dyonysius Areopagita.

ANNOTATIONS
CHAP. XVII.

The people may not iudge of the sense of Scriptures.

11. *Searching the Scriptures.*) The Heretikes vse this place to proue that the hearers must trie and iudge by the Scriptures, vvhether their teachers and preachers doctrine be true, and so reiect that that they find not in the Scriptures. as though here the sheepe vvere made iudges of their Pastors, the people of the Priests, and men and vvomen of al sortes, euen of S. Paules doctrine it self: Which vvere the most folish disorder in the vvorld. And they did not therfore read the Scriptures of the old Testament (for none of the nevv vvere yet extant commonly) to dispute vvith the Apostle, or to trie and iudge of his doctrine, or vvhether they should beleeue him or no: for they vvere bound to beleeue him and obey his vvord, vvhether he alleaged Scripture or no, and vvhether they could reade or vnderstand the Scriptures or no. but it vvas a great comfort and confirmation for the Ievves that had the Scriptures, to finde euen as S. Paul said, that Christ vvas God, crucified, risen, and ascended to heauen: vvhich by his preaching and expounding they vnderstood, and neuer before, though they read them, and heard them read euery Sabboth. As it is a great comfort to a Catholike man, to heare the Scriptures declared & alleaged most euidently for the Churches truth against Heretikes, in Sermons or othervvise. And it doth the Catholikes good & much confirmeth them; to vew diligently the places alleaged by the Catholike preachers. Yet they must not be iudges for al that, ouer their ovvne Pastors, vvhom Christ commaundeth them to heare and obey, and by vvhom they heare the true sense of Scriptures.

The comfort of Christian men by hearing or reading the Scriptures.

The Protestâts call deuotion, superstition.

22. *Superstitious.*) S. Paul calleth not them superstitious for adoring the true and only God vvith much deuotion or many ceremonies or in comely prescribed order, or for doing due reuerence to holy Sacraments, to Saincts and their memories, Images, or Monuments: or for keeping the prescribed lavves, daies, and fastes of the Church, or for fulfilling vovves made to God, or for blessing vvith the signe of the Crosse, or for capping and kneeling at the name of IESVS, or for religiously vsing creatures sanctified in the same name, or any other Christian obseruation, for vvhich our nevv Maisters cõdemne the Catholike people of Superstition: them selues vvholy voide of that vice by al vvise mens iudgement, because they haue in maner taken avvay al religiõn, and are become Epicureians and Atheists: vvho are neuer troubled vvith superstition, because it is a vice consisting in excesse of vvorship or religion, vvhereof they are void. but the Apostle calleth them superstitious for vvorshipping the Idols and goddes of the Heathen, and * for the feare that they had, lest they should leaue out any God that vvas vnknovven to them: for thus their Altar vvas inscribed: *Dijs Asiæ, Europæ, & Lybiæ, Deo ignoto & peregrino.* that is, To the gods of Asia, Europe, and Lybia: to the vnknovven and strange God. This superstition (saith S. Augustine) is vvholy taken avvay from the Church by Christs incarnation, and by the Apostles preaching, and by Martyrs holy life and death. Neither doth the Catholike Church allovv this or any other kinde of superstitious obseruation. Only vve must take heede that vve beleeue not her Aduersaries definition of superstition, for they vvould imply therein al true religion.

The Apostle speaketh of the Heathens superstition.

* Δεισιδαίμονας

Aug. de cõs. Euãg. li. 1 c. 26.

The Catholike Church alloweth no superstition.

29. *The Diuinitie to be like.*) Nothing can be made by manshand of vvhat forme or sort so euer, that is like to Gods essence, or to the forme or shape of his Godhead or Diuinitie. therfore hovvsoeuer the Heathens did paint or graue their Idols, they vvere nothing like to God. And this also is impertinently alleaged by Heretikes against the Churches images: Vvhich are not made, either

to

to be adored vvith godly honour, or to be any resemblance of the Diuinitie or any of the three persons in Godhead, but only of Christ as he vvas in forme of man, vvho in that respect may be truely expressed, as other men by their purtraites: and of the Holy Ghost, not as he is in him self, but as he appeared in firy tongues or in the similitude of a dooue, or such like. And so to paint or graue any of the three persons as they appeared visibly and corporally, is no more inconuenient or vnlavvful, then it vvas vndecent for them to appeare in such formes. And therfore to paint or portraite the Father also being the first person, as he hath shevved him self in vision to any of the Prophetes of the old or nevv Testament (namely to Daniel as an old man) or the three Angels representing the three Persons to Abraham, or the one Angel that vvrastling vvith Iacob bare our Lords Person, no such thing is any vvhere forbidden, but is very agreable to the peoples instruction. In vvhich sort the Angels vvere commonly pourtered (and namely the Cherubins ouer the Propitiatorie) as they be novv in the Church, not in their natural forme, but vvith corporal vvinges (as the Seraphins appeared to Esay the Prophete) to expresse their qualitie and office of being Gods Angels, that is, *Messengers*: and God the Father vvith the vvorld in his hand, to signifie his creation and gouernement of the same, and such like: Vvhereof the people being vvel instructed may take much good, and no harme in the vvorld, being novv through their faith in Christ far from al fond imagination of the false gods of the Pagans. And therfore S. Gregorie saith of the Churches Images, *That vvhich scripture or vvriting doth to the readers, the same doth the picture to the simple that looke therevpon. for in it euen the ignorant see vvhat they ought to folovv, in it they do read, that knovv no letters.* Vvhere he calleth it a matter of antiquitie and very conuenient, that in holy places Images vvere painted to the peoples instruction, so they be taught that they may not be adored vvith diuine honour. and he in the same place sharply rebuketh Serenus the Bishop of Massilia, that of indiscrete zele he vvould take avvay Images, rather then teach the people hovv to vse them.

Dan. 7, 22. *Gen. 18, 2.* *Gen. 32, 24* *Exo. 37, 7.* *Esa. 6, 2.* *Grego. li. 9 ep. 9.*

How there may be Images or resemblaces of the thre persons in Trinitie, and of Angels.

Images are for the peoples instruction.

34. *Dionysius Areopagita.*) This is that famous Denys that first conuerted France, and vvrote those notable and diuine vvorkes *de Ecclesiastica & cælesti hierarchia, de diuinis nominibus*, and others, in vvhich he confirmeth and proueth plainely almost al things that the Church novv vseth in the ministration of the holy Sacraments, and affirmeth that he learned them of the Apostles, giuing also testimonie for the Catholike faith in most things novv controuersed, so plainely, that our Aduersaries haue no shift but to deny this Denys to haue been the author of them, feyning that they be an others of later age. Vvhich is an old flight of Heretikes, but most proper to these of al others. Vvho seeing al antiquitie against them, are forced to be more bold or rather impudent then others in that point.

S. Dionysius Areopagita is al for the Catholikes.

CHAP. XVIII.

At Corinth in Achaia, he vvorketh vvith his ovvne hands, preaching IESVS *to be* CHRIST, *vnto the Ievves vpon their Sabboths. 6 But they being obstinate and blaspheming, he in plaine termes forsaketh them, and turneth to the Gentils, among vvhom according to a vision that he had to embolden him, he planteth the Church in great numbers, 12 the obstinat Ievves in vaine soliciting the Proconsul against him. 18 From thence at length departing he returneth 19 by Ephesus (vvhere he promiseth the Ievves to returne to them) 22 and so to Antioch in Syria (from vvhence he began his iourney Act. 15) 23 but not resting, by and by he goeth againe to visite the nevv Churches that he planted Act. 16 in Galatia and Phrygia: 24 Apollo in his absence mightily confounding the Ievves at Ephesus, 27 and aftervvard at Corinth.*

1 AFTER these things, departing from Athens, 2 he came to Corinth. † and finding a certaine Ievv, named Aquila, borne in Pontus, vvho of late vvas come out of Italie, and Priscilla his vvife (because Claudius had commaunded al 3 Ievves to depart from Rome,) he came to them. † And because he vvas of the same craft, he remained vvith them, and 4 vvrought, (and they vvere tentmakers by their craft.) † And

 he

he disputed in the synagogue euery Sabboth, interposing the name of our Lord IESVS, and he exhorted the Ievves and the Greekes. † And vvhen Silas and Timothee vvere come 5 from Macedonia, Paul vvas instant in preaching, testifying to the Ievves that IESVS is CHRIST. † But they contradi- 6 cting and blaspheming, he shaking his garmēts, said to them, Your bloud vpon your ovvne head: I being cleane, from hence forth vvil goe to the Gentiles. † And departing thēce, 7 he entred into the house of a certaine man, named Titus Iustus, one that serued God, vvhose house vvas adioyning to the synagogue. † And Crispus the prince of the Synagogue 8 beleeued our Lord, vvith al his house: and many of the Corinthians hearing beleeued, and vvere baptized. † And our 9 Lord said in the night by a vision to Paul, Doe not feare, but speake, and hold not thy peace, † for-because I am vvith 10 thee: and no man shal set vpon thee to hurt thee: for I haue much people in this citie. † And he sate there a yere & sixe 11 moneths, teaching among them the vvord of God.

† But Gallio being Proconsul of Achaia, the Ievves vvith 12 one accord rose vp against Paul, and brought him to the iudgement seate, † saying, That this man contrarie to the Lavv 13 persuadeth men to vvorshippe God. † And Paul beginning 14 to open his mouth, Gallio said to the Ievves, If it vvere some vniust thing, or an heinous facte, O you men Ievves, I should by reason beare you. † But if they be questions of vvord & 15 names, and of your lavv, your selues looke vnto it: I vvil not be iudge of these things. † And he droue them from the 16 iudgement seate. † And al apprehēding Sósthenes the prince 17 of the synagogue, strooke him before the iudgement seate: and Gallio cared for none of those things

† But Paul vvhen he had staied yet many daies, taking his 18 leaue of the brethren, sailed to Syria, (and vvith him Priscilla and Aquila,) vvho had shorne his head in Cenchris. for he had * a vovv. † And he came vnto Ephesus, and them he 19 left there. But him self entring into the synagogue, disputed vvith the Ievves. † And vvhen they desired him, that he 20 vvould tarie a longer time, he consented not, † but taking 21 his leaue, and saying, I vvil returne to you againe God vvilling, he departed from Ephesus. † And going dovvne to 22 Cæsaréa, he vvent vp, and saluted the Church, and came dovvne to Antioche.

Nu. 6, 18. Act. 21, 24.

23 † And hauing taried there a certaine time, he departed, vvalking in order through the countrie of Galatia and Phrygia, confirming al the disciples.

24 † And a certaine Ievv, named Apollo, borne at Alexandria, an eloquent man, came to Ephesus, mighty in the scriptures. 25 † This man vvas taught the vvay of our Lord: and being feruent in spirit he spake, and taught diligently those things that pertaine to IESVS, knovving only the baptisme 26 of Iohn. † This man therfore began to deale confidently in the synagogue. Vvhom vvhen Priscilla and Aquila had heard, they tooke him vnto them, and expounded to him the 27 vvay of our Lord more diligently. † And vvhereas he vvas desirous to goe to Achaia, the brethren exhorting vvrote to the disciples to receiue him. Vvho, vvhen he vvas come, pro-28 fited them much that had beleeued. † For he vvith vehemencie conuinced the Ievves openly, shevving by the scriptures, that IESVS is CHRIST.

Apollo.

CHAP. XIX.

Hovv Paul began the Church of Ephesus, first in 12 that vvere baptized vvith Iohns baptisme, 8 then preaching three moneths in the Synagogue of the Ievves, vntil for their obstinacie and blaspheming, he forsooke them, disputing aftervvard in a certaine schoole for tvvo yeres space to the maruelous increase of the Church, specially through his great miracles also, in healing diseases vvith the touche of his clothes, and expelling diuels, 13 vvho yet contemned the Exorcists of the Ievves. 18 Hovv the Christians there confesse their actes, and burne their vnlavvful bookes: 21 and hovv he foretold that after he had been at Hierusalem, he must see Rome. 23 and vvhat a great sedition vvas raised against him at Ephesus, by them that got their liuing of vvorking to the idolatrous Temple of Diana.

1 AND it came to passe vvhen Apollo vvas at Corinth, that Paul hauing gone through the higher partes came to Ephesus, and found certaine disciples: 2 † and he said to them, Haue you receiued the holy Ghost, beleeuing? But they said to him, Nay, neither haue vve heard Whe-3 ther there be a holy Ghost. † But he said, In vvhat then vvere 4 you baptized? Vvho said, [c] In Iohns baptisme. † And Paul said: * Iohn baptized the people vvith the baptisme of penance, saying: That they should beleeue in him that vvas to 5 come after him, that is to say, [c] in IESVS. † Hearing these things, they vvere baptized in the name of our Lord IESVS.

The Epistle vpō Whitson-eue.

Mt, 3, 11. Mr. 1, 8. Lu. 3, 16.

c Iohns baptisme not sufficiēt.

c Christs baptisme necessarie.

:: S. Paul ministred the Sacrament of Cōfirmatiō. *See añot, c. 8, 17.*

† And vvhen Paul had :: imposed hands on them, the holy Ghost came vpon them, and they spake vvith tongues, and prophecied. † And all the men vvere about tvvelue. 6 7

† And entring in to the synagogue, he spake confidently for three moneths, disputing and exhorting of the kingdom of God. ⊣ † But vvhen certaine vvere indurate, and beleeued not, il-speaking the vvay of our Lord before the multitude, departing from them, he separated the disciples, daily disputing in the schole of one Tyrannus. † An this vvas done for the space of tvvo yeres, so that al vvhich dvvelt in Asia, heard the vvord of our Lord, Ievves and Gentils. 8 9 10

† And God vvrought by the hand of Paul miracles not common: † so that there vvere also brought from his body "napkins or handkerchefs vpon the sicke, and the diseases departed from them, and the vvicked spirits vvent out. † And certaine also of the Iudaical exorcists that vvent about, assaied to inuocate vpon them that had euil spirits, the name of our Lord IESVS, saying, I adiure you by IESVS vvhom Paul preacheth. † And there vvere certaine sonnes of Sceua a Ievve, cheefe priest, seuen, that did this. † But the vvicked spirit ansvvering, said to them, IESVS I knovv, and "Paul I knovv: but you, vvhat are ye? † And the man in vvhom the vvicked spirit vvas, leaping vpon them, and mastring both, preuailed against them, so that they fled out of that house naked and vvounded. † And this vvas made notorious to al the Ievves and the Gentiles that dvvelt at Ephesus: and feare fel vpon al them, and the name of our Lord IESVS vvas magnified. † And many of them that beleeued, came confessing and declaring :: their deedes. † And many of them that had folovved "curious things, brought together their "bookes, and burnt them before al: and counting the prices of them, they found the money to be fiftie thousand pence. † So mightely increased the vvord of God and vvas confirmed. 11 12 13 14 15 16 17 18 19 20

them

:: They made not only a general confessiō wherein al mē shew thē selues alike to be sinners, as our Protestants do: but euery one confessed his owne proper deedes and faultes.

The 6 part. :: Of taking avvay the Gospel frō Hierusalem the head citie of the Iewes, and giuing it to ROME the head citie of the Gentils.

† And vvhen these things vvere ended, Paul purposed in the Spirit, vvhen he had passed through Macedonia and Achaia, to goe to Hierusalem, saying, After I shall haue been there, I must see :: Rome also. † And sending into Macedonia tvvo of them that ministred vnto him, Timothee and Erastus, him self remained for a time in Asia. 21 22

† And at that time there vvas made no litle trouble about 23

the

24 the vvay of our Lord. † For one named Demetrius, a ſiluerſmith, that made ſiluer [c] temples of Diána, procured to the ar-
25 tificers no ſmal gaine: † vvhom calling together and them that vvere the ſame kinde of vvorkemen, he ſaid, Sirs, you
26 knovv that our gaine is of this occupation: † and you ſee, and heare that this ſame Paul by perſuaſion hath auerted a great multitude not only of Epheſus, but almoſt of al Aſia, ſaying, That they are not gods vvhich be made by handes.
27 † And not only vnto vs is this part in danger to be reproued, but alſo the temple of great Diana ſhal be reputed for nothing, yea & her maieſtie ſhal begin to be deſtroied, vvhom
28 al Aſia & the vvorld vvorſhippeth. † Hearing theſe things, they vvere repleniſhed vvith anger, and cried out ſaying,
29 Great is Diana of the Epheſians. † And the vvhole citie vvas filled vvith confuſion, & they ranne violently vvith one accord into the theátre, catching Gaius and Ariſtarchus Ma-
30 cedonians, Paules companions. † And vvhen Paul vvould haue entred in to the people, the diſciples did not permit him.
31 † And certaine alſo of the Princes of Aſia that vvere his frendes, ſent vnto him, deſyring that he vvould not aduéture
32 him ſelf into the theátre: † and others cried an other thing. For the aſſemblie vvas confuſe, & the more part knevv
33 not for vvhat cauſe they vvere aſſembled. † And of the multitude they drevv forth Alexander, the Ievves thruſting him forvvard. But Alexander vvith his hand deſiring ſilence,
34 vvould haue giuen the people ſatisfaction. † Vvhom as ſoone as they perceiued to be a Ievve, there vvas made one voice of al, almoſt for the ſpace of tvvo houres crying out,
35 Great is Diana of the Epheſians. † And vvhen the Scribe had appeaſed the multitudes, he ſaith, Ye men of Epheſus, for vvhat man is there that knovveth not the citie of the Epheſians to be a vvorſhipper of great Diana, & [c] Iupiters childe?
36 † Foraſmuch therfore as theſe things can not be gainſaid, you
37 muſt be quieted, and doe nothing raſhly. † For you haue brought theſe men, being neither ſacrilegious, nor blaſphe-
38 ming your Goddeſſe. † But if Demetrius and the artificers that are vvith him, haue matter to ſay againſt any man, there are Courtes kept in the common place, & there are Procon-
39 ſuls, let them accuſe one an other. † And if you aſke any
40 other matter: it may be reſolued in a lavvful aſſemblie. † For vve are in danger alſo to be accuſed for this daies ſedition:

c ναοὺς

c The Proteſtants tranſlate, *ſhrines*, in the bible an. 1577: to make the people thinke that it toucheth the holy ſhrines of Saincts: moſt corruptly, the greeke ſignifying plainly, *temples*, and that of heathé gods.

c τοῦ διοπετοῦς.

c Here the Heretikes adde to the text this word, *image*, more then is in the greeke, to put a ſcruple into the peoples minde concerning holy Images.

vvhereas there is no man guilty by vvhom vve may giue an account of this concourse. And vvhen he had said these things, he dimissed the assemblie.

ANNOTATIONS CHAP. XIX.

Touching of Relikes, & miracles done by the same.

12. *Napkins.*] The napkins that had touched S. Paules body, vvrought miracles, and it vvas no superstition to attribute that vertue to them vvhich God gaue to them in deede: nor to seeke to touch them for health, vvas any dishonour to God, but it much proued Christes religiõ to be true, and him to be the only God, vvhose seruants, yea vvhose seruants *shades and napkins could do such vvonders, as S. Chrysostome (*to. 5. cont. Gentiles, quòd Christus sit Deus, in vit. Babylæ.*) shevveth in a vvhole booke to that purpose, against the Pagans, prouing hereby and by the like vertue of other Saincts and their Relikes, that Christ their Lord and Maister is God. for it is al one concerning the bodies of Saincts, reliques, garments, staues, bookes, or any thing that belonged to them, al which may and haue done and yet doe (vvhen it is necessarie to our edification) the like vvonders to Gods great honour: not only in their life time, but after their death much more. for S. Paules napkins had as great force vvhen he vvas dead, as vvhen he liued, and so much more, as his grace and dignitie vvith God is greater then before. Vvhich S. Chrysostom in the place alleaged proueth at large by the shrine of S. Babylas the Martyr: and to thinke the contrarie, is the Heresie of Vigilantius, condemned so long since as S. Hieroms time, and by him refuted aboundantly.

Act. 5, 15.

The name, or presence, or Reliques of Saincts & holy men, confound the Diuel.

16. *Paul I knovv.*] Both the said napkins taken from S. Paules body, and his name also, vvere dreadful and able to expel diuels. Vvhereby vve learne that not only Christes name, vvhich is the principal, but his seruãts names also inuocated vpon the possessed, haue povver ouer diuels: vvhich is a maruelous honour to Saincts, and nothing diminisheth the glorie of Christ, but excedingly increaseth the same, not only him self, but his seruants also being able to do such things, and to be stronger then any Diuel in Hel. So vve read in * S. Hierom that many did inuocate the name of S. Hilarion vpon the possessed, and the Diuels straight departed. so did the Diuel knovv *S. Babylas and other Saincts, euen after they vvere dead, vvhen they could not speake for the presence of their Relikes, and vvhen they vvere tormented and expelled by them: vvhereof al antiquitie is ful of testimonies. But our Heretikes Luther and Caluin and their Scholers attempting to cast out Diuels, sped much like as these good fellovves did.

In vit. Hilarionis. *Chrys. loco citato.*

Superstitious, heretical, and al hurtful bookes must be made avvay.

19. *Curious things.*] Curious and vnlavvful sciences, as Vvitchcraft, Necromancie, and other meanes of diuination by southsaying, figure-casting, interpretation of dreames, or any vvay not allovved by God and his Church, must much more be abhorred of old Christians, vvhen these so lately conuerted vvere so zelous and diligent to leaue them And by this example al that are nevvly reconciled to the Church, are taught, the first thing they do, to burne their heretical and naughtie bookes.

Decrees and penal lavves against heretical bookes.

19. *Bookes.*] A Christian man is bound to burne or deface al vvicked bookes of vvhat sort so euer, specially Heretical bookes. Vvhich though they infect not him alvvaies that keepeth them, yet being furth comming, they may be noisom and pernicious to others that shal haue them and read them after his death, or othervvise. Therfore hath the Church taken order for condemning al such bookes, and against the reading of them, vvhere danger may ensue: and the Christian Emperours, Constantinus Magnus, Valentinian, Theodosius, Martian, Iustinian, made penal lavves for the burning or defacing of them. *Sozom. li. 1 c. 20. li. 2 c. 31. Conc. Chalc. act. 3. in fine, cap. Ampla. & in fine totius Conc. c. Imperator. Conc. Constantinop. 2. conses. 5. cap. Debitam. & Act. 1 cap. 1. & cap. Rem.* See Eusebius *li. 3 de vita Constant. c. 61. 62. 63. 64.* The danger of reading them, as it is manifest, so it is signified by Euseb. *li. 7 c. 6.* S. Augustine *li. 3 de bapt. c. 14.* S. Greg. *li. 5 ep. 64.*

CHAP. XX.

Hauing visited the Churches of Macedonia and Achaia (as he purposed Act. 19) and novv about to saile from Corinth tovvard Hierusalem, because of the Ievves lying in vvaite for him, he is constrained to returne into Macedonia. 6 And so at Philippos taking boate, commeth to Troas, vvhere vpon the Sunday, vvith a sermon, and a miracle, he greatly confirmeth that Church. 13 Thence comming to Milétum, 17 he sendeth to Ephesus for the Clergie of those partes: to vvhom he maketh a Pastoral sermon, committing vnto their charge the flocke begũne by him there, and novv like to be seen of him no more, considering the troubles that by reuelation he looketh for at Hierusalem.

AND

1 ND after that the tumult vvas ceased, Paul calling the disciples, and exhorting them, tooke his leaue, and set forvvard to goe into Macedonia. 2 † And vvhen he had vvalked through those partes, & had exhorted them vvith much speach, he came to Greece: 3 † vvhere vvhen he had spent three moneths, the Ievves laid vvait for him as he vvas about to saile into Syria: and he had councel to returne through Macedonia. 4 † And there accompanied him Sosipater of Pyrrhus, of Berœa: and of Thessalonians, Aristarchus, and Secundus: and Caius of Derbè, and Timothee: and of Asia, Tychicus and Tróphimus. 5 † These going before, staied for vs at Troas: 6 † but vve sailed after the daies of Azymes from Philippi, and came to them vnto Troas in fiue daies, vvhere vve abode seuen daies.

7 † And in the first of the Sabboth vvhen vve vvere assembled to ∷ breake bread, Paul disputed vvith them, being to depart on the morovv, and he continued the sermon vntil midnight. 8 † And there vvere a great number of lampes in the vpper chamber vvhere vve vvere assembled. 9 † And a certaine yong man named Eútychus, sitting vpon the vvindovv, vvhereas he vvas oppressed vvith heauy sleepe (Paul disputing long) driuẽ by sleepe, fel from the third loft downe, 10 and vvas taken vp dead. † To vvhom vvhen Paul vvas gone dovvne, he lay vpon him: and embracing him he said, 11 Be not troubled, for his soule is in him. † And going vp and breaking bread and tasting, and hauing talked sufficiently to 12 them vntil day light, so he departed. † And they brought the lad aliue, and vvere not a litle comforted.

∷ S. Paul did here breake bread on the Sunday as it is broken in the Sacramẽt of the body of Christ, and had both before & after the celebrating of the Sacramẽt a sermon to the people. *Aug. ep. 86 ad Casulanũ. Vener. Beda in 20 Act.*

13 † But vve going vp into the ship, sailed to Asson, from thence meaning to receiue Paul. for so he had ordained, him 14 self purposing to iourney by land. † And vvhen he had found vs in Asson, taking him vvith vs vve came to Mitylé-15 ne. † And sailing thence, the day folovving vve came ouer against Chios: and the other day vve arriued at Samos: and 16 the day folovving vve came to Milétum. † for Paul had purposed to saile leauing Ephesus, lest any stay should be made him in Asia. For he hastened, if it vvere possible for him, to keepe the day of ″ Pentecost at Hierusalem.

17 † And sending from Milétum to Ephesus, he called the 18 [c] Auncients of the Church. † Vvho being come to him, and assembled

c πρεσβυτέρους

c That is, *Priests* as *Act. 15, 4.* See the marginal annot. there.

assembled together, he said to them, You knovv * from the first day that I entred into Asia, in vvhat maner I haue been vvith you al the time, † seruing our Lord vvith al humilitie and teares, and tentations that did chaunce to me by the conspiracies of the Ievves: † Hovv I haue vvithdravven nothing that vvas profitable, but that I preached it to you, & taught you openly and from house to house, † testifying to Ievves and Gentils ∷ penance tovvard God and faith in our Lord IESVS CHRIST. † And novv behold, being bound by the spirit, I goe to Hierusalem: not knovving vvhat things shal befall me in it, † but that the Holy Ghost through out al cities doth protest to me, saying: that bands and tribulations abide me at Hierusalem. † But I feare none of these things, neither doe I make my life more pretious thẽ my self, so that I may cõsũmat my course & ministerie vvhich I receiued of our Lord IESVS, to testifie the Gospel of the grace of God. † And novv behold I doe knovv, that you shal no more see my face al you, through vvhom I haue passed preaching the kingdom of God. † Vvherefore I take you to witnesse this present day that I am cleere from the bloud of al. † For I haue not spared to declare vnto you al the counsel of God. † Take heede to your selues and to the vvhole flocke vvherein the ∷ Holy Ghost hath placed you bishops, to rule the Church of God vvhich he hath purchased with his ovvne bloud. † I knovv that after my departure there vvil " rauening vvolues enter in among you, not sparing the flocke. † and out of your ovvne selues shal arise men speaking peruerse things, to dravv avvay disciples after them selues. † For the vvhich cause be vigilant, keeping in memorie that for three yeres night and day I ceased not vvith teares to admonish euery one of you. † And novv I commend you to God and to the vvord of his grace, vvho is able to edifie, and to giue inheritance in al the sanctified. † No mans siluer and gold or garment haue I coueted. † Your selues knovv that for such things as vvere needful for me and them that are vvith me, these hands haue ministred. † I haue shevved you al things, that so labouring, you must receiue the vveake, and remember the vvord of our Lord IESVS, because he said, " It is a more blessed thing to giue rather then to take.

† And vvhen he had said these things, falling on his knees he praied vvith al them. † And there vvas great vveeping

made

Margin: Act. 19, 1

Verse numbers: 19, 20, 21, 22, 23, 24, 25, 26, 27, 28, 29, 30, 31, 32, 33, 34, 35, 36, 37

∷ Apostolike preaching commendeth not faith only but penance also to the people.

∷ Bishops or Priests (for then these names Were sometime vsed indifferẽtly) gouernours of the Church of God, & placed in that roome & high functiõ by the Holy Ghost.

made of al, and falling vpon the necke of Paul, they kiſſed
38 him, † being ſorie moſt of al for the vvord vvhich he had ſaid, that they ſhould ſee his face no more. And they brought him going vnto the ſhippe.

ANNOTATIONS
CHAP. XX.

16. Pentecoſt.] Though the Apoſtles might deſire to come to the Ievves Feſtiuities, by reaſon of the general concourſe of people to the ſame, the better to deale for their ſaluation and to ſpred the Goſpel of Chriſt, yet it is like that they novv kept ſolemly the Chriſtian Pentecoſt or vvhitſontide, for memorie of the Holy Ghoſt, and that S. Paul vvent to that Feaſt of the Chriſtians rather then the other of the Ievves. And Ven. Bede ſaith here, *The Apoſtle maketh haſt to keepe the fifteth day, that is, of remiſſion and of the Holy Ghoſt.* For, that the Chriſtians already kept the eight day, that is, the Sunday or our Lordes day, and had altered already the ordinarie Sabboth into the ſame, it is plaine by the Scriptures(*1 Cor. 16,2. Apoc. 1,10.*)and by antiquitie. *Iuſtin. Mart. Apolog. 2 ad Anton. Pium in fine.* And it is as like that they changed the Ievves Paſche and Pentecoſt as that, ſpecially vvhen it is euident that * theſe Feſtiuities be kept by Apoſtolike tradition, and approued by the vſe of al auncient Churches and Councels.

The Chriſtian Pentecoſt.

Sunday.

Aug. ep. 118 c. 1.

29. Rauening vvolues.] The gouernours of the Church are foretold of the great danger that ſhould fall to the people by vvolues, that is to ſay, by Heretikes, vvhoſe cruelty tovvard the Catholikes is noted by this terme. They be knovve by the forſaking the vnitie of the Church vvhereof they vvere before, by going out and dravving many diſciples after them, and by their peruerſe doctrine. Such vvolues came aftervvard in deede in diuers ages, Arius, Macedonius, Neſtorius, Eutyches, Luther, Caluin, great bloudſucking vvolues, and vvaſters of the flocke of Chriſt.

Rauening vvolues are the Heretikes of al ages.

35. More bleſſed to giue.] Among many other infinite goodly things and ſpeaches vvhich Chriſt ſpake and be not vvritten in the Goſpels, this ſentence is one: vvhich S. Paul heard of ſome of the Apoſtles daily conuerſant vvith him, or els learned of Chriſt him ſelf, or of the Holy Ghoſt. And it ſignifieth, that vvhereas the vvorld commonly counteth him happie that receiueth any benefite, as almes either temporal or ſpiritual, yet in deede he that giueth or beſtovveth, is more happie. Vvhich if the vvorld did vvel conſider, men vvould giue almes faſter then they do, if it vvere but for their ovvne benefite.

Chriſts ſpeaches not vvritten in the Goſpel.

Great almeſmen bleſſed.

CHAP. XXI.

From Milétum going on his iourney, 4 he can not be diſſuaded neither at Tyre, 8 nor at Cæſarea (in both vvhich places the Holy Ghoſt reueled hovv he ſhould be handled in Hieruſalem, 10 the Prophet Agabus expreſly foretelling that the Ievves there ſhould deliuer him to the Gentils) 15 but to Hieruſalem he cometh: vvhere being vvelcome to the Chriſtians, and namely to Iames the Biſhop, and to the Prieſts, vvhile he goeth about to ſatisfie the Chriſtian Ievves there, vvho had been miſinformed of him as if he had taught it to be vnlaWful for the IeWes to keepe Moyſes Lavv: 27 he is inuaded by the infidel Ievves, and ready to be murdered by them, vntil the Romane ſouldiars do reſcue him.

1 AND vvhen it came to paſſe that vve ſailed, being caried from them, vvith a ſtraight courſe vve came to Cóos, and the day folovving to
2 Rhodes, and from thence to Pátara. † And vvhen vve had found a ſhip that paſſed ouer to
3 Phœníce, going vp into it vve ſailed. † And vvhen vve vvere in the ſight of Cypres, leauing it on the left hand, vve ſailed

into Syria, and came to Tyre: for there the ſhip vvas to diſcharge her lode. † And finding diſciples, vve taried there ſeuen daies: vvho ſaid to Paul by the Spirit, that he ſhould not goe vp to Hieruſalem. † And the daies being expired, departing vve vvent forvvard, al bringing vs on the vvay, vvith their vviues and children, til vve vvere out of the citie: and falling vpon our knees on the ſhore, vve praied. † And vvhen vve had bid one an other farevvel, vve vvent vp into the ſhip: and they returned vnto their ovvne. † But vve hauing ended the nauigation, from Tyre came dovvne to Ptolomáis: and ſaluting the brethren, vve taried one day vvith them. † And the next day departing, vve came to Cęſarêa. And entring into the houſe of * Philip the Euangeliſt, vvho vvas one of the ſeuen, vve taried vvith him. † And he had ∷ foure daughters virgins, that did prophecie.

4 5 6 7 8 9

Act. 6,5

∷ As S. Peter had a wife, but vſed her not after his calling, as it is noted els where out of S. Hierom *Luc. 4, 38*: ſo may it be ſaid of S. Philip being Deacon.

† And as vve abode there for certaine daies, there came a certaine prophet from Ievvrie, named Agabus. † He, vvhẽ he vvas come to vs, tooke Paules girdle: and binding his ovvne handes & feete, he ſaid, Thus ſaith the holy Ghoſt: The man vvhoſe girdle this is, ſo ſhal the Ievves binde in Hieruſalem, & ſhal deliuer him into the handes of the Gentiles. † Vvhich when vve had heard, vve & they that vvere of the ſame place, deſired him that he would not goe vp to Hieruſalem. † Then Paul anſvvered, and ſaid, Vvhat doe you, vveeping and afflicting my hart? for I am ready not only to be bound, but to die alſo in Hieruſalem for the name of our Lord IESVS. † And vvhen vve could not perſuade him, we ceaſed, ſaying, The vvil of our Lord be done.

10 11 12 13 14

† And after theſe daies, being prepared, vve vvent vp to Hieruſalem. † And there came alſo of the diſciples from Cæſarêa vvith vs, bringing vvith them one Iaſon a Cyprian (vvith vvhom vve ſhould lodge) an old diſciple. † And vvhen vve vvere come to Hieruſalem, the brethren receiued vs gladly. † And the day folovving Paul vvent in vvith vs to Iames, and al the Auncients vvere aſſembled. † Vvhom vvhen he had ſaluted, he told particularly vvhat God had done among the Gentiles by his miniſterie. † But they hearing it, magnified God, and ſaid to him: Thou ſeeſt (brother) hovv many thouſands there are among the Ievves that haue beleeued: and al are zelátours of the Lavv. † But they haue heard of thee that thou doeſt teach thoſe Ievves

15 16 17 18 19 20 21

that

that are among the Gentiles, to depart from Moyses: saying that they ought not to circumcise their children, nor vvalke according to the custome. † Vvhat is it then? needes must the multitude assemble: for they vvil heare that thou art come. † Doe this therfore vvhich vve tel thee, There are vvith vs foure men, that haue a vovve on them. † Taking these vnto thee, sanctifie thy self vvith them: and bestovv on them, that they may * shaue their heads: and al shal knovv that the things vvhich they heard of thee, are false: but that thy self also vvalkest" keeping the Lavv. † But concerning them that beleeue of the Gentils, * vve haue written, decreeing that they should refraine them selues from the immolated to Idols, and bloud, and suffocated, and fornication.

(22, 23, 24, 25)

Nu. 6, 18.

Act. 15, 20.

26 † Then Paul taking the men vnto him, the next day being purified vvith them entred into the temple, shevving the accomplishment of the * daies of the purification, vntil an oblation vvas offered for euery one of them.

Nu. 6, 13

27 † But vvhiles the seuen daies vvere a finishing, those Ievves that vvere of Asia, vvhen they had seen him in the temple, stirred vp al the people, and laid handes vpon him, 28 † crying, Ye men of Israël, help: this is the man that against the people & the Lavv and this place teaching al men euery vvhere, hath also moreouer brought in Gentiles into the temple, and hath violated this holy place. 29 († For they had seen Tróphimus the Ephesian in the citie vvith him, vvhom they supposed that Paul had brought into the temple.) 30 † And the vvhole citie vvas in an vproare: and there vvas made a concourse of the people. And apprehending Paul, they drevve him forth of the temple: and immediatly the doores vvere shut. 31 † And as they sought to kil him, it vvas told the Tribune of the band, That al Hierusalem is in a confusion. 32 † Vvho forthvvith taking vnto him souldiars & Centurions, ranne dovvne to them. Who, vvhē they had seen the Tribune and the souldiars, ceased to strike Paul. 33 † Then the Tribune comming neere apprehended him, and commaunded him to be bound vvith tvvo chaines: and he demaunded vvho he vvas, and vvhat he had done. 34 † And some cried one thing, some an other, in the multitude. And vvhereas he could not knovv the certaintie for the tumult, he commaunded him to be led [c] into the castel. 35 † And vvhen he vvas come to the staires, it chaunced that he vvas caried of the souldiars because

c In castra. *So in the places folovving.*

of the violence of the people. † For the multitude of the 36 people folovved, crying, Avvay vvith him. † And vvhen 37 Paul began to be brought into the castel, he saith to the Tribune, Is it lavvful for me to speake some thing to thee? Vvho said, Canst thou speake Greeke? †. Art not thou the Ægyp- 38 tian that before these daies did raise a tumult, and didst lead forth into the desert foure thousand men that vvere murderers? † And Paul said to him, * I am a man truely a Ievve of 39 Tarsus, a citizen not of an obscure citie of Cilicia. And I desire thee, permit me to speake to the people. † And vvhen he 40 had permitted him, Paul stãding on the staiers, beckened with his hand to the people. and great silence being made, he spake vnto them in the Hebrevv tongue, saying.

Act. 22, 3.

ANNOTATIONS
Chap. XXI.

Virgins.

9. *Virgins.*] S. Luke noteth specially that his daughters vvere Virgins, meaning (no doubt) that they vvere of the state, profession, or purpose of perpetual virginitie, not only that they vvere yong maides vnmaried: and that they vvere the rather for that, endued vvith the gift of prophecie, as S. Hierom saith *li. 1 adu. Iouin. c. 24. See Oecum. c. 29 in hunc locum.*

Auoiding of scãdal in things not vnlavvful.

24. *Keeping the Lavv.*] Al the obseruations of the Lavv vvere novv in them selues dead and vnprofitable, yet til further propagation of the Gospel, they vvere not damnable to the keepers, nor offensiue to God, but might be obserued euen of the Christian Ievves. and for feare of scandalizing the vveake of that nation, nevvly conuerted or prone to receiue the faith, the Apostles by Gods suggestion did thinke it good to obserue them as occasion required.

Chap. XXII.

Being licensed by the Tribune to speake to the people, he shevveth them that he vvas once as earnest on that side as they novv be: 6 and hovv strange and miraculous his conuersion vvas. 17 They heare him quietly, vntil he began to make mention of a vision that sent him avvay from them to the Gentils. 22 Then they crie out vpon him so, 23 that for their crying the Tribune commaundeth him to be scourged. 25 Which yet by his vvisedom he escapeth.

MEN brethren and fathers, heare vvhat 1 account I doe render novv vnto you. † (And vvhen they had heard 2 that he spake to them in the Hebrevv tongue, they did the more keepe silẽce. † And he saith,) * I am a man a Ievve, 3 borne at Tarsus in Cilicia, but brought vp in this citie, at the feete of Gamaliel instructed according to the veritie of the lavv of the fathers, an

Act. 21, 39.

4 an emulátour of the Lavv as alſo al you are this day: † vvho * perſecuted this vvay vnto death, binding & deliuering into 5 cuſtodies men & vvomē, † as the high Prieſt doth giue me te- 6 ſtimonie, and al the auncients. † of vvhom * receiuing letters alſo to the brethren, I vvent to Damaſcus, that I might bring them thence bound to Hieruſalem, to be puniſhed. 7 And it came to paſſe as I vvas going, and dravving nigh to Damaſcus at midday, ſodēly from heauen there ſhone round 8 about me much light: † and falling on the ground, I heard a voice ſaying to me, Saul, Saul, vvhy perſecuteſt thou me? 9 † And I anſvvered, Vvho art thou Lord? And he ſaid to me, 10 I am IESVS of Nazareth, vvhom thou perſecuteſt. † And they that vvere vvith me, ſavv the light in deede, but the 11 voice they heard not of him that ſpake vvith me. † And I ſaid, Vvhat ſhal I doe Lord? And our Lord ſaid to me, Ariſe and goe to Damaſcus: and there it ſhal be told thee of al 12 things that thou muſt doe. † And vvhereas I did not ſee for the brightneſſe of that light, being led of my companions by 13 the hand, I came to Damaſcus. † And one Ananias, a man according to the Lavv hauing teſtimonie of al the Ievves in- 14 habitants, † comming to me, and ſtanding by me, ſaid to me, Brother Saul, looke vp. And I the ſelf ſame houre looked vp 15 on him. † But he ſaid, The God of our fathers hath preördained thee, that thou ſhouldeſt knovv his vvil, and ſee the 16 Iuſt one, and heare a voice from his mouth: † becauſe thou ſhalt be his vvitnes to al men, of thoſe things vvhich thou 17 haſt ſeen and heard. † And novv vvhat tarieſt thou? Riſe vp, and be baptized, & :: vvaſh avvay thy ſinnes inuocating his 18 name. † And it befel me returning into Hieruſalem, and 19 praying in the temple, that I vvas in a traunce, † and ſavv him ſaying vnto me, Make haſt, and depart quickely out of Hieruſalem: becauſe they vvil not receiue thy teſtimonie of 20 me. † And I ſaid, Lord, they knovv that I did caſt into priſon and beate in euery ſynagogue them that beleeued in thee. 21 † And vvhen the bloud of Steuen thy [c] vvitnes vvas ſhed, :: I ſtoode by and conſented, and kept the garments of them 22 that killed him. † And he ſaid to me, Goe, for into the Gentiles a farre vvil I ſend thee.

23 † And they heard him vntil this vvord, and they lifted vp their voice, ſaying, Avvay vvith ſuch an one from the earth: 24 for it is not meete he ſhould liue. † And vvhen they cried

Act. 8,3

Act. 9,2

c μάρ-τυρος

Act. 7, 38.

:: The Sacramēt of Baptiſme doth it ſelf vvaſh avvay ſinnes as here is plaine, & therfore doth not only ſignifie (as the Heretikes affirme) that our ſinnes be forgiuen before, or othervviſe by faith only remitted. Vvhereby the Churches doctrine is proued to be fully agreable to the Scriptures, that the Sacraments giue grace *ex opere operato*, that is, by the force & vertue of the vvorke and vvord, done & ſaid in the Sacrament.

:: Not only the Principals but al that conſent to the death or vexation of Chriſtian men for the Catholike faith, do highly offend. vvhich the Apoſtle confeſſeth here, that Gods mercie may be more notoriouſly glorified in him hereby.

out, and threvv of their garments, and cast dust into the aire, † the Tribune commaunded him to be caried into the castel, 24 and to be beaten vvith vvhippes, and that he should be tormented: to knovv for vvhat cause they did so crie at him. † And vvhen they had bound him very straight vvith thõgs, 25 Paul saith to the Centurion standing by him: Is it lavvful for you to vvhippe a man that is a Romane and vncondemned? † Vvhich the Centurion hearing, vvent to the Tribune, and 26 told him, saying, Vvhat vvilt thou doe? for this man is a citizen of Rome. † And the Tribune comming, said to him, 27 Tel me, art thou a Romane? But he said, Yea. † And the Tri- 28 bune ansvvered, I obtained this citie vvith a great summe. And Paul said, But I vvas also borne to it. † Immediatly ther- 29 fore they departed from him that vvere to torment him. The Tribune also feared after he vnderstoode that he was a citizẽ of Rome, and because he had bound him. † But the next 30 day meaning to knovv more diligently for vvhat cause he vvas accused of the Ievves, he loosed him, and commaunded the [c]Priests to come together and al the Councel: & bringing forth Paul, he set him among them.

[c] ἀρχιερεῖς

CHAP. XXIII.

As the people in the tumult, so also the very cheefe of the Ievves in their Councel shevv them selues obstinate, and vvilful persecutors of the truth in S. Pauls person. Whose behauiour tovvardes them is ful of constancie, modestie, and vvisedom. 11 (Christ also by a vision encouraging him, and foretelling that he shal to Rome.) 12 Yea they conspire vvith 40 men to kil him traiterously. 16 But the matter being detected, the Romane Tribune conueigheth him strongly to Cæsaréa.

AND Paul looking vpon the Councel, 1 said, Men brethren, I vvith al good conscience haue conuersed before God, vntil this present day. † And the high Priest 2 Ananias commaunded them that stoode by him, to smite him on the mouth. † Then Paul said to him, ⁘ God shal 3 strike thee, thou vvhited vvall. And thou sitting iudgest me according to the lavv, and contrarie to lavv doest thou commaund me to be smitten? † And they that stoode by, said, 4 Doest thou reuile the high Priest of God? † And Paul said, 5 "I knevve not, brethren, that he is the high Priest. For it is vvritten: *The prince of thy people thou shalt not misspeake.* † And Paul 6 knovving

⁘ He said not this through perturbation of minde or of a passion, but by way of prophecie, that this figuratiue high priesthod then trimmed like a vvhited vvall, was to be destroied, vvhereas now the true priesthod of Christ was cõe. *Beda in hunc lo.*

Exo. 22, 28.

knovving that the one part vvas of Sadducees, and the other of Pharisees, :: he cried out in the Councel, Men brethren, *I am a Pharisee, the sonne of Pharisees: of the hope and resurrection of the dead am I iudged. 7 † And vvhen he had said these things, there rose dissension betvvene the Pharisees 8 and Sadducees, and the multitude vvas diuided. † For the "Sadducees say * there is no resurrection, nor Angel, nor spirit: but the Pharisees confesse both. 9 † And there vvas made a great crie. And certaine of the Pharisees rising vp, stroue saying, Vve finde no euil in this man. vvhat if a spirit hath spoken to him, or an Angel? 10 † And vvhen there vvas risen great dissensiō, the Tribune fearing lest Paul should be torne in peeces by them, cōmaunded the souldiars to goe dovvne, and to take him out of the middes of them, and to bring him into the castel. 11 † And the night folovving our Lord standing by him, said, Be constant: for as thou hast testified of me in Hierusalem, so :: must thou testifie at Rome also.

Phil. 3, 5.

Mt. 22, 23.

:: Such prudent euasions from danger are lawful. vvhich S. Chrysostōe calleth (specially in this Apostle) the wisdom of the serpēt, as otherwise in his teaching and preaching & patiēce he vsed the simplicitie of a dooue.

12 † And vvhen day vvas come, certaine of the Ievves gathered them selues together, &" vovved them selues, saying, that they vvould neither eate nor drinke til they killed Paul. 13 † And they vvere more then fourtie men that had made this 14 conspiracie: † vvho came to the cheefe priests and the auncients, and said, By execration vve haue vovved our selues, 15 that vve vvil eate nothing, til vve kill Paul. † Novv therfore giue you knovvledge to the Tribune vvith the Coūcel, that he bring him forth to you, as if you meant to knovv some more certaintie touching him. But we, before he come neere, 16 are ready for to kil him. † Vvhich vvhen Paules sisters sonne had heard, of their lying in vvaite, he came and entred 17 into the castel and told Paul. † And Paul calling to him one of the Centurions, said, Bring this yong man to the Tribune, 18 for he hath some thing to tel him. † [c] And he taking him, brought him to the Tribune, and said, The prisoner Paul desired me to bring this yong man vnto thee, hauing some 19 thing to say to thee. † And the Tribune taking him by the hand, vvent aside vvith him apart, and asked him, Vvhat is 20 it that thou hast to tel me? † And he said, The Ievves haue agreed to desire thee, that to morovv thou vvilt bring forth Paul into the Councel, as though they meant to inquire some 21 more certaintie touching him. † But doe not thou credite them, for there lie in vvaite for him more then fourtie men of

:: Though God who could not lie, had promised Paul that he should goe to Rome: yet the Apostle omitted not humane meanes to defend him self from his enemies and otherwise. neither said he as the Heretikes called Predestinates, Let them do what they wil, they cā not hurt me, for I am predestinate to goe to Rome. See his doings and sayings to saue him self, in the chap. folowing.

c See the curtesie & equitie of Heathen Officers tovvard their prisoners, to saue them from al iniurie and villanie.

of them, vvhich haue vovved neither to eate nor to drinke, til they kil him: and they are novv ready, expecting thy promisse. 22 † The Tribune therfore dimissed the yong man, commaunding that he should speake to no man that he had notified these things vnto him. 23 † And calling tvvo Centurions, he said to them, Make ready tvvo hundred souldiars, to goe as farre as Cæsaréa, and seuentie horsemen, and launces tvvo hundred, from the third houre of the night: 24 † and prepare beasts. that setting Paul on, they might bring him safe to Felix the President (25 † For he feared lest perhaps the Ievves might take him avvay, and kil him, and him self aftervvard should sustaine reproche, as though he vvould haue taken money) 26 † vvriting a letter conteining this much.

Claudius Lysias to the most excellent President Felix, greeting. 27 † This man being apprehended of the Ievves, and ready to be killed of them, I comming in vvith the band deliuered him, vnderstanding that he is a Romane: 28 † and meaning to knovv the cause that they obiected vnto him, I brought him downe into their Councel. 29 † Vvhom I found to be accused concerning questions of their lavv: but hauing no crime vvorthie of death or of bandes. 30 † And vvhen it vvas told me of embushments that they had prepared against him, I sent him to thee, signifying also to the accusers, to speake before thee. Fare vvel. 31 † And the souldiars according as it vvas commaunded them, taking Paul, brought him by night to Antipatris. 32 † And the next day sending avvay the horsemen to goe vvith him, they returned to the castel. 33 † Vvho vvhen they vvere come to Cæsaréa, and had deliuered the letter to the President, they did set Paul also before him. 34 † And vvhen he had read, and had asked of vvhat prouince he vvas: and vnderstanding that of Cilicia: 35 † I vvil heare the, said he, vvhen thy accusers are come. And he commaunded him to be kept in Herods palace.

ANNOTATIONS
CHAP. XXIII.

The honour of Priesthod.

5. I knevv not.] *Our Lord* (saith S. Cyprian) *in the Gospel, When it Was said to him, AnsWerest thou the high Priest so? teaching that the honour of Priesthod must be kept, said nothig to the high Priest, but only purging his innocencie, said, If I haue spoken euil, beare Witnes of euil: but if Wel, Why smitest thou me? Also the blessed Apostle vvhen it vvas said to him, Doest thou assaile the high Priest so With il Wordes? spake not any thing cōtumeliously against the Priest, Whereas he might haue put forth him self stoutly against them Which had*

Cypr. ep. 65. 69. nu. 2.

had both crucified our Lord, and vvhich had novv also lost their God and Christ, Temple and Priesthod. but though in false and spoiled Priests, yet cōsidering the very bare shadovv of the name of Priests, he said, I knew not brethren that he vvas high Priest. By vvhich vvordes of the Apostle, either it may be thought he knevv not in deed that he vvas in that function, because he had not beene of long time in those partes: or els that he so said in respect of the abrogation of the high Priesthod of the Ievves, vvhereby he knevv this man not to be truely any Priest, as also because at this time they came not orderly to it by succession of Aaron and Lavv of Moyses, but by the Roman Emperours fauour, * as is said before. though (as it is lavvful in such a case) the lesse to irritate them, he frameth his speach so as they might not take occasion of further accusation against him.

See Annot. Io. c. 11, 51.

8. *The Sadducees.*] This vvas the vvorst Heresie among the Ievves, denying that there be any Angels, or spirits, the Resurrectiō also of the bodies: & consequētly (as it may very vvel be gathered by the booke of the Machabees) they denied praier for the dead. for to offer or pray for the dead, & to thinke rightly & religiously of the Resurrectiō, are made there sequels one of an other. Of this sect of Sadducees vvas (as Eusebius vvriteth *li. 2 c. 22. Ec. hist.*) this Ananias the High Priest, that caused Paul to be smitten. for their Priesthod had novv no more the protection of God to preserue it in truth and right iudgement, the Christian Priesthod being then established.

Mac. li. 2. c. 12, 43.

The Sadducees (as it seemeth) denied praier for the dead.

12. *Vovved them selues.*] Such vovves, othes, or execrations as this, binde no man before God, yea they must in no vvise be obserued. It is a great offence either to vovv voluntarily, or to take any such thing vpon a man, for feare or by commaundement. For example, if thou haue rashly by promes, vow, or othe, appointed to be reuenged vpon any man, thou bindest not thy self thereby, neither must thou keepe thy promes. If thou be put to an othe to accuse Catholikes for seruing God as they ought to do, or to vtter any innocent man to Gods enemies and his, thou oughtest first to refuse such vnlavvful othes: but if thou haue not constancie and courage so to do, yet know thou that such othes binde not at al in conscience and Lavv of God, but may and must be broken vnder paine of damnation. For to make or take such vowes or othes, is one sinne, aud to keepe them, is an other far greater. as vvhen Herode, to keepe his othe, killed Iohn Baptist. And such vowes and othes to God as these, are vnlavvful & must be broken: and not the vowes of Chastitie and Religion, as our nevv Ministers teach by their vvordes and vvorkes.

Vnlawful othes & vovves must not be kept.

Mat. 14, 9.

CHAP. XXIIII.

They prosecute him to Cæsarea, bringing vvith them an oratour, vvho before the President Felix accuseth him. 10 He ansvvereth, defending him self from the crimes they charged him vvith, but confessing his religion plainly. 22 The Iudge perceiuing his religion to be irreprehensible, yeldeth not to condemne him at their pleasure, 24 yea he oftentimes vvith his vvife heareth his preaching, 27 but yet doth not his dutie to deliuer him out of prison.

1 ND after fiue daies the high priest Ananias descended, vvith certaine auncients and one Tertullus an oratour, vvho vvent to the President against Paul. 2 † And Paul being cited, Tertullus began to accuse, saying.

Vvhereas vve liue in much peace by thee, & many things are corrected by thy prouidence: 3 † vve doe alvvaies and in al places receiue it, most excellent Felix, vvith al thanks-geuing. 4 † But lest I hinder thee any longer, I desire thee of thy clemencie breifely to heare vs. 5 † Vve haue found this man pestiferous, and raising seditiōs to al the Ievves in the vvhole vvorld, and authour of the sedition [c] of the secte of the Nazarenes, 6 † vvho also hath attempted to violat the temple,

ςτῆς αἱρέσεως

vvhom also being apprehended vve vvould haue iudged according to our lavv. † But Lysias the Tribune comming in, 7 vvith great force tooke him avvay out of our handes, † commaunding 8 his accusers to come to thee, of vvhom thou maiest thy self iudging, vnderstand of al these things, vvhereof vve accuse him. † And the Ievves also added, saying that 9 these things vvere so.

† But Paul ansvvered, (the President making a signe vnto 10 him for to speake.)

Knovving that of many yeres thou art iudge ouer this nation, I vvil vvith good courage ansvver for my self. † For 11 thou maiest vnderstand that it is not aboue tvvelue daies to me, since I vvent vp to adore in Hierusalem. † and neither 12 in the temple did they finde me disputing vvith any man, or causing concourse of the multitude, neither in the synagogs, nor in the citie: † neither can they proue vnto thee the things 13 vvhereof they novv accuse me. † But this I confesse to thee, 14 that [c] according to the :: secte, vvhich they call heresie, I doe so serue ' the father my God', beleeuing al things that are vvritten in the Law & the Prophets: † hauing hope in God, 15 the vvhich these also them selues expect, that there shal be a resurrectiō of iust and vniust. † In this my self also doe studie 16 to haue a cōscience vvithout offense tovvard God & toward 17 men alvvaies. † And after many yeres * I came to bestovv almes vpon my nation, & oblations, and vovves. † In the 18 vvhich they foūd me * purified in the tēple: not vvith multitude nor vvith tumult. † But certaine Ievves of Asia, vvho 19 ought to be present before thee and to accuse, if they had any thing against me: † or let these men thē selues say, if they haue 20 found in me any iniquitie, forasmuch as I stād in the Councel, 21 † but of this one voice only that I cried stāding among them, That * of the resurrection of the dead am I iudged this day of you. † And Felix differred them, knovving most certainely of 22 this vvay, saying, Vvhen Lysias the Tribune is come dovvne, I vvil heare you. † And he commaunded the Centurion to 23 keepe him, and that he should haue rest, neither to prohibit any of his to minister vnto him.

† And after some daies, Felix comming vvith Drusilla 24 his vvife, vvhich vvas a Ievve, called Paul, and heard of him the faith that is in Christ IESVS. † And he disputing of 25 :: iustice and chastitie, and of the iudgement to come, Felix being

:: Because Tertull' the Iewes orator called Christian religion the sect or (as it is there vers. 5 in the Greeke) the heresie of the Nazarens: S. Paul ansvvereth and shevveth that it is no heresie. And as for the word, *Sect*, in this place: it is in the Greeke, *According to the vvay, vvhich they call heresie*, as also Act. 9, 2. 24, 22. And therfore the vvord sect here is so taken. See *Annot. c. 28, 22.*

:: The Apostolike teaching was not of only or special-faith, but of iustice, & chastitie, & iudgement, that is to say, of the terrour of Hel and other Gods iudgements in the next life ansvverable to our deedes in this vvorld: by vvhich the hearers vvere first terrified, and so induced to penance. Hovv say Heretikes then that such things make men hypocrites?

c κατὰ τὴν ὁδὸν
' *the God of my fathers.*

Ro. 15, 28

Act. 21, 26.

Act. 23, 6.

being terrified, anſvvered, For this time, goe thy vvay: but in time conuenient I vvil ſend for thee. 26 † hoping alſo vvithal, that money vvould be giuen him of Paul, for the vvhich cauſe alſo oftentimes ſending for him, he ſpake vvith him. 27 † But vvhen tvvo yeres vvere ended, Felix had a ſucceſſour Portius Feſtus. And Felix being vvilling to ſhevv the Ievves a pleaſure, left Paul in priſon.

CHAP. XXV.

After tvvo yeres empriſonment the Ievves continevv their ſute againſt him, ſoliciting the nevv Preſident Feſtus, 6 firſt at Hieruſalem, then at Caſarea: 9 vvhere through the Ievves partialitie he is faine to appeale vnto the Emperour: 13 and is in the meane time brought forth by Feſtus (giuing him good teſtimonie, notvvithſtanding the exclamations of the Ievves againſt him) vnto king Agrippa and his Queene Bernice.

1 FESTVS therfore vvhen he vvas come into the prouince, after three daies vvent vp to Hieruſalem from Cæſaréa. 2 † And the cheefe prieſts, & principal men of the Ievves vvent vnto him againſt Paul: and they deſired him, 3 † requeſting fauour againſt him, that he vvould commaund him to be brought to Hieruſalem, laying vvaite for to kil him in the vvay. 4 † But Feſtus anſvvered, that Paul is in Cæſaréa: and that he vvould very ſhortly goe thither. 5 † They therfore, ſaith he, that are of abilitie among you, going dovvne vvith me, if there be any crime in the man, let them accuſe him.

6 † And hauing taried among them not aboue eight or ten daies, he vvent dovvne to Cæſaréa, and the next day he ſate in the iudgement ſeate: and he commaunded Paul to be brought. 7 † Vvho being brought, there ſtoode about him the Ievves that vvere come dovvne from Hieruſalem, obiecting many and greuous [c] cauſes vvhich they could not proue, 8 † Paul making anſvver, That neither againſt the lavv of the Ievves, nor againſt the temple, nor againſt Cæſar haue I any thing offended. 9 † But Feſtus vvilling to ſhevv the Ievves a pleaſure, anſvvering Paul, ſaid, Vvilt thou goe vp to Hieruſalem, and there be iudged of theſe things before me? 10 † And Paul ſaid, At Cæſars iudgemēt ſeate doe I ſtand, vvhere I ought to be iudged: the Ievves I haue not hurt, as thou very

[c] crimes as v. 27.

vvel knovvest. † For if I haue hurt them, or done any thing 11 vvorthie of death, I refuse not to die. but if none of those things be, vvhereof these accuse me, no man can giue me to them. ∴ I appeale to Cæsar. † Then Festus hauing conferred 12 vvith the Councel, ansvvered, Hast thou appealed to Cæsar? to Cæsar shalt thou goe.

∴ If S. Paul both to saue him self from vvhipping and from death sought by the Ievves, doubted not to crie for succour of the Romane lawes, and to appeale to Cæsar the Prince of the Romans not yet Christened: hovv much more may vve call for aide of Christian Princes and their lavves, for the punishment of Heretikes, and for the Churches defense against them? S. *Augustine ep. 50.*

† And vvhen certaine daies vvere passed, king Agrippa & 13 Bernice came dovvne to Cæsaréa to salute Festus. † And as 14 they taried there a good many daies, Festus signified to the king, of Paul, saying, A certaine person vvas left prisoner by Felix, † concerning vvhom, vvhen I vvas at Hierusalem, the 15 cheefe priests and the auncients of the Ievves came vnto me, desyring condemnation against him. † To vvhom I ansvve- 16 red, That it is not the Romanes custome to yeld vp any man before that he vvhich is accused haue his accusers present and take place to make his ansvver for to cleere him self of the crimes. † Vvhen they therfore vvere assembled hi- 17 ther, vvithout any delaie, the day folovving, sitting in the iudgement seat, I commaunded the man to be brought. † Of 18 vvhom, vvhen the accusers stoode vp, they brought no cause vvhich I thought il of: † but certaine questions of their 19 ovvne superstition they had against him, and of ∴ one IESVS deceased, vvhom Paul affirmed to liue. † Doubting therfore 20 of this kinde of question, I said, vvhether he vvould goe to Hierusalem, & there be iudged of these things. † But Paul ap- 21 pealing to be kept vnto the knovvledge of Augustus, I commaunded him to be kept, til I send him to Cæsar. † And Agrippa said to Festus, My self also vvould heare the man. To 22 morovv, said he, thou shalt heare him.

∴ This vvhom he termeth by contempt, one IESVS, hath novv made al the Romane Emperours and Princes of the World to know him, and hath giuen the seate of the Cæsars to his poore seruants, Peter & his successors.

† And the next day vvhen Agrippa and Bernice vvere come vvith great pompe, and had entred into the hall of au- 23 dience vvith the Tribunes and principal men of the citie, at Festus commaundement Paul vvas brought. † And Festus saith, King Agrippa, and al ye men that are present together vvith vs, you see this man, concerning vvhom al the multi- 24 tude of the Ievves called vpon me at Hierusalem, requesting and crying out that he ought not to liue any longer. † Yet haue I found nothing that he hath committed vvorthie of 25 death. But forasmuch as he him self appealed to Augustus, I haue determined to send him. † Of vvhom vvhat to vvrite 26 for certaintie to my lord, I haue not. For the vvhich cause I haue

haue brought him forth to you, and especially to thee, king Agrippa, that examination being made, I may haue vvhat to vvrite.

27 † For it seemeth to me vvithout reason, to send a prisoner, & not to signifie [c] his causes.

c τὰς κατ' αὐτοῦ αἰτίας.

CHAP. XXVI.

In that honorable Audience being permitted to speake, 2 he declareth to the king vvhat he first vvas, 12 and hovv miraculously he vvas conuerted, 19 and that he hath preached since, as he vvas commaunded from heauen, and as the Prophets had foretold of Christ. 24 Which strange tale Festus the Heathen President hearing, saith that he is mad. 25 But he ansvvereth, and exhorteth them al to be Christians as he is. 30 They finally pronounce that he might be set at libertie, but only for his appeale.

1 BVT Agrippa said to Paul, Thou art permitted to speake for thy self. Then Paul stretching forth his hand, began to make his ansvver.

2 † Touching al things vvhereof I am accused of the Ievves, king Agrippa, I account my self happie for that I am to defend my self this day before thee,

3 †, especially vvhereas thou knovvest al things that are among the Ievves, customes and questions: for the vvhich cause I beseeche thee, heare me patiently.

4 † And my life truely from my youth, vvhich vvas from the beginning in my nation in Hierusalem, al the Ievves doe knovv:

5 † knovving me before from the beginning (if they vvil giue testimonie) that according to

6 the most sure [c] secte of our religion I liued a Pharisee. † And novv for the hope of the promisse that vvas made of God to

7 our fathers, doe I stand subiect to iudgement. † [b] the vvhich, our tvvelue tribes [c] seruing night and day, hope to come vnto. Of the vvhich hope, o king, I am accused of the Ievves.

8 † Vvhat incredible thing is it iudged vvith you, if God raise

9 the dead? † And my self truely had thought that I ought to doe against the name of IESVS of Nazareth many contrarie

10 things. † Vvhich also I * did at Hierusalem, and many of the saincts did I shut vp in prisons, hauing receiued authoritie of the cheefe priests: and vvhen they vvere put to death,

11 [c] I brought the sentence. † And through out al the synagogs often times punishing them, I cōpelled them to blaspheme:

c αἰρεσιν

b in quā

c λατρεύ-

Act. 8,3.

c detuli sententiam.

and yet more mad against them, I persecuted them euen vnto foraine cities. † Among vvhich things vvhiles* I vvent to Damascus vvith authoritie and permission of the cheefe priests, 12 † at midday, in the vvay, I savv (o king) from heauen a light 13 to haue shined round about me and them that vvere in companie vvith me, aboue the brightnes of the sunne. † And 14 vvhen al vve vvere fallen dovvne on the ground, I heard a voice speaking to me in the Hebrew tongue: Saul, Saul, vvhy persecutest thou me? It is hard for thee to kicke against the pricke. † And I said, Vvho art thou Lord? And our Lord 15 ansvvered, I am IESVS vvhom thou doest persecute. † But 16 rise vp and stand vpon thy feete: for to this end haue I appeared to thee, that I may ordaine thee a minister and vvitnes of those things vvhich thou hast seen, and of those things vvherein I vvil appeare to thee, † deliuering thee out of the 17 peoples & natiõs vnto the vvhich novv I send thee, † to opẽ 18 their eies, that they may be conuerted from darkenes to light, and from the povver of Satan to God, that they may receiue remission of sinnes and lot among the saincts by the faith that is in me. † Vvherevpon, king Agrippa, I vvas not in- 19 credulous to the heauenly vision: † but to them first that are 20 at Damascus, and at Hierusalem, and vnto al the countrie of Ievvrie, and to the Gentiles * did I preach that they should doe :: penãce, and turne to God, doing vvorkes vvorthie of penance. † For this cause the Ievves, vvhen I vvas in the 21 temple,* apprehending me, attẽpted meaning to kil me. † But 22 aided by the help of God, I stand vntil this day, testifying to small and to great, saying nothing beside those things vvhich the Prophets did speake should come to passe, & Moyses, † if 23 CHRIST vvere passible, if the first of the resurrection from the dead, he vvere to shevv light to the people and to the Gentiles.

Act. 9, 3.

:: Penãce often inculcated, and vvorkes agreable to the same.

Act. 9, 20.

Act. 23, 30.

† As he spake these things and made his ansvver, Festus 24 vvith a loud voice said, Thou art mad, Paul: much learning turneth thee to madnesse. † And Paul said, I am not mad, 25 most excellent Festus: but I speake vvordes of veritie and sobrietie. † for the king knovveth of these things, to vvhom al- 26 so I speake constantly. for I thinke none of these things to be vnknovven to him. For neither vvas any of these things done in a corner. † Beleeuest thou the prophets, king Agrip- 27 pa? I knovv that thou beleeuest. † And Agrippa said to Paul: 28

A litle

29 A litle thou perſuadeſt me to become a CHRISTIAN. † And Paul ſaid, I vviſh of God, both in litle, and in much, not only thee, but alſo al that heare this day, to become ſuch as I am
30 alſo, except theſe bandes. † And the king roſe vp, and the
31 Preſident, and Bernice, and they that ſate by them. † And going a ſide, they ſpake among them ſelues, ſaying, That this man hath done nothing vvorthie of death or bandes.
32 † And Agrippa ſaid to Feſtus, This man might be releaſed, if he had not appealed to Cæſar.

CHAP. XXVII.

What a dangerous nauigation he had tovvards Rome: and that by his prediction and counſel the [ſh]ip might haue been ſaued. And for his ſake (as God alſo reuealed to him bef[o]re) al the companie vvas preſerued, being 276 perſons.

1 AND after it vvas decreed that he ſhould ſaile into Italie, and that Paul vvith other priſoners ſhould be deliuered to a Centurion named Iulius, of the band Auguſta,
2 † vve going vp into a ſhip of Adrumétum, beginning to ſaile about the places of Aſia, looſed from the land, Ariſtarchus
3 the Macedonian of Theſſalonica continuing vvith vs. † And the day folovving vve came to Sidon. And Iulius intreating Paul courteouſly, permitted him to goe to his frendes, and
4 to take care of him ſelf. † And vvhen vve had looſed thẽce, vve ſailed vnder Cypres: becauſe the vvindes vvere cõtrarie.
5 † And ſailing the ſea of Cilicia and Pamphilia, vve came to
6 Lyſtra', vvhich is in Lycia: † and there the Centurion finding a ſhip of Alexandria ſailing into Italie, remoued vs into
7 it. † And vvhereas many daies vve ſailed ſlovvly, & vvere ſcarſe come ouer againſt Gnidus, the vvinde hindering vs,
8 vve ſailed neere Crete by Salmóne: † and vvith much a doe ſailing by it, vve came into a certaine place that is called Good-hauens, nigh to the vvhich vvas a citie Thalaſſa.
9 † And vvhen much time vvas ſpent, and vvhereas novv it vvas not ſafe ſailing, becauſe the ∷ faſt novv vvas paſt, Paul
10 comforted them, † ſaying to them, Ye men, I ſee that the sailing beginneth to be vvith hurt and much damage not only
11 of the lading and the ſhip, but alſo of our liues. † But the Centurion

Myra' (margin at v. 6)

∷ It may ſignifie the Ievves faſt of the ſeuenth moneth Septẽber, after vvhich the nauigation vvas perilous, vvinter approching.

Centurion beleeued the gouernour and maiſter of the ſhip, more then thoſe things vvhich vvere ſaid of Paul. † And 12 vvhereas it vvas not a commodious hauen to vvinter in, very many taking counſel appointed to ſaile thence, if by any meanes they might comming to Phœníce, vvinter there, a hauen of Crete looking tovvard the [c] Afrike and the Chore. † And the ſouthvvinde blovving, they thinking that they 13 had obteined their purpoſe, vvhen they had parted from Aſſon, ſailed along by Crete. † But not long after, a tempeſtuous 14 vvinde that is called Euro-aquilo, droue againſt it. † And 15 vvhen the ſhippe vvas caught and could not make vvay againſt the vvinde, giuing vp the ſhip to the vvindes, vve vvere driuen. † And running vpon a certaine iland, that 16 is called [c] Cauda, vve could ſcarſe get the cock-boate. † Vvhich being taken vp, they vſed helps, girding the 17 ſhip, and fearing leſt they ſhould fall into [c] the Syrte, letting dovvne the veſſel, ſo vvere they caried. † And vvhen vve 18 vvere mightily toſſed vvith the tempeſt, the next day they caſt forth, † And the third day vvith their ovvne handes 19 they threvve forth the tacklinges of the ſhip. † And neither 20 ſunne, nor ſtarres appearing for many daies, and no ſmal ſtorme being tovvard, al hope vvas novv taken avvay of our ſauing.

c names of vvindes.

c Græc. Clauda.

c a place of quicke ſandes.

† And vvhen there had been long faſting, then Paul ſtan- 21 ding in the middes of them, ſaid, You ſhould in deede, O ye men, haue heard me, and not haue parted from Crete, & haue gained this hurt and loſſe. † And novv I exhort you to be 22 of good cheere. for there ſhal be no loſſe of any ſoule amõg you, but of the ſhip. † For "an Angel of the God vvhoſe I 23 am, and [c] vvhom I ſerue, ſtoode by me this night, † ſaying, 24 Feare not Paul, thou muſt appeare before Cæſar: and behold God hath ∷ giuen thee al that ſaile vvith thee. † For the 25 vvhich cauſe be of good cheere ye men: for I beleeue God, that it ſhal ſo be, as it hath been ſaid to me. † And vve muſt 26 come vnto a certaine iland. † But after the fourtenth night 27 vvas come on vs, as vve vvere ſailing in Adria about midnight, the ſhipmen deemed that there appeared ſome countrie to them. † Vvho alſo ſounding, found tvventie fadomes: 28 and being parted a litle from thence, they found fiftene fadomes. † And fearing leſt vve ſhould fall into rough pla- 29 ces, caſting out of the ſterne foure ankers, they vviſhed that

∷ Paul (ſaith S. Hierom) had ſo many ſoules in the ſhip giuen him, that is, ſo many men ſaued for his ſake: and after he is vvith Chriſt, ſhal he ſhut his mouth, and not be able once to ſpeake for them that haue beleeued in his Goſpel? *Hiero. adu. vigil.* Vvhereby he proueth that if God do much for the merits of Saincts in this life, much more at their interceſſion & praier in heauen.

c ᾧ λατρεύω.

30 that day vvere come. † But as the ſhipmen ſought to flee out of the ſhip, hauing let dovvne the cock-boate into the ſea, preteding as if they vvere about to caſt out ankers out of
31 the fore part of the ſhip, † Paul ſaid to the Centurion and to the ſouldiars, " Vnles theſe tarie in the ſhip, you can not be
32 ſaued. † Then the ſouldiars cut of the ropes of the cock-boate: and ſuffered it to fal avvay.

33 † And vvhen it began to be light, Paul deſired all to take meate, ſaying, This day is the fourtenth day that you expect
34 and remaine faſting, taking nothing. † For the vvhich cauſe I deſire you to take meate for your health ſake: for there ſhal
35 not an heare of the head periſh of any of you. † And vvhen he had ſaid theſe things, taking bread, he gaue thankes to God in the ſight of them al: and vvhen he had broken it, he
36 began to eate. † And being al made of better cheere, they
37 alſo tooke meate. † And vve vvere in al in the ſhip, ſoules
38 tvvo hundred ſeuentie ſixe. † And being filled vvith meate,
39 they lighted the ſhip, caſting the vvheat into the ſea. † And vvhen day vvas come, they knevv not the land: but they ſpied a certaine creeke that had a ſhore, into the vvhich they
40 minded, if they could, to caſt a land the ſhip. † And vvhen they had taken vp the ankers, they committed them ſelues to the ſea, looſing vvithal the rudder bands: and hoiſing vp the maine ſaile according as the vvinde blevve, they vvent on
41 tovvard the ſhore. † And vvhen vve vvere fallen into a place betvvene tvvo ſeas, they graueled the ſhip: and the fore-part truly ſticking faſt remained vnmoueable: but the
42 hinder part vvas broken by the violence of the ſea. † And the counſel of the ſouldiars vvas, that they ſhould kil the
43 priſoners: leſt any ſvvimming out, might runne avvay. † But the Centurion vvilling to ſaue Paul, forbade it to be done: & he commaunded them that could ſvvimme, to caſt out them
44 ſelues firſt, and eſcape, and goe forth to land: † and the reſt, ſome they caried on bordes, and ſome vpon thoſe things that vvere of the ſhip. And ſo it came to paſſe, that al the ſoules eſcaped to land.

ANNOTATIONS
CHAP. XXVII.

23. An Angel.] S. Paul had many visions, specially to assure him that he should to Rome and stand before Cæsar, our Lord him self before (23, 11) appearing to him, and here an Angel, for that purpose. Vvhereby vve plainely see the special prouidence of God tovvard that See, vvhere his tvvo principal Apostles vvere designed to preach, plant the faith, liue, die, be buried, and honoured til the vvorldes end.

Gods prouidẽce to the See of ROME.

31. Vnles these tarie] Vvhen God reuealeth to vs any thing, or assureth vs of any euent to come, he dischargeth vs not thereby of our requisite endeuours and labours for atcheiuing the same, not executing ordinarily his designements tovvards men othervvise then by their ovvne free vvil and actions. S. Paul said not here, Let vs do vvhat vve list: vvorke vve or sit vve stil, vvhether the mariners goe out or tarie vvithin, vve are al sure to be saued, for so God hath reuealed to me, and he can not lie, neither can it fall othervvise. but contrarievvise saith he, If these mariners leaue the ship, you can not be saued. So say al true Catholike preachers to Christian people, Vvhat prouidence, predestination, or foresight so euer God haue of your saluation, you are not thereby constrained any vvay, you haue free vvil stil, and can not be saued (though you be predestinate) except you keepe Gods commaundements, repent you of your sinnes, beleeue, liue and die vvel. And if it vvere reuealed to any mã, that he vvere one of Gods electe, & that he should finally die in grace and be saued, yet he vvere bound to vvorke his saluation vvith feare and trembling, as S. Paul both did, and taught, lest he become reprobate: no lesse then the same Apostle here and his fellovves, though they had their life promised to them of God, yet vvere bound to labour and vse al possible diligence that they might not be drovvned.

Gods predestination and appointment taketh not avvay mans free vvil and endeuours.

1 Cor. 9, 27
Philip. 2, 12.

CHAP. XXVIII.

After their shipvvracke hauing vvintered in the Iland (novv named Malta) vvhere many miracles vvere vvrought by Paul, they take ship againe, and so by Sicile they come to Puteoli in Italie, the Christian Romans comming a great vvay to meete him, to his great ioy. 16 Finally being come to Rome, in his lodging he declareth to the Ievves his cause, 23 and on a day appointed preacheth IESVS *vnto them. 25 And seeing their incredulitie, he shevveth hovv it vvas foretold by Esay: 28 but that the Gentils vvil not be incredulous. 30 To vvhom he there preacheth tvvo vvhole yeres vvithout prohibition.*

AND vvhen vve had escaped, then vve knevv 1 that the :: iland vvas called Mityléne. But the Barbarous shevved vs no smal courtesie. † For, 2 kindling a fire they refreshed vs al, because of the imminent raine and the colde. † And 3 vvhen Paul had gathered together some number of stickes, and had laide them on the fire, a viper issuing out of the heate, inuaded his hand. † But as the Barbarous savv the 4 beast hanging on his hand, they said one to an other, Vndoubtedly this man is a murderer, vvho being escaped out of the sea, c Vengeance doth not suffer him to liue. † And he in 5 deede shaking of the beast into the fire, suffred no harme. † But they supposed that he should be turned into a svvel- 6 ling, and that he vvould sodenly fall and die. But expecting long and seeing that there vvas no harme done on him, being changed they said, that he vvas a God. † And in those pla- 7 ces vvere lands of the prince of the ile, named Publius, vvho receiuing

:: This iland (novv Malta) is the seate of the knightes of the Rhodes. the inhabitãts vvherof haue a special deuotion to S. Paul: to vvhõ both the cheefe Church (being the Bishops Seate) is dedicated, and the vvhole Iland (as they count it) consecrated. Where the people shevv yet to strãgers, his prison and other memories of his miracles.

Melita

c ἡ δίκη

8 receiuing vs, for three daies intreated vs courteouſly. † And it chaunced that the father of Publius lay vexed vvith feuers and the bloudy flixe. Vnto vvhom Paul entred: and vvhen he had praied, and impoſed hands on him, he healed him.
9 † Vvhich being done, al in the ile alſo that had infirmities,
10 came, and vvere cured: † vvho alſo honoured vs vvith many honours, and vvhen vve vvere ſailing avvay, laded vs vvith neceſſaries.

11 † And after three moneths, vve ſailed in a ſhip of Alexandria, that had vvintered in the iland, vvhoſe ſigne vvas the
12 Caſtors. † And vvhen vve vvere come to Syracûſa, vve ta-
13 ried there three daies. † Thence compaſſing by the ſhore, vve came to Rhegium: and after one day the Southvvinde
14 blovving, vve came the ſecond day to Putéoli, † vvhere finding brethren, vve vvere deſired to tarie vvith them ſeuen
15 daies: and ſo vve came to Rome. † And from thence, vvhen the brethren had heard, they came to meete vs vnto *Apij-forum*, and the Three-tauerns. Vvhom vvhen Paul had ſeen, giuing
16 thanks to God, he tooke courage. † And vvhen vve vvere come to Rome, Paul vvas permitted to remaine to him ſelf
17 vvith a ſouldiar that kept him. † And after the third day he called together the cheefe of the Ievves. And vvhen they vvere aſſembled, he ſaid to them,

Men brethren, I doing nothing againſt the people, or the cuſtome of the fathers, vvas deliuered priſoner from Hie-
18 ruſalem into the hands of the Romanes, † vvho vvhen they had examined me, vvould haue releaſed me, for that there
19 vvas no cauſe of death in me. † But the Ievves contradicting it, I vvas compelled to appeale vnto Cæſar, not as hauing any
20 thing to accuſe my nation. † For this cauſe therfore I deſired to ſee you and to ſpeake to you. for, becauſe of the hope of Iſraël, am I compaſſed vvith this" chaine.

21 † But they ſaid to him, Vve neither receiued letters concerning thee from Ievvrie, neither did any of the brethren
22 that came hither, report or ſpeake any euil of thee. † But vve deſire of thee to heare vvhat thou thinkeſt: for" concerning this [c] ſecte, it is knovvē to vs that it is gaineſaid euery vvhere.
23 † And vvhen they had appointed him a day, they came to him vnto his lodging very many: to vvhom he expounded, teſtifying the kingdom of God, and vſing perſuaſion to them

c αἱρέσεως

of IESVS out of the lavv of Moyses and the Prophets, from morning vntil euening. † And certaine beleeued those things 24 that vvere said: but certaine beleeued not. † And vvhereas 25 they did not agree among them selues, they departed, Paul saying one vvord: That vvel did the holy Ghost speake by Esaie the prophet to our fathers, † saying, *Goe to this people, and* 26 *say to them, Vvith the eare you shal heare, and shal not vnderstand: and seeing you shal see, and shal not perceiue.* † *For the hart of this people is* 27 *vvaxen grosse, and vvith their eares haue they heauily heard, and their eies* ∷ *they haue shut: lest perhaps they may see vvith their eies, and heare vvith their eares, and vnderstand vvith their hart, and be conuerted, and I heale them.* † Be it knovven therfore to you, that this Saluation of 28 God is sent to the Gentiles, and they vvil heare.

Esa 6,9. Mat. 13, 14. Mr. 4,12. Lu. 8,10 Io.12,40 Ro. 11,8

∷ Here also (*as Mat. 13.*) it is plaine that they would not see, nor heare, & that their excecatiō is to be attributed to thē selues & not to God. *See annota. Io. 12, 40.*

† And vvhen he had said these things, the Ievves vvent 29 out from him, hauing much questioning among them selues. † And he taried ful tvvo yeres in his hired lodging: and he 30 receiued al that came into him, † preaching the kingdom of 31 God, and teaching the things that concerne our Lord IESVS CHRIST vvith al confidence, vvithout prohibition.

ANNOTATIONS
CHAP. XXVIII.

5. Shaking of the beast.] The promes of Christ (*Marc. 16*) that venemous serpents should not hurt them that beleeue in him, is fulfilled not in al beleuers, but in such as had the gift of miracles, as S. Paul had. Vvhom here a viper by nature so venemous that the people thought he should haue died out of hand, did no vvhit annoy: he extinguishing by the povver of Christ al the poison of the beast. Yea and (as the Christian people there til this day beleeue) by S. Paules praiers the Iland vvas deliuered for euer from al such venemous serpents, in so much that children there play vvith scorpions euer since that time, and Pilgrimes daily carie vvith them peeces of stones out of the place vvhere S. Paul abode, by vvhich they affirme that they heale them vvhich in other countries adioyning are bitten of scorpions, the medicine therfore being called, *S. Paules grace.* The Heretikes that knovv not the povver of God, nor the miraculous vertues giuen to his Saincts, maruel and blaspheme, vvhen they heare such things as be proper to certaine countries, attributed sometimes to Gods miracles done by his Saincts: as though that vvere not possible, or vvere not as much to Gods honour, and more, then things proceding only of natural causes. Such profane men vvould not haue attributed the holsomnes of the vvaters of Iericho to Eliseus his vertue and miracles, amending them by casting salt into them, if the Scripture had not expresly testified the same. It is the part of al faithful men to referre such things to God, vvhen any iust occasion is giuen therevnto, rather then to nature: though the incredulous doe alvvaies contrarie, for feare of superstition & dishonouring God. As though this escape of drovvning, might better and more to Gods glorie, be referred to chaunce and the mariners industrie, then to S. Paules praiers and extraordinarie vvorking.

Malta hath S. Paules blessing and grace vntil this day.

Tho. Fazellus de rebus Siculis decad. 1 li. 16. 1.

Gods miraculous vertue in certaine countries and creatures, by his Saincts.

4 Reg. 2, 19

20. Chaine.] I vvould vvish novv (saith S. Chrysostome) to be for a time in the place vvhere these chaines remaine, and to see the fetters vvhich Diuels feare, and Angels reuerence. *homil. 5 ad populum Antiochenum.* See also S. Gregorie *lib. 3 episto. 30.* of the miracles done by S. Paules chaines, and that he sendeth to the Emperesse Constantia some dust thereof filed of, for a great Relike and holy gift.

S. Pauls chaines honoured.

21. Concerning.

22. *Concerning this sect.*] The Heretikes of al sortes comfort them selues much, vvhen they finde here or els vvhere the Christian faith called of the Ievves or incredulous persons, a Sect or an Heresie, & sometimes in contempt of Christes person the Maister of the same, the Secte of the Nazarens: as though the Church of God might as vvel erre in naming their doctrine Heresie, as the Ievves and Pagans might and did misse in condemning Christian religion for an Heresie: or as though the Protestants doctrine vvere as vvel proued and tried to be no Heresie, by the Prophets and other Scriptures, miracles, and consent of al Nations and ages, as Christes blessed doctrine is. Vvhereas in deed the Protestants doctrine is euidently conuinced to be heretical, by the same arguments that Christes religion is proued to be the only true doctrine of saluation, and not an heresie. And vvhosoeuer can deduce the Christian faith from Adam to this day, through out al the Fathers, Patriarches, Prophetes, Priests, Apostles, and Bishops, by descent and succession of al lavves and states of true vvorshippers and beleeuers (vvhich is the only or special vvay to proue that the Christian faith is no heresie) he shal by the same meanes al at once proue the Protestants doctrine to be an heresie and a false secte. That the Ievves therfore and il men in al places contradicted the Christian religion, calling it an Heresie or a Sect, as though it had a beginning of some certaine Sect-Maister other then God him self, they vvere deceiued: and the Church of God neuerthelesse calling the Protestants doctrine Heresie in the vvorst part that can be, and in the vvorst sort that euer vvas, doth right and most iustly.

The name of Sect is vvel giuen to al Heresies, though the Christian religion at the first vvas falsely so called.

The end of the Actes of the Apostles.

Vvhereunto we ioyne for the readers behalfe, tvvo Tables of the tvvo cheefe Apostles, and a note of the rest, as an abridgement of the said booke, and a supply of some things not there mentioned.

THE SVMME OF THE ACTES OF THE APOSTLES, CONTEINING SPECIALLY THE GESTES OF THE TVVO PRINCIPAL *Apostles, SS. Peter and Paul, in such order of time and yeres of the Emperours, and from Christs Natiuitie, and Ascension, as they vvere done: so far as by holy Scriptures or Ecclesiastical vvriters may be gathered. Wherein though it be not possible to set dovvne the precise and vndoubted time or yere of euery thing, because neither S. Luke nor others do note particularly and orderly the moments of euery action of the said Apostles: yet vve folovv the most probable and plaine plat that vve finde in holy Scripture and auncient vvriters. Whereby the studious reader may easily discouer the folly of the Protestants, that can finde no time When * Peter might possibly come to Rome, be Bishop, and die there: diuers things in S. Paules actes being no lesse hard to reconcile to the course of S. Lukes narration, then any thing touching the historie of S. Peter, namely his * three yeres preaching in Arabia: al vvhich must needes be true, vvhether vve hit the very iust time or no, and hovv so euer authors differ about the same.*

See the annot. Rom. 16, 15.

Gal. 1.

A TABLE OF S. PETER.

Tiberij	*Nat. Dñi.*	*Ascen*	
18	34	1	PETER causeth the Disciples to procede to the election of an other Apostle in Iudas roome. *Act. 1.*
			Receiuing vvith the rest the gifts of the Holy Ghost on Vvhit-sunday, he made the first Sermon, and conuerted 3000. *Act. 2.*
			He cureth one borne lame, preacheth Christ and penance to the Ievves: so that 5000 beleeued. *Act. 3 & 4.*
			He is imprisoned, released againe, threatened and commaunded to preache no more: but he vvith Iohn ansvvereth, that they must obey God more then man. *Act. 4.*
			He striketh to death vvith a vvord, Ananias and Saphîra, for sacrilege. *Act. 5.*
			He is sent vvith Iohn to Samari- , to confirme the nevvly baptized, vvhere he reproueth Simon Magus. *Act. 8.*
			He healeth Æneas at Lydda, and raiseth Tabitha from death at Ioppè. *Act. 9.*
19	35	2	He is vvarned and taught by a vision, to preach to Cornelius a Gentil. *Act. 10.* He defendeth his receiuing of the Gentiles *Act. 11.* and recordeth (*Act. 15*) that God called the first Gentiles by his ministerie. so that Paules first preaching to them, and his going to Arabia, must be after this. See *S. Chrys. in Act. ho. 22. Euseb. li. 2 c. 3.*
20	36	3	He continueth preaching in diuers partes of Iurie and the prouinces adioyning. About tvvo yeres after this, S. Paul visiteth him at Hierusalem. *Gal. 1.*
			He preacheth in Syria and the Prouinces of Asia minor, Bythynia, Pontus, Galatia, Cappodocia, ordaining Bishops and Priests in diuers places. *1 Pet. 1. Nicepho. li. 2 c. 35. Platina in Petro.*
23	39	6	He goeth to Antioche, preaching there, and making that his Seate, yet not remaining there continually, but for the affaires of the Church, departing thence, sometime to Hierusalem, sometime to other places. *Hiero. in Catalogo. Ignat. ad Magnesianos.*
			At Hierusalem he is cast into prison after the putting of S. Iames to death, by the commaundement of Herod. he is praied for by the vvhole Church, & deliuered out of prison by an Angel. *Act. 12.*
Claudij 2	44	11	Auoiding the furie of Herod, he leaueth Iurie againe. He appointeth Euodius Bishop in Antioche. *Euseb. in Chron. & li. 3 c. 16. Suidas. Ignat. ad Antiochen.* And passing by Corinth, HE CAME TO ROME, to conuince Simon Magus. *Hiero. in Catalogo. Euseb. li. 2 c. 12. 13. 24. Concil. to. 1.*
			He approueth & declareth the Gospel of S. Marke to be Canonical. *Hiero. in Catalo. Euseb. li. 2 c. 14.*
			Hauing founded the Church at Rome, and planted his Apostolical Seate there, aftervvard absent from the citie (either expelled thence vvith other Ievves, *Cornel. Tacit. in Claudio*: or rather according to the office of his Apostleship) leauing it for a time, he visited other Churches, and came to Hierusalem againe, vsing both in his absence and presence, Linus and Cletus for his coadiutors. *To. 2 Concil. pag. 656. Epiph. to. 2. Hæres. 27.*
	51	18	He holdeth the first Councel. *Act. 15.* He is reprehended at Antioche by S. Paul. *Galat. 1.* except that difference fell before the Councel, as some thinke. *August. ep. 19.*
			He returneth to Rome againe, the Romane faith by his diligence novv made famous through the vvorld. *Ro. 1. & 15. Theodoret. in 16. Ro.* Thence he vvriteth his first epistle. *1 Pet. 5. Euseb. li. 2 c. 14. Hiero. in Catalogo.*
			He sendeth S. Marke to Alexandria, and others to plant the faith in diuers partes of the vvorld. *Grego. li. 5 ep. 60. & li. 6 ep. 37. Nicepho. li. 2 c. 35.*
			He vvriteth his second epistle a litle before his death, vvhich Christ reuealed to him to be at hand. *2 Pet. 1.* He taketh order for his successor.
Neronis 14	70	37	He vvas finally crucified at Rome. *See the last Annot. Ioan. c. 21.*

FOELIX

FOELIX ECCLESIA cui totam doctrinam Apostoli cum suo sanguine profuderunt: vbi PETRVS Passioni Domini adæquatur, vbi PAVLVS Ioannis (Baptistæ) exitu coronatur. *Tertul. de Præscript.*

NON ita cœlum splendescit, quando radios sol demittit, quemadmodum ROMANORVM VRBS duas illas lampades vbique terrarum effundens. *Chrys. in ep. Ro. hom. 32 in moral.*

Prudent. in Hymno de S. Laurent.

Hic nempe iam regnant duo
Apostolorum principes:
Alter vocator Gentium,
Alter cathédram possidens
Primam, recludit creditas
Æternitatis ianuas.

Merita Petri & Pauli propter eundem Passionis diem celebrius & solenniter Roma commendat. *S. Aug. de cons. Euang. li. 1 c. 10.*

A TABLE OF S. PAVL.

Tiberij	*Natiuit.*	*Ascen.*	
18	34	1	SEVEN Deacons are elected and ordered by imposition of handes. *Act. 6.*
			Steuen the principal of them maketh a blessed sermon, for vvhich he vvas stoned to death, Saul (aftervvard Paul) consenting and aiding therevnto. *Act. 7.*
19	35	2	Saul by commission persecuteth. *Act. 9.*
			In his iourney to Damascus he is conuerted. *Ibid.*
			He goeth into Arabia and preacheth there. *Galat. 1.*
21	38	5	Paul returneth to Damascus, vvhere being in danger he escapeth, let dovvne in a basket by the vvall. *Act. 9.*
			Thence he commeth to Hierusalem to see Peter, *Galat. 1.* Vvhere being in danger of his life, the brethren conuey him out of the citie to Cæsaréa, and thence to Tarsus. *Act. 9.*
			He preacheth in the partes of Syria and Cilicia. *Galat. 1.* and at Antioche, vvhere the Christians vvere first called by that name. *Act. 11.*
			He and Barnabas being seuered from the rest of the Disciples by the appointmēt of the holy Ghost, and after fasting and praier, by imposition of handes consecrated Apostles and Bishops, they comme to Cypres, vvhere he conuerted the Proconsul. *Act. 13.*
			He preacheth in Lycaonia, and at Lystra is almost stoned to death. He appointeth Priests in euery Church, and returning by Pisidia, came agaİne to Antioche vvhence they first departed. *Act. 14.*
Claudij 9	51	18	At Antioche and there about he remaineth (*Act. 14*) vntil the controuersie touching the obseruation of Moyses lavv, for resolution vvhereof he and Barnabas ascend to Hierusalem. Vvhere they are appointed to bring the determination of the Councel to Antioche. And from thence passing through Syria and Cilicia, they teach the Christians to obserue the decrees of the Apostles and Auncients. *Act. 15.*
			Doing the same in the cities of Lycaonia and others adioining, by a vision he is vvarned to passe ouer the sea, and so commeth into Macedonia, vvhere he planteth the Gospel. *Act. 16.*
			Hence forvvard S. Luke pursueth S. Pauls storie, chapter by chapter, vntil his apprehension in Hierusalem, and arriual at Rome, in this order.
			He returneth from Macedonia by Thessalonica to Athens, vvhere he conuerteth many, namely S. Denys Areopagita. *Act. 17.*
			From Athens he commeth to Corinth, vvhere he remaineth 18 moneths. *Act. 18.* and hauing visited the Churches of Asia *Act. 19*) he commeth backe to Corinth *Act. 20.* Vvhence he vvriteth his epistle to the Romanes. *Ro. 15.*
			From Corinth he saileth to Tróas in Asia, vvhere vpon a Sunday he raised Eutychus from death, preaching til midnight. from Tróas he commeth to Milétum by sea, and there sendeth for the Bishops and Auncients of Ephesus, and exhorteth them. *Act. 20.*
Neronis 2	58	25	Thence comming to Hierusalem he is taken, *Act. 21*: and from the Tribune Lysias deliuered to Felix the Gouernour, *Act. 23*: and by him left to Festus, *Act. 24.* he appealeth to Cæsar, *Act. 25*: and so is SENT TO ROME, *Act. 27*: vvhere he arriueth. *Act. 28.*
			At Rome he remaineth in free prison tvvo yere, *Act. 28.* and then is deliuered, *2 Tim. 4.*
			After his deliuerie he preached in sundrie countries of the vvest, namely in Spaine. *Hiero. in Catalogo. Epiph. Hæres. 27.* Him self vvriteth that he purposed so to doe. *Ro. 15.*
			In his Epistle to the Philippians (c. 1) he minded to visite the Churches of Asia, vvhich also he did. *Genebrard. in Chron.*
			He vvriteth last of al, his second Epistle to Timothee a litle before his death. *2 Tim. 4.* being novv the second time apprehended and in bandes at Rome. *Theodoret.*
14	70	37	He vvas beheaded at Rome, the same day that Peter vvas crucified. *S. Ambros. ser. 66. 68. S. Maximus.*

OF THE OTHER APOSTLES.

Genebr. out of diuers authors.

THE Actes of the rest of the tvvelue Apostles be not much vvritten of in this booke: but as * other Ecclesiastical writers do testifie, they preached specially in these nations, as foloVveth. *Andrevv in Achaia, Iohn in Asia. Philip in Phrygia, Iames in Ievvrie, Bartholomevv in Scythia, Thomas in India, Matthevv in Aethiopia, Simon in Persia, Thaddæus in Mesopotamia, the other Iames in Spaine, Matthias in Palestine.* So distributing them selues through out the vvorld, to gather one Catholike Church of al Nations, according as Christ gaue them commission *Mat.* 28, 19: and as it vvas prophecied of them before Psal. 18. *Their sound is gone forth into euery countrie, and their wordes into the endes of the whole world.* But before they departed one from an other (the time vvhereof is not certainely knovven) * al Tvvelue assembling together, & ful of the Holy Ghost, eche laying dovvne his sentence, agreed vpon tvvelue principal articles of the Christian faith, and appointed them for a rule to al beleeuers: Vvhich is therfore called and is THE APOSTLES CREDE: *Not vvritten in paper,* as the Scripture, *but from the Apostles deliuered by tradition.* Ruff. & Hiero. locis citatis. Vvhich, as of old (*Hiero. cont. Lucifer*) so at this day al solemnely professe in their Baptisme, either by them selues or by others: and al that be of age and capacitie, are bound to know and beleeue euery article of the same. Vvhich are these that folovv.

Ruffi. in expos. Symb. Apost. Ambr. ser. 38. Hiero. ep. 61 c. 9. aduers erro. Io. Hieros.

THE APOSTLES CREDE, or SYMBOLVM APOSTOLORVM.

1 I *Beleeue* in God the Father, *almightie, creator of heauen and earth.*

2 *And in* IESVS CHRIST, *his only Sonne, our Lord.*

3 *Vvho vvas conceiued by the Holy Ghost; borne of the Virgin* MARIE.

4 *Suffered vnder Pontius Pilate, was crucified, dead, and buried: Descended into Hel.*

5 *The third day he rose againe from death:*

6 *Ascended into heauen: Sitteth at the right hād of God the Father almightie.*

7 *From thence he shal come to iudge the quicke and the dead.*

8 *I beleeue* in the Holy Ghost.

9 *The holy* Catholike Church: *the communion of saincts.*

10 *Forgiuenesse of sinnes.*

11 *Resurrection of the flesh.*

12 *Life euerlasting. Amen.*

THE

THE ARGVMENT OF THE EPISTLES IN GENERAL.

AFTER the Gospels, *vvhich is a storie of Christ himselfe, and after* the Actes of the Apostles, *Vvhich is a storie of Christes Church : novv folovv* the Epistles of the Apostles, *vvhich they vvrote of such matters, as they had then occasion to vvrite of. For being the founders and the Doctors of the Church, they did in their time, as the Doctors that succeded them, did after them: vvho from the beginning vnto this day, haue vvritten Epistles & Bookes against heresies, euer as they arose, and of al other Ecclesiastical matters, as they had occasion ministred vnto them. Of vvhich their doing the Apostles first gaue here the ensample: as also S. Luke in the Actes of the Apostles, led the vvay to al the writers of the Ecclesiastical Historie after him. For al though there be no comparison betvvene them for authoritie, forasmuch as these are* Canonical Scripture, *and so are not any vvritings of their successors: yet the occasions and matters (as I haue said) are like.*

Most of these Epistles *are* S. Paules *Epistles: the rest are called* * Catholicæ Epistolæ, *the* Epistles Catholike. *For S. Paul vvriteth not any Epistle to al (hovvbeit euery one of them is for al the Church:) but some to particular Churches of the Gentils, as to the Romanes, to the Corinthians, to the Galatians, to the Ephesians, to the Philippians, to the Colossians, to the Thessalonians: some to particular persons, as to Timothee, to Tite (vvho vvere Bishops among the Gentiles, to vvit, of Ephesus, and of Crete) and to Philemon, and then one to the Hebrevves, vvho vvere the Ievves of Hierusalem and Iurie. But the Epistles of the other Apostles, that is, of S. Iames, S. Peter, S. Iohn, and S. Iude, are not so intituled to any one Church or person (except S. Iohns tvvo later short Epistles, vvhich yet might not be separated from his first, because they vvere al of one Author) and therefore they are termed* Catholike, *that is,* vniuersal. *For so vvriteth S. Iames:* To the tvvelue tribes that are in dispersion, greeting. *and S. Peter in his first Epistle, thus:* To the elect strãgers of the dispersion of Pontus, Galatia, Cappadocia, Asia, & Bithynia. *in his second, thus:* To them that haue obteined equal faith vvith vs. *likevvise S. Iude:* To them that are in God the father beloued, and in Iesus Christ preserued, and called. *S. Iohns first is vvithout title.*

Eusebius li. 2. Eccl. hist. c. 22.

Novv, for the occasions of their vvriting, vvhereby vve shal perceiue the matters or arguments that they handle: it must be remembred (as the Storie of that time in the Actes of the Apostles doth at large declare) that the Church then beginning, vvas planted by the Apostles not onely in the Ievves, but also in the Gentiles: yea and specially in the Gentiles. Vvhich thing offended the Ievves many waies. For, they could not abide to see, so much as their owne Countrie to receiue him for CHRIST, *vvhom they had reiected and crucified: much lesse, to see, them preach him to the Gentiles also. that offended euen those Ievves also, that beleeued him to be Christ. Hovvbeit such of them as vvere Catholikes, and therefore not obstinat, vvere satisfied vvhen they vnderstood by the Apostles that it vvas Gods pleasure, as Act. 11. vve reade. But others of thē became heretikes, & preached to the Christian Gentiles, that it vvas necessary for them to receiue also the Ievves religion. Of such vve reade Act. 15.* Vnles you be circumcised, you can not be saued. *And as these did so preach against the truth, so did the vnchristened Ievves not onely themselues persecute, but also stirre vp the Idolatrous Gentiles euery vvhere to persecute the Christians: by such obstinacie prouoking God to reprobate theire Nation: vvhich yet they thought vnpossible to be done, because they vvere the seede of Abraham, and vvere circumcised, and had receiued the Lavv by Moyses. for such carnal respects they trusted in themselues, as though God and Christ vvere vnseparably bound vnto them: attributing also so much to their ovvne vvorkes, (vvhich they thought they did of them selues, being holpē with the knovvledge of their lavv,) that they vvould not acknovvledge the death of Christ to be necessarie for their saluation: but looked for such a Christ, as should be like other princes of this vvorld, and make them great men temporally.*

Herevpon did S. Paul vvrite his Epistles, to shevv both the vocation of the Gentiles, and the reprobation of the Ievves. Moreouer, to admonish both the Christian Gentiles, not to receiue Circumcision and other ceremonies of Moyses lavv, in no vvise: and the Ievves also, not to put their trust in the same, but rather to vnderstand, that novv, Christ being come, they must cease. Againe, to shevv the necessitie of Christs comming and of his death: that vvithout it neither the Gentiles could be saued: no nor the Ievves, by no vvorkes that they could doe of themselues, although they vvere also holpen by the Lavv, telling them vvhat vvas good & vvhat vvas bad: for so much as al vvere sinners, and therfore also impotent or infirme: and the Lavv could not take avvay sinne, and infirmitie, and giue strength to fulfil that vvhich it gaue knovvledge of. but this vvas God onely able to doe, and for Christs sake onely vvould he doe it. Therfore it is necessarie for al to beleeue in Christ, and to be made his members, being incorporat into his Body vvhich is his Catholike Church. For so (although they neuer yet did good vvorke, but al il) they shal haue remission of their sinnes, and nevv strength vvithal, to make them able to fulfil the cōmaūdemēts of Gods lavv, yea & their vvorkes after this shal be so gracious in Gods sight, that for them he vvil giue them life euerlasting. This is the necessitie, this is also the fruite of Christian Religion. And therfore he exhorteth al, both Gentils and Ievves, as to receiue it humbly, so also to perseuere in it constantly vnto the end, against al seduction of heresie, and against al terror of persecution: and to vvalke al their time in good vvorkes, as novv God hath made them able to doe.

The doctrine of the Cath. Church concerning good vvorkes.

The same doctrine doth the Catholike Church teach vnto this day most exactly: to vvit, that no vvorkes of the vnbeleeuing or vnbaptized, vvhether they be Ievves or Gentiles, can saue them: no nor of any Heretike, or Schismatike, although he be baptized, because he is not a member of Christ: yea more then that, no vvorke of any that is not a liuely member of Christ, although othervvise he be baptized, and continue vvithin his Church, yet because he is not in grace but in mortal sinne, no vvorke that he doth, is meritorious or able to saue him.

S. Paules doctrine concerning faith and good vvorkes.

This very same is S. Paules doctrine: he denieth to the vvorkes of such as haue not the Spirit of Christ, al vertue to iustifie or to saue: neither requireth he a man to haue had knovvledge of the Lavv, or to haue kept it afortime, as though othervvise he might not be saued by Christ: but yet vvhen he is Christened, he requireth of necessitie, that he keepe Gods commaundements, by auoiding of al sinne, and doing good vvorkes: and to such a mans good vvorkes he attributeth as much vertue as any Catholike of this time.

Neuertheleſſe there vvere certaine at that time (as alſo al the Heretikes of this our time) vvhom S. Peter termeth vnlearned and vnſtable, *vvho reading S. Paules* Epiſtles, *did miſconſter his meaning, as though he required not good vvorkes no more after Baptiſme, then before Baptiſme: but held that onely Faith did iuſtifie and ſaue a man. Therevpon the other Apoſtles vvrote their Epiſtles, as S. Auguſtine noteth in theſe vvordes:* Therfore becauſe this opinion (*Ad ſalutem obtinendam ſufficere Solam fidem,* that onely faith is ſufficient to obteine ſaluation) was then riſen: the other Apoſtolical Epiſtles, of Peter, Iohn, Iames, Iude, do againſt it ſpecially direct theire intention: to auouch vehemently, *fidem ſine operibus nihil prodeſſe,* that faith vvithout vvorkes profiteth nothing. As alſo Paul him ſelfe did not define it *to be quamlibet fidem, qua in Deum creditur,* whatſoeuer maner of faith, vvherevvith vve beleeue in God, but that holeſome & expreſſe Euangelical faith, vvhoſe vvorkes procede from loue, and *the faith* (quoth he) *that vvorketh by loue.* vvherevpon that faith, vvhich ſome thinke to be ſufficient to ſaluation, he ſo affirmeth to profite nothing, that he ſaith, *If I ſhould haue al faith ſo that I could remoue mountaines, and haue not charitie, I am nothing.*

2. Pet. 3.

Aug. de fide & oper. ca. 14. Et præf. pſal. 31.

Gal. 5.

1. Cor. 13.

He therfore that vvill not erre in this point, nor in any other, reading either S. Paules Epiſtles, or the reſt of the holy Scriptures, muſt ſticke faſt to the doctrine of the Catholike Church, vvhich Church S. Paul termeth the piller and ground of the truth: *aſſuring him ſelf that if any thing there ſound to him as contrarie herevnto, he faileth of the right ſenſe: and bearing alvvaies in his minde the admonition of S. Peter, ſaying:* As alſo our moſt deere brother Paul according to the vviſedom giuen to him, hath vvritten to you: as alſo in al his Epiſtles, ſpeaking in them of theſe things, in the vvhich are certaine things hard to vnderſtand, vvhich the vnlearned and vnſtable depraue, as alſo the reſt of the Scriptures, to theire ovvne perdition. You therfore brethren, foreknovving, take heede leſt ye be led amis by the error of the vnvviſe, and fall avvay from your ovvne ſtedfaſtnes.

1. Tim. 3.

2. Pet. 3.

THE TIME VVHEN THE EPISTLE TO THE ROMANES VVAS VVRITTEN, and the Argument thereof.

THE *hiſtorie of S. Paul, vntil he came to Rome, S. Luke in the Actes of the Apoſtles vvrote exactly: and though vvithout any mention of his* Epiſtles, *yet certaine it is, that ſome of them he vvrote before he came there, to vvit, the tvvo vnto the Corinthians, and this to the Romanes: & (* as it ſeemeth) before them al, the Epiſtle to the Galatians. Vvherein yet becauſe he maketh mention of the foureteenth yere after his conuerſion, it appeareth, that he preached ſo long vvithout any vvriting.*

Gal. 2.

And this order may thus brieſely be gathered. Firſt he preached to the Galatians Act. 16: and paſſing through Phrygia and the countrey of Galatia. *Vvhereof he maketh mention him ſelfe alſo, Gal. 1:* Vve euangelized to you. *and Gal. 4:* I euangelized to you heretofore. *After vvhich the falſe Apoſtles came and perſuaded them to receiue Circumciſion. Vvherevpon he ſaith Gal. 1:* I maruel that thus ſo ſoone you are trasferred from him that called you to the grace of Chriſt, vnto an other Goſpel. *and vviſheth therfore*

 Gal. 4:

Gal. 4. *saying*: And I vvould I vvere vvith you novv. *And accordingly he came vnto them aftervvard, as vve reade Act.* 18. Vvalking in order through the countrie of Galatia and phrygia, confirming al the Disciples. *At vvhich time also it seemeth, that he tooke order vvith them about those contributions to helpe the neede of the Christians in Hierusalem, vvhereof he speaketh* 1. *Cor.* 16: And concerning the collections that are made for the saincts, as I haue ordeined to the Churches of Galatia, so doe you also. *By vvhich vvordes also it is euident, that the Corinthians had not as then made their gathering. But vvhen he vvrote the Second to them (vvhere in the* 11 *chapter he maketh mention of* 14 *yeres, not onely after his Conuersion, as to the Galatians, but also after his Rapte, vvhich seemeth to haue bene vvhen he vvas at Hierusalem Act.* 9. *foure yeres after his Conuersion*, in a traunce, *as he calleth it Act.* 22, 17) *then vvere they readie. For so he saith* 2. *Cor.* 8: You haue begone from the yere past. *and* 2. *Cor.* 9: For the vvhich I doe glorie of you to the Macedonians: that also Achaia is ready from the yere past. *hovvbeit it folovveth there*: But I haue sent the brethren, that (as I haue said) you may be ready: lest vvhen the Macedonians come vvith me, and find you vnready, vve be ashamed. *But vvhen he vvrote to the Romanes, then vvas he novv come to Corinth for the purpose, and had receiued theire contribution, and vvas readie to goe vvith it vnto Hierusalem. For so he saith Rom.* 15. Novv therfore I vvil goe vnto Hierusalem to minister to the saincts. For Macedonia and Achaia haue liked vvel to make some cōtribution vpō the poore saincts that are in Hierusalem.

The argument of the Epistle to the Romanes.

So then, the Epistle to the Romanes vvas not the first that he vvrote. But yet it is * *and alvvaies vvas set first, because of the primacie of that Church. for vvhich cause also he handleth in it, such matters as perteined not to them alone, but to the vniuersal Church, and specially to al the Gentiles: to vvit, the very frame (as it vvere) of the Church of Christ. Tanquam enim* a *pro ipso Domino legatione fungens, hoc est, pro* b *lapide angulari, vtrumque populum tam ex Iudæis quàm ex Gentibus connectit in Christo per vinculum gratiæ. so saith S. Augustine, giuing vs briefly the argument. in english thus*: As being a legate for our Lord him self, that is, for the corner stone, he knitteth together in Christ by the bād of Grace, both peoples, as vvel of the Ievves as of the Gentils. *Shevving, that neither of them had in their Gentilitie or Iudaisme any vvorkes to bragge of, or to chalenge to them selues iustificatiō or saluation thereby, but rather sinnes they had to be sorie for, and to humble them selues to the faith of Christ, that so they might haue remission of them, and strength to doe meritorius vvorkes aftervvard. In vvhich sort, because the Gentils did humble them selues, therefore had they found mercy, though they neuer vvist of the Lavv of Moyses. But the Ievves, because they stoode vpon their ovvne vvorkes, vvhich they did by their ovvne strength, vvith the knovvledge of the Lavv (being therefore also called* the vvorkes of the Lavv,) *& so would not humble themselues to beleeue in Christ crucified, they missed of mercy, and became reprobate, excepting a few* Reliquiæ *that God of his goodnes had reserued to him self. Hovvbeit in the end, vvhen the fulnes of the Gentils is come into the Church, then shal the fulnes of the Ievves also open their eies, acknow ledge their errour, and submit themselues to Christ and his Church, in like maner. In the meane time, those that haue found the grace to be Christians, he exhorteth to perseuērāce (as it vvas specially needeful in those times of persecutions) and to leade their whole life now after Baptisme in good workes: and to be careful of vnitie, bearing therefore one with an other, both Iew and Gentil, al that they may,*

* Epih. Hær. 42 Marcionis.
Aug. in Expos. incho. Ep. ad Rom.
a 2. Cor. 5.
b Ephes. 2.

The vvorkes of the Lavv.

may, and geuing no offence to them that are weake. Thus he disputeth, and thus he exhorteth through the whole Epistle: though, if we wil diuide it by that which is principal in ech parte, vve may say, that vnto the 12 *chapter is his disputation: and from thence to the end, his exhortation.*

Novv, in these points of faith, and in al others (as also in example of life) the commendation that he giueth to the Church of Rome, is much to be noted. Your faith is renoumed in the vvhole vvorld. and your obediéce is published into euery place. I reioyce therfore in you. *And againe:* you haue obeied from the hart vnto that forme of doctrine, vvhich hath been deliuered to you. *And therevpon againe:* I desire you brethren, to marke them that make dissensions and scandals contrarie to the doctrine vvhich you haue learned, and auoide them. For such doe not serue Christ our Lord, but theire ovvne belly: and by svveete speaches ad benedictions seduce the harts of innocents. *Therfore to shunne* Luther *and* Caluin, *and al their crewes, vve haue iust reason and good vvarrant. They make dissensions and scandals against the doctrine of the Romane* Church. *Let no man therefore be seduced by their sugred vvordes.*

Rom. 1. Rom. 16. Rom. 6. Rom. 16.

The church readeth S. Pauls epistles at Mattins frō Sunday in Christmas vnto Septuagesme.

THE EPISTLE OF PAVL THE APOSTLE TO THE ROMANES.

Chap. I.

The foundation of his Apostleship being laid, 8 he highly commendeth the Romanes, and protesteth his affection tovvardes them. and so coming to the matter, saith, our Christian Catholike doctrine (that teacheth al to beleeue) to be the vvay to saluation: 18 because the Gentiles (first of al) could not be saued by their Philosophie, vvhereby they knevv God, for so much as they did not serue him, but Idols: he therfore iustly permitting them to fall into al kind of most damnable sinne.

The Epistle vpō Christmas eue.

PAVL the seruant of IESVS CHRIST, 1 called to be an Apostle, * separated into the Gospel of God, † vvhich 2 before he had promised by his Prophets in the holy Scriptures, † of 3 his sonne, (vvho vvas made to him of the seede of Dauid according to the flesh, † vvho vvas predestinate 4 the sonne of God in povver, according to the spirit of sanctification, by the resurrectiō of our Lord IESVS CHRIST from the dead, † by vvhom vve haue receiued grace and 5 Apostleship [c] for obedience to the faith ⁘ in al Nations for the name of him, † among vvhom are you also the called of 6 IESVS CHRIST:) ✠ † to al that are at Rome the be- 7 loued of God, called to be saincts. Grace to you and peace from God our father, and our Lord IESVS CHRIST.

† First I giue thankes to my God through IESVS CHRIST 8 for al you, because " your faith is renoumed in the vvhole vvorld. † For God is my vvitnes, [c] vvhom I serue " in my 9 spirit in the Gospel of his Sonne, that ⁘ vvithout intermission I make " a memorie of you † alvvaies in my praiers, besee- 10 ching, if by any meanes I may sometime at the length haue a prosperous iourney by the vvil of God, to come vnto you.

† For

Act. 13, 2.

c Faith must not be subiect to sense, reason, arguing or vnderstāding, but must cōmaund & be obeied in humilitie and simplicitie.

⁘ S. Augustine vseth this place and the like agaīst Heretikes, vvhich vvould dravv the common Catholike faith of al natiōs, to some certaine countries or corners of the World. *Aug. ep. 161.*

c εἰς ὑπακοὴν πίστεως.

⁘ He praieth without intermission that omitteth no day certaine times of praier. *Aug. heres. 57.*

c ᾧ λατρεύω

11 † For I desire to see you, that I may imparte vnto you some
12 spiritual grace, to ∷ confirme you: † that is to say, to be comforted together in you by that vvhich is cōmon to vs both,
13 your faith and mine. † And I vvil not haue you ignorant (brethren) that I haue often purposed to come vnto you (and haue been staied hitherto) that I may haue some fruite in you,
14 as also in the other Gentiles. † To the Greekes and the Bar-
15 barous, to the vvise and the vnvvise I am detter. † so (as much as is in me) I am ready " to euangelize to you also that are at Rome.

∷ The Romanes vvere conuerted and taught by S. Peter before. therefore he vseth that speach, to confirme them in their faith. Author *Com. apud Hierony. Theodoret. in 16. Rom. & Chrys.*

16 † For I am not ashamed of the Gospel. For it is the povver of God, vnto saluation to euery one that beleeueth, to the
17 Ievve first and to the Greeke. † For ∷ the iustice of God is reuealed therein by faith into faith: as it is vvritten: *And the iust " liueth by faith.*

Abac. 2, 4.

18 † For the vvrath of God from heauen " is reuealed, vpon al impietie and iniustice of those men that deteine the veritie
19 of God in iniustice: † because, that of God vvhich is knovvē, is manifest in them. For God hath manifested it vnto them.
20 † For his inuisible things, from the creation of the vvorld are seen, being vnderstoode by those things that are made: his eternal povver also & Diuinitie: so that they are inexcusable.

∷ He meaneth not Gods ovvne iustice in him self, but that iustice vvhervvith God endueth man vvhen he iustifieth him. *Aug. de Sp. & lit. c. 9.* Whereby you may gather the vanitie of the Heretical imputatiue iustice.

21 † Because, vvhereas they knevve God, they haue not glorified him as God, or giuē thankes: but are become vaine in their
22 cogitations, and their folish hart hath been darkened. † for,
23 saying them selues to be vvise, they became fooles. † And they changed the glorie of the incorruptible God, into a c similitude of the image of a corruptible man, and of foules
24 and foure-footed beastes and of them that creepe. † (For the vvhich cause God ∷ hath deliuered them vp vnto the desires of their hart, into vncleannesse, for to abuse their owne bodies
25 among them selues ignominiously.) † vvho haue changed the veritie of God into lying: and haue vvorshipped & c serued the creature rather then the creator, vvho is blessed
26 for euer. Amen. † Therfore " God hath deliuered them into passions of ignominie. For their vvomen haue changed the
27 natural vse, into that vse that is contrarie to nature. † And in like maner the men also, leauing the natural vse of the vvoman, haue burned in their desires one tovvard an other, men vpon men vvorking turpitude, & the revvard of their errour
28 (vvhich they should) receauing in them selues. † And as they

ἐσεβάσθησαν

c Lo these and the like are the Images or Idols so often condēned in the scriptures, and not the holy Images of Christ and his Saincts.

∷ Eph. 4, 19. he saith, *They haue deliuered or giuen vp them selues to al vncleannesse.* By vvhich cōferēce of scripturs vve learne that them selues are the cause of their ovvne sinne and damnation, God of his iustice permitting & leauing them to their ovvne vvil, and so giuing them vp into passions &c.

they liked not to haue God in knovvledge: God deliuered them vp into a reprobate sense: to doe those things that are not conuenient: † replenished vvith al iniquitie, malice, 29 fornication, auarice, vvickednes, ful of enuie, murder, contention, guile, malignitie, vvhisperers, † detractours, odible 30 to God, contumelious, proude, hautie, inuentours of euil things, disobedient to parents, † folish, dissolute, vvithout 31 affection, vvithout fidelitie, vvithout mercie. † Who vvhereas 32 they knevv the iustice of God, did not vnderstand that they vvhich doe such things, are" vvorthie of death: not only they that doe them, but they also that consent to the doers.

ANNOTATIONS. CHAP. I.

Apostolical salutation or blessing. The same vsed of Heretikes.

7. *Grace to you and peace.*] It is a kind of blessing rather then a prophane salutation, proper to the Apostles, of greater vertue then the benedictions of the fathers in the old Testament. The holy fathers of the Church seemed to absteine from it for their reuerence to the Apostles. * The Manichees (*August. cont. ep. funda. c. 5. 6.*) and other Heretikes (as also these of our time) because they vvould be counted Apostles, often vse it.

Epiph. hæres. 66.

The Romane faith highly commended. It can not faile, nor be corrupted.

8. *Your faith renoumed.*] The holy Doctors vpon these vvordes of the Apostle, and specially by our Maisters promis * made to Peter, that his faith should not faile, giue great testimonie for the prouidence of God in the preseruation of the Romane faith. S. Cyprian thus: ep 55. nu. 6. *They are so bold to cary letters from prophane Schismatikes to the chaire of Peter and the principal Church vvhence Priestly vnitie rose: not considering the Romanes to be them vvhose faith (the Apostle being the commender) vvas praised, to vvhom misbeleefe can not haue accesse.* So S. Hierom Apolog. adu. Ruff. li. 3 c. 4. to. 2. *Knovv you, that the Romane faith commended by the Apostles mouth, vvil receiue no such deceites, nor can be possibly changed, though an Angel taught othervvise, being fensed by S. Paules authoritie.* Againe ep. 65. ad Pammach. & Oceanum. c. 4. to. 2. *Whatsoeuer thou be that auouchest nevv sectes, I pray thee haue respect to the Romane eares, spare the faith vvhich vvas praised by the Apostles voice.* And in an other place: *Wil ye knovv ô Paula and Eustochium, hovv the Apostle hath noted euery prouince vvith their proprieties? the faith of the people of Rome is praised. Where is there so great concourse to Churches and Martyrs sepulchres? Where soundeth Amen like thunder from heauen, or vvhere are the temples (void of Idols) so shaken as there? Not that the Romanes haue an other faith then the rest of the Christian Churches, but that there is in them more deuotion and simplicitie of faith.* In an other place the same holy Doctor signifieth that it is al one to say, the Romane faith, and, the Catholike. *Apolog. 1 adu. Ruff. c. 1.* So doth S. Cyprian *ep. 52. num. 1. ad Antonianum*: and S. Ambrose *de obitu fratris, in med.* Vvherevpon, this vvord, *Romane*, is added to, *Catholike*, in many countries vvhere Sectes do abound, for the better distinction of true beleeuers from Heretikes: vvhich in al ages did hate and abhorre the Romane faith and Church, as al malefactors do their Iudges and correctors.

Luc. 22.

The Romane statiōs, a token of greater faith and deuotion. The Catholike and Romane faith al one.

Proœm. li. 2. Com. in ep. ad Gal.

Hovv God is serued in spirit.

9. *Serue in spirit.*] Diuerse Heretikes vvhen they heare that God is a spirit, and must be serued and adored in spirit, imagine, that he must be honoured only invvardly, vvithout ceremonies and external vvorkes: vvhich you see is othervvise, for that the Apostle serued God in spirit, by preaching the Gospel. To serue God then in spirit, is to serue him vvith faith, hope, and charitie, and vvith al vvorkes proceding of them: as to serue him carnally, is, vvith vvorkes external, vvithout the said internal vertues.

Praier for conuersion of soules.

9 *A memorie of you.*] A great example of charitie for al men, specially for Prelates and Pastors, not only to preach, but to pray continually for the conuersion of people to Christes faith: Vvhich the Apostle did for them vvhom he neuer knevv, in respect of Gods honour only and the zeale of soules.

The Gospel is not only the Written Word.

15. *To euangelize.*] The Gospel is not only the life of our Sauiour vvritten by the foure Euangelistes, nor only that vvhich is vvritten in the nevv Testamēt: but their vvhole course of preaching and teaching the faith. Vvhich faith commeth ordinarily of preaching and hearing, and not of vvriting or reading. And therfore S. Paul thought not him self discharged by vvriting to the Romanes, but his desire vvas to preach vnto them: for that vvas the proper commission giuen to the

Apostles

Mat. 28. Apostles, * to preach to al nations. The vvriting of the bookes of the Testament, is an other part of Gods prouidence, necessary for the Church in general, but not necessarie for euery man in particular: as to be taught and preached vnto, is for euery one of age and vnderstanding. And therfore S. Peter (vvho vvas the cheefe of the Commission) vvrote litle: many of them vvrote nothing at al: and S. Paul that vvrote most, vvrote but litle in comparison of his preaching: nor to any but such as vvere conuerted to the faith by preaching before.

The Apostles vvriting, and preaching, vvhether more necessarie, and hovv.

17. *Liueth by faith.*] In the 10. to the Hebrevves, he shevveth by this place of the Prophete (*Abacuc 2*) that the iust though he liue here in peregrination, and seeth not presently nor enioyeth the life euerlasting promised to him, yet holdeth fast the hope thereof by faith. In this place he applieth the Prophetes vvordes further to this sense, That it is our faith, that is to say, *the Catholike beleefe* (saith S. Augustine *li. 3 cont. 2 ep. Pelag.*) *Which maketh a iust man, and distinguisheth betvvene the iust and vniust*, and that by the lavv of faith, and not by the lavv of vvorkes. Vvhereof it riseth, that the Ievv, the Heathen Philosopher, and the Heretike, though they excelled in al vvorkes of moral vertues, could not yet be iust: and a Catholike Christian man liuing but an ordinarie honest life, either not sinning greatly, or supplying his faults by penance, is iust. And this difference riseth by faith. not that faith can saue any man vvithout vvorkes, *For it is not a reprobate faith that vve speake of*, (as the holy Doctor saith) *but that vvhich vvorketh by charitie*, and therfore remitteth sinnes and maketh one iust. See S. Augustines place.

The Catholike or Christian faith with good vvorkes iustifieth. & vvithout this faith, no vvorkes whatsoeuer.

18. *Is reuealed.*] By al the passage folovving you may see, that the Gospel and Christs lavv consisteth not only in preaching faith, (though that be the ground, and is first alvvaies to be done:) but to teach vertuous life and good vvorkes, and to denounce damnation to al them that commit deadly sinnes and repent not. And againe vve see that not only lacke of faith is a sinne, but al other actes done against Gods commaundements.

Not only faith.

26. *Hath deliuered them vp.*] As he saith here, God deliuered them vp, so to the Ephesians (c. 4, 19) he saith of the same persons and things, They deliuered them selues vp to al vncleannesse. So that it is not meant here that God doth driue, force, or cause any man to sinne, as diuers blasphemous Heretikes do hold: but only that by his iust iudgement, for their ovvne deseruing, and for due punishment of their former greuous offenses, he vvithholdeth his grace from them, and so suffereth them to fall further into other sinnes. As, for their crime of Idolatrie, to suffer them to fall into vnnatural abominations: as novv for heresie, he taketh his grace and mercie from many, and so they fall headlong into al kind of turpitude. as contrarievvise, for il life, he suffereth many to fall into heresie. And for Christes sake let euery one that is entangled vvith the Idolatrie of this time, that is to say, vvith these nevv sectes, looke vvel into his ovvne conscience, vvhether his forsaking the true God, may not come vnto him for a punishment of his former or present il life vvhich he liueth.

God is not the author of sinne.

God punisheth sinne by permitting men to fall further and further.

32. *Worthy of death.*] Here you see vvhy the Church taketh some sinnes to be deadly, and calleth them mortal: to vvit, because al that doe them, are vvorthy of damnation: others be venial, that is to say, pardonable of their ovvne nature and not vvorthy of damnation.

Sinnes mortal and venial.

CHAP. II.

Novv also he shevveth that neither the Ievves could be saued by the knovvledge of the Lavv, of the vvhich they did so much bragge against the Gentils, seing they did notvvithstanding sinne as the Gentils did. 14 And therfore that the true Ievv is the Christian (though he be a Gentil) vvho by grace in his hart doeth the good vvorkes that the Lavv commaundeth.

1 FOR the vvhich cause thou art inexcusable ô man vvhosoeuer ″ thou be that iudgest. For vvherein thou iudgest an other, thou condemnest thy self. for thou doest the same things 2 vvhich thou iudgest. † For vve knovv that the iudgement of God is according to veritie vpon them 3 that doe such things. † And doest thou suppose this ô man that iudgest them which doe such things, and doest the same, 4 that thou shalt escape the iudgement of God? † Or ″ doest

thou contemne the riches of his goodnes, and patience, and longanimity, not knovving that the benignity of God bringeth thee to penance? † But according to thy hardnes and 5 impenitent hart, thou heapest to thy self vvrath, in the day of vvrath and of the reuelation of the iust iudgement of God, † vvho vvil * render to euery man " according to his vvorkes. 6 † to them truely that according to patience in good vvorke, 7 seeke glorie and honour and incorruption, life eternal. † but 8 to them that are of contention, and that obey not the truth, but giue credite to iniquitie, vvrath and indignation. † Tribulation 9 and anguish vpon euery soul of man that vvorketh euil, of the Ievve first and of the c Greeke: † but glorie and 10 honour and peace to euery one that vvorketh good, to the Ievv first and to the Greeke. † for * there is no acception of 11 persons vvith God. † For vvhosoeuer haue sinned vvithout 12 the Lavv, vvhithout the Lavv shal perish: and vvhosoeuer haue sinned in the Lavv, by the Lavv shal be iudged. † For 13 * " not the hearers of the Lavv are iust vvith God: but the doers of the Lavv " shal be iustified. † For vvhen the Gentiles 14 vvhich haue not the Lavv, naturally doe those things that are of the Lavv: the same not hauing the Lavv, them selues are a lavv to them selues: † vvho shevv the vvorke of the Lavv 15 vvritten in their hartes, their conscience giuing testimonie to them, and among them selues mutually their thoughtes accusing, or also defending, † in the day vvhen God shal iudge 16 the secretes of men, according to my Gospel, by IESVS CHRIST.

† But if thou be surnamed a Ievv, and restest in the Lavv, 17 and doest glorie in God, † and knovvest his vvil, and 18 approuest the more profitable things, instructed by the Lavv, † presumest that thy self art a leader of the blinde, a light of 19 them that are in darknes, † a teacher of the folish, a maister of 20 infants, hauing the forme of science & of veritie in the Lavv. † Thou therfore :: that teachest an other, teachest not thy 21 self: that preachest, men ought not to steale, thou stealest: † that saiest men should not commit aduoutrie, thou com- 22 mittest aduoutrie: that abhorrest idols, thou doest sacrilege: † that doest glorie in the Lavv, thou by preuarication of the 23 Lavv doest dishonour God. († *For* c *the name of God through you is* 24 *blasphemed among the Gentiles*, as it is vvriten.) † Circumcision in 25 deede profiteth, if thou obserue the Lavv: but if thou be a preuaricatour

Good men also according to the merits of their good vvil shal haue their reward. *Aug. ep.* 47.

c That is, *the Gentile.*

:: It is a shameful and damnable thing for preachers, teachers, or other guides of mens life, to commit the same things them selues which they reproue in other.

c It is a great sinne that by the il life of the faithful, our Lordes name should be il spoken of amōg the misbeleuers, & many vvithdravven from the true religiō thereby

Ps. 61, 13

Deu. 10, 17. *Act.* 10, 34.

Mt. 7, 21 *Ia.* 1, 22

Es. 52, 5. *Ez.* 36, 20.

preuaricatour of the Lavv, thy circumcision is become :: prepuce. 26 † If then the prepuce " keepe the iustices of the Lavv: 27 shal not his prepuce be reputed for circumcision? † and shal not that vvhich of nature is prepuce, fulfilling the Lavv, iudge thee, that by the letter and circumcision art a preuaricatour 28 of the Lavv? † For not he that is in open shevv, is a Ievv, nor that vvhich is in open shevv, in the flesh, is circumcision: 29 † but he that is in secrete, is a Ievv: and the circumcision of the hart, " in spirit, not in the letter: vvhose praise is not of men, but of God.

:: Prepuce is the foreskinne not circumcised, & therfore signifieth the Gentiles, or the state and conditiō of the Gentiles: as circumcisiō, the Ievves and their state.

ANNOTATIONS
CHAP. II.

1. Thou that iudgest.) Such as by publike authoritie either spiritual or temporal haue to punish offenders, be not forbidden to iudge or condemne any for their offenses, though them selues be sometimes guilty in their conscience of the same or greater: yet may it be matter of aggrauating sinnes before God, vvhen they vvil not repent of those offenses them selues, for the vvhich they punish others. but if they be open offenders them selues, in the same sort for vvhich they iudge other, they giue scandal, and thereby aggrauate their sinnes very much. Proprely here he forbiddeth to charge an other falsely or truely vvith these crimes vvhereof him self is as farre guilty or more then the other, as the Ievves specially did the Gentils, to vvhom he speaketh here.

Iudging other men.

4. Doest thou contemne?) This proueth that God offereth his grace and mercie to many, and by long patience and sufferance expecteth their repētance, differring their punishment of purpose that they may amend, and that he is not delighted in their perdition, nor is the cause of their sinne: but contrariewise that they harden their ovvne hartes, and of their ovvne free vvil reiect his grace and contemne his benignitie.

Gods long suffering is for our repentance.

6. According to his vvorkes.) Though the holy Apostles special purpose be in this Epistle, to commend vnto the Gentiles that trusted so much in their moral vvorkes, the faith in Christ: yet lest any man should thinke or gather vntruely of his vvordes, that Christian mens vvorkes vvere not meritorious or the cause of Saluation, he expresly vvriteth, that God giueth as vvel euerlasting life and glorie to men, for and according to their good vvorkes, as he giueth damnation for the contrarie vvorkes. And hovv so euer Heretikes fondly flee from the euidence of these places, yet S. Augustine saith, Life euerlasting to be rendered for good vvorkes according to this manifest Scripture, *God shal render to euery man according to his vvorkes.*

Good vvorkes meritorious.

Li. de grat. & lib. arb. c. 8.

13. Not the hearers.) This same sentence agreable also to Christes vvordes (*Mat. 7, 21*) is the very ground of S. Iames disputation, that not faith alone, but good vvorkes also do iustifie. Therfore S. Paul (hovvsoeuer some peruersly conster his vvordes in other places) meaneth the same that S. Iames. And here * he speaketh not properly of the first iustification, vvhen an Infidel or il man is made iust, vvho had no acceptable vvorkes before to be iustified by (of vvhich kind he specially meaneth in other places of this Epistle) but he speaketh of the second iustification or increase of former iustice, vvhich he that is in Gods grace, daily proceedeth in, by doing al kind of good vvorkes, vvhich be iustices, and for doing of vvhich, he is iust in deede before God. and of this kinde doth S. Iames namely treate. Vvhich is directly against the Heretikes of this time, vvho not only attribute nothing to the vvorkes done in sinne and infidelitie, but esteeme nothing at al of al Christian mens vvorkes tovvard iustification and saluation, condemning them as vncleane, sinful, hypocritical, Pharisaical: vvhich is directly against these & other Scripture, and plaine blaspheming of Christ and his grace, by vvhose spirit and cooperation vve doe them.

Aug. de Sp. & lit. c. 26. to. 3.

The first, iustification, vvithout vvorkes: the second, by vvorkes

S. Paul speaketh of the first specially, S. Iames of the second.

13. Shal be iustified.) Of al other Articles deceitfully handled by Heretikes, they vse most guile in this of Iustification: and specially by the equiuocation of certaine vvordes, vvhich is proper to al contentious vvranglers, and namely in this vvord, *Iustifie*, Vvhich because they finde sometime to signifie the acquiting of a guilty man of some crime vvhereof he is in deede guilty, & for vvhich he ought to be condemned, (as by mans iudgement either of ignorance or of purpose often a very malefactor is deemed or declared and pronounced innocent) they falsly make it so signifie in this place and the like, vvheresoeuer man is said to be iustified of God for his vvorkes or othervvise: as though it vvere said, that God iustifieth man, that is to say, imputeth to him the iustice of Christ,

Against imputatiue iustice.

 though

though he be not in deede iust: or of fauour reputeth him as iust, vvhen in deede he is vvicked, impious, and vniust. Vvhich is a most blasphemous doctrine against God, making him either ignorant vvho is iust, and so to erre in his iudgement, or not good, that can loue and saue him vvhom he knovveth to be euil. And a maruelous pitieful blindnes it is in the Churches Aduersaries, that they should thinke it more to Gods glorie, and more to the commendation of Christes iustice, merites, and mercie, to call and count an il man so continuing, for iust: then by his grace and mercie to make him of an il one, iust in deede, and so truely to iustifie him, or as the vvord doth here signifie, to esteeme and approue for iust in deede, him, that by his grace keepeth his lavv and commaundements. For, that the keepers or doers of the commaundements be iust and so reputed, it is plaine by the correspondence to the former vvordes, *Not the hearers are iust, but the doers.* Vvherevpon S. Augustine *de Sp. & lit. c. 26. to. 3.* hath these vvordes, *When it is said, The doers of the Lavv shalbe iustified, vvhat other thing is said, then, The iust shalbe iustified? for the doers of the Lavv verily are iust.*

True inherent iustice more for gods glorie, & for the commendation of Christs merites.

26. *Keepe the iustices.*) If a Gentil either novv since Christ, by his grace and faith, or any other before Christ, not of the stocke of Abraham, through the Spirit of God keepe the iustices of the Lavv, he is iust no lesse then if he had been outvvardly circumcised, and shal condemne the circumcised Ievv not keeping the Lavv, vvithout vvhich, his outvvard Sacrament can not serue him, but shal be much to his condemnation, that hauing the Lavv and peculiar Sacraments of God, he did not keepe the Lavv, nor invvardly exercise that in his hart vvhich the outvvard signe did import. And al this is no more but to insinuate that true iustice is not in faith only or knovvledge of the Lavv, or in the name either of Ievv or Christian, but in doing good vvorkes and keeping the Lavv by Gods grace.

True iustice both in Ievv and Gentile, is by keeping the Lavv.

29. *In spirit, not letter.*] The outvvard ceremonies, Sacraments, threates, and commaundements of God in the Lavv, are called the *letter*: the invvard vvorking of God in mens hart, and enduing him vvith faith, hope, and charitie, and vvith loue, liking, vvil, and abilitie to keepe his commaundements by the grace and merites of Christ, are called the *spirit.* In vvhich sense, the carnal Ievv vvas a Ievv according to the letter, and he vvas circumcised after the letter: but the true beleeuing Gentil obseruing by Gods grace in hart and in Gods sight, that vvhich vvas meant by that carnal signe, is a Ievv according to the spirit, and iustified by God. Of the spirit and letter S. Augustine made a famous vvorke, very necessarie for the vnderstanding of this Epistle. *de sp. & lit. to. 3.*

The letter, and the spirit. The carnal, and spiritual Ievve.

CHAP. III.

He graunteth that the Ievves did passe the Heathen Gentils, in Gods benefits, 9 but not in their ovvne vvorkes, concluding, that he hath shevved, both Ievv and Gentil to be sinners: 18 and therfore (inferring) that there must be some other vvay to Saluation, indifferent to both, vvhich is to beleeue in IESVS CHRIST, *that for his sake their sinnes may be forgiuen them.*

WHAT preeminence then hath the Ievv, or what 1 is the profit of circumcision? † Much by al 2 meanes. First surely because the vvordes of God vvere cōmitted to them. † for vvhat if certaine 3 of them haue not beleeued? Hath their incredulitie made the faith of God frustrate? † God forbid. but * God is true: & 4 * :: euery man a lyer, as it is vvritten: *That thou maiest be iustified in thy vvordes, and ouercome vvhen thou art iudged.* † But" if our iniqui- 5 tie commend the iustice of God, vvhat shal vve say? Is God vniust that executeth vvrath? (I speake according to man) † God forbid. othervvise hovv shal God iudge this vvorld? 6 † For if the veritie of God hath abounded in my lie, vnto 7 his glorie, vvhy am I also yet iudged as a sinner, † and not 8 (as vve are blasphemed, and as some report vs to say) let vs doe

Io. 3, 33. Ps. 115, 11. Ps. 50, 6.

:: God only by nature is true, al mere men by nature may lie, deceiue and be deceiued: yet God by his grace & spirit may and doth preserue the Apostles and principal gouerners of his people & the Church and Councels in al truth, though they vvere and are mere men.

doe euil, that there may come good? vvhose damnation is iust.

9 † Vvhat then? do vve excel them? No, not so. For vve haue argued the Ievves and the Greekes, al to be vnder sinne:

Ps. 13, 1. 52, 3.

10 † as it is vvritten: *That* " *there is not any man iust,* † *there is not that vnder-*11 *standeth, there is not that seeketh after God.* † 12 *Al haue declined, they are become vnprofitable together: there is not that doeth good, there is not so much as* 13 *one.* † *Their throte is an open sepulchre, vvith their tonges they dealt de-*14 *ceitefully. The venim* [c] *of aspes vnder their lippes.* † 15 *Vvhose mouth is ful of malediction and bitternes:* † 16 *Their feete svvift to shede bloud.* † *De-struction and infelicitie in their vvaies:* † 17 *and the vvay of peace they haue not knovven.* † 18 *There is no feare of God before their eies.* † And vve 19 knovv that vvhatsoeuer the Lavv speaketh, to them it speaketh that are in the Lavv: that euery mouth may be stopped, 20 and al the vvorld may be made subiect to God: † because * " by the vvorkes of the Lavv no flesh shal be iustified before him. For by the Lavv is the knovvledge of sinne.

Ps. 5, 11. Ps. 139, 4. Ps. 9, 7. Es. 19, 7. Pro. 1, 16. Ps. 35, 2.

c *Aspidum.* A kinde of litle serpents.

Gal. 2, 16.

21 † But novv vvithout the Lavv " the iustice of God is ma-22 nifested: testified by the lavv and the Prophets. † And the iustice of God by faith of IESVS CHRIST, vnto al and 23 vpō al that [c] beleeue in him. For there is no distinction. † For 24 al haue sinned: and doe neede the glorie of God. † Iustified :: gratis by his grace, by the redemption that is in CHRIST 25 IESVS, † vvhom God hath proposed a ' propitiation ', by faith in his bloud, to the shevving of his iustice, for the re-26 mission of former sinnes, † in the toleration of God, to the shevving of his iustice in this time: that he may be iust, and iustifying him that is of the faith of IESVS CHRIST.

c To beleeue in him, here comprisech not only the act of faith, but of hope & charitie, as the Apostle explicateth him self. *Galat.* 5, 6.

propiti-atour

:: No man atteineth his first iustification by the merites either of his faith or workes, but merely by Christes grace and mercie: though his faith & workes procedīg of grace be dispositiōs & preparations therevnto.

27 † Vvhere is then thy boasting? it is excluded. by vvhat 28 lavv? of deedes? No, but by the lavv of faith. † For vve account a man to be iustified " by faith vvithout the vvorkes 29 of the Lavv. † Is he God of the Ievves only? is he not also 30 of the Gentiles? Yes of the Gentiles also. † For it is one God, that iustifieth circumcision by faith, and prepuce by 31 faith. † Do vve then destroy the Lavv by faith? God forbid. but vve do establish the Lavv.

ANNOTATIONS
CHAP. III.

5. If your iniquitie.) No maruel that many novv a daies deduce false and detestable conclusions out of this Apostles high and hard vvritings, seeing that S. Peter noted it in his daies, and him self here confesseth that his preaching and speaches vvere then falsely misconstrued: as though he had

2. Pet. 3.

S. Paules speaches mistaken of the vvicked

had taught that the Ievves and Gentils il life and incredulity had been directly the cause of Gods more mercie, and that therfore sinne commeth of God to the aduancement of his glorie, and consequently that men might or should doe il, that good might ensue thereof. Vvhich blasphemous constructions they tooke of these and the like vvordes: *vvhere sinne abounded, there did grace more abound.* and, *The Lavv entered in, that sinne might abound.* and out of the Psalme 50. *That thou maiest be iustified in thy vvordes, and ouercome vvhen thou art iudged.* As though he meant that men do sinne, to the end that God may be iustified. And at al these and the like places of the Apostle though forevvarned by S. Peter, and by the Apostles ovvne defense and Protestation, that he neuer meant such horrible things, yet the vvicked also of this time do stumble and fall. But the true meaning is in al such places, that God can and doth vvhen it pleaseth him, conuert those sinnes vvhich man committeth against him and his commaundements, to his glorie: though the sinnes them selues stand not vvith his vvil, intention, nor honour, but be directly against the same, and therfore may not be committed that any good may fall. for, vvhat good so euer accidentally falleth, it procedeth not of the sinne, but of Gods mercie that can pardon, and of his omnipotencie that can turne il to good. And therfore against those carnal interpretations, S. Paul very carefully & diligently giueth reason also in this place v. 6, that it is impossible: because God could not iustly punish any man, nor sit in iudgement at the later day for sinne vvithout plaine iniurie, if either him self vvould haue sinne committed, or man might doe it to his glorie. Therfore let al sincere readers of the Scriptures, and specially of S. Pauls vvritings, hold this for a certaintie, as the Apostles ovvne defense (vvhatsoeuer he seeme to say hereafter sounding in their sense, that sinne commeth of God, or may therfore be committed that he may vvorke good thereof) that the Apostle him self condemneth that sense as slaunderous and blasphemous.

Ro. 5, 20.
Ro. 3, 4.

The sense of the places that sound, as if God caused sinne.

10. *Not any iust*] These general speaches, that both Ievv and Gentile be in sinne, and none at al iust, are not so to be taken, that none in neither sort vvere euer good: the Scriptures expresly saying that Iob, *Zacharie, Elisabeth, and such like, vvere iust before God, & it vvere blasphemie to say that these vvordes alleaged out of the 13 Psalme, vvere meant in Christes mother, in S. Iohn the Baptist, in the Apostles &c. For, this only is the sense: that neither by the lavv of nature, nor lavv of Moyses, could any man be iust or auoid such sinnes as here be reckened, but by faith and the grace of God, by vvhich there vvere a number in al ages (specially among the Ievves) that vvere iust and holy, vvhom these vvordes touch not, being spoken only to the multitude of the vvicked, vvhich the Prophet maketh as it vvere a seueral body conspiring against Christ, and persecuting the iust and godly, of vvhich il companie he saith, that none vvas iust nor feared God.

Hovv it is said, *none iust.*

Iob. 1.
* Luc. 1.

20. *By the vvorkes of the Lavv.*) S. Hierom and S. Chrysostom expound this of the ceremonial vvorkes only, and in that sense the Apostle specially prosecuteth this proposition in his Epistle to the Galatians. but it is true also of al mans moral vvorkes done vvithout faith & the grace of God: vvhich can not be acceptable or auailable in Gods sight, to iustifie any man, And so S. Augustine taketh it *de Sp. & lit. c. 8. to. 3.*

No vvorkes auaile vvithout faith and grace.

22. *Iustice of God.*) Bevvare of the vvicked and vaine commentarie of the Caluinistes, glosing, the iustice of God to be that vvhich is resident in Christ, apprehended by our faith: and so that imputed to vs vvhich vve in deede haue not. Vvherein at once they haue forged them selues against Gods manifest vvord, a nevv no iustice, a phantastical apprehension of that vvhich is not, a false faith and vntrue imputation. vvhereas the iustice of God here, is that vvherevvith he endueth a man at his first conuersion, and is novv in a man, and therfore mans iustice: but yet Gods iustice also, because it is of God. Of this iustice in vs, vvhereby vve be truely iustified and in deede made iust, S. Augustine speaketh thus: *The grace of Christ doth vvorke our illumination and iustification invvardly also.* And againe, *He giueth to the faithful the most secrete grace of his Spirit, vvhich secretly he povvreth into infants also.* And againe, *They are iustified in Christ that beleeue in him through the secrete communication and inspiration of spiritual grace, vvhereby euery one leaneth to our Lord.* And againe, *He maketh iust renevving by the Spirit, and regeneration by grace.*

The Heretikes phantastical or imputatiue iustice.

True inhærent iustice.

De pec. mer. li. 1 c. 9. 10.

28. *By faith, vvithout vvorkes.*) This is the place vvherevpon the Protestants gather falsly their only faith, and vvhich they commonly auouch, as though the Apostle said, that only faith doth iustifie. Vvhere he both in vvordes and meaning excepteth only the vvorkes of the Lavv done vvithout Christ before our conuersion: neither excluding the Sacraments of Baptisme or Penance, nor hope and charitie, or other Christian vertues, al vvhich be the iustice of faith. as the good vvorkes proceding thereof, be likevvise the lavv and iustice of faith. Al vvhich the Aduersaries vvould exclude by foisting in the terme, only. Of vvhich kind of men S. Augustine vpon this place saith thus: *Men not vnderstanding that vvhich the Apostle saith, (vve counte a man to be iustified by faith vvithout the vvorkes of the Lavv) did thinke that he said, faith vvould suffise a man though he liued il and had no good vvorkes. Which God forbid the vessel of election should thinke: vvho in a certaine place after he had said, * In Christ* IESVS *neither circumcision nor prepuce auaileth any vvhit, he straight added, but faith vvhich vvorketh by loue.*

Vvhat vvorkes are excluded from iustification.

de grat. & lib. arb. c. 7

Gal. 5.

CHAP. IIII.

That Abraham vvas not iustified by his ovvne povver, but by Gods grace, in vvhom he beleeued (6 vvhich is a vvay for the sinner also to come to iustice.) 9 And that, seing he vvas not as then circumcised, not only the circumcised Ievv, but also the vncircumcised Gentil may by beleeuing the Christian faith, come to iustice, as Abraham did: 11 specially considering also, that Abraham vvas promised to be Father of the vvhole vvorld, and not only of the Ievves, to vvhom onely the Lavv vvas giuen: and that, not to fulfil the promise, but for an other cause.

1 VVHAT shal vve say then that " Abraham did finde, our father according to the flesh? 2 † For if Abraham vvere iustified "by vvorkes: he hath glorie, but not vvith God. 3 † For vvhat saieth the Scripture? *Abraham beleeued God, and it vvas reputed him to iustice.* 4 † But " to him that vvorketh, the revvard is not [c] imputed according to grace, but according to dette. 5 † But "to him that vvorketh not, yet beleeueth in him that iustifieth the impious, his faith is [c] reputed to iustice according to the purpose of the grace of God. 6 † " As Dauid also termeth the blessednes of a man, to vvhom God reputeth iustice vvithout vvorkes, 7 † *Blessed are they, vvhose iniquities be forgiuen, and vvhose sinnes be " couered.* 8 † *Blessed is the man to vvhom our Lord hath not imputed sinne.*

Gen. 5, 6
Gal. 3, 6
Ia. 2, 23.

c λογίζεται

c λογίζεται

Ps. 31, 1.

9 † This blessednes then doth it abide in the circumcision, or in the prepuce also? For vve say that vnto Abraham faith vvas :: reputed to iustice. 10 † Hovv vvas it reputed? in circumcision, or in prepuce? Not in circumcision, but in prepuce. 11 † And * he receiued [c] the signe of circumcision, " a seale of the iustice of faith that is in prepuce: that he might be the father of al that beleeue by the prepuce, that vnto them also it may be reputed to iustice: 12 † and might be father of circumcision, not to them only that are of the circumcision, but to them also that folovv the steppes of the faith that is in the prepuce of our father Abraham. 13 † For not by the Lavv vvas the promisse to Abraham, or to his seede, that he should be heire of the vvorld: but by the iustice of faith. 14 † For if they that are of the Lavv, be heires: faith is made voide, the promisse is abolished. 15 † For the Lavv vvorketh vvrath. For vvhere is no lavv, neither is there preuarication. 16 † Therfore of faith: that according to grace the promisse may be firme to al the seede, not to that only vvhich is of the Lavv, but to that also vvhich is of the faith of Abraham, vvho is the

Gen. 17, 10.

:: The vvord, *Reputed*, doth not diminish the truth of the iustice, as though it vvere reputed for iustice, being not iustice in deede, but signifieth, that as it vvas in it self, so God esteemed & reputed it, as the same greeke vvord must needes be taken *v. 4* next going before, & 1 *Cor.* 4, 1. and els vvhere.

c Our Sacraments of the nevv Lavv giue *ex opere operato* that grace and iustice of faith vvhich here is commended. vvhereas circũcisiõ vvas but a signe or marke of the same.

the father of vs al, (as it is vvritten: † *For, a father of many nations haue I appointed thee*) before God, vvhom ` thou didst beleeue', vvho quickeneth the dead: and calleth those things that are not, as those things that are. 17 † Vvho contrarie to hope beleeued in hope: that he might be made the father of many nations, according to that vvhich vvas * said to him: *So shal thy seede be*, as the starres of heauen, and the sand of the sea. 18 † And he vvas not vveakened in faith: neither did he cõsider his ovvne body novv quite dead, vvhereas he vvas almost an hundred yeres old, and the dead matrice of Sara. 19 † In the promisse also of God he staggered not by distrust: but vvas strengthened in faith, giuing glorie to God: 20 † most fully knovving that vvhatsoeuer he promised, he is able also to doe. 21 † Therfore vvas it also reputed him to iustice. 22

† And it is not vvritten only for him, that it vvas reputed him to iustice: 23 † but also " for vs, to vvhom it shal be reputed beleeuing in him, that raised vp IESVS CHRIST our Lord from the dead, 24 † vvho vvas deliuered vp for our sinnes, and rose againe for our iustification. 25

Gen. 17, 4.
` he beleeued,
Gen. 15, 5

ANNOTATIONS
CHAP. IIII.

Abrahams Workes before faith.

1. *Abraham.*] The Apostle disputing in this chapter, as before, against them that thought they might be iustified by their vvorkes done vvithout the grace of Christ and faith in him, proposeth Abraham for an example, and proueth that he had no iustice nor estimation of iustice before God by any vvorkes done before he had faith, or that proceded not of faith and Gods grace.

Iustice before men, and iustice before God.

2. *By vvorkes.*] If Abraham did any commendable vvorkes before he beleeued Christ, as many Philosophers did, men might count him iust therfore, but in gods sight (vvho accepteth nothing vvithout faith in him, or that procedeth not from his grace) he should neuer haue had the estimation of a iust man. Therfore God in the Scriptures reputing him as a iust man, giueth the cause thereof, saying, *Abraham beleeued God, and it vvas reputed to him for iustice.*

Not vvorkes, but mere grace is cause of our first iustificatiõ.

4. *To him that vvorketh.*] That is to say, He that presumeth of his ovvne vvorkes as done of him self vvithout faith, Gods helpe, and grace: and saying, that grace or iustification vvere giuen to him for his vvorkes: this man doth chalenge his iustification as dette, and not as of fauour and grace.

5. *To him that vvorketh not*] He vvorketh not (in this place) that hath no vvorkes or alleageth not his vvorkes done in his infidelitie as cause of his iustification, but faith in Christ, and that proceding of mere grace. Vvherevpon S. Augustine saith: *Knovv thou that faith found thee vniust. And if faith giuen to thee, made thee iust, it found thee a vvicked one vvhom it might make iust. If it found thee vvicked, and of such an one made thee iust, vvhat vvorkes hadst thou being then vvicked? None couldest thou haue (nor canst haue) before thou beleeuedst. Beleeue then in him that iustifieth the impious, that thy good vvorkes may be good vvorkes in deede.* August. in Psal. 31.

Heretical translation.

6. *As Dauid termeth.*] The Protestants for, c *termeth*, translate, *describeth*, for that they vvould haue the ignorant beleeue, the vvhole nature & definition of Iustification to be nothing els but remission of sinnes, and no grace or inherent iustice giuen from God at al. Vvhen the Apostle vvould say nothing els, but that in the first iustificatiõ God findeth no good vvorkes or merites to revvard, but only sinnes to forgiue vnto such as haue faith in him.

c λέγει

Vvhat is, *Sinnes couered or not imputed.*

7. *Couered.* 8. *not imputed.*] You may not gather (as the Heretikes doe) of these termes, *couered*, and, *not imputed*, that the sinnes of men be neuer truely forgiuen, but hidden only. for that derogateth much to the force of Christes bloud and to the grace of God, by vvhich our offences be truely

Io. 1, 29. 2 Cor. 6, 11. Apoc. 1, 5.

truly remitted. He is the Lambe that *taketh avvay* the sinnes of the vvorld, *that vvasheth*, and *blotteth out* our sinnes. therfore to couer them, or, not to impute them, is, not to charge vs vvith our sinnes, because by remission they be cleane taken avvay: othervvise it vvere but a feined forgiuenesse. *See S. Augustine in psal. 31 enarrat. 2.*

11. A seale.] The Heretikes vvould proue hereby, that the Sacraments of the Church giue not grace or iustice of faith, but that they be notes, markes, and badges only of our remission of sinnes had by faith before: because Abraham vvas iust before, and tooke this Sacrament for a seale thereof only. To vvhich must be ansvvered, that it folovveth not that it is so in al, because it vvas so in the Patriarch, vvho vvas iust before, and vvas therfore as it vvere the founder of Circumcision, or he in vvhom God vvould first establish the same: no more then it folovveth that, because the Holy Sacrament of the Altar remitted not sinnes to Christ nor iustified him, therefore it hath that effect in none. Looke S. Augustine *de baptismo contra Donatistas li. 4. c. 24.* Vvhere you shal see that (though not in Abraham) yet in Isaac his sonne, and so consequently in the rest, the Sacrament vvent before, and iustice folovved.

The Sacraméts are not mere markes, but causes of iustification.

24. For vs, to vvhom it shal be reputed.] By this it is most plaine against our Aduersaries, that the faith vvhich vvas reputed for iustice to Abraham, vvas his beleefe of an Article reuealed to him by God, that is to say, his assent and credit giuen to Gods speaches: as in vs his posteritie according to the spirit, it is here plainely said, that iustice shal be reputed to vs by beleeuing the Articles of Christes death and Resurrection, and not by any fond special faith, *fiducia* or confidence of eche mans ovvne saluation. to establish the vvhich fiction, they make no account of the faith Catholike, that is, vvherevvith vve beleeue the Articles of the faith, vvhich only iustifieth, but call it by contempt, an historical faith: so as they may terme Abrahams faith, and our Ladies faith, of vvhich it vvas * said, Beata quæ credidisti, *Blessed art thou that hast beleeued.* And so in truth they deny as vvel the iustification by faith, as by vvorkes.

By vvhat faith vve are iustified.

Luc. 1, 45.

CHAP. V.

Hauing therfore through faith in Christ, obteined the beginning, he shevveth vvhat great cause vve haue to hope for the accomplishment. 12 And then he procedeth in his arguing, and shevveth that as by one, al vvere made sinners, so by one, al must be made iust.

1 BEING iustified therfore by faith, "let vs haue peace tovvard God by our Lord IESVS CHRIST: 2 † by vvhō also vve haue" accesse through faith into this grace vvherein vve stand, and glorie, ∴ in the hope of the glorie of the sonnes of God. 3 † And not only this: but also vve glorie in tribulations, knovving 4 that tribulation vvorketh patience: † and patience, probation: 5 and" probation, hope. † and hope confoundeth not: because" the charitie of God is povvred forth in our hartes, 6 by the holy Ghost vvhich is giuen vs. ⁋ † For vvhy did Christ, vvhen vve as yet vvere [c] vveake, according to the time 7 die for the impious? † For, scarse for a iust man doth any die: 8 for perhaps for a good man durst some man die. † But God commendeth his charitie in vs: because, vvhen as yet vve 9 vvere sinners, Christ died for vs. † Much more therfore now being iustified in his bloud, shal vve be saued from vvrath

The Epistle on Imber Saturday in vvhitson-vveeke, And for many Martyrs.

∴ Christian mē do not vaunt thē selues of the certaītie of their saluatiō, but glorie in the hope thereof onely, vvhich hope is here insinuated to be giuen in our iustificatiō, & is aftervvard to be cōfirmed by probation in tribulation.

ἀσθενῶν

c The Heretikes falsely translate, *of no strength*, to take avvay al free vvil. *Nu. Test. 1580.*

by him. 10 † For if, vvhen vve vvere enemies, vve vvere recōciled to God by the death of his Sonne: much more being reconciled, ſhal vve be ſaued in the life of him. 11 † And not only this: but alſo vve glorie in God through our Lord IESVS Chriſt, by vvhom novv vve haue receiued reconciliation.

12 † Therfore, as ″by one man ſinne entred into this vvorld, and by ſinne death: and ſo vnto al men death did paſſe, in vvhich al ſinned. 13 † For euen vnto the Lavv ſinne vvas in the world: but ſinne was not imputed, when the law was not. 14 † But death reigned from Adam ″ vnto Moyſes, euen on them alſo that ſinned not after the ſimilitude of the preuarication of Adam, vvho is a figure of him to come. 15 † But not as the offence, ſo alſo the gift. for if by the offence of one, many died: much more the grace of God and the gift, in the grace of one man IESVS Chriſt, hath abounded vpon many. 16 † And not as by one\` ſinne', ſo alſo the gift. for iudgemēt in deede is of one, to condemnatiō: but grace is of many offences, to iuſtificatiō. 17 † For if in the offēce of one, death reigned by one: much more they that receiue the aboundance of grace and of donation & of iuſtice, ſhal reigne in life by one, IESVS Chriſt. 18 † Therfore as by the offence of one, vnto al men to condemnation: ſo alſo by the iuſtice of one, vnto al men to iuſtification of life. 19 † For as by the diſobedience of one man, many vvere made ſinners: ſo alſo by the obedience of one, many ∴ ſhal be made iuſt. 20 † But the Lavv entred in, that ſinne might abound. And vvhere ſinne abounded, grace did more abound. 21 † that as ſinne reigned to death: ſo alſo grace may reigne by iuſtice to life euerlaſting, through IESVS Chriſt our Lord.

ſinner;

∴ Here vve may ſee againſt the Heretikes, that they vvhich be borne of Chriſt and iuſtified by him, be made & conſtituted iuſt in deede, & not by imputation only: as al that be borne of Adam, be vniuſt and ſinners in truth, & not by imputation.

ANNOTATIONS
CHAP. V.

Againſt the Heretikes ſpecial faith and ſecuritie.

1. *Let vs haue.*) Vvhether vve read, *Let vs haue peace*, as diuerſe alſo of the Greeke Doctors (*Chryſoſt. Orig. Theodor. Oecum. Theophyl.*) doe, or, *We haue peace*: it maketh nothing for the vaine ſecuritie and infallible certaintie vvhich our Aduerſaries ſay, euery man ought to haue vpon his preſumed iuſtification by faith, that him ſelf is in Gods fauour, and ſure to be ſaued: *peace tovvards God*, being here nothing els, but the ſincere reſt, tranquillitie and comfort of minde and conſcience, vpon the hope he hath, that he is reconciled to God. Sure it is that the Catholike faith, by vvhich, and none other, men be iuſtified, neither teacheth nor breedeth any ſuch ſecuritie of ſaluation. And therfore they haue made to them ſelues an other faith vvhich they call *Fiduciam*, quite vvithout the compaſſe of the Creede and Scriptures.

ἔχωμεν
ἔχομεν

Iuſtificatiō attributed much

2. *Acceſſe through faith.*) Iuſtification, implieth al grace and vertues receiued by Chriſtes merites, but the entrance and acceſſe to this grace and happy ſtate is by faith, becauſe faith is the ground and

and first foundation to build on, and port to enter into the rest. Vvhich is the cause that our iustification is attributed to faith, namely in this Epistle, though faith it self be of grace also.

to faith as to the fundation.

4. Probation hope.) This refelleth the errour also of the Protestants, that vvould haue our hope to hold only on Gods promises, and not a vvhit on our doings. Vvhere vve see that it standeth (and is strengthened also) vpon patience and constancie, and good probation and trial of our selues in aduersities: and that so grounded vpon Gods promises and our ovvne doings, it neuer confoundeth.

Our hope is strengthened by vvel doing.

5. Charitie is povvred.) Charitie also is giuen vs in our first iustification, and not only imputed vnto vs, but in deede invvardly povvred into our hartes by the Holy Ghost, vvho vvith and in his giftes & grace is bestovved vpon vs. for this Charitie of God is not that vvhich is in God, but that vvhich he giueth vs, as S. Augustine expoundeth it: *li. de Sp. & lit. c. 32.* Vvho referreth this place also to the grace of God giuen in the Sacrament of Confirmation. *de bapt. cont. Donat. li. 3 c. 16.*

Charitie is a qualitie in vs.

12. By one man sinne entred.) By this place specially the Church of God defendeth and proueth against the old Heretikes the Pelagians, that denied children to haue any original sinne, or to be baptized for the remission thereof: that in and by Adam al be conceiued, borne, and constituted sinners. Which no lesse maketh against the Caluinists also, that affirme, Christiā mens children to be holy from their mothers vvombe. And the same reason vvhich S. Augustine deduceth (*li. 1 c. 8. 9. de pec. meritis.*) out of this text, to proue against the said Pelagians, that the Apostle meaneth not of the general imitation of Adam in actual sinnes, serueth against Erasmus and others, inclining rather to that nevv exposition, then to the Churches and fathers graue iudgement herein. *Conc. Mileuitanum c. 2.*

Conc. Tri. sess. 5 decr. de pec. orig.

Al by Adam borne in original sinne.

14. vnto Moyses.) Euen in the time of the Lavv of nature, vvhen men knevv not sinne, and therfore it could not by mans iudgement be imputed: and in the time of Moyses Lavv, vvhen the commaundement taught them to knovv it, but gaue them no strength nor grace to auoid it, sinne did reigne, and therevpon death and damnation, euen til Moyses *inclusiue*, that is to say, euen til the end of his Lavv. And that not in them onely vvhich actually sinned, as Adam did, but in infants vvhich neuer did actually offend, but onely vvere borne and conceiued in sinne, that is to say, hauing their natures defiled, destitute of iustice, and auerted from God in Adam, and by their descent from him: Christ onely excepted, being conceiued vvithout mans seede, and his mother for his honour and by his special protection (as many godly deuout men iudge) preserued from the same.

Christ only not conceiued in sinne, and (as it is thought) our B. Lady.

20. That sinne might abound.) *That*, here hath not the signification of causalitie, as though the Lavv vvere giuen for that cause to make sinne abound: but it noteth the sequele, because that folovved thereof, and so it came to passe, that by the prohibition of sinne, sinne increased: by occasion vvhereof, the force of Christes grace is more amply and aboundantly bestovved in the nevv Testament.

The Lavv did not cause more sinne, though that vvere the sequele thereof.

CHAP. VI.

He exhorteth vs, novv after Baptisme, to liue no more in sinne, but to vvalke in good vvorkes: because there vve died to the one, and rose againe to the other 14 (grace also giuing vs sufficient strength) 16 and vvere made free to the one, and seruants to the other, 21 and specially because of the fruite here, and the end aftervvard, both of the one and of the other.

b The *Epistle* vpō the 6 Sūday after Pentecost.

1 VVHAT shal vve say then? Shal vve continue in 2 sinne that grace may abound? † God forbid. For vve that are dead to sinne, hovv shal vve yet liue 3 therein? † b Are you ignorant that al vve vvhich are baptized in Christ IESVS, in his death vve are baptized? 4 † For :: vve are buried together vvith him by Baptisme into death: that as Christ is risen from the dead by the glorie of 5 the father, so vve also may vvalke in nevvnesse of life. † For if vve be become complanted to the similitude of his death,

:: Remission of sinne, nevv life, sanctification, and iustificatiō, are giuen by baptisme, because it resembleth in vs and applieth to vs Christes death and resurrectiō, and engraffeth vs into him.

vve ſhal be alſo of his reſurrection. † Knovving this, that 6 our old man is crucified vvith him, that the body of ſinne may be deſtroied, to the end that vve may ſerue ſinne no longer. † For he that is dead, is iuſtified from ſinne. † And 7 if vve be dead vvith Chriſt, vve beleeue that vve ſhal liue 8 alſo together vvith Chriſt. knovving that Chriſt riſing 9 againe from the dead, novv dieth no more, death ſhal no more haue dominion ouer him. † For that he died, " to ſinne he 10 died once: but that he liueth, he liueth to God. † So thinke 11 you alſo, that you are dead to ſinne, but aliue to God in Chriſt IESVS our Lord. ⊣

† Let not " ſinne therfore reigne in your mortal body, that 12 you obey the concupiſcences thereof. † But neither doe ye 13 exhibite your members inſtruments of iniquitie vnto ſinne: but exhibite your ſelues to God as of dead men, aliue: and your members inſtruments of iuſtice to God. † For ſinne 14 ſhal not haue dominion ouer you. for you are not vnder the Lavv, but vnder grace.

† Vvhat then? ſhal vve ſinne, because vve are not vnder 15 the Lavv, but vnder grace? God forbid. † * Knovv you not 16 that to vvhom you exhibite your ſelues ſeruants to obey, you are the ſeruants of him vvhom you obey, vvhether it be of ſinne, to death, or of obedience, to iuſtice. † But thankes be to 17 God, that you vvere the ſeruants of ſinne, but ∷ haue obeied from the hart, vnto that " forme of doctrine, into the vvhich you haue been deliuered. † And being made free from ſinne, 18 you vvere made ſeruants to iuſtice. † I ſpeake an humane 19 thing, becauſe of the infirmitie of your fleſh. for as you haue exhibited your members to ſerue vncleanneſſe and iniquitie, vnto iniquitie: ſo now exhibite your mẽbers to ſerue iuſtice, ∷ vnto ſanctification. † For when you vvere ſeruants of ſinne, 20 you were free to iuſtice. † What fruite therfore had you then in 21 thoſe things, for vvhich novv you are aſhamed? for the end of them is death. † But novv being made free from ſinne, 22 and become ſeruants to God, you haue your fruite vnto ſanctification, but the end, life euerlaſting. † For the ſtipends 23 of ſinne, death. but " the grace of God, life euerlaſting in Chriſt IESVS our Lord. ⊣

∷ Here againe is ſignifi d, that our diſcharge frõ the bõdage of ſinne, is by the Chriſtian faith, & by obedience to the vvhole doctrine of Chriſts religion: in that the Apoſtle attributeth this their deliuerance frõ ſinne, to their humble receiuing of the Catholike faith.

The Epiſtle vpõ the 7 Sunday after Pentecoſt.

∷ He ſignifieth that as vvhen they vvere ſubiect to ſinne by cõtinual & oftẽ vvorking vvickednes, they increaſed their iniquitie: that ſo alſo novv being iuſtified, they may & ſhould by external vvorkes of iuſtice, increaſe their iuſtice and ſanctification.

Io. 8, 34. 2. Pet. 2, 19.

ANNOT.

ANNOTATIONS
CHAP. VI.

3. We that are baptized.) That vvhich before he chalenged from the Lavv of Moyses, to faith, is novv attributed to baptisme, vvhich is the first Sacrament of our faith and the entrance to Christian religion. Whereby it is plaine that he meaneth not onely faith to iustifie, but the Sacraments also, and al Christian religion, vvhich he calleth the Lavv of spirit, grace, and faith.

Not only faith.

6. Old man, body of sinne.) Our corrupt state subiect to sinne and concupiscence, comming to vs from Adam, is called the *Old man:* as our person reformed in & by Christ, is named the *Nevv man.* And the lumpe and masse of sinnes vvhich then ruled, is called the corps or body of sinne.

The old man, & the nevv.

10. To sinne he died.) Christ died to sinne; vvhen by his death he destroied sinne: Vve die to sinne, in that vve be discharged of the povver thereof, vvhich before vvas as it vvere the life of our persons, and commaunded al the partes and faculties of our soule and body: as contrarievvise vve liue to God, vvhen his grace ruleth and vvorketh in vs, as the soule doth rule our mortal bodies.

Dying to sinne. Liuing to God.

12. Sinne reigne.) Concupiscence is here named sinne, because it is the effect, occasion, and matter of sinne, and is as it vvere a disease or infirmitie in vs, inclining vs to il, remaining also after Baptisme according to the substance or matter thereof: but it is not properly a sinne, nor forbidden by commaundement, til it reigne in vs, and vve obey and folovv the desires thereof. *August. li. de nupt. & concupisc. c. 23. Cont. 2 epist. Pelag. li. 1 c. 13. Conc. Trident. Sess. 5. decret. de pec. orig.*

Hovv concupiscéce is called sinne.

17. Forme of doctrine,) At the first conuersion of euery nation to the Catholike faith, there is a forme & rule of beleefe set dovvne, vnto vvhich vvhen the people is once put by their Apostles, they must neuer by any persuasion of men alter the same, nor take of man or Angel, any nevv doctrine or Analogie of faith, as the Protestants call it.

The doctrine of our first Apostles.

23. The grace of God, life euerlasting.) The sequele of speache required, that as he said, death or damnation is the stipend of sinne, so life euerlasting is the stipend of iustice. and so it is, and in the same sense he spake in the last chapter: *that as sinne reigneth to death, so grace reigneth by iustice to life euerlasting.* but here he changed the sentence somevvhat, calling life euerlasting *grace,* rather then *revvard:* because the merites by vvhich vve attaine vnto life, be al of Gods gift and grace. *August. Ep. 105 ad Sixtum.*

Life euerlasting a stipend, and yet grace.

CHAP. VII.

Our former husband (sinne) vvith his lavv, is dead in Baptisme: and novv vve are maried to an other husband (to Christ) to bring forth children to God, that is, good vvorkes. 7 And hovv the Lavv being good, vvas yet to vs the lavv of sinne and death, because concupiscence reigned in vs. 17 But novv by Baptisme grace reigneth in vs. though also concupiscence doth remaine and tempt vs still.

1 ARE you ignorant brethren (for I speake to them that knovv the Lavv) that the Lavv hath dominion ouer a man as long time as he liueth? 2 † for *the vvoman that is vnder a husband: ∷ her husband liuing is bound to the lavv. but if her husband be dead, she is loosed from the lavv of her husband. 3 † Therfore her husband liuing, she shal be called an aduouteresse if she be vvith an other man: but if her husband be dead, she is deliuered from the lavv of her husband: so that she is not an aduouteresse if she be

* 1. Cor. 7, 39.

∷ Nothing but death dissolueth the band betvvixt man & vvife: though for fornication one may depart from an others companie. therfore to mary againe is aduoutrie, during the life of the partie separated.

:: Being novv baptised and dead to sinne, & engraffed in Christs mystical body, you are discharged of the Lavv of Moyses, and are free in Christ.

vvith an other man. † Therfore my brethren :: you also are 4 made dead to the Lavv by the body of Christ: that you may be an other mans vvho is risen againe from the dead, that vve may fructifie to God. † For vvhen vve vvere in the flesh, 5 the passions of sinnes, that vvere by the Lavv, did vvorke in our members, to fructifie vnto death. † but novv vve are 6 loosed from the lavv of death, vvherein vve vvere deteined: c in so much vve serue in :: nevvnesse of spirit, and not in the oldnes of the letter.

:: By Baptisme vve haue not Christes iustice imputed to vs, but an invvard nevvnesse of spirit giuen vs and resident in vs.

c ὥστε δου-λεύειν

† Vvhat shal vve say then? is the Lavv sinne? God for- 7 bid. But sinne I did not knovv, but by the Lavv. for concu-piscēce I knevv not, vnlesse the lavv did say: "*Thou shalt not couet.* † But :: occasion being taken, sinne by the commaundement 8 vvrought in me al cōcupiscence. For vvithout the Lavv sinne vvas dead. † And I liued vvithout the Lavv sometime. But 9 vvhen the commaundement vvas come, sinne reuiued. † And 10 I vvas dead: and the commaundement, that vvas vnto life, the same to me vvas found to be vnto death. † For sinne 11 taking occasion by the commaundement, seduced me, and by it killed me. † Therfore * the Lavv in deede is holy, and the 12 commaundement holy, and iust, and good.

Exo. 20, 17. Deu. 5, 21.

:: Sinne or concupiscēce vvhich vvas a sleepe before, vvas vvakened by prohibition, the Lavv not being the cause thereof, nor giuing occasion therevnto, but occasion being taken by our corrupt nature to resist that vvhich vvas commaunded.

1. Tim. 1, 8.

† That thē vvhich is good, to me vvas it made death? God 13 forbid. but sinne, that it may appeare sinne, by the good thing vvrought me death: that sinne might become sinning aboue measure by the cōmaundemēt. † For vve knovv that the Law 14 is spiritual, but I am carnal, sold vnder sinne. † For "that vvhich 15 I vvorke, I vnderstand not. for" not that vvhich I vvil, the same do I: but vvhich I hate, that I doe. † And if that vvhich 16 I vvil not, the same I doe: I cōsent to the Lavv, that it is good.

† But novv, not I vvorke it any more, but the sinne that 17 dvvelleth in me. † For I know that there dvvelleth not in me, 18 that is to say, in my flesh, good. For to vvil, is presēt vvith me, but to accomplish that vvhich is good, I finde not. † For 19 "not the good vvhich I vvil, that doe I: but the euil" vvhich I vvil not, that I doe. † And if that vvhich I vvil not, the 20 same I doe: novv not I vvorke it, but the sinne that dvvel-leth in me. † I finde therfore, the Lavv, to me hauing a vvil 21 to doe good, that euil is present vvith me. † For I am de- 22 lighted vvith the lavv of God according to the invvard man: † but I see an other lavv in my members, repugning to the 23 lavv of my minde, and captiuing me in the lavv of sinne that is

The Epistle in a Votiue Masse for sinnes.

24 is in my members. † Vnhappie man that I am, vvho ſhal 25 deliuer me from the body of this death? † The grace of God by IESVS Chriſt our Lord. ⊣ Therfore I my ſelf " vvith the minde [c] ſerue the lavv of God, but vvith the fleſh, the lavv of ſinne.

c δουλεύω

ANNOTATIONS
CHAP. VII.

7. *Thou ſhalt not couet.*) It is not the habitual concupiſcence or infirmitie of our nature or ſenſual deſire or inclination to euil, coueting againſt the ſpirit, that is forbidden properly in this precept: but the conſent of our reaſon and minde vnto it, to obey and folovv the luſtes thereof, that is a ſinne and prohibited.

Actual concupiſcence forbidden, not habitual.

15. *That vvhich I vvorke.*) This being vnderſtood of S. Paul him ſelf or any other iuſt perſon, the ſenſe is, that the fleſh and inferiour part ſtirreth vp diuerſe diſordered motions and paſſions or perturbations againſt the minde, and vpon ſuch a ſoden ſometimes inuadeth the ſame, that before it attēdeth, or reaſon can gather it ſelf to deliberate, mā is in a ſort (though vnvvittingly) entangled. Vvhich as ſoone as it is perceiued, being of the iuſt condemned, reiected, and reſiſted, neuer maketh him a ſinner.

Soden inuoluntarie motions are no ſinne.

15. *Not that vvhich I vvil*) He meaneth not, that he can do no good that he vvilleth or deſireth, or that he is euer forced to do that vvhich his vvill agreeth not vnto: but that by reaſon of the forcibleneſſe of concupiſcence, vvhereof he can not rid him ſelf during life, he can not accompliſh al the deſires of his ſpirit and minde, according as he ſaith to the Galatians, *The fleſh coueteth againſt the ſpirit, and the ſpirit againſt the fleſh, that not vvhatſoeuer you vvill, you can do.*

G. 5, 17.

Concupiſcence taketh not avvay free vvil.

19. *Not the good vvhich I vvill.*) So may the iuſt alſo be forced by the rage of concupiſcence or ſenſual appetite, to do or ſuffer many things in his inferiour part or external members, vvhich his vvill conſenteth not vnto. And ſo long it is ſo farre from ſinne, that (as * S. Auguſtine ſaith) he neede neuer ſay to God, *forgiue vs our ſinnes*, for the ſame. for, ſinne is voluntarie, and ſo be not theſe paſſions.

ep. ad Aſelicum 200.

Sinne is voluntarie, and otherwiſe it is no ſinne.

19. *Which I vvil not.*) It maketh not any thing againſt free vvill that the Apoſtle ſaith, that good men do or ſuffer ſometimes in their bodies, that vvhich the vvill agreeth not vnto: but it proueth plainely free vvil. becauſe the proper act thereof, that is, to vvill or nill, to conſent or diſſent, is euer (as you may ſee here) free in it ſelf: though there may be internal or external force to ſtay the members of a man, that they obey not in euery act, that vvhich the vvill commaundeth or preſcribeth. And therfore that is neuer imputed to mā vvhich he doth in his external or internal faculties, vvhen vvil concurreth not. Yea aftervvard (v, 20) the Apoſtle ſaith, *Non ego operor*, man doeth not that vvhich is not done by his vvill: vvhich doth moſt euidently proue free vvill.

25. *With the minde, vvith the fleſh.*) Nothing done by concupiſcence (vvhich the Apoſtle here calleth ſinne) vvherevnto the ſpirit, reaſon, or minde of man conſenteth not, can make him guilty before God. Neither can the motions of the fleſh in a iuſt man euer any vvhit deefile the operatiōs of his ſpirit, as the Lutherans do hold: but make them often more meritorious, for the continual combat that he hath vvith them. for it is plaine that the operations of the fleſh and of the ſpirit do not concurre together to make one acte, as they imagine: the Apoſtle concluding cleane contrarie, That in minde he ſerueth the Lavv of God, in fleſh the lavv of ſinne, that is to ſay, concupiſcence.

Concupiſcence defileth not a iuſt mans actiōs as the Lutherās ſay.

CHAP. VIII.

That novv after Baptiſme vve are no more in ſtate of damnation, becauſe by the grace vvhich vve haue receiued, vve are able to fulfil the Lavv: vnles vve do vvilfully giue the dominion againe to concupiſcence. 18 Then (becauſe of the perſecutions that then vvere) he comforteth and exhorteth them vvith many reaſons.

THERE

HERE is novv therfore no damnation 1 to them that are in Christ IESVS: that walke not according to the flesh. † For the 2 lavv of the spirit of life in Christ IESVS, hath deliuered me from the lavv of sinne and of death. † For that vvhich vvas 3 impossible to the Lavv, in that it vvas vveakened by the flesh: God sending his sonne in the similitude of the flesh of sinne, euen of sinne damned sinne in the flesh, † that :: the iustification of the lavv might be ful- 4 filled in vs, vvho vvalke not according to the flesh, but according to the spirit. † For they that are according to the 5 flesh, are affected to the things that are of the flesh, but they that are according to the spirit: are affected to the things that are of the spirit. † For the vvisedom of the flesh, is death: 6 but the vvisedom of the spirit, life and peace. † Because the 7 vvisedom of the flesh, is "an enemie" to God: for to the law of God it is not subiect, neither can it be. † And they that are 8 in the flesh, can not please god. † But you are not in the flesh, 9 but in the spirit, yet if the Spirit of God dvvel in you. But if any man haue not the Spirit of Christ, the same is not his. † But if Christ be in you: the body in deede is dead because 10 of sinne, but the spirit liueth because of iustification. † And 11 if the Spirit of him that raised vp IESVS from the dead, dvvel in you: he that raised vp IESVS CHRIST from the dead, shal quicken also your mortal bodies, because of his Spirit dvvelling in you. † Therfore brethren, vve are detters: not to the 12 flesh, to liue according to the flesh. † For if you liue accor- 13 ding to the flesh, you shal die. but if by the spirit, you mortifie the deedes of the flesh, you shal liue. † For vvhosoeuer 14 :: are ledde by the spirit of God, they are the sonnes of God. † For *you haue not receiued the spirit of seruitude againe in 15 feare: but *you haue receiued the spirit of adoption of sonnes, vvherein vve crie: Abba, (father). † For" the Spirit him self, 16 giueth testimonie to our spirit, that we are the sonnes of God. 17 † And if sonnes, heires also: heires truly of God, and coheires of Christ: ‡ " yet if vve suffer vvith him, that vve may be also glorified vvith him.

† For I thinke that the passions of this time are not" con- 18 digne to the glorie to come that shal be reuealed in vs. † For 19 the expectation of the creature, expecteth the reuelation of the

:: This conuinceth against the Churches aduersaries, that the lavv, that is, gods cōmaundemēts may be kept, & that the keeping thereof is iustice, & that in christian men that is fulfilled by Christs grace vvhich by the force of the Lavv could neuer be fulfilled.

The Epistle vpō the 8 Sunday after Pentecost.

:: He meaneth not that the Childrē of God be violently cōpelled against their vvilles, but that they be svveetly dravvē, moued, or induced to do good. *Aug. Enchirid. c. 64. De verb. Do. ser. 43 c. 7. et de verb. Apost. ser. 13 c. 11. 12.*

The Epistle vpō the 4 Sunday after Pentecost, and for many Martyrs.

" *enmitie*

2. Tim. 1, 7, Gal. 4, 5.

condignæ ad gloriam

20 the sonnes of God. † For the creature is made subiect to vanitie, not vvilling, but for him that made it subiect in hope: 21 † because the creature also it self shal be deliuered from the seruitude of corruption, into the libertie of the glorie of the 22 children of God. † For vve knovv that euery creature gro-23 neth, and trauaileth euen til novv. † And not only it, but vve also our selues hauing the first fruites of the spirit, vve also grone vvithin our selues, expecting the adoption of the 24 sonnes of God, the redemption of our body. ⊣ † For ″by hope vve are saued. But hope that is seen, is not hope. for that 25 vvhich a man seeth, vvherfore doth he hope it? † But if vve hope for that vvhich vve see not: vve expect by patience. 26 † And in like maner also the Spirit helpeth our infirmitie. For, vvhat vve should pray as vve ought, vve knovv not: but the Spirit him self requesteth for vs vvith gronings vnspea-27 keable. † And he that searcheth the hartes, knovveth vvhat ″ the Spirit desireth: because according to God he requesteth 28 for the sainctes. † And vve knovv that to them that loue God, al things cooperate vnto good, to such as according to 29 purpose are called to be sainctes. † For vvhom he hath forknowen, he hath also predestinated to be made conformable to the image of his sonne: that he might be the first-borne in 30 many brethren. † And ″ vvhom he hath predestinated: them also he hath called. and vvhom he hath called: them also he hath iustified. and vvhom he hath iustified: them also hath he 31 glorified. † What shal vve then say to these things? If God 32 be for vs, vvho is against vs? † He that spared not also his ovvne sonne, but for vs al deliuered him: hovv hath he not 33 also vvith him giuen vs al things? † Who shal accuse against 34 the elect of God? God that iustifieth. † Who is he that shal condemne? Christ IESVS that died, yea that is risen also againe, vvho is on the right hand of God, vvho also maketh 35 intercession for vs. † Who then shal separate vs from the charitie of Christ? tribulation? or distresse? or famine? or 36 nakednes? or danger? or persecution? or the svvord? († as it is vvritten, *For vve are killed for thy sake al the day: vve are esteemed as sheepe of slaughter.*) † But in al these things we ouercome because 37 38 of him that hath loued vs. [c] † For ″I am sure that neither death, nor life, nor Angels, nor Principalities, nor Povvers, neither 39 things present, nor things to come, neither might, † nor height, nor depth, nor other creature, shal be able to

Ps. 43, 22.

c πέπεισμαι γὰρ

The Epistle for S. Ignatius Febr. 1.

separate vs from the charitie of God vvhich is in Christ IESVS our Lord.

ANNOTATIONS
CHAP. VIII.

The testimonie of the Spirit.

16. *The spirit giueth testimonie.*) This place maketh not for the Heretikes special faith, or their presumptuous certainty that euery one of them is in grace: the testimonie of the Spirit being nothing els, but the invvard good motions, comfort, and contentment, vvhich the children of God do daily feele more and more in their hartes by seruing him: by vvhich they haue as it vvere an attestation of his fauour tovvardes them, vvhereby the hope of their iustification and saluation is much corroborated and strengthened.

Novvithstandig Christs satisfaction and Passion, yet ours also is required.

17. *Yet if they suffer.*) Christes paines or passions haue not so satisfied for al, that Christian men be discharged of their particular suffering or satisfying for eche mans ovvne part: neither be our paines nothing vvorth to the attainement of heauen, because Christ hath done ynough. but quite contrarie: he vvas by his passion exalted to the glorie of heauen: therfore vve by compassion or partaking vvith him in the like passions, shal attaine to be fellovves vvith him in his kingdom.

Al suffering in this life is nothing in comparison of the heauenly glorie: and yet it is meritorious & vvorthy of the same.

Heretical trāslation.

18. *Condigne.*) Our Aduersaries ground hereon, that the vvorkes or sufferances of this life be not meritorious or vvorthy of life euerlasting, vvhere the Apostle saith no such thing, no more then he saith that Christs Passions be not meritorious of his glorie, vvhich I thinke they dare not much auouch in our Sauiours actions. He expresseth onely, that the very afflictions of their ovvne nature, vvhich vve suffer vvith or for him, be but short, mometanie & of no account in comparison of the recompense vvhich vve shal haue in heauen. no more in deede vvere Christes paines of their ovvne nature, compared to his glorie, any vvhit comparable: yet they vvere meritorious or vvorthy of heauen, & so be ours. And therfore to expresse the said cōparison, here he saith, *They are not condigne * to the glorie.* He saith not, *of the glorie*, as the Heretikes falsly trāslate: though the Scripture speaketh so also, vvhen it signifieth only a cōparison, as *Prou. 3.* in the greeke, *Omne pretiosum non est* illa dignū.* S. Augustine, *illi dignum.* S. Hierom, *non valet huic comparari.* that is, No pretious thing is vvorthie of vviedom, or to be compared vvith it. See the like *Eccle. 26, 20. Tob. 9, 2.* But vvhen the Apostle vvil expresse that they are condigne, vvorthy, or meritorious of the glorie, he saith plainely, *That our tribulation vvhich presently is momentanie and light, vvorketh aboue measure exceedingly an eternal vveight of glorie in vs.* The valevv of Christes actions riseth not of the length or greatnes of them in them selues, though so also they passed al mens doings: but of the vvorthines of the person. And so the value of ours also riseth of the grace of our adoption, vvhich maketh those actiōs that of their natures be not meritorious nor ansvverable to the ioyes of heauen in them selues, to be vvorthy of heauen. And they might as vvel proue that the vvorkes of sinne do not demerite damnation. for, sinne in deede for the quantity and nature of the vvorke, is not ansvverable in pleasure to the paine of Hel: but because it hath a departing or an auersion from God, be it neuer so short, it deserueth damnation, because it alvvaies procedeth from the enemy of God, as good vvorkes that be meritorious, procede from the childe of God.

*ad gloriā πρὸς τὴν δόξαν.

* ἄξιον αὐτῆς

2. Cor. 4, 17

Vvhence the merite of vvorkes riseth.

As sometime faith only is named, so els vvhere only hope, and only charitie, as the cause of our saluation.

24. *By hope saued*) That vvhich in other places he attributeth to faith, is here attributed to hope. for vvhensoeuer there be many causes of one thing, the holy vvriters (as matter is ministred and occasion giuen by the doctrine then handled) sometimes referre it to one of the causes, sometime to an other: not by naming one alone, to exclude the other, as our Aduersaries captiously and ignorantly do argue: but at diuers times and in sundrie places to expresse that, vvhich in euery discourse could not, nor needed not to be vttered. In some discourse, faith is to be recommended: in others, charitie: in an other, hope: sometimes, almes, mercie: els vvhere, other vertues. One vvhile, *Euery one that beleeueth, is borne of God. 1 Io. 5, 1.* An other vvhile, *Euery one that loueth, is borne of God. 1 Io. 4, 7.* Sometimes, faith purifieth mans hart. *Act. 15, 9.* And an other time, Charitie remitteth sinnes. *1 Pet. 4, 8.* Of faith it is said, *The iust liueth by faith. Ro. 1, 17.* Of charitie, *We knovv that vve are transferred from death to life, because vve loue &c. 1 Io. 3, 14.*

Scripture abused against the Godhead of the Holy Ghost.

27. *The Spirit desireth.*) Arius and Macedonius old Heretikes had their places to contend vpon, against the Churches sense, as our nevv Maisters novv haue. They abused this text to proue the Holy Ghost not to be God, because he needed not to pray or aske, but he might commaund if he vvere God. Therfore S. Augustine expoundeth it thus, *The Spirit prayeth.* that is, *causeth and teacheth vs to pray, and vvhat to pray or aske.* August. de anima & eius orig li. 4, c. 9. & ep. 121. c. 15.

The doctrine of predestination, hovv to be re-

30. *Whom he hath predestinated.*) Gods eternal foresight, loue, purpose, predestination, and election of his deere children, and in time their calling, iustifying, glorifying by Christ, as al other actes and intentions of his diuine vvil and prouidence tovvardes their saluation, ought to be reuerenced of al men vvith dreadful humilitie, and not to be sought out or disputed on vvith presump-

tuous

tuous boldnes and audacitie. for it is the gulfe that many proud persons, both in this age and alvvaies, haue by Gods iust iudgement perished in, founding thereon most horrible blasphemies against Gods mercie, nature, and goodnes, and diuers damnable errours against mans free vvil, and against al good life and religion. This high conclusion is here set dovvne for vs, that vve may learne to knovv of vvhom vve ought to depend in al our life, by vvhom vve expect our saluatiõ, by vvhose prouidence al our graces, giftes, and vvorkes do stand: by vvhat an euerlasting gratious determination, our redemption, vvhich is in Christ IESVS, vvas designed: & to giue God incessable thankes for our vocation and preferment to the state vve be in, before the Ievves, vvho deserued no better then they, before the light of his mercie shining vpon vs accepted vs, and reiected them. But this said eminent truth of Gods eternal predestination standeth (as vve are bound to beleeue vnder paine of damnation, vvhether vve vnderstand hovv or no) & so S. Augustine in al his diuine vvorkes vvritten of the same (*De gratia & lib. arb. De corrept. & gratia. Ad articulos falsò impositos.*) defendeth, declareth, proueth, and conuinceth, that it doth stand (I say) vvith mans free vvil and the true libertie of his actions, and forceth no man to be either il or good, to sinne or vertue, to saluation or damnatiõ, nor taketh avvay the meanes or nature of merites, and cooperation vvith God to our ovvne and other mens saluation.

uerenced, and vvhat it teacheth vs.

Gods predestition taketh not avvay free Wil.

38. I am sure.) This speache is cõmon in S. Paul according to the latin translation, vvhen he had no other assured knovvledge but by hope: as *Ro. 15, 14. 2 Tim. 1, 5. Heb. 6, 9*: Vvhere the Greeke vvord signifieth only a probable persuasion. And therfore except he meane of him self by special reuelation, or of the predestinate in general, (in vvhich tvvo cases it may stand for the certitude of faith or infallible knovvledge) othervvise that euery particular man should be assured infallibly that him self should be iustified, and not that onely, but sure also neuer to sinne, or to haue the gift of perseuerance, and certaine knovvledge of his predestination: that is a most damnable false illusion and presumption, condemned by the Fathers of the holy Councel of Trent. *Sess. 6. c. 9. 12. 13.*

πέπεισμαι, *Confido. Hier. q. 9 ad Algas.*

No man ordinarily is sure of his saluation, but only in hope.

CHAP. IX.

With a protestation of his sorow for it (lest they should thinke him to reioyce in their perdition) he insinuateth the Iewes to be reprobate, although they come of Abrahams flesh, 6 saying, to be the sonnes of God, goeth not by that, but by Gods grace: 19 considering that al vvere one damned masse. 24 by which grace the Gentils to be made his people: and so the prophets to haue foretold of them both. 30 And the cause hereof to be, that the Gentils submit them selues to the faith of Christ, vvhich the Iewes vvil not.

1 I SPEAKE the verity in Christ, I lie not, my conscience bearing me vvitnes in the holy Ghost, 2 † that I haue great sadnesse & continual sorovv in my hart. 3 † For I vvished, my self to be an ″ anáthema from Christ for my brethren, vvho are my kinsmen according to the flesh, 4 † vvho are Israëlites, vvhose is the adoption of sonnes, and the glorie, and the testament, and the lavv giuing, and [c] the seruice, and the promisses: 5 † vvhose are the fathers, & of vvhom Christ is according to the flesh, vvho is aboue al things God blessed for euer. Amen.

[c] λατρεία,

6 † But not that the vvord of God is frustrate. For, ″not al that are of Israël, they be Israëlites: 7 † nor they that are the seede of Abrahã, al be children: ″*but in Isaac shal the seede be called vnto thee:* † that is to say, not they that are the childrẽ of the flesh, they are the children of God: but they that are the children of the promisse, are esteemed for the seede. 8 † For the vvord of the

Gen. 21, 12.

promisse is this, *According to this time vvil I come: and Sara shal haue a sonne.* † And not only she, But * Rebecca also conceiuing 10 " of one copulation, of Isaac our father. † For vvhen they 11 vvere " not yet borne, nor had done any good or euil (that the purpose of God according to election might stand) † not of vvorkes, but of the caller it vvas said to her: *That* 12 *the elder shal serue the yonger,* † as it is vvritten: *Iacob I loued, but Esau I* 13 *hated.*

Gen. 18, 10.
Gen. 25, 21.
Gen. 25, 23.
Mal. 1, 2.

S. Hierom. q. 10. ad Hedibiam.
Al the epistle surely to the Romanes needeth interpretatiō, and is enwrapped with so great obscurities that to vnderstād it we neede the helpe of the Holy Ghost, who by the Apostle did dictat these same things: but especially this place. Howbeit nothīg pleaseth vs but that which is Ecclesiastical, that is, the sense of the Church.

† Vvhat shal vve say then?" Is there iniquitie vvith God? 14 God forbid. † For to Moyses he saith, *I vvil haue mercie on vvhom* 15 *I haue mercie: and I vvil shevv mercie to vvhom I vvil shevv mercie.* † Ther- 16 fore it is " not of the vviller, nor the runner, but of God that shevveth mercie. † For the Scripture saith to Pharao: *That* 17 " *to this very purpose haue I raised thee, that in thee I may shevv my povver: and that my name may be renovvmed in the vvhole earth.* † Therfore on 18 vvhom he vvil, he hath mercie: and vvhom he vvil, he doth indurate.

Exo. 33, 19.
Exo. 9, 16.

† Thou saiest therfore vnto me: Vvhy doth he yet com- 19 plaine? for vvho resisteth his vvil? † O man, " vvho art 20 thou that doest ansvver God? Doth the vvorke say to him that vvrought it: Vvhy hast thou made me thus? † Or hath 21 not " the potter of clay, povver, of the same masse to make one vessel vnto honour, and an other vnto cōtumelie? † And 22 if God vvilling to shevv vvrath, and to make his might knovven, ∷ susteined in much patience the vessels of vvrath 'apte' to destruction, † that he might shevv the riches of 23 his glorie vpon the vessels of mercie vvhich he prepared vn- to glorie.

∷ That God is not the cause of any mans reprobation or damnation, othervvise then for punishment of his sinnes, he shevveth by that he expecteth al mens amendement vvith great patience, and consequently that they haue also free vvil.

'apted, fitted'

† Vvhom also he hath called, vs, not only of the Ievves, 24 but also of the Gentiles, † as in Osee he saith, *I vvil call that* 25 *vvhich is not my people, my people: and her that vvas not beloued, beloued: and her that hath not obteined mercie, hauing obteined mercie.* † *And it shal be, in* 26 *the place vvhere it vvas said to them, you are not my people: there they shal be called the sonnes of the liuing God.* † And Esaie crieth for Israel, *If the* 27 *number of the children of Israel be as the sand of the sea, the remaines shal be saued.* † *For, consummating a vvord, and abbridging it in equitie: because a* 28 *vvord abbridged shal our Lord make vpon the earth.* † And as Esay fore- 29 told, *Vnles the Lord of Sabaoth had left vs seede: vve had been made like Sodom, and vve had been like as Gomorrha.*

Os. 2, 23.
Os. 1, 10
Es. 10, 22.
Es. 1, 9.

† What shal vve say then? That the Gentiles vvhich pur- 30 sued not after iustice, haue apprehended iustice, but the iustice that is of faith. † But Israel in pursuing the lavv of iu- 31 stice, is not come vnto the lavv of iustice. † Vvhy so? Be- 32 cause

Es.8,14. 28,16.

cause not of faith, but as it vvere of vvorkes. for [c] they haue 33 stombled at the stone of stombling, † as it is vvritten, *Behold I put in Sion a stone of stombling, and a rocke of scandal: and vvhosoeuer beleeueth in him, shal not be confounded.*

c Here vve see that they are the cause of their ovvne damnation by infidelity.

ANNOTATIONS
CHAP. IX.

3. *Anáthema.*] *Anáthema*, by vse of Scripture is either that vvhich by separation from profane vse, and by dedication to God, is holy, dreadful, and not vulgarly to be touched: or contrariewise, that which is reiected, seuered, or abandoned from God, as cursed and detested, and therfore is to be auoided. And in this later sense (according as S. Paul taketh it 1 Cor. 16. *If any loue not our Lord* IESVS CHRIST, *be he Anathema*, that is to say, Avvay vvith him, Accursed be he, Bevvare you company not vvith him) the Church and holy Councels vse the vvord for a curse and excommunication against Heretikes and other notorious offenders and blasphemers. Novv hovv the Apostle, vvishing him self to be Anathema from Christ to saue his Countrie mens soules, did take this vvord, it is a very hard thing to determine. Some thinke, he desired onely to die for their saluation. Others, that being very loth to be kept from the fruition of Christ, yet he could be content to be so still for to saue their soules. Others, that he vvished vvhat malediction or separation from Christ so euer that did not imply the disfauour of God tovvards him, nor take avvay his loue tovvard God. This only is certaine that it is a point of vnspeakable charitie in the Apostles breast, and a paterne to al Bishops and Priests, hovv to loue the saluation of their flocke. As the like vvas vttered by Moyses vvhen he said: *Either forgiue this people, or blot me out of thy booke.*

Anáthema.

In vvhat sense S. Paul vvisheth to be anáthema.

Exo.32,32.

6. *Not al of Israel.*] Though the people of the Ievves vvere many vvaies honoured and priuileged, and namely by Christes taking flesh of them: yet the promis of grace and saluation vvas neither onely made to them, nor to al them that carnally came of them or their fathers: Gods election and mercie depending vpon his ovvne purpose, vvil, and determination, and not tied to any nation, familie, or person.

Gods promis not made to carnal Israel.

7. *But in Isaac.*] The promise made to Abraham vvas not in Ismael, vvho vvas a sonne borne onely by flesh and nature: but in Isaac, vvho vvas a sonne obtained by promisse, faith, and miracle: and vvas a figure of the Churches children borne to God in Baptisme.

Isaac preferred before Ismael.

10. *Of one copulation.*] It is proued also by Gods choosing of Iacob before Esau (vvho vvere not onely brethren by father and mother, but also tvvinnes, and Esau the elder of the tvvo, vvhich according to carnal count should haue had the preeminence) that God in giuing graces folovveth not the temporal or carnal prerogatiues of men or families.

Iacob before Esau.

11. *Not yet borne.*] By the same example of those tvvinnes, it is euident also, that neither nations nor particular persons be elected eternally, or called temporally, or preferred to Gods fauour before others, by their ovvne merites: because God, vvhen he made choise, and first loued Iacob, and refused Esau, respected them both as il, and the one no lesse then the other guilty of damnation for original sinne, vvhich vvas alike in them both. And therfore vvhere iustly he might haue reprobated both, he saued of mercie one. Vvhich one therfore, being as il and as void of good as the other, must hold of Gods eternal purpose, mercie, and election, that he vvas preferred before his brother vvhich vvas elder then him self, and no vvorse them him self. And his brother Esau on the other side hath no cause to complaine, for that God neither did nor suffered any thing to be done tovvards him, that his sinne did not deserue. for although God elect eternally & giue his first grace vvithout al merites, yet he doth not reprobate or hate any man but for sinne, or the foresight thereof.

By the example of Iacob and Esau, is shevved gods mere mercie in the elect, and iustice in the reprobate.

14. *Is there iniquitie?*] Vpon the former discourse that of tvvo persons equal, God calleth the one to mercie, and leaueth the other in his sinne, one might inferre that God vvere vniust and an accepter of persons. To vvhich the Apostle ansvvereth, that God vvere not iust nor indifferent in deede, so to vse the matter vvhere grace or saluation vvere due. As if tvvo men being Christened, both beleeue vvel, & liue vvel: if God should giue heauen to the one, & should damne the other, then vvere he vniust, partial, & forgetful of his promisse: but respecting or taking tvvo, Who both be vvorthy of damnation (as al are before they be first called to mercie) then the matter standeth on mere mercie, and of the giuers vvil and liberalitie, in vvhich case partialitie hath no place. As for example.

That God is not vniust, or an accepter of persons, is declared by familiar examples.

S. Augustines example is of tvvo debters: the one forgiuē all, and the other put to pay all, by the same creditor. *li. de predest. & gra. cap. 4.*

1	Tvvo malefactors being condemned both for one crime, the Prince pardoneth the one, and letteth the lavv procede on the other.	1	So likevvise, God seing al mankind and euery one of the same in a general condemnation, and masse of sinne, in and by Adam, deliuereth some, and not othersome.
2	The theefe that is pardoned, can not attribute his escape to his ovvne deseruings, but to the Princes mercie.	2	Al that be deliuered out of that cōmon damnation, be deliuered by grace and pardon, through the meanes and merits of Christ.
3	The theefe that is executed, can not chalenge the Prince that he vvas not pardoned also: but must acknowledge that he hath his deseruing.	3	Such as be left in the common case of damnation, can not complaine, because they haue their deseruing for sinne.
4	The standers by, must not say, that he vvas executed because the Prince vvould not pardon him. for that vvas not the cause, but his offense.	4	Vve may not say that such be damned, because God did not pardon them, but because they had sinne, and therfore deserued it.
5	If they aske further, vvhy the Prince pardoned not both, or executed not both: the ansvver is, that as mercie is a goodly vertue, so iustice is necessarie and commendable.	5	That some should be damned, and not al pardoned, and other some pardoned rather then al condemned, is agreable to Gods iustice & mercie: both vvhich vertues in Gods prouidence tovvards vs are recommended.
6	But if it be further demaunded vvhy Iohn rather then Thomas vvas executed: or Thomas rather then Iohn pardoned: ansvver, that (the parties being othervvise equal) it hangeth merely and vvholy vpon the Princes vvil and pleasure.	6	That Saul should be rather pardoned them Caiphas (I meane vvhere tvvo be equally euil and vndeseruing) that is onely Gods holy wil and appointment, by vvhich many an vnvvorthy man getteth pardon, but no good or iust or innocent person is euer damned.

Predestination and reprobatiō take not avvay free vvil, neither must any man be retchlesse & desperate.

In al this mercie of God tovvards some, and iustice tovvards other some, both the pardoned vvorke by their ovvne free vvil, and thereby deserue their saluation: and the other no lesse, by their ovvne free vvil, vvithout al necessitie, vvorke vvickednes, & them selues and only of them selues procure their ovvne damnation. Therfore no man may vvithout blasphemie say, or can truely say, that he hath nothing to doe tovvards his owne saluation, but vvil liue, and thinketh he may liue vvithout care or cogitation of his end the one vvay or the other, saying, If I be appointed to be saued, be it so: if I be one designed to damnation, I can not helpe the matter: come vvhat come may. Al these speaches and cogitations are sinful & come of the enemie, and be rather signes of reprobation, then of election. Therfore the good man must vvithout searche of Gods secretes, vvorke his ovvne saluation and (as S. Peter saith) *make his election sure by good vvorkes,* vvith continual hope of Gods mercie, being assured that if he beleeue vvel and doe vvel, he shal haue vvel. for example, if a husband man should say, If God vvil, I shal haue corne ynough: if not, I can not make it, and so neglect to till his ground: he may be sure that he shal haue none, because he wrought not for it. An other man vseth his diligence in tilling and ploughing, and committeth the rest to God, he findeth the fruite of his labours.

2. Pet. 1. 10.

Our election or cōuersion is not of our selues, but of Gods grace and mercie.

16. *Not of the vviller.*] If our election, calling, or first comming to God, lay vvholy or principally vpon our ovvne vvil or vvorkes: or if our vvilling or endeuouring to be good, vvould serue vvithout the helpe and grace of God, as the Pelagians taught, then our election vvere vvholy in our selues, vvhich the Apostle denieth. and then might Pharao and other indurate persons (vvhom God hath permitted to be obstinate, to shevv his povver and iust iudgement vpon them) be conuerted vvhen them selues list, vvithout Gods helpe and assistance: vvhereas vve see the contrarie in al such obstinate offenders, vvhom God for punishment of former sinnes, visiteth not vvith his grace, that by no threates, miracles, nor persuasion, they can be conuerted. Vvherevpon vve may not vvith Heretikes inferre, that man hath not free vvil, or that our vvill vvorketh nothing in our conuersion or comming to God: but this onely, that our vvilling or vvorking of any good to our saluation, commeth of Gods special motion, grace, and assistance, and that it is the secondary cause, not the principall.

17. *To this purpose haue I raised.*] He doth not say, that he hath of purpose raised or set him vp to sinne, or that he vvas the cause of the same in Pharao, or that he intended his damnation directly or absolutely, or any othervvise but in respect of his demerits: but rather (as the Apostle saith straight after in this chapter of such hardened & obstinate offenders) that he vvith long patience & toleration expected his conuersion, and (as S. Chrysostome

interpreteth

interpreteth this word, *Excitaui*) preserued him aliue to repent, vvhom he might iustly haue condemned before. In the 9 of Exodus, vvhence this allegation is, vve reade, *Posui te, I haue put* or *set thee vp*, as here, *I haue raised thee.* that is to say, I haue purposely aduanced thee to be so great a king, and chosen thee out to be a notorious example both of the obdurate obstinacie that is in such vvhom I haue for so great sinnes forsaken, and also to shevv to the vvorld, that no obstinacie of neuer so mightie offenders can resist me to doe any thing vvhich shal not fall to my glorie. Vvhich is no more to say, but that God often for the punishment of Nations, and to shevv his iustice and glorie, giueth vvicked Princes vnto them, and indueth them vvith povver and al prosperitie, and taking his grace from them vpon their deserts, hardeneth their hartes so, as they vvithstand and contemne God, and afflict his people. in vvhose end and fall, either temporal or eternal, at the length God vvil euer be glorified. Neither vvould he either raise or suffer any such, or giue them povver and prosperitie in this life, vvherevpon he knovveth they vvil be vvorse, but that he can vvorke al that to his honour and glorie. mary, that he vseth not such rigorous iustice on al that deserue it, that is his great grace and mercie. And that he exerciseth his iustice vpon some certaine persons, rather then vpon other some of equal deserts, that lieth vvholy vpon his vvil, in vvhose iudgements there be many things secrete, but nothing vniust.

Exo. 9, 16.

In vvhat sense, God raised vp Pharao &c.

20. Who art thou?] Here the Apostle staieth the rashnes and presumption of such poore vvormes, as take vpon them to question vvith God of their election or reprobation: as certaine impious Heretikes of our time haue done, setting out bookes farsed vvith most blasphemous and erroneous doctrine cōcerning this high and hidden mysterie, and haue giuen occasion to the ignorant vvhich alvvaies be curious, to iangle, and perniciously to erre in these things, that are impossible to be vnderstood of any, or vvel thought of, but of the obedient and humble.

Heretical bookes concerning predestination.

21. The potter.] This example of the pot and potter reacheth no further but to declare, that the creature may not reason vvith God his maker, vvhy he giueth not one so great grace, as an other, or vvhy he pardoneth not one as vvel as an other: no more then the chamber pot may chalenge the Potter vvhy he vvas not made a drinking pot, as vvel as an other. And therfore the Heretikes that extend this similitude to proue that man hath no free vvil no more then a peece of clay, doe vntruely and deceitfully apply the example. specially vvhen vve may see expresly in the booke of Exodus, that Pharao notvvithstāding his indurate hart, had free vvil: vvhere both it is said, *He vvould not dismisse the people:* and, *He indurated his oWne hart him self. Exo. c. 8, 15.* and (in the *Hebrue*) *v. 32. & c. 9. 35. 1 Reg. 6, 6.* And this Apostle also vvriteth, that ★ a man may *cleanse him self* from the filthy, and so become a vessel of honour in the house of God.

The example of the pot and the potter.

2 Tim. 2, 21.

CHAP. X.

The Lavv vvas not (as the Ievves ignorant zeale supposed) for them to iustifie them selues by it (considering that they could not fulfil it:) but to bring them to Christ, to beleeue in him, and so for his sake to be iustified by the grace of God: 5 according to Moyses saying, and the Apostles preaching: 11 that so the Gentils also (according to the Prophets) hearing and beleeuing might come to iustice: the Ievves in the meane time (though inexcusably) remaining incredulous.

1 BRETHREN, the vvil of my hart surely and praier to God, is for them vnto saluation. 2 † For I giue them testimonie that they haue zeale of God, but not according to knovvledge. 3 † For, not knovving "the iustice of God, & seeking to establish their ovvne, they haue not been subiect to the iustice of God. 4 † For, :: the end of the Law is Christ: vnto iustice to euery one that beleeueth.

:: The Lavv vvas not giuē to make a mā iust or perfect by it self, but to brīg vs to Christ to be iustified by him.

:: The iustice of the Law of Moyses Went no further of it self, but to saue a man from the temporal death and punishmét prescribed to the trásgressors of the same.

beleeueth. † for Moyses vvrote, :: that, the iustice vvhich is 5 of the Lavv, *the man that hath done it, shal liue in it.* † But " the iustice 6 vvhich is of faith, saith thus, *Say not in thy hart, Vvho shal ascend into heauen?* that is to bring Christ dovvne. † *Or vvho descendeth into* 7 *the depth?* that is to call Christ againe from the dead. † But 8 vvhat saith the Scripture? *The vvord is nigh, in thy mouth, and in thy hart.* this is the vvord of faith vvhich vve preach. † For if 9 thou confesse vvith thy mouth our Lord IESVS, and in thy hart beleeue that God hath raised him vp from the dead, thou shalt be saued. † For vvith the hart vve beleeue vnto iustice: 10 but vvith the mouth confession is made to saluation.

Leu. 18, 5. Deu. 30, 12.

The Epistle vpó S. Andrevves day, Nouemb. 30.

† For the Scripture saith: *Vvhosoeuer beleeueth in him, shal* 11 *not be confounded.* † For there is no distinction of the Iew 12 and the Greeke: for one is Lord of al, riche tovvard al that inuocate him. † *For euery one* :: *vvhosoeuer shal inuocate the name of our* 13 *Lord, shal be saued.* † " Hovv then shal they inuocate in vvhom 14 they haue not beleeued? Or hovv shal they beleeue him vvhom they haue not heard? And hovv shal they heare without a preacher? † But hovv shal they preach " vnles they 15 be sent? as it is vvritten: *Hovv beautiful are the feete of them that euangelize peace, of them that euangelize good things?* † But al :: do not obey 16 the Gospel. For Esay saith, *Lord, vvho hath beleeued the hearing of vs?* † Faith then, is by hearing: and hearing is by the vvord of 17 Christ. † But I say, haue they not heard? And certes *into al the* 18 *earth hath the sound of them gone forth: and vnto the endes of the vvhole vvorld the vvordes of them.* ⊣

Es. 28.16

:: To beleeue in him & to inuocate him, is to serue him With al loue and sincere affectió. Al that so doe, shal doubtlesse be saued & shal neuer be confounded.

Ioel. 2, 32.

Es. 52, 7.

Es. 53, 1.

:: We see then that it is in a mans free Wil to beleeue or not to beleeue, to obey or disobey the Gospel or truth preached.

Ps. 18, 5.

† But I say, hath not Israel knovven? Moyses first saith, 19 *I vvil bring you to emulation in that vvhich is not a nation: in a folish nation, I vvil driue you into anger.* † But Esay is bold, and saith, *I vvas* 20 *found of them that did not seeke me: openly I appeared to them " that asked not of me.* † But to Israel he saith, *Al the day haue I spred my handes to a people* 21 *that beleeueth not, and contradicteth me.*

Deu. 32, 21. Es. 65, 1. Es. 65, 2.

ANNOTATIONS
CHAP. X.

Gods iustice, & the Ievves ovvne iustice.

3. *The iustice of God.*] The iustice of God, is that vvhich God giueth vs through Christ. the Ievves ovvne or proper iustice, is that vvhich they had or chalenged to haue of them selues and by their ovvne strength, holpen onely by the knovvledge of the Lavv vvithout the helpe or grace of Christ.

Iustice of faith.

6. *The iustice of faith*] The iustice vvhich is of faith, reacheth to the life to come, making man assured of the truth of such Articles as concerne the same. as, of Christs Ascension to heauen, of his Descending to Hel, of his comming dovvne to be Incarnate, and his Resurrection and returne againe to be glorified: by vvhich his actions vve be pardoned, iustified, and saued, as by the Lavv vve could neuer be.

8. The

8. The vvord of faith.] The vvord of faith is the vvhole Lavv of Christ, concerning both life and doctrine, grounded vpon this, that Christ is our Sauiour, & that he is risen againe. Vvhich point (as al other) must both be beleeued in hart, and also be confessed by mouth. for though a man be iustified invvardly vvhen he hath the vertues of faith, hope, and charitie from God: yet if occasion be giuen, he is also bound to confesse vvith his mouth, and by al his external actions, vvithout shame or feare of the vvorld, that vvhich he invvardly beleeueth: or els he can not be saued. Vvhich is against certaine ⋆ old Heretikes that taught, a man might say or doe vvhat he vvould, for feare or danger, so that he kept his faith in hart.

Open cōfession & protestation of our faith is somtime necessarie.

Euseb. li. 6 c. 31 histor. Eccles.

14. Hovv shal they inuocat?] This maketh not (as Heretikes pretend) against inuocatiō of Saincts: the Apostle saying nothing els, but that they can not inuocate Christ as their Lord and Maister, in vvhom they do not beleeue, and vvhom they neuer heard of. For he speaketh of Gentils or Pagans, vvho could not inuocate him, vnlesse they did first beleeue in him. To the due inuocation of Christ, vve must knovv him and our duties to him. And so is it true also that vve can not pray to our B. Ladie nor any Sainct in heauen, til vve beleeue and knovv their persons, dignitie, and grace, and trust that they can helpe vs. But if our aduersaries thinke that vve can not inuocate them, because vve can not beleeue in them: let them vnderstand that the Scripture vseth also this speach, to beleeue in men: and it is the very Hebrevv phrase, vvhich they should not be ignorant of that bragge thereof so much. *Exod. 14, 31. They beleeued in God and in Moyses.* and *2 Paral. 20, 20.* in the Hebrevv. *Ep. ad Philem. v. 5.* And the ancient fathers did read in the Crede indifferently, *I beleeue in the Catholike Church.* and, *I beleeue the Catholike Church. Conc. Nicen. apud Epiphan. in fine Ancorat. Hieron. contr. Lucif. Cyril. Hierosf. Cathec. 17.*

The place alleaged against inuocatiō of Saincts, ansvvered.

15. vnlesse they be sent.) This place of the Apostle inuincibly condemneth al the preachings, vvritings, ordinances, innouations and vsurpations of Church, pulpit, & vvhatsoeuer our nevv Euangelists haue intruded them selues and entered into by the vvindovv: shevving that they be euery one from the highest to the lovvest, false prophets, running and vsurping, being neuer lavvfully called. Vvhich is so euident in the Heretikes of our daies that the Caluinists confesse it in them selues, and say that there is an exception to be made in them, because they found the state of the Church interrupted.

Preachers not lavvfully called nor sent.

Confes. des Eglis. de France.

20. That asked not.] That Christ vvas found of those that neuer asked after him, it proueth that the first grace and our first iustification is vvithout merites. That God called so continually and earnestly by his Prophets and by other his signes and vvonders, vpon the Ievves, and they vvithstood it: free vvil is proued, and that God vvould haue men saued, and that they be the cause of their ovvne damnation them selues.

The first iustification of mere grace.

Free vvil.

CHAP. XI.

Not al the Ievves vvere reprobate, but some electe: and they by grace obtained iustice, the rest (according to the Prophets) being excecated. 11 Against vvhom notvvithstanding the Christian Gentils (to vvhom by that occasion Christ is come) must not insult: but rather feare euery man him self to be likevvise cut of the tree (vvhich is the Catholike Church) 25 and knovv that vvhen al the Gentils are brought into the Church, then (about the end of the vvorld) shal the multitude of the Ievves also come in: 33 according to the disposition of the vvonderful vvisedom of God.

1 I Say then: Hath God reiected his people? God forbid. for I also am an Israëlite, of the seede of Abraham, of the tribe of 2 Ben-iamin. † God hath not reiected his people vvhich he foreknevve. Or knovv you not in Elias vvhat the Scripture saith: hovv he requesteth God against Israël? 3 † *Lord, they haue slaine thy Prophets, they haue digged dovvne thine altares: and* 4 *I am left alone, and they seeke my life.* † But vvhat saith the diuine

3. reg. 19. 10.

ansvver vnto him? *I haue left me seuen* " *thousand men, that haue not bovved their knees to* c*Baal?* † So therfore at this time also, there 5 are remaines saued according to the election of grace. † And 6 if by grace: " not novv of vvorkes. othervvise grace novv is not grace.

c The Heretikes adde here also, *Image*, to the text. as *Act. 19, 35.*

† Vvhat then? that vvhich Israel sought, the same he hath 7 not obtained: but the election hath obtained: and the rest vvere blinded. † as it is vvritten: " *God hath giuen them the spirit* 8 *of compunction: eies, that they may not see: and eares, that they may not heare: vntil this present day.* † And Dauid saith: *Be their table made for a snare* 9 *and for a trappe and for a scandal and for a retribution vnto them.* † *Be their eies* 10 *darkened, that they may not see: and their backe make thou alvvaies crooked.* † I say then, haue they so stombled, ∴ that they should fall? 11 God forbid. but by their offence, saluation is to the Gentils, that they may emulate them. † And if the offence of them 12 be the riches of the vvorld, and the diminution of them ∴ the riches of the Gentils: hovv much more the fulnesse of them?

Es. 6, 9.

Ps. 68, 23

∴ The Ievves are not reiected vvholy & incurably for euer: but for a part, and for a time suffered to fall. Which God did turne to the Gentils general good.

∴ If God could and did turne their fall and sinne into the good of the Gentils, much more vvil he vvorke good of their general conuersion, vvhich shalbe at length the accomplishmēt of the Church consisting of both the Nations.

† For to you Gentils I say, as long verely as I am the 13 Apostle of the Gentils, I vvil honour my ministerie, † if by 14 any meanes I may prouoke my flesh to emulation, and may saue some of them. † For if the losse of them be the recon- 15 ciliation of the vvorld: vvhat shal the receiuing be, but life from the dead? † And if the first fruite be holy, the masse also: 16 and if the roote be holy, the boughes also. † And if some 17 of the boughes be broken, and thou vvhereas thou vvast a vvilde oliue, art graffed in them, and art made partaker of the roote and of the fatnesse of the oliue, † glorie not against the 18 boughes. And if thou glorie: not thou bearest the roote, but the roote thee. † Thou saiest then: The boughes vvere 19 broken, that I might be graffed in. † Vvel: " because of 20 incredulitie they vvere broken, but thou by faith doest stand: be not to highly vvise, but ∴ feare. † For if God hath not 21 spared the natural boughes: lest perhaps he vvil not spare thee neither. † See then the goodnes and the seueritie of God: vpō 22 them surely that are fallen, the seueritie: but vpon thee the goodnes of God, if thou abide in his goodnesse, othervvise thou also shalt be cut of. † But they also, if they do not 23 abide in incredulitie, shal be graffed in. for God is able to graffe them in againe. † For if thou vvast cut out of the 24 natural vvild oliue, and contrarie to nature vvast graffed into the good oliue: hovv much more they that are according to

∴ We see that he vvhich standeth by faith, may fall from it, and therfore must liue in feare, and not in the vaine presumption and securitie of the Heretikes.

25 nature, shal be graffed into their ovvne oliue? † For I vvil not haue you ignorant, brethren, of this mysterie (that you be not vvise in your selues) that blindnes in part hath chaunced in Israël, vntil the fulnes of the Gentiles might enter:

Esa. 59, 20.

26 † and so al Israël might be saued, as it is vvritten: *There shal come out of Sion, he that shal deliuer, and shal auert impietie from Iacob.* 27 † *And this to them the testament from me:* vvhen I shal haue taken avvay their sinnes. 28 † "According to the Gospel in deede enemies for you: but according to the election, most deere for the fathers. 29 † for vvithout repentance are the giftes and the vocation of God. 30 † for "as you also sometime did not beleeue God, but novv haue obteined mercie because of their incredulitie: 31 † so these also novv haue not beleeued, for your mercie, that they also may obteine mercie. 32 † For God hath "cōcluded al into incredulitie, that he may haue mercie on al.

The Epistle vpō Trinitie Sunday.

33 † "O depth of the riches of the vvisedom and of the knowledge of God: hovv incomprehensible are his iudgements, and his vvaies vnsearcheable? 34 † for * vvho hath knovven the minde of our Lord? or vvho hath been his cōseler? 35 † Or vvho hath first giuen to him, and retribution shal be made him? 36 † For of him, and by him, and in him are al things: to him be glorie for euer. Amen. ⊣

Esa. 40, 13.

ANNOTATIONS
CHAP. XI.

4. *Seuen thousand.*] The Heretikes alleage this place and example very impertinently to proue that the Church may be vvholy secrete, hid, or, vnknovven. for though the faithful vvere forced to keepe close in that persecution of Achab and Iezabel, vvhich vvas onely in the kingdom of the ten tribes, that is, of Israel: yet at the very same time, in Hierusalem and al the kingdom of Iuda, the external vvorship and profession of faith vvas open to al the vvorld, and vvel knovven to Elias & the faithful, so many, that * the very souldiars only vvere numbered aboue ten hundred thousand. besides that there is a great difference betvvene the Christian Church and the Ievves, ours resting vpon better promisses then theirs. And vve vvil not put the Protestants to proue that there vvere 7000 of their Sect, vvhen their nevv Elias Luther began: but let them proue that there were seuē, or any one, either then or in al ages before him, that vvas in al pointes of his beleefe. Heretikes there vvere before him, as Iouinian, Vigilantius, Heluidius, Vvicleffe &c. and vvith him, Zuinglius, Caluin, &c. Vvho beleeued as he did in some things, but not in al.

2 Par. 17.

Gods ansWer to Elias of 7000, maketh nothīg for the Protestants inuisible Church.

6. *Not novv of vvorkes.*] If saluation be attributed to good vvorkes done of nature vvithout faith & Gods helpe, the same can not be of grace. for such vvorkes exclude grace, fauour, and mercie: and chalenge onely of dette, and not of gift. Therfore take heede here of the Heretikes exposition, that vntruely exclude Christian mens vvorkes from necessity or merite of saluation, vvhich are done vvith and by Gods grace, and therfore euidētly consist vvith the same, and be ioyned vvith Gods grace as causes of our saluation. Our Aduersaries are like il Potecaries, euer taking *quid pro quo*, either of ignorance, or of intent to deceiue the simple.

What Workes are not, & What are the cause of saluation.

 5. *God*

God is not author of sinne.

8. God hath giuen.] It doth not signifie his vvorking or action, but his permission. *Chrys. ho. 19 in ep. Ro.* And S. Augustine saith, not by putting malice into them, but by not imparting his grace vnto them, and that through their ovvne deserts alvvaies, and their ovvne willes euer properly working the same. See *Annot. Mat. c. 13, 14. Ro. c. 1, 24.*

Aug. Ep. 105. ad Sixtum.

A paraphrastical explication of the text, concerning the Iewes and Gentils, their standing, falling, rising againe, &c.

20. Because of incredulity.] He represseth the pride of the Gentils vaunting them selues of their receiuing, and of the Ievves reiection, namely in that they thought the Ievves to be forsaken for no other cause, but that they might come into their roomes: declaring that the direct and proper cause of their forsaking, vvas their incredulity, exhorting the Gentiles to bevvare of the same, because they may fall as vvel as the other, and that God is as like to execute iustice against them as against the Ievves, as he hath done in many nations falling to heresie.

28. According to the Gospel.] In respect, or, as concerning beleefe in Christ and receiuing the Gospel, they are Gods enemies: by occasion of vvhich their incredulity, the Gentiles found mercie: othervvise in respect of his special election of that nation, and the promisses made to the Patriarches, the Ievves are deere to him still. for God neuer promiseth but he performeth, nor repenteth him self of the priuileges giuen to that nation.

30. For as you.] As the Gentiles vvhich before beleeued not, found mercie and came to faith, vvhen the Ievves did fall: so the Ievves not novv beleeuing, vvhen al the Gentils haue obtained mercie, shal in the end of the vvorld by Gods disposition obtaine grace and pardon as the Gentiles haue done.

32. Concluded al.] That so God taking al Nations and al men in sinne (vvhich they fell into, not by his drift or causing, but of their ovvne free vvil) may of his mercie call and conuert vvhom and in vvhat order he vvill: and the parties haue no cause to bragge of their deseruings: but both countries and particular men may referre their eternal election and their first calling and conuersion to Christ, and to his mercie only: no vvorkes vvhich they had before in their incredulity, deseruing any such thing, though their vvorkes aftervvard proceding of faith and grace doe merite heauen.

How far to deale and to know, in the doctrine of predestination.

33. O depth] The Apostle concludeth that no man ought to search further into Gods secrete and vnsearcheable counsels of the vocation of the Gentils, and reiecting the Ievves, othervvise then this, that al vvhich be reiected, for their sinnes be iustly reiected: and al that be saued, by Gods great mercie and Christs grace be saued. And vvhosoeuer seeketh among the people to spred contagion of curiosity by seeking further after things past mans & Angels reache, they ouerreache & ouerthrovv them selues. If thou vvilt be saued, beleeue, obey the Church, feare God and keepe his commaundements: that is thy part and euery mans els. Thou maist not examine vvhether thou be predestinate or reprobate, nor seeke to knovv the vvaies of Gods secrete iudgement tovvard thy self or other men. It is the common enemy of our soules, that in this vnhappy time hath opened blasphemous tongues, and directed the proude pennes of Caluin, Beza, Verone, and such reprobates, to the discussing of such particulars, to the perdition of many a simple man, and specially of yong Scholers in Vniuersities, which with lesse studie may learne to be provvd and curious, then to be humble, wise, and obedient.

The Heretikes writings of predestination.

The second part of this Epistle, moral.

CHAP. XII.

He exhorteth them to mortification of the body, 2 to renouation of the minde, 3 to keeping of vnitie by humilitie, 6 to the right vsing of their gifts and functions, 9 to many other good actions, 17 and specially to louing of their enemies.

The Epistle vpō the 1 Sunday after the Epiphanie.

I BESECH you therfore brethren by the 1 mercie of God, * that you exhibite your bodies " a liuing host, holy, pleasing God, your reasonable seruice. † And be not conformed 2 to this vvorld: but be reformed in the newnes of your minde, * that you may proue vvhat the good, and acceptable, and perfect vvil of God is. † for I say by the 3 grace that is giuen me, to al that are among you, ∴ not to be more

Phil. 4, 18.

Eph. 5, 17. 1. Th. 4, 3.

∴ None must presume to medle aboue the measure of gods gift, or out of the compasse of his state and vocation.

more vvise then behoueth to be vvise, but to be vvise vnto sobrietie, * to euery one as God hath deuided the measure of
4 faith. † For as in one body vve haue many members, but al
5 the members haue not one action: † so vve being many, are
6 one body in Christ, & eche one an others members. ⊣ † And hauing giftes, according to the grace that is giuen vs, differēt,
7 either ∷ prophecie " according to the rule of faith, † or mini-
8 sterie in ministring, or he that teacheth in doctrine, † he that exhorteth in exhorting, he that giueth in simplicitie, he that ruleth in carefulnes, he that shevveth mercie in cheerefulnes.
9 † c Loue vvithout simulation. Hating euil. cleauing to good.
10 † Louing the charitie of the brotherhod one toward an other.
11 Vvith honour preuenting one an other. † In carefulnes not
12 slouthful. In spirit feruent. Seruing our Lord. † Reioycing in
13 hope. Patient in tribulation. Instant in praier. † Communicating to the 'necessities' of the saincts. Pursuing hospitalitie.
14 † Blesse them that persecute you: blesse, and ∷ curse not. † To
15 reioyce vvith them that reioyce, to vveepe vvith them that
16 vveepe. † Being of one minde one tovvard an other. Not minding high things, but cōsenting to the humble. ⊣ b Be not
17 vvise in your ovvne conceite. † To no man rendring euil for euil. Prouiding good things not only before God, but
18 also before al men. † If it may be, as much as is in you, ha-
19 uing peace vvith al men. † Not reuenging your selues my deerest, but giue place vnto vvrath, for it is vvritten: *Reuenge*
20 *to me: I vvil revvard,* saith our Lord. † but *if thine enemie hunger, giue him meate: if he thirst, giue him drinke. for, doing this, thou shalt heape coales of fire vpon his head.*
21 † Be not ouercome of euil, but ouercome in good the euil. ⊣

1 Cor. 12, 11. Eph. 4, 7.

c *dilectio*

memories

Deu. 32, 35. Pro. 25, 21.

The Epistle vpō the 2 Sunday after the Epiphanie.

∷ Prophecie is interpretatiō of the Scriptures, which is according to the rule of faith, when it is not against the right faith, or when it is profitable to edifie charitie, as S. Augustine speaketh *li. 3. Doct. Chr. c. 27* and *li. 1. c. 36.* and in effect he saith the same *li. 12. Confess. c. 18 vnto c. 32.*

∷ Cursing is a vice whereunto the common people is much giuen, who often curse thē on whom they can not otherwise be reuenged. they may see here that it is a great fault.

b The Epistle vpō the 3 Sūday after the Epiphanie.

ANNOTATIONS
CHAP. XII.

1. *A liuing host.*] Lest men should thinke by the former discourse of Gods eternal predestination, that no reward were to be had of good life and workes, the Apostle now earnestly recommendeth to them holinesse of life.

1. *A liuing host.*] Man maketh his body a sacrifice to God by giuing it to suffer for him, by chastising it vvith fasting, vvatching, and such like, and by occupying it in workes of charitie and vertue to Gods honour. Whereby appeareth how acceptable these workes are to God and grateful in his sight, being compared to a sacrifice, which is an high seruice done to him.

The body chastised by penāce is a grateful sacrifice.

6. *According to the rule of faith.*] By this, and many places of holy Write, we may gather, that the Apostles by the holy Ghost, before they were sundered into diuers Nations, set downe among them selues a certaine Rule and forme of faith and doctrine, conteining not onely the Articles of the Crede, but al other principles, groundes, and the whole platforme of al the Christian religion. Which Rule was before any of the bookes of the new Testament were written, & before

The Apostolical rule or analogie of faith.

before the faith was preached among the Gentiles: by vvhich not onely euery other inferiour teachers doctrine was tried, but al the Apostles, and Euangelistes preaching, vvriting, interpreting (which is here called prophecying) were of Gods Church approued and admitted, or disproued and reiected. This forme, by mouth and not by Scripture, euery Apostle deliuered to the countrie by them conuerted. For keeping of this forme, the Apostle before praised the Romanes, and afterward earnestly warneth them by no mans plausible speache to be drawen from the same. This he commendeth to Timothee, calling it his *Depositum*. For not holding this fast and sure, he blameth the Galatians, further also denouncing to him self or an Angel that should write, teach, or expound against that which they first receiued, Anathema, and commaunding alwaies to bevvare of them that taught otherwise. For feare of missing this line of truth, him self notwithstanding he had the Holy Ghost, yet lest he might haue preached in vaine and lost his labour, he went to conferre with Peter and the rest. for the fast keeping of this Rule of truth, the Apostles held Councels, and their successors by their example. For the holding of this Rule, and by the measure thereof, were al the holy Scriptures written. for and by the same, al the glorious doctors haue made their sermons, commentaries, and interpretations of Gods vvord: al vvritings and interpretatiōs no otherwise admitted nor deemed to be of God, but as they be agreable to this Rule.

c. 6, 17. *c. 16, 17.* *1. Tim. 6, 20.* *Gal. 1, 6.* *Gal. 2, 1.* *Act. 15, 6.*

The Heretikes phãtastical rule, or rather rules of faith, many and diuers one from an other.

And this is the sure Analogie and measure of faith, set downe and commended to vs euery where for the Apostles tradition: and not the phantastical rule or square that euery Sectmaister pretendeth to gather out of the Scriptures falsely vnderstood and wrested to his purpose, by which they iudge of doctor, Scripture, Church, and al. Arius had by that meanes a rule of his owne, Luther had his false weightes, and Caluin his owne also. According to which seueral measure of euery *Sect*, they haue their expositions of Gods word: and in England (as in other infected Countries) they kept of late an apish imitation of this prophecying which S. Paul here and in other places speaketh of, and which was an exercise in the primitiue Church, measured not by euery mans peculiar spirit, but by the former Rule of faith first set downe by the Apostles. And therfore al this new phantastical Prophecying & al other preaching in Caluins schoole, is iustly by this note of the Apostle condemned, for that it is not according to, but quite against the Rule of faith.

CHAP. XIII.

To yeld obedience and al other duties vnto Potestats: 8 to loue their neighbour vvhich is the fulfilling of the Lavv: 11 and specially to consider, that novv being the time of grace, vve must doe nothing that may not beseeme day light.

LET "euery soul be subiect to higher powers, for there is "no povver but of God. And those that are, of God are ordeined. † Therfore he that resisteth the povver, resisteth the ordinance of God. And "they that resist, purchase to them selues damnatiō. † for princes are no feare to the good worke, but to the euil. But wilt thou not feare the povver? Doe good: and thou shalt haue praise of the same. † for he is gods minister vnto thee for good. But if thou doe euil, feare. for he "beareth not the svvord without cause. For he is Gods minister: a reuēger vnto vvrath, to him that doeth euil. † Therfore be subiect of necessitie, not only for vvrath, but also for conscience sake. † For therfore "you giue tributes also. for they are the ministers of God, seruing vnto this purpose. † Render therfore to al men their devv: * to vvhom tribute, tribute: to vvhom custom, custom: to whom feare, feare: to vvhō honour, honour. † Ovve no

1 2 3 4 5 6 7 8

Tit. 3, 1. *1. Pet. 2, 13.* *Mt. 22, 21.*

The Epistle vpō the 4 Sunday after the Epiphanie.

no man any thing: but, that you loue one an other. For he that
9 loueth his neighbour, hath ∷ fulfilled the lavv. † For, *Thou shalt not commit aduoutrie, Thou shalt not kil, Thou shalt not steale, Thou shalt not beare false vvitnes, Thou shalt not couet*, and if there be any other commaundement: it is comprised in this vvord, *Thou shalt*
10 *loue thy neighbour as thy self.* † The loue of thy neighbour, vvorketh no euil. Loue therfore is the fulnesse of the lavv. ⊣
11 † And that knovving the season, that it is novv the houre for vs to rise from sleepe. For novv our saluation is neerer
12 then vvhen vve beleeued. † The night is passed, and the day is at hand. Let vs therfore cast of the vvorkes of darknesse,
13 and doe on the armour of light. † As in the day let vs vvalke honestly: not in banketings and drunkennes, not in chamberings and impudicities, not in contention and emulation:
14 † but doe ye on our Lord IESVS Christ, ⊣ and make not prouision for the flesh in concupiscences.

Exo. 20, 13.

Leu. 19, 18.

∷ Here vve learne that the Law may be & is fulfilled by loue in this life: against the Aduersaries saying it is impossible to keepe the commaundements.

The Epistle vpon the 1 Sunday in Aduent.

ANNOTATIONS
CHAP. XIII.

1. *Euery soul be subiect.*] Because the Apostles preached libertie by Christ from the yoke of the Law and seruitude of sinne, and gaue al the faithful both example and commaundement to obey God more then men, and withal euer charged them expresly to be obedient and subiect to their Prelates as to them which had cure of their soules and were by the Holy Ghost placed ouer the Church of God: there were many in those daies newly conuerted, that thought them selues free from al temporal Potestats, carnal Lordes, and humane creatures or powers: wherevpon the bondman tooke him self to be loose from his seruitude, the subiect from his Soueraine, were he Emperour, King, Duke, or what other secular Magistrate so euer, specially the Princes of those daies being Heathens and persecutors of the Apostles, and of Christes religion. for which cause and for that the Apostles were vntruely charged of their Aduersaries, that they withdrevve men from order and obedience to Ciuil lavves and Officers: S. Paul here (as S. Peter doth 1 Chap. 2.) cleereth him self, and expresly chargeth euery man to be subiect to his temporal Prince and Superiour: Not euery man to al that be in Office or Superiority, but euery one to him whom God hath put in authoritie ouer him, by that he is his Maister, Lord, king, or such like: Neither to them in matters of religion or regiment of their soules (for most part vvere Pagans, whom the Apostle could not vvill men to obey in matters of faith) but to them in such things onely as concerne the publike peace & Policie, and what other causes so euer consist vvith Gods holy vvill and ordinance. for * against God no power may be obeied.

Obedience to teporal rulers, & in what cases.

Act. 4, 19. 5, 29.

1. *No povver but of God.*] S. Chrysostome here noteth, that power, rule, & Superioritie, is Gods ordinance, but not eftsones al Princes: because many may vsurpe, who reigne by his permission onely, and not by his appointment: nor al actions that euery one doeth in and by his soueraine povver, as Iulians apostasie and affliction of Catholikes, Pharaos tyrannical oppression of the Israelites, Achabs persecution of the Prophets, Neros executing of the Apostles, Herods and Pilats condemning of Christ: al which things God permitted them, by the abuse of their power to accomplish, but they vvere out of the compasse of his causing and ordinance.

Chrys. in ep. Ro. ho. 23.

In what sense, al power or superioritie is of God.

2. *They that resist.*] Vvhosoeuer resisteth or obeieth not his lavvful Superior in those causes vvherein he is subiect vnto him, withstandeth Gods appointment, & sinneth deadly, and is vvorthy to be punished both in this vvorld by his Superior, and by God in the next life. for in temporal gouernement and causes, the Christians vvere bound in conscience to obey their Heathen Emperours: though on the other side, they were bound vnder paine of damnation to obey their Apostles and Prelates, and not to obey their kings or Emperours

In things lawfully comaunded it is mortal sinne not to obey our Superiors.

Emperours, in matters of religion. Vvhereby it is cleere that vvhen vve be commaunded to obey our Superiors, it is meant alvvaies and onely in such things as they may lawfully commaund, and in respect of such matters vvherein they be our Superiors.

4. Beareth not the sword.] That the Apostle meaneth here specially of temporal povvers, vve may see by the svvord, tribute, & external compulsion, vvhich he here attributeth to them. And the Christian men then had no doubt vvhether they should obey their Spiritual povvers. but novv the disease is cleane contrarie. for al is giuen to the secular povver, and nothing to the spiritual, vvhich expresly is ordained by Christ and the Holy Ghost: and al the faithful are commaunded to be subiect thereunto, as to Christs ovvne vvord and vvill. There vvere Heretikes called *Begardi*, that tooke avvay al rule and Superioritie: The Wiclefists vvould obey nor Prince nor Prelate, if he vvere once in deadly sinne. The Protestants of our time (as vve may see in al Countries vvhere the secular svvord is dravven against their Sectes) care neither for the one nor for the other, though they extol onely the secular vvhen it maketh for them. The Catholikes onely most humbly obey both, euen according to Gods ordinance, the one in temporal causes, and the other in Spiritual: in vvhich order both these States haue blessedly florished in al Christian countries euer since Christes time, and it is the very vvay to preserue both, as one day al the vvorld shal confesse vvith vs.

The Apostle speaketh of temporal powers.

Heresies against rule and Superioritie.

The obedience of Catholikes both to Spiritual and temporal Superiors.

6. You giue tributes.] Though euery man ought to be ready to serue his temporal Prince vvith his goods, by tributes or vvhat other lavvful taxes and subsidies soeuer: yet they may exempt by priuileges vvhom they thinke good. As in al countries Christian: Priests for the honour of Christ, vvhose Ministers they be, haue by the grauntes and auncient charters of kings bene excepted and exempted. Notvvithstanding they vvere neuer vnready to serue voluntarely their Soueraine, in al common causes, vvith vvhatsoeuer they had. See *Annot. in Mat. 17, 26.*

The Clergie exempted from tribute.

Hiero. in Mat. 17.

13. Not in banketings.] This vvas the very place vvhich S. Augustine, that glorious Doctor, vvas by a voice from heauen directed vnto, at his first miraculous and happy conuersion, not only to the Catholike faith, but also to perpetual continencie, by this voice comming from heauen, *Tolle, lege: Tolle, lege.* Take vp and read, take vp and read. as himself telleth *li. 8 Confes. c. 12.*

S. Augustines conuersion.

CHAP. XIIII.

Like a moderator and peacemaker betvvene the firme Christians (vvho vvere the Gentils) and the infirme (vvho vvere the Christian Ievves, hauing yet a scruple to cease from keeping the ceremonial meates and daies of Moyses Lavv) he exhorteth the Ievv not to condemne the Gentil vsing his libertie: and the Gentil againe, not to condemne the scrupulous Iew: but rather to abstaine from vsing his libertie, then offending the Ievv, to be an occasion vnto him of apostating.

AND him that is vveake in faith, take vnto you: not in disputations of cogitatiõs. 1 † For one beleeueth that he may "eate al things: but he that is vveake, `let him eate' herbes. 2 † Let not him that eateth, despise him that eateth not: and he that eateth not: let him not iudge him that eateth. for God hath taken him to him. 3 † Vvho art thou that iudgest an other mans seruant? To his ovvne Lord he standeth or falleth. and he shal stand: for God is able to make him stand. 4 † For one iudgeth "betvveene day and day: and an other iudgeth euery day. let euery one abound" in his ovvne sense. 5 † He that respecteth the day, respecteth to our Lord. 6

` eateth

Lord. And he that eateth, eateth to our Lord: for he giueth thankes to God. And he that eateth not, to our Lord he eateth 7 not, and giueth thankes to God. † For none of vs liueth to 8 him self: & no man dieth to him self. † For whether vve liue, we liue to our Lord: or vvhether we die, we die to our Lord. Therfore vvhether vve liue, or vvhether vve die, vve are our 9 Lords. † For to this end Christ died and rose againe: that he may haue dominion both of the dead and of the liuing. 10 † But thou, vvhy iudgest thou thy brother? or thou, vvhy doest thou despise thy brother? For * vve shal al stand before 11 the iudgement seate of Christ. † For it is vvritten, *Liue I*, saith our Lord, *that euery knee shal bovve to me: and euery tongue shal confesse to* 12 *God*. † Therfore euery one of vs for him self shal render ac-13 count to God. † Let vs therfore no more iudge one an other. but this iudge ye rather, that you put not a stumbling 14 blocke or a scandal to your brother. † I knovv and am persuaded in our Lord IESVS Christ, that nothing is :: cōmon of it self, but to him that supposeth, any thing to be cōmon, 15 to him it is common. † For if because of meate thy brother be greeued: novv thou vvalkest not according to charitie. * Do not vvith thy meate destroy him for vvhom Christ 16 died. † Let not then our good be blasphemed. † For the 17 kingdom of God is " not meate and drinke: but iustice, and 18 peace, and ioy in the holy Ghost. † for he that in this serueth 19 Christ, pleaseth God, and is acceptable to men. † Therfore the things that are of peace let vs pursue: and the things that 20 are of edifying one tovvard an other let vs keepe. † Destroy not the vvorke of God for meate. * Al things in deede are cleane: but it is il for the man that eateth by giuing offence. 21 † It is good not to eate flesh, and not to drinke vvine, nor that vvherein thy brother is offended, or scandalized, or 22 vveakened. † Hast thou faith? " haue it vvith thy self before God. Blessed is he that iudgeth not him self in that vvhich he 23 approueth. † But " he that discerneth, if he eate, is damned: because not of faith. for " al that is not of faith, is sinne.

2. Cor. 5, 10.

Es. 45, 23.

1. Cor. 8.

Tit. 1, 15

:: *Common*, that is, *vncleane*. See Annot. Marc. 7, 2.

Though he vvish the vveake to be borne vvithal, yet he vttereth his minde plainly, that in deede al the meates forbidden and vncleane in the Lavv, are novv through Christ cleansed & lawful for euery mā to vse.

ANNOTATIONS
CHAP. XIIII.

2. *Eate al things*.] By similitude of vvordes the simple are soone deceiued, and Heretikes make their vauntage of any thing to seduce the vnlearned. There vvere diuers meates forbidden in the Lavv of Moyses, and for signification, made and counted vncleane, vvhereof

The Apostles meaning about eating or not eating certaine meates.

the Ievves might not eate at al, as porke, hare, conny, and such like, both of fishes, foules, and beasts, a great number. Christ discharged al them that became Christians, after his Passion, of that obseruance and al other ceremonies of the old Lavv: Notvvithstanding, because diuers that vvere brought vp in the Lavv, had a religion and conscience, sodenly to forsake their former maner, the Apostle here admonisheth such as be stronger and better instructed in the case, to beare vvith the vveaker sort, that being Christians could not yet finde in their hartes to eate and vse the meates forbidden by God in the Lavv: as on the other side he vvarneth the vveake that vvould not eate, not to take offence or scandal at them that did eate vvithout scruple, any of the irregular or forbidden meates in the Lavv, nor in any vvise to iudge or condemne the eater, but to commit that to God, and finally that neither nother should condemne the other for eating or not eating. Now the Protestants fondly apply al this to the fastes of the Church, and differences of meates in the same: as though the Church did forbid any meate vvholy neuer to be eaten or touched, or made any creatures vncleane, or othervvise prescribed any abstinence, then for chastising of mens bodies and seruice of God. It is a great blindnesse that they can put no difference betvvixt Christes fast of fourtie daies, *Mat. 4.* Iohns abstaining from al delicate meates and drinkes, *Mat. 3, 11.* the vvidovv Annes, *Luc. 2, 37.* the Nazareites, *Num. 6.* the Recabites, *Ierem. 35, 14.* the Niniuites, *Ion. 3.* S. Paules, *2 Cor. 11, 27.* S. Timothees, *1 Tim. 5, 23.* Iohns Disciples and Christs Disciples fast *Mat. 9, 14. 15.* (Which he said they should keepe after his departure from them:) and the ceremonial distinction of creatures and meates, cleane and vncleane, in the old Lavv. of vvhich it is euident the Apostle treateth in al this chapter, & of none other at al. Therfore vvhen the Protestants by the vvordes of this place vvould proue, that vve be either made free from fasting and from obeying the Churches commaundement or folovving Christes example in that matter, or that the obseruers of Christian fastes be vveake in faith, & ought not in any vvise cõdemne of sinne the breakers of the prescribed fastes of the holy Church, they doe abuse ignorantly or vvilfully the Apostles vvordes and discourse.

The Heretikes fondly abuse this place agaist the fastes of the Church.

Folish Heretikes see not the differẽces of things.

Distinction of daies.

5. *Betvvene day and day.*] By the like deceite they abuse this place against the Holydaies of Christ and his B. mother and Saincts, vvhich concerneth onely the Ievves festiuities and obseruation of times, vvhereof in the Epistle to the Galatians c. 4. 10.

The text explicated concerning euery mans cõscience in Iudaical meates and drinkes.

6. *Euery one in his ovvne sense.*) The Apostle doth not giue freedom, as the Churches enemies vvould haue it, that euery man may doe or thinke vvhat he list. but in this matter of Iudaical obseruation of daies and meates, & that for a time onely, til the Christian religion should be perfectly established, he would haue no restrainte made, but that euery one should be borne vvithal in his ovvne sense: yet so, that they should not condemne one an other, nor make necessitie of saluation in the obseruation of the Iudaical rites of meates, daies, &c.

Not eating, but disobedience damnable.

17. *Not meate and drinke.*] The substance of religion or the kingdom of God standeth not in meate or drinke, and therfore the better might they vse indifferencie and toleration in that point for a time, for peace sake and to auoid scandal. but if the precept of Moyses Lavv had bound still as before, then (not for the meates sake, but for the disobedience) it had been damnable to haue eaten the vncleane meates.

22. *Haue it vvith thy self.*] Thou that art perfect, and beleeuest or knovvest certainely that thou art free from the Lavv concerning meates and festiuities, yet to the trouble and hinderance of the feeble that can not yet be brought so far, be discrete & vtter not thy self out of season.

To doe against our conscience, is sinne.

23. *He that discerneth.*] If the vveake haue a conscience, and should be driuen to eate the things vvhich in his ovvne hart he thinketh he should not doe, he committeth deadly sinne, because he doth against his conscience, or against his ovvne pretensed knovvledge.

Vvhat actions of infidels are sinne, and what are not.

Chrys. ho. 26. in ep. Ro.

23. *Al this is not of faith.*] The proper sense of this speach is, that euery thing that a man doeth against his knovvledge or conscience, is a sinne, for so by the circumstance of the letter, faith must here be taken. though S. Augustine sometimes applieth it also to proue that al the actions of infidels (meaning those vvorkes vvhich directly procede of their lacke of faith) be sinnes. But in any vvise take heede of the Heretikes commentarie, vvho hereby vvould proue that the infidel sinneth in honouring his parents, fighting for his countrie, tilling his ground, and in al other vvorkes. And no maruel that they so hold of infidels, vvho maintaine * that Christian men also offend deadly in euery good deede.

Luther.

CHAP.

CHAP. XV.

He proceedeth to make peace betvvene the Christian Gentils and Ievves. 8 vvith this resolution, that the Ievves vocation is of promis in deede, but the Gentils also of mercie, and foretold by the Scriptures. 14 Then dravving to an ende, he excuseth him self to the Romanes for vvriting thus vnto them, 21 hoping novv at length to see them, after that he hath been at Hierusalem, 29 vvherevnto also he requesteth their praiers.

1 AND vve that are the strōger, must susteine the infirmities of the vveake, & not please our selues. 2 † Let euery one of you please his neighbour vnto good, to edification. 3 † For, Christ did not please him self, but as it is vvritten, *The reproches of them that reproched thee, fel vpon me.* 4 † For :: vvhat things soeuer haue been vvritten, to our learning they are vvritten: that by the patience and consolation of the Scriptures, vve may haue hope. 5 † And the God of patience and of comfort giue you to be of one minde one tovvard an other according to IESVS Christ: 6 † that of [c] one minde, vvith one mouth you may glorifie God and the Father of our Lord IESVS Christ. 7 † For the vvhich cause receiue one an other: as Christ also hath receiued you vnto the honour of God. 8 † For I say Christ IESVS to haue been :: minister of the circumcision for the veritie of God to confirme the promisses of the fathers. 9 † But the Gentils to honour God for his mercie, as it is vvritten: *Therfore vvil I confesse to thee in the Gentils ô Lord, and vvil sing to thy name.* 10 † And againe he saith, *Reioyce ye Gētils vvith his people.* 11 † And againe, *Praise al ye Gentils our Lord: and magnifie him al ye peoples.* 12 † And againe Esaie saith, *There shal be the roote of Iesse: and he that shal rise vp to rule the Gentils, in him the Gentils shal hope.* 13 † And the God of hope replenish you vvith al ioy and peace in beleeuing: that you may abound in hope, and in the vertue of the holy Ghost. ⊣

14 † And I my self also, my brethren, am assured of you, that you also are ful of loue, replenished vvith al knowledge, so that you are able to admonish one an other. 15 † But I haue vvritten to you (brethren) more boldly in part, as it were putting you in remembrance: for the grace vvhich is giuen me 16 of God, † to be the minister of Christ IESVS in the Gētils: sanctifying the Gospel of God, that the oblation of the Gentils may be made acceptable and sanctified in the holy

Psa. 68, 10.

Psa. 17, 50.

Deu. 32, 43.

Psa. 116, 1.

Esa. 11, 10.

The Epistle vpō the 2. Sunday in Aduent.

:: He meaneth al that is vvritten in the old Testamēt: much more al things vvritten in the nevv Testamēt, are for our learning and comfort.

c Vnitie in religion commended.

:: Christ did execute his office and ministerie onely tovvards the people of Circumcision, that is, the Ievves.

Ghoſt. † I haue therfore glorie in Chriſt IESVS tovvard God. † For I dare not ſpeake any of thoſe things vvhich Chriſt vvorketh not by me for the obedience of the Gentils, by vvord and deedes, † in the vertue of ſignes and vvõders, in the vertue of the holy Ghoſt: ſo that from Hieruſalem round about vnto Illyricum I haue repleniſhed the Goſpel of Chriſt. † And I haue ſo preached this Goſpel, not vvhere Chriſt vvas named, leſt I ſhould build vpon an other mans foundation: † but as it is vvritten, *They to vvhom it hath not been preached of him, ſhal ſee: and they that haue not heard, ſhal vnderſtand.* † For the vvhich cauſe alſo I vvas hindred very much from comming vnto you. † But novv hauing no longer place in theſe countries, and hauing a deſire to come vnto you theſe many yeres novv paſſed: † vvhen I ſhal begin to take my iourney into Spaine, I hope that as I paſſe, I ſhal ſee you, and be brought thither of you, if firſt in part I ſhal haue enioyed you. † Novv therfore I vvil goe vnto Hieruſalem to miniſter to the :: ſaincts. † For Macedonia and Achaia haue liked vvel to make ſome contribution vpon the poore ſaincts that are in Hieruſalem. † For it hath pleaſed them: and they are their detters. For if the Gentiles be made partakers of their ſpiritual things: they ought alſo in carnal things to miniſter vnto them. † This therfore vvhen I ſhal haue accõpliſhed, and ſigned them this fruite, I vvil goe by you into Spaine. † And I knovv that comming to you, I ſhal come in aboundance of the bleſſing of Chriſt. † I beſeeche you therfore brethren by our Lord IESVS Chriſt, and by the charitie of the holy Ghoſt, that you :: helpe me in your praiers for me to God, † that I may be deliuered from the infidels that are in Ievvrie, and the oblation of my ſeruice may become acceptable in Hieruſalem to the ſaincts, † that I may come to you in ioy by the vvil of God, that I may be refreſhed vvith you. † And the God of peace be vvith you all. Amen.

17 18 19 20 21 22 23 24 25 26 27 28 29 30 31 32 33

Eſ. 52, 15

:: He meaneth the holy perſons that hauing forſaken al their goods for Chriſt, vvere vvholy conuerted to ſerue our Lord vvith al their minde. *S. Hiero. againſt Vigilantius* the Heretike reprehending the almes giuen to ſuch, as do the Heretikes alſo of our time.

:: In that the Apoſtle deſired to be praied for, vve may be moued to ſeeke the ſame as a great benefite.

CHAP. XVI.

He commendeth the bearer Phœbè to the Romanes, 3 and him ſelf to many there by name. 17 he declareth the doctrine vvhich the Romanes had learned, to be the touchſtone to knovv Seducers. 21 he doth vnto them the commendations of al the Churches and of certaine perſons by name: 25 and concludeth.

AND

1 AND I commend to you Phœbè our sister, vvho is in the ministerie of the Church that is 2 in Cenchris: † that you receiue her in our Lord as it is vvorthie for saincts: and that you assist her in whatsoeuer busines she shal neede you. for she also hath assisted many and my self.

3 † [c] Salute Prisca and Aquila my helpers in Christ IESVS, 4 († vvho for my life haue laid dovvne their neckes: to vvhō not I only giue thankes, but also al the Churches of the Gentiles) 5 † and their ⁘ domestical Church. Salute Epænetus my 6 beloued: vvho is the first fruite of Asia in Christ. † Salute 7 Marie vvho hath laboured much about vs. † Salute Andrónicus and' Iulia' my cosins and fellovv captiues: vvho are noble among the Apostles, vvho also before me vvere in 8 Christ. † Salute Ampliátus my best beloued in our Lord. 9 † Salute Vrbánus our helper in Christ IESVS, and Stachys 10 my beloued. † Salute Apelles [c] approued in Christ. Salute 11 them that are of Aristóbolus house. † Salute Herodion my kinsman. Salute them that are of Narcissus house, that are in 12 our Lord. † Salute Tryphæna and Tryphósa: vvho labour in our Lord. Salute Persis the beloued, vvho hath much la-13 boured in our Lord. † Salute Rufus the elect in our Lord 14 and his mother and mine. † Salute Asyncritus, Phlegon, Hermas, Pátrobas, Hermes: and the brethren that are vvith 15 them. † Salute Philólogus and Iulia, Nereus, and his sister and Olympias: and al the saincts that are vvith them. 16 † " Salute one an other in a " holy kisse. Al the churches of Christ salute you.

17 † And I desire you brethren, " to marke them that make dissensions and scandals contrarie to the doctrine vvhich you 18 haue [c] learned, and auoid them. † For such doe not serue Christ our Lord, " but their ovvne belly: and ⁘ by svveete speaches and benedictions seduce the hartes of innocents. 19 † For " your obedience is published into euery place. I reioyce therfore in you. But I vvould haue you to be vvise in 20 good, and simple in euil. † And the God of peace crush Satan vnder your feete quickely. The grace of our Lord IESVS Christ be vvith you.

21 † Timothee my coadiutor saluteth you, and Lucius, and 22 Iason, and Sosipater, my kinsmen. † I Tertius salute you, 23 that vvrote the epistle, in our Lord. † Caius mine host, and

Iunia

ἐν τῷ δοκίμῳ

c The onely salutation of so vvorthy a man is sufficient to fil him vvith greate grace that is so saluted. *Chrys. in 2. Tim. 4.*

⁘ This domestical Church vvas either that faithful and Christiā houshold, or rather the Christians meeting together there & in such good houses to heare diuine seruice and the Apostles preaching in those times of persecution.

The Protestants here reasō thus, Peter is not here saluted, therfore he vvas neuer at Rome. See the Annotation.

c Of the Prince of the Apostles, saith Theodorete vpon this place.

⁘ The special vvay that Heretikes haue euer had to beguile, vvas and is by svveete vvordes & gay speaches. Which their sheepes cote see before described particularly in the Annotations vpon S. Matthevv. c. 7, 15.

the whole Churches, saluteth you. Erastus the Cofferer of the citie saluteth you, and Quartus, a brother. † The grace of our 24 Lord IESVS Christ be vvith al you, Amen.

† And to him that is able to confirme you according to 25 my Gospel and preaching of IESVS Christ, according to the reuelation of the mysterie from eternal times kept secrete, † vvhich novv is opened by the Scriptures of the prophets 26 according to the precept of the eternal God, to the obediēce of faith knovven in al Gentiles, † to God the only vvise 27 through IESVS Christ, `to vvhom' be honour & glorie for euer and euer. Amen.

ANNOTATIONS
CHAP. XVI.

16. Salute one an other.] Neuer Sectmaisters made more foule or hard shifts to proue or defend falsehod, then the Protestants: but in tvvo points, about S. Peter specially, they passe euen them selues in impudencie. The first is, that they hold he vvas not preferred before the other Apostles, vvhich is against al Scriptures most euidently. The second is, that he vvas neuer at Rome, vvhich is against al the Ecclesiastical histories, al the Fathers Greeke and Latine, against the very sense and sight of the monuments of his Seate, Sepulcher, doctrine, life, and death there. Greater euidence certes there is thereof and more vveighty testimonie, then of Romulus, Numas, Cæsars, or Ciceros being there: yet vvere he a very brutish man that vvould deny this to the discredite of so many vvriters and the vvhole vvorld. Much more monstruous it is, to heare any deny the other. Theodorete saith he vvas there, vvriting vpon this chapter. Prosper also *carmine de ingratis in principio.* S. Leo *de natali Petri.* S. Augustine *to. 6 c. 4. cont. ep. fund.* Orosius *li. 7 c. 6.* S. Chrysostome *in ps. 48.* S. Epiphanius *har. 27.* Prudentius *in hymno 2. S. Laurentij, & hymno 12.* Optatus *li. 2. contra Donatistas.* S. Ambrose *li. 5. ep. de Basilicis tradendis.* S. Hierome *in Catalogo.* Lactantius *li. 4. c. 21, de vera sapientia.* Eusebius *hist. Eccl. li. 2, c. 13, 15.* S. Athanasius *de fuga sua.* S. Cyprian. *ep. 55. nu. 6.* Tertullian *de præscriptionibus nu. 14.* and *li. 4, contra Marcionem nu. 4.* Origen *in Genes. apud Euseb. li. 3, c. 1.* Irenæus *li. 3, c. 3.* Hegesippus *li. 3, c. 2 de excid. Hierosolym,* Caius and Papias the Apostles ovvne scholers, and Dionysius the B. of Corinth, alleaged by Eusebius *li. 2, c. 14 & 24.* Ignatius *ep. ad Romanos.* The holy Councel of Chalcedon, and many other affirme it. yea Peter him self (according to the iudgement of the aūcient Fathers) confesseth he vvas at Rome, calling it Babylon *1. ep. c. 5. Euseb. li. 2. c. 14. hist. Ec.* Some of these tel the time and cause of his first going thither: some, hovv long he liued there: some, the maner of his death there: some, the place of his burial: and al, that he vvas the first Bishop there. Hovv could so many of such vvisedom and spirit, so neere the Apostles time deceiue or be deceiued? how could Caluin and his, after fiftene hundred yeres knovv that vvhich none of them could see?

That S. Peter vvas at Rome.

Chalced. conc. act. 3.

See the Annotations 1 *Pet. c. 5, 13.*

Some great argument must they needes haue to controule the credite of the vvhole vvorld. This of truth is here their argument, neither haue they a better in any place, to vvit, If S. Peter had bene at Rome, S. Paul vvould haue saluted him, as he did others here in the end of his letter to the Romanes. Is not this a high point to disproue al antiquitie by? Any man of discretion may straight see, that S. Peter might be knovven vnto S. Paul to be out of the Citie, either for persecution or busines, vvhen this epistle vvas vvritten, (for he vvent often out as S. Epiphanius declareth) & so the omitting to salute him, can proue no more, but that then he vvas not in Rome. but it proueth not so much neither, because the Apostle might for respect of his dignitie and other the Churches affaires, vvrite vnto him special letters, and so had no cause to salute him in his common Epistle. Or hovv knovv they that this Epistle vvas not sent inclosed to S. Peter, to be deliuered by his meanes to the vvhole Church of the Romanes in some of their assemblies? it is very like it vvas recommended to some one principal man or other that is not here named: and tvventy causes there may be vnknovven to vs, vvhy he saluted him not: but no cause vvhy our Aduersaries vpon such friuolous reasons should reproue an approued truth. For euen as vvel might they say that S. Iohn vvas neuer at Ephesus, because S. Paul in his Epistle to the Ephesians doth not salute him. And plaine it is, that it is the Romane seate and faith of Peter, vvhich they (as all Heretikes before them)

The Protestants great argument, that Peter vvas neuer at Rome.

Epiph. har. 27.

them) do feare and hate, and vvhich wil be their bane: and they knovv that there is no argument vvhich conuinceth in their conscience, that Peter vvas neuer at Rome. Therfore to conclude, vve say to them in S. Augustines vvordes, *Why call you the Apostolike chaire, the chaire of pestilence? What hath the Church of Rome done against you, in vvhich S. Peter did sit, and from vvhich by nefarious furie you haue separated your selues?*

The Heretikes hatred of the Romane see.

li. 2. cont. lit. Petil. c. 51.

16. *Holy kisse.*] Hereof, and by the common vsage of the first Christians, vvho had special regard of vnitie and peace among them selues, and for signe and protestation thereof, kissed one an other, came our holy ceremonie of giuing the *Pax*, or kissing one an other in the Sacrifice of the *blessed* Masse.

Orig. in 16. ad Ro.

Kissing the Pax.

17. *To marke them.*] He carefully warneth them to take heede of seditious sovvers of Sectes and dissension in religion, and this euer to be their marke, if they should teach or moue them to any thing vvhich vvas not agreable to that vvhich they had learned at their conuersion: not bidding them to examine the case by the Scriptures, but by their first forme of faith and religion deliuered to them before they had or did read any booke of the nevv Testament.

Against Sect-maisters hovv to examine our faith.

18. *But their ovvne belly.*] Hovvsoeuer Heretikes pretend in vvordes and external shew of their sheepes cote, in deede they seeke but after their ovvne profite and pleasure, & by the Apostles ovvne testimonie we be vvarranted so to iudge of them as of men that in deede haue no religion nor conscience.

Heretikes giuen to voluptuousnes.

19. *Your obedience.*] Against Heretikes and their illusions, there is no better way then in simplicitie to cleaue vnto that vvhich hath bene taught before: for the vvhich the Romane obedience is much commended. *See Annot.* vpon the first *chap. vers. 8.*

THE

THE ARGVMENT OF THE FIRST EPISTLE TO THE CORINTHIANS.

OVV S. Paul planted the Church at Corinth, cōtinuing there a yere and an halfe together, vve reade Act. 18. After that, vvhen he vvas at Ephesus Act. 19, about the end of the three yeres that he abode there, he vvrote this first Epistle to the Corinthians. For euen as S. Luke there vvriteth, vvhen these things vvere ended, Paul purposed in the Spirit, when he had gone ouer *Macedonia* and *Achaia*, to goe to Hierusalem: *so likevvise doth S. Paul himselfe vvrite here*: I vvil come to you *in Achaia*, when I shal haue gone ouer Macedonia, for I vvill go ouer Macedonia. but I vvil tarie at Ephesus vntil Pentecost,

Act. 19, 21.

1 Cor. 16, 5.

The matter that he vvriteth of, is not one, as in the Epistle to the Romanes, but diuers. partly such faultes of theirs, as vvere signified vnto him by them that vvere of Chloë 1 *Cor.* 1, 11. *partly such questions as them selues vvrote to him of*, And concerning the things that you vvrote to me. 1 *Cor.* 7, 1. *for so vve may (as it seemeth) deuide the Epistle into these tvvo partes. Or, to put al together, he vvriteth of eight things*: 1 *Of certaine Schismes beginning among them, by occasion of certaine preachers, vvhom in the Second Epistle he toucheth more plainely as being False apostles. chap.* 1. 2. 3. 4. 2 *Of an incestuous fornicator, and some that vvent to lavv before infidel iudges. chap.* 5. 6. 3 *Of Matrimonie and Continencie. chap.* 7. 4 *Of meates sacrificed to Idols. chap.* 8. 9. 10. 5 *Of his Traditions. chap.* 11. 6 *Of the Giftes of the Holy Ghost. chap* 12. 13. 14. 7 *of the Resurrection. chap.* 15. 8 *of the Contributions that he gathered of the Gentiles, to succour the Christian Ievves at Hierusalem. chap.* 16.

THE

THE FIRST EPISTLE OF PAVL TO THE CORINTHIANS.

CHAP. I.

After salutation, 4 hauing acknovvledged the graces of their Churche, 10 he dehorteth them from their Schismatical boasting against one an other in their baptizers (telling them that they must boast onely in Christ for their Baptisme) 17 and in their preachers, vvho had the vvisedom of vvordes: telling them that it is the preaching of the Crosse, vvhereby God saueth the vvorld, and vvherein onely Christians should boast: 26 seing God of purpose chose the contemptible, that so him self might haue the glorie.

The I. part, Of Schismes that vvere about their baptizers & preachers.

1 PAVL called to be an Apostle of IESVS Christ, by the vvil of God, 2 and Sósthenes a brother, † to the Church of God that is at Corinth, to the sanctified in Christ IESVS, called to be saincts, vvith al that inuocate the name of our Lord IESVS Christ in euery place of theirs and ours. 3 † Grace to you and peace from God our father and our Lord IESVS Christ.

4 † I giue thankes to my God alvvaies for you for the grace 5 of God that is giuen you in Christ IESVS, † that in al things you be made riche in him, in al vtterance, and " in al knovvledge, 6 († as the testimonie of Christ is confirmed in you,) 7 † so that nothing is vvanting to you in any grace, expecting 8 the reuelation of our Lord IESVS Christ, † vvho also vvil confirme you vnto the end vvithout crime, in the day of 9 the comming of our Lord IESVS Christ. † God is faithful: by vvhom you are called into the societie of his sonne IESVS Christ our Lord.

10 † And I beseeche you brethren by the name of our Lord IESVS Christ, that you al say one thing, and that there be no schismes among you: but that you be perfect in one sense, &

in one knovvledge. † For it is signified vnto me (my brethren) of you, by them that are of Chloë, that there be contentions among you. † And I meane this, for that euery one of you saith, ∷ I certes am Paules, & I Apollos, but I Cephas, and I Christs. † Is Christ deuided? Vvhy, vvas Paul crucified for you? or in the name of Paul vvere you baptized? † I giue God thankes, that I baptized none of you, but * Crispus and Caius: † lest any man say that in my name you vvere baptized. † And I baptized also the house of Stéphanas. But I know not if I haue baptized any other.

11 12 13 14 15 16

∷ The beginning of al Schismes is ouer much admiring & addicting mens selues to their owne particular Maisters.

Act. 18, 8.

† For Christ sent me not to baptize, but to euangelize: not in vvisedom of speache, that the crosse of Christ be not made void. † For the vvord of the crosse, to them in deede that perish, is folishnes: but to them that are saued, that is, to vs, it is the povver of God. † For it is vvritten, *I vvil destroy the vvisedom of the vvise: and the prudence of the prudent I vvil reiecte.* † *Vvhere is the vvise? vvhere is the Scribe? vvhere is the disputer of this vvorld?* Hath not God made the vvisedom of this vvorld folish? † For because in the vvisedom of God the vvorld did not by vvisedom knovv God: it pleased God by the folishnes of the preaching to saue them that beleeue. † For both the Ievves aske signes, and the Greekes seeke vvisedom: † but vve preach Christ crucified, to the Ievves certes a scandal, and to the Gentiles, folishnes: † but to the called Ievves & Greekes, Christ the povver of God and the vvisedom of God. † For that vvhich is the folish of God, is vviser then men: and that vvhich is the infirme of God, is stronger then men. † For see your vocation brethren, that not many vvise according to the flesh, not many mightie, not many noble: † but the folish things of the vvorld hath God chosen, that he may confound the vvise: and the vveake things of the vvorld hath God chosen, that he may confound the strong: † and the base things of the vvorld and the contemptible hath God chosen, and those things vvhich are not, that he might destroy those things vvhich are: † that no flesh may glorie in his sight. † And of him you are in Christ IESVS, " vvho is made vnto vs vvisedom from God, & iustice, & sanctificatiõ, and redemption: † that as it is vvritten, *He that doth glorie, may glorie in our Lord.* ⁜

17 18 19 20 21 22 23 24 25 26 27 28 29 30 31

Es. 33, 18

The Epistle for S. Agatha, *Febr. 5.*

Ier. 9, 23

ANNOT.

ANNOTATIONS
CHAP. I.

5. In al knovvledge.] Obſerue that the Apoſtles neuer vvrote their letters but to ſuch as vvere conuerted to Chriſtes faith before. for men can not lightly learne the Chriſtian religion by reading Scriptures, but by hearing, and by the preſence of their teachers, which may inſtruct them at large and particularly of euery Article, as clerely & breefely by letters they could not doe. Neither doth novv any man learne his faith firſt, but by hearing of his parents and Maiſters. for if vve ſhould vvhen vve come to yeres of diſcretion, be ſet to picke our faith out of the Scriptures, there vvould be a madde vvorke and many faithes among vs.

Faith cōmeth by hearing rather then reading.

30. Who is made.] He meaneth not, as our Aduerſaries captiouſly take it, that vve haue no iuſtice, ſapience, nor ſanctity of our ovvne, other then Chriſtes imputed to vs: but the ſenſe is, that he is made the author, giuer, and meritorious cauſe of al theſe vertues in vs. for ſo the Apoſtle interpreteth him ſelf plainely in the 6 Chapter folovving, vvhen he vvriteth thus, *You be vvaſhed, you be iuſtified, you be ſanctified in the name of our Lord* IESVS CHRIST *and in the Spirit of our God.*

Chriſt is made our iuſtice, becauſe he is the author of the iuſtice in vs.

CHAP. II.

That his ovvne preaching among them, vvas in humble maner in the ſight of man. 5 Hovvbeit it is moſt profound vviſedom (as they ſhould and vvould perceiue, if they vvere not carnal) vvhich is taught in the Church of Chriſt.

1 AND I (brethren) vvhen I came to you, I came not in loftineſſe of ſpeache or of vviſedom, preaching to you the teſtimonie of Chriſt. 2 † For I iudged not my ſelf to knovv any thing among you but IESVS Chriſt, and him crucified. 3 † And *I vvas vvith you in infirmitie, and feare and much trembling: 4 † and my ſpeache and my preaching vvas not in the perſuaſible vvordes of humane vviſedom, but in ſhevving of ſpirit and povver: 5 † that your faith might not be in the vviſedom of men, but in the povver of God.

*Act. 18, 1.

6 But vve ſpeake vviſedom among the perfect. † but the vviſedom not of this vvorld, neither of the princes of this 7 vvorld, that come to naught: † but vve ſpeake the vviſedom of God in a myſterie, which is hid, vvhich God did predeſti- 8 nate before the worlds, vnto our glorie: † which none of the princes of this vvorld did knovv: for if they had knovven, 9 they vvould neuer haue crucified the Lord of glorie. † But as it is vvritten, *That vvhich eie hath not ſeen, nor eare hath heard, neither hath it aſcended into the hart of mā, vvhat things God hath prepared for them that* 10 *loue him.* † but to vs God hath reuealed by his Spirit. For the

Iſa. 64, 4.

Spirit searcheth al things, yea the profoundities of God. † For vvhat man knovveth the things of a man, but " the spi- 11 rit of a man that is in him? so the things also that are of God no man knovveth, but the spirit of God.

† And vve haue receiued not the spirit of this vvorld, but 12 the spirit that is of God; " that vve may knovv the things that of God are giuen to vs. † vvhich also vve speake not in 13 learned vvordes of humane vvisedom: but in the doctrine of the Spirit, comparing spiritual things to the spiritual. † But 14 " the sensual man perceiueth not those things that are of the spirit of God. for it is folishnes to him, and he can not vnderstand: because he is spiritually examined. † But the spi- 15 ritual man iudgeth al things: and him self is iudged of no man. † For * vvho hath knovven the sense of our Lord that 16 may instructe him? But vve haue the sense of Christ.

Esa. 40, 13.

ANNOTATIONS
CHAP. II.

Hovv Angels and Saincts & mortal men knovv our cogitations.

11. *But the spirit of man.*] One man can not knovv an others cogitations naturally: but God giueth to Prophets and other, euen in this vvorld oftentimes, by extraordinary grace to knovv mens secretes. As he did to S. Peter, to knovv the fraude of Ananias and Saphira: and to Eliseus, his seruants bribery in his absence, and vvhat vvas done in the king of Syria his chamber. and as he giueth to al * Angels and Saincts (so far as is conuenient to our necessities and their heauenly glorie) to vnderstand not onely our vocal praiers, but our invvard repentance and desires.

*Act. 5. 4. reg. 5 & 6. * Luc. 15, 7.*

The Heretikes allegatiō for their vaine securitie, ansvvered.

12. *That vve may knovv.*] The Protestants that chalenge a particular spirit reuealing to eche one his ovvne predestination, iustification, and saluation, vvould dravv this text to that purpose. Vvhich importeth nothing els (as is plaine by the Apostles discourse) but that the holy Ghost hath giuen to the Apostles, & by them to other Christian men, to knovv Gods ineffable gifts bestovved vpon the beleeuers in this time of grace: that is, Christes Incarnation, Passion, presence in the Sacrament, & the incomprehensible ioyes of heauen, vvhich Pagans, Ievves, and Heretikes deride.

The sensual man.

14. *The sensual man.*] The sensual man is he specially, that measureth these heauenly mysteries by natural reason, humane prudence, external sense, and vvorldly affection, as the Ievv, Pagane, and Heretike doe: and sometime both here and els vvhere, the more infirme and ignorant sort of Christian men be called sensual or carnal also, vvho being occupied in secular affaires, and giuen to sensual ioy and vvorldlines, haue no such sense nor feeling of these great gifts of God, as the perfecter sort of the faithful haue. Vvho trying these high pointes of religion, not by reason and sense, but by grace, faith, and Spirit, be therfore called spiritual. The spiritual then is he, that iudgeth and discerneth the truth of such things as the carnal can not attaine vnto: that doth by the spirit of the Church, vvhereof he is partaker in the vnitie of the same, not onely see the errours of the carnal, but condemneth them and iudgeth euery povver resisting Gods spirit and vvord: the carnal Ievv, Heathen, or Heretike, hauing no meanes nor right to iudge of the said spiritual man. For vvhen the spiritual is said to be iudged of none, the meaning is not that he should not be subiect or obedient to his Pastors and spiritual Povvers and to the vvhole Church, specially for the trial or examination of al his life, doctrine, and faith: but that a Catholike man and namely a teacher of Catholike doctrine in the Church, should not be any vvhit subiect to the iudgement of the Heathen or the Heretike, nor care vvhat of ignorance or infidelitie they say against him. for such carnal men haue no iudgement in such things, nor can attaine to the Churches vvisedom in any ceremonie, mysterie, or matter vvhich they condemne.

The spiritual man.

Hovv the spiritual man iudgeth al, & is iudged of none.

Therfore

Therfore S. Irenæus excellently declaring that the Church and euery ſpiritual childe thereof, iudgeth and condemneth al falſe Prophets and Heretikes of vvhat ſort ſo euer, at length he concludeth vvith theſe notable vvordes: *The ſpiritual ſhal iudge alſo all that make ſchiſmes, vvhich be cruel, not hauing the loue of God, and reſpecting their ovvne priuate, more then the vnitie of the Church: mangle, deuide, and (as much as in them lieth) kill for ſmal cauſes the great and glorious body of Chriſt, ſpeaking peace, and ſeeking battaile. He ſhal iudge alſo them that be out of the truth, that is to ſay, out of the Church: vvhich Church ſhal be vnder no mans iudgement. for to the Church are al things knovvn, in vvhich is perfect faith of the Father, and of al the diſpenſation of Chriſt, and firme knovvledge of the Holy Ghoſt that teacheth all truth.*

Iren. li. 4. c. 62.

The Church is vnder no mans iudgement.

CHA. III.

If they vvil not be carnal ſtil, they muſt boaſt in God only, & not in their preachers, Which are but his miniſters, 10 and neede to looke vvel hovv they preach: 12 becauſe not al preaching, though it be Catholike, is meritorious: but rather it buildeth matter to be purged by fire, vvhen it is vaine and vnfruitful (as alſo any other like vvorkes of other Catholikes.) marie if it be heretical, deſtroying the temple of God, then it vvorketh damnation. 18 The remedie is, to humble them ſelues and referre al to God.

1 AND I, brethren, could not ſpeake to you as to ſpiritual, but as to carnal. As it vvere to litle 2 ones in Chriſt, † I gaue you ∷ milke to drinke, not meate: for you could not as yet. but neither can you novv verely, for yet you are car-3 nal. † For vvhereas there is among you emulation and contention, are you not carnal, and vvalke according to man? 4 † For vvhen one ſaith, I certes am Paules, & an other, I Apollos: are you not ʻmenʼ? Vvhat is Apollo then? and vvhat is 5 Paul? † The miniſters of him vvhom you haue beleeued, & 6 to euery one as our Lord hath giuen. † I planted, Apollo 7 vvatered: but God gaue the increaſe. † Therfore neither he that planteth is any thing, nor he that vvatereth: but he 8 that giueth the increaſe, God. † And he that planteth and he that vvatereth are one. And ″ euery one ſhal receiue his ovvne 9 reward according to his ovvne labour. † For vve are Gods ᶜ coadiutors: you are Gods huſbandrie, you are Gods buil-10 ding. † According to the grace that is giuen me, as a vviſe vvorkemaſter haue I laid the foundation: and an other buildeth therevpon. but let euery one looke hovv he buildeth 11 thereon. † For other foundation no man can lay, beſide that 12 vvhich is laid: vvhich is Chriſt IESVS. † And if any man build ″ vpon this foundation, gold, ſiluer, pretious ſtones, 13 vvood, hay, ſtubble, † the vvorke of euery one ″ ſhal be manifeſt: for ″ the day of our Lord vvil declare, becauſe it ſhal be reuealed in fire: and the vvorke of euery one of vvhat

ʻ carnal

∷ The Church onely hath truth both in her milke and in her bread: that is, vvhether ſhe inſtruct the perfect, or the imperfect who are called carnal. *Aug. li. 15. c. 5. cont. Fauſt.*

c συνεργοί

c A maruelous dignitie of ſpiritual paſtors, that they be not onely the inſtruments or miniſters of Chriſt, but alſo Gods coadiutors in the vvorke of our Saluation.

kinde it is, the fire ſhal trie. † If any mans vvorke abide, 14 vvhich he built therevpon: he ſhal receiue revvard. † If 15 any mans vvorke burne, he ſhal ſuffer detriment: but him ſelf ſhal be ſaued: yet ſo [a] as by fire. † Knovv you not that 16 you are the temple of God: and the Spirit of God dvvelleth in you? † But if any violate the temple of God, God vvil 17 deſtroy him. For the temple of God is holy: vvhich you are. † Let no man ſeduce him ſelf: if any man ſeeme to be vviſe 18 among you in this world, let him become a foole that he may be vviſe. † For the vviſedom of this vvorld is foliſhnes 19 vvith God. For it is vvritten, *I vvil compaſſe the vviſe in their ſubteltie.* † And againe, *Our Lord knovveth the cogitations of the vviſe that they be* 20 *vaine.* † Let no man therfore glorie in men. For al things are 21 yours: † vvhether it be Paul, or Apollo, or Cephas, or the 22 vvorld, or life, or death, or things preſent, or things to come, for al are yours: † and you are Chriſts, and Chriſt is Gods. 23

Iob 5, 13. Pſ. 93, 11

ANNOTATIONS
CHAP. III.

8. *Euery man ſhal receiue according.*] A moſt plaine text for proofe that men by their labours, and by the diuerſities thereof, ſhal be diuerſly revvarded in heauen: and therfore that by their vvorkes proceding of grace, they do deſerue or merite heauen, and the more or leſſe ioy in the ſame. for though the holy Scripture cõmonly vſe not this vvord merite, yet in places innumerable of the old and nevv Teſtament, the very true ſenſe of merite is conteined, and ſo often as the vvord, *merces*, and the like be vſed, they be euer vnderſtood as correlatiues or correſpondent vnto it. for if the ioy of heauen be retribution, repaiment, hire, vvages for vvorkes (as in infinite places of holy Scripture,) then the vvorkes can be none other but the valure, deſert, price, vvorth, and merite of the ſame. And in deede this vvord, *revvard*, vvhich in our Engliſh tonge may ſignifie a voluntary or bountiful gift, doth not ſo vvel expreſſe the nature of the* Latin vvord, or the Greeke, vvhich are rather the very ſtipend that the hired vvorkeman or iournieman couenanteth to haue of him vvhoſe vvorke he doth, and is a thing equally and iuſtly anſvvering to the time and vveight of his trauels and vvorkes (in vvhich ſenſe the Scripture ſaith, *Dignus eſt operarius mercede ſua.* the vvorkeman is vvorthy of his hire) rather then a free gift. though, becauſe faithful men muſt acknovvledge that their merites be the giftes and graces of God, they rather vſe the vvord revvard, then hire, ſtipend, or repaiment. though in deede it be al one, as you may ſee by diuers places of holy vvrite. as, * *My merces* (revvard) *is vvith me to render to euery one * according to his vvorkes.* And *Our Lord vvil render vnto me according to my iuſtice.* Pſ. 17. And *the very vvord it ſelf* merite (equiualent to the Greeke) is vſed thus, *Mercie ſhal make a place to euery one * according to the merite of Workes.* Eccli 16, 15. And *If you doe your iuſtice before men, you ſhal not haue reward in heauen.* Mat. 6, 1. Vvhere you ſee that the revvard of heauen is recompenſe of iuſtice. And the euaſion of the Heretikes is friuolous and euidently falſe, as the former and like vvordes do conuince, for they ſay heauen is our *Merces* or revvard, not becauſe is is due to our vvorkes, but to the promes of God: vvhere the vvordes be plaine, *According to euery mans vvorkes* or *labours*. vpon vvhich vvorkes, and for vvhich vvorkes conditionally, the promes of heauen vvas made.

Good vvorkes meritorious, and the revvardes in heauẽ are different according to the ſame.

Merces μισθὸς.

1. Tim. 5, 18.

Apoc. 22, 12. Mat. 16, 27. Ro. 2, 6.

κατὰ τὰ ἔργα.

12. *Vpon this foundation.*] The foundation is Chriſt, and faith in him vvorking by charitie. The vpper building may be either pure and perfect matter of gold, ſiluer, and pretious ſtone, vvhich (according to the moſt authentical and probable expoſition) be good vvorkes of charitie and al Chriſtian iuſtice done by Gods grace: or els, vvood, hay, ſtubble, vvhich ſignifie the manifold actes of mans infirmitie and his venial ſinnes. Vvhich more or leſſe mixed and medled vvith the better matter aforeſaid, require more or leſſe puniſhmẽt or purgation at the day of our death. At vvhich

Building of gold, or ſtubble.

day

day, if by penance or other meanes in the Church, the said venial sinnes be before hand cleansed, there shal neede no purging at al, but they shal straight receiue the reward due to them.

13. Shal be manifest.] Vvhether our life and workes be pure and neede no cleansing, novv in this vvorld is hard to iudge: but the day of our Lord, vvhich is at our death, vvil make it plaine in vvhat termes euery mans life is tovvards God. for then Purgatorie fire shal reueale and proue it. for, vvhosoeuer hath any impure matter of venial sinnes or such other dettes, to Gods iustice paiable and purgable, must into that fire, and after due paiment and cleansing, be saued through the same. Vvhere the vvorkes of the perfect men and such as died vvith al dettes paied, cleansed, or forgiuen, are quitted from the fire, and neuer incurre damage, paine, or losse thereby. The places of fathers expounding this for Purgatorie, be very many most euident, vvhich are cited in the last Annotation folovving.

Our vvorkes shal be manifested by fire.

13. The day of our Lord shal declare.] That this purgation rather signifieth the place of Gods iustice after our death, then any affliction in this life, the Apostles precise specifying of fire declareth, and of reuealing and notifying the difference of mens vvorkes by the same: vvhich is not done euidently euer in this life: and namely the vvord, *day of our Lord:* vvhich commonly and properly signifieth in Scripture and namely in this Apostle (*1 Cor. 5, 5. 2 Cor. 1, 13. Philip. 1, 10. 6. 1 Thes. 5, 2. 2 Thes. 2, 2.*) either the particular, or the general iudgement: and therfore that the trial spoken of, is not properly nor litterally meant any affliction or aduersitie of this life, as Caluin also cõfesseth, coyning a folish nevv construction of his ovvne. Vvhere you may note also in that mans Commentarie, that this vvord, *dies Domini*, vvas so preiudicial against him and al other expositions of the trial to be made in this vvorld, that he vvould gladly haue (*Domini*) out, reading thus, *A day shal come vvhich shal open &c.* Vvhere vnderstand, that if it vvere only *Dies* (as * in the Greeke) yet thereby also the Scripture is vvont to signifie the selfsame thing: as, *2 Tim. 1, 12. 18.* and *2 Tim. 4, 8.* and *Heb. 10, 25. the day*, as in this place, vvith the greeke article only, vvhich is al one vvith *Dies illa*, or *Dies Domini*.

Calu. in hunc locum.

* ἡ ἡμέρα

Vvhat is signified by, *the day of our Lord.*

15. As by fire.] S. Augustine vpon these vvordes of the Psalme 37. *Lord rebuke me not in thine indignation, nor amend me in thy vvrath.* For it shal *come to passe* (saith he) *that some be amended in the vvrath of God, and be rebuked in his indignation. And not al perhaps that are rebuked, shalbe amended, but yet some there shal be saued by amending. It shalbe so surely, because amending is named: yet so as by fire. but some there shalbe that shalbe rebuked, and not amended. to vvhom he shal say, Goe ye into euerlasting fire. Fearing therfore these more greuous paines, he desireth that he may neither be rebuked in indignation by eternal fire, nor amended in his vvrath. that is to say, Purge me in this life, and make me such an one as shal not neede the amending fire, being for them vvhich shalbe saued, yet so as by fire. Wherfore? but because here they build vpon the foundation, vvood, hay, stubble? for if they did build gold, siluer, and pretious stones, they should be secure from both fires, not onely from that eternal vvhich shal torment the impious eternally: but also from that vvhich shal amend them that shalbe saued by fire. for it is said,* he shal be safe, yet so as by fire. *And because it is said, he shalbe safe, that fire is cõtemned. Yea verely though safe by fire, yet that fire shalbe more greuous, then vvhatsoeuer a man can suffer in this life. And you knovv hovv great euils the vvicked haue suffered, and may suffer: yet they haue suffered such as the good also might suffer. for vvhat hath any malefactor suffered by the lavves, that a Martyr hath not suffered in the confession of Christ? These euils therfore that are here, be much more easie, and yet see hovv men, not to suffer them, doe vvhatsoeuer thou cõmaundest. Hovv much better doe they that vvhich God commaundeth, that they may not suffer those greater paines?* Thus far. S. Augustine. See S. Ambr. vpon this place *1 Cor. 3. & Ser. 20 in Psal. 118.* Hiero. *li. 2 c. 13 adu. Iouinianum.* Greg. *li. 4. Dialog. c. 39. & in Psal. 3. Pœnit. in principio.* Origen. *ho. 6 in c. 15. Exod.* and *ho. 14 in c. 24. Leuit.*

Tvvo fires after this life: one eternal, the other temporal, that is, the purging or amending fire.

Purgatorie fire passeth al the paines of this life.

CHAP. IIII.

He requireth to be esteemed for his office, but regardeth not to be praised of man for his vertue: considering that neither his ovvne conscience is a sufficient iudge thereof, but onely God vvho seeth al. 8 He toucheth them for contemning in their pride, the Apostles them selues as miserable: 18 threatening to come to those proude Falseapostles vvho vvere the authors of al these schismes.

So

The Epistle vpon the 4 Sunday of Aduent.

O let a man esteeme vs as the ministers of 1 Christ, and the dispensers of the mysteries of God. † Here novv is required among the 2 dispensers that a man be found faithful. † But 3 to me it is a thing of lest account, to be iudged of you, or of mans day: but I iudge not my self neither. † For I am not guilty in conscience of 4 any thing: "but I am not iustified herein: but he that iudgeth me, is our Lord. † Therfore iudge not before the time: vntil 5 our Lord do come, vvho also wil lighten the hiddē things of darkenes, and vvil manifest the counsels of the hartes: & then the praise shal be to euery man of God. ⊣

:: Loe vvhen he named him self, and Apollo, & Cephas: he meāt other seditious and factious preachers vvhose names he spared.

† But these things, brethren, :: I haue transfigured into 6 my self and Apollo, for you: that in vs you may learne, one not to be puffed vp against an other, aboue that is vvritten. † For vvho discerneth thee? Or vvhat hast thou that thou 7 hast not receiued? And if thou hast receiued, what doest thou glorie as though thou hast not receiued? † Now you are filled, 8 now are you become riche: without vs you reigne: & I would to God you did reigne, that vve also might reigne vvith you.

a The Epistle vpon S. Iames day, *Iul.* 25. b The Epistle for a Confessor that is not a Bishop.

† a For I thinke that God hath shevved vs Apostles the last, 9 as it vvere deputed to death: because b vve are made a spectacle to the vvorld, and to Angels and men. † Vve are 10 fooles for Christ: but you vvise in Christ. vve vveake: but you strong. you noble, but vve base. † Vntil this houre we 11 doe both hunger, and thirst, and are naked, and are beaten vvith buffets, and are vvanderers, † and labour vvorking 12 vvith our ovvne handes. vve are cursed: and do blesse. vve are persecuted: and susteine it. † vve are blasphemed: and vve 13 beseeche. vve are made the refuse of this vvorld, the drosse of al euen vntil novv. † Not to confound you, do I vvrite these 14 things: but as my deerest children I admonish you. ⊣ † For 15

c So may S. Augustine our Apostle say to vs English men.

c if you haue ten thousand pædagoges in Christ: yet not many fathers. For in Christ IESVS by the Gospel I begat you. ⊣ † I beseeche you therfore be folovvers of me. 16 † Therfore haue I sent to you Timothee, vvho is my deerest 17 sonne and faithful in our Lord: vvho vvil put you in minde of my vvaies that are in Christ IESVS, as euery vvhere in euery Church I teach. † As though I vvould not come to 18 you, so certaine are puffed vp. † But I vvil come to you 19 quickly, if our Lord vvil: and vvil knovv not the vvordes

20 of them that be puffed vp, but the povver. † For the king-
21 dom of God is not in vvordes, but in povver. † Vvhat vvil you? "in rodde that I come to you: or in charitie, and the ſpirit of mildnes?

ANNOTATIONS
CHAP. IIII.

4. But not iuſtified.] The Heretikes are certaine that they be in Gods grace, but S. Paul though guiltie of no crime in his conſcience, durſt not aſſure him ſelf that he vvas iuſtified, neither could take vpon him to be iudge of his ovvne hart and cogitations, vvhether they vvere pure or no: but the trial thereof he left onely to Gods iudging day.

No man ſure of grace or iuſtification.

21. In rodde.] The Apoſtles haue povver of diſcipline and cenſures againſt offenders, and povver of gentlenes, meekenes, and indulgence alſo: to vſe either puniſhing or pardoning, according to their wiſedom, and according to the occaſions of time and place.

Spiritual povver to puniſh or pardon.

The ſecond part of the Epiſtle: of the inceſtuous fornicator: & lavving before Infidels.

CHAP. V.

Sharply rebuking their Clergies negligence, 3 him ſelf abſent excommunicateth that publike inceſtuous perſon: 6 commaunding that hereafter no Chriſtian be ſo tolerated in any open crime, but excommunicated.

1 THERE is plainely heard fornication among you, and ſuch fornication, as the like is not among the heathen, ſo
2 that one hath his * fathers vvife. † And you are puffed vp: and :: haue not mourned rather, that he might be taken avvay from amõg you, that hath done
3 this deede. † "I in deede abſent in body, but preſent in ſpirit, haue already iudged, as preſent, him
4 that hath ſo done, † in the name of our Lord IESVS Chriſt, "you being gathered together and my ſpirit, "vvith the ver-
5 tue of our Lord IESVS † to deliuer ſuch an one" to Satan for the deſtruction of the fleſh, that the ſpirit may be ſaued
6 in the day of our Lord IESVS Chriſt. † Your glorying is not good. Knovv you not that a litle leauen corrupteth the
7 vvhole paſte? † Purge the old leauen, that you may be a nevv paſte, as you are azymes. For our Paſche, Chriſt, is im-
8 molated. † Therfore "let vs feaſt, not in the old leauen, nor in the leauen of malice and vvickednes, but in the azymes of ſinceritie and veritie. ┤

Leu. 18, 8. 20, 11

:: Chriſtian men ſhould be ſorovvful to ſee greuous offences borne vvithal, and ought zelouſly to ſeeke the offenders puniſhment by excõmunication.

The Epiſtle vpon Eaſter day.

9 † I vvrote to you in c an epiſtle, Not to keepe companie
10 vvith fornicatours. † I meane not the fornicatours of this

c Either this Epiſtle in the vvordes before, or ſome other.

vvorld, or the couetous, or the extorsioners, or seruers of Idols: othervvise you should haue gone out of this vvorld. † But novv I vvrote to you, not to keepe companie, if he 11 that is named a brother, be a fornicatour, or a couetous person, or [c] a seruer of Idols, or a railer, or a drunkarde, or an extorsioner: vvith such an one " not so much as to take meate. † For vvhat is it to me to iudge of them that are vvithout? 12 Do not you iudge of them that are vvithin? † for them that 13 are vvithout, God vvil iudge. Take away " the euil-one from among your selues.

c A notorious wilful corruption in the bible 1562: translating in the verse before, *Idolaters*: and here, *vvorshipper of images*: the Apostles vvord being one, εἰδωλολάτρης, *Idolater*.

ANNOTATIONS
CHAP. V.

3. I absent.] S. Paul here vseth his Apostolike povver, of binding this incestuous person, excommunicating him by his letters and *Mandatum*, though absent.

The authoritie of Ecclesiastical censures is in the Clergie only, and is executed in the name of Christ.

4. You being gathered.] Though he commaunded the acte should be done in the face of the Church, as such sentences and censures be at this day executed also, yet the iudgement and authoritie of giuing sentence vvas in him self, and not in the vvhole multitude, as the Protestants and the popular Sectaries affirme. for the povver of binding and loosing vvas not giuen to the vvhole Church, but as in the persons of the Prelats, & to them for the benefite of the vvhole. Vvherevpon S. Chrysostome vpon those vvordes, *Dic Ecclesiæ, Tel the Church.* Mat. 18: *Complaine to the Church, that is*, saith he, *to the Prelats and Presidents thereof.*

4. With the vertue.] Al such great povver ouer sinners, is holden and exercised in the name and vertue of CHRIST IESVS. And vvhosoeuer setteth light by it, despiseth our Lordes name and povver.

The terrible sentence of excómunication.

5. To Satan.] To assure vs that al excommunicate persons be in the povver and possession of the Diuel, and quite out of Christes protection as soone as they be separated by the Churches sentence, from her body and the Sacraments and felovvship of Christian Catholike men: it pleased God to giue povver to the Apostles and Prelates in the primitiue Church, to cause the Diuel straight vpon their sentence of excommunication, to inuade the body of the excommunicate, and to torment him corporally. so Christ excommunicated Iudas, and the Diuel entered into him, and he vvent forth of the happie felovvship of the Apostles. *Io. 13, 27.* so this Apostle excommunicated Alexander and Hymenæus, and Satan straight tooke them: *1 Tim. 1* Yea it is thought that S. Peter excommunicated Ananias and Sapphira, and for signe of his povver and terrour of the sentence, strooke them both starke dead. *De mirabil. S. Scriptura li. 3 c. 16 apud D. August.* Vvhich miraculous povver though it be not ioyned novv to that sentence, yet as far as concerneth the punishment spiritual, vvhich it specially appartaineth vnto, it is as before, and is by the iudgement of the holy Doctors (*Cypr. ep. 62. nu. 3. Chrys. in 1 Tim. 1. ho. 5. Ambros. in 1 Tim. 1. Hiero. ep. ad Heliod. c. 7. August. de cor. & gra. c. 11.*) the terriblest and greatest punishment in the vvorld, yea far passing al earthly paine and torment of this life, and being a very resemblance of damnation, and so often called by the Fathers, namely by S. Augustine. *And by this spiritual svvord* (saith S. Cyprian) *al must die in their soules, that obey not the Priests of Christ in the nevv lavv, as they that vvere disobedient to the iudges of the old lavv, vvere slaine vvith the corporal svvord.* Vvould God the vvorld knevv vvhat a maruelous punishment Christ hath appointed the Priests to execute vpon the offenders of his lavves, and specially vpon the disobedient, as Heretikes namely.

Act. 5.

locis citatis.

Puritie in receiuing the B. Sacrament.

8. Let vs feast.] The Paschal lambe, vvhich vvas the most expresse figure of Christ euery vvay, * vvas first sacrificed and aftervvard eaten vvith azymes or vnleauened bread. so Christ our Paschal, being then nevvly sacrificed on the Crosse, is recommended to them as to be eaten vvith al puritie and sinceritie, in the holy Sacrament. Vvhich mysterie the holy Church in these vvordes commendeth to the faithful euery yere at the feast of Easter.

Exo. 12.

Vve are boūd to auoid, not al sinners, but

11. Not to take meate.] It is not meant that vve should separate our selues corporally from al sinners, or that vve might refuse to liue in one Church or felovvship of Sacraments vvith them, vvhich vvas the errour and occasion of the Donatistes great schisme: nor that euery man is straight after he hath committed any deadly sinne, excommunicated, as some Lutherans hold: but that vve

should

ſhould auoid them vvhen the Church hath excommunicated them for ſuch, though in minde, and condemnation of their faults; euery one ought to be alvvaies far from them. As for the Heathen and Pagans, vvhich be not vnder the Churches diſcipline, and at that time in external vvorldly affaires dealt vvith Chriſtians and liued amongeſt them vvhether they vvould or no, the Apoſtle did not forbid Chriſtians their companie.

the excommunicate only, & them, except in certaine caſes.

13. *The euil one.*] He concludeth that though they can not, nor him ſelf neither, cut of the Heathen that be publike offenders, yet the il perſon by him excommunicated being one of their ovvne body, they may cut of, as is aforeſaid, and auoid his company. Vpon vvhich commaundement of the Apoſtle, vve ſee that vve are bound by Gods vvord to auoid al companie and conuerſation vvith the excommunicate, except in caſes of neceſſitie, and the ſpiritual profite of the perſon excommunicated.

CHAP. VI.

He rebuketh them for going to lavv before Iudges that vvere not Chriſtians, 9 telling that extorſion (as many other offenſes likevviſe) is a mortal ſinne. 12 And vvith diuers reaſons he inueigheth againſt fornication, bidding alſo to flee al occaſion thereof.

1 DARE any of you hauing a matter againſt an other, to be iudged before the vniuſt, and not before the ſainctes? 2 † Or knovv you not that ∷ the ſaincts ſhal iudge of the vvorld? And if the vvorld ſhal be iudged by you: are you vnvvorthie to iudge of the leſt things? 3 † Knovv you not that vve ſhal iudge Angels? hovv much more ſecular things? 4 † If therfore you haue ſecular iudgements: the contemptible that are in the Church, ſet them to iudge. 5 † I ſpeake to your ſhame. So is there not among you any vviſe man, that can iudge betvvene his brother? 6 † but brother vvith brother" contendeth in iudgement: and that before infidels? 7 † Novv certes there is plainely "a fault in you, that you haue iudgements amõg you. Vvhy do you not rather take vvrong? vvhy do you not rather ſuffer fraude? 8 † But your ſelues doe vvrong and defraude: and that to the brethren. 9 † Knovv you not that the vniuſt ſhal not poſſeſſe the kingdom of God? Do not erre, Neither fornicatours, nor [c] ſeruers of Idols, 10 nor aduouterers, nor the effeminat, nor the liers vvith mankinde, † nor theeues, nor the couetous, nor drunkards, nor 11 railers, nor extorſioners ſhal poſſeſſe the kingdom of God. † And theſe things certes you vvere: but you are vvaſhed, but you are ſanctified, but you are iuſtified in the name of our Lord IESVS Chriſt, and in the Spirit of our God.

∷ The faithful iudge and giue ſentence vvith God at the later day, ſpecially the Apoſtles and the perfect Chriſtiãs that haue forſaken al for Chriſts ſake.

εἰδωλολάτραι

c For this, the Engliſh bible 1562 falſely tranſlateth, *vvorſhippers of images.*

12 † Al things are lavvful for me, but al things are not expedient. Al things are lavvful for me, but I vvil be brought 13 vnder the povver of none. † The meate to the belly, and

the belly to the meates: but God vvil destroy both it and them: and the body not to fornication, but to our Lord, and our Lord to the body. † But God both hath raised vp our 14 Lord, and vvil raise vp vs also by his povver. † Knovv you 15 not that your bodies are the members of Christ? Taking therfore the members of Christ, shal I make them the members of an harlot? God forbid. † Or knovv you not, that he 16 which cleaueth to an harlot, is made one body? *For they shal be,* saith he, *tvvo in one flesh.* † But he that cleaueth to our Lord, is one 17 spirit. † Flee fornication. Euery sinne vvhatsoeuer a man 18 doeth, is vvithout the body: but he that doth fornicate, sinneth ∷ against his ovvne body. † Or knovv you not that 19 your members are the temple of the holy Ghost vvhich is in you, vvhom you haue of God, and you are not your ovvne? † For you are bought vvith a great price. Glorifie and beare 20 God in your body.

Gen. 2, 24.

∷ Fornication is not onely enemy to the soule, but wasteth, weakeneth, corrupteth and defileth the body, more properly and directly then any other sinnes doe.

ANNOTATIONS
CHAP. VI.

Going to law before heathen or heretical iudges.

6. Contendeth in iudgement.] To be giuen much to brabling and litigiousnes for euery trifle, to spend a pound rather then lose a peny, the Apostle much reprehendeth in Christian men. For a Christian man to dravv an other to the iudgements seates and courtes of Heathen Princes (vvhich then onely reigned) and not to suffer their controuersies and quarels to be taken vp among them selues brotherly and peaceably, was a great fault: as, for one Catholike to draw an other for mere trifles, before secular or heretical Officers, is a very vnchristian part.

Going to lavv not forbiddē: but to agree othervvise, better.

7. A fault.] He forbade not al iudgements of controuersies, but onely signified that it was a fault, and that it proceded of some iniuries done one to an other, and imperfections, that they so molested one an other: and that it had been more agreable to Christian perfection and charitie, rather to tolerate and suffer a smal iniurie, then to draw his fellow to iudgement seates.

CHAP. VII.

The 3. part. Of Mariage and continencie.

That maried folke may aske their debt, and must pay it, though it be better for them to conteine, 8 as also for the vnmarried and vvidovves to continevv single, though they may marrie. 10 That the married may not depart from one an other (nor in any case marrie an other, during the life of the former) 12 vnles it be from one that is vnbaptized, vvhich yet he dissuadeth: 17 counseling also euery one to be content vvith his state vvherein he vvas Christened. 25 Virginitie is not commaunded, but counseled as the better and more meritorious then Mariage, 39 as also vvidovvhod.

AND

1 AND concerning the things vvhereof you vvrote to me: It is good for a man not to touch a vvoman. 2 † But becauſe of fornication let euery man haue "his ovvne vvife, and let euery vvoman haue her ovvne huſband. 3 †. "Let the huſband [c] render his dette to the vvife: and the vvife alſo in like maner to her huſband. 4 † The vvoman hath not povver of her ovvne body: but her huſband. And in like maner the man alſo hath not povver of his ovvne body: but the vvoman. 5 † Defraude not one an other, except perhaps by conſent for a time, ∷ that you may" giue your ſelf' to praier': and returne againe together, leſt Satan tempt you for your incontinencie. 6 † But I ſay this "by indulgence, not by commaundement. 7 † For I vvould al men to be as my ſelf: but euery one hath "a proper gift of God: one ſo, and an other ſo.

c debitũ reddat

to faſting & praier:

∷ If the lay man can not pray, vnles he abſtaine from his vvife: the Prieſt that alwaies muſt offer ſacrifices, and alvvaies pray, muſt therfore alvvaies be free from matrimonie. *Hiero. li. 1 c. 19 aduer. Iouin.*

8 † ∷ But I ſay to the vnmaried and to vvidovves: it is good for them if they ſo abide euen as I alſo. 9 † But "if they doe not conteine them ſelues, let them marie. For it is" better to marie then [c] to be burnt.

∷ Before he treated of the continencie of ſuch as vvere married, novv he giueth leſſons for the vnmarried alſo.

c Gr. πυροῦσθαι.

10 † But to them that be ioyned in matrimonie, not I giue commaundement, but our Lord, * that the vvife depart not 11 from her huſband: † and if ſhe depart, "to remaine vnmaried, or to be recõciled to her huſband. And let not the huſband put avvay his vvife.

Mt. 5,32 19,9. Mr. 10, 9. Lu. 16,18.

12 † For to the reſt, "I ſay, not our Lord. If any brother haue a vvife an infidel, and ſhe conſent to dvvel with him: let him 13 not put her avvay. † And if any vvoman haue a huſband an infidel, and he conſent to dvvel vvith her: let her not put 14 avvay her huſband. † For the man an infidel is ſanctified by the faithful vvoman: and the vvoman an infidel "is ſanctified by the faithful huſband: otherwiſe your children ſhould 15 be vncleane: but novv they are holy. † But if the infidel depart, let him depart. for the brother or ſiſter is not ſubiect 16 to ſeruitude in ſuch. but in peace hath God called vs. † For how knoweſt thou woman, if thou ſhalt ſaue thy huſbãd? or how 17 knoweſt thou man, if thou ſhalt ſaue the vvoman? † But to euery one as our Lord hath deuided, as God hath called euery 18 one, ſo let him vvalke, and as in al Churches I teach. † Is any man called being circumciſed? let him not procure prepuce. Is any man called in prepuce? let him not be circumciſed.

 † Circumciſion

† Circumcision is nothing, and prepuce is nothing: but the 19 obseruation of the commaundements of God. † Euery one 20 in the vocation that he vvas called, in it let him abide. † Vvast 21 thou called being a bondman? care not for it: but and if thou canst be made free, vse it rather. † For he that in our Lord is 22 called, being a bondman, is the [c] franchised of our Lord. likevvise he that is called, being free, is the bondman of Christ. † You vvere bought vvith price, be not made the :: bõdmen 23 of men. † Euery `brother' vvherein he vvas called, in that 24 let him abide before God.

[c] libertus

` one, brethren,

:: You must not serue men so that you obey & please them more then God.

The Epistle for holy Virgins not Martyrs.

† And as concerning virgins, a commaundement of our 25 Lord I haue not: but " counsel I giue, as hauing obteined mercie of our Lord to be faithful. † I thinke therfore that 26 this is good for the present necessitie, because it is good for a man so to be. † Art thou tied to a vvife? seeke not to be 27 loosed. Art thou loose from a vvife? seeke not a vvife. † But 28 if thou take a vvife, :: thou hast not sinned. And " if a virgin marie, she hath not sinned. neuerthelesse " tribulation of the flesh shal such haue. but I spare you. † This therfore I say 29 brethren, the time is short, it remaineth, that they also which haue vviues, be " as though they had not: † and they that 30 vveepe, as though they vvept not: and they that reioyce, as though they reioyced not: and they that bye, as though they possessed not: † and they that vse this vvorld, as though they vsed it not. for the figure of this vvorld passeth avvay. 31 † But I vvould haue you to be vvithout carefulnes. He that is 32 without a vvife, is " careful for the things that pertaine to our Lord, hovv he may please God. † But he that is vvith a vvife, 33 is careful for the things that pertaine to the vvorld, hovv he may please his vvife: and he is deuided. † And the vvoman 34 vnmaried & the virgin, thinketh on the things that pertaine to our Lord: that she may be holy both in body and in spirit. † But she that is maried, thinketh on the things that pertaine to the vvorld, hovv she may please her husband. † And 35 this I speake to your profit: not to cast a snare vpon you, but to that vvhich is honest, & that may giue you povver vvithout impediment to attend vpon our Lord. † But if any 36 man thinke that he seemeth dishonoured vpon his virgin, for that she is past age, and if it must so be, let him doe that he vvil. He sinneth not if she marie. † For he that hath de- 37 termined in his hart being settled, not hauing necessitie, but

:: Virginitie counseled as the better: Mariage not forbidden, because it is no sinne.

hauing

hauing povver of his ovvne vvil, and hath iudged this in his
38 hart, to keepe his virgin, doeth vvel. † Therfore both he that ioyneth his virgin in matrimonie, doeth vvel: & he that ioyneth not, doeth better.

Ro. 7, 2.

39 † * A vvoman is bound to the lavv so long time as her husband liueth: but if her husband sleepe, she is at libertie:
40 let her marie to vvhom she vvil: only in our Lord. † But [c] more blessed shal she be if she so remaine, according to my counsel. and I thinke that I also haue the Spirit of God.

c The state of vvidovvhod more blessed, then the state of matrimonie.

ANNOTATIONS
CHAP. VII.

τὴν ἑαυτοῦ

2. *His ovvne vvife.*] He saith not, as the Protestants here pretend to excuse the vnlavvful coniunction of Votaries, *Let euery one mary*: but, let euery one haue, keepe, or vse his ovvne vvife to vvhom he vvas maried before his conuersion. for the Apostle ansvvereth here to the first question of the Corinthians, vvhich vvas not, vvhether it vvere lavvful to mary, but vvhether they vvere not bound vpon their conuersion, to absteine from the company of their vviues married before in their infidelitie, as some did persuade them that they ought to doe. *Hiero. li. 1 cont. Iouin. c. 4. Chrys. in hunc locum ho. 19.*

The Apostle biddeth not al to marie, but to keepe their vviues before maried.

3. *Let the husband render.*] These vvordes open the Apostles intention and talke to be onely of such as are already maried, and to instruct them of the bond and obligation that is betvvene the maried couple for rendring of the dette of carnal copulation one to an other: declaring that the maried persons haue yelded their bodies so one to an other, that they can not vvithout mutual consent, neither perpetually, nor for a time, defraude one the other.

5. *Giue your self to praier.*] This time, & the Heretikes doctrine, and high estimatiō of matrimonial actes, are far from the puritie of the Apostolike and primitiue Church, vvhen the Christians to make their praiers and fastings more acceptable to God, abstained by mutual consent euen from their lavvful vviues. our nevv Maisters not much absteining (as it may be thought) from their vviues for any such matter. And yet S. Augustine saith, the Prelate should passe other in this case, and thinke that not to be lavvful for him, that may be borne in others, because he must daily supply Christes roome, offer, baptize, and pray for the people. So saith he *li. 1. q. ex vtroque test. q. 127 in fine. See S. Hiero. li. 1 c. 19. aduers. Iouin. S. Ambr. li. 1 Offic. c. vlt.* But alas for the people, vvhose maried Pastors are in this point far vvorse then the vulgar folke, neither teaching continencie, nor giuing good example.

Continence in maried folkes for praier sake.

6. *By indulgence, not commaundement.*] Lest some might misconstre his former vvordes, as though he had precisely commaunded maried persons not to abstaine perpetually from carnal copulation, or not to giue their consent one to an other of continencie but for a time onely: he declareth plainely that he gaue no rule or precept absolutely therein, but that he spake al the foresaid, condescending to their infirmities onely, insinuating that continencie from carnal copulation is much better, and that him self kept it continually. *Aug. de bon. coniug. c. 10. Enchirid. c. 78.*

Perpetual continencie, euen in maried folkes, better then carnal copulation.

7. *A proper gift.*] To such as may lavvfully mary, or be already maried, God giueth not alvvaies that more high and special gift or grace of continencie, though euery one of them al that duely aske and labour for it, might haue it: but such are not bound to endeuour or seeke for it alvvaies, and therfore can not be commaunded to abstaine further then they like. but vvhensoeuer a man is bound to abstaine, either by vovv or any other necessarie occasion (as if one of the parties be in prison, vvarre, banishment, siknes, or absent perpetually by lavvful diuorce) the other must needes in paine of damnation abstaine, and can not excuse the vvant of the gift of chastitie. for * he is bound to aske it and to seeke for it of God by fasting, praying, and chastising his body: and so labouring duely for it, God vvil giue the grace of chastitie. So had S. Paul it, and so had al the holy men that continued chast. Therfore detest the doctrine of the Protestants in this point, that vvhen they did not fast nor pray for it, say they haue not the gift. And it vvere a great maruel vvhy so fevv of the nevv Sectes or rather none novv a daies haue that gift, but that vve see it is obtained by those meanes vvhich our forefathers vsed, & they vse not at al. To liue in mariage continently vvithout

Who are boūd to liue continently: and that God giueth this gift to al that aske it.

* See S. Augustine li. 2. c. 19. 20. de Adult. Coniug. to

vvithout the breach of coniugal fidelitie, is a gift of God also, but men must not breake their faith of vvedlocke for vvant of it, but must knovv that God giueth that gift to such as humbly aske it of him. *August. de grat. & lib. arbitrio c. 4. De continent. c. 1.*

The Apostle permitteth mariage to them that be free, not to vovved persons.

9. *If they conteine not.*] He meaneth of such as be free; for if they marry after they haue made vow or promes to God of chastitie, they are vvorthely damned, such being bound to conteine, and so may conteine if they list. *August. de bono viduit. c. 8. 9. & de adult. coniug. li. 1. c. 15. & de fide ad Petrum c. 3. in fine. Ambros. ad virg. lapsam c. 5.*

9. *Better to marry.*] It is better to marry for the said persons that be free, then to be ouerthrovven and fall into fornication. for, *to burne*, or, *to be burnt*, is not to be tempted onely (as the Protestants thinke that picke quarels easely to marry) but it signifieth * to yeld to concupiscence either in minde or external vvorke. Vve say also, for such as be free. for concerning others lavvfully made Priests, and such as othervvise haue made vow of chastitie, they can not marry at al, and therfore there is no comparison in them betvvixt mariage and fornication or burning. for their mariage is but pretensed, and is the vvorst sort of continencie and fornication or burning.

Theodoret in hunc locum.

After diuorce not to marie.

11. *To remaine vnmarried.*] Neither partie may dimisse the other and mary an other for any cause. for though they be separated for fornication, yet neither may marry againe. *August. de adult. coniug. li. 1 c. 8. 9.* and *li. 2 c. 5. 19.* See *Annotat. Mat. 19.* and S. Augustine in his vvhole bookes *de adulter. coniugijs to. 6.*

The Apostles precepts.

12. *I say, not our Lord.*] By this vve learne, that there vvere many matters ouer and aboue the things that Christ taught or prescribed, left to the Apostles order and interpretation: vvherein they might, as the case required, either commaund or counsel, and vve bound to obey accordingly.

Hovv the infidel, or infidels childe, are sanctified by the Christian.

14. *Sanctified.*] Vvhen the infidel partie is said to be cleane or sanctified by the faithful, or the children of their mariage to be cleane, vve may not thinke that they be in grace or state of saluation thereby, but onely that the mariage is * an occasion of sanctification to the infidel partie and to the children. for S. Augustine (*li. 3 de pec. mer. & remis. c. 12.*) concludeth against the Pelagians, as vve may doe against the Caluinists, holding Christian mens children to be holy from their mothers vvombe and not to neede Baptisme, that vvhat other sanctification soeuer it be that is here meant, it can not be ynough to saluation vvithout faith, Baptisme, &c.

Hiero. li. 1 c. 5 aduers. Iouin.

19. *But the obseruation.*] Neither to be Ievv nor Gentil, bond or free, maried or single, nor the faith it self vvhich is proper to Christian men, vvil serue to saluation, vvithout good vvorkes and keeping the commaundements. S. Hierom *adu. Iouin. li. 1 c. 16.*

The differēce of counsels & precepts.

25. *Counsel I giue.*] A counsel is one thing, a commaundement is an other. To doe that vvhich is counseled, is not necessarie, because one may be saued notvvithstanding. but he that vvil doe that vvhich he is counseled vnto, shal haue a higher degree of glorie. He that fulfilleth not a cōmaundement, except he doe penance, can not escape punishment. *August. li. de virg. c. 13. & 14.*

A professed virgin may not marrie.

28. *If a virgin marrie.*] He speaketh not of that virgin vvhich hath dedicated her self to God. (for if any such mary, she shal be damned for breaking her first vow) but onely of yong maides vnmaried in the vvorld. *Hiero. adu. Iouin. li. 1 c. 7. Chrys. ho. 20.* Theodorete, Photius, and the other Greeke Doctors vpon this place *apud Oecum. Epiph. hæres. 61.*

Virginitie counseled as more meritorious.

28. *Tribulation of the flesh.*] They are maruelously deceiued (saith S. Augustine *li. de virg. c. 13*) that thinke the Apostle counseleth virginitie rather then mariage, onely for that mariage hath many miseries and molestations ioyned vnto it, which by virginitie shal be auoided, & not in respect of the greater reward in heauen. for the Apostles prouident counseling to virginitie, is for the next life, and he alleageth these troubles of mariage in that sense specially as they be a hinderance from the seruice of God here, and therfore an impediment to vs toward the next life and the more ample ioyes thereof.

The continencie of married folke.

Their perpetual continencie, best.

29. *As though they had not.*] He exhorteth that such as haue vviues, should not vvholy bestovv them selues in the vaine transitorie pleasure and voluptuousnes of their flesh, but liue in such moderation, that their mariage hinder them as litle as may be, from spiritual cogitatiōs. Vvhich is best fulfilled of them that by mutual consent do vvholy conteine, vvhether they haue had children or none, contemning carnal issue for the ioyes of heauen. And these mariages be more blessed then any other, saith S. Augustine *de Ser. Do. in monte li. 1 cap. 14.*

Virginitie preferred, and vvhy.

Vvhy continencie is required in the clergie.

32. *Careful for the things of our Lord.*] The Protestants might here learne if they list, first that virginitie is not onely preferred before mariage, for that it is a more quiet state of life in this world, but for that it is more conuenient for the seruice of God. Secondly that virginitie hath a grateful puritie and sanctitie both of body & soule, vvhich mariage hath not. Thirdly, they may learne the cause why the Church of God requireth chastitie in the clergie, and forbiddeth not onely fornication, but al carnal copulation euen in lavvful vvedlocke: Vvhich is not onely to the end that Gods Priests be not diuided from him by the clogges of mariage, but also that they be cleane and pure from the fleshly actes of copulation.

CHAP. VIII.

He rebuketh the learned vvho in pride of their knovvledge did eate Idolothyta, that is things offered to Idols, vsing (as they said) their libertie: but not considering that the ignorant tooke their doing as an example for them to frequent such meates so, as they did before in their Paganisme, vvith opinion that they did sanctifie the eaters.

The 4 part. Of meates sacrificed to Idols.

1 AND concerning those things that are sacrificed to Idols, vve knovv that "vve al haue knovvledge. :: Knovvledge puffeth 2 vp: but charitie edifieth. † And if any man thinke that he knoweth something, he hath not yet knovven, as he ought to 3 knovv. † But if any man loue God, the 4 same is knovven of him. † But as for the meates that are immolated to Idols, vve knovv that an Idol is nothing in 5 the vvorld, and that there is no God, but one. † For although there be that are called gods, either in heauen, or in 6 earth (for there are many gods, and many lordes) † yet to vs there is one God, the Father, of vvhom al things, and vve vnto him: and one Lord, IESVS Christ, by vvhom al things, 7 and vve by him. † But there is not knovvledge in al. For "some vntil this present vvith a conscience of the Idol, eate as a thing sacrificed to Idols: and their conscience being 8 vveake, is polluted. † But meate doth not commend vs to God. For neither if vve eate, shal vve abound: nor if vve 9 eate not, shal vve lacke. † But take heede lest perhaps this 10 your libertie be an offense to the vveake. † For if a man see him that hath knovvledge, sit at table "in the Idols temple: shal not his conscience, being vveake, be edified, to eate 11 things sacrificed to Idols? † And through thy knovvledge shal the* vveake brother perish, for whom Christ hath died? 12 † But sinning thus against the brethren, and striking their 13 vveake conscience: you sinne against Christ. † Vvherfore if* meate scandalize my brother: I vvil neuer eate flesh, lest I scandalize my brother.

:: Knowledge vvithout charitie puffeth vp in pride, and profiteth nothing at al. vvhē it is ioyned vvith charitie, then it edifieth. *Aug. li. 9 ciu. Dei c. 20.*

Ro. 14, 15

Ro. 14, 21.

ANNOTATIONS
CHAP. VIII.

1. *Vve al haue knovvledge.*] The spiritual and perfectly instructed Christians knevv no meates, novv to be vncleane, neither for signification, as in the Lavv of Moyses: nor alwaies

No meates vncleane.

by nature and creation, as the Manichees thought: nor by any other pollution, as in that they vvere offered to Idols: and therefore they did eate boldly of such meates as vvere sacrificed, contemning and condemning their Idols as mere nothing, and the vvorship of them as the honour of things imaginarie. vvhich their facte, for their vvant of discretion and charitie, and for the vse of that their libertie to the offense and scandal of the vveake, the Apostle doth here reprehend.

Giuing of scandal reprehended.

7. Some vvith a conscience.] The perfecter mens fault vvas, that they gaue offense by their eating, to the vveaker Christians. Who seeing them vvhom they reputed vvise and learned, to eate the meates offered to Idols, conceiued that there vvas some vertue and sanctificatiō in those meates, from the Idol to vvhich they vvere offered: and though that such things vvere or might be eaten vvith the same conscience and deuotion as before their conuersion.

The Heretikes ridiculously apply S. Paules wordes agaist the Churches fastes and abstinence.

Therefore the case standing thus, and the Apostles discourse of eating or not eating meates being so as is declared (a thing so euident that it admitteth no other interpretation) if the Protestants apply any of this admonition against our fastes in the Cath. Church, they be too to ridiculous.

10. In the Idols temple.] Like as novv, some Catholikes haue said, they knovv that Caluins communion is but as other bread and vvine. But yet the ignorant seing such goe to the Communion, thinke that it is a good act of Religion. Yea vvhatsoeuer they pretend, it must needes seeme an honour to Caluins Communion, when they are seen in the Idols temple solemnly sitting or communicating at the abominable table.

Going to the Communion, vvhat a sinne in Catholikes.

CHAP. IX.

To them that so vaunted their libertie about Idolothyta, he bringeth his ovvne example, to vvit, that he also had libertie to liue by the Gospel, but yet that he vsed it not, so to auoid scandal of the infirme, and because it vvas more meritorious. 24 Declaiming against their securitie, and shevving them by similitudes and examples, 24 both of himself, 1 And of the Israelites, that saluation is not so lightly come by: 14 and so concludeth againe against eating of Idolothyta, because it is also to commit idolatrie, 22 and not onely to giue il example to the infirme.

1 AM I not free? Am I not an Apostle? Haue I not seen Christ IESVS our Lord? Are not you " my vvorke in our Lord? 2 † And if to others I be not an Apostle, but yet to you I am. for you are the seale of my Apostleship in our Lord. 3 † my defense to them that examine me is this: 4 † Haue not vve povver to eate and drinke? 5 † Haue vve not povver to lead about " a vvoman a sister, as also the rest of the Apostles, and our Lordes brethren, and ∴ Cephas? 6 † Or I only and Barnabas haue not vve povver to doe this? 7 † " Vvho euer plaieth the souldiar at his ovvne charges? Vvho planteth a vine, and eateth not of the fruite thereof? Vvho feedeth a flocke, and eateth not of the milke of the flocke? 8 † Speake I these things according to man? Or doth not the Lavv also say these things? 9 † For it is vvritten in the Lavv of Moyses, *Thou shalt not moosel the mouth of the oxe that ∴ treadeth out the corne.* Vvhy, hath God care of oxen? 10 † Or for vs certes doth he say it? For they are vvritten for vs. because he that eareth, ought

∴ He nameth Cephas (that is Peter) to proue his purpose by the example of the cheefe and Prince of the Apostles. *S. Ambro. S. Chrys. Oecum.* vpon this place.

∴ In that coūtrie they did tread out their corne vvith oxen, as vve do thresh it out.

Deu. 25, 4.

ought to eare in hope: and he that treadeth, in hope to receiue fruite. 11 † If vve haue sovven vnto you spiritual things, 12 is it a great matter if vve reape your carnal things? † If other be partakers of your povver: vvhy not vve rather? Hovvbeit vve haue not vsed, this povver: but vve beare al things, lest vve should giue any offence to the Gospel of Christ. 13 † Knovv you not *that they which vvorke in the holy place, eate the things that are of the holy place: and they that serue [c] the altar, participat with the altar? 14 † So also our Lord ordained for them that preach the Gospel, to liue of the Gospel.

Deu. 18, 1.

c τῷ θυσιαστηρίῳ,

c The English bible (1562) here and in the next chapter, saith thrise for *altar, temple*: most falsely & heretically, against holy altars, vvhich about the time of that translation were digged dovvne in England.

15 † But I haue vsed none of these. Neither haue I vvritten these things, that they should be so done in me: for it is good for me to die rather, then that any man should make 16 my glorie void. † For and " if I euangelize, it is no glorie to me: for necessitie lieth vpon me: for vvoe is to me if I 17 euangelize not. † For if I doe this vvillingly, I haue revvard: but if against my vvil, a charge is committed to me. 18 † Vvhat is my revvard then? That preaching the Gospel, I yeld the Gospel vvithout cost, that I abuse not my povver in 19 the Gospel. † For vvhereas I vvas free of al, I made my self 20 the seruant of al: that I might gaine the moe. † And I became to the Ievves as a Ievv, that I might gaine the Ievves. 21 † to them that are vnder the Lavv, as though I vvere vnder the Lavv (vvhereas my self vvas not vnder the Lavv) that I might gaine them that vvere vnder the Lavv. to them that vvere vvithout the Lavv, as though I vvere vvithout the Lavv (vvhereas I vvas not vvithout the lavv of God, but vvas in the lavv of Christ) that I might gaine them that 22 vvere vvithout the Lavv. † To the vveake I became weake, that I might gaine the weake. To al men :: I became al things, 23 that I might saue al. † And I doe al things for the Gospel, " that I may be made partaker thereof.

:: Not by fiction or simulation, but by compassion of the infirmities of al sortes. *Aug. ep. 9.*

The Epistle vpon the Sunday of Septuagesme.

24 † Knovv you not that they that runne in the race, al rūne in deede, but one receiueth the price? " So runne that you 25 may obteine. † And euery one that striueth for the maistrie, refraineth him-self from al things: and they certes, that they may receiue a corruptible crovvne: but vve an incorruptible. 26 † I therfore so runne, not as it vvere at an vncertaine thing: 27 so I fight, not as it vvere beating the aire: † but " I chastise my body, and bring it into seruitude, " lest perhaps vvhen I haue preached to others, my self become reprobate.

ANNOTATIONS
CHAP. IX.

The Heretikes fond pretense of Gods honour.

1. *My vvorke.*] As he called him self before Gods coadiutor, so here he boldly also chalengeth the Corinthians conuersion to be his handy worke in our Lord: nothing derogating thereby frō Christ, as the Protestants rudely charge the Fathers & Catholike men (vnder pretense of Gods honour) for vsing such phrases or speaches in the Apostles sense, of the Saincts or Sacraments.

Heretical trāslation.

5. *A vvoman a sister.*] The Heretikes peruersely (as they do al other places for the aduantage of their Sect) expound this of the Apostles wiues, and for, *vvoman*, translate, *vvife*, al belles sounding vvedding to them. Vvhere the Apostle meaneth plainely the deuout vvomen that after the maner of Ievvrie * did serue the preacher of necessaries, of vvhich sort many folovved Christ, and sustained him and his of their substance. So doth S. Chrysostome, Theodorete, and al the Greekes (*Oecu. in collect. super hunc lo.*) take it. So doth S. Augustine *De op. Monach. c. 4.* and S. Hierom *li. 1 adu. Iouinianum c. 14.* both disputing and prouing it by the very vvordes of the text. S. Ambrose also vpon this place. And the thing is most plaine, for to vvhat end should he talke of burdening the Corinthiās vvith finding his vvife, vvhen him self (c. 7, 7. 8.) clerely saith that he vvas single?

New Test. 1580.

Mat. 27, 55.

Pastors and preachers due.

7. *Who plaieth the souldiar?*] He proueth by the Scriptures and natural reasons that Preachers and Pastors may chalenge their finding of their flocke, though him self for causes had not, nor intended not to vse his right and libertie therein.

Vvorke of supererogation.

16. *If I Euangelize.*] If I should preach either of compulsion and seruil feare, or mere necessitie, not hauing othervvise to liue and sustaine my self in this vvorld, I could not looke for revvard in heauen. but novv doing it, not onely as enioyned me, but also as of loue and charitie, and freely vvithout putting any man to cost, and that voluntarely and of very desire to saue my hearers, I shal haue my revvard of God, yea and a revvard of Supererogation, vvhich is giuen to them that of aboundant charitie do more in the seruice of God then they be commaunded, as S. Augustine expoundeth it. *De op. Mon. c. 5.*

Doing vvel in respect of reward.

23. *That I may be partaker.*] A singular place to conuince the Protestants, that vvil not haue men vvorke vvel in respect of revvard at Gods hand: the Apostle confessing expresly, that al this that he doth either of duety or of Supererogation aboue duety (as to preach of freecost, and to vvorke vvith his ovvne hands to get his ovvne meate and his fellovves, and to abstaine from many lavvful things) al is, the rather to attaine the revvard of heauen.

Running for the game.

24. *So runne.*] If such as runne for a price, to make them selues more svvift, and to vvinne the game, abstaine from many meates and pleasures: vvhat should not vve doe or suffer to vvinne the crovvne of glorie, proposed and promised to none but such as runne, trauel, and endeuour for it?

Penance meritorious.

27. *I chastise.*] The goale of euerlasting glorie is not promised nor set forth for onely-faith men, for such runne at randon: but it is the price of them that chastise and subdue their bodies and fleshly desires by fasting, vvatching, voluntary pouertie, and other afflictions. Lord, hovv farre is the carnal doctrine of the Sectaries and the maners of these daies from the Apostles spirit. Vvherein euen vve that be Catholikes, though vve do not condemne vvith the Protestants these voluntarie afflictions as superfluous (much lesse as superstitious or iniurious to Christs death,) but much cōmend them, yet vve vse nothing the zeale and diligence of our first Christian aunceters herein, and therfore are like to be more subiect to Gods temporal chastisments, at the least in the next life, then they vvere.

S. Paul had not the Protestants securitie of saluation.

27. *Lest perhaps.*] Here may vve lambes tremble (saith a holy father) vvhen the ramme, the guide of the flocke, must so labour and punish him self (besides al his other miseries adioyned to the preaching of the Gospel) lest perhaps he misse the marke. A man might thinke S. Paul should be as sure and as confident of Gods grace & saluation as vve poore vvretched caitiues: but the Heretikes vnhappy securitie, presumption, and faithles persuasion of their saluation is not *fides Apostolorum* but *fides dæmoniorum, not the faith of the Apostles*, but *the faith of Diuels.*

Aug. apud Pet. Lomb. in hunc locum.

CHA. X.

See the argument of the 9 Chapter, vvhich comprehendeth the contents of this also.

FOR

Exo. 13, 21. Nu. 8, 18

Exo. 14, 22.

Exo. 16, 15.

Exo. 17, 6. Nu. 20, 10.

Nu. 26, 63.

Nu. 11, 4

Exo. 32, 6.

Nu. 25, 1

Nu. 21, 5

Nu. 11, 23. 14, 37.

1 FOR I vvil not haue you ignorant brethren, that our fathers vvere al * vnder the cloude, & al * passed through the sea, 2 † and al in Moyses vvere baptized in the cloude and in the sea: 3 † and * al did eate " the same spiritual foode, 4 † and al * drunke the same spiritual drinke (and they * drunke of the spiritual rocke that folovved them, and the rocke vvas Christ,) 5 † but in the more part of them God vvas not vvel pleased. ⊣ for they 6 * vvere ouerthrovven in the desert. † And these things vvere done in a figure of vs, that vve be not coueting euil things, as * they also coueted. 7 † Neither become ye Idolaters, as certaine of them: as is vvritten: *The people sate dovvne to eate and drinke, and rose vp to play.* 8 † Neither let vs fornicate, * as certaine of them did fornicate, and there fel in one day three and tvventie thousand. 9 † Neither let vs tempt Christ: as certaine of them tempted, and * perished by the serpents. 10 † Neither doe you murmure: as * certaine of them murmured, and perished by the destroyer. 11 † And al these things chaunced to them in figure: but they are vvritten to our correption, vpon vvhom the endes of the vvorld are come. 12 † Therfore he that thinketh him self to stand, let him take heede :: lest he fall. 13 † 'Let not tentation apprehend' you, but humane. and God is faithful, vvho vvil not suffer you to be tempted aboue that vvhich you are able: but vvil make also vvith tentation [c] issue, that you may be able to susteine. ⊣

The Epistle vpon the 9 Sunday after Pentecost.

'Tentation hath not apprehended

c ἔκβασιν

:: It is profitable to al, or in a maner to al, for to keepe them in humilitie, not to knovv vvhat they shal be: saith S. Augustine. Vvhich maketh agaist the vaine securitie of the protestants.

14 † For the vvhich cause, my deerest, flee from the seruing 15 of Idols. † I speake " as to vvise men: your selues iudge 16 vvhat I say. † The chalice of benediction " vvhich vve do blesse: is it not the cõmunication of the bloud of Christ? and the bread vvhich vve breake, is it not " the participation 17 of the body of our Lord? † For being many, vve are " one 18 bread, one body, al that participate of one bread. † Behold Israël according to the flesh: " they that eate the hostes, are 19 they not partakers of the altar? † Vvhat then? do I say that that vvhich is immolated to Idols, is any thing? or that the 20 Idol is any thing? † But the things that the heathen do immolate, to deuils they do immolate, and not to God. And " I 21 vvil not haue you become fellovves of deuils. † " You can not drinke the chalice of our Lord, and the chalice of deuils:

 you

you can not be" partakers of the table of our Lord, and of the table of deuils. † Or do vve emulate our Lord? Vvhy, are we 22 stronger then he?

" Al things are lavvful for me, but al things are not expedient. † Al things are lavvful for me, but al things do not 23 edifie. † Let no man seeke his ovvne, but an other mans. 24 † Al that is sold in the shambles, eate: asking no question for 25 conscience. † *The earth is our Lordes, and the fulnes thereof.* † If any 26 inuite you of the infidels, and you vvil goe: eate of al that is 27 set before you, asking no question for conscience. † But if 28 any man say, This is immolated to Idols: do not eate for his sake that shevved it, and for conscience: † conscience I say 29 not thine but the others. For vvhy is my libertie iudged of an other mans conscience? † If I participate vvith thankes: 30 vvhy am I blasphemed for that vvhich I giue thankes for? † Thersore vvhether you eate, or drinke, or do any other 31 thing: doe al things vnto the glorie of God. † Be vvithout 32 offense to the Ievves and to the Gentiles, and to the Church of God: † as I also in al things doe please al men, not see- 33 king that vvhich is profitable to my self, but vvhich is to many: that they may be saued.

Ps. 23, 1.

ANNOTATIONS
CHAP. X.

The old figures of our Sacraments.

3. *The same.*] The red sea and the cloud, a figure of our Baptisme: the Manna from heauen and vvater miraculously dravven out of the rocke, a figure of the holy Sacrament of Christes body and bloud: our Sacraments containing the things and graces in truth, vvhich theirs only signified. And it is an impudent forgerie of the Caluinists, to vvrite vpon this place, that the Ievves receiued no lesse the truth and substance of Christ and his benefites in their figures or Sacraments, then vve do in ours: and that they and vve al eate and drinke of the self same meate and drinke: the Apostle saying onely, that they among them selues did al feede of one bread, & drinke of one rocke: vvhich vvas a figure of Christ, therein especially, that out of Christes side pearced vpon the Crosse, gushed out bloud and vvater for the matter of our Sacraments.

Vve receiue greater benefites by our Sacraments thē the Iewes did by theirs.

Calu. in hunc loc.

The Apostle and auncient fathers speake couertly of the B. Sacrament.

15. *As to vvise men.*] To cause them to leaue the sacrifices and meates or drinkes offered to Idols, he putteth them in minde of the onely true Sacrifice and meate and drinke of Christes body and bloud: of vvhich and the sacrifice of Idols also, they might not be in any case partakers. Vsing this terme, *vt prudentibus loquor*, in the same sense (as it is thought) as the Fathers of the primitiue Church did giue a vvatch vvord of keeping secrete from the Infidels and vnbaptized, the mysterie of this diuine Sacrifice, by these vvordes, *Norunt fideles, norunt qui initiati sunt.* *August. in Ps. 39. & 33. Conc. 1. 2. & Ps. 109. Ho. 42. c. 4. in lib. 50 hom. Orig. in Leuit. ho. 9. Chrys. ho. 27 in Gen. in fine ho. 31 ad po. Antioch. ho. 5. in 1 Tim.* S. Paul saith, I speake to you boldly of this mysterie as to the vvises and better instructed in the same.

The Apostles blessed the Chalice, & so consecrated.

16. *Which vve blesse.*] That is to say, the Chalice of Consecration vvhich vve Apostles and Priests by Christes commission do consecrate, by vvhich speach as vvel the Caluinists (that vse no consecration of the cuppe at al, blasphemously calling it magical murmuration, and peruersely referring the benediction to thankes giuing to God) as also the Lutherans be refuted, vvho affirme Christes body and bloud to be made present by receiuing & in the receiuing onely. for the Apostle expresly referreth the benediction to the chalice, and not to God, making the holy bloud and the communicating thereof the effect of the benediction.

Calix cui benedicimus. ὃ εὐλογοῦμεν.

16. The participation of the body.] The holy Sacrament and Sacrifice of Christs body and bloud being receiued of vs, ioyneth vs in soul and body and engraffeth vs into Christ him self, making vs partakers and as a peece of his body and bloud. *For not by loue or spirit onely* (saith S. Chrysostom) *but in very deede vve are vnited in his flesh, made one body vvith him, members of his flesh and boones.* Chrys. ho. 45 in Io. sub finem. And S. Cyril, *Such is the force of mystical benediction that it maketh Christ corporally by communicating of his flesh to dvvel in vs.* Cyril li. 10. in Io. c. 13.

Our vniting to Christ by the B. Sacrament.

17. One bread, one body.] As vve be first made one vvith Christ by eating his body and drinking his bloud, so secondly are vve conioyned by this one bread vvhich is his body, and cuppe vvhich is his bloud, in the perfect vnion and felovvship of al Catholike men, in one Church vvhich is his body Mystical. Vvhich name of Body mystical is specially attributed and appropriated to this one commonvvealth and Societie of faithful men, by reason that al the true persons and true members of the same, be marueulously knit together by Christes ovvne one body, and by the self same bloud in this diuine Sacrament. See *S. August. li. 21, c. 25 de ciu. Dei. Hilar. li. 8 de Trin. circa med.*

Our vnion among our selues by the B. Sacrament.

18. They that eate the hostes.] It is plaine also by the example of the Ievves in their Sacrifices, that he that eateth any of the host immolated, is partaker of the Sacrifice, and ioyned by office and obligation to God, of vvhose sacrifice he eateth.

20. I vvil not haue you.] I conclude then (saith the Apostle) thus: that as the Christian vvhich eateth and drinketh of the sacrifice or Sacrament of the altar, by his eating is participant of Christes body, and is ioyned in felovvship to al Christian people that eate and drinke of the same, being the host of the nevv Lavv: and as al that did eate of the hostes of the Sacrifices of Moyses Lavv, vvere belonging and associated to that state and to God to vvhom the Sacrifice vvas done: euen so vvhosoeuer eateth of the meates offered to Idols, he shevveth and professeth him self to be of the Communion and Societie of the same Idols.

Participation in Sacrament or sacrifice, shevveth of vvhat societie vve are.

21. You can not drinke.] Vpon the premisses he vvarneth them plainely, that they must either forsake the sacrifice and fellovvship of the Idols and Idolaters, or els refuse the Sacrifice of Christs body and bloud in the Church. In al vvhich discourse vve may obserue that our bread and chalice, our table and altar, the participation of our host and oblation, be compared or resembled point by point, in al effects, conditions, and proprieties, to the altars, hostes, sacrifices and immolations of the Ievves and Gentils. Vvhich the Apostle vvould not, nor could not haue done in this Sacrament of the Altar, rather then in other Sacraments or seruice of our religion, if it onely had not bene a Sacrifice and the proper vvorship of God among the Christians, as the other vvere among the Ievves and Heathen. And so do al the Fathers acknovvledge, calling it onely, & continually almost, by such termes as they do no other Sacrament or ceremonie of Christes religion: *The lambe of God laid vpon the table*: Conc. Nic. *the vnbloudy seruice of the Sacrifice*, In Conc. Ephes. ep. ad Nestor. pag. 605. *the Sacrifice of sacrifices*: Dionys. Ec. Hier. c. 3. *the quickening holy sacrifice: the vnbloudy host and victime*: Cyril. Alex. in Conc. Ephes. Anath. 11. the propitiatorie sacrifice both for the liuing and the dead: Tertul. de cor. Milit. Chrys. ho. 41 in 1 Cor. Ho. 3. ad Philip. Ho. 66 ad po. Antioch. Cypr. ep. 66. & de cœn. Do. nu. 1. August. Ench. 109. Quæst. 2. ad Dulcit. to. 4. Ser. 34. de verb. Apost. *the Sacrifice of our Mediator: the sacrifice of our price: the Sacrifice of the nevv Testament: the sacrifice of the Church*: August. li. 9. c. 13. & li. 3 de bapt. c. 19. *the one onely inconsumptible victime vvithout vvhich there is no religion*: Cyprian. de cœn. Do. nu. 2. Chrys. ho. 17 ad Hebr.* *The pure oblation, the nevv offering of the nevv Lavv: the vital and impolluted host: the honorable and dreadful Sacrifice: the Sacrifice of thankes giuing or Eucharistical: and the Sacrifice of Melchisedec.* Vvhich Melchisedec by his oblation in bread and vvine did properly and most singularly prefigurate this office of Christes eternal Priesthod and sacrificing him self vnder the formes of bread and vvine: vvhich shal continevv in the Church through out al Christian Nations in steed of al the offerings of Aarons Priesthod, as the * Prophete Malachie did foretel, as S. Cyprian, S. Iustine, S. Irenæus and others the most auncient Doctors and Martyrs do testifie. *Cypr. ep. 63. nu. 2. Iustin. Dial. cum Trypho. post med. Irenæ. li. 4 c. 32.* And S. Augustine *li. 17 c. 20 de ciu. Dei. & li. 1 cont. adu. leg. & proph. c. 18. & li. 3 de bapt. c. 19*: S. Leo *ser. 8 de Passione*: and others do expresly auouch that this one Sacrifice hath succeded al other and fulfilled al other differences of sacrifices, that it hath the force and vertue of al other, to be offered for al persons and causes that the others, for the liuing and the dead, for sinnes and for thankes giuing, and for vvhat other necessitie so euer of body or soule.* Vvhich holy action of Sacrifice they also call the MASSE in plaine vvordes. *August. ser. 251. 91. Con. Carthag. 2, c. 3. 4. c. 84. Mileuit. c. 12. Leo ep. 88. 81 c. 2. Grego. li. 2. ep. 9 93. &c.* This is the Apostles and Fathers doctrine. God graunt the Aduersaries may find mercie to see so euident and inuincible a truth.

* *Cypr. Iustin. Irenæ. infra.*

* *Malac. 1, 11.*

* *Ambros. ep. 33.*

The sacrifice of the altar is proued, by the Apostles comparison with the sacrifices of Iewes and Gentils.

It is proued to be a sacrifice, out of the fathers.

The fathers called this sacrifice, the MASSE.

21. Partakers of the table.] Though the faithful people be many vvaies knovven to be Gods peculiar, and be ioyned both to him & among them selues, and also seuered and distinguished from al others that pertaine not to him, as vvel Ievves and Pagans, as Heretikes and Schismatikes, by sundry other external signes of Sacraments, doctrine, and gouernement: yet the most proper and substantial vnion or difference consisteth in the Sacrifice and Altar: by vvhich God so specially bindeth his Church vnto him, and him self vnto his Church, that he acknovvledgeth none to be his

The distinctiō of Christian Catholikes frō the rest, is by not comunicating with thē.

specially in their sacrifices, and at the Communion table.

his, that is not partaker of his one onely Table and Sacrifice in his Church: and acquitteth him self of al such as ioyne in felovvship vvith any of the Heathen at their Idolatrie, or vvith the Ievves at their Sacrifices, or vvith Heretikes and Schismatikes at their prophane and detestable table. Vvhich because it is the proper badge of their separation from Christ and his Church, and an altar purposely erected against Christes Altar, Priesthod, and Sacrifice, is in deede a very sacrifice, or (as the Apostle here speaketh) a table and cuppe of Diuels, that is to say, wherein the Diuel is properly serued, and Christes honour (no lesse then * by the altars of Ieroboam or any prophane superstitious rites of Gentilitie) defiled. And therfore al Catholike men, if they looke to haue felovvship with Christ and his members in his body and bloud, must deeme of it as of Idolatrie or sacrilegious superstition, and abstaine from it and from al societie of the same, as good Tobie did from Ieroboams calues and the altars in Dan and Bethel: and as the good faithful did from the Excelses, and from the temple and sacrifices of Samaria. Novv in the Christian times vve haue no other Idols, but heresies, nor Idolothytes, but their false seruices shifted into our Churches in steede of Gods true and onely vvorship. *Cypr. de vnit Ec. nu. 2. Hiero. in 11 Osee. & 8. Amos. & in 2. Habac. Aug. in ps. 80. v. 10. De Ciu. Dei li. 18. c. 51.*

The heretikes Communiō is the very table and cup of Diuels.

* 3. reg. 12.

Tob. 1.

3. reg. 12.

22 *Al things are lavvful.*] Hitherto the Apostles arguments and examples vvhereby he vvould auert them from the meates offered to Idols, seeme plainly to cōdemne their fact as Idololatrical, or as participant & accessory to Idolatrie, & not onely as of scādal giuen to the weake brethren: and so no doubt it vvas in that they went into the very temple of the Idols, and did vvith the rest that serued the Idols, eate and drinke of the flesh and libaments directly offered to the Idol, yea and feasted together in the same bankets made to the honour of the same Idols: vvhich could not but defile them and entangle them vvith Idolatrie: not for that the meate it self vvas iustly belonging to any other but to God, or could be defiled, made noisome or vnlawful to be eaten, but for and in respect of the abuse of the same and detestable dedicating of that to the diuel, vvhich belonged not to him, but to God alone. Of vvhich sacrilegious act they ought not to be partakers, as needes they must, entering and eating with them in their solemnities. to this end hath S. Paul hitherto admonished the Corinthians. Novv he declareth that othervvise in prophane feasts it is lavvful to eate vvithout curious doubting or asking vvhether this or that vvere offered meates, and in markettes to bye vvhatsoeuer is there sold, vvithout scruple and vvithout taking knovvledge vvhether it be of the Idolothytes or no: vvith this exception, first, that if one should inuite him to eate, or bye this or that as sacred and offered meates, that then he should not eate it, lest he should seeme to approue the offering of it to the Idol, or to like it the better for the same. Secondly, vvhē the vveake brother may take offence by the same. For though it be lavvful in it self to eate any of these meates vvithout care of the Idol: yet al lavvful things be not in euery time and place expedient to be done.

Hovv by participatiō with idolaters, idolatrie is committed.

How to auoid scandal in things indifferent.

CHAP. XI.

The 5. part. Of his Traditions.

He commendeth them for keeping his Traditions generally. 2 and in particular for this, that a man praied and prophecied bareheaded, a vvoman veiled, he bringeth many reasons. 17 About another, he reprehendeth the riche that at the Charitable supper supped vncharitably, 23 telling them that they receiued therfore vnvvorthely the B. Sacrament, and shevving them vvhat an heinous sinne that is, seeing it is our Lordes body and the representation of his death, as he by tradition had taught them.

BE ye folovvers of me, as I also of 1 Christ. † And I praise you brethren, 2 that in al things you be mindeful of me: and as I haue deliuered vnto you, you keepe [a] my [c] precepts.

c In the greeke, *Traditions*, παραδόσεις.

† And I vvil haue you knovv, 3 that the head of euery man, is Christ: and the head of the vvoman, is the man: and the head of Christ, is God.

† Euery

4 † Euery man praying or prophecying vvith his head coue-
5 red: dishonesteth his head. † But " euery vvoman praying or prophecying vvith her head not couered: dishonesteth
6 her head: for it is al one as if she vvere made balde. † For if a vvoman be not couered, let her be polled. but if it be a foule thing for a vvoman to be polled or made balde: let her
7 couer her head. † The man truely ought not to couer his head, because he is the image and glorie of God, but the vvo-
8 man is the glorie of the man. † For the man is not of the
9 vvoman, but the vvoman of the man. † For * the man vvas not created for the vvoman, but the vvoman for the man.
10 († Therfore ought the vvoman to haue povver vpon her
11 head for the Angels.) † But yet neither the man vvithout the vvoman: nor the vvoman vvithout the man, in our Lord.
12 † For as the vvoman is of the man, so also the man by the
13 vvoman: but al things of God. † Your selues iudge: doth
14 it become a vvoman not couered to pray vnto God? † Neither doth nature it self teache you, that a man in deede if he
15 nourish his heare, it is an ignominie for him: † but if a vvoman nourish her heare, it is a glorie for her, because heare is
16 giuen her for a veile? † But if any man seeme to be contentious, vve haue no such " custome, nor the * CHVRCH of God.

Gen. 2, 21.

* churches.

17 † And this I commaund: not praising it that you come
18 together not to better, but to vvorse. † First in deede vvhen you come together into the Church, I heare that there are
19 schismes among you, and in part I beleeue it. † For " there must be heresies also: that they also vvhich are approued,
20 may be made manifest among you. † Vvhen you come therfore together in one, is it not novv to eate " our Lordes sup-
21 per. † For euery one taketh his ovvne supper before to eate.
22 And one certes is an hungred, and an other is drunke. † Vvhy, haue you not houses to eate and drinke in? or contemne ye the Church of God: and confound them that haue not? Vvhat shal I say to you? praise I you in this? I do not praise you.

The Epistle vpon Maundy Thursday.

a The Epistle vpon CORPVS Christi day.

∴ The Apostles drift in al that he saith here of the Sacrament, is against vnvvorthy receiuing (as S. Augustine also noteth *Ep. 118. c. 3.*) and not to set out the vvhole order of ministratiō, as the heretikes do ignorantly imagine.

23 † a For I receiued of our Lord that vvhich also " I haue de-
24 liuered vnto you, ∴ that our Lord IESVS " in the night that he vvas betraied, " tooke " bread: † and giuing thankes brake, and said: " Take ye & eate, " THIS IS " MY BODY VVHICH SHAL BE DELIVERED FOR YOV: " this doe ye for

Mat. 26, 26. Mr. 14, 22. Luc. 22, 19.

the commemoration of me. † In like maner also the chalice 25 after he had supped, saying, THIS CHALICE IS THE NEVV TESTAMENT IN MY BLOVD. this doe ye, as often as you shal drinke, for the comemoration of me. † For 26 as often as you shal eate this bread, and drinke the chalice, "you shal shevv the death of our Lord, vntil he come. † Ther- 27 fore vvhosoeuer shal eate this bread, or drinke the chalice of our Lord vnvvorthily, he shal be "guilty of the body and of the bloud of our Lord. † But let a man proue him self: 28 and so, let him eate of that bread, and drinke of the chalice. † For he that eateth and drinketh vnvvorthily: eateth and 29 drinketh iudgement to him self, "not discerning the body of our Lord. ⁜ † Therfore are there among you many weake 30 and feble, and "many sleepe. † But if vve did "iudge our 31 selues: vve should not be iudged. † But vvhiles vve are 32 iudged, of our Lord vve are chastised: that vvith this world vve be not damned. ⁜ † Therfore my brethren, vvhen you 33 come together to eate, "expect one an other. † If any man 34 be an hungred, let him eate at home: that you come not together vnto iudgement. And the rest "I vvil dispose, vvhen I come.

ANNOTATIONS
CHAP. XI.

2. *My precepts.*] Our Pastors and Prelates haue authoritie to commaund, and vve are bound to obey. And the Gouerners of the Church may take order and prescribe that vvhich is comely in euery state, as time and place require, though the things be not of the substance of our religion.

5. *Euery vvoman.*] Vvhat gifts of God so euer vvomen haue, though supernatural, as some had in the Primitiue Church, yet they may not forget their vvomanly shamefastnes, but shevv them selues subiect and modest, and couer their heads vvith a veile.

The Custome of the Church, is a good answer against al vvranglers.

16. *Custome.*] If vvomen or other, to defend their disorder & malipertnes, dispute or alleage Scriptures and reasons, or require causes of their preachers vvhy & by vvhat authoritie they should be thus restrained in things indifferent, make them no other ansvver but this, This is the custome of the Church, this is our custome. Vvhich is a goodly rule to represse the saucinesse of contentious ianglers, vvhich being out of al modestie and reason, neuer vvant vvordes and replies against the Church. Vvhich Church if it could then by prescription of tvventy or thirty yeres, and by the authority of one or tvvo of their first preachers, stoppe the mouthes of the seditious: vvhat should not the custome of fiftene hundred yeres, & the decrees of many hundred Pastors, gaine of reasonable, modest, and humble men?

That heresies shal come, and vvherfore.

19. *There must be heresies*] Vvhen the Apostle saith, *Heresies must be*: He shevveth the euent, and not that God hath directly so appointed it as necessarie. for, that they be, it commeth of mans malice and free vvil: but that they be conuerted to the manifestation of the good and constant in faith & the Churches vnitie, that is Gods special vvorke of prouidence that vvorketh good of euil. And for that there should fall Heresies and Schismes, specially concerning the Article and vse of the B. Sacrament of the Altar, vvhereof he novv beginneth to treate, it may make vs maruel the lesse, to see so great dissensions, Heresies, and Schismes of the vvicked and vveake in faith concerning the same. Such things then vvil be, but vvo to him by vvhom scandals or Sectes do come. *Let vs vse Heretikes,* saith S. Augustine, *not to that end to approue their errours, but that by defending the*

Vvhat commoditie vve may make of heresies.

Catholike doctrine against their deceites, vve may be more vvatchful and vvary: because it is most truely vvritten. There must be heresies that the tried and approued may be manifested or discouered from the holovv hartes among you. Let vs vse this benefite of Gods prouidence. for Heretikes be made of such as vvould erre or be naught, though they vvere in the Church: but being out, they profite vs excedingly, not by teaching the truth vvhich they knovv not, but by stirring vp the carnal in the Church to seeke truth, and the spiritual Catholikes, to cleere the truth. for there be innumerable holy approued men in the Church, but they be not discerned from other among vs, nor manifest, so long as vve had rather sleepe in darknes of ignorance, then behold the light of truth. therfore many are raised out of their sleepe by Heretikes to see the day of God, and are glad thereof. August. c. 8. de vera relig.

20. *Our Lordes supper.*] The Christians at or about the time of the Churches onely Sacrifice and their communicating there of, kept great feastes: vvhich continued long, for that the reliefe of the poore vpon the common charges of the richer sort, and the charitie and vnitie of al sortes vvere much preserued thereby, for vvhich cause they vvere called ἀγάπαι, that is, *Charities*, of the auncient Fathers, and vvere kept commonly in Church houses or porches adioyning, or in the body of the Church (vvhereof see Tertullian *Apolog. c. 39.* Clemens Alexand. S. Iustine, S. Augustine *cont. Faust. li. 20 c. 20.*) after the Sacrifice and Communion vvas ended, as S. Chrysostom *ho. 27. in 1 Cor. in initio* iudgeth. Those feastes S. Paul here calleth *Cœnas Dominicas*, because they vvere made in the Churches vvhich then vvere called *Dominicæ*, that is, *Our Lordes houses*. The disorder therfore kept among the Corinthians in these Church-feastes of Charitie, the Apostle seeketh here to redresse, from the foule abuses expressed here in the text. And as S. Ambrose *in hunc locum*, and most good authors novv thinke, this vvhich he calleth *Dominicam cœnam*, is not meant of the B. Sacrament, as the circunstances also of the text do giue, namely, the reiecting of the poore, the rich mens priuate deuouring of al, not expecting one an other, glottony and drunkennesse in the same, vvhich can not agree to the holy Sacrament. And therfore the Heretikes haue smal reason, vpon this place, to name the said holy Sacramēt, rather, *the Supper of the Lord*, then after the maner of the primitiue Church, the *Eucharist*, MASSE, or *Liturgie*. But by like they vvould bring it to the supper againe or Euening seruice, vvhen men be not fasting, the rather to take avvay the old estimation of the holines thereof.

Coc. Gang. can. 11. Conc. Loadic. can. 27. 28.

Agapæ or suppers of charitie.

Vvhether the Apostle meane by *our Lords supper*, the B. Sacrament.

23. *I haue deliuered.*] As al other partes of religion vvere first deliuerd by preaching and vvord of mouth to euery Nation conuerted, so this holy order and vse of the B. Sacrament vvas by S. Paul first giuen vnto the Corinthians by tradition. Vnto vvhich as receiued of our Lord he reuoketh them by this Epistle, not putting in vvriting particularly al things pertaining to the order, vse, and institution, as he aftervvard saith: but repeating the summe and substance thereof, and leauing the residue to his returne. But his vvordes and narration here vvritten vve vvil particularly prosecute, because the Heretikes make profession to folovv the same in their pretended reformation of the MASSE.

Traditiō vvithout vvriting.

Whether the catholikes or Protestants doe more imitate Christs institution of the B. Sacrament.

23. *In the night.*] First the Aduersaries may be here conuinced that al the circunstāces of time, person, & place vvhich in Christes action are noted, neede not to be imitated. As, that the Sacramēt should be ministred at night, to men onely, to onely tvvelue, after or at supper, & such like: because (as S. Cyprian *ep. 63. nu. 7.* & S. Augustine *ep. 118. c. 6.* note) there vvere causes of those accidents in Christ that are not novv to be alleaged for vs. He instituted then this holy act: vve do not. he made his Apostles Priests, that is to say, gaue them commission to do and minister the same: vve do not. he vvould haue this the last act of his life & vvithin the bounds of his Passion: it is not so vvith vs. he vvould eate and make an end of the Paschal to accomplish the old Lavv: that can not be in our action. therfore he must needes doe it after supper and at night: vve may not do so. he excluded al vvomen, al the rest of his Disciples, al lay men: vve inuite al faithful, men & vvomen. In many circunstances then, neither vve may imitate Christes first action, nor the Heretikes as yet do: though they seeme to encline by abandoning other names sauing this (calling it Supper) to haue it at night and after meate. though (as is before noted) they haue no iust cause to call it so vpon Christs fact, seeing the Euangelists do plainely shevv *that the Sacrament vvas instituted after Supper, as the Apostle him self here recordeth of the later part in expresse speach. And most men thinke, a long sermon and the vvashing of the Apostles feete came betvvene, yea and that the supper vvas quite finished, & grace said. But in al these and such like things, the Catholike Church onely, by Christes Spirit can tel, vvhich things are imitable, vvhich not, in al his actions.

Io. 13, 2.

Al circunstāces in our Sauiours action about the B. Sacramēt, neede not be imitated.

23. *Tooke.*] Christ tooke bread into his hands, applying this ceremonie, action, and benediction to it, and did blesse the very element, vsed povver and actiue vvord vpon it, *as he did ouer the bread and fishes vvhich he multiplied: and so doth the Church of God: and so do not the Protestants, if they folovv their ovvne booke and doctrine, but they let the bread & cuppe stand a loofe, and occupie Christes vvordes by vvay of report and narration, applying them not at al to the matter proposed to be occupied: and therfore hovvsoeuer the simple people be deluded by the rehersal of the same vvordes vvhich Christ vsed, yet consecration, benediction, or sanctification of bread and vvine they professe they make none at al. At the first alteration of religion, there vvas a figure of the Crosse at this vvord, *He blessed*: and at the vvorde, *He tooke*, there vvas a glosse or

Luc. 9, 16.

The Protestants imitate not Christ in blessing the bread and vvine.

rubrike that appointed the Minister to imitate Christs action, and to take the bread into his hands: aftervvard that vvas reformed and Christes actiou abolished, and his blessing of bread turned to thankes giuing to God.

They imitate him not in vnleauened bread, and mingling water with wine.

23. *Bread.*] Christ made the holy Sacrament of vnleauened bread, and al the Latin Church imitateth him in the same, as a thing much more agreable to the signification both in it self and in our liues, then the leauen. Yet our Aduersaries neither folovv Christ, S. Paul, nor the vvest Church, in the same: but rather purposely make choise of that kind that is in it self more vnseemely, and to the first institution lesse agreable. In the other part of the Sacrament they contemne Christ and his Church much more impudently and damnably. For Christ and al the Apostles and al Catholike Churches in the vvorld haue euer mixed their wine vvith water, for great mysterie and signification, specially for that water gushed together vvith bloud out of our Lordes side. *This our Lord did* (saith S. Cyprian *Ep. 63 ad Cecilium. nu. 4, 7.*) *and none rightly offereth, that folovveth not him therein.* Thus Irenæus (*li. 5. c. 1.*) Iustine (*Apolog. 2. in fine.*) and al the Fathers testifie the Primitiue Church did, and in this sort it is done in al the MASSES of the Greekes, S. Iames, S. Basils, S. Chrisostoms: and yet our Protestants pretending to reduce al to Christ, vvil not doe as he did, and al the Apostles and Churches that euer vvere.

The vvordes of consecration, to be said ouer the bread and vvine. the vvhich the Protestants do not.

24. *This is.*] These vvordes being set dovvne, not in the person of the Euangelistes or Apostles, but expressed as in Christes ovvne person, to be said ouer the bread, and the like ouer the vvine, are the formes of the Sacrament and vvordes of consecration: neither is it a Sacrament but (as S. Augustine saith) vvhen the vvordes come, that is to say, actiuely and presently be applied to the elements of the same. Therfore the Protestants neuer applying these vvordes more then the vvhole narration of the institution, nor reciting the vvhole (as is said) othervvise then in historical maner, (as if one vvould minister Baptisme & neuer apply the wordes of the Sacramēt to the childe, but onely read Christes speaches of the same) make no Sacrament at al. And that these proper vvordes be the onely forme of this Sacrament, and so to be spoken ouer or vpon the bread and vvine, S. Ambrose plainly and precisely vvriteth, recording hovv far the Euangelists narratiue vvordes do goe, and vvhere Christes ovvne peculiar mystical vvordes of consecration begin: and so the rest of the fathers. *Ambro. li. 4. de Sacr. c. 4. & c. 9. de init. Myster. Iusti. Apolog. 2. in fine. Cypr. de Cœn. Do. nu. 1. 2. Aug. Ser. 28. de verb. Do. sec. Mat. Tertul. li. 4. cont. Marc. Chrys. ho. 2. in 2. ad Tim. in fine. & ho. de prodit. Iuda to. 3. Grego. Nyss. in orat. Catech. Damasc. li. 4. c. 14.*

tract. 80 in Io.

The Protestants haue taken away the B. Sacrament altogether.

24. *My body.*] Vvhen the vvordes of Consecration be by the said impietie of the Protestants, thus remoued from the elements: no maruel if Christes holy body and bloud be not there, or that it is novv no more a Sacrament, but common bread and vvine. So they that vniustly charge the Cath. Church vvith defrauding the people of one peece of the Sacramēt, haue in very deede left no part nor spice of Sacrament, neither folovving Christ, as they pretend, nor S. Paul, nor any Euangelist, but their owne detestable Secte, hauing boldly defaced the vvhole institution, not in any accidental indifferent circunstances, but in the very substance and al. The right name is gone, the due elements both gone, no blessing or consecration, or other action ouer them, the formes be gone: and consequently the body and bloud, the Sacrament and the Sacrifice.

The povver to consecrate giuen to Priests onely.

24. *This doe.*] By these vvordes, authoritie and povver is giuen to the Apostles, and by the like, in the Sacrament of Orders, to al lavvful Priests onely. No maruel then that the nevv heretical Ministers being lay men, giue the people nothing but bare bread and vvine, profane, naked, and natural elements void of Sacrament and al grace. See the Annotation vpon S. Luke chap. 22, 19.

The Sacramēt consisteth not in the receiuing.

24. *Take and eate.*] This pertaineth to the receiuing of those things vvhich by consecration are present and sacrificed before: as vvhen the people or Priests in the old Lavv did eate the hostes offered or part thereof, they vvere made partakers of the sacrifice done to God before. And this is not the substance, or being, or making of the Sacrament or Sacrifice of Christes body and bloud: but it is the vse and application to the receiuer, of the things vvhich vvere made and offered to God before. There is a difference betvvixt the making of a medecine or the substance and ingredience of it, and the taking of it. Novv the receiuing being but a consequence or one of the endes vvhy the Sacrament vvas made, & the meane to apply it vnto vs: the Aduersaries vnlearnedly make it al and some, ad therfore improperly name the vvhole Sacrament and ministration thereof, by calling it the Communion. Vvhich name they giue also rather then any other, to make the ignorant beleeue that many must communicate together: as though it vvere so called for that it is common to many. By which collusion they take avvay the receiuing of the Priest alone, of the sicke alone, of reseruing the consecrated Host and the vvhole Sacrament. Against vvhich deceite, knovv that this part of the MASSE is not called Communiō, for that many should concurre together alwaies in the external Sacrament: but for that vve do communicate

Vvhy the Protestants call it the Communion.

Communion, vvhich is a part of the

nicate or ioyne in vnitie and perfect felovvship of one body, vvith al Christian men in the vvorld, vvith al (vve say) that eate it through the vvhole Church, and not vvith them onely vvhich eate vvith vs at one time. And this fellovvship riseth of that, that vve be, euery time vve receiue either alone or vvith companie, partakers of that one body vvhich is receiued through out al the vvorld. *It is called cõmunion* (saith S. Damascene) *& so in deede it is, for that by it vve cõmunicate vvith Christ, & be partakers of his flesh & diuinitie, & by it doe cõmunicate and are vnited one vvith an other. onely let vs take heede that vve de not participat vvith heretikes.* And vvhen the Apostle saith, that al be one bread and one body that are partakers of one Bread, he meaneth not of them onely that communicate at one time and place: but that al be so, that communicate in vnitie through the whole Church. Thẽ the name Communion is as ignorantly vsed of them, as the name of Supper.

MASSE, what it signifieth.

li. 4. c. 14. de orthod. fide.

26. You shal shevv.] Vpon this vvord the Heretikes fondly ground their false supposition, that this Sacrament can not rightly be ministred or made vvithout a sermon of the death of Christ: and that this and other Sacraments in the Church, be not profitable, when they be ministred in a strange language. As though the grace, force, operation, & actiuitie, together vvith the instruction and representation of the things which they signifie, vvere not in the very substance, matter, forme, vse, and vvorke it self of euery of the Sacraments: and as though preaching vvere not one vvay to shevv Christes Passion, and the Sacraments an other vvay: namely this Sacrament, conteining in the very kindes of the elements and the action, a most liuely representation of Christes death. As vvisely might they say that neither Abels sacrifice nor the Paschal lambe could signifie Christes death vvithout a Sermon.

Hovv Christs death is shewed by the B. Sacrament it self, vvithout sermon or othervvise.

27. Guilty of the body.] First herevpon marke vvel, that il men receiue the body and bloud of Christ, be they infidels or il liuers. For in this case they could not be guilty of that vvhich they receiue not. Secondly, that it could not be so heinous an offense for any man to receiue a peece of bread or a cuppe of vvine, though they vvere a true Sacrament. For it is a deadly sinne to receiue any Sacramẽt with vvil & intentiõ to cõtinevv in sinne, or vvithout repentance of former sinnes: but yet by the vnvvorthy receiuing of no other Sacrament is man guilty of Christes body and bloud, but here, vvhere the vnvvorthy (as S. Chrysostom saith) doth vilany to Christes ovvne person, as the Ievves or Gentiles did, that crucified it. *Chrys. ho. de non contemn. Ec. &c. Ho. 60 & 61 ad po. Antioch.* Vvhich inuincibly proueth against the Heretikes that Christ is really present.

The vvicked receiue the body & bloud. The real presence is proued by the heinous offẽse of vnvvorthy receiuing.

28. Let him proue.] A man must examine his life diligently vvhether he be in any mortal sinne, and must confesse him self of euery offense vvhich he knovveth or feareth to be deadly, before he presume to come to the holy Sacrament. For so the Apostles doctrine here, vvith the continual custom of the Cath. Church and the Fathers example, binde him to doe. *Cypr. de lapsi. nu. 7. Aug. Eccl. dog. c. 53.*

Confessiõ before receiuing the B. Sacrament.

29. Not discerning the body.] That is, because he putteth no difference nor distinction betvvixt this high meate and others. and therfore S. Augustine saith ep. 118. c. 3. *that it is he that the Apostle saith shal be damned, that doth not by singular veneration or adoration make a difference betvvene this meate and al others.* And againe *in Psal. 98. No man eateth it before he adore it.* And S. Ambrose *li. 3, c. 12 de Sp. San. We adore the flesh of Christ in the Mysteries.* S. Chrysostome *ho. 24 in 1 Cor. We adore him on the altar, as the Sages did in the manger.* S. Nazianzene *in Epitaph. Gorgoniæ. My sister called on him vvhich is vvorshipped vpon the altar.* Theodorete *Dial. 2 Inconf. The Mystical tokens be adored.* S. Denys, this Apostles scholer, made solemne inuocation of the Sacrament after Consecration. *Ecclesiast. Hier. c. 3 part. 3 in princip.* and before the receiuing, the vvhole Church of God crieth vpon it, * *Domine non sum dignus, Deus propitius esto mihi peccatori. Lambe of God that takest avvay the sinnes of the vvorld, haue mercie on vs.* And for better discerning of this diuine meate, vve are called from common profane houses to Gods Church: for this, vve are forbidden to make it in vulgar apparel, and are appointed sacred solemne vestiments. *Hiero. in Epitaph. Nepot. & li. 2 adu. Pelag. c. 9. Paulinus ep. 12 ad Seuer. Io. Diaco. in vit. D. Greg. li. 3, c. 59.* For this, is the halovving of Corporals and Chalices, *Ambr. 2 Off. c. 28. Nazianz. Orat. ad Arianos. Optatus li. 6 in initio.* for this, profane tables are remoued and altars consecrated: *August. Ser. de temp. 255.* for this, the very Priests them selues are honorable, chast, sacred, *Hiero. ep. 1 ad Heliodorum c. 7. Li 1 adu. Iouin. c. 19. Ambros. in 1 Tim. 3.* for this, the people is forbidden to touch it vvith cõmon hands. *Nazianz. orat. ad Arianos in initio.* for this, great care and solicitude is taken that no part of either kinde fall to the ground, *Cyril. Hieros. mystag. 5 in fine. Orig. ho. 13 in c. 25 Exod.* for this, sacred prouision is made that if any hosts or parts of the Sacrament do remaine vnreceiued, they be most religiously reserued vvith al honour and diligence possible. and for this, examination of consciences, confession, continencie, & (as S. Augustine saith) receiuing it fasting. Thus do vve Catholikes and the Church of God discerne the holy Body and bloud by S. Paules rule, not onely from your profane bread and vvine (vvhich not by any secrete abuse of your Curats or Clerkes, but by the very order of your booke, the Minister, if any remaine after your Communion, may take home vvith him to his ovvne vse, and

Adoration of the B. Sacrament.

* *See the Annot. Mat. 8, 8.*

The manifold honour and discerning of Christes body in the Cath. Church.

ep. 118, c. 6.

The Profane bread of the Protestants.

and therfore is no more holy by your ovvne iudgement then the rest of his meates) but from al other either vulgar or sanctified meates, as* the Catechumens bread, and our vsual holy bread. If al this be plaine and true, and you haue nothing agreable to the Apostles nor Christes institution, but al cleane contrarie: then *imperet vobis Deus* and confound you for not discerning his holy Body, and for conculcating the bloud of the nevv Testament.

Holy bread.

*Aug. de pec. merit. li. 2. c. 26. Ep. Iude.

Vnvvorthie receiuing.

30. Many sleepe.] Vve see here by this, it is a fearful case and crime to defile by sinne (as much as in vs lieth) the body of Christ in the Sacrament. seeing God strooke many to death for it in the Primitiue Church, and punished others by greuous sicknes. No maruel that so many strange diseases and deaths fall vpon vs novv in the vvorld.

Penance and satisfaction.

31. Iudge your selues.] Vve may note here that it is not ynough, onely to sinne no more, or to repent lightly of that vvhich is past: but that vve should punish our selues according to the vveight of the faults past and forgiuen: and also that God vvil punish vs by temporal scourges in this life or the next, if vve do not make our selues very cleane before vve come to receiue his holy Sacrament. vvhose heauy hands vve may escape by punishing our selues by fasting and other penance.

33. Expect one an other.] Returning novv to their former fault and disorder for the vvhich he tooke this occasion to talke of the holy Sacrament, and hovv great a fault it is to come vnvvorthely to it: he exhorteth them to keepe their said suppers or feastes in vnitie, peace, and sobrietie, the riche expecting the poore &c.

The Masse is agreable to the Apostles vse and tradition: the Communion is not.

34. I vvil dispose.] Many particular orders & decrees, moe then be here or in any other booke of the nevv Testament expresly vvritten, did the Apostles, as we see here, and namely S. Paul to the Corinthians, set dovvne by tradition, vvhich our vvhole ministration of the MASSE is agreable vnto, as the substance of the Sacrifice and Sacrament is by the premisses proued to be most consonant: Caluins supper and Communion in al points vvholy repugnant to the same. And that it agreeth not to these other not vvritté traditions, they easely confesse. The* Apostles deliuered vnto the Church to take it onely fasting: they care not for it. The Apostles taught the Church to consecrate by the vvordes and the signe of the Crosse, vvithout vvhich (saith S. Augustine *tract. in Io. 118. Ser. 75. in append. Chrys. ho. 55 in 16 Mat.*) no Sacrament is rightly perfited: the Protestants haue take it avvay. The Apostles taught the Church to keepe * a Memorie or inuocatió of Saincts in this Sacrifice: the Caluinists haue none. The Apostles decreed that in this Sacrifice there should be special praiers for the dead, *Chrys. ho. 3 in ep. ad Philip. Aug. de cur. pro mort. c. 1*: they haue none. Likewise that water should be mixed with the wine, and so forth. See *Annot. in c. 11, v. 21. Bread.* Therfore if Caluin had made his new administration according to all the Apostles written wordes, yet not knovving how many things beside, the Apostle had to prescribe in these wordes, *Cætera cum venero disponam* (the rest I wil dispose, when I come) he could not haue satisfied any wise man in his new chaunge. But now seeing they are fallen to so palpable blindnes, that their doing is directly opposite to the very Scripture also, which they pretend to folow onely, and haue quite destroied both the name, substance, and al good accidents of Christes principal Sacrament, we trust al the world wil see their folly and impudencie.

*Aug. ep. 118 c. 6.

*Aug tract 84 in Io. & Chrys. ho. 21 in Act.

CHAP. XII.

They must not make their diuersitie of Giftes an occasion of Schisme, considering that al are of one Holy Ghost, and for the profit of the one body of Christ vvhich is the Church: 12 Vvhich also could not be a body, vvithout such varietie of members. 12 Therfore neither they that haue the inferiour giftes, must be discontent, seing it is Gods distribution: nor they that haue the greater, contemne the other, considering they are no lesse necessarie: 25 but al in al ioyne together, 28 and euery one knovv his ovvne place.

The 6. part. As touching the Giftes of the Holy Ghost.

The Epistle vpon the 10 Sunday after Pentecost.

Nd concerning spiritual things, I vvil not haue you ignorát, brethren. † You know that vvhen you vvere heathen, you vvent to dumme Idols according as you vvere ledde. † Therfore I doe you to vnderstand that no má speaking in the Spirit of God, saith anáthema to IESVS. And no man can say, Our Lord IESVS: but in the holy Ghost. 1 2 3

† And

4 † And there are diuisions of graces, but one Spirit. † And
5 there are diuisions of ministrations: but one Lord. † And
6 there are diuisions of operations, but one God, vvhich vvor-
7 keth al in al. † And the manifestation of the Spirit is giuen
8 vnto euery one to profit. † To one certes by the Spirit is giuen :: the vvord of vvisedom: and to an other, the vvord of
9 knovvledge according to the same Spirit: † to an other,
" faith in the same Spirit: to an other, the grace of doing cu-
10 res in one Spirit: † to an other, the vvorking of miracles: to
an other, prophecie: to an other, discerning of spirites: to an
other, kindes of tonges: to an other, interpretation of lan-
11 guages. † And al these things vvorketh one and the same
Spirit, diuiding to euery one according as he vvil. ✠

:: Al these Giftes be those vvhich the learned call *Gratias gratis datas*: vvhich be bestovved often euen vpon il liuers, vvhich haue not the other graces of God whereby their persons should be grateful, iust & holy in his sight.

Ro. 12, 4
Eph. 4, 7.

12 † For * as the body is one, and hath many members, and
al the members of the body vvhereas they be many, yet are
13 :: one body: so also Christ. † For in one Spirit vvere vve
al baptized into one, vvhether Ievves, or Gentiles, or bond-
men, or free: and in one Spirit vve vvere al made to drinke.
14 † For the body also is not one member, but many. † " If
15 the foote should say, because I am not the hand, I am not of
16 the body: is it therfore not of the body? † And if the eare
should say, because I am not the eie, I am not of the body:
17 is he therfore not of the body? † If the vvhole body vvere
the eie: vvhere is the hearing? If the vvhole vvere the hea-
18 ring: vvhere is the smelling? † But novv God hath set
the members, euery one of them in the body as he vvould.
19 † And if al vvere one member, vvhere vvere the body? † But
20 novv there are many members in deede, yet one body. † And
the eie can not say to the hand: I neede not thy helpe. or
againe the head to the feete, You are not necessarie for me.
21 † But much more those that seeme to be the more vveake
22 members of the body, are more necessarie: † and such as
vve thinke to be the baser members of the body, vpon them
vve put more aboundant honour: and those that are our vn-
23 honest partes, haue more aboundant honestie. † And our
honest partes neede nothing: but God hath tempered the
body, giuing to it that vvanted, the more aboundant honour,
24 † that there might be no " schisme in the body, but the mem-
25 bers together might be careful one for an other. † And if
one member suffer any thing, al the members suffer vvith it.
or if one member do glorie, al the members reioyce vvith it.

" one body,

:: A maruelous vniō betwixt Christ & his Church & a great cōfort to al Catholikes being members therof, that the Church and he, the head & the body, make & be called one Christ. *Aug. de vnit. Ec.*

† And

:: S. Augustine ep. 137 giueth the same reason, vvhy miracles & cures be done at the memories or bodies of some Saincts more then at others: & by the same Saincts in one place of their memories rather then at other places.

† And you are the body of Christ, and members of member. 26

† And * some verily God hath set in the Church first Apostles, secondly prophets, thirdly doctors, next miracles, thē the graces of doing cures, helpes, gouernements, kindes of tonges. 27 † Are al Apostles? are al prophets? are al doctors? 28 † :: are al miracles? haue al the grace of doing cures? do al 29 speake vvith tonges? do al interpret? † But pursue the better 30 giftes. And yet I shevv you a more excellent vvay.

Eph. 4, 11.

ANNOTATIONS
CHAP. XII.

Zealous faith.

9. *Faith in the same.*] This faith is not an other in substance then the common faith in Christ, but is of an other accidental qualitie onely, that is, of more feruor, deuotiō, zeale, and confident trust, specially for doing of miracles.

Vnitie.

15. *If the foote.*] The Church is of exceding great distinctiō of members, giftes, orders, and offices: yet of great concord, concurrence, mutual communion and participation in al actions of her members among them selues, and vvith Christ the head of the Body.

Schisme.

25. *Schisme in the body.*] As Charitie and vnitie of spirit, is the proper bond and vveale of the common Body: so is diuision or Schisme, vvhich is the interruption of peace and mutual Societie betvvene the partes of the same, the special plague of the Church, and as odious to God as rebellion to the temporal Soueraine.

CHAP. XIII.

That aboue al other Giftes they should seeke after Charitie: as that vvithout vvhich nothing profiteth, 4 and vvhich doth al as is to be done, and remaineth also in heauen.

The Epistle vpon the Sunday of Quinquagesme, called Shroue-sunday.

:: This proueth that faith is nothing vvorth to saluatiō vvithout vvorkes, and that there may be true faith vvithout Charitie.

IF I speake vvith the tonges of men and of Angels, and haue " not charitie: I am become as sounding brasse, or a tinkling cymbal. 1 † And if I should haue prophecie, and knevv al mysteries, and al knovvledge, and if I should :: haue al faith so that I could remoue mountaines, and haue not charitie, I am nothing. 2 † And if I should distribute al my goods to be meate for the poore, and if I should " deliuer my body so that I burne, and haue not charitie, it doth profit me nothing. 3

† Charitie is patient, is benigne: Charitie enuieth not, 4 dealeth not peruersly: is not puffed vp, † is not ambitious, 5 seeketh not her ovvne, is not prouoked to anger, thinketh not euil: † reioyceth not vpon iniquitie, but reioyceth 6 vvith

7 vvith the truth: † suffereth al things, beleeueth al things, ho-
8 peth al things, beareth al things. † Charitie neuer falleth
auvay: vvhether prophecies shal be made voide, or tonges
9 shal cease, or knovvledge shal be destroied. † For in part
10 vve knovv, and in part vve prophecie. † But ∷ vvhen that
shal come that is perfect, that shal be made voide that is in
11 part. † Vvhen I vvas a litle one, I spake as a litle one, I vnderstood as a litle one, I thought as a litle one. But vvhen I vvas
made a man, I did avvay the things that belōged to a litle one.
12 † Vve see novv by a glasse in a darke sort: but then face to
face. Novv I knovv in part: but then I shal knovv as also I
13 am knovven. † And novv there remaine, faith, hope, charitie,
"these three. but the ∷ greater of these is charitie.

∷ By this text S. Augustine *li. 22. Ciu. c. 29* proueth that the Saints in heauen haue more perfect knovvledge of our affaires here, then they had vvhen they liued here.

∷ Charitie is of al the three the greatest. Hovv then doth onely faith, being inferior to it, saue & iustifie, and not Charitie?

ANNOTATIONS CHAP. XIII.

1. Not Charitie.] Vvithout Charitie, both tovvard euery particular person, and specially tovvard the common body of the Church, none of al the giftes and graces of God be profitable.

Charitie.

3. Deliuer my body.] *Beleeue* (saith S. Augustine) *assuredly and hold for certaine, that no Heretike and Schismatike that vniteth not him self to the Catholike Church againe, hovv great almes so euer he giue, yea or shede his bloud for Christes name, can possibly be saued. For, many Heretikes by the cloke of Christes cause, deceiuing the simple, suffer much. But vvhere true faith is not, there is no iustice, because the iust liueth by faith. So it is also of Schismatikes, because vvhere charitie is not, iustice can there be none: vvhich if they had, they vvould neuer plucke in peeces the body of Christ vvhich is the Church.* Aug. seu Fulg. de fid. ad Pet. c. 39. So saith S. Augustine in diuers places, not onely of Heretikes that died directly for defense of their heresie, as the Anabaptistes and Caluinists novv a daies do (for that is more damnable:) but of some Heretikes and Schismatikes that may die among the Heathen or Turkes for defense of truth or some Article of Christes religion. *Aug. de verb. Do. ser. 50 c. 2. & in Ps 34 conc. 2 prope finem. Cypr. de vnit. Ec. nu. 8.*

False Martyrs.

13. These three.] These are the three vertues Theological, eche one by nature and definition distinct from an other. and faith is by nature the first, and may be and often is before, and vvithout Charitie: and truely remaineth in diuers after they haue by deadly sinne lost Charitie. Bevvare therfore of the Heretikes opinion, which is, that by euery mortal sinne faith is lost no lesse then charitie.

The 3 vertues theological. Charitie is lost by mortal sinne, not faith.

CHAP. XIIII.

Against their vaine childishnes, that thought it a goodly matter to be able to speake (by miracle) strange languages in the Church," preferring their languages before prophecying, that is, opening of Mysteries: he declareth that this Gift of languages is inferior to the Gift of prophecie. 26 Giuing order also hovv both giftes are to be vsed, to vvit, the Prophet to submit him self to other Prophets: and the Speaker of languages not to publish his inspiration, vnles there be an interpreter. 34 Prouided alvvaies, that vvomen speake not at al in the Church.

" Much like to some fond Linguists of our time, who thinke them selues better then a doctor of Diuinitie that is not a Linguist.

OLOVV Charitie, earnestly pursue 1 spiritual things: but " rather that you may prophecie. † For he that speaketh 2 vvith tongue, speaketh " not to men, but to God: for no man heareth. But in spirit he speaketh mysteries. † For he that 3 prophecieth, speaketh to men vnto edification, and exhortation, and consolation. † He that speaketh vvith tongues, edifieth him self: but 4 he that prophecieth, edifieth the Church. † And I would haue 5 you al to speake vvith tongues, but rather to prophecie. For greater is he that prophecieth, then he that speaketh vvith tongues: vnlesse perhaps he interpret, that the Church may take edification. † But novv brethren " if I come to you spea- 6 king vvith tongues: vvhat shal I profit you, vnlesse I speake to you either in reuelation, or in knovvledge, or in prophecie, or in doctrine? † Yet the things vvithout life that giue a 7 sound, be it pipe or harpe, vnlesse they giue a distinction of sou͂des, hovv shal that be knovven which is piped, or which is harped? † For " if the trumpet giue an vncertaine voice, vvho 8 shal prepare him self to battel? † So you also by a tōgue vnlesse 9 you vtter manifest speach, hovv shal that be knovven that is said? for you shal be speaking into the aire. † There are (for 10 example) so many kindes of tongues in this vvorld, & none is vvithout voice. † If then I knovv not the vertue of the 11 voice, I shal be to him to vvhom I speake, barbarous: and he that speaketh, barbarous to me. † So you also, because you 12 be emulators of spirites: seeke to abound vnto the edifying of the Church. † And therfore he that speaketh vvith the 13 tongue, " let him pray that he may interpret. † For if I pray 14 vvith the tongue, " my spirit praieth, but my vnderstanding is vvithout fruite.

† Vvhat is it then? I vvil pray in the spirit, I vvil pray also 15 in the vnderstanding: I vvil sing in the spirit, I vvil sing also in the vnderstanding. † But if thou blesse in the spirit: he 16 that supplieth the place [c] of the vulgar hovv shal he say, Amen, vpon thy blessing? because he knovveth not vvhat thou saiest. † For thou in deede giuest thankes vvel: but the 17 other is not edified. † I giue my God thankes, that I 18 speake [*] vvith the tongue of you al [*]. † But in the Church I vvil 19 speake fiue vvordes vvith my vnderstanding that I may instruct

[c] By this word are meant al rude vnlearned men, but specially the simple which vvere yet vnchristened, as the Catechumens, vvhich came in to those spiritual exercises, as also infidels did at their pleasures.

[c] idiotæ

[*] vvith tongues more the͂ you all.

ſtruct others alſo : rather then ten thouſand vvordes in a
20 tongue. † Brethren, be not made children in ſenſe, but in
21 malice be children : and in ſenſe be perfect. † In the Lavv it
Es.28,11 is vvritten, *That in other tongues and other lippes I vvil ſpeake to this peo-*
22 *ple :and neither ſo vvil they heare me, ſaieth our Lord.* † Therfore languages are for" a ſigne not to the faithful,but to infidels : but
23 prophecies,not to infidels,but to the faithful. † If therfore the vvhole Church come together in one,and al ſpeake with tongues,and there enter in vulgar perſons or "infidels, vvil
24 they not ſay that you be madde? † But if al prophecie,and there enter in any infidel or vulgar perſon, he is conuinced
25 of al, he is iudged of al. † the ſecrets of his hart are made manifeſt, and ſo falling on his face he vvil adore God, pronouncing that God is in you in deede.

26 † Vvhat is it then brethren? vvhen you come together, euery one of you hath" a pſalme, hath a doctrine, hath a reuelation,hath a tongue,hath an interpretation : let al things
27 be done to edification. † Vvhether a man ſpeake with tõgue, by tvvo, or at the moſt by three, and" in courſe, and let
28 one interpret. † But if there be not an interpreter, let him hold his peace in the Church,and ſpeake to him ſelf and to
29 God. † And let prophets ſpeake tvvo or three, and let the
30 reſt iudge. † But if it be reuealed to an other ſitting, let the
31 firſt hold his peace. † For you may al prophecie one by one:
32 that al may learne,and al may be exhorted, † and the ſpirites
33 of prophets are ſubiect to prophets. † For God is not the God of diſſenſion,but of peace : as alſo in all the Churches of the ſaincts I teache.

1. Tim. 2, 12.
34 † "Let * vvomen hold their peace in the Churches : for it is not permitted them to ſpeake, but to be ſubiect, as alſo
Gen. 3, 16.
35 * the Law ſaith. † But if they learne any thing,let them aſke their ovvne huſbands at home. For it is a foule thing for a
36 vvoman to ſpeake in the Church. † Or did the vvord of
37 God proceede from you? came it vnto you onely? † If any man ſeeme to be a prophet, or ſpiritual, let him knovv the things that I vvrite to you, that they are the cõmaundements
38 of our Lord. † But if any man knovv not, he ſhal not be
39 knovven. † Therfore,brethren,be earneſt to prophecie:and
40 to ſpeake vvith tongues prohibit not. † But let al things be done honeſtly and according to order among you.

ANNOTATIONS
CHAP. XIIII.

A paraphrastical exposition of this Chapter concerning vnknovven tongues.

1. *Rather prophecie.*] The gift of prophecying, that is, of expounding the hard points of our religion, is better then the gift of strange tonges, though both be good.

2. *Not to men.*] To talke in a strange language, vnknovven also to him self, profiteth not the hearers, though in respect of God vvho vnderstandeth al tonges and thinges, and for the mysteries vvhich he vttereth in his spirit, and for his ovvne edification in spirit and affection, there be no difference: but the Prophet or Expositor treating of the same matters to the vnderstanding of the vvhole assemblie, edifieth not him self alone but al his hearers.

6. *If I come.*] That is, If I your Apostle and Doctor should preach to you in an vnknovven tongue, and neuer vse any kinde of exposition, interpretatiō, or explication of my strange vvordes, vvhat profite could you take thereby?

8. *If the trumpet.*] As the Trumpeter can not giue vvarning to or from the fight, vnles he vse a distinct & intelligible sound or stroke knovven to the souldiars: euen so the preacher that exhorteth to good life, or dehorteth from sinne, except he doe it in a speach vvhich his hearers vnderstand, can not attaine to his purpose, nor doe the people any good.

13. *Let him pray that.*] He that hath onely the gift of strange tonges, let him pray to God for the gift of interpretation: that the one may be more profitable by the other. for, to exhort or preach in a strange, tongue vvas not vnlavvful nor vnprofitable, but glorious to God, so that the speach had bene either by him self, or by an other, aftervvard expounded.

14. *My spirit praieth.*] Also vvhen a man praieth in a strange tongue vvhich him self vnderstandeth not, it is not so fruitful for instruction to him, as if he knevv particularly vvhat he praied. Neuertheles the Apostle forbiddeth not such praying neither, confessing that his spirit, hart, and affection praieth vvel tovvardes God, though his minde and vnderstanding be not profited to instruction, as othervvise it might haue bene if he vnderstood the vvordes. Neither yet doth he appoint such an one to get his strange praier translated into his vulgar tongue, to obteine thereby the foresaid instruction. See the Declaration folovving of this Chapter.

22. *A signe.*] The extraordinarie gift of tonges vvas a miraculous signe in the primitiue Church, to be vsed specially in the Nations of the Heathen for their conuersion.

23. *Infidels.*] In the primitiue Church, vvhen Infidels dvvelt neere or among Christians, and often times came vnto their publike preaching & exercises of exhortation and exposition of Scriptures and the like: it vvas both vnprofitable and ridiculous to heare a number talking, teaching, singing Psalmes & the like, one in this language, & an other in that, al at once like a blacke-saunts, and one often not vnderstood of an other, sometime not to them selues, and to strangers or the simple standers by, not at al. Vvhere othervvise if they had spoken either in knovven tonges, or had done it in order, hauing an expositor or interpreter vvithal, the Infidels might haue bene conuinced.

Of vvhat spiritual exercise the Apostle speaketh.

26. *A Psalme.*] Vve see here that those spiritual exercises consisted specially, first, in singing or giuing forth nevv Psalmes or praiers and laudes: secondly, in Doctrine, teaching, or reading lectures: thirdly, in Reuelation of secrete things either present or to come: fourthly, in speaking Tonges of strange Nations: lastly, in translating or Interpreting that vvhich vvas said, into some common knovven language, as into Greeke, Latin, &c. Al vvhich gifts they had among them by miracle from the holy Ghost.

The disorders in the same.

27. *In course.*] Al these things they did vvithout order, of pride and contention they preached, they prophecied, they praied, they blessed, vvithout any seemely respect one of an other, or obseruing of turnes and entercourse of vttering their Giftes. Yea vvomen vvithout couer or veile, and vvithout regard of their sexe or the Angels or Priests or their ovvne husbands, malepartly spake tonges, taught, or prophecied vvith the rest. This vvas then the disorder among the Corinthians, vvhich the Apostle in this vvhole chapter reprehendeth and sought to redresse, by forbidding vvomen vtterly that publike exercise, and teaching men, in vvhat order and course as vvel for speaking in tonges, as interpreting and prophecying, it should be kept.

A MORE AMPLE DECLARATION OF THE sense of this 14 Chapter.

That S. Pauls place maketh nothing agaīst the seruice in the latin tōge.

This then being the scope and direct drift of the Apostle, as is most cleere by his vvhole discourse, and by the record of al antiquitie: let the godly, graue, and discrete Reader take a tast in this one point, of the Protestants deceitful dealing, abusing the simplicitie of the popular, by peruerse application of Gods holy vvord, vpon some smal similitude and equiuocation of certaine termes,

against

againſt the approued godly vſe and truth of the vniuerſal Church, for the ſeruice in the Latin or Greeke tongue: Which they ignorantly, or rather vvilfully, pretend to be againſt this diſcourſe of S. Paul touching ſtrange tonges. Know therfore, firſt, that here is no vvord Written or meant of any other tongues but ſuch as men ſpake in the Primitiue Church by miracle. and that nothing is meant of thoſe tongues vvhich Were the common languages of the vvorld or of the Faithful, vnderſtood of the learned and ciuil people in euery great citie, and in Which the Scriptures of the Old or neW Teſtament vvere Written, as, the Hebrevv, Greeke, and Latin. for though theſe alſo, might be giuen by miracle & Without ſtudy, yet being knovven to the IeWes, Romans, or Greekes in euery place, they be not counted among the differences of barbarous and ſtrange tonges here ſpoken of, Which could not be interpreted commonly, but by the miraculous gift alſo of interpretation. And therfore this Apoſtle (as the Euangeliſts alſo and others did their bookes) vvrote his Epiſtles in Greeke to the Romans and to al other Churches. Vvhich vvhen he vvrote, though he penned them not in the vulgar language peculiar to euery people, yet he vvrote them not in Tongue, that is, in any ſtrange tongue not intelligible vvithout the gift of interpretation, vvhereof he ſpeaketh here: but in a notable knovven and learned ſpeach interpretable of thouſands in euery countrie. No more did S. Auguſtine our Apoſtle, ſpeaking in Latin, & bringing in the Scriptures and Seruice in Latin, preach and pray in Tonges according to the Apoſtles meaning here. for the Latin vvas not, nor is not, in any part of the Vveſt, either miraculous or ſtrange, though it be not the National tongue of any one countrie this day. And therfore S. Bede ſaith, (*li. 1 hiſt. Angl. c. 1.*) that being then foure diuers vulgar languages in our countrie, the Latin vvas made common to them al. And in deede of the tvvo (though in truth neither ſort be forbidden by this paſſage of S. Paul) the barbarous languages of euery ſeueral prouince in reſpect of the vvhole Church of Chriſt, are rather the ſtrange Tonges here ſpoken of, then the common Latin tongue, vvhich is vniuerſally of al the Vveſt Church more or leſſe learned, and pertaineth much more to vnitie and orderly coniunction of al Nations in one faith, Seruice, and vvorſhip of God, then if it vvere in the ſundry barbarous ſpeaches of euery Prouince. Vvherein al Chriſtians that trauel about this part of the vvorld or the Indes either, vvhere ſo euer they come, ſhal finde the ſelf ſame Maſſe, Mattins, and Seruice, as they had at home. Vvhere novv, if vve goe to Germanie, or the Germans or Geneuians come to vs, eche others Seruice ſhal be thought ſtrange and barbarous. Yea and the Seruice of our ovvne language vvithin a fevv hundreth yeres (or rather euery age) ſhal vvholy become barbarous and vnknovven to our ſelues, our tongue (as al vulgar) doth ſo often change.

By ſtrange tonges the Apoſtle meaneth not the latin, Greeke, or Hebrue.

S. Auguſtine our Apoſtle brought in the Seruice in the latin tongue.

The latin ſeruice one and the ſame in al countries and ſtrange to none.

The ſeruice in vulgar tóge ſtrange and barbarous to euery ſtráger.

And for edification, that is, for increaſe of faith, true knovvledge, and good life, the experience of a fevv yeres hath giuen al the vvorld a ful demonſtration vvhether our forefathers vvere not as vviſe, as faithful, as deuout, as fearful to breake Gods lavves, and as likely to be ſaued, as vve are in al our tongues, tranſlations, and Engliſh praiers. Much vanitie, curioſitie contempt of Superiors, diſputes, emulations, contentions, Schiſmes, horrible errors, profanation and diuulgation of the ſecrete Myſteries of the dreadful Sacraments, * vvhich of purpoſe vvere hidden from the vulgar (as S. Denys *Eccl. Hier. c. 1.* and S. Baſil *de Sp. Sanct. c. 27.* teſtifie) are fallen by the ſame, but vertue or ſound knovvledge none at al.

Vvhether the ſeruice in vulgar tonges do more edifie.

* See Annot 1. Cor. 10. 16.

Vvherein this alſo is a groſſe illuſion and vntruth, that the force and efficacie of the Sacraments, Sacrifice, and common praier, dependeth vpon the peoples vnderſtanding, hearing, or knovvledge: the principal efficacie of ſuch thinges and of the vvhole miniſterie of the Church, conſiſting ſpecially of the very vertue of the vvorke, and the publike office of the Prieſts, Who be appointed in Chriſtes behalfe to diſpoſe theſe Myſteries to our moſt good: the infant, innocent, idiote and vnlearned, taking no leſſe fruite of Baptiſme and al other diuine offices, meete for euery ones condition, then the learnedſt Clerke in the Realme: and more, if they be more humble, charitable, deuout, and obedient, then the other, hauing leſſe of theſe qualities and more learning.

The vertue of the Sacramēts and Seruice conſiſteth not in the peoples vnderſtáding.

Vvhich vve ſay not, as though it Were inconuenient for the people to be vvel inſtructed in the meaning of the Sacraments and holy ceremonies and Seruice of the Church (for, that to their comfort and neceſſarie knovvledge, both by preaching, Catechizing, and reading of good Catholike bookes, Chriſtian people do learne in al Nations much more in thoſe countries vvhere the Seruice is in Latin, then in our Nation, God knovveth:) But We ſay that there be other Waies to inſtruct them, and the ſame leſſe ſubiect to danger and diſorder, then to turne it into vulgar tongues. Vve ſay, the ſimple people and many one that thinke them ſelues ſome body, vnderſtand as litle of the ſenſe of diuers Pſalmes, Leſſons, and Oraiſons in the vulgar tongue, as if they vvere in Latin: yea and often take them in a vvrong, peruerſe, and pernitious ſenſe, vvhich lightly they could not haue done in Latin. Vve ſay, that ſuch as vvould learne in deuotion and humilitie, may and muſt rather vvith diligence learne the tongue that ſuch Diuine things be vvritten in, or vſe other diligence in hearing ſermons and inſtructions: then for a fevv mens not neceſſarie knovvledge, the holy vniuerſal order of Gods Church ſhould be altered. For if in the kingdom of England onely, it be not conuenient, neceſſarie, nor almoſt poſſible, to accommodate their Seruice booke to euery prouince and people of diuers tongues: hovv much leſſe ſhould the vvhole Church ſo do, conſiſting of ſo many differences? Neither doth the Apoſtle in al this Chapter appoint any ſuch

The people is to be taught the meaning of Sacraments & ceremonies, and are taught in al Catholike coūtries.

thing to be done, but admonisheth them to pray and labour for the grace of vnderstanding and interpretation, or to get others to interprete or expound vnto them. And that much more may vve doe concerning the Seruice in Latin, vvhich is no strange nor miraculously gotten or vnderstood tongue, but common to the most and cheefe churches of the vvorld, and hath bene, since the Apostles time, daily vvith al diligence through out al these partes of Christendom, expounded in euery house, schole, church, and pulpit: and is so vvel knovven for euery necessarie part of the diuine Seruice, that by the diligence of parents, Maisters, and Curates, euery Catholike of age almost, can tel the sense of euery ceremonie of the Masse, vvhat to ansvver, vvhen to say *Amen* at the Priestes benediction, vvhen to confesse, vvhen to adore, vvhen to stand, vvhen to kneele, when to receiue, vvhat to receiue, vvhen to come, vvhen to depart, and al other dueties of praying and seruing, sufficient to saluation. And thus is it euident that S. Paul speaketh not of the common tonges of the Churches Seruice.

Catholike people in euery countrie vnderstandeth euery ceremonie, and can behaue them selues accordingly.

Secondly, it is as certaine, that he meaneth not nor vvriteth any vvord in this place of the Churches publike Seruice, praier, or ministration of the holy Sacrament, vvherein the Office of the Church specially consisteth: but onely of a certaine exercise of mutual conference, wherein one did open to an other and to the assemblie, miraculous giftes and graces of the Holy Ghost, and such Canticles, Psalmes, secrete Mysteries, sorts of Languages, and other Reuelations, as it pleased God to giue vnto certaine both men and vvomen in that first beginning of his Church. In doing of this, the Corinthians cōmitted many disorders, turning Gods gifts to pride and vanitie, and namely that gift of tonges: vvhich being in deede the least of al giftes, yet most puffed vp the hauers, and novv also doth commonly puffe vp the professors of such knovvledge, according as S. Augustine vvriteth thereof. This exercise and the disorder thereof vvas not in the Church (for any thing we can reade in antiquitie) these fourtene hundreth yeres: and therfore neither the vse nor abuse, nor S. Paules reprehēsion or redressing thereof, can concerne any vvhit the Seruice of the Church. Furthermore this is euident, that the Corinthians had their Seruice in Greeke at this same time, and it vvas not done in these miraculous tonges. Nothing is meant then of the Church Seruice. Againe the publike Seruice had but one language: in this exercise they spake in many tonges. In the publike Seruice euery man had not his ovvne special tongue, his special Interpretation, special Reuelation, proper Psalmes: but in this they had. Againe, the publike Seruice had in it the ministration of the holy Sacrament principally: vvhich vvas not done in this time of conference. For into this exercise vvere admitted Catechumens and Infidels and vvhosoeuer vvould: in this vvomen, before S. Paules order, did speake and prophecie: so did they neuer in the Ministration of the Sacrament. vvith many other plaine differences, that by no meanes the Apostles vvordes can be rightly and truely applied to the Corinthians Seruice then, or ours novv. Therfore it is either great ignorance of the Protestants, or great guilfulnes, so vntruely and peruersly to apply them.

Aug. doct. Chr. li. 2. c. 13.

That he speaketh not of the Churches seruice, is proued by inuincible arguments.

Neither is here any thing meant of the priuate praiers which deuout persons of al sortes and sexes haue euer vsed, specially in Latin, as vvel vpon their Primars as Beades. For, the priuate praiers here spoken of, vvere psalmes or hymnes and sonnets nevvly inspired to them by God, and in this conference or prophecying, vttered to one an others comfort, or to them selues and God onely. But the praiers, psalmes, and holy vvordes of the Christian people vsed priuately, are not composed by them, nor diuersely inspired to them selues, nor novv to be approued or examined in the assemblies: but they are such as vvere giuen and vvritten by the Holy Ghost, and prescribed by Christ and his Church for the faithful to vse, namely the *Pater noster*, the *Aue Maria*, and the *Creede*, our *Ladies Mattins*, the *Litanies*, and the like. Therfore the Apostle prescribeth nothing here thereof, condemneth nothing therein, toucheth the same nothing at al. But the deuout people in their aūcient right may and ought stil vse their Latin primars, beades, and praiers, as euer before. Vvhich the wisedom of the Church for greate causes hath better liked and allowed of, then that they should be in vulgar tonges, though she wholy forbiddeth not, but sometimes graunteth to haue them translated, and vvould gladly haue al faithful people in order and humilitie learne, as they may, the contents of their praiers: and hath commaunded also in some Counceis, that such as can not learne distinctly in Latin (specially the *Pater noster* & the *Creede*) should be taught them in the vulgar tōgue. And therfore as vve doubt not but it is acceptable to God, & auailable in al necessities, & more agreable to the vse of al Christian people euer since their conuersion, to pray in Latin, then in the vulgar, though euery one in particular vnderstand not vvhat he saith: so it is plaine that such pray vvith as great consolation of spirit, vvith as litle tediousnes, vvith as great deuotion and affection, and oftentimes more, then the other: and alvvaies more then any Schismatike or Heretike in his knovven language. Such holy Oraisons be in maner consecrated

The Apostle speaketh not of the peoples priuate praiers in latin, as vpon primmars, beades, or othervvise.

Latin praiers translated, or the people taught the cōtents thereof.

The peoples deuotion nothing the lesse, for praying in Latin.

secrated and sanctified in and by the Holy Ghost that first inspired them. and there is a reuerence and Maiestie in the Churches tongue dedicated in our Sauiours Crosse, and giueth more force and valure to them said in the Churches obedience, then to others. The children cried * *Hosanna* to our Sauiour, and vvere allovved, though they knevv not vvhat they said. It is vvel neere a thousand yeres that * our people vvhich could nothing els but *barbarum frendere*, did sing *Alleluia*, and not, *Praise ye the Lord.* and longer agoe since the poore husband men sang the same at the plough in other Countries. *Hiero. to. 1 ep. 58.* And *Sursum corda*, and *Kyrie eleison*, and the Psalmes of Dauid sung in Latin in the Seruice of the Primitiue Church, haue the auncient and flat testimonies of S. Cyprian, S. Augustine, S. Hierom and other Fathers. *Grego. li. 7 ep. 63. Cypr. exp. orat. Do. nu. 13. August. c. 13 de dono perseuer. & de bono vid. c. 16.* and *ep. 178. Hiero. præfat. in Psal. ad Sophron. Aug. de Catechiz. rud. c. 9. de Doct. Chr. li. 2 c. 13.* See *ep. 10. August.* of S. Hieroms latin translation readde in the Churches of Africa. Praiers are not made to teache, make learned, or increase knovvledge, though by occasion they sometimes instruct vs. but their special vse is, to offer our hartes, desires, and vvants to God, and to shevv that vve hang of him in al things: and this euery Catholike doth for his condition, vvhether he vnderstand the vvordes of his praier or not. The simple sort can not vnderstand al Psalmes, nor scarse the learned, no though they be translated or read in knovven tonges: men must not cease to vse them for al that, vvhen they are knovven to containe Gods holy praises. The simple people vvhen they desire any thing specially at Gods hand, are not bound to knovv, neither can they tel, to vvhat petition or part of the *Pater noster* their demaund pertaineth, though it be in English neuer so much. they can not tel no more vvhat is, *Thy kingdom come*, then *Adueniat regnum tuum.* nor vvhether their petition for their sicke children or any other necessitie, pertaine to this part, or to *Fiat voluntas tua*, or *Ne nos inducas*, or to vvhat other part els. It is ynough that they can tel, this holy Oraison to be appointed to vs, to call vpon God in al our desires. more then this, is not necessarie. And the translation of such holy things often breedeth manifold danger and irreuerence in the vulgar (as to thinke God is author of sinne, vvhen they read, *Leade vs not into tentation*) and seldom any edification at al. For, though vvhen the prayers be turned and read in English, the people knovveth the vvordes, yet they are not edified to the instruction of their minde and vnderstanding, except they knevv the sense of the vvordes also and meaning of the holy Ghost. For if any man thinke that S. Paul speaking of edification of mans minde or vnderstanding, meaneth the vnderstanding of the vvordes onely, he is fouly deceiued. for, vvhat is a childe of fiue or sixe yeres old edified or increased in knovvledge by his *Pater noster* in English? It is the sense therfore, vvhich euery man can not haue, neither in English nor Latin, the knovvledge vvhereof properly and rightly edifieth to instruction. and the knovvledge of the vvordes onely, often edifieth neuer a vvhit, and sometimes buildeth to error and destruction: as it is plaine in al Heretikes and many curious persons besides. finally both the one and the other vvithout charitie and humilitie maketh the Heretikes and Schismatikes vvith al their English and vvhat other tonges and intelligence so euer, to be *as sonans & cymbalum tinniens*, sounding brasse and a tinkling cymbal.

Mat. 21. * *Greg. li. 27. Moral. c. 6.* *1 Cor. 13.*

The seruice alvvaies in Latin through out the vvest Church.

It is not necessarie to vnderstand our praiers.

Hovv far is sufficient for the people to vnderstand.

Hovv the mind or vnderstāding is edified.

To conclude, for praying either publikly or priuately in Latin vvhich is the common sacred tōgue of the greatest part of the Christiā World, this is thought by the vvisest & godliest to be most expedient, and is certainely seen to be nothing repugnant to S. Paul. If any yet vvil be contentious in the matter, vve must ansvver them vvith this same Apostle, *The Church of God hath no such custome.* and vvith this notable saying of S. Augustine, *ep. 118. c. 5. Any thing that the vvhole Church doth practise and obserue through out the vvorld, to dispute thereof as though it vvere not to be done, is most insolent madnesse*

1 Cor. 11, 16.

A notable rule of S. Augustine.

34. Let vvomen hold their peace.] There be, or vvere, certaine Heretikes in our Countrie (for such euer take the Scriptures diuersely for the aduantage of time) that denied vvomen to hold lavvfully any kingdom or temporal Souerainty: but that is false and against both reason & the Scriptures. This onely in that sexe is true, that it is not capable of holy orders, spiritual Regiment or Cure of soules: and therfore can not doe any function proper to Priests and Bishopes: not speake in the Church, and so not preach, nor dispute, nor haue or giue voice either deliberatiue or definitiue in Councels and publike Assemblies, concerning matters of Religiō, nor make Ecclesiastical lavves concerning the same, nor binde, nor loose, nor excōmunicate, nor suspend, nor degrade, nor absolue, nor minister Sacramēts, other then Baptisme in the case of mere necessitie, when neither Priest nor other man can be had: much lesse prescribe any thing to the Clergie, how to minister them, or giue any mā right to rule, preach, or execute any spiritual function as vnder her and by her authoritie: no creature being able to impart that vvhereof it self is incapable both by nature and Scriptures. This Regiment is expresly giuen to the Apostles, Bishopes, and Prelates: they onely haue authoritie to bind and loose, *Mat. 18*: they onely are set by the Holy Ghost to gouerne the Church, *Act. 20.*: they onely haue cure of our soules directly, and must make account to God for the same, *Hebr. 13.*

Vvomen may haue any temporal Soueraintie, but no Ecclesiastical function.

CHAP. XV.

The 7 part. Of the resurrection of the dead.

He proueth the Resurrection of the dead by the Resurrection of Christ, and vvith many other arguments: and 31 ansvvereth also obiections made against it. 49 And then exhorteth in respect of it, vnto good life.

The Epistle vpō the 11 Sūday after Pentecost.

AND I do you to vnderstand, brethren, 1 the Gospel vvhich I preached to you, which also you receiued, in the vvhich also you stand, † by the vvhich also you are 2 saued, after vvhat maner I preached vnto you if you keepe it, vnlesse you haue beleeued in vaine. † For [c] I deliuered vnto you first of al vvhich 3 I also receiued: that Christ died for our sinnes * according to the Scriptures: † and that he vvas buried, and that he rose 4 againe the third day, * according to the scriptures: † and 5 that he vvas * seen of Cephas: and after that of the eleuen. † Then vvas he seen of moe thē fiue hundred brethren to- 6 gether: of vvhich many remaine vntil this present, & some are a sleepe. † Moreouer he vvas seen of Iames, then of al 7 the Apostles. † And last of al, as it vvere of [c] an abortiue * he 8 vvas seen also of me. † For I am the least of the Apostles, 9 vvho am not worthy to be called an Apostle, because I persecuted the Church of God. † But by the grace of God I am 10 that vvhich I am: & his grace in me hath not been ∷ void, but I haue laboured more aboundantly then al they: yet not I, but the grace of God " vvith me. † For vvhether I, or 11 they, so vve preach, and so you haue beleeued.

† But if Christ be preached that he is risen againe from 12 the dead: hovv doe certaine among you say, that there is no resurrection of the dead? † And if there be no resurrection 13 of the dead, neither is Christ risen againe. † And if Christ 14 be not risen againe, then vaine is our preaching, vaine also is your faith. † and vve are found also ∷ false witnesses of God: 15 because vve haue giuen testimonie against God, that he hath raised vp Christ, vvhom he hath not raised vp, if the dead rise not againe. † For if the dead rise not againe, neither is 16 Christ risen againe. † And if Christ be not risen againe, 17 vaine is your faith, for yet you are in your sinnes. † Then 18 they also that are a sleepe in Christ, are perished. † If in this 19 life onely vve be hoping in Christ, vve are more miserable then al men.

† But

[c] This deliuerie in the latin & greeke importeth *tradition*. so by Tradition did the Apostles plant the Church in al truth, before they vvrote any thing.

∷ In him Gods grace is not void, that worketh by his free vvil according to the motion and direction of the same grace.

∷ So may we say, If the Cath. faith in al pointes be not true, then our first Apostles vvere false vvitnesses then hath our Countrie beleeued in vaine al this while, then are al our forefathers

c tradidi παρέδωκα

Es. 53, 8. Dan. 9, 26.

Ps. 15, 10 Ion. 2, 2. Lu. 24.

Act. 9, 3

c one borne out of time

Col.1, 18 Ap.1, 5. Ro.5 12. 1.Thes. 4, 15.

20 † But novv Christ is risen againe from the dead, the 21 *first fruites of them that sleepe: † for * by a man death: and 22 by a man the resurrection of the dead. † And as in Adam al 23 die, so also in Christ al shal be made aliue. † But * euery one in his ovvne order: the first fruites Christ, then they that are 24 of Christ, that beleeued in his comming. † Then the ende, vvhen he shal haue deliuered the kingdom to God and the Father, vvhen he shal haue abolished al principalitie and authoritie and povver. † And he must reigne, *Vntil he put al his* 26 *enemies vnder his feete.* † And the enemie death shal be destroied last. *For he hath subdued al things vnder his feete.* And vvhereas he 27 saith, † *Al things are subdued to him*: Vndoubtedly, except him 28 that subdued al things vnto him. † And vvhen al things shal be subdued to him: then the Sonne also him self shal be subiect to him that subdued al things vnto him, that God may be al in al.

dead in their sinnes and perished. Which (presupposing Christ to be God) vvere the greatest absurditie in the vvorld.

Ps. 109. 1. Ps. 8, 8.

29 † Otherwise what shal they do that are baptized for the dead, 30 if the dead rise not againe at al? † vvhy also are they baptized 31 for them? vvhy also are vve in danger euery houre? † I die daily by your glorie brethren, vvhich I haue in Christ IESVS 32 our Lord. † If (according to man) I fought vvith beastes at Ephesus, vvhat doth it profit me, if the dead rise not againe? 33 *Let vs eate and drinke, for to morovv vve shal die.* † Be not seduced, 34 *Euil communications corrupt good maners.* † Avvake ye iust, and sinne not. for some haue not the knovvledge of God, I speake to your shame.

Esa. 22, 13. Menander.

35 † But some man saith, Hovv doe the dead rise againe? and 36 vvith vvhat maner of body shal they come? † Foole, that vvhich thou sovvest is not quickened, vnlesse it die first. 37 † And that vvhich thou sovvest, not the body that shal be, doest thou sovv: but bare graine, to vvit, of vvheate, or of 38 some of the rest. † And God giueth it a body as he vvil: and 39 to euery seede his proper body. † Not al flesh, is the same flesh: but one of men, an other of beastes, an other of birdes, 40 an other of fishes. † And bodies celestial, and bodies terrestrial: but one glorie of the celestial, and an 41 other of the terrestrial. † One glorie of the sunne, an other glorie of the moone, and an other glorie of the starres. For 42 ∴ starre differeth from starre in glorie: † so also the resurrection of the dead It is sovven in corruption, it shal rise in in- 43 corruptiō. † It is sovvē in dishonour, it shal rise in glorie. It is

∴ The glorie of the bodies of Saincts shal not be al alike, but differēt in heauen according to mens merits.

44 sovven in infirmitie, it shal rise in povver. † It is sovven a natural body: it shal rise a ∴ spiritual body. If there be a natural body, there is also a spiritual, † as it is vvritten, *The first man Adam vvas made into a liuing soul:* the last Adam into a quickening spirit. † Yet that is not first vvhich is spiritual, but that vvhich is natural: aftervvard that vvhich is spiritual. † The first man of earth, earthly: the second man from heauen, heauenly. † Such as is the earthly, such also are the earthly. and such as the heauenly, such also are the heauenly. † Therfore as vve haue borne the image of the earthly, let vs beare also the image of the heauenly. † This I say brethren, that ∴ flesh and bloud can not possesse the kingdom of God: neither shal corruption possesse incorruption.

45 Gen. 2, 7

46 47 48 49 50

∴ As to become spiritual doth not take away the substance of the body glorified: no more vvhen Christes body is said to be in spiritual sort in the Sacrament, doth it import the absence of his true body and substance.

∴ Flesh and bloud signifie not here the substance of those things, but the corrupt qualitie incident to them in this life by the fall of Adam.

51 † [b] Behold I tel you a mysterie. Vve shal al in deede rise againe: but vve shal not al be changed. † In a moment, in the tvvinkling of an eie, at the * last trompet (for * the trompet shal sound) and the dead shal rise againe incorruptible: and vve shal be changed. † For this corruptible must doe on incorruption: & this mortal doe on immortalitie. † And vvhen this mortal hath done on immortalitie, then shal come to passe the saying that is vvritten, *Death is svvallovved vp in victorie.* † *Death vvhere is thy victorie? Death vvhere is thy sting?* † And the sting of death, is sinne: and the povver of sinne is the Lavv. † But thankes be to God that hath giuen vs the victorie by our Lord IESVS Christ. ⊣ † Therfore my beloued brethren, be stable & vnmoueable: abounding in the worke of our Lord alvvaies, knovving that your labour is not vaine in our Lord.

52 53 54 55 56 57 58

Ap. 8, 2. 11, 15.

Os. 13, 14.

b The Epistle vpō Al-soules day.

ANNOTATIONS
CHAP. XV.

Free vvil vvith grace.

11 *Vvith me.*) God vseth not man as a brute beast or a blocke: but so vvorketh in him and by him that free wil may concurre in euery action vvith his grace, vvhich is alvvaies, the principal. The heretikes to auoid this concurrence in vvorking & labouring, translate, *vvhich is vvith me*: vvhere the Apostle rather saith, *vvhich laboureth vvith me.*

Heret. translation.

Fasting is meritorious.

32 *Let vs eate and drinke.*] S. Ambrose applieth these vvordes to our Christian Epicurians that taks avvay fasting, and deny the merite thereof: *Hovv can vve be saued* (saith he) *if we vvash not avvay our sinnes by fasting, seeing the scriptures say, fasting and almes deliuer from sinne? Vvhat are these nevv maisters then that exclude al merite of fasting? is not this the very voice of the heathen saying, Let vs eate and drinke, to morovv vve shal die? li. 10. epist. ep. 82.*

CHAP.

CHAP. XVI.

He prescribeth an order for their contributing to the Christians at Hierusalem, 3 promising to come vnto them. 10 Of Timothee, and of Apollos comming thither. 13 and so vvith exhortation, and diuers commendations, he endeth.

The 8 part. Of the contributions.

1 AND concerning the collections that are made for the saincts, as I haue ordeined to the Churches of Galatia, so doe ye also. 2 † In :: the first of the Sabboth let euery one of you put a part vvith him self, laying vp vvhat shal vvel like him: that not vvhen I come, then collections be made. 3 † And vvhen I shal be present: vvhom you shal approue by letters, them vvil I send to carie your grace into Hierusalem. 4 † And if it be vvorthie that I also goe, they shal goe vvith me.

:: That is Sūday. *Hiero. q. 4. Hedibia.* So quickly did the Christians keepe Sunday, holiday, and assembled to Diuine Seruice on the same.

5 † And I vvil come to you, vvhen I shal haue passed through Macedonia. for I vvil passe through Macedonia. 6 † And vvith you perhaps I vvil abide, or vvil vvinter also: that you may bring me on my vvay vvhithersoeuer I goe. 7 † For I vvil not novv see you by the vvay, for I hope that I shal abide vvith you some litle time, if our Lord wil permit. 8 † But I vvil tarie at Ephesus vntil :: Pentecost. 9 † For a great doore and euident is opened vnto me: and many aduersaries. 10 † And if Timothee come, see that he be vvithout feare vvith you, for he vvorketh the vvorke of our Lord, as also I. 11 † Let no mā therfore despise him, but cōduct ye him in peace: that he may come to me. for I expect him vvith the brethren. 12 † And of brother Apollo I doe you to vnderstand, that I much intreated him, to come vnto you vvith the brethren: & [c] at all it vvas not his minde to come novv. but he vvil come vvhen he shal haue leisure.

:: The Heretikes & other nevv fangled striue among them selues, vvhether Pentecost signifie here the terme of fiftie daies, or els the Ievves holy day so called. But it cōmeth not to their mindes that it is most like to be the feast of Whitsontide kept & instituted euē thē by the Apostles, as appeareth by the Fathers *See S. Aug. ep. 119 c. 15 & 16. Ambr. in c. 17. Luca.*

c πάντως

13 † Vvatch ye, stand in the faith, doe manfully, & be strengthened. 14 † Let al your things be done in charitie. 15 † And I beseeche you brethren, you knovv the house of Stéphanas, and of Fortunátus, that they are the first fruites of Achaia, & haue ordeined them selues to the ministerie of the saincts: 16 † that you also be subiect to such, and to euery one that helpeth and laboureth with vs. 17 † And I reioyce in the presence of Stephanas and Fortunatus and Achaicus, because [c] that 18 vvhich you vvanted, they haue supplied. † For they haue refreshed both my spirit and yours. Knovv them therfore that are such.

c τὸ ὑμῶν ὑστέρημα

† The churches of Asia salute you. Aquila and Priscilla 19 vvith their domestical church salute you much in our Lord. † Al the brethren salute you. Salute one an other in a [c] holy 20 kisse. † The salutation vvith mine ovvne hand Paules. † If 21 any man loue not our Lord IESVS Christ, be he *anáthema.* [c] *Maran atha.* 22 † The grace of our Lord IESVS Christ be vvith 23 you. † My charitie be vvith you al in Christ IESVS. 24 Amen.

c *See Ro. 16,16.*

c מרן אתא

c That is, *our Lord is come.* Hiero. ep. 173. Therfore *anathema* to al that loue him not, or beleue not. *Theophyla. upon this place.*

THE ARGVMENT OF THE SECOND EPISTLE TO THE CORINTHIANS.

1. Cor. 11. 2. Gal. 2. 1.

FOR the time vvhen this Epistle vvas vvritten, looke the Argument of the epistle to the Romanes: to vvit, about the eightenth yere after his conuersion, & our Lordes passion. because in the 11 chapter he maketh mention of 14 yeres, not only after his Conuersion, as to the Galatians, but also after his rapte, vvhich seemeth to haue bene vvhen he vvas at Hierusalem Act. 9, 26. foure yeres after his Conuersion (Gal. 1, 18) in a traunce or excesse of minde, as he calleth it, Act. 22, 17. It vvas vvritten at Troas (it is thought) and sent by Titus, as vve reade chap. 8.

It is for the most part against those false Apostles vvhom in the first part of the first to the Corinthians, he noted, or rather spared, but novv is constrained to deale openly against them, & to defend both his ovvne person vvhich they sought to bring into contempt, making vvay thereby to the corruption of the Corinthians, and vvithall to mainteine the excellencie of the Ministerie and Ministers of the nevv Testament, aboue vvhich they did magnifie the Ministerie of the old Testament: bearing them selues very high because they vvere Ievves.

Against these therefore S. Paule auoucheth the preeminent povver of his Ministerie, by vvhich povver also he giueth a pardon to the incestuous fornicator vvhom he excommunicated in the last Epistle, seeing novv his penance, and againe threateneth to come & excommunicate those that had greuously sinned and remained impenitent. Tvvo chapters also he interposeth of the contributions to the church of Hierusalem, mentioned in his last, exhorting them to doe liberally, and also to haue all in a readines against his comming.

THE

THE SECOND EPISTLE OF PAVL TO THE CORINTHIANS.

CHAP. I.

By his troubles in Asia he comforteth them, and (against his Aduersaries the false apostles of the Ievves) alleageth to them the testimonie of his ovvne and also of their conscience, 17 ansvvering them that obiected lightnes against him, for not comming to Corinth according to his promis.

1 PAVL an Apostle of IESVS Christ by the vvil of God, and Timothee our brother: to the Church of God that is at Corinth, vvith al the saincts 2 that are in al Achaia. † Grace vnto you and peace from God our father, and from our Lord IESVS Christ.

3 † Blessed be the God and father of our Lord IESVS Christ, the fa- 4 ther of mercies, and God of al comfort, † vvho comforteth vs in al our tribulation: that vve also may be able to comfort them that are in all distresse, [c] by the exhortation vvherevvith 5 vve also are exhorted of God. † For as the ‖ passions of Christ abound in vs: so also by Christ doth our ‖ comfort 6 abound. † And vvhether vve be in tribulation, for your exhortation and saluation: vvhether vve be exhorted, for your exhortation and saluation, vvhich vvorketh the tolera- 7 tion of the same passions vvhich vve also doe suffer: † and our hope is firme for you: knovving that as you are partakers of the passions, so shal you be of the consolation also. ⊣

8 † For vve vvil not haue you ignorant brethren: concerning our tribulation, vvhich happened in Asia, that vve vvere pressed aboue measure aboue our povver, so that it vvas te- 9 dious vnto vs euen to liue. † But vve in our selues had the ansvver of death, that vve be not trusting in our selues, but in

The Epistle for a Martyr that is a Bishop.

c διὰ τῆς παρακλήσεως ἧς παρακαλούμεθα

God vvho raiseth vp the dead, † vvho hath deliuered and 10 doth deliuer vs out of so great dangers: in vvhom vve hope that he vvil yet also deliuer vs, † you" helping vvithal in 11 praier for vs, that" by many mens persons, thankes for that gift vvhich is in vs, may be giuen by many in our behalfe. † For our glorie is this, the testimonie of our conscience, that 12 in simplicity and sincerity of God, and not in carnal vvisedō, but in the grace of God vve haue conuersed in this vvorld: and more aboundantly tovvards you. † For vve vvrite no 13 other things to you, then that you haue read and knovv. And I hope that you shal knovv vnto the ende: † as also you 14 haue knovven vs in part, that vve are " your glorie, as you also ours in the day of our Lord IESVS Christ. † And in 15 this confidence I vvould first haue come to you, that you might haue a second grace: † and by you passe into Mace- 16 donia, and againe from Macedonia come to you, and of you be brought on my vvay into Ievvrie.

† Vvhereas then I vvas thus minded, did I vse lightenes? 17 Or the things that I minde, do I minde according to the flesh, that there be vvith me, *It is* and *It is not*? † But God is faithful, 18 because our preaching vvhich vvas to you, there is not in it, " *It is*, and, *It is not*. † For the Sonne of God IESVS Christ, 19 vvho by vs vvas preached among you, by me and Syluanus and Timothee, vvas not, *It is*, and, *It is not*. but, *It is*, vvas in him. † For al the promises of God that are, in him *It is*: therfore 20 also by him, Amen to God, vnto our glorie. † And he that 21 confirmeth vs vvith you in Christ, and that hath anointed vs, God: † vvho also " hath sealed vs, and giuen the pledge 22 of the Spirit in our hartes. † And I call God to vvitnesse vpon 23 my soul, that sparing you, I came not any more to Corinth, † " not because vve ouerrule your faith: but, vve are helpers 24 of your ioy. for in the faith you stand.

ANNOTATIONS
CHAP. I.

Al our afflictions, be Christs afflictions, for the coniunction betwene the head & body.

3. *Passions of Christ.*] Al the afflictions of the faithful be called Christes ovvne passions, not onely because they be suffered for him, but for that there is so straite coniunction and communion betvvixt him being the head, and euery of the liuing members of his body, vvhich is the Church, that vvhatsoeuer is suffered by any one of the same, is counted as a peece of his ovvne Passion. As likevvise vvhatsoeuer good vvorkes be done to any of them or by any of them, be accepted as done to or by Christ him self. Vvhich thing if the Protestants vvel vveighed, they vvould not

maruel

maruel that the Catholike Church attributeth such force of merite and satisfaction to the vvorke of holy men.

Merite and satisfaction.

5. The comfort abound.] Vvorldly men that see onely the exterior miseries and afflictions that Catholikes do suffer, being persecuted by the Heathen or Heretikes, deeme them exceding miserable. but if they felt or could conceiue the aboundance of consolation vvhich Christ euer giueth according to the measure of their afflictions, they vvould neuer vvonder at the voluntary toleration of vvhat torments so euer for Christes sake, but vvould vvish rather them selues to be in any dungeon in England vvith the comfort that such haue from God, then to liue out of the Church in al the vvealth of the vvorld.

Vvorldly men feele not the comfort of afflicted Catholikes.

11. You helping in praier.] S. Paul knevv that the helpe of other mens praiers vvas nothing derogatorie to the office of Christes mediation or intercession for him, nor to the hope that he had in God: and therfore he craueth the Corinthians aide herein as a support and succours for him self in the sight of God. Vvith vvhat reason or Scripture then, can the Protestants say that the praiers of Sainctes be iniurious to Christ, or not to stand vvith the confidence vve haue in him? As though it vvere more dishonour to God that vve should vse the aide of Sainctes in heauen, then of sinners in earth: or * that the intercession of these our fellovves beneath, vvere more auailable then the praiers of those that be in the glorious sight of God aboue.

Intercessiō of Saincts or holy men for vs, no derogation to Christ.

Hiero. cōt. Vigil.

11. By many mens.] He meaneth, that as the praiers of many ioyned together for him, shal be rather heard, then of any alone: so their common thankes giuing to God for graunting their request, shal be more acceptable and glorious to God, then any one mans thankes alone. Vvhich thing doth much commend the holy Churches publike praiers, processions, stations, and pilgrimages, vvhere so many meete and vniformely ioyne their praiers and laudes together vnto God.

Publike praiers & fastes.

14. Your glorie.] The Apostles, teachers, and preachers, that conuert countries or particular persons to Christ, and the peoples or parties by them conuerted, shal in the day of iudgement haue much mutual ioy and glorie of and for eche other, one giuing to the other great matter of merite in this life, and of revvard in the next. See 1 *Thess. 2. v. 19.*

Their glorie in heauen that conuert other.

18. It is, it is not.] As he dischargeth him self of al other leuitie touching his promis or purpose of comming to them, so much more of al inconstancie in preaching Christes doctrine and faith. Vvherein, one day to affirme, an other day to deny, to dissent from his fellovves or from him self, to change euery yere or in euery epistle the forme of his former teaching, to come daily vvith nevv deuises repugnant to his ovvne rules, vvere not agreable to an Apostle and true teacher of Christ, but proper to false prophets and Heretikes. Vvhereof vve haue notorious examples in the Protestants: vvho being destitute of the spirit of peace, concord, constancie, vnitie, and veritie, as they varie from their ovvne vvritings vvhich they retract, reforme or deforme continually, so both in their preachings, & forme of Seruice, they are so restles, changeable, and repugnant to them selues, that if they vvere not kept in avve vvith much a do, by temporal lavves or by the shame and rebuke of the vvorld, they vvould coine vs euery yere or euery Parliament, nevv Communions, nevv faithes, and nevv Christes, as you see by the manifold endeuours of the Puritans. And this to be the proper note of false Apostles and Heretikes, see *in S. Irenæus li. 1 c. 18.* and *Tertul. de prascript. S. Basil. ep. 82.*

The Protestants inconstancie in chāging their writings, translations, seruice bookes, &c.

Eph. 4, 30.

22. Hath sealed.] The learned Diuines proue by this place and by the like in the fourth to the Ephesians, that the Sacrament of Baptisme doth not onely giue grace, but imprinteth and sealeth the soule of the baptized, vvith a spiritual signe, marke, badge, or token, vvhich can neuer be blotted out, neither by sinne, heresie, apostasie, nor other vvaies, but remaineth for euer in man for the cognisance of his Christendom, and for distinction from others vvhich vvere neuer of Christes fold. by vvhich also he is as it vvere consecrated and deputed to God, made capable and partaker of the rightes of the Church, and subiect to her lavves and discipline. See S. Hierom *in 4. Ephes.* S. Ambrose *li. 1 de Sp. sancto cap. 6* S. Cyril Hierosol. *Catechesi 17* at the end, and S. Dionysius Areopag. *c. 2. Eccl. Hierarch.* The vvhich fathers expresse that spiritual signe by diuers agreable names, vvhich the Church and most Diuines, after S. Augustine, call the *character* of Baptisme. by the truth and force of vvhich spiritual note or marke of the soul, he specially conuinceth the Donatistes, that the said Sacrament though giuen and ministred by Heretikes or Schismatikes or vvho els so euer, can neuer be reiterated. See *ep. 57. & li. 6 cont. Donatist. cap. 1. & li. 2 cont. Parmenianum c. 11.* As the like indeleble characters giuen also by the Sacraments of Confirmation and Orders, do make those also irreiterable and neuer to be receiued but once. Vvhereas al other Sacraments sauing these three, may be often receiued of the self same person. And that holy Orders can not be iterated, see S. Augustine *li. 2 cont. Parmen. c. 13. li. de bono coniug. c. 24.* and S. Gregorie *li. 2 Regist. ep. 32.* The like of Confirmation is decreed in the most aūcient Councel Tarracon. *cap. 6.* Finally that this character is giuen onely by these said three Sacraments, and is the cause that none of them can be in any man repeated or reiterated, see the decrees of the Councels Florentine and Trent. Vvhich yet is no nevv deuise of them, as the Heretikes falsely affirme, but agreable (as you see) both to the Scriptures and also to the auncient fathers and Councels.

The indeleble character of Baptisme, Cōfirmatiō, Holy Orders.

See Conc. Tarraco. to. 2. Concil.

24. Not because vve ouerrule.] Caluin and his seditious Sectaries vvith other like *vvhich despise*

dominion

The Caluinistes vvil be subiect to no tribunal in earth, for trial of their religiō.

dominion, as S. Iude describeth such, vvould by this place deliuer them selues from al yoke of spiritual Magistrates and Rulers: namely that they be subiect to no man touching their faith, or for the examination and trial of their doctrine, but to God and his vvord onely. And no maruel that the malefactors and rebelles of the Church vvould come to no tribunal but Gods, that so they may remaine vnpunished at least during this life. for though the Scriptures plainely condemne their heresies, yet they could vvrithe them selues out by false gloses, constructions, corruptions, and denials of the bookes to be Canonical, if there vvere no lavves or iudicial sentence of men to rule and represse them.

Tyrannical dominiō is forbid in Prelates, not Ecclesiastical Soueraintie for examination of faith or maners.

Notvvithstanding then these vvordes of S. Paul, vvhereby onely tyrannical, insolent, and proud behauiour and indiscrete rigor of Prelates or Apostles tovvards their flockes is noted, as also in the first of S. Peter *cap. 5.* (the Greeke vvord in these places, and in the Gospel *Mt. 20, 25. Mr. 10, 42.* κατακυριεύειν signifying lordly and insolent dominion:) yet he had and exercised iust rule, preeminence, and prelacie ouer them, not onely for their life, but also and principally touching their faith. for he might & did call them to account for the same, and excōmunicated heretikes for foresaking their faith. *1 Cor. 4, 5. 2 Cor. 10, 4. 13, 10. 1 Tim. 1, 20. Tit. 1, 11.* And al Christian men are bound to obey their lavvful Prelates in matters of faith and doctrine specially, and must not vnder that ridiculous pretence of obeying Gods vvord onely (vvhich is the shifte of al other Heretikes, as Anabaptistes, Arians, and the like, as vvel as the Protestants) disobey Gods Church, Councels, and their ovvne Pastors and Bishops, vvho by the Scriptures haue the regiment of their soules, and may examine and punish as vvel Iohn Caluin as Simon Magus, for falling from the Catholike faith. for though God alone be the Lord, author and giuer of faith, yet they are his * cooperators and coadiutors by vvhom the faithful do beleeue and be preserued in the true faith, and be defended from vvolues, vvhich be Heretikes seeking to corrupt them in the same. And this same Apostle * chalengeth to be their father as he that begat and formed them by his preaching in Christ.

* συνεργοί *1 Cor. 3, 9.*

* *1 Cor. 4, 15.*

CHAP. II.

Prosecuting the true cause vvhich in the last chapter he gaue of his not comming, 6 he pardoneth novv after some part of penance, him that for incest he excommunicated in the last epistle, requiring them obediently to consent therevnto. 12 Then, of his going from Troas into Macedonia, God euery vvhere giuing him the triumph.

AND I haue determined vvith my self 1 this same thing, not to come to you againe in sorovv. † For if I make you sorie: 2 and who is it that can make me glad, but he that is made sorie by me? † And 3 this same I vvrote to you: that I may not, vvhen I come, haue sorovv vpon sorovv, of the vvhich I ought to reioyce: trusting in you al, that my ioy is the ioy of you al. † For of much tribulation and anguish of hart I vvrote to you by many teares: 4 not that you should be made sorie: but that you may knovv vvhat charitie I haue more aboundantly tovvard you. † And if any 5 man hath made sorovvful, not me hath he made sorovvful, but in part, that I burden not al you. † To him that is such a 6 one, "this rebuke sufficeth that is giuen of many: † so that 7 cōtrariewise you should rather pardon and comfort him, lest perhaps such an one be svvallovved vp vvith ouer great sorovv. † For the vvhich cause "I beseeche you that you con- 8 firme

9 firme charitie tovvard him. † For therfore alſo haue I written that I may knovv the experiment of you, vvhether in al
10 things you be" obedient. † And vvhom you haue pardoned any thing," I alſo. For, my ſelf alſo that vvhich [c] I pardoned, if I pardoned any thing, "for you" in the perſon of Chriſt,
11 † that vve be not "circumuented of Satan. for vve are not ignorant of his cogitations.
12 † And vvhen I vvas come to Troas for the Goſpel of
13 Chriſt, and a doore vvas opened vnto me in our Lord, † I had no reſt in my ſpirit, for that I found not Titus my brother, but bidding them fare vvel, I vvent forth into Macedo-
14 nia. † And thankes be to God, vvho alvvaies triumpheth vs in Chriſt IESVS, and manifeſteth the odour of his knovv-
15 ledge by vs in euery place. † For vve are the good odour of Chriſt vnto God in them that are ſaued, and in them that pe-
16 riſh. † To ſome in deede the odour of death vnto death: but to others the odour of life vnto life. And to theſe things
17 vvho is ſo ſufficient? † For vve are not as very many," adulterating the vvord of God, but of ſinceritie, and as of God, before God, in Chriſt vve ſpeake.

[c] κεχάρισμαι. Though he did great Penance (ſaith Theodorete) yet he calleth this pardoning, χάριν, *a grace*, becauſe his ſinne vvas greater then his penance.

ANNOTATIONS
CHAP. II.

6. This rebuke ſufficeth.] This Corinthian for inceſt vvas excommunicated and put to penance by the Apoſtle, as appeareth in the former Epiſtle c. 5. And here order is giuen for his abſolution and pardoning. Vvherein firſt vve haue a plaine example and proofe of the Apoſtolike povver, there of binding, and here of looſing: there of puniſhing, here of pardoning: there of retaining ſinnes, here of remiſsion. Secondly vve may hereby proue that not onely amendment, ceaſing to ſinne, or repentance in hart and before God alone, is alvvaies ynough to obteine ful reconcilement, vvhereas vve ſee here his ſeparation alſo from the faithful, and the Sacraments, and from al companie or dealing vvith other Chriſtian men, beſides other bodily affliction: al vvhich called of the Apoſtle before *interitus carnis, the deſtruction of the fleſh*, and named here, *Rebuke*, or (as the * Greeke vvord alſo importeth) mulct, penaltie, correction, chaſtiſment, vvere enioyned him by the Apoſtles commaundement in the face of the Church, and by the offender patiently ſuſteined ſo long. Thirdly vve ſee that it lieth in the handes of the Apoſtles, Biſhops, and ſpiritual Magiſtrates, to meaſure the time of ſuch penance or diſcipline, not onely according to the vveight of the offence committed, but alſo according to the vveaknes of the perſons puniſhed, and other reſpectes of time and place, as to their vviſedom ſhal be thought moſt agreable to the parties good, and the Churches edification. Laſtly by this vvhole handling of the offenders caſe, vve may refute the vvicked hereſie of the Proteſtants, that vvould make the ſimple beleeue, no puniſhment of a mans ovvne perſon for ſinnes cōmitted, nor penance enioyned by the Church, nor any paines temporal or ſatisfaction for our life paſt, to be neceſſarie, but al ſuch things to be ſuperfluous, becauſe Chriſt hath ſatisfied ynough for all. Vvhich Epicurian doctrine is refelled, not onely hereby, but alſo by the Prophets, Iohn the Baptiſtes, Chriſtes, and the Apoſtles preaching of penance and condigne vvorkes or fruites of repentance, to euery man in his ovvne perſon, and not in Chriſtes perſon onely: and by the vvhole life and moſt plaine ſpeaches and penitential canons

Margin: The Apoſtle excommunicateth, enioyneth penance: and aftervvard pardoneth & abſolueth.

Margin: 1. Cor. 5, 5. * ἐπιτιμία.

Margin: Pardon or remiſsion of penance enioyned.

Margin: Penance and ſatisfaction euidently proued againſt the Proteſtants.

Margin: Ioel 2, 12. Mt. 3. et 4. Act. 2. et 26.

canons of the holy doctors and Councels prescribing times of penance, commending penance, enioyning penance, and continually vsing the word satisfaction in this case through out al their vvorkes, as our Aduersaries them selues can not but confesse.

Zeale against the excommunicate.

8. I beseeche you.] They vvhich at the beginning did beare to much vvith the offender, and seemed loth to haue him excommunicated in so austere maner: yet through their obedience to the Apostle became on the other side so rigorous, and so farre detested the malefactor after he vvas excommunicated, that the Apostle novv meaning to absolue him, vvas glad to intreate and commaund them also to accept him to their companie and grace againe.

The Apostle chalengeth their obediēce to his Ecclesiastical authoritie.

9. Obedient.] Though in the last chapter he discharged him self of tyrannical dominion ouer them, yet he chalengeth their obedience in al things as their Pastor and Superior, and consequently in this point of receiuing to mercie the penitent Corinthian. Vvhereby vve see, that as the power and authoritie of excommunicating, so of absoluing also vvas in S. Paules person, though both vvere to be done in the face of the Church: els he vvould not haue commaunded or required their obedience.

The authoritie of Indulgences vvherupō it is groūded.

10. I also.] The Heretikes and others not vvel founded in the Scriptures and antiquitie, maruel at the Popes pardons, counting them either fruitles or vnlavvful or no elder then S. Gregorie. But in deede the authoritie, power, and right of them is of Christes ovvne vvord and commission, principally giuen to Peter, and so aftervvard to al the Apostles, and in their persons to al the cheefe Pastors of the Church, vvhen it vvas said, *Whatsoeuer you loose in earth, shal be loosed in heauen.* (Mat. 18, 18.) By vvhich commission the holy Bishops of old did cut of large peeces of penance enioyned to offenders, and gaue peace, grace, or indulgence, *before they had accomplished the measure of their appointed or deserued punishment. (Cypria. ep. 13. 14. 15.) and that is to giue pardon. And so S. Paul here did tovvardes the Corinthian, vvhom he assoiled of mere grace and mercie, as the vvord *donare* or *condonare* doth signifie, (κεχάρισμαι. See Theodoret in hūc loc.) when he might longer haue kept him in penance and temporall affliction for his offence. Vvherof though he had already before God invvardly repented, yet vvas he iustly holden vnder this correction for some satisfaction of his fault past, during the Apostles pleasure.

Vvhat is a pardon or indulgence.

To remit then the temporal punishment or chastisment due to sinners after the offence it self and the guilt therof be forgiuen of God, is an Indulgence or pardon. vvhich the principal Magistrates of Gods Church by Christes vvarrant and the Apostles example, haue euer done, being no lesse authorised to pardon then to punish, and by imitation of our Maister (vvho forgaue *the aduoutresse and diuers other offenders, not only their sinnes, but also often the temporal punishments due for the same) (Io. 8, 11.) are as much giuen to mercie as to iustice.

Indulgences or pardons in the primitiue Church.

10. For you.] Theodorete vpon this place saith that the Apostle gaue this pardon to the Corinthian at the intercession of the blessed men Timotheus and Titus. And we may read in sundrie places, of S. Cyprian namely, (Cypr. locis citatis.) that Indulgences or remissions vvere giuen in the primitiue Church by the mediation of holy Confessors or Martyrs, and by cōmunicating the satisfactorie vvorkes of one to another, to vvhich end they gaue their letters to Bishops in the behalfe of diuers their Christiā brethrē, a thing most agreable to the mutual entercourse that is betvvene the members of Christes mystical body, and very ansvverable to Gods iustice, * vvhich by supply of the one sort that aboundeth, standeth entire in respect of the other sort also that wanteth. (2 Cor. 8.) In vvhich kinde the Apostle confesseth that him self by his suffering and tribulations, supplieth the vvantes of such passions as Christ hath to suffer, (Col. 1, 24.) not in his ovvne person, but in his body, vvhich is his Church. Vvherevpon vve inferre most assuredly, that the satisfactorie and penal vvorkes of holy Sainctes suffered in this life, be communicable and applicable to the vse of other faithful men their fellovv-members in our Lord, and to be dispensed according to euery ones necessitie and deseruing, by them vvhom Christ hath constituted ouer his familie, and hath made the dispensers of his treasures.

Al pardon and remission is in the vertue and name of Christ.

10. In the person of Christ.] For that many might of ignorance or pride reproue the practise of Gods Church and her Officers, or deny the Apostles authoritie to be so great ouer mens soules as to punish and pardon in this sort, S. Paul doth purposely and precisely tell them that he doth giue pardon as Christes Vicar, or as bearing his person in this case: and therfore that no man may maruel of his povver herein, except he thinke that Christes povver, authoritie, and commission is not sufficient to release temporal punishment due to sinners.

Heretical trāslation.

And this to be the proper meaning of these vvordes, *In the person of Christ*, (ἐν προσώπῳ Χριστοῦ.) and not as the Protestants vvould haue it (the better to auoid the former conclusion of the Apostles giuing indulgence) *In the face or sight of Christ*, you may easily vnderstand by the Apostles like insinuation of Christes povver, vvhen he committed this offender to Satan, (1 Cor. 5, 4.) affirming that he gaue that sentence in the name and vvith the *vertue* or *povver of our Lord* IESVS CHRIST. In al vvhich cases the Protestants blindnes is exceding great,

vvho

vvho can not see that this is not the vvay to extol Christes povver, to deny it to his Priests, seing the Apostle chalengeth it by that that Christ hath such povver, & that him self doth it in his name, vertue, and person. So novv in this, and in no other name, giue Popes and Bishops their pardons. Vvhich pertaining proprely to releasing onely of temporal punishment due after the sinne and the eternal punishment be forgiuen, is not so great a matter as the remission of the sinne it self: vvhich yet the Priests * by expresse commission do also remitte.

Io. 20, 23.

11. *Circumuented of Satan.*] Vve may see hereby, that the dispensation of such discipline, and the releasing of the same, be put into the povver and handes of Gods ministers, to deale more or lesse rigorously, to pardon sooner or later, punish longer or shorter vvhile, as shal be thought best to their vvisedom. for the end of al such correction or pardoning must be the saluation of the parties soul, as the Apostle noted 1 *Cor. 5, 5.* Vvhich to some, and some certaine times, may be better procured by rigour of discipline then by indulgence, to some others, by lenitie and humane dealing (so pardoning of penance is called in old Councels) rather then by ouermuch chastisemēt. for consideration vvhereof, in some ages of the Church, much discipline, great penance and satisfaction vvas both enioyned and also vvillingly susteined, and then vvas the lesse pardoning and fevver indulgences, because in that voluntary vse and acceptation of punishment, and great zeale and feruor of spirit, euery man fulfilled his penance, and fevv asked pardon. Novv in the fall of deuotion and lothsomnes that men commonly haue to do great penance, though the sinnes be far greater then euer before, yet our holy mother the Church knovving vvith the Apostle the cogitations of Satan, hovv he vvould in this delicate time, driue men either to desperation, or to forsake Christ and his Church and al hope of saluation, rather then they vvould enter into the course of canonicall discipline, enioyneth small penance, and seldom vseth extremitie vvith offenders as the holy Bishops of the primitiue Church did, but condescending to the vveaknes of her children, pardoneth exceding often and much, not onely al enioyned penance, but also al or great partes of vvhat punishment temporal so euer due or deserued, either in this vvorld or in the next. As for the Heretikes vvhich neither like the Churches lenitie and pardoning in these daies, nor the old rigor of the primitiue Church, they be like to the Ievves * that condemned Iohn the Baptist of austeritie, and Christ of to much freedom and libertie: not knovving nor liking in deede either Christes ordinance and commission in binding or loosing, or his prouidence in the gouernement of the Church.

Conc. Nic. can. 12. Ancyran. can. 2 & 5.

Mat. 11, 18.

Al binding & loosing must be vsed to the parties saluation.

The great penance of the primitiue Church.

Vvhy more pardons and Indulgences now then in old time.

17. *Adulterating.*] The Greeke vvord signifieth to make commoditie of the vvord of God, as vulgar Vinteners do of their vvine. Vvhereby is expressed the peculiar trade of al Heretikes, and exceding proper to the Protestants, that so corrupt Scriptures by mixture of their ovvne phantasies, by false trāslations, glosses, colorable and pleasant commentaries, to deceiue the tast of the simple, as tauerners and tapsters do, to make their vvines salable by manifold artificial deceites. The Apostles contrarievvise, as all Catholikes, deliuer the Scriptures and vtter the vvord of God sincerely and entirely, in the same sense and sort as the fathers left them to the Church, interpreting them by the same Spirit by vvhich they vvere vvritten or spoken.

καπηλεύοντες.

The Heretikes corrupting of the Scripture.

CHAP. III.

Lest the Iudaical false Apostles should obiect againe that he praiseth him self, he saith that the Corinthians are his commendation: and they in their hartes being iustified by his ministerie, he thereof inferreth that the ministers of the nevv Testament are farre more glorious then they of the old, 12 and our people more lightened then theirs.

1 BEGIN we againe to commend our selues? or do vve neede (as certaine) epistles of commendation to you, or from you? 2 † Our epistle you are, vvritten in our hartes, vvhich is knovven and read of al men: 3 † being manifested that you are " the epistle of Christ, ministred by vs, & vvritten not vvith inke, but vvith the Spirit

of the liuing God: not in tables of ſtone, but in the tables carnall of the hart. † And ſuch confidence vve haue by 4 Chriſt to God: † not that vve be ſufficient to thinke any 5 thing" of our ſelues, as of our ſelues: but our ſufficiencie is of God. † Vvho alſo hath made vs meete miniſters of the 6 nevv teſtament: not in the letter, but in the Spirit. For" the letter killeth: but the Spirit quickeneth. † And if the mini- 7 ſtration of death with letters figured in ſtones, vvas in glorie, ſo that the children of Iſraël could not behold the face of Moyſes, for the glorie of his countenãce, that is made voide: 8 † how ſhal not the miniſtration of the Spirit be more in glo- 9 rie? † For if the miniſtratiõ of damnation be in glorie:" much more the miniſterie of iuſtice aboundeth in glorie. ⊣ † For 10 neither vvas it glorified, vvhich in this part vvas glorious, by reaſõ of the excelling glorie. † For if that vvhich is made void, 11 is by glorie: much more that vvhich abideth, is in glorie.

The Epiſtle vpon the 12 Sunday after Pentecoſt.

† Hauing therfore ſuch hope, vve vſe much confidence: 12 † and not* as Moyſes put a vele vpon his face, that the chil- 13 dren of Iſraël might not behold his face, vvhich is made voide, † but their ſenſes vvere dulled. For vntil this preſent 14 day," the ſelf ſame vele in the lecture of the old teſtament re- maineth vnreuealed (becauſe in Chriſt it is made voide) † but 15 vntil this preſent day, vvhen Moyſes is read, a vele is put vpõ their hart. † But vvhen he ſhal be conuerted to our Lord, 16 the vele ſhal be taken avvay. † And* our Lord is a Spirit. And 17 vvhere the Spirit of our Lord is, there is" libertie. † But vve 18 al, beholding the glorie of our Lord vvith face reuealed, are transformed into the ſame image from glorie vnto glorie, as of our Lordes Spirit.

Exo. 34, 33.

Io. 4, 24

ANNOTATIONS
CHAP. III.

The Apoſtles vvrote the Goſpel in mens hartes much more then in paper.

1. *The Epiſtle of Chriſt.*] S. Paul and other holy vvriters of Scriptures did ſet dovvne many thinges in vvriting, by penne, inke, and paper, al vvhich be of the Holy Ghoſt: but the ſpecial and proper booke of Chriſtes truth and Goſpel, is not the external vvriting in thoſe dead creatures, but in the hartes of the faithful, being the proper ſubiecte of theſe truthes and graces preached in the nevv Teſtament, and the habitacle of the Holy Ghoſt. In the vvhich booke of faithful mens hartes S. Paul vvrote diuers thinges not vttered in any Epiſtle: as ſundrie of the Apoſtles vvrote the Chriſtian religion in the hartes of their hearers onely, and in other material bookes not at all. Vvhereof S. Irenæus *li. 3. c. 4.* ſaith, *What and if the Apoſtles alſo had left no Scriptures, ought vve not to folovv the order of the tradition, vvhich they deliuered vnto them to vvhom they committed the Churches? to the vvhich ordinance many nations of thoſe barbarous people that haue beleeued in Chriſt, do conſent, vvithout letter or inke, hauing ſaluation vvritten in their hartes, and keeping diligently the tradition of the elders.* And S. Hierom, (*cont. Io. Hieroſ. c. 9. ad Pam.*) *In the Creede of our faith and hope, vvhich being deliuered by tradition from*

Scripture vvritten, and Tradition vnvvritten.

the Apostles, is not vvritten in paper and inke, but in the tables carnal of the hart. And this is the Churches booke also, vvhereby and vvherein she keepeth faithfully al truth vvritten in the hartes of those to vvhom the Apostles did preach, vvith the like diligence as she keepeth and preserueth the other booke vvhich is of holy Scriptures, from al corruption of Heretikes and other iniuries.

Gods grace & free will both must cōcurre.

5. Of our selues.] This maketh first against the Heretikes called Pelagians, that hold our meritorious actions or cogitations to be of free vvil onely, and not of Gods special grace. Secondly against the Protestantes, vvho on the contrarie side referre al to God, and take avvay mans freedom and proper motion in his thoughtes and doings: the Apostle confessing our good cogitations to be our ovvne, but not as comming of our selues, but of God.

The letter killeth both Ievv and Heretike.

6. The letter killeth.] As the letter of the old Lavv not truely vnderstood, nor referred to Christ, commaunding and not giuing grace and spirit to fulfil that vvhich vvas commaunded, did by occasiō kill the carnal Iew: so the letter of the nevv Testamēt not truely taken nor expounded by the Spirit of Christ (vvhich is onely in his Church) killeth the Heretike: vvho also being carnal and void of spirit, gaineth nothing by the external precepts or good lessons of the Scriptures, but rather taketh hurt by the same. See S. Augustine *to. 10. Ser. 70 & 100 de tempore. & li. de Sp. & lit. c. 5. 6. & seq.*

The preeminence of the new Testamēt, Sacraments, &c.

9 Much more.] The preeminence of the new Testament and of the priesthod or Ministerie thereof before the old, is, that the nevv, by al her Sacraments and Priests as ministers immediate of grace and remission of sinnes, doth so *ex opere operato* giue the spirit of life and charitie into the hartes of the faithful, as the old did giue the letter or external act of the Lavv.

The heretikes more blinde in not seing the Church, then the Iewes in not seing Christ.

Aug. in Psal. 30. Conc. 2.

14. The selfsame vele.] As the Ievves reading the old Testament, by reason of their blindnes (vvhich God for the punishment of their incredulitie suffereth to remaine as a couer vpon their eies and hartes) can not see Christ in the Scriptures vvhich they daily heare read in their Synagogs, but shal, vvhen they beleeue in him and haue the couer remoued, perceiue al to be most plainely done and spoken of him in their law & Scriptures: euen so Heretikes hauing (as S. Augustine noteth) a farre greater couer of blindnes and incredulitie ouer their hartes in respect of the Catholike Church vvhich they impugne, then the Iewes haue concerning Christ, can not see, though they read or heare the Scriptures read neuer so much, the maruelous euidence of the Catholike Church and truth in al pointes: but vvhen they shal returne againe to the obedience of the same Church, they shal finde the Scriptures most cleere for her and her doctrine, and shal vvonder at their former blindnes.

True Christiā libertie.

1. Pet. 2, 16.

17. Libertie.] The Spirit and grace of God in the nevv Testament dischargeth vs of the bondage of the Lavv and sinne, but is not a vvarrant to vs of fleshly licence, as S. Peter vvriteth: nor dischargeth Christians of their obedience to order, lavv, and power of Magistrates spiritual or temporal, as some Heretikes of these daies do seditiously teach.

CHAP. IIII.

That according as so glorious a ministerie requireth, he liueth and preacheth sincerely. 7 the vvhich glorie his Aduersaries can not count vaine, considering his persecutions, because persecution is to Gods glorie, and to our humilitie and hope, and meritorious of increase of grace in this life, and of most glorious bodies and soules aftervvard.

1 THERFORE hauing this ministration: according as vve haue obteined mercie, vve faile not, 2 † but vve renounce the secrete things of dishonestie, not walking in craftines, nor "adulterating the vvord of God, but in manifestation of the truth commending our selues to euery conscience of men

before God. † And if our Gospel be also hidde, in them 3 that perish it is hidde, † in vvhom the God of this vvorld 4 hath blinded the mindes of the infidels, that the illumination of the Gospel of the glorie of Christ vvho is the image of God, might not shine to them. † For vve preache not our selues, but IESVS Christ our Lord: and vs, your seruants by IESVS, † because God that commaunded light to shine 6 of darkenes, he hath shined in our hartes to the illumination of the knovvledge of the glorie of God, in the face of Christ IESVS. † But vve haue this treasure in earthen 7 vessels, that the excellencie may be of the povver of God, and not of vs. † In al things vve suffer tribulation, but are 8 not in distresse: [c] vve vvant, but are not destitute: † vve 9 suffer persecution, but are not forsaken: vve are cast dovvne, but vve perish not: † alvvaies bearing about in our body 10 the mortification of IESVS, that the life also of IESVS may be manifested in our bodies. † For vve that liue, are alvvaies 11 deliuered vnto death for IESVS: that the life also of IESVS may be manifested in our mortal flesh. † Death then vvor- 12 keth in vs, but life in you. † And hauing the same spirit of 13 faith, as it is vvritten, *I beleeued, for the vvhich cause I haue spoken,* vve also beleeue, for the vvhich cause vve speake also: † knovving 14 that he vvhich raised vp IESVS, vvil raise vp vs also vvith IESVS and set vs vvith you. ⁜ † For al things are for you: 15 that the grace abounding by many in giuing of thankes, may abound vnto the glorie of God. † For vvhich cause vve 16 faile not: but although that our man vvhich is vvithout, [b] corrupte: yet that vvhich is vvithin, is renevved from day to day. † For that our tribulation vvhich presently is momen- 17 tanie & light, " [c] vvorketh aboue measure excedingly an eternal vveight of glorie in vs, † we not cōsidering the things that 18 are seen, but that are not seen. For the things that be seen, are temporal: but those that be not seen, are eternal.

The Epistle for S. Athanasius. Mai. 2. (margin, at v. 5)

[c] The English Bible 1577, doth falsely translate, *prepareth.*

[c] *aporiamur.* See S. Ambr. Theoph.

Ps. 115, 10.

[b] *corrumpitur.*

c κατεργάζεται.

ANNOTATIONS
CHAP. IIII.

Heretikes corrupters of Gods word: Catholike Doctors, right handlers therof.

2. *Adulterating.*] He giueth often vvarning of false teachers, whose special and proper studie is to falsifie and adulterate by deceitful constructions, interpretations, and applications, the word of God: hauing no other end but to make their aduantage of the Scriptures, and to gaine glorie and estimation among the sinful and simple, by new deuised expositions. Vvherein the Protestants do excel the auncient Heretikes, none euer more impurely handeling the vvord of God then they do. Origen calleth such *Scripturarum fures & adulteros* in 2 ad Rom.

See Iren. li. 1. c. 1.

& adulteros, theeues and adulterers of the Scriptures. S. Cyprian (*de vnit. Ec. nu.* 7.) calleth them, corrupters of the Gospel, false interpreters, artificers and craftesmasters in corrupting the truth. On the other side, for special reuerence and sinceritie of dealing in those matters, the fathers and al Catholike preachers or Expositors vvere of old called according to S. Paules vvordes to Timothee, *Recte tractantes verbum Dei*, right handlers of the vvord of God.

2. *Tim.* 2.

17. *Worketh.*] The temporal and short tribulations vvhich vve patiently and willingly suffer for Christ, do winne vs euerlasting ioy and glorie. And it is here to be noted against the Heretikes, that tribulations do vvorke or cause the said saluation, which they deny to be giuen for such thinges, but for or by faith onely. S. Augustine maketh such tribulations for Christ so much the meritorious cause of euerlasting life and rest, that he saith it is salable and bought thereby. And it is written. Sap. 10, *God rendreth or repaieth to iust men the hire of their labours.*

Tribulations meritorious of glorie.

Aug. in ps. 93. *prope finem.*

CHAP. V.

That after death of the body the soule may to heauen: therfore, although naturally vve abhorre death, by grace he desireth it rather: 9 in consideration of Christes iust iudgement, liuing as in the sight of God, yea and of their consciences. 12 Which he speaketh not to praise him self, but because of his Aduersaries vvho did glorie in carnal respectes: but he and the other Apostles regard nothing but their reconciliation vnto God by Christ, and to reconcile others also, as being his legates for that purpose.

1 FOR vve knovv that if our earthly house of this habitation be dissolued, that vve haue a building of God, a house not made vvith hand, eternal in 2 heauen. † For in this also do vve grone, desirous to be ouerclothed with our ha- 3 bitation that is from heauen: † yet so, if 4 vve be found clothed, not naked. † For vve also that are in this tabernacle, grone being burdened: because vve would not be spoiled, but ouerclothed, that that 5 vvhich is mortal, might be svvallovved vp of life. † And he that maketh vs to this same, is God, vvho hath giuen vs the 6 pledge of the Spirit. † Being bold therfore alvvaies, and knovving that vvhile vve are in the body, vve are pilgrimes 7 from God, († for vve vvalke by faith and not by sight) 8 † but vve are bold, and haue a good vvil to be pilgrimes ra- 9 ther from the body, & :: to be present vvith our Lord. † And therfore vve endeuour, vvhether absent or present, to please 10 him. † For * vve must al be manifested before the iudgemēt seate of Christ, that euery one may receiue" the proper things of the body, according as he hath done, " either good or euil. 11 † Knovving therfore the feare of our Lord vve vse persuasion to men: but to God vve are manifest. † And I hope 12 also that in your consciences vve are manifest. † Vve commend

:: This place proueth that the Saincts departed novv since Christ, sleepe not til the day of iudgement, and that they be not holden in any seueral place of rest from the fruition of God til the resurrection of their bodies, but that they be present vvith God in their soules.

Ro. 14, 10.

mend not our selues againe to you, but giue you occasion to glorie for vs: that you may haue against them that glorie in face, and not in hart. † for vvhether vve excede in minde, to 13 God: or vvhether vve be sober, to you. † For the charitie 14 of Christ vrgeth vs: iudging this, that if one died for al, then al vvere dead. † and Christ died for al: that they also vvhich 15 liue, may not novv liue to them selues, but to him that died for them and rose againe. † Therfore vve from hence forth 16 knovv no man according to the flesh. And if vve haue knovven Christ according to the flesh: but novv vve know him no more.

† If then any be in Christ a nevv creature: the old are 17 passed, behold * al things are made nevv. † but al of God, 18 vvho hath reconciled vs to him self by Christ: and hath giuen " vs the ministerie of reconciliation. † For God in 19 deede vvas in Christ reconciling the vvorld to him self, not imputing to them their sinnes, and hath put in vs the vvord of reconciliation. † For Christ therfore vve are legates, God 20 as it vvere exhorting by vs. For Christ vve beseeche you, be reconciled to God. † Him that knevv no sinne, for vs he 21 made [c] sinne: that vve might be made " the iustice of God in him

Esa. 43, 19. Apoc. 21, 5.

c That is to say, a sacrifice and an host for sinne. *See the last annot. of this chapter.*

ANNOTATIONS
CHAP. V.

The obiection against praiers for the dead, ansvvered by S. Augustine.

10. *The proper things of his body.*] S. Augustine (*Enchirid. c. 110.*) obiecteth this speach of the Apostle, as in the person of such as deny the praiers, almes, and sacrifices of the liuing to be auailable for the dead, and he ansvvereth as folovveth. *This practise* (saith he) *of Gods Church in the commendation of the dead, is nothing repugnant to the sentence of the Apostle, vvhere he saith, that vve shal al stand before the iudgement seate of Christ, that euery one may receiue according to his deserts in the body, either good or euil. For, in his life and before death he deserued this, that these vvorkes after his death might be profitable vnto him. for in deede they be not profitable for al men. and vvhy so? but because of the difference and diuersitie of mens liues vvhiles they vvere in flesh.* The like he hath in diuers other places. August. li. de Præd. Sanct. c. 12. & ad Dulcit. q. 2. *And so hath S. Denys* c. 7. Ec. Hierarch.

Vvorkes meritorious and demeritorious.

10. *Either good or euil.*] Heauen is as vvel the revvard of good vvorkes, as Hel is the stipend of il vvorkes. Neither is faith alone sufficient to procure saluation, nor lacke of faith the onely cause of damnation: by good deedes men merite the one, and by il deedes they deserue the other. This is the Apostles doctrine here and in other places, hovv so euer the Aduersaries of good life and vvorkes teach othervvise.

Bishops and Priests vnder Christ ministers of our reconciliatiō.

18. *The ministerie of reconciliation.*] Christ is the cheefe Minister, according to his manhod, of al our reconcilement to God: and for him, as his ministers, the Apostles and their successors the Bishops and Priests of his Church, in vvhom the vvord of reconcilement, as vvel by ministring of the Sacrifice and Sacraments for remission of sinnes, as by preaching and gouernement of the vvorld to saluation, is placed. And therfore their preaching must be to vs, as if Christ him self did preach: their absolution and remission of sinnes, as Christes ovvne pardon: their vvhole office being nothing els (as vve see by this passage) but the Vicarship of Christ.

21. *The iustice of God.*] *Euen as* (saith S. Augustine) *vvhen vve reade, Saluation is our Lordes, it is not meant that saluatiō Whereby our Lord is saued, but vvhereby they are saued vvhō he saueth: & vvhē it is said,*

said, Gods iustice, that is not to be vnderstood vvherevvith God is iust, but that vvherevvith men are iust vvhom by his grace he iustifieth. See S. Augustine *de Sp. & lit. c. 18. & ep. 120 ad Honoratum.* and abhorre Caluins vvicked and vnlearned glose on this place, that teacheth iustice no othervvise to be in man, then sinne in Christ. Vvhereas the Scriptures call man iust, because * *he doth* iustice: but not so call they Christ sinne, because he doth sinne, but because he taketh avvay sinne, and is a sacrifice for sinne, as the Heretikes knovv very vvel, that knovv the vse and signification of the Hebrevv vvord in al the old Testament, namely *Psal. 39, 8.* and in the booke of *Leuiticus* very often, *c. 5. 6. 9. 12. 14. 16.* and *Numer. c. 29.*

1. Io. 3, 7.

Gods iustice, wherewith he maketh vs iust.

CHAP. VI.

That he helpeth vvith his exhortations, and in al things behaueth him self as becommeth a minister of God. 11 Which he speaketh so openly, because his hart is open vnto them: exhorting them to be likevvise open-harted tovvardes him, 14 and to auoid those Infidels.

1 AND vve "helping do exhorte, that you receiue not the " grace of God in vaine. 2 († For he saith, *In time accepted haue I heard thee: and in the day of saluation haue I holpen thee.* Behold, novv is the time acceptable: behold novv the day of saluation.) 3 † to no man giuing any offence, that our ministerie be not blamed: 4 † but in al things let vs exhibite our selues as the ministers of God, in much patience, in tribulations, in necessities, in distresses, 5 † in stripes, in prisons, in seditions, in labours, 6 " in vvatchings, in fastings, † in chastitie, in knovvledge, in lõganimitie, in svveetenes, in the holy Ghost, in charitie not feined, 7 † in the vvord of truth, in the vertue of God, by the armour of iustice on the right hand, and on the left, 8 † by honour and dishonour, by infamie and good fame: as seducers, and true: as they that are vnknovven, and knovven: 9 † as dying, and behold vve liue: as chastened, & not killed: 10 † as sorovvful, but alvvaies reioycing: as needie, but enriching many: as ∷ hauing nothing, and possessing al things. ⊣

11 † Our mouth is open to you ô Corinthians, our hart is dilated. 12 † You are not straitened in vs: but in your ovvne bovvels you are straitened. 13 † But hauing the same revvard (I speake as to my children) be you also dilated. 14 † ∷ Beare not the yoke vvith infidels. For vvhat participation hath iustice vvith iniquitie? or " vvhat societie is there betwene light and darkenes? 15 † And vvhat agreement vvith Christ and Belial? or vvhat part hath the faithful vvith the infidel? 16 † And vvhat agreement hath the temple of God vvith Idols? For

Es. 49, 8

The Epistle vpon the first Sunday of Lent.

The Epistle for many Martyrs.

∷ S. Augustine (in ps. 113) gathereth hereby, that the Apostles did vovv pouertie.

∷ It is not lawful for Catholikes to marie vvith Heretikes or Infidels. *See S. Hierom. cont. Iouinian. li. 1. Cont. Laod. c. 10 & 31.*

you are the temple of the liuing God. as God saith, *That I vvil dvvel, and vvalke in them, and vvil be their God: and they shal be my people.* *Leu. 26, 11.*

† For the vvhich cause, *Goe out of the middes of them, and separate your selues*, saith our Lord, *and touch not the vncleane: and I vvil receiue you.* 17 *Es. 52, 11*

† *and I vvil be a father to you: and you shal be my sonnes and daughters, saith our Lord omnipotent.* 18 *Hier. 31, 1.*

ANNOTATIONS
CHAP. VI.

Gods Ministers are his coadiutors.

1. *Helping.*] For that he declared before the Ministers of the nevv Testament to be Christes deputies, and that vvhen they preach or do any function, God as it vvere speaketh or doeth it by them, he boldly novv saith, *Helping therfore*: that is to say, ioyning or vvorking together vvith God, vve do exhort. *συνεργοῦντες*

Gods grace forceth no mā against his vvil.

1. *Grace in vaine.*] The grace of God vvorketh not in man against his vvill, nor forceth any thing vvithout his acceptation and consent: and therfore it lieth in mans vvill to frustrate or to folovv the motion of God, as this text plainely proueth.

Voluntarie penance.

5. *In Watchings.*] Vvhen in the middes of many miseries and persecutions, the Apostles yet of their ovvne accord added and required voluntarie vigils, fastings, and chastitie, vve may vvel perceiue these vvorkes to be vvonderful grateful to God, and specially needful in the Clergie.

Not to communicate with Heretikes in any acte of religion.

14. *What societie.*] Generally here is forbidden conuersation and dealing vvith al Infidels, and consequently vvith Heretikes, but specially in praiers, or meetings at their Schismatical Seruice, preaching, or other diuine office vvhatsoeuer. Vvhich the Apostle here vttereth in more particular and different termes, that Christian folke may take the better heede of it. No societie (saith he) nor felovvship, no participation nor agreement, no consent betvvene light and darknes, Christ and Baal, the temple of God and the temple of Idols: al Seruice, as pretended vvorship of God set vp by Heretikes or Schismatikes, being nothing els but Seruice of Baal and plaine Idolatrie, and their conuenticles nothing but conspirations against Christ. from such therfore specially vve must seuer our selues alvvaies in hart and mind, and touching any act of religion in body also, according as the children of Israel vvere commaunded by God to separate them selues from the Schismatikes Corè, Dathan, and Abiron, and their tabernacles, by these vvordes: *Depart from the tabernacles of the impious men, and touch ye not those things vvhich pertaine to them, lest you be envvrapped in their sinnes.* *Num. 16, 26.*

CHAP. VII.

He procedeth to exhorte them to puritie, and to receiue him into their charitie. 3 Which lest they should thinke he speaketh to accuse them, he commendeth them highly, both for their behauiour tovvard Titus, and for their penance vvhich they had done vpon his other epistle.

HAVING therfore these promisses, my deerest, let vs cleanse our selues from al inquinatiō of the flesh and spirit, perfiting sanctification in the feare of God. 1 † Receiue vs. Vve haue hurt no man, vve haue corrupted no man, vve haue circumuented no man. 2 † I speake not to your cōdemnation. for I said before that you are in our hartes to die together and to liue together. 3 † Much is my confidence vvith you, much is my glorying for you: I am replenished vvith consolation 4 consolation: I do excedingly abound in ioy in al our tribulation. 5 † For also vvhen vve vvere come into Macedonia, our flesh had no rest, but vve suffered al tribulatiō: vvithout, 6 combats: vvithin, feares. † But God that comforteth the 7 humble, did comforte vs, in the comming of Titus. † And not only in his comming, but also in the consolation, vvhervvith he vvas comforted among you, reporting to vs your desire, your vveeping, your emulation for me, so that I re-8 ioyced the more. † For although I made you sorie in an epistle, it repenteth me not: albeit it repented me, seing that the same epistle (although but for a time) did make you sorie. 9 † Novv I am glad: not because you vvere made sorie, but because you vvere made "sorie to penance. For you vvere made sorie according to God, that in nothing you should 10 suffer detriment by vs. † For ∵ the sorovv that is according to God, vvorketh penance vnto saluation that is stable: but the 11 sorovv of the vvorld vvorketh death. † For behold this very thing, that you vvere made sorie according to God, hovv great carefulnes it vvorketh in you: yea defense, yea indignation, yea feare, yea desire, yea emulation, yea reuenge. in al things you haue shevved your selues to be vndefiled in 12 the matter. † Therfore although I vvrote to you, not for him that did the iniurie, nor for him that suffered: but to manifest 13 our carefulnes that vve haue for you before God, † therfore vve are comforted. But in our consolation, vve did the more aboundantly reioyce vpon the ioy of Titus, because his spi-14 rit vvas refreshed of al you. † And if to him I gloried any thing of you, I am not cōfounded: but as vve spake al things to you in truth, so also our glorying that vvas to Titus, is 15 made a truth, † and his bovvels are more aboundantly toward you: remembring the obedience of you al, hovv vvith 16 feare and trembling you receiued him. † I reioyce that in al things I haue confidence in you.

∵ Contrition or sorovvful lamenting of our offenses, is the cause of saluation. Not onely faith then saueth, as the Heretikes affirme.

ANNOTATIONS
CHAP. VII.

9. *Sorie to penance.*] The sorovv vvhich a man taketh for vvorldly losses or any temporal aduersitie, is not here commended, but that vvhich is and ought to be in al men for their sinnes past, vvhich is called here, Sorovv tovvardes God and for penance, othervvise called Contrition, and is a thing excedingly requisite and much praised, the fruites vvhereof are these that the Apostle reckeneth, vvorking saluation. Vvhich doctrine is farre distant from * Luthers, and Caluins, and such vvicked Libertines, that teach contrition to be al together a meanes to make sinners either hypocrites, or to put them in despaire.

Contrition for a mans sinne vvorketh saluatiō.

* *To. 2. in assert. art. 6. a Leone damnat.*

CHAP. VIII.

By the example of the poore Macedonians he exhorteth them to contribute largely vnto the Church of Hierusalem, 7 and by praising of them, 9 and by the example of Christ. 14 and by their ovvne spiritual profite in being partakers of that Churches merites, 16 and by commending the collectors that he sendeth.

AND vve doe you to vnderstand, brethren, the 1 grace of God, that is giuen in the churches of Macedonia, † that in much experience of tri- 2 bulation they had aboundance of ioy, & their very deepe pouertie abounded vnto the riches of their simplicitie, † for according to their povver (I giue 3 them testimonie) and aboue their povver they vvere willing, † vvith much exhortation requesting vs the grace and com- 4 munication of the ministerie that is done tovvard the saincts. † And not as vve hoped, but their ovvne selues they gaue, 5 first to our Lord, ∷ then to vs by the vvil of God: † in so 6 much that vve desired Titus, that as he began, so also he vvould perfit in you this grace also. † But as in al things you 7 abound in faith, and vvord, and knovvledge, & al carefulnes, moreouer also in your charitie tovvard vs, that in this grace also you may abounde. † I speake not as commaunding: but 8 by the carefulnes of others, approuing also the good dispo- sition of your charitie. † For you knovv the grace of our 9 Lord IESVS Christ, that for you he vvas made poore, wher- as he vvas riche: that by his pouertie you might be riche. † And in this point I giue counsel: for this is profitable for 10 you, vvhich haue begõne not only to doe, but also to be wil- ling, from the yere past: † but novv perfourme ye it also in 11 deede: that as your minde is prompt to be vvilling, so it may be also to perfourme, of that vvhich you haue. † For if the 12 vvil be prompt: it is accepted according to that vvhich it hath, not according to that vvhich it hath not. † For not 13 that other should haue ease, and you tribulation: but by an equalitie. † Let in this present time your " aboundance sup- 14 plie their vvant: that their aboundance also may supplie your vvant, that there be an equalitie, † as it is vvritten: *He that had* 15 *much, abounded not: and he that had litle, vvanted not.* ⁊

† And thankes be to God, that hath giuen the self same 16 carefulnes for you in the hart of Titus, † for that he admitted 17 in deede exhortation: but being more careful, of his ovvne vvil

∷ The principal respecte next after God, is to be had of our maisters in religion, in al temporal and spiritual dueties.

The Epistle for S. Paulinus, *Iun.* 22.

Exo. 16, 28.

The Epistle vpon S. Lukes day, *Octob.* 18.

18 vvil he vvent vnto you. † Vve haue ſent alſo vvith him the brother, vvhoſe praiſe is in the Goſpel through al the 19 churches: † & not only that, but alſo he vvas ordeined of the churches fellovv of our peregrination, for this grace vvhich is miniſtred of vs to the glorie of our Lord, and our deter- 20 mined vvil: † auoiding this, leſt any man might reprehend 21 vs in this fulnes that is miniſtred of vs. † For vve prouide good things * not only before God, but alſo before men. 22 † And vve haue ſent vvith them our brother alſo, vvhom vve haue proued in many things often to be careful: but now 23 much more careful, for the great confidence in you, † either for Titus vvhich is my fellovv and coadiutor tovvard you, or our brethren Apoſtles of the churches, the glorie of 24 Chriſt. † The declaration therfore vvhich is of your charitie and our glorying for you, declare ye tovvard them in the face of the churches. ⊣

Ro. 12, 17.

ANNOTATIONS CHAP. VIII.

14. *Aboundance ſupply.*] He meaneth that ſuch as abound in vvorldly riches, ſhould communicate for ſupply of other their brethrens neceſſities, vvhatſoeuer they may: that on the other ſide they vvhom they helpe in temporals, may impart to them againe ſome of their ſpiritual riches, as praiers, and other holy vvorkes and graces, vvhich is a happie change and entercourſe for the vvelthy men, if they could ſee it. And this place proueth plainely that the faſtings and ſatisfactorie deedes of one man, be auailable to others, yea and that holy Sainctes or other vertuous perſons may in meaſure and proportion of other mens neceſſities and deſeruings, allotte vnto them, as vvel the ſupererogation of their ſpiritual vvorkes, as theſe that abound in vvorldly goods, may giue almes of their ſuperfluities, to them vvhich are in neceſſitie. Vvhich enterchange and proportion of things the Apoſtle doth euidently ſet dovvne.

Temporal benefites vpon ſpiritual perſons.

One may ſatisfie and ſupererogate for an other.

CHAP. IX.

He procedeth exhorting them to the foreſaid contribution, 3 to verifie his commending of them. 6 and to do it liberally, that ſo they may merite the more, and God be the more praiſed.

1 FOR concerning the miniſterie that is done ″ tovvard the ſainctes, it is ſuper- 2 fluous for me to vvrite vnto you. † For I know your prompt minde: for the which I glorie of you to the Macedonians: That Achaia alſo is ready from the yere paſt, and your emulation hath prouoked very ma- 3 ny. † But I haue ſent the brethren, that the thing vvhich vve glorie of you, be not made voide in this behalfe, that (as I

haue ſaid) you may be ready: † leſt vvhen the Macedoniãs 4 ſhal come vvith me, and finde you vnready, vve (that vve ſay not, ye) may be aſhamed [c] in this ſubſtance. † Therfore I 5 thought it neceſſarie to deſire the brethren that they vvould come to you, and prepare this bleſſing before promiſed, to be ready ſo, as a bleſſing, " not as auarice. † And this I ſay, he 6 that " ſovveth ſparingly, ſparingly alſo ſhal reape: and he that ſovveth in bleſſings, of bleſſings alſo ſhal reape. † Euery 7 one as he hath determined in his hart, not of ſadnes or of neceſſitie. † for *God loueth a cheereful giuer.* † And God is able to 8 make al grace abound in you: that in al things alvvaies ha- 9 uing al ſufficiencie, you may abound vnto al good vvorkes, † as it is vvritten: *He diſtributed, he gaue to the poore:* ∴ *his iuſtice remaineth for euer.* † And he that miniſtreth ſeede to the ſovver, 10 vvil giue bread alſo for to eate: & vvil multiplie your ſeede, and vvil augmẽt the increaſes of the fruites of your iuſtice: † that being enriched in al things, you may abound vnto 11 al ſimplicitie, vvhich vvorketh by vs thankes-giuing to God. † Becauſe the miniſterie of this office " doth not only ſupplie 12 thoſe things that the Saincts vvant, but aboundeth alſo by many thankes-giuings in our Lord, † by the proofe of this 13 miniſterie, glorifying God in the obedience of your confeſſion vnto the Goſpel of Chriſt, and in the ſimplicitie of communicating vnto them, and vnto al, † and in their praying 14 for you, being deſirous of you becauſe of the excellẽt grace of God in you. † Thankes be to God for his vnſpeake- 15 able gift.

c That is, in this matter of almes. Chryſ. Theophyl.

The Epiſtle for S. Laurence, Aug. 10

∴ The fruite of almes is the encreaſe of grace in al iuſtice and good workes to life euerlaſting: God giuing theſe things for revvard & recompenſe of charitable vvorkes, which therfore be called the ſeed or meritorious cauſe of theſe ſpiritual fruites.

Eccl. 35, 11.

Pſ. 111, 9

ANNOTATIONS
CHAP. IX.

Procters for Catholike priſoners.

1. *Tovvard the Saincts.*] By the Apoſtles earneſt and often calling vpon the Corinthians to giue almes for relieuing the faithful in diſtreſſe, the Paſtors of Gods Church may learne, that it ſpecially pertaineth to their office to be procters for holy men in priſon, pouertie, and al other neceſſitie, ſpecially vvhen their vvant commeth for confeſſion of their faith.

Cheereful giuing.

5. *Not as auarice.*] The couetous man that parteth vvith his peny painefully and vvith ſorovv as though he loſt a limme of his body, is noted, and cheereful, ready, voluntarie, and large contribution is commended.

The greater almes, the greater merite and revvard.

6. *Sovveth ſparingly.*] Almes is compared to ſeede. for as the ſeede throvven into the ground, though it ſeme to be caſt avvay, yet is not loſt, but is laid vp in certaine hope of great encreaſe: ſo that vvhich men giue in almes, though it ſeeme to be caſt avvay and to periſh in reſpect of the giuer, yet in deede it is moſt fruitful, the benefite thereof manifoldly returning to him againe. Vvherevpon the Apoſtles cõcluſion is cleere, that according to the meaſure of the almes or ſeeding (vvhich is more or leſſe in reſpect of the vvil and abilitie of the giuer) the encreaſe and aboundance of harueſt, that is, of grace and glorie ſhal enſue. See S. Auguſtine *in Pſal. 49 circa med. & q. 4. ad Dulcitium.*

12. *Doth not onely supply.*] Vvhen almes are giuen, specially to holy men, not onely the giuers obtaine great benefite thereby, and the vvantes of others be supplied, but God also by the receiuers continual praiers and thankes giuing therfore, is excedingly honoured: so that charitie bestovved in this sort, is an acte of Gods vvorship and of religion.

Almes redoūd to Gods honour.

CHAP. X.

Against the false Apostles, graunting the infirmitie of his person, he doth notvvithstanding set out the povver of his Apostleship, 12 reprehending them also for chalenging to them selues the praise of other mens labours.

1 AND I Paul my self beseeche you by the mildenes and modestie of Christ, vvho in presence in deede am humble amōg you, 2 but absent am bold on you. † But I beseeche you, that being present I neede not be bold by that confidence vvhervvith I am thought to be bold against some: vvhich thinke vs as though vve vvalke according to the 3 flesh. † For vvalking in the flesh, vve vvarre not accor- 4 ding to the flesh. † For the" vveapons of our vvarfare are not carnal: but mightie to God vnto the destruction of mu- 5 nitions, destroying counsels, † and al loftinesse extolling it self against the knovvledge of God, and bringing into capti- 6 uitie al vnderstanding vnto the obedience of Christ, † and hauing in a readinesse" to reuenge al disobediēce, vvhen your 7 obedience shal be fulfilled. † See the things that are according to appearance. If any man haue affiance in him self, that he is Christs: let him thinke this againe vvith him self, that 8 as he is Christs, so vve also. † For and if I should glorie somevvhat more of our povver, vvhich our Lord hath giuen vs"vnto edification and not to your destruction: I shal not 9 be ashamed. † But that I may not be thought as it vvere to 10 terrifie you by epistles († for his epistles in deede, say they, are sore and vehement: but his bodily presence vveake, and 11 his speache contemptible) † let him this thinke that is such a one, that such as vve are in vvord by epistles, absent: such 12 also vve are in deede, present. † For vve dare not matche or compare our selues vvith certaine, that commend them selues: but vve measure our selues in our selues, and compare 13 our selues to our selues. † But vve vvil not glorie aboue our measure: but according to the measure of the rule, vvhich God hath measured to vs, a measure to reache euen vnto you.

† For

† For not, as though vve reached not vnto you, doe vve extend our selues beyond. For vve are come as farre as to you in the Gospel of Christ. † not glorying aboue measure in other mens labours: but hauing [c] hope of your faith increasing, to be magnified in you according to our rule aboūdantly, † yea vnto those places that are beyond you, to euangelize, not in an other mans rule, to glorie in those things that are prepared before. † But he that glorieth, let him glorie in our Lord. † For not he that commendeth him self, the same is approued: but vvhom God commendeth.

14 15 16 17 18

c ἐλπίδα αὐξομένης τῆς πίστεως ὑμῶν,

Ier. 9, 23

ANNOTATIONS
CHAP. X.

Punishing of Heretikes.

4. Vveapons.] He meaneth the ample spiritual and Apostolical povver giuen by Christ for the punishment of false Apostles, Heretikes, and rebelles to Gods Church, vvho are here noted specially by pride and insolence (vvhich is the proper marke of such fellovves) to extoll them selues aboue the measure of the science of God, vvhich consisteth in humble obedience to the faith and the preachers of the same.

Their pride.

The spiritual povver of Bishops against Heretikes.

6. To reuenge.] You may see hereby, that the spiritual povver of Bishops is not onely in preaching the Gospel, and so by persuasion and exhortation onely (as some Heretikes hold) to remitte or retaine sinnes, but that it hath authoritie to punish, iudge, and condemne Heretikes and other like rebelles: vvhich povver * one of the principal rebelles of this time being conuinced by the euidence of the place, acknovvledgeth to be grounded vpon Christes vvord, *Vvhatsoeuer you binde in earth, shal be bound in heauen: Mat. 18, 18.* applying also the vvordes spoken to Hieremie (c. 1, 10.) *Behold I appoint thee ouer Nations and kingdoms, that thou plant, plucke vp, build and destroy:* to confirme and explicate the povver Apostolike here alleaged by S. Paul. Mary they vvould gladly dravv this povver from the lavvful successors of the Apostles, to them selues, their ministers and consistories, vvhich are nothing els but the shoppes and Councels of sedition and al the conspiracies of this time, against the lavvful Princes of the vvorld.

Caluin. vpon this place.

Heretical Cōsistories.

Ecclesiastical censures (namely Excommunication) whē & where to be executed.

8. Vnto edification.] This great povver of the Churches censures, specially of Excommunication, as it vvas giuen for the good and saluation of the people, so it must not be vsed against the innocent: no nor yet vpon Heretikes or other offenders, but vvhere and vvhen it may by likelihod benefite either the parties, or the people, or may be executed vvithout the hurt or perturbation of the vvhole Church, as often times it can not be, by reason of the multitude of offenders. Vvhich caused the Apostle here to signifie that he vvould not vse his vttermost authoritie against the false Apostles vvhich disturbed them, till them selues vvere in perfect obedience vnto him. lest by punishing the principal offenders, a greater disturbance and reuolt might fall among the people, if they vvere not before in perfect obedience.

CHAP. XI.

He reasoneth the matter vvith the Corinthians, vvhy they should preferre the false Apostles before him. 16 And because they giue them leaue to bragge and commend them selues, and to abuse them so miserably, he trusteth they vvil also giue him the hearing: 21 and so he beginneth, and first shevving him self in al Iudaical respectes (vvherein onely stood al their boasting) to be as they are, he addeth afteruvard such a long roll of his sufferings for Christ, as is incomparable.

Vvould

1 VVould God you could beare some litle of 2 my folly: but do ye also support me: † for I emulate you vvith the emulation of God. For I haue ∴ despoused you to one man, to present you a chaste virgin vnto Christ. 3 † But I feare lest, as the serpent seduced Eue by his subteltie, so your senses may be corrupted, & fall" from 4 the simplicitie that is in Christ. † For if he that ∴ commeth, preache an other Christ vvhō we haue not preached, or you receiue an other spirit vvhom you haue not receiued: or an other Gospel vvhich you haue not receiued: you might vvel 5 suffer it. † For I suppose that I haue done nothing lesse then 6 the great Apostles. † For although" rude in speache, yet not in knovvledge. but in al things we are made manifest to you. 7 † Or did I commit a sinne, humbling my self, that you might be exalted? because I euāgelized vnto you the Gospel of God 8 gratis? † Other churches I spoiled, taking a stipend, for your 9 ministerie. † And vvhen I vvas vvith you, and had neede, I vvas burdenous to none: for that vvhich I vvanted, the brethren supplied that came from Macedonia: & in al things I haue kept my self vvithout burden to you, and vvil keepe. 10 † The truth of Christ is in me, that this glorying shal not 11 be infringed tovvard me in the countries of Achaia. † Vvher-12 fore? because I loue you not? God doth knovv. † But that vvhich I doe, I vvil also doe, that I may cut avvay the occasion of them that desire occasion: that, in that vvhich they 13 glorie, they may be found euen like vs. † For such false apostles are ∴ craftie vvorkers, trāsfiguring them selues into Apo-14 stles of Christ. † And no maruel: for Satan him self trans-15 figureth him self into an Angel of light. † It is no great matter therfore if his ministers be trāsfigured as the ministers of iustice: vvhose ende shal be according to their vvorkes.

16 † Againe I say, (let no man thinke me to be foolish: othervvise take me as foolish, that I also may glorie a litle,) 17 † that vvhich I speake, I speake not according to God, but 18 as it vvere in foolishnes, in this substance of glorying. † Because many glorie according to the flesh, I also vvil glo-19 rie. † For you do gladly suffer the foolish: vvhereas your 20 selues are vvise. † For you suffer if a man bring you into seruitude, if a man deuoure, if a man take, if a man be extol-21 led, if a man strike you on the face. † I speake according

Gen. 3,4

∴ The Apostles and their successors did despouse the people vvhom they conuerted, to Christ, in al puritie & chastitie of truth, and vvholy vndefiled and void of errour and heresie.

∴ The note of a false teacher, *to come:* that is, vvithout lavvful calling or sending to thrust and intrude him self into an other mans charge.

∴ A proper terme for Heretikes that shape thē selues into the habit of true teachers, specially by often allegation and commendatiō of the Scriptures. Reade the notable admonition of the auncient vvriter *Vincentius Lirinensis* in his golden booke *Against the Prophane nouelties of al heresies.*

The Epistle vpon the Sunday of Sexagesme.

to dishonour, as though vve had been vveake in this part. Vvherein any man dare (I speake folishly) I dare also. † * They are Hebrevves: and I. They are Israëlites: and I. 22 They are the seede of Abraham: and I. † They are the mini- 23 sters of Christ: and I. (I speake as one scarse vvise) more I: in many moe labours, in prisons more aboundantly, in stripes aboue measure, in deathes often. † Of the Ievves fiue times, 24 did I receiue * fourtie, sauing one. † Thrise vvas I beaten 25 * vvith roddes, * once I vvas stoned, thrise I suffred * ship- vvracke, night and day haue I been in the depth of the sea, † in iourneying often, perils of vvaters, perils of theeues, pe- 26 rils of my nation, perils of Gentiles, perils in the citie, perils in the wildernes, perils in the sea, perils among false brethren, † in labour and miserie, in much vvatchings, in hunger and 27 thirst, in fastings often, in colde and nakednes, † beside those 28 things which are outwardly: my daily [b] instance, the careful- nes of al churches. † Vvho is vveake, and I am not vveake? 29 vvho is scandalized, and I [c] am not burnt? † If I must glorie: 30 I vvil glorie of the things that concerne my infirmitie. † The 31 God and Father of our Lord IESVS Christ, vvho is blessed for euer, knovveth that I lie not. † * At Damascus the Gouer- 32 nour of the nation vnder Aretas the king, kept the citie of the Damascenes, for to apprehend me: † and through a 33 vvindovv in a basket vvas I let dovvne by the vvall, and so escaped his handes.

Phil. 3, 5

Deu. 25, 3. Act. 16, 23. 14, 18. 27, 15.

b ἐπισύστασις. S. Chrysostom and Theophylacte interpret it of daily conspiracie against him. others, of multitude of cares instât & vrgêt vpô him.

c πυροῦμαι?

Act. 9, 24.

ANNOTATIONS
CHAP. XI.

As Eue by the Serpent, so the people are seduced by Heretikes.

3. *From the simplicitie.*] People fall from their first faith, virginitie, and simplicitie in Christ, not by sodê reuolt, but by litle & litle, in giuing eare to the subtil persuasiô of the Serpent, speaking to thê by the svveete mouthes & illurementes of Heretikes, of vvhich kind of seductiô, he giueth Eue for an example, vvho vvas by her greedy desire of knovvledge and the Diuels promis of the same, dravven from the natiue simplicitie and obedience to God. as at this day, promis and pretense of knovvledge driueth many a poore soul from the sure, true, sincere, and onely beleefe of Gods Church.

Heretikes sometime eloquent.

Knovvledge better then gay wordes.

Yong orators among heretikes preferred before the auncient Doctors.

6. *Rude in speach.*] Hereby vve see that the seditious and false teachers haue often the gift of eloquence vvhereby the simple be easily beguiled. Such vvere Corè and Dathan, as Iosephus vvriteth *Antiq. li. 4 c. 2.* for the same, S. Augustine (*li. 5 Confes. c. 3. et 13.*) calleth the Heretike Faustus Manichæus, *magnum laqueum Diaboli*, *a great snare of the Diuel*, saying that he passed the glorious Doctor S. Ambrose in shevv of vvordes, but farre inferior to him (vvithout al comparison) in substance and matter. In vvhich sort the Apostle here is glad to compare him self vvith the false Apostles, vvhom the Corinthians did folovv and extoll farre aboue him by reason of their eloquence, graunting to them that gift, but chalenging to him self superioritie in knovvledge, vvhich al vvise men preferre before vaine vvordes. And it is the bane of our poore countrie, that the people novv a daies giue credit rather to nevv orators and folish yonkers, for their svveete speaches: then to the glorious Doctors of Christes Church, for their singular knovvledge and more graue eloquence.

CHAP. XII.

He telleth of his incomparable visions, 5 but for humilitie liketh better to talke of his infirmities: 11 putting the fault in the Corinthians for that he is faine thus to rehearse his ovvne commendations. 13 Vvhere againe he reasoneth the matter vvith them like a father, vvhy they should preferre those false Apostles before him. 20 And feareth lest at his comming he shal be compelled to excommunicate many of them.

1 IF I must glorie (it is not expedient in deede) but I vvil come to the" visions and reuelatiõs 2 of our Lord. † I knovv a man in Christ aboue fourtene yeres agoe (vvhether in the body, I knovv not: or out of the body, I knovv not: God doth knovv) such a one :: rapt euen to the third heauẽ. 3 † And I knovv such a man (vvhether in the body, or out of 4 the body, I knovv not: God doth know) † that he vvas rapt into Paradise: & heard secrete vvordes, which it is not lavvful 5 for a man to speake. † For such an one I vvil glorie: but for 6 my self I vvil glorie nothing, sauing in my infirmities. † For and if I vvil glorie, I shal not be foolish: for I shal say truth. but I spare, lest any mã should esteeme me aboue that vvhich 7 he seeth in me, or heareth any thing of me. † And lest the greatnes of the reuelations might extoll me, there vvas giuen me a pricke of my flesh, an angel of Satan, to buffet 8 me. † For the vvhich thing thrise I besought our Lord, 9 that it might depart from me: † and he said to me, My grace sufficeth thee, for povver is perfited in infirmitie. Gladly therfore vvil I glorie in mine infirmitie, that the povver of 10 Christ may dvvel in me. ⌐ † For the vvhich cause I please my self in infirmities, in contumelies, in necessities, in persecutions, in distresses for Christ. for vvhen I am vveake, then am I mightie.

:: By this vve may proue that it is neither impossible, incredible, nor vndecent, that is reported by the auncient fathers of some that haue been rauished or rapt (whether in body or out of body God knovveth) & brought to see the state of the next life, as vvel of the saued as damned.

11 † I am become foolish: you haue compelled me. For I ought to haue been commended of you: for I haue been nothing lesse then they that are aboue measure Apostles, al-12 though I am nothing. † Yet the signes of my Apostleship haue been done vpon you in al patience," in signes & vvõders 13 and mighty deedes. † For vvhat is there that you haue had lesse then the other churches: but that I my self haue not 14 burdened you? Pardon me this iniurie. † Behold, novv the third time I am ready to come to you: and I vvil not be burdenous vnto you. For I seeke not the things that are

yours: but you. For neither ought the childrē lay vp treasures for the parents, but the parents for the children. † But I most 15 gladly vvil bestovv, & vvil my self moreouer be bestovved for your soules: although louing you more, I am loued lesse.

† But be it so: I haue not burdened you: but being craf- 16 tie, I tooke you by guile. † Haue I circumuented you by 17 any of them vvhom I sent to you? † I requested Titus, and 18 I sent vvith him a brother. Did Titus circumuent you? vvalked vve not vvith one spirit? not in the self same steppes? † Of old thinke you that vve excuse our selues to you? 19 *Againe* Before God, in Christ vve speake: but al things (my deerest) for your edifying. † For I feare lest perhaps vvhen I come, 20 I finde you not such as I vvould: and I be found of you, such an one as you vvould not. lest perhaps cōtentions, emulatiōs, stomakings, dissensions, detractions, vvhisperings, svvellings, seditions be among you. † lest againe vvhen I come, God 21 humble me among you: & I mourne many of them that sinned before, & ∷ haue not done penāce for the vncleannes & fornication and incontinencie that they haue committed.

∷ τῶν μὴ μετανοησάντων. Vvhich S. Augustine saith (ep. 108) is spoken here of doing great penance for heinous sinnes, as *Pœnitentes* did in the primitiue Church. So that it is not onely to repent or to amend their liues, as the Protestants translate it.

ANNOTATIONS
CHAP. XII.

Visiōs haue no credite with heretikes.

1. *Visions.*] S. Cyprian (*ep. 69. nu. 4.*) complaineth that the Aduersaries of Gods Church and Priestes, giue no credit to visions. but their incredulitie is much more in our daies, that condemne al such reuelations, though they be reported and recorded for most certaine, of holy S. Gregorie, S. Bede, or vvho els so euer. Yea they are so vvicked in this case, that the vision vvhich the holy author of the booke of Machabees * calleth *fide dignum*, vvorthy of credit, is one cause vvhy they deny the vvhole booke to be Canonical: and as vvel might they for this vision deny al S. Paules Epistles, and for the like, the Actes of the Apostles, *Act. 9. 10. 11. 12. 27*: and the Gospel it self, *Mat. 1, 20. 2, 13, 19.*

2. Macha. 15, 11.

The Apostles some greater then other.

11. *Aboue measure Apostles.*] Though al vvere in that they vvere Apostles, of one and the same order, yet vve may see that some had maruelous great preeminence and priuilege aboue others in the same office: specially S. Peter and S. Iohn, vvhom S. Paul often calleth *great Apostles, aboue measure or passing Apostles, the pillers, &c.* 2 Cor. 11, 5. 12, 11. Gal. 2, 9.

We must sticke to the faith first planted by miracles.

12. *In signes.*] Miracles be necessarie, and be great signes of truth, vvhen it is first nevvly taught. And therfore let al Catholike men hold fast that faith vvhich vvas first preached and confirmed by miracles. as in England by S. Augustine, and in other nations by other holy Apostolike men. And let the Heretikes that preach extraordinarily, nevvly, and othervvise then vve receiued at our first conuersion, shevv their calling and doctrine by miracles, or els let them be taken for false Apostles as they be.

CHAP. XIII.

He driueth into them the feare of excommunication: to the end that they doing penance beforehand, he may not be compelled to vse his authoritie vvhen he commeth, and as he hath threatened. 11 And so vvith a general exhortation he endeth.

LO

Deu. 19, 15.

1 LO this the third time I come vnto you: * In the mouth of tvvo or three vvitnesses ſhal euery vvord ſtand. 2 † I foretold and doe foretel as preſent, and novv abſent, to them that ſinned before, and al the reſt, that if I come againe, I vvil not ſpare. 3 † Seeke you an experiment of him that ſpeaketh in me, Chriſt: vvho in you is not vveake, but is mightie in you? 4 † For although he vvas crucified of infirmitie: yet he liueth by the povver of God. For vve alſo are vveake in him: but vve ſhal liue vvith him by the povver of God on you. 5 † " Trie your ovvne ſelues if you be in the faith: proue ye your ſelues. Knovv you not your ſelues that Chriſt IESVS is in you, vnleſſe 6 perhaps you be reprobates. † But I hope, you ˋknovv' 7 that vve are not reprobates. † And vve pray God, that you doe no euil, not that vve may appeare approued, but that you may doe that vvhich is good, and vve be as reprobates. 8 † For vve can not any thing againſt the truth: but for 9 the truth. † For vve reioyce, for that vve are vveake, & you are mightie. This alſo vve pray for, your conſummation. 10 † Therfore theſe things I vvrite abſent: that being preſent I may not deale hardly according to the [c] povver vvhich our Lord hath giuen me vnto edification and not vnto deſtruction.

ˋſhal knovv

c Eccleſiſtical power to puniſh offenders by the cēſures of the Church.

11 † For the reſt brethren, reioyce, be perfect, [c] take exhortation, be of one minde, haue peace, and the God of peace & 12 of loue ſhal be vvith you. † Salute one an other in a * holy 13 kiſſe. Al the ſaincts ſalute you. † The grace of our Lord IESVS Chriſt, and the charitie of God, and the communication of the holy Ghoſt be vvith you all. Amen.

c παρακαλεῖσθε, Ro. 16, 16. 1. Co. 16, 20.

The Epiſtle in a votiue Maſſe of the B. Trinitie.

ANNOTATIONS
CHAP. XIII.

5. Trie your ſelues.] The Heretikes argue herevpõ, that euery man may knovv him ſelf certainely to be in grace: vvhere the Apoſtle ſpeaketh expreſly and onely of faith. the act vvhereof a man may knovv and feele to be in him ſelf, becauſe it is an act of vnderſtanding, though he can not be aſſured that he hath his ſinnes remitted, and that he is in al pointes in ſtate of grace and ſaluation: becauſe euery man that is of the Catholike faith, is not alvvaies of good life agreable therevnto, nor the actes of our vvil ſo ſubiect to vnderſtanding, that vve can knovv certainely vvhether vve be good or euil. See S. Auguſtine *to. 7 de perfect. iuſtitia c. 15. Li. de Cor. et grat. c. 13.* & S. Thomas 1.2, q. 112. art. 5.

Vve may knovv that we haue faith, but not that vve are in grace.

THE ARGVMENT OF THE EPISTLE OF S. PAVL TO THE GALATIANS.

HAT this Epistle may seeme to be the first that S. *Paul vvrote, vvas declared in the Argument of the Epistle to the Romanes, notvvithstanding that in the second chapter it is euidét to haue bene vvritten* 14 *yeres at the least after his Conuersion, and (as it is said) from Ephesus, belike at that time of his being there, vvhich is mentioned Act.* 18.

The occasion of it vvere such False apostles, as vve reade of, Act. 15. *Et quidam descendentes, &c.* And certaine comming dovvne from Ievvrie, taught the brethren (*that is the Christian Gentiles at Antioche*) that vnles you be circumcised according to the manner of Moyses, you can not be saued. *Such commers also to the Galatians (vvhom* S. *Paul had conuerted Act.*16, *as him self mentioneth Gal.* 1. *and* 4.) *did seduce them, saying, that al the other Apostles to vvhom they should rather harken, then to Paul (vvho came they knevv not from vvhence) did vse Circumcision: yea and that Paul himself, vvhen he came among them, durst do none other. And to vvinne them more easily, they did not lay on them the burden of the vvhole Lavv, but of Circumcision only.*

Against these deceiuers, S. *Paul declareth, that he receiued his Apostleship and learned the Gospel that he preacheth, of Christ him self after his Resurrection: and that the other Apostles (although he learned nothing of them) receiued him into their societie, and allovved vvel of his preaching to the Gentiles, though them-selues being Ievves, and liuing among the Ievves, had not yet left the ceremonies of the Lavv: hovvbeit they did not put in them any hope of iustification, but in Christ alone vvithout them. He declareth moreouer, that the said Falseapostles belyed him, in saying that he also preached Circumcision sometimes. Againe, that they them-selues in preaching no more but Circumcision, did against the nature of Circumcision, because it is a profession to obserue the vvhole Lavv: finally, vvhatsoeuer they pretended, that in deede they did it onely to please the Ievves, of vvhom othervvise they should be persecuted.*

*So that in this Epistle he handleth the same matter, vvhich in the Epistle to the Romanes: but here lesse exactly and more briefly, because the Galatians vvere very rude, and the Romanes contrarivvise, repleti omni scientia (Rom.*15) replenished vvith al knovvledge.

THE

THE EPISTLE OF PAVL TO THE GALATIANS.

CHAP. I.

After the foundation laide in the salutation, 6 he exclaimeth against the Galatians, and their false apostles, 11 considering that the Gospel vvhich he preached to thē, he had it immediatly of Christ him self. 13 Vvhich to shevv he beginneth to tel the storie of his conuersion and preaching since then, that as he learned nothing of the other Apostles, so yet he had their approbation.

1 PAVL an Apostle not of men, " neither by man, but by IESVS Christ, and God the Father that raised him from the dead, 2 † and al the brethren that are vvith me: to the churches of Galatia. 3 † Grace to you and peace from God the Father and our Lord 4 IESVS Christ, † vvho gaue him self for our sinnes, that he might deliuer vs from this present vvicked vvorld, according to the vvil of 5 our God and father: † to vvhom is glorie for euer and euer. Amen.

6 † I maruel that thus so soone you are transferred from him that called you into the grace of Christ, vnto an other Go-7 spel: † vvhich is not an other, vnles there be some that trou-8 ble you, and vvil :: inuert the Gospel of Christ. † But although we, " or an Angel from heauen, euāgelize to you beside that vvhich vve haue euangelized to you, be he anáthe-9 ma. † As vve haue said before, so novv I say againe, If any euangelize to you, beside that vvhich you haue receiued, 10 be he anáthema. † For do I novv vse persuasion to men, or to God? Or do I seeke to please men? If I yet did please men, I should not be the seruant of Christ.

11 † c For I doe you to vnderstand, brethren, the Gospel that vvas

:: New Gospellers that peruert, corrupt, or alter the one onely true and first deliuered Gospel, are to be auoided. See S. Augustine *Cont. Faustum li. 32. c. 27.*

c The Epistle vpon the Commemoration of S. Paul, Iun. 30.

vvas euangelized of me, that it is not according to man.
† For neither did I receiue it of man, nor learne it: but by the 12 reuelation of IESVS Christ.
† For you haue heard my cõuersation sometime in Iudaisme, 13 that aboue measure I persecuted the Church of God, and expugned it, † and profited in Iudaisme aboue many of mine 14 equales in my nation, being more aboundantly an emulator of the traditions of my fathers. † But vvhen it pleased him 15 that separated me from my mothers vvombe, and called me by his grace, to reueale his sonne in me, † that I should euan- 16 gelize him among the Gentils, incontinent I condescended not to flesh and bloud, † neither came I to Hierusalem to 17 the Apostles my antecessors: but I vvent into Arabia, and againe I returned to Damascus. † Then, after three yeres I 18 came to Hierusalem " to see Peter: and taried with him fiftene daies. † But other of the Apostles savv I none: sauing Iames 19 :: the brother of our Lord. † And the things that I vvrite to 20 you: behold before God, that I lie not. ꝗ † After that, I came 21 into the partes of Syria and Cilicia. † And I vvas vnknowen 22 by sight to the churches of Ievvrie, that vvere in Christ: † but they had heard only, That he vvhich persecuted vs 23 sometime, doth novv euangelize the faith vvhich sometime he expugned: † and in me they glorified God. 24

Act. 9, 1.

:: S. Iames was called our Lordes brother after the hebrew phrase of the Iewes, by vvhich mere kinsmen are called brethrẽ. for they were not brethren in deede, but rather sisters children.

ANNOTATIONS
CHAP. I.

S. Paul sent to preache by ordinarie impositiõ of hãdes.

1. *Neither by man.*] Though he vvere not first by mans election, nomination, or assignement, but by Gods ovvne special appointmẽt, chosen to be an Apostle: yet by the like expresse ordinance of God he tooke orders or imposition of hands of men, as is plaine *Act. 13.* Let vs bevvare then of such false Apostles, as novv a daies intrude them selues to the office of Ministerie and preaching, neither called of God, nor rightly ordered of men.

No shevv of learning or vertue must moue vs from the faith.

8. *Or an Angel.*] Many vvorthie obseruations are made in the fathers vvritings, of the earnest admonition of the Apostle, and much may vve gather of the text it self. first, that the credit of any man or Angel for vvhat learning, eloquence, shevv of grace or vertue so euer, though he vvrought miracles, should not moue a Christian man from that truth vvhich he hath once receiued in the Catholike Church: of vvhich point Vincentius Lirinensis excellently treateth. *li. cont. profan. hæres. Nouitates.* Vvhereby vve may see that it is great pitie and shame, that so many folovv Luther and Caluin and such other leude fellovves, into a nevv Gospel, vvhich are so farre from Apostles and Angels, that they are not any vvhit comparable vvith the old Heretikes in giftes of learning or eloquence, much lesse in good life.

Preaching cõtrarie to the faith receiued is forbidden, not other preaching.

Secondly S. Augustine noteth vpon the vvord, *Beside*, that not al other teaching, or more preaching then the first, is forbidden, but such as is contrarie and disagreing to the rule of faith. *The Apostle did not say*, saith he, *If any man euangelize to you more then you haue receiued, but, beside that you receiued. for if he should say that, he should be preiudicial to him self, vvho coueted to come to the Thessalonians, that he might supply that vvhich vvas vvanting to their faith. Novv he that supplieth,* addeth

Tract. 98 in Ioan.

addeth that vvhich vvas lacking, taketh not avvay that vvhich vvas, &c. By vvhich vve see hovv friuolously and calumniously the Heretikes charge the Church vvith addition to the Scriptures.

Thirdly, as vvel by the vvord *euangelizamus* (vve euangelize) as the vvord *accepistis* (you haue receiued) vve may note that the first truth, against vvhich no second Gospelling or doctrine may be admitted, is not that onely vvhich he vvrote to the Galatians, or vvhich is conteined either in his or any other of the Apostles or Euãgelistes vvritings, but that vvhich vvas by vvord of mouth also preached, taught, or deliuered them first, before he Wrote to them. Therfore the Aduersaries of the Church that measure the Word of God or Gospel by the Scriptures onely, thinking them selues not to incurre S. Paules curse, except they teach directly against the vvritten vvord, are fouly beguiled. As therein also they shamfully erre, When they charge the Catholikes With adding to the Gospel, When they teach any thing that is not in expresse Wordes Written by the Apostles or Euangelistes: not marking that the Apostle in this Chapter, and els Where, commonly calleth his & his fellovves Whole preaching, the Gospel, be it Written or vnvvritten.

The Gospel is not onely in the Written Word of scripture, but in vnWritten tradition also.

Fourthly, by the same Wordes We see condemned al after-preachings, later doctrines, neW sectes and authors of the same: that onely being true, Which Was first by the Apostles and Apostolike men as the lavvful husbandmen of Christes fild, sovved and planted in the Church: and that false, Which Was later and as it vvere ouersovven by the enemie. By Which rule not onely Tertullian (*de præscript. nu. 6 & 9.*) but all other aũcient Doctors, and specially S. Irenæus (*li. 3. c. 2. 3. 4.*) tried truth from falsehod, and condemned old Heretikes, prouing Marcion, Valentine, Cerdon, Menander, and such like, false Apostles, because they came in With their noueltios long after the Church Was setled in former truth.

After-preaching & ouersowing of nouelties, argueth false doctrine.

Sixthly, This curse or execration pronounced by the Apostle, toucheth not onely the Galatians, or those of the Apostles time, that preached othervvise then they did, but it perteineth to al times, preachers, and teachers, vnto the Worldes end, and it concerneth them (as Vincentius Lirinensis saith) that preach a neW faith, or change that old faith Which they receiued in the vnitie of the Catholike Church. *To preach any thing to Christian Catholike men* (saith he) *besides that vvhich they haue receiued, neuer vvas it lavvful, neuer is it, nor neuer shal it be lavvful. to say anáthema to such, it hath been, and is, and shal be alvvaies behooful.* So S. Augustine by this place holdeth al accursed, that draW a Christian man from the societie of the Whole Church, to make the seueral part of any one sect: that call to the hidden conuenticles of Heretikes, from the open and knovven Church of Christ: that allure to the priuate, from the common: finally al that draW With chatting curiositie the children of the Catholike Church, by teaching any thing besides that they found in the church. *ep. 48. Psal. 103. Con. 2.* *mentioning also that a Donatist feined an Angel to haue admonished him to call his frende out of the Communion of the Catholike Church into his sect. and he saith, that if it had been an Angel in deede, yet should he not haue heard him. Lastly S. Hierom vseth this place, Wherein the Apostle giueth the curse or anáthema to al false teachers not once but tvvise, to proue that the zeale of Catholike men ought to be so great tovvard al Heretikes and their doctrines, that they should giue them the anáthema, though they vvere neuer so deere vnto them. In Which case, saith this holy Doctor, I Would not spare mine ovvne parents. *Ad Pammach. c. 3. cont. Io. Hieros.*

Li. cont. proph. har. nouit.

* *Aug. ep. 165.*

The Apostles curse vpon al that teache nevv doctrine, and dravv men from the Cath. Church.

Zeale against heretikes.

18. To see Peter.] In What estimation S. Peter Was With this Apostle, it appeareth: seing for respect and honour of his person, and of duety as Tertullian *de præscript.* saith (notvvithstanding his great affaires Ecclesiasticall) he vvent so farre to see him. not in vulgar maner, but (as S. Chrysostom noteth the Greeke Word to import) to behold him as men behold a thing or person of name, excellencie, and maiestie. for vvhich cause, and to fill him self With the perfect vew of his behauiour, he abode With him fiftene daies. See S. Hierom *ep. 103 ad Paulinum. to. 3.* Who maketh also a mysterie of the number of daies that he taried With S. Peter. See S. Ambrose *in Comment. huius loci*, and S. Chrysostome vpon this place, and *ho. 87 in Ioan.*

ἱστορῆσαι

B. Paul doth visite S. Peter of honour and reuerence tovvard him.

CHAP. II.

He telleth furth the storie begonne in the last chapter, and hovv he reprehended Peter, 15 and then specially vrgeth the ensample of the Christian Ievves, vvho sought vnto Christ for iustification, and that by vvarrant also of their Lavv it self, as also because othervvise Christs death had been needles.

HEN after fourtene yeres I vvent vp 1 againe to Hierusalem vvith Barnabas, taking Titus alſo vvith me. † And I 2 vvent vp according to reuelation: and " cōferred with them the Goſpel which I preach among the Gentiles, but apart with thē that ſeemed to be ſomething, leſt perhaps " in vaine I ſhould runne or had runne. † But neither Titus which vvas with me, vvhere- 3 as he vvas a Gentil, vvas compelled to be circumciſed: † but 4 becauſe of the falſe brethren craftely brought in, vvhich craf- tely came in to eſpie our libertie that vve haue in Chriſt IESVS, that they might bring vs into ſeruitude. † To 5 vvhom vve yelded not ſubiection no not for an houre, that the truth of the Goſpel may remaine vvith you. † But of 6 them that ſeemed to be ſomething, (vvhat they vvere ſome- time, it is nothing to me. * God accepteth not the perſon of man) for to me, they that ſeemed to be ſomething, " added nothing. † But contrarievviſe vvhen they had ſeen, that to 7 me vvas committed the Goſpel of the [c] prepuce, as " to Peter of the circumciſion († for he that vvrought in Peter to the 8 Apoſtleſhip of the circumciſion, vvrought in me alſo among the Gentils) † and vvhen they had knovven the grace that 9 vvas giuen me, Iames and Cephas and Iohn, vvhich ſeemed to be pillers, " gaue to me and Barnabas the right handes of ſocietie: that vve vnto the Gentiles, & they vnto the circum- 10 ciſion: † only that vve ſhould be mindeful of the poore: the vvhich ſame thing alſo I vvas careful to doe.

† And vvhen Cephas vvas come to Antioche, " I reſiſted 11 him [c] in face, becauſe he vvas " reprehenſible. † For before 12 that certaine came from Iames, he did eate vvith the Gentiles: but vvhen they vvere come, he vvithdrevv and ſeparated him ſelf, fearing them that vvere of the circumciſion. † And 13 to his ſimulation cōſented the reſt of the Ievves, ſo that Bar- nabas alſo vvas ledde of them into that ſimulation. † But 14 vvhen I ſavv that they vvalked not rightly to the veritie of the Goſpel, I ſaid to Cephas before them al: If thou being a Ievve, liueſt Gentile-like & not Iudaically: hovv doeſt thou compel the Gentils to Iudaize.

† Vve are by nature Ievves, and not of the Gentils, ſin- 15 ners. † But knovving that * man is not iuſtified by the 16 vvorkes

Marginal notes:

Deu. 10, 17.

c See the marginal Annotation *Rom. 2. v. 25.*

c That is, *in preſence, before them al*, as Beza him ſelf expoundeth it. Yet the Engliſh Bezites to the more diſgracing of S. Peter, tranſlate, *to his face*, No. Teſt. an. 1580.

c κατὰ πρόσωπον

Ro. 3, 19. 20.

vvorkes :: of the Lavv, but by the faith of IESVS Christ: we also beleeue in Christ IESVS, that we may be iustified by the faith of Christ, and not by the vvorkes of the Lavv: for the vvhich cause, by the workes of the Law no flesh shal be iusti-
17 fied. † But if seeking to be iustified in Christ, our selues also be found sinners: is Christ then a minister of sinne? God for-
18 bid. † For if I build the same things againe vvhich I haue de-
19 stroied, I make my self a preuaricatour. † For I by the Lavv, am dead to the Law, that I may liue to God: vvith Christ I am
20 nailed to the crosse. † And I liue, novv not I: but Christ liueth in me. And that that I liue novv in the flesh, I liue in the faith of the sonne of God, who loued me, & deliuered him self for
21 me. † I cast not avvay the grace of God. For if iustice be by the Lavv, then Christ died in vaine.

:: By this and by the discourse of this whole epistle, you may perceiue, that when iustification is attributed to faith, the vvorkes of Charitie be not excluded, but the vvorkes of Moyses law: that is, the ceremonies, sacrifices and sacramẽts thereof principally, and consequently al workes done merely by nature and free wil, without the faith, grace, spirit, & aide of Christ.

ANNOTATIONS
CHAP. II.

1. *Conferred vvith them.*] Though S. Paul vvere taught his Gospel of God and not of man, and had an extraordinarie calling by Christ him self, yet by reuelation he vvas sent to Hierusalem to conferre the said Gospel which he preached, vvith his elders the ordinarie Apostles and Rulers of the Church, to put both his vocation and doctrine to their trial and approbation, and to ioyne in office, teaching, and societie or communion vvith them. For there is no extraordinarie or miraculous vocation, that can seuer or separate the person so called, in doctrine or fellovvship of Christian life and religion, from the ordinarie knowen societie of Gods people and Priestes. Therfore vvhosoeuer he be (vpon vvhat pretence so euer) that vvil not haue his calling and doctrine tried by the ordinarie Gouerners of Gods Church, or disdaineth to go vp to the principal place of our religion, to conferre vvith Peter and other pillers of the Church, it is euident that he is a false teacher, a Schismatike, and an Heretike. By vvhich rule you may trie al your nevv teachers of Luthers or Caluins schoole: vvho neuer did nor euer durst put their preaching to such conference or trial of holy Councel or Bishops, as they ought to do, and vvould do, if it vvere of God, as S. Paules vvas.

S. Paul conferreth vvith S. Peter and the rest, for trial of his doctrine.

The heretikes submit their doctrine to no trial of Bishops or Coũcel.

2. *In vaine.*] Though S. Paul doubted not of the truth of the Gospel vvhich he preached, knovving it to be of the holy Ghost: yet because other men could not, nor vvould not acknovvledge so much, til it vvere allovved by such as vvere vvithout al exception knovven to be Apostles & to haue the spirit of truth, to discerne vvhether the vocation, spirit, & Gospel of Paul vvere of God, he knevv he should othervvise vvithout conferẽce vvith them, haue lost his labour, both for the time past and to come. *He had not had* (saith S. Hierom) *securitie of preaching the Gospel, if it had not been approued by Peters sentence and the rest that vvere vvith him. Hiero. ep. 89. c. 2. See Tertul. li. 4 Cont. Marc. nu. 3.* Therfore by reuelation he vvent to conferre with the Apostles at Hierusalem, that by them hauing his Apostleship and Gospel liked and approued, he might preach vvith more fruite. Vvherein vve see, this holy Apostle did not as the seditious proud Heretikes do novv a daies, vvhich refusing al mans attestation or approbation, vvil be tried by Scriptures onely. As also vve may learne that it is no such absurditie as the Aduersaries vvould make it, to haue the Scriptures approued by the Churches testimonie. Seing the Gospel vvhich S. Paul preached (being of as much certaintie and of the same Holy Ghost that the Scriptures be) vvas to be put in conference and examination of the Apostles, vvithout al derogation to the truth, dignitie, or certaintie of the same. And the cauilling of Heretikes, that we make subiect Gods Oracles to mans censure, and the Scriptures to haue no more force then the Church is content to graunt vnto them, is vaine and false. For, to beare vvitnes or to giue euidence or attestation that the preaching or vvriting of such, is true and of the Holy Ghost, is not to make it

The approbation of S. Paules doctrine by Peter & the rest, vvas very requisite.

No absurditie that the Scriptures be approued by the Churches testimonie.

The Church maketh not

Canonical Scripture, but declareth that it is so.

it true: no more then the Goldsmith or touch-stone that trie and discerne vvhich is true gold, make it good gold, but they giue euidence to man that so it is. And therfore that disputation also, vvhether the Scripture or the Church be of greater authoritie, is superfluous: either giuing testimonie to the other, and both assured by the Holy Ghost from al error: the Church yet being before the Scriptures, the spouse of Christ, and proper dwelling, temple, or subiect of God and his graces: for the vvhich Church the Scriptures vvere, and not the Church for the Scriptures. In vvhich Church there is iudicial authoritie by office and iurisdiction to determine of doubtful questions touching the sense of the Scriptures and other controuersies in religion, & to punish disobedient persons. Of which iudicial power the Scriptures be not capable, as neither the truthes & determinations of the same can be so euident to men, nor so agreable and fit for euery particular resolution, as diuersitie of times and persons requireth. Certaine is the truth, and great is the authoritie of both: but in such diuers kindes, as they can not be vvell compared together. The controuersie is much like as if a man touching the ruling a case in lavv or giuing sentence in a matter of question, should aske, vvhether the iudge, or the euidēce of the parties, be of more authoritie or credit. vvhich vvere as friuolous a dispute, as it were a disordered part for any man to say, he vvould be tried by no other iudge but by his owne vvritings or euidences. Vvith such triflers and seditious persons haue vve to do now a daies in diuinitie, as vvere intolerable in any prophane science or facultie in the vvorld.

The Scripture & Church cōpared together for antiquitie, authoritie, &c.

The Scriptures alvvaies true in them selues, are so knovven to be by the Church.

6. Added nothing.] The Gospel and preaching of S. Paul vvas wholy of God, & therfore though it vvere put to the Churches probation, as gold is to the touch stone: yet being found in al pointes pure, nothing could be altered or amended therein by the Apostles. Euen so the Scriptures vvhich are in deede vvholy of the Holy Ghosts enditing, being put to the Churches trial, are found, proued, and testified vnto the vvorld to be such, and not made true, altered, or amended by the same. Vvithout vvhich attestation of the Church, the holy Scriptures in them selues vvere alvvaies true before: but not so knowen to be, to al Christians, nor they so bound to take them. And that is the meaning of the famous sentence of S. Augustine *Cont. ep. fund. c. 5.* vvhich troubleth the Heretikes so much. *I vvould not beleeue the Gospel* (saith he) *vnles the authoritie of the Church moued me.*

The Apostles commissiō general through the vvorld, & yet peculiar to certaine prouinces.

7. To Peter of the circumcision.] Vve may not thinke, as the Heretikes deceitfuly teach, that the charge of the Apostles vvas so distincted, that none could preach or exercise iurisdiction but in those seueral places or towardes those peoples or prouinces onely, vvhereunto by Gods appointment or their ovvne lot or election, they vvere specially designed. For, euery Apostle might by Christes commission (*Mat. 28. Goe, and teach al nations*) vse al spiritual functiō through the vvhole vvorld: yet for the more particular regard & care of prouinces, & for peace & order sake, some were appointed to one countrie, & some to an other: as, of the other Apostles, we see in the Ecclesiastical histories, and for S. Peter & S. Paul, it is plaine by this place & other, that to them as to the tvvo cheefe and most renovvmed Apostles, the Church of al Nations vvas giuen, as deuided into two partes, that is, Ievves and Gentiles: the first and principal being S. Peters lot, that herein also he might resemble our Sauiour, vvho vvas sent namely * *to the lost sheepe of Israel*, and vvas properly * *the Minister of the Circumcision*: the second being S. Paules, vvhom Christ chose specially to preach to the Gentiles: Not so for al that, that either he vvas limited to the Gentils onely, (vvhō the Actes of the Apostles report, in euery place, first to haue entered into the Synagogs & preached Christ to the Ievves, as he vvrote also to the Hebrues & euer had special regard & honour to thē:) or Peter so boūd to the Ievves only, that he could not meddle vvith the Gentiles: seing he vvas * the man chosen of God, by whom the Gentils should first beleeue, vvho first baptized them, and first gaue order concerning them. Therfore the treacherie of Caluin is intolerable, that vpon this distinction of the Apostles charge, vvould haue the simple suppose, that S. Peter could not be Bishop of Rome (so might he barre S. Iohn from Ephesus also) nor deale among the Gentiles, as a thing against Gods ordinance and the appointment betvvene him and S. Paul: as though thereby the one had bound him self to the other, not to preach or meddle vvithin his fellovves compasse. And vvhich is further most seditious, he exhorteth al men to keepe fast the foresaid compact, and rather to haue respect to S. Paules Apostleship, then to S. Peters: as though the preaching, authoritie, and Apostleship of both vvere not a like true, and al of one holy Spirit, vvhether they preached to Iewes or Gentiles, as both did preach vnto both peoples, as is already proued, and at length, partly by the daily decay of the Ievvish state and their incredulitie, and partly for that in Christianitie the distinction of Iew & Gentil ceased after a season: both vvent to the cheefe citie of the Gentiles, and there founded the Church common to the Hebrues and al nations, Peter first, and Paul aftervvard. And therfore Tertullian saith, *de præscript nu. 14. O happie Church, to vvhich the Apostles povvred out al doctrine vvith their bloud. Where Peter suffereth like to our Lordes passion, vvhere Paul is crovvned*

Mat. 15.

Ro. 15.

Act. 10. & 15. v. 7.

Calu. li. 4. c. 6. nu. 15. Instit.

Iewes and Gentiles specially committed to the two principal Apostles.

Neither Peter only of the Ievves, nor Paul Apostle of the Gētiles only.

Caluins folish reason that Peter vvas not B. of Rome, & his derogatiō from Peters Apostleship.

The Church founded at Rome by S. Peter and S. Paul.

crovvned vvith Iohn(Baptists)death.

9. Gaue the right handes of societie.] There is and alwaies ought to be, a common fellowship and fraternitie of al Pastors and preachers of the Church. Into vvhich societie who so euer entereth not, but standeth in Schisme and separation from Peter and the cheefe Apostolike Pastors, what pretence so euer he hath, or vvhence so euer he chalengeth authoritie, he is a vvolfe, and no true Pastor. Vvhich vnion and communion together was so necessarie euen in S. Paules case, that, notvvithstanding his special calling of God, yet the Holy Ghost caused him to go vp to his elder Apostles, to be receiued into their felovvship or brotherhod. for it is to be noted, that SS. Peter, Iames, and Iohn vvere not sent to S. Paul, to ioyne vvith him or to be tried for their doctrine and calling, by him: but contrariewise he vvas sent to them as to the cheefe and knovven ordinarie Apostles. They therfore gaue Paul their handes, that is to say, tooke him into their societie, and not he them. And S. Hieroms rule concerning this, shal be found true to the vvorldes end, speaking of S. Peters successor: *He that gathereth not vvith thee, scattereth. Ep. 57.* And in an other place for the same cause he calleth Rome, *tutissimum Communionis portum*, the most safe and sure hauen of communion or Societie. *Ep. 16. c. 3.* And vvhereas the Heretikes by this also vvould proue that Peter had no preeminẽce aboue Paul being his fellovv Apostle, it is ridiculous. As though al of one fellowship or brotherhod be alvvaies equal, or as though there vvere not order and gouernement, superioritie and inferioritie, in euery societie vvel appointed. And they might perceiue by this vvhole passage, that Peter vvas the special and in more singular sort, the Apostle of the Ievves, though Iames and Iohn vvere also: as S. Paul is also called in more singular sort the Apostle aud doctor of the Gentiles then S. Barnabas, and yet they vvere both alike taken here into this societie, as they were both at once and alike segregated into this ministerie, and ordered together *Act. 13.* It is a poore reason then to say or thinke, S. Peter not to be aboue S. Barnabas neither, because of this societie and fellovvship vnto vvhich he vvas receiued together vvith S. Paul.

Al Catholike preachers and Pastors must communicate vvith Peter & his successors.

The heretikes ridiculous argumẽt against Peters preeminence.

11. I resisted him.] Vvicked Porphyrie (as S. Hierom vvriteth) chargeth S. Paul of enuie and malepart boldnes, and S. Peter of errour. *Proœm. Comment. in Galat.* Euen so the like impious sonnes of Cham, for this, and for other things, gladly charge S. Peter, as though he had committed the greatest crimes in the vvorld. for, it is the propertie of Heretikes and il men, to be glad to see the Saincts reprehended and their faultes discouered, as vve may learne in the vvritings of S. Augustine against Faustus the Manichee, vvho gathered out al the actes of the holy Patriarches, that might seeme to the people to be vvorthy blame. Vvhom the said holy Doctor defendeth at large against him. as both he, and before him S. Cyprian, finde here vpon this Apostles reprehension, much matter of praising both their vertues: S. Paules great zeale, and S. Peters vvonderful humilitie: that the one in the cause of God vvould not spare his Superior, and that the other, in that excellent dignitie, vvould not take it in il part, nor by allegation of his Supremacie disdaine or refuse to be controvvled by his iunior. vvhich of the tvvo they count the greater grace and more to be imitated. *For neither Peter* (saith S. Cyprian) *Whom our Lord chose the first and vpon vvhom he built the Church, vvhen Paul disputed vvith him of circumcision, chalenged insolently or arrogantly tooke any thing to him self, saying that he had the Primacie, and therfore the later Disciples ought rather to obey him.* ep. 71 ad Quintum. nu. 2. And S. Augustine ep. 19 c. 2 in fine. *That* (saith he) *vvhich vvas done of Paul profitably by the libertie of charitie, the same Peter tooke in good part by holy and benigne godlines of humilitie, and so he gaue vnto posteritie a more rare and holy example, if at any time perhaps they did amis, to be content to be corrected of their iuniors, then Paul, for to be bold and confident: yea the inferiors to resist their betters for defending the truth of the Gospel, brotherly charitie alvvaies preserued.* By vvhich notable speaches of the Doctors vve may also see, how friuolously the Heretikes argue herevpon, that S. Peter could not be Superior to S. Paul, being so reprehended of him: vvhereas the Fathers make it an example to the Superiors, to beare vvith humilitie the correption or controulement euen of their inferiors. Namely by this example S. Augustine (*li. 2 de bapt. c. 1.* excellently declareth, that the B. Martyr S. Cyprian, vvho vvalked avvry touching the rebaptizing of them that vvere christened of Heretikes, could not, nor vvould not haue been offended to be admonished & reformed in that point by his fellovves or inferiors, much lesse by a vvhole Councel. *We haue learned*, saith he, *that Peter the Apostle, in vvhom the Primacie of the Apostles by excellent grace is so preeminent, vvhen he did othervvise concerning circumcision then the truth required, vvas corrected of Paul the later Apostle. I thinke (vvithout any reproch vnto him) Cyprian the Bishop may be compared to Peter the Apostle. hovvbeit I ought rather to feare lest I be iniurious to Peter. for vvho knovveth not that the principalitie of Apostleship it to be preferred before any dignitie of Bishop vvhatsoeuer? but if the grace of the Chaires or Sees differ, yet the glorie of the Martyrs is one.* And vvho is so dull that can not see, that the inferior, though not by office and iurisdiction, yet by the law of brotherly loue and fraternal correption, may reprehend his superior? Did euer any man vvonder that a good Priest or any vertuous person should tell the Pope, or any other great Prelate or greatest Prince in earth, their faultes? Popes may be reprehended, and are iustly admonished of their faultes, and ought to take it in good part, and

The heretikes malitiously derogate from S. Peter.

Paules reprehension of Peter, teacheth vs the zeale of the one, and humilitie of the other.

It proueth nothing agaist Peters superioritie, that he vvas reprehended.

The superior may be reprehended or admonished of the inferior.

Heretikes reprehension of Catholike Bishops is rather railing.

& so they do and euer haue done, vvhen it commeth of zeale & loue, as of S. Paul, Irenæus, Cyprian, Hierom, Augustine, Bernard: but of Simon Magus, Nouatus, Iulian, Wicleffe, Luther, Caluin, Beza, that do it of malice, & raile no lesse at their vertues then their vices, of such (I say) Gods Prelates must not be taught nor corrected, though they must patiently take it, as our Sauiour did the like reproches of the malitious Ievves, and as Dauid did the malediction of Semei. *2 Reg. 16.*

S. Peters errour vvas not in faith, but in conuersation or behauiour.

11. Reprehensible.] The Heretikes hereof againe inferre, that Peter then did erre in faith, and therfore the Popes may faile therein also. To vvhich vve ansvver, that hovvsoeuer other Popes may erre in their priuate teachings or vvritings, vvhereof vve haue treated before in the Annotation vpon these vvordes, *That thy faith faile not*: (Luc. 22, 32.) it is certaine that S. Peter did not here faile in faith, nor erre in doctrine or knovvledge. for it vvas *conuersationis non prædicationis vitium*, as Tertullian saith. *de præscript. nu. 7.* It vvas a default in conuersation, life, or regiment, Which may be committed of any man, be he neuer so holy, and not in doctrine. S. Augustine and vvhosoeuer make most of it, thinke no othervvise of it. But S. Hierom and * many other holy fathers deeme it to haue been no fault at all, nor any other thing then S. Paul him self did vpon the like occasion: & that this vvhole combat vvas a set thing agreed vpon betvvene them. It is a schoole point much debated betvvixt S. Hierom and S. Augustine *ep. 9. 11. 19. apud August.*

* *See S. Chrysost. Theophyl. &c.*

Chap. III.

By their ovvne conuersion at the first, 6 and by the example of Abraham, and promise made to him, he shevveth that the vvay to obtaine the benediction, is to seeke vnto God by faith in Christ. 10 Seing also that the Lavv curseth euery one that hath not euermore kept the Lavv. 15 And, that the Lavv vvas not giuen to alter Gods testament, 19 but to conuince the Ievves of sinne, 23 and so to be their pædagogue or leader vnto Christ, 25 and then to cease.

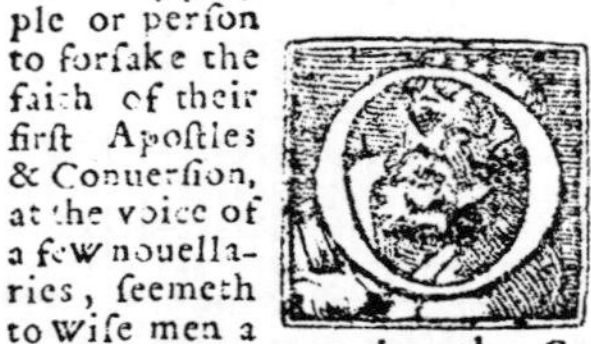

1 O Sensles Galatians, vvho hath :: bevvitched you, not to obey the truth, before vvhose eies IESVS Christ vvas proscribed, being crucified among you? 2 † This only I vvould learne of you, By the vvorkes of the Lavv, did you receiue the Spirit, or by the hearing of the faith? 3 † Are you so foolish, that vvhereas you began vvith the spirit, now you vvil be consummate vvith the flesh? 4 † Haue you suffered so great things vvithout cause? if yet vvithout cause. 5 † He therfore that giueth you the Spirit, and vvorketh miracles among you: by the vvorkes of the Lavv, or by the hearing of the faith doeth he it? 6 † As, *Abraham beleeued God, and it vvas reputed to him vnto iustice.* (Gen. 15, 6. Ro. 4, 3.)

7 † Knovv ye therfore that they that are :: of faith, the same are the children of Abraham. 8 † And the Scripture foreseing that God iustifieth the Gentils by faith, shevved vnto Abraham before, *That in thee shal al nations be blessed.* (Gen. 12, 3.) 9 Therfore they that are of faith, shal be blessed vvith the faithful Abraham. 10 † For vvhosoeuer are of the vvorkes of the Lavv, are vnder curse. For it is vvritten: " *Cursed be euery one that abideth not in al things that be vvritten in the booke of the Lavv, to doe them.* (Deu. 27, 26.) 11 † But that in the Lavv no man is iustified vvith God, it is manifest, because the

:: For any people or person to forsake the faith of their first Apostles & Conuersion, at the voice of a few nouellaries, seemeth to wise men a very bewitching & sensles brutishnes. Such is the case of our poore coūtrie, Germanie, and others.

:: This faith whereby Abraham was iustified, and his children the Gentils beleeuing in Christ, implieth al Christian vertues, of which the first is faith, the groūd & foundation of al the rest, and therfore here and els where often named of the Apostle.

Abac. 2. Ro. 1. Leu. 18. Deu. 21.

12 *The iust" liueth by faith.* † But the Lavv is not by faith: but, *He that*
13 *doeth those things, shal liue in them.* † Christ hath redeemed vs from the curse of the Lavv, being made a curse for vs (because it is
14 vvritten, *Cursed is euery one that hangeth on a tree*) † that on the Gentiles the blessing of Abraham might be made in Christ IESVS: that vve may receiue the promisse of the Spirit by faith.

15 † Brethren (I speake according to man) yet a mans testamēt being confirmed no man despiseth, or further disposeth.

The Epistle vpō the 13 Sūday after Pētecost.

16 † To Abraham vvere the promises said, and to his seede. He saith not, *And to seedes*, as in many: but as in one, *And to thy seede,*

Gen. 22, 18.

17 vvhich is Christ. † And this I say, the testament being confirmed of God, the Lavv vvhich vvas made after foure hundred and thirtie yeres, maketh not void to frustrate the pro-
18 mise. † For if the inheritance be of the Lavv, novv not of
19 promise. But God gaue it to Abraham by promise. † Vvhy vvas the Lavv then? It vvas put for transgressions, vntil the seede came to vvhom he had promised: ordeined by Angels
20 in the hand of a mediatour. † And a mediatour is not of one:
21 but God is one. † Vvas the Lavv then against the promises of God? God forbid. For if there had been a Lavv giuen that could iustifie, vndoubtedly iustice should be of the Lavv.

Ro. 3, 9. 21, 32.

22 † But the Scripture * hath concluded al things vnder sinne: that the promise by the faith of IESVS Christ might be gi-
23 uen to them that beleeue. ⊣ † But before the faith came, vnder the Lavv we vvere kept shut vp, vnto that faith which
24 vvas to be reuealed. † Therfore the Lavv vvas our Peda-
25 gogue in Christ: that vve may be iustified by faith. † But vvhē
26 the faith came, novv vve are not vnder a pædagogue. † For you are al the children of God by faith in Christ IESVS.
27 † For as many of you as are baptized in Christ, " haue put
28 on Christ. † There is not Ievve nor Greeke, there is not bond nor free, there is not male nor femal. For al you are one
29 in Christ IESVS. † And if you be Christs, then are you the seede of Abraham, heires according to promise.

ANNOTATIONS
CHAP. III.

10. *Cursed be.*] By this place the Heretikes vvould proue that no man is iust truely before God, al being guiltie of damnation and Gods curse, because they keepe not euery iote of the Lavv. Vvhere in deede the Apostle meaneth not such as offend venially (as it is plaine by the place of

NotWithstanding venial sinnes, men

Deuteronomie

are truely iust, and may keepe the cōmaundements.

Deuteronomie vvhence he reciteth this text)but onely such as commit great and damnable crimes, and so by greeuous and mortal transgressions vvholy breake Gods precepts, and thereby incurre the curse of the Lavv, from vvhich the said Lavv could not deliuer them of it self, nor by any other meanes,but by the faith and grace of CHRIST IESVS.

Not only faith.

11. Liueth by faith.] It is neither the Heretikes special presumption and confidence, nor the faith of Diuels, nor faith vvithout vvorkes vvhich is dead in it self as S. Iames saith, that can giue life to the iust. for that vvhich is dead, can not be the cause of life. but it is the Catholike faith, as S. Augustine vvriteth,vvhich vvorketh by charitie (according to the Apostles ovvne explication of this vvhole passage) by vvhich the iust liueth. *Li. 3. c. 5. cont. duas ep. Pelag.* See the Annotation vpon the same vvordes. *Rom. 1.* Iac. 2.

Baptisme giueth grace and iustification, not faith only.

27. Haue put on Christ.] Here the Aduersaries might haue seen, if they vvere not blinded by contentious striuing against Gods Church, that vvhen Iustification is attributed to faith vvithout mention of good vvorkes or other Christian vertues & Sacraments, it is not meant to exclude any of the same from the vvorking of iustice or saluation. for here vve learne that by the Sacrament of Baptisme also vve put on Christ, vvhich is to put on faith, hope, charitie, and al Christian iustice. By the same vve proue also that the Sacraments of the nevv lavv giue grace, for that the receiuers thereof put on Christ. And the Aduersaries euasion, that it is faith vvhich vvorketh in the Sacrament, and not the Sacrament it self, is plainely false: Baptisme giuing grace and faith it self to the infant that had none before.

CHAP. IIII.

That the Lavv vvas fit for the time of nonnage: but being novv come to ful age, to desire such seruitude is absurd, specially for Gentils. 12 And that he vvriteth this not of any displeasure, but to tel them the truth, remembring hovv passingly they honoured him vvhen he vvas present, and exhorting them therfore not to harken to the false Apostles in his absence. 21 By the allegorie also of Abrahams tvvo sonnes, shevving, that the children of the Ievves Synagogue shal not inherite, but vve vvho are the children of the free vvoman: that is, of the Cath. Church of Christ.

The Epistle vpon Twelfth eue.

AND I say, as long as the heire is a litle one, he differeth nothing from a seruant, although he be lord of al, 1 † but is vnder tutors and gouernours vntil the time limited of the father: 2 † so vve also, vvhen vve vvere litle ones, vvere " seruing vnder the :: elemētes of the vvorld. 3 † But vvhen the fulnes of time came, God sent his sonne made of a vvoman, made vnder the Lavv: 4 † that he might redeeme them that vvere vnder the Lavv, that vve might receiue the adoption of sonnes. 5 † And because you are sonnes, * God hath sent the Spirit of his sonne into your hartes crying: Abba, Father. 6 † Therfore novv he is not a seruant, but a sonne. And if a sonne, an heire also by God. 7 ¶ † But then in deede not knowing God, you serued them that by nature are not Gods. 8 † But novv vvhen you haue knovven God, or rather are knovven of God: hovv turne you againe to the " vveake & poore elements, vvhich you vvil serue againe? 9 † " You obserue daies, and moneths, and times, and yeres. 10 † I feare you, 11 lest

:: That is, the rudiments of religiō, wherin the carnal Iewes vvere trained vp: or the corporal creatures, wherein their manifold sacrifices, sacraments, and rites did consist.

Ro. 8, 15.

12 lest perhaps I haue laboured in vaine among you. † Be ye as I, because I also am as you: brethren, I beseeche you, you
13 haue hurt me nothing. † And you knovv that by infirmitie
14 of the flesh I euangelized to you heretofore: † and your tentation in my flesh you despised not, neither reiected, but :: as an Angel of God you receiued me, as Christ IESVS.

:: So ought al Catholike people receiue their teachers in religion, vvith al duetie, loue, & reuerence.

15 † Vvhere is then your blessednes? for I giue you testimonie that if it could be done, you vvould haue plucked out your
16 eies and haue giuen them to me. † Am I then become your
17 enemie, telling you the truth? † They emulate you not vvel: but they vvould exclude you, that you might emulate them.
18 † But do you emulate the good in good alvvaies: and not only vvhen I am present vvith you.
19 † My litle children, vvhom I trauail vvithal againe, vntil
20 Christ be formed in you. † And I vvould be vvith you now and chaunge my voice: because I am confounded in you.

The Epistle vpon the 4 Sũday in Lent.

21 † Tel me you that vvil be vnder the Lavv, haue you not read
22 the Lavv? † For it is vvritten that * Abraham had tvvo sonnes: one of the bond-vvoman, and one of the free-vvo-
23 man. † But he that of the bond-vvoman, vvas borne according to the flesh: and he that of the free-vvoman, by the
24 promisse. † vvhich things are said "by an allegorie. For these are the tvvo testaments. The one from mount Sina, gendring
25 vnto bondage: vvhich is Agar, († for Sina is a mountaine in Arabia,[c] vvhich hath affinitie to that vvhich novv is Hie-
26 rusalem) and serueth vvith her children. † But that Hieru-
27 salem vvhich is aboue, is free: vvhich is our mother. † For it is vvritten: *Reioyce thou barren, that bearest not: breake forth and crie, that trauailest not: because many are the children of the desolate, more then of her that*
28 *hath a husband.* † But * we brethren, according to Isaac, are the
29 children of promis. † But :: as then he that vvas borne according to the flesh, persecuted him that vvas after the spirit:
30 so novv also. † But vvhat saith the Scripture? *Cast out the bond-vvoman and her sonne. for the sonne of the bond-vvoman shal not be heire vvith*
31 *the sonne of the free-vvoman.* † Therfore brethren vve are not the children of the bond-vvoman, but of the free: by the "freedom vvherevvith Christ hath made vs free. ⊣

Gen. 16, 15. 21, 2.

c συστοιχεῖ

Es. 54, 1.

Ro. 9, 8.

Gen. 21, 10.

:: This mutual persecution, is a figure also of the Church iustly persecuting Heretikes, & contrarivvise of Heretikes (vvhich be the childrẽ of the bondvvoman) vniustly persecuting the Catholike Church. *Aug. ep. 48.*

ANNOTATIONS
CHAP. IIII.

External vvorship of God by vse of creatures, necessarie: & hovv the Heathen, Ievves, & Christians differ in the same.

The vse of external elemẽts in the Sacraments.

3. Seruing.] There can be no external vvorship of God nor association of men in religion, either true or false, vvithout the vse of corporal things or elements. The Heathen so vsed the creatures of elements that they serued them as their goddes. The Ievves, of vvhom the Apostle here speaketh, serued not the creatures them selues vvhich they occupied in their ceremonies, but they serued the only true God vnder the elements: that is to say, being seruilely clogged, yoked, kept occupied and in avve, vvith innumerable fleshly, grosse, and combersom offices about creatures. The Christians neither serue elements, as the one, nor be kept in seruile thraldom thereby, as the other: but occupie only a fevv exceding easie, svvete, seemely, and significant, for an agreable exercise both of body and minde. Vvhereof S. Augustine saith thus, li. 3. c. 9 de doct. Christ. *Some fevv for many, most easie to be done, most honorable for signification, and most cleane and pure for to be obserued and kept, hath our Lord him self and the Apostolical discipline deliuered.* And li. de ver. relig. c. 17. *Of the vvisedom of God it self mans nature being taken, vvhereby vve vvere called into libertie, a fevv Sacraments most holsom vvere appointed and instituted, vvhich might conteine the societie of Christian people, that is, of the free multitude vnder one God.* And againe, cont. Faust. li. 19. c 13. *The Sacraments are changed, they are made easier, fevver, holsommer, happier.* the same he hath in the 118 epistle c. 1. and many other places besides. By vvhich you may see, it is not al one to vse elements, visible Sacraments or ceremonies, and to serue them as the Pagans do, or to serue vnder them as the Ievves did, vvherevvith the Heretikes calumniously charge the Christians. And as touching the small number, facilitie, efficacie, and signification, vvherein the said holy father putteth the special difference: vvho seeth not that for so many busie sacrifices, vve haue but one: for Sacraments vvel nere infinite, but seuen: al so easie, so ful of grace, so significant, as can be possible, as of euery one in their seueral places is proued?

Our Sacraments fevv & easie in respect of the Ievves.

S. Augustine falsely alleaged of the Heretikes for tvvo Sacraments only.

The other Sacraments proued out of S. Augustine.

Here, let the good Readers take heede of a double deceite vsed by the Aduersaries about S. Augustines places alleaged. first, in that they say he made but tvvo Sacraments, vvhich is vntrue. for, although treating of the difference betvvene the Ievvish Sacraments and ours, he namely giueth example in Baptisme and the Eucharist (as sometimes also for example he nameth but one) yet he hath no vvord nor signe at al that there should be no moe. but contrarievvise in the foresaid epistle 118 he insinuateth, that besides those tvvo, there be other of the same sort in the Scriptures. Yea, vvith Water and bread, Which be the elements of the tvvo foresaid Sacraments, he expresly nameth oile also (*li. 2 cont. lit. Petil. c. 104.*) the element or matter of the Sacrament of Confirmation: Which in the same place he maketh to be a Sacrament as Baptisme is. So doth he affirme of the Sacrament of Orders *li. 1 de bapt. c* 1. and also of Matrimonie *li. de bono coniug. c.24.* of Penance likevvise, he speaketh as of Baptisme, Which he calleth Reconciliation, *li. 1 de adult. coniug. c. 28.* Lastly, by the booke *de visitatione infirmorum* in S. Augustine, *li. 2 c. 4.* by *Prosper de prædictionibus p. 2. c. 29.* S. Innocentius ad Eugubinum *to. 1. Conc. ep. ad Eugub. c.* 8. S. Cyril *li. 2 in Leuiticum,* and S. Chrysostom *li. 3 de Sacerdotio,* * *Extreme vnction* is proued to be a Sacrament. It is false then that the Heretikes affirme of S. Augustine, by vvhose doctrine it is plaine, that though the elements or Sacraments of the nevv lavv be but fevv and very fevv in comparison of those in the old lavv, yet there be no fevver then seuen specified by him. Vvhich number of seuen the holy Councels of Florence and Trent do expresly define to haue been instituted by Christ, against these late Heretikes. See more of these Sacraments in their places. Act. 8. 1 Tim 4. Io. 20. Ia. 5. *Ephes. 5.*

ep. 118. c. 1. & in ps. 103. conc. 1

* *Aug. ser. 215 de tēp. & de recti- tud. Cath. conuersat.*

S. Augustine falsely alleaged against the ceremonies of the Church.

The other forgerie of the Aduersaries concerning the elements or ceremonies, is, that S. Augustine (ep. 119. c. 19.) should affirme, that the Church and Christian people in his daies (vvherevpon they inferre that it is so much more novv) vvere so loden vvith obseruation of vnprofitable ceremonies, that they vvere in as great seruilitie and subiection to such things as the Ievves. He saith so in deede of some particular presumptions, inuentions, and vsages of certaine persons, as that some made it a heinous matter to touch the groũd vvith their bare feete vvithin their ovvne octaues, and such like vanities. Whereby some simple folkes might be infected, vvhich this holy Doctor specially misliked, and vvisheth such things (as they may, vvithout scandal) to be taken avvay. But that he vvrote or meant so of any ceremonie that the Church vseth, either appointed by Scripture, or Councel, or custom of the Catholike Church, him self denieth it in expresse termes in the same place, and in sundrie other: vvhere he allovveth al the holy ceremonies done in the ministration of the Sacraments and els vvhere. Vvhereby it is cleere, that the Churches most comely orders and significant rites pertaine not to the yoke of the old lavv, much lesse to the superstition of Gentilitie, as Heretikes affirme: but to the svveete yoke of Christ and light burden of his lavv, to order, decencie, and instruction of the faithful, in al libertie, loue, faith, grace, and spirit.

9. Vveake and poore.] Vvhether he meane of the creatures vvhich the Gentils serued (as it may seeme by the vvordes before of seruing strange gods) so the elements vvere

most

most base and beggerly: or of the Iudaical ceremonies and sacraments (as most expound it) euen so also their elements vvere vveake and poore in them selues, not giuing life, saluation, and remission of sinnes, nor being instruments or vessels of grace, as the 7 Sacraments of the nevv lavv be.

The Heathenish and Iudaical obseruatiō of daies heretically cōpared vvith the Christian obseruation of festiuities and holy daies &c.

10. You obserue daies.] That vvhich S. Paul speaketh against the Idololatrical obseruation of daies, moneths, and times, dedicated by the Heathen to their false goddes, and to vvicked men or spirites, as to Iupiter, Mercurie, Ianus, Iuno, Diana, and such like, or against the superstitious differences of daies, fatall, fortunate, or dismol, and other obseruations of times for good lucke or il lucke in mans actions, gathered either by particular fansie, or popular obseruation, or curious and vnlavvful artes, or (lastly) of the Iudaical festiuities that vvere then ended and abrogated, vnto vvhich notvvithstanding certaine Christian Ievves vvould haue reduced the Galatians against the Apostles doctrine: al that (I say) do the Heretikes of our time falsely and deceitfully interprete against the Christian holidaies, and the sanctification and necessarie keeping of the same. Vvhich is not only contrarie to the Fathers exposition, but against the very Scriptures, and the practise of the Apostles & the vvhole Church. *Aug. cont. Adimāt. c. 16. Ep. 118. c. 7. Hiero. in hunc locum.* In the Apocalypse c. 1. there is plaine mention of the Sunday, that is, our Lordes day (*Dominicus dies*) vnto vvhich the Ievves Sabboth vvas altered, their Pasche into our Easter, their Pētecost into our Vvhitsontide: vvhich vvere ordained & obserued of the Apostles them selues. And the antiquitie of the feastes of Christes Natiuitie, Epiphanie, & Ascēsion is such, that they cā be referred to no other origine but the Apostles institution: vvho (as S. Clement testifieth *li. 8. const. Apost. c. 39.*) gaue order for celebrating their fellovv Apostles, S. Steuens, and other Martyrs daies after their death: and much more no doubt did they giue order for Christes festiuities. According to vvhich, the Church hath kept not only his, but S. Steuens and the B. Innocents, euen on the same daies they be novv solemnely kept, & his B. mothers, and other Saincts, (as the Aduersaries them selues confesse) aboue 1300 yeres, as appeareth in the barbarous combattes betvvene Vvestphalus the Lutheran, & Caluin, and by the vvritings betvvixt the Puritans and Protestants.

Sūday, Easter, vvhitsontide.

Orig. ho. 3. in diuers. Aug. ep. 28. et Ser. de Sāctis. Fulgent. Leo.

The festiuities of Christ.

Other holidaies of Saincts.

For vvhich purpose, see also hovv old the holiday of S. Polycarpe is *in Eusebius li. 4 c. 14*: of the * Assumptiō of our Ladie or her dormition in S. Athanasius, S. Augustine, S. Hierom. S. Damasc. & both of that feast and of her Natiuitie in S. Bernard, vvho professeth *he receiued them of the Church, & that they ought to be most solemnely kept.* ep. 174. Vvherein vve can not but vvonder at the nevv Church of England, that (though against the pure Caluinistes vvil and doctrine) keepe other Saincts and Apostles daies of their death, and yet haue abolished this special feast of our Ladies departure, vvhich they might keepe, though they beleeued not her Assumption in body (vvhereof yet S. Denys giueth so great testimonie) being assured she is departed at the least: except they either hate her, or thinke her vvorthy of lesse remembrance then any other Saint, * her self prophecying the contrarie of al Catholike generations, that they should blesse her. And in deede the Assumption is her proper day, as also the feast of her Natiuitie: the other of the Purification and the Annunciation, vvhich they keepe in England, being not so peculiar to her, but belonging rather to Christes Presentation in the Temple, and his Conception. To conclude, vve may see in S. Cyprian *ep. 34.* Origen *ho. 3. in diuers.* Tertullian *de cor. mil.* S. Gregorie Nazianzene *de amore pauperum.* the Councel of Gangres, yea and in the councel of Nice it self giuing order for Easter and the certaine celebrating thereof, that Christian Festiuities be holy, aūcient, and to be obserued on prescript daies and times, and that this is not Iudaical obseruation of daies, as Aërius taught, for vvhich he vvas condemned of Heresie, as S. Epiphanius vvitnesseth. But of holidaies S. Augustine sheweth both the reason and his liking, in these memorable vvordes. First for the feastes belonging to our Lord, thus: *We dedicate and consecrate the memorie of Gods benefites vvith solemnities, feastes, and certaine appointed daies, lest by tract of times there might creepe in ingrateful and vnkinde obliuion.* Of the festiuities of Martyrs thus: *Christian people celebrate the memories of Martyrs vvith religious solemnitie, both to moue them selues to imitation of them, and that they may be partakers of their merites, and be holpen vvith their praiers. Cont. Faust. li. 20 c. 21.* And of al Saincts daies, thus: *Keepe ye and celebrate vvith sobrietie the Natiuities of Saincts, that vve may imitate them vvhich haue gone before vs, and they may reioyce of vs vvhich pray for vs. In ps. 88. Conc. 2. in fine.*

** See the Annotation, Act. 1. v. 14.*

Festiuities of our B. Ladie.

ep. ad Timotheū.

Luc. 1. v. 48.

See S. Grego. li. 7. ep. 29. of Martyrs feasts al the yere, and Masses in the same.

Cōc. Gāgr. c. 20

Epiphan. Hær. 75.

Aug. de Ciuit. Dei li. 10. c. 16.

S. Augustines vvordes of Festiuities and holy daies.

And as is said of prescript daies of feastes, so the like is to be said * of fastes, vvhich els vvhere vve haue shewed to be of the Apostles ordinance. And so also of the Ecclesiastical diuision of the yere into Aduent, Septuagesme, &c. the vveeke into so many Feries, the day into Houres of praiers, as the Prime, the Third, the Sixth, the None &c. Vvhereof see * S. Cyprian, vvho deriueth these things by the Scriptures from the Apostles also, and counteth these things vvhich the vvicked Heretikes reproue, to be ful of mysterie. Like vnto this also is it, that the holy Scriptures vvere so disposed of, and deuided, that certaine peeces (as is alvvaies obserued and practised vntil this day) should be read at one time, and others at other times and seasons, through out the yere, according to the diuersitie of our Lordes actions and benefites, or the Saincts stories then recorded. Vvhich the Puritane Caluinists also condemne of superstition, desiring to bring in hellish horrour and al disorder. See conc. Carthag. 3. c. 47. & pag. 288 of this booke.

** Hilar. prolog. in psal. explan. Epip. hær. 75. & in fine. li. 3 cont. hær.*

** Cypri. de orat. Do. nu. 15.*

Prescript fasting daies.

Canonical houres.

Reading of the Scriptures according to the time of the yere.

The Scriptures haue an allegorical sense beside the litteral.

24. By an allegorie.] Here vve learne that the holy Scriptures haue beside the litteral sense, a deeper spiritual and more principal meaning: which is not only to be taken of the holy vvordes, but of the very factes and persons reported: both the speaches and the actions being significatiue ouer and aboue the letter. Vvhich pregnancie of manifold senses if S. Paul had not signified him self in certaine places, the Heretikes had bene lesse vvicked and presumptuous in condemning the holy fathers allegorical expositions almost vvholy: who now shew them selues to be mere brutish and carnal men, hauing no sense nor feeling of the profunditie of the Scriptures, vvhich our holy fathers the Doctors of Gods Church savv.

True Christiā libertie.

31. Freedom.] He meaneth the libertie and discharge from the old ceremonies, sacraments, and the vvhole bondage of the Lavv, and from the seruitude of sinne, and the Diuel, to such as obey him: but not libertie to do vvhat euery man list, or to be vnder no obedience of spiritual or temporal lavves and gouerners: not a licence neuer to pray, fast, keepe holyday, or vvorkday, but vvhen and hovv it seemeth best to euery mans phantasie. Such a dissolute licentious state is farre from the true libertie vvhich Christ purchased for vs.

CHAP. V.

Against the lie of the false Apostles, he protesteth his mind of Circumcision. 13 and testifieth, that they are called to libertie. But yet lest any misconster Christian libertie, he telleth them that they shal not inherite the kingdom, vnles they abstaine from the vvorkes of the flesh, vvhich are al mortal sinnes: and do the fruitful vvorkes of the Spirit, fulfilling al the commaundements of the Lavv by Charitie.

1 STAND, and be not holden in againe vvith the yoke of seruitude. 2 † Behold I Paul tel you that if you be circumcised, Christ shal profite you nothing. 3 † And I testifie againe to euery man circumciding him self, that he is a detter to doe the vvhole Lavv. 4 † You are euacuated from Christ, that are iustified in the Lavv: you are fallē from grace. 5 † For vve in spirit, by faith, expect the hope of iustice. 6 † For in Christ IESVS* neither circumcision auaileth ought, nor prepuce: but "faith that vvorketh by charitie. 7 † You ranne vvel, vvho hath hindered you not to obey the truth? 8 † The persuasion is not of him that calleth you. 9 *† A litle leauen corrupteth the vvhole paste. 10 † I haue confidence in you in our Lord: that you vvil be of no other minde: but he that troubleth you, shal beare the iudgement, vvhosoeuer he be. 11 † And as for me, brethren, if as yet I preach circumcision, vvhy doe I yet suffer persecution? then is the scandal of the crosse euacuated. 12 † I Would they vvere also cut of that trouble you.

13 † For you, brethrē, are called into libertie: only make not this "libertie an occasion to the flesh, but by charitie serue one

Gal. 6, 15.

1 Cor. 5, 6.

14 one an other. † For al the Lavv is fulfilled in one vvord: *Leu. 19, 18.* 15 *Thou shalt loue thy neighbour as thy self.* † But if you bite and eate one an other: take heede you be not consumed one of an 16 other. † And I say, vvalke in the spirit, and the lustes of the 17 flesh you shal not accomplish. † For the flesh lusteth against the spirit: and the spirit against the flesh. for these are aduersaries one to an other: ∴ that not vvhat things soeuer you 18 vvil, these you doe. † But if you be ledde by the spirit, you are not vnder the Lavv.

19 † And the vvorkes of the flesh be manifest, vvhich are, 20 fornication, vncleannes, impudicitie, lecherie, † seruing of Idols, vvitch-craftes, enmities, cōtentions, emulations, angers, 21 bravvles, dissensions, sectes, † enuies, murders, ebrieties, commessations, and such like. vvhich I foretel you, as I haue foretold you, that they vvhich doe [c] such things, shal not ob-22 teine the kingdom of God. † But the fruite of the Spirit is, Charitie, ioy, peace, patience, benignitie, goodnes, longani-23 mitie, † mildnes, faith, modestie, cōtinencie, chastitie. Against 24 such there is no lavv. † And they that be Christs, haue cru-25 cified their flesh vvith the vices and concupiscences. ⊣ † [b] If 26 vve liue in the spirit, in the spirit also let vs vvalke. † Let vs not be made desirous of vaine glorie, prouoking one an other, enuying one an other.

The Epistle vpō the 14 Sūday after Pentecost.

∴ Here men thinke (saith S. Augustine) the Apostle denieth that vve haue free libertie of vvil: not vnderstanding that this is said to them, if they vvil not hold fast the grace of faith conceiued, by vvhich only they cā vvalke in the spirit, & not accōplish the concupiscences of the flesh. *in c. 5. Gal.*

c S. Augustine shevveth hereby that not only infidelitie is a damnable sinne.

b The Epistle vpō the 15 Sūday after Pentecost.

ANNOTATIONS
CHAP. V.

6. Faith.] This is the faith vvorking by charitie, vvhich S. Paul meaneth els vvhere, vvhen he saith that faith doth iustifie. And note vvel that by these termes circumcision & prepuce not auailable to iustification, it is plaine that in other places he meaneth the vvorkes of Circumcision and Prepuce (that is, of the Ievves and the Gentils) vvithout faith, vvhich auaile not, but faith vvorking by charitie: as vvho should say, faith and good vvorkes, not vvorkes vvithout faith.

Iustificatiō by faith only, disproued by conference of Scriptures.

Againe note here, that if the Protestants vvho pretend conference of places to be the best or only vvay to explicate hard speaches of the holy Scriptures, had folovved but their ovvne rule, this one text vvould haue interpreted & cleared vnto them al other vvhereby iustice and saluation might seeme to be attributed to faith alone: the Apostle here so expresly setting dovvne, the faith vvhich he commendeth so much before, not to be alone, but vvith charitie: not to be idle, but to be vvorking by Charitie: as S. Augustine noteth. *de fid. & op. c. 14.* Further the good Reader must obserue, that vvhereas the Protestants some of them confesse, that Charitie and good vvorkes be ioyned and requisite also, and that they exclude them not, but commend them highly, yet so that the said Charitie or good vvorkes are no part of our iustice or any cause of iustification, but as fruites and effectes of faith onely, vvhich they say doth all, yea though the other be present: this false glose also is reproued euidently by this place, vvhich teacheth vs cleane contrarie: to vvitte, that faith hath her vvhole actiuitie and operation tovvard iustice and saluation, of charitie, and not contrariewvise: vvithout vvhich it can not haue any act meritorious or agreable to God for our saluation. for vvhich cause S. Augustine saith, *li. 15 de Trin. c. 18. Fidem non facit vtilem nisi charitas. nothing maketh faith profitable but charitie.* But the Heretikes ansvver, that vvhere the Apostle saith, faith

Hovv the Protestants admit charitie and good vvorkes to iustificatiō.

Charitie is more principal then faith in iustificatiō.

faith vvorketh by charitie, he maketh charitie to be the instrument only of faith in vvel vvorking, and therfore the inferior cause at the least. but this also is easily refuted by the Apostles plaine testimonie, affirming that charitie is * the greater vertue, & that if a man had al faith and lacked charitie, he vvere vvorth nothing. And againe, * that Charitie is the perfection and accõplishment of the Lavv (as faith is not) vvhich can not agree to the instrumental or inferior cause. And therfore vvhen it is said that faith vvorketh by charitie, it is not as by an instrument, but as the body vvorketh by the soul, the matter by the forme, vvithout vvhich they haue no actiuitie. Vvherevpon the the Schooles call Charitie, the forme or life of faith, that is to say, the force, actiuitie, & operatiue qualitie thereof, in respect of merite and iustice. Vvhich S. Iames doth plainely insinuate, vvhen he maketh faith vvithout Charitie, to be as a dead corps vvithout soul or life, and therfore vvithout profitable operation. c. 2. v. 26.

(Margin: Cor. 13. Rom. 13. 1 Tim. 1.)

(Margin: Hovv faith vvorketh by charitie.)

(Margin: True libertie, not carnal and fleshly.)

13. Libertie an occasion.] They abuse the libertie of the Gospel to the aduantage of their flesh, that vnder pretense thereof, shake of their obedience to the lavves of man, to the decrees of the Church and Councels, that vvil liue and beleeue as they list, and not be taught by their Superiors, but fornicate vvith euery Sect-maister that teacheth pleasant & licentious things: and al this vnder pretence of spirit, libertie, and freedom of the Gospel. Such must learne that al heresies, schismes, and rebellions against the Church and their lavvful Prelates, be counted here among the vvorkes of the flesh. See S. Augustine *de fid. & op. c. 24. 25.*

CHAP. VI.

If any do sinne, the rest that do the vvorkes of the Holy Ghost, must not therfore take pride in them selues, but rather make humilitie of it, partly by fearing their ovvne fall, partly by looking straitly to their ovvne vvorkes. 6 He exhorteth earnestly to good vvorkes, assuring them that they shal reape none other then here they sovv. 11 With his ovvne hand he vvriteth, telling them, the true cause vvhy those false Apostles preach circumcision, to be only to please the Ievves: 17 and a plaine argument that he preacheth it not, to be thus, that he is persecuted of the Ievves.

BRETHREN, and if a man be preoccupated in any fault, you that are spiritual, instruct such an one in the spirit of lenitie, considering thine ovvne self, lest thou also be tempted. 1

† Beare ye one an others burdens: & so you shal fulfil the lavv of Christ. 2

† For if any man esteeme him self to be something, vvhereas he is nothing, he seduceth him self. 3

† But let euery one proue his ovvne vvorke, & so in him self only shal he haue the glorie, and not in an other. 4

† For euery one shal beare his ovvne burden. 5

† And let * him that is catechized in the vvord, communicate to him that catechizeth him, in al his goods. 6

(Margin: 1. Cor. 9, 7.)

† Be not deceiued, God is not mocked. 7

† For what things a mã shal sow, those also shal he reape. For he that sovveth in his flesh, of the flesh also shal reape corruptiõ. but he that soweth in the spirit, of the spirit shal reape life euerlasting. 8

(Margin: ⁘ The Workes of mercie be the seede of life euerlasting, and the proper cause thereof, and not faith only.)

† And * doing good, let vs not faile. For in due time vve shal ⁘ reape not 9

(Margin: 2. Thes. 3, 13.)

10 not failing. † Therfore vvhiles vve haue time, let vs vvorke good to al, but " especially to the domesticals of the faith. ⊣

b The Epistle for S. Francis, Octob. 4.

11 † See vvith vvhat maner of letters I haue written to you vvith mine ovvne hand. 12 † Vvhosoeuer vvil please in the flesh, they force you to be circumcised, only that they may not suffer the persecution of the crosse of Christ. 13 † For neither they that are circumcised, do keepe the Lavv: but they vvil haue you to be circumcised, that they may glorie in your flesh. 14 † b But ∵ God forbid that I should glorie, sauing in the crosse of our Lord IESVS Christ: by vvhom the vvorld is crucified to me, and I to the vvorld. 15 † For in Christ IESVS neither circumcision auaileth ought, nor prepuce, but " a nevv creature. 16 † And vvhosoeuer shal folovv this rule, peace vpō them, and mercie, and vpon the Israël of God. 17 † From hencefurth let no man be troublesome to me. for I beare the markes of our Lord IESVS in my body. 18 The grace of our Lord IESVS Christ be vvith your spirit brethren. Amen. ⊣

∵ Christ (saith S. Augustine) chose a kinde of death, to hang on the Crosse and to fixe or fasten the same crosse in the foreheads of the faithful, that the Christian may say, God forbid that I should glorie sauing in the crosse of our Lord IESVS CHRIST. *Expos. in Euang. Io. tract. 43.*

ANNOTATIONS
CHAP. VI.

6. Communicate] The great duety & respect that vve ought to haue to such as preach or teach vs the Cath. faith. and not in regard onely of their paines taken vvith vs, and vvel-deseruing of vs by their doctrine: but that vve may be partakers of their merites, vve ought specially to do good to such, or (as the Apostle speaketh) cōmunicate vvith them in al our temporal goods, that vve may be partakers of their spiritual. See S. Augustine *li. 2. Euang. quæst. q.* 8.

Duety to our spiritual teachers.

10. Especially.] In giuing almes, though vve may do vvel in helping al that are in necessitie, as farre as vve can, yet vve are more bound to succour Christians, then Ievves or Infidels: and Catholikes, then Heretikes. See S. Hierom *q. 1. ad Hedibiam.*

In almes whom to preferre.

15. A nevv creature.] Note vvel that the Apostle calleth that here a nevv creature, vvhich in the last chapter he termed, *faith vvorking by charitie*, & (1 Cor. 7, 19) *the obseruatiō of the cōmaundemēts of God*. Vvhereby vve may learne that vnder the name of faith is conteined the vvhole reformation of our soules and our nevv creation in good vvorkes. and also that Christian iustice is a very qualitie, condition and state of vertue and grace resident in vs, and not a phantastical apprehension of Christes iustice only imputed to vs. Lastly, that the faith vvhich iustifieth, ioyned vvith the other vertues, is properly the formal cause, and not the efficient or instrumental cause of iustification. that is to say, these vertues put together, being the effect of Gods grace, be our nevv creature and our iustice in Christ.

Iustice an inherent qualitie in vs.

Faith with the other vertues is the formal cause of iustification.

THE

THE ARGVMENT OF THE EPISTLE OF S. PAVL TO THE EPHESIANS.

F S. Paules first comming to Ephesus, and short abode there, vve reade Act. 18. *And immediatly Act.* 19. *of his returning thither according to his promise vvhat time he abode there* three moneths, speaking to the Ievves in the Synagogue. *Act.* 19. *v.* 8. *and aftervvard apart from them (because they vvere obstinate)* tvvo yeres *in a certaine schoole,* so that al that dvvelt in Asia, heard the vvord of our Lord, Ievves and Gentiles. *Act.* 19. *v.* 10. *The vvhole time himself calleth* three yeres, *in his exhortation at Milétum to the Cleargie of Ephesus. Act.* 20. *v.* 31.

After all this he vvriteth this Epistle vnto them from Rome (as it is said) being then prisoner *and* in chaines. *and that as it seemeth, not the first time of his being in bonds there, vvhereof vve reade Act.* 28 *: but the second time, vvhereof vve reade in the Ecclesiasticall Stories afterv vard : because he saith in this Epistle c.* 6. *v.* 21. Tychicus vvil certifie you of al things, vvhom I haue sent to you. *Of vvhom againe in the* 2. *to Tim. c.* 4. *v.* 12. *he saith*: Tychicus I haue sent to Ephesus. *And the said* 2. *Epistle to Timothee (no doubt) vvas vvritten very litle before his death : for in it thus he saith:* I am euen novv to be sacrificed, & the time of my resolution is at hand. 2. *Tim.* 4, 6.

Eph. 3. v. 1. & 4. v. 1. Eph. 6. v. 20.

*In the three first chapters, he commendeth vnto them the grace of God, in calling of the Gentiles no lesse then the Ievves, and making one blessed Church of both. Vvherein his intention is to moue them to perseuére (for othervvise they should be passing vngratefull) and specially not to be moued vvith his trouble, vvho vvas their Apostle : knovving (belike) that * it vvould be a great tentation vnto them, if they should heare soone after, that he vvere executed : therfore also arming them in the end of the Epistle, as it vvere in complete harnesse.*

* See Act. 20. v. 25. 32.

In the other three chapters he exhorteth them to good life, in all pointes, and all states, as it becommeth Christians : and afore all other things, that they be most studious to continue in the vnitie of the Church, and obedience of the pastors thereof, vvhom Christ hath giuen to continue and to be our stay against all Heretikes, from his Ascension, euen to the full building vp of his Church in the end of the vvorld.

THE EPISTLE OF PAVL TO THE EPHESIANS.

CHAP. I.

He magnifieth the grace of Gods eternal predestination and temporal vocation, 11 both of the Ievves, 13 and also of the Ephesians being Gentils. 13 for vvhose excellent faith and charitie he reioyceth, and continually praieth for their increase, that they may see more cleerely the greatnes both of the inheritance in heauen, and also of Gods might vvhich helpeth them thereunto: 20 an example of vvhich might they may behold in the supereminent exalting of Christ.

1 PAVL an Apostle of IESVS Christ by the vvil of God: to al the sainctes that are at Ephesus: and to the faithful in Christ IESVS. 2 † Grace to you and peace from God our father, and our Lord IESVS Christ.

3 † Blessed be God and the Father of our Lord IESVS Christ, vvhich hath blessed vs in al spiritual blessing, in cœlestials, in Christ: 4 † as he chose vs in him before the constitution of the vvorld, that vve should be holy and immaculate ∷ in his sight in charitie. 5 † Vvho hath predestinated vs vnto the adoption of sonnes, by IESVS Christ, vnto him self: 6 according to the purpose of his vvil: † vnto the praise of the glorie of his grace, vvherein he hath ᵃgratified vs in his beloued sonne. 7 † In vvhom vve haue redemption by his bloud (the remission of sinnes) according to the riches of his grace. 8 † Vvhich hath superabounded in vs in al vvisedō 9 and prudence, † that he might make knovven vnto vs the sacrament of his vvil, according to his good pleasure, vvhich 10 he purposed in him self, † in the dispensation of the fulnes of times, to ᶜperfit al things in Christ, that are in heauen and in 11 earth, in him. † In vvhom vve also are called by lot: prede-

∷ Vve learne here that by Gods grace men be holy and immaculate, not onely in the sight of men, nor by imputation, but truely and before God: contrarie to the Doctrine of the Caluinistes.

ᵃ ἐχαρίτωσεν

ᶜ ἀνακεφαλαιώσασθαι

ſtinate according to the purpoſe of him that vvorketh al things, according to the counſel of his vvil: † that vve may 12 be vnto the praiſe of his glorie, vvhich before haue hoped in Chriſt: † in vvhom you alſo, vvhen you had heard the 13 vvord of truth (the Goſpel of your ſaluation:) in vvhich alſo beleeuing you vvere ∵ ſigned vvith the holy Spirit of promis, † vvhich is the pledge of our inheritance, to the 14 redemption of acquiſition, vnto the praiſe of his glorie.

∵ Some referre this to the grace of Baptiſme: but to many learned it ſeemeth that the Apoſtle alludeth to the giuing of the Holy Ghoſt in the Sacrament of Confirmation, by ſigning the baptized with the ſigne of the Croſſe & holy Chriſme. For that vvas the vſe in the Apoſtles time, as els where we haue prooued. Annot. *Act.* 8.

† Therfore I alſo hearing your faith that is in our Lord 15 IESVS, and loue tovvard al the ſainctes: † ceaſe not to giue 16 thankes for you, making a memorie of you in my praiers, † that God of our Lord IESVS Chriſt, the father of glorie, 17 giue you the ſpirit of vviſedom and of reuelation, in the knovvledge of him, † the eies of your hart illuminated, 18 that you may knovv vvhat the hope is of his vocation, and vvhat are the riches of the glorie of his inheritance in the ſainctes, † and vvhat is the paſſing greatnes of his povver 19 tovvard vs that beleeue: according to the operation of the might of his povver, † vvhich he vvrought in Chriſt, rai- 20 ſing him vp from the dead, and ſetting him on his right hand in celeſtials, † aboue ″al Principalitie & Poteſtate & Power, 21 and Domination, and euery name that is named not only in this vvorld, but alſo in that to come. † And he hath *ſubdued 22 al things vnder his feete: and hath made him ″head ouer al the CHVRCH, † vvhich is his body, the ∵ fulnes of him 23 vvhich is filled al in al.

* Pſ. 8, 8.

∵ Chriſt is not ful, vvhole, and perfect without the church no more then the head without the body,

---

ANNOTATIONS
CHAP. I.

21. Al Principalitie.] The Fathers vpon this, and other places of the old and new Teſtament, vvhere they finde the orders of holy Angels or ſpirites named, agree that there be nine orders of them. Of vvhich ſome be here counted and called, as vve ſee: in the Epiſtle to the Coloſsians, the order of Thrones is ſpecified, vvhich maketh fiue: to vvhich if vve adde theſe foure, Cherubim, Seraphim, Angels, and Archangels, vvhich are commonly named in holy vvrite, in al there be nine. *S. Denys cœl. Hier. c. 7. 8. 9. & Ec. Hier. c. 1. S. Athanaſ. li. de Communi eſſent. in fine. Gregor. Moral. li. 32. c. 18.* Therfore, good Reader, make no accompt of * Caluins and others infidelitie, vvhich blaſphemouſly blame and condemne the holy doctors diligence in this point, of curioſitie and impietie. The vvhole endeuour of theſe heretikes is, to bring al into doubt, and to corrupt euery Article of our Religion.

Nine orders of Angels.

* *Cal. vpon this place.*

22. Head.] It maketh a high proofe among the Proteſtants, that no man can be head of the Church, becauſe it is a calling and dignitie proper to Chriſt. But in truth by as good reaſon there ſhould be no king nor lord, becauſe, *He is king and lord.* neither ſhould there be Biſhop or Paſtor, becauſe he is *the Biſhop and Paſtor of our ſoules*: nor Pontifex nor Apoſtle, for by thoſe titles S. Paul termeth him Hebr. 3: none ſhould be piller, foundation

As Chriſt is king, and yet men are kings alſo: ſo Chriſt is head of the

Apoc. 19. 1 Pet. 2, 25.

dation, rocke, light, or maister of the Church or truth, because Christ is properly al these. And yet our nevv doctors (though they be exceding seditious and vvould for the aduantage of their sect be gladly ridde of kings and al other Superiors temporal, if they feared not the svvord more then God, and vvould finde as good Scriptures to be deliuered of them, as they now finde to discharge them selues of obedience to Popes:) yet (I say) they vvil not deny, al the former titles and dignities (notvvithstanding Christes soueraine right in the same) to be giuen and communicated to the Princes and Magistrates of the earth both spiritual and temporal. though Christ in a more diuine, ample, absolute, excellent, and transcendent sort, haue al these things attributed or appropriated to him self. So then, though he be the head of the Church, and the onely head in such soueraine and principal maner, as no earthly man or mere creature euer is or can be, and is ioyned to the Church in a more excellent sort of coniunction, then any king is to his subiects or Countrie, or any Pope or Prelate to the Church vvhereof he is gouernour, euen so farre that it is called his body Mystical: life, motion, spirit, grace issuing dovvne from him to it and the members of the same, as from the head to the natural body. though in this sort (we say) no man can be head but Christ, nor the Church be body to any but to Christ: yet the Pope may be the ministerial head, that is to say, the cheefe Gouernour, Pastor, and Prelate of the same, and may be his Vicar or Vicegerent in the regiment of that part vvhich is in earth. as S. Hierom calleth Damasus the Pope, *Summum Sacerdotem, the cheefe and highest Priest*: and the Apostle saith of this ministerial head, *The head can not say to the feete, you are not necessarie for me.* For therein also is a great difference betvvene Christ and euery mortal Prelate, that (as the Apostle here saith) he is head of the vvhole Church, meaning of the triumphãt (& of al Angels also though in an other sort) no lesse thẽ of the Church militãt. So Peter vvas not, nor any Pope, nor any man can be. Where you must obserue, that for this soueraine preeminence of Christ in this case, the Church is not called the body mystical of any Gouernour, Peter, Paul, or vvhat Prelate or Pope so euer.

Church, and yet man may be head thereof also.

Christ is head of his Church in a far more excellent sort, then any man can be.

Hiero. ep. 123.

1. Cor. 12, 21.

CHAP. II.

He putteth them in minde of their vnvvorthines before they vvere Christians: that al the praise may be giuen to the grace of God: 11 and of the enmitie that vvas then betvvene the Ievv and the Gentil: 13 until novv that Christ by his Crosse hath made both one, taking avvay the ceremonies of the Lavv, and making one body, and building one holy Temple of al, in his Catholike Church.

1 AND you vvhen you vvere dead by your 2 offenses & sinnes, † vvherein sometime you vvalked according to the course of this vvorld, according to the * prince of the povver of this aire, of the spirit that novv 3 vvorketh on the childrẽ of diffidence, † in vvhom also vve al conuersed sometime in the desires of our flesh, doing the vvil of the flesh and of thoughtes, and vvere 4 by nature the children of vvrath as also the rest: † but God (vvhich is riche in mercie) for his exceding charitie vvher5 vvith he loued vs, † euen vvhen vve vvere dead by sinnes, quickened vs together in Christ, (by vvhose grace you are 6 saued,) † and raised vs vp vvith him, and hath made vs sit 7 vvith him in the celestials in Christ IESVS, † that he might shevv in the vvorldes succeding, the aboundant riches of his 8 grace, in bountie vpon vs in Christ IESVS. † For by " grace you are saued through faith (and that not of your selues,

Eph. 6, 12.

:: It is said, not of workes as thine, of thy self being vnto thee, but as those in which God hath made, formed, and created thee. *Aug. de gr. & lib. arbit. c. 8. & seq.*

for it is the gift of God) † :: not of vvorkes, that no man 9 glorie † For vve are his vvorke, created in Christ IESVS in 10 good vvorkes, vvhich God hath prepared that vve should vvalke in them.

† For the vvhich cause be mindeful that sometime you 11 vvere Gentils in the flesh, vvho vvere * called prepuce, of that vvhich is called circumcision in the flesh, made vvith 12 hand: † vvho vvere at that time vvithout Christ, alienated from the conuersation of Israël, and * strangers of the testaments, hauing no hope of the promis, and vvithout God in 13 this vvorld. † But novv in Christ IESVS, you that sometime vvere farre of, are made nigh in the bloud of Christ. † For 14 he is our peace, vvho hath made both one, and dissoluing the middle vvall of the partition, the enmities in his flesh: † eua- 15 cuating the lavv of cōmaundements [c] in decrees: that he may create the tvvo in him self into one new man, making peace, † and may reconcile both in one body to God by the crosse, 16 killing the enmities in him self.

1. reg. 17, 26. Ezec 44, 7.

Ro. 9, 4.

c ἐν δόγμασι

The Epistle for S. Thomas the Apostle, Decemb. 21.

† And comming he euangelized peace to you that vvere 17 farre of, and peace to them that vvere nigh. † For * by him 18 vve haue accesse both in one Spirit to the Father. † Novv 19 then you are not strangers and forreiners: but you are [c] citizens of the saincts, and the domesticals of God, † ″ built 20 vpon the foundation of the Apostles and Prophets, IESVS Christ him self being the highest corner stone: † in vvhom 21 al building framed together, grovveth into an holy temple in our Lord, † in vvhom you also are built together into an 22 habitation of God in the holy Ghost. ⊣

Ro. 5, 2.

c συμπολῖται

ANNOTATIONS
CHAP. II.

Our first iustificatiō of mere grace, & faith the foundatiō therof.

8. *By grace you are saued through faith.*] Our first iustification is of Gods grace, and not of our deseruings: because none of al our actions that vvere before our iustification, could merite or iustly procure the grace of iustification. Againe, he saith, *through faith*: for that faith is the beginning, foundation, and roote of al iustification, and the first of al other vertues, vvithout which it is impossible to please God.

The Church builded vpon Christ, and yet vpon the Apostles also.

20. *Built vpon the foundation.*] Note against the Heretikes that thinke it dishonorable to Christ, to attribute his titles or callings to mortal men, that the faithful (though builded first, principally, and properly vpon Christ) yet are said here to be built also vpon the Apostles and Prophets. Vvhy may not the Church then be builded vpon Peter?

CHAP. III.

For vvitnessing the vocation of the Gentils, as being the Apostle of the Gentils, he is in prison: 13 Wherein the Gentils therfore haue cause to reioyce, rather then to shrinke. So he saith, 14 and also praieth to God (vvho is almightie) to confirme their invvard man, though the outvvard be infirmed by persecutions.

1 FOR this cause, I Paul the prisoner of IESVS Christ, for you Gentiles: 2 † if yet you haue heard the dispensation of the grace of God, vvhich is giuen me tovvard you, 3 † because according to reuelation the sacrament vvas made knovven to me, as I haue vvrittẽ before in breife: 4 † according as you reading may vnderstand my vvisedom in the mysterie of Christ, 5 † vvhich vnto other generations vvas not knovven to the sonnes of men, as novv it is reuealed to his holy Apostles & Prophets in the Spirit. 6 † The Gentils to be coheires & concorporat and comparticipant of his promis in Christ IESVS by the Gospel: 7 † vvhereof I am made a minister according to the gift of the grace of God, which is giuen me according to the operation of his povver. 8 † To me ★ the least of al the saincts is giuen this grace, among the Gentils to euangelize the vnsearcheable riches of Christ; 9 † and to illuminate al men vvhat is the dispensatiõ of the sacrament hidden [c] from vvorldes in God, vvho created al things: 10 † that the manifold vvisedom of God, may be notified to the Princes and Potestats in the celestials by the Church, 11 † according to the [c] prefinitiõ of worldes, vvhich he made in Christ IESVS our Lord. 12 † In vvhom vve haue affiance and accesse in confidence, by the faith of him. 13 † [b] For the vvhich cause I desire that you faint not in my tribulations for you, vvhich is your glorie.

14 † For this cause I bovve my knees to the Father of our Lord IESVS Christ, 15 † of vvhom al paternitie in the heauens 16 and in earth is named, † that he giue you according to the riches of his glorie, povver to be fortified by his Spirit in the 17 inner man. † Christ :: to dvvel by faith in your hartes, 18 rooted and founded [c] in charitie, † that you may be able to comprehend vvith al the saincts, vvhat is the bredth, and 19 length, and height, and depth, † to knovv also the charitie of

★ 1. Cor. 15, 9.

c ἀπὸ τῶν αἰώνων

c that is, the eternal prefinitiõ

c That is, *for euer before.*

b The Epistle vpon the 16 Sunday after Pentecost.

:: Christ dvvelleth in vs by his giftes, and vve be iust by those his giftes remaining and resident in vs, & not by Christes proper iustice onely, as the Heretikes affirme.

c Not faith only must be in vs, but charitie vvhich accõplisheth al vertues.

Christ, surpassing knovvledge, that you may be filled vnto al the fulnes of God. † And * to him that is able to doe al 20 things more aboundantly then vve desire or vnderstand, according to the povver that vvorketh in vs: † to him be 21 glorie in the CHVRCH, and in Christ IESVS, vnto al generations vvorld vvithout end. Amen.

Ro. 16, 25.

CHAP. IIII.

He exhorteth them to keepe the vnitie of the Church most carefully vvith al humilitie bringing them many motiues therevnto: 7 and ansvvering that euen the diuersitie it self of offices is not for diuision, as being the gift of Christ him self, but to build vp the Church, and to hold al in the vnitie thereof against the suttle circumuentions of Heretikes: that vnder Christ the head, in the Church being the body, euery member may prosper. 17 Neither (as touching life) must vve liue like the Heathen, but as it becommeth Christians, laying of al our old corrupt maners, and increasing daily in al goodnes.

The Epistle vpon the 17 Sunday after Pentecost. And in a Votiue Masse against Schisme.

I Therfore prisoner in our Lord, beseeche you, 1 that you vvalke vvorthy of the vocation in vvhich you are called, † vvith al humilitie & 2 mildenes, vvith patience, supporting one an other in charitie, † careful to keepe the 3 vnitie of the spirit in the bond of peace. † One body and 4 one spirit: as you are called in one hope of your vocation. † One Lord, " one faith, one baptisme. † * One God and 5 6 Father of al, vvhich is ouer al, and by al, and in al vs. ⊣ † But 7 * to euery one of vs is giuen grace according to the measure of the donation of Christ. † For the vvhich he saith, *Ascending* 8 *on high, he ledde captiuitie captiue: he gaue giftes to men.* († And that he 9 ascended, vvhat is it, but because he descended also first into the c inferiour partes of the earth? † He that descended, the 10 same is also he that is ascended aboue al the heauens, that he might fill al things.) † And * he gaue, " some Apostles, and 11 some Prophets, and othersome Euangelists, and othersome pastors and doctors, † to the consummation of the sainctes, 12 vnto the vvorke of the ministerie, vnto the edifying of the body of Christ: † " vntil vve meete al into the vnitie of faith 13 and knovvledge of the sonne of God, into a perfect man, into the measure of the age of the fulnes of Christ: ⊣ † that 14 novv vve be not children vvauering, and caried about " vvith euery vvinde of doctrine in the vvickednes of men, in craftines to the circumuention of errour. † But doing the truth 15 in charitie, let vs in al things grow in him, vvhich is the head,

The Epistle vpō Ascension eue. And vpon SS. Simon and Iudes day.

c He meaneth specially of his descending to Hel.

Malac. 2, 10. Ro. 12, 4 1. Cor. 12, 4. Ps. 67, 19.

1. Cor. 12, 28.

Christ:

16 Christ: † of vvhom the vvhole body being compacte and knit together by al iuncture of subministration, according to the operation in the measure of euery member, maketh the increase of the body vnto the edifying of it self in charitie.

17 † This therfore I say and testifie in our Lord: that novv you vvalke not as also the * Gentiles vvalke in the vanitie of 18 their sense, † hauing their vnderstanding obscured vvith darkenes, alienated from the life of God by the ignorance 19 that is in them, because of the blindenes of their hart, † vvho despairing, * haue giuen vp them selues to impudicitie, vnto 20 the operation of al vncleannes, vnto auarice. † But you haue 21 not so learned Christ: † if yet you haue heard him, and haue 22 been taught in him, (as the truth is in IESVS.) ⁊ † * Lay you avvay, according to the old conuersation the old man, vvhich 23 is corrupted according to the desires of errour. † And ∷ be 24 renevved in the spirit of your minde: † and put on the nevv man vvhich according to God is created in iustice, and holi-25 nesse of the truth. † For the vvhich cause laying avvay lying, * speake ye truth euery one vvith his neighbour, because vve are members one of an other.

26 † * Be angrie and sinne not. let not the sonne goe dovvne 27 vpon your anger. † Giue not place to the Deuil. † He that 28 stole, let him novv not steale: but rather let him labour in vvorking vvith his handes that vvhich is good, that he may 29 haue vvhence to giue vnto him that suffereth necessitie. † Al naughtie speache let it not proceede out of your mouth: but if there be any good to the edifying of the faith, that it may 30 giue grace to the hearers. † And contristate not the holy Spi-rit of God: in vvhich you are signed vnto the day of redemp-31 tion. † Let al bitternes, and anger, and indignation, and cla-mour, and blasphemie be taken avvay from you vvith al ma-32 lice. † And be gentle one to an other, merciful, pardoning one an other, as also God in Christ hath pardoned you.

Margin: 1 Pet. 4, 3. Ro. 1, 21. — Ro. 1, 24. — Colos. 3, 8. Heb. 12, 1. — Zach. 8, 16. — Ps. 4, 5.

Margin note: ∷ The Apostle teacheth vs not to apprehēd Christs iustice by faith only, but to be renevved in our selues truly, & to put on vs the nevv mā formed & created in iustice and holines of truth. By the which, free vvil also is proued to be in vs, to worke With God, or to consent vnto him in our sanctification.

ANNOTATIONS
CHAP. IIII.

5. *One faith.*] As rebellion is the bane of ciuil Commonvvealths and kingdoms, and peace and concord, the preseruation of the same: so is Schisme, diuision, and diuersitie of faiths or felovvships in the seruice of God, the calamitie of the Church: and peace, vnitie, vniformitie, the special blessing of God therein. and in the Church aboue al Commonvvealths, because it is in al pointes a Monarchie tending euery vvay to vnitie. but one God, but one Christ, but one Church, but one

Margin: Vnitie of the Cath. Church.

one hope, one faith, one baptisme, one head, one body. Vvhereof S. Cyprian *li. de unit. Ec. nu. 3.* saith thus: *One Church the Holy Ghost in the person of our Lord designeth & saith, One is my doue. This vnitie of the Church he that holdeth not, doth he thinke he holdeth the faith? He that vvithstandeth and resisteth the Church, he that forsaketh Peters chaire vpon vvhich the Church vvas built, doth he trust that he is in the Church? When the blessed Apostle S. Paul also shevveth this Sacrament of vnitie, saying, One body and one spirit &c. Which vnitie vve Bishops specially that rule in the Church, ought to hold fast and maintaine, that vve may proue the Bishoply function also it self to be one and vndiuided, &c.* And againe, *There is one God, and one Christ, and one Church, and one Chaire, by our Lordes voice founded vpon Peter. An other altar to be sette vp, or a nevv Priesthod to be made, besides one altar, & one Priesthod, is impossible. Whosoeuer gathereth els vvhere, scattereth. It is adulterous, it is impious, it is sacrilegious, vvhatsoeuer is instituted by mans furie to the breach of Gods diuine disposition. Get ye far from the contagion of such men, & flee from their speaches as a canker and pestilense, our Lord hauing præmonished and vvarned before hand, They are blind, leaders of the blind, &c.* Vvhereby vve learne that this vnitie of the Church commended so much vnto vs, consisteth in the mutual fellovvship of al Bishops vvith the See of Peter. S. Hilarie also (*li. ad Constantium Augustum*) thus applieth this same place of the Apostle against the Arians, as vve may do against the Caluinists. *Perilous and miserable it is*, saith he, *that there are novv so many faithes as vvilles, and so many doctrines as maners, vvhiles either faithes are so vvritten as vve vvill, or as vve vvil, so are vnderstood: and vvhereas according to one God, and one Lord, and one Baptisme, there is also one faith, vve fall avvay from that vvhich is the only faith, and vvhiles moe faithes be made, they beginne to come to that, that there is none at al.*

Ep. 40.

Schisme detestable.

Among heretikes as many faithes as willes.

11. *Some Apostles.*] Many functions that vvere euen in the Apostles time, are not here named: vvhich must be noted against the Aduersaries that call here for Popes. as though the names of Bishops, Priests, or Deacons vvere not as vvel least out as Popes: vvhom yet they can not deny to haue been in vse in S. Paules daies. And therfore they haue no more reason, out of this place to dispute against the Pope, then against the rest of the Ecclesiastical functions. Neither is it necessarie to reduce such as be not specified here, to these here named: though in deede both other Bishops and Prelates and specially Popes may be conteined vnder the names of Apostles, Doctors, and Pastors. Certes the roome and dignitie of the Pope is a very continual Apostleship, and S. Bernard calleth it *Apostolatum. Bernard. ad Eugen. li. 14. c. 4. & c. 6 in fine.*

The heretikes folish negatiue argument against the Pope, ansvvered.

The Popes office is called an Apostleship.

13. *Until vve meete.*] The Church of God shal neuer lacke these spiritual functions, or such as be ansvverable to them, according to the time and state of the Church, til the vvorldes end. Vvhereby you may proue, the Catholike Church, that is to say, that visible companie of Christians vvhich hath euer had, and by good records can proue they haue had, a continual ordinarie succession of Bishops, Pastors, and Doctors, to be the onely true Church: and these other good fellovves that for many vvorldes or ages together can not shevv that they had any one Bishop, or ordinarie yea or extraordinarie officer for them and their sect, to be an adulterous Heretical generation. And this place of the Apostle assuring to the true Church a perpetual visible continuance of Pastors and Apostles or their successors, vvarranted the holy fathers to trie al Heretikes by the most famous succession of the Popes of Rome. So did S. Irenæus, *li.* 3 c. 3. Tertullian, *in præscript.* Optatus, *li. 2 cont. Parm.* S. Augustine, *in ps. cont. part. Donat. et cont. ep. Manich. c. 4. et ep. 165. Epiph. hær. 27.* and others.

Continual succesion of Bishops, an euident argument of the true visible Church.

The fathers refuted heretikes by the succession of the Bishops of Rome.

14. *With euery vvinde.*] The special vse of the spiritual Gouernours is, to keepe vs in vnitie and constancie of the Catholike faith, that vve be not caried avvay vvith the blast or vvind of euery heresie. Vvhich is a very proper note of sectes and nevv doctrines that trouble the infirme vveaklings of the Church, by certaine seasons of diuerse ages: as sometime the Arians, then the Manichees, an other time the Nestorians, then the Lutherans, Caluinists, and such like: vvho at diuers times in diuers places haue blovven diuers blastes of false doctrine.

Heretical blastes carie avvay the inconstant only.

CHAP. V.

He continueth his exhortation to good life, 5 assuring them against al deceiuers, that no committer of mortal sinne shal be saued: considering that for such sinnes it is that the Heathen shal be damned: 8 & that Christians must rather be the light of al others. 22 Then he commeth in particular and exhorteth husbands and vviues to do their duety one tovvardes the other, by the example of Christ and his obedient and beloued spouse the Church.

BE

1 BE ye therfore folovvers of God, as most deere children: † and * walke in loue, as Christ also loued vs, and deliuered him self for vs an oblation and host to God in an odour of sv vetenes. † But * fornication and al vncleannes, or auarice, let it not so much as be named among you, as it becommeth saincts: † or filthines, or foolish talke, or scurrilitie, being to no purpose: but rather giuing of thankes. † For vnderstanding knovv you this, that no fornicatour, or vncleane, or couetous person (vvhich is ∷ the seruice of Idols) hath inheritance in the kingdom of Christ and of God.

The epistle vpon the 3 Sūday in Lent.

Io.13,34

Col.3,5.

∷ See the heretical corruption of this place in the Annotation Col.3. v. 5.

6 † Let no man seduce you vvith vaine vvordes. For, for these things commeth the anger of God vpō the children of diffidence. 7 † Become not therfore partakers vvith them. 8 † For you vvere sometime darkenes, but novv light in our Lord. 9 Vvalke as children of the light, († for the fruite of the light is in al goodnes, and iustice, and veritie) ⊣ 10 † prouing vvhat is vvel pleasing to God: 11 † and communicate not vvith the vnfruitful vvorkes of darkenes, but rather reproue them. 12 † For the things that are done of them in secrete, it is shame euen to speake. 13 † But al things that are reproued, are manifested by the light. 14 for al that is manifested, is light. † for the vvhich cause he saith: *Rise thou that sleepest, and arise from the dead: and Christ vvil illuminate thee.* 15 † See therfore, brethren, how 16 you vvalke vvarily. not as vnvvise, but * as vvise: † 17 redeeming the time, because the daies are euil. † Therfore become not vnvvise, but * vnderstanding vvhat is the vvil of God. 18 † And be not drunke vvith vvine vvherein is rioteousnes, 19 but be filled vvith the Spirit, † speaking to your selues in psalmes & hymnes, and spiritual canticles, chaūting 20 and singing in your hartes to our Lord: † giuing thankes alvvaies for al things, in the name of our Lord IESVS Christ 21 to God & the Father. † Subiect one to an other in the feare of Christ.

Es.9,60

Col.4,5.

Ro.12,2.

The Epistle vpon the 20 Sunday after Pentecost.

22 † Let * vvomen be subiect to their husbandes, as to 23 our Lord: † because * the man is the head of the woman: as Christ is the head of the ∷ CHVRCH. Him self, " the sa- 24 uiour of his body. † But as the CHVRCH is subiect to

Col.3,18.
Tit.2,5.
1 Per.3,1.
Ge.3,16.
1 Cor.11,3.

The Epistle in a votiue masse for mariage.

∷ It is much to be noted, that in the first

Vvu Christ

English Bibles there is not once the name of CHVRCH in al the Bible, but in steede thereof, *Congregatiõ*. vvhich is so notorious a corruption, that thẽ selues in the later bibles correct it for shame, but yet suffer the other to be read and vsed still. See the Bible printed in the yere 1562.

Christ, so also the vvomen to their husbands in al things. † Husbands, loue your vviues, as Christ also "loued the CHVRCH, and deliuered him self for it: † that he might sanctifie it, cleansing it by the lauer of vvater in the vvord, † that he might present to him self a glorious CHVRCH, not hauing spot, or wrinkle, or any such thing, but that it may be holy and vnspotted. † So also men ought to loue their vviues as their ovvne bodies. He that loueth his vvife, loueth him self. † For no man euer hated his ovvne flesh: but he nourisheth & cherisheth it, "as also Christ the CHVRCH: † because vve be the members of his body, of his flesh & of his bones. † *For this cause shal mã leaue his father & mother: and shal cleaue to his vvife, and they shal be tvvo in one flesh.* † "This is a great sacramẽt. but I speake in Christ and in the CHVRCH † Neuertheles you also euery one, let eche loue his vvife as him self: and let the vvife feare her husband. ⊣

25 26 27 28 29 30 31 32 33

Gen. 2, 24. Mat. 19, 5.

ANNOTATIONS
CHAP. V.

No saluation out of the cath. CHVRCH.

23. *Sauiour of his body.*] None hath saluation or benefite by Christ, that is not of his body the Church. And vvhat Church that is, S. Augustine expresseth in these vvordes. *The Catholike Church onely is the body of Christ, vvhereof he is head. out of this body the Holy Ghost quickeneth no man.* And a litle after, *He that vvil haue the Spirit, let him bevvare he remaine not out of the* CHVRCH, *let him bevvare he enter not into it feinedly.* August. ep. 50 ad Bonifacium comitem in fine.

The CHVRCH neuer erreth.

24. *Subiect to Christ.*) The CHVRCH is alvvaies subiect to Christ, that is, not onely vnder him, but euer obedient to his vvordes and commaundement. Vvhich is an euident and inuincible demonstration that she neuer rebelleth against Christ, neuer falleth from him by error, Idolatrie, or false vvorship, as the Heretikes novv, and the Donatistes of old did teach.

Christs loue tovvard his Church.

The Church triumphant vvithout spot and vvrinkle.

25. *Loued the Church.*] Loe Christes singular loue of the CHVRCH, for vvhich onely & the members thereof he effectually suffered his Passion, and for vvhose continual cleansing and purifying in this life, he instituted holy Baptisme and other Sacraments: that at length in the next life it may become vvithout al spot, vvrinkle, or blemish. for, in this vvorld by reason of the manifold infirmities of diuers her members, she can not be vvholy vvithout sinne, but must say alvvaies, *Dimitte nobis debita nostra, Forgiue vs our debtes.* August. li. 2. Retract. c. 18.

The manifold dignitie of the Church

29. *As Christ the Church.*] It is an vnspeakable dignitie of the CHVRCH, vvhich the Apostle expresseth often els vvhere, but specially in this vvhole passage, to be that creature onely for vvhich Christ effectually suffered, to be vvashed and embrued vvith vvater and bloud issuing out of his holy side, to be nourished vvith his ovvne body (for so doth S. Irenæus expound li. 5. in principio) to be his members, * to be so ioyned vnto him as the body and members of the same flesh, bone, and substance to the head, to be loued and cherished of him as vvife of husband, yea to be his vvife and most deere spouse, taken and formed (as S. Augustine often saith) out of his ovvne side vpon the Crosse, as Eue our first father Adams spouse vvas made of his ribbe. *In Psal. 126. & in Psal. 127. & tract. 9 in Ioan. & tract.* 120. In respect of vvhich great dignitie and excellencie, the same holy father affirmeth the CHVRCH to be the principal creature, and therfore named in the Creede next after the Holy Ghost. and he proueth against the Macedonians, the Holy Ghost to be God, because he is named before the Church in the confession of our faith. Of vvhich incomparable excellencie of the Church, so beloued of Christ and so inseparatly ioyned in mariage vvith him, if the Heretikes of our time had any sense or consideration, they vvould neither thinke their cõtemptible companie or cõgregation to be the glorious spouse of our Lord, nor teach that the Church may erre, that is to say, may be diuorced from her spouse for Idolatrie, superstition, Heresie, or other abominations: Vvherevpon one of these absurdities vvould ensue, that either Christ

* Aug. li. 1 de Symb. ad Catech. c. 9.

The Church is the principal creature.

The Church can not erre.

Christ may sometimes be vvithout a Church & spouse in earth (as he vvas al the vvhile there vvere no Caluinists, if their Church be the spouse of Christ) or els if the Catholike Church onely is and hath been his vvife, and the same haue such errors as the Heretikes falsely pretend, that his vvife so deere and so praised here, is notvvithstanding a very vvhoore. Vvhich horrible absurdities proue and conuince to any man of common sense, both that the Catholike Church alvvaies is, and that it teacheth truth alvvaies, and to honour God truely and sincerely alvvaies: vvhatsoeuer the adulterous generation of Heretikes thinke or blaspheme.

Absurdities that folow, if the Church may erre.

32. *This is a great Sacrament.*] Mariage a great Sacramēt of Christ and his Church prefigured in the first parēts. *Adam* (saith S. Augustine *tract.* 15 *in Io.*) *vvho vvas a forme or figure of him that vvas to come, yea rather God in him, gaue vs a great token of a Sacrament. For both he deserued sleeping to take a vvife, and of his ribbe his vvife vvas made vnto him: because of Christ sleeping on the Crosse the Church vvas to be made out of his side.* In an other place he maketh Matrimonie a Sacramēt of Christ and his Church: in that, that as the maried mā must forsake father & mother and cleaue vnto his vvife, so Christ as it vvere left his father, exinaniting him self by his incarnatiō, & left the Synagogue his mother, & ioyned him self to the Church. *Li.* 12 *c.* 8. *cont. Faustum* In diuers other places he maketh it also a Sacrament, specially in that it is an inseparable bond betvvixt tvvo, and that can neuer be dissolued but by death: signifying Christs perpetual and indissoluble coniunction vvith the Church his one onely spouse. *de Gen. ad lit. li.* 9 *c.* 7. *Cont Pelag. de pec. orig. li.* 2 *c.* 34. *De fid. et op. c.* 7. *De bono coniug. c.* 7. & 18. And in an other place, *The good of Mariage* (saith he) *among the people of God is in the holines of a Sacrament.* De bono cōiugali *c.* 24.

MATRIMONIE a Sacrament.

Vvho vvould haue thought such mysteries and Sacramēts to be in Mariage, that the ioyning of man & vvife together should represent so great a mysterie, if the Apostle him self, & after him this holy father and others, had not noted it? or vvho can maruel that the holy Church taketh this to be a Sacrament, and to giue grace of sanctification to the parties maried, that they may liue together in mutual fidelitie, bring vp their children in faith and feare of God, and possesse their vessel (as the Apostle speaketh) in sanctification and honour, and not in passion of lust and ignominie, as the Heathen do vvhich knovv not God, and as our brutish nevv Maisters seeme to do that commend mariage aboue al things so farre as it feedeth their concupiscences, but for grace, Sacrament, mysterie, or sanctification thereby, they care no more then the Heathen or brute beastes do? And thus vve gather that matrimonie is a Sacrament, and not of the Greeke vvord *Mysterie* onely, as Caluin falsely saith, nor of the Latin vvord *Sacrament*, both vvhich vve knovv haue of their nature a more general signification, and that in the Scriptures also: but vvhereas these names are here giuen to Matrimonie by the Apostle, & are not giuen in the Scriptures to Baptisme and the Eucharist, let them tel vs vvhy they also apply these vvordes from their general signification to signifie specially and peculiarly those tvvo Sacramēts neuer so named expresly in Scripture, and do not likevvise folovv the Catholike Church in calling matrimonie by the same name, vvhich is here so called of the Apostle, specially vvhereas the signification in it, is as great as in any other of the Sacraments, and rather greater.

1 Thes. 4.

The grace giuen by this Sacrament.

The protestāts fleshly estimation of mariage.

μυστήριον *Sacramentum.*

CHAP. VI.

Likevvise children and parents he exhorteth, 5 *item seruants and maisters.* 10 *Then, that al take courage in the might of God, but so, that vvithal they arme them selue (considering vvhat mightie enemies they haue) vvith al peeces of spiritual armour,* 18 *praying alvvaies feruently, and for him also.*

Col. 3, 20 Exo. 20, 12. Deu. 5, 16.

1 HILDREN, obey your parents in our Lord. for this is iust. 2 † *Honour thy father and thy mother* (vvhich is the first commaundement in the promis,) 3 † *that it may be vvel vvith thee, and thou maiest be long-liued vpon the earth.* 4 † And you fathers, prouoke not your children to anger: but bring them vp in the discipline and correption of our Lord.

Col. 3, 22 Tit. 2, 9. 1 Pet. 2, 18.

5 † * Seruants, be obedient to your lordes according to

the fleſh, with feare and trembling, in the ſimplicitie of your hart, as to Chriſt: † not ſeruing to the eie, as it vvere pleaſing 6 men, but as the ſeruants of Chriſt, doing the vvil of God frō the hart, † vvith a good vvil ſeruing, as to our Lord and not 7 to men. † Knovving that euery one vvhat good ſoeuer he 8 ſhal doe, that ſhal he [c] receiue of our Lord, vvhether he be bond, or free. † And you maiſters, doe the ſame things to 9 them, [b] remitting threatenings: knovving that both their Lord and yours, is in heauen: and * acception of perſons is not vvith him.

c God leaueth no good worke vnrewarded.

b ἀνιέντες

Deu. 10, 17.

The Epiſtle vpon the 21 Sunday after Pentecoſt.

† Hence forth brethren, be ſtrengthened in our Lord, & 10 in the might of his povver. † Put you on the [c] armour of 11 God, that you may ſtand againſt the deceites of the Deuil. † For our vvreſtling is not againſt fleſh and bloud: but 12 againſt Princes and Poteſtats, againſt the * rectors of the vvorld of this darkenes, againſt the ſpirituals of vvickednes in the celeſtials. † Therfore take the armour of God, that 13 you may reſiſt in the euil day, and ſtand in al things perfect. † Stand therfore hauing your loines girded in truth, and 14 ∴ clothed with the breaſt-plate of iuſtice, † & hauing your 15 feete ſhod to the preparation of the Goſpel of peace: † in 16 al things taking the ſhield of faith, vvherevvith you may extinguiſh al the firie dartes of the moſt vvicked one. † and 17 take vnto you the * helmet of ſaluation: and the ſvvord of the ſpirit (vvhich is the vvord of God) ⁜ † in al praier 18 and ſupplication praying at al time in ſpirit: and in the ſame vvatching in al inſtance and ſupplication for al the ſaincts: † and for me, that ſpeache may be giuen me in 19 the opening of my mouth vvith cōfidence, to make knowen the myſterie of the Goſpel, † for the vvhich I am a legate 20 in this chaine, ſo that in it I may be bold according as I ought, to ſpeake.

c πανοπλίαν

Eph. 2, 2.

∴ If mā could not be truely iuſt or haue iuſtice in him ſelf, hovv could he be clothed vvith iuſtice?

Eſ. 59, 17. 1. Theſ. 5, 8

† And that you alſo may knovv the things about me, 21 vvhat I doe: Tychicus my deereſt brother and faithful miniſter in our Lord, vvil make you vnderſtād al things: † vvhom 22 I haue ſent to you for this ſame purpoſe, that you may know the things about vs, and he may comfort your hartes. † Peace 23 to the brethren and ∴ charitie vvith faith from God the Father, and our Lord IESVS Chriſt. † Grace with al that loue 24 our Lord IESVS Chriſt in incorruption. Amen.

∴ S. Auguſtine noteth in ſundrie places vpō this ſame text, that faith without charitie ſerueth not to ſaluation. li. 50. ho. 7.

THE ARGVMENT OF THE EPISTLE OF S. PAVL TO THE PHILIPPIANS.

H*OVV S. Paul vvas called by a viſion into Macedonia, vve reade Act. 16. and hovv he came to Philippi being the firſt citie thereof, and of his preaching, miracles, and ſuffering there. And againe Act.* 19. Paul purpoſed in the Spirit, vvhen he had paſſed through Macedonia and Achaia, to goe to Hieruſalem, ſaying: After I haue been there, I muſt ſee Rome alſo. *Vvhich purpoſe he executed Act.* 20. *taking his leaue at Epheſus. And being aftervvard come into Achaia,* he had counſel to returne through Macedonia, *and ſo at length from Philippi he began his nauigation tovvard Hieruſalem, and from Hieruſalem being caried priſoner to Rome (Act.* 28.) *he vvrote from thence this Epiſtle to the Philippians: or rather in his ſecond apprehenſion, about* 10 *yeres after the firſt.*

In it he confirmeth them (as he did the Epheſians alſo about the ſame time) againſt the tentatiō that they might haue in hearing that he vvere executed. therfore he firſt ſaith:* And I vvil haue you knovv brethren, that the things about me, are come to the more furtherance of the Goſpel: ſo that my bandes vvere made manifeſt in Chriſt in al the Court &c. *Secondly he ſignifieth that his deſire is,* to be diſſolued and to be vvith Chriſt. *but yet (leſt they ſhould be diſcomforted) that he hopeth* to come againe *to them. Vvhereof notvvithſtanding, that he hath yet no certaintie, he ſignifieth in ſaying:* I hope to ſend Timothee vnto you, immediatly as I ſhal ſee the things that concerne me. *Thirdly therefore he prepareth them againſt the vvorſt, ſaying:* I hope to come againe to you: but and if I be immolated, vpon the ſacrifice and ſeruice of your faith, I reioyce and congratulate vvith you al, and the ſelf ſame thing do you alſo reioyce and congratulate vvith me.

Eph. 5.
Phil. 1. v. 12. 23. 26.
Phil. 2. v. 23. 24. 17.

Moreouer he partly vvarneth them (as he had done before) of thoſe Iudaical Falſe-apoſtles vvho preached circumciſion & Moyſes lavv to the Chriſtian Gentils: partly he exhorteth them to ſuffer perſecution, to liue vvel, and ſpecially to humble them ſelues one to an other, rather then by any pride to breake the peace & vnitie of the Church.

Phil. 3.

THE EPISTLE OF PAVL TO THE PHILIPPIANS.

CHAP. I.

Hauing signified that he vseth to thanke God for their vertue, 9 and also to pray for their encrease: 12 he certifieth them (for their confirmatiõ & comfort) vvhat good was come through his trouble at Rome, 24 & that he doubteth not (though he rather desire martyrdom) but to come againe vnto them, 27 exhorting them to liue as they ought to do, 28 and namely not to shrinke for persecution.

PAVL and Timothee the seruants of IESVS Christ: to al the sainctes in Christ IESVS that are at Philippi, vvith the "Bishops and Deacons. † Grace to you and peace from God our father, and our Lord IESVS Christ. 1 2

† I giue thankes to my God in al memorie of you († alvvaies in al my praiers for al you, vvith ioy making petition) † for your communicating in the Gospel of Christ from the first day vntil novv. † trusting this same thing, that he which hath begõne in you a good worke, vvil perfit it vnto the day of Christ IESVS. † as it is reason for me, this to thinke for al you, for that I haue you in hart, & in my bandes, and in the defense, and the confirmation of the Gospel, al you to be partakers of my ioy. † For God is my vvitnes, hovv I couet you al in the bowels of IESVS Christ. † And this I pray, that your charitie may more and more abound in knovvledge and in al vnderstanding: † that you may approue the better things, that you may be sincere and vvithout offence vnto the day of Christ, † replenished vvith the fruite of iustice by IESVS Christ, vnto the glorie and praise of God. ⊣ 3 4 5 6 7 8 9 10 11

The Epistle vpon the 22 Sunday after Pentecost.

† And I vvil haue you knovv brethren, that the things about me are come to the more furtherance of the Gospel: 12

† so

13 † ſo that my bandes vvere made manifeſt in Chriſt in al the
14 court, and in al the reſt, † that many of our brethren in our Lord, hauing confidence in my bandes, vvere bold more aboundantly vvithout feare to ſpeake the vvord of God.
15 † Some in deede euen for enuie and contention: but ſome al-
16 ſo for good vvil preache Chriſt. † Some of charitie: knovv-
17 ing that I am ſet vnto the defenſe of the Goſpel. † And ſome of contention preache Chriſt not ſincerely: ſuppoſing that
18 they raiſe affliction to my bandes. † But vvhat? So that by al meanes, vvhether by occaſion, or by truth, Chriſt be prea-
19 ched: in this alſo I reioyce, yea & vvil reioyce. † For I knovv that this ſhal fall out to me vnto ſaluatiõ by your praier and
20 the ſubminiſtration of the Spirit of IESVS Chriſt, † according to my expectation & hope, becauſe in nothing ſhal I be confounded, but in al confidence as alvvaies, novv alſo ſhal Chriſt be magnified in my body, vvhether it be by life,
21 or by death. † For vnto me, to liue is Chriſt: and to die is
22 gaine. † And if to liue in the fleſh, this vnto me be the fruit
23 of the vvorke, and vvhat I ſhal chooſe I knovv not. † And I am ſtraitened of the tvvo: hauing deſire to be diſſolued & to be vvith Chriſt, a thing much more better. † but to abide
24 in the fleſh, \`neceſſarie' for you. † And truſting this, I know that I ſhal abide and continue vvith you al, vnto your fur-
25 therance and ioy of the faith: † that your gratulation may abound in Chriſt IESVS in me, by my comming againe to you.

more neceſſarie

26 † Only * conuerſe ye vvorthie of the Goſpel of Chriſt: that vvhether vvhen I come and ſee you, or els be abſent, I may heare of you that you ſtand in one Spirit, of one minde
27 labouring together to the faith of the Goſpel. † And in nothing be ye terrified of the aduerſaries, vvhich to them is [b] cauſe of perdition: but to you of ſaluation, & this of God:
28 † for to you [c] it is giuen for Chriſt, not only that you beleeue
29 in him, but alſo that you ſuffer for him, † hauing the ſame combat like as you haue ſeen in me, and novv \`haue heard' of me.

Eph. 4,1

[c] ἐχαρίσθη

\` *doe heare*

[b] ἔνδειξις, A manifeſt proofe and euidence.

ANNOTATIONS
CHAP. I.

2. *Biſhops*

Bishops and Priests alwais distinct functions.

2. Bishops and deacons.] Vvicleffe and other Heretikes vvould proue by this that Priests are not here named, and for that there could not be many Bishops of this one tovvne, that there is no difference betvvixt a Bishop and a Priest; vvhich vvas the old heresie of Aerius, of vvhich matter,* in other places: for this present it is ynough to knovv that in the Apostles time there vvere not obserued alvvaies proper distinct names of either function, as they vvere quickly aftervvard, though they vvere alvvaies diuers degrees & distinct functions. *See S. Chrysostom, Oecumenius, Theophylactus, and the rest of the Græcians vpon this place.*

* *See Annot. Tit. 1. v. 5.*

CHAP. II.

He exhorteth them most instantly to keepe the vnitie of the Church, and to humble them selues for that purpose one to an other, 5 by the example of the maruelous humilitie of Christ, 9 specially seing hovv maruelously he is novv exalted for it. 12 Item to obedience, feare, and perseuerance. 17 Insinuating (lest it should aftervvardes trouble them) that he may be martyred at this time. 19 Timothee he hopeth to send, vvhom he highly commendeth: 25 as also Epaphroditus, vvhom he presently sendeth.

IF therfore there be any consolation in 1 Christ, if any solace of charitie, if any societie of spirit, if any bovvels of commiseration: † fulfil my ioy, that you be of 2 one meaning, hauing the same charitie, of one minde, agreing in one. † nothing 3 by contentiō, neither by vaine glorie: but in humilitie, * eche coūting other better then them selues: † * euery one not cōsidering the things that are their ovvne, 4 but those that are other mens. † For this thinke in your 5 selues, vvhich also in Christ IESVS, † vvho vvhen he vvas 6 in the forme of God, thought it no robberie, him self to be equal to God, † but he exinanited him self, taking the forme 7 of a seruant, made into the similitude of men, and in shape found as man. † He * humbled him self, made obediēt vnto 8 death: euen the death of the crosse. † " For the vvhich thing 9 God also hath exalted him, and hath giuen him a name which is aboue al names: † that * in the " name of IESVS euery knee 10 bovve of the celestials, terrestrials, and infernals: † and eue- 11 ry tongue cōfesse that our Lord IESVS Christ is in the glorie of God the Father. ¶

The Epistle vpon Palme Sunday. And vpon Holy Roode day, Mai. 3.

The Epistle vpon Holy Roode day Septemb. 14. And in a Votiue Masse of the Holy Crosse.

Ro. 12, 10.
1 Cor. 10, 24.
Heb. 2, 9.
Es. 45, 14. Ro. 14, 11.

† Therfore my deerest, (as you haue alvvaies obeied) 12 not as in the presence of me only, but much more novv in my absence, " vvith feare and trembling vvorke your saluation. † For it is God that " vvorketh in you both to vvil 13 and to accomplish, according to his good vvil. † And doe 14 ye al things vvithout murmurings and staggerings: † that 15 you may be vvithout blame, and the simple children of God,

vvithout

vvithout reprehension in the middes of a crooked and peruerse generation. among vvhom you shine as lightes in the
16 vvorld: † conteining the vvord of life ∷ to my glorie in the daie of Christ, because I haue not runne in vaine, nor in
17 vaine laboured. † But and if I be ∷ immolated, vpon the " sacrifice and seruice of your faith, I reioyce and congratulate
18 vvith you al. † And the self same thing doe you also reioyce, and congratulate vvith me.

19 † And I hope in our Lord IESVS, to send Timothee vnto you quickly, that I also may be of good comfort, when
20 I knovv the things pertaining to you. † For I haue no mã so of one minde that vvith sincere affection is careful for you.
21 † For ∷ al seeke the things that are their ovvne: not the
22 things that are IESVS Christs. † And knovv ye an experiment of him, that as a sonne the father, so hath he serued
23 vvith me in the Gospel. † This man therfore I hope to send vnto you, immediatly as I shal see the things that concerne
24 me. † And I trust in our Lord that my self also shal come to
25 you quickly. † But I haue thought it necessarie to send to you Epaphroditus my brother and coadiutor and fellovv souldiar, but your Apostle, and minister of my necessitie.
26 † Because in deede he had a desire tovvard you al: and vvas
27 pensife, for that you had heard that he vvas sicke. † For in deede he vvas sicke euen to death: but God had mercie on him: and not only on him, but on me also, lest I should haue
28 sorovv vpon sorovv. † Therfore I sent him the more spedily: that seeing him, you may reioyce againe, and I may be
29 vvithout sorovv. † Receiue him therfore vvith al ioy in
30 our Lord: and such intreate vvith honour. † because for the vvorke of Christ, he came to the point of death: yelding his life, that he might fulfil that vvhich on your part vvanted tovvard my seruice.

∷ Such as haue by their preaching gained any to Christ, shal ioy and glorie therein exceedingly at the day of our Lord.

∷ Pastors ought to be so zelous of the saluation of their flocke, that vvith S. Paul they should offer them selues to death for the same.

∷ Many forsake their teachers vvhen they see them in bandes and prison for their faith, because most mẽ preferre the vvorld before Christs glorie.

ANNOTATIONS
CHAP. II.

9. *For the vvhich.*] Caluin doth so abhorre the name of merite in Christian men tovvard their ovvne saluation, that he vvickedly and vnlearnedly denieth Christ him self to haue deserued or merited any thing for him self: though these vvordes (vvhich he shamefully vvritheth from the proper and plaine sense, to signifie a sequele and not a cause of his exaltation) and diuers other in holy vvrite, proue that he merited for him self according to al learned mens iudgement. As Apoc 5. *The lambe that vvas slaine, is vvorthie to receiue povver and Diuinitie.* And Heb. 2. *We see* IESVS *for the passion of death, crovvned vvith glorie and honour.* See S. Augustine vpõ these vvordes of the Psalme 109. *propterea exaltabit caput.*

Caluins blasphemie agaĩst Christs ovvne merites.

The Protestants vvill haue no reuerence done at the name of IESVS.

10. *Name of* IESVS.] By the like vvickednes they charge the faithful people for capping or kneeling vvhen they heare the name of IESVS. as though they vvorshipped not our Lord God therein, but the syllables or letters or other material elemẽts vvhereof the vvord vvritten or spoken consisteth, and al this, by sophistications to dravv the people from due honour and deuotion tovvard CHRIST IESVS, vvhich is Satans drift by putting scruples into poore simple mens mindes about his Sacraments, his Saincts, his Crosse, his name, his image, & such like, to abolish al true religiõ out of the vvorld, and to make them plaine Atheists. But the Church knovveth Satans cogitations, and therfore by the Scriptures and reason, vvarranteth and teacheth al her children to do reuerence vvhen so euer IESVS is named.

Hovv Catholikes honour the name of IESVS, and other things pertaining to him.

because Catholikes do not honour these things nor count them holy, for their matter, colour, sound, and syllables, but for the respect and relation they haue to our Sauiour, bringing vs to the remembrance and apprehension of Christ, by sight, hearing, or vse of the same signes. els vvhy make vve not reuerence at the name of Iesus the sonne of Sirach, as vvel as of IESVS CHRIST? And it is a pitieful case to see these prophane subtelties of Heretikes to take place in religion, vvhich vvere ridiculous in al other trade of life. Vvhen vve heare our Prince or Soueraine named, vve may vvithout these scruples doe obeisance, but tovvardes Christ it must be superstitious.

Vaine securitie of saluatiõ.

12. *With feare and trembling.*] Against the vaine presumption of Heretikes that make men secure of their predestination and saluation, he vvilleth the Philippians to vvorke their saluation vvith feare and trembling, according to that other Scripture, *Blessed is the man that alvvaies is fearful.* Prouerb. 28, v. 14.

S. Augustine ansvvereth the obiectiõ agaist free vvil.

13. *Worketh in you.*] Of this thus saith S. Augustine, *Not because the Apostle saith, it is God that vvorketh in you both to vvil and vvorke, must vve thinke he taketh avvay our free vvill. For if it vvere so, then vvould he not a litle before haue vvilled them to vvorke their ovvne saluation vvith feare and trembling. For vvhen they be commaunded to vvorke, their free vvil is called vpon: but, vvith trembling and feare, is added, lest by attributing their vvel vvorking to them selues, they might be proud of their good deedes as though they vvere of them selues.* August. de gratia & lib. arbit. c. 9.

Martyrdom.

17. *The sacrifice.*] The obedience of faith and martyrdom be so acceptable actes to God, vvhen they be voluntarily referred to his honour, that by a metaphore they be called sacrifice and pleasant hostes to God.

CHAP. III.

He vvarneth them of the False-apostles, 4 shevving that him self had much more to bragge of in Iudaisme then they: but that he maketh price of nothing but only of Christ, and of Christian iustice, and of suffering vvith him (12 vvherein yet he acknovvledgeth his imperfection) 17 exhorting them to beare Christes Crosse vvith him, and not to imitate those bellygods.

FROM hence forth my brethren, reioyce in our Lord. To vvrite the same things vnto you, to me surely it is not tedious, and to you it is necessarie. 1

† See the dogges, see the euil vvorkers, see the [c] concisiõ. 2

† For vve are the [c] circumcision, vvhich in spirit serue God: and vve glorie in Christ IESVS, and not hauing confidence in the flesh, 3

† albeit I also haue confidence in the flesh. 4

† If any other man seeme to haue confidence in the flesh, I more, 5

† circumcised the eight day, of the stocke of Israël, of the tribe of Beniamin, * an Hebrevv of Hebrevves: * according to the Lavv, a Pharisee: 6

† according to emulation, persecuting the Church of God: according to the iustice that is in the Lavv, conuersing vvithout blame. 7

† But the

c By allusiõ of vvords, he calleth the carnal Christiã Iews that yet boasted in the circũcision of the flesh, *concisiõ*: & him self & the rest that circũcided their hart and senses spiritually, the true *circumcision*. S. Chrys. Theophylact.

c κατατομὴ et περιτομὴ

2. Cor. 11, 22.

Act. 23, 6.

the things that vvere gaines to me, those haue I esteemed for Christ, detriments. 8 † Yea but I esteeme al things to be detriment for the passing knovvledge of IESVS Christ my Lord: for vvhom I haue made al things as detriment, and do esteeme them as dung, that I may gaine Christ: 9 † and may be found in him not hauing ″ my iustice vvhich is of the Lavv, but that vvhich is of the faith of Christ, vvhich is of God iustice in faith: 10 † to knovv him, and the vertue of his resurrection, and the societie of his passions, configured to his death, 11 † ∷ if by any meanes I may come to the resurrection vvhich is from the dead. 12 † ″ Not that novv I haue receiued, or novv am perfect: but I pursue, if I may comprehend vvherein I am also comprehended of Christ IESVS. ⊣ 13 † Brethren, I do not account that I haue comprehended. Yet one thing: forgetting the things that are behinde, but stretching forth my self to those that are before, 14 † I pursue to the marke,[c] to the price of the supernal vocation of God in Christ IESVS. 15 † Let vs therfore as many as are perfect, be thus minded: and if you be any ″ othervvise minded, this also God `hath reuealed' to you. 16 † Neuerthelesse vvherevnto we are come, that vve be of the same minde, let vs continue in the same rule.

17 †[a] Be folovvers ∷ of me brethren: & obserue them that vvalke so as you haue our forme. 18 † For * many vvalke vvhom often I told you of (and novv vveeping also I tel you) the enemies of the crosse of Christ: 19 † vvhose end is destruction: vvhose God, is the belly: and their glorie in their confusion, vvhich minde vvorldly things. 20 † But our conuersation is in heauen: vvhence also vve expect the Sauiour, our Lord IESVS Christ, 21 † vvho vvil reforme the body of our humilitie, configured to the body of his glorie, according to the operation vvhereby also he is able to subdue al things to him self.

c *ad brauium*

` vvil reueale'

Ro. 16, 17.

The Epistle for a Confessor that is not a Bishop.

∷ If S. Paul ceased not to labour still, as though he vvere not sure to come to the marke vvithout continual endeuour: vvhat securitie may vve poore sinners haue of Heretikes persuasions & promises of securitie and saluation by onely faith?

a The Epistle vpon the 23 Sunday after Pentecost. And for S. Clemēt, Nouemb. 23.

∷ It is a goodly thing vvhen the Pastor may so say to his flocke. Neither is it any derogatiō to Christ, that the people should imitate their Apostles life & doctrine, & other holy men, *S. Augustine, S. Benedict, S. Dominike, S. Francis.*

ANNOTATIONS CHAP. III.

9. *My iustice.*] Diuers Lutherans in their translations do shamfully mangle this sentence by transposing the vvordes, and false pointing of the partes thereof, to make it haue this sense, that the Apostle vvould haue no iustice of his ovvne, but onely that iustice vvhich is in Christ. Vvhich is a false and heretical sense of the vvordes, and not meant by S. Paul: vvho calleth that a mans ovvne iustice, vvhich he chalengeth by the vvorkes of the Lavv or nature vvithout the grace of Christ: and that Gods iustice (as S. Augustine expoundeth this place) not vvhich is in God, or by

Magdeburg. cent. 1. li. 2 c. 4. *pag.* 222.

The obiection against inherent iustice, ansvvered.

vvhich God is iust, but that vvhich is in man from God and by his gift. *li. 3 cont. 2 ep. Pelag. c. 7. de Sp. & lit. c. 9.*

Double perfection: here, and in the life to come.

12. *Not that novv.*] No man in this life can attaine the absolute perfectnes either of iustice or of that knovvledge, vvhich shal be in heauen: but yet there is also an other perfectnes, such as according to this state a man may reach vnto, vvhich in respect of the perfection in glorie, is small, but in respect of other lesser degrees of mans iustice and knovvledge in this life, may be called perfectnes. And in this sense the Apostle in the next sentence calleth him self and others perfect, though in respect of the absolute perfectnes in heauen, he saith here, he is not yet perfect nor hath yet attained therevnto.

The heretikes folish defense of their dissensions and diuisions among them selues.

15. *Othervvise minded.*] Vvhen Catholike men novv a daies charge Heretikes vvith their horrible diuisions, dissensions, combattes, contentions, and diuersities among them selues, as the Catholikes of al other ages did chalenge their Aduersaries most truely and iustly for the same, (both because vvhere the Spirit of God is not, nor any order or obedience to Superiors, there can be no peace nor vnitie, and specially for that it is, as S. Augustine saith (*li. de agone Christ. c. 29*) the iust iudgement of God that they vvhich seeke nothing els but to diuide the Church of Christ, should them selues be miserably diuided among them selues) therfore (I say) vvhen men charge the Protestants vvith these things, they flee for their defence to this, that the old Fathers vvere not al of one iudgement in euery point of religion: that S. Cyprian stood against others, that S. Augustine and S. Hierom vvrote earnestly in a certaine matter one against an other, that our Dominicans and Franciscans, our Thomists and Scotists be not al of one opinion in diuers matters, and therfore diuisions and contentions should not be so preiudicial to the Zuinglians and Lutherans, as men make it. Thus they defend them selues: but ridiculously and against the rule of S. Paul here, acknovvledging that in this imperfection of mens science in this life, euery one can not be free from al error, or thinke the same that an other thinketh: vvherevpon may rise differences of vnderstanding, opinion, and iudgement, in certaine hard matters vvhich God hath not reuealed or the Church determined, and therfore that such diuersitie is tolerable and agreable to our humane condition and the state of the vvay that vve be in: alvvaies prouided, that the controuersie be such and in such things, as be not against the set knovven rule of faith, as he here speaketh, and such as breake not mutual societie, fellovvship, and communion in praier, seruice, Sacraments, and other offices of life and religion. for such diuisions and differences come neuer but of Schisme or Heresie, and such are among the Heretikes, not onely in respect of vs Catholikes, but among them selues: as they knovv that be acquainted vvith the vvritings of Luther against Zuinglius, or Vvestphalus against Caluin, or the Puritans against the Protestants, not onely charging one an other vvith Heresie, Idolatrie, Superstition, and Atheisme, but also condemning ech others ceremonies or maner of administrations, til it come to excommunication, and banishment, yea sometimes burning one of an other. Thus did not S. Cyprian, S. Augustine, S. Hierom, the Dominicans, Franciscans, Thomists, Scotists, vvho al agree in one rule of faith, al of one communion, al most deere one to an other in the same, al (thankes be to God) come to one holy Masse, and receiue the same Sacraments, and obey one head through out al the vvorld. S. Augustine *li. 2 de bapt. c. 5.* shal make vp this matter vvith this notable sentence: *We are men* (saith he) *and therfore to thinke somevvhat othervvise then the thing is, is an humane tentation: but by louing our ovvne sentence to much, or by enuying our betters, to procede vnto the sacrilege of deuiding the mutual societie and of making schisme or heresie, is diuelish presumption: in nothing to haue other opinion then the truth is, that is Angelical perfection.* And a litle after, *If you be any other vvise minded, this God vvil reueale: but to them only* (saith he) *that vvalke in the vvay of peace, and that stray a side into no diuision or separation.* Vvhich saying vvould God al our deere countrie men vvould marke, and come into the Church, vvhere onely, God reuealeth truth.

The difference betvvene the disagreing of auncient fathers or other Catholikes, & the Heretikes dissensions among them selues.

The spiteful vvritings of Heretikes, one Secte against an other.

A notable place of S. Augustine.

CHAP. IIII.

He exhorteth them to perseuerance, 2 and certaine by name to vnitie, 5 to modestie, 6 to peace vvithout solicitude or careful anxietie, 8 to al that good is, 9 to such things as they see in him self. 10 that he reioyced in their contribution, not for his ovvne neede, but for their merite.

Therefore

1 THERFORE, my ʺdeerest brethren and most desired, my ʺioy and ʺmy crovvne: so stand in our Lord, my 2 deerest. † \`Euchodia' I desire & Syntyché I beseeche to be of one minde in 3 our Lord. † Yea and I beseeche thee my ʺsincere companion, helpe those vvomen that haue laboured vvith me in the Gospel vvith ∴ Clement, and the rest my coadiutors, 4 vvhose names are in the booke of life. ⊣ † [b] Reioyce in our 5 Lord alvvaies: againe I say reioyce. † Let your modestie 6 be knovven to al men. Our Lord is nigh. † Be nothing careful: but [c] in euery thing by praier & supplicatiō vvith thākes-7 giuing let your petitions be knovven vvith God. † And the peace of God vvhich passeth al vnderstanding, keepe your hartes and intelligences in Christ IESVS. ⊣

\`Euodia

[c] ἐν παντὶ τῇ προσευχῇ

∴ This Clement vvas aftervvard the 4 Pope of Rome from S. Peter, as S. Hierom vvriteth according to the cōmon supputation.

b The Epistle vpon the 3 Sunday in Aduent.

8 † For the rest brethren, vvhat things so euer be true, vvhatsoeuer honest, whatsoeuer iust, vvhatsoeuer holy, whatsoeuer amiable, vvhatsoeuer of good fame, if there be any vertue, if any praise of discipline, these things thinke vpon. 9 † Vvhich you haue both learned, and receiued, and heard, & seen in me: these things doe ye, and the God of peace shall 10 be vvith you. † And I reioyced in our Lord excedingly, that once at the length you haue [c] reflorished to care for me, 11 as you did also care: but you vvere occupied. † I speake not as it vvere for penurie. for I haue learned, to be cōtent vvith 12 the things that I haue. † I knovv both to be brought lovv, I knovv also to abound: (euery vvhere, and in al things I am instructed) both to be ful, & to be hungrie, both to abound, 13 and to suffer penurie. † I can al things in him that streng-14 theneth me. † Neuerthelesse you haue done vvel, communicating to my tribulation.

c This reflorishing is the reuiuing of their old liberalitie, vvhich for a time had been slacke & dead. S. Chrys.

15 † And you also knovv ô Philippians, that in the beginning of the Gospel, vvhen I departed from Macedonia, no church communicated vnto me in the account of gift and 16 ∴ receite, but you only: † for vnto Thessalonica also, once 17 and tvvise you sent to my vse. † Not that I seeke the gift, but 18 I seeke the fruite abounding in your account. † But I haue al things, and abound: I vvas filled after I receiued of Epaphroditus the things that you sent, an odour of svveetenes, 19 an ʺacceptable host, pleasing God. † And my God supply

∴ He counteth it not mere almes or a free gift that the people bestovveth on their Pastors or preachers, but a certaine mutual traffike as it vvere, and enterchange: the one giuing spiritual, the other rēdering tēporal things for the same.

al your [c] lacke according to his riches in glorie, in Christ IESVS. † And to God & our father be glorie vvorld vvithout end. Amen. 20

c. χρείαν

† Salute ye euery saincte in Christ IESVS. † The brethren that are vvith me, salute you. Al the sainctes salute you: but especially they that are of Cæsars house. † The grace of our Lord IESVS Christ be vvith your spirit. Amen. 21 22

ANNOTATIONS
CHAP. IIII.

The revvard of preachers.

1. *My ioy.*] He calleth them his ioy and crovvne, for that he expected the crovvne of euerlasting life as a revvard of his labours tovvardes them. Vvhereby vve may learne also, that besides the essential glorie vvhich shal be in the vision and fruition of God, there is other manifold felicitie incident in respect of creatures.

Suspitious translation.

S. Paul had no vvife.

3. *Sincere companion.*] The English Bibles vvith one consent interprete the Greeke vvordes, *faithful yokefellovv*, perhaps to signifie (as some vvould haue it) that the Apostle here speaketh to his vvife: but they must vnderstand that their Maisters Caluin and Beza mislike that exposition, and * al the Greeke fathers almost much more reiect it, and it is against S. Paules ovvne vvordes speaking to the vnmaried, That it is good for them to remaine so, euen as him self did. 1 *Cor.* 7, 8. Vvhereby it is euident he had no vvife, and therfore meaneth here some other his coadiutor and fellovv-labourer in the Gospel.

S. Chrys. Theodore. Oecum. Theophyl.

Almes giuen religiously.

18. *Acceptable.*] Hovv acceptable almes are before God, vve see here: namely vvhen it is giuen for religion to deuout persons for a recompense of spiritual benefites. for so it putteth on the condition of an oblation or sacrifice offered to God, and is most acceptable and svvete in his sight.

THE

THE ARGVMENT OF THE EPISTLE OF S. PAVL TO THE COLOSSIANS.

HE Epistle to the Colossians is not only in sense, but almost in vvordes also, all one vvith the Epistle to the Ephesians, and vvas sent also by the same messenger Tychicus. c. 4. v. 7. And in it he maketh like mention of his bandes and sufferings. c. 1. v. 24. and c. 4. v. 3, 18. And therfore no doubt it vvas vvritten at Rome at the same time, to vvitte, in his last apprehension, yet before he knevv of his martyrdom.

This difference there is, that he had himself preached to the Ephesians, but vvith the Colossians he had neuer bene, as he signifieth c. 2. v. 1. Therefore although in matters of exhortation he be here briefer then to the Ephesians, yet in matters of doctrine he is longer. And generally he assureth them, that to be the truth, vvhich their Apostle Epaphras had taught them, but namely he giueth them vvarning both of the Iudaical False-apostles, vvho sought to corrupt them vvith some ceremonies of Moyses lavv: and also of the Platonike Philosophers, vvho reiected Christ; (vvho is in deede the head of the Church and Mediator to bring vs to God) and in steed of him, brought in certaine Angels as more excellēt then he, vvhom they termed, Minores dij, *teaching the people to sacrifice vnto them (calling that, humilitie) that they might bring them to the great God. Vvith vvhich falsehod the heresie of Simon Magus a long time deceiued many, as vve reade in Epiph. hær. 21.*

Against such therefore S. Paul telleth the Colossians, that Christ is the Creator of all the Angels, God in person, the head of the Church, the principall in all respects: that he is the Redeemer, Mediator, and pacifier betvvene God and men, and therefore by him vve must goe to God, so that vvhether vve pray our selues, or desire any other in earth or in heauen to pray for vs, al must be done (as the Cath. Church in euery Collect doth) Per Christum dominum nostrum, *that is,* through Christ our Lord *or,* per Do. nostrum Iesum Christum filium tuum, qui tecum viuit & regnat, &c. *Vvhereby the Church professeth cōtinually against such seductions, both the Mediatorship, and the Godhead of Christ.*

THE

THE EPISTLE OF PAVL TO THE COLOSSIANS.

Chap. I.

Saying, that he thanketh God for their excellent faith and charitie, and continually praieth for their encrease, he doeth vvithal giue vvitnes to the preaching of their Apostle Epaphras, and extolleth the grace of God in bringing them to Christ, vvho is cheefe aboue al, and peacemaker by his bloud. This is the Gospel not of Epaphras alone, but of the vniuersal Church, and of Paul him self vvho also suffereth for it.

PAVL an Apostle of IESVS Christ 1 by the vvil of God, and brother Timothee: † to them that are at Colossa sainctes and faithful brethren in 2 Christ IESVS. † Grace to you and 3 peace from God our Father and our Lord IESVS Christ.

Vve giue thankes to God and the Father of our Lord IESVS Christ alvvaies for you, praying: † hearing your faith in Christ 4 IESVS, and the loue vvhich you haue tovvard al the saincts, † for the hope that is laid vp for you in heauen, vvhich you 5 haue heard in the vvord of the truth of the Gospel, † that 6 is come to you, as also ∷ in the vvhole vvorld it is, and fructifieth, and grovveth, euen as in you, since that day that you heard & knevv the grace of God in truth, † as you learned 7 of Epaphras our deerest fellovv-seruant, vvho is a faithful minister of IESVS Christ for you, † vvho also hath mani- 8 fested to vs your loue in spirit. † Therfore [b] vve also from 9 the day that vve heard it, cease not praying for you and desiring, that you may be filled vvith the knovvledge of his vvil, in al vvisedom, and spiritual vnderstanding: † that you may 10 vvalke [c] vvorthie of God, in al things pleasing: Fructifying in

∷ He shevveth that the Churche and Christes Gospel should daily grovv and be spred at length through the vvhole vvorld. Which can not stand vvith the heretikes opinion of the decay thereof so quickly after Christes time, nor agree by any meanes to their obscure Conuenticles. See S. Augustine ep. 80. *in fine.*

b The Epistle vpon the 24 Sunday after Pentecost.

c So S. Ambr. & the Gr. Doctors. or thus: *vvorthily, pleasing God &c.*

c ἀξίως κυρίου

in [c] al good vvorke, & increasing in the knovvledge of God: 11 † in al povver strengthened according to the might of his 12 glorie, in al patience and longanimitie vvith ioy † giuing thankes to God and the Father, vvho hath made vs :: vvorthy 13 vnto the part of the lot of the sainctes in the light: † vvho hath deliuered vs from the povver of darkenes, and hath 14 translated vs into the kingdom of the sonne of his loue, † in vvhom vve haue redemption, the remission of sinnes: ┤ 15 † vvho is the * image of the inuisible God, the first-borne of 16 al creature: † because * in him vvere created al things in heauen, and in earth, visible, and inuisible, vvhether Thrones, or Dominations, or Principalities, or Potestates: † al by him, 17 & in him vvere created: † and he is before al, and al consist in 18 him. † And he is the head of the body, the CHVRCH, vvho is the beginning, first-borne of the dead: that he may be in al 19 things holding the primacie: † because in him it hath vvel 20 pleased, al fulnes to inhabite: † and by him to reconcile al things vnto him self, pacifying by the bloud of his crosse, vvhether the things in earth, or the things that are in heauen.

21 † And you, vvhereas you vvere sometime alienated and 22 enemies in sense, in euil vvorkes: † yet novv he hath reconciled in the body of his flesh by death, to present you holy 23 & immaculate, and blameles before him: † if yet ye cõtinue in the faith, grounded and stable, and vnmoueable from the hope of the Gospel vvhich you haue heard, vvhich is preached among al creatures that are vnder heauen, vvhereof I 24 Paul am made a minister. † Vvho novv reioyce in suffering for you, and " do accomplish those things that vvant of the passions of Christ, in my flesh for his body, vvhich is the 25 CHVRCH: † vvhereof I am made a minister according to the dispensation of God, vvhich is giuen me tovvard you, that I 26 may fulfil the vvord of God, † the mysterie that hath been hidden from vvorldes and generations, but novv is mani-27 fested to his sainctes, † to vvhõ God vvould make knovven the riches of the glorie of this sacrament in the Gentiles, 28 vvhich is Christ, in you the hope of glorie, † vvhom vve preache, admonishing euery man, and teaching euery man in al vvisedom, that vve may present euery man perfect in 29 Christ IESVS. † Vvherein also I labour striuing according to his operation vvhich he vvorketh in me in povver.

Hebr. 1, 3

Io. 1, 3.

c Many things requisite, and diuers things acceptable to God beside faith.

:: We are not onely by acceptation or imputation partakers of Christes benefites, but are by his grace made worthie thereof, and deserue our saluation condignely.

ANNOTATIONS
CHAP. I.

There is no want in Christes passions vvhich he suffred in him self as head: but there is vvant in those passions of Christ vvhich he daily suffereth in his body the Church, and the members thereof.

24. *Do accomplish that vvanteth.*] As Christ the head and his body make one person mystical and one full Christ, the Church being therfore his plenitude, fulnes, or complement *Ephes.* 1: so the passions of the head and the afflictions of the body and members make one complete masse of passions. Vvith such difference for al that, betvvene the one sort and the other, as the preeminence of the head (and specially such a head) aboue the body, requireth and giueth. And not only those passions vvhich he suffered in him self, vvhich vvere fully ended in his death, and vvere in them selues fully sufficient for the redemption of the vvorld & remission of al sinnes, but al those vvhich his body and members suffer, are his also, and of him they receiue the condition, qualitie, and force to be meritorious and satisfactorie. for though there be no insufficiencie in the actions or passions of Christ the head, yet his vvisedom vvil, and iustice requireth and ordaineth,* that his body and members should be fellovves of his passions, as they looke to be fellovves of his glorie: that so suffering vvith him and by his example, they may applie to them selues and others the general medicine of Christes merites and satisfactions, as it is effectually also applied to vs by Sacraments, sacrifice, and other vvaies also: the one sort being no more iniurious to Christes death then the other, notvvithstanding the vaine clamours of the Protestants, that vvould vnder pretence of Christes Passion, take avvay the valure of al good deedes. Herevpon it is plaine novv, that this accomplishment of the vvants of Christes Passions, vvhich the Apostle and other Saincts make vp in their flesh, is not meant but of the penal and satisfactorie vvorkes of Christ in his members, euery good man adding continually (and specially Martyrs) somevvhat to accomplish the full measure thereof: and these be the plenitude of his passions and satisfactions, as the Church is the plenitude of his person: & therfore these also through the communion of Saincts and the societie that is not onely betvvene the head and the body, but also betvvene one member and an other, are not only satisfactorie and many vvaies profitable for the sufferers them selues, but also for other their fellovv-members in Christ. for though one member can not merite for an other properly, yet may one beare the burden and discharge the debt of an other, both by the lavv of God and nature. and it vvas a ridiculous Heresie of Vvicleffe to deny the same. Yea (as vve see here) the passions of Saincts are alvvaies suffered for the common good of the vvhole body, and sometimes vvithal by the sufferers special intention they are applicable to special persons one or many: as here the Apostle ioyeth in his passions for the Collossians, in an other place his afflictions be for the saluation of the Corinthians, sometimes he vvisheth to be *Anathema*, that is according to Origens exposition (*in li. nu. ho.* 10 & 24.) a sacrifice for the Ievves, and he often speaketh of his death as of a libation, host, or offering, as the fathers do of al Martyrs passions. Al vvhich dedicated and sanctified in Christes bloud and sacrifice, make the plenitude of his Passion, and haue a forcible crie, intercession, and satisfaction for the Church and the particular necessities thereof. In vvhich, as some do abound in good vvorkes and satisfactions (as S. Paul, vvho reckeneth vp his afflictions and glorieth in them 2 *Cor.* 11: and Iob, vvho auoucheth that his penalties farre surmounted his sinnes: and our Ladie much more, vvho neuer sinned, and yet suffered so great dolours) so other some do vvant, and are to be holpen by the aboundance of their fellovv-members.

Ro. 8, 17. *Leo ser.* 19. *de passio.*

How Christs merites are applied to vs, vvithout any iniurie to his death.

The vvorkes of one may satisfie for an other.

2. *Cor.* 1, 6. *Ro.* 9, 3. *Phil.* 2. 2 *Tim.* 4. *Iob* 6.

The ground of Indulgēces or pardons.

Vvhich entercourse of spiritual offices and the recompense of the vvants of one part by the store of the other, is the ground of the old libels of Indulgence vvhereof is treated before out of S. Cyprian (See the Annotations 2 *Cor.* 2. v. 10) and of al indulgences or pardons, vvhich the Church daily dispenseth vvith great iustice and mercie, by their hands in vvhom Christ hath put the vvord of our reconcilement, to vvhom he hath committed the keies to keepe and vse, his sheepe to feede, his mysteries and al his goods to dispense, his povver to binde and loose, his commission to remitte and reteine, and the stevvardship of his familie to giue euery one their meate and sustenance in due season.

CHAP. II.

He is careful for them, though he vvere neuer vvith them: that they rest in the vvonderful vvisedom vvhich is in Christian religion, and be not caried avvay either vvith Philosophie, to leaue Christ and to sacrifice to Angels: or vvith Iudaisme, to receiue any ceremonies of Moyses lavv.

FOR

1 FOR I vvil haue you knovv brethren, vvhat maner of care I haue for you and for them that are at Laodicia, and vvhosoeuer haue not seen my face in the flesh: 2 † that their hartes may be comforted, instructed in charitie, & vnto al the riches of the fulnes of vnderstãding, vnto the knovvledge of the mysterie of God 3 the Father of Christ IESVS, † in vvhom be al the treasures of vvisedom and knovvledge hidde. 4 † But this I say :: that 5 no man deceiue you in loftines of vvordes. † For although I be absent in body, yet in spirit I am vvith you: reioycing, & seeing your order, & the constancie of that your faith which 6 is in Christ. † Therfore as you haue receiued IESVS Christ 7 our Lord, vvalke in him, † rooted and built in him, and confirmed in the faith, as also you haue learned, abounding ˋin him' in thankes-giuing.

ˋin it

8 † Bevvare lest any man deceiue you " by philosophie, and vaine fallacie: according to the tradition of men, according to the elements of the vvorld, and not according to Christ. 9 † For in him dvvelleth al the fulnesse of the Godhead cor-10 porally: † and you are in him replenished, vvho is the head 11 in al Principalitie and Povver: † in vvhom al you are circumcised vvith circumcision not made by hand in spoiling 12 of the body of the flesh, in the circumcision of Christ, † buried vvith him in Baptisme: in vvhõ also you are risen againe by the faith of the operation of God, vvho raised him vp 13 from the dead. † And you *vvhen you vvere dead in the offenses and the prepuce of your flesh, did he quicken toge-14 ther vvith him: pardoning you al offenses, † vvyping out the hand vvriting ˋof decree' that vvas against vs, vvhich vvas contrarie to vs. and the same he hath taken out of the 15 vvay, fastening it to the crosse: † and spoiling the Principalities and Potestats, [c] hath ledde them confidently in open 16 shevv, triumphing them in him self. † Let no man therfore iudge you " in meate or in drinke, or in part of a festiual day, 17 or of the Nevv-moone, or of Sabboths: † vvhich are a shadovv of things to come, but the body Christs.

18 † Let no man seduce you, [b] vvilling in the humilitie and "religion of Angels, vvalking in the things vvhich he hath 19 not seen, in vaine puffed vp by the sense of his flesh, † and

Eph. 2, 1.

ˋby decrees

c ἐν αὐτῷ / δόγμασιν,

:: Heretikes do most commonly deceiue the people with eloquẽce namely such as haue it by the gift of nature, as the Heretikes of al ages had, & lightly al seditious persons, vvhich dravv the vulgar sort to sedition by the allurement of their tongue. Nothing (saith S. Hierom. *ep. 2. ad Nepotian.*) is so easie as vvith volubilitie of tongue to deceiue the vnlearned multitude, which whatsoeuer it vnderstandeth not, doth the more admire and wonder at the same. The Apostle here calleth it, πιθανολογίαν, persuasible speache.

b That is, wilful or selfwilled in voluntarie religiõ. for that is, θέλων ἐν θρησκείᾳ, whereof commeth the word folowing ἐθελοθρησκείᾳ, *Superstitiõ. v. 23. See Annot. v. 21.*

c ἐπιχορηγούμενον. That is, taking subministration of spiritual life and nourishment by grace from Christ the head.

"not holding the head, vvhereof the vvhole body by ioyntes and bandes being c serued & compacted, grovveth to the increase of God. † If then you be dead vvith Christ, from the 20 elements of this vvorld:" vvhy do you yet c decree as liuing in the vvorld? † Touch not, tast not, hãdle not: † which 21 things are al vnto destruction by the very vse, according to 22 the precepts and doctrines of men. † vvhich are in deede 23 "hauing a shevv of vvisedom in superstition and humilitie, and not to spare the body, not in any honour to the filling of the flesh.

c δογματίζεσθε

ANNOTATIONS
CHAP. II.

Philosophie and other humane sciences hovv profitable or hurtful to the Church of God.

8. *By Philosophie.*] Philosophie and al humane science, so long as they be subiect and obedient to Christ (as they be in the Schooles of Christian Catholike men) be not forbidden, but are greatly commended and be very profitable in the Church of God. Othervvise vvhere secular learning is made the rule of religion and commaundeth faith, there it is pernicious and the cause of al heresie and infidelitie. for the vvhich, S. Hierom and before him Tertullian call Philosophers, *the Patriarkes of Heretikes*, and declare that al the old heresies rose onely by to much admiring of prophane Philosophie. *Hiero. ad Ctesiph. cont. Pelag. c. 1. Tertul. de præscr. & cont. Hermog. & cont. Marcio. li. 5.* And so do these nevv sectes no doubt in many things. for, other arguments haue they none against the presence of Christ in the B. Sacrament but such as they borovv of Aristotle and his like, concerning quantitie, accidents, place, position, dimensions, senses, sight, tast, and other straites of reason, to vvhich they bring Christes mysteries. Al Philosophical arguments therfore against any article of our faith be here condemned as deceitful, and are called also here, *the tradition of men, and the elements of the vvorld.* The better to resist vvhich fallacies and traditions of Heathen men, the Schoole learning is necessarie, vvhich keepeth Philosophie in avve and order of faith, and vseth the same to vvithstand the Philosophical and sophistical deceites of the Heretikes and Heathen. So the great Philosophers S. Denys, S. Augustine, Clemens Alexandrinus, Iustine, Lactantius and the rest, vsed the same to the great honour of God and benefite of the Church. So came S. Cyprian, S. Ambrose, S. Hierom, and the Greeke fathers, furnished vvith al secular learning vnto the studie of Diuinitie, vvhereof see S. Hierom *ep. 84 ad Magnum Oratorem.*

The Protestants abuse Philosophie against the B. Sacrament.

Schoole learning.

16. *In meate.*] The Protestants vvilfully or ignorantly applie al these kindes of forbearing meates, to the Christian fastes: but it is by the circunstance of the text plaine (as S Augustine also teacheth) that the Iudaical obseruation and distinction of certaine cleane and vncleane meates is forbidden to the Colossians, vvho vvere in danger to be seduced by certaine Ievves, vnder pretence of holines to keepe the Lavv touching meates and festiuities and other like, vvhich the Apostle shevveth vvere onely shadovves of things to come: vvhich things are come, and therfore the said shadovves to cease. Vvhere he nameth the Sabboths and feastes of the nevv moone, that no man neede to doubt but that he speaketh onely of the Ievvish daies and kindes of fastes and feastes, and not of Christian holidaies or fasting daies at all.

Scriptures abused by the Protestants against Christian fasting & holydaies.

Aug. ep. 59. ad Paulinum in solut. 7. quæst.

18. *Religion of Angels.*] By the like false application of this text as of the other before, the Heretikes abuse it against the inuocation or honour of Angels vsed in the Catholike Church, vvhere the Apostle noteth the vvicked doctrine of Simon Magus and others (See S. Chrys. *ho. 7 in hunc locum.* and *Epiph. hær. 21.*) vvho taught, Angels to be our mediators and not Christ, *non tenens caput, not holding the head*, as the Apostle here speaketh, & prescribed sacrifices to be offered vnto them, meaning indifferently as vvel the il Angels as the good. Vvhich doctrine the said Heretike had of Plato, vvho taught, that spirites (vvhich he calleth *dæmones*) vvere to be honoured as mediators next to God. Against vvhich S. Augustine disputeth *li. 8. 9. & 10 de ciuit.* as the condemneth also the same vndue vvorship *li. 10 Confess. cap. 42.* S. Hierom (q. 10 ad Algasiam) expoundeth this also of il spirites or diuels, vvhom he proueth (out of S. Steuens sermon *Act. 7*) that the Ievves did vvorship, auouching that they serue them still, so many of them and so often as they obserue the Lavv. Of vvhich idolatrie also to Angels Theodorete speaketh vpon this place, declaring that the Ievves defended their superstition tovvardes Angels by that, that the Lavv vvas giuen by them,

S. Paules place cõcerning religion of Angels, explicated: and that

deceitfully

deceitfully at once inducing the Colossiãs, both to keepe the lavv, & to honouring of the Angels as the giuers of the same. Vvhereby diuers of the faithful vvere so seduced, that they forsooke Christ and his Church and seruice, and committed idolatrie to the said Angels. Against vvhich abominations the Counceel of Laodicia Cap. 35 tooke order, accursing all that forsooke our Sauiour and committed idolatrie to Angels, and contemning Christ, kept conuenticles in the name of spirites and Idols. of vvhich kinde of vvorship of Angels and Diuels see Clemens Alexand. Strom. 3. Tertulliã (*li. 5. cont. Marcion.*) expoundeth this place of the false teachers that feined them selues to haue reuelatiõ of Angels, that the Lavv should be kept touching differẽce of cleane & vncleane meates. Vvhich is very agreable to that * in the Epistle to Timothee, vvhere S. Paul calleth abstaining from meates after the Ievvish or heretical maner, *the doctrine of Diuels*: vvhereof see more in the annotation vpon that place. Haimo a godly aũcient vvriter, vpon this place, saith further, that some Philosophers of the Gentils and some of the Ievves also taught, that there vvere foure Angels Presidents of the foure elements of mans body, and that in feined hypocrisie (vvhich the Apostle here calleth humilitie) they pretended to vvorship by sacrifice the said Angels. Theophylacte expoundeth this feined humilitie, of certaine Heretikes, that pretending the mediatorship to be a derogation to Christs maiestie, vvorshipped Angels as the only mediators. Al vvhich vve set dovvne vvith more diligẽce, that the Heretikes may be ashamed to abuse this place against the due reuerence and respect or praiers made to the holy Angels. Vvhom the Scriptures record so often to offer our praiers vp to God, and to haue been lavvfully reuerenced of the Patriarkes, neuer as gods, but as Gods ministers and messengers. *Iosu.* 5, 14. *Tob.* 12, 12. *Gen.* 48, 16. *Angelus qui eruit me.* 1 *Tim.* 5, 21. And that they may be praied vnto, & can helpe & heare vs, see S. Hierom *in cap.* 10 *Danielis.* S. Ambrose *in Psal.* 118. *ser* 1. S. Augustine *li.* 10 *de ciuit. Dei c.* 12. Bede *li.* 4 *in Cantica c.* 24.

1. Tim. 4, 1.

the Protestants vvickedly abuse it against the due honour & inuocation of Angels.

19. *Not holding the head.*] Because he hath much a do vvith such false preachers as taught the people to preferre the Angels vvhich gaue the Lavv, or other vvhatsoeuer, before Christ: in this Epistle, and to the Ephesians, he often affirmeth Christ to be our head, yea and to be exalted far aboue al creatures, Angels, Potestats, Principalities, or vvhatsoeuer.

20. *Why doe you.*) A maruelous impudent translation of these vvordes in the English Bibles thus, *Why are you burdened vvith traditions?* Vvhereas the Greeke hath not that signification: but to make the name of Tradition odious, here they put it of purpose, not being in the Greeke: and in other places Where Traditions are cõmended (1 *Cor.* 11. *and* 2 *Thes.* 2.) and Where the Greeke is so most flatly (παραδόσεις) there they translate it, *Instructions, ordinances*, &c.

δογματίζεσθε

Heretical translation.

21. *Touch not.*] The Heretikes (as before and alvvaies) very vainely alleage this against the Catholike fastings: vvhen it is most cleere that the Apostle reprehendeth the foresaid false teachers that thought to make the Christians subiect to the obseruation of the ceremonies of the old Lavv, of not eating hogges, conies, hares flesh, and such like, not to touch a dead corps nor any place vvhere a vvomã in her floures had sittẽ, & other infinite doctrines of touching, tasting, vvashing, eating, and the rest, either commaunded to the old people by God, or (as many things vvere) voluntarily taken vp by them selues, sometime cleane against Gods ordinance, and often friuolous and superstitious. Vvhich sort as Christ in the Gospel, so here S. Paul calleth the precepts and doctrines of men, and superstition, and (as the Greeke vvord signifieth) * voluntarie vvorship, that is inuented by Heretikes of their ovvne head vvithout the vvarrant of Christ in the Scriptures, or the Holy Ghost in the Church, or any lavvful authoritie of such vvhom Christ commaundeth vs to obey. Against such Sect-Maisters therfore as vvould haue yoked the faithful againe vvith the Ievvish or Heretical fastes of Simon Magus and the like, S. Paul speaketh, and not of the Churches fastes or doctrines.

Scripture abused against the Churches fastes.

* ἐθελοθρησκεία

23. *Hauing a shevv.*] Againe the Heretikes of our time obiect, that these foresaid false teachers pretended holines, vvisedom, and chastisement of their bodies (for so S. Paul saith) by forbidding certaine meates according to the Ievves obseruation, euen as the Catholikes do. It is true they did so, and so do most vices imitate vertues. for if chastising of mens bodies and repressing their concupiscences and lustes vvere not godly, and if abstinence from some meates vvere not laudably and profitably vsed in the Church for the same purpose, no Heretikes (to induce the abolished obseruations and differences of meates of the Ievves, or the condemnation of certaine meates and creatures as abominable according to others) vvould haue falsely pretented the chastisement of their flesh, or made other shevv of vvisedom and pietie, to found their vnlavvful Heretical or Iudaical superstition concerning the same. The Catholike Church & her children, by the example of Christ, S. Iohn Baptist, the Apostles and other blessed men, do that lavvfully, godly, religiously, and sincerely in deede to the end aforesaid, vvhich these false Apostles onely pretended to do. So * S. Paul did chastise his body in deede, by vvatching, fasting, and many other afflictons, and that vvas lavvful and vvas true vvisedom and pietie in deede. The foresaid Heretikes not so, but to induce the Colossians to Iudaisme and other abominable errors, did but pretend these things in hypocrisie.

The hypocritical abstinẽce of old Heretikes, maketh nothĩg against true and sincere fasting, but cõmendeth it.

1 Cor. 9, 27. 2 Cor. 11, 27.

CHAP. III.

He exhorteth to mortifie and put of al corrupt maners of the old man, and to put on such vertues as are for the nevv man. 18 In particular also, vviues and husbands, children and parents, seruants and maisters, ech sort to do their duetie.

The Epistle vpon Easter eue.

HERFORE if you be risen vvith 1 Christ, seeke the things that are aboue: vvhere Christ is sitting on the right hand of God. † Minde the things that are 2 aboue, not the things that are vpon the earth. † For you are dead: and your life 3 is hidde vvith Christ in God. † Vvhen 4 Christ shal appeare, your life: then you also shal appeare vvith him in glorie. ⊣

† * Mortifie therfore your members that are vpon the 5 earth, fornication, vncleannesse, lust, euil concupiscence, and " auarice, vvhich is [c] the seruice of Idols. † for vvhich things 6 the vvrath of God commeth vpon the children of incredulitie. † in vvhich you also vvalked sometime, vvhen you 7 liued in them. † But novv lay you also al avvay: anger, indig- 8 nation, malice, blasphemie, filthie talke out of your mouth. † Lie not one to an other: * spoiling your selues of the old 9 man vvith his actes, † and " doing on the nevv, him that is 10 renevved vnto knovvledge, * according to the image of him that created him. † vvhere there is not, Gentile and 11 Ievve, circumcision and prepuce, Barbarous and Scythian. bonde and free: but al, and in al Christ.

Eph. 5, 3.

" εἰδωλολατρεία.

Eph. 4, 22.

Gen. 1, 26.

The Epistle vpon the 5 Sunday after the Epiphanie.

† Put ye on therfore as the elect of God, holy, and be- 12 loued, * the bovvels of mercie, benignitie, humilitie, modestie, patience, † supporting one an other: and pardoning 13 one an other, if any haue a quarel against any man. as also our Lord hath pardoned vs: so you also. † But aboue al these 14 things haue charitie, vvhich is the band of perfectiō: † & let 15 the peace of Christ [c] exult in your hartes, vvherein also you are called in one body: and be thankeful. † Let the vvord of 16 Christ dvvel in you aboundantly, in al vvisedom: teaching and admonishing your ovvne selues, vvith psalmes, hymnes, and spiritual cãticles, in grace singing in your hartes to God. 17 † Al vvhatsoeuer you doe in vvord or in vvorke, al things in the name of our Lord IESVS Christ, giuing thankes to God and the Father by him. ⊣

Eph. 4, 32.

" βραβευέτω, triumph and haue the victorie

† * Vvomen

Eph. 5, 22. 1.Pet. 3, 7. Eph.6,1. Eph. 6,5 Tit.2. 9. 1. Pet.2, 18.

18 † * Vvomen be subiect to your husbands, as it behoueth 19 in our Lord. † * Men, loue your vviues: and be not bitter 20 tovvard them. † * Children obey your parents in al things: 21 for that is vvel pleasing to our Lord. † Fathers, prouoke not your children to indignation: that they become not discou- 22 raged. † * Seruants, obey in al things, your maisters according to the flesh, not seruing to the eie, as pleasing men, 23 but in simplicitie of hart, fearing God. † Vvhatsoeuer you doe, vvorke it from the hart as to our Lord, and not to men: 24 † knovving that you shal receiue of our Lord the :: retri- 25 bution of inheritance. Serue our Lord Christ. † For he that doeth iniurie, shal receiue that vvhich he hath done vniustly: and * there is not acceptiō of persons vvith God.

:: Retribution or revvard for good vvorkes: ἀνταπόδοσις, vvhich signifieth rendering one for an other.

Deu.10, 17. Ro. 2, 11. Gal.2,6.

ANNOTATIONS
CHAP. III.

5. Auarice, vvhich is the seruice of idols.] Here is a maruelous impudent and folish corruption in the vulgar English Bible printed the yere 1577 and (as it seemeth) most authorised. Vvhere for their errour against the Images of Christ and his Saincts, and to make image and idol, al one: the translator, for that vvhich the Apostle saith in Greeke, *Couetousnes is idolatrie*, maketh him to say in English, *Couetousnes is vvorshipping of images*: as also *Eph. 5, 4* he translateth thus, *The couetous person is a vvorshipper of images*: for that vvhich the Apostle saith, *The couetous man is an idolater*, meaning spiritual idolatrie, because he maketh money his God. In vvhich sense to call this spiritual idolatrie, vvorshipping of images, is to ridiculous, and must needes procede of blinde heresie.

Heretical and foolish translation.

9. Doing on the nevv.] By this and the vvhole discourse of this chapter conteining an exhortation to good life, and to put on the habite of the nevv man vvith al vertues: vve may see, our iustice in Christ to be a very qualitie and forme inherent in our soul, adorning the same, and not an imputation onely of Christes righteousnes, or a hiding onely of our sinnes and vvickednes, vvhich the Heretikes falsely affirme to remaine in vs after baptisme and alvvaies during life. See S. Augustine *de pec. mer. & remis. li. 2 c. 7. & cont, Iulian. li. 6 c. 7.*

Iustice an inherent qualitie in vs.

CHAP. IIII.

He exhorteth to instance in praier, 5 and to vvisedom in behauiour. 7 He sendeth Tychicus. 10 He doeth commendations, 15 and inioyneth to be done.

1 YOV Maisters, that vvhich is iust and equal, doe to your seruants: knovving that you also haue a 2 Maister in heauen. † * Be instant in praier: vvat- 3 ching in it in thankes giuing, † * praying vvithal :: for vs also, that God may opē vnto vs the doore of speache to speake the mysterie of Christ (for the vvhich also I am 4 bound) † that I may manifest it, so as I ought to speake. 5 † * Vvalke vvith vvisedom tovvard them that be vvithout: redeeming

Luc.18,1 Eph. 6, 18. 2. Thes. 3,1

:: S. Paul euer much desireth the praiers of the faithful: vvhereby vve learne the great efficacie of them.

Eph. 5, 15.

redeeming the time. † Your talke alvvaies, in grace let it be 6 seasoned vvith salte: that you may knovv hovv you ought to ansvver euery man.

† The things that are about me, Tychicus our deerest 7 brother, and faithful minister, & fellovv-seruant in our Lord, vvil make you vnderstand al, † vvhom I haue sent to you 8 for this same purpose, that he may know the things that concerne you, and may comfort your hartes, † vvith * Onesi- 9 mus the most deere and faithful brother vvho is of you. Al things that are done here, shal they doe you to vnderstand.

Phile. 10.

† Aristarchus my fellovv-prisoner saluteth you, & Marke 10 the cosin-german of Barnabas (concerning vvhom you haue receiued commaundements, If he come to you, receiue him) † and Iesus that is called Iustus: vvho are of the Circumci- 11 sion. these only are my coadiutors in the kingdom of God: vvhich haue been a comfort to me. † Epaphras saluteth you 12 vvho is of you, the seruant of Christ IESVS, alvvaies careful for you in praiers, that you may stand perfect and ful in al the vvil of God. † For I giue him testimonie that he hath 13 much ∷ labour for you, and for them that be at Laodicia, and that are at Hierapolis. † * Luke the most deere physició salu- 14 teth you: and Demas. † Salute the brethren that are at 15 Laodicia: and Nymphas and the Church that is in his house. † And vvhen the epistle shal be read vvith you, make that 16 it be read also in the Church of the Laodicians: and that you read that vvhich is of the Laodicians. † And say to Ar- 17 chippus, See the ministerie vvhich thou hast receiued of our Lord, that thou fulfil it. † The salutation: vvith mine owne 18 hand, Paules. Be mindeful of my bandes. Grace be vvith you. Amen.

∷ He did not only pray, but tooke other great paines to procure Gods grace for the Colossians: perhaps by watching, fasting, and doing other penance of body: that God would not suffer them to fall from their receiued faith to the secte of Simon Magus or the Iudaizing christiās.

2 Tim. 4, 10. 11

THE

THE ARGVMENT OF THE FIRST EPISTLE OF S. PAVL TO THE THESSALONIANS.

HOVV S. Paul vvith Silas (or Siluanus) and Timothee according to a vision calling him out of Asia into Macedonia, came to Philippi being the first citie thereof, vve reade Act. 16. And hovv againe from Philippi, after scourging and imprisoning there, he came to Thessalonica *being the head citie of that countrie, vve reade Act. 17. vvhere after 3 vveekes preaching, the Ievves stirred the citie against them, and pursued them also to Beræa: so that Paul vvas conueied from thence to Athens, vvhere he expected the cōming of Silas & Timothee from the foresaid Beræa in Macedonia, but receiued them (as vve haue Act. 18.) at Corinth in Achaia.*

Hauing therefore left the Thessalonians in such persecution, and being careful to knovv hovv they did in it, he vvas desirous to returne vnto them, as he signifieth in the 2 chapter of this Epistle v. 17. But (as he there addeth) Satan hindered vs. *therefore tarying himself at Athens, he sendeth Timothee vnto them. at vvhose returne vnderstanding their constancie, he is much comforted, as he declareth c. 3. So then they are all three together at the vvriting of this Epistle, as also vve haue in the title of it:* Paul and Siluanus and Timothee to the Church of the Thessalonians. *And therefore it seemeth to haue bene vvritten at Corinth, not at Athens: because after the sending of Timothee to Thessalonica, they mette not at Athens againe, but at Corinth.*

The first three chapters of it are, to confirme and comfort them against the tentations of those persecutions. The other tvvo are of exhortation, to liue according to his preceptes, namely in sanctification of their bodies, and not in fornication: to loue one an other: to comfort one an other about their frendes departed, vvith the doctrine of the Resurrection, and vvith continuall preparation to die: the laietie to obey, and the Cleargie to be diligent in euery point of their office.

THE FIRST EPISTLE OF PAVL TO THE THESSALONIANS.

Chap. I.

He thanketh God for them, 4 and gathereth that they are elect, because his preaching at their first conuersion vvas vvith diuine povver, and they on the other side receiued it vvith al ioy, notvvithstanding the great persecution that vvas raised against them.

PAVL and Siluanus and Timothee to the 1 Church of the Thessalonians in God the Father, & our Lord IESVS Christ. Grace to you and peace.

The Epistle vpon the 6 Sunday after the Epiphanie.

† Vve giue thankes to God alvvaies 2 for al you: making a memorie of you in our praiers without intermissiō, † mindeful 3 of the vvorke of your faith and labour, and of the charitie, & of the enduring of the hope of our Lord IESVS Christ, before God and our father: † knovving brethren 4 beloued of God, your election: † that our Gospel hath not 5 been to you in word only, but in povver and the holy Ghost, and in much fulnesse, as you knovv vvhat maner of men vve haue been among you for your sakes. † And you became 6 "folovvers of vs, & of our Lord: receiuing the vvord in much tribulation, vvith ioy of the holy Ghost: † so that you were 7 made a paterne to al that beleeue in Macedonia & in Achaia. † For from you vvas bruited the vvord of our Lord: not on- 8 ly in Macedonia and in Achaia, but in euery place, your faith vvhich is to God vvard, is proceded, so that it is not necessarie for vs to speake any thing. † For they them selues re- 9 port of vs vvhat maner of entring vve had to you: and how you are turned to God :: from Idols, to serue the liuing and true God, † and to expect his Sonne from heauen (vvhom 10 he

:: In this and the like places the Heretikes malitiously & most falsely translate, construe, & apply al things meāt of the Heathē idols, to the memories and images of Christ and his saincts, namely the English Bibles of the yeres 1562. 1577. See the Annotatiō 1 Io. 5, 21.

he raised vp from the dead) IESVS, vvho hath deliuered vs from the vvrath to come. ⊣

ANNOTATIONS
CHAP. I.

6. Folovvers of vs.] S. Paul is bold to commend them for imitation of him, yea and to ioyne him self in that point vvith Christ, to be their paterne to vvalke after. Vvhere without curiositie he nameth him self first, and our Lord aftervvard, because he vvas a more neere and ready obiect then Christ, vvho vvas not nor could not be folovved but through the preaching and conuersation of the Apostle, vvho vvas in their sight or hearing. And this imitation of some holy man or other, hath made so many Religious men of diuers orders and rules, al tending to the better imitation of Christ our Lord. See the like vvordes of the Apostle, 1 Cor. 11, 1. *and Philip.* 3,17.

Religious persons imitation of diuers holy men is the imitatiō of Christ him self.

CHAP. II.

He calleth euen them selues to vvitnes, that his preaching vnto them vvas as he said, in most commendable maner. 13 And againe on the other side he thanketh God for their maner of receiuing it: that is, vvith al ioy, notvvithstanding the persecution of their ovvne citizens.

1 FOR your selues knovv, brethren, our entrance vnto you, that it vvas not vaine: 2 † but [c] hauing suffered before and * been abused vvith contumelies (as you knovv) at Philippi, vve had confidence in our God, to speake vnto you the Gospel of God in much carefulnes. 3 † For our exhortation vvas not of errour, nor of vncleannesse, nor in deceite: 4 † but as vve vvere approued of God that the Gospel should be committed to vs, so vve speake: not as pleasing men, but God, vvho proueth our hartes. 5 † For neither haue we been at any time in the vvord of adulation, as you knovv: nor in occasion of auarice, God is vvitnes: 6 † nor seeking glorie of men, neither of you, nor of others. 7 † Vvhereas vve might haue been a burdē to you, as the Apostles of Christ: but vve became 'children' in the middes of you, as if a nource should cherish her children: 8 † so hauing a desire to you, vve would gladly deliuer vnto you not only the Gospel of God, but also our ovvne soules: because you are become most deere vnto vs. 9 † For you are mindeful, brethren, of * our labour and toile, day & night vvorking, lest vve should charge any of you, vve preached among you the Gospel of God. 10 † You are

Act. 16, 12. 23.

c A notable example for Catholike preachers, and passing comfortable, whē in the middes of persecutiōs and reproches they preache sincerely, to please God & not men.

milde

Act. 20, 34. 1. Cor. 4, 12. 2. Thes. 3,

are vvitnesses and God, hovv holily and iustly and vvithout blame, vve haue been to you that did beleeue. † as you 11 knovv in vvhat maner we desiring and comforting you, haue adiured euery one of you (as a father his children) that you vvould vvalke vvorthie of God, vvho hath called you into his kingdom and glorie.

† Therfore vve also giue thankes to God vvithout in- 12 termission: because that vvhen you had receiued of vs the vvord of the hearing of God, you receiued it not as the vvord of men, but (as it is in deede) " the vvord of God, who vvorketh in you that haue beleeued. † For you, brethren, 13 are become folovvers of the churches of God that be in Iewrie, in Christ IESVS: for you also haue suffered the same things of your ovvne lineage, as they also of the Ievves, † vvho 14 both killed our Lord IESVS, and the Prophets, and haue persecuted vs, and please not God, and are aduersaries to al men, † prohibiting vs to speake to the Gentiles that they may be 15 saued, to make vp their sinnes alvvaies. for the vvrath of God is come vpon them euen to the end. † But vve, brethren, [c] de- 16 priued of you for a short time, in sight, not in hart: haue hastened the more aboundantly to see your face vvith much desire. † For vve vvould haue come to you, I Paul certes, 17 once and againe: but Satan hath hindered vs. † For vvhat is 18 our hope, or ioy, or crovvne of glorie? ∴ Are not you before our Lord IESVS Christ in his comming? † For you are 19 our glorie and ioy.

∴ If the Apostle vvithout iniurie to god, in right good sense call his scholers the Thessaloniãs, his hope, ioy, glorie: vvhy blaspheme the Protestãts the Cath. Church & her childrẽ for terming our B. Ladie or other Sainctes, their hope, for the special confidẽce they haue in their praiers?

c ἀπορφανισθέντες

ANNOTATIONS
CHAP. II.

Not only the vvrittẽ vvord, is the vvord of God.

12. *The vvord of God.*] The Aduersaries vvil haue no vvord of God but that vvhich is vvritten and conteined in the Scripture: but here they might learne that al Paules preaching before he vvrote to them, vvas the very vvord of God. They might also learne that vvhat so euer the lavvful Apostles, Pastors, and Priestes of Gods Church preach in the vnitie of the same Church, is to be taken for Gods ovvne vvord, and ought not to be reputed of them for doctrines of men or Pharisaical traditions, as they falsly call canons, precepts, and decrees of holy Church.

CHAP. III.

Because he could not come him self, as he desired, he sent Timothee. 6 At vvhose returne novv vnderstanding that they stand stil stedfast, notvvithstãding al those persecutions, he reioyceth excedingly: 10 praying that he may see them againe, 12 and for their increase in charitie.

FOR

1 FOR the vvhich cause forbearing no longer, it pleased vs to remaine at Athens, alone. 2 † And vve sent Timothee our brother, & the minister of God in the Gospel of Christ, to confirme you and exhort you for your faith, 3 † that no man be moued in these tribulations, for your selues knovv, that vve are appointed to this. 4 † For euen vvhẽ vve vvere vvith you, vve foretold you that vve should suffer tribulatiõs, as also it is come to passe, & you knovv. 5 † Therfore I also forbearing no lõger, sent to knovv your faith: lest perhaps he that tempteth, hath tempted you, & our labour be made vaine. 6 † But now *Timothee cõming vnto vs frõ you, & reporting to vs your faith & charitie, and that you haue a good remẽbrance of vs alvvaies, desiring to see vs, as vve also you: 7 † therfore vve are cõforted, brethrẽ, in you, in al our necessitie & tribulation, by your faith, 8 † because novv vve liue, if you stand in our Lord. 9 † For vvhat thankes-giuing can vve render to God for you, in al ioy vvherevvith vve reioyce for you before our God, 10 † night and day more aboundantly praying that vve may ⁖see your face, and may accomplish those things that vvant of your faith.

Act. 18, 5.

⁖ Though letters or epistles in absẽce giue great comfort and confirmation in faith, yet it is preaching in presence by vvhich the faith of Christ and true religion is alvvais both begunne and accomplished.

11 † And God him self and our Father, and our Lord IESVS Christ direct our vvay to you. 12 † And our Lord multiplie you, and make your charitie abound one to an other, & tovvard al men: as vve also in you, 13 † to cõfirme your hartes vvithout blame, in holinesse, before God and our Father, in the comming of our Lord IESVS Christ vvith al his Saincts. Amen.

CHAP. IIII.

He exhorteth them to liue as he taught them: and namely to absteine from al fornicatiõ, 9 to loue one an other, 11 to meddle onely vvith their ovvne matters, 12 to behaue them selues vvel tovvard the Infidels. 13 Touching their frendes departed, he comforteth them, shevving that they shal meete againe at the Resurrection, and be vvith Christ for euer.

The Epistle vpon the 2 Sunday in Lent.

1 FOR the rest therfore, brethren, vve desire & beseeche you in our Lord IESVS, that as you haue receiued of vs hovv you ought to vvalke, and to please God, as also you doe vvalke, that you abounde more. 2 † For you knovv vvhat precepts I haue giuen

uen to you by our Lord IESVS. † For this is the vvil of 3 God, your sanctificatiō: that you abstaine from fornication, † that euery one may knovv to possesse his vessel in sanctifi- 4 cation and honour: † not in the passion of lust, as also the 5 Gentiles that knovv not God, † and that no man ouergoe, 6 nor circumuent his brother in businesse: because our Lord is reuenger of al these things, as vve haue foretold you & haue testified. † For God hath not called vs into vncleannesse: 7 but into sanctification. ⁋ † Therfore he that despiseth these 8 things, despiseth" not man but God, vvho also hath giuen his holy Spirit in vs.

c Al Catholike Christians make one fraternitie or brotherhod.

† But concerning the charitie of the[c] fraternitie, vve haue 9 no neede to vvrite to you: † for * your selues haue learned of God to loue one an other. † Yea and you doe it tovvard 10 al the brethren in al Macedonia. But vve desire you brethrē, 11 that you :: aboūd more: † & that you employ your indeuour to be quiet, & that you doe your ovvne businesse, & vvorke vvith your ovvne handes, as we haue cōmaunded you: † and 12 that you vvalke honestly tovvard them that are vvithout: and neede nothing of any mans.

Io. 13,34 15, 17. Heb. 13,1

:: Christian men ought to procede and profite continually in good vvorkes and iustification.

The Epistle in a Masse for the dead vpon the day of the burial or deposition.

† And vve vvil not haue you ignorant, brethren, concer- 13 ning them that" sleepe, that you be not sorovvful, as also others that haue no hope. † For if vve beleeue that IESVS 14 died and rose againe, so also God them that haue slept by IESVS vvil bring vvith him. † For this vve say to you in 15 the vvord of our Lord, * that :: vve vvhich liue, vvhich are remaining in the aduent of our Lord, shal not preuent them that haue slept. † For our Lord him self in commaundement 16 and in the voice of an * Archangel and in the trōpet of God vvil descend from heauen: and the dead that are in Christ, shal rise againe first. † Then vve that liue, that are left, vvith- 17 al shal be taken vp vvith them in the cloudes to meete Christ, into the aire, and so alvvaies vve shal be vvith our Lord. † Therfore cōfort ye one an other in these vvordes. ⁋ 18

:: He speaketh in the person of those that shal be aliue vvhen our Sauiour returneth to iudgement.

1. Cor. 15, 23.

Mt. 24, 31. 1. Cor. 15, 52.

ANNOTATIONS
CHAP. IIII.

The precepts of the Church.

8. *Not man but God.*] He that despiseth the Churches or her lavvful Pastors precepts, offendeth no lesse then if he contemned Gods expresse commaundements. For they be of the holy Ghost, and are not to be counted among the commaundements of men onely.

13. *Sleepe.*] Some Heretikes peruersly inferred of this that the soules did sleepe til the day of iudgement: vvhere it is meant of the bodies onely.

CAHP.

CHAP. V.

To talke of the time of the Resurrection is not necessarie, but to prepare our selues against that time so sodaine and so terrible to the vnprepared. 12 He beseecheth the laietie to be obedient, 14 and the Clergie to be vigilant, vvith many short precepts moe.

1 AND of the times and momentes, brethren, 2 you neede not that vve vvrite to you. † For your selues knovv perfectly that the day of our Lord shal so come, as * a theefe in the night. 3 † For vvhen they shal say, peace & securitie: then shal sodaine destruction come vpon them, as the paines to her that is vvith childe, and they shal not escape. 4 † But you brethren are not in darknesse: that the same day may, as a theefe ouertake you.

Mt. 24, 44. 2 Pet. 3, 10 Apoc. 3, 3 16, 15.

5 † For al you are the children of light, and children of the 6 day: vve are not of the night nor of darknesse. † Therfore let vs not sleepe as also others: but let vs vvatch and be 7 sober. † For they that sleepe, sleepe in the night: & they that 8 be drunke, be drunke in the night. † But vve that are of the day, are sober, * hauing on the breast-plate of faith and ∷ charitie, and a helmet, the hope of saluation. 9 † For God hath not appointed vs vnto vvrath, but vnto the purchasing of 10 saluation by our Lord IESVS Christ, † vvho died for vs: that vvhether vve vvatch, or sleepe, vve may liue together 11 vvith him. † For the vvhich cause comfort one an other: & edifie one an other, as also you doe.

Esa. 59, 17. Eph. 6, 17.

∷ A christian mans vvhole armour is not faith only, but al the three vertues here named.

12 † And vve beseeche you brethren, that you vvil knovv them that labour among you, and that gouerne you in our 13 Lord, and admonish you: † that you haue them more aboudātly in charitie for their vvorke. haue peace vvith them. 14 † [b] And vve beseeche you brethren, admonish the vnquiet, comfort the vveake-minded, beare vp the vveake, be patient 15 to al. † See that * none render euil for euil to any man: but 16 alvvaies that vvhich is good pursue tovvards eche other, and 17 tovvards al. † Alvvaies reioyce. † [c] Pray * vvithout inter-18 mission. † In al things giue thankes. for this is the vvil of 19 God in Christ IESVS in al you. † The Spirit extinguish not. 20 † Prophecies despise not. † But " prooue al things: hold that 21 which is good. † From al appearance of euil refraine your 22 selues.

Pro. 17, 13. Ro. 12 1. Pet. 3, 9. Luc. 18, 1.

b The Epistle vpō the Imber Saturday in Lent.

c To desire eternal life of him that onely can giue it, is to pray vvithout intermission: but because that desire is oftē by worldly cares cooled, certaie houres and times of vocal praier vvere appointed. *See S. Aug. ep. 121 ad Probam.*

23 † And the God of peace him self sanctifie you in al things: that

that your vvhole spirit, and soule and body vvithout blame may be preserued in the comming of our Lord IESVS Christ. ⊣ † He is faithful, that hath called you, vvho also 24 vvil doe it. † Brethren pray for vs. † Salute al the brethren 25 in a holy kisse. † I adiure you by our Lord that this epistle 26 be read to al the holy brethren. † The grace of our Lord 27 IESVS Christ be vvith you. Amen. 28

ANNOTAT. CHAP. V.

Not rashly to credite euery spirit.

10 *But prooue.*] Though vve may not extinguish the spirit, nor cōtemne the prophets, yet vve must bevvare vve be not deceiued by geuing to light credite to euery one that vaūteth him self of the spirit, as Arch-heretikes euer did. vve must trie thē by the doctrine of the Apostles & the Spirit of the Catholike Church, vvh ich can not beguile v

THE ARGVMENT OF THE SECOND EPISTLE OF S. PAVL TO THE THESSALONIANS.

THE second to the Thessalonians hath in the title as the first: Paul and Siluanus and Timothee, *&c. And therfore it seemeth to haue bene vvritten in the same place, to vvitte, at Corinth, vvhere they remained* *a yere and sixe moneths, *& straight vpon their ansvver to the first epistle.*

Act. 18. v. 11.

First he thanketh God for their increase, and perseuērance (comforting them againe in those persecutions) and praieth for their accomplishment. Secondly he assureth them that the day of Iudgement is not at hand, putting them in remembrāce vvhat he told them thereof by vvord of mouth, vvhen he vvas present (as therfore he biddeth them aftervvard * *to hold his Traditions vnvvritten, no lesse then the vvritten,) to vvitte, that all those persecutions and heresies, raised then, and aftervvard against the Catholike Church, vvere but the mysterie of Antichrist, and not Antichrist him self. but that there should come at length a plaine Apostasie, & thē (the vvhole forerunning mysterie being once perfitly vvrought) should follovv the reuelation of Antichrist him self in person (as after all the mysteries of the old Testament, Christ* IESVS *our Lord came him self in the fulnes of time.) And then at length after all this the day of Iudgement and second comming of Christ shal be at hand, and not before, vvhatsoeuer pretense of vision, or of some speach of mine (saith S. Paul) any make to seduce you vvithal, or of my former epistle, or any other. For vvhich cause also in the end of this epistle, he biddeth them to knovv his hand,* vvhich is a signe in euery epistle.

* c. 2. v. 15.

Lastly he requesteth their praiers, and requireth them to keepe his commaundements and Traditions, namely that the poore vvhich are able get their ovvne liuing vvith vvorking, as he also gaue them example, though he vvere not bound thereto.

THE

THE SECOND EPISTLE OF PAVL TO THE THESSALONIANS.

Chap. I.

He thanketh God for their increase in faith and charitie, and constancie in persecution (assuring them that they merite thereby the kingdom of God, as their persecutors do damnation:) 11 and also praieth for their accomplishment.

1 PAVL and Siluanus and Timothee: to the churche of the Thessalonians in God our Father and our Lord IESVS Christ. 2 † Grace to you and peace from God our Father and our Lord IESVS Christ.

3 † Vve ought to giue thankes alvvaies to God for you brethren, so as meete is, because your faith increaseth excedingly, and the charitie of euery one of you 4 aboundeth tovvards eche other: † so that vve our selues also glorie in you in the churches of God, for your patience, and faith in al your persecutions and tribulations, vvhich 5 you sustaine † for an example of the iust iudgemét of God, that :: you may be [c] counted vvorthie of the kingdom of 6 God, for the vvhich also you suffer. † if yet it be iust vvith 7 God to repay tribulation, to them that vexe you: † and to you that are vexed, rest with vs in the reuelation of our Lord 8 IESVS from heauen vvith the Angels of his povver, † in flame of fire, giuing reuenge to them that knovv not God, & 9 that obey not the Gospel of our Lord IESVS Christ. † vvho shal suffer eternal paines in destruction, from the face of our 10 Lord and from the glorie of his povver: † vvhen he shal come to be :: glorified in his sainctes, and to be made maruelous in al them that haue beleeued, because our testimonie

c καταξιωθῆναι ὑμᾶς

1. Thes. 4, 16.

:: Note that by constant and patient suffering of afflictiós for christmen are made vvorthie (so the Greeke signifieth, as the Aduersaries them selues trãslate v. 11.) of the crowne or kingdom of heauen, and so do merite and deserue the same. See Anno. Luc. 20, 35. And the Apostle here saith that it is Gods iustice no lesse to repay glorie to the afflicted, then to render punishmét to them that afflict, because of their contrarie deserts or merites.

:: Christ shal be glorified in his Sainctes, that is, by the

concerning you vvas credited in that day. † Vvherein also 11 vve pray alvvaies for you, that our God [c] make you vvorthie of his vocation, and accomplish al the good pleasure of his goodnesse & the vvorke of faith in povver, † that the name 12 of our Lord IESVS Christ may be glorified in you, and you in him, according to the grace of our God, and of our Lord IESVS Christ.

great and vnspeakable honour & exaltatiō of them he shal be honoured, as now he is: the honour vvhich the Church doth to them, not diminishing Christs glorie (as the Aduersaries folishly pretēd) but excedingly augmenting the same.

[c] ἀξιώσῃ

CHAP. II.

He requireth them, in no case to thinke that Domesday is at hand, 3 repeating vnto them, that there must before come first a reuolt, secondly the reuelation also of Antichrist him self in person, and that Antichrist shal not permit any God to be vvorshipped but onely him self: that also vvith his lying vvonders he shal vvinne to him the incredulous Ievves. But Christ shal come then immediatly in maiestie, and destroy him and his. 13 Therfore he thanketh God for the faith of the Thessalonians, 15 and biddeth them sticke to his Traditions both vvritten and vnvvritten, & praieth God to cōfirme them.

The Epistle in the Imber Saturday of Aduent.

ND vve desire you, brethren, by the cō- 1 ming of our Lord IESVS Christ, and of our congregatiō into him: † that you be 2 not easily moued from your sense, nor be terrified, neither by spirit, nor by word, nor by epistle as sent by vs, "as though the day of our Lord vvere at hand. † Let 3 no man seduce you by any meanes, for " vnlesse there come [c] a reuolt first, and " the man of sinne be reuealed, the sonne of perdition, † vvhich is an aduersarie & is" extolled :: aboue 4 al that is called God, or that is vvorshipped, so that he sitteth " in the temple of God, shevving him self as though he were God. † Remember you not, that vvhen I vvas yet vvith 5 you, I told you these things? † And novv " vvhat letteth, you 6 knovv: that he may be reuealed in his time. († For novv the 7 mysterie of iniquitie vvorketh: only that he vvhich novv holdeth, doe hold, vntil he be taken out of the vvay.) † And 8 then that vvicked one shal be reuealed * vvhom our Lord IESVS shal kil vvith the spirit of his mouth: & shal destroy vvith the manifestation of his aduent, him, † vvhose com- 9 ming is according to the operatiō of Satan," in al povver, and lying signes and vvonders, † and in al seducing of iniquitie 10 to them that perish, for that they haue not receiued the charitie of the truth that they might be saued. † Therfore 11 :: God vvil send them the operation of errour, to beleeue lying:

:: Hovv then can the Pope be Antichrist, as the Heretikes fondly blaspheme, vvho is so far from being exalted aboue God, that he praieth most humbly not onely to Christ, but also to his B. mother and al his Saincts.

:: *Deus mittet* (saith S. Aug. *li. 20. de Ci. c. 19.*) *quia Deus Diabolum facere ista permittet. God wil send, because God wil pmit the Diuel to do these things.* Whereby vve may take a general rule that Gods action or working in such things is his permissiō. *See Annot. Ro. 1, 24.*

[c] ἀποστασία

* *Es. 11, 4.*

12 lying: † that al may be iudged vvhich haue not beleeued the truth, but haue consented to iniquitie.

13 † But vve ought to giue thãkes to God alvvaies for you, brethrẽ beloued of God, that he hath chosen you first-fruites vnto saluation, in sanctification of spirit and faith of the

14 truth: † into the vvhich also he hath called you by our Gospel, vnto the purchasing of the glorie of our Lord IESVS

15 Christ. † Therfore brethren stand: and hold [c] the " traditiõs vvhich you haue learned, vvhether it be by vvord, or by our

16 epistle. † And our Lord IESVS Christ him self, and God & our father vvhich hath loued vs, and hath giuen eternal con-

17 solation, and good hope in grace, † [c] exhort your hartes, and confirme you in euery good vvorke and vvorde.

c τὰς παραδόσεις

c παρακαλέσαι

c This vvord of exhorting implieth in it comfort and consolation: as 2. Cor. 1. v. 4. & 6.

ANNOTATIONS
CHAP. II.

2. *As though the day.*] The curiositie of man fed by Satans deceites, hath sought to knovv and to giue out to the vvorld, such things as God vvil not impart to him, nor be necessarie or profitable for him to knovv: so farre, that both in the Apostles daies and often aftervvard, some haue feined reuelations, some falsely gathered out of the Scriptures, some presumed to calculate and coniecte by the starres, and giuen furth to the vvorld a certaine time of Christes coming to iudgement. Al vvhich seducers be here noted in the person of some that vvere about to deceiue the Thessalonians therein. And S. Augustine (in his 80 Epistle ad Hesychium) proueth that no man can be assured by the Scriptures of the day, yere, or age, that the end of the vvorld or the second Aduent shal be.

The day of iudgment vncertaine, and to be left to Gods secretes.

3. *Vnles there come a reuolt first.*] Though vve can not be assured of the moment, houre, or any certaine time of our Lordes cõming, yet he vvarranteth vs that it vvil not be before certaine things be fulfilled, vvhich must come to passe by the course of Gods prouidence and permission before, vvhich are diuers, vvhereof in other places of Scriptures vve be forevvarned. Here he vvarneth vs of tvvo specially, of a reuolt, defection or an apostasie, and of the comming or reuelation of Antichrist. Vvhich tvvo pertaine in effect both to one, either depending of the other, and shal fall (as it may be thought) neere together, and therfore S. Augustine maketh them but one thing.

Two special signes before the later day: a general apostasie, and the comming of Antichrist.

This apostasie or reuolt, by the iudgement in maner of al auncient vvriters, is the general forsaking & fall of the Romane empire. So Tertullian *li. de resur. carnis.* S. Hierom *q.* 11 *ad Algasiam.* S. Chrysostom *ho.* 4. and S. Ambrose vpon this place, S. Augustine *De Ciuit. Dei li.* 20 *c.* 19. Al vvhich fathers and the rest * Caluin presumptuously condemneth of errour and follie herein, for that their exposition agreeth not vvith his and his fellovves blasphemous fiction that the Pope should be Antichrist. To establish vvhich false impietie, they interprete this reuolt or apostasie to be a general reuolt of the visible Church from God, vvhose house or building (they say) vvas sodenly destroied, and lay many yeres ruined, and ruled onely by Satan and Antichrist. So saith the foresaid Arch-heretike here, though for the aduantage of his defence and as the matter els vvhere requireth, he seemeth (as al their fashion is) to speake in other places quite contrarie: but vvith such colour and collusion of vvordes, that neither other men nor him self can tell vvhat he vvould haue or say. And his fathers Vvicleffe and Luther, his fellovves and folovvers Illyricus, Beza, and the rest, are (for the time of the Churches falling from Christ) so various among them selues, and so contrarie to him, that it is horrible to see their confusion, and a pitieful case that any reasonable man vvil folovv such companions to euident perdition.

Caluin. in hunc locũ.

The heretikes interpretatiõ of this apostasie, & their cõdéning of the fathers.

But concerning this errour and falshod of the Churches defection or reuolt, it is refuted sufficiently by S. Augustine against the Donatistes in many places. Vvhere he proueth that the Church shal not faile to the vvorldes end, no not in the time of Antichrist: affirming them to deny Christ, and to robbe him of his glorie & inheritance bought vvith his bloud, vvhich teach that the Church may faile or perish. *Li. de vnit. Ec. c.* 12. 13. *De Ciuit. li.* 20 *c.* 8. *In Psal.* 85 *ad illud, Tu solus Deus*

There can be no apostasie of the visible Churche from God.

magnus.ps.70 Conc. 2.& Psal. 60. De vtil.cred. c. 8. S. Hierom refuteth the same vvicked Heresie in the *Luciferians, prouing against them, that they make God subiect to the Diuel, and a poore miserable Christ, that imagine the Church his body may either perish or be driuen to any corner of the vvorld. both of them ansvver to the Heretikes arguments grounded on Scriptures falsely vnderstood, vvhich vvere to long here to rehearse. It is ynough for the Christian reader to knovv, that it is an old deceite and excuse of al Heretikes and Schismatikes, for defence of their forsaking Gods Church, that the Church is perished, or remaineth hidden, or in them selues onely and in those places vvhere they and their folovvers dvvel: to knovv also, that this is reproued by the holy Doctors of the primitiue Church, and that it is against Christes honour, povver, prouidence, and promis.

Dialog. adu. Lucifer. c. 6.

If the Aduersaries had said that this reuolt vvhich the Apostle foretelleth shal come before the vvorldes end, is meant of great numbers of Heretikes & Apostataes reuolting from the Church, they had said truth of them selues and such others, vvhom S. Iohn calleth Antichristes. And it is very like (be it spoken vnder the correction of Gods Church and al learned Catholikes) that this great defection or reuolt shal not be onely from the Romane empire, but specially from the Romane Church, and vvithal from most points of Christian religion. not that the Catholike Christians, either in the time of Antichrist or before, shal refuse to obey the same, but for that neere to the time of Antichrist and the consummation of the vvorld, there is like to be a great reuolt of kingdoms, peoples, and Prouinces from the open external obedience and communion thereof. Vvhich reuolt hauing been begunne and continued by Heretikes of diuers ages, resisting & hating the Seate of Peter (vvhich they called *cathedram pestilentiæ, the chaire of pestilence,* * in S. Augustines daies) because it is Christes fort erected against Hel gates and al Heretikes, and being novv vvonderfully increased by these of our daies the next precursors of Antichrist as it may seeme, shal be fully atchieued a litle before the end of the vvorld by Antichrist him self. though euen then also, vvhen for the fevv daies of Antichristes reigne the external state of the Romane Church and publike entercourse of the faithful vvith the same may cease, yet the due honour and obedience of the Christians tovvard it, and communion in hart vvith it, and practise thereof in secrete, and open confessing thereof if occasion require, shal not cease; no more then it doth novv in the Christians of Cypres and other places vvhere open entercourse is forbidden.

1 Io. 2, v. 18.

It is very like, the Apostle speaketh of a great apostasie frō the See of Rome, and from most articles of the Catho. faith.

li. 2. cont. lit. Petil. c. 51.

This is certaine and vvonderful in al vvise mens eies, and must needes be of Gods prouidence, & a singular prerogatiue, that this Seate of Peter standeth, vvhen al other Apostolike Sees be gone: that it stood there for certaine ages together vvith the secular seate of the Empire: that the Popes stood vvithout vvealth, povver, or humane defense, the Emperours knovving, vvitting, and seeking to destroy them, and putting to the svvord aboue thirtie of them one after an other, yea and being as much afraid of them as if they had been *æmuli imperij, Competitors of their Empire,* as S. Cyprian noteth (*epist. 52 ad Antonianum. num. 3*) of S. Cornelius Pope in his daies, and Decius then Emperour: againe, that the Emperours aftervvard yelded vp the citie vnto them, continuing for al that in the Emperial dignitie stil: that the successors of those that persecuted them, laid dovvne their crovvnes before their Seate and sepulcres, honouring the very memories and Relikes of the poore men vvhom their predecessors killed: that novv vvel neere these 1600 yeres this Seat standeth, as at the beginning in continual miserie, so novv of long time for the most part in prosperitie, vvithout al mutation in effect, as no other kingdom or State in the vvorld hath done, euery one of them in the said space being manifoldly altered. It standeth (vve say) al this vvhile (to vse S. Augustines vvordes *de vtil. cred. c. 17.*) *Frustra circumlatrantibus hæreticis, the Heretikes in vaine barking about it,* not the first Heathen Emperours, not the Gothes and Vandals, not the Turke, not any sackes or massakers by Alaricus, Gensericus, Attila, Borbon, and others, not the emulation of secular Princes, vvere they kings or Emperours, not the Popes ovvne diuisions among them selues and manifold difficulties and dangers in their elections, not the great vices vvhich haue been noted in some of their persons, not al these nor any other endeuour or scādal could yet preuaile against the See of Rome, nor is euer like to preuaile til the end of the vvorld dravv neere, at vvhich time this reuolt (here spoken of by the Apostle) may be in such sort as is said before, and more shal be said in the Annotations next folovving.

The wonderful prouidēce of God in preseruing the See of Rome more then al other states, notwithstanding manifold dangers and scandals.

3. The man of sinne.] There vvere many euen in the Apostles time (as vve see by the 4 Chapter of S. Iohns first epistle and in the vvritings of the aūcient fathers) that vvere forerunners of Antichrist, and for impugning Christes truth and Church vvere called antichristes, vvhether they did it by force and open persecution, as Nero and others either Heathen or Heretical Emperours did, or by false teaching and other deceites, as the Heretikes of al ages. in vvhich common and vulgar acception S. Hierom saith, al belonged to Antichrist that vvere not of the communion of Damasus then Pope of Rome. *Hiero. ep. 57 ad Damas.* and in an other place, al that haue nevv names after the peculiar calling of Heretikes, as Arians, Donatistes (and as vve say novv, Caluinistes, Zuinglians, &c.) al such (saith he) be Antichristes. *Dial. cont. Lucifer, c. 9.* Yea these later of our time much more then any of the former, for diuers causes vvhich shal aftervvard be set dovvne. Neuerthelesse they nor none of them are that great Aduersarie, enemie, and impugner of Christ, vvhich is by a peculiar distinction and special signification named, *the Antichrist,* 1 Io. 2. and *the man of sinne.* the

Many Antichrists, as fore runners of the great Antichrist.

The great Antichrist shal be one special and notorious man.

the sonne of perdition, the Aduersarie, described here & els vvhere, to oppose him self directly against God & our Lord IESVS CHRIST. The Heathen Emperours vvere many, Turkes be many, Heretikes haue been and novv are many, therfore they can not be that one great Antichrist vvhich here is spoken of, and vvhich by the article alvvaies added in the Greeke, is signified to be one special and singular man: as his peculiar & direct opposition to Christs person in the 5 chapter of S. Iohns Gospel v. 43: the insinuation of the particular stocke and tribe vvhereof he should be borne, to wit, of the Ievves (for of them he shal be receiued as their Messias *Io. 5. v. 43.*) and of the tribe of Dan. *Iren. li. 5. Hieron. com. in c. 11 Dan. August. q. in Iosu. q. 22*: the note of his proper name *Apoc. 13*: the time of his appearing so neere the vvorldes end: his short reigne, his singular vvast and destruction of Gods honour and al religion, his feined miracles, the figures of him in the Prophets and Scriptures of the nevv & old Testament: al these & many other arguments proue him to be but one special notorious Aduersarie in the highest degree, vnto vvhom al other persecutors, Heretikes, Atheistes, and vvicked enemies of Christ and his Church, are but members and seruants.

ὁ ἀντίχριστος. ὁ υἱὸς ἀπωλείας. ὁ ἄνθρωπος ἁμαρτίας, ὁ ἀντικείμενος.

Gen. 49, 17.

And this is the most common sentence also of al aũcient fathers. Onely Heretikes make no doubt but Antichrist is a vvhole order or succession of men. vvhich they hold against the former euident Scriptures and reasons, onely to establish their folish and vvicked paradoxe, that Christes cheefe Minister is Antichrist, yea the vvhole order. Vvherein Beza specially pricketh so high, that he maketh Antichrist (euen this great Antichrist) to haue been in S. Paules daies, though he vvas not open to the vvorld. Vvho it should be (except he meane S. Peter, because he vvas the first of the order of Popes) God knovveth. And sure it is, except he vvere Antichrist, neither the vvhole order, nor any of the order can be Antichrist, being al his lavvful successors both in dignitie and also in truth of Christes religion. Neither can al the Heretikes aliue proue that they or any of them vsed any other regiment or iurisdiction Ecclesiastical in the Church, or forced the people to any other faith or vvorship of God, then Peter him self did preach and plant. Therfore if the rest be Antichrist, let Beza boldly say that S. Peter vvas so also, and that diuers of the aũcient Catholike fathers did serue and vvorke (though vnvvares) tovvardes the setting vp of the great Antichrist, for so doth that blasphemous penne boldly vvrite in his Annotations vpon this place: and an English printed booke of late comming forth out of the same schoole, hath these vvordes: *As for Leo and Gregorie Bishops of Rome, although they vvere not come to the ful pride of Antichrist, yet the mysterie of iniquitie hauing vvrought in that Seate neere fiue or sixe hundred yeres before them, and then greatly increased, they vvere deceiued vvith the long continuance of errour.* Thus vvriteth a malapert scholer of that impudent schole, placing the mysterie of Antichrist as vvorking in the See of Rome euen in S. Peters time, and making these tvvo holy fathers great vvorkers and furtherers of the same. vvhereas an other English Rabbine doubted not at Paules crosse to speake of the self same fathers as great Doctors aud Patrones of their nevv Gospel, thus: *O Gregorie, ô Leo, if vve be deceiued, you haue deceiued vs.* Vvhereof vve giue the good Christian Reader vvarning more diligently, to bevvare of such damnable bookes and Maisters, carying many vnaduised people to perdition.

Beza in hoc cap.

The Caluinistes place Antichrist in the See of Rome, in S. Paules daies.

Against D. Sanders rocke pag. 248. & pag. 178.

They make S. Leo & S. Gregorie, great furtherers of Antichristes pride.

Iuel.

4. *Extolled.*] The great Antichrist vvhich must come neere the vvorldes end, shal abolish the publike exercise of al other religions true and false, and pull dovvne both the B. Sacrament of the altar, vvherein cõsisteth specially the vvorship of the true God, and also al Idols of the Gentils, and sacrifices of the Ievves, generally al kinde of religious vvorship, sauing that vvhich must be done to him self alone. vvhich vvas partly prefigured in such kings as published that no God nor man but them selues should be praied vnto for certaine daies, as * Darius and such like. Hovv can the Protestants then for shame and vvithout euident cõtradiction, auouch the Pope to be Antichrist, vvho (as vve say) honoureth Christ the true God vvith al his povver, or (as they say) honoureth Idols, and chalengeth no diuine honour to him self, much lesse to him self onely, as Antichrist shal do? He hũbly praieth to God, & lovvly kneeleth dovvne in euery Church at diuers altars erected to God in the memories of his Saincts, and praieth to them. He saieth or heareth Masse daily vvith al deuotiõ, he cõfesseth his sinnes to a Priest as other poore men do, he adoreth the holy Eucharist vvhich Christ affirmed to be his ovvne body, the Heretikes call it an Idol (no maruel if they make the Pope his Vicar Antichrist, vvhen they make Christ him self an Idol:) These religious dueties doth the Pope, vvhereas Antichrist shal vvorship none, nor pray to any, at the least openly.

Antichrist shal suffer no vvorship or adoration, but of him self only. therfore the Pope can not be Antichrist.

Dan. 6, 6.

4. *In the temple.*] Most auncient vvriters expound this of the Temple in Hierusalem, vvhich they thinke Antichrist shal build vp againe, as being of the Ievves stocke, and to be acknovvledged of that obstinate people (according to our Sauiours prophecie Io. 5) for their expected and promised Messias. *Iren. li. 5 in fine. Hyppolyt. de consum. mundi. Cyril. Hieros. Catech. 15. Author op. imp. ho. 49. in Mat.* See S. Hierom *in 11 Dan. Grego. li. 31. Moral. c. 11.* Not that he shal suffer them to vvorship God by their old maner of sacrifices, (al vvhich he vvil either abolish, or conuert to the onely adoration of him self: though at the first to apply him self to the Ievves, he may perhaps be circumcised and keepe some part of the law) for it is here said that he shal sitte in the Temple as God, that is, he shal be adored there by sacrifice and diuine honour, the name and vvorship of the true God vvholy defaced. And this they thinke to be *the abominatiõ of desolation* foretold by Daniel, mentioned by our Sauiour, prefigured and resembled by Antiochus and others, that defaced the

In vvhat temple Antichrist shal sitte.

Dan. 9. Mat. 24. 1 Mach. 1.

vvorship

The abomination of desolation consisteth cheefely in abolishing the sacrifice of the altar.

worship of the true God by prophanation of that Temple, specially by abrogating the daily sacrifice, which was a figure of the only sacrifice and continual oblation of Christes holy body and bloud in the Church, as the abolishing of that, vvas a figure of the abolishing of this, vvhich shal be done principally & most vniuersally by Antichrist him self (as novv in part by his forerunners) through out al Nations and Churches of the vvorld (though then also Masse may be had in secret, as it is novv in nations vvhere the secular force of some Princes prohibiteth it to be said openly.) For although he may haue his principal seate and honour in the Temple and citie of Hierusalem, yet he shal rule ouer the vvhole vvorld, and specially prohibite that principal vvorship instituted by Christ in his Sacraments, as being the proper Aduersarie of Christes person, name, lavv, and Church. the prophanation and desolation of vvhich Church by taking avvay the sacrifice of the altar, is the proper abomination of desolation, and the vvorke of Antichrist onely.

Hovv Antichrist shal sit in the Church.

S. Augustine therfore *li. 20 de ciuit. c. 19.* and S. Hierom *q. 11 ad Algasiam.* do thinke, that this sitting of Antichrist in the temple, doth signifie his sitting in the Church of Christ, rather then in Salomons temple. Not as though he should be a cheefe member of the Church of Christ, or a special part of his body mystical, and be Antichrist and yet vvithal continuing vvithin the Church of Christ, as the Heretikes feine, to make the Pope Antichrist (vvhereby they plainely confesse and agnise that the Pope is a member of the Church, *& in ipso sinu Ecclesiæ, and in the very bosome of the Church,* say they:) for that is ridiculous, that al Heretikes vvhom S. Iohn calleth Antichristes as his precursors, should go out of the Church, and the great Antichrist him self should be of the Church, & in the Church, & cōtinevv in the same. and yet to them that make the vvhole Church to reuolt from God, this is no absurditie. But the truth is, that this Antichristian reuolt here spoken of, is from the Catholike Church: and Antichrist, if he euer vvere of or in the Church, shal be an Apostata and a renegate out of the Church, and shal vsurpe vpon it by tyrannie, and by chalenging vvorship, religion, & gouernement thereof, so that him self shal be adored in al the Churches of the vvorld vvhich he list to leaue standing for his honour. And this is to sitte in the temple or ⋆ against the Temple of God, as some interprete. If any Pope did euer this, or shal do, then let the Aduersaries call him Antichrist.

Beza.

Neither Antichrist nor his precursors, are mēbers of the Church.

⋆ εἰς τὸν ναὸν

Antichrist (by interpretatiō, *One against Christ*) why so called.

And let the good Reader obserue, that there be tvvo special causes vvhy this great man of sinne is called Antichrist. The one is, for impugning Christes kingdom in earth, that is to say, his spiritual regiment vvhich he constituted and appointed in his Church, and the forme of gouernement ordained therein, applying al to him self by singular tyrannie and vsurpation. in vvhich kinde S. Athanasius (*ep. ad Solit. vit. degentes,*) is bold to call the Emperour Constantius being an Arian Heretike, Antichrist, for making him self *Principem Episcoporum*, *Prince ouer the Bishops and President of Ecclesiastical iudgements &c.* The other cause is, for impugning Christes Priesthod, vvhich is only or most properly exercised in earth by the sacrifice of the holy Masse, instituted for the commemoration of his death, & for the external exhibition of godly honour to the B. Trinitie, vvhich kinde of external vvorship by sacrifice no lavvful people of God euer lacked. And by these tvvo things you may easily perceiue, that the Heretikes of these daies do more properly and neerely prepare the vvay to Antichrist and to extreme desolation, then euer any before, their special heresie being against the spiritual Primacie of Popes and Bishops, and against the sacrifice of the altar, in vvhich tvvo the souerainitie of Christ in earth consisteth.

Protestants & Caluinists the neere forerūners of Antichrist.

S. Augustins humilitie in interpreting the scriptures

6. *What letteth.*] S. Augustine (*li. 20 c. 19 de ciuit dei.*) professeth plainely that he vnderstandeth not these vvordes, nor that that folovveth of the mysterie of iniquitie, and least of al that vvhich the Apostle addeth, *Only that he vvhich holdeth novv, do hold &c.* Vvhich may humble vs al and stay the confident rashnes of this time, namely of Heretikes, that boldly feine hereof vvhatsoeuer is agreable to their heresie and phantasie. The Apostle had told the Thessalonians before by vvord of mouth a secret point vvhich he vvould not vtter in vvritting, and therfore referreth them to his former talke. The mysterie of iniquitie is cōmonly referred to Heretikes, vvho vvorke to the same, and do that that Antichrist shal do, but yet not openly, but in couert and vnder the cloke of Christes name, the Scriptures, the vvord of the Lord, shevv of holines, &c. Vvhereas Antichrist him self shal openly attempt and atchieue the foresaid desolation, and Satan novv seruing his turne by Heretikes vnderhand, shal tovvard the last end vtter, reueale, & bring him forth openly. and that is here, *to be reuealed,* that is, to appeare in his ovvne person.

The mysterie of iniquitie is the couert working of heretikes toward the manifest reuelation of Antichrist himself.

These other vvordes, *Only that he vvhich novv holdeth, hold*: Some expound of the Emperour, during vvhose continuance in his state, God shal not permit Antichrist to come, meaning that the very Empire shal be vvholy desolate, destroied, and taken avvay before or by his comming: vvhich is more then a defection from the same, vvhereof vvas spoken before: for there shal be a reuolt from the Church also, but it shal not be vtterly destroied. Others say, that it is an admonition to al faithful, to hold fast their faith and not to be beguiled by such as vnder the name of Christ or Scriptures seeke to deceiue them, til they that novv pretend religion and the Gospel, end in a plaine breach, reuolt, and open apostasie by the appearance of Antichrist, vvhom al Heretikes serue in mysterie, that is, couertly and in the Diuels meaning, though the vvorld seeth it not, nor them selues at the beginning thought it, as novv euery day more & more al men perceiue they tend to plaine Atheisme and Antichristianisme.

9. *In al povver.*] Satan vvhose povver to hurt is abridged by Christ, shal then be let loose, and shal assist Antichrist in al maner of signes, vvonders, and false miracles, vvhereby many shal be seduced, not only Ievves: But al such as be deceiued and caried avvay by vulgar speache only, of Heretikes that can vvorke no miracles, much more shal folovv this man of sinne doing so great vvonders. And such both novv do folovv Heretikes, and then shal receiue Antichrist, that deserue so to be forsaken of God, by their forsaking of the vnitie and happie fellovvship of Saincts in the Catholike Church, vvhere onely *is the Charitie of truth*, as the Apostle here speaketh.

What kinde of men shal folow Antichrist.

15. *Traditions.*] Not onely the things vvritten and set dovvne in the holy Scriptures, but al other truthes and pointes of religion vttered by vvord of mouth and deliuered or giuen by the Apostles * to their scholers by tradition, be so here approued and els vvhere in the Scripture it self, that the Heretikes purposely, guilfully, and of il cõscience (that belike reprehendeth them) refraine in their translations, from the Ecclesiastical and most vsual vvord, *Tradition*, euer-more vvhen it is taken in good part, though it expresse most exactly the signification of the Greeke vvord: but vvhen it soundeth in their fond phantasie against the traditions of the Church (as in deede in true sense it neuer doth) there they vse it most gladly. Here therfore and * in the like places, that the reader might not so easily like of Traditions vnvvritten, here commended by the Apostle, they translate it, *Instructions*, *Constitutions*, *Ordinances*, and vvhat they can inuent els, to hide the truth from the simple or vnvvarie Reader, vvhose translations haue no other end but to beguile such by art and conueiance.

* See S. Denys Areopag. Ec. Hier. c. 1. παράδοσις

* 1. Cor. 11. 2. Thes. 3.

Hereticaltrãslation.

Traditions vnvvritten.

But S. Chrysostom (*ho. 4 in 1 Thes. 2.*) and the other greeke scholies or commentaries say herevpon, both vvritten and vnvvritten precepts the Apostles gaue by tradition, and both be vvorthy of obseruation. S. Basil (*De Sp. Sancto c. 29 in principio.*) thus, *I account it Apostolike to continevv firmely euen in vnvvritten traditions.* and to proue this, he alleageth this place of S. Paul. In the same booke c. 17 he saieth, *If vve once go about to reiect vnvvritten customs as things of no importance, vve shal, ere vve be avvare, doe damage to the principal partes of the faith, and bring the preaching of the Gospel to a naked name.* And for example of these necessarie traditions, he nameth the signe of the Crosse, praying tovvards the east, the vvords spoken at the eleuatiõ or shevving of the holy Eucharist, vvith diuerse cerimonies vsed before & after the consecration, the halovving of the font, the blessing of the oile, the anointing of the baptized vvith the same, the three immersions into the font, the vvordes of abrenuntiatiõ and exorcismes of the partie that is to be baptised &c. *Vvhat scripture* (saith he) *taught these and such like? none truly, al comming of secret and silent tradition, vvherevvith our fathers thought it meete to couer such mysteries.*

Their authoritie & estimation, & examples of some peculiar traditions out of the fathers.

S. Chrysostom

S. Basil.

S. Hierom (*Dialog. cont. Lucif. c. 4. et ep. 28 ad Liciniũ.*) reckeneth vp diuers the like traditiõs, vvilling men to attribute to the Apostles such customs as the Church hath receiued in diuers christian countries. S. Augustine esteemeth the Apostolike traditions so much, that he plainely affirmeth in sundrie places, not onely the obseruation of certaine festiuities, fastes, ceremonies, & vvhatsoeuer other solemnities vsed in the Catholike Church, to be holy, profitable, and Apostolike, though they be not vvritten at al in the scriptures: but he often also vvriteth, that many of the articles of our religion and pointes of highest importance, are not so much to be proued by scriptures, as by tradition. namely auouching that in no vvise vve could beleeue that children in their infancie should be baptized, *if it vvere not an Apostolical tradition. De Gen. ad lit. li. 10 c. 23.* Tradition caused him to beleeue that the baptized of heretikes should not be rebaptized, notvvithstanding S. Cyprians authoritie and the manifold scriptures alleaged by him, though they seemed neuer so pregnant. *De bap. li. 2. c. 7.* By tradition onely, he and others condemned Heluidius the heretike for denying the perpetual virginitie of our Lady. And vvithout this, be the Scriptures neuer so plaine, no Arian, no Macedonian, no Eutychian, no Pelagian, no Zuinglian vvil yeld. *We must vse tradition*, (saith S. Epiphanius *har. 61 Apostolicorum.*) *For the Scripture hath not al things: and therfore the Apostles delivered certaine things in vvritting, certaine by tradition.* and for that he alleageth this place also of S. Paul. And againe *har. 55. Melchised. There be boundes set dovvne for the foundation and building vp of our faith, the tradition of the Apostles, and holy Scriptures, and succession of doctrine, so that truth is euery vvay fensed.*

S. Hierom.

S. Augustine.

S. Epiphanius.

S. Irenæus (*li. 3. c. 4.*) hath one notable chapter, that in al questions vve must haue recourse to the traditions of the Apostles: teaching vs vvithal, that the vvay to trie an Apostolical tradition and to bring it to the fountaine, is by the Apostolike succession of Bishops, but specially of the Apostolike See of Rome: declaring in the same place that there be many barbarous people, simple for learning, but for constancie in their faith most vvise, vvhich neuer had Scriptures, but learned onely by tradition. Tertullian. (*li. de corona militis. nu. 3.*) reckeneth vp a great number of Christian obseruations or customs (as S. Cyprian in many places doth in maner the same) vvhereof in fine he concludeth, *Of such and such if thou require the rule of Scriptures, thou shalt finde none. Tradition shal be alleaged the author, custom the confirmer, and faith the obseruer.* Origen also of this matter vvriteth in plaine termes, that

S. Irenæus.

Tertullian.

S. Cyprian.

Origen.

that there be many thinges done in the Church (vvhich he there nameth) vvhereof there is no easier reason to be giuen then tradition from Christ and the Apostles. *ho. 5. in Numer.* S. Dionysius Areopagita referreth the praying and oblation for the dead in the Liturgie or Masse, to an Apostolical tradition. *in fine Ec. Hierarch. c. 7. parte 3.* So doth Tertullian *De coron. militis.* S. Augustine *De cura pro mortuis* c. 1. S. Chrysostom *ho. 3. in ep. ad Philip. in Moral.* S. Damascene *Ser. de defunctis in initio.*

The Scriptures giuen vs by tradition, and the sense thereof.

Vve might adde to al this, that the Scriptures them selues, euen al the bookes and partes of the holy Bible, be giuen vs by tradition: els vve should not nor could not take them (as they be in deede) for the infallible vvord of God, no more then the vvorkes of S. Ignatius, S. Clement, S. Denys, and the like. The true sense also of the Scriptures (vvhich Catholikes haue & heretikes haue not) remaineth stil in the Church by tradition. The Crede is an Apostolike traditiõ. *Ruffin. in expo. Symb. in principio. Hiero. ep. 61. c. 9. Ambros. Ser. 38. Aug. de Symb. ad Catechum. li. 3. c. 1.* And vvhat Scriptures haue they to proue that vve must accept nothing not expresly vvritten in Scriptures? Vve haue to the contrarie, plaine Scriptures, al the fathers, most euident reasons, that vve must either beleeue traditions or nothing at al. And they must be asked vvhether, if they vvere assured that such and such things (vvhich be not expressed in Scriptures) vvere taught and deliuered by vvord of mouth from the Apostles, they vvould beleeue them or no? If they say no, then they be impious that vvil not trust the Apostles preaching: if they say they vvould, if they vvere assured that the Apostles taught it: then to proue vnto them this point, vve bring them such as liued in the Apostles daies, and the testimonies of so many fathers before named neere to those daies, and the vvhole Churches practise and asseueratiõ descending dovvne from man to man to our time. vvhich is a sufficient proofe (at least for a matter of fact) in al reasonable mens iudgement. specially vvhen it is knovven that S. Ignatius the Apostles equal in time, vvrote a booke of the Apostles traditions, as Eusebius vvitnesseth *li. 3. Ec. hist. c. 30.* And Tertullians booke of prescriptiõ against Heretikes, is to no other effect but to proue that the Church hath this vantage aboue Heretikes, that she can proue her truth by plaine Apostolike tradition, as none of them can euer do.

The Creede an Apostolical tradition.

An inuincible argument for the credite of Traditions.

CHAP. III.

He desireth their praiers, 4 and inculcateth his precepts and traditions, namely of vvorking quietly for their ovvne liuing, commaunding to excommunicate the disobedient.

FOR the rest, brethren, pray for vs, that 1 the vvord of God may haue course and be glorified, as also vvith you: † and 2 that vve may be deliuered from importunate and naughtie men. for al men haue not faith. † But our Lord is faith- 3 ful, vvho vvil confirme and keepe you from euil. † And vve haue confidence 4 of you in our Lord, that the things vvhich vve commaund, both you doe, and vvil doe. † And our Lord direct your 5 hartes in the charitie of God, and patience of Christ.

Ep. 6, 18. Col. 4, 3.

† And vve denounce vnto you, brethren, in the name of 6 our Lord IESVS Christ, that you vvithdravv your selues frõ euery brother vvalking inordinatly, and not according to the [c] traditiõ vvhich they haue receiued of vs. † For your selues 7 knovv hovv you ought to imitate vs: for vve haue not been vnquiet

c Here also (as is noted before 2 *Thess.* 2. 15) the aduersaries in their translatiõs auoid the vvord, *Tradition*, being plaine in the Greeke, lest them selues might seeme to be noted as men vvalking inordinately, and not according to Apostolical Tradition, as al Schismatikes, Heretikes, and rebels to Gods Church doe.

c παράδοσιν

Act. 20. 1. Cor. 4. 1. Th. 2. 1. Cor. 9, 6.

8 vnquiet among you: † * neither haue vve eaten bread of any man gratis, but in labour & in toile night and day vvorking, lest vve ſhould burden any of you. 9 † * Not as though vve had not authoritie: but that vve might giue our ſelues a paterne vnto you for to imitate vs. 10 † For alſo vvhen vve vvere vvith you, this vve denounced to you, that if any vvil not vvorke, " neither let him eate. 11 † For vve haue heard of certaine amõg you that vvalke vnquietly, vvorking nothing, but curiouſly meddling. 12 † And to them that be ſuch vve denounce, & beſeeche them in our Lord IESVS Chriſt, that vvorking vvith ſilence, they eate their ovvne bread.

Gal. 6, 9.

13 † But you brethren * fainte not vvel-doing. 14 † And if any " obey not our vvord, " note him by an epiſtle: 15 † and do not companie vvith him, that he may be confounded: and do not eſteeme him as an enemie, but admoniſh him as a brother. 16 † And the Lord of peace himſelf giue you euerlaſting peace in euery place. Our Lord be vvith you al. 17 † The ſalutation, vvith mine ovvne hand, Paules: vvhich is a ſigne in euery epiſtle. ſo I vvrite. 18 † The grace of our Lord IESVS Chriſt be vvith you al. Amen.

ANNOTATIONS
CHAP. III.

10. *Neither let them eate.*] It is not a general precept or rule, that euery man ſhould liue by his handvvorke, as the Anabaptiſtes argue falſely againſt Gentlemen, and the Caluiniſtes applie it peruerſely againſt the vacant life of the Clergie, ſpecially of Monkes and other Religious men. But it is a natural admonitiõ onely, giuen to ſuch as had not vvherevvith to liue of their ovvne, or any right or good cauſe vvhy to chalenge their finding of others, and to ſuch as vnder the colour of Chriſtian libertie did paſſe their time idly, curiouſly, vnprofitably, and ſcandalouſly, refuſing to do ſuch vvorkes as vvere agreable to their former calling and bringing vp. Such as theſe, vvere not tolerable, ſpecially there and then, vvhen the Apoſtle and others (that might lavvfully haue liued of the altar and their preaching) yet to diſburden their hearers, and for the better aduancement of the Goſpel, vvrought for their liuing: * proteſting neuertheles continually, that they might haue done othervviſe, as vvel as S. Peter and the reſt did, vvho vvrought not, but vvere found othervviſe iuſtly and lavvfully, as al ſortes of the Clergie preaching or ſeruing the Church and the altar, be and ought to be, * by the lavv of God and nature. Vvhoſe ſpiritual labours far paſſe al bodily trauailes, vvhere the dueties and functions of that vocation be done accordingly: as S. Auguſtine affirmeth of his ovvne extraordinarie paines incident to the Eccleſiaſtical affaires and regiment: in ſteede of vvhich, if the vſe of the Church and his infirmitie vvould haue permitted it, he vviſheth he might haue laboured vvith his handes ſome houres of the day. as ſome of the Clergie did euer voluntarily occupie them ſelues in teaching, vvriting, grauing, painting, planting, ſovving, embrodering, or ſuch like ſeemely and innocent labours. *See S. Hierom ep. 114. ſeu præf. in Iob. and in vit. Hilario.*

The heretikes cauillation againſt Religious mẽ that vvorke not, anſvvered.

1 Cor. 9.

** See S. Cypr. ep. 66.*

The ſpiritual trauailes of the Clergie.

Religious mẽ working with their handes.

And Monkes for the moſt part in the primitiue Church (fevv of them being Prieſts, and many taken from ſeruile vvorkes and handicraftes, yea often times profeſſed of bondmen, made free by their maiſters to enter into religiõ) vvere appointed by their Superiors to vvorke certaine houres of the day, to ſupply the lackes of their Monaſteries: as yet the

Religious do (vvomen specially) in many places, vvhich standeth vvell vvith their profession. And S. Augustine vvriteth a vvhole booke (*de opere Monachorum to. 3.*) against the errour of certaine disordered Monkes that abused these vvordes, (*Nolite esse soliciti, be not careful &c.* and *Respicite volatilia cœli, behold the foules of the aire &c.*) to proue that they should not labour at al, but pray only and commit their finding to God: not only so excusing their idlenes, but preferring them selues in holines aboue other their fellowes that did worke, and erroneously expounding the said Scriptures for their defence: as they did other Scriptures, to proue they should not be shauen after the maner of Monkes. Vvhich letting their heads to grow he much blameth also in them. *See li. 2. Retract. c. 21. & de op. Monach. c. 31.* and S. Hierom *ep. 48. c. 3.* of Nonnes cutting their heare.

Monkes were shauen in the primitiue Church, and Nonnes clipped of their heare.

Vvhere by the vvay you see that the Religious vvere shauen euen in S. Augustines time, vvho reprocheth them for their heare, calling them *Crinitos, Hearelings,* as the Heretikes novv contrarievvise deride them by the vvord *Rasos, Shauelings.* So that there is a great difference betvvene the auncient Fathers and the nevv Protestants. And as for hand labours, as S. Augustine in the booke alleaged, would not haue Religious folke to refuse them, vvhere necessitie, bodily strength, and the order of the Church or Monasterie permit or require them: so he expresly vvriteth, that al can not nor are not bound to vvorke, and that vvho so euer preacheth or ministreth the Sacraments to the people or serueth the altar (as al Religious men commonly now do) may chalenge their liuing of them vvhom they serue, and are not bound to vvorke, * no nor such neither as haue been brought vp before in state of Gentlemen, and haue giuen avvay their lands or goods, and made them selues poore for Christes sake. Vvhich is to be noted, because the Heretikes affirme the said Scripture and S. Augustine to condemne al such for idle persons.

S. Augustines opinion concerning Religious mens working or not working.

li. de op Monach. c. 21.

14. *Obey not.*] Our Pastors must be obeied, and not onely secular Princes. and such as vvill not be obedient to their spiritual gouernours, the Apostle (as S. Augustine saith) giueth order and commaundement that they be corrected by correption or admonition, *By degradation, excommunication, and other lavvful kindes of punishments. Cont. Donatist. post collat. c. 4. 20.* Read also this holy fathers answer to such as said, *Let our Prelates commaund vs onely vvhat vve ought to do, and pray for vs that vve may do it: but let them not correct vs.* Vvhere he proueth that Prelates must not onely commaund and pray, but punish also if that be not done vvhich is commaunded. *Li. de correp. & grat. c. 3.*

Ecclesiastical censures against the disobedient.

14. *Note him.*] Disobedient persons to be excommunicated, and the excommunicated to be separated from the companie of other Christians, and the faithful not to keepe any companie or haue conuersation vvith excommunicated persons, neither to be partaker vvith them in the fault for vvhich they are excommunicated, nor in any other act of religion or office of life, except cases of mere necessitie and other prescribed and permitted by the law: al this is here insinuated, and that al the Churches censures be grounded in Scriptures and the examples of the Apostles.

Not to communicate with excōmunicate persons but in certaine cases.

THE

THE ARGVMENT OF THE FIRST EPISTLE OF S. PAVL TO TIMOTHEE.

AFTER the Epistles to the Churches, novv folovv his Epistles to particular persons, as to Timothee, to Titus, vvho vvere Bishops: and to Philémon.

Of Timothee vve reade Act. 16. hovv S. Paul in his visitation tooke him in his traine at Lystra, circumciding him before, because of the Ievves. he vvas then a Disciple, that is to say, a Christian man. Aftervvard the Apostle gaue him holy Orders, and consecrated him Bishop, as he testifieth in both these Epistles vnto him. 1. Tim. 4. v. 14. and 2. Tim. 1. v. 6.

He vvriteth therfore vnto him as to a Bishop, and him self expresseth the scope of his first Epistle, saying: These things I vvrite to thee, that thou maiest knovv hovv thou oughtest to conuerse in the House of God, vvhich is the Church. *And so he instructeth him (and in him, al Bishops) hovv to gouerne both him self, & others. and touching him self, to be an example & a spectacle to al sortes, in al vertue. as touching others, to prohibit al such as goe about to preach othervvise then the Catholike Church hath receiued, and to inculcate to the people the Catholike faith: to preach vnto yong and old, men and vvomen: to seruants, to the riche, to euery sort conueniently. Vvith vvhat circumspection to giue orders, & to vvhat persons: for vvhom to pray: vvhom to admit to the vovv of vvidovvhod &c.*

1 Timoth. 3.

This Epistle vvas vvritten, as it seemeth, after his first emprisonmēt in Rome, vvhen he vvas dismissed and set at libertie. and thervpon it is, that he might say here, I hope to come to thee quickly. *to vvit vnto Ephesus, vvhere * he had desired him to remaine. although in his voiage to Hierusalem, before his being at Rome, he said at Milétum to the Clergie of Ephesus, vpō probable feare:* And now behold I knovv, that you shal no more see my face.

1 Timoth. 3.
* 1 Tim. 1.
Act. 20. v. 25. 38.

Vvhere it vvas vvritten, it is vncertaine: though it be commonly said, at Laodicia. Vvhich seemeth not, because it is like he vvas neuer there, as may be gathered by the Epistle to the Colossians, vvritten at Rome in his last trouble, vvhen he vvas put to death.

Col. 2. v. 1.

THE FIRST EPISTLE OF PAVL TO TIMOTHEE.

CHAP. I.

He recommendeth vnto him, to inhibite certaine Ievves vvho iangled of the Lavv as though it vvere contrarie to his preaching. 11 Against vvhom he auoucheth his ministerie, though he acknovvledge his vnvvorthines.

PAVL an Apostle of IESVS Christ according to the commaundement of God our sauiour, and of Christ IESVS our hope: † to Timothee his beloued sonne in the faith. Grace, mercie, and peace from God the father, and from Christ IESVS our Lord. 1 2

† As I desired thee to remaine at Ephesus vvhen I vvent into Macedonia, that thou shouldest denounce to certaine "not to teache othervvise, † nor to attend" to fables and genealogies hauing no ende: vvhich minister " questions rather then the edifying of God vvhich is in faith. † But" the ende of the precept is charitie from a pure hart, and ∷ a good conscience, and a faith not feined. † From the vvhich things certaine straying, are turned into c vaine talke, † " desirous to be doctors of the Lavv, not vnderstanding neither vvhat things they speake, nor of vvhat they affirme. † But vve know that * the Lavv is good, if a man vse it lavvfully: † knovving this that " the Lavv is not made to the iust man, but to the vniust, and disobedient, to the impious and sinners, to the vvicked and contaminate, to killers of fathers and killers of mothers, to murderers, † to fornicatours, to lyers vvith mākinde, to man-stealers, to liers, to periured persons, and vvhat other thing soeuer is contrarie to sound doctrine, † vvhich is 3 4 5 6 7 8 9 10 11

∷ S. Augustine saith, He that list to haue the hope of heauē let him looke that he haue a good cōsciēce. to haue a good conscience, let him beleeue & vvorke vvel. for that he beleueth, he hath of faith: that he vvorketh, he hath of charitie. Præfat. in Psa. 31.

c ματαιολογίαν.

Ro. 7, 12.

is according to the Gospel of the glorie of the blessed God, vvhich is committed to me.

12 † I giue him thankes vvhich hath strengthened me, Christ IESVS our Lord, because he hath esteemed me faithful, put-
13 ting me in the ministerie. † vvho before vvas blasphemous and a persecutor & contumelious. but I obteined the mercie
14 of God, because I did it being ignorant in incredulitie. † And the grace of our Lord ouer-abounded vvith faith and loue,
15 vvhich is in Christ IESVS. † A faithful saying, & vvorthie of al acceptatiō, that Christ IESVS came into this vvorld * to
16 saue sinners, of vvhom I am the cheefe. † But therfore haue I obtained mercie: that in me first of al Christ IESVS might shevv al patience, [c] to the information of them that shal
17 beleeue on him vnto life euerlasting. † And to the king of the vvorldes, immortal, inuisible, onely God, honour & glorie for euer and euer. Amen.
18 † This precept I commend to thee ô Timothee: according to the prophecies going before [c] on thee, that thou warre
19 in them a good vvarfare, † hauing faith and a good conscience, ∴ vvhich certaine repelling, haue made shipvvracke
20 about the faith. † Of vvhom is Hymenæus & Alexander: vvhom I haue " deliuered to Satan, that they may learne not to blaspheme.

Mt. 9, 13. Mr. 2, 17.

c πρὸς ὑποτύπωσιν

c ἐπί σε

∴ Euil life and no good conscience is often the cause that men fall to Heresie from the faith of the Catholike Church. Againe, this plainely reproueth the heretikes false doctrine, saying, that no man can fall from the faith that he once truely had.

ANNOTATIONS
CHAP. I.

3. *Not to teach othervvise.*] The proper marke of Heretikes & false preachers, is, to teach othervvise or contrarie to that vvhich they found taught and beleeued generally in the vnitie of the Catholike Church before their time: al doctrine that is odde, singular, new, differing from that vvhich vvas first planted by the Apostles, and descēded downe from them to al nations and ages folowing vvithout contradiction, being assuredly erroneous. * The Greeke vvord vvhich the Apostle here vseth, expresseth this point so effectually, that in one compound terme he giueth vs to vvit, that an Heretike is nothing els but an after-teacher, or teacher-otherwise. vvhich euen it self alone is the easiest rule euen for the simple to discerne a false Prophet or preacher by, specially vvhen an heresie first beginneth. Luther found al Nations Christian at rest and peace in one vniforme faith, and al preachers of one voice and doctrine touching the B. Sacrament and other Articles: so that vvhat so euer he taught against that vvhich he found preached and beleeued, must needes be an other doctrine, a later doctrine, an after-teaching or teaching-othervvise, and therfore consequently must needes be false. And by this admonitiō of S. Paul, al Bishops are vvarned to take heede of such, and specially to prouide that no such odde teachers arise in their dioceses.

*ἑτεροδιδασκαλεῖν

Teaching othervvise then the doctrine receiued, is a special marke of Heretikes.

Luthers teaching othervvise.

4. *To fables.*] He speaketh specially of the Iewes after-doctrines and humane constitutions repugnant to the lawes of God, vvhereof Christ giueth warning *Mt.* 23 and in other places, vvhich are conteined in their Cabala and Talmud: generally of al heretical doctrines, vvhich in deede, how so euer the simple people be beguiled by thē, are nothing but fabulous inuentions, as vve may see in the Valentinians, Manichees, and others of old: by the brethren of loue, Puritans, Anabaptistes, and Caluinistes of our time. For

Al heretical doctrine is fables.

which cause Theodorete entitleth his booke against Heretikes, *Hereticarum fabularum, Of Heretical fables.*

Curious questioning in religion.

4. *Questions.*] Let our louing brethren consider vvhether these contentious and curious questionings and disputes in religion, vvhich these vnhappie heresies haue ingendered, haue brought forth any increase of good life, any deuotion, or edification of faith and religion in our daies. and then shal they easily iudge of the truth of these new opinions, and the end that wil folovv of these innouations. In truth al the world now seeth they edifie to Atheisme and no othervvise.

Charitie the very formal cause of our iustification.

5. *The end Charitie.*] Here againe it appeareth, that Charitie is the cheefe of al vertues, and the end, consummation, and perfection of al the law and precepts. and yet the Aduersaries are so fond as to preferre faith before it, yea to exclude it from our iustification. Such obstinacie there is in them that haue once in pride & stubbernes forsaken the euident truth. Charitie doubtles which is here commended, is iustice it self, and the very formal cause of our iustification, as the vvorkes proceding thereof, be the vvorkes of iustice. *Charitas inchoata* (saith S. Augustine) *inchoata iustitia: Charitas prouecta, prouecta iustitia: Charitas magna, magna iustitia: Charitas perfecta, perfecta iustitia est. Charitie novv beginning, is iustice beginning: Charitie grovven or increased, is iustice grovven or increased: great Charitie, is great iustice: perfect Charitie, is perfect iustice. Li. de nat. & grat. c. 70.*

Heretikes great boasters, but vnlearned.

7. *Desirous to be Doctors.*] It is the proper vice both of Iudaical and of Heretical false teachers, to professe knowledge and great skill in the Lavv and Scriptures, being in deede in the sight of the learned most ignorant of the vvord of God, not knowing the very principles of diuinitie, euen to the admiration truely of the learned that reade their bookes or heare them preach.

Libertines alleage scripture.

9. *The lavv not made to the iust.*] By this place and the like, the Libertines of our daies vvould discharge them selues (vvhom they count iust) from the obedience of lawes. But the Apostles meaning is that the iust man doth vvel, not as compelled by lavv or for feare of punishment due to the transgressors thereof, but of grace & mere loue tovvard God & al goodnes, most vvillingly, though there were no law to commaund him.

Excommunication of Heretikes, and the effect thereof.

20. *Deliuered to Satan.*] Hymenæus and Alexander are here excõmunicated for falling from their faith & teaching heresie: an example vnto Bishops to vse their spiritual power vpon such. In the primitiue Church, corporal affliction through the ministerie of Satan vvas ioyned to excommunication. Vvhere we see also the diuels readines to inuade them that are cast out by excommunication, from the fellowship of the faithful, and the supereminent povver of Bishops in that case. Vvhereof S. Hierom (*ep. 1. ad Heliod. c. 7*) hath these memorable vvordes: *God forbid* (saith he) *I should speake sinistrously of them, vvho succeding the Apostles in degree, make Christes body vvith their holy mouth, by vvhom vve are made Christians: vvho hauing the keies of heauen, do after a sort iudge before the day of iudgement: vvho in sobrietie and Chastitie haue the keeping of the spouse of Christ.* And a litle after, *They may deliuer me vp to Satan, to the destruction of my flesh, that the spirit may be saued in the day of our Lord Iesus. And in the old Lavv vvhosoeuer vvas disobedient to the Priests, Was either cast out of the campe and so stoned of the people, or laying dovvne his necke to the svvord, expiated his offense by his bloud: but novv the disobedient is cut of vvith the spiritual svvord, or being cast out of the Church, is torne by the furious mouth of Diuels.* So saith he. Vvhich vvordes vvould God euery Christiã man vvould vveigh.

The Priests high authoritie of Excommunication.

The terrible effect thereof.

CHAP. II.

By his Apostolike authoritie he appointeth publike praiers to be made for al mẽ vvithout exception. 8 also men to pray in al places: 9 and vvomen also in semely attire, 11 to learne of men, and not to be teachers in any vvise, but to seeke saluation by that vvhich to them belongeth.

I Desire therfore first of al things that " obsecrations, praiers, postulations, thankesgeuings be made for al men, † ∷ for kings and al that are in preeminence: that vve may leade a quiet and a peaceable life in al pietie and chastitie. † For this is good and acceptable before our Sauiour God, vvho

∷ Euen for heathen kings & Emperours by vvhom the Church suffereth persecution: much more for al faithful Princes & powers

4 † " vvho vvill al men to be saued, and to come to the knovv-
5 ledge of the truth, † For there is one God," one also media-
6 tour of God and men, man Christ IESVS: † vvho gaue him self a redemption for al, vvhose testimonie in due times is cõ-
7 firmed. † * vvherein I am appointed a preacher & an Apo-stle (I say the truth, I lie not) doctor of the Gentiles in faith and truth.

2.Tim.1, 11.

8 † I vvil therfore that men pray in euery place: lifting vp
9 pure handes, vvithout anger and altercation. † In like maner * vvomen also in comely attire: vvith demurenesse and sobrietie adorning them selues, not in plaited heare, or gold,
10 or pretious stones, or gorgeous apparel, † but that vvhich
11 becõmeth vvomen professing pietie by good vvorkes. † Let
12 a vvoman learne in silence, vvith al subiection. † But * to teach " I permit not vnto a vvoman, nor to haue dominion
13 ouer the man: but to be in silẽce. † For * Adam vvas formed
14 first: then Eue. † and Adam vvas not seduced: but the
15 vvoman being seduced, vvas in preuarication. † Yet she shal be saued by generation of children: if 'they' continue in faith & loue and sanctification vvith sobrietie.

1.Pet.3, 3.

1. Cor. 14,34.

Gen. 1, 27. 3, 6.

'she

and people both spiritual and temporal, for vvhom as members of Christes body, and therfore ioyning in praier & oblation vvith the ministers of the Church, the Priestes more properly and particularly offer the holy Sacrifice. See S. Augustine *de orig. anima li.1.c.9.*

ANNOTATIONS
CHAP. II.

1. *Obsecrations.*] This order of the Apostle S. Augustine (*ep.59*) findeth to be fulfilled specially in the holy celebration of the Masse, vvhich hath al these kindes, expressed here in foure diuers vvordes pertaining to foure sortes of praiers. the difference vvhereof he exactly seeketh out of the proper signification and difference of the Greeke vvordes. And he teacheth vs that the first kind of praiers vvhich here be called, *obsecrations*, are those that the Priest saith before the consecration: that the second called, *Praiers*, be al those vvhich are said in and after the Consecration, & about the Receiuing, including specially the *Pater noster*, vvherevvith the vvhole Church (saith he) in maner endeth that part. as S. Hierom also affirmeth, that Christ taught his Apostles to vse the *Pater noster* in the Masse. Sic docuit, & c. *So taught he his Apostles, that daily in the Sacrifice of his body the faithful should be bold to say, Pater noster &c. Li.3 cont. Pelag. cap.5.* Where he alludeth to the very vvordes novv vsed in the preface to the said *Pater noster* in the said Sacrifice, *audemus dicere, Pater noster.* The third sort called here in the text, *Postulatiõs*, be those vvhich are vsed after the Cõmunion, as it vvere for dimissing of the people vvith benediction, that is, vvith the Bishops or Priests blessing. Finally the last kinde, vvhich is *Thankes-giuings*, concludeth al, * vvhen the Priest and people giue thankes to God for so great a mysterie then offered and receiued. Thus the said holy father handleth this text ep. 59 to Paulinus.

δεήσεις. προσευχαί. ἐντεύξεις. εὐχαριστίαι. * Theoph. in hunc loc.

The praiers & petitions in the Masse, deduced out of the Apostles vvordes by S. Augustine, & other fathers.

PATER NOSTER in the Masse.

S. Epiphanius also insinuateth these vvordes of the Apostle to pertaine to the Liturgie or Masse, vvhen he thus vvriteth to Iohn Bishop of Hierusalem. *Vvhen vve accomplish our praiers after the rite of the holy Mysteries, vve pray both for al others, and for thee also.* ep.60 c. 2 ad Io. Hierosolym. apud Hieronymum. And most of the other fathers expoũd the foresaid vvordes, of publike praiers made by the Priest, vvhich are said in al Liturgies or Masses both Greeke and Latin, for the good estate of al that be in high dignitie, as kings and others. *See S. Chrys. ho. 6. in 1 Tim. & S. Ambr. in hunc loc. Prosper de vocat. li. 1. c. 4.* So exactly doth the practise of the Church agree vvith the Precepts of the Apostle and the Scriptures, and so profoũdly do the holy fathers seeke out the proper sense of the Scriptures, vvhich our Protestants do so prophanely, popularely, and lightly skimme ouer, that they can neither see nor endure the truth.

Praier in the Masse for kings and other.

4 *Vvho vvil al men*] The perishing or damnation of men must not be imputed to God, vvho delighteth not in any mans perdition, but hath prouided a general medicine & redemption to saue al from perishing that vvil accept it, or that haue it applied vnto them by his Sacraments and other meanes by him ordained, and so vvould haue al saued by his conditional vvil and ordinance: that is, if men vvil them selues, by accepting, doing, or hauing done vnto them al things requisite by Gods lavv. for God vseth not his absolute vvil or povver tovvardes al in this case. But he that list see the manifold senses (al good and true) that these vvordes may beare, let him see S. Augustine, *Ad articul. sibi falso impos. resp. 2. to. 7. Ench. c. 103. Ep. 107. De cor. & grat. c. 15*, and *S. Damascene li. 2 de orthod. fide c. 29.*

God vvil no mans perditiō but the saluation of al.

5 *One mediator.*] The Protestants are to peuish and pitifully blind, that charge the Catholike Church & Catholikes, vvith making moe Mediators then one, vvhich is Christ our Sauiour, in that they desire the Saincts to pray for them, or to be their patrones and intercessors before God. Vve tel them therfore that they vnderstand not vvhat it is to be a Mediator, in this sense that S. Paul taketh the vvord, and in vvhich it is properly and onely attributed to Christ. For, to be thus a Mediator, is, * by nature to be truely both God and man, to be that one eternal Priest and Redeemer, vvhich by his sacrifice and death vpon the Crosse hath reconciled vs to God, and paied his bloud as a full and sufficient raunsom for al our sinnes, him self vvithout neede of any redemption, neuer subiect to possibilitie of sinning: againe, to be the singular Aduocat and Patrone of mankind, that by him self alone and by his ovvne merites procureth al grace & mercie to mankind in the sight of his Father, none making any intercession for him, nor geuing any grace or force to his praiers, but he to al: none asking or obtaining either grace in this life, or glorie in the next, but by him. In this sort then (as S. Augustine truely saith, Cont. ep. Parm. li. 2. c. 8.) neither Peter nor Paul, no nor our B. Lady, nor any creature vvhatsoeuer, can be our Mediator. The aduersaries thinke to basely of Christes mediation, if they imagine this to be his onely prerogatiue, to pray for vs, or that vve make the saincts our Mediators in that sort as Christ is, vvhen vve desire them to pray for vs. vvhich is so far inferior to the singular mediation of him, that no Catholike euer can or dare thinke or speake so basely vnto him, as to desire him to pray for vs: but vve say, *Lord haue mercie vpō vs, Christ haue mercie vpon vs*: & not, *Christ pray for vs*, as vve say to our Ladie and the rest. Therfore to inuocate Saincts in that sort as the Catholike Church doth, can not make them our Mediators as Christ is, vvhom vve must not inuocate in that sort. And as vvel make vve the faithful yet liuing, our Mediators (by the Aduersaries arguments) vvhen vve desire their praiers, as the departed Saincts.

Hovv there is but one Mediator, Christ: and vvhat it is to be such a Mediator.

* *Aug. li. 9. de Ciu. cap. 15. De fid. ad Pet. c. 2.*

The different maner of praying to Christ, and to Saincts.

Kyrie eleison. Christe eleison.

But novv touching the vvord *Mediator*, though in that singular sense proper to our Sauiour, it agreeth to no mere creature in heauen or earth, yet taken in more large and common sort by the vse of Scriptures, doctors, and vulgar speach, not onely the Saincts, but good men liuing, that pray for vs and help vs in the vvay of saluation, may and are rightly called Mediators. As S. Cyril li. 12 Thesaur. c. 10 proueth, that Moyses according to the Scriptures and Ieremie and the Apostles and others be Mediators. Read his ovvne vvordes, for they plainely refute al the Aduersaries cauillations in this case. And if the name of * sauiour and redeemer be in the Scriptures giuen to men, vvithout derogation to him that is in a more excellent and incomparable maner the onely Sauiour of the vvorld: vvhat can they say, vvhy there may not be many Mediators, in an inferior degree to the onely and singular Mediator? S. Bernard saith, *Opus est mediatore ad Mediatorem Christum, nec alter nobis vtilior quam Maria.* that is, *We haue neede of a mediator to Christ the Mediator, and there is none more for our profite then our Ladie.* Bernard. Ser. qui incipit, *Signum magnum apparuit &c. post Ser. 5 de Assumpt.* S. Basil also in the same sense, vvriting to Iulian the Apostata, desireth the mediation of our Ladie, of the Apostles, Prophets, and Martyrs, for procuring of Gods mercie and remission of his sinnes. His vvordes are cited in *Conc. Nic. 2. act. 4. pag. 110 & 111.* Thus did and thus beleeued al the holy fathers, most agreably to the Scriptures, and thus must al the children of the Church do, be the Aduersaries neuer so importunate and vvilfully blinde in these matters.

Hovv there be many mediators, as there be many sauiours, and redeemers, euē in the Scriptures.

Iud. 3, 9. 2 Esd. 9, 27. Act. 7, 35.

12 *I permit not.*] In times of licentiousnes, libertie, and heresie, vvomen are much giuen to reading, disputing, chatting, and iangling of the holy Scriptures, yea and to teach also if they might be permitted. but S. Paul vtterly forbiddeth it, and the * Greeke Doctors vpon this place note that the vvoman taught but once, that vvas vvhen after her reasoning vvith Satan, she persuaded her husband to transgression, and so she vndid al mankind. And in the Ecclesiastical vvriters vve find that vvomen haue been great promoters of euery sort of heresie (vvhereof see a notable discourse in S. Hierom *ep. ad Ctesiph. cont. Pelag. c. 2.*) vvhich they vvould not haue done, if they had according to the Apostles rule, folovved pietie and good vvorkes, and liued in silence and subiection to their husbands.

Women great talkers of Scripture, and promoters of heresie.

* *S. Chrys. Ho. 9. in 1. Tim.*

CHAP. III.

Of vvhat qualitie they must be, vvhom he ordaineth Bishops, 8 and Deacons. 14 and the cause of his vvriting to be, the excellencie of the Catholike Church, and of Christ, vvho is the obiect of our religion.

1 A Faithful saying. If a man desire a Bishops office, he desireth "a good worke. † * It behoueth therfore "a Bishop to be irreprehensible, the husband "of one vvife, sobre, vvise, comely, chast, a man of hospitalitie, a teacher, † not giuen to vvine, no fighter, but modest, no quareler, not couetous, † vvel ruling his ovvne house, [c] hauing his children subiect vvith al chastitie. † But if a man knovv not to rule his ovvne house: hovv shal he haue care of the Church of God? † "Not [b] a neophyte: lest puffed into pride, he fall into the iudgment of the Deuil. † And he must haue also good testimonie of them that are vvithout: that he fall not into reproch and the snare of the Deuil.

Tit. 1, 6.

c He saith, *hauing children*, not, *getting children. S. Ambr. Ep. 82.*

b νεόφυτον

b *Neophytus* is he that vvas lately christened or nevvely planted in the mystical body of Christ.

8 † Deacons in like maner [c] chast, not double-tonged, not giuen to much vvine, not folovvers of filthie lucre: † hauing the mysterie of faith in a pure cōscience. † And let these also be proued first: & so let them minister, hauing no crime. † The vvomen in like maner chast, not detracting, sober, faithful in al things. † Let deacons be the husbandes of one vvife: vvhich rule vvel their children, & their houses. † For they that haue ministred vvel, shal purchase to them selues a good degree, and much confidence in the faith vvhich is in Christ IESVS.

c σεμνούς

14 † These things I vvrite to thee, hoping that I shal come to thee quickly. † but if I tary long, that thou maiest knovv hovv thou oughtest to conuerse "in the house of God, vvhich is the CHVRCH of the liuing God, "the piller and ground of truth. † And manifestly it is a great sacrament of pietie, vvhich vvas manifested in flesh, vvas iustified in spirit, appeared to Angels, hath beene preached to gentils, is beleeued in the vvorld, is assumpted in glorie.

ANNOTATIONS
CHAP. III.

The great charge, & great merite, of Ecclesiastical functions.

1. *A good vvorke.*] *Nothing* (saith S. Augustine) *in this life, and specially in this time, is easier, pleasanter, or more acceptable to men, then the office of a Bishop, Priest, or Deacon, if the thing be done onely for fashion sake and flatteringly; but nothing before God more miserable, more lamentable, more damnable.* Againe, *There is nothing in this life, and specially at this time, harder, more laborious, or more dangerous, then the office of a Bishop, Priest, or Deacon: but before God nothing more blessed, if they vvarre in such sort as our Captaine commaundeth.* August. ep. 148.

The Apostle vnder the name of Bishop instructeth Priestes also.

2. *A Bishop.*] That vvhich is here spoken of a Bishop (because the vvordes Bishop & Priest in the nevv Testament be often taken indifferently for both or either of the tvvaine, as is noted in an other place) the same is meant of euery Priest also: though the qualities here required, ought to be more singular in the Bishop, then in the Priest, according to the difference of their degrees, dignities, and callings.

The heretikes opinion cocerning Priests mariage.

2. *Of one vvife.*] Certaine Bishops of Vigilantius sect (vvhether vpon false construction of this text, or through the filthines of their fleshly lust) vvould take none to the Cleargie, except they vvould be maried first, *not beleeuing* (saith S. Hierom aduers. Vigilant. c. 1.) *that any single man liueth chastly, shevving hovv holily they liue them selues, that suspect il of euery man, and vvil not giue the Sacrament* (of Order) *to the Cleargie, vnles they see their vviues haue great bellies, and children vvalling at their mothers breastes.* Our Protestants though they be of Vigilantius sect, yet they are scarse come so farre, to commaund euery Priest to be maried. Neuertheles they mislike them that vvil not marrie, so much the vvorse, and they suspect il of euery single person in the Church, thinking the gift of chastitie to be very rare among them, & they do not onely make the state of mariage equal to chast single life, vvith the Heretike Iouinian, but they are bold to say sometimes, that the Bishop or Priest may do his duety and charge better maried, then single: expresly against S. Paul, vvho affirmeth that the vnmaried thinke of the things that belong to God, and that the maried be diuersely distracted and intangled vvith the vvorld. 1 *Cor.* 7.

S. Paules place, *of one vvife*, excludeth bigamos from holy Orders.

The Apostle then, by this place vve novv treate of, neither commaundeth, nor counselleth, nor vvisheth, nor vvould haue Bishops or Priests to marrie, or such onely to be receiued as haue been maried: but, that such an one as hath been married (so it vvere but once, and that to a virgin) may be made Bishop or Priest. Which is no more then an inhibition that none hauing been tvvise maried or being *bigamus*, should be admitted to that holy Order. And this exposicion onely is agreable to the practise of the vvhole Church, the definition of aucient Councels, the doctrine of al the fathers vvithout exception, and the Apostles tradition. Vvhich sense S. Chrysostom vvholy folovveth vpon the Epistle to Titus (though here he folovv not vvholy the same sense.) *Ho. 2 in ep. ad Tit.* S. Ambrose also vpon this place, and most plainely and largely in his 82 Epistle *post med.* giuing the cause why *bigamus* can not be made Bishop or Priest, in fine affirmeth, not onely the Apostle but the holy Councel of Nice to haue taken order that none should be receiued into the Cleargie, that vvere tvvise maried. S. Hierom *Ep. 83. ad Oceanum c. 2. & ep. 2. c. 18. ep. 11. c. 2* expresly vvriteth that the Cleargie is made of such as haue had but one vvife, at least after Baptisme: for he thought that if one vvere often maried vvhen he vvas yet no Christian, he might notvvithstanding be ordered Bishop or Priest. But S. Ambrose ep. 82. S. Augustine *de bono Coniug. c. 18.* S. Innocentius the first *ep. 2. c. 5. 6. to. 1. Concil.* S. Leo, *ep.* 87* S. Gregorie, & after them the vvhole Church, exclude those also vvhich haue been tvvise maried vvhen so euer. vvhereof S. Augustine giueth goodly reason and example in the place alleaged. S. Leo *ep.* 87 addeth further, & proueth that the mã is couted bigamus, & not the husband of one vvife, in respect of holy Orders, not onely if he hath had tvvo vviues, but if his one vvife vvere not a virgin. vvhich being obserued in the high Priests of the old lavv, must needes be much rather kept novv. See also the booke *de Ecclesiasticis dogmatibus c.* 72, in S. Augustines vvorkes. * *li.* 2 *ep.* 25. *Leuit.* 21.

Vvho are counted *bigami*.

The Heretical clergie nothing regardeth the Apostles prescription of one vvife.

And by these fevv you may see hovv shamefully the state of the nevv heretical Cleargie of our time is fallen from the Apostolike and al the fathers practise and doctrine herein. Vvho do not onely take men once or twise maried before, but (vvhich vvas neuer heard of before in any person or part of the Catholike Church) they marie after they be Bishops or Priests, once, tvvise, and as often as their lustes require. Whereas it vvas neuer lawful in Gods Church to marrie after Holy Orders. Neither is there one authentical example thereof in the world. For those of vvhom Nice Councel speaketh, vvere maried before, & were but tolerated onely to vse their wiues: the fathers in the same Councel prouiding expresly at the same time, that none from thence forth should marrie after they came to holy Orders, *and that according to the aucient tradition of the Church*, as Socrates and Sozomenus declare in most plaine vvordes. See Suidas in the vvord *Paphnutius*. And in vvhat countrie so euer they haue been permitted to haue carnal dealing euen vvith their vviues whom they had before, it was not according to the exact rule of the Apostles & Churches tradition, by vvhich al that be in holy Orders, should wholy abstaine, not onely from marying, but euen from their wiues before maried. Vvhereof thus vvriteth S. Epiphanius

None euer maried after holy Orders.

They that vvere made Priests of maried men, absteined from their vviues.

Socrat. li. 1 *c.* 8. *Sozom. li.* 1 *c.* 22

nius hæres. 59 cont. Catharos. The holy preaching of God receiueth not, after Christ, them that marrie againe after their vviues departure, by reason of the great dignitie and honour of Priesthod. And this the holy Church of God obserueth vvith al sinceritie. Yea she doth not receiue the once maried person that yet vseth his vvife and begetteth children: but onely such an one she taketh to be Deacon, Priest, Bishop, or Subdeacõ, as abstaineth from his one vvife, or is a vvidovver, specially vvhere the holy canõs be sincerely kept. But thou vvilt say vnto me, that in certaine places Priests, Deacons, and Subdeacons do yet beget children (belike this holy father neuer heard of any Bishop that did so, and therfore he leaueth out that order, vvhich he named vvith the other in the former part of the sentence) *but that is not done according to order and rule, but according to mans minde, vvhich by time slacketh, and for the great multitude* (of Christian people) *vvhen there vvere not found sufficient for the ministerie. &c.* the rest of his vvordes be goodly for that purpose.

S. Epiphanius.

Mariage of Priests is contrarie to the aũcient canõs.

Eusebius also *Euang. demonst. li. 1. c. 9* saith, that such as be consecrated to the holy ministerie, should abstaine vvholy from their vviues vvhich they had before. S. Hierom *Apolog. ad Pammach. c. 8* proueth, that such of the Apostles as were maried, did so, and that the Clergie ought to do the same by their example. Yea in his time he testifieth (*Cont. Vigil. c. 1.*) that they did liue single in maner through the world, euẽ in the East Church also. *What,* saith he, *shal the Churches of the East do, vvhat they of Ægypt, of the See Apostolike: vvhich take to the Clergie, either virgins, or the continent and vnmaried, or such as if they haue vviues, cease to be husbands?* And againe he saith *in Apolog. ad Pãmach c. 3.* (See also c. 8.) *If maried men like not vvel of this, let them not be angrie vvith me, but vvith the holy Scriptures, vvith al Bishops, Priests, Deacons, and the vvhole companie of Priests and Leuites, that knovv they can not offer sacrifices if they vse the act of mariage.* S. Augustine *de adult. Coniug. li. 2. c. 20.* maketh it so plaine a matter that al Priests should liue chast, that he writeth, that euen such as vvere forced (as many vvere in the primitiue Church) to be of the Clergie, vvere bound to liue chast, yea and did it vvith great ioy and felicitie, neuer complaining of these necessities and intolerable burdens, or impossibilities of liuing chast, as our fleshly companie of new Ministers and Superintendents do novv, that thinke it no life vvhithout vvomen. much like to S. Augustine before his conuersion, vvhen he vvas yet a Manichee, vvho (as him self reporteth *Confess. li. 6. c. 3*) admiring in S. Ambrose al other his incomparable excellencies, yet counted al his felicities lesse, because he lacked a vvoman, vvithout vvhich he thought (in time of his infidelitie) no man could liue. But after his conuersion thus he said to God of S. Ambrose: *What hope he had, and against the tentations of his excellencie vvhat a fight he felt, or rather vvhat a comfort and solace in tribulation, and his secrete mouth vvhich vvas vvithin in his hart, vvhat sauourie and svveete ioyes it tasted of thy bread, neither could I coniecture, neither had I tried.*

Eusebius.

S. Hierom.

S. Augustine.

See S. Leo ep. 92. c. 3.

S. Ambrose.

See Tertullian *li. 1 ad vxorem.* S. Cyprian *de singul. Clericor.* the first Councel of Nice *can. 3. Conc. Tolet. 2 can. 3. Conc. Aurelian. 3 can. 2.* of Carthage the second cap. 2, of Neocæsarea cap. 1, of Ancyra cap. 10. and you shal find that this vvas generally the Churches order euen from the Apostles time, though in some places by the licentiousnes of many, it vvas sometime not so religiously looked vnto. Vvhereby you may easily refute the impudent clamors of Heretikes against Siricius, Gregorie 7, and others, vvhom they falsely make the authors of the Cleargies single life.

Tertullian.
S. Cyprian.

Councels.

6. Not a Neophyte.] That vvhich is spoken here properly and principally of the nevvly baptized (for so the vvord Neophyte doth signifie) the fathers extend also to al such as be but nevvly retired from prophane occupations, ciuil gouernement, vvarfare, or secular studies, of vvhom good trial must be taken before they ought to be preferred to the high dignitie of Bishop or Priest. though for some special prerogatiue and excellencie, it hath in certaine persons been othervvise, as in S. Ambrose and some other notable men. Tertullian (*li. de præscript.*) noteth Heretikes for their lightnes in admitting euery one vvithout discretion to the Cleargie. *Their Orders* (saith he) *are rash, light, incõstant: novv they place Neophytes, then secular men, then our Apostataes, that they may tie them by glorie and preferment, Whom vvith the truth they can not. No vvhere may a man sooner prosper and come forvvard, then in the campe of rebelles, vvhere to be onely, is to deserue much. therfore one to day a Bishop, to morovv somevvhat els: to day a Deacon, to morovv Lector, that is, a Reader: to day a Priest, to morovv a lay man. for to laie men also they enioyne the functions of Priestes.* And S. Hierom *ep. 83 ad Oceanum c. 4.* saith of such, *Yesterday a Catechumene or nevvly conuerted, to day a Bishop: yesterday in the theatre, to day in the Church: at night in the place of games and maisteries, in the morning at the altar: a vvhile ago a great patrone of stageplaiers, novv a consecrator of holy virgins.* And in an other place, *Out of the bosome of Plato and Aristophanes they are chosen to a Bishoprike, vvhose care is, not hovv to sucke out the marovv of the Scriptures, but hovv to soothe the peoples eares vvith florishing declamations.* Dialog. cont. Lucifer. c. 5.

None rashly to be admitted to the Clergie

Heretikes admit al sortes vvithout exception.

8. Deacons.] Vnder the name of Deacons are here conteined Subdeacons, as before vnder the name of Bishop, Priests also vvere comprehended. for to these foure pertaineth the Apostles precept and order touching one vvife, and touching continẽcie and chastitie, as by the alleaged Councels and fathers (namely by the vvordes of S. Epiphanius) doth appeare. for they onely be in holy Orders, as seruing by their proper function about the Altar and the B. Sacrament: in respect

Leo ep. 92. c. 3. Greg. li. 1, ep. 42.

The three holy orders, only bound to chastitie.

vvhereof, the law of chastitie pertaineth to them, and not to the foure inferior Orders of *Acolyti, Exorcistæ, Lectores*, and *Ostiarij*. Vvho neither by precept nor vovv be bound to perpetual chastitie, as the others of the holy and high Orders be bound, both by precept and promis or solemne assent made vvhen they tooke Subdeaconship.

The 4 inferiour orders not bound to chastitie.

Al these degrees and orders to haue been euer since Christes time in the Church of God, it might be proued by al antiquitie: but for as much as the Apostles purpose is not here to recken vp al the Ecclesiastical Hierarchie, it neede not be treated of in this place. But we vvish the learned to reade the 3.4.5.6.7.8.9 chapters of the 4 Councel of Carthage, vvhereat S. Augustine vvas present: vvhere they shal see the expresse callings, offices, and maner of ordering or creating al the said sortes, and shal vvel perceiue these things to be most auncient and venerable. Let them read also Eusebius historie, the 35 Chapter of the 6 booke, vvhere for al these orders he reciteth Cornelius epistle to Fabius, concerning Nouatus. Likewise S. Cyprian in many places, namely *ep. 55. nu. 1.* Where see the notes vpon the same. *S. Hiero. ep. 2. c. 6.* Of Subdeacon there is mention in S. Augustine. *ep. 74 and ep. 20 de epistolis 22 in edit. Paris. S. Epiph. hær.* 59. S. Cyprian *ep. 24.* S. Ignatius *ep. 9* ad Antiochenos. and in the 43 canon of the Apostles. *Conc. Tolet. 2. can. 1 & 3. Conc. Laodicen. can. 21. Epist. Epiph. apud Hiero. 60. c. 1.*

Al the seuen orders auncient, euē from Christ and the Apostles time.

15. *In the house of God.*] *Al the vvorld being Gods, yet the Church onely is his house, the Rector or Ruler vvhereof at this day.* (saith S. Ambrose vpon this place) *is damasus.* Where let our louing brethren note vvel, how cleere a case it vvas then, that the Pope of Rome vvas not the Gouernour onely of one particular See, but of Christes vvhole house, vvhich is the Vniuersal Church, vvhose Rector this day is Gregorie the thirtenth.

S. Ambrose calleth the B. of Rome Rector of the vvhole Church.

15. *The piller of truth.*] This place pincheth al Heretikes vvonderfully, and so it euer did, and therfore they oppose them selues directly against the very letter and confessed sense of the same, that is, cleane contrarie to the Apostle. some saying, the Church to be lost or hidden: some, to be fallen avvay from Christ these many ages: some, to be driuen to a corner onely of the vvorld: some, that it is become a stewes and the seate of Antichrist: lastly the Protestants most plainely and directly, that it may and doth erre, and hath shamefully erred for many hundred yeres together. And they say herein like them selues, and for the credit of their ovvne doctrine, vvhich can not be true in very deede, except the Church erre, euen the Church of Christ, vvhich is here called the house of the liuing God.

The heretikes say directly cōtrarie to the Apostle, that the Church is not the piller of truth.

But the Church vvhich is the house of God, whose Rector (saith S. Ambrose) in his time was Damasus, and novv Gregorie the thirtenth, and in the Apostles time S. Peter, is the piller of truth, the establishement of al veritie: therfore it can not erre. It hath the Spirit of God to lead it into al truth till the vvorldes end: therfore it can not erre. It is builded vpon a rocke, hel gates shal not preuaile against it: therfore it can not erre. Christ is in it til the end of the vvorld, he hath placed in it Apostles, Doctors, Pastors, and Rulers, to the consummation and ful perfection of the whole body, that in the meane time we be not caried about vvith euery blast of doctrine: therfore it can not erre. He hath praied for it, that it be sanctified in veritie, that the faith of the cheefe Gouernour therof faile not: it is his house, his spouse, his body, his lotte, kingdom and inheritance, giuen him in this vvorld: he loueth it as his ovvne flesh, and it can not be diuorced or separated from him: therfore it can not erre. the nevv Testament, Scriptures, Sacraments, and sacrifice can not be changed, being the euerlasting dourie of the Church, continued and neuer rightly occupied in any other Church but in this our Catholike Church: therfore it can not erre. And therfore al those pointes of doctrine, faith, and vvorship, vvhich the Arians, Manichees, Protestants, Anabaptistes, other old or new Heretikes, vntruely thinke to be errors in the Church, be no errors in deede, but them selues most shamfully are deceiued, and so shal be still, til they enter againe into this house of God, vvhich is the piller and ground of al truth: that is to say, not onely it self free from al error in faith and religion, but the piller and stay to leane vnto in al doubtes of doctrine, and to stand vpon against al heresies and errors that il times yeld, without vvhich there can be no certaintie nor securitie. And therfore the holy Apostles, and Councels of Nice and Constantinople, made it an article of our *Creede*, to beleeue the CATHOLIKE and APOSTOLIKE CHVRCH. Vvhich is, not onely to acknowledge that there is such a Church, as heretikes falsely say: but that that Which is called the Catholike Church, & knovven so to be, and communicateth vvith the See Apostolike, is the Church: and that vve must beleeue, heare, and obey the same, as the touch stone, piller, and firmament of truth. For, al this is comprised in that principle, *I beleeue the Catholike Church.* And therfore the Coūcel of Nice said, *I beleeue in the Church*, that is, I beleeue and trust the same in al things.

Io. 14. 16. Mat. 16. Mat. 28. Eph. 4. Io. 17. Luc. 22. Psal. 2. Eph. 5.

That the Church is the piller of truth and can not erre, is proued by many reasons.

The meaning of this article, *I beleeue the Cath. Church.*

τιςεύω εἰς τὴν ἐκκλησίαν

Neither can the Heretikes escape by fleing from the knovven visible Church, to the hid congregation or companie of the Predestinate. For that is but a false phantastical apprehension

apprehension of Vvicleffe and his folowers. The companie of the Predestinate maketh not any one Societie among them selues, many of them being yet vnborne, and many yet Infidels and heretikes, and therfore be not of the one house of God vvhich is here called, *the piller of truth.* And those of the Predestinate that be already of the Church, make not a seueral companie from the knovven Catholike Church, but are baptized, houseled, taught, they liue and die in the common Catholike visible Church, or els they can neither receiue Sacraments, nor saluation. S. Paul instructeth not Timothee hovv to teach, preach, correct, and conuerse in the inuisible societie of the Predestinate, but in the visible house of God. So that it must needes be the visible Church which can not erre.

It is the visible Church that is the piller of truth and can not erre.

If any make further question, how it can be that any companie or societie of men (as the Church is) can be void of error in faith, seing al men may erre: he must knovv that it is not by nature, but by priuilege of Christes presence, of the Holy Ghosts assistance, of our Lordes promis and praier. See S. Augustine vpon these vvordes of the 118 Psalme *Conc. 13. Ne auferas de ore meo verbum veritatis vsquequaque.* Vvhere he hath goodly speaches of this matter. For the same purpose also these vvordes of Lactantius are very notable. *It is the Catholike Church onely, that keepeth the true vvorship of God, this is the fountaine of truth, this the house of faith, this the Temple of God: vvhither if any man enter not, or from vvhich if any man go out, he is an aliene and stranger from the hope of euerlasting life and saluation. No man must by obstinate contention flatter him self, for it standeth vpon life and saluation. &c.* S. Cyprian saith, *The Church neuer departeth from that vvhich she once hath knovven. Ep. 55 ad Cornel. nu. 3.* S. Ireneus saith, *That the Apostles haue laid vp in the Church as in a rich treasurie, al truth.* And, *that she keepeth With most sincere diligence, the Apostles faith and preaching. li. 3 c. 4. & 40. & li. 1. c. 3.* It vvere an infinite thing to recite al that the fathers say of this matter, al counting it a most pernicious absurditie to affirme, that the Church of Christ may erre in religion.

Vvhence the Church hath this priuilege neuer to erre.

S. Augustine.

Lactantius.

S. Cyprian.

S. Irenæus.

CHAP. IIII.

He prophecieth that certaine should depart from the Catholike faith, vvilling Timothee therfore to inculcate to the people those articles of the said faith. 7 Item to exercise him self in spiritual exercise, 12 to gette authoritie by example of good life, 13 to studie, to teach, to increase in the grace giuen him by holy orders.

2 Tim. 3
3 Pet. 3.
Iude v. 18.

1 AND the Spirit manifestly saith that in the last times certain " shal depart from the faith attending to spirites of errour, and 2 doctrines of diuels, † speaking lies in hypocrisie, and hauing their conscience seared, 3 † " forbidding to marie, to abstaine from meates vvhich God created to receaue vvith thankes-giuing for the faithful, and them that 4 haue knovven the truth. † For ⁘ euery creature of God is good, and nothing to be reiected that is receiued " vvith 5 thankes-giuing. † For it is " sanctified by the vvord of God and praier.

6 † These things proposing to the brethren, thou shalt be a good minister of Christ IESVS, nourished in the vvordes of the faith and the good doctrine vvhich thou hast at-7 tained vnto. † But folish and old vviues fables auoid: and

⁘ we see plainely by these vvordes such abstinence only to be disalovved as condemneth the creatures of God to be naught by nature & creation.

:: Some (saith S. Chrysost.) expound this of fasting, but they are deceiued. for fasting is a spiritual exercise. See a goodly commentarie of these vvordes in S. August. *li. de mor. Eccl. Cath. c. 33.*

exercise thy self to pietie. † For :: corporal exercise is profitable to litle: but pietie is profitable to al things: hauing promisse of the life that novv is, and of that to come. † A faithful saying and vvorthie of al acceptation. † For to this purpose vve labour and are reuiled, because vve hope in the liuing God vvhich is the Sauiour of al men, especially of the faithful. † Commaund these things and teach.

1. *Tim.* 1, 4. *Tit.* 3, 9.

† Let no man contemne thy youth: but be an example of the faithful, in vvord, in conuersation, in charitie, in faith, in chastitie. † Til I come, attend vnto reading, exhortation, doctrine. † Neglect not "the grace that is in thee: vvhich is giuen thee by prophecie, vvith imposition of the handes" of priesthod. † These things doe thou meditate, be in these things: that thy profiting may be manifest to al. † Attend to thy self, and to doctrine: be earnest in them. For, this doing, thou shalt " saue both thy self and them that heare thee.

ANNOTATIONS
CHAP. IIII.

Al Heretikes are apostataes from the faith.

1. *Shal depart.*] It is the proper description of Heretikes, to forsake their former faith, and to be Apostataes, as the Greeke vvord importeth: to giue eare to particular spirites of error & deception, rather then to the Spirit of Christ in his Church, to folovv in hypocrisie and shevv of vertue the pernicious doctrine of Diuels, vvho are the suggesters and prompters of al Sectes, and are lying spirites in the mouthes of al Heretikes and false preachers: men that haue put their conscience to silence and made it sensles to the holy Churches admonition: the Apostle noting * once before also in this same Epistle, that Heretikes haue no conscience, vvhich is the cause both of their fall and of their obduration in heresie.

ἀποστῆσονται

cap. 1, 19.

The old Heresies against matrimonie.

3. *Forbidding to marrie.*] He speaketh (saith S. Chrysostom) of the Manichees, Encratites, and Marcionistes. *ho.* 12 *in* 1 *Tim.* S. Ambrose vpon this place, addeth to these the Patritians also. S. Irenæus *li.* 1 *c.* 30. S. Epiphanius *hær.* 45. 26. 61. 30. S. Hierom 1 *cont. Iouin. c.* 1. *& ep.* 50 *c.* 1 *&* 3. S. Augustine *hær.* 25. 40. and generally al antiquitie affirme the same both of them, and also of the Heretikes called Apostolici, Ebionitæ, and the like. Their heresie about mariage vvas, that to marrie or to vse the act of matrimonie, is of Satan, as S. Irenæus vvitnesseth *li.* 1 *c.* 22: and that the distinction of male and femal and the creation of man and vvoman for generation, came of an il God. They taught their hearers, * saith S. Augustine, that if they did vse vvomen, they should in any vvise prouide that they might not conceiue or beare children. Clemens Alexandrinus (*li.* 3. *Strom. in principio*) vvriteth, that such admit no mariage nor procreation of children, lest they should bring into the vvorld creatures to suffer miserie and mortalitie. And this is the damnable opinion concerning mariage, noted here by the Apostle.

* *Aug. hær.* 46.

The old Heresies about abstinẽce from meates.

For the second point consisting in the prohibition of meates or vse of certaine creatures made to be eaten, the said Heretikes or diuers of them (for they vvere not al of one sect touching these points) taught, that men might not eate certaine sortes of meates, specially of beastes and liuing creatures, for that they vvere not made (say they) of the good God, but of the euil. And vvine they called the gall of the Prince of darkenes, and not to be drunke at al, and the Vine vvhereof it came, to be of the Diuels creation. And diuers other creatures they cõdemned as things by nature and creation polluted and abominable. *August. hær. Manich.* 46. *& hær.* 25 *Tatian. & toto libro de mor. Manich. to.* 1. Lo these vvere the Heretikes and their heresies vvhich S. Paul here prophecieth of, that forbid mariage and meates as you haue heard, for vvhich they and their folovvers vvere condemned in diuers Councels.

:: The Catholikes impudently charged vvith the said old heresies.

Is it not novv an intolerable impudencie of the Protestants, vvho for a smal similitude of vvordes in the eares of the simple, apply this text to the fastes of the Church, and the chastitie of of Priests and Religious? As though either by appointing or vsing some daies of abstinence from certaine meates, the Church or any Catholike man condemned the said meates. vnles the Rechabites *Hierem.* 35. or the Nazarites *Num.* 6. or the Niniuites *Ion.* 3. or Moyses *Exod.* 34. or Elias 3 *Reg.* 19. or holy Anna the vvidow *Luc.* 2 or Iohn Baptist *Mat.* 3 & 9. or Christ him self *Mt.* 4. commending, vsing, and folovving a prescript number of fasting daies, or God him self that in the very beginning, in Paradise, prescribed abstinence from the fruite of one certaine tree, and after appointed so many fastes in the Lavv, vnles he therfore, condẽned his ovvne creatures, & the rest, those creatures from vvhich they abstained. No, there be many good and lavvful causes to forbid some or to abstaine frõ some meates: as, for obedience, as in Paradise: for significatiõ, as the Ievves: for that they haue been offered to Idols, as in the Epistle to the Corinthians: for chastening the bodie and penance. for health also: and onely those causes are vnlavvful for vvhich the Manichees and other Heretikes abstained.

Abstinence from certaine meates is no condemnation of the meates.

Diuers good causes of abstinence.

Concerning mariage likewise, they may as vvel charge God or the Church for forbidding the father to marrie the daughter, or the brother the sister, or other prohibited persons in the Lavv: as vvel might they charge Christ and the Apostle for prohibiting the man to marrie, during his vviues life: and appointing vvidowes that serue the Church, to liue vnmaried, and not admitting a maried woman as vvel as vvidovv, nor her that hath had moe husbands, as vvel as her that hath beẽ maried but once: as they charge the Church for not admitting maried persons to the altar, and for forcing them & Religious persons to keepe their promis of chastitie. No, the holy Church is so farre from condemning Wedlocke, that she honoureth it much more then the Protestants, accounting it an holy Sacrament, vvhich they do not, who onely vse it to lust as the Heathen doe, and not to religion.

Forbidding certaine persons to marrie is no condemnation of matrimonie.

Catholikes esteeme matrimonie more then the Protestants doe.

But it is an old deceitful practise of Heretikes to charge Catholike men vvith old condemned heresies. The Eutychians slaundered the Councel of Chalcedon and S. Leo to be Nestorians, and to make two persons in Christ, because they said there vvere tvvo natures. *Vigilius li. 5. cont. Eutychen.* Arius charged Alexander his Bishop of Sabellianisme, for auouching the vnitie of substance in Trinitie. *Socrat. li. 1. c. 3.* Iulianus accused S. Augustine of the heresie of Apollinaris. *li. 5. cont. Iulian. c. 15.* Other Pelagians chalenged him for condemning mariage. *Retract. li. 2. c. 53.* And that our Protestants bragge not to much of their goodly inuention, Iouinian the old Heretike, their Maister in this point, accused * the holy doctors and Catholikes vpon this same place, to be Manichees, and to condemne meates and mariage, as both S. Hierom and S. Augustine do testifie. And they both answer to the Heretike, that the Church in deede & Catholikes do abstaine frõ some for euer, and some for certaine daies, and euery Christian man lightly al the 40 daies of Lent fast: not for that they thinke the meates vncleane, abominable, or of an il creation, as the Manichees do: but for punishment of their bodies and taming their concupiscences. *Hiero. li. 2. cont. Iouin. c. 11. Aug. cont. Adimantum c. 14. Li. de mor. Cath. Ec. Hiero. in c. 4. ad Galat.* And as for mariage, the said doctors answer, that no Catholike man condemneth it for vnlavvful, as the old Heretikes did, but onely preferreth virginitie and continencie before it, as a state in it self more agreable to God and more meete for the Cleargie. See S. Augustine against Faustus the Manichee *li.* 30 *c.* 5. 6. and *har.* 25 in the name, *Apostolici.* S. Hierom *ep.* 50. *c.* 1. & 3. Al this the Catholikes continually tel the Aduersaries, and they can not but see it. Yet by accustomed audacitie and impudencie they beare it out still.

* *Aug. li. 2 c. 5 de nupt. & concupisc.*

The Protestants obiectiõs answered long ago by S. Hierom and S. Augustine.

4. *With thankes giuing.*] By the most aũcient custom of the faithful both before Christ and sithence, men vse to blesse their table and meates, by the hand and word of a Priest, if any be present, othervvise by such as can conueniently do it. And in husbandmens houses vvhere they haue no other meanes, they should at least blesse Gods giftes and them selues vvith a *Pater noster* or the signe of the Crosse: not onely to acknowledge from whom they haue their continual sustenance, but also to blesse their meate and sanctifie it. For the Greeke vvord vsed of S. Paul, by Ecclesiastical vse, vvhẽ it cõcerneth meates, signifieth not onely thankes giuing, but blessing or sanctifying the creatures to be receiued, as being al one vvith εὐλογία, and in English vve call it grace, not onely that after meate, which is onely thankes to God, but that before meate, vvhich is alvvaies a benediction of the creatures, as it is plaine in the prescript and vsual formes of grace. For vvhich cause a Priest should euer do it rather then a lay man or any of inferior order in the Cleargie. In so much that S. Hierom (ep. 85) reprehendeth certaine Deacons vvhom he savv say grace or blesse the meate and the companie, in the presence of a Priest. Vvho also recordeth (in the life of S. Paul the holy Eremite) the great curtesie and humilitie of him and S. Antonie, yelding one to the other the preeminence of blessing their poore dinner. For to blesse is a great thing, and a Priestly prerogatiue, as the Apostle vvitnesseth, declaring the preeminence of Melchisedec in that he blessed Abraham. Read the note folowing.

μετὰ εὐχαριστίας.

Blessing of the table or of meates, specially by a Priest.

To blesse is a preeminence of the better person.

Hebr. 7.

5. *Sanctified*

No creature il by nature, yet one more sanctified then an other.

5. Sanctified.] Al creatures be of Gods creation, none of the Diuel, or of any other cause and beginning, as the Manichees blasphemed: and therfore none are il, abominable, or vncleane by creation, nature, and condition, but al good and made for mans vse, though al be not alike holy nor equally sanctified. God made seuen daies, but he sanctified onely one of them. he made al places, but he sanctified none but the Temple and such like deputed to his seruice, as the Arke, the altar, and the rest vvhich vvere by sacred vse both holy them selues, and gaue also holines and sanctification to things that touched them or vvere applied vnto them. So our Sauiour saith, that the Temple sanctified the gold, and the altar the gift, and generally al creatures seuered from common and profane vse, to religion and vvorship of God, are made sacred thereby. So the places and daies of Gods apparition or vvorking some special vvonders or benefites tovvard the people, vvere holy, as Bethel, Sinai, and others. And much more those times and places of Christes Natiuitie, Passion, burial, Resurrection, Ascension: vvhich is so plaine a case, that the hil vvhere he vvas transfigured onely, is called therfore by S. Peter, *the holy mount.*

Holy times and places, & euery thing deputed to the seruice of God, holy.

Mat. 23.

2. Pet. 1.

These therfore be holy memories and monuments of al sortes sanctified, besides that creatures (as vve see here) be sanctified also by the vvord of God and praier, that is to say, by benediction & inuocation of our Lordes holy name vpon them, specially by the signe of the Crosse, as S. Chrysostom noteth on this place, *ho. 12 in 1 ad Tim.* by the vvhich the aduersarie povver of Satan vsurping vniustly vpon Gods creatures through mans sinne, and seeking deceitfully in or by the same to annoy mans body or soule, is expelled, and the meates purged from him and made holesom. S. Gregorie (*li. 1 Dialog. c. 4.*) recordeth that the Diuel entered into a certaine religious vvoman by eating the herbe lettice vnblessed. And S. Augustine *li. 18 de ciu. Dei c. 18.* shevveth at large, vvhat vvaies he hath by meates and drinkes and other vsual creatures of God, to annoy men: though his povver be much lesse then it vvas before Christ. but still much desire he hath on al sides to molest the faithful by abusing the things most neere and necessarie vnto them, to their hurt both bodily and Ghostly. for remedie vvhereof, this sanctification vvhich the Apostle speaketh of, is very soueraine, pertaining not onely to this common and more vulgar benediction of our meates and drinkes, but much more (as the proprietie of the Greeke vvord vsed by the Apostle for sanctification, doth import) to other more exact sanctifying and higher applying of some creatures, and blessing them to Christes honour in the Church of God, and to mans spiritual and corporal benefites.

Creatures hallovved by the signe of the Crosse.

The blessing of our meate vvhat a vertue it hath.

ἁγιάζεται

For as S. Augustine vvriteth *li. 2 de pec. merit. c. 26.* besides this vsual blessing of our daily foode, the Cathecumens (that is, such as vvere taught tovvard Baptisme) are sanctified by the signe of the Crosse, and the bread (saith he) vvhich they receiue, though it be not the body of Christ, yet is holy, and more holy then the vsual bread of the table. He meaneth a kinde of bread then halovved, specially for such as vvere not yet admitted to the B. Sacrament: either the same, or the like to our holy bread, vsed in the Church of England and France on Sundaies. And it vvas a common vse in the primitiue Church to blesse loaues, and send them for sacred tokens from one Christian man to an other. and that not among the simple and superstitious (as the Aduersaries may imagine) but among the holiest, learnedst, and vvisest. Such halovved breads did S. Paulinus send to S. Augustine and Alipius, and they to him againe, calling them blessings. Read S. Hierom in the life of Hilarion (*post medium:*) hovv Princes and learned Bishops & other of al sortes came to that holy man for holy bread, *panem benedictum.* In the primitiue Church the people commonly brought bread to the Priests to be halovved. *Author op. imp. ho. 14 in Mt.* The 3 Coũcel of Carthage cap. 24. maketh mention of the blessing of milke, honie, grapes, and corne. See the 4 Canon of the Apostles. And not onely diuers other creatures vsed at certaine times in holy Churches seruice, as vvaxe, fire, palmes, ashes, but also the holy oile, Chrisme, and the vvater of Baptisme, that also vvhich is the cheefe of al Priestly blessing of creatures, the bread and vvine in the high Sacrifice, be sanctified. for vvithout sanctification, yea (as S. Augustine affirmeth *tract. 118 in Ioan.*) vvithout the signe of the Crosse, none of these things can rightly be done.

Holy bread.

August. ep. 31. 34 35. 36.

The signe of the crosse vsed in blessing.

Can any man novv maruel that the Church of God by this vvarrãt of S. Paules vvord expoũded by so long practise and tradition of the first fathers of our religion, doth vse diuers elements and blesse them for mans vse and the seruice of God, expelling by the inuocatiõ of Christes name, the aduersarie povver from them, according to the authoritie giuen by Christ, *Super omnia dæmonia, ouer al Diuels*: and *by praier*, vvhich importeth as the Apostle here speaketh, desire of help, as it vvere by the vertue of Christ to combat vvith the Diuel, and so to expel him out of Gods creatures, vvhich is done by holy exorcisme, and euer beginneth, *Adiutorium nostrum in nomine Domini*, as vve see in the blessing of holy vvater and the like sanctification of elements. Vvhich exorcismes, namely of children before they come to Baptisme, see in S. Augustine *li. 6 cont. Iulian. c. 5. & de Ec. dogmat. c. 31. De nupt. & concupis. li. 1 c. 20.* and of holy vvater, that hath been vsed these 1400 yeres in the Church by the institution of Alexander the first, in al Christian countries, and of the force thereof against Diuels, see a famous historie in Eusebius *li. 5 c. 21.* and in Epiphanius *hær.* 30 Ebionitarum. See S. Gregorie to S. Augustine our Apostle, of the vse thereof in halovving the Idolatrous temples to be made the Churches of Christ. *apud Bedam li. 1 c. 30 hist. Angl.* Remember hovv the Prophet Eliseus applied salt to the healing and purifying of vvaters, 4 *Reg.* 2: hovv the

The Churches exorcismes.

Luc. 9.

Holy vvater.

Angel

Angel Raphael vsed the liuer of the fish to driue avvay the Diuel, *Tob. 6. 8*: hovv Dauids harp and Psalmodie kept the euil spirit from Saul, *1 Reg. 16*: hovv a peece of the holy earth saued such a mans chamber from infestatiõ of Diuels, *August. de Ciuit. dei li. 22 c. 8*: how Christ him self, both in Sacramẽts, & out of them, occupied diuers sanctified elements, some for the health of the body, some for grace and remission of sinnes, and some to vvorke miracles by. See in S. Hierom against Vigilantius c. 2. hovv holy Relikes tormẽt them. * In the historie of Iulianus the Apostata, hovv the signe of the Crosse: in the Actes (cap. 19) hovv the name of IESVS yea and of Paul putteth them to flight.

Theodoret. li. 3 c. 3.

The force of sanctified creatures. The holy land. Relikes. The crosse. The name of IESVS.

Furnish your selues vvith such examples and groundes of Scriptures and antiquitie, and you shal contemne the Aduersaries cauillations and blasphemies against the Churches practise in such things, and further also finde, these sacred actions and creatures, not only by increase of faith, feruor, and deuotion, to purge the impuritie of our soules, and procure remission of our daily infirmities, but that the cheefe Ministers of Christes Church, by their soueraine authoritie graunted of our Lord, may ioyne vnto the same, their blessing and remission of our venial sinnes or spiritual dettes: as vve see in S. Iames, remission of al sinnes to be annexed to the vnction vvith holy oile, vvhich to the Catholikes is a Sacrament, but to the Protestants vvas but a temporal ceremonie, and to some of them not of Christes institution, but of the Apostles onely. In their ovvne sense therfore they should not maruel that such spiritual effectes should procede of the vse of sanctified creatures, vvhereas venial trespasses be remitted many vvaies, though mortal ordinarily by the Sacraments onely. S. Gregorie did commonly send his benediction and remission of sinnes, in and vvith such holy tokens as vvere sanctified by his blessing and touching of the Apostles bodies and Martyrs Relikes, as novv his successors do in the like halovved remembrances of religion. See his 7 booke, epistle 126: and 9 booke, epistle 60. Thus therfore and to the effectes aforesaid the creatures of God be sanctified.

Ia. c. 5.

Remission of venial sinnes annexed to halovved creatures.

S. Gregorie.

If any man obiect that this vse of creatures is like coniuration in Necromancie, he must knovv the difference is, that in the Churches sanctifications and exorcismes, the Diuels be commaunded, forced, and tormented by Christes vvord and by praiers: but in the other vvicked practises, they be pleased, honoured, and couenanted vvithal: and therfore the first is godly and according to the Scriptures, but Necromancie abominable and against the Scriptures.

The difference betvvene the Churches exorcismes & other coniurations.

14. *The grace.*] S. Augustine declareth this grace to be the gift of the holy Ghost giuen vnto him by receiuing this holy Order, vvhereby he vvas made fitte to execute the office to his ovvne saluation and other mens. And note vvithal, that grace is not onely giuen in or vvith the Sacraments, by the receiuers faith or deuotion, but by the Sacrament, *per impositionem, by imposition of handes*. for so he speaketh 2 *Tim.* 1. Which is here said, *cum impositione, vvith imposition.*

Grace giuen in the Sacramẽt of Orders.

14. *With imposition.*] S. Ambrose vpon this place, implieth in the vvord *Imposition of hands*, al the holy action and sacred vvordes done and spoken ouer him vvhen he vvas made Priest. *Whereby* (saith he) *he vvas designed to the vvorke, and receiued authoritie, that he durst offer sacrifice in our Lordes steede vnto God.* So doth the holy Doctor allude vnto the vvordes that are said novv also in the Catholike Church to him that is made Priest: *Accipe potestatem offerendi pro viuis & mortuis in nomine Domini.* that is, *Take or receiue thou authoritie to offer for the liuing and the dead in the name of our Lord.* for the vvhich S. Hierom also (as is noted before) saith, that the ordering of Priests is, *by imposition of handes and imprecation of voice.*

Consecratiõ of Priests by imposition of handes.

In Esa. c. 58.

14. *Of Priesthod.*] The practise of the Church giueth vs the sense of this place, vvhich the auncient Councel of Carthage doth thus set dovvne. *When a Priest taketh orders, the Bishop blessing him and holding his hand vpon his head, let al the Priests present lay also their hands on his head by the Bishops hands &c.* Vvho seeth not novv, that holy Orders giuing grace by an external ceremonie and vvorke, is a Sacrament? So al the old Church counteth it. And S. Augustine (*cont. ep. Parmen. li. 2 c. 13.*) plainely saith that no man doubteth but it is a Sacrament. and lest any man thinke that he vseth not the vvord Sacrament proprely and precisely, he ioyneth it in nature and name vvith Baptisme. Againe vvho seeth not by this vse of imposition of hands in giuing Orders and other Sacraments, that Christ, the Apostles, and the Church may borovv of the Ievvish rites, certaine conuenient ceremonies and Sacramental actions, seing this same (as * the Heretikes can not deny) vvas receiued of the maner of Ordering Aaron and the Priests of the old lavv or other heads of the people? See *Exod.* 39. *Num.* 27, 23.

Conc. Carth. 4 c. 3.

Beza in cap. 6. Act.

Holy Orders a Sacrament.

16. *Saue both thy self.*] Though Christ be our onely Sauiour, yet the Scriptures forbeare not to speake freely and vulgarly and in a true sense, that man also may saue him self and others. But the Protestants notvvithstanding folovv such a captious kind of Diuinitie that if a man speake any such thing of our Lady or any Saint in heauen, or other meane of procuring saluation, they make it a derogation to Christes honour. Vvith such hypocrites haue vve novv a daies to do.

Men also are called sauiours vvithout derogatiõ to Christ.

CHAP. V.

Hovv to behaue him self tovvardes yong and old. 3 to bestovv the Churches oblations vpon the needy vvidovves, 9 and not to admitte the said Churches vvidovves vnder threescore yeres old. 17 In distribution to respect vvel the Priests that are painful. 19 and hovv in his Consistorie to heare accusations against Priests. 22 to be straite in examining before he giue Orders. to be chast, and to remitte somevvhat of his drinking vvater.

A Seniour rebuke not: but beseeche as a father: 1 yong men, as brethren: † old vvomen, as 2 mothers: yong vvomen, as sisters, in al chastitie.

The Epistle for holy vvidovves.

† Honour vvidovves: vvhich are " vvidovves in deede. † But if any vvidovv haue children or nephevves: let her learne first to rule her ovvne house, and to render mutual dutie to her parents. for this is acceptable before God. † But she that is a vvidovv in deede and desolate: let her hope in God, and continue in obsecrations & :: praiers night and day. † For she that is in deliciousenes, liuing is dead. † And this commaund that they be blamlesse. † But if any man haue not care of his ovvne, and especially of his domesticals, " he hath denied the faith, and is vvorse then an infidel. † " Let a vvidovv be chosen of no lesse thē three score yeres, vvhich hath been the " vvife of one husband, † hauing testimonie in good vvorkes, if she haue brought vp her children, if she haue receiued to harbour, if she haue vvashed the Saincts feete, if she haue ministred to them that suffer tribulation, if she haue folovved euery good vvorke. ⊣ † But the yonger vvidovves auoid. For vvhen they shal be " vvanton in Christ, " they vvil marie: † " hauing damnation, because they haue made void " their first faith. † and vvithal idle also they learne to goe about from house to house: not only idle, but also ful of vvordes and curious, speaking things vvhich they ought not. † " I vvil therfore the yonger to marie, to bring forth children, to be housevviues: to giue no occasion to the aduersarie for to speake euil. † For novv certaine are turned backe " after Satan. † If any faithful man haue vvidovves, let him minister to them, and let not the Church be burdened: that there may be sufficient for them that are vvidovves in deede.

(3) (4) (5) (6) (7) (8) (9) (10) (11) (12) (13) (14) (15) (16)

:: Because of this continual praier vvhich standeth not vvith cōiugal & carnal actes of matrimonie (as the Apostle signifieth 1 Cor. 7, 5) therfore vvere these vvidovves to liue in the state of perpetual continencie.

† The priestes that rule vvel, let them be esteemed c vvorthie of double honour: especially they that labour " in the vvord and doctrine. † For the Scripture saith: *Thou shalt not moosel the mouth to the oxe that treadeth out the corne* and, *The vvorke man is vvorthie of his hire.* † :: Against a priest receiue not accusation: but vnder tvvo or three vvitnesses. † Them that sinne, reproue before al: that the rest also may haue feare.

(17) (18) (19) (20)

c Double honour and liuelihod due to good Priestes.

:: Here the Apostle vvil not haue euery light felovv to be heard against a priest. so S. Augustin for the like reuerence of priesthod, admonisheth Pācarius that in no vvise he admitte any testimonies or accusations of Heretikes against a Catholike priest. ep. 212.

Deu. 25. 1. Cor. 9. Mat. 10, 10.

† I testifie before God and Christ IESVS, and the elect 21 Angels, that thou keepe these things vvithout preiudice,

doing

22 doing nothing by declining to the one part. † Impose hãdes on no man :: lightly, neither do thou communicate vvith other mens sinnes. Keepe thy self chast. † Drinke not yet " vvater: but vse a litle vvine for thy stomake, and thy often
24 infirmities. † Certaine mens sinnes be manifest, going before
25 to iudgement: and certaine men they folovv. † In like maner also good deedes be manifest, & they that are othervvise, can not be hidde.

:: Bishops must haue great care that they giue not orders to any that is not wel tried for his faith, learning, and good behauiour.

ANNOTATIONS
CHAP. V.

Ambr. in hunc loc. *Luc.* c. 2, 37.

3. *Widovves in deede.*] S. Ambrose calleth them vvidovves and desolate in deede, that might marie, but to make them selues better and more vvorthy of God, refuse mariage, vvhich they knovv to be but once blessed, imitating * holy Anne, vvho in fasting and praiers serued God night and day, neuer knovving but one husband. Such professed vvidovves then are to be honoured and succoured. Neither doth he speake onely of the Churches vvidovves (of vvhom specially aftervvard) but of al that by profession kept their vvidovvhod, exhorting them to passe their time in praier and fasting, v. 5. Vvhich vvas an honorable and holy state much vvritten of, and commended in the primitiue Church, namely by S. Ambrose and by S. Augustine, vvho vvrote bookes intitled thereof, and make it next to virginitie. *Ambr. de viduis. August. de bono viduitatis.*

Widowhod.

8. *He hath denied.*] Not that by this or by any other deadly sinne (except incredulitie or doubtfulnes in beleefe) they lose their faith: but that their factes be not ansvverable to their faith and to Christian religion, vvhich prescribeth al such duties.

9. *Let a vvidovv be chosen.*] Novv he speaketh more particularly and specially of such vvidovves as vvere nourished and found by the oblations of the faithful & the almes of the Church, and did vvithal some necessarie seruices about vvomen that vvere to be professed or baptized, for their instruction and addressing to that and other Sacraments, and also about the sicke and impotent: and vvithal sometimes they had charge of the Church goods or the disposition of them vnder the Deacons: in respect vvhereof they also and the like are called *Diaconissæ.* Eusebius li 6 c 35 reciteth out of Cornelius Epistle, that in the Church of Rome there is one Bishop, 40 Priests, sixe Deacons, seuen Subdeacons, Acoluthi 42, Exorcistes, Lectors, and Ostiarij 52, vvidovves together vvith the poore 150, al vvhich God nourisheth in his Church. See *Act. Apost. c. 6.* S. Chrysostom *li. 3 de Sacerdotio propius finem.* S. Epiphanius *in hæresi 79 Collyridianorum.* Novv then, vvhat maner of vvomen should be taken into the fellovvship of such as vvere found of the Church, he further declareth.

Widowes called *Diaconissæ*, & their office.

9. *The vvife of one husband.*] If you vvould haue a plaine paterne of Heretical fraude, corruption, and adulteration of the natiue sense of Gods vvord, and an inuincible demonstration that these nevv Glosers haue their consciences seared and hartes obdurated, vvillingly peruerting the Scriptures against that vvhich they knovv is the meaning thereof, to the maintenance of their sectes: marke vvel their handling of this place about these vvidovves of the Church. S. Paul prescribeth such onely to be admitted as haue been the vviues of one husband, that is to say, once onely maried, not admitting any that hath been tvvise maried. By vvhich vvordes the Catholikes proue first, that the like phrase * vsed before of Bishops and Deacons, that they should be the husbands of one vvife, must needes signifie that they can not be tvvise maried, nor admitted to these and the like functions, if they vvere more then once maried before. Secondly, vve proue by this place against the Aduersaries, that the state of vvidovvhod is more vvorthy, honorable, decent, and pure in respect of the seruice of the Church, and more to be relieued of the reuenues thereof, then the state of maried folkes. and that not onely (as the Aduersaries perhaps may ansvver) for their greater necessitie, or more leisure, freedom, or expedition to serue, in that they be not combered vvith husband and houshold, but in respect of their vidual continencie, chastitie, and puritie. for els such as vvere vvidovves vvith intention and freedom to marie aftervvard, might haue been admitted by the Apostle, as vvel as those that vvere neuer to marie againe.

These widowes must haue had but one husbãd: wherof many Catholike cõclusiõs are deduced.

c. 3, 2. — 1 — 2

3 Thirdly, vve proue that second mariage not onely after admission to the almes or seruice of the Church, but before also, is disagreable and a signe of incontinencie or more lust and fleshlines then is agreable or comely for any person belonging to the Church: and consequently, that the

Apostle in the last chapter treating of the holy functions of Bishops, Priests, Deacons, and of the Churches refusing generally *bigamos* or twise maried persons, must needes much more meane that no man twise maried should be receiued to holy Orders: and further, that as none were admitted to be widowes of the Church, that euer intended to marie againe, so none should euer be receiued to minister the Sacraments (which is a thing infinitely more, and requireth more puritie, and continencie, then the office or state of the said widowes,) that intended to marie againe. To receiue the body of Christ (saith S. Hierom *in Apolog. pro lib. cont. Iouin. ep.* 50. *c.* 6.) is a greater and holier thing then praier, and therfore Priests that must both continually pray and also be occupied about the receiuing or ministring the holy Sacrament daily, must liue continently.

4 Fourthly, we proue that it is not vnlawful to annexe, by precept or the parties promis, single life or chastitie to a whole state or order of the faithful, because the Apostle & the whole Church in his time ioyned to this state of the Churches widowes, perpetual cõtinencie. 5 Fifthly, we proue hereby that to refuse and not to accept the twise maried or such as wil not liue single, into the state of widowes or holy Orders, is not to condemne or forbid second mariage, or once & often marying, with the Manichees according to the doctrine of Diuels, as the Protestants (and before them the old condemned Iouinianistes) do blaspheme the Church. for then did S. Paul allow and teach doctrine of Diuels, who refuseth a twise maried woman, and bindeth others by their entering into this state, neuer to marie againe: as no doubt he did the Cleargie men much more in the 3 chapter before. Thus loe we Catholikes cõferre & conster the Scriptures, & for this meaning we haue al the Doctors without exception. What shift then haue the Heretikes here? for marie and remarie they must, let the Scriptures & al the Doctors in the world say nay to it. In truth they do not expound the word of God, but flee from the euidence of it, some one way & some an other.

Beza vpon this place.

And of al other, their extremest and most shameful tergiuersation is, that the Apostle here forbiddeth * not the admission of such widowes as haue been twise maried, but onely them that haue had two husbands at once. which was a very vnprobable and extorted exposition before, concerning Bishops and Deacons, c. 3. and (as S. Hierom saith ep. 83.) *malo nodo malus cuneus*: but here that an exception should be made onely against widowes that had had two husbands together (which was a thing neuer lawful nor neuer heard of) that is a most intolerable impudencie, and a cõstruction that neuer came to any wise mans cogitation before: and yet these their fansies must be Gods word, and *bigamus* or *bigamia* must against their old natures and vse of al writers, be al one with *Polygamus* and *Polygamia*. They giue an example of such widowes, in women diuorced iustly from their husbands in the old law. As though S. Paul here tooke order for the Iewes widowes onely, or that had been such a cõmon case among the Iewes also, that the Apostle needed to take so careful order for it. finally, they let not to say that if the Apostle should be vnderstood to refuse a widow twise maried at sundrie times, it were vnreasonable & iniurious to second mariages, which haue no more indecencie or signe of incontinencie (say they) then the first. Thus bold they are with the Apostle and al antiquitie.

The Caluinists most absurd exposition of the Apostles wordes.

Their blaspheme against the plaine text.

11. *Wanton in Christ.*] Widowes waxing warme, idle, and wel fedde by the Church, lust after husbands, as also Apostate-Priests and Superintendents marie, specially after they haue gotten good Ecclesiastical liuings. Which is to waxe wanton in Christ, or against Christ, καλὰ χριστοῦ. * The Greeke word signifieth to cast of the raines or bridle, that is, the bond or promis of continencie which they had put vpon them.

* καταστρηνιᾶν

11. *They wil.*] *In the chastitie of widowhed or Virginitie* (saith S. Augustine) *the excellencie of a greater gift is sought for. Which being once desired, chosen, and offered to God by vow, it is not onely damnable to enter afterward into mariage, but though it come not actually to mariage, onely to haue the wil to marie is damnable.* Aug. li. de bono viduit. cap. 9.

The very wil to breake the vow of chastitie, is damnable.

12. *Hauing damnation.*] It signifieth not blame, checke, or reprehension of men, as some to make the fault seeme lesse, would haue it: but * iudgement or eternal damnatiõ, which is a heauy sentence. God graunt al maried Priests and Religious may consider their lamentable case. What a greuous sinne it is, see S. Ambrose *ad virginem lapsam cap.* 5 & 8.

* κρίμα

12. *Their first faith.*] Al the auncient fathers that euer wrote commentaries vpon this Epistle, Greeke and Latin, as S. Chrysostom, Theodorete, Oecumenius, Theophylactus, Primasius, S. Ambrose, Ven. Bede, Haimo, Anselme, and the rest: also al others that by occasion vse this place, as the 4 Councel of Carthage ca. 104. and the 4 of Toleto c. 55. S. Epiphanius *hær.* 48. S. Hierom *cont. Iouinianum li.* 1. *c.* 7. & S. Athanasius *li. de virginitate*. S. Augustine in exceding many places: al these expound the Apostles wordes of the vow of Chastitie or the faith and promis made to Christ to liue continently. *What is to breake their first faith?* saith S. Augustine. *They vowed, and performed not.* In ps. 75. *prope finem.* Againe in an other place, *They breake their first faith, that stand not in that which they vowed.* *Li. de Sancta virgin. c.* 33. Againe he and al the fathers with him in Carthage Councel before named: *If any widowes, how yong so euer they were left of their husbands deceased, haue vowed them selues to God, left their laical habite, and vnder the testimonie of the Bishop and Church haue appeared in religious weede, and afterward goe any more to secular mariage, according to the Apostles sentence*

Breaking of their first faith, is (by the consent of al antiquitie) whẽ they breake their vow of chastitie.

sentence they shal be damned, because they vvere so bold to make void the faith or promis of Chastitie which they vovved to our Lord. So saith he and 215 fathers moe in that Councel.

And this promis of chastitie is called, *faith*, because the fidelitie betvvixt maried persons is ordinarily called of holy writers, *faith*: and the vovv of chastitie made to God, ioyneth him & the persons so vovving, as it vvere in mariage, so farre, that if the said persons breake promis, they are counted and called in the last alleaged Councel, *Gods adulterers*. In the 3 to the Romanes also and often els vvhere, faith is taken for promis or fidelitie. And that it is so taken here, the vvordes *irritum facere* (to frustrate and make void) do proue. for that terme is commonly vsed in matter of vovv, promis, or compacte. *Gen. 17. Num. 30.* This promis is called here *prima fides* (the first faith) in respect of the later promis vvhich vovvbreakers make to them vvith vvhom they pretend to marrie. So saith S. Augustine *li. de bono viduit. c. 8. & 9.* and Innocentius *1 ep. 2. cap. 13. to. 1. Conc.* And this is the onely natiue, euident, and agreable sense to the circumstance of the letter. And the vaine euasion of the Heretikes to saue the Apostate-Monkes, Friers, Nunnes, and Priests from damnation for their pretended mariages, is friuolous: to vvit, that *first faith* here signifieth the faith of Baptisme or Christian beleefe, & not the promis or vovv of Chastitie. But vve aske them if this faith of Baptisme be broken by mariage or no. For the text is plaine that by intending to marie, they breake their faith, and by breaking their faith they be damned, if they die vvithout repentance. In truth vvhich vvay so euer they writhe them selues to defend their sacrilege or pretended mariages, they lose their labour and struggle against their ovvne conscience and plaine Scripture.

Why this vow is called faith or fidelitie.

Vvhy the first faith.

The heretikes exposition of this first faith, imposible & against the text.

14. *I vvil the yonger.*] He speaketh of such yong ones as vvere yet free. For such as had already made vovv, neither could they vvithout damnation marie, were they yong or old, nor he vvithout sinne commaund or counsel them to it. Neither (as S. Hierom proueth to * Gerontia, and S. Chrysostom vpon this place) doth he precisely commaund or counsel the yong ones. that vvere free, to marie, or absolutely forbid them to vovv chastitie: God forbid, say they. But his speach conteineth onely a vvise admonition to the frailer sort, that it vvere farre better for them not to haue vowed at all, but to haue maried againe, then to haue fallen to aduoutrie and Apostasie after profession. Vvhich is no more but to preferre second mariage before fornication: and a good warning, that they vvhich are to professe, looke wel vvhat they do. S. Paules experience of the fall of some yong ones to mariage, caused him to giue this admonition here: as also that before, that none should be receiued to the Churches almes vnder threescore yeres of age. Not forbidding the Church for euer, to accept any vovves of vvidowes or virgins til that age, as the Heretikes falsely affirme: but shewing vvhat vvas meete for that time and the beginning of Christianitie, vvhen as yet there vvere no Monasteries builded, no prescript rule, no exact order of obedience to Superiors: but the professed (as S. Paul here noteth) coursed & wandered vp and downe idly, as novv our professed virgins or Nunnes do not, neither can do. Of vvhom therfore, vvhere discipline is obserued, there is no cause of such danger. Besides that vvidowes hauing had the vse of carnal copulation before, are more dangerously tempted, then virgins that are brought vp from their tender age in pietie and haue no experience of such pleasures. See S. Ambrose *li. de viduis*, prouing by the example of holy Anna, vvho liued a vvidow euen from her youth til 80 yeres of age, in fasting and praying night and day, that the Apostle doth not here without exception forbid al yong vvidowes to vow, yea he esteemeth that profession in the yonger women much more laudable, glorious, and meritorious. See his booke *de Viduis in initio*.

* otherwise Ageruchia ep. 11.

S. Paul meaneth not that vvidovves professed should marie.

It is better for the frailer sort, that are in danger of falling, to marie rather then to vow.

Yong vvomen may be professed & taken into religion.

15. *After Satan.*] Vve may here learne, that for those to marie vvhich are professed, is to turne backe after Satan. For he speaketh of such as vvere maried cōtrarie to their vow. And herevpon vve call the Religious that marie (as Luther, Bucer, Peter martyr and the rest) Apostataes. More vve learne, that such yong ones haue no excuse of their age, or that they be vehemently tempted and burne in their concupiscences, or that they haue not the gift of Chastitie. For notvvithstanding al these excuses, these yong professed vvidowes if they marie, go backvvard after Satan, and be Apostataes, & damned, except they repent. For as for the Apostles vvordes to the Corinthians, *It is better to marie then to burne*, Vve haue before declared out of the fathers, and here vve adde, that it pertaineth onely to persons that be free and haue not vowed to the contrarie. as S. Ambrose *li. ad virg. laps. c. 5.* S. Augustine *de bono vid. c. 8.* and S. Hierom *li. 1. cont. Iouin. c. 7.* expound it.

To marie after the vovv of Chastitie, is to goe after Satan.

1 Cor. 7.

The Heretikes of our time thinke there is no remedie for fornication or burning, but mariage. and so did S. Augustine vvhen he was yet a Manichee. *Putabam me miserum &c. I thought* (saith he *li. 6. Confes. c. 11.*) *that I should be an vnhappie and miserable man if I should lacke the companie of a vvoman, and the medicine of thy mercie to heale the same infirmitie I thought not vpon, because I had not tried it: and I imagined that continencie vvas in a mans ovvne povver and libertie, vvhich in my self I did not feele: being so foolish not to vnderstand that no man can be continent vnles thou*

The heretikes only remedie against concupiscence is mariage.

giue it. Verely thou vvouldest giue it, if vvith invvard mourning I vvould knocke at thy eares, and vvith sound faith vvould cast my care vpon thee.

The vow of chastitie lawful, possible to be kept, more grateful to God.

By al vvhich you may easily proue, that chastitie is a thing that may lavvfully be vowed, that it is not impossible to be fulfilled by praier, fasting, and chastisement of mens concupiscence, that it is a thing more grateful to God then the condition of maried persons: for els it should not be required either in the Cleargie or in the Religious. finally, that it is most abominable to persuade the poore virgins or other professed to such sacrilegious vvedlocke, which S. Augustine auoucheth to be vvorse then aduoutrie. *de bon. vidu. c.* 4. 11. Iouinian vvas the first that euer made mariage equal vvith virginitie or chast life, for vvhich he vvas condemned of heresie. *Aug. in argumento li. de bono Coniugali. De pec. merit li.* 3. *c.* 7. *Li. de hæres. hær.* 82. He vvas the first that persuaded professed virgins to marie, which S. Augustine saith vvas so clerely and vvithout question vvicked, that it could neuer infect any Priest, but certaine miserable Nunnes. Yea for this strange persuasion he calleth Iouinian a monster, saying of him thus *Li.* 2. *Retract. cap.* 22. *The holy Church that is there* (at Rome) *most faithfully and stoutly resisted this monster.* S. Hierom calleth the said Heretike and his complices, *Christian epicures. li* 2 *cont. Iouin. c.* 19. See S. Ambrose *ep.* 82 *ad vercellensem episcopum in initio.* But vvhat vvould these holy doctors haue said, if they had liued in our doleful time, vvhen the Protestants go quite avvay vvith this vvickednes, and call it Gods vvord?

Iouinians heresie in this point, cōdemned of old, is called of the Protestants, Gods vvord.

17. *In vvord and doctrine.*] Such Priests specially and Prelates are vvorthy of double, that is, of the more ample honour, that are able to preach and teach, and do take paines therein. Vvhere vve may note, that al good Bishops or Priests in those daies vvere not so vvel able to teach as some others, and yet for the ministerie of the Sacraments, and for vvisedom and gouernement, vvere not vnmeete to be Bishops and Pastors. for though it be one high commendation in a Prelate, to be able to teach, as the Apostle before noted: yet al can not haue the like grace therein, and it is often recompensed by other singular giftes no lesse necessarie. S. Augustine laboured in vvord and doctrine, Alipius and Valerius vvere good Bishops, and yet had not that gift. *Posid. in vit. Aug. c.* 5. And some times and countries require preachers more then other. Al vvhich vve note, to discouer the pride of Heretikes, that contemne some of the Catholike Priests or Bishops, pretending that they can not preach as they do, vvith meretricious and painted eloquence.

Many good & vvorthie Bishops, that haue not the gift of preaching and teaching.

23. *Water.*] You see hovv lavvful and hovv holy a thing it is, to fast from some meates or drinkes, either certaine daies, or alvvaies, as this B. Bishop Timothee did: vvho vvas hardly induced by the Apostle to drinke a litle vvine vvith his vvater in respect of his infirmities. And marke vvithal, vvhat a calumnious and stale cauillation it is, that to abstaine from certaine meates and drinkes for punishment of the body or deuotion, is to condemne Gods creatures. See an homilie of S. Chrysostom vpon these vvordes, to. 5.

CHAP. VI.

Vvhat to teach seruants. 3 If any teach against the doctrine of the Church obstinately, he doth it of pride and for lucre. 11 But the Catholike Bishop must folovv vertue, hauing his eie alvvaies to life euerlasting and to the cōming of Christ. 17 Vvhat to commaund the riche. 20 Finally, to keepe most carefully the Catholike Churches doctrine, vvithout mutation.

1 WHOSOEVER are seruantes vnder yoke, let them counte their maisters vvorthie of al honour: lest the name of our Lord and his doctrine be blasphemed. 2 † But they that haue faithful maisters, let them not contemne them because they are brethren, but serue the rather, because they be faithful and beloued, vvhich are partakers of the benefite. These things teache and exhort.

3 † If any man ᶜ teach othervvise, and consent not to the sound vvordes of our Lord IESVS Christ, and to that doctrine

c See the anotation before cap. 1, 3. 4.

ἑτεροδιδασκαλεῖ

4 ctrine vvhich is according to pietie: † he is proude, knowing nothing, but " languishing about questions and strife of vvordes: of vvhich rise enuies, contentions, blasphe-
5 mies, euil suspicions, † conflictes of men corrupted in their minde, and that are depriued of the truth, that esteeme gaine
6 to be pietie. † But [b] pietie vvith sufficiencie is great gaine.
7 † For vve * brought nothing into this vvorld: doubtlesse,
8 neither can vve take avvay any thing. † But * hauing foode, and vvhervvith to be couered, vvith these vve are content.
9 † For they that vvil be made riche, fall into tentation & the snare of the deuil, & many desires vnprofitable and hurteful,
10 vvhich drovvne men into destruction and perdition. † For the roote of al euils is couetousenes: :: vvhich certaine desiring haue erred from the faith, and haue intangled them selues in many sorovves.

11 † But thou, ô man of God, flee these things: and [b] pursue
12 iustice, pietie, faith, charitie, patience, mildenes. † Fight the good fight of faith: apprehend eternal life, ⊣ vvherein thou art called and hast confessed a good confession before many
13 vvitnesses. † I commaund thee before God vvho quickeneth al things, and Chirst IESVS vvho * gaue testimonie
14 vnder Pontius Pilate a good confession: † that thou keepe the commaundement vvithout spotte, blamelesse vnto the
15 comming of our Lord IESVS Christ. † vvhich in due times the Blessed & onely Mightie vvil shevv, the * King of kings
16 and Lord of lordes, † vvho only hath immortalitie, and inhabiteth light not accessible, * vvhom no man hath seen, yea neither can see, to vvhom be honour and empire euerlasting. Amen. ⊣

17 † Commaund the riche of this vvorld not to be high minded, nor to trust in the vncertaintie of riches, but in the liuing God (vvho giueth vs al things aboundantly to enioy)
18 † to doe wel, to become riche in good workes, to giue easily,
19 to communicate, † to heape vnto them selues a good :: foundation for the time to come, that they may apprehend the true life.

20 † O Timothee, keepe the " *depositum*, auoiding the " profane [c] nouelties of voices, & oppositions of " falsely called knovv-
21 ledge. † Vvhich certaine promising, haue erred about the faith. Grace be vvith thee: Amen.

ANN

Marginal notes:

Iob 1, 21.

Mat. 6, 25.

Io. 18, 37

Apoc. 17, 14. 19, 16.

Io. 1, 18.

c καινοφωνίας. *S. Chrysostom.*

b The epistle for S. Alexius *Iul.* 17.

:: As in the 1. chap. lacke of faith and good conscience, so here couetousnes or desire of these temporal things, & in the end of this chap. presumption and boasting of knowledge, are causes of falling from the faith: heresie often being the punishmēt of former sinnes.

b The epistle for S. Timothee, *Ian.* 24.

:: Almes dedes and good workes laide for a foūdatiō and ground to attaine euerlasting life. So say the doctors vpō this place.

ANNOTATIONS
CHAP. VI.

4. *Languiſhing.*] Euen theſe be the good diſputes of our nevv Sect-maiſters, and the vvorld hath to long proued theſe inconueniences here named, to be the fruites of ſuch endles altercations in religion as theſe vnhappie ſectes haue brought forth.

20. *Depoſitum.*] The vvhole doctrine of our Chriſtianitie being taught by the Apoſtles, and deliuered to their ſucceſſors, and comming dovvne from one Biſhop to an other, is called the *Depoſitum*, as it vvere a thing laid into their hands, and committed vnto them to keepe. Vvhich becauſe it paſſeth from hand to hand, from age to age, from Biſhop to Biſhop vvithout corruption, change, or alteration, is al one vvith Tradition, and is the truth giuen vnto the holy Biſhops to keepe, and not to lay men. See the notable diſcourſe of Vincentius Lirinenſis vpon this text. *li. cont. profan. hær. Nouationes.* And it is for this great, old, and knovven treaſure committed to the Biſhops cuſtodie, that S. Irenæus calleth the Catholike Church *Depoſitorium diues*, *the rich treaſurie of truth.* li. 3 c. 4. And as Clemens Alexandrinus vvriteth *li. 2 Strom.* this place maketh ſo much againſt al Heretikes vvho do al change this *Depoſitum*, that for it onely ſuch men in his daies denied this Epiſtle. The Heretikes of our daies chalenge alſo the truth, and ſay it is the old truth. but they leape 14 or 15 hundreth yeres for it ouer mens heads to the Apoſtles. But vve call for the *Depoſitum*, and aſke them in vvhoſe hands that truth vvhich they pretend, vvas laid vp, and hovv it came dovvne to them. for it can not be Apoſtolical, vnles it vvere Depoſitum in ſome Timothees hand, ſo to continevv from one Biſhop to an other vntil our time and to the end.

Depoſitum, is the Catholike truth deſcending from the Apoſtles by ſucceſsion of Biſhops, euen vnto the end.

The Proteſtãts can ſhew no ſuch *depoſitum.*

20. *Profane nouelties.*] *Non dixit antiquitates* (ſaith Vincentius Lirinenſis) *non dixit vetuſtates, ſed prophanas nouitates. Nam ſi vitanda eſt nouitas, tenenda eſt antiquitas: ſi prophana eſt nouitas, ſacrata eſt vetuſtas.* that is, *He ſaid not*, ANTIQVITIES: *he ſaid not*, AVNCIENTNES: *but* PROFANE NOVELTIES. *For if noueltie is to be auoided, antiquitie is to be kept: if noueltie be profane, auncientnes is holy and ſacred.* See his vvhole booke againſt the profane nouelties of hereſies.

Vve may not meaſure the nevvnes or oldnes of Wordes and termes of ſpeaking in religion, by holy Scriptures only: as though all thoſe or only thoſe Were new and to be reiected, that are not expreſly found in holy vvrite: but vve muſt eſteeme them by the agreablenes or diſagreablenes they haue to the true ſenſe of Scriptures, to the forme of Catholike faith and doctrine, to the phraſe of the old Chriſtians, to the Apoſtolike vſe of ſpeache come vnto vs by tradition of all ages and Churches, and to the preſcription of holy Councels and Schooles of the Chriſtian World: vvhich haue giuen out (according to the time and queſtions raiſed by heretikes and contentious perſons) very fit, artificiall, and ſignificant vvordes, to diſcerne and defend the truth by, againſt falſhod.

Prophane nouelties of vvordes how to be tried and examined.

Theſe termes, *Catholike, Trinitie, Perſon, Sacrament, Incarnation, Maſſe,* and many moe, are not (in that ſenſe vvherein the Church vſeth them) in the Scriptures at all, and diuers of them Were ſpoken by the Apoſtles before any part of the nevv Teſtament vvas vvritten, ſome of them taken vp ſtraight after the Apoſtles daies in the vvrittings and preachings of holy Doctors, and in the ſpeach of all faithfull people, and therfore can not be counted Nouelties of vvordes. Others beſide theſe, as, *Conſubſtantial, Deipara, Tranſſubſtantiation,* and the like, vvhich are neither in expreſſe termes found in Scriptures, nor yet in ſenſe (if vve ſhould folovv the iudgement of the ſpeciall ſectes againſt vvhich the ſaid vvordes Were firſt inuented, the Arians crying out againſt Nicene Councel, for the firſt: the Neſtorians againſt the Epheſine Coũcel, for the ſecond: the Lutherans & Caluiniſts againſt the Laterã and the later Councels, for the third) theſe vvordes alſo notWithſtanding, by the iudgemẽt of holy Church and Councels approued to be conſonant to Gods vvord, and made authenticall among the faithfull, are ſound and true vvordes, and not of thoſe kinde vvhich the Apoſtle calleth *Nouelties.*

Catholike termes not expreſly in the Scriptures, but in ſenſe, are no ſuch nouelties of vvordes.

The vvordes then here forbidden, are the neW prophane termes and ſpeaches inuented or ſpecially vſed by heretikes, ſuch as S. Irenee recordeth the Valentinians had a number moſt-monſtruous: as the Manichees had alſo diuers, as may be ſeene in S. Auguſtine: The Arians had their **Similis ſubſtantiæ*, and Chriſt to be *ex non exiſtentibus*: the other heretikes after thoſe daies had their * *Chriſtiparam*, and ſuch like, agreable to their ſectes. But the Proteſtants paſſe in this kinde, as they excede moſt heretikes in the number of neW opinions: as their *Seruum arbitrium*, their *ſole faith*, their *fiduce*, their *apprehenſion of Chriſtes iuſtice*, their *imputatiue righteouſnes*: their horrible termes of terrors, anguiſhes, diſtreſſes, diſtruſt, feares and feeling of hell paines in the ſoule of our Sauiour, to expreſſe their blaſphemous fiction of his temporall damnation, vvhich they call his deſcending to hell: Their *markes, tokens,* and *badges Sacramentall*, their *Companation, Impanation, Circumpanation,* to auoid the true conuerſion in the Eucharist: their preſence *in figure, in faith, ſigne, ſpirit, pleadge, effect,*

Heretical nouelties of vvordes.

The Proteſtãts prophane nouelties of vvordes.

* ὁμοιούσιον.

* Χριστοτόκον.

effect, to auoid the reall presence of Christes body. These and such like innumerable vvhich they occupie in euery part of their false doctrine, are in the sense that they vse them, all false, captious and deceitfull vvordes, and are *nouitates vocum* here forbidden.

And though some of the said termes haue been by some occasion obiter vvithout il meaning spokē by Catholikes before these Heretikes arose, yet now knovving thē to be the propre speaches of Heretikes, Christiā men are boūd to auoid them. Wherein the Church of God hath euer been as diligent to resist Nouelties of vvordes, as her Aduersaries are busy to inuent them. for vvhich cause she vvil not haue vs cōmunicate vvith them, nor folow their fashion and phrase nevvly inuented, though in the nature of the vvordes sometime there be no harme. In S. Augustines daies vvhen Christiā men had any good befallē them, or entered into any mans house, or met any frind by the vvay, they vsed alvvaies to say, *Deo gratias*. The Donatistes and Circumcellions of that time being nevvfangled, forsooke the old phrase and vvould alvvaies say, *Laus Deo*: from vvhich the Catholike men did so abhorre (as the said Doctor vvriteth) that they had as leefe mette a theefe as one that said to them, *Laus Deo*, in steede of *Deo gratias*. As novv vve Catholikes must not say, *The Lord*, but, *Our Lord*: as vve say, *Our Lady*, for his mother, not, *The Lady*. Let vs keepe our forefathers vvordes, and vve shal easily keepe our old and true faith that vve had of the first Christians. Let them say, *Amendement, abstinence, the Lordes Supper, the Communion table, Elders, Ministers, Superintendent, Congregation, so be it, praise ye the Lord, Morning-Praier, Euening-praier*, and the rest, as they vvill: Let vs auoid those Nouelties of vvordes, according to the Apostles prescript, and keepe the old termes, *Penance, Fasting, Priest, Church, Bishop, Masse, Mattins, Euensong, the B. Sacrament, Altar, Oblation, Host, Sacrifice, Alleluia, Amen, Lent, Palme-Sunday, Christmas*, & the very vvordes vvil bring vs to the faith of our first Apostles, and condemne these nevv apostataes nevv faith and phrases.

in Ps. 132.

Catholikes must abhorre from heretical phrases and vvordes.

20. *Falsely called knovvledge.*] It is the propertie of al Heretikes to arrogate to them selues great knovvledge, and to condemne the simplicitie of their fathers the holy Doctors and the Church. but the Apostle calleth their pretended skill, a knovvledge falsely so called, being in truth high and deepe blindnes. *Such* (saith S. Irenæus *li. 5 c. 17.*) *as forsake the preaching of the Church, argue the holy Priests of vnskilfulnes, not considering hovv far more vvorth a religious idiote is, then a blasphemous and impudent sophister, such as al Heretikes be.* And againe Vincentius Lirinensis speaking in the person of Heretikes saith, *Come ô ye folish and miserable men, that are commonly called Catholikes, and learne the true faith vvhich hath been hid many ages heretofore, but is reuealed and shevved of late, &c.* See his vvhole booke concerning these matters.

Heretikes arrogate knowledge falsely so called.

THE ARGVMENT OF THE SECOND EPISTLE OF S. PAVL TO TIMOTHEE.

THE cheefe scope of this second to Timothee, is, to open vnto him that his martyrdom is at hand. Vvhich yet he doth not plainely before the end: preparing first his minde vvith much circumstance, because he knevv it vvould greiue him sore, and also might be a tentation vnto him. Therfore he talketh of the cause of his trouble, & of the revvard: that the one is honorable, and the other most glorious: and exhorteth him to be constant in the faith, to be ready alvvaies to suffer for it, to fulfil his ministerie to the end, as him self novv had done his.

Vvhereby it is certaine, that it vvas vvritten at Rome, in his last apprehension and emprisonment there: as he signifieth by these vvordes Cap. 1: Onesiphorus vvas not ashamed of my chaine, but when he was come to Rome, carefully sought me, &c. *And of his martyrdom, thus:* For I am novv ready to be offered, and the time of my resolution (*or death*) is at hand. *cap. 4.*

THE SECOND EPISTLE OF PAVL TO TIMOTHEE.

CHAP. I.

Vvith his praises he couertly exhorteth him not to be dismaied for his trouble, 6 (hauing grace giuen in Orders to helpe him, 8 and knovving for vvhat cause he is persecuted) and namely vvith the example of Onesiphorus.

PAVL an Apostle of IESVS Christ 1 by the vvil of God, according to the promisse of the life which is in Christ IESVS: † to Timothee my deerest 2 sonne, grace, mercie, peace from God the father, and Christ IESVS our Lord.

† I giue thankes to God, vvhom 3 I serue from my progenitours in a pure conscience, that vvithout intermission I haue a memorie of thee in my praiers, night and day † desiring to see thee, 4 mindeful of thy teares, that I may be filled vvith ioy, † cal- 5 ling to minde that faith vvhich is in thee not feined, vvhich also dvvelt first "in thy grandmother Loïs, and thy mother Eunîce, and I am sure that in thee also. † For the vvhich 6 cause I admonish thee that thou resuscitate the ∴ grace of God, vvhich is in thee by the imposition of my handes. † For God hath not giuen vs the spirit of feare: but of 7 povver, and loue, and sobrietie. † Be not therfore ashamed 8 of the testimonie of our Lord, nor of me his prisoner: but trauail vvith the Gospel according to the povver of God, † vvho hath deliuered and called vs by his holy calling, *not 9 according to our vvorkes, but according to his purpose and grace, vvhich vvas giuen to vs in Christ IESVS* before the secular times. † But it is manifested novv by the illumination 10 of

∴ Here againe it is plaine that holy Orders giue grace, & that euen by and in the external ceremonie of imposing the Bishops hands. And it is a maner of speach specially vsed in this Apostle and S. Luke, that Orders giue grace to the ordered, & that to take orders or authoritie to minister Sacramēts or preach, is, to be giuen or deliuered to Gods grace. *Act.* 14, 25.

Tit. 3, 5.

Tit. 1, 3.

of our Sauiour IESVS Christ, vvho hath destroied death, & 11 illuminated life and incorruption by the Gospel: † vvherein * I am appointed a preacher and Apostle and Maister of the 12 Gentiles. † For the vvhich cause also I suffer these things: but I am not cōfounded. For I know whom I haue beleeued, & I am sure that he is able to keepe my " *depositum* vnto that day. 13 † Haue thou " a forme of sound vvordes, vvhich thou hast 14 heard of me in faith & c in the loue in Christ IESVS. † Keepe the good *depositum* by the holy Ghost, vvhich dvvelleth in vs. 15 † Thou knovvest this, that al vvhich are in Asia, be auerted from me: of vvhom is Phigelus and Hermogenes. 16 † Our Lord giue mercie to * the house of Onesiphorus: because he hath often refreshed me, and hath :: not been a-17 shamed of my chaine. † but vvhen he vvas come to Rome: 18 he sought me carefully, and found me. † " Our Lord graunt him to finde mercie of our Lord in that day. And how many things he ministred to me at Ephesus, thou knovvest better.

1 Timo. 2, 7.

ἐν ἀγάπῃ τῇ ἐν Χριστῷ

2 Tim. 4, 19.

c Faith and loue coupled commonly together in this Apostles vvritings.

:: Vvhat a happie & meritorious thig it is to relieue the afflicted for religiō, & not to be ashamed of their disgrace, yrōs or What miseries soeuer.

ANNOTATIONS
CHAP. I.

5. *In thy grandmother.*] Though God shevv mercie to many that be of incredulous, heretical or il parents, yet it is a goodly benediction of God to haue good education and to haue good faithful progenitors and Catholike parents. And it is a great sinne to forsake the faith of our fathers that be Catholikes, or contrarie to our education in the Church to folovv strange doctrines, abandoning not onely our next natural parents faith, but the aūcient faith and beleefe of al our progenitors for many hundred yeres together. And if to folovv the faith of mother and grandmother onely, the Christian religion being then but nevvly planted, vvas so commendable euen in a Bishop, hovv much more is it novv laudable to cleaue fast to the faith of so many our progenitors and ages that continued in the same Christian religion vvhich they first receiued?

A great blessing, to haue Catholike progenitors: and very cōmendable to cleaue fast to their faith.

Our Protestants in their great vvisedom laugh at good simple men vvhen they talke of their fathers faith. But S. Hierom, *I am a Christian*, saith he, *and borne of Christian parents, and carie the signe of the crosse in my forehead.* And againe ep. 65. c. 3. *Until this day the Christian vvorld hath been vvithout this doctrine. that faith vvil I hold fast being an old man, vvherein I vvas borne a child.* And the holy Scriptures set vs often to schole to our fathers. *Aske thy fathers, and they vvil shevv thee, thy auncetours, and they vvil tel thee.* And againe, *Our fathers haue shevved vnto vs.* And cōmonly the true God is called the God of the faithful and of their forefathers. *Dan.* 2. 3. And false Gods and nevv doctrines or opinions be named, *Nevv and fresh, such as their fathers vvorshipped not. Deut.* 32. Finally S. Paul both here and * often els alleageth for his defense and commendation, that he vvas of faithful progenitors. And it is a case that Heretikes can not lightly bragge of, no one sect commonly during so long vvithout intermission, that they can haue many progenitors of the said sect. Vvhich is a demonstration that their faith is not true. and that it is impossible our Catholike faith to be false, supposing the Christian religion to be true.

Apol. cōt. Ruff. li. 1. c. 8.

Deut. 32. & Ps. 43.

* Act. 24. 2 Cor. 11.

The peoples speaches of their fathers faith, is very Christian and laudable.

12. *Depositum.*] A great comfort to al Christians, that euery of their good deedes and sufferings for Christ, and al the vvorldly losses susteined for defense or confession of their faith, be extant vvith God, and kept as *depositum*, to be repaied or receiued againe in heauen. Vvhich if the vvorldlings beleeued or considered, they vvould not so much maruel to see Catholike men so vvillingly to lose land, libertie, credit, life and al for Christes sake and the Churches faith.

Al our good deedes are laid vp vvith God, to be revvarded

13. *A forme.*] The Apostles did set dovvne a platforme of faith, doctrine, & phrase of Catholike speach and preaching, & that not so much by vvriting (as here vve see) as by vvord of mouth: to vvhich he referreth Timothee ouer and aboue his Epistles vnto him. And hovv precisely Chri-

We must speake in Catholike termes, after a certaine rule of faith, and forme of vvordes.

stian Doctors ought to keepe the forme of vvordes auncienctly appropriated to the mysteries and matters of our religion, S. Augustine expresseth in these vvordes *li. 10 de ciuit. c. 23. Philosophers speake vvith freedom of vvordes &c. but vve must speake according to a certaine rule, lest licentious libertie of vvordes breede an impious opiniõ of the things also that are signified by the same.* Trinitie, person, essence, Consubstantial, Transsubstantiation, Masse, Sacrament, and such like, be *verba sana* (as the Apostle speaketh) *sound vvordes*, giuen to expresse certaine high truthes in religion, partly by the Apostles and first founders of our religion vnder Christ, and partly very aptly inuented by holy Councels and fathers, to expresse as neere as could be the high ineffable or vnspeakable veritie of some points, and to stoppe the Heretikes audacitie and inuention of nevv vvordes and prophane speaches in such things, vvhich the Apostle vvarneth Timothee to auoid 1 *ep. c.* 6, 20. and 2 *ep.* 2, 16. See the Annotations there.

Relieuers of Cath. prisoners.

18. *Our Lord.*] To haue this praier of an Apostle, or any Priest or poore Cath. man so relieued, giueth the greatest hope at the day of our death or general iudgemẽt, that can be: and it is worth al the landes, honours, and riches of the vvorld.

CHAP. II.

He exhorteth him to labour diligently in his office, considering the revvard in Christ, and his denial of them that deny him. 14 Not to contend, but to shunne heretikes: neither to be moued to see some subuerted, considering that the elect continue Catholikes, and that in the Church be of al sortes. 24 Yet vvith al svveetenes to reclaime the deceiued.

THOV therfore my sonne, be strong in the grace vvhich is in Christ IESVS: 1 † & the things vvhich thou hast heard of me by many witnesses, these cõmend to faithful men, vvhich shal be fit to teach others also. 2 † Labour thou as a good souldiar of Christ IESVS. 3 † "No man being a souldiar to God, intãgleth him self vvith secular businesses: that he may please him to vvhom he hath approued him self. 4 † For he also that striueth for the maisterie, is not crovvned vnlesse he striue lavvfully. 5 † The husbandman that laboureth, must first take of the fruites. 6 † Vnderstand vvhat I say: for our Lord vvil giue thee in al things vnderstanding 7 † Be mindeful that our Lord IESVS Christ is risen againe from the dead, of the seede of Dauid, according to my Gospel, 8 † vvherein I labour euen vnto bandes, as a malefactour: but the vvord of God is not tied. 9 † Therfore ∴ I sustaine al things for the elect, that they also may obtaine the saluation, vvhich is in Christ IESVS, vvith heauenly glorie. 10 † A faithful saying. For if vve be dead vvith him, vve shal liue also together. 11 † If vve shal sustaine, vve shal also reigne together. 12 * If vve shal deny, he also vvil denie vs. † * If vve beleeue not: he continueth faithful, he can not denie him self. 13 † These things admonish: 14 testifying before our Lord.

∴ Marke here that the elect (though sure of saluation) yet are saued by meanes of their preachers & teachers, as also by their ovvne endeuours.

Mat. 10, Ro. 3, 3.

Contend

Contend not in vvordes, for it is profitable for nothing, 15 but for the subuersion of them that heare. † Carefully prouide to present thy self approued to God, a vvorkeman not to be confounded, " rightly handling the vvord of truth. 16] † But [c] profane and vaine speaches auoid: for they doe much 17 grovv to impietie: † & " their speache spreadeth as a canker: 18 of vvhom is Hymenæus and Philêtus: † vvho haue erred from the truth, saying that the resurrection is done already, and haue subuerted the faith of some.

c See the Annotatiõ before 1 Tim.6.v.20.

19 † But the sure foundation of God standeth, hauing this seale, Our Lord knovveth, vvho be his, and let euery one de-20 part from iniquitie that nameth the name of our Lord. † But " in a great house there are not only vessels of gold and of siluer, but also of vvood and of earth: and certaine in deede 21 vnto honour, but certaine vnto contumelie. † If any man therfore shal " cleanse him self from these, he shal be a vessel vnto honour, sanctified & profitable to our Lord, prepared to euery good vvorke.

22 † But youthful desires flee: and pursue iustice, faith, charitie, & peace vvith them that inuocate our Lord from a pure 23 hart. † And * foolish and vnlearned questiõs auoid, knovv-24 ing that they ingender braules. † But the seruant of our Lord must not vvrangle: but be milde tovvard al men, 25 apt to teache, patient, † vvith modestie admonishing them that resist the truth: lest sometime :: God giue them repen-26 tance to knovv the truth: † and they recouer them selues from the snares of the deuil, of vvhom they are held captiue at his vvil.

Tit.3, 9.

:: Conuersion from sinne and heresie is the gift of God and of his special grace: yet here vve see, good exhortations and praier and such other helpes of man be profitable thereunto. Vvhich could not be, if vve had not free vvill.

ANNOTATIONS
CHAP. II.

4 *No man being a souldiar.*] First of al, the Apostle (1 *Cor.* 7.) maketh mariage & the needful cares, solicitude, and distractions therevpon euer depending, special impediments of al such as should employ them selues vvholy to Gods seruice, as Bishops & Priests are bound to do. *He that is vvith a vvife* (saith he) *is careful for the vvorld, hovv to please his vvife, and is distracted or deuided.* 1 Cor. 7.

Vvhat secular affaires do not agree nor cõsist vvith spiritual mens function.

Secondly, the practise of Physicke, merchandise, or any other profane facultie and trade of life to gather riches, and much more to be giuen to hunting, hauking, gamening, shevves, enterludes, or the like pastimes, is here forbidden.

Thirdly, the seruices of Princes and manifold base offices done to them for to obtaine dignities and promotions, are disagreable to Priestly functions, not so, to be their chaplens for this purpose to preach vnto them, to heare their confessions, to minister the Sacraments vnto them, to say Diuine seruice before them, and such other spiritual dueties. for, al such seruices done to principal persons both of the Clergie and Laitie, be godly and cõsonant to Priestly vocation. As also seruing of Princes and Commonvveales in ciuil causes and matters of state, in making peace and quietnes

Hovv spiritual men may serue secular Princes, & deale in ciuil causes.

among the people, by deciding or compounding their controuersies, and al such like affaires tending to the honour of God and good of men, and to the vpholding of true religion, vvhen they may be done vvithout notorious damage or hinderance of their spiritual charge, or vvhen the hurtes thereof be aboundantly recompensed by the necessarie dueties done for the general good of kingdom or Countrie: al such things (I say) be lavvful and often very requisite. And S. Augustine, S. Ambrose, S. Bernard, and other holy Bishops of old vvere much occupied therein, as vve see in S. Augustines booke *de opere Monachorum c. 29. & Posid. in vit. c. 19.*

in vit. S. Ambr. & Bern.

Catholikes only, right hãdlers of the Scripture.

15. *Rightly.*] The Scriptures or chalenge of the vvord of God is common to Catholikes and Heretikes, but al is in the handling of them. these later handle them guilefully, adultering the vvord of God, as* els vvhere the Apostle speaketh: the other sincerely after the maner of the Apostles and doctors of Gods Church: Vvhich the Greeke expresseth by a significant vvord of cutting a thing straight by a line, ὀρθοτομοῦντα.

2 Cor. 2 & 4.

Heretical bookes and sermõs are to be auoided.

17. *Their speache.*] The speaches, preachings, and vvritings of Heretikes be pestiferous, cõtagious, and creeping like a canker. therfore Christian men must neuer heare their sermons nor read their bookes. For such men haue a popular vvay of talke vvhereby the vnlearned, and specially vvomen loden vvith sinne, are easily beguiled. *Nothing is so easy* (saith S. Hierom) *as vvith voluble and rolling tong to deceiue the rude people, vvhich admire vvhatsoeuer they vnderstand not. Ep. 2. ad Nepot. c. 10.*

Who are out of the Church or vvithin it.

20. *In a great house*] He meaneth not that Hymenæus and Philétus (of vvhõ he spake immediatly before) or other heretikes, be properly vvithin the Church, as catholike men are, though greuous sinners: but that euil men vvho for the punishment of their sinnes become heretikes, vvere before they fell from their faith as vessels of contumelie, vvithin the Church. Yea and often also after they be seuered in hart and in the sight of God, so long as they stand in external profession and vse of the same Sacraments, and in the outvvard fellovvship of Catholikes, not yet either separated of them selues, nor cast out by the gouernours of the Church, so long (we say) they be after a sort in the Church: though properly and in deede they be out of the compasse of Gods house. Mary of those that are openly seuered in Sacraments, Seruice, and communion, there is no question but they are out of the Church.

Free vvil.

21. *Cleanse him self.*] Man then hath free vvil to make him self a vessel of saluation or damnation: though saluation be attributed to Gods mercie principally, the other to his iust iudgement: neither of both being repugnant to our free vvil, but vvorking vvith and by the same, al such effectes in vs as to his prouidence and our deserts be agreable.

CHAP. III.

He prophecieth of Heretikes to come, 6 and noteth certaine then also for such, bidding him to auoid them, 10 and (vvhat so euer persecution befall for it) to cõtinue constant in the Catholike doctrine, both because of his Maister (S. Paul him self) 15 and also because of his ovvne knovvledge in the Scriptures.

AND this knovv thou, that *in the last daies shal approche perilous times. 2 † and " men shal be louers of them selues, couetous, hautie, proud, blasphemous, not obedient to their parents, vnkinde, vvicked, 3 † vvithout affection, vvithout peace, accusers, incontinent, vnmerciful, vvithout benignitie, 4 † traitours, stubburne, puffed vp, and louers of voluptuousnes more then of God: 5 † hauing an appearance in deede of pietie, but denying the vertue thereof. And these auoid. 6 † For of these be they that craftely enter into houses: and leade captiue seely " vvomen loden vvith sinnes,

1 Timot. 4, 1.

7 sinnes, vvhich are ledde vvith diuers desires: † alvvaies learning, and neuer attaining to the knovvledge of the truth.
8 † But as :: Iannes & Mambres * resisted Moyses, so these also
9 resist the truth, men corrupted in minde, reprobate cōcerning the faith. † But they shal prosper no further: for their " folly shal be manifest to al, as theirs alsovvas.

10 † But thou hast attained to my doctrine, institution, pur-
11 pose, faith, longanimitie, loue, patience, † persecutions, passions: vvhat maner of things vvere done to me at Antioche, at Iconium, at Lystra: vvhat maner of persecutiōs I sustained.
12 and out of al our Lord deliuered me. † And " al that vvil liue
13 godly in Christ IESVS, shal suffer persecution. † But euil men and seducers shal prosper to the vvorse: erring, and dri-
14 uing into errour. † But thou, :: continue in those things vvhich thou hast learned, and are committed to thee: know-
15 ing of vvhom thou hast learned: † and because from thine infancie thou hast knovven the holy Scriptures, vvhich can instruct thee to saluation, by the faith that is in Christ IESVS.
16 † " * All Scripture inspired of God, is profitable to teach,
17 to argue, to correct, to instruct in iustice: † that the man of God may be perfect, instructed to euery good vvorke.

Exo. 7. 2. Pet. 1, 21.

:: That those Magicians vvhich resisted Moyses, were thus called, it is not written in al the old Testamēt, therfore it came to the Apostles knowledge by tradition, as the Church novv hath the names of the 3 kings, of the penitēt theefe, of the souldiar that pearced Christes side on the Crosse, and of the like.

:: In al danger and diuersitie of false sectes, S. Paules admonition is, euer to abide in that vvas first taught & deliuered, neuer to giue ouer our old faith for a new fansie. This is it which before he calleth *depositum*. 1. *Tim.* 6. *and* 2. *Tim.* 1.

ANNOTATIONS
CHAP. III.

2. *Men shal be.*] Al these wordes S. Cyprian expoundeth of such as by pride and disobedience resist Gods Priests. Let no faithful man, saith he, that keepeth in minde our Lordes and the Apostles admonition, maruel if he see in the later times some proud and stubburne fellowes and the enimies of Gods Priests, goe out of the Church or impugne the same: vvhen both our Lord and the Apostle foretold vs that such should be. *Cypr. ep.* 55. *nu.* 3.

6. *Women loden.*] Women loden with sinnes, are for such their deseruings, and through the frailtie of their sexe, more subiect to the heretikes deceites, then men: the enemie attempting (as he did in the fall of our first parents) by them to ouerthrovv men. See S. Hierom vpon the 3 chapter of Ieremie. Where he addeth that euery heresie is first broched *propter gulam & ventrem*, for gluttonie and belly-cheere.

Women easily seduced by heresie.

9. *Folly manifest.*] Al heretikes in the beginning seeme to haue some shew of truth, God for iust punishment of mens sinnes permitting them for some vvhile in some persons and places to preuaile: but in short time God detecteth them, and openeth the eies of men to see their deceites: in so much that after the first brunt they be mainteined by force onely, al wise men in maner seing their falshod, though for troubling the state of such common weales vvhere vnluckely they haue been receiued, they can not be so sodenly extirped.

The folly of Heretikes in time appeareth.

12. *Al that vvil liue.*] Al holy men suffer one kinde of persecutiō or other, being greeued and molested by the vvicked, one way or an other: but not al that suffer persecution, be holy, as al malefactors. The Church and Catholike Princes persecute heretikes, and be persecuted of them againe, as S. Augustine often declareth. *See ep.* 48.

Persecution.

13. *Prosper.*] Though heresies and the authors of them be after a while discouered & by litle and litle forsaken generally of the honest, discrete, and men careful of their owne saluation

saluation, yet their authors and other great sinners proceede from one errour and heresie to an other, and finally to plaine Atheisme and al Diuelish disorder.

16. Al Scripture.] Besides the Apostles teaching and tradition, the reading of holy Scriptures is a great defense and helpe of the faithful, aud specially of a Bishop, not onely to auoid and condemne al heresies, but to the guiding of a man in al iustice, good life and vvorkes. Vvhich commendation is not here giuen to the bookes of the new Testament onely (vvhereof he here speaketh not, as being yet for a great part not vvritten) but to the Scripture of the old Testament also, yea and to euery booke of it. For there is not one of them, nor any part of them, but it is profitable to the end aforesaid, if it be read and vnderstood according to the same Spirit vvherewith it vvas vvritten.

The great profit of reading the Scriptures.

The Heretikes vpon this commendation of holy Scriptures, pretend (very simply in good sooth) that therfore nothing is necessarie to iustice and saluation but Scriptures. As though euery thing that is profitable or necessarie to any effect, excluded al other helpe, and vvere onely ynough to attaine the same. By vvhich reason a man might as vvel proue that the old Testament vvere ynough, and so exclude the new: or any one peece of al the old, and thereby exclude the rest. For he affirmeth euery Scripture to haue the foresaid vtilities. and they might see in the very next line before, that he requireth his constant perseuerance in the doctrine vvhich he had taught him ouer and aboue that he had learned out of the Scriptures of the old Testament, vvhich he had read from his infancie, but could not thereby learne al the mysteries of Christian religion therein. Neither doth the Apostle affirme here that he had his knowledge of Scriptures, by reading onely, vvithout helpe of maisters and teachers, as the Aduersaries herevpon (to committe the holy Scriptures to euery mans presumption) do gather: but affirmeth onely that Timothee knevv the Scriptures and therfore had studied them by hearing good readers and teachers, as S. Paul him self did of Gamaliel and the like, and as al christian students doe, that be trained vp from their youth in Catholike vniuersities in the studie of Diuinitie.

The Heretikes folish argumēt: Al Scripture is profitable, ergo only Scripture is necessarie & sufficient.

CHAP. IIII.

He requireth him to be earnest vvhile he may, because the time vvil come vvhen they vvil not abide Catholike preaching, 5 and to fulfil his course, as him self novv hath done. 9 and to come vnto him vvith speede, because the rest of his traine are dispersed, and he dravveth novv to heauen.

The Epistle for holy Doctors, and for S. Dominike *August.* 4.

I Testifie before God and IESVS Christ 1 vvho shal iudge the liuing and the dead, and by his aduent, and his kingdom: † Preach the vvord. vrge in season, out of 2 season, reproue, beseeche, rebuke in al patience and doctrine. † For "there shal be 3 a time vvhen they vvil not beare sound doctrine: but according to their ovvne desires they vvil heape to them selues maisters, hauing itching eares, † and 4 from the truth certes they vvil auert their hearing, and to fables they vvil be conuerted. † But be thou vigilant, labour 5 in al things, doe the vvorke of an Euangelist, fulfil thy ministerie. Be sober. † For I am euen novv ⁚⁚ to be sacrificed: & 6 the time of my resolutiō is at hand. † I haue fought a good 7 fight, I haue consummate my course, I haue kept the faith. † Concerning the rest, there is laid vp for me "a crovvne of 8 iustice, vvhich our Lord vvil render to me in that day, a iust iudge:

⁚⁚ The martyrdom of saincts is so acceptable to God, that it is counted as it vvere a sacrifice in his sight, and therfore hath many effectes both in the partie that suffereth it, and in others that are partakers of the merite as of a sacrifice: vvhich name it hath by a Metaphore.

iudge: and not only to me, but to them also that loue his comming. ⁋

9 † Make hast to come to me quickly. 10 † For Demas hath left me, louing this vvorld, and is gone to Thessalonica: Crescens into Galatia, Titus into Dalmatia. 11 † * Luke only is vvith me. Take Marke, and bring him vvith thee: for he is profitable to me for the ministerie. 12 † But Tychicus I haue sent to Ephesus. 13 † The cloke that I left at Troas vvith Carpus, cōming bring vvith thee, and the bookes, especially the parchement. 14 † Alexander the Coppersmith hath shevved me much euil, our Lord vvil revvard him according to his 15 vvorkes: † vvhom doe thou also auoid, for he hath greatly 16 resisted our vvordes. † In my first ansvver no man vvas with 17 me, but al did forsake me: be it not imputed to them. † But our Lord stoode to me, and strengthened me, that by me the preaching may be accomplished, and al Gentiles may heare: and I was deliuered from the mouth of the lion. 18 † Our Lord 'hath deliuered' me from al euil vvorke: and vvil saue me vnto his heauenly kingdom. to vvhom be glorie for euer & euer. Amen.

Col. 4, 14

' vvil deliuer

19 † Salute Prisca and Aquila, and * the house of Onesiphorus. 20 † Erastus remained at Corinth. And Trophimus I 21 left sicke at Milētum. † Make hast to come before vvinter. Eubūlus and Pudens and [c] Linus and Claudia, and al the brethren, salute thee. 22 † Our Lord IESVS Christ be vvith thy spirit. Grace be vvith you. Amen.

2 Timo. 1, 16.

c This Linus vvas coadiutor vvith & vnder S. Peter, & so counted secōd in the number of Popes.

ANNOTATIONS
CHAP. IIII.

3. *There shal be a time.*] If euer this time come (as needes it must that the Apostle foresavv and foretold) novv it is vndoubtedly. for the properties fall so iust in euery point vpon our nevv Maisters and their Disciples, that they may seeme to be pourtered out, rather then prophecied of. Neuer vvere there such delicate Doctors that could so pleasantly clavv and so svveetly rubbe the itching eares of their hearers, as these, vvhich haue a doctrine framed for euery mans phansie, lust, liking, and desire. the people not so fast crying, *Speake placentia, things that please*: but the Maisters as fast vvarranting them to doe *placentia*.

The Apostle prophecied of our nevv delicate preachers.

Esa. 30. v. 10.

8. *A crovvne of iustice.*] This place conuinceth for the Catholikes, that al good vvorkes done by Gods grace after the first iustification, be truely and properly meritorious, and fully vvorthy of euerlasting life: and that therevpon heauen is the due and iust stipend, crovvne, or recompense, vvhich God by his iustice ovveth to the persons so vvorking by his grace. for he rendreth or repaieth heauen as a iust iudge, and not onely as a merciful giuer. and the crovvne vvhich he paieth, is not onely of mercie or fauour or grace, but also of iustice. It is his merciful fauour and grace, that vve vvorke vvel & merite heauen: it is his iustice, for those merites to giue vs a crovvne correspondent in heauen. S. Augustine vpon these vvordes of the Apostle, expresseth both breifely thus,

Vvorkes meritorious.

How heauen is due both of iustice and mercie.

Hovv should he repay as a iust iudge, vnles he had first giuen as a merciful father? Li. de grat. & lib. arbit. c. 6.

And vvhen you heare or read any thing in the Scriptures, that may seeme to derogate from mans vvorkes in this case, it is alvvaies meant of vvorkes considered in their ovvne nature and valure, not implying the grace of Christ, by vvhich grace it cometh, & not of the vvorke in it self that vve haue a right to heauen & deserue it vvorthily: vvhich the Apostle in the 6 to the Hebrues more then insinuateth, saying these vvordes, *God is not vniust, to forget your vvorke & loue vvhich you haue shevved in his name &c.* As though he vvould say, that he vvere vniust if he did forget to recompense their vvorkes.* The parable also of the men sent into the vineyard, proueth that heauen is our ovvne right, bargained for and vvrought for, and accordingly paid vnto vs as our hire at the day of iudgement, for that is *merces* and μισθὸς vvhereby the Scripture so often calleth it. It is the goale, the marke, the price, the hire, of al striuing, running, labouring, due both by promis and by couenant and right dette. See a notable place in S. Augustine *in Psal.* 83 *in fine:* and 100 *in initio, & ho.* 14 *c.* 2. *li.* 50 *hom:* S. Cyprian also, and namely the later end of his booke *de opere & eleemosyna:* and thou shalt easily contemne the contrarie falshod, vvhich doth not so much derogate from mans vvorkes, as from Gods grace vvhich is the cause and ground of al vvorthines in mans merites. S. Augustines vvordes be these, *Marke that he to vvhom our Lord gaue grace, hath our Lord also his detter. He found him a giuer, in the time of mercie: he hath him his detter in the time of iudgement.* See the place and the rest here coted, vvhere he examineth and explicateth the matter at large.

It is not of vs, but of Gods grace, that vvorkes be meritorious.

To such good vvorkes heauē is due: to say the contrarie, is to derogate from Gods grace.

Mat. 20.

In Ps. 100.

THE ARGVMENT OF THE EPISTLE OF S. PAVL TO TITVS.

HAT Titus vvas a Gentil, and not a Ievv, and that he vvas in S. Paules traine, at the least the 14 yere after his conuersion, if not before, vve vnderstand by the Epistle to the Galatians c. 2. And that he continued vvith him to the very end, appeareth in the second to Timothee c. 4. Vvhere he maketh mention that he sent him from Rome into Dalmatia, vvhen him self vvas shortly after to be put to death.

And therefore although S. Luke neuer name him in the Actes, as neither him self, yet no doubt he comprehendeth him commonly, vvhen he speaketh thus in the first person plurall: Forthvvith vve sought to goe into Macedonia. Act, 16. *For S. Paul also sent him to Corinth, betvvene the vvriting of his 1 & 2 to the Corinthians (vvhich time concurreth vvith Act. 19) by occasion vvhereof he maketh much and honorable mention of him in the said second Epistle c 2. & c. 7. and againe* ★ *he sent him vvith the same Epistle: both times about great matters: so that no doubt he vvas euen then also a Bishop, and receiued accordingly of the Corinthians,* vvith feare and trembling 2. *Cor.* 7, *v.* 15. *But the same is plainer in this Epistle to him self c* 1. *v.* 5. *Vvhere the Apostle saith:* for this cause I left thee at Crete, &c. *By vvhich vvordes it is manifest also, that this Epistle vvas not vvritten during the storie of the Actes (seing that no mention is there of S. Paules being in the ile of Crete) but after his dismission at Rome out of his first trouble, and before his second or last trouble there, as is euident by these vvordes:* Vvhen I shall send to thee Artemas or Tychicus, make hast to come to me to Nicopolis, for there I haue determined to vvinter. *Tit.* 3.

2 Corinth. 8.

Therefore he instructeth him (and in him, all Bishops) much like as he doth Timothee, vvhat qualities he must require in them that he shall make priests and Bishops, in vvhat sort to preach, and to teach al sortes of men, to commend good vvorkes vnto them: finally, him self to be their example in all goodnes.

THE EPISTLE OF PAVL TO TITVS.

CHAP. I.

Of vvhat qualitie the Priests and Bishops must be: 9 namely learned, considering the Iudaical seducers of that time. 12 That the Cretensians must be roughly vsed, to haue them continue sound in faith.

1 PAVL the seruant of God, and an Apostle of IESVS Christ according to the faith of the elect of God and knowledge of the truth: vvhich is according to pie-
2 tie †into the hope of life euerlasting, vvhich he promised that lieth not, God,
3 * before the secular times: † but hath manifested in due times his vvord in preaching, vvhich is cōmitted to me according to the precept of our Sauiour God:
4 † to Titus my beloued sonne according to the cōmon faith, grace and peace from God the father, and Christ IESVS our Sauiour.

2.Tim.1, 9.

5 † For this cause left I thee in Crete, that thou shouldest reforme the things that are vvanting, and shouldest " ordaine priestes by cities, as I also appointed thee:
6 † * if any be vvithout crime, the husband " of one vvife, hauing faithful children, not in the accusation of riote, or not
7 obedient. † For a Bishop must be vvithout crime, as the stevvard of God: not proud, not angrie, not giuen to vvine,
8 no striker, not couetous of filthy lucre: † but giuen to hos-
9 pitalitie, gentle, sober, iust, holy, continent: † embracing that faithful vvord vvhich is according to doctrine, that he may be able to exhort in sound doctrine, & to reproue them that gainesay it.

1.Tim.3, 2.

10 † For there be many disobedient, vaine-speakers, and se-
11 ducers, especially they that are of the Circumcision. † vvho

must be controuled. vvho subuert vvhole houses, teaching the things they ought not, for filthie lucre. † One of 12 them said, their ovvne proper prophete, *The Cretensians alvvaies liers, naughtie beastes, slouthful bellies.* † This testimonie is true. For 13 the vvhich cause rebuke them sharpely, that they may be sound in the faith, † not attending to Ievvish fables, and 14 commaundements of men auerting them selues from the truth.

Epimenides.

† * Al things are :: cleane to the cleane: but to the pol- 15 luted and to infidels nothing is cleane: but polluted are both their minde and conscience. † They confesse that 16 they knovv God: but in their vvorkes they deny, vvhereas they be abominable and incredulous and to euery good vvorke reprobate.

Rom. 14, 20.

:: He speaketh not of the Churches abstaining from meates some times, vvhich is not for any vncleannes in the creatures, but for chastening their bodies: but he meaneth the Ievvish superstition, vvho novv being Christians, vvould not cease to put difference of cleane and vncleane according to their old lavv. See S. Augustine *Cont. Faust. li. 31. c. 4.*

ANNOTATIONS
CHAP. I.

Priests must be consecrated by Bishops only.

5. *Ordaine Priests.*] Though Priests or Bishops may be nominated and elected by the Princes, people, or Patrons of places, according to the vse of the time and diuersitie of Countries and fashions, yet they can not be ordered and consecrated but by a Bishop vvho vvas him self rightly ordered or consecrated before, as this Titus vvas by S. Paul. And here it seemeth that he did not onely consecrate them vvhom the people had elected before, but him self also made choise of the persons, no mention being here made of any other election popular. Vvhich though it vvere long vsed in the primitiue Church, yet for diuers causes and specially for continual tumultes, partialities, and disorders vvhich S. Augustine much complaineth of in his time, vvas iustly taken avvay, and other better meanes of their designement appointed. See *Conc. Laodic. cap. 12. 13.* S. August. *de adult. coniug. li. 2. c. 20. Ep.* 110. and *Possid. in vita Aug. c.* 8.

The popular election of the Cleargie taken avvay.

The preeminẽce of a Bishop aboue a Priest.

And that the ordering of Priests or imposition of hands to that purpose, belongeth onely to Bishops, and to no inferior Priests or other persons, it is plaine by the Apostolike practise set dovvne in the Scriptures, namely in the Actes, and in the Epistles to Timothee and Titus. And S. Hierom, vvho seemeth sometimes to say that in the primitiue Church there vvas no great difference betvvixt a Bishop and Priest, yet he euer excepteth giuing holy Orders, vvhich preeminence he attributeth to Bishops onely. *ep.* 85. as he doth also Confirming the Baptized by giuing them the holy Ghost through imposition of hand and holy Chrisme. *Dial. cont. Lucifer. c.* 4. Note also that Aërius vvas of old condemned of heresie, for holding that there vvas no difference betvvixt a Priest and a Bishop. *Epiph. har.* 75. *August. har.* 53. Note lastly the fraudulent translation of the Heretikes alvvaies, turning for *Priests* (vvhich here is euident to be a calling of Order and office) *elders*, saying, *That thou ordaine Elders.* vvhich in our vulgar tonge signifieth the age, and not the Office properly: and al this for hatred of Priests.

To put no differẽce betvvene them is Aërius heresie.

Heret. translation.

6. *Of one vvife.*] To that vvhich is said vpon the like vvordes 1 *Tim.* 3: adde this testimonie of S. Epiphanius *li. 3. to. 2. cont. hareses in fine. Holy Priesthod*, saith he, *for the most part procedeth of Virgins: and if not of virgins, yet of them that liue a sole or single life: but and if the single and sole persons suffice not to the Ministerie, of such as conteine from their vviues, or after once marying remaine vvidovves. For, him that hath been maried tvvise, it is not lavvful to take to Priesthod &c.* If you list to see the causes vvhy bigamie is forbidden them that are to be Priests, and continencie required of the Clergie, see the same author *li. 2. to. 1. hares.* 59. S. Ambrose *li. 1. Offic. c.* 50. and vpon 1 *Tim.* 3. S. Augustine *de bono Coniugal. c.* 18. S. Hierom *ep.* 50 *c.* 5 *ad Pammachium*, and against Iouinian *li.* 1 *c.* 19. S. Leo *ep.* 87. and other auncient authors.

Bigami excluded from holy Orders, and the causes thereof.

The notable men of both Testamẽts, that liued cõtinẽtly from vviues.

And if the studious reader peruse al antiquitie, he shal finde al notable Bishops and Priests of Gods Church to haue been single, or continent from their vviues, if any vvere maried before they came to the Clergie. So vvas S. Paul, and exhorteth al men to the like. 1 *Cor.* 7, 7. So vvere al the Apostles after they folovved Christ, as S. Hierom vvitnesseth, affirming that our Lord loued

Iohn

Iohn specially for his virginitie. *Apol. ad Pammach. c. 8. & li. 1 cont. Iouin. c.* 14. S. Ignatius *ep. 6 ad Philadelph.* saith of the said Iohn, and of Timothee, Titus, Euodius, Clement, that they liued and died in chastitie, reckening vp of the old Testament diuers notable personages that did the same, as Elias, Iesus Naue (othervvise called Iosue) Melchisedec, Elisæus, Hieremie, Iohn Baptist. No man is ignorant that al the notable fathers of the Greeke and Latin Church liued chast: Athanasius, Basil, Nazianzene, Chrysostom, Cyprian, Hilarie (vvho entered into holy Orders after his vviues death) Ambrose, Hierom, Augustine, Leo, Gregorie the great. Certaine other notable fathers had once vviues, but no holy men euer vsed them, much lesse maried, after they vvere in holy Orders. A maruelous thing, that so many heretofore should haue the gift of chastitie then, and novv so fevv, if the Protestants say true, that skarse one among them in our age of al their sectes, euen of their principal Superintendents, hath had it.

Only the Protestants complaine that they haue not the gift of chastitie.

CHAP. II.

Vvhat to preach both to old and yong (not onely vvith vvord but vvith example also) and to seruants. 11 For there are of al sortes in the Church, and they must be instructed accordingly.

1 BVT doe thou speake the things that become sound doctrine. 2 † Old men that they be sober, [c]chast, vvise, sound in the faith, in loue, in patience. 3 † Old women in like maner, in holy attire, not il speakers, not giuen to much wine: teaching vvel, 4 † that they may teach the yong women vvisedom, to loue their husbands, to loue their children, 5 † vvise, chast, sober, hauing a care of the house, gentle, subiect to their husbandes, that the vvord of God be not blasphemed. 6 † Yong men in like maner exhort that they be sober. 7 † In al things shevv thy self an example of good vvorkes, in doctrine, in integritie, in grauitie, 8 † the vvord sound, irreprehensible: that he vvhich is on the contrarie part, may be afraid, hauing no euil to say of vs. 9 †* Seruants to be subiect to their maisters, in al things pleasing, not gainsaying: 10 † not defrauding, but in al things shevving good faith, that they may adorne the doctrine of our Sauiour God in al things.

c σεμνοὺς pudicos

Eph. 6, 5. Col. 3, 22. 1. Pet. 2, 18.

11 † For the grace of God our Sauiour hath appeared to al men: 12 † instructing vs that denying impietie & worldly desires, vve liue soberly, and iustly, and godly in this vvorld, 13 † expecting the blessed hope and [c] aduent of the glorie of the great God and our Sauiour IESVS Christ, 14 † vvho gaue him self for vs, that he might redeeme vs from al iniquitie, and might cleanse to him self a people acceptable, a pursuer of

The Epistle at the first Masse on Christmas day, and vpon the Circumcision of our Lord.

c ἐπιφάνειαν

:: Bishops must be stout and cōmaund in Gods cause, and the people must in no vvise disobey or contemne them.

good vvorkes. † These things speake, and exhort ⊣ and rebuke :: vvith al authoritie. Let no man contemne thee. 15

CHAP. III.

To teach them obedience vnto Princes, and meekenes tovvardes al men, considering that vve also vvere as they, til God of his goodnes brought vs to Baptisme. 8 To teach good vvorkes, 9 and to auoid vaine questions, 10 and obstinate Heretikes.

DMONISH them to be subiect to Princes and Potestates, to obey at a vvord, to be ready to euery good vvorke, † to blaspheme no mā, not to be litigious, but modest: shevving al mildenes tovvard al men. † for we also vvere sometime vnvvise, incredulous, erring, seruing diuerse desires & voluptuousnesses, liuing in malice & enuie, odible, hating one an other. † But vvhen [b] the benignitie and [c] kindnes tovvard man of our Sauiour God appeared: † * not by the vvorkes of iustice vvhich vve did, but according to his mercie he hath saued vs :: by the lauer of regeneratiō and renouation of the holy Ghost, † vvhom he hath povvred vpon vs aboundantly by IESVS Christ our Sauiour: † that being iustified by his grace, vve may be heires according to hope of life euerlasting. ⊣ 1 2 3 4 5 6 7

b The Epistle at the 2 Masse on Christmas day, and in the Votiue Masse of our B. Lady betvvene Christmas and Candlemas.

:: As before in the Sacrament of holy Orders (1. Tim. 4. and 2 Tim. 1) so here it is plaine that Baptisme giueth grace, & that by it as by an instrumental cause we be saued.

c φιλανθρωπία

2. Tim. 1, 9.

† * It is a faithful saying, and of these things I vvil haue thee auouch earnestly: that they vvhich beleeue in God, be careful to excell in good vvorkes. These things be good and profitable for men. † But * foolish questions, and genealogies, and cōtentions, and controuersies of the Lavv auoid. For they are vnprofitable and vaine. 8 9

1 Tim. 4. 2. Tim. 2, 23.

† A man that is " an heretike after the first and second :: admonition auoid: † knovving that he that is such an one, is " subuerted, and sinneth, being condemned " by his ovvne iudgement. 10 11

:: These admonitions or corrections must be giuen to such as erre, by our Spiritual Gouernours and Pastors: to vvhom if they yeld not, Christian men must auoid them.

† Vvhen I shal send to thee Artemas or Tychicus, hasten to come vnto me to Nicopolis. for there I haue determined to vvinter. † Set forvvard Zenas the lavvyer and Apollos carefully, that nothing be vvanting to them. † And let our men also learne [c] to excel in good vvorkes to necessarie vses: that they be not vnfruiteful. Al that are vvith me, salute thee: 12 13 14 15

c προΐστασθαι praeesse.

thee: salute them that loue vs in the faith. The grace of God be vvith you al. Amen.

ANNOTATIONS
CHAP. III.

10. *A man that is an Heretike.*] Not euery one that erreth in religion, is an Heretike, but he onely that after the Churches determination, vvilfully and stubburnely standeth in his false opinion, not yelding to decree of Councel or the cheefe Pastors of the Church therein. *They* (saith S. Augustine *ep. 162.*) *that defend their sentence (though false and peruerse) vvith no stubburne stomake or obstinate hart, specially if it be such as them selues by bold presumption broched not, but receiued it of their deceiued parents, and do seeke the truth vvarily and carefully, being ready to be reformed if they finde it, such are not to be reputed among Heretikes.* And againe, *li. 18 de Ciuit. c. 51.* *They that in the Church of Christ haue any erased or peruerse opinion, if being admonished to be of a sound and right opinion, they resist obstinatly, and vvil not amend their pestiferous opinions, but persist in defense of them, are thereby become Heretikes, and going forth out of the Church, are counted for enimies that exercise vs.* Againe *li. 4 de Bapt. cont. Donat. c. 16.* *He is an Heretike that, vvhen the doctrine of the Catholike faith is made plaine and manifest vnto him, had rather resist it, and choose that vvhich him self held &c.* And in diuers places he declareth that S. Cyprian, though he held an errour, yet vvas no Heretike, because he vvould not haue defended it after a general Councel had declared it to be an errour. *li. 2 de bapt. c. 4.* So Possidonius in the life of S. Augustine reporteth, hovv, after the determination of the See Apostolike that Pelagius opinion vvas heretical, al men esteemed Pelagius an Heretike, and the Emperour made lavves against him as against an Heretike. Againe S. Augustine saith, *He is an Heretike in my opinion, that for some temporal commoditie, and specially for his glorie and principalitie, coineth or els folovveth false or nevv opinions.* de vtilit. credendi cap. 1.

> *Vvho is properly an Heretike, & vvho is not.*
>
> *Descriptions or markes hovv to knovv an Heretike.*
>
> *vit. Aug. c. 18.*

Let our Protestants behold them selues in this glasse, and vvithal let them marke al other properties that old Heretikes euer had, and they shal finde al definitions and markes of an Heretike to fall vpon them selues. And therfore they must not maruel if vve vvarne al Catholike men by the vvordes of the Apostle in this place, to take heede of them, and to shunne their preachings, bookes, conuenticles and companies. Neither neede the people be curious to knovv vvhat they say, much lesse to confute them: but they must trust Gods Church, vvhich doth refute and condemne them. And it is ynough for them to knovv that they be condemned, as S. Augustine noteth in the later end of his booke de heresibus. And S. Cyprian saith notably to Antonianus demaunding curiously vvhat heresies Nouatianus did teach: *No matter,* ꝙ he, *What heresies he hath or teacheth, vvhen he teacheth vvithout.* that is to say, out of the Church.

> *The former markes agree to the Protestants.*
>
> *Their bookes, seruice, & preaching must be auoided.*
>
> *Ep. 52. nu. 7.*

11. *Subuerted.*] Heretikes be often incorrigible, yet the Church of God ceaseth not by al meanes possible to reuoke them. therfore S. Augustine saith *ep. 162.* *The Heretike him self though svvelling vvith odious and detestable pride, and madde vvith the frovvardnes of vvicked contention, as vve admonish that he be auoided lest he deceiue the vveaklings and litle ones, so vve refuse not by al meanes possible to seeke his amendment and reformation.*

> *The Church seeketh the amendement of the most obstinate Heretikes.*

11. *By his ovvne iudgement.*] Other greuous offenders be separated by excommunication from the cōmunion of Saincts and the fellovvship of Gods Church, by the sentence of their Superiors in the same Church: but Heretikes more miserable and infortunate then they, runne out of the Chutch of their ovvne accord, and so giue sentence against their ovvne soules to damnation.

> *Heretikes cut them selues frō the Church.*

THE EPISTLE OF PAVL TO PHILEMON.

THE ARGVMENT.

Hearing of Philémons vertue, vvho vvas a Colosian, he vvriteth a familiar letter from Rome (being prisoner there) about his fugitiue seruant Onesimus: not doubting but that he might commaund him, yet rather requesting that he vvil forgiue him, yea and receiue him as he vvould Paul him self, vvho also hopeth to come vnto him.

PAVL

PAVL the prisoner of Christ IESVS, 1 and brother Timothee: to Philémon the beloued and our coadiutor, † & 2 to Appia our deerest sister, & to Archippus our felovv-souldiar and to the church vvhich is in thy house. † Grace to you and peace from God 3 our father, and our Lord IESVS Christ.

† I giue thankes to my God, alvvaies making a memorie 4 of thee in my praiers, † hearing thy ∷ charitie and faith 5 vvhich thou hast in our Lord IESVS, and" tovvard al the saincts: † that the communication of thy faith may be 6 made euident in the agnition of al good that is in you in Christ IESVS. † For I haue had great ioy and consolation 7 in thy charitie, because the bovvels of the saincts ∷ haue rested by thee brother.

∷ Faith and charitie commẽded alwais together, both necessarie to make a complete Christiã man, and to iustification & saluation.

∷ The dueties of charitie and mercie done to Christes prisoners, are exceding acceptable to God and al good men.

† For the vvhich thing hauing great cõfidence in Christ 8 IESVS to commaund thee that vvhich pertaineth to the purpose: † for charitie rather I beseeche, vvhereas thou art 9 such an one, as Paul being old and novv prisoner also of IESVS Christ. † I beseeche thee for my sonne vvhom I haue 10 begotten in bandes, * Onesimus, † vvho hath been some- 11 time vnprofitable to thee, but novv profitable both to me & thee, † vvhom I haue sent backe to thee. And ∷ do thou re- 12 ceiue him as mine ovvne bovvels. † vvhom I vvould haue 13 reteined vvith me, that for thee he might minister to me in the bandes of the Gospel: † but vvithout thy counsel I 14 vvould doe nothing: that thy good might be not as it vvere of necessitie, but voluntarie. † For perhaps therfore he de- 15 parted for a season from thee, that thou mightest take him againe for euer. † novv not as a seruant, but for a seruant, 16 a most deere brother, especially to me, but hovv much more to thee both in the flesh and in our Lord? † If therfore thou 17 take me for thy fellovv: receiue him as my self. † And if he 18 hath hurt thee any thing or is in thy dette, that impute to me. † I Paul haue vvritten vvith mine ovvne hand: I vvil repay 19 it: not to say to thee, ∷ that thou ovvest me thine ovvne self also. † Yea brother. [c] God graunt I may enioy thee in 20 our Lord. Refresh my bovvels in our Lord. † Trusting in 21 thy obedience I haue vvritten to thee, knovving that thou vvilt

Col. 4, 9.

∷ Al Spiritual men ought to be exceding propense and ready to procure mens pardon, and recõciliation to al penitents.

∷ The great debt & duetie that vve owe to such as be our spiritual parents in Christ.

[c] ὀναίμην

22 vvilt doe aboue that also vvhich I do say. † And withal prouide me also a lodging. for I hope by your praiers that I shal be giuen to you.

23 † There salute thee Epaphras my fellovv-prisoner in

24 Christ IESVS, † Marke, Aristarchus, Demas and Luke my

25 coadiutors. † The grace of our Lord IESVS Christ be with your spirit. Amen,

ANNOT.

5. *Tovvard al the sainctes.*] The Apostle sticketh not to say, Charitie and faith in Christ and al his Saincts, vvhich our captious Aduersaries count in Catholike mens speaches and vvritings, very absurd, feining that in al such vve make no difference betvvixt the loue vve beare to Christ, and the loue vve owe to our neighbours: betvvixt the trust or beleefe vve haue in God, and that vvhich vve haue in his holy Saincts. Malice and contention doth so blinde al Heretikes.

Faith and beleefe in Saincts.

THE ARGVMENT OF THE EPISTLE OF S. PAVL TO THE HEBREVVES.

HAT the Hebrevves vvere not all the Ievves, but only a part of them, it is manifest Act. 6: vvhere the primitiue Church of Hierusalem, although it consisted of Ievves only, as vve reade Act. 2, yet is said to consist of tvvo sortes, Greekes & Hebrues. Vvhich againe is manifest Phil. 3. vvhere S. Paul cōparing him self with the Iudaical false-Apostles, saith, that he also is, an Hebrue of Hebrues. *Finally, they seeme to haue been those Ievves vvhich vvere borne in Iurie, vvhich for the most part dwelled also there. Therefore to the Christian Ievves in Hierusalem and in the rest of Iurie, S. Paul vvriteth this Epistle, out of Italie: saying therevpon,* The brethrē of Italie salute you. *Heb. 13. By vvhich vvordes, & by these other in the same place,* Knovv ye our brother Timothee to be dimissed, vvith vvhom (if he come the sooner) I vvil see you, *it is euident, that he vvrote this, not only after he vvas brought prisoner to Rome, vvherein S. Luke endeth the Actes of the Apostles: but also after he vvas set at libertie there againe.*

Many causes are giuen of the Doctors, vvhy vvriting to the Ievves, he doth not put his name in the beginning, Paul an Apostle &c. *as he doth lightly in* *his Epistles to the Churches and Bishops of the Gentils. The most likely cause is, for that he vvas* the preacher and Apostle and Maister of the Gentils. *And againe in an other place he saith, that him self vvas appointed the Apostle of the Gentils, as Peter of the Ievves. Gal. 2. Only S. Peter therfore vvriting to the Ievves, doth vse this stile:* Peter an Apostle of IESVS Christ &c. *because he vvas more peculiarly their Apostle, as being the vicar of Christ, vvho vvas also him self* * *more specially* the minister of the Circumcision, *that is (as him self speaketh)* not sent but to the sheepe vvhich vvere lost of the house of Israël. *Mat. 15.*

2. Tim. 1.
1. Tim. 2.
1. Pet. 1.
Rom. 5.

* Yet vvas Christ head of the Gentils also. So likevvise his vicar S. Peter, notwithstādig his more peculiar Apostleship ouer the Iewes.

The Argument of the Epistle S. Paul him self doth tell vs in tvvo vvordes, calling it verbum solatij, the vvord of solace and comfort. *Vvhich also is plaine in the vvhole course of the Epistle, namely in the tenth chapter. v. 32. &c. Vvhere he exhorteth them to take great comfort and confidence in their manifold tribulations sustained of their ovvne countrie men the Ievves, vvhereof the Apostle also maketh mention to the Thessalonians. 1. Thess. 2. v. 14. Those persecutions then of the obstinate incredulous Ievves their countrie men, vvas one great tentation vnto them. An other tentation vvas, the persuasions that they brought vnto them out of Scriptures, to cleaue vnto the Lavv, and not to beleeue in* IESVS *the dead man.*

Heb. 13.

And vvhereas the Ievves did magnifie their lavv, by the Prophetes, and by the Angels by vvhom it vvas giuen, and by Moyses, and by their land of promise, into vvhich Iosue brought them, and by their father Abraham, and by their Aaronicall or Leuitical priesthod and sacrifices, by their Tabernacle, & by their Testament: he shevveth, that our Lord IESVS, *as being the natural sonne of God, passeth incomparably the Prophetes, the Angels, and Moyses: that the Rest or quietnes vvhich God promised, vvas not in their earthly land, but in heauen: that his figure Melchisedec far passed Abraham: and that his priesthod, Sacrifice, Tabernacle, and testament, far passed theirs. In al vvhich he shooteth often at these three markes: to take avvay the scandal of Christes death, by giuing them sundrie good reasons & testimonies of it: to erect their mindes from visible and earthly promises (to vvhich only, the Ievves vvere vvholy bent) to inuisible and heauenly: and to insinuate that the Ceremonies should novv cease, the time of their correction by Christ being novv come.*

The Epistle may be deuided into these partes: the first, Of Christes excellencie aboue the Prophetes, Angels, Moyses, and Iosue: c. 1. 2. 3. 4. The second, of his priesthod and excellencie thereof aboue the priesthod of the old Testament: c. 5. vnto the middest of the 10. The last part is of exhortation c. 10. v. 9. to the end of the Epistle.

THE

THE EPISTLE OF PAVL THE APOSTLE TO THE HEBREVVES.

Let the Christian Reader note the corruption and impudent boldnes of our Aduersaries, that vpon a false priuate persuasion of their ovvne, that S. Paul vvas not the author of this Epistle, * leaue out his name in the title of the same, contrarie to the authentical copies both Greeke and Latin. In old time there vvas some doubt vvho should be the vvriter of it, but then, vvhen it vvas no lesse doubted vvhether it vvere Canonical Scripture at al. Aftervvard the vvhole Church (by vvhich onely vve knovv the true Scriptures from other vvritings) held it and deliuered it, as novv she doth, to the faithful, for Canonical, and for S. Paules Epistle. Notvvithstanding the Aduersaries vvould haue refused the Epistle, as vvel as they do the Author, but that they falsely imagine certaine places thereof to make against the Sacrifice of the Masse.

** In the English Bible of the yere 1579.*

Heretical corruption.

The Epistle to the Hebrues, is S. Paules.

CHAP. I.

God spake to their fathers by the Prophets: but to them selues by his ovvne Sonne, 14 vvho incomparably passeth al the Angels.

1 DIVERSELY and many vvaies in times past God speaking to the fathers in the prophets: 2 † last of al in these daies hath spoken to vs in his Sonne, vvhom he hath appointed heire of al, by vvhom he made also the vvorldes. 3 †* Vvho being the [c] brightnesse of his glorie, and " the [b] figure of his substance, & carying al things by the vvord of his povver, making purgation of sinnes, sitteth on the right hand of the Maiestie in the high places: 4 † being made so much better then Angels, as he hath inherited a more excellent name aboue them.

5 † For to vvhich of the Angels hath he said at any time, *Thou art my sonne, to day haue I begotten thee?* and againe, *I vvil be to him a father, and he shal be to me a sonne.* 6 † And vvhen againe he bringeth in

The Epistle at the third masse on Christmas day.

Sap. 7, 26.

c ἀπαύγασμα

b χαρακτὴρ ὑποστάσεως

The excellencie of Christ aboue Angels.

Ps. 2, 7. 2. reg. 7, 14.

in the first begotten into the vvorld, he saith, *And* [n] *let al the Angels of God adore him.* † And to the Angels truely he saith, *He that maketh his Angels, spirites: and his ministers, a flame of fire.* † But to the Sonne: *Thy throne ô God for euer & euer: a rod of equitie, the rod of thy kingdom.* † *Thou hast loued iustice, and hated iniquitie: therfore thee, God, thy God hath anointed vvith the oile of exultation aboue thy fellovves.* † And, *Thou in the beginning ô Lord didst found the earth: and the vvorkes of thy handes are the heauens.* † *They shal perish, but thou shalt continue: and they shal al vvaxe old as a garment.* † *And as a vesture shalt thou chaunge them, & they shal be changed: but thou art the self same, and thy yeres shal not faile.* † But to vvhich of the Angels said he at any time: *Sit on my right hand, vntil I make thine enemies the footestoole of thy feete?* † Are they not al, :: ministring spirits: sent to minister for them vvhich shal receiue the inheritance of saluation?

(7) (8) (9) (10) (11) (12) (13) (14)

Ps. 96, 8. — Ps. 103, 4. — Ps. 44, 7. — Ps. 101, 26. — Ps. 109, 1. — 1. Cor. 15, 25.

: The holy Angels (saith S. Augustine) to the societie of vvhom vve aspire in this our peregrination, as they haue eternitie to continue, so also facilitie to knovv, and felicitie to rest: for they do helpe vs vvithout al difficultie, because vvith their spiritual motions pure and free, they labour or trauel not. *De Ciuit. li. 11. c. 31.*

ANNOTATIONS
CHAP. I.

3. *The figure.*] To be the figure of his substance, signifieth nothing els but that vvhich S. Paul speaketh in other vvordes to the Philippians c. 2. v. 6. that he is the forme and most expresse resemblance of his fathers substance. So S. Ambrose and others expound it, and the Greeke vvord *Character* is very significant to that purpose. Note also by this place, that the Sonne, though he be a figure of his Fathers substance, is notvvithstanding of the same substance. So Christes body in the Sacrament and his mystical death and sacrifice in the same, though called a figure, image, or representation of Christes visible body and sacrifice vpon the Crosse, yet may be and is the self same in substance.

μορφή — χαρακτὴρ

The B. Sacrament a figure, and yet the true body.

6. *Let al the Angels adore.*] The Heretikes maruel that vve adore Christ in the B. Sacrament, vvhen they might learne by this place, that vvheresoeuer his person is, there it ought to be adored both of men and Angels. And vvhere they say it vvas not made present in the Sacrament nor instituted to be adored, vve ansvver that no more vvas he incarnate purposely to be adored: but yet straight vpon his descending from heauen, it vvas the duety both of Angels and al other creatures to adore him.

The adoratiõ of Christ in the B. Sacrament.

CHAP. II.

He inferreth of the foresaid, that it shal be incomparably more damnable for them to neglect the nevv Testament then the old, 3 considering the irrefragable authoritie of the Apostles also. 5 Then he prosecuteth the excellencie of Christ aboue the Angels, 9 vvho neuertheles, vvas made lesser then Angels, to suffer and die for men, to destroy the dominion of the Diuel, 15 to deliuer men from feare of death, 17 and to be a fitte Priest for men.

THERFORE more aboundantly ought vve to obserue those things vvhich vve haue heard: [c] lest perhaps vve runne out. † For if the vvord that vvas spoken by Angels, became sure, and al preuarication and disobedience hath receiued a iust retribution of revvard: † hovv shal vve escape

(1) (2) (3)

c As that vvhich runneth out of a broken vessel, or that rũneth by, is lost.

c μή ποτε παραῤῥυῶμεν

escape if vve neglect so great saluation? vvhich vvhen it vvasbegonne to be declared by our Lord, of them that heard vvas confirmed on vs, † * God vvithal testifying by signes, & vvonders, and diuers miracles, & distributions of the holy Ghost according to his vvil. † For not to Angels hath God made subiect the world to come, whereof vve speake. † But one hath testified in a certaine place, saying: *Vvhat is man, that thou art mindeful of him: or the sonne of man, that thou visitest him?* † *Thou didst minish him litle lesse then Angels: with glorie and honour thou hast crovvned him, and constituted him ouer the vvorkes of thy handes.* † *Al things hast thou made subiect vnder his feete.* For in that he subiected al things to him, he left nothing not subiect to him. But novv vve see not as yet al things subiected to him. † But * him that vvas a litle lessened vnder the Angels, vve see IESVS, ∴ because of the passion of death, crovvned vvith glorie and honour: that through the grace of God he might tast death for al. † For it became him for vvhom al things, and by vvhom al things, that had brought many children into glorie, to consummate the author of their saluation, by his passion. † For he that sanctifieth, and they that be sanctified: al of one. For the which cause he is not ashamed to call them brethrē, † saying, *I vvil declare thy name to my brethren: in the middes of the Church vvil I praise thee*. And againe, *I vvil haue affiance in him.* And againe, *Behold here am I and my children: vvhom God hath giuen me.* † Therfore because the children haue communicated vvith flesh & bloud, him self also in like maner hath been partaker of the same: that * by death he might destroy him that had the empire of death, that is to say, the Deuil: † and might deliuer them that by the feare of death through al their life vvere subiect to seruitude.

† For no vvhere doth he take Angels: but [c] the seede of Abraham he taketh. † Vvherevpon he ought in al things to be like vnto his brethren: that he might become a merciful and faithful high Priest before God, that he might repropitiate the sinnes of the people. † For in that vvherein him self suffered and vvas tempted: he is able to helpe them also that are tempted.

Margin verse numbers: 4, 5, 6, 7, 8, 9, 10, 11, 12, 13, 14, 15, 16, 17, 18.

Marginal references: *Mar. 16, 20.* — *Ps. 8, 5.* — *1 Cor. 15* — *Eph. 1.* — *Philip. 2, 8.* — *Ps. 21, 23* — *Ps. 17, 3.* — *Es. 8, 18.* — *Ose. 13, 14. 1 Cor. 15, 54.*

∴ This proueth against the Caluinists that Christ by his Passiō merited his owne glorification. Which they would not for shame deny of Christ, but that they are at a point to deny al meritorious workes, yea euē in Christ also. and therfore they translate also this sentēce heretically, by transposing the wordes. *In the Bible printed the yere 1579.*

c The dignitie of man, in that Christ tooke our nature vnto his person in Deitie, and not the nature of Angels.

CHAP. III.

By example of Christ (vvho is incomparably more excellent then Moyses also) he exhorteth them to be faithful vnto God. 7 Their revvard shal be, to enter into euerlasting rest, if they perseuere, as contrarievvise to be excluded (as vvas shadovved in their forefathers in the vvildernes) if they sinne and become incredulous.

WHEREFORE holy brethren, partakers of the 1 heauenly vocation, consider the Apostle, & high priest of our confession IESVS: † vvho is faith- 2 ful to him that made him, as also * Moyses in al his house. † For, this man is esteemed vvorthie of more 3 ample glorie aboue Moyses, by so much as more ample glorie then the house, hath he that framed it. † For euery 4 house is framed of some man. but he that created al things, is God. † And Moyses in deede vvas faithful in al his house 5 as a seruant, for a testimonie of those things vvhich vvere to be said: † but Christ as the Sonne in his ovvne house: which 6 house are vve, if vve keepe firme the confidence and glorie of hope vnto the end.

The excellencie of Christ aboue Moyses.

Nu. 12, 7

† Vvherefore, as the holy Ghost saith, *To day if you shal heare* 7 *his voice,* † *harden not your hartes as in the exacerbation according to the day* 8 *of tentation in the desert,* † *vvhere your fathers tempted me: proued & savv* 9 *my vvorkes* † *fourtie yeres. For the vvhich cause I vvas offended vvith this ge-* 10 *neration, and said, They doe alvvaies erre in hart. And they haue not knovven my vvaies.* † *to vvhom I svvare in my vvrath, if they shal enter into my rest.* 11

Ps. 94, 8

† Bevvare brethren, lest perhaps there be in some of you 12 an euil hart of incredulitie, to depart from the liuing God. † but exhort your selues euery day, vvhiles *to day* is named, 13 that none of you be obdurate vvith the fallacie of sinne, † For vve be made partakers of Christ: yet so if vve keepe 14 the ∷ beginning of his substance firme vnto the end. † Vvhile 15 it is said, *To day if you shal heare his voice, do not obdurate your hartes as in that exacerbation.* † For some hearing did exasperate: but not al 16 they that vvent out of Ægypt by Moyses. † And vvith 17 vvhom vvas he offended fourtie yeres? vvas it not with them that sinned, * vvhose carcasses vvere ouerthrovven in the desert? † And to vvhom did he svveare that they should not 18 enter into his rest: but to them that were incredulous? † And 19 vve see that they could not enter in, because of incredulitie.

∷ Faith is the groundworke of our creatiō in Christ, which if we hold not fast, al the building is lost.

Nu. 14, 37. 21, 23.

CHAP. IIII.

That they must feare to be excluded out of the foresaid rest (vvhich he proueth out of the psalme) 12 considering that Christ seeth their most invvard secretes. 14 And that he (as their Priest vvho also him self suffered) is able and ready to strengthen them in confession of their faith.

LET

1 LET vs feare therfore lest perhaps forsaking the promis of entring into his rest, some of you be thought to be vvanting. 2 † For to vs also it hath been denounced, as also to them. but the vvord of hearing did not profit them, not mixt vvith faith of those things vvhich they heard. 3 † For vve that haue beleeued, shal enter into the rest: as he said, *As I svvare in my vvrath, if they shal enter into my rest*: and truely the vvorkes from the foundation of the vvorld being perfited. 4 † For he said in a certaine place of the :: seuenth day, thus: *And God rested the seuenth day from al his vvorkes*. 5 † And againe in this, *If they shal enter into my rest*. 6 † Because then it remaineth that certaine enter into it, and they to vvhom first it vvas preached, did not enter because of incredulitie: 7 † againe he limiteth a certaine day: *To day*, in Dauid saying, after so long time, as is aboue said, *To day if you shal heare his voice: doe not obdurate your hartes*. 8 † For if [c] Iesus had giuen them rest: he vvould neuer speake of an other day aftervvard. 9 † Therfore there is left a sabbatisme for the people of God. 10 † For he that is entred into his rest, the same also hath rested frō his vvorkes, as God from his.

11 † Let vs hasten therfore to enter into that rest: that no man fal into the same example of incredulitie. 12 † For :: the vvord of God is liuely and forcible, and more persing then any tvvo edged svvord: and reaching vnto the diuision of the soule and the spirit, of the ioyntes also and the marowes, and a discerner of the cogitations and intentes of the hart. 13 † And there is no creature inuisible in his sight. but al things are naked and open to his eies, to vvhom our speache is.

14 † Hauing therfore a great high Priest that hath entred the heauens, IESVS the sonne of God, let vs hold the confession. 15 † For vve haue not a high priest that can not haue compassion on our infirmities: but tempted in al things by similitude, except sinne. 16 † "Let vs goe therfore vvith confidence to the throne of grace: that vve may obteine mercie, and finde grace in seasonable aide.

Margin: Ps. 94, 11 — Gen. 2, 2. — Heb. 3, 7.

[c] So Iosue is called in Greeke.

:: If the Apostle had not euidently here shevved that the Sabboths rest vvas a figure of the eternal repose in heauen, vvho durst to haue applied that Scripture of Gods rest the seuenth day, to that purpose? Or hovv can our Aduersaries now reprehend the like applicatiō manifoldly vsed in al holy auncient vvriters to the like end?

:: Whatsoeuer God threateneth by his vvord concerning the punishment of sinne and incredulitie, shal be executed, be the offense neuer so secrete, deepe, or hidden in our harts. because Gods speach passeth easily and searcheth throughly euery part, power, and facultie of mans soul.

The Epistle in a Masse for the election of the Pope.

ANNOTATIONS
CHAP. IIII.

16. *Let vs go vvith confidence.*] The Aduersaries go about to proue by these vvordes that vve neede no helpe of Saincts to obtaine any thing, Christ him self being so readie, and vve being admonished

Scripture abused against inuocation of Saincts.

monished to come to him vvith confidence as to a most merciful Mediator and Bishop. But by that argument they may as vvel take avvay the helpes and praiers of the liuing one for an other. And vve do not require the helpe either of the Saincts in heauen, or of our brethren in earth, for any mistrust of Gods mercie, but for our ovvne vnvvorthines: being assured that the praier of a iust man auaileth more vvith him, then the desire of a greuous sinner: and of a number making intercession together, rather then of a man alone. vvhich the Heretikes can not deny except they reproue the plaine Scriptures. Neither do vve come lesse to him, or vvith lesse confidence, vvhen vve come accompanied vvith the praiers of Angels, Saincts, Priests, or iust men ioyning vvith vs, as they fondly imagine and pretend: but vvith much more affiance in his grace, mercie, and merites, then if vve praied our selues alone.

CHAP. V.

That Christ being a man and infirme, vvas therein but as al Priests. and that he also vvas called of God to this office: offering as the others: 8 and suffered obediently for our example. 11 Of vvhose Priesthod he hath much to say, but that the Hebrues haue neede rather to heare their Catechisme againe.

The Epistle for a Bishop that is a Confessor, and for S. Thomas of Canterburie.

OR "euery high Priest taken from amõg men, is appointed for mẽ in those things that pertaine to God: that he may offer giftes and sacrifices for sinnes: 1 † that cã haue compassion on them that be ignorant and do erre: because him self also is cõpassed vvith infirmitie: 2 † & therfore he ought, as for the people, so also for him self to offer for sinnes. 3 † *Neither doth any man "take the honour to him self, but he that is called of God, * as Aaron. 4 ⊣ † So Christ also "did not glorifie him self that he might be made a high priest: but he that spake to him, *My Sonne art thou, I this day haue begottẽ thee.* 5 † As also in an other place he saith, *Thou art "a priest for euer, according to the order of Melchisedec.* 6 ⊣ † Vvho in the daies of his flesh, "vvith a strong crie and teares, offering praiers and supplications to him that could saue him from death, vvas heard "for his reuerence. 7 ⊣ † And truely vvhereas he was the Sonne, he learned by those things vvhich he suffered, obedience: 8 † and being consummate, 9 "vvas made to al that obey him, cause of eternal saluation, † called of God a high priest according to the order of Melchisedec. 10

† Of vvhome vve haue great speache and "inexplicable to vtter: because you are become vveake to heare. 11 † For vvhereas you ought to be maisters for your time, you neede to be taught againe your selues vvhat be the elements of the beginning of the vvordes of God: and you are become such 12

2 Par. 26, 18.
1 Par. 23, 13.
Ps. 2, 7.
Ps. 109, 4.

as

13 as haue neede of milke, & not of strong meate. † For euery one that is partaker of milke, is vnskilful of the vvord of iu-
14 stice: for he is a childe. † But strong meate is for the perfect, them that by custome haue their senses exercised to the discerning of good & euil.

ANNOTATIONS
CHAP. V.

The description of a Priest, and his office.

1. *Euery high Priest.*] By the description of a Priest or high Priest (for to this purpose al is one matter) he proueth Christ to be one in most excellent sort. First then, a Priest must not be an Angel, or of any other nature but mans. Secondly, euery man is not a Priest, but such an one as is specially chosen out of the rest, and preferred before other of the community, seuered, assumpted, and exalted into a higher state and dignitie then the vulgar. Thirdly, the cause and purpose vvhy he is so sequestred and piked out from the residue, is to take charge of Diuine things, to deale as a mediator betvvixt God and the people, to be the Deputie of men in such things as they haue to craue or to receiue of God, and to present or giue to him againe. Fourthly, the most proper and principal part of a Priests office is, to offer oblations, giftes, and sacrifices to God for the sinnes of the people: vvithout vvhich kind of most soueraine dueties, no person, people, or Commonvvealth can appertaine to God: and vvhich can be done by none, of vvhat other dignitie or calling soeuer he be in the vvorld, that is not a Priest: diuers Princes (as vve read in the Scriptures) punished by God, and king Saul deposed from his kingdom, specially for attempting the same.

3. Reg. 13. 2. Par. 26. 1. Reg. 13.

The Princes temporal authoritie how far it extendeth.

And generally vve may learne here, that *in ijs quæ sunt ad Deum*, in al matters touching God, his seruice, and religion, the Priest hath onely charge and authority: as the Prince temporal is the peoples gouernour, guider, and soueraine, in the things touching their vvorldly affaires: Vvhich must for al that by him be directed and manneged no othervvise, but as is agreable to the due vvorship and seruice of God. against vvhich if the terrene Povvers commit any thing, the Priests ought to admonish them from God.

There is a peculiar order & calling of Priests of the new Testament.

Priests and sacrifice necessarie in the new Testament, & nothing derogatorie to Christs priesthod or sacrifice.

Vve learne also hereby, that euery one is not a Priest, and that the people must alvvaies haue certaine persons chosen out from among them, to deale in their sutes and causes vvith God, to pray, to minister Sacraments, and to sacrifice for them. And vvhereas the Protestants vvil haue no Priest, Priesthod, nor sacrifice, but Christ and his death, pretending these vvordes of the Apostle to be verified onely in the Priesthod and Seruice of the old lavv, and Christes person alone, and after him of no moe: therein they shevv them selues to be ignorant of the Scriptures, and of the state of the nevv Testament, and induce a plaine Atheisme and Godlesnesse into the vvorld. for, so long as man hath to doe vvith God, there must needes be some deputed, and chosen out from among the rest, to deale according to this declaration of the Apostle, in things pertaining to God, and those must be Priests. for els, if men neede to deale no more, but immediatly vvith Christ, vvhat doe they vvith their Ministers? Vvhy let they not euery man pray, and minister for him self, and to him self? Vvhat doe they vvith Sacraments, seing Christes death is as vvel sufficient vvithout them, as vvithout sacrifice? Vvhy standeth not his death as vvel vvith Sacrifice, as vvith Sacraments: as vvel vvith Priesthod, as vvith other Ecclesiastical functiō? There is no other cause in the vvorld, but that (Sacrifice being the most principal act of religion that man ovveth to God, both by his Lavv, and by the lavv of nature) the Diuel by these his ministers, vnder pretence of deferring or attributing the more to Christes death, vvould abolish it.

The difference and excellencie of Christs Priesthod.

This definition of a Priest and his function, vvith al the properties thereto belonging, holdeth not onely in the lavv of Moyses, and order of Aarons Priesthod, but it vvas true before, in the lavv of nature, in the Patriarches, in Melchisedec, and novv in Christ, and all his Apostles, and Priests of the nevv Testament: sauing that it is a peculiar excellencie in Christ, that he onely offered for other mens sinnes, and not at all for his ovvne, as all other doe.

Al true priests and preachers must be lawfully called thereto.

4. *Taketh to him self.*] A special prouiso for all Priests, preachers, and such as haue to deale for the people in things pertaining to God, that they take not that honour or office at their ovvne hands, but by lavvful calling and consecration, euen as Aaron did. By vvhich clause if you examine Luther, Caluin, Beza, and the like, or if al such as novv a daies intrude them selues into sacred functions, looke into their consciences, great and foul matter of damnation vvil appeare.

The dignitie & function of Priesthod is

5. *Did not glorifie him self.*] The dignity of Priesthod must needes be passing high and soueraine, vvhen it vvas a promotion and preferment in the sonne of God him self according to his manhod, and vvhen he vvould not vsurpe, nor take vpon him the same, vvithout his fathers ex-

not to be vsurped.

presse commission and calling therevnto. An eternal example of humility, and an argument of condemnation to al mortal men, that arrogate vniustly any function or povver spiritual, that is not giuen them from aboue, and by lavvful calling, and commission of their superiors.

Christ both Priest & king: but his Priesthod more excellent of the two.

Christ a Priest as he is man, not as he is God.

6. *A Priest for euer.*] In the 109 Psalme, from vvhence this testimonie is taken, both Christes kingdom and Priesthod are set fourth. but the Apostle vrgeth specially his Priesthod, as the more excellent and preeminent state in him, our Redemption being vvrought & atchieued by sacrifice, vvhich vvas an act of his Priesthod, and not of his kingly povver. though he vvas properly a king also, as Melchisedec vvas both Priest, and king, being a resemblance of Christ in both, but much more in his Priesthod. And our Lord had this excellent double dignitie (as appeareth by the discourse of S. Paul, and his allegations here out of the Psalmes) at the very first moment of his conception or incarnation. for you must bevvare of the vvicked heresie of the Arians and Caluinists (except in these later it be rather an errour proceding of ignorance) that sticke not to say, that Christ vvas a Priest, or did sacrifice, according to his Godhead. Vvhich is to make Christ, God the fathers Priest, and not his sonne, and to doe sacrifice and homage to him as his Lord, and not as his equal in dignity and nature. Therfore S. Augustine saith *in Psal.* 109. *That as he vvas man, he vvas Priest: as God, he vvas not Priest.* And Theodorete in Psal 109. *As man, he did offer sacrifice: but as God, he did receiue sacrifice.* And againe, *Christ touching his humanity vvas called a Priest, and he offered no other host but his ovvne body. &c.* Dialog. 1 circa med. Some of our nevv Maisters not knovving so much, did let fall out of their pennes the contrarie, and being admonished of the errour, and that it vvas very Arianisme, yet they persist in it of mere ignorance in the groundes of Diuinitie.

Psal. 2. 109.

Retent. pag. 89.

The sacrifice on the Crosse, vvas the principal acte of Christs priesthod.

7. *With a strong crie.*] Though our Sauiour make intercession for vs, according to his humane nature, cōtinually in heauen also: yet he doth not in any external creatures make sacrifice, nor vse the praiers sacrificall, by vvhich our redemption vvas atchieued, as he did in the time of his mortal life, and in the act of his Passion, and most principally, vvhen vvith a loud voice, and vvith this praier, *In manus tuas commendo spiritum meum*, he voluntarily deposed his soul, yelding it in most proper sort for a sacrifice. for in that last point of his death, consisteth specially his high Priestly office, and the very vvorke and consummation of our redemption.

Luc. 23, 46.

Priests praiers more effectual.

Obserue more ouer, that though commonly euery faithful person pray both for him self and others, and offer his praiers to God, yet none offereth by office, and special deputation, and appointment, in the person of the vvhole Church and people, sauing the Priest. Vvhose praiers therfore be more effectual in them selues, for that they be the voice of all faithful men together, made by him that is appointed and receiued of God for the peoples legate. And of this kind vvere all Christes praiers, in all his life and death, as all his other actions vvere: his fasting, vvatching, preaching, instituting, ministring, or receiuing Sacraments: euery one being done as Priestly actions.

Christs Priestly actions.

Notorious Heretical trāslatiō to mainteine Caluins horrible blasphemie.

7. *For his reuerence.*] These vvordes haue our English Translators perniciously and most presumptuously corrupted, turning them thus, *In that vvhich he feared*, contrarie to the version and sense of al antiquity, and to Erasmus also, and contrarie to the ordinarie vse of the Greeke vvord, as Beza him self defineth it *Luc. 2 v. 25*: and contrarie to the propriety of the Greeke phrase, as not onely the Catholikes, but * the best learned Lutherans do shevv and proue by many examples. They folovv herein the singular presumption of Caluin, vvho vvas the first (as his fellovv Beza confesseth) that euer found out this interpretation. Vvhich neither S. Chrysostom, nor any other, as perfect Græcians as they vvere, could euer espie. Vvhere, onely to haue made choise of that impious and arrogant Sectaries sense, before the said fathers and all the Churches besides, had been shameful ynough: but to set the same dovvne for very Scripture of Gods blessed vvord, that is intolerable, and passeth al impiety. And vve see plainely that they haue no conscience, indifferencie, nor other purpose, but to make the poore Readers beleeue, that their opinions be Gods ovvne vvord, and to dravv the Scriptures to sound after the fantasie of their heresies. But if the good Reader knevv, for vvhat point of doctrine they haue thus framed their translation, they vvould abhorre them to the depth of Hel. forsooth it is thus: they vvould haue this Scripture meane, that Christ vvas in horrible feare of damnation, and that he vvas not onely in paines corporal vpon the Crosse (vvhich they hold, not to haue been sufficient for mans redemption) but that he vvas in the very sorovves & distresses of the damned, vvithout any difference, but that it vvas not euerlasting, as theirs is.

ἀπὸ εὐλαβείας

Flac. Illyr. vpon this place.

Caluins blasphemie that Christ suffered hel paines vpō the crosse, and that his death othervvise were insufficient.

For this horrible blasphemie (vvhich is their interpretation of Christes descending into Hel) Gods holy vvord must be corrupted, and the sacrifice of Christes death (vvhereof they talke so presumptuously) must not be ynough for our redemption, except he be damned for vs also to the paines of Hel. Vvo be to our poore Countrie, that must haue such bookes, and read such translations. See Caluin and Beza in their Commentaries and Annotations vpon this place, and you shal see, that for defense of the said blasphemies they haue thus translated this text. See the Annotations before, *Act. 2, 27* and *Mat. 27, 46.*

Christ yelding vp the Ghost, accomplished our redemption.

9. *Consummate.*] The ful vvorke of his sacrifice, by vvhich vve vvere redeemed, vvas vvholy consummate and accomplished, at the yelding vp of his spirit to God the Father, vvhen he said, *Consummatum est.* though for to make the same effectual to the saluation of particular men, he him

Io. 19. 30.

self

ſelf did diuers things, and novv doth in heauen, and our ſelues alſo muſt vſe many meanes, for the application thereof to our particular neceſſities. See the next Annotation.

9. *Was made to all.*] The Proteſtants vpon pretence of the ſufficiencie of Chriſtes Paſſion, and his onely redemption, oppoſe them ſelues guilefully in the ſight of the ſimple, againſt the inuocation of Saincts, and their interceſſion, and help of vs, againſt our penitential vvorkes or ſuffering for our ovvne ſinnes, either in this life or the next: againſt the merites of faſting, praying, almes, and other things commended to vs in holy Vvritte, and againſt moſt things done in the Church, in ſacrifice, Sacrament, and ceremonie. But this place and many other ſhevv, that Chriſtes Paſſion, though it be of it ſelf far more ſufficient and forcible, then the Proteſtants in their baſeneſſe of vnderſtanding can conſider, yet profiteth none but ſuch, as both doe his commaundements, and vſe ſuch remedies and meanes to apply the benefite thereof to them ſelues, as he appointeth in his vvord, or by the Holy Ghoſt in his Church. And the Heretikes that ſay, faith onely is the thing required to apply Chriſtes benefites vnto vs, are hereby alſo eaſily refuted. for vve do not obey him onely by beleeuing, but by doing vvhatſoeuer he commaundeth. Laſtly, vve note in the ſame vvordes, that Chriſt appointeth not by his abſolute and eternal election, men ſo to be partakers of the fruite of his redemption, vvithout any condition or reſpect of their ovvne vvorkes, obedience, or free vvil: but vvith this condition alvvaies, if men vvil obey him, and do that vvhich he appointeth. See S. Auguſtine (or Proſper) to. 7 Reſponſ. Proſperi *li.* 2. *articulo* 1 *ad obiectiones Vincentij*, vvhere he ſaith of the cup of Chriſtes paſſion, *It hath in deede in it ſelf, to profite al: but if it be not drunken, it healeth not.*

Chriſts Paſsiō ſufficient for al, but profitable to them only vvhich obey, not by faith only, but by doing as he and his Church commaund.

11 *Inexplicable.*] Intending to treate more largely and particularly of Chriſtes or Melchiſedeks Prieſthod, he forvvarneth them that the myſterie thereof is far paſſing their capacitie, and that through their feeblenes in faith and vveakenes of vnderſtanding, he is forced to omit diuers deepe points concerning the Prieſthod of the nevv lavv. Among vvhich (no doubt) the myſterie of the Sacrament and Sacrifice of the altar, called MASSE, vvas a principal & pertinent matter: vvhich the Apoſtles and Fathers of the primitiue Church vſed not to treate of ſo largely and particularly in their vvritings, vvhich might come to the hands of the vnfaithful, vvho of al things tooke ſooneſt ſcandal of the B. Sacrament, as vve ſee Io. 6. *He ſpake to the Hebrues* (ſaith S. Hierom ep 126) *that is, to the Ievves, and not to faithful men, to vvhom he might haue been bold to vtter the Sacrament.* And in deede it vvas not reaſonable to talke much to them of that ſacrifice vvhich vvas the reſemblance of Chriſtes death, vvhen they thought not right of Chriſtes death it ſelf. Vvhich the Apoſtles vviſedom and ſilence our Aduerſaries vvickedly abuſe againſt the holy Maſſe.

The Apoſtle omitteth to ſpeake of the B. Sacrament as a myſterie then to deepe for the Ievves capacitie.

CHAP. VI.

He exhorteth them to be perfect ſcholers, and not to neede to be Catechumens againe, 4 *conſidering they can not be baptized againe:* 9 *and remembring their former good vvorkes, for the vvhich God vvil not faile to performe them his promis, if they faile not to imitate Abraham by perſeuerance in the faith vvith patience.* 20 *And ſo endeth his digreſsion, and returneth to the matter of Chriſtes Prieſthod.*

1 VHERFORE intermitting the vvord of the beginning of Chriſt, let vs proceede to perfection, not againe laying " the foundatiō of penance from dead vvorkes, and of faith 2 tovvard God, † of the doctrine of baptiſmes, and of impoſition of handes, and of the reſurrection of the 3 dead, and of eternal iudgement. † And this ſhal vve doe, if 4 God vvill permit. † For * it is " impoſſible for them that were once illuminated, haue taſted alſo the heauenly gift, and 5 vvere made partakers of the holy Ghoſt, † haue moreouer taſted the good vvord of God, and the povvers of the world

* Heb. 10, 26.

to come, † and are fallen: to be renevved againe to penāce, 6 crucifying againe to them selues the sonne of God, and making him a mockerie. † For the earth drinking the raine 7 often cōming vpon it, & bringing forth grasse commodious for them by vvhom it is tilled, receiueth blessing of God. † but bringing forth thornes and bryers, it is reprobate, and 8 very neere a curse, vvhose end is, to be burnt.

:: It is euident by these vvordes, against the Nouatians and the Caluinists, that S. Paul meant not precisely, that they had done, or could do any such sinne, vvhereby they should be put out of all hope of saluation, and be sure of damnation, during their life.

† But :: vve confidently trust of you, my best beloued, 9 better things and neerer to saluation: although vve speake thus. † For" God is not vniust, that he should forget your 10 vvorke & loue which you haue shevved in his name, vvhich haue ministred to the sainctes and do minister. † And our 11 desire is that euery one of you shevv forth the same carefulnesse to the accomplishing of hope vnto the end: † that 12 you become not slouthful, but imitatours of them vvhich by faith and patience shal inherite the promisses. † For God 13 promising to Abraham, because he had none greater by vvhō he might sweare, he sware by him self, † saying, *Vnles bles- 14 sing I shal blesse thee, and multiplying shal multiplie thee. † And so patiently enduring he obtained the promise. † For mē 15 svveare by a greater then them selues: and the end of al their 16 controuersie, for the confirmation, is an othe. † Vvherein 17 God meaning more aboundantly to shevv to the heires of the promise the stabilitie of his coūsel, he interposed an othe: † that by tvvo things vnmoueable, vvhereby it is impossible 18 for God to lie, vve may haue a most strong comfort. vvho haue fled to hold fast the hope proposed, † vvhich vve haue 19 as an anker of the soule, sure and firme, and going in into the inner partes of the vele, † vvhere IESVS the precursor for 20 vs is entered, made a high priest for euer according to the order of Melchisedec.

Gen. 22, 16.

ANNOTATIONS
CHAP. VI.

The Apostles forme of Catechisme, and the poīts therof.

1. *The foundation of penance.*] Vve see hereby, vvhat the first groundes of Christian institution or Catechisme vvere in the primitiue Church, and that there vvas euer a necessarie instruction and beleefe of certaine points had by vvord of mouth and tradition, before men came to the Scriptures: vvhich could not treate of things so particularly, as vvas requisite for the teaching of al necessarie groundes. Among these points vvere the 12 Articles conteined in the Apostles Creede: the doctrine of penance before Baptisme: the maner and necessitie of Baptisme: the Sacrament of Imposition of hands after Baptisme, called Confirmation: the articles of the Resurrection, Iudgement, and such like. Vvithout vvhich things first laid, if one should be sent to picke his faith out of the Scripture, there vvould

be

be madde rule quickly. See S. Augustine *in exposit, inchoat. ep. ad Ro. versus finem.*

4. *Impossible.*] How hard the holy Scriptures be, and how dangerously they be read of the vnlearned, or of the proud be they neuer so vvel learned, this one place might teach vs. * VVhereat the Nouatians of old did so stumble, that they thought, and heretically taught, that none falling into any mortal sinne after Baptisme, could be receiued to mercie or penance in the Church: and so to a contentious man, that vvould folow his owne sense, or the bare vvordes, vvithout regard of the Churches sense and rule of faith (after vvhich euery Scripture must be expounded) the Apostles speach doth here sound. Euen as to the simple, and to the Heretike that submitteth not his sense to the Churches iudgement, certaine places of this same Epistle, seeme at the first sight, to stand against the daily oblation or sacrifice of the Masse: vvhich yet in truth make no more for that purpose, then this text we now stand on, serueth the Nouatians: as vvhen we come to the places, it shal be declared.

Ambr. de pœnit. li. 2. c. 2.

The Nouatians (as al Heretikes) made Scripture the groũd of their heresie.

Other places make no more for the Protestants then this doth for Nouatus.

And let the good Readers beware here also of the Protestants exposition, for they are herein vvorse then Nouatians, specially such as precisely folovv Caluin: holding impiously, that it is impossible for one that forsaketh entirely his faith, that is, becommeth an Apostata or an Heretike, to be receiued to penance or to Gods mercie. To establish vvhich false and damnable sense, these fellowes make nothing of S. Ambroses, S. Chrysostoms, and the other fathers exposition, vvhich is the holy Churches sense, That the Apostle meaneth of that penance vvhich is done before and in Baptisme. vvhich is no more to say, but that it is impossible to be baptized againe, and thereby to be renouated and illuminated, to die, be buried, and rise againe the second time in Christ, in so easie and perfect penance and cleansing of sinnes, as that first sacrament of generation did yeld: vvhich applieth Christes death in such ample maner to the receiuers, that it taketh avvay al paines due for sinnes before committed: and therfore requireth no further penance aftervvard, for the sinnes before committed, al being vvashed away by the force of that Sacrament duely taken. S. Augustine calleth the remission in Baptisme, *Magnam indulgentiam*, a great pardon. *Enchirid. c. 64.*

Ambr. loco cit. & in ep. ad Heb. Chry. ho. 9 in c. 6 ad Hebr.

Caluins heresie vpon this place, vvorse then the Nouatians.

The fathers exposition of this place.

The Apostle therfore warneth them, that if they fall from their faith, and from Christes grace and lavv vvhich they once receiued in their Baptisme, they may not looke to haue any more that first great and large remedie applied vnto them, nor no man els that sinneth after Baptisme: though the other penance, vvhich is called the *Second table after shipvvracke*, vvhich is a more paineful medicine for sinne then Baptisme, requiring much fasting, praying, and other afflictions corporal, is open not onely to other sinners, but to al once baptized, Heretikes, or oppugners of the truth malitiously and of purpose or what way so euer, during this life. See S. Cyprian *ep. 52.* S. Ambrose vpon this place. S. Augustine *cont. ep. Parm. li. 2. c. 13.* and *ep. 50.* S. Damascene *li. 4. c. 10.*

Hiero. ep. 8 ad Demetriad. c. 6.

The Sacramẽt of penance is ready for al sinners vvhatsoeuer.

10. *God is not vniust.*] It is a vvorld to see, vvhat vvringing & vvrithing the Protestants make, to shift them selues from the euidence of these vvordes, vvhich make it most cleere to all not blinded in pride and contention, that good vvorkes be meritorious, and the very cause of saluation, so far that God should be vniust, if he rendered not heauen for the same. *Reuera grandis iniustitia Dei* (saith S. Hierom) *Si tantum peccata puniret, & bona opera non susciperet.* That is, *In deede great vvere Gods iniustice, if he vvould onely punish sinnes, and vvould not receiue good vvorkes. Li. 2. cont. Iouin. c. 2.*

Gods iustice in revvarding meritorious vvorkes.

CHAP. VII.

To proue the Priesthod of Christ incomparably to excel the priesthod of Aaron (and therfore, that Leuitical priesthod novv to cease, and that lavv also vvith it) he scanneth euery vvord of the verse alleaged out of the Psalme, Our Lord hath svvorne: thou art a Priest for euer, according to the order of Melchisedec.

1 FOR this [a] Melchisedec, the king of Salem, Priest of the God most high, * vvho mette Abraham returning from the slaughter of the kings, and blessed him: 2 † to vvhom also Abrahã deuided tithes of al: first in deede by in-

Gen. 14, 18.

terpretation, ∷ the king of iustice: & then also king of Salem, vvhich is to say, king of peace, † " vvithout father, without mother, vvithout genealogie, hauing neither beginning of daies nor end of life, but likened to the sonne of God, continueth a priest for euer. 3

† And " behold hovv great this man is, to vvhom also Abraham the Patriarke gaue " tithes of the principal things. 4 † And certes * they of the sonnes of Leui that take the priesthod, haue commaundement to take tithes of the people according to the Lavv, that is to say, of their brethren: albeit them selues also issued out of the loines of Abraham. 5 † but he vvhose generation is not numbered among them, tooke tithes of Abraham, and blessed him that had the promises. 6 † But vvithout al contradiction, that vvhich is lesse, " is blessed of the better. 7 † And here in deede, ∷ men that die, receiue tithes: but there he hath vvitnes, that he liueth. 8 † And (that it may so be said) by Abraham Leui also, which receiued tithes, vvas tithed. 9 † for as yet he vvas in his fathers loines, vvhen Melchisedec mette him. 10 † If then consummation vvas by the Leuitical priesthod (for vnder it the people receiued the Lavv) " vvhat necessitie vvas there yet an other priest to rise according to the order of Melchisedec, and not to be called according to the order of Aaron? 11 † For the priesthod being " translated, it is necessarie that a translation of the Lavv also be made. 12 † For he on vvhom these things be said, is of an other tribe, of the vvhich, none attended on the altar. 13 † For it is manifest that our Lord sprung of Iuda: in the which tribe Moyses spake nothing of ' priestes'. 14 † And yet it is much more euident: if according to the similitude of Melchisedec there arise an other priest, 15 † vvhich vvas not made according to the Lavv of the carnal commaundement, but according to the povver of life indissoluble. 16 † For he vvitnesseth, *That thou art " a priest for euer, according to the order of Melchisedec.* 17 † Reprobation certes is made " of the former cōmaundement, because of the vveakenesse and vnprofitablenesse thereof. 18 † For the Lavv brought nothing to perfection, but an introduction of a better hope, by the vvhich vve approche to God. 19 † And in as much as it is not vvithout an othe, (the other truely vvithout an othe vvere made priestes: 20 † but this " vvith an othe, by him that said vnto him: *Our Lord hath svvorne, and it shal not repent him: thou art a priest for euer*) 21

† by

∷ When the fathers & catholike expositours pike out allegories and mysteries out of the names of mē, the Protestāts not endued vvith the Spirit vvherby the scriptures vvere giuē, deride their holy labours in the search of the same: but the Apostle findeth high mysterie in the very names of persons and places, as you see.

∷ The tithes giuen to Melchisedech were not giuē as to a mere mortal mā, as al of the tribe of Leui & Aarons order were: but as to one representing the Sonne of God, vvho now liueth and reigneth and holdeth his priesthod & the functions therof for euer.

* Nu. 18, 21. Deu. 18, 1. Ios. 14, 4.

Priesthod.

Ps. 109, 4.

Ps. 109, 4.

22 † by so much, is IESVS made a suretie of a better testamẽt.
23 † And the other in deede vvere made priestes," being many, because that by death they vvere prohibited to continue:
24 † but this, for that he continueth for euer, hath an euerlasting
25 priesthod. † vvhereby he is able to saue also for euer \`going' by him self to God: ∵ alvvaies liuing to make intercession for vs.
26 † For it vvas seemely that vve should haue such a high priest, holy, innocent, impolluted, separated from sinners, and
27 made higher then the heauens. † vvhich hath not necessitie daily (as the priestes) first * for his ovvne sinnes to offer hostes, then for the peoples. for " this he did once, in offering
28 him self. ⁋ † For the Lavv appointeth priestes them that haue infirmitie: but the vvord of the othe vvhich is after the Lavv, the Sonne for euer perfected.

them that goe

Leu. 9, 7. 16, 6.

The Epistle for a Cõfessor that is a Bishop.

∵ Christ according to his humane nature praieth for vs, & continually representeth his former passion and merites to God the Father.

ANNOTATIONS
CHAP. VII.

1. *Melchisedec.*] The excellencie of this person vvas so great, that some of the antiquity tooke him to be an Angel, and some the holy Ghost. Vvhich opinion not onely the Hebrues, that auouch him to be Sem the sonne of Noë, but also the cheefe fathers of the Christians do condemne: not doubting but he vvas a mere man and a Priest and a king, vvhosoeuer he vvas. for els he could not in office and order and sacrifice haue been so perfect a type and resemblance of our Sauiour, as in this Chapter and other is shevved.

3. *Without father.*] Not that he vvas vvithout father and mother, saith S. Hierom *ep.* 126: for Christ him self vvas not vvithout father, according to his diuinity, nor vvithout mother, in his humanity: but for that his petigree is not set out in the Genesis, as the genealogie of other Patriarches is, but is sodenly induced in the holy historie, no mention made of his stocke, tribe, beginning, or ending, and therfore in that case also resembling in a sort the sonne of God, vvhose generation vvas extraordinarie, miraculous, and ineffable, according to both his natures, lacking a father in the one, and a mother in the other. his person hauing neither beginning nor ending, and his kingdom, and Priesthod specially, in him self and in the Church, being eternall, both in respect of the time past, and the time to come: as the said Doctor in the same epistle vvriteth.

The resemblãce of Melchisedec to Christ, in many points.

4. *Behold.*] To proue that Christes Priesthod farpasseth the Priesthod of Aaron: and the Priesthod of the nevv Testament, the Priesthod of the old lavv: and consequently that the sacrifice of our Sauiour and the sacrifice of the Church doth much excel the sacrifices of Moyses lavv, he disputeth profoundly of the preeminences of Melchisedec aboue the great Patriarch Abraham, vvho vvas father of the Leuites.

By the sundrie excellencies of Melchisedecks Priesthod is proued the excellẽcie of the Priesthod & sacrifice of the nevv Testament.

4. *Tithes.*] The first preeminence, that Abraham paied tithes, and that of the best and most cheefe things that he [illegible], vnto Melchisedec, as a duety and homage, not for him self onely in person, but for Leui, vvho yet vvas not borne, and so for the vvhole Priesthod of Leuies stocke, acknovvledging thereby, Melchisedec not onely to be a Priest, but his Priest and Superior, and so of al the Leuitical order. And it is here to be obserued, that vvhereas in the 14 of Genesis, vvhence this holy narration is taken, both in the Hebrue, and in the 70, it standeth indifferent or doubtfull, vvhether Melchisedec paied tithes to Abraham, or tooke tithes of him: the Apostle here putteth al out of controuersie, plainely declaring that Abraham paied tithes to the other, as the inferiour to his Priest and Superior. And touching paiment of tithes, it is a natural duety, that men ovve to God in al lavves, and to be giuen to his Priests in his behalfe, for their honour and liuelihod. Iacob promised or vovved to pay them, Gen. 28. Moyses appointed them *Leuit.* 27. *Num.* 18. *Deut.* 12. 14. 26. Christ confirmeth that duety *Mat.* 23: and Abraham specially here giueth them to Melchisedec

He receiued tithes of Abrahã, & consequently of Leui & Aarõ.

Tithes.

sedec: plainely thereby approuing them or their equiualent to be due to Christ and the Priesthod of the nevv Testament, much more then either in the lavv of Moyses, or in the lavv of Nature. Of vvhich tithes due to the Clergie of Christes Church see S. Cyprian *ep. 66.* S. Hierom *ep. 1 c. 7.* and *ep. 2 c. 5.* to Heliodorus and Nepotianus. S. Augustine *ser. 119 de tempore.*

He blessed Abraham.

Blessing a great preeminéce, specially in Priests.

7. *Is blessed of the better.*] The second preeminence is, that Melchisedec did blesse Abraham: vvhich vve see here S. Paul maketh a great and soueraine holy thing, grounding our Sauiours prerogatiue aboue the vvhole order of Aaron therein: and vve see that in this sort it is the proper act of Priesthod: and that vvithout al controuersie as the Apostle saith, he is greater in dignitie, that hath authority to blesse, then the person that hath not, and therfore the Priests vocation to be in this behalfe far aboue any earthly king, vvho hath not povver to giue benediction in this sacred maner, neither to man, nor other creature. As here Melchisedec, so Christ blessed much more, and so haue the Bishops of his Church done, and do. Vvhich no man can maruel that our forefathers haue so highly esteemed and sought for, if he marke the vvonderful mysterie and grace thereof here expressed. This Patriarch also vvhich here taketh blessing of Melchisedec, him self (though in an inferior sort) blessed his sonnes, as the other Patriarches did, and fathers do their children by that example.

The ful accomplishment of mans redéption vvas not by Aarons but by Melchisedecks Priesthod.

11. *If consummation.*] The principal proposition of the vvhole epistle and al the Apostles discourse, is inferred & grounded vpon the former prerogatiues of Melchisedec aboue Abraham and Leui: that is, that the end, perfection, accomplishment, and consummation of al mans dueties and debtes to God, by the general redemption, satisfaction, full price and perfect ransom of al mankind, vvas not atchieued by any or al the Priests of Aarons order, nor by any sacrifice or act of that Priesthod, or of al the lavv of Moyses, vvhich vvas grounded vpon the Leuitical Priesthod, but by Christ and his Priesthod, vvhich is of the order and rite of Melchisedec.

The Apostle to confute the Ievves false persuasion of Aarons Priesthod and sacrifices, speaketh altogether of the sacrifice of the Crosse.

11. *What necessitie.*] This disputation of the preeminence of Christes Priesthod aboue the Leuitical order, is against the erroneous persuasion of the Ievves, that thought their lavv, Priesthod, and sacrifices to be euerlasting, and to be sufficient in them selues, vvithout any other Priest then Aaron and his successors, and vvithout al relation to Christes Passion or any other redemption or remission, then that vvhich their Leuitical offices did procure: not knovving that they vvere all figures of Christes death, and to be ended and accomplished in the same. Vvhich point vvell vnderstood and kept in mind, vvill cleere the vvhole controuersie betvvixt the Catholikes and Protestants, concerning the sacrifice of the Church. for, the scope of the Apostles disputation being, to auouch the dignity, preeminence, necessitie, and eternal fruite and effect of Christes Passion, he had not to treate at all of the other, vvhich is a sacrifice depending of his Passion, specially vvriting to the Hebrues, that vvere to be instructed and reformed first touching the sacrifice of the Crosse, before they could fruitfully heare any thing of the other. though in couert and by most euident sequele of disputation, the learned and faithfull may easily perceiue vvherevpon the said Sacrifice of the Church (vvhich is the Masse) is grounded. And therfore S. Hierom saith, *ep. 126:* that al these commendations of Melchisedec are in the type of Christ, *cuius profectus Ecclesiæ sacramenta sunt.*

No lavvful state of people vvith out an external Priesthod.

12. *Translated.*] Note vvel this place, and you shal perceiue thereby, that euery lavvful forme and manner of lavv, state, or gouernement of Gods people dependeth on Priesthod, riseth, standeth, falleth, or altereth vvith the Priesthod. In the lavv of Nature, the state of the people hanged on one kind of Priesthod: in the lavv of Moyses, of an other: in the state of Christianity, of an other: and therfore in the former sentence the Apostle said, that the Ievvish people or Commonvvealth had their lavv vnder the Leuitical Priesthod, and the Greeke more properly expresseth the matter, that they vvere *legitimated,* that is to say, made a lavvful people or communitie vnder God, by the Priesthod. for there is no iust nor lavvful Commonvvealth in the vvorld, that is not made legal and Gods peculiar, and distinguished from vnlavvful Commonvveales that hold of false goddes, or of none at al, by Priesthod. Vvherevpon it is cleere, that the nevv lavv, and al Christian peoples holding of the same, is made lavvful by the Priesthod of the nevv Testament, and that the Protestants shamefully are deceiued, and deceiue others, that vvould haue Christian Commonvveales to lacke an external Priesthod, or Christes death to abolish the same. for, this is a demonstration, that if Christ haue abolished Priesthod, he hath abolished the nevv lavv, vvhich is the nevv Testament and state of Grace, vvhich al Christian Commonvvealths liue vnder. Neither vvere it true, that the Priesthod vvere trãslated vvith the Lavv, if al external Priesthod ended by Christes death, vvhere the nevv lavv began. for so the lavv should not depend on Priesthod, but dure vvhen al Priesthod vvere ended: vvhich is against S. Paules doctrine.

νενομοθέτηto

External Priesthod necessarie for the state of the nevv Testament.

External sacrifice also necessarie for the same.

Furthermore it is to be noted, that this legitimation or putting Communities vnder lavv, and Priesthod, of vvhat order soeuer, is no othervvise, but by ioyning one vvith an other in one homage of sacrifice external, vvhich is the proper act of Priesthod. for, as no lavvful state can be vvithout priesthod, so no priesthod can be vvithout sacrifice. And vve meane alvvaies of Priesthod & sacrifice taken in their ovvne proper signification, as here S. Paul taketh them. for, the constitution difference, alteration, or trãslation of states and lavves rise not vpon any mutation of spiritual or metaphorically taken Priesthod, or sacrifice: but vpon those things in proper acception, as it is most plaine.

Lastly

Lastly, it foloweth of this, that though Christ truely sacrificed him self vpon the Crosse (there also a Priest according to the order of Melchisedec) and there made the ful redemption of the vvorld, confirmed, and consummated his compact, and Testament, and the lavv and priesthod of this his nevv and eternal state, by his bloud: yet that can not be the forme of sacrifice into vvhich the old Priesthod and sacrifices vvere translated, vvhere-vpon the Apostle inferreth the translation of the Law. For they all vvere figures of Christes death, and ended in effect at his death, yet they vvere not altered into that kind of sacrifice, vvhich vvas to be made but once, and vvas executed in such a sort, that peoples and nations Christened could not meete often to vvorship at it, nor haue their law and Priestes constituted in the same. though for the honour and duety, remembrance and representatiõ thereof, not onely vve Christians, but also al peoples faithful both of Iewes & Gentiles, haue had their priesthod and sacrifices according to the difference of their states. Vvhich kind of Sacrifices vvere translated one into an other: and so no doubt is the Priesthod Leuitical properly turned into the Priesthod and sacrifice of the Church, according to Melchisedecks rite, and Christes institution in the formes of bread and vvine. See the next note.

The translation of the old Priesthod & sacrifices, must needes be into the said Priesthod and sacrifice of the Church.

17. *A Priest for euer.*] Christ is not called a Priest for euer, onely for that his person is eternal, or for that he sitteth on the right hand of God, and perpetually praieth or maketh intercession for vs, or for that the effect of his death is euerlasting: for al this proueth not that in proper signification his Priesthod is perpetual: but according to the iudgement of al the fathers grounded vpon this deepe and diuine discourse of S. Paul, and vpon the very nature, definition, and propriety of Priesthod, and the excellent act and order of Melchisedec, and the state of the new law, he is a Priest for euer according to Melchisedecks order, specially in respect of the sacrifice of his holy body and bloud, instituted at his last supper, and executed by his commission, commaundement, and perpetual concurrence vvith his Priests, in the formes of bread and vvine: in vvhich things onely the said high Priest Melchisedec did sacrifice. For though S. Paul make no expresse mention hereof, because of the depth of the mysterie, and their incredulity or feeblenesse to vvhom he vvrote: yet it is euident in the iudgement of all the learned fathers (vvithout exception) that euer vvrote either vpon this epistle, or vpon the 14 of Genesis, or the Psalme 109, or by occasion haue treated of the sacrifice of the altar, that the eternity and proper act of Christes Priesthod, and consequently the immutability of the new law, consisteth in the perpetual offering of Christes body and bloud in the Church.

Hovv Christ is a Priest for euer.

Christs eternal Priesthod consisteth in the perpetual sacrifice of his body & bloud in the Church.

Which thing is so vvell knowen to the Aduersaries of Christes Church and Priesthod, and so graunted, that they be forced impudently to cauill vpon certaine Hebrue particles, that Melchisedec did not offer in bread and vvine: yea and vvhen that vvill not serue, plainely to deny him to haue been a Priest: vvhich is to giue checkmate to the Apostle, and to ouerthrow all his discourse. Thus vvhiles these vvicked men pretend to defend Christes onely Priesthod, they in deede abolish as much as in them lieth, the vvhole order, office, and state of his eternall law and Priesthod.

The Protestãts cauilling vpon particles, agaĩst Melchisedecks sacrifice & Priesthod, directly against the Apostle.

Arnobius saith, *By the mysterie of bread and vvine he vvas made a Priest for euer.* And againe, *The eternal memorie, by vvhich he gaue the food of his body to them that feare him: in psal.* 109. 110. Lactantius, *In the Church he must needes haue his eternal Priesthod according to the order of Melchisedec. Li.* 14. *Institut.* S. Hierom to Euagrius, *Aarons Priesthod had an end, but Melchisedecks, that is, Christes and the Churches is perpetuall,* * *both for the time past and to come.* S. Chrysostom therfore calleth the Churches sacrifice, *hostiam inconsumptibilem, an host or sacrifice that can not be consumed. ho.* 17 *in* 9 *Hebr.* S. Cyprian, *hostiam qua sublata, nulla esset futura religio*, an host vvhich being taken away, there could be no religion. *de Cœna Domini. nu* 2. Emissenus, *perpetuam oblationem & perpetuò currentem redemptionem, a perpetual oblation and a redemption that runneth or continueth euerlastingly. ho.* 5 *de Pasch.* And our Sauiour expresseth so much in the very institution of the B. Sacrament of his body and bloud: specially vvhen he calleth the later kind, *the nevv Testament in his bloud*, signifying that as the old law vvas established in the bloud of beastes, so the new (vvhich is his eternal Testament) should be dedicated and perpetual in his owne bloud: not onely as it vvas shed on the Crosse, but as giuen in the Chalice. And therfore into this sacrifice of the altar (saith S. Augustine *li.* 17 *de Ciuit. c.* 20. S. Leo *ser.* 8 *de Passione*, and the rest) vvere the old sacrifices to be translated. See S. Cyprian *ep.* 63 *ad Cecil. nu.* 2. S. Ambrose *de Sacram. li.* 5. *c.* 4. S. Augustine *in Psal.* 33. *Conc.* 2. and *li.* 17. *de Ciuit. c.* 17. S. Hierom *ep.* 17. *c.* 2. *& ep.* 126. Epiph. *hær.* 55. Theodoret *in Psal.* 109. Damascene *li.* 4. *c.* 14.

Ep. 126.

* *That is, from Adã to the end of the vvorld, represented by sacrifice.*

Christs eternal Priesthod and sacrifice in the Church is proued out of the fathers.

Finally if any of the fathers, or all the fathers, had either vvisedom, grace, or intelligence of Gods vvorde and mysteries, this is the truth. If nothing vvil serue our Aduersaries, Christ Iesus confound them, and defend his eternal Priesthod, and state of his new Testament established in the same.

The old commaundement, and the new.

18. *Of the former commaundement.*] The vvhole law of Moyses conteining all their old Priesthod, sacrifice, sacraments, and ceremonies, is called the *Old commaundement*: and the new Testament conteining the sacrifice of Christes body and bloud, and al the sacraments and graces giuen by the same, is named the *Nevv mandatum*: for vvhich our forefathers called the Thursday in the holy vveeke, *Maundy thursday*, because that in it, the new law and Testament was dedicated in the Chalice of his bloud: the old *mandatum*, law, Priesthod, and sacrifices, for that they vvere insufficient and vnperfect, being taken avvay: and this new sacrifice, after the order of Melchisedec, giuen in the place thereof.

Maundy thursday vvhy so called.

The introduction of a new Priesthod.

19. *The introduction.*] Euer obserue, that the abrogation of the old law, is not an abolishing of al Priesthod, but an introductiõ of a new, conteining the hope of eternal things, vvhere the old had but temporal.

The eternitie of the new Priesthod confirmed by the fathers othe, & Christs passion.

21. *With an othe.*] This othe signifieth the infallible and absolute promis of the eternitie of the new Priesthod and state of the Church: Christ by his death, and bloud shed in the sacrifice of the Crosse, confirming it, sealing it, and making him self the surety and pledge therof. For though the new Testament vvas instituted, giuen, and dedicated in the Supper, yet the vvarrant, confirmation, and eternal operation therof, vvas atchieued vpon the Crosse, in the one oblation and one general and euerlasting redemption there made.

By the comparison of many priests, & one, is not meant that there is but one Priest of the new Testament.

23. *Being many.*] The Protestants not vnderstanding this place, seine very folishly, that the Apostle should make this difference betvvixt the old state and the new: that, in the old, there were many Priests: in the new, none at all but Christ. Which is against the Prophet Esay, specially prophecying of the Priests of the new Testament (as S. Hierom declareth vpon the same place) in these vvordes, *You shal be called the * Priests of God: the *ministers of our God, shal it be said to you*: & it taketh away al visible Priesthod, & consequently the lawful state that the Church and Gods people haue in earth, vvith al Sacraments and external vvorship.

Esa. c. 61.
* ἱερεῖς
* λειτουργοί.

The meaning is, that the absolute sacrifice of eternal redẽption could not be done by those many Aaronical priests but by one onely, Christ Iesus: vvho liueth a Priest for euer, hath no successor, and as cheefe priest, worketh and concurreth vvith al Priests in their priestly functions.

The Apostle then meaneth first, that the absolute sacrifice of cõsummation, perfection, and vniuersal redemption, vvas but one, once done, and by one onely Priest done, and therfore it could not be any of the sacrifices, or al the sacrifices of the Iewes law, or vvrought by any or by all of them, because they vvere a number at once, and succeding one an other, euery of their offices and functions ending by their death, and could not vvorke such an eternal redemption as by Christ onely vvas vvrought vpon the Crosse. Secondly, S. Paul insinuateth therevpon, that Christ neuer loseth the dignitie or practise of his eternal Priesthod, by death nor othervvise, neuer yeldeth it vp to any, neuer hath successors after him, that may enter into his roome or right of Priesthod, as Aaron and al other had in the Leuitical Priesthod, but that him self vvorketh and concurreth vvith his ministers the Priests of the new Testament, in al their actes of Priesthod, as vvel of sacrifice as Sacrament, blessing, preaching, praying, and the like vvhat so euer.

This therfore vvas the fault of the Hebrues, that they did not acknowledge their Leuitical sacrifices and Priesthod to be reformed and perfited by Christes sacrifice on the Crosse: and against them the Apostle onely disputeth, and not against our Priests of holy Church, or the number of them, vvho al confesse their Priesthod and al exercises of the same, to depend vpon Christes onely perpetual Priesthod.

27. *This did he once.*] This is the special preeminence of Christ, that he offereth for other mens sinnes onely, hauing none of his owne to offer for, as al other Priests both of the old and new law haue. And this againe is the special dignitie of his owne person, not communicable to any other of vvhat order of Priesthod so euer, that he by his death (which is the onely oblation that is by the Apostle declared to be irreiterable in it self) paied the one full sufficient ransom for the redemption of all sinnes.

CHAP. VIII.

Out of the same Psalme 109 he vrgeth this also, Sit thou on my right hand, *shevving that the Leuitical tabernacle on earth, vvas but a shadovv of his true Tabernacle in heauen: vvithout vvhich he should not be a Priest at all: 6 Vvhereas he is of a better Priesthod then they, as also he proueth by the excellencie of the nevv Testament aboue the old.*

BVT

1 BVT the ſumme concerning thoſe things vvhich be ſaid, is: Vve haue ſuch an high prieſt, vvho is ſette on the right hand of the ſeate of maieſtie in the heauens, 2 † a ∷ miniſter of the holies, and of the true tabernacle, vvhich our Lord pight & not man. 3 † For euery high prieſt is appointed to offer giftes and hoſtes, vvherfore it is ″ neceſſarie that he alſo haue ſome thing that he may offer: 4 † ″ if then he vvere vpon the earth, neither vvere he a prieſt: vvhereas there vvere that did offer giftes according to the Lavv, 5 † that c ſerue the exampler & ſhadovv of ″ heauenly things. As it vvas anſvvered Moyſes, vvhen he finiſhed the tabernacle, * See (quod he) that thou make al things according to the exampler vvhich vvas ſhevved thee in the mount.

∷ Chriſt liuing and reigning in heauē, continueth his prieſtly functiō ſtil, and is miniſter not of Moyſes Sancta & tabernacle, but of his ovvne body & bloud, vvhich be the true holies, and tabernacle, not formed by mā, but by Gods ovvne hand.

c λατρεύουσι

Exo, 25, 9. 40.

6 † But novv he hath obtained a better miniſterie, by ſo much as he is mediatour of a better teſtament, vvhich is eſtabliſhed in better promiſes. 7 † For ∷ if that former had been void of fault, there ſhould not certes a place of a ſecōd been ſought. 8 † For blaming them, he ſaith: *Behold the daies ſhal come, ſaith our Lord: and I vvil conſummate vpon the houſe of Iſrael, and vpon the houſe of Iuda a nevv Teſtament:* 9 † *not according to the teſtament vvhich I made to their fathers in the day that I tooke their hand to bring them out of the land of Ægypt: becauſe they did not continue in my teſtament: and I neglected them, ſaith our Lord.* 10 † *For this is the teſtament vvhich I vvil diſpoſe to the houſe of Iſrael after thoſe daies, ſaith our Lord: Giuing my lavves ″ into their minde, & in their hart vvil I ſuperſcribe them: and I vvil be ″ their God, and they ſhal be my people:* 11 † *and euery one ″ ſhall not teach his neighbour, and euery one his brother, ſaying, Knovv our Lord: becauſe al ſhal knovv me from the leſſer to the greater of them:* 12 † *becauſe I wil be merciful to their iniquities, & their ſinnes I wil not novv remember.* 13 † And in ſaying a nevv, the former he hath made old. And that vvhich grovveth auncient and vvaxeth old, is nigh to vtter decay.

∷ The promiſes and effectes of the Lavv vvere temporal, but the promiſes and effectes of Chriſtes Sacraments in the Church be eternal.

Hier. 31, 31.

ANNOTATIONS
CHAP. VIII.

3. *Neceſſarie that he alſo.*] Euen now being in heauen, becauſe he is a Biſhop and Prieſt, he muſt needes haue ſomewhat to offer, and vvherein to do ſacrifice: and that not in ſpiritual ſort onely, for that could not make him a Prieſt of any certaine order. And it is moſt falſe and vvicked, to hold vvith the Caluiniſtes, * that Melchiſedecks Prieſthod vvas vvholy ſpiritual. For then Chriſts death vvas not a corporal, external, viſible, and truely named ſacrifice: neither could Chriſt or Melchiſedec be any otherwiſe a Prieſt, then euery

* *Beza in ſchol. Teſt. Græcolat. in c. 7 Heb. num. 8.*

Chriſts prieſthod & ſacrifice is external, not ſpiritual only.

faithful man is: vvhich to hold (as the Caluinists folowing their owne doctrine must needes do) is directly against the Scriptures, and no lesse against Christes one oblation of his body vpon the Crosse, then it is against the daily sacrifice of his body vpon the altar. Therfore he hath a certaine host in external and proper maner, to make perpetual oblation thereby in the Church: for, visible and external act of sacrificing in heauen he doth not exercise.

How Christes body is made fit to be sacrificed and eaten perpetually.

4. *If vpon the earth.*] It is by his death, and resurrection to life againe, that his body is become apt and fitte in such diuine sort to be sacrificed perpetually. For if he had liued in mortal sort still, that vvay of mystical representation of breaking his body and separating the bloud from the same, could not haue been agreable. and so the Church and Christian people should haue lacked a priesthod and sacrifice, & Christ him self should not haue been a Priest of a peculiar order, but either must haue offered in the things that Aarons Priests did, or els haue been no Priest at all. For, to haue offered onely spiritually, as all faithful men do, that could not be ynough for his vocation, and our redemption, and state of the new Testament. How his flesh vvas made fit to be offered and eaten in the B. Sacrament, by his death, see Isychius *li.* 1 *in leuit. cap.* 2.

Kingdom of heauen, and *heauēly things*, spokē of the Church.

5. *Heauenly things.*] As the Church or state of the new Testament is commonly called *Regnum cœlorum & Dei*, in the Scriptures, so these heauenly things be probably taken by learned men, for the mysteries of the new Testament. And it seemeth that the paterne giuen to Moyses to frame his tabernacle by, vvas the Church, rather then the heauens them selues: al S. Paules discourse tending to shew the difference betwixt the new Testament and the old, and not to make comparison betwene the state of heauen and the old law. Though incidently, because the condition of the new Testament more neerely resembleth the same, then the old state doth, he sometime may speake somewhat therof also.

Grace, the effect of the new Testament.

10. *Into their minde.*] This also and the rest folowing is fulfilled in the Church, and is the proper effect of the new Testament, vvhich is the grace and spirit of loue, graffed in the hartes of the faithful by the holy Ghost, vvorking in the Sacraments and sacrifice of the new law to that effecte.

The new Testamēt or couenant betwene God & man.

10. *Their God.*] This mutual couenant made betwixt God and the faithful, is that vvhich vvas dedicated and established, first in the chalice of his bloud, called therfore *the nevv Testament in his bloud*: and vvhich vvas straight after ratified by the death of the testator, vpon the Crosse. *Luc.* 22.

Scriptures abused for phātastical inspirations.

11. *Shal not teach.*] So it vvas in the primitiue Church, in such specially as vvere the first founders of our new state in Christ. And that vvhich vvas verified in the Apostles and other principal men, the Apostle speaketh generally as though it vvere so in the vvhole. as S. Peter applieth the like out of Ioël, and our Sauiour so speaketh, vvhen he saith that such as beleeue in him, shal worke miracles of diuers sortes. Christian men then must not abuse this place to make chalenge of new inspirations and so great knowledge that they neede no Scriptures or teaching in this life, as some Heretikes doe: vvith much like reason and shew of Scriptures as the Protestants haue to refuse external sacrifice. And it is no lesse phantastical madnesse to deny external sacrifice, sacraments, or Priesthod, then it is to abolish teaching and preaching. *Act.* 2. *Io.* 14. *v.* 12.

CHAP. IX.

In the old Testament, that secular Sanctuarie had tvvo partes: the one signifying that time, vvith the ceremonies therof for the emundation of the flesh: the other signifying heauen, vvhich then vvas shut, vntil our High priest Christ entered into it, and that vvith his ovvne bloud, shed for the emundation of our consciences. Wherevpon he concludeth the excellencie of his tabernacle and host aboue the old. 25 Noting also the difference, that he entered but once (so effectual vvas that one blouddy offering of him self, for euer) vvheras the Leuitical High priest entered euery yere once.

THE

Exo. 25. 26,1.36. a λατρείας

The Epistle vpon Imber saturday in Septemb.

1 THE former also in deede had iustificatiōs c of seruice, and a secular sanctuarie. 2 † For the tabernacle vvas made, the first, vvherin vvere, the candlestickes, and the table, and the proposition of loaues, vvhich is called Holy. 3 † But after the second vele, the tabernacle, vvhich is called *Sancta Sanctorum*: 4 † hauing a golden censar, and the arke of the testamēt couered about on euery part vvith gold, in the vvhich vvas " a golden potte hauing Manna, and the rod of Aaron that had blossomed, & * the tables of the testament, 5 † and ouer it vvere * the " Cherubins of glorie ouershadovving the propitiatorie. of vvhich things it is not needeful to speake novv particularly. 6 † But these things being so ordered, in the first tabernacle in deede the priests alvvaies entered, accōplishing offices of the sacrifices. 7 † But in the second, * once a yere the high priest only: not vvithout bloud vvhich he offereth for his ovvne and the peoples ignorance: 8 † the holy Ghost signifying this, that the vvay of the holies was :: not yet manifested, the former tabernacle as yet standing. 9 † vvhich is a c parable of the time present: according to vvhich are offered giftes and hostes, vvhich can not concerning the conscience make perfect c him that serueth, 10 † onely in meates and in drinkes, and diuerse baptismes, and iustices of the flesh laid on them " vntil the time of correction.

3 Reg. 8. 2 Par. 5. Exo. 25, 22.

Exo 30, 10. Leu. 16, 2. 30.

:: The vvay to heauē vvas not open before Christs passion. & therfore the Patriarches and good men of the old Testament vvere in some other place of rest vntil then.

c τὸν λατρεύοντα

c Al things done in the old Testament and priesthod were figures of Christes actions.

b The Epistle vpon Passion Sunday.

11 † But b Christ assisting an high Priest of the good things to come, by a more ample and more perfect tabernacle not made vvith hand, that is, not of this creation: 12 † neither by the bloud of goates or of calues, but by his ovvne bloud entered in once into the Holies, " eternal redemption being found. 13 ⊣ † For * if the bloud of goates and of oxen & the ashes of an heifer being sprinkled, sanctifieth the polluted to the cleansing of the flesh: 14 † hovv much more ` hath' the bloud of Christ vvho by the holy Ghost offered him self vnspotted vnto God, ` cleansed' our conscience from dead vvorkes, to serue the liuing God? 15 † And therfore he is the mediatour of the nevv Testament: that death being a meane, vnto the redemption " of these preuarications vvhich vvere vnder the former testament, they that are called may receiue the promise of eternal inheritance. 16 ⊣ † For * vvhere there is a testament: the death of the testatour must of neces-

Leu. 9, 8 16, 6. 14 Nu. 19. ` shal cleanse

Gal. 3, 15

 sitie

ſitie come betvvene. † For a teſtament is confirmed in the 17 dead: othervviſe it is yet of no value, vvhiles he that teſted, liueth. † Vvherevpon neither vvas the firſt certes dedicated 18 vvithout bloud. † For al the commaundement of the Lavv 19 being read of Moyſes to al the people: he taking the bloud of calues and goates vvith ∷ vvater and ſcarlet vvool and hyſſope, ſprinkled the very booke alſo it ſelf and al the people, † ſaying, *" This is the bloud of the Teſtament, vvhich 20 God hath commaunded vnto you. † The tabernacle alſo & 21 al the veſſel of the miniſterie he in like maner ſprinkled with bloud. † And al things almoſt according to the lavv are 22 cleanſed with bloud: and vvithout ſheading of bloud there is not remiſſion.

∷ Here we may learne that the Scriptures conteine not al neceſſarie rites or truthes, whẽ neither the place to which the Apoſtle alludeth, nor any other, mentioneth half theſe ceremonies, but he had them by tradition.

Exo. 24, 8.

† It is neceſſarie therfore that " the examplers of the cœleſtials be cleanſed vvith theſe: but the celeſtials them ſelues 23 vvith better hoſtes then theſe. † For IESVS is not entred 24 into Holies made vvith hand, examplers of the true: but into heauen it ſelf, that he may appeare novv to the countenance of God for vs. † Nor that he ſhould " offer him ſelf often, 25 as the high prieſt entereth into the Holies, euery yere in the bloud of others: † othervviſe he ought to haue ſuffered 26 often from the beginning of the vvorld: but novv once in the cõſummation of the vvorldes, to the deſtructiõ of ſinne, he hath appeared by his ovvne hoſt. † And as it is appointed 27 to men to die once, and after this, the iudgement: † ſo alſo 28 Chriſt vvas offered once c to exhauſt the ſinnes of many. the ſecond time he ſhal appeare vvithout ſinne to them that expect him, vnto ſaluation.

c By this word vvhich ſignifieth to emptie or draw out euen to the botom, is declared the plentiful and perfect redẽption of ſinne by Chriſt.

c *ad exhaurienda peccata.*

ANNOTATIONS
CHAP. IX.

Relikes.

4 *A golden potte.*] The Proteſtants count it ſuperſtitious to keepe vvith honour and reuerence the holy memories or monuments of Gods benefites and miracles, or the tokens of Chriſtes Paſſion, as his Croſſe, garments, or other things appertaining to him or his Saincts, and thinke it impoſſible that ſuch things ſhould dure ſo long: vvhen they may here ſee the reuerent and long reſeruation of Manna, vvhich of it ſelf vvas moſt apt to putrifie, and of Aarons rodde, onely for that it ſodenly floriſhed by miracle, the tables of the Teſtament &c. See a notable place in S. Cyril *li. 6 cont. Iulian.* vvhere he defendeth againſt Iulian the Apoſtataes blaſphemie, the keeping and honouring of that Croſſe or vvood vvhich Chriſt died on. See alſo S. Paulinus *ep.* 11. and vvhat reuerence S. Hierom and the faithful of his time did to the ſepulchres of Chriſt and his Martyrs, and to their relikes. ***We reuerence and vvorſhip*** (ſaith he) ***euery vvhere Martyrs ſepulchres, and putting the holy aſhes to our eies, if vve may, vve touch it vvith our mouth alſo: and do ſome thinke, that the monument vvherein our Lord vvas buried, is to be neglected?*** But our Proteſtants can not ſkill of this. they had rather

They cõtinue vvithout putrefaction.

The holy CROSSE.

The ſepulchres of Chriſt and his Saincts.

ep. 17. c. 5

rather folovv Vigilantius, Iulianus the Apostata, and such Maisters, then the holy Doctors and euident practise of the Church in al ages.

5. *Cherubins.*] You see it is a fond thing, to conclude vpon the first or second commaundement, that there should be no sacred images in the Church, vvhen euen among these people that vvere most prone to idolatrie, and grosse in imagination of spiritual things such as Angels are, and to vvhom the precept vvas specially giuen, the same God that forbade them grauen idols, did commaund these images of Angels to be made and set in the soueraine holiest place of al the Tabernacle or Temple. By vvhich it is plaine, that much more the images of Christ and his B. mother and Saincts, that may be more truely pourtered then mere spiritual substances can be, are not contrarie to Gods cōmaundement, nor against his honour, or repugnant to any other Scripture at all, vvhich condemne onely the Idols or pourtraitures of the Heathen made for adoration of false Gods.

Images in Salomons temple commaunded by God.

10. *Until the time of correction.*] Al those grosse and carnal sacrifices, ceremonies, and obseruations instituted to cleanse and purifie the flesh from legal irregularities and impurities onely, and not reaching to the purging of the soules & consciences of men, being commaunded not for euer, but till Christes comming, ceased then: and better, more forcible, and more spiritual Sacraments vvere instituted in their place. For vve may not imagine Christ to haue taken avvay the old, and put none in their place: or to alter the sacraments onely into other sacraments external, and not also to translate the sacrifices to some other more excellent. for it is called, *tempus correctionis, non abolitionis sacrificij aut legis: the time of correction not of abolishing sacrifice or lavv.* Neither haue they more reason to affirme Christes one oblation vpon the Crosse to haue rather taken avvay al kind of sacrifice, then al manner of Sacraments. The time and state of the nevv Testament is not made lavvlesse, hostlesse, or vvithout sacrifice, but it is the time of correction or reformation and abettering al the foresaid things.

Sacrifice not taken avvay by the nevv Testament, but changed into a better.

12. *Eternal redemption.*] No one of the sacrifices, nor al the sacrifices of the old lavv, could make that one general price, ransom, and redemption of all mankind, and of al sinnes, sauing this one highest Priest Christ, and the one sacrifice of his bloud once offered vpon the Crosse. Vvhich sacrifice of redemption can not be often done, because Christ could not die but once. though the figures also thereof in the lavv of nature and of Moyses, vvere truely called sacrifices, as specially this high and maruelous commemoration of the same in the holy Sacrament of the altar, according to the rite of the nevv Testament, is most truely and singularly (as S. Augustine calleth it) a sacrifice. But neither this sort, nor the other of the old lavv, being often repeated and done by many Priests (al vvhich vvere and are sinners them selues) could be the general redeeming and consummating sacrifice: nor any one of those Priests, nor al the Priests together, either of the lavv of Nature, or of Aarons, or Melchisedecks order (except Christ alone) coulde be the general redeemers of the vvorld.

Li. de Sp. & lit. c. 11.

One only sacrifice on the Crosse the redēption of the vvorld: and one onely Priest (Christ) the redeemer thereof.

And this is the Apostles meaning in al this comparison and opposition of Christes death to the old sacrifices, and of Christ to their Priests: and not that Christes death or sacrifice of the Crosse should take avvay al sacrifices, or proue that those Aaronical offices vvere no true sacrifices at al, nor those Priests, verily Priests. They vvere true Priests & true sacrifices, though none of those sacrifices vvere the high, capital, and general sacrifice of our price and redemption: nor none of them, or of those Priests, could vvithout respect to this one sacrifice of Christes death, vvorke any thing to Gods honour, or remission of sinnes, as the Ievvves did falsely imagine, not referring them at al to this general redemption and remission by Christ, but thinking them to be absolute sacrifices in them selues. And that to haue been the errour of the Hebrues, you may read in S. Augustine *li. 3. doct. Christ. c. 6.* And this, vve tel the Protestants, is the onely purpose of the Apostle.

But they be so grosse, or ignorant in the Scriptures, and so maliciously set against Gods and the Churches truth, that they peruersely and folishly turne the vvhole disputation against the sacrifice of the B. Masse, and the Priests of the new Testament: as though vve held, that the sacrifice of the altar vvere the general redemption or redeeming sacrifice, or that it had no relation to Christes death, or that it vvere not the representation and most liuely resemblance of the same, or vvere not instituted and done, to apply in particular to the vse of the partakers, that other general benefite of Christes one oblation vpon the Crosse. Against the Ievves then onely S. Paul disputeth, and against the false opinion they had of their Priests and sacrifices, to vvhich they attributed al remission and redemption, vvithout respect of Christes death.

The Apostles disputatiō being only against the errour of the Iewes cōcerning their sacrifices and priests: the Protestants applying it against the sacrifice of the Masse & priestes of the new Testament.

15. *Of those preuarications.*] The Protestants do vnlearnedly imagine, that because al sinnes be remitted by the force of Christes passion, that therfore there should be no other sacrifice after his death. Vvhereas in deede they might as vvell say, there ought neuer to haue been sacrifice appointed by God, either in the lavv of Nature, or of Moyses: as al their argumēts made against the Sacrifice of the Church vpon the Apostles discourse, proue as vvel, or rather onely, that there vvere no sacrifices of Aarons order or Leuitical lavv at all. For against the Ievves false opinion concerning them, doth he dispute, and not a vvord touching the sacrifice of the Church, vnto vvhich

in

in al this discourse he neuer opposeth Christes sacrifice vpon the Crosse: al Christian men vvel knovving that the host & oblation of those tvvo, though they differ in maner and external forme, yet is in deede al one.

The Apostle then shevveth here plainely, that al the sinnes that euer vvere remitted since the beginning of the vvorld, vvere no otherwvise forgiuen, but by the force and in respect of Christes Passion. Yet it folovveth not therevpon, that the oblations of Abel, Abraham, Aaron, &c vvere no sacrifices, as by the Heretikes foolish deduction it should do: S. Paul not opposing Christes Passion to them, for the intent to proue them to haue been no sacrifices, but to proue, that they vvere not absolute sacrifices, nor the redeeming or consummating Sacrifice, vvhich could not be many, nor done by many Priests, but by one, and at one time, by a more excellent Priest thé any of them, or any other mere mortal man.

Caluins argumét against the sacrifice of the altar, maketh no lesse against the sacrifices of the old Lavv.

And that you may see the blasphemous pride and ignorance of Caluin, and in him, of al his fellovves: read (so many as may read Heretical bookes) his commentarie vpon this place, and there you shal see him gather vpon this, that Christes death had force from the beginning & vvas the remedie for al sinnes since the creation of the vvorld, therefore there must be no moe but that one sacrifice of Christes death. Vvhich must needes by his deduction hold (as it doth in deede) no lesse against the old sacrifices then the nevv sacrifice of the Church, and so take avvay al, vvhich is against the Apostles meaning and al religion.

The correspondéce of vvordes in dedicating both Testamēts proueth the real presence of bloud in the Chalice.

20. *This is the bloud.*] Christes death vvas necessarie for the full confirmation, ratification, and accomplishement of the nevv Testament, though it vvas begonne to be dedicated in the sacrifice of his last supper, being also vvithin the compasse of his Passion. Vvhich is euident by the vvordes pronounced by Christ ouer the holy chalice, vvhich be correspondent to the vvordes that vvere spoken (as the Apostle here declareth) in the first sacrifice of the dedication of the old lavv, hauing also expresse mention of remission of sinnes thereby, as by the bloud of the nevv Testament. Vvhereby it is plaine, that the B. Chalice of the altar hath the very sacrificall bloud in it that vvas shed vpon the Crosse, in & by vvhich, the nevv Testament (vvhich is the lavv of spirit, grace, and remission) vvas dedicated, and doth consist. And therfore it is also cleere, that many diuine things, vvhich to the Heretikes or ignorant may seeme to be spoken onely of Christes sacrifice vpon the Crosse, be in deede verified & fulfilled also in the sacrifice of the altar. Vvhereof S. Paul for the causes aforesaid vvould not treate in plaine termes See Isychius *li. 1 in Leuit. c. 4 paulo post initium,* applying al these things to the immolation of Christ also in the Sacrament.

In the old Testament vvere figures of the nevv: in the nevv, is resemblance of the heauenly state.

23. *The examplers.*] Al the offices, places, vessels, and instruments of the old lavv, vvere but figures and resemblances of the state and sacraments of the nevv Testament, vvhich are here called *celestials*, for that they are the liuely image of the heauenly state next ensuing: vvhich be therfore specially dedicated and sanctified in Christes bloud, sacrificed on the altar, and sprinkled vpon the faithful, as the old figures and people vvere cleansed by the bloud of beasts. And therfore by a transition vsual in the holy Scriptures, the Apostle sodenly passeth in the sentéce immediatly folovving, and turneth his talke to Christes entrance into heauen, the state vvhereof, both by the Sacraments of the old lavv, and also more specially by them of the nevv, is prefigured.

Christ once offered in blouddy sort, but vnblouddily ofté, namely in the sacrifice of the altar.

25. *Offer him self often.*] As Christ neuer died but once, nor neuer shal die againe, so in that violent, painful, and blouddy sort he can neuer be offered againe, neither needeth he so to be offered any more: hauing by that one action of sacrifice vpon the Crosse, made the full ransom, redemption, and remedie for the sinnes of the vvhole vvorld. Neuerthelesse, as Christ died and vvas offered after a sort in all the sacrifices of the Lavv and Nature, since the beginning of the vvorld (al vvhich vvere figures of this one oblation vpon the Crosse) so is he much rather offered in the sacrifice of the altar of the nevv Testament, incomparably more neerely, diuinely, and truely expressing his death, his body broken, his bloud shed, then did any figure of the old lavv, or other sacrifice that euer vvas: as being in deede (though in hidden, sacramental, and mysticall, and vnblouddy maner) the very selfsame B. body and bloud, the self same host, oblation and sacrifice, that vvas done vpon the Crosse.

The sacrifice of the altar & that on the Crosse, both one.

And this truth is most euident by the very forme of vvordes vsed by our Sauiour in the institution and consecration of the holy Sacrament, and by the profession of all the holy Doctors. *Our sacrifice,* saith S. Cyprian, *is correspondent to the Passion of Christ.* And, *The sacrifice that vve offer, is the Passion of Christ.* ep. 63. nu. 4. & nu. 7. S. Augustine de fid. ad Pet. c. 19. *In those carnal sacrifices vvas the prefiguring of the flesh of Christ, vvhich he vvas to offer for sinnes, and of the bloud, vvhich he vvas to sheade. but in this Sacrifice is the commemoration of the flesh of Christ vvhich he hath novv giuen, and of the bloud vvhich he hath shed:* in illis prænuntiabatur occidendus, in hoc annuntiatur occisus. *In them he vvas forshevved as to be killed: in these he is shevved, as killed.* And S. Gregorie Nazianzene saith, *orat. in morbum*, that the Priest in this sacrifice, *immiscet se magnis Christi Passionibus.* S. Ambrose *li. 1 Offic. c. 48, Offertur Christus in imagine quasi recipiens passionem.* Alexander the first, *ep. ad omnes Orthodox. nu. 4. to. 1. Conc. Cuius corpus & sanguis conficitur, passio etiam celebratur.* S. Gregorie, *ho. 37 in Euang. So often as vve offer the host of his Passion, so often vve renevve his Passion.* And, *He suffereth for vs againe in mysterie.* And Isychius, *li. 2 c. 8 in Leuit. post med. By the sacrifice of*

the

the onely-begotten many thinges are giuen unto vs, to vvitte, the remißion or pardoning of al mankinde, and the singular introduction or bringing in of the mysteries of the nevv Testament.

And the said fathers and others, by reason of the difference in the maner of Christes presence and oblation in respect of that on the Crosse, called this *the vnbloudy sacrifice*, as* Caluin him self confesseth, but ansvvereth them in the pride of hereticall spirit, vvith these vvordes: *Nihil moror quòd sic loquantur vetusti scriptores.* that is, *I passe not for it, that the auncient vvriters do so speake*: calling the distinction of bloudy and vnbloudy sacrifice, scholasticall and friuolous, and *diabolicum commentum, a diuelish deuise.* Vvith such ignorant and blasphemous men vve haue to do, that thinke they vnderstand the Scriptures better then all the fathers.

Comment. in 9 Hebr.

The fathers call it the vnbloudy sacrifice of the altar.

Caluins contept of the fathers.

CHAP. X.

Because in the yerely feast of Expiation vvas only a commemoration of sinnes, therfore in place of al those old sacrifices the Psalme telleth vs of the oblation of Christes body. 10 Vvhich he offered bloudily but once (the Leuitical Priests offering so euery day) because that once vvas sufficient for euer, 15 in that it purchased (as the prophet also vvitnesseth) remißion of sinnes. 19 After al this he prosecuteth and exhorteth them vnto perseuerance, partly vvith the opening of Heauen by our high-priest, 26 partly vvith the terrour of damnation if they fall againe: 32 bidding them remember hovv much they had suffered already, and not lose their revvard.

1 FOR the lavv hauing" a shadovv of good things to come, not the very image of the things: euery yere vvith the self same hostes vvhich they offer incessantly, can neuer make the commers thereto 2 perfect: † othervvise" they should haue ceased to be offered, because the vvorshippers once cleansed should haue no 3 conscience of sinne any longer. † but in them there is 4 made a cõmemoration of sinne euery yere. † for it is" impossible that vvith the bloud of oxen and goates sinnes should 5 be taken avvay. † Therfore comming into the vvorld he saith:" *Host and oblation thou vvouldest not:" but a body thou hast fitted to me:* 6 † *Holocaustes and* c *for sinne did not please thee.* 7 † *Then said I, Behold I come: in the head of the booke it is vvritten of me: That I may doe thy vvil ô God.* 8 † Saying before, *Because hostes and oblations, & holocaustes, & for sinne thou vvouldest not," neither did they please thee,* vvhich are offered accor- 9 ding to the lavv, † *then said I, Behold I come that I may doe thy vvil ô God*: he taketh avvay the first, that he may establish that that 10 folovveth. † In the vvhich vvil, vve are sanctified by the 11 oblation of the body of IESVS Christ once. † And euery priest in deede is ready daily ministring, and" often offering 12 the same hostes, vvhich can neuer take avvay sinnes: † but this man offering one host for sinnes, for euer * sitteth on

Leu. 16, 14.

Ps. 39, 7.

Ps. 109. Cor. 15, 25.

c *For sinne*, is the proper name of a certaine sacrifice called in Hebrue חטאה: as Holocaust is an other kinde. *See the Annot. 2 Cor. 5. v. 21.*

the right hand of God, † hence forth expecting, vntil his 13 enemies be put the footestoole of his feete. † For by one 14 oblation hath he consummated for euer them that are sancti-fied. † And the holy Ghost also doth testifie to vs. For after 15 that he said: † *And this is the Testament vvhich I vvil make to them after* 16 *those daies, saith our Lord, giuing my lavves* ∴ *in their hartes, & in their mindes vvil I superscribe them:* † *and their sinnes and iniquities I vvil novv remember* 17 *no more.* † But vvhere there is remission of these," novv there 18 is not an oblation for sinnes.

Hier. 31, 33. 34. Heb. 8, 8.

∴ This is partly fulfilled in & by the grace of the new testament, but it shal be perfectly accomplished in heauen.

† Hauing therfore brethren confidence in the entring of 19 the holies in the bloud of Christ: † vvhich c he hath dedi-20 cated to vs a nevv and liuing vvay by the vele, that is, his flesh, † and a high priest ouer the house of God, † let vs 21 approche vvith a true hart in fulnesse of faith, hauing our 22 hartes sprinkled from euil conscience, and our body vva-shed vvith cleane vvater, † let vs hold the confession of our 23 hope vndeclining (for he is faithful that hath promised) † and let vs consider one an other vnto the prouocation of 24 charitie and of good vvorkes: † not forsaking our assem-25 blie as some are accustomed, but comforting, and so much the more as you see the day approching. † * For "if vve 26 sinne vvillingly after the knovvledge of the truth receiued, novv there is not left an host for sinnes, † but a certaine 27 terrible expectation of iudgement and rage of fire, vvhich shal consume the aduersaries. † A man making the lavv of 28 Moyses frustrate: vvithout any mercie * dieth vnder tvvo or three vvitnesses. † ∴ hovv much more thinke you, doth 29 he deserue vvorse punishements vvhich hath troden the sonne of God vnder foote, and estemed" the bloud of the te-stament polluted, vvherein he is sanctified, and hath done contumelie to the spirit of grace? † For vve knovv him that 30 said, *Reuenge to me, I vvil repay.* And againe, *That our Lord vvil iudge his people.* † " It is horrible to fal into the handes of the liuing 31 God.

c ἐνεκαίνισεν

c To dedicat, is to be authour & beginner of a thing. The Protestants trãslate, *he hath prepared,* for their heresie that Christ vvas not the first mã that entered into heauen.

Heb. 6, 4.

∴ Heresie and Apostasie from the Catholike faith, punishable by death.

Deu. 19, 15. Mat. 18, 16. to. 8, 17.

Deu. 32, 35. Rom. 12, 19. Ps. 134, 14.

† But call to minde the old daies: vvherein being illu-32 minated, you sustained a great fight of passions. † and on the 33 one part certes by reproches and tribulations made a specta-cle: and on the other part made companions of them that conuersed in such sort. † For, "you both had compassion 34 on them that vvere in bondes: and the spoile of your ovvne goodes you tooke" vvith ioy, knovving that you haue a bet-

The Epistle for many Martyrs.

ter

35 ter and a permanent substāce. † Do not therfore leese your 36 c confidence, vvhich hath a great remuneration. † For patience is necessarie for you: that doing the vvil of God, you 37 may receiue the promise. † For * yet a litle and a very litle vvhile, he that is to come, vvil come, and vvil not slacke. 38 † and my iust " liueth of faith. ‡ but if he vvithdravv him 39 self, he shal not please my soule. † But vve are not the children of vvithdravving vnto perdition: but of faith to the vvinning of the soule.

Abac, 2, 3. Ro. 1, 17. Gal. 3, 12.

c Good vvorkes make great cōfidence of saluation, & haue great revvard.

ANNOTATIONS
CHAP. X.

1. *A shadovv.*] The sacrifices and ceremonies of the old law, vvere so far from the truth of Christs Sacraments, and from giuing spirit, grace, remission, redemption, and iustification, and therevpon the entrance into heauen and ioyes celestiall, that they vvere but mere shadowes, vnperfectly and obscurely representing the graces of the new Testament and of Christes death: vvhereas all the holy Churches rites and actions instituted by Christ in the Priesthod of the new law, conteine and giue grace, iustification, and life euerlasting to the faithful and vvorthy receiuers: and therfore they be not shades or darke resemblances of Christes passion, vvhich is the fountaine of all grace and mercie, but perfect images and most liuely representations of the same, specially the sacrifice of the altar, vvhich because it is the same oblation, the same host, and offered by the same Priest Christ IESVS (though by the ministerie of man and in mysterie) is the most pure and neere image, character, and correspondence to the sacrifice of Christes passion, both in substance, force, and effect, that can be.

The old sacrifices obscurely shadovved, but the sacrifice of the altar most plainely representeth the sacrifice on the Crosse.

2. *They should haue ceased.*] If the hostes and offerings of the old law had been of them selues perfect to all effectes of redemption and remission, as the Hebrues (against vvhom the Apostle disputeth) did thinke, and had had no relation to Christes sacrifice on the Crosse or any other absolute and vniuersal oblation or remedie for sinne, but by and of their owne efficacie could haue generally purged and cleansed man of all sinne and damnation: then they should neuer haue needed to be so often repeated and reiterated. For being both generally auailable for all, by their opinion, and particularly applied (in as ample sort as they could be) to the seueral infirmities of euery offender, there had been no sinnes left. But sinnes did remaine, euen those sinnes for vvhich they had offered sacrifices before, notvvithstanding their sacrifices vvere particularly applied vnto them. For, offering yerely they did not onely offer sacrifices for the new committed crimes, but euen for the old, for vvhich they had often sacrificed before: the sacrifices being rather recordes and attestations of their sinnes, then a redemption or full remission, as Christes death is. Vvhich being once applied to man by Baptisme, vvipeth away all sinnes past, God neuer remembring them any more, nor euer any sacrifice or sacrament or ceremonie being made or done for them any more, though for new sinnes other remedies be daily requisite. Their sacrifices then could not of them selues remitte sinnes, much lesse make the general redemption vvithout relation to Christes Passion. And so you see it is plaine euery vvhere, that the Apostle proueth not by the often repetition of the Ievvish sacrifices, that they vvere no sacrifices at all, but that they vvere not of that absolute force or efficacie, to make redemption or any remission, vvithout dependance of the one vniuersal redemption by Christ: his vvhole purpose being, to inculcate vnto them the necessitie of Christes death, and the oblation of the new Testament. As for the Churches holy sacrifice, it is cleane of an other kinde then those of the Iewes, and therfore he maketh no opposition betwixt it, and Christes death or sacrifice on the Crosse, in all this Epistle: but rather as a sequele of that one general oblation, couertly alvvaies inferreth the same: as being in a different maner the very self same host and offering that vvas done vpon the Crosse, and continually is vvrought by the self same Priest.

The Ievves sacrifices vvere not absolute & independēt, because they vvere often repeated.

The Apostle proueth by the often repeating of the Ievves sacrifices, not that they vvere none, but that they vvere not absolute & sufficient.

4. *Impossible.*] The hostes and sacrifices of the old law, vvhich the carnal Iewes made all

The old sacrifices remitted not sinnes, but vvere only signes therof.

all the count of, vvithout relation to Christes death, vvere not onely not perfect and absolute sufficient in them selues, but they did not, nor could not remit any sinnes at all, being but onely signes therof, referring the offenders for remission in deede, to Christes Passion. For the bloud of bruit beastes could haue no other effect, nor any other element or creature, before Christes death. the fruite vvhereof, before it vvas extant, could be no othervvise properly applied vnto them, but by beleefe in him.

God refuseth the Iewes sacrifices, not al sacrifice.

5. *Host and oblation.*] He meaneth not that God vvould no host nor sacrifice any more, as the Protestants falsely imagin: for that vvere to take away not onely the sacrifice of Christes body vpon the altar, but the sacrifice of the same body vpon the Crosse also. Therfore the Prophet speaketh onely of the legal and carnal sacrifices of the Iewes, signifying that they did neuer of them selues please God, but in respect of Christ, by vvhose oblation of his owne body they should please.

That Christ should haue a body, vvas necessarie for his Priesthod, and sacrifice.

5. *But a body.*] If Christ had not had a body, he could not haue had any vvorthy matter or any matter at all to sacrifice in visible maner, other then the hostes of the old law. Neither could he either haue made the general redemption by his one oblation vpon the Crosse, nor the daily sacrifice of the Church: for both vvhich, his body vvas fitted by the diuine vvisedom. Which is an high conclusion, not vnderstood of Ievves, Pagans, nor the Heretikes of our time, that Christes humane nature vvas taken to make the Sonne of God (vvho in his diuine nature could not be either Priest or host) fitte to be the sacrifice and Priest of his father, in a more vvorthy sort, then all the Priests or oblations of the old law. And that this body vvas giuen him, not onely to be the sacrifice vpon the Crosse, but also vpon the altar, S. Augustine affirmeth in these vvordes. *The table vvhich the Priest of the nevv Testament doth exhibit, is of his body and bloud: for that is the sacrifice vvhich succeded al those sacrifices that vvere offered in shadovv of that to come. For the vvhich also vve acknovvledge that voice of the same Mediatour in the psalme,* BUT A BODY THOU HAST FITTED TO ME, *because in steede of all those sacrifices and oblations his body is offered, and is ministred to the partakers or receiuers. Li. 17 Ciuit. Dei. c. 20.* And againe *li. 4 de Trin. c. 14. Who so iust and holy a Priest, as the onely sonne of God? What might so conueniently be offered for men, of men, as mans flesh? and vvhat so fitte for this immolation or offering, as mortal flesh? vvhat so cleane for clearsing the vices of mortal men, as the flesh borne of the virgins vvombe? and vvhat can be offered and receiued so gratefully, as the flesh of our sacrifice, made the body of our Priest?*

The body of Christ is the sacrifice of the altar.

Ps. 39.

The Ievves sacrifices refused, not al sacrifice.

8. *Neither did they please thee*] By that he saith, the things offered in the Lavv, did not please God, and likevvise by that he saith, the former to be taken avvay, that the second may haue place, it is euident, that all hostes and sacrifices be not taken avvay by Christ, as the Heretikes folishly conceiue: but that the old hostes of brute beastes be abrogated to giue place to that vvhich is the proper host of the nevv lavv, that is, Christes ovvne body.

We must often note that the Apostles speache of many Priests and often sacrificing, concerneth only the Iewes Priests and sacrifices, not the Priests and sacrifice of the new Testament.

11. *Often offering the same hostes.*] As S. Paul is forced often to inculcate that one principle of the efficacie and sufficiencie of Christes death, because of the Hebrues to much attributing to their legal sacrifices, and for that they did not referre them to Christes onely oblation: so vve, through the intolerable ignorance and importunity of the Heretikes of this time (abusing the vvordes of the Apostle spoken in the devve defence and declaration of the valure and efficacie of Christes Passion aboue the sacrifices of the Lavv) are forced to repeat often, that the Apostles reason of many Priests and often repetition of the self same sacrifices, concerneth the sacrifices of the Lavv onely, vnto vvhich he opposeth Christes sacrifice and Priesthod: and speaketh no vvord of or against the Sacrifice of the nevv Testament, vvhich is the sacrifice of Christes ovvne Priesthod, Lavv, and institution, yea the same sacrifice done daily vnblouddily, that once vvas done blouddily: made by the same Priest Christ Iesus, though by his ministers hands: and not many hostes, as those of the old lavv vvere, but the very self same in number, euen Christes ovvne body that vvas crucified. And that you may see that this is the iudgement of all antiquity, and their exposition of these and the like vvordes of this Epistle, and that they seeing the very same arguments that the Protestants novv make so much a doe vvithall among the simple and vnlearned, yet vvel perceiued that they made nothing against the daily oblation or sacrifice of the altar, and therfore ansvvered them before the Protestants vvere extant, 1200 yeres: vve vvil set dovvne some of their vvordes, vvhose authoritie and exposition of the Scriptures must preuaile in all that haue vvisedom or the feare of God, aboue the false and vaine gloses of Caluin and his folovvers.

The Caluinists arguments against Christs body often offered, and in many places, ansvvered by the fathers long agoe.

Thus then first saith S. Ambrose: *Quid ergo nos &c. What vve then? do not vve offer euery day? vve offer surely: but this sacrifice is an exampler of that: for vve offer alvvaies the self same, and not novv one lambe, to morovv an other, but alvvaies the self same thing: therfore it is one sacrifice. othervvise, by this reason because it is offered in many places, there should be many Christes. not so, but it is one Christ in euery place, here vvhole, and there vvhole, one body. But this vvhich vve doe, is done for a commemoration of that vvhich vvas done. for vve offer not an other sacrifice, as the high Priest of the old lavv, but alvvaies the self same. &c.* Primasius S. Augustines scholer doth also preoccupate these Protestants obiections thus: *What shal vve say then? do not our Priests daily offer*

in 10 cap. Hebr.

ibidem.

offer sacrifice? they offer surely, because vve sinne daily, and daily haue neede to be cleansed: and because he can not die, he hath giuen vs the sacrament of his body and bloud: that as his Passion vvas the redemption and absolution of the vvorld, so also this oblation may be redemption and cleansing to all that offer it in truth and veritie. So saith this holy father, to vvitte, that as the sacrifice of the Crosse vvas a general redemption, so this of the altar is, to all that vse it, a particular redemption or application of Christes redemption to them. In vvhich sense also V. Bede calleth the holy Masse, *redemptionem corporis & animæ sempiternam, the euerlasting redemption of body and soul.* li. 4 c. 22. histor. Againe the same Primasius, *The diuinity of the Word of God vvhich is euery vvhere, maketh that there are not many sacrifices, but one, although it be offered of many, and that as it is one body vvhich he tooke of the Virgins vvombe, not many bodies, euen so also one sacrifice, not diuers, as those of the Ievves vvere.*

The general redemption vpon the Crosse is particularly applied in the sacrifice of the altar.

Primas. loco citato.

ho. 17 in ep. ad Heb.

* S. Chrysostom also, and after him Theophylacte, and Oecumenius, and of the Latines, Haimo, Paschasius, Remigius, and others, obiect to them selues thus: *Do not vve also offer euery day? vve offer surely. but this sacrifice is an exampler of that, for vve offer alvvaies the self same: and not novv one lambe, to morovv an other, but the self same: therfore this is one sacrifice. Othervvise, because it is offered in many places, there should be many Christes.* And a litle after, *Not an other sacrifice, as the high Priest of the old Lavv, but the self same vve do alvvaies offer, rather vvorking a remembrance or commemoration of the sacrifice.* See the Annotation Luke 22, 19. vpon these vvordes, *A commemoration.* Thus did al the auncient fathers Greeke and Latin treate of these matters, and so they said Masse, and offered daily, and many of them made such formes of celebrating the diuine sacrifice, as the Greekes and Latines do vse in their Liturgies and Masses, and yet they savv these places of the Apostle and made commentaries vpon them, and vnderstood them (I trovv) as vvel as the Protestants.

He that for his further confirmation or comfort list see vvhat the aűcient Councels and Doctors beleeued, taught, and practised in this thing, let him read the first holy Councel of Nice *cap.* 14: *& in fine Conc. ex Græco.* the Councel of Ephesus Anathematis. 11. the Chalcedon Councel *act.* 3. *pag.* 112. *Conc. Ancyran. c.* 1. 4. & 5. Neocæsar. *can.* 13. Laodic. *can.* 19. Carthag. 2 *cap.* 8. Carthag. 3 *cap.* 24. & Carthag. 4 *cap.* 33. *& c.* 41. S. Denys *cap.* 3 *Eccl. hier.* S. Andrevve *in historia Passionis.* S. Ignatius *ep. ad Smyrnenses.* S. Martialis *ep. ad Burdegalenses.* S. Iustine *Dialog. cum Triphone.* S. Ireneus *li.* 4 *cap.* 32. 34. Tertullian *de cultu fœminarum, & de corona milit.* Origen *homil.* 13 *in Leuit.* S. Cyprian *ep. ad Cecilium. nu.* 2. *& de Cœna Domini. nu.* 14. & Eusebius *demonst. Euang. li.* 1 *cap.* 10. and the rest vvhich vve haue cited by occasion before, & might cite but for tediousnes: a truth most knovven and agreed vpon in the Christian religion.

Councels and fathers.

18. *Novv there is not.*] Christes death can not be applied vnto vs in that full and ample sort as it is in baptisme, but once: Christ appointing that large remission and application to be made but once in euery man, as Christ died but once. for it is not meant, that all sinne shal cease after Christes sacrifice vpon the Crosse, nor that there should be no oblation for sinnes committed after Baptisme, or that a man could not sinne at al after Baptisme, or that if he sinned aftervvard, he could haue no remedie or remission by Gods ordinance in the Church, vvhich diuers falsehods sundrie Heretikes gather of this and such like places: but onely the Apostle telleth the Hebrues, as he did before chap. 6, and as he doth straight aftervvard, that if they fall novv (vvhereunto they seemed very prone) to their old lavv, and voluntarily after the knovvledge and profession of the Christian faith by Baptisme, commit this sinne of incredulitie and apostasie, they can neuer haue that abundant remission applied vnto them by Baptisme, vvhich can neuer be ministred to them againe. And that general full pardon he calleth here, *oblation*, and aftervvard in the 26 verse, *hostiam pro peccato, an host for sinne.*

When the Apostle seemeth to say, there is no remission or oblation for sinne, he alvvaies meaneth that ful remission by Baptisme.

26. *If vve sinne vvillingly.*] As the Caluinists abuse other like places against the holy sacrifice of the Masse, so they abuse this as the Nouatians did before them, to proue that an Heretike, Apostata, or any that vvilfully forsaketh the truth, can neuer be forgiuen. Vvhich (as is before declared in the 6 chapter) is most vvicked blasphemie: the meaning hereof being, as is there said, onely to terrifie the Hebrues, that falling from Christ they can not so easily haue the host of Christes death applied vnto them, because they can not be baptized any more, but must passe by sacramental penance, and satisfaction, and other hard remedies vvhich Christ hath prescribed after Baptisme in the Churches discipline. Therfore S. Cyril saith, *li.* 5 *in Io. cap.* 17. *Penance is not excluded by these vvordes of Paul, but the renevving by the lauer of regeneration. He doth not here take avvay the second or third remission of sinnes (for he is not such an enemy to our saluation) but the host vvhich is Christ he denieth that it is to be offered againe vpon the Crosse.* So saith this holy Doctor. And by this place & the like you see, hovv perilous a thing it is for Heretikes & ignorant persons to read the Scriptures. Vvhich by folovving their ovvne fantasie* they peruert to their damnation.

The Caluinists heresie against remission of sinnes.

Al sinnes may be remitted by penāce, but not so fully as by Baptisme.

Perilous reading of the Scriptures.

2 Pet. 3.

29. *The bloud of the Testament.*] Vvhosoeuer maketh no more account of the bloud of Christes sacrifice, either as shed vpon the Crosse, or as in the holy Chalice of the altar (for our Sauiour calleth that also* the bloud of the nevv Testament) then he doth of the bloud of calues and goates, or of other common drinkes, is vvorthy death, and God vvil in the next life, if it be not punished here, reuenge it vvith greuous punishment.

Luc. 22.

Contempt of Christs bloud in the Sacramēt.

31. *It is horrible.*] Let al Christian people do satisfaction and penance for their sinnes in this life. for the iudgemēts of God in the next life done by God him self, of vvhat sort soeuer, vvhether temporall as in Purgatorie, or eternal as in Hell, be exceding greuous.

Penance.

34. *You had compassion.*] To be mercifulto the afflicted for religion, & to be partakers of their miseries, is a very meritorious vvorke, and giueth great confidence before God in the day of repaiment or remuneration for the same.

Mercie to the emprisoned for religion.

34. *With ioy.*] If all Christian men vvould consider this, they vvould not thinke it so great a matter to lose their land or goods for defense of the Catholike faith.

Losse of goods for religion.

38. *Liueth of faith.*] Faithful men afflicted in this life, haue their comfort in their assured faith and hope of Christes comming to deliuer them once from all these miseries: & so by that faith and comfort they liue, vvhereas othervvise this miserable life vvere a death.

Faith is the cōfort of the afflicted.

CHAP. XI.

He exhorteth them by the definition of faith, to sticke vnto God, though they see not yet his revvard: shevving that all the Saincts aforetime did the like, being all constant in faith, though not one of them receiued the promis, that is, the inheritance in heauen: but they and vve novv after the comming of Christ receiue it together.

AND "faith is, :: the substance of things to be hoped for, c the argument of things "not appearing. † For in this the old men obtained testimonie. 1 2

:: By this vvord substāce is meant, that faith is the ground of our hope.

c ἔλεγχος

† * By faith, vve vnderstand that the vvorldes vvere framed by the vvord of God: that of inuisible things visible things might be made. 3

Gen. 1, 13

† * By faith, Abel offered a greater hoste to God thē Cain: * by vvhich he obtained testimonie that he vvas iust, God giuing testimonie to his giftes, & by it, he being dead, yet speaketh. † * By faith :: Henoch vvas translated, that he should not see death, and he vvas not found: because God translated him. for before his translation he had testimonie that he had pleased God. † But vvithout faith it is impossible to please God. For " he that commeth to God, must beleeue that he is, and is a :: revvarder to them that seeke him. 4 5 6

Gen. 4, 4 Mat. 23, 35. Gen. 5, 24. Eccl. 44, 16.

:: Here it appeareth that Henoch yet liueth and is not dead: against the Caluinists. See the annot. Apocal. chap. 11.

:: Vve must beleeue that God vvill revvard all our good vvorkes: for he is a revvarder of true iustice, not an accepter or imputer of that that is not.

† * By faith, Noë hauing receiued an ansvver concerning those things vvhich as yet vvere not seen, fearing, framed the arke for the sauing of his house, by the vvhich he condemned the vvorld: and vvas instituted heire of the iustice vvhich is by faith. 7

Gen. 6, 13. Eccl. 44, 17.

† * By faith, he that is called, Abraham, obeied to goe forth into the place vvhich he vvas to receiue for inheritāce: and he vvent forth, not knovving vvhither he vvent. † By faith, he abode in the land of promise, as in a strāge lād, dvvelling 8 9

Gen. 12, 4. 13, 1.

ling in cottages vvith Isaac & Iacob the coheires of the same
10 promise. † For he expected the citie that hath foundations: vvhose artificer and maker is God.

Gen. 17, 19. 18, 10.21,2. Eccl. 44 22.

11 † * By faith, Sara also her self being barren, receiued vertue in conceauing of seede, yea past the time of age: because she beleeued that he vvas faithful which had promised.
12 † For the vvhich cause euen of one (and him quite dead) there rose as the starres of heauen in multitude, & as the sand that is by the sea shore innumerable.

13 † According to faith died al these, not hauing receiued the promises, but beholding them a farre of, and saluting them, and cõfessing that they are pilgrimes & strangers vpon
14 the earth. † for they that say these things, doe signifie that
15 they seeke a countrie. † And in deede if they had been mindeful of the same from vvhence they came forth, they had
16 time verely to returne. † but novv they desire a better, that is to say, a heauenly. Therfore God is not confounded to be called their God. for he hath prepared them a citie.

Gen. 22, 9. Gen. 21, 12. Rom. 9,7: Gen. 27, 27.36. Gen. 48, 15. Gen. 47, 31. Gen. 50, 24, 25.

17 † * By faith, Abraham offered Isaac, vvhen he vvas tempted: and his onlie-begotten did he offer vvho had receiued
18 the promises: († to vvhom it vvas said, *That in Isaac shal seede*
19 *be called to thee.*) † accounting that God is able to raise vp euen from the dead. wherevpõ he receiued him also [c] for a parable.
20 † * By faith, also of things to come, Isaac blessed Iacob and Esau.
21 † * By faith, Iacob dying, blessed euery one of the sonnes of Ioseph: * and " adored the toppe of his rodde
22 † * By faith, Ioseph dying, made mention of the going forth of the children of Israël: and gaue commaundement :: concerning his bones.

c That is, in figure and mysterie of Christ dead, & aliue againe.

:: The translation of Relikes or Saincts bodies, & the due regard and honour vve ought to haue to the same, are proued hereby.

Exo. 2, 2. Exo. 1, 16 Exo. 2, 11

23 † * By faith, Moyses being borne, vvas hidde three monethes by his parents: because they savv him a proper infant, and they feared not * the kings edict.
24 † * By faith, Moyses being made great, denied him self to
25 be the sonne of Pharaos daughter: † rather chosing to be afflicted vvith the people of God, then to haue the pleasure
26 of temporal sinne, † esteeming the reproche of Christ, greater riches then the treasure of the Ægyptians. for :: he
27 looked vnto the remuneration. † * By faith, he left Ægypt: not fearing the fiercenes of the king. for him that is inuisible
28 he susteined as if he had seen him. † By faith, he celebrated the

Exo. 12, 37.

:: The Protestants that deny vve may or ought to doe good in respect or for revvard in heauen, are hereby cõfuted.

the Pasche, & the sheading of the bloud: that he vvhich destroied the first-borne, might not touche them. † * By faith 29 they passed the redde sea as it vvere by the drie land: vvhich the Ægyptians assaying, vvere deuoured.

Gen. 14, 22.

† * By faith the vvalles of Iericho fel dovvne, by the 30 circuting of seuen daies.

Iosue 6, 20

† * By faith, Rahab the harlot perished not vvith the incredulous, receiuing the spies vvith peace. 31

Iosue 6, 23 25. 2, 3.

† And vvhat shal I yet say? For the time vvil faile me 32 telling of Gedeon, Barac, Sampson, Iephtè, Dauid, Samuël, & the prophets: † vvho by faith ouercame kingdōs, " vvrought 33 iustice, obteined promises, stopped the mouthes of lions, † extinguished the force of fire, repelled the edge of the 34 svvord, recouered of their infirmitie, vvere made strong in battel, turned avvay the campe of forainers: † vvomen re- 35 ceiued of resurrection their dead. and others vvere racked, not accepting redemption, that they might finde a better resurrection. † And others had trial of mockeries and stripes, 36 moreouer also of bādes & prisons: † they vvere stoned, they 37 vvere hevved, they vvere tempted, they died in the slaughter of the svvord, they vvent about in sheep-skinnes, in goates skinnes, needy, in distresse, afflicted: † of vvhom the vvorld 38 vvas not vvorthie. vvandering in desertes, in mountaines and dennes, and in caues of the earth. † And al these being ap- 39 proued by the testimonie of faith, ⊣ receiued not the promise, † God for vs prouiding some better thing, that they 40 vvithout vs should not be consummate.

The Epistle for many Martyrs.

ANNOTATIONS
CHAP. XI.

Not only or a special faith.

1. *Faith is.*] By this description of faith, and by all the commendation therof through the vvhole chapter, you may vvell perceiue that the Apostle knevve not the forged special faith of the Protestants, vvhereby euery one of these new Sectmasters & their folovvers beleeue their sinnes are remitted, and that them selues shal be saued, though their sectes be cleane contrarie one to an other.

Faith is of things not seen: as in the B. Sacrament.

1. *Not appearing*] *This is the praise of faith*, saith S. Augustine, *if that vvhich is beleeued, be not seen. For vvhat great thing is it, if that be beleeued, vvhich is seen? according to that sentence of our Lord vvhen he rebuked his disciple, saying: Because thou hast seen me Thomas, thou hast beleeued: blessed are they that haue not seen and haue beleeued. Aug. in euang. Io. tract. 79.* Vvhich may be a rebuke also and a checke to al those faithles speaches, I vvould see him, tast him, touch him and feele his very flesh in the Sacrament, othervvise I vvil not beleeue.

Nothing profitable or meritorious with out faith.

6. *He that commeth.*] Faith is the foundation and ground of all other vertues and vvorship of God, vvithout vvhich no man can please God. Therfore if one be a Iewe, a Heathen, or an heretike, that is to say, be vvithout the Catholike faith, al his vvorkes shal profit him no vvhit to saluation.

21. *Adored*

21. *Adored the toppe of his rod.*] The learned may see here that the Apostle doth not tie him self to the Hebrue in the place of Genesis vvhence it is alleaged, but folovveth the Septuaginta, though it differ from the Hebrue, as also the other Apostles and Euangelists and our Sauiour him self did: neither vvere they curious (as men novv a daies) to examine all by the Hebrue only, because they vvriting and speaking by the holy Ghost, knevve very vvell that this translation * is the sense of the holy Ghost also, and as true, and as directly intended as the other: and therfore also that translation continued alvvaies authentical in the Greeke Church, notvvithstanding the diuersitie thereof from the Hebrue. Euen so vve that be Catholikes, folovv vvith al the Latin fathers the authentical Latin translation, though it be not alvvaies agreable to the Hebrue or Greeke that novv is. But Caluin is not onely very saucie, but very ignorant, vvhen he saith that the Septuaginta vvere deceiued, and yet that the Apostle vvithout curiosity vvas content to folovv them: because it is euident, that *the Hebrue being thẽ vvithout pointes, *might be trãslated the one vvay as vvel as the other. Vvhich they vnderstood so vvel (and therfore vvere not deceiued) that vvithin three lines after, in the beginning of the next chapter, they translate the same vvord, as he vvould haue it in this place.

Gen. 47. v. 31.

* Aug. de ciu. Dei li. 15 c. 14.

* מטה

* ῥάβδος, rod. κλίνη, bed.

The citatiõs in the nevv Testament, not only according to the Hebrue, but to the Septuagita.

The vulgar latin translation.

Againe obserue in those vvordes, *He adored the toppe of his rod*, that adoration (as the Scripture vseth this vvord) may be done to creatures, or to God at and before a creature: as, at or * before the Arke of the Testament in old time, novv at or before the crucifixe, relikes, images: and in the Psalmes 98.131. *Adore ye his footestoole. Adore ye tovvard his holy mount. We vvil adore tovvard the place vvhere his feete stoode*: or (vvhich by the Hebrue phrase is al one) *Adore ye his holy mount. We vvill adore the place vvhere his feete stood.* as also * the Greeke fathers, S Damascene *li. 1 de imaginibus*, and Leontius cited of him, yea S. Chrysostom also do handel these places, and namely that of the Apostle vvhich vve novv speake of, interpreting the Greeke as our Latin hath, and as vve do, He adored the rod or the toppe of his rod, that is, the scepter of Ioseph novv Prince of Ægypt, so fulfilling Iosephs dreames vvhich foretold the same *Gen.* 37: and vvithal signifying as it vvere by this propheticall fact, * the kingdom of Israel or of the ten tribes that vvas to come of Ioseph by Ephraim his yonger sonne in the first king Ieroboam. thus the Greeke fathers. Vvherevnto may be added, that al this vvas done in type and figure of Christes scepter and kingdom, vvhom he adored by and in his Crosse, as he did Ioseph by or in his rod and scepter: and therfore the Apostle saith, he did it by faith, as hauing respect tovvard things to come. By al vvhich it is euident, that it is false vvhich the Caluinists teach, that vve may not adore image, crucifixe, or any visible creature, that is, vve may not adore God at or by such creatures, nor kneele before them: and therfore their corrupt translation of this place for the same purpose is intolerable, saying thus, (LEANING) *vpon his staffe he adored* (GOD), adding no lesse then tvvo vvordes more then is in the Greeke. Which though it might be the sense of the place, and S. Augustine so expoundeth it, yet they should not make his exposition the text of holy Scripture, specially vvhereas he only of al the auncient fathers (as Beza confesseth) so expoundeth it.

* Ios. 7, 6.

* Oecum. in collect.

* 3 Reg. 11. 12.

Adoration of creatures, and namely of holy things.

Corrupt translation against Dulia.

33. *Wrought iustice.*] Men are not iust by beleefe onely, as the Protestants affirme, but by vvorking iustice. And vve may note that in all this long commendation of faith in the fathers and holy persons, their good vvorkes are also specially recounted, as Rahabs harbouring the spies, Abrahams offering his sonne (vvhich their vvorkes S. Iames doth inculcate:) Noës making the Arke *Gen.* 6. Abels better oblation then Cains *Gen.* 4. & *Hebr.* 11. *v.* 4 and so forth. therfore S. Clement Alexandrinus saith, that the said persons and others vvere iust by faith and obedience, by faith and hospitality, by faith and patience, by faith and humility.

Ias. 2.

Li. 4 Stro. pag. 240.

Not faith onely.

The Apostles purpose then is nothing els, but to proue to the Hebrues (vvho made so great account of their Patriarches and forefathers and their famous actes) that all these glorious personages and their vvorkes vvere commendable and acceptable onely through the faith they had of Christ, vvithout vvhich faith none of all their liues and vvorkes should haue profited them any vvhit: the Gentiles doing many noble actes (as Heretikes may also doe) vvhich are of no estimatiõ before God, because they lacke faith. And that is the scope of S. Paules Epistle to the Romanes, and of al other passages vvhere he commendeth faith: further prouing specially in this Epistle to the Hebrues, that all their sacrifices vvere nothing els but figures and attestations of the Christian faith in Christ and his death. Al vvhich high resolution & conclusion against the Ievves and Gentiles, that the Christian faith is the true faith & religion, the Heretikes of our time ignorantly and brutishly abuse against Christian vvorkes, sacrifice, and Sacraments, vvhich the Apostle meant specially to commend and establish by his high commendation of the faith in Christ.

No vvorkes of the Patriarkes or any other profitable, but by their faith in Christ. Which is alvvaies the Apostles meaning in cõmending faith.

40. *Without vs should not.*] The fathers before Christ could not be accomplished, that is, not admitted to the heauenly ioyes, vision, and fruition of God, till the Apostles and other of the nevv lavv vvere associate to them, and the vvay to euerlasting glorie opened by our Lordes death and Ascension. Neither shal either they or vve be fully perfected in glorie both of body and soul, till the general resurrection: Gods prouidence being so, that vve should not one be consummated vvithout an other, all being of one faith, and redeemed by one Lord Christ.

The Patriarkes and other iust not in heauen before Christ.

LIII CHAP.

CHAP. XII.

By the foresaid examples he exhorteth them to patience, 2 and by example of Christ him self crucified, 5 and because this discipline is an argument that they be Gods children, 9 vvith vvhose rodde they should be much more content then vvith that of their carnal fathers: and because it bringeth iustification. 12 Exhorting them therfore to plucke vp their hartes, and to take faster footing: 18 considering that all being novv so svveete, and not terrible as in the old Testament, their damnation, if they refuse to heare, vvil be so much the greater.

AND therfore vve also hauing so great a cloud 1 of vvitnesses put vpon vs: * laying avvay al vveight and sinne that compasseth vs, by patience let vs runne to the fight proposed vnto vs, † looking on the author of faith, and the 2 consummator IESVS, vvho, ioy being proposed vnto him, sustained the crosse, contemning confusion, and sitteth on the right hand of the seate of God.

Col. 3, 8.
1 Pet. 2, 1.

† For, thinke diligently vpon him vvhich sustained of 3 sinners such contradiction against him self: that you be not vvearied, fainting in your mindes. † For you haue not yet 4 resisted vnto bloud, repugning against sinne: † and you haue 5 forgotten the consolatiō, vvhich speaketh to you, as it vvere to children, saying, *My sonne, neglect not the discipline of our Lord: neither be thou vvearied vvhiles thou art rebuked of him.* † *For vvhom our* 6 *Lord loueth, he chasteneth: and" he scourgeth euery childe that he receiueth,*

Prou. 3, 11.
Apoc. 3, 19.

† Perseuêre ye in discipline. As vnto children doth God 7 offer him self to you. for vvhat sonne is there, vvhom the father doth not correct? † But if you be vvithout discipline, 8 vvhereof al be made partakers: then are you bastards, & not children. † Moreouer the fathers in deede of our flesh 9 vve had for instructors, and vve did reuerence them: shal vve not much more obey the Father of spirites, & liue? † And 10 they in deede for a time of fevv daies, according to their vvil instructed vs: but he, to that vvhich is profitable in receiuing of his sanctification. † And al discipline for the present cer- 11 tes seemeth not to be of ioy, but of sorovv: but aftervvard it vvil render to them that are exercised by it, most peaceable fruite of iustice.

† For the vvhich cause stretch vp the slacked handes and 12 the loose knees: † and make straight steppes to your feete: 13 that no man halting erre, but rather be healed. † * Folovv 14 peace vvith al men, and holinesse: vvithout vvhich no man shal

Rom. 12, 18.

15 shal see God: † looking diligently lest any man ∷ be vvanting to the grace of God: lest any' roote of bitternes springing vp do hinder, and by it many be polluted. † Lest there 16 be any fornicator or prophane person [c] as Esau: * vvho for one dish of meate sold his first-birth-rightes. † For knovv 17 ye that aftervvard also desiring to inherite the benediction, he vvas reprobated: * for " he found not place of repẽtance, although vvith teares he had sought it.

Gen. 25, 33.

Gen. 27, 38.

∷ That vve be not good, there is no lacke on Gods part, vvho offereth his grace to vs: but the defect is in our selues that are not ansvverable to Gods calling of vs and grace tovvards vs.

c Such as forsake their saluation and religion to saue their lands and goods, are like Esau.

18 † For you are not come to * a palpable mount, and an accessible' fire, and vvhirlevvinde, and darkenes, and storme, 19 † and the soũd of trompet, & voice of vvordes, vvhich they that heard, excused them selues, that the vvord might not be 20 spokẽ to them, († for they did not beare that vvhich was said, 21 *And if a beast shal touche the mount, it shal be stoned.* † And so terrible vvas it vvhich vvas seen, Moyses said: *I am frighted and tremble.*

Exo. 19. 20.

' kindled (or) burning.

Exo. 19, 12.

22 † But ∷ you are come to mount Sion, and the citie of the liuing God, heauenly Hierusalem, and the assemblie of 23 many thousand Angels, † & the Church of the first-borne, vvhich are vvritten in the heauens, and the iudge of all, God: 24 and the spirites of the iust [c] made perfect, † and the mediator of the nevv Testament IESVS, and the sprinkling of bloud speaking better then * Abel.

∷ The faithful are made fellovves of Angels & of al the perfect soules departed since the beginning of the vvorld, and of Christ him self.

c τετελειωμένων

Gen. 4, 10.

25 † See that you refuse him not speaking. for if they escaped not, refusing him that spake vpon the earth: much more vve, that turne avvay from him speaking to vs from heauen. 26 † Vvhose voice moued the earth then: but novv he promiseth, saying, *Yet once: and I vvil moue not only the earth, but heauen also.* 27 † And in that he saieth, *Yet once*, he declareth the translation of moueable things as being made, that those things 28 may remaine vvhich are vnmoueable. † Therfore receiuing an vnmoueable kingdom, vve haue grace: by the vvhich [c] let 29 vs serue pleasing God, vvith feare & reuerence. † For * our God is a consuming fire.

Ag. 2, 7.

c λατρεύωμεν

Deu. 4, 24.

ANNOTATIONS
CHAP. XII.

6. *He scourgeth.*] By this vve proue that God often punisheth the sinnes euen of his louing children, though not vvith eternal damnation, yet vvith temporall chastisement and correction: & that he doth not alvvaies together vvith the remission of deadly sinnes & eternal punishment, exempt the offender receiued to his grace, from al fatherly correction either in this life or in the next. Neither haue the Heretikes of this time any reason or scripture in the vvorld, vvhy they should

Temporal punishment after remissiõ of sinnes, either here, or in purgatorie.

ſhould take avvay Gods chaſtiſement of his children in the next life, more then in this vvorld.

17. *He found not.*] It is not meant, that Eſau could not find remiſſion of his ſinne at Gods hand: but that, hauing once ſold and yelded vp the right of his firſt-birth to his yonger brother, it vvas to late to be ſorie for his vnaduiſed bargaine.

CHAP. XIII.

He commendeth vnto them mutual loue, 2 hoſpitality, 3 compaſſion, 4 chaſtitie, 5 contentation, 7 imitation of the faith of their Catholike Prelates and Martyrs (not harkening to the doctrines of Heretikes, nor fearing the caſting out of the Ievves ſynagogue) 17 and obedience to their preſent paſtors. 18 And ſo vvith requeſting their praiers, and praying for them, he endeth the Epiſtle.

ἡ φιλαδελφία

LET c the charitie of the fraternitie abide in you. 1 † And " hoſpitalitie do not forget, for by this, certaine being not avvare, * haue receiued Angels to harbour. 2 † Remember them in bondes, as if you vvere boũd vvith them: and them that labour, as your ſelues alſo remaining in bodie. 3 † " Mariage honorable in all, and the bed vndefiled. For, fornicatours & aduouterers God vvil iudge. 4 † Let your maners be vvithout auarice: contented vvith things preſent. For he ſaid, *I vvil not leaue thee, neither vvil I forſake thee.* 5 † ſo that vve do confidently ſay: *Our Lord is my helper: I vvil not feare vvhat man ſhal doe to me.* 6

Rom. 12. 10. 1 Pet. 4. Gen. 18, 3. 19, 2. 3.

Deu. 31. Ioſ. 1. Pſal. 55, 12. 117, 6.

The epiſtle for a Confeſſor that is a Biſhop.

† " Remember your Prelates, vvhich haue ſpoken the vvord of God to you: the end of vvhoſe conuerſation beholding, imitate their faith. 7 † IESVS Chriſt yeſterday, and to day: the ſame alſo for euer. 8 † Vvith ∷ various & ſtrãge doctrines be not led avvay. For it is beſt that the hart be eſtabliſhed vvith grace, " not vvith meates: vvhich haue not profited thoſe that vvalke in them. 9

∷ Nevv, diuers, changeable, & ſtrange doctrines to be auoided, for ſuch be hereticall. Againſt vvhich the beſt remedie or preſeruatiue is, alvvaies to looke backe to our firſt Apoſtles, & the holy fathers doctrine.

† " Vve haue an altar: vvhereof they haue not povver to eate vvhich ſerue the tabernacle. 10 † For * the bodies of thoſe beaſtes, vvhoſe bloud for ſinne is caried into the holies by the high prieſt, are burned vvithout the campe. 11 † For the vvhich thing IESVS alſo, that he might ſanctifie the people by his ovvne bloud, ſuffered vvithout the gate. 12 † Let vs goe forth therfore to him vvithout the campe: carying his reproche. 13 † For vve haue not here a permanent citie: but vve ſeeke that vvhich is to come. 14 † By him therfore let vs offer " the hoſt of praiſe alvvaies to God, that is to ſay, * the fruite of lippes confeſſing to his name. 15

Leu. 16, 27.

Oſe. 14, 3.

† And

16 † And beneficence aud communication do not forget. 17 for vvith such hostes" God is promerited. † " Obey your Prelates, and be subiect to them. For they vvatch as being to render account for your soules: ꝗ that they may doe this vvith ioy, and not mourning. for this is not expedient for 18 you. † Pray for vs. for vve haue confidence that vve haue a 19 good conscience, vvilling to conuerse vvel in all. † And I beseeche you the more to doe this, that I may the more spe- 20 dily be restored to you. † And the God of peace vvhich brought out from the dead the great Pastor of the sheepe, in the bloud of the eternal testamēt, our Lord IESVS Christ: 21 † [c]fitte you in al goodnes, that you may doe his vvil, doing in you that vvhich may please before him by IESVS Christ: to vvhom is glorie for euer and euer. Amen.

22 † And I desire you brethren that you suffer the vvord of consolation. For in very fevv vvordes haue I vvritten to 23 you. † Knovv you our brother Timothee to be dismissed: 24 vvith vvhom (if he come the sooner) I vvil see you. † Salute al your prelates, and al the sainctes. The brethren of 25 Italie salute you. † Grace be vvith you al. Amen.

c aptet vos

c καταρτίσαι, that is, *make you perfect and absolute in al goodnes.*

ANNOTATIONS
CHAP. XIII.

2. *Hospitality.*] Hospitality, that is, receiuing and harbouring of poore pilgrimes, persecuted and desolate persons, is so acceptable to God and so honorable, that often-times it hath been mens good happe to harbour Angels in steede of poore folke vnawares. Vvhich must needes be euer a great benediction to them and their families, as vve see by Abraham and Lot *Gen. 18. & 19.* (and the like fell also to S. Gregorie, as Io. Diaconus vvriteth, to vvhose ordinarie table of poore men, not onely Angels but Christ also came in Pilgrimes vveede. *In vit. li. 1. c. 10. & li. 2. c. 22. 23.*) vvherof if vve had not example and vvarrant by S. Paules vvordes in this place, and many other expresse Scriptures of the old Testament, these scorneful miscreants of this time making so litle account both of good vvorkes and such miraculous enterance of Christ and his Angels into holy mens harbour, vvould make this also seeme fabulous, as they do other like things.

Hospitalitie.

Angels harboured.

4. *Mariage honorable.*] *The Apostle* (saith a holy doctor) *saith, Mariage honorable in all, and the bed vndefiled. And therfore the seruants of God in that they are not maried, thinke not the good of mariage to be a fault, but yet they doubt not perpetual continencie to be better then good mariage, specially in this time vvhen it is said of continencie, He that can take, let him take. De fid. ad Pet. c. 3. apud Aug. in fine.* Marke the doctrine of the fathers and of the Catholike Church concerning matrimonie, that it is honorable, and so honorable, that it is a holy sacrament, but yet * inferiour to virginity and perpetual continencie: honorable in all, that is, all such as may lawfully marie and are lawfully maried: not in brother and sister, not in persons that haue vowed the contrarie, to vvhom the same Apostle saith it is damnable. *1. Tim. 5. v. 11.* And this vvere the meaning of this place, if it vvere to be read thus, *Mariage is honorable.*

* 1 Cor. 7. v. 38.

Hovv mariage is honorable in al, if the Apostle did so say, as he doth not.

But to see how the Protestants in all their translations, to abuse the simple, do falsifie this sentence of the Apostle, to make it serue for the mariage of Votaries, it is notorious. First, they vse deceit in supplying the verbe substantiue that vvanteth, making it the Indicatiue moode thus, *Mariage is honorable &c.* as though the Apostle affirmed al mariage to be honorable

One short place manifoldly corrupted by the Protestants.

They restraīe the sense to their Heretical fansie.

honorable or lavvful, vvhere the verbe to be supplied ought rather to be the Imperatiue moode, *Let mariage be honorable*, that so the speache may be an exhortation or commaundement to them that be or vvil be maried, to vse them selues in that state in al fidelity, cleanlinesse, and coniugal continencie one tovvard an other: as vvhen S. Peter also and this Apostle exhorte maried men to giue honour to their vviues as to the vveaker vessels, and to possesse their vessel in honour, not in the passions of ignominie and vncleanlinesse: this is honorable or chast mariage, to vvhich he here exhorteth. And that it is rather an exhortation, then an affirmation, it is euident by the other partes and circumstances of this place both before & after: al vvhich are exhortations in their owne translations. this only being in the middes, and as indifferent to be an exhortation as the rest (by their owne confession) they restraine of purpose. Our text therfore and al Catholike translatiõs leaue the sentence indifferent * as it is in the Greeke, and as true translatours ought to do, not presuming to addict it to one side, lest they should restraine the sense of the holy Ghost to their owne particular fantasie.

1 Pet. 3.
1 Thes. 4.

* τίμιος ὁ γάμος ἐν πᾶσι.

Againe, * our new Translatours corrupt the text in that they translate, *in omnibus, among al men*, because so they thinke it vvould sound better to the ignorant, that Priests, Religious, and al vvhosoeuer, may marie: vvhere they can not tell either by the Greeke or Latin, that *in omnibus* should be the masculine gendre, rather then the neutre (as not only Erasmus, but * the Greeke doctors also take it) to signifie that mariage should be honorably kept betweene man and vvife in al pointes and in al respectes. *See S. Chrys. and Theophyl. in hunc locum*. For there may be many filthy abuses in vvedlocke, vvhich the Apostle vvarneth them to take heede of, and to keepe their mariage-bed vndefiled. But the third corruption for their purpose aforesaid, and most impudent, is, * that some of the Caluinistes for, *in omnibus*, translate, *inter quosuis*, vvith a marginal interpretation to signifie al orders, conditions, states, and qualities of men. So boldly they take away al indifferencie of senses, and make Gods vvord to speake iust that vvhich them selues vvould, and their heresie requireth, in vvhich kind they passe al impudencie and al heretikes that euer vvere.

* The Eng. Bib. 1577.
* Oecum. in Collect.
* Beza in no. Test. Græcolat. an. 1565.

Vve must haue regard to the faith & doctrine of the fathers.

7. *Remember your Prelates.*] Vve be here vvarned to haue great regard in our life and beleefe, to the holy fathers, Doctors, & glorious Bishops gone before vs in Gods Church, not doubting but they being our lawful Pastors, had and taught the truth: of vvhom S. Augustine said, *That vvhich they found in the Church, they held fast: that vvhich they learned, they taught: that vvhich they receiued of their fathers, the same they deliuered to their children. Cont. Iulian. li. 2 c. 10.* Vvhich respect to our holy forefathers in faith, is now in this vvicked contempt of the Heretikes, so much the more to be had. See the said holy doctors second booke against Iulian the Pelagian throughout, vvhat great account he maketh of them in the confutation of heresies, and hovv far he preferreth them aboue the proud Sectmaisters of that time: as vve must now doe against our new doctors. This place also is rightly vsed to proue that the Church of God should keepe the memories of Saincts departed, by solemne holidaies and other deuout vvaies of honour.

Memories and feastes of Saīcts.

Iudaical abstinence from meates.

9. *Not vvith meates.*] He speaketh not of Christian fastes, but of the legal difference of meates, vvhich the Hebrues vvere yet prone vnto: not considering that by Christes faith they vvere made free from al such obseruations of the Law.

Material altars for the sacrifice of christs body.

10. *We haue an altar.*] He putteth them in minde by these vvordes, that in folowing to much their old Iewish rites, they depriued them selues of an other maner and a more excellent sacrifice and meate: meaning, of the holy altar, and Christes ovvne blessed body offered and eaten there. of vvhich, they that continue in the figures of the old Law, could not be partakers. *This altar* (saith Isychius) *is the altar of Christes body, vvhich the Ievves for their incredulity must not behold. Li. 6 c. 21 in Leuit.* And the Greeke vvord (as also the Hebrue ansvvering thereunto in the old testament) signifieth properly an altar to sacrifice on, and not a metaphorical and spiritual altar. Vvhereby vve proue against the Heretikes, that vve haue not a common table or profane communion borde, to eate mere bread vpon, but a very altar in the proper sense, to sacrifice Christes body vpon: and so called of the fathers in respect of the said body sacrificed. *Greg. Nazianz. in orat. de sorore Gorgonia. Chrys. demonst. quod Christus sit Deus. Socrat. li. 1. c. 20. 25. Aug. ep. 86. De ciu. Dei. li. 8. c. 27. & li. 22. c. 10. Confess. li. 9 c. 11. 13. Cont. Faust. Manich. li. 20. c 21. Theophyl. in 23. Mat.* And vvhen it is called a table, it is in respect of the heauenly foode of Christs body and bloud receiued.

θυσιαστήριον.
מזבח

The Sacrifice of the altar is the principal host of praise and thankes giuing, therfore called, *Eucharistia*.

15. *The hoste of praise.*] Though it may signifie the spiritual sacrifices of praise and thankesgiuing of vvhat sort soeuer: yet it specially may be thought to signifie the great Sacrifice of the B. body and bloud of Christ: not as vpon the Crosse, vvhich vvas but once done in bloudy sort, but as in the Church, and new Testament, vvhere it is daily done vnbloudily, being the proper host of laude and thankes giuing, and therfore called the *Eucharist*, and being the fruite and effecte of Christ and his Priests lippes or vvordes, that is, of consecration: because this sacrifice is made by the force of the holy vvordes. And vvhen vve reade in the psalme and other places of the olde

Test.

Testament, of the host of praise, it may be thought to be a prophecie of the nevv Sacrifice, & not of euery vulgar thankes giuing. And so the old fathers in the primitiue Church to hide the mysteries from the vnvvorthy or heathen, often speake. *What is* (saith S. Augustine) *a more holy sacrifice of praise, then that vvhich consisteth in thankes giuing, all vvhich the faithful do knovv in the sacrifice of the Church. Li. 1. cont. aduers. leg. & proph. c. 18.* Againe, *c. 20. The Church from the times of the Apostles by the most certaine successions of Bishops, offereth to God in the body of Christ the Sacrifice of praise.* And a litle aftervvard, *Novv Israel according to the spirit, that is, the Church offereth a singular Sacrifice according to the spirit: of vvhose house he vvil not take calues nor goates, but vvil take the Sacrifice of praise, not according to the order of Aaron, but according to the order of Melchisedec. See ep. 120. c. 19. & ep. 57. ad q. 1. in fine.* Thus you see, vvhen the holy fathers handle the Scriptures, they finde Masse and Sacrifice in many places, vvhere the ignorant heretikes or the simple might thinke they speake onely of a common thankes giuing.

16. *God is promerited.*] This latin vvord *promeretur*, cannot be expressed effectually in any one English vvord. It signifieth, Gods fauour to be procured by the foresaid vvorkes of almes and charitie, as by the deserts and merites of the doers. Which doctrine and vvord of merites the Aduersaries like so il, that they flee both here and els vvhere from the vvord, translating here for, *promeretur Deus, God is pleased*, more neere to the Greeke, as they pretend. Which in deede maketh no more for them then the latin, vvhich is agreable to most auncient copies, as vve see by Primasius S. Augustines scholer. For if God be pleased vvith good vvorkes and shew fauour for them, then are they meritorious, and then only faith is not the cause of Gods fauour to men.

εὐαρεστεῖται

The Protestants auoid the vvord merite.

Good vvorkes meritorious.

17. *Obey your Prelates.*] There is nothing more inculcated in the holy Scriptures, then obedience of the lay people to the Priests and Prelates of Gods Church, in matters of soule, conscience, and religion. Vvhereof the Apostle giueth this reason, because they haue the charge of mens soules, and must ansvver for them: vvhich is an infinite preeminence and superiority, ioyned vvith burden, and requireth maruelous submission and most obedient subiection of al that be vnder them and their gouernement. From this obedience there is no exception nor exemption of kings nor Princes, be they neuer so great. If they haue soules, and be Christian men, they must be subiect to some Bishop, Priest, or other Prelate. And vvhatsoeuer he be (though Emperour of all the vvorld) if he take vpon him to prescribe and giue lawes of religion to the Bishops and Priests, vvhom he ought to obey and be subiect vnto in religion, he shal be damned vndoubtedly, except he repent, because he doth against the expresse vvord of God and law of nature. And by this you may see the difference of an heretical and a disordered time, from other Catholike Christian daies. For heresie and the like damnable reuoltes from the Church of God, is no more but a rebellion and disobedience to the Priests of Gods Church, vvhen men refuse to be vnder their discipline, to heare their doctrine, and interpretation of Scriptures, to obey their lawes and counsels. This disobedience and rebellion from the Spiritual Gouernour, vnder pretence of obedience to the Temporal, is the bane of our daies, and specially of our Countrie, vvhere these new Sectes are properly mainteined by this false principle, That the Prince in matters of soule and religion may commaund the Prelate: vvhich is directly and euidently against this Scripture and all other, that commaund the sheepe of Christes fold to obey their spiritual Officers.

The Apostle doth inculcate obedience to the Priests and Bishops of Gods Church.

No person exempted from this obediēce, in matters of religion.

THE

THE ARGVMENT OF THE EPISTLE OF S. IAMES.

HIS Epistle (as the rest folovving) is directed specially, as S. Augustine saith, against the errour of only faith, vvhich some held at that time also, by misconstruing S. Paules vvordes. Yea not only that, but many other errours (vvhich then also vvere annexed vnto it, as they are novv) doth this Apostle here touche expresly.

He saith therfore, that not only faith, but also good vvorkes are necessarie: that not only faith, but also good vvorkes do iustifie: that they are actes of Religion, or seruice and vvorship of God: that to keepe al the commaundements of God, and so to abstaine from al mortal sinne, is not impossible, but necessarie: that God is not author of sinne, no not so much as of tentation to sinne: that vve must stay our selues from sinning, vvith feare of our death, of the Iudgement, of hel: and stirre our selues to doing of good, vvith our revvard that vve shall haue for it in heauen. These pointes of the Catholike faith he commendeth earnestly vnto vs, inueighing vehemently against them that teach the cōtrarie errors. Hovvbeit he doth vvithal admonish not to neglect such, but to seeke their conuersion, shevving them hovv meritorious a thing that is. Thus then he exhorteth generally to all good vvorkes, & deborteth from al sinne. but yet also namely to certaine, & from certaine: as, from acception of persons, from detraction and rash iudging, from concupiscēce and loue of this vvorld, from svvearing: and, to praier, to almes, to humilitie, confession and penance: but most copiously to patience in persecution.

Vvhich Iames vvrote this epistle.

Novv, vvho this Iames vvas: It is not he, vvhose feast the Church keepeth the 25 of Iulie, vvhich vvas S. Iohns brother, and vvhose martyrdom vve haue Act. 12, but he, vvhom the Church vvorshippeth the first of Maie, vvho is called Frater Domini, our lordes brother, *and brother to Iude, and vvhich vvas the first Bishop of Hierusalem, of vvhom vve reade Act. 15 & 21. and also Gal. 2. of vvhose vvonderful austeritie and puritie of life, the Ecclesiasticall stories do report.* Euseb. li. 2. c. 22. Hiero. in Catalogo.

Therfore as the old High-priest had povver and charge ouer the Ievves, not only in Hierusalem and Iurie, but also dispersed in other Countries (as vve vnderstand Act. 9. v. 1, & 2.) so S. Iames likevvise, being Bishop of Hierusalem, and hauing care not only of those Ievves vvith vvhom he vvas resident there in Iurie, but of al the rest also, vvriteth this Epistle, To the tvvelue tribes that are in dispersion. *and in them, to al Christians vniuersally dispersed through the vvorld.*

Ia. 1.

THE

THE CATHOLIKE EPISTLE OF IAMES THE APOSTLE.

The Church readeth these Catholike or Canonical Epistles in order at Mattins, frõ the 4 Sũday after Easter vntil VVhitsunday.

Catholike Epistle.] The vvord Catholike though in the title of this Epistle & the rest folovving (called The Catholike Epistles) it be not vvholy in the same sense, as it is in the Creede: yet the Protestants so feare and abhorre the vvord altogether, that in some of their Bibles they leaue it cleane out, although it be in the Greeke, and in some they had rather translate ridiculously thus, *The general Epistle &c.* vvhereas these are famously knovven and * specified in antiquitie, by the name of Catholike Epistles, for that they are vvritten to the vvhole Church, not to any peculiar people or person, as S. Paules are.

Euseb. li. 2. hist. c. 22.

The Protestants abhorre the vvord *Catholike.*

CHAP. I.

Vve haue to reioyce in persecution (but if vve be patient, and vvithal absteine from al mortal sinne) 9 considering hovv vve shal be exalted and crovvned for it, vvhen the persecutor (vvho enricheth him self vvith our spoiles) shal fade avvay. 13 But if any be tempted to fall, or to any other euil, let him not say, God is the author of it, vvho is the author of al good onely. 19 Such points of the Cath. faith vve must be content to learne vvithout contradiction and anger, and to doe accordingly. 26 Because othervvise vve may talke of Religion, but in deede it is no Religion.

1 IAMES the seruant of God and of our Lord IESVS Christ, to the tvvelue tribes that are in dispersion, greeting.

2 † Esteeme it, my brethren, al ioy, vvhen you shal fall into diuers tentatiõs: 3 † knovving that * the probatiõ of your faith vvorketh patience. 4 † And let patience haue a perfect vvorke: that you may be perfect & entire, failing in nothing. 5 † But if any of you lacke vvisedom, let him aske of God vvho giueth to al men aboundantly, and vpbraideth not: and it shal be giuen him. 6 † But * let him " aske in faith nothing doubting. for he that doubteth, is like to a vvaue of the sea, vvhich is moued & caried about by the vvinde. 7 † therfore let not that man thinke that he shal

The Epistle for a Martyr.

Ro. 5, 3.

Mat. 21, 22.
Mar. 11, 24.

receiue any thing of our Lord. † A man double of minde 8 is inconſtant in al his vvaies.

† But let the humble brother glorie, in his exaltation. 9 † and the riche, in his humilitie, becauſe * as the floure of 10 graſſe ſhal he paſſe: † for the ſunne roſe vvith heate, & par- 11 ched the graſſe, and the floure of it fel avvay, and the beautie of the ſhape thereof periſhed: ſo the riche man alſo ſhal vvither in his vvaies. † Bleſſed is the man that ſuffereth ten- 12 tation: for vvhen he hath been proued, he ſhal receiue the crovvne of life, vvhich God hath promiſed to them that loue him. ⊣

Pſ. 102, 15. Eccl. 14,18. Eſ. 4, 6. 1 Pet. 1, 24. Iob 5,17.

The Epiſtle for a Martyr that is a Biſhop.

† " Let no man vvhen he is tempted, ſay that he is temp- 13 ted of God. for " God is not a tempter of euils, and he temp- teth no man. † But ∷ euery one is tempted of his ovvne cõ- 14 cupiſcence abſtracted and allured. † Aftervvard " concupiſ- 15 cence vvhen it hath cõceiued, bringeth forth ſinne. but " ſinne vvhen it is conſummate, ingendreth death.

∷ The groũd of tẽtation to ſinne, is our cõcupiſcence, & not God.

The Epiſtle on the 4 Sunday after Eaſter.

† Do not erre therfore my deereſt brethren. † Euery beſt 16 gift, and euery perfect gift, is from aboue, deſcending from 17 the Father of lightes, vvith vvhom is no tranſmutation, nor ſhadovving of alteration. † Voluntarily hath he begotten 18 vs by the vvord of truth, that vve may be ſome beginning of his creature. ⊣ You knovv my deereſt brethren, And *let eue- 19 ry man be ſvvift to heare: but ſlovv to ſpeake, and ſlovv to anger. † For the anger of man vvorketh not the iuſtice of 20 God.

Prou. 17 27.

The Epiſtle on the 5 Sunday after Eaſter.

† For the vvhich thing caſting avvay al vncleanneſſe and 21 aboundance of malice, in meekeneſſe receiue the engraffed vvord, vvhich is able to ſaue your ſoules. ⊣ † But * be doers 22 of the vvord, and not hearers only, deceauing your ſelues. † For if a man be a hearer of the vvord, and not a doer: he ſhal 23 be compared to a man beholding the countenance of his na- tiuitie in a glaſſe. † For he conſidered him ſelf, and vvent 24 his vvay, and by and by forgat vvhat an one he vvas. † But 25 he that hath looked in " the lavv of perfect libertie, and hath remained in it, not made a forgetful hearer, but a doer of the vvorke: this man ſhal be ∷ bleſſed in his deede. † And if 26 any man thinke him ſelf to be religious, not bridling his tong, but ſeducing his hart: this mans religion is vaine. † " Religion cleane and vnſpotted vvith God and the Father, 27 is

Mat. 7, 21. Ro. 2, 13.

∷ Beatitude or ſaluation conſiſteth in vvel vvorking.

is this, to visite pupilles and vvidovves in their tribulation: & to keepe him self vnspotted from this vvorld. ┤

ANNOTATIONS
CHAP. I.

6. *Aske in faith nothing doubting.*] The Protestants vvould proue by this, that no man ought to pray vvithout assurance that he shal obtaine that vvhich he asketh. Where the Apostle meaneth nothing els, but that the asker of lavvful things may not either mistrust Gods povver and hability, or be in diffidence and despaire of his mercie: but that our doubt be onely in our ovvne vnWorthinesse or vndue asking.

Vvhat faith is required in praier.

13. *Let no man say that he is tempted of God.*] Vve see by this, that vvhen the Scriptures (as in the *Pater noster* and other places) seeme to say, that God doth sometimes tempt vs, or leade vs into tentation: they meane not, that God is any vvaies the author, causer, or mouer of any man to sinne, but onely by permission, and because by his gratious povver he keepeth not the offender from tentations. Therfore the blasphemie of Heretikes, making God the author of sinne, is intolerable. See *S. August. ser. 9 de diuers. c. 9.*

God is not author of euil.

13. *God is not a tempter of euils.*] The Protestants as much as they may, to diminish the force of the Apostles conclusion against such as attribute their euil tentations to God (for other tentations God doth send to trie mens patience and proue their faith) take and translate the vvord passiuely, in this sense, that God is not tempted by our euils. Vvhere more consonantly to the letter and circumstance of the vvordes before & after, & as agreably * to the Greeke, it should be taken actiuely as it is in the Latin, that God is no tempter to euil. for being taken passiuely, there is no coherence of sense to the other vvordes of the Apostle.

Partial and vvilful translation.

* ἀπείραστος κακῶν.

15. *Concupiscence vvhen it hath conceiued.*] Concupiscence (vve see here) of it self is not sinne, as Heretikes falsely teach: but vvhen by any consent of the minde vve do obey or yeld to it, then is sinne ingendred and formed in vs.

Concupiscēce of it self no sinne.

15. *Sinne consummate ingendreth death.*] Here vve see that not al sinne nor al consent vnto concupiscence is mortal or damnable, but vvhen it is consummate, that is, vvhen the consent of mans minde fully and perfectly yeldeth to the committing or liking of the acte or motion vvherevnto concupiscence moueth or inciteth vs.

Not euery sinne mortal.

25. *The lavv of perfect libertie.*] The lavv of the Gospel and grace of Christ, is called the lavv of libertie, in respect of the yoke and burden of the old carnal ceremonies, and because Christ hath by his bloud of the nevv Testament deliuered all that obey him, from the seruitude of sinne and the Diuel. But not as the Libertines and other Heretikes of this time vvould haue it, that in the nevv Testament euery man may follovv his ovvne liking and conscience, & may choose vvhether he vvil be vnder the lavves and obedience of Spiritual or Temporal Rulers, or no

Vvhat is the lavv of libertie in the Nevv Testament.

27. *Religion cleane.*] True religion standeth not onely in talking of the Scriptures, or onely faith, or Christes iustice: but in puritie of life, and good vvorkes, specially of charitie and mercie done by the grace of Christ. This is the Apostolical doctrine, and far from the Heretical vanitie of this time.

Good vvorkes a part of mans iustice.

CHAP. II.

Against acception of persons. 10 From al and euery sinne vve must absteine, hauing in al our vvordes and deedes, the Iudgement before our eies: vvherein vvorkes of mercie shal be required of vs, 14 and onely faith shal not auaile vs. 18 And that the Catholike by his vvorkes shevveth that he hath faith: vvhereas the Heretike hath no more faith then the Diuel, talke he of faith neuer so much, and of iustification thereby onely, by the example of Abraham Ro. 4. For Abraham in deede vvas iustified by vvorkes also, 25 and likevvise Rahab.

Y brethren, Haue not the faith of our 1 Lord IESVS Christ of glorie " in acception of persons. † For if there 2 ſhal enter into your aſſemblie a man hauing a golden ring in goodly appareil, and there ſhal enter in a poore man in homely attire, † & you haue 3 reſpect to him that is clothed vvith the goodly appareil, and ſhal ſay to him, Sitte thou here vvel: but ſay to the poore man, Stand thou there: or ſitte vnder my foote-ſtoole: † do you not 4 iudge vvith your ſelues, and are become iudges of vniuſt cogitations? † Heare my deereſt brethren: hath not God cho- 5 ſen the poore in this vvorld, riche in faith, and heires of the kingdom vvhich God hath promiſed to them that loue him? † But you haue diſhonoured the poore mā. Do not "the riche 6 oppreſſe you by might: and them ſelues dravv you to iudgements? † Doe not they blaſpheme the good name that is 7 inuocated vpon you? † If not-vvithſtanding you fulfil the 8 roial lavv according to the ſcriptures, *Thou ſhalt loue thy neighbour as thy ſelf*, you doe vvel: † but if you accept perſons, you 9 vvorke ſinne, reproued of the Lavv as tranſgreſſours. † And 10 ⋆ vvhoſoeuer ſhal keepe the vvhole Lavv, but offendeth in one: "is made guilty of al. † For he that ſaid, Thou ſhalt 11 not commit aduoutrie, ſaid alſo, Thou ſhalt not kil. And if thou doe not commit aduoutrie, but ſhalt kil: thou art made a tranſgreſſour of the Lavv. † So ſpeake ye, and ſo doe, as 12 beginning to be iudged by the lavv of libertie. † For "iudge- 13 ment vvithout mercie to him that hath not done mercie. And mercie • exalteth it ſelf aboue iudgement.

† " Vvhat ſhal it profit my brethren, if a man ſay he hath 14 faith: but hath not vvorkes? Shal faith be able to ſaue him? † And ⋆ if a brother or ſiſter be naked, & lacke daily foode: 15 † and one of you ſay to them, Goe in peace, be vvarmed & 16 filled: but you giue them not the things that are neceſſarie for the bodie: vvhat ſhal it profit? † So faith alſo, if it haue 17 not vvorkes, is dead in it ſelf. † But ſome man ſaith, Thou 18 haſt faith, and I haue vvorkes: ſhevv me thy faith vvithout vvorkes: & I vvil ſhevv thee by vvorkes my faith. † Thou 19 beleeueſt that there is one God. Thou doeſt vvel: the deuils alſo

Leu. 19, 15. Deu. 1, 16. Pro. 24, 23. Eccl. 42, 1.

Leu. 19, 18. Mat. 22, 39. Rom. 13.

Leu. 19, 37. Deu. 1, 18.

• κατακαυχᾶται

Io. 3, 17

20 also beleeue and tremble. † But vvilt thou knovv ∴ ô vaine 21 man, that faith vvithout vvorkes is 'idle'? † "Abraham our father vvas he not iustified by vvorkes, * offering Isaac his 22 sonne vpon the altar? † Seest thou that" faith did vvorke vvith his vvorkes: and by the vvorkes the faith vvas con- 23 summate? † And the Scripture vvas fulfilled, saying, *Abraham beleeued God, and it vvas reputed him to iustice, and he vvas called" the freende of God.* 24 † Do you see that by vvorkes a man is iustified: &" not by faith only? 25 † And in like maner also *" Rahab the harlot, vvas not she iustified by vvorkes, receiuing the messengers, and putting them forth an other vvay? 26 † For euen as the bodie vvithout the spirit is dead: so also "faith vvithout vvorkes is dead.

dead

Gen. 22, 10.

Gen. 15, 6. Ro. 4, 3. Gal. 3

Ios. 2, 1. 18. and 6, 22.

∴ He speaketh to al heretikes that say, faith onely without vvorkes doth iustifie, calling them vaine men, and comparing them to Diuels.

ANNOTATIONS
CHAP. II.

1. *In acception of persons.*] The Apostle meaneth not, as the Anabaptists and other seditious persons sometime gather hereof, that there should be no difference in Commonvveales or assemblies, betvvixt the Magistrate and the subiect, the free man and the bond, the riche and the poore, betvvixt one degree and an other. for, God and nature, and the necessitie of man, haue made such distinctions, and men are bound to obserue then. But it is meant onely, or specially, that in spiritual giftes and graces, in matters of faith, Sacraments, and saluation, and bestovving the spiritual functions and charge of soule, vve must esteeme of a poore man or a bond man, no lesse then of the rich man and the free, then of the Prince or the Gentleman: because as Christ him self calleth all, and endueth al sorts vvith his graces: so in such and the like things vve must not be partial, but count al to be fellovves, brethren, and members of one head And therfore the Apostle saith vvith a special clause, That vve should not hold or haue the Christian faith vvith or in such differences or partialities.

Scripture abused by the Anabaptistes to make no distinction of persons.

Vvhat the Apostle meaneth by acception of persons.

10. *Is made guilty of al.*] He meaneth not, that vvhosoeuer is a theefe, is also a murderer, or that euery murderer is an aduouterer also: or that al sinnes be equal, according to the Stoïkes and the Heresie of Iouinian: much lesse, that he shal haue as great damnation that transgresseth one commaundement, as if he had offended against euery precept. but the sense is, that it shal not auaile him to saluation, that he seemeth to haue kept certaine and not broken al the commaundements: seeing that any one transgression of the Lavv, proueth that he hath not obserued the vvhole, vvhich he vvas bound to do, so far as is required, and as is possible for a man in this life. S. Augustine disputing profoundly in his 29 Epistle to S. Hierom, of this place of S. Iames, expoundeth it thus: that he vvhich offendeth in one, that is, against the general and great commaundement of loue or charitie (because it is in maner al, as being the summe of al, the plenitude of the lavv, and the perfection of the rest) breaketh after a sort and transgresseth al, no sinne being committed but either against the loue of God, or of our neighbour.

How he that offendeth in one commaundement, is guilty of al.

13. *Iudgement vvithout mercie.*] Nothing giueth more hope of mercie in the next life, then the vvorkes of almes, charitie, and mercie, done to our neighbours in this life. Neither shal any be vsed vvith extreme rigour in the next vvorld, but such as vsed not mercie in this vvorld. *August. de pec. merit. li.* 2 *c.* 3. Vvhich is true, not onely in respect of the iudgement to euerlasting damnation, but also of the temporal chastisement in Purgatorie, as S. Augustine signifieth, declaring that our venial sinnes be vvashed avvay in this vvorld vvith daily vvorkes of mercie, vvhich othervvise should be chastised in the next. See *epist.* 29 aforesaid *in fine.* and *li.* 21 *de Ciu. Dei c.* 27 *in fine.*

Vvorkes of mercie exceding grateful to God.

14. *What shal it profite, if a man say he hath faith?*] This vvhole passage of the Apostle is so cleere against iustification or saluation by onely faith, damnably defended by the Protestants, and so euident for the necessitie, merite, & concurrence of good vvorkes, that their first author Luther and such as exactly folovv him, boldly (after the maner of Heretikes) vvhen they can make no shift nor false glose for the text, deny the booke to be Canonical Scripture. But Caluin and his companions disagreing vvith their Maisters, confesse it to be holy Scripture. but their shiftes and

The proud & impudent dealing of the heretikes against this Epistle, because it is so plaine against only faith.

fond gloses for ansvver of so plaine places, be as impudent as the denying of the Epistle vvas in the other. vvho vvould neuer haue denied the booke, thereby to shevv them selues Heretikes, if they had thought those vulgar euasions that the Zuinglians and Caluinists do vse (vvhereof they vvere not ignorant) could haue serued. In both sortes the Christian Reader may see, that al the Heretikes vaunting of expresse Scriptures & the vvord of God, is no more but to delude the vvorld. vvhereas in deede, be the Scriptures neuer so plaine against them, they must either be vvrested to sound as they say, or els they must be no Scriptures at all. And to see Luther, Caluin, Beza, & their fellovves, sitte as it vvere in iudgement of the Scriptures, to allovv or disallovv at their pleasures, it is the most notorious example of Heretical pride & miserie that can be. See their prefaces and censures vpon this Canonical Epistle, the Apocalypse, the Machabees, and other.

Only faith, an old heresie.

21. *Abraham vvas he not iustified by vvorkes?*] It is much to be noted that S. Augustine in his booke *de fide & operibus c.* 14 vvriteth, that the heresie of onely faith iustifying or sauing, vvas an old Heresie euen in the Apostles time, gathered by the false interpretation of some of S. Paules profound disputation in the Epistle to the Romans, vvherein he commended so highly the faith in Christ, that they thought good vvorkes vvere not auailable: adding further, that the other three Apostles, Iames, Iohn, and Iude, did of purpose vvrite so much of good vvorkes, to correct the said errour of onely faith, gathered by the misconstruction of S. Paules vvordes. Yea vvhen S. Peter (*Ep. 2 c. 3.*) vvarneth the faithful that many things be hard in S. Paules vvritings, and of light vnlearned men mistaken to their perdition: the said S. Augustine affirmeth, that he meant of his disputation concerning faith, vvhich so many Heretikes did mistake to condemne good vvorkes. And in the preface of his commentarie vpon the 31 Psalme, he vvarneth al men, that this deduction vpon S. Paules speache, *Abraham vvas iustified by faith, therfore vvorkes be not necessarie to saluation:* is the right vvay to the gulfe of Hel and damnation.

S. Iames & the rest inculcate good vvorkes against the errour of only faith falsely gathered of S. Paules vvordes.

loco citato.

S. Augustines vvhole disputation in this poīt very notable, & directly against only faith.

And lastly (vvhich is in it self very plaine) that vve may see this Apostle did purposely thus commend vnto vs the necessitie of good vvorkes, and the inanity aud insufficiencie of onely faith, to correct the errour of such as misconstrued S. Paules vvordes for the same: * the said holy Doctor noteth that of purpose he tooke the very same example of Abraham, vvhom S. Paul said to be iustified by faith, and declareth that he vvas iustified by good vvorkes, specifying the good vvorke for vvhich he vvas iustified and blessed of God, to vvitte, his obedience and immolation of his onely sonne. But hovv S. Paul saith that Abraham vvas iustified by faith, see the Annotations vpon that place. *Ro.* 4. *v.* 1.

* *Li.* 83 *q. q.* 76.

Heresies against good vvorkes.

22. *Faith did vvorke vvith.*] Some Heretikes hold, that good vvorkes are pernicious to saluation and iustification: other, that though they be not hurtful but required, yet they be no causes or vvorkers of saluation, much lesse meritorious, but are as effectes and fruites issuing necessarily out of faith. Both vvhich fictions, falshods, and flightes from the plaine truth of Gods vvord, are refuted by these vvordes, vvhen the Apostle saith, That faith vvorketh together vvith good vvorkes: making faith to be a coadiutor or cooperator vvith vvorkes, and so both ioyntly concurring as causes and vvorkers of iustification: yea aftervvard he maketh vvorkes the more principal cause, vvhen he resembleth faith to the body, and vvorkes to the spirit or life of man.

Workes cōcurre vvith faith as cause of iustification.

Workes make vs iust in deede before God.

23. *The freend of God.*] By this also an other false and friuolous euasion of the Heretikes is ouertaken, vvhen they feine, that the Apostle here vvhen he saith, vvorkes do iustifie, meaneth that they shevv vs iust before men, and auaile not to our iustice before God. For the Apostle euidently declareth that Abraham by his vvorkes vvas made or truely called the freend of God, and therfore vvas not (as the Heretikes say) by his vvorkes approued iust before man onely.

The Protestants say, *by faith only*: S. Iames cleane contrarie, *Not by faith only*.

24. *Not by faith onely.*] This proposition or speache is directly opposite or contradictorie to that vvhich the Heretikes hold. For the Apostle saith, Man is iustified by good vvorkes, and not by faith only. but the Heretikes say, Man is not iustified by good vvorkes, but by faith only. Neither can they pretend that there is the like contradiction or contrarietie betvvixt S. Iames speache and S. Paules. for though S. Paul say, man is iustified by faith, yet he neuer saith, by faith onely, nor euer meaneth by that faith vvhich is alone, but alvvaies by that faith vvhich vvorketh by charitie, * as he expoundeth him self. Though concerning vvorkes also, there is a difference betvvixt the first iustification, vvhereof S. Paul specially speaketh: and the second iustification, vvhereof S. Iames doth more specially treate. Of vvhich thing * els vvhere there is ynough said.

* *Gal.* 5.

* See the annot. vpon the epistle to the Romans *c.* 2. *v.* 13.

The manifold meaning of certaine fathers, vvhen they say, *Only faith.*

The fathers in deede vse sometimes this exclusiue, *sola*, *onely*: but in far other sense then the Protestants. For some of them thereby exclude only the vvorkes of Moyses law, against the Iewes: some, the vvorkes of nature and moral vertues vvithout the grace or knowledge of Christ, against the Gentiles: some, the necessitie of external good vvorkes vvhere the parties lacke time and meanes to doe them, as in the case of the penitent theefe: some, the false opinions, sectes, and religions contrarie to the Catholike faith, against Heretikes and miscreants: some exclude reason, sense, and arguing in matters of faith and mysterie, against such as vvil beleeue nothing but that they see or vnderstand: some, the merite

merite of vvorkes done in sinne before the first iustification: some, the arrogant Pharisaical vaunting of mans ovvne proper vvorkes and iustice, against such as referre not their actions and good deedes to Gods grace. To these purposes the holy Doctors say sometimes, that only faith saueth and serueth: but neuer (as the Protestants vvould haue it) to exclude from iustification and saluation, the cooperation of mans free vvil, dispositions and preparations of our hartes by praiers, penance, and sacraments, the vertues of hope and charitie, the purpose of vvel-vvorking and of the obseruation of Gods commaundements: much lesse, the vvorkes and merites of the children of God, proceding of grace and charitie, after they be iustified and are now in his fauour: vvhich are not only dispositions and preparations to iustice, but the meritorious cause of greater iustice, and of saluation.

25. *Rahab.*] This Apostle alleageth the good vvorkes of Rahab by vvhich she vvas iustified, and S. Paul (11 Hebr.) saith she vvas iustified by faith. Vvhich are not contrarie one to the other. for both is true, that she vvas saued by faith, as one saith: and that she vvas saued by her vvorkes, as the other saith. But it vvere vutruely said, that she vvas saued either by onely faith, as the Heretikes say: or by onely good vvorkes, as no Catholike man euer said. But because some Ievves and Gentil Philosophers did affirme: they, that they should be saued by the vvorkes of Moyses lavv: these, by their moral vvorkes: therfore S. Paul to the Romans disputed specially against both, prouing that no vvorkes done vvithout or before the faith of Christ, can serue to iustification or saluation.

S. Paul nameth faith, & S. Iames vvorkes, causes of iustification: but neither the one, faith only: nor the other, vvorkes only.

26. *Faith vvithout vvorkes is dead.*] S. Iames (as the Protestants feine) saith that faith vvithout good vvorkes is no faith, and that therfore it iustifieth not, because it is no faith. for he saith that it is dead vvithout vvorkes, as the body is dead vvithout the soule, and therfore being dead hath no actiuity or efficacie to iustifie or saue. But it is a great difference, to say that the body is dead, and to say that it is no body. euen so it is the like difference, to say that faith vvithout vvorkes is dead, and to say that faith vvithout vvorkes is no faith. And if a dead body be notvvithstanding a true body, then according to S. Iames comparison here, a dead faith is notvvithstanding a true faith, but yet not auailable to iustification, because it is dead, that is, because it is onely faith vvithout good vvorkes.

Faith vvithout vvorkes is a true faith, but not auailable: as the body vvithout the spirit is a true body, though it be dead.

And therfore it is a great impudencie in Heretikes, and a hard shift, to say that the faith of vvhich the Apostle disputeth al this vvhile, is no true or proprely called faith at all. It is the same faith that S. Paul defined and commended in al the 11 chapter to the Hebrues, and the same vvhich is called the Catholike faith, and the same vvhich being formed & made aliue by charitie, iustifieth. Mary true it is, that it is not that special faith vvhich the Heretikes feine onely to iustifie, to vvit, vvhen a man doth firmely beleeue as an article of his faith, that him self shal be saued. this special faith it is not vvhereof the Apostle here speaketh. for neither he, nor S. Paul, nor any other sacred vvriter in al the holy Scriptures euer speake or knevve of any such forged faith.

Vvhat faith the Apostle speaketh of: & that he knevv no special faith.

CHAP. III.

Against proud Maisters and authors of Sectes. 5 Of the manifold sinnes of the vnbrideled tongue. 13 The difference betvvixt proud, cötentious, and vvorldly vvisedom, and that vvisedom vvhich is heauenly, peaceable, modest, and so forth.

Mat. 23, 8.

Eccl. 14, 1. 19, 16.

1 BE yee not" many maisters my brethren, knovving that you receiue the greater iudgement, 2 † For in many things vve offend al.* If any man offend not in vvord: this is a perfect man. he is able also vvith bridle to 3 turne about the whole body. † And if vve put bittes into the mouthes of horses that they may obey vs, vve 4 turne about al their body also. † And behold, the shippes, vvhereas they be great, and are driuen of strong vvindes: yet are

are they turned about vvith a litle sterne whither the violẽce of the director vvil. † So the tongue also is certes a litle mẽ- 5 ber, & c vaunteth great things. Behold hovv ˋmuch' fire what a great vvood it kindleth? † And the tongue, is fire, a vvhole 6 vvorld of iniquitie. The tongue is set amoug our members, vvhich defileth the vvhole bodie, & inflameth the vvheele of our natiuitie, inflamed of hel. † For al nature of beastes & fou- 7 les and serpents & of the rest is tamed & hath been tamed by the nature of man. † but the tongue no man can tame, an vn- 8 quiet euil, ful of deadly poison. † By it vve blesse God & the 9 Father: & by it vve curse men vvhich are made after the simi- litude of God. † Out of the self same mouth procedeth bles- 10 sing & cursing. These things must not be so done my brethrẽ. † Doth the fountaine giue forth out of one hole svveete & 11 soure water? † Can, my brethren, the figge tree yeld grapes: 12 or the vine, figges? So neither ˋcan the salt water yeld' sweete.

c μεγαλαυχεῖ.

litle

can it yeld salt and svveete vvater.

† Vvho is vvise and hath knowledge among you? Let him 13 shevv by good conuersation his vvorking in mildenesse of vvisedom. † But if you haue bitter zeale, and there be con- 14 tentions in your hartes: glorie not and be not liers against the truth. † for this is not ⁚⁚ vvisedom descending from 15 aboue: but earthly, sensual, diuelish. † For vvhere zeale and 16 contention is: there is inconstancie, and euery peruerse vvorke. † But the vvisedom that is from aboue, first certes is 17 chast: then peaceable, modest, suasible, cõsenting to the good, ful of mercie and good fruites, not iudging, vvithout simu- lation. † And the fruite of iustice, in peace is sovved, to them 18 that make peace.

⁚⁚ The diffe- rence betwixt the humane vvisedom, spe- cially of here- tikes: and the vvisedom of the Catholike Church & her children.

ANNOTATIONS
CHAP. III.

1. *Many maisters.*] He meaneth principally Sect-maisters that make them selues seue- ral Ringleaders in sundry sortes of new deuised doctrines: euery one arrogating to him self to be maister, and none so humble as to be a scholer, either to Gods Church and true Pastors, or to other guides and authors of the said sectes. So did Zuinglius disdaine to be Luthers scholer, and Caluin to be the folower of Zuinglius.

Many maisters are many proud Sect- maisters.

CHAP. IIII.

By concupiscence and loue of this vvorld, vve are made enemies to God: but vve should rather humble vs to him, punishing our selues for our sinnes. 11 Against detraction, and rash iudging. 13 To remember alvvaies the vncertentie of our life.

FROM

1 FROM vvhence are vvarres & contentions among you? Are they not hereof? of your concupiscences vvhich vvarre in your members? 2 † You couet: and haue not. you kil, & enuie: and can not obtaine. you contend and vvarre: and you haue not, because you aske not. 3 † You aske, and receiue not: because you aske amisse: that you may consume it on your cōcupiscences. 4 † Aduouterers, know you not that the * frendship of this vvorld, is the enemie of God? Vvhosoeuer therfore vvil be a frende of this vvorld: is made an enemie of God. 5 † Or do you thinke that the Scripture saieth in vaine: *To enuie doth the spirit couet vvhich dvvelleth in you?* 6 † And :: giueth greater grace. For the which cause it saith, *God resisteth the proud, & giueth grace to the humble.*

1. Io. 2, 15.

:: The boldnes of Hæretikes adding here the vvord *Scripture* to the text thus, *And the Scripture giueth greater grace.*

Prou. 3, 35. 1 Pet. 5, 5.

7 † Be subiect therfore to God, but resist the Deuil, and he 8 vvil flee from you. † c Approche to God, & he vvil approche to you. Cleanse your handes, ye sinners: and" purifie your 9 hartes, ye double of minde. † Be miserable, and mourne, & vveepe: let your laughter be turned into mourning: and ioy, 10 into sorovv. † * Be humbled in the sight of our lord, and he 11 vvil exalt you. † c Detracte not one frō an other my brethrē. He that detracteth from his brother, or he that iudgeth his brother, detracteth from the Law, and iudgeth the Law. But if thou iudge the Lavv, thou art not a doer of the Lavv, but a 12 iudge. † For there is one lavv-maker, and iudge that can de-13 stroy and deliuer. † But thou, * vvhat art thou that iudgest thy neighbour?

c Free vvil & mans owne endeuour necessarie in comming to God.

1 Pet. 5, 6.

c μὴ καταλαλεῖτε ἀλλήλων

c He forbiddeth detractiō, euil speaking, slaundering.

Ro. 14, 4.

Behold novv you that say, To day or to morovv vve vvil goe into that citie, and there certes vvil spend a yere, and 14 vvil traficke, and make our gaine († vvho are ignorāt vvhat shal be on the morovv. For vvhat is your life? It is a vapour appearing for a litle vvhile, and aftervvard it shal vanish 15 avvay) † for that you should say, :: If our Lord vvil: and, 16 If vve shal liue, vve vvil doe this or that. † But novv you reioyce in your arrogancies. Al such reioycing, is vvicked. 17 † To one therfore knovving to doe good, and not doing it: to him it is sinne.

:: Al promises and purposes of our worldly affaires are to be made vnder condition of Gods good liking & pleasure: and it becommeth a Christian man to haue vsually this forme of speache in that case, *If God vvil, if God otherWise dispose not.*

ANNOTATION
CHAP. IIII.

Mans vvorking vvith Gods grace, is no derogation therevnto.

8. *Purifie your hartes.*] Man (vve see here) maketh him self cleane and purgeth his owne hart. Vvhich derogateh nothing to the grace of God being the principal cause of the same. Yet Protestants thinke vve derogate from Christs Pasſion, vvhen vve attribute ſuch effects to our owne vvorkes, or to other ſecundarie helpes and cauſes.

CHAP. V.

By the damnatiō to come vpon the vnmerciful riche, he exhorteth the perſecuted to patience and by their ovvne revvard, and by examples. 12 Not to ſvveare at all in common talke. 13 In affliction, to pray: in proſperitie, to ſing: in ſicknes, to call for the Prieſts, and that they pray ouer them and anoile them vvith oile: and that the ſicke perſons confeſſe their ſinnes. 19 Finally, hovv meritorious it is, to conuert the erring vnto the Catholike faith, or the ſinner to amendment of life.

:: A feareful deſcription of the miſeries that ſhal befall in the next life to the vnmerciful couetous men.

GOE to novv ye riche men, vveepe, :: hovvling 1 in your miſeries vvhich ſhal come to you. † Your 2 riches are corrupt: and your garmentes are eaten of mothes. † Your gold and ſiluer is ruſted: and 3 their ruſt ſhal be for a teſtimonie to you, and ſhal eate your fleſh as fire. You haue ſtored to your ſelues vvrath in the laſt daies. † Behold" the hire of the vvorkemen that haue rea- 4 ped your fields, vvhich is defrauded of you, crieth: and their crie hath entred into the eares of the Lord of Sabboth. † You 5 haue made merie vpon the earth: and in riotouſnes you haue nouriſhed your hartes in the day of ſlaughter. † You haue 6 ' preſented, and ſlaine the iuſt one: and he reſiſted you not.

condemned

† Be patient therfore brethren, vntil the comming of our 7 Lord. Behold, the huſband man expecteth the pretious fruite of the earth: patiently bearing til he receiue c the timely and the latevvard. † Be you alſo patient, and confirme your 8 hartes: because the comming of our Lord ' vvil approche'. † Grudge not brethren one againſt an other: that you be not 9 iudged. Behold, the iudge ſtandeth before the gate. † Take 10 an example, brethren, of labour and patience, the prophetes: vvhich ſpake in the name of our Lord. † Behold vve accoūt 11 them bleſſed that haue ſuffered. The ſufferance of Iob you haue heard, and the end of our Lord you haue ſeen, becauſe our Lord is merciful and pitiful. † But before al things 12 my brethren, *" ſvveare not, neither by heauen, nor by earth, nor other othe whatſoeuer. But let your talke be, yea, yea: no, no:

c He meaneth either fruite or raine.

' is at hand.

Mt. 5, 34

no: that you fall not vnder iudgement.

The Epistle in a votiue Masse for the sicke.

13 † Is any of you in heauinesse? let him pray. Is he of a 14 cheereful hart? let him sing. † Is any man sicke amõg you? "let him bring in the priestes of the Churche, and let them pray ouer him, *"anoiling him vvith oile in the name of our 15 Lord. † and "the praier of faith" shal saue the sicke: and our Lord "shal lift him vp: and if he be in sinnes, "they shal 16 be remitted him. † [b]" Confesse therfore your sinnes one to an other: & pray one for an other that you may be saued. ⫞ 17 for the continual praier of a iust man auaileth much. † *Elias vvas a man like vnto vs passible: and vvith praier "he praied that it might not raine vpon the earth, and it rained not for 18 three yeres and sixe monethes. † And *he praied againe: and the heauen gaue raine, and the earth yelded her fruite.

Mr. 6, 13

b The Epistle in *Maioribus Litaniis* on S. Markes day, and in the Rogation daies.

3 reg. 17. Eccl. 48. Lu. 4, 25

3. reg. 18, 41.

b the heretikes translate, *Acknovvledge your sinnes. &c.* So litle they can abide the very vvord of confession.

19 † My brethren, if any of you shal erre from the truth, & 20 a man conuert him: † he must know that he vvhich maketh a sinner to be conuerted from the errour of his vvay, "shal saue his soule from death, and :: couereth a multitude of sinnes. ⫞

:: He that hath the zeale of conuerting sinners, procureth thereby mercie and remission to him self: vvhich is a singular grace.

ANNOTATIONS
CHAP. V.

4. *The hire.*] To vvithhold from the poore or labourer the hire or vvages that is due or promised to him for his seruice or vvorke done, is a great iniquitie, and one of those fiue sinnes vvhich in holy Vvrite be said to call for vengeance at Gods hand, as vve see here. They be called in the Catechisme, *Sinnes crying to heauen.* The other foure be, Murder, *Gen.* 18. v. 20. Vsurie, *Exod.* 22. v. 27. The sinne against nature, *Gen.* 18. v. 20. The oppression and vexation of vvidovves, pupilles, strangers, and such like. *Ib. & Exod.* 3. v. 9.

The sinnes crying to heauen.

12. *Svveare not.*] He forbiddeth not al othes, as the Anabaptists falsely say. for in iustice and iudgement vve may be by our lavvful Magistrate put to svveare, and may lavvfully take an othe, as also for the aduantaging of any necessarie truth vvhen time and place require. but the custom of svvearing, and al vaine, light, and vnnecessarie othes in our daily speache do displease God highly, and are here forbidden by the Apostle, as also by our Sauiour. *Mat.* 5.

Vvhat othes are lavvful, vvhat are not.

14. *Let him bring in the Priests.*] The Protestants for their special hatred of the holy order of Priesthod, as els vvhere often, so here they corrupt the text euidently, translating *Presbyteros,* elders. As though the Apostle had meant men of age, and not such as vvere by holy office, Priests. S. Chrysostom vvho knevv the sense and signification of the Greeke vvord according to the Ecclesiastical vse and the vvhole Churches iudgement, better then any Protestant aliue, taketh it plainely for *Sacerdotes,* that is, Priests *li.* 3 *de Sacerdotio prope initium.* And if they confesse that it is a vvord of office vvith them also, though they call them Elders, and not Priests: then vve demaund vvhether the Apostle meane here men of that function vvhich they in their nevv Churches call Elders. If they say no, as they must needes (for Elders vvith them are not deputed specially to publike praying or administration of the Sacraments, such as the Apostle here requireth to be sent for) then they must needes graunt, that their Elders ansvver not to the function of those vvhich in the nevv Testament are called *Presbyteri* in Greeke and Latin, and therfore both their translation to be false and fraudulent, and also their naming of their nevv degrees or orders to be fond and incongruous.

Heretical trãslation against Priesthod.

Neither their *Elders* (so called) nor their Ministers, can be those vvhõ the Apostle here calleth *Presbyteros.*

If they say their Ministers be correspondent to such as vvere called *Presbyteri* in holy vvrite and in the Primitiue Church, and that they are the men vvhom the Apostle villeth to be called for to anoile the sicke & to pray for him, vvhy do they not then translate *Presbyteros*, Ministers? Which they might doe vvith as good reason, as call such as they haue taken in steede of our Catholike Priests, Ministers. Vvhich vvord being in large acception common to all that haue to doe about the celebration of diuine things, vvas neuer appropriated by the vse either of Scripture or of the holy Church, to that higher function of publike administration of the Sacraments and Seruice, vvhich is Priesthod: but to the order next vnder it, vvhich is Deaconship. And therfore if any should be called Ministers, their Deacons properly should be so termed. And the Protestants haue no more reason to keepe the aũcient Greeke vvord of Deacon, appropriated to that office by the vse of antiquity, then to keepe the vvord Priest, being made no lesse peculiar to the state of such onely as minister the holy Sacraments, & offer the Sacrifice of the Altar. But these fellovves folovv neither Gods vvord nor Ecclesiastical vse, nor any reason, but mere phantasie, noueltie, and hatred of Gods Church. And hovv litle they folovv any good rule or reason in these things may appeare by this, that here they auoid to translate *Priests*, and yet in their Cõmunion booke, in their order of visiting the sicke, they commonly name the Minister, *Priest*.

They haue no reason to call their Ministers by that name.

Their Deacõs should rather be called Ministers.

They should keepe the name Priest, as vvel as deacon.

14. *Anoiling vvith oile.*] Here is the Sacrament of extreme Vnction so plainely promulgated (for it vvas instituted, as al other Sacraments of the nevv Testament, by our Sauiour Christ him self, and, as Venerable Bede thinketh and other auncient vvriters, the anoiling of the sicke vvith oile *Marc. 6.* pertaineth therevnto) that some Heretikes, for the euidence of this place also (as of the other for good vvorkes) deny the Epistle. Other (as the Caluinists) through their confidence of cunning shiftes and gloses, confessing that S. Iames is the author, yet condemne the Church of God for vsing and taking it for a Sacrament. But vvhat dishonour to God is it (vve pray them) that a Sacrament should be instituted in the matter of oile, more then in the element of vvater? Vvhy may not grace & remission of sinnes be annexed to the one as vvel as to the other, vvithout derogation to God?

The Sacramẽt of EXTREME VNCTION.

But they say, Sacraments endure for euer in the Church, this but for a season in the Primitiue Church. Vvhat Scripture telleth them that this general and absolute prescription of the Apostle in this case, should endure but for a season? vvhen vvas it taken avvay, abrogated, or altered? They see the Church of God hath alvvaies vsed it vpon this vvarrant of the Apostle, vvho knevve Christs meaning and institution of it better then these deceiued men, vvho make more of their ovvne fond ghesses and cõiectures, grounded neither on Scripture nor vpon any circumstance of the text, nor any one authentical author that euer vvrote, then of the expresse vvord of God. It vvas (say they) a miraculous practise of healing the sicke, during onely in the Apostles time, and not long after. Vve aske them vvhether Christ appointed any certaine creature or external element vnto the Apostles generally to vvorke miracles by. Him self vsed sometimes clay and spittle, sometimes he sent them that vvere diseased, to vvash them selues in vvaters. but that he appointed any of those or the like things for a general medicine or miraculous healing onely, that vve reade not. for in the beginning, for the better inducing of the people to faith and deuotion, Christ vvould haue miracles to be vvrought by sundry of the Sacraments also. Vvhich miraculous vvorkes ceasing, yet the Sacraments remaine still vnto the vvorldes end.

The heretikes obiections against the said Sacrament, ansvvered: and vvithal it is proued to be a Sacrament.

Againe vve demaund, vvhether euer they read or heard that men vvere generally commaunded to seeke for their health by miraculous meanes. Thirdly, vvhether al Priests, or (as they call them) Elders, had the gift of miracles in the primitiue Church? No, it can not be, for though some had, yet al these indifferently of vvhom the Apostle speaketh, had not the gift: and many that vvere no Priests, had it, both men and vvomen, vvhich yet could not be called for, as Priests vvere in this case. And though the Apostle and others could both cure men and reuiue them againe, yet there vvas no such general precept for sicke or dead men, as this, to call for the Apostles to heale or restore them to life againe. Lastly, had any external element or miraculous practise, vnles it vvere a Sacrament, the promisse of remission of al kinde of actual sinnes ioyned vnto it? or could S. Iames institute such a ceremonie him self, that could saue both body and soule, by giuing health to the one, and grace and remission to the other? At other times these contentious vvranglers raile at Gods Church, for annexing only the remission of venial sinnes to the element of vvater, made holy by the Priests blessing thereof in the name of Christ, and his vvord: and loe here they are driuen to hold that S. Iames prescribed a miraculous oile or creature vvhich had much more povver and efficacie. Into these straites are such miscreants brought that vvil not beleeue the expresse vvord of God, interpreted by the practise of Gods vniuersal Church.

Remission of sinnes annexed to creatures.

Holy vvater.

Venerable Bede in 9 Luc. saith thus. *It is cleere that this custome vvas deliuered to the holy Church by the Apostles them selues, that the sicke should be anointed vvith oile consecrated by the Bishops blessing.* See for this, and for the assertion & vse of this Sacrament, S. Innocentius *ep. 1 ad Decentium Eugubinum cap. 8. to. 1. Conc. & Lib. 2. de visitatione infirmorum* in S. Augustine *cap. 4. Concil. Cabilonense 2. cap. 48. Conc. Wormatiense cap. 72. to. 3. Conc. Aquisgra. c. 8. Florentinum,* and other later Councels. S. Bernard in the life of Malachie *in fine.* This holy oile because the faithful savv to haue such vertue in the primitiue Church, diuers caried it home and occupied it in their infirmities, not vsing it in the Sacramental sort vvhich the Apostle prescribeth, as the Aduersaries vnlearnedly obiect

Holy oile blessed by the Bishop.

The peoples deuotion tovvard such hallowed creatures.

vnto

vnto vs: but as Christians novv do (and then also did) concerning the vvater of Baptisme, vvhich they vsed to take home vvith them after it vvas hallovved, and to giue it their diseased to drinke

The sacramental vvordes.

15. *The praier of faith.*] He meaneth the forme of the Sacrament, that is, the vvordes spoken at the same time vvhen the partie is anoiled, vvhich no doubt are most auncient and Apostolike. Not that the vvord or praier alone should haue that great effect here mentioned, but ioyned vvith the foresaid vnction, as is plaine.

The three effects of this Sacrament.

15. *Shal saue.*] The first effect of this Sacrament is, to saue the soule, by giuing grace and comfort to vvithstand the terrours and tentations of the enemie, going about (specially in that extremitie of death) to driue men to desperation or distresse of minde and other damnable inconueniences. the vvhich effect is signified in the matter of this Sacrament specially.

15. *Shal lift him vp.*] Vvhen it shal be good for the saluation of the partie, or agreable to Gods honour, this Sacramét restoreth also a man to bodily health againe, as experience ofté teacheth vs. Vvhich yet is not done by vvay of miracle, to make the partie sodenly vvhole, but by Gods ordinarie prouidence and vse of second causes, vvhich othervvise should not haue had that effect, but for the said Sacrament. This is the second effect.

Priests (and not Elders) are the ministers of this sacrament.

15. *They shal be remitted him.*] Vvhat sinnes soeuer remaine vnremitted, they shal in this Sacrament and by the grace thereof be remitted, if the persons vvorthely receiue it. this is the third effect. S. Chrysostom of this effect saith thus: *They* (speaking of Priests) *do not onely remit sinnes in baptisme, but aftervvard also, according to the saying of S. Iames, If any be sicke, let him bring in the Priests &c. Li. 3 de Sacerd. prope initiũ.* Let the Protestãts marke that he calleth *Presbyteros, sacerdotes*: that is, *Priests*, and maketh them the onely ministers of this Sacrament, and not elders or other lay men. By al vvhich you see this Sacrament of al other to be maruelous plainely set forth by the Apostle. Onely sicke men and (as * the Greeke vvord giueth) men very vveake must receiue it: onely Priests must be the ministers of it: the matter of it is holy oile: the forme is praier, in such sort as vve see novv vsed: the effects be as is aforesaid. Yet this so plaine a matter and so profitable a Sacrament, the enemie by Heretikes vvould vvholy abolish.

* ἀσθενοῦντας

Confession

In hunc locum.

16. *Confesse therfore.*] It is not certaine that he speaketh here of sacramental Confession: yet the circumstance of the letter vvel beareth it, and very probable it is that he meaneth of it: and Origen doth so expound it *ho. 2 in Leuit.* & Venerable Bede vvriteth thus, *In this sentence* (saith he) *there must be this discretion, that our daily and litle sinnes vve confesse one to an other, vnto our equals, and beleeue to be saued by their daily praier. but the vncleannes of the greater leprosie let vs according to the lavv open to the Priest, and at his pleasure in vvhat maner and hovv long time he shal commaund, let vs be careful to be purified.* But the Protestants fleing from the very vvord confession in despite of the Sacrament, translate thus, *Acknovvledge your faultes one to an other* They do not vvel like to haue in one sentence, Priests, praying ouer the sicke, anoiling them, forgiuing them their sinnes, confession, and the like.

Truthes vnvvritten and knovven by tradition.

17. *He praied.*] The Scriptures to vvhich the Apostle alludeth, make no métion of Elias praier. therfore he knevv it by tradition or reuelation. Vvhereby vve see that many things vnvvritten be of equal truth vvith the things vvritten.

Conuerting of soules

20. *Maketh to be conuerted.*] Here vve see the great revvard of such as seeke to conuert Heretikes or other sinners from errour and vvickednes: and hovv necessarie an office it is, specially for a Priest.

Our saluation attributed to men, vvithout derogation to Christ.

20. *Shal saue.*] Vve see, it derogateth not from God, to attribute our saluation to any man or Angel in heauen or earth, as to the vvorkers thereof vnder God, by their praiers, preaching, correction, counsel, or othervvise. Yet the Heretikes are so folish and captious in this kinde, that they can not heare patiently, that our B. Lady or others should be counted meanes or vvorkers of our saluation.

THE ARGVMENT OF BOTH THE EPISTLES OF S. PETER, THE FIRST, AND THE SECOND.

F S. Peter vve reade at large, both in the Gospels, and in the Actes of the Apostles: and namely, that Christ designed him, and also made him his vicar (as S. Mathevv for that cause in the catalogue of the Apostles, calleth him Primus, the first, *and all antiquitie,* Princeps Apostolorum, the Prince of the Apostles) *and that he accordingly executed that office after Christes departure, plāting the Church first among the Ievves in Hierusalem and in al that countrey and coastes about, as Christ also him self before had preached to the Ievves alone.*

c. 10. v. 2.

*But preaching at length to the Gentiles also, according to Christes commission (Mat. 28. v. 19.) and being novv come to Rome, the head citie of the Gentiles, from thence he vvriteth this Epistle to his Christian Ievves hauing care of them in his absence, no lesse then vvhen he vvas present: and not to the Ievves that vvere at home, (belike because they had S. Iames, or his successor S. Simon Cleophæ, resident vvith them) but * to them that vvere dispersed in Pontus, Galatia, Cappadocia, and Bithynia.*

1 Pet. 1.

And that he vvriteth it from Rome, him self signifieth, saying: The Church that is in Babylon saluteth you. ** Vvhere by Babylon he meaneth Rome, as al antiquitie doth interpret him: not, that he so calleth the Church of Rome, but the heathen state of the Romane empire, vvhich then, and 300 yeres after, vnto the conuersion of Constantinus the Emperour, did persecute the elect Church of Rome, in so much that the first 33 Bishops thereof vnto S. Siluester, vvere al Martyrs.*

1 Pet. 5.

* See the Annotation 1 Pet. 5. v. 13.

For the matter vvhereof he vvriteth, him self doth signifie it in these vvordes: This loe the second Epistle I vvrite to you, my deerest, in vvhich (Epistles) I stirre vp by admonition, your sincere minde, that you may be mindeful of those vvordes &c. *So he saith there of both together. And againe of the first to the same purpose, in an other place:* I haue breefely vvritten, beseeching and testifying that this is the true grace of God, vvherein you stand. *For, there vvere at that time certaine Seducers (as * S. August. also hath told vs) vvho vvent about to teach* Onely faith, *as though good vvorkes vvere not necessarie, nor meritorious. there vvere also great persecutions, to compel them vvith terrour to denie Christ & al his religiō He therfore exhorteth thē accordingly, neither for persecution neither by seduction to forsake it: though in the first, his exhortation is more principally against persecution: and in the second, more principally against seduction. The first epistle is noted to be very like to S. Paules epistle to the Ephesians, in vvordes also, and so thicke of Scriptures, as though he spake nothing els.*

2 Pet. 3.

1 Pet. 5.

* See the Annotatiō vpon S. Iames epistle c. 2. v. 21.

The time vvhen the first vvas vvritten, is vncertaine: the second vvas vvrittē a litle before his death, as is gathered by his vvordes in the same. c. 1. v. 14.

THE

THE FIRST EPISTLE OF PETER THE APOSTLE.

CHAP. I.

He comforteth them in their persecutions (being novv by Baptisme made the children of God) vvith the hope of their heauenly inheritance: 6 shevving hovv meritorious it is for them to be so constant in faith, 10 and confirming them therein vvith the authoritie of the Prophets and of the Holy Ghost. 15 Exhorting them to liue also accordingly in al holines, 15 considering the holines of God, the vprightnes of his iudgement, the price of their redemption by Christ, 22 and the vertue of the seede in them (Which is grace regeneratiue in Baptisme) foretold by the Prophet also.

The Epistle *In Cathedra S. Petri Romæ.* Ian. 18.

1 PETER an Apostle of IESVS Christ, to the electe strangers of the dispersion of Pontus, Galatia, Cappadocia, Asia, and Bithynia, 2 † according to the prescience of God the Father, into sanctification of the Spirit, vnto the obedience and sprinkling of the bloud of IESVS Christ: Grace to you and peace be multiplied.

The Epistle for many martyrs.

2 Cor. 1, 3. Eph. 1, 3.

3 † Blessed be God and the father of our Lord IESVS Christ, vvho according to his great mercie hath regenerated vs vnto a liuely hope, by the resurrection of IESVS Christ from the dead, 4 † vnto an inheritance incorruptible, and incontaminate, and that can not fade, conserued in the heauens in you, 5 † (vvho in the vertue of God are kept by faith vnto saluatiõ) ready to be reuealed in the last time. 6 † wherin you shal reioyce, a litle novv if you must be made heauy in diuerse tentations: 7 † that the probation of your faith much more pretious then gold (vvhich is proued by the fire) may be found vnto praise and glorie and honour in the reuelatiõ of IESVS Christ: ⁋ 8 † vvhom hauing not seen, you loue: in vvhom novv also not seing you beleeue: and beleeuing you reioyce vvith ioy vnspeakable and glorified, 9 † receiuing the end of your faith, the saluation of your soules

soules. † Of the vvhich saluation the Prophetes inquired & searched, vvhich prophecied of the grace to come in you, 10 † searching vnto vvhich or vvhat maner of time the Spirit 11 of Christ in them did signifie: foretelling those passions that are in Christ and the glories folovving: to vvhom it vvas re- 12 uealed, that not to thẽ selues, but to you they ministred those things vvhich novv are told you by them that haue euangelized to you, the holy Ghost being sent from heauen, on vvhom the Angels desire to looke.

† For the vvhich cause hauing the loines of your ∵ minde 13 girded, sober, trust perfectly in that grace vvhich is offered you, in the reuelation of IESVS Christ, † as children of o- 14 bedience, not configurated to the former desires of your ignorance: † but according to him that hath called you, the 15 Holy one, be you also in al conuersation holy: † because 16 it is vvritten: *You shal be holy, because I am holy.* † And if you in- 17 uocate the Father, him vvhich * vvithout acception of persons iudgeth according to euery ones [c] vvorke: in feare conuerse ye the time of your peregrination. † Knovving that 18 * not vvith corruptible things, gold or siluer, you are redeemed from your vaine conuersation of your fathers ∵ tradition: † but vvith the pretious bloud as it vvere of an im- 19 maculate and vnspotted lambe, Christ, † * foreknovven 20 in deede before the constitution of the vvorld, but manifested in the last times for you, † vvhich by him are faithful 21 in God vvho raised him from the dead, and hath giuen him glorie, that your faith and hope might be in God. † Making 22 your soules chaste in obedience of charitie, in the sincere loue of the fraternitie from the hart loue ye one an other 23 earnestly: † borne againe not of corruptible seede, but incorruptible by the vvord of God vvho liueth and remaineth for euer. † For *al flesh is as grasse: and al the glorie thereof as the* 24 *floure of grasse. the grasse is vvithered, and the floure thereof is fallen avvay.* † But the vvord of our Lord remaineth for euer, and this 25 is the vvord that is euangelized among you.

∵ Chastitie not onely of body but also of minde, is required. *S. Bede vpon this place.*

c God vvil iudge men according to euery ones vvorkes, and not by faith onely.

∵ He meaneth the errours of Gentility. or if he vvrite to the Iewes dispersed, he meaneth the yoke of the Law vvith the fond and heauy additiõs of their later Maisters, called *Deuterôses.* The heretikes, to make it sound to the simple against the traditions of the Churche, corrupt the text thus. *Which you haue receiued by tradition of the fathers.*

Leu. 11, 19. 20, 7

Deu. 10.

Ro. 2.

Gal. 2.

1 *Cor.* 6, 20. 7, 23.

Ro. 16, 25. *Col.* 1, 26. *Tit.* 1, 2.

Esa. 40, 6.

CHAP. II.

Novv

Novv after their Baptisme, vvhat must be their meate: 4 and being come to Christ, hovv happie they be aboue their incredulous brethren, according to the Scriptures also. 11 Wherevpon he beseecheth them to shine in good life among the Heathen, so to procure their conuersion: 13 to be obedient subiects to higher Povvers (hovvsoeuer some misconster Christian libertie) 14 and seruants to obey their Maisters. 19 And so, doing vvel, though they suffer for it, it is very meritorious, 21 vvhereas Christ also not onely gaue them example, 24 but also by his death hath made them able to liue iustly.

1 LAYING avvay therfore al malice, and al guile, and simulations, and enuies, and al detractions, 2 † as infants euen novv borne, reasonable, milke vvithout guile desire ye, that in it you may grovv vnto saluatiō. 3 † if yet you haue tasted that our Lord is svveete.

The Epistle vpon Saturday in Easter weeke.

4 † Vnto vvhom approching, a liuing stone, of men in deede reprobated, but of God elect and made honorable: 5 † be ye also your selues superedified as it vvere liuing stones, 'spiritual houses', a holy priesthod, to offer "spiritual hostes, acceptable to God by IESVS Christ. 6 † For the vvhich cause the Scripture conteineth, *Behold I put in Sion a principal corner stone elect, pretious. and he that shal beleeue in him, shal not be confounded.* 7 † To you therfore that beleeue, honour: but to them that beleeue not, *the stone vvhich the builders reiected, the same is made into the head of the corner:* 8 † and * a stone of offense, and a rocke of scandal, to them that stumble at the vvord, neither doe beleeue 'wherin also they are put'. 9 † But you are an * elect generation, a c kingly priesthod, a holy nation, a people of purchase: that you may declare his vertues vvhich from darkenesse hath called you into his marueulous light. 10 † *Vvhich sometime not a people: but novv the people of God. Vvhich not hauing obtained mercie: but novv hauing obtained mercie.*

a spiritual house,

Es. 28, 16.

Ps. 117. *Mt.* 21. *Act.* 4.

Es. 8. *Ro.* 9, 33.

Exo. 19. *Apoc.* 1.

Ose. 2. *Ro.* 9.

Gal. 5, 16.

c The Protestants can no more gather of this, that al Christians be Priests: then, that al be kings: as is most plaine *Apocalyp.* 1, 6. and 5, 10. *Thou hast made vs a kingdom (or kings) & priests.*

` *vvhereto also they are ordeined.*

11 † My deerest I beseche you as strangers & pilgrimes, * to refraine your selues from carnal desires which vvarre against the soule, 12 † hauing your conuersation good among the Gentiles: that in that vvherein they misreport of you as of malefactors, by the good vvorkes considering you, * they may glorifie God in the day of visitation. 13 † * " Be subiect therfore to euery :: humane c creature for God: vvhether it be " to king, as excelling: 14 † or to rulers as sent by him to the reuenge of malefactors, but to the praise of the good: 15 † for so is the vvil of God, that doing vvel you may make the ignorance of vnvvise men to be dumme: 16 † as free, & " not

Mt. 5, 16

Ro. 13, 1.

κτίσει

The Epistle vpō the 3 Sunday after Easter.

:: So is the Greeke, but the Protest. in fauour of temporal lawes made against the Cath. religion, translate it very falsely thus, *to al maner ordināce of man:* the selues boldly reiecting Ecclesiastical decrees as mēs ordinances.

as hauing the freedom for a cloke of malice, but as the seruants of God. † Honour al men. [c] Loue the fraternitie. Feare 17 God. Honour the king.

c In this speache is often commẽded the vnitie of al Christians among them selues.

† Seruants be subiect in al feare to your maisters, not only 18 to the good & modest," but also to the vvaivvard. † For this 19 is thanke, if for cõscience of God a man sustaine sorovves, suffering vniustly. † For vvhat glorie is it; if sinning, and buf- 20 feted you suffer? but if doing vvel you sustaine patiently: this is thanke before God. † For vnto this are you called: 21 because Christ also suffred for \`vs', leauing \`you' an example that you may folovv his steppes. † *vvho did no sinne, neither vvas* 22 *guile found in his mouth.* † vvho vvhen he vvas reuiled, [c] did not 23 reuile: vvhen he suffred, he threatened not: but deliuered him self to him that iudged him vniustly. † vvho him self* bare 24 our sinnes in his body vpon the tree: that dead to sinnes, we may liue to iustice. by vvhose stripes you are healed. † For 25 you vvere as sheepe straying: but you be conuerted novv to the Pastor and Bishop of your soules. ⊣

The Epistle vpõ the 2 Sunday after Easter.

\`you \`vs
Es. 53, 9.
c οὐκ ἀντελοιδόρει
Es. 53, 4. Mt. 8, 17.

ANNOTATIONS
CHAP. II.

Spiritual hostes and Priests.

5. *Spiritual hostes.*] Here vve see, that as he speaketh of spiritual hostes, vvhich euery Christian man offereth, so he speaketh not properly of priesthod, vvhen he maketh al Priests, but of a spiritual priesthod. Which spiritual priesthod vvas also in al the Ievves: but the priesthod (properly so called) vvas onely in the sonnes of Aaron, and they offered the sacrifices (properly so called) vvhich none besides might offer.

Obedience to temporal princes.

13. *Be subiect.*] Not onely our Maister Christ, but the Apostles and al Christians vvere euer charged by such as thought to bring them in hatred vvith Princes, vvith disobedience to kings and temporal Magistrates. therfore both * S. Paul and this Apostle do specially vvarne the faithful, that they giue no occasiõ by their il demeanure to secular Princes, that the Heathen should count them disobedient or seditious vvorkers against the States of the vvorld.

Ro. 13.

God instituted the Spiritual gouernemẽt in more excellẽt maner then the temporal.

13. *To euery humane creature.*] So he calleth the temporal Magistrate elected by the people, or holding their Soueraintу by birth & carnal propagation, ordained for the vvorldly vvealth, peace, and prosperitie of the subiects: to put a difference betvvixt that humane Superiority, and the spiritual Rulers and regiment, guiding and gouerning the people to an higher end, and instituted by God him self immediatly. for Christ did expresly constitute the forme of regiment vsed euer since in the Church. He made one the cheefe, placing Peter in the Supremacie: he called the Apostles and Disciples, giuing them their seueral authorities. Aftervvard * God guided the lot for choise of S. Matthias in Iudas place: and the Holy Ghost expresly and namely seuered and chose Paul and Barnabas vnto their Apostolical function: and generally the Apostle saith of al spiritual Rulers, *The holy Ghost hath placed you to rule the Church of God.*

Act. 1.
Act. 20.

And although al povver be of God, and kings rule by him, yet that is no othervvise, but by his ordinarie concurrence, and prouidence, vvhereby he procureth the earthly cõmodity or vvealth of men, by maintaining of due superiority and subiection one tovvards an other, and by giuing povver to the people and Commonvvealth to choose to them selues some kinde or forme of Regiment, vnder vvhich they be content to liue for their preseruation in peace and tranquillity. But Spiritual superiority is far more excellent, as in more excellent sort depending, not of mans ordinance, election, or (as this Apostle speaketh) creation, but of the Holy Ghost, vvho is alvvaies resident in the Church (vvhich is Christs body mystical, and therfore an other manner of Com-

monWealth

monvvealth then the earthly) concurring in singular sort to the creation of al necessarie Officers in the said Church, euen to the vvorlds end, as S. Paul vvriteth to the Ephesians.

Eph. 4.

Lest therfore the people, being then in so precise sort alvvaies vvarned of the excellencie of their Spiritual gouernours * and of their obedience tovvard them, might neglect their dueties to Temporal Magistrates, specially being infidels, and many times tyrants and persecutors of the faith, as Nero and other vvere then: therfore S. Peter here vvarneth them to be subiect, for their bodies and goods and other temporal things, euen to the vvorldly Princes both infidels and Christians, vvhom he calleth humane creatures.

Hebr. 13.

13. *To the king as excelling.*] Some simple heretikes & others also not vnlearned, at the begining, for lacke of better places, vvould haue proued by this, that the king vvas head of the Church, and aboue al Spiritual rulers: and to make it sound better that vvay, they falsely translated it, *To the king as to the cheefe head.* in the Bible of the yere 1562. But it is euident that he calleth the king, the precellent or more excellent, in respect of his Vicegerents vvhich he calleth Dukes or Gouernours that be at his appointment: and not in respect of Popes, Bishops, or Priests, as they haue the rule of mens soules: vvho could not in that charge be vnder such Kings or Emperours as the Apostle speaketh of: no more then the kings or Emperours then, could be heads of the Church, being Heathen men and no members thereof, much lesse the cheefe members. See a notable place in S. Ignatius ep. ad Smyrnenses, vvhere he exhorteth them first to honour God, next the Bishop, & then the king.

Heret. translation.

The Kings excellencie of power is in respect of the nobilitie and lay magistrates vnder him.

This is an inuincible demonstration, that this text maketh not for any spiritual claime of earthly kings, because it giueth no more to any Prince then may and ought to be done and graunted to a Heathen Magistrate. Neither is there any thing in al the nevv Testament that proueth the Prince to be head or cheefe gouernour of the Church in spiritual or Ecclesiastical causes, more then it proueth any heathen Emperour of Rome to haue been. for they vvere bound in temporal things to obey the heathen being lavvful kings, to be subiect to them euen for conscience, to keepe their temporal lavves, to pay them tribute, to pray for them, and to doe al other natural duties: and more no scriptures binde vs to doe to Christian kinges.

Christiã Princes haue no more right to be supreme heads in spiritual causes, then the Heathen.

16. *Not as hauing.*] There vvere some Libertines in those daies, as there be novv, that vnder pretence of libertie of the Gospel, sought to be free from subiection and lawes of men as novv vnder the like vvicked pretence, Heretikes refuse to obey their spiritual rulers and to obserue their lawes.

Libertines.

18. *But also the vvaivvard.*) The Vviclefistes and their folovvers in these daies, sometimes to moue the people vnto sedition, hold and teach that maisters and magistrates lose their authoritie ouer their seruants and subiects, if they be once in deadly sinne, and that the people in that case neede not in conscience obey them. Vvhich is a pernicious and false doctrine, as is plaine by this place, vvhere vve be expresly commaunded to obey euen the il-conditioned. vvhich must be alvvaies vnderstood, if they commaund nothing against God. for then this rule is euer to be folovved. *Vve must obey God rather then men.* Act. 5, 29.

Deadly sinnes of Princes or Superiors exempt not the subiectes frõ obedience, as Wicleffe held.

CHAP. III.

The dutie of vviues and husbands to ech other. 9 None to doe or speake euil by their persecutors, 15 but to ansvver them alvvaies vvith modestie, and specially vvith innocencie, after the example of Christ most innocet: vvhose body though they killed, yet his soule liued and preached aftervvard to the soules in Hel (namely to those in the time of Noes floud being a figure of our Baptisme) rose againe, and ascended.

1 IN like maner also * let the vvomen be subiect to their husbandes: that if any beleeue not the vvord, by the conuersation of the 2 vvomen vvithout the vvord they may be vvonne, † considering your chast conuer-3 sation in feare. † Vvhose trimming let it not be outvvardly the plaiting of heare, or laying on gold round about, or of putting on vestures: 4 † but the man of the hart that is hidden, in the incorruptibi-

Eph. 5, 28. Col. 3, 18.

1 Tim. 2, 9.

Hovv vviues should behaue them selues tovvard their husbands.

Against the proud, curious and costly attire of vvomẽ, vvherein this il time of ours exceedeth.

litie of a quiet and a modeſt ſpirit, vvhich is riche in the ſight of God. † For ſo ſometime the holy vvomen alſo that truſted in God, adorned them ſelues, ſubiect to their ovvne huſbandes. † As *Sara obeied Abraham, calling him lord: ᶜvvhoſe daughters you are, doing vvel, and not fearing any perturbation. † Huſbandes likevviſe, dvvelling vvith them according to knovvledge, as vnto the vveaker feminine veſſel imparting honour, as it vvere to the coheires alſo of the grace of life: that your praiers be not hindered. 5 6 7

Gen. 18.

c is

Hovv huſbands ſhould behaue them ſelues tovvard their vviues.

† And ˋin fineˊ al of one minde, hauing compaſſion, louers of the fraternitie, merciful, modeſt, humble. † * not rendering euil for euil, nor curſe for curſe: but contrariewiſe, bleſſing: for vnto this are you called, that you may by inheritāce poſſeſſe a benediction. † *For he that vvil loue life, and ſee good daies: let him refraine his tong from euil, and his lippes that they ſpeake not guile. † Let him decline from euil, and doe good: let him enquire peace, and folovv it: † becauſe the eies of our Lord are vpon the iuſt, and his eares vnto their praiers: but the countenance of our Lord vpon them that doe euil things.* † And vvho is he that can hurt you, if you be emulators of good? † But* & if you ſuffer ought for iuſtice, bleſſed are ye. And the feare of them feare ye not, & be not troubled. † But ſanctifie our Lord Chriſt in your hartes, ready alwaies to ſatiſfie euery one that aſketh you a reaſon of that hope vvhich is in you: † but vvith modeſtie and feare, hauing a good conſcience: that in that vvhich they ſpeake il of you, they may be confounded vvhich calumniate your good conuerſation in Chriſt. † For it is better to ſuffer as doing vvel (if the vvil of God vvil haue it ſo) then doing il. 8 9 10 1 112 13 14 15 16 17

ˋ*in faith*

Pro. 17, 13. Mat. 5, 44.

Pſ. 33, 13

Mat. 5, 10.

The Epiſtle vpon friday in Eaſter vveeke.

† Becauſe Chriſt alſo died once for our ſinnes, the iuſt for the vniuſt: that he might offer vs to God, mortified certes in fleſh, but quickened in ſpirit. † In the vvhich ſpirit comming he preached "toˋ themˊ alſo that vvere in priſon: † vvhich had been "incredulous ſometime, * vvhen they expected the patience of God in the daies of Noë, vvhen the arke vvas a building: in the vvhich, fevv, that is, * eight ſoules vvere ſaued by vvater. † Vvherevnto Baptiſme being" of the like forme novv ſaueth ˋyouˊ alſo: not the laying avvay of the filth of the fleſh, but "the examination of a good conſcience tovvard God by the reſurrection of IESVS Chriſt. † vvho is on the right hand of God, ⊣ ſvvallovving death, that vve might be made heires of life euerlaſting: being gone into heauen, Angels and Potentates and Povvers ſubiected to him. 18 19 20 21 22

ˋ*thoſe ſpirites*

Gen. 6. Mat. 24 Gen. 7, 7

ˋ*vs*

AN

ANNOTATIONS
CHAP. III.

19. *To them that vvere in prison.*] S. Augustine in his 99 Epistle *in principio*, confesseth this place to be exceding hard to vnderstand, & to haue many difficulties vvhich he could neuer explicate to his ovvne satisfaction. Yet vnto Heretikes this and al other textes be easie, not doubting but that is the sense vvhich them selues imagin, vvhatsoeuer other men deeme thereof. S. Augustine onely findeth him self sure of this, that Christs descending into Hel in soule after his death, is plainely proued hereby. Vvhich thing he declareth there, to be conformable to diuers other expresse vvordes of holy Vvrite, and namely to this same Apostles sermon *Act.* 2. And at length he concludeth thus, *Quis ergo nisi infidelis negauerit fuisse apud inferos Christum?* that is, *Therfore vvho but an infidel, vvil deny that Christ vvas in Hel?* Caluin thẽ (you see) vvith al his folovvers are infidels, vvho in steede of this descending of Christ in soule after his death, haue inuented an other desperate kinde of Christs being in Hel, vvhẽ he vvas yet aliue on the Crosse. S. Athanasius also in his epistle cited by S. Epiphanius *har.* 77 *in principio*, and in his booke *de Incarnatione Verbi propius initio*, S. Cyril *de recta fide ad Theodosium*, Oecumenius, and diuers others vpon this place, proue Christs descending to Hel. As they likevvise declare vpon the vvordes folovving, that he preached to the spirites or soules of mẽ deteined in Hel or in Prison.

Christ in soule descẽded vnto hel, vvhiles his body lay in the graue.

The Caluinists denying the same, are (by S. Augustines iudgement) infidels.

But vvhether this vvord *Prison* or *Hel* be meant of the inferiour place of the damned, or of *Limbus patrum* called Abrahams bosome, or some other place of temporal chastisement: and, to vvhom he preached there, and vvho by his preaching or presence there vvere deliuered, and vvho they vvere that are called, *Incredulous in the daies of Noë*: al these things S. Augustine calleth great profundities, confessing him self to be vnable to reache vnto it: onely holding fast and assured this article of our faith, that he deliuered none deputed to damnation in the lovvest hel, and yet not doubting but that he released diuers out of places of paines there. vvhich can not be out of any other place then Purgatorie. See the said Epistle, vvhere also he insinuateth other expositions for explication of the manifold difficulties of this hard text, vvhich vvere to long to reherse, our special purpose being onely to note briefely the things that touche the controuersies of this time.

Certaine difficulties vvhereof S. Augustine doubteth.

Purgatorie.

20. *Incredulous sometime.*] They that take the former vvordes, of Christs descending to Hel, and deliuering certaine there deteined, do expound this, not of such as died in their infidelitie or vvithout al faith in God, for such vvere not deliuered: but either of some that once vvere incredulous, and aftervvard repented before their death: or rather and specially of such as othervvise vvere faithful, but yet trusted not Noës preaching by his vvorke and vvord, that God vvould destroy the vvorld by vvater. Vvho yet being othervvise good men, vvhen the matter came to passe, vvere sorie for their errour, and died by the floud corporally, but yet in state of saluation, and being chastised for their fault in the next life, vvere deliuered by Christs descending thither. and not they onely, but al others in the like conditiõ. For the Apostle giueth these of Noës time but for an example.

Vvhat vvere the incredulous persons of vvhom the Apostle here speaketh.

21. *Of the like forme.*] The vvater bearing vp the Arke from sinking, and the persons in it from drowning, vvas a figure of Baptisme, that likewise saueth the vvorthie receiuers from euerlasting perishing. *As Noë* (saith S. Augustine) *vvith his, vvas deliuered by the vvater and the vvood, so the familie of Christ by Baptisme signed vvith Christs Passion on the Crosse. Li.* 12. *Cont. Faustum c.* 14. Againe he saith, that as the vvater saued none out of the Arke, but vvas rather their destruction: so the Sacrament of Baptisme receiued out of the Catholike Church at Heretikes or Schismatikes hands, though it be the same vvater and Sacrament that the Catholike Church hath, yet profiteth none to saluation, but rather vvorketh their perdition. Vvhich yet is not meant in case of extreme necessitie, vvhen the partie should die vvithout the said Sacrament, except he tooke it at an Heretikes or Schismatikes hand. Neither is it meant in the case of infants, to vvhom the Sacrament is cause of saluation, they being in no fault for receiuing it at the hands of the vnfaithful, though their parents and frendes that offer them vnto such to be baptized, be in no small fault. S. Hierom to Damasus Pope of Rome, compareth that See to the Arke, & them that communicate vvith it, to them that vvere saued in the Arke: al other Schismatikes and Heretikes, to the rest that vvere drowned.

Ibid. c. 17.

Ep. 57.

Noës Arke & the vvater, a figure of christs Crosse & Baptisme.

Baptisme receiued of Heretikes or Schismatikes, vvhen damnable, vvhen not.

21. *The examination of a good conscience.*) The Apostle seemeth to allude here to the very forme of Catholike Baptisme, conteining certaine interrogatories and solemne promises made of the articles of the Christian faith, and of good life, and of renouncing Satan and al his pompes and vvorkes. vvhich (no doubt) hovvsoeuer the Caluinists esteeme of them, are the very Apostolike ceremonies vsed in the ministration of this Sacrament. *See S. Denys in fine Ec. hierarchia. S. Cyril li.* 12 *in Io. c.* 64. *S. Augustine ep.* 23. *S. Basil de Sp. sancto c.* 12 and 15. *S. Ambrose de ijs qui mysterijs initiantur c.* 2. 3. 4.

The ceremonies of Baptisme, namely *Abrenuntio. &c.*

CHAP. IIII.

That they arme them selues to sinne no more after Baptisme, against the tentations of the Heathen, considering that the general end novv approcheth. 8 specially tovvard their euen-Christians to shevv their charitie, hospitalitie, and grace, doing al to the glorie of God. 12 And as for being persecuted because they are Christians, to reioyce, considering the revvard that they shal haue vvith Christ, and damnation that they auoid thereby.

HRIST therfore hauing suffered in the flesh, be you also armed vvith the same cogitation. because he that hath suffered in the flesh, hath ceased from sinnes: † that novv not after the desires of men, but according to the vvil of God he liue the rest of his time in the flesh. † For the time past sufficeth (to accomplish the vvil of the Gentiles) them that haue vvalked in riotousnes, desires, excesse of wine, banketings, potations, and vnlavvful seruices of Idols. † Vvherein they maruel blaspheming, you not concurring into the same confusion of riotousnes. † vvho shal render account to him, vvhich is ready to iudge the liuing and the dead. † For, for this cause also vvas ∴ it euangelized to the dead: that they may be iudged in deede according to men, in the flesh: but may liue according to God in the Spirit. † And the end of al 'shal approche'. 1 2 3 4 5 6 7

∴ It hath the same difficulty and sense that the other like wordes haue before, *Chap.* 3. See the annotation there *v.* 19. and S. Aug. *ep.* 69. & Oecumenius *vpon this place.*

is at hand.

The Epistle vpon Sunday next after the Ascension.

† Be vvise therfore: and vvatch in praiers. † But before al things, hauing mutual charitie cõtinual among your selues: because* "charitie couereth the multitude of sinnes. † * Vsing hospitalitie one tovvard an other vvithout murmuring. † * Euery one as he hath receiued grace, ministring the same one tovvard an other: as good dispensers of the manifold grace of God. † If any man speake, as the vvordes of God. if any man minister: as of the povver, vvhich God administreth. that in al things God may be honoured by IESVS Christ: ✠ to vvhom is glorie and empire for euer and euer. Amen. 8 9 10 11

Prou. 10 *Ro.* 12, *Heb.* 13. *Ro.* 12, 6.

† My deerest, thinke it not strange in the feruour vvhich is to you for a tẽtation, as though some nevv thing happened to you: † but communicating vvith the passions of Christ, be glad, that in the reuelation also of his glorie you may be glad reioycing. † * If you be reuiled in the name of Christ, you shal be blessed: because that vvhich is of the honour, glorie, 12 13 14

The Epistle for a Martyr.

Mt. 5, 11.

glorie, and vertue of God, and the Spirit vvhich is his, ſhal
15 reſt vpon you. † But let none of you ſuffer as a murderer, or a theeſe, or a railer, or a coueter of other mens things.
16 † But if as a Chriſtian, let him not be aſhamed, but let him
17 glorifie God in this name. † for * the time is "that iudgement begin of the houſe of God. And if firſt of vs: vvhat ſhal be the end of them that beleeue not the Goſpel of God?
18 † And * "if the iuſt man ſhal ſcarſe be ſaued: where ſhal the
19 impious and ſinner appeare? † Therfore they alſo that ſuffer according to the vvil of God, let them commend their ſoules to the faithful creator, in good deedes. ⁊

Hier. 25, 29.

Prou. 11, 31.

ANNOTATIONS
CHAP. IIII.

9. *Charitie couereth.*] Faith onely cannot iuſtifie, ſeeing that charitie alſo doth cauſe remiſsion of ſinnes. And ſaying charitie, he meaneth loue and charitable vvorkes tovvard our neighbours, vnto vvhich vvorkes of mercie the Scriptures do ſpecially attribute the force to extinguiſh al ſinnes. See S. Auguſtine *c. 69 Enchiridij and tract. 1. in ep. 1. Io. c. 1.* and venerable Bede *vpon this place.* And in the like ſenſe the holy Scriptures commonly commend vnto vs almes and deedes of mercie for redemption of our ſinnes. *Prouerb. c. 10. Eccleſiaſtici 12. v. 2. Danielis c. 4. v. 24.*

Not only faith.
Vvorkes of mercie.

17. *That iudgement begin.*] In this time of the new Teſtament, the faithful and al thoſe that meane to liue godly (ſpecially of the Clergie) muſt firſt and principally be ſubiect to Gods chaſtiſement and temporal afflictions, vvhich are here called iudgement. Vvhich the Apoſtle recordeth for the comfort and confirmation of the Catholike Chriſtians, vvho vvere at the time of the vvriting hereof, excedingly perſecuted by the heathen Princes & people.

The better mē moſt afflicted in this life.

18. *If the iuſt.*] Not that a man dying iuſt and in the fauour of God, can afterward be in doubt of his ſaluation, or may be reiected of God: but that the iuſt being both in this life ſubiect to aſſaults, tentations, troubles, and dangers of falling from God and loſing their ſtate of iuſtice, & alſo oftentimes to make a ſtraite count, & to be temporally chaſtiſed in the next life, cannot be ſaued vvithout great vvatch, feare, and trembling, and much labouring and chaſtiſement. And this is far contrarie to the Proteſtants doctrine, that putteth no iuſtice but in faith alone, maketh none iuſt in deede and in truth, teacheth men to be ſo ſecure and aſſured of their ſaluation, that he that hath liued vvickedly al his life, if he onely haue their faith at his death, that is, if he beleeue ſtedfaſtly that he is one of the elect, he ſhal be as ſure of his ſaluation immediatly after his departure, as the beſt liuer in the vvorld.

The iuſt man him ſelf is hardly ſaued.

Againſt the vaine ſecuritie of only faith.

CHAP. V.

He exhorteth Prieſts to feede their flockes, onely for Gods ſake and revvard of heauen, vvithout al lordlines. 5 the laie to obey: al to be humble one towards an other: 8 to be conſtant in the Catho. faith, conſidering it is not man, but that lion the Diuel that perſecuteth them, 9 as he doth the vvhole Church alſo, & that God vvil after a vvhile make them ſecure in heauen.

THE

The Epistle for S. Apollinaris Iul. 23.

THE" seniors therfore that are among 1 you, I beseche, my self a fellovv senior vvith them and a vvitnesse of the passions of Christ, vvho am also partaker of that glorie vvhich is to be reuealed in time to come: † feede the flocke of 2 God vvhich is among you [c] prouiding not by constrainte, but vvillingly according to God: :: neither for filthie lucre sake, but voluntarily: † neither as" ouerruling" the Clergie, but made exam- 3 ples of the flocke from the hart. † And vvhen the prince of 4 pastors shal appeare, you shal receiue the incorruptible " crovvne of glorie.

[c] ἐπισκοποῦντες

:: Desire of lucre, or to exercise holy functions for gaine, is a filthy fault in the Clergie, and therfore much to be auoided.

† In like maner ye yong men be subiect to the seniors. 5 And do ye al insinuate humilitie one to an other, because *God resisteth the proude: and to the humble he giueth grace.* † * Be ye 6 humbled therfore vnder the mightie hand of God, that he may exalt you in the time of visitation: † * casting al your 7 carefulnes vpon him, because he hath care of you. † Be so- 8 ber and vvatch: because your aduersarie the Deuil as a roaring lion goeth about, seeking vvhom he may deuoure. † vvhom 9 resist ye, strong in faith: knovving that the self same affliction is made to that your fraternitie vvhich is in the vvorld. † But the God of al grace, vvhich hath called vs vnto his e- 10 ternal glorie in Christ IESVS, he vvil perfite you hauing suffered a litle, and confirme, and stablish you. † To him be 11 glorie and empire for euer and euer. Amen. ꟼ

The Epistle vpon the 3 Sunday after Pentecost.

Prou 3. Iac. 4.

Iac. 4. Psa. 54. Mt. 6, 25

† By Syluanus a faithful brother to you, as I thinke, I 12 haue breefely vvritten: beseching and testifying that this is the true grace of God, vvherein you stand. † The Church 13 saluteth you," that is in Babylon, coëlect: and Marke my sonne. † * Salute one an other in a holy kisse. Grace be to 14 al you vvhich are in Christ IESVS. Amen.

Ro. 16, 16. 1 Cor. 16, 20. 2 Cor. 13, 12.

ANNOTATIONS
CHAP. V.

Senior in the vulgar translation is often Priest or Bishop. *See Act.* 15.

1. *Seniors.*] Though the Latin, *Senior*, be not appropriated to holy order by vse of speache, neither in the Latin nor in our language: yet it is plaine that the Greeke vvord *Presbyter*, vvhich the Apostle here vseth, is here also (as commonly in other places of the new Testament) a vvord of Ecclesiastical office, and not of age, and is as much to say as *Priest* or *Bishop*. For the Apostle him self being of that order, speaketh (as by his vvordes it is plaine), to such as had charge of soules, saying, *Feede the flocke of God vvhich is among you.*

Because

Becauſe vve folow the vulgar latin tranſlation, vve ſay *Seniors* and *Senior*: vvhereas other-vviſe vve might and ſhould ſay according to the Greeke, *The Prieſts therfore I beſeech, my ſelf a fellovv-prieſt vvith them.* So doth S. Hierom read (*Preſbyteros compreſbyter*) and expound ep. 85. So tranſlateth Eraſmus, and Beza him ſelf.

3. *Ouerruling.*] Not ſuperiority, preeminence, ſoueraintie, or rule on the one ſide, nor obedience, ſubiection, and inferiority on the other ſide, be forebidden in the Clergie: but tyrannie, pride, and ambitious domination be forbidden, and humility, meekenes, moderation are commended in Eccleſiaſtical Officers. the Greeke vvord here of ruling or ouerruling, being the ſame that our Sauiour vſeth in the Goſpel of the tyrannical rule of ſecular Heathen Princes, ſaying to his Apoſtles, that it ſhal not be ſo among them: according as here the prince of the Apoſtles teacheth his brethren the Eccleſiaſtical rulers.

κατακυριεύοντες. *Mat.* 20. *v.* 25.

Not Superioritie but tyrannie and lordlines is forbidden in the Clergie.

3. *The Clergie.*] Some of the Engliſh nevv tranſlations turne it corruptly, *Pariſhes*: others, *heritages*: both, to auoid the moſt knovven, true, and common vvord in al Chriſtian languages, to vvit, *Clergie*, a vvord, by vſe of al antiquity, & agreably to the holy Scriptures, made proper to the Spiritualty or Clergie. though in an other more vulgar acception it may agree to al Chriſts choſen heritage, as vvel of lay people as Prieſts. vvhich the Proteſtants had rather folovv, becauſe they vvill haue no difference betvvene the laity & the Clergie. But the holy fathers far othervviſe euen from the beginning. Vvhereof ſee S. Cyprian *ep.* 4. 5. 6. &c. And S. Hierom *ep.* 2 to Nepotianus *c.* 5. vvhere he interpreteth this vvord. *Therfore* (ſaith he) *Clericus*, that is, *a Clergie man, vvhich ſerueth the Church of Chriſt, let him firſt interprete his name, and the ſignification of the name being declared, let him endeuour to be that vvhich he is called.* If κλῆρος (Clerus) *in Greeke, be called in Latin, Sors, therfore are they called* Clerici, *that is, Clergie men, becauſe they are of the lot of our Lord, or becauſe our Lord him ſelf is the lot or portion of Clergie men &c.*

Heret. tranſlation.

The name of Clergie and Clerke.

Vvhich calling no doubt vvas taken out of the holy Scriptures, *Numer.* 18. and *Deutero.* 18. vvhere God is called the inheritance, lot, and portion of the Prieſts and Leuites: and novv vvhen men be made of the Clergie, they ſay, *Dominus pars hæreditatis meæ.* that is, *Our Lord is the portion of mine inheritance.* but ſpecially out of the nevv Teſtament, *Act.* 1, 17. 25. and 8, 21. Vvhere the lot or office of the Eccleſiaſtical miniſterie is called by this vvord κλῆρος, Clerus. See in Venerable Bede the cauſes vvhy this holy ſtate being ſeuered by name from the Laity, doth vveare alſo a crovvne on their head for diſtinction. *Lib.* 5. *hiſt. Angl. c.* 22.

κληρονομία. κλῆρος. μερίς.

Prieſts crovvnes.

4. *Crovvne of glorie.*] As life euerlaſting ſhal be the revvard of al the iuſt, ſo the preachers & Paſtors that doe vvel, for their doing ſhal haue that revvard in a more excellẽt degree, expreſſed here by theſe vvordes, *Crovvne of glorie.* according to the ſaying of Daniel c. 12. *They that ſleepe in the duſt of the earth, ſhal avvake, one ſort to life euerlaſting, others to euerlaſting rebuke. but ſuch as be learned, ſhal ſhine as the brightnes of the firmament: and ſuch as inſtruct many to iuſtice, ſhal be as ſtarres, during al eternitie.*

The heauenly crovvne of Doctors and preachers.

13. *That is in Babylon.*] The Proteſtants ſhevv them ſelues here (as in al places vvhere any controuerſie is, or that maketh againſt them) to be moſt vnhoneſt and partial handlers of Gods vvord. The aũcient fathers, namely S. Hierom *in Catalogo de ſcriptoribus Eccleſiaſticis, verbo Marcus*: Euſebius *li.* 2 *c.* 14 *hiſt.* *Oecumenius* vpon this place: and many moe agree, that Rome is meant by the vvord Babylon, here alſo as in the 16 and 17 of the Apocalypſe: ſaying plainely, that S. Peter vvrote this Epiſtle at Rome, vvhich is called Babylon for the reſemblance it had to Babylon that great citie in Chaldæa (vvhere the Ievves vvere captiues) for magnificence, Monarchie, reſort and confuſion of al peoples and tongues, and for that it vvas before Chriſt and long after, the ſeate of al Ethnike ſuperſtition & idolatrie, & the ſlaughter houſe of the Apoſtles & other Chriſtian men, the Heathen Emperours thẽ keeping their cheefe reſidẽce there. See S. Leo *Ser.* 1 *in Nati. Petri & Pauli.*

S. Peter vvriteth from Babylon, that is, Rome.

Vvhy Rome vvas called Babylon.

This being moſt plaine, and cõſonant to that vvhich folovveth of S. Marke, vvhom al the Eccleſiaſtical hiſtories agree to haue been Peters ſcholer at Rome, and that he there vvrote his Goſpel: yet our Aduerſaries fearing hereby the ſequele of Peters or the Popes ſupremacie at Rome, deny that euer he vvas there, or that this Epiſtle vvas vvritten there, or that Babylon doth here ſignifie Rome: but they ſay that Peter vvrote this Epiſtle at Babylon in Chaldæa, though they neuer reade either in Scriptures or other holy or profane hiſtorie, that this Apoſtle vvas euer in that tovvne. but ſee their ſhameles partiality. here Babylon (ſay they) is not taken for Rome, becauſe it vvould folovv that Peter vvas at Rome &c. but in the Apocalypſe vvhere al euil is ſpoken of Babylon, there they vvill haue it ſignifie nothing els but Rome, and the Romane Church alſo, not (as the fathers interprete it) the temporal ſtate of the Heathen Empire there. So do they folovv in euery vvord no other thing but the aduantage of their ovvne hereſie. See the Annotation vpon the laſt of the Romans v. 16. and vpon the 17 of the Apocalypſe. v. 5.

The Proteſtãts vvil haue Babylon to ſignifie Rome in other places but not here.

And as for their vvrangling vpon the ſupputation of the time of his going thither, and the number of yeres that he vvas there, & the diuerſitie that ſeemeth to be in the Eccleſiaſtical vvriters concerning the ſame, read B. Fiſher and other that ſubſtantially anſvver al ſuch cauils. And if ſuch contentious reaſoning might take place, vve ſhould hardly beleeue the principal things recorded either in Eccleſiaſtical hiſtories, or in the Scriptures them ſelues. Concerning the time of

The Proteſtants vvrãgle about the time of Peters being at Rome.

Christs fleing into Ægypt, of the comming of the Sages to adore him, yea of the yeres of his age, & time of his death, al aűcient vvriters do not agree. and concerning the day of his last supper and institution of the holy Sacrament, there is diuersitie of opinions. Shal vve therfore inferre that he neuer died, and that the other things neuer vvere? Can the Heretikes accord al the histories that seeme euen in holy Scripture to haue contradiction? Can they tel vs certainely, vvhen Dauid first came to Saul, and the like? doubt they vvhether the vvorld vvas euer created, because the count of the yeres is diuers? Do they not beleeue that Paradise euer vvas, because no man knovveth vvhere it is? and such other like things infinite to rehearse? Vvhich vvhen they vvere done, vvere plaine and knovven things in the vvorld: and novv for vs to call them to an account, after so many yeres, ages, and vvorldes, is but sophistication and plaine infidelitie. And this sect of the Protestants standing onely vpon destruction, and negatiues, & dealing vvith our religion euen as Iulian, Porphyrie, and Lucian did, it is an easie thing for them to bestovv their time in picking of quarels.

Many things most true (euen in the Scriptures) are not agreed vpon concerning the time.

THE SECOND EPISTLE OF PETER THE APOSTLE.

CHAP. I.

Hovv much God hath done for them, making them Christians: 5 and that they againe must doe their part, not hauing onely faith, but al other vertues also and good vvorkes, that so they may haue the more assurance to enter into the kingdom of heauen. 13 And that he is so careful to admonish them, knovving that his death is at hand, knovving also most certainely the comming of Christ by the vvitnes of the Father him self, as also by the Prophets. Concerning vvhom he vvarneth them that they folovv not priuate spirites, but the holy Ghost (speaking novv in the Church.)

1 SIMON PETER seruant and Apostle of IESVS Christ, to them that haue obtained equal faith vvith vs in the iustice of our God and Sauiour IESVS Christ. 2 † Grace to you and peace be accomplished in the knovvledge of God and Christ IESVS our Lord: 3 † as al things of his diuine povver vvhich pertaine to life and godlines, are giuen vs by the knovvledge of him vvhich hath called vs by his ovvne propre glorie and vertue, by vvhom he hath giuen vs most great and pretious promises: that by these you may be made

made partakers of the diuine nature, fleeing the corruption
5 of that concupiscence vvhich is in the vvorld. † And you
employing al care, minister ye in your faith, vertue: and in
6 vertue, knovvledge: † and in knovvledge, abstinence: and in
7 abstinence, patience: and in patience, pietie: † and in pietie,
loue of the fraternitie: and in the loue of the fraternitie,
8 charitie. † For if these things be present vvith you, & abound:
they shal make you not vacant, nor vvithout fruite in the
9 knovvledge of our Lord IESVS Christ. † For he that hath
not these things ready, is blinde, and groping vvith his hãd,
hauing forgotten the purging of his old sinnes.

10 † Vvherfore, brethren, labour the more that " by good
vvorkes you may make sure your vocation and election. for,
11 doing these things, you shal not sinne at any time. † For so
there shal be ministred to you aboundantly an entrance into
the euerlasting kingdom of our Lord and Sauiour IESVS
12 Christ. † For the vvhich cause I wil begin to admonish you
alvvaies of these things: and you in deede knovving & be-
13 ing confirmed in the present truth. † But I thinke it meete
as long as I am in this tabernacle, to stirre you vp by admo-
14 nition: † being certaine that the laying avvay of my tabernacle is at hand, according as our Lord IESVS Christ also signi-
15 fied to me. † And I vvil doe my diligence, you to haue often
" after my decease also, that you may keepe a memorie of
these things.

16 † For, not hauing folovved vnlearned fables, haue vve
made the povver and ` presence' of our Lord IESVS Christ
knovven to you: but [c] made beholders of his greatenesse.
17 † For, * he receiuing from God his father honour and glorie,
this maner of voice comming dovvne to him from the mag-
nifical glorie, *This is my beloued sonne in vvhom I haue pleased my self,
18 heare him.* † And this voice vve heard brought from heauen,
19 vvhen vve vvere vvith him in the :: holy mounte. † And we
haue the prophetical vvord more sure: vvhich you doe vvel
attending vnto, as to a candel shining in a darke place, vntil
the day davvne, and the day starre arise in your hartes: ꟻ
20 † vnderstanding this first that no prophecie of scripture is
21 made by " priuate interpretation. † For, * not by mans vvil
vvas prophecie brought at any time: but the holy men of
God spake, inspired vvith the holy Ghost.

presci- ence

Mt.17,5

2 Tim 3, 17.

The Epistle in the *Transfiguration* of our Lord, *Aug.6.*

c By this it is plaine, that either Iohn, Iames, or Peter must be the author of this epistle. for these three onely vvere present at the Trãsfiguration. *Mat.17,1.*

:: You see that places are made holy by Christs presence, & that al places be not alike holy. See Annot, *Act.7,33.*

ANNOTATIONS
CHAP. I.

Good vvorkes must concurre vvich Gods predestination to the effecte thereof.

10. *By good vvorkes.*] Here vve see, that Gods eternal predestination and election consisteth vvith good vvorkes: yea that the certainty and effect thereof is procured by mans free vvill and good vvorkes, and that our vvel doing is a meane for vs to attaine to the effect of Gods predestination, that is, to life euerlasting. and therfore it is a desperate folly and a great signe of reprobate persons, to say, If I be predestinate, doe vvhat I vvil, I shal be saued. Nay, the Apostle saith, If thou hope to be one of the predestinate (for knovv it thou canst not) do vvel, that thou maist be the more assured to attaine to that thou hopest: or, make it sure by good vvorkes. The Protestāts in such cases not much liking these vvordes, *by good vvorkes*, though the Latin haue it vniuersally, and some Greeke copies also, as Beza confesseth, leaue them out in their translations, by their vvonted pollicie.

διὰ τῶν καλῶν ἔργων.

The heretikes (according to their custom) exclude this sense altogether by their false translation.

15. *After my decease also.*] These vvordes though they may be easily altered by cōstruction into diuers senses not vntrue, yet the correspondēce of the partes of the sentēce going before and folovving, giue most plaine this meaning, that, as during his life he vvould not omit to put them in memorie of the things he taught them, so after his death (vvhich he knew should be shortly) he vvould not faile to endeuour that they might be mindeful of the same. Signifying that his care ouer them should not cease by death, & that by his intercession before God after his departure, he vvould doe the same thing for them, that he did before in his life by teaching and preaching. This is the sense that the * Greeke Scholies speake of, and this is most proper to the text, and consonant to the old vse of this Apostle and other Apostolike Saincts and fathers of the primitiue Church.

Oecum. in hunc loc. Gagn.

S. Peters Pastoral care & protection of the Church after his death.

S. Clement in his Epistle to S. Iames our Lordes brother, vvitnesseth, that S. Peter encouraging him to take after his decease the charge of the Apostolike Romane See, promised that after his departure he vvould not cease to pray for him & his flocke, thereby to ease him of his Pastoral burden. *To. 1 Concil. ep. 1. S. Clem. in initio.* And S. Leo the Great one of his successors in the said See, often attributeth the good administration and gouernement thereof to S. Peters praiers and assistance: namely in these goodly vvorkes *Ser. 3 in anniuers. die assumpt. ad Pontif. We are much bound* (saith he) *to giue thankes to our Lord and Redeemer Iesus Christ, that hath giuen so great povver to him vvhom he made the Prince of the vvhole Church: that if in our time also any thing be done vvel & be rightly ordered by vs, it is to be imputed to his vvorkes and his gouernement, to vvhom it vvas said,* And thou being conuerted, confirme thy brethren: *and to vvhom our Lord after his resurrection said thrise,* Feede my sheepe. *Which novv also vvithout doubt the godly Pastor doth execute, confirming vs vvith his exhortations, and not ceasing to pray for vs, that vve be ouercome vvith no tentation. &c.*

Luc. 22. Io. 21.

The Saincts in heauen pray for the liuing.

Yea it vvas a common thing in the primitiue Church among the auncient Christians, and alvvaies since among the faithful, to make couenant in their life time, that vvhether of them vvent to heauen before the other, he should pray for his frende and fellovv yet aliue. See the Ecclesiastical historie of the holy virgin and Martyr Potamiæna, promising at the houre of her Martyrdom, that after her death she vvould procure mercie of God to Basilides one of the souldiars that ledde her to execution, and so she did. *Euseb. li. 6. c. 4.* Also S. Cyprian *ep. 57 in fine. Let vs,* (saith he) *pray mutually one for an other, and vvhether of vs tvvo shal by Gods clemencie be first called for, let his loue continue, and his praier not cease for his brethren and sisters in the vvorld.* So said this holy Martyr at that time vvhen Christiās vvere so far from Caluinisme (vvhich abhorreth the praiers of Saincts & praying to them) that to be sure, they bargained before hād to haue the martyrs & other Saincts to pray for them. The same S. Cyprian also in his booke *De disciplina & habitu virginum, in fine,* after a godly exhortation made to the holy Virgins or Nonnes in his time, speaketh thus vnto them: *Tantùm tunc mementote nostri, cùm incipiet in vobis virginitas honorari.* that is, *Onely then haue vs in remembrance, vvhen your virginitie shal begin to be honoured.* that is, after their departure. Vvhere he insinuateth the vse of the Catholike Church in keeping the festiual daies and other dueties tovvard the holy Virgins in heauen. S. Hierom also in the same manner speaketh to Heliodorus, saying, that vvhen he is once in heauen, then he vvil pray for him that exhorted and incited him to the blessed state of the Monastical life. *Ep. 1. c. 2.*

Feastes of holy Virgins.

Inuocation of Saincts.

And so doth he speake to the vertuous matrone Paula after her death, desiring her to pray for him in his old age, affirming that she shal the more easily obtaine, the neerer she is novv ioyned to Christ in heauen. *in Epitaph. Paulæ in fine.* It vvere to long to report, hovv S. Augustine desireth to be holpen by S. Cyprians praiers (then and long before a Sainct in heauen) to the vnderstanding of the truth concerning the peace and regiment of the Church. *li. 5 de Bapt. cont. Donatistas c. 17.* And in an other place the same holy Doctor alleageth the said S. Cyprian saying, that great num-

bers

bers of our parents, brethren, children, frendes, and other, expect vs in great solicitude and carefulnes of our saluation, being sure of their ovvne. *li. 1 de predest. Sanctorum c.* 14. S. Gregorie Nazianzene in his orations of the praise of S. Cyprian *in fine*, and of S. Basil also *in fine*, declareth hovv they pray for the people. vvhich tvvo Saincts he there inuocateth, as al the auncient fathers did, both generally al Saincts, and (as occasion serued) particularly their special Patrones. Among the rest see hovv holy Ephrem (*in orat. de laud. S. Deipara*) praied to our B. Ladie vvith the same termes of *Aduocate*, *Hope*, *Reconciliatrix*, that the faithful yet vse, and the Protestants can not abide. S. Basil *ho. de* 40 *Martyribus in fine.* S. Athanasius *Ser. in Euang. de S. Deipara in fine.* S. Hilarie *in Psal.* 124. S. Chrysostom *ho.* 66 *ad po. Antiochenum in fine.* Theodorete *de curat. Græcorum affectuum li.* 8 *in fine.* Finally al the fathers are ful of these things: vvho better knevv the meaning of the Scripture and the sense of the Holy Ghost, then these nevv interpreters doe.

Priuate phantastical interpretations.

20. *Priuate.*] The Scriptures can not be rightly expounded of euery priuate spirit or phantasie of the vulgar reader: but by the same spirit vvherevvith they vvere vvritten, vvhich is resident in the Church.

CHAP. II.

As not onely Prophets, but also false-prophets vvere in the old Testament, so novv likevvise there shal be Maisters of Heresie, to the damnation of them selues, and of their folovvers. 4 And of their damnation he pronounceth by examples (as he comforteth the vertuous Catholikes or true beleeuers vvith the example of Lot) because of their railing at their Superiors and Prelates, their blaspheming of Catholike doctrine, their voluptuous liuing, their lecherie, their couetousnes, their maner of seducing, and the persons seduced, 20 for vvhom it had been lesse damnable, if they had neuer been Christians.

1 BVT there vvere also false-prophets in the people, as also in you there *shal be lying maisters vvhich shal bring in sectes of perdition, & denie him that hath bought them, [c] the Lord: bringing vpon them selues speedie perdition. 2 † And :: many shal folovv their riotousnesses, by vvhom the vvay of truth shal be blasphemed. 3 † and in auarice shal they [c] vvith feined vvordes make merchandise of you. vnto vvhom the iudgement novv long since ceaseth not: and their perdition slumbereth not. 4 † For if God spared not Angels sinning: but with the ropes of Hel being dravven dovvne into Hel deliuered them to be tormented, that they should be reserued vnto iudgemēt: 5 † & he spared not the original vvorld, but *kept the eight, Noë, the preacher of iustice, bringing in the deluge vpon the vvorld of the impious. 6 † And * bringing the cities of the Sodomites and of the Gomorrheites into ashes, he damned them vvith subuersion, putting an example of them that shal doe impiously: 7 † and * deliuered iust Lot oppressed by the iniurie and luxurious conuersation of the

1 Tim. 4. Iude.

c δεσπότην

Gen. 7.

Gen. 19.

Gen. 19, 16.

:: Heretikes (of whom he prophecieth here) do gaine scholers, by preaching libertie, and by their owne licentious life, which is specially ioyned to the heresie of these daies.

c Al the sweete wordes of heretikes, speaking much of the vvord of the Lord, the Gospel, IESVS CHRIST &c. are but termes of art to bie and sel poore mens soules.

abominable men. † for in sight and * hearing he vvas iust: 8 dvvelling vvith them vvho from day to day vexed the iust soule vvith vniust vvorkes.

† Our Lord knovveth to deliuer the godly from tentation, 9 but to reserue the vniust vnto the day of iudgement to be tormented: † and especially them vvhich vvalke after 10 the flesh in concupiscence of vncleannesse, and cōtemne dominion, bold, self-pleasers: they :: feare not to bring in sectes, blaspheming. † Vvhereas Angels being greater in strength 11 and povver, beare not the execrable iudgemēt * against them. † But these men as vnreasonable beastes, naturally tending 12 to the snare and into destruction, :: in those things vvhich they know not, blaspheming, shal perish in their corruption, † receiuing the revvard of iniustice, esteeming for a pleasure 13 the delightes of a day: [b] coinquinations and spottes, flovving in delicacies, in their feastings rioting vvith you, † hauing 14 eies ful of adulterie and incessant sinne: alluring vnstable soules, hauing their hart exercised vvith auarice, the children of malediction: † leauing the right vvay they haue erred, 15 hauing folovved the vvay of Balaam of Bosor, vvhich loued the revvard of iniquitie, † but * had a checke of his madnesse. 16 the dumme beast vnder the yoke, speaking vvith mans voice, prohibited the folishnes of the prophet.

† These are fountaines vvithout vvater, and cloudes, tossed 17 vvith vvhirlevvindes, to vvhom the mist of darkenesse is reserued. † For, speaking the proud things of vanitie, they 18 allure in the desires of fleshly riotousnes, those that escape a litle, vvhich conuerse in errour, † :: promising them libertie, 19 vvhereas them selues are the slaues of corruption. for * vvherevvith a man is ouercome: of that he is the slaue also. † For if fleeing from the coinquinations of the vvorld in 20 the knovvledge of our Lord and Sauiour IESVS Christ, they againe intangled vvith the same be ouercome: * the later things are become vnto them vvorse then the former. † For 21 it vvas better for them not to knovv the vvay of iustice, then after the knovvledge, to turne backe from that holy cōmaundement vvhich vvas deliuered to them. † For, that of 22 the true prouerbe is chaunced to them, * The dogge returned to his vomite: and, The sovve vvashed [c] into her vvallovving in the mire.

The special properties of heretikes.

:: So heretikes blaspheme the highest mysteries of our faith through ignorance.

:: Vvho euer promised more libertie to their folowers then Luther, Caluin, & the like, taking avvay penance, fasting, continencie or chastitie, keeping of vowes, necessitie of good vvorkes (because faith doeth al) obedience to Ecclesiastical pastors and Coūcels, and such like?

* from our Lord

b coinquinationes & macula,

Nu. 22, 23.

Io. 8, 34. Ro. 6, 16

Mt. 12, 45.

Pro. 26, 11.

c εἰς κύλισμα

CHAP.

CHAP. III.

These tvvo Epistles he vvriteth to confirme them in the Apostles doctrine, and vvarneth them of scorners that shal come, and denie Domesday. 5 Whose vaine argument he ansvvereth, and giueth the reason of Gods so long patience, 10 exhorting to al holines of life in respect of that terrible day. 16 Finally giuing vvarning of such as misinterprete S. Paules Epistles & the other Scriptures, and that vve must not for any thing fall from the true faith.

1 THIS loe the second epistle I vvrite to you my deerest, [c] in vvhich I stirre vp by 2 admonition your sincere minde: † that you may be mindeful of those vvordes vvhich I told you before from the holy Prophetes, and of your Apostles, of the preceptes of our Lord and Sauiour. 3 † Knovving this first, that * in the last daies shal come mockers in deceit, vvalking according to their ovvne concupiscences, 4 † saying, Vvhere is his promise or his cõming? For 5 since the time that the fathers slept, al things do so perseuêre from the beginning of creature. for they are vvilfully ignorant of this, that the heauens vvere before, & the earth, out of vvater, and through vvater, consisting by the vvord of God: 6 † by the vvhich, that vvorld then, being ouerflovved vvith 7 vvater perished. † But the heauens vvhich novv are, & the earth, are by the same word kept in store, reserued to fire vnto the day of iudgemẽt & of the perdition of the impious men. 8 † But this one thing be not ignorãt of, my deerest, that * one day with our Lord is as a thousand yeres, & a thousand yeres 9 as one day. † Our Lord slacketh not his promis, as some do esteeme it: but he doth patiently for you, * not vvilling that 10 any perish, but that al returne to penance. † And * the day of our Lord shal come as a theefe in the vvhich the heauens shal passe vvith great violence, but the elementes shal be resolued vvith heate, and the earth and the vvorkes vvhich are in it, shal be burnt.

11 † Therfore vvhereas al these thinges are to be dissolued: vvhat maner of men ought you to be in holy conuersations 12 and godlinesses, † expecting and hasting vnto the cõming of the day of our Lord, by vvhich the heauens burning shal be resolued, and the elementes shal melt vvith the heate of 13 fire? † But vve expect * nevv heauens and a nevv earth according

c in quibus

2 Tim. 3, 1. Iude, 18.

Ps. 89, 4

Ezec. 33. 1 Tim. 2. Mt. 24. 1 Thes. 5. Apoc. 3.

Esa. 65, 17. Apo. 21, 1.

cording to his promises, in vvhich iustice inhabiteth.

† For the vvhich cause my deerest, expecting these things, 14 labour earnestly to be found immaculate and vnspotted to him in peace: † and * the longanimitie of our Lord, do ye 15 account saluation, as also our most deere brother Paul according to the vvisdom giuen him hath vvritten to you: † as al- 16 so in al epistles, speaking in them of these things, in the vvhich are" certaine things hard to be vnderstoode, vvhich the vnlearned and vnstable depraue, as also the rest of the Scriptures, to their ovvne perdition. † You therfore brethrē, 17 foreknovving, take heede lest ledde aside by the errour of the vnwise you fal away from your owne stedfastnes. † but 18 grovv in grace and in knovvledge of our Lord and sauiour IESVS Christ. To him be glorie both novv and vnto the day of eternitie. Amen.

Ro. 2, 4.

ANNOTATIONS
CHAP. III.

The heretical proud spirit of priuate interpretation of Scriptures.

16. *Certaine things hard.*] This is a plaine text to conuince the Protestants, vvho (as al heretikes lightly doe and did from the beginning) say the Scriptures be easie to vnderstand, and therfore may be not onely read safely, but also expounded boldly of al the people, as vvel vnlearned as learned: and consequently euery one by him self and his priuate spirit, vvithout respect of the expositions of the learned fathers, or expectation of the Churches, their Pastors and Prelates iudgment, may determine and make choise of such sense as him self liketh or thinketh agreable. For this is partly their saying, partly the necessarie sequele of their folish opinion, vvhich admitteth nothing but the bare Scriptures. And Luther said that the Scriptures vvere more plaine then al the fathers commentaries: and so al to be superfluous but the Bible. *Præfat. assert. art. damnat.*

The Scriptures be hard, namely S. Paules epistles, specially vvhere he speaketh of iustificatiō by faith.

Against al vvhich Diuelish & seditious arrogācie, tending to make the people esteeme them selues learned or sufficient vvithout their Pastors and spiritual rulers helpe, to guide them selues in al matters of doctrine & doubtes in religion: the holy Apostle here telleth and forevvarneth the faithful, that the Scriptures be ful of difficultie, & specially S. Paules epistles of al other partes of holy vvrite, and that ignorant men ad vnstable or phātastical fellovves puffed to & fro vvith euery blast of doctrine and hæresie, abuse, peruert, and misconster them to their ovvne damnation. And * S. Augustine saith, that the special difficulty in S. Paules epistles, vvhich ignorant and euil men do so peruert and vvhich S. Peter meaneth, is his hard speache and much commendation of that faith vvhich he saith doth iustifie. vvhich the ignorant euen from the Apostles time, and much more novv, haue and do so misconster, as though he had meant that onely faith vvithout good vvorkes could iustifie or saue a man. Against vvhich vvicked collection and abuse of S. Paules vvordes, the said father saith, al these Canonical or Catholike epistles vvere vvritten.

* De fid. & op. c. 14.

The Protestāts idle distinctiō betvvene difficultie in the Epistles and difficultie in the things.

But the Hæretikes here to shift of the matter, and to creepe out after their fashion, ansvver, that S. Peter saith not, S. Paules epistles be hard, but that many things in them are hard. Vvhich may be to the Catholikes an example of their sophistical euasions from the euidence of Gods vvord. As though it vvere not al one to say, *Such an author or vvriter is hard*: and, *There be many things in that vvriter hard to be vnderstood.* For, vvhether it be that the argument and matter be high and past vulgar capacitie, as that of prædestination, reprobation, vocation of the Gentiles, and iustifying faith: or vvhether his manner of stile and vvriting be obscure: al proue that his epistles be hard, and other Scriptures also: because

S. Peter

S. Peter here affirmeth that by reason of the difficulties in them, vvhether in the style, or in the depth of the matter, the ignorant and vnstable (such as Heretikes be) do peruert his vvritings, as also other Scriptures, to their ovvne damnation. Vvhereby it is plaine that it is a very dangerous thing for such as be ignorant, or for vvilde vvitted fellovves, to reade the Scriptures. For such conditioned men be they that become Heretikes, and through ignorance, pride, and priuate phantasie, meeting vvith hard places of S. Paules epistles or other Scriptures, breede Hæresies.

The Greeke copies, haue both, some ἐν οἷς, *in vvhich things:* some ἐν αἷς, *in vvhich epistles.*

And that not onely the things treated of in the holy Scriptures, but also that the very manner of vvriting and enditing thereof, is high and hard, and purposely by Gods prouidence appointed to be vvritten in such sort, see S. Augustine li. 2 de doct. Christ. c. 6. and ep. 119. S. Ambrose ep. 44 in principio. S. Hierom to Paulinus ep. 103 c. 5. 6. 7. vvho also (ep. 65. c. 1.) saith, that in his old age vvhen he should rather haue taught then be taught, he vvent as far as Alexandria, onely to heare Didymus, and to haue his helpe for the vnderstanding of the Scriptures, and confesseth vvith great thankes to the said Didymus, that he learned of him that vvhich before he knevve not. Dauid saith, *Giue me vnderstanding, and I vvil searche thy lavv.* The Eunuch in the Actes said, Hovv can I vnderstand vvith out an interpreter? The Apostles, til Christ opened their sense to vnderstand the scriptures, could not vnderstand them. The holy Doctors by continual studie, vvatching, fasting, and praying, had much a doe to vnderstand them: that great clerke S. Augustine cōfessing in the foresaid epistle 119. c. 21. that there vvere many moe things that he vnderstood not, then that he vnderstood. The Heretikes say the fathers did commonly erre. and hovv could such great vvise learned men be deceiued in reading and expounding the Scriptures, if they vvere not hard? and if they vvere hard to them, hovv are they easie to these nevv maisters the Hæretikes? finally, vvhy do they vvrite so many nevv glosses, scholies, commentaries, as a cart cannot carrie? Vvhy do Luther, Zuinglius, Caluin, and their Companions agree no better vpon the interpretation of the Scriptures, if they be not hard? vvhereat stumbled al the old heretikes & the nevv, Arius, Macedonius, Vigilantius, Nestorius, Eutyches, Berengarius, Vvicleffe, Protestants, Puritanes, Anabaptists, and the rest, but at the hardnes of the Scriptures? They be hard then to vnderstand, and Heretikes peruert them to their ovvne damnation.

Not only the matter, but the style of the Scriptures is hard.

Ps. 118. Act. 8. Luc. 24. v. 45.

THE ARGVMENT OF S. IOHNS THREE EPISTLES.

*F S. Iohn vvas said in the Argument before his Gospel. Novv herefolovv his three Epistles: one to al Catholikes (though * some auncients do cal it,* Ad Parthos: *) the other tvvo being very short, vnto a certaine Ladie, & to one Gaius. The effect of al is, to vvitnes vnto them the certaintie of the Catholike faith, and to exhort them to continue still in it: also to loue the Catholike Church. and so, neither to become heretikes, nor Schismatikes: but rather to auoid al such, as the forerunners of Antichrist, and to remember, that Catholikes neede not to goe to schole to any such Masters, hauing at home in the Catholike Church, the doctrine of the holy Ghost him self, vvho vvas giuen to the Church visibly in the beginning, to leade her into al truth, and to continue vvith her for euer. Therfore he saith:* That vvhich you haue heard from the beginning, let it abide in you. *Likevvise a litle after. v.27. and ep. 2. v.6.* This is the commaundement, that as you haue heard from the beginning, you vvalke in the same, because many seducers are gone out into the vvorld. *and v. 8. & 9.*

* Higinus ep. 1. to. 1. Cōcil. August. li. 2. Euang. quæst. q. 39.

1. Ioh. 2. v.24.

And not only thus in general, but also in particular he expresseth the pointes vvhich the heretikes did then call in question. Some vvere about Christ him self. for they denied that IESVS *is Christ, that he is the very sonne of God, that he is incarnate. Ep. 1. c. 2. v. 22. and Ep. 2. v. 7. And against such it vvas that he vvrote his Gospel also, as he there signifieth. Ioh. 20. v. 31. Other pointes are about our iustification, against onely faith, and for good vvorkes, as also S. Aug. noted, vvhose vvordes vvere cited before. Herevpon he saith:* If vve say vve haue societie vvith God, and vvalke in darkenes, vve lie. *Ep. 1. c. 1. Againe,* He that saith he knovveth God, and keepeth not his commaundements, is a lier. *Againe,* This is the charitie of God, that vve keepe his cōmaundements, and his commaundements are not heauie. *Finally,* Children let no man seduce you, he that doth iustice, is iust, euen as he is iust. *Ep. 1. c. 3. v. 7. 8. 9. likevvise c. 2. v. 29. and in deede in all the three Epistles through out, he doth inculcate good vvorkes and keeping the commaundements, against the heresie of only faith.*

De fid. & op. c. 14.

1. Ioh. 2 & 5.

THE

THE FIRST EPISTLE OF IOHN THE APOSTLE.

CHAP. I.

Good cause there is to beleeue the Apostles preaching. 5 And this is one point of their preaching, that to haue participation vvith God, vve must not onely beleeue, but also abstaine from al mortal sinne, 8 though vve al sinne venially.

1 THAT vvhich vvas from the beginning, vvhich vve haue heard, vvhich vve haue seen vvith our eies, vvhich vve haue looked vpon, and our handes haue handled of the vvord of life: 2 († and the life vvas manifested: and vve haue seen, and do testifie, and declare vnto you the life eternal vvhich vvas vvith the Father, and hath appeared to vs) 3 † that vvhich vve haue seen and haue heard, vve declare vnto you, that "you also may haue societie vvith vs, and our societie may be vvith the Father and vvith his Sonne IESVS Christ. 4 † And these things vve vvrite to you, that you may reioyce, and your ioy may be ful.

5 † And this is the annuntiation vvhich vve haue heard of him, and declare vnto you, That * God is light, and in him there is no darkenesse. 6 † If vve shal say that we haue societie vvith him, and vvalke in darkenesse: vve lie, and do not the truth. 7 † But if we vvalke in the light, as he also is in the light: vve haue societie one tovvard an other, and * "the bloud of IESVS Christ his sonne cleanseth vs "from al sinne. 8 † * If vve shal say "that vve haue no sinne, vve seduce our selues, and the truth is not in vs. 9 † If vve confesse our sinnes: he is faithful & iust, for to forgiue vs our sinnes, and to cleanse vs

Io. 8, 12.

Heb. 9. 1 Pet. 1. Apo. 1. 3 Reg. 8, 46. 2 Par. 6, 36.

from al iniquitie. † If vve shal say that vve haue not sin- 10 ned: vve make him a lier, and his vvord is not in vs.

ANNOTATIONS
CHAP. I.

No saluatiõ but in the Societie of the Church.

3. *You may haue societie.*] S. John shevveth manifestly, that vvhosoeuer desire to be partakers vvith God, must first be vnited to the Churches societie, learne that faith, and receiue those Sacraments, vvhich the Disciples receiued of the Truth it self, conuersant vvith them in flesh. So saith Venerable Bede vpon this place. Vvhereby vve see there is no societie vvith God in sectes or schismes, nor any vvhere but in the vnitie, fellovvship, and communion of that Church vvhich can proue it self to descend from the Apostles.

Many meanes & instruments of remitting sinne, but al by the force & merite of Christs bloud applied by them.

7. *The bloud of Iesus.*] Vvhether sinnes be remitted by praiers, by fasting, by almes, by faith, by charitie, by sacrifice, by Sacraments, & by the Priests, (as the holy Scriptures do plainely attribute remissiõ to euery of these) yet none of al these do othervvise remit, but in the force, by the merite & vertue of Christs bloud: these being but the appointed meanes & instruments by vvhich Christ vvil haue his holy bloud to vvorke effectually in vs. vvhich meanes vvhosoeuer contemneth, depriueth him self of the cõmoditie of Christs ovvne bloud, & continueth still in sinne and vncleannesse, vaunt he him self neuer so much of Christs death. Vvhich point let the Protestants marke vvel, and cease to beguile their poore deceiued folovvers, persuading them, that the Catholikes derogate from Christs bloud, or seeke remission othervvise then by it, for that they vse humbly the meanes appointed by Christ to apply the benefite of his holy bloud vnto them.

Al remission of sinnes is by the Passiõ of Christ though by secũdarie meanes also.

7. *From al sinne.*] From original and actual, venial and mortal, *a culpa & pœna*, that is, from the fault and the paine due for the same. V. Bede saith, that Christs Passion doth not onely remit in Baptisme the sinnes before committed, but al other aftervvard also done by frailtie: yet so, if vve vse for the remission of them, such meanes as be requisite and as Christ hath appointed, vvhereof he reckeneth some. *Bede vpon this place.* See S. Augustine also vpon this place *to.* 9. and S. Hierome *li.* 2 *con. Pelag. c.* 3.

Some sinnes venial.

A man may be truely iust, notvvithstanding venial sinnes.

S. Augustine excepteth our B. Ladie from sinners.

Examples of venial sinnes.

8. *That vve haue no sinne.*] Vve gather by these vvordes and the former, that there be tvvo sortes of sinnes: one mortal, excluding vs from light and the societie of God: an other venial, vvhich is found euen in those that vvalke in the light, and are in the societie of God. Also vve note against the Pelagians, that vve be truely called the sonnes of God, and so iust in deede, though vve be not vvithout al sinnes, euery one of vs, as vvel iust as vniust, being taught and bound to confesse our offenses, and to aske pardon daily of God, by this petition of the *Pater noster, Forgiue vs our debtes.* Therfore S. Augustine *li. de natura & grat. c.* 36. reckeneth vp al the holy Patriarches, Prophets, and renovvmed iust persons, to haue been sinners, euen vvhen they vvere in grace and iustice: excepting alvvaies our B. Ladie, *de qua propter honorem Domini, nullam prorsus, cùm de peccatis agitur, habere volo quæstionem. of vvhom,* saith he, *for the honour of our Lord, vvhen vve talke of sinnes, I vvil haue no question.* And Pelagius asking vvhat sinnes Abel & such iust men did commit, *S. Augustine ãsvvereth, that they might laugh sometime immoderately, or iest to much, or couet somevvhat intẽperatly, or plucke fruite ouer greedily, or in eating take somevvhat more then aftervvard vvas vvel digested, or haue their intention in time of praier somevvhat distracted, and such like. thus in sense S. Augustine. Vvhereby vve may learne vvhich be venial sinnes, that consist vvith true iustice & * can not alvvaies be auoided euen of holy men in this life. In the booke *de fide ad Petrum c.* 41. are excepted from this common rule of sinners, the children vvhich be nevvely baptized and haue not yet vse of reason to sinne either mortally or venially.

* *c.* 38.

* *de dono perseuerãt. c.* 2.

CHAP. II.

If any sinne mortally, he must not dispaire. 3 To knovv God rightly, is not to beleeue onley, but to keepe his commaundements: 7 and that this is no nevv doctrine, but the very primitiue, though a nevv life it is. 9 Therfore he that beleeueth must also loue his brethren: 12 and that men must not loue the vvorld, but doe that vvhich God vvilleth. 18 Many are gone out of the Church and become Seducers, al the ministers of Antichrist: but true Christians must continue in their old faith, considering the revvard, and that they neede not goe to schole to any Heretike, the Holy Ghost himself being the scholemaster of the Church. 29 he doth earnestly inculcate iustice and good vvorkes.

MY

1 My litle children, these things I vvrite to you, "that you sinne not. But & if any man shal sinne, vve haue "an [c] aduocate vvith the Father, IESVS Christ 2 the iust: † and he is the propitiation for our sinnes: and not for ours only, but also " for the vvhole vvorldes. 3 † And in this vve know that vve haue 4 knovven him, if vve obserue his commaundements. † "He that saith he knovveth him, and keepeth not his cõmaundements: is a lier and the truth is not in him: 5 † But he that keepeth his vvord, in him in very deede the charitie of God is 6 perfited: in this vve knovv that vve be in him. † He that saith he abideth in him: ought euen as he walked, him self also to vvalke.

ὁ παράκλητον

7 † My deerest, I vvrite not a nevv cõmaundement to you, but an old cõmmaundemẽt vvhich you had from the beginning. The old cõmaundement is the vvord vvhich you haue 8 heard. † Againe * a nevv commaundement vvrite I to you, vvhich thing is true both in him and in you: because the 9 darkenesse is passed, and the true light novv shineth. † He that saith he is in the light, and hateth his brother: is in the 10 darkenesse euen vntil novv. † * He that loueth his brother, 11 abideth in the light, and scandal is not in him. † But he that hateth his brother: is in the darkenesse, and vvalketh in the darkenesse, and knovveth not vvhither he goeth, because the darkenes hath blinded his eies.

Io. 13, 34 15, 12.

1 Io. 3, 14.

12 † I vvrite vnto you litle children, because your sinnes are 13 forgiuen you for his name. † I vvrite vnto you fathers, because you haue knovven him vvhich is from the beginning. I vvrite vnto you yong men, because you haue ouercome the 14 vvicked one. † I vvrite to you infantes, because you haue knovven the Father. I vvrite vnto you yong men, because you are strong, and the vvord of God abideth in you, & you 15 haue ouercome the vvicked one. † Loue not the vvorld, nor those things vvhich are in the vvorld. If any man loue the 16 vvorld, the charitie of the Father is not in him. † because ∷ al that is in the vvorld, is the concupiscence of the flesh, & the concupiscence of the eies, and the pride of life, vvhich is not 17 of the Father, but is of the vvorld. † And the vvorld passeth

∷ Hovv al sinne & tentation procede of these three, see S. Thomas Summe. 1. 2. quæst. 77. art. 5.

and the concupiscence thereof. But he that doeth the vvil of God, abideth for euer.

18 † Litle children, it is the last houre, & as you haue heard, that c Antichrist commeth: now there are become " many antichristes: vvhereby vve knovv, that it is the last houre. 19 † "They vvent out from vs: but" they :: vvere not of vs. for if they had been of vs, they vvould surely haue remained with vs: but" that they may be manifest that they are not al of vs. 20 † But you haue c the vnction from the Holy one, and "knovv al things. 21 † I haue not vvritten to you as to them that knovv not the truth, but as to them that knovv it: and that no lie is of the truth. 22 † Vvho is a lier, but he vvhich denieth that IESVS is not Christ? This is Antichrist vvhich denieth the Father and the Sonne. 23 † Euery one that denieth the Sonne, neither hath he the Father. He that confesseth the Sonne, hath the Father also. 24 † You, that vvhich you haue :: heard from the beginning, let it abide in you. If that abide in you vvhich you haue heard from the beginning, you also shal abide in the Sonne & the Father. 25 † And this is the promis vvhich he promised vs, life euerlasting.

26 † These things haue I vvritten to you concerning them that seduce you. 27 † And you, the vnction vvhich you haue receiued from him, let it abide in you. And you haue no neede that any man teache you: but as his vnction teacheth you of al things, and it is true, and it is no lie. And as it hath taught you, abide c in him. 28 † And now litle children abide in him: that vvhen he shal appeare, vve may haue confidence, and not be cōfounded of him in his cōming. 29 † If you know that he is iust, knovv ye that euery one also :: vvhich doeth iustice, is borne of him.

:: They vvere of vs for the time, that is, of and in the Church: otherwise they could not haue gone out. but they vvere not of the cōstāt sort, or of the elect & predestinat: for then they had taried within, or returned before their death.

:: Keepe that firmely & constantly vvhich you haue heard euen from the beginning, by the mouth of the Apostles: & not that only vvhich you haue receiued by vvriting.

:: Vve see it is Apostolical doctrine, that men may do or vvorke iustice, and that so doing they be iust by their workes proceding of Gods grace, & not, by faith or imputation onely.

c ὁ ἀντίχριστος

c χρίσμα Chrisma. whereof Christ & Christiās

c or, in it.

ANNOTATIONS
CHAP. II.

1. *That you sinne not.*] S. Iohn (saith V. Bede vpon this place) is not contrarie to him self, in that he seeketh here to make them vvithout sinne, vvhom he said in the last chapter could not be vvithout al sinnes. but in the former place he vvarned vs only of our frailety, that vve should not arrogate to our selues perfect innocencie: here he prouoketh vs to vvatchfulnes and diligence in resisting and auoiding sinnes, specially the greater, vvhich by Gods grace may more easily be repelled.

Hovv Christ is our only Aduocate.

1. *An aduocate.*] The calling and office of an Aduocate, is in many things proper to Christ, and in euery condition more singularly and excellently agreing to him then to any Angel, Sainct, or creature liuing. though these also be rightly and truely so called, & that not onely vvithout al derogation, but much to the honour of Christs aduocation. To him

him soly and onely it agreeth to procure vs mercie before Gods face, by the general ransom, price, & paiment of his bloud for our deliuerie, as is said in the sentence folovving, *And he is the propitiation for our sinnes, and not for ours onely, but for the vvhole vvorlds.* In vvhich sort he is our onely aduocate, because he is our onely redeemer. and herevpon he alone immediatly, by and through him self, and vvithout the aide or assistance of any other, man or Angel, in his ovvne name, right, and merites, confidently dealeth in our causes before God our iudge, & so procureth our pardon, vvhich is the highest degree of aduocation that can be.

Al vvhich notvvithstanding, yet the Angels, and Saincts, and our fellovves aliue, may and do pray for vs, and in that they deale vvith God by intercession to procure mercie for vs, may iustly be called our aduocates: not so as Christ is, vvho demaundeth al things immediatly by his ovvne merites, but as secondary intercessors, vvho neuer aske nor obtaine any thing for vs, but *per Christum Dominum nostrum*, by and through Christ our common Lord, Aduocate, and Redeemer of mankinde. And behold hovv S. Augustine (*tract. 1 in ep. Io.* vpon these very vvordes) preuented the Heretikes cauillations. *Sed dicit aliquis &c. But some man vvil say, Do not the Saincts then pray for vs? do not Bishops then or Prelates and Pastors pray for the people? Yes*, saith he: *Marke the Scriptures, and you shal finde that the Apostles praied for the people, and againe desired the people to pray for them, and so the head praieth for al, and the members one for an other.* And likevvise (lest the Heretikes should say, there is a difference betvvixt the liuing and the dead in this case) thus the same holy father vvriteth vpon the 85 Psalme in fine. *Our Lord Iesus Christ doth yet make intercession for vs, al the Martyrs that be vvith him, pray for vs: neither vvil their intercession cease, til vve cease our gronings.*

How Angels, Saincts, & men aliue are our aduocates.

Sainctes in heauen pray for vs.

In this sense therfore vvhosoeuer praieth for vs, either aliue or dead, is our aduocate. as S Augustine (*ep. 59 to Paulinus circa med.*) calleth Bishops, the peoples aduocates, vvhen they giue them their benediction or blessing. So doth the holy Church call our B. Lady our aduocate, by the very vvordes of S. Irenæus, that you may see such speaches be no nevv inuentions of the later ages, but Apostolical. *The obedient Virgin* MARIE (saith he) *is made the aduocate of the disobedient virgin Eue.* And to confound the Protestãts plainely, in that they thinke or pretend that the aduocation or patronage of Saincts should be iniurious to Christ, remẽber that * our Sauiour acknovvledgeth Angels to be deputed for the protection (vvhich is nothing els but aduocation) of infants before the face of God, besides the plaine examples in the old Testament *Gen. 48. v. 16. Tob. 5. v. 27. & c. 12. v. 12. Dan. 10.* And this not onely the Catholike Church, but the very English Protestants them selues in their seruice booke and in the Collect of Michelmas day, professe, and pray for the same protection or aduocation of Angels, and defend the same against their yonger brethren the Puritanes.

Iren. li. 3. c. 33. & li. 5 post med.

D. Hiero. in Mat. c. 18.

The B. virgin is our aduocate.

Angels are our protectors.

2. *For the vvhole vvorlds.*] S. Augustine gathereth hereof against the Donatistes, and al other Heretikes, that vvould driue the Church into corners or some certaine countries, from the vniuersalitie of al Nations (vvhereof it vvas named by the Apostles, Catholike) that the true religion, and Church, and consequently the effect of Christs propitiation, death, and aduocation, pertaineth not to one age, nation, or people, but to the vvhole vvorld. S. Augustine vpon this place *to. 9. tract. 1 in ep. Io.*

The Catholike Church is the only true Church.

4. *He that saith he knovveth.*] To knovv God here, signifieth (as it doth often in the Scriptures) to loue, that is, as in the last chapter, to be in societie vvith him, and to haue familiar and experimental knovvledge of his graces. If any vaunt them selues thus to knovv God, and yet keepe not his commaundements, he is a lier, as al Caluinistes and Lutherans, that professe them selues to be in the fauour of God by onely faith: affirming, that they neither keepe, nor possibly can keepe his commaundements.

Not only faith.

18. *Many antichrists.*] *The holy Apostle S Iohn* (saith S. Cyprian) *did not put a difference betvvixt one heresie or schisme and an other, nor meant any sort that specially separated them selues, but generally called al vvithout exception*, antichristes, *that vvere aduersaries to the Church, or vvere gone out from the same.* And a litle after, *It is euident that al be here called antichristes, that haue seuered them selues from the charitie and vnitie of the Catholike Church.* So vvriteth he *ep. 76. nu. 1 ad Magnum.* Vvhereby vve may learne, that al Heretikes, or rather Arch-heretikes be properly the precursors of that one and special Antichrist, vvhich is to come at the last end of the vvorld, & vvhich is called here immediatly before, ὁ ἀντίχριστος, *that peculiar and singular Antichrist.*

Al Heretikes are antichristes the forerũners of the great Antichrist.

19. *They vvent out from vs.*] An euident note and marke, vvhereby to conuince al Heretikes and false teachers, to vvit, that being once of the common Catholike Christian fellovvship, they forsooke it, and vvent out from the same. Simon Magus, Nicolas the Deacon, Hymenæus, Alexander, Philétus, Arîus, Macedonius, Pelagius, Nestorius, Eutyches, Luther, Caluin, and the like, vvere of the common societie of al vs that be Christian Catholikes, they vvent out from vs vvhom they savv to liue in vnitie of faith and religion together, and made them selues nevv conuenticles. therfore they vvere (as the Apostle here shevveth) antichristes, and vve and al that abide in the auncient fellovvship of Christian religion, that vvent not out of their fellovvship, in vvhich vve neuer vvere, nor out of any other societie of knovven Christians, can not be Schismatikes or Heretikes, but must needes be true Christian Catholike men. Let our aduersaries tel vs, out of vvhat

The marke of al heretikes is, their going out of the Catholike societie.

Church

The Catholikes can not be proued to haue gone out.

Church vve euer departed, vvhen, and vvhere, and vnder vvhat persons it vvas that vve reuolted, as vve can tel them the yere, the places, the Ringleaders of their reuolt.

Hovv Heretikes are of the Church, before they fall.

19. *They vvere not of vs.*] He meaneth not, that Heretikes vvere not, or could not be in or of the Church, before they vvent out or fel into their heresie or schisme: but partly that many of them vvhich aftervvard fall out, though they vvere before vvith the rest, and partakers of al the Sacraments vvith other their fellovves, yet in deede vvere of naughtie life and conscience vvhen they vvere vvithin, and so being rather as il humors and superfluous excrements, then true and liuely partes of the body, after a sort may be said not to haue been of the body at al. So S. Augustine expoundeth these vvordes in his commentarie vpon this place. *tract.* 3. but els vvhere, more agreably as it seemeth, that the Apostle meaneth, that such as vvil not tarie in the Church, but finally forsake it to the end, in the prescience of God, and in respect of the smal benefite they shal haue by their temporal smal abode there, be not of or in the Church, though according to this present state, they are truely members thereof. *Li. de corrept. & gr. c.* 9 & *de dono perseuer.* c. 8.

By heresies constãt Catholikes are knovven.

19. *That they may be manifest*] God permitteth heresie to be, that such as be permanent, constant, and chosen members and children of the Catholike Church, onely knovven to God before, may novv also be made manifest to the vvorld, by their constant remaining in the CHVRCH, vvhen the vvinde and blast of euery heresie or tentation driueth out the other light and vnstable persons.

Euery good Catholike is sufficiently taught by the Church to saluation.

20. *Knovv al things.*] They that abide in the vnitie of Christes Church, haue *the vnction*, that is, the Holy Ghost, vvho teacheth al truth. not that euery member or man thereof hath al knovvledge in him self personally, but that euery one vvhich is of that happie societie to vvhich Christ promised and gaue the Holy Ghost, is partaker of al other mens giftes and graces in the same holy Spirit, to his saluation. Neither neede any to seeke truth at Heretikes handes or others that be gone out, vvhen it is vvithin them selues and onely vvithin them selues in Gods Church. *If thou loue vnitie* (saith S. Augustine) *for thee also hath he, vvhosoeuer hath any thing in it. take avvay enuie, it is thine vvhich I haue, it is mine vvhich thou hast. &c.* Tract. 32 in Euang. Ioan.

CHAP. III.

It is not for the sonnes of God, to sinne mortally, but for the sonnes of the Diuel, vvherby they are knovven one from an other, & not by onely faith. 11 True faith is, that vve also loue our brethren, giuing both our life and substance for them. 19 Such vnfeined loue may haue great confidence before God. 23 because the keeping of his cõmaundements doth much please him, vvhich consist in faith and charitie.

:: Not by nature, as Christ is: but by grace and adoption.

c Hovv we shal see God, & be like vnto him in the next life, see S. Augustine *ep.* 111.112. *& li.* 12. *de ciuit. Dei c.* 29.

:: This teacheth vs that mã sanctifieth him self by his free wil working together with Gods grace. S. Augustine *vpon this place.*

1 SEE vvhat maner of charitie the Father hath giuẽ vs, that vve should be named and be :: the sonnes of God. For this cause the World doth not knovv vs, because it hath not knovven him. 2 † My deerest, novv vve are the sonnes of God: & it hath not yet appeared vvhat we shal be. Vve know that whẽ he shal appeare, we shal be like to him: because vve shal [c] see him as he is. 3 † And euery one that hath this hope in him, :: sanctifieth him self, as he also is holy. 4 † Euery one that committeth sinne, committeth also iniquitie: and " sinne is iniquitie. 5 † And * you knovv that he appeared to take away our sinnes: * and sinne in him there is none. 6 † Euery one that abideth in him, " sinneth not: and euery one that sinneth, hath not seen him, nor knovven him. 7 † Litle children, let no mã seduce you. " He that doeth iustice, is iust: euen as he also is iust. 8 † * He that committeth sinne, is of

Es. 53, 4.

1 Pet. 2, 24.

Io. 8, 44

is of the deuil: because the deuil " sinneth from the beginning. For this, appeared the Sonne of God, that he might dissolue the vvorkes of the deuil. † Euery one that is borne of God, committeth not sinne: because his seede abideth in him, and he can not sinne because he is borne of God. † In this are the children of God manifest, and the children of the deuil. Euery one that is not iust, is not of God, and he that loueth not his brother. † because this is the annuntiation, vvhich you haue heard from the beginning, * That you loue one an other. † Not as * Cain, vvho vvas of the vvicked, and killed his brother. And for vvhat cause killed he him? Because his vvorkes vvere vvicked: but his brothers, iust.

(9) (10) (11) (12)

The Epistle for S. Polycarpus, Ian. 26.

Io. 13. 15 Gen. 4, 8

(13) † Maruel not brethren, if the vvorld hate you. (14) † Vve knovv that vve are translated from death to life, because vve loue the brethren. He that loueth not, abideth in death. (15) † Vvhosoeuer hateth his brother: is a murderer. And you knovv that no murderer hath life euerlasting abiding in him self. (16) † * In this vve haue knovven the charitie of God, because he hath yelded his life for vs: and vve ought to yeld our liues for the brethren. ⊣ (17) † * He that shal haue the substance of the vvorld, and shal :: see his brother haue neede, and shal shut his bovvels from him: hovv doth the charitie of God abide in him?

The Epistle vpon the 2 Sunday after Pentecost.

Io. 15, 13

Io. 2, 15.

:: Euery man is bound to giue almes according to his abilitie, when he seeth his brother in great necessitie.

(18) † My litle children, let vs not loue in word, nor in tongue, (19) but in deede and truth. ⊣ † in this vve knovv that vve are of the truth: and in his sight vve shal persuade our hartes. (20) † For if our hart do reprehend vs: God is greater then our (21) hart, and knovveth al thinges. † My deerest, if our hart do (22) not reprehend vs, vve haue confidence tovvard God. † and * vvhatsoeuer vve shal aske, " vve shal receiue of him: because vve keepe his commaundementes, and doe those (23) thinges vvhich are pleasing before him. † And * this is his commaundement, that vve beleeue in the name of his sonne IESVS Christ: and :: loue one an other, as he hath giuen (24) cōmaundement vnto vs. † And * he that keepeth his commaundementes, abideth in him, and he in him. And in this vve knovv that he abideth in vs, by the Spirit vvhich he hath giuen vs.

Mat. 21. Io. 14. 1 Io. 5. Io. 17, 3. 13, 34. Io. 14, 23.

:: Lest any mā should thinke by the wordes next before, onely faith in Christ to be commaunded or to please God, he addeth to faith the cōmaundemēt of charitie or loue of our neighbour.

ANNOTATIONS
CHAP. III.

Concupiscence remaining after Baptisme is no sinne, vvithout consent.

4. *Sinne is iniquitie.*] Iniquitie is not taken here for vvickednes, as it is commonly vsed both in Latin and in our language, as is plaine by the Greeke vvord ἀνομία, signifying nothing els but a svvaruing or declining from the straight line of the lavv of God or nature. So that the Apostle meaneth, that euery sinne is an obliquitie or defect from the rule of the lavv: but not contrarie, that euery such svvaruing from the lavv, should be properly a sinne, as the Heretikes do vntruely gather, to proue that concupiscence remaining after Baptisme is a very sinne, though vve neuer giue our consent vnto it. And though in the 5 chapter folovving vers. 17. the Apostle turne the speache, affirming euery iniquitie to be a sinne, yet there the Greeke vvord is not the same as before, ἀνομία, but ἀδικία. by vvhich it is plaine that there he meaneth by *iniquitie*, mans actual and proper transgression vvhich must needes be a sinne. See S. Augustine *cont. Iulian. li.* 5 *c.* 3. S. Ambr. *li. de Apologia Dauid c.* 13.

Heretical exposition of Scriptures.

No man in grace sinneth mortally.

6. *Sinneth not.*] Iouinian & Pelagius falsely (as Heretikes vse to doe) argued vpon these vvordes, and those that folovv vers. 9: the one, that the baptized could sinne no more: the other, that no man being or remaining iust could sinne. But among many good senses giuen of this place, this seemeth most agreable, that the Apostle should say, that mortal sinne doth not consist together vvith the grace of God, & therfore can not be committed by a man continuing the sonne of God. and so is the like speache in the 9 verse folovving to be taken. See S. Hierom *li.* 2 *cont. Iouinianum c.* 1.

True iustice.

7. *He that doeth iustice.*] He doth inculcate this often, that mans true iustice or righteousnes consisteth in doing or vvorking iustice, and that so he is iust, and biddeth them not to be seduced by Heretikes, in this point.

Hovv the Diuel sinned from the beginning.

8. *Sinneth from the beginning.*] The Diuel vvas created holy and in grace, and not in sinne: but he fel of his ovvne free vvil from God. Therfore these vvordes, *from the beginning*, may be interpreted thus, from the beginning of sinne, and so the Apostle vvil say, The Diuel committed the first sinne. So S. Augustine *li.* 11 *de ciu. Dei c.* 15 expoundeth it. The most simple meaning seemeth to be, that he sinned from the beginning of the vvorld, not taking the beginning precisely for the first instant or moment of the creation, but straight vpon the beginning, as it must needes also be taken in S. Iohns Gospel c. 8, 44.

Not only faith.

22. *Vve shal receiue, because.*] Let the Protestants be ashamed to say, that vve obtaine al of God by onely faith, the Apostle here attributing it to the keeping of Gods commaundements. Note here also that Gods commaundements are not impossible to be kept, but vvere then, and are novv obserued of good men.

CHAP. IIII.

Vve may not beleeue al that boast of the spirit, but trie them, vvhether they teach Catholike articles of the faith (namely the incarnation of Christ:) vvhether their doctrine be not vvorldly, and them selues disobedient hearers of the Apostles. 7 *Vve must loue one an other, considering the exceding loue of God in sending his sonne to saue vs.* 17 *An argument of perfect charitie is, if vve haue nothing in our conscience to feare in the day of Iudgement.* 19 *And an argument that vve loue God is, if vve loue our brethren.*

1 MY deerest, "beleeue not euery spirit, but " proue the spirites if they be of God: because many false prophetes are gone out into the vvorld † 2 In this is the spirit of God knovven. " euery spirit that confesseth IESVS Christ to haue come in flesh, is of God: † 3 and euery spirit "that dissolueth IESVS, is not of God: and this is [c] antichrist, of vvhom you haue heard that he commeth, and novv he is in

c τὸ τοῦ ἀντιχρίστου

4 in the vvorld. † You are of God, litle children, and haue ouercome him. because greater is he that is in you, then he 5 that is in the vvorld. † They are of the vvorld: therfore of 6 the vvorld they speake, and the vvorld heareth them. † Vve are of God. * He that knovveth God, heareth vs. he that is not of God, heareth vs not. "in this vve knovv the spirit of truth, and the spirit of errour.

Io. 8, 47. 10, 27.

7 † My deerest, let vs loue one an other: because charitie is of God. And euery one that loueth, is borne of God, & knovv-8 eth God. † He that loueth not, knovveth not God: because 9 God is charitie. † * In this hath the charitie of God appeared in vs, because God hath sent his only-begotten sonne into the 10 vvorld, that vve may liue by him. † In this is charitie: not as though vve haue loued him, but because he hath loued vs, and sent his sonne a propitiation for our sinnes.

Io. 3, 16.

The Epistle vpon the first Sunday after Pentecost.

11 † My deerest, if God hath so loued vs: vve also ought to 12 loue one an other. † * God :: no man hath seen at any time. If vve loue one an other, God abideth in vs, and his charitie 13 in vs is perfited. † In this vve knovv that vve abide in him, 14 and he in vs: because he of his Spirit hath giuen to vs. † And vve haue seen, and doe testifie, that the Father hath sent his 15 Sonne the Sauiour of the vvorld. † Vvhosoeuer shal confesse that IESVS is the Sonne of God, God abideth in him, 16 and he in God. † And vve haue knovven and haue beleeued the charitie, vvhich God hath in vs. God is charitie: and he 17 that abideth in charitie, abideth in God, and God in him. † In this is charitie perfited vvith vs, "that vve may haue confidence in the day of iudgement: because as he is, vve also are 18 in the vvorld. † "Feare is not in charitie: but perfect charitie casteth out feare, because feare hath painefulnes. and he that 19 feareth, is not perfect in charitie. † Let vs therfore loue God, 20 because God first hath loued vs. † If any man shal say, that I loue God: and hateth his brother, he is a lier. For he that loueth not his brother vvhom he seeth: God vvhom he seeth 21 not, hovv can he loue? † * And this commaundement vve haue from God: that he vvhich loueth God, loue also his brother. ✠

Io. 1, 18. 1 *Tim.* 6, 16.

:: No man in this life, nor with corporal eies, cá see the proper essence or substáce of the Deitie. *See S. August. ad Paulin. de vidēdo Deo. ep. 112.*

Io. 13, 34. 15, 12.

ANNOTATIONS
CHAP. IIII.

Heretical boasting of the spirit.

1. *Beleeue not euery spirit.*] That is, Receiue not euery doctrine of such as boast them selues to haue the spirit. For there be many false prophets, that is to say, Hæretikes, which shal goe out of the Church, and chalenge the spirit, and vaunt of Gods word, Scripture, and Gospel, vvhich in deede be seduceers.

The Church only, not euery priuate man, hath to proue and discerne spirites.

1. *Proue the spirites.*] It is not meant by this place, as the Protestants vvould haue it, that euery particular person should of him self examine, trie, or iudge who is a true or false doctor, and which is true or false doctrine. But the Apostle here would euery one to discerne these diuersities of spirites, by taking knovvledge of them to vvhom God hath giuen the gift of discerning spirites and doctrines (vvhich S. Paul expresly saith is giuen but to some, and not to euery one, 1 *Cor.* 12.) and by obeying the Church of God, to whom Christ hath giuen * the Spirit of truth. And this is onely the sure way to proue the spirites and doctrines of these daies. And al they that would bring vs from our Pastors and the Churches iudgement, to our owne priuate trial, seeke nothing els but to driue vs to miserable vncertainty in al our beleefe. as Caluin doth, who vpon this place saith, that priuate men may examine the general Councels doctrines.

Io. 14, 16.

Caluin.

To confesse or deny any article which the Cath. Church teacheth, is at al times a certaine marke of Catholike or heretike.

2. *Euery spirit that confesseth.*] The Apostle speaketh according to that time, and for that part of Christian doctrine which then vvas specially to be confessed, taught, & mainteined against certaine vvicked Hæretikes, Cerinthus, Ebion, and the like, that taught wickedly against the person and both natures of Christ IESVS. The Apostle therfore giueth the faithful people this token to knovv the true teachers of those daies from the false. Not that this marke vvould serue for al times, or in case of al other false doctrines, but that it vvas then a necessarie note. As if a good Catholike vvriter, Pastor, or parents would vvarne al theirs, now in these daies, to giue eare onely to such teachers as acknowledge Christ our Sauiour to be really present, and sacrificed in the B. Masse, & that al such are true preachers and of God, the rest to be of the Diuel, or to be counted the spirit of Antichrist. Vvhich spirit of Antichrist (he saith) was come euen then, and is no doubt much more novv in al Hæretikes, al being precursors of that great Antichrist vvhich shal come tovvards the later end.

Many old heresies that dissolued Christ.

3. *That dissolueth.*] To dissolue, loose, or separate IESVS a sunder, vvas proper to al those old Heretikes that taught either against his Diuinitie, or Humanitie, or the Vnitie of his person, being of two natures, as Cerinthus, Ebion, Nestorius, Eutyches, Manes or Manichæus, Cerdon, Apelles, Apollinaris and the like. And this is one place by vvhich vve may see that the common Greeke copies be not euer authentical, and that our old approued translation may not alvvaies be examined by the Greeke that novv is, vvhich the Protestants onely folow: but that it is to be presupposed, vvhen our old Latin text differeth plainely from the Greeke, that in old time either al or the more approued Greeke reading was othervvise, and that often the said Greeke was corrupted then or since by Heretikes or otherwise. For of the Greekes, S. Irenæus *li.* 3. *c.* 18: among the Latin fathers, S. Augustine *tract.* 6. *in fine*, S. Leo *ep.* 10. *c.* 5, and Venerable Bede did reade as we doe. and this reading maketh more against the said Heretikes, then that vvhich the common Greeke novv hath, to vvit, *Euery spirit that confesseth not Christ to haue come in flesh, is not of God.* vvhich is also in effect said before vers. 2. And that therfore it vvas corrupted and altered by Heretikes, see the vvordes of Socrates also a Greeke vvriter, very agreable to this purpose. *Nestorius* (saith he) *being eloquent by nature,* vvhich is often in Heretikes, *accounted him self therfore learned, & disdained to study the old interpreters, counting him self better then them al: being ignorant that in S. Iohns Catholike epistle the old* (Greeke) *copies had,* EVERY ONE THAT DISSOLVETH IESVS, IS NOT OF GOD. So saith he, adding moreouer that such as vvould separate the diuinitie from the dispensation of Christs humanitie, tooke out of the old copies this sense. for vvhich the old expositours noted that these which would loose IESVS, had corrupted this Epistle. See also the Tripartite li. 12. c. 4.

The Greeke text corrupted by old heretikes.

li. 7. c. 32.

A sure marke of true or false teachers.

6. *In this vve knovv.*] This is the most sure & general marke to knovv the true spirites and prophets from the false: that those vvhich be of God, wil heare and obey their Apostles and lavvful pastors succeding the Apostles, and submit them selues to the Church of God: the other, that be not of God, wil not heare either Apostle, pastor, or Church, but be their ovvne iudges.

Against the Protestāts special faith and

17. *That vve may haue confidence.*] Confidence called in Latin *Fiducia*, is neither al one with faith, nor a persuasion infallible that maketh a man no lesse secure and certaine of his saluation, then of the things that vve are bound to beleeue, as the Protestants falsely teach;

teach: but it is onely a hope wel corroborated, confirmed, and strengthened vpon the promises and grace of God, and the parties merites. And the vvordes both folowing & going before, proue also euidently against the Protestants, that our confidence and hope in the day of iudgement dependeth not onely vpon our apprehension of Christs merites by faith, or vpon his grace and mercie, but also vpon our conformitie to Christ in this life, in charitie and good vvorkes. And that is the doctrine of S. Peter vvhen he said, *Labour, that by good vvorkes you may make sure your vocation and election.* and S. Paules meaning, vvhen he said, *I haue fought a good fight, there is laid vp for me a crovvne of iustice, vvhich our Lord vvil render to me in that day, a iust iudge.*

presumptuous securitie of saluation.

2 Pet. 1, 10.
2 Tim. 4, 7.

18. *Feare is not in charitie.*] The Heretikes very falsly vnderstand this place so, that Christian godly men ought to haue no doubt, mistrust, or feare of hel and damnation. Vvhich is most euidently against the Scriptures, commending euery where vnto vs the awe and feare of God and his iudgements. *Feare him* (saith our Sauiour Mat. 10) *that can cast body and soul into hel.* And Psal. 118. *Pearse my flesh vvith thy feare.* Vvhich feare of Gods iudgements caused S. Paul & al good men to chastise their bodies, lest they should be reprobate and damned. And the vvise man for this cause affirmeth him to be happie, *that is euer fearful.* And holy Iob saith, *I feared al my vvorkes.* And the Apostle, *Vvith feare and trembling vvorke your saluation.* Vvhich kinde of feare is euen in the iustest men and most ful of charitie, consisting wel with the same vertue, and is called *Filialis timor*, because it is such as the good childe ought to haue toward his father.

The feare of God in iust men, cōsisteth with charitie.

1 Cor. 9.
Prou. 28.
Iob. 9.
Phil. 2.

But there is a kinde of feare vvhich standeth not with charitie, and is cleane against hope also, that vvhich bringeth such perplexitie and anxietie of conscience, that it induceth a man to mistrust or despaire of Gods mercies. That seruile feare also vvhich maketh a man often to leaue sinning and to doe the external vvorkes of iustice, not for any loue or delight he hath in God or his lawes, but onely for feare of damnation, though it be not il in it self, but very profitable, as that vvhich helpeth toward the loue of God, yet it standeth not with charitie neither, but is daily more and more lessened, and at length quite driuen out by charitie. Of these kinde of feares then the Apostle speaketh, and (as some expound) of the feare of men also, of vvhich our Sauiour saith, *Feare not them that kil the body.*

Vvhat feare agreeth not with charitie.

Seruile feare is not il.

Mat. 10.

CHAP. V.

They that loue God, must loue his natural sonne IESVS, *and his sonnes by adoption, and keepe his commaundements, vvhich to the regenerate are light.* 4 *But not, vnles they continue in the Catholike faith, namely of this article, that* IESVS *is the sonne of God, and therfore able to giue vs life euerlasting,* 14 *and al our petitions,* 16 *and our praiers for al our brethren that sinne not vnto death, dying in their mortal sinnes by impenitence. Last of al, he vvarneth them not to communicate vvith Idols.*

1 WHOSOEVER beleeueth that IESVS is Christ, is borne of God. And euery one that loueth him vvhich begat: loueth him also vvhich vvas borne of him. 2 † In this vve knovv that vve loue the children of God: vvhen as vve loue God, and keepe his commaundementes. 3 † For this is the charitie of God, that vve keepe his commaundementes: * and " his commaundementes are not heauy. 4 † Because al that is borne of God, ouercommeth the vvorld. and this is the victorie vvhich ouercommeth the vvorld, our faith. 5 † Vvho is he * that ouercōmeth the vvorld, but he that beleeueth that IESVS is the sonne of God? 6 † This is he that came by vvater and bloud IESVS Christ: not in vvater only, but in vvater and bloud. And it is

Mat. 11, 30.
1 Cor. 15, 57.

The Epistle vpon *Dominica in albis* or Low Sunday.

the Spirit vvhich testifieth, that Christ is the truth.

† For there be" three vvhich giue testimonie in heauen, the 7 Father, the Vvord, and the Holy Ghost. and these three be one. † And there be three vvhich giue testimonie in earth: 8 the spirit, vvater, and bloud. ˋand these three be one'. † If vve 9 receiue the testimonie of men, the testimonie of God is greater. because this is the testimonie of God vvhich is greater, that he hath testified of his sonne. † * He that beleeueth in 10 the sonne of God, hath the testimonie of God in him self. † He that beleeueth not the Sōne, maketh him a lier: because he beleeueth not in the testimonie vvhich God hath testified of his sonne. † And this is the testimonie, that God hath giuen 11 vs life euerlasting. And this life is in his sonne. † He that 12 hath the Sonne, hath life. he that hath not the sonne of God, hath not life.

† These thinges I vvrite to you, that you may knovv that 13 you haue eternal life which beleeue in the name of the sonne of God. † And this is the confidence which vve haue toward 14 him: that, * vvhatsoeuer vve shal aske according to his vvill, he heareth vs. † And [c] vve knovv that he heareth vs vvhat- 15 soeuer vve shal aske: vve knovv that vve haue the petitions vvhich vve request of him.

† He that knoweth his brother to sinne a sinne not to 16 death, let him aske, and life shal be giuen him, sinning not to death. There is " a sinne to death: " for that I say not that any man aske. † Al [c] iniquitie, is sinne. And there is a sinne ˋto 17 death'. † Vve know that euery one vvhich is borne of God, 18 sinneth not: but the generation of God preserueth him, and the vvicked one toucheth him not. † Vve knovv that vve 19 are of God, and the vvhole vvorld is set in vvickednesse. † And vve knovv that the sonne of God commeth: and he 20 * hath giuen vs vnderstanding, that vve may knovv the true God, & may be in his true sonne. This is the true God, & life euerlasting. † My litle children, keepe your selues " from 21 Idols. Amen.

Io.3,36.

Mt.7,7. 21,22. 1 Io.3, 22.

c or, *if vve knovv*

c ἀδικία. ˋ*not to death.*

Luc.24, 45. ἀπὸ τῶν εἰδώλων.

ANNOTATIONS
CHAP. V.

The cōmaundements possible to be kept.

3. *His commaundements are not heauie.*] Hovv can the Protestants say that Gods commaundements can not possibly be fulfilled or kept in this life, seing the Apostle saith, *they be not heauie:* and Christ saith, *his yoke is svveete, and his burden light?* See for the ful vnderstanding of this place. *Mat.11.* S.Aug *v.30.*

S. Augustine *de perfectione iustitiæ c.10.* The Heretikes in fauour of their foresaid errour, rather translate, *His commaundements are not* * *greuous*: then, *are not heauie*.

* *baqua*

7. *Three vvhich giue testimonie.*] An expresse place for the distinction of three persons, & the vnitie of nature and essence in the B. Trinitie: against the Arians and other like Heretikes, vvho haue in diuers ages found them selues so pressed vvith these plaine Scriptures, that they haue (as it is thought) altered and corrupted the text both in Greeke and Latin many vvaies: euen as the Protestants handle those textes that make against them. But because vve are not novv troubled vvith Arianisme so much as vvith Caluinisme, vve neede not stand vpon the varietie of readings or expositions of this passage. See S. Hierom in his epistle put before the 7 Canonical or Catholike Epistles.

Heret. translation.

Three persons & one substãce in the B. Trinitie.

The Arians corrupt the text of Scripture.

16. *A sinne to death.*] A sinne to death is an other thing then a mortal sinne. for it is that mortal sinne onely, vvhereof a man is neuer penitent before his death, or in vvhich he continueth til death, and dieth in it. *I affirme* (saith S. Augustine de correp. & grat. c. 12) *that a sinne to death is to leaue faith vvorking by charitie euen til death.* So likevvise in the vvordes before, *a sinne not to death*, is not that vvhich vve call a venial sinne, but any that a man committeth and continueth not therin til death.

Vvhat is a sinne to death.

16. *For that I say not.*] If the sinne to death vvhereof he speaketh, be the sinne vvherein a man dieth vvithout repentance, according to S. Augustines vvordes before rehearsed: then the praier vvhich he speaketh of, must needes be praier for the dead. because he speaketh of praying, or not praying, for them that died in deadly sinne, exhorting vs to pray, and encouraging vs to doe it vvith confidence to be heard, if vve pray, for them that departed this life not in deadly sinne: and contrarivvise in maner dissuading & discouraging vs from praying for such as continued in vvickednes euen til their liues end. And S. Augustine setteth dovvne the Churches practise agreable to the Apostles meaning, li. 21 c. 24 de Ciuit. Dei. *If there be any* (saith he) *that persist til death in impenitence of hart, doth the Church novv pray for them, that is, for the soules of them that so are departed?* So saith he. And this is the cause, that *Concilium Bracharense primum cap.* 34 forbiddeth to pray for such as die in desperation, or kil them selues: and the reason, vvhy the Church forbeareth to pray for Heretikes that die in their heresie, or mainteine heresie vnto death and by their death.

Praier for the dead.

Some of the dead may not be praied for.

And that the place is most properly or onely meant of praying for the departed, this conuinceth, that neither the Church nor any man is dehorted here from praying for any sinner yet liuing, nor for the remission of any sinne in this life: al sinnes (of vvhat sort soeuer) being pardonable, so long as the committers of them be in case and state to repent: as they be, so long as they be in this vvorld. And vve see that the Church praieth, and is often heard, for Heretikes, Ievves, Turkes, Apostataes, and vvhat other infidels or il men soeuer, during their liues. And it is great blasphemie that the Caluinistes vtter vpon this place: to vvit, that Apostasie and certaine other sinnes of the reprobate, can not be forgiuen at al in this life. Vvhich they hold, onely to auoid the sequele of praying for the dead vpon these vvordes of S. Iohn. besides that they must take vpon them presumptuously, to knovv and discerne of Gods secretes, vvho be reprobate, and vvho be not, and according to that, pray for some, and not for othersome. al vvhich is most vvicked and absurd presumption.

It is proued that the Apostle speaketh of praying for the dead.

The Caluinists blasphemie, to auoid this sense of the Apostle.

As for their allegation, that S. Ieremie the Prophet vvas forbidden to pray for the Ievves, and vvarned that he should not be heard, Chap. 7. 11. 14: there is great difference. first, he had a reuelation by the vvordes of God, that they vvould continue in their vvickednes, as vve haue not of any certaine person, vvhereof S. Iohn here speaketh. secondly, Ieremie vvas not forbidden to pray for the remission of their sinnes, nor had denial to be heard therein for any mans particular case, vvhereof the Apostle here speaketh: but he vvas told that they should not escape the temporal punishment and affliction vvhich he had designed for them, and that he vvould not heare him therein.

21. *From idols.*] It is so knovven a treacherie of Heretikes to trãslate *idola* images (as here and in a number of places, specially of the English Bible printed the yere 1562) that vve neede not much to stand vpon it. As this also is seen to al the vvorld, that they doe it of purpose to seduce the poore ignorant people, and to make them thinke, that vvhatsoeuer in the Scriptures is spoken against the idols of the Gentiles (vvhich the Prophet calleth *Simulachra Gentium*) is meant of pictures, sacred images, & holy memories of Christ and his Saincts. Against such seducers the second sacred Councel of Nice, called the seuenth Synode, decreeth thus Act. 4. pag. 122. *Quicunque sententias sacræ scripturæ de Idolis, contra venerandas imagines adducunt, anáthema. Qui venerandas imagines idola appellant, anáthema. Qui dicunt quod Christiani adorant imagines vt Deos, anathema.* that is, *Anáthema to al them that bring the sentences of holy Scripture touching Idols, against the venerable images. Anáthema to them that call the venerable images, idols. Anáthema to them that say, Christians adore images as gods.*

Heret. translation against sacred images.

Psal. 113.

Edit. Colo. an. 1567.

The 2 Councel of Nice pronoũceth anáthema, that is, a curse against the Caluinists.

Novv in their later translations the Heretikes perceiuing that the vvorld seeth their vnhonest dealing, corrected them selues in some places, and in this place haue put, *idols*, in the text: but to giue the people a vvatchvvord that the Churches images are to be comprised in the vvord,

idols,

idols, * they haue put, *images*, in the margent. But concerning this matter, it is most euident that neither euery idol is an image, nor euery image an idol: and that, hovvsoeuer the origine or etymologie of the vvord, *idol*, may be taken in the Greeke, yet both the vvordes and the things be in truth and by the vse of al tonges, far differing. The great dragon that the Babylonians adored (*Dan.* 14) vvas an idol, but not an image: the Cherubins in Salomons temple vvere images, but not idols. and the face of the Queene in her coine or els vvhere, as Cæsars face vpon the coine that Christ called for, is an image, but not an idol. and the Heretikes dare not translate that text of Scripture thus, *Vvhose idol is this superscription?* nor call the Queenes image, the idol of the Queene: nor Christ, the idol of his father: nor vvoman, the idol of the man: nor man, the idol of God. al vvhich in Scripture be named images for al that, and be so in deede, and not idols. vvhich conuinceth, that the Heretikes be false & corrupt translatours in this place and other the like, confounding these tvvo vvordes as if they vvere al one.

The great difference of idol & image.

** The Bible of the yere 1577.*

But as for the hauing of images or purtraites of holy things, not onely in priuate houses, but also in Churches, God him self doth vvarrant vs, vvho * cōmaunded euen the Ievves them selues (a people most prone to idolatrie, and that after he had giuen them a special precept of not hauing, making, or vvorshipping of idols) to make the images of Angels (the Cherubins) and that in the soueraine holiest place of adoration that vvas in the Temple, & about the Arke. yea and in respect of vvhich sacred images partly, they did (as S. Hierom saith *ep.* 17 *c.* 3) so great reuerence to the holy place called *Sancta sanctorum.* If they then vvere vvarranted and commaunded to make and haue in so great reuerēce the images of mere spirites or Angels, vvhose natural shape could not be expressed: hovv much more may vve Christians haue and reuerence the images of Christ, his B. mother, the Apostles, and other Saincts, being men, vvhose shape may be expressed? So doth the said Nicene Councel argue against the Heretikes vvhich at that time vvere the Aduersaries of images.

Sacred images in Churches, by Gods ovvne vvarrant.

** Exod.* 25.

The 2 Councel of Nice vvas gathered against Imagebreakers.

And note here, that eight hundred yeres agoe, they vvere straight counted Heretikes, that began to speake against images, and that Councel vvas called purposely for them, and condemned them for Heretikes, & confirmed the former auncient reuerence and vse of sacred images. vvhich began euen in our Sauiours time or litle after, vvhen good religious folke for loue and reuerence made his image, namely the vvoman that he healed of the blouddy fluxe. vvhich image vvas also approued by miracles, as the Ecclesiastical historie telleth, and namely Eusebius *Eccl. hist. li.* 7 *c.* 14.* vvho also vvitnesseth that the images of Peter and Paul vvere in his daies. as you may see also in S. Augustine (*li. d. consens. Euangelist. c.* 10) that their pictures commonly stoode together in Rome, euen as at this day. Of our Ladies image see S. Gregorie *li.* 7 *ep.* 5. *indict.* 2 *ad Ianuar.* & *ep* 53. In vvhom also (*li.* 7. *ep.* 109) you may see the true vse of images, & that they are the bookes of the vnlearned, and that the people ought to be instructed and taught the right vse of them, euen as at this day good Catholike folke doe vse them to helpe & increase their deuotion, in al Catholike Churches: yea the Lutherans them selues reteine them still. S. Damascene vvrote three bookes in defense of sacred images against the foresaid Heretikes.

The antiquitie of holy images.

** Loco citato.*

The vse and fruite of holy images.

THE SECOND EPISTLE OF IOHN THE APOSTLE.

He commendeth the lady and her sonnes for continuing in the old faith, bidding them so to doe hereafter also, lest they lose the revvard of their vvorkes in the day of iudgement: and to loue the true beleeuers, but vvith Heretikes to haue no societie: expressing also the points then in controuersie.

THE Senior to the lady Elect and her 1 children, vvhom I loue in truth, and not I onely, but also al that haue knowen the truth, † for the truth vvhich 2 abideth in vs, and shal be vvith vs for euer. † Grace be vvith you, mercie, 3 peace from God the Father, and from Christ IESVS the sonne of the Father in truth, and charitie.

4 † I vvas exceding glad, because I haue found of thy children vvalking in truth, as vve haue receiued commaundement of the Father. 5 † And novv I beseeche thee Lady, not as vvriting a nevv commaundement to thee, but that vvhich vve haue had "from the beginning, * that vve loue one an other. 6 † And this is charitie, that vve vvalke according to his commaundements. For this is the commaundement, that as you haue heard from the beginning, you walke in the same: 7 † because many seducers are gone out into the vvorld, which do not confesse IESVS Christ to haue come into flesh: this is a seducer and an antichrist.

Io. 15, 12. 1 Io. 3, 11.

8 † Looke to your selues, that you lose not the thinges vvhich you haue vvrought: but that you may receiue a ful 9 ∷ revvard. † Euery one that [c] reuolteth, and persisteth not in in the doctrine of Christ: hath not God. He that persisteth in the doctrine: the same hath both the Father, and the Sonne. 10 † If * any man come to you, and bring not "this doctrine: "receiue him not into the house," nor say, *God saue you*, vnto 11 him. † For he that saith vnto him, *God saue you*, communicateth vvith his vvicked vvorkes.

∷ Revvard for keeping fast the Catholike faith.

c To goe backe or reuolt from the receiued truth and doctrine Apostolical, is damnable.

Ro. 16, 17.

12 † Hauing moe thinges to vvrite vnto you: I vvould not by paper and inke: for I hope that I shal be vvith you, and 13 speake mouth to mouth: that your ioy may be ful. † The children of thy sister electe salute thee.

ANNOT.

6. *From the beginning.*] This is the rule of a Christian Catholike man, to vvalke in that faith and vvorship of God vvhich he hath receiued from the beginning. Vvhich is that vvhich vve novv call according to the Scriptures, *the tradition of the Apostles*: that vvhich is come to vs from man to man, from Bishop to Bishop, and so from the Apostles. So shal a faithful man auoid seducers that rise vp in euery age, teaching nevv doctrine.

To hold fast the old receiued faith.

10. *This doctrine.*] The Apostles, and true Pastors their lavvful successors, and the Church of God in holy Councel, vse to set dovvne the true doctrine in those pointes vvhich Heretikes call into controuersie. Vvhich being once done and declared to the faithful, they neede no other marke or description to knovv an Heretike or false teacher by, but that he commeth vvith an other doctrine then that vvhich is set dovvne to them. Neither can the Heretikes shift them selues, as novv a daies they vvoulddoe, saying, ô let vs first be proued Heretikes by the Scriptures, let them define an Heretike. No, this is not the Apostles rule. Many a good honest shepheard knovveth a vvoolfe, that can not define him. but the Apostle saith, If he bring not this set doctrine, he is a seducer. So holy Church saith novv, Christ is really in the B. Sacrament, vnder forme of bread and vvine &c. If therfore he bring not this doctrine, he is a seducer, and an Heretike: and vve must auoide him, vvhether in his ovvne definitions and censures he seeme to him self an Heretike or no.

To bring vvilfully an other doctrine then the Catholike Church setteth dovvne, is alvvaies a marke of seducers and Heretikes.

10. *Receiue him not.*] Though in such times and places vvhere the communitie or most part be infected, necessitie often forceth the faithful to conuerse vvith such in vvorldly affaires, to salute them, to eate and speake vvith them, and the Church by decree of Councel, for the more quietnes of timorous consciences prouideth, that they incurre not excommunication or other censures for communicating in vvorldly affaires vvith any in this kinde, except they be by name excommunicated

Vvhen & wherein to couerse With Heretikes, is tolerable: vvhen.

vvhen & where-in, it is damnable.

cated or declared to be Heretikes: yet euen in vvorldly conuersatiō and secular actes of our life, vve must auoid them as much as vve may, because their familiaritie is many vvaies contagious and noisome to good men, namely to the simple: but in matter of religion, in praying, reading their bookes, hearing their sermons, presence at their seruice, partaking of their Sacraments, and al other communicating vvith them in spiritual things, it is a great damnable sinne to deale vvith them.

S. Iohn vvould not be in one bath vvith Cerinthus the Heretike.

10. *Nor say, God saue you.*] S. Irenæus (*li. 3 c. 3*) reporteth a notable storie of this holy Apostle touching this point, out of S. Polycarpus, vvhich is this. *There be some* (saith he) *that haue heard Polycarpe say, that vvhen Iohn the disciple of our Lord vvas going to Ephesus, into a bath, to vvash him self, and savv Cerinthus the Heretike vvithin the same, he sodenly skipt out, saying that he feared lest the bath should fall, because Cerinthus the enemie of truth vvas vvithin.* So saith he of S. Iohn, and addeth also a like vvorthie example of S. Polycarpe him self: vvho on a time meeting Marcion the Heretike, and the said Marcion calling vpon him, and asking him vvhether he knew him not: *Yes,* quoth Polycarpe, *I knovv thee for Satans sonne and heire. So great feare* (saith S. Irenæus) *had the Apostles and their disciples to communicate in vvord onely, vvith such as vvere adulterers or corrupters of the truth, as S. Paul also vvarned, vvhen he said, A man that is an Heretike, after the first and second admonition auoid.* So far Irenæus. If then, to speake vvith them or salute them, is so earnestly to be auoided according to this Apostles example & doctrine: vvhat a sinne is it to flatter them, to serue them, to marie vvith them, and so forth?

The like zeale of S. Polycarpe, and other Apostolike men in not communicating vvith Heretikes.

Tit. 3.

THE THIRD EPISTLE OF IOHN THE APOSTLE.

He commendeth Gaius, for continuing in the truth, and for susteining or succouring true preachers, 9 noting Diotrepes for the contrarie, and praising Demetrius.

HE Seniour to Gaius the deerest, whom I loue in truth. 1

† My deerest, concerning al thinges I make my praier that thou procede prosperously, and fare vvel, as thy soule doth prosperously. 2 † I vvas exceding glad vvhen the brethren came, and gaue testimonie to thy truth, euen as thou vvalkest in truth. 3 † Greater ˋthankeˊ haue I not of them, then that I may heare my children do vvalke in truth. 4 † My deerest, thou doest faithfully vvhatsoeuer thou vvorkest on the brethren, ∴ and that vpon strangers. 5 † they haue rendred testimonie to thy charitie in the sight of the Church: vvhō, thou shalt doe vvel, bringing on their vvay in maner vvorthie of God. 6 † For, for his name did they depart, taking nothing of 7

pleasure χαρὰν, χάριν

∴ A great grace to be beneficial to strangers, specially to them that be of our Catholike faith and suffer for the same.

8 of the Gentiles. † Vve therfore ought to receiue such : that vve may be coadiutors of the truth.

9 † I had vvritten perhaps to the Church: but he that loueth to beare [b] primacie among them, Diótrepes, doth not

10 receiue vs. † For this cause, if I come,[c] I vvil aduertise his vvorkes vvhich he doeth : vvith malicious vvordes chatting against vs. and as though these thinges suffise him not : neither him self doth receiue the brethren, and them that do re-

11 ceiue, he prohibiteth, and casteth out of the Church. † My deerest, do not imitate euil, but that vvhich is good . He that doeth vvel , is of God : he that doeth il , hath not seen God.

12 † To Demetrius testimonie is giuen of al , and of the truth it self, yea and vve giue testimonie: and thou knovvest that our testimonie is true.

13 † I had many thinges to vvrite vnto thee : but I vvould

14 not by inke and penne vvrite to thee. † But I hope forthvvith to see thee, and vve vvil speake mouth to mouth. Peace be to thee. The freendes salute thee. Salute the freendes by name.

c commonebo. ὑπομνήσω

b It seemeth (saith S. Bede) he vvas an Arch-heretike or proud Sectmaister.

c That is, *I vvil rebuke them and make them knovven to be vvicked.* Bede.

THE ARGVMENT OF THE EPISTLE OF S. IVDE.

N *the Goſpel theſe are called* Fratres Ieſu, the brethren of Ieſus: *Iames and Ioſeph, and Simon, and Iude. Their father is called Alphæus, vvhere Iames is termed,* Iames of Alphæus: *and their mother,* Maria Iacobi minoris. Marie the mother of Iames the yonger and of Ioſeph. *Vvhich Marie in an other place being called* Maria Cleophæ, *vve perceiue their father vvas named both Alphæus and alſo Cleophas. And that this Cleophas vvas brother to Ioſeph our Ladies huſband,* * *Hegeſippus telleth vs. Therfore becauſe Ioſeph vvas called the father of Chriſt, his brothers children, vvere called the brethren, that is (according to the cuſtom of the ſcripture alſo) the kinſmen of our Lord: and not becauſe they vvere the children of Ioſeph him ſelf by an other vvife, much leſſe (as Heluidius the heretike did blaſpheme) by our B Ladie the perpetual virgin* MARIE. *Hovvbeit ſome good authors ſay, that their mother Marie vvas the natural ſiſter of our Ladie, and that therfore they are called,* Fratres Domini, the brethren of our Lord.

Mat. 13
Mat. 10.
Mat. 1[illegible]
Ioh. 19.

* Euſeb. hiſt. li. 3. c. 10.

Hovvſoeuer that be, three of them are reckened amōg the 12. *Apoſtles, Iames, and Simon Cananæus, and Iude. Yea and that they vvere ſomevvhat more then Apoſtles, though leſſe then Peter, S. Paul ſignifieth, vvhere he ſaith ſpeaking of him ſelf and Barnabas:* As alſo the other Apoſtles, and the brethren of our Lord, and Cephas. 1. *Cor.* 9.

Luc. 6.
Mat. 10.

And as S. Luke calleth this Iude, Iude of Iames, *ſo he calleth him ſelf in this Epiſtle of his,* Iude the ſeruant of Ieſus Chriſt, and the brother of Iames. *S. Mathevv and S. Marke do call him* Thaddæus, *as* Lebbæus *alſo in the Greeke. His feaſt and his brother Simons together, the Church keepeth Octob.* 28. *called* Simon and Iudes day.

Mat. 10.
Mar. 3.

His Epiſtle is an Inuectiue againſt al heretikes (as it vvere a Commentarie of 2 *Pet.* 2.) *and namely (as* * *S. Aug. hath told vs) againſt thoſe, vvhich miſconſtred S. Paules Epiſtles and held* Only faith, *vvhom he calleth therfore,* Men that transferre or peruert the grace of God into riotouſnes, *v.* 4. *exhorting Catholikes to be conſtant and vnmoueable from their old faith, and to contend for the keeping thereof, v.* 3. *and v.* 20. *For, heretikes (ſaith he)* ſegregate them ſelues *from the Church and from her faith. v.* 19.

pag. 379. 646.

THE

THE CATHOLIKE EPISTLE OF IVDE THE APOSTLE.

He exhorteth them to stand to their old faith, shevving them by examples, that it is damnable not to continue and be constant: 8 inueighing against the lecherie, blasphemie, apostasie, banketing of the heretikes, 14 and that their damnation vvas long foretold. 17 Catholikes therfore to be vnmoueable, to reproue the obstinate, to recouer al not desperate, to confirme the vveake, and to liue them selues vertuously and vvithout mortal sinne, vvhich by Gods grace they may doe.

1 IVDE the seruant of IESVS Christ, and brother of Iames: to them that are in God the Father beloued, and in IESVS Christ preserued, and called. 2 † Mercie to you, and peace and charitie be accomplished.

3 † My deerest, taking al care to vvrite vnto you of your common saluation, I thought it necessarie to vvrite vnto you: beseeching you to contend for the faith once deliuered to the saincts. 4 † For there are certaine men secretely entred in (vvhich vvere long ago prescribed vnto this iudgement) impious, transferring the grace of our God ∷ into riotousnes, and denying the onely Dominator, and our Lord IESVS Christ. 5 † * But I vvil admonish you, that once knovv al things, that [c] IESVS, sauing the people out of the land of Ægipt, * secondly destroied them vvhich beleeued not. 6 † But the Angels vvhich kept not their principalitie, but forsooke their owne habitation, he hath reserued vnder darkenesse in eternal bondes vnto the iudgment of the great day. 7 † As * Sodom and Gomorrhe, and the cities adioyning in like maner hauing [c] fornicated, and going after other flesh, vvere made an example, sustaining the paine of eternal fire. 8 † In like maner these also defile the flesh, and ∷ despise dominion, & blaspheme maiestie. † Vvhen Michael the Archangel, disputing vvith the Diuel, made altercation

2 Pet. 2.

Nu. 14, 37.

Gen. 19.

c exfornicata.

∷ Diuers Heretikes abuse the libertie of Christes grace and Gospel, to the fulfilling of their carnal lustes and cōcupiscēces.

c This is our Sauiour, not Iosuè, as S. Hierom noteth ep. 17. see Abac. c. 3. v. 18.

∷ Such be heretikes, that wil not be subiect to any superior, or that

for

refuse to obey the lawes either of Spiritual or Temporal rulers. in vvhich kinde (specially in blaspheming the supreme Spiritual Magistrate) the Protestants do passe.

" for the body of Moyses: he durst not inferre iudgment of blasphemie, but said, Our Lord `commaund' thee. † But 10 these, vvhat things so euer certes they are ignorant of, " they blaspheme: and vvhat things so euer naturally, as dumme beastes, they knovv, in those they are corrupted.

rebuke

† Vvo vnto them, `vvhich' haue gone in the vvay of 11 * " Cain: and vvith the errour of * Balaam, haue for revvard povvred out them selues, and haue perished in the contradiction of Corè. † These are in their bankets, spottes, 12 feasting together vvithout feare, feeding them selues, cloudes vvithout vvater vvhich are caried about of vvindes, trees of autumne, vnfruiteful, tvvise dead, plucked vp by the rootes, † raging vvaues of the sea, foming out their ovvne confusions, 13 vvandering starres: to vvhom the storme of darkenesse is reserued for euer. † And of these prophecied Enoch, the seuenth 14 from Adam, saying, Behold our Lord is come in his holy thousandes, † to doe iudgement against al, and to reproue 15 al the impious, of al the vvorkes of their impietie vvherby they haue done impiously, and of al the hard thinges vvhich impious sinners haue spoken against him. † These 16 are murmurers, ful of complaintes, vvalking according to their ovvne desires, and their mouth speaketh pride, admiring persons for gaine sake.

`because they

Gen. 4, 8
Nu. 22.
Nu. 16.

† But you my deerest, be mindeful of the vvordes vvhich 17 haue been spoken before by the Apostles of our Lord IESVS Christ, † vvho told you, * that in the last time shal come 18 mockers, according to their ovvne desires vvalking in impieties. † " These are they vvhich segregate them selues, sen- 19 sual, hauing not the Spirit. † But you my deerest, building 20 your selues vpon `our' most holy faith, in the holy Ghost, praying, † keepe your selues in the loue of God, expecting the 21 mercie of our Lord IESVS Christ vnto life euerlasting. † And these certes reproue being iudged: † but them saue, 22 pulling out of the fire. And on other haue mercie in feare: 23 hating also that vvhich is carnal, the spotted cote.

1 Tim. 4
2 Tim. 3.
2 Pet. 3.

your

† And to him that is able to preserue you vvithout sinne, 24 and to sette you immaculate before the sight of his glorie in exultation in the comming of our Lord IESVS Christ, † to 25 the onely God our Sauiour by IESVS Christ our Lord be glorie and magnificēce, empire and power before al worldes, and novv and for al vvorldes euermore. Amen.

ANNOT.

9. *For the body of Moyses.*] Vvhen, why, or hovv this altercation or combat was betwene S. Michael and the Diuel about Moyses body, no man can declare. only this vve see that many truthes and stories vvere kept in the mouthes and hartes of the faithful, that vvere not written in Scriptures canonical, as this vvas among the Ievves.

Truthes vnwritten, and knowen by tradition.

10. *They blaspheme.*] He speaketh of Heretikes, who being ignorant in Gods mysteries and the diuine doctrine of his Church, vvhen they can not reproue the things, then they fall to execrations, irrisions, and blasphemies against the Priests, Church, and Sacraments, and vvhatsoeuer is godly.

Ignorãce maketh Heretikes blaspheme.

11. *Cain, Balaam, Corè.*] The Apostle vvould haue Heretikes specially to be knowen by the resemblance they haue, first to Cain, in that for enuy that his brothers seruice and sacrifice was accepted and his reiected, slewe his said brother, and was a fugitiue from the face and citie of God, vvhich is the Church. Secondly, by their resemblance to Balaam, who for money was induced to curse Gods people, as couetousnes is commonly the cause that first maketh Heretikes and false Prophets. wherevpon S. Augustine saith, *He is an Heretike that for temporal commodities sake either coineth or folovveth nevv opinions. S. August. li. de Vtil. cred. cap.* 1. And lastly by the resemblance they haue vvith the auncient and notorious Schismatike Corè, and his companions, vvho forsooke the ordinarie Priesthod appointed by God, and would needes doe sacrifice them selues without lavvful calling.

Heretikes resembled to Cain, Balaam, and Corè.

Such in deede be al Heretikes, and such be al their sacraments, seruice, and offices in their Church, as Cores vvere in his schismatical tabernacles. And as pride vvas the cause of his reuolting from the obedience of Moyses and Aaron his Priests and true Gouernours: so is intolerable pride the cause of al Heretikes forsaking their lavvful Pastors and Rulers, and namely of forsaking Christes owne Vicar in earth, our true Aaron, as S. Bernard calleth him. *De consid. li. 2. cap.* 8. To al such forsakers the Apostle here giueth the curse and *Va* due to the said three, Cain, Balaam, and Corè, and telleth them that the storme of darkenes and eternal damnation is prouided for them: most liuely describing al Heretikes (as in some vve to our woe haue experience by their maners in our daies) in al this passage euen to the end of the epistle.

19. *These are they vvhich segregate them selues.*] The conditions of Heretikes in the later daies, that is, euer since Christs time, not of these onely of our age. For there were many that forsooke Gods Church and *segregated them selues* from the fellowship of the faithful euen in the primitiue Church: that vve may the lesse maruel at these mens segregating them selues, and going out from the rest into seueral sectes, which S. Augustine therfore calleth *Segregations.*

Al Heretikes segregate them selues.

THE

THE ARGVMENT OF THE APOCALYPSE OF S. IOHN.

THAT vvhich the old Testament foretold of Christ him self, the Apostles could report the fulfilling thereof in the nevv Testament, by vvay of an historie, euen from his Conception to his Glorification. But of his Church, they could not doe the like: because in their time it did but beginne: being to continue long after them, euen to the end of the vvorld, and then at length to be glorified, as Christ her Spouse alreadie is. Herevpon God vvould haue S. Luke to report in the Actes of the Apostles, the storie of the Churches beginning. and for the rest of it to the end, (that vve might receiue this benefite also by the Apostles handes) he vvould S. Iohn to tell vs of it in this booke by vvay of a prophecie.

Hier. ad Paulin.

Of vvhich booke S. Hierome saith: The Apocalypse of S. Iohn hath as many sacraments or mysteries, as vvordes. *Yea more then that,* In euery vvord there are hid manifold and sundrie senses. *Therfore it is very litle that can here be noted, in respect. Yet to giue the good Catholike (vvhose comfort is here) some litle helpe, the booke may be deuided into fiue partes.*

Ca. 1. 2. 3. — 1 part.

The first (after the Proœme) conteineth seuen Epistles from Christ novv in glorie, to seuen Churches of Asia, or (for, these he maketh al one) to the seuen Bishops of those Churches: meaning not to those only, but to al his Churches & Bishops throughout the vvorld: saying therefore in euery one of them, to al in general: He that hath an eare, let him heare vvhat the Spirit saith to the Churches. *As also in euery one he exhorteth vs to fight manfully (in this spiritual vvarfare of ours against sinne) for the victorie, and in euery one accordingly promiseth vs a revvard in heauen. But before this, in the beginning of euery one, he partly commendeth, partly reprehendeth, and exhorteth to penance. Vvhere this is much to be noted, and feared, that among so many, he reproueth somevvhat in al, saue only in tvvo, vvhich are the second & the sixt. In the beginning also of euery one, he taketh some peece out of the apparition going before, to frame thereof his style agreably to the matter of eche Epistle.*

Ca. 4. to the 8. — 2

After this admonition to Pastors and their flockes: the second part folovveth, vvherein the Church and vvhole course thereof from the beginning to the end, is expressed in the opening of a booke in Gods hand, and the seuen seales thereof, by Christ. for the vvhich, he seeth praise sung novv in heauen and earth, not only to the Godhead, as before, but also (after a nevv manner) to Christ according to his Manhod. And here, vvhen he is come to the opening of the last seale, signifying Domesday, he letteth that matter alone for a vvhile, and to speake more fully yet of the said course of the Church, he bringeth in an other pagent (as it vvere) of seuen Angels vvith seuen Trumpets. The effect of both the Seales & Trumpets, is this: That the Church beginning and proceding, there should be raised against it, cruel persecutions, and pestilent heresies: and at length after al heresies, a certaine most blasphemous Apostasie, being the next preparatiue to the

Ca. 8. to the 12

comming

comming of Antichrist: After al vvhich, Antichrist him self in person shal appeare in the time of the sixt seale, and sixt trumpet, persecuting and seducing (for the short time of his reigne) more then al before him. The Church notvvithstading shal still continue, and vvade through al, because Christ her Spouse is stronger then al these aduersaries. vvho also straight after the said sixt time, shal in the seuenth, come in maiestie and iudge al.

3 *Of the vvhich iudgement, differring yet a vvhile to speake at large, he doth first in the third part intreate more fully of the Deuils vvorking by Antichrist and his companie against the Church, that the iustice of Christ aftervvard in iudging, may be more manifest.* C. 12.13.14.

4 *At length therefore in the fourth part he commeth to the seuen last plagues, the seuenth of them conteining the final damnation of the vvhole multitude, societie or corps of the vvicked, from the beginning of the vvorld to the end. Vvhich multitude, in the Gospel and first Epistle of this same S. Iohn (as also in the other Scriptures commonly) is often called* Mundus, the vvorld. *and here he calleth it partly,* Meretricem, a vvhore or harlot, *because vvith her concupiscence she entiseth the carnal and earthly men avvay from God: partly,* Ciuitatem Babylon, the Citie of Babylon, *because it maketh vvarre against Hierusalem the Citie of God, and laboureth to hold Gods people captiue in sinne, as it vvas shadovved in Nabuchodonosor & his Babyloniās, leading and holding the* Ievves *vvith their Hierusalem, in captiuitie, vntil Cyrus (in figure of Christ) deliuered them. But vvhether al these seuen plagues should be vnderstood (as the seuenth) of Domesday it self, it is hard to define. More like it is, that the first sixe are to goe before Domesday: but vvhether corporally and literally, (so as Moyses plagued Egypt) or rather spiritually, it is more hard to define. Yet it seemeth more easie, to vnderstand them corporally, as also the plagues vvherevvith Elias and his fellovv shal in the time of Antichrist plague the vvicked (vvhich peraduenture shal be the same last plagues) vvhereof vve reade in this booke c. 11. v. 6. But not content to haue described thus the damnation of the vvhole adulterous & bloudy societie, he doth also expresly report of their three grād Captaines damnation, vvhich are these, Antichrist, and his Falseprophet, and the Deuil him self the author of al this mischiefe.* C. 15. to the 21. 1 Io. 2. Apoc. 17.

5 *Finally, on the other side, in the fifth part he reporteth the vnspeakeable and euerlasting glorie, that the Church after al this suffering, shal by Christ her glorious Spouse be assumpted vnto. And so he concludeth the booke.* C. 21. 22.

The Church readeth this booke at Mattins frō the 3 Sūday after Easter vnto the 4.

THE APOCALYPSE OF IOHN THE APOSTLE.

Chap. I.

The 1 part. Seuen epistles to the Churches.

9. S. Iohn being banished in the ile Patmos, is commaunded to vvrite to the seuen Churches of Asia (signified by the seuen candlestickes) that vvhich he savv vpon a Sunday, round about the Sonne of man: 13 vvhose maner of apparition is described.

The Epistle vpon Michelmas day Septemb. 29, & on the Apparition of S. Michael Mai. 8.

1 THE " Apocalypse of IESVS Christ vvhich God gaue him, to make manifest to his seruants the thinges vvhich must be done quickly: and signified, sending by his Angel to his seruant Iohn, 2 † vvho hath giuen testimonie to the vvord of God, and the testimonie of IESVS Christ, vvhat things soeuer he hath seen. 3 † Blessed is he that readeth and heareth the wordes of this prophecie: and ∴ keepeth those thinges Which be vvritten in it. for the time is nigh.

∴ There be many (specially novv a daies) that be great readers, hearers and talkers of Scriptures. but that is not ynough to make them good or blessed before God, except they keepe the things prescribed and taught therein, according to our Sauiours saying (*Luc. 11.*) Blessed are they that heare the vvord of God, and keepe it.

4 † Iohn " to the seuen churches vvhich are in Asia. Grace to you and peace from * him that is, and that vvas, and that shal come, and " from the seuen spirites vvhich are in the sight of his throne, 5 † and from IESVS Christ vvho is the faithful vvitnes, the * first-borne of the dead, & the prince of the kings of the earth, vvho hath loued vs, and * vvashed vs from our sinnes in his bloud, ⊣ 6 † and hath made vs * " a kingdom and priestes to God and his father, to him be glorie and empire for euer and euer. Amen. 7 † Behold he commeth vvith the cloudes, and euery eie shal see him, and * they that pricked him. And al the tribes of the earth shal bevvaile them selues vpon him. yea, Amen. 8 † * I am Alpha and Omega, the beginning and end, saith our Lord God, vvhich is, and vvhich vvas, and vvhich shal come, the omnipotent.

Exo. 3, 14. *Col. 1.* *Heb. 9.* *1 Pet. 1.* *1 Pet. 2.* *Zach. 12.* *Esa. 44.* *Apo. 21. 22, 13.*

9 † I Iohn your brother and partaker in tribulation, and
the kingdom, and patience in Christ IESVS, vvas in :: the
Iland, vvhich is called Patmos, for the vvord of God and the
10 testimonie of IESVS. † I vvas c in spirit " on the Dominical day, and heard behind me a great voice as it vvere of a
11 trompet † saying, That vvhich thou seest, vvrite in a booke:
and send to the seuen churches vvhich are in Asia, to Ephesus, and Smyrna, and Pergamus, and Thiatîra, and Sardis, and
12 Philadelphia, and Laodicia. † b And I turned, to see the voice
that spake vvith me. And being turned I savv seuen candle-
13 stickes of gold: † & in the middes of the seuen candlestickes
of gold, one :: like to the Sonne of man, " vested in a c priestly
garment to the foote, and girded about neere to the pappes
14 vvith a girdle of gold. † and his head and heares vvere
vvhite, as vvhite vvool, & as snovv, and his eies as the flame
15 of fire. † and his feete like to latten, as in a burning fornace.
16 and his voice as the voice of many vvaters: † and he had
in his right hand seuen starres. and from his mouth proceded a sharpe tvvo edged svvord: and his face, as the sunne
17 shineth in his vertue. † And vvhen I had seene him, I fel at
his feete as dead. And he put his right hand vpon me, saying,
18 Feare not. * I am the first and the last, † and aliue, and vvas
dead, and behold I am liuing for euer and euer, and haue the
19 keies of death and of hel. † Vvrite therefore the thinges
vvhich thou hast seene, and that are, and that must be done
20 after these. † The sacrament of the seuen starres, vvhich
thou hast seene in my right hand, and the seuen candlestickes
of Gold. " the seuen starres, are " the angels of the seuen
churches. and :: the seuen candlestickes, are the seuen
churches.

Marginal notes (left): c podére Sap. 18, 24. — Esa. 41, 4. 44, 6.

Marginal notes (right):

:: Banished thither for religion by Nero, or rather by Domitian, almost 60 yeres after Christes Ascensiõ.

c I had a visiõ, and not with my corporal eies, but in spirit I beheld the similitudes of the thinges folovving.

b The 1 GENERAL VISION of the 7 according to S. Ambrose.

:: It seemeth not to be Christ him self, but an Angel bearing Christes person, & vsing diuers speaches proper to Christ.

:: S. Irenæus alluding to this saith, *The Church euery vvhere preacheth the truth, and this is the seuenfold candlesticke, bearing the light of Christ* &c. Li. 5. aduers. hær.

ANNOTATIONS
CHAP. I.

1. APOCALYPSE.] Of the Apocalypse thus vvriteth the auncient father Denys, Bishop of Corinth, as Eusebius alleageth him li. 7. c. 20 hist. Eccl. *Of this booke* (saith he) *this is my opinion, that the matter thereof is far more profound then my vvit can reache vnto, and I doubt not but almost in euery sentence of it, there lieth hidden a certaine sense exceding mystical and maruelous, vvhich though I vnderstand not, yet I conceiue that vnder the vvordes there is a deepe meaning, and I measure not the matter by reason, but attribute al to faith, taking it to be more high and diuine, then I can by cogitation comprise: not reprouing that vvhich I vnderstand not, but therfore I admire vvith reuerẽce, because my vvit can not attaine to it.* Againe S. Augustine saith, *that in the Apocalypse many things are obscurely spoken, to exercise the minde of the reader: and yet some fevv things left euident, that through them a man may vvith labour searche out the rest. specially for that the author so repeateth the same things in diuers sortes, that seeming to speake of sundry matters, in deede is found but to vtter the same things diuers vvaies.* li. 20. de Ciuit. Dei c. 17.

Marginal note: An admonition to the reader concerning the difficultie of this booke.

Vvhich vve set dovvne here in the beginning, to vvarne the good Christian reader, to be humble and vvise in the reading both of al other holy Scriptures, and namely of this diuine and deepe prophecie: giuing him further to vnderstand, that vve vvil in our Annotations, according to our former trade and purpose, onely or cheefely note vnto the studious, such places as may be vsed by Catholikes, or abused by Heretikes, in the controuersies of this time, and some other also that haue special matter of edification, and that as breefely as may be, for that the volume grovveth great.

Numbers mystical.

4. *To the 7 Churches.*] That certaine numbers may be obserued as significatiue and mystical, it is plaine by many places of holy Scripture, and by the auncient Doctors special noting of the same to many purposes. Vvhereby vve see the rashnes of our Aduersaries, in condemning generally al religious respect of certaine numbers in our praiers, fastes, or actions. Namely the number of *Seuen*, is mystical, and prophetical, perfect, and vvhich (as S. Augustine saith.) the Church knovveth by the Scriptures, to be specially dedicated to the Holy Ghost: and to appertaine to spiritual mundation, as in the Prophets appointing of Naaman to vvash seuen times in Iordan, and the sprinkling of the bloud seuen times against the tabernacle. *li. 4 quæst. in numer. q.* 33. See *li. 5. c. 5 de Gen. ad lit. & li. 5 quæst in Deuter. q.* 42. Al these visions stand vpon Seuens, seuen Churches, seuen Angels, seuen starres, seuen spirites, seuen candlestickes, seuen lampes, seuen trumpets, seuen vials, seuen hornes of the Lambe, seuen hilles, seuen thunders, seuen heades of the Dragon, signifying the Diuel: seuen of the beast that is Antichrist: seuen of the beast that the harlot rid vpon: finally the number also of the visions is specially marked to be seuen, in this booke. and euery time that this number is vsed in this prophecie, it hath a mysterie & a more large meaning, then the nature of that number is precisely and vulgarly taken for. As vvhen he vvriteth to seuen Churches, it is to be vnderstood of al the Churches in the vvorld: as the seuen Angels, for al the Angels or gouernours of the vvhole Catholike Church: and so forth in the rest, because the number of *Seuen*, hath the perfection of vniuersalitie in it, as S. Augustine saith *li. 5 quæst. in Deuter. q.* 42.

The number of Seuen mystical: specially in this booke.

4. *From the 7 spirites,*] The Holy Ghost may be here meant, and so called for his seuenfold giftes and graces, as some expositours thinke. but it seemeth more probable that he speaketh of the holy Angels, by comparing this to the like in the 5 Chapter folovving: vvhere he seemeth to call these, the seuen spirites sent into al the vvorld, as S. Paul to the Hebrues (c. 1, 14) speaketh of Angels. and so the Protestants take it in their cõmentaries: vvhich vve note, because therevpon they must needes confesse that the Apostle here giueth or vvisheth grace and peace, not from God onely, but also from his Angels: though that benediction commeth one vvay of God, and an other vvay of his Angels or Saincts, being but his creatures. And so they may learne, that the faithful often ioyning in one speache, *God and our Lady, our Lord and any of his Saincts,* to helpe vs or blesse vs, is not superstitious, but an Apostolical speache. and so the Patriarch said (Gen. 48. v. 16.) *The Angel that deliuereth me from al euils, blesse these children.* See the Annot. *Act.* 15, 28.

Grace & peace from God & the holy Angels.

God and our Ladie saue vs, and the like.

6. *A kingdom and Priests.*] As al that truely serue God, and haue the dominion and superioritie ouer their concupiscences and vvhatsoeuer vvould induce them to sinne, be kings: so al that employ their vvorkes and them selues to serue God & offer al their actions as an acceptable sacrifice to him, be priests. Neuerthelesse, as if any man vvould therevpon affirme that there ought to be no other earthly povvers or kings to gouerne in vvorldly affaires ouer Christians, he vvere a seditious Heretike, euen so are they that vpon this or the like places vvhere al Christians be called priests in a spiritual sort, vvould therfore inferre, that euery one is in proper signification a Priest, or that al be Priests alike, or that there ought to be none but such spiritual priests. for it is the seditious voice of Corè, saying to Moyses and Aaron, *Let it suffice you, that al the multitude is of holy ones, and the Lord is in them. Vvhy are you extolled ouer the people of the Lord?* Num. 16.

Hovv al Christians be both kings & Priests.

10. *On the Dominical day.*] Many notable pointes may be marked here. first, that euen in the Apostles time there vvere daies deputed to the seruice of God, and so made holy and different, though not by nature, yet by vse and benediction, from other profane or (as vve call them) vvorke-daies.

Difference of holy daies and vvorkedaies.

Secondly, that the Apostles and faithful abrogated the Sabboth vvhich vvas the seuenth day, and made holy day for it, the next day folovving, being the eight day in count from the creation: and that vvithout al Scriptures, or cõmaundement of Christ that vve reade of, yea (vvhich is more) not onely othervvise then vvas by the Lavv obserued, but plainely othervvise then vvas prescribed by God him self in the second commaundement, yea and othervvise then he ordained in the first creatiõ, vvhen he sanctified precisely the Sabboth day, & not the day folovving. Such great povver did Christ leaue to his Church, and for such causes gaue he the holy Ghost to be resident in it, to guide it into al truthes, euen such as in the Scriptures are not expressed. And if the Church had authoritie & inspiration from God, to make Sunday (being a vvorke-day before) an euerlasting holy day: and the Saturday, that before vvas holy day, novv a common vvorkeday: vvhy may not the same Church prescribe & appoint the other holy feasts of Easter, Vvhitsuntide, Christmas, and the rest? for the same vvarrant she hath for the one, that she hath for the other.

Sunday made holiday by the Apostles & the Churches authoritie.

Other feastes ordained by the Church.

Thirdly, it is to be noted that the cause of this change vvas, for that novv vve Christians esteeming more our redemption, then our first creation, haue the holy day vvhich vvas before for the

As Saturday vvas in memorie of the creation, so Sunday of Christs resurrection.

the remembrance of Gods accomplishment of the creation of things, novv for the memorie of the accomplishment of our redemption. Vvhich therfore is kept vpon that day on vvhich our Lord rose from life to death, vvhich vvas the day after the Sabboth, being called by the Ievves, *vna* or *prima Sabbathi*, *the first of* or *after the Sabboth*. *Mat* 28. *Act*. 20. 1 *Cor*. 16. Fourthly, it is to be marked, that this holy day by the Apostles tradition also, vvas named *Dominicus dies*, *our Lordes day*, or, *the Dominike*, vvhich is also an old Ecclesiastical vvord in our language. for the name Sunday is a heathenish calling, as al other of the vveeke daies be in our lãguage: some imposed after the names of planets, as in the Romans time: some by the name of certaine Idols that the Saxons did vvorship, & to vvhich they dedicated their daies before they vvere Christians. Vvhich names the Church vseth not, but hath appointed to call the first day, *the Dominike*, after the Apostle here: the other by the name of *Feries*, vntil the last of the vveeke, vvhich she calleth by the old name, *Sabboth*, because that vvas of God, and not by imposition of the heathen. See the marginal Annotation *Luc*. 24, 1.

The Church vseth not the Heathenish names of daies: but *Dies Dominicus*, *feria*, *Sabbatum*.

Lastly obserue, that God reuealeth such great things to Prophets, rather vpon holy daies, and in times of contemplation, sacrifice, and praier, then on other profane daies. and therfore as S. Peter (*Act*. 10) had a reuelation at the sixt houre of praier, and Zacharie (*Luc*. 1) at the houre of incense, and Cornelius (*Act*. 10) vvhen he vvas at his praiers the ninthe houre, so here S. Iohn noteth that he had al these maruelous visions vpon a Sunday.

God giueth greater grace at holy times of praier & fasting.

13. *Vested in a Priestly garment*.] He appeared in a long garment or vestment proper vnto Priests (for so the vvord, *podéres*, doth signifie, as *Sap*. 18, 24) and that vvas most agreable for him that represented the person of Christ the high Priest, and appeared to Iohn being a most holy Priest, and vvho is specially noted in the Ecclesiastical historie for his Priestly garment called, *pétalon* or *lámina*. *Euseb*. *li*. 3 *hist*. *Eccl*. *c*. 25. & *li*. 5 *c*. 23.

Priestly garments

20. *The seuen starres*.] The Bishops are the starres of the Church, as the Churches them selues are the golden candlestickes of the vvorld: no doubt to signifie, that Christ preserueth the truth onely in and by the lavvful Bishops and Catholike Church, and that Christs truth is not to be sought for, in corners or conuenticles of Heretikes, but at the Bishops handes, and * vpon the candlesticke vvhich shineth to al in the house.

The true religiõ manifest as the light on a candlesticke.

Mat. 5, 15

20. *The Angels of the Churches*.] The vvhole Church of Christ hath S. Michael for her keeper and Protector, and therfore keepeth his holy day onely by name, among al Angels. And as earthly kingdoms haue their special Angels Protectors, as vve see in the 10 Chapter of Daniel: so much more the particular Churches of Christẽdom. See S. Hierom *in* 34 *Ezech*. But of those Angels it is not here meant, as is manifest. And therfore Angels here must needes signifie the Priests or Bishops specially of the Churches here, and in them, al the gouernours of the vvhole & of euery particular Church of Christendom. They are called Angels, for that they are Gods messengers to vs, interpreters of his vvil, our keepers and directors in religion, our intercessors, the cariers and offerers of our praiers to him, and mediators vnto him vnder Christ, and for these causes and for their great dignitie they are here and in * other places of Scripture called Angels.

Angels Protectors.

Bishops & Priests are called Angels.

Malach. 2, 7.

CHAP. II.

He is commaunded to vvrite diuers things to the churches of Ephesus, Smyrna, Pergamus, and Thyatira: praising them that had not admitted the doctrine of the Heretikes called Nicolaita, 22 and calling others by threates vnto penance: 26 and promising revvard to him that manfully ouercommeth.

1 AND ⁞ to the Angel of the Church of Ephesus vvrite, Thus saith he vvhich ″ holdeth the seuen starres in his right hand, vvhich vvalketh in the middes of the seuen candlestickes of gold, 2 † I knovv ″ thy vvorkes and labour, and thy patience: and that thou canst not beare euil men, and hast tried them which say them selues to be Apostles, and are not, and hast found them liars: 3 † and thou hast patience, and hast borne for my

⁞ That vvhich before he vvilled him to vvrite to the church, he novv vvilleth to be vvritten to the Angels or Bishops of the same onely. vvhere vve see, it is al one, to the Church, and to the head or gouernour therof.

name, and hast not fainted. † But I haue against thee a fevv 4 thinges, bicause ∷ thou hast left thy first charitie. † Be mindeful 5 therfore from vvhence thou art fallen: and doe penance, and doe the first vvorkes. But if not: I come to thee, and " vvil moue thy candlesticke out of his place, vnlesse thou doe penance. † but this thou hast, " because thou hatest 6 the factes " of the Nicolaïtes, vvhich I also hate. † He that 7 hath an eare, let him heare vvhat the Spirit saith to the Churches, To him that ouercommeth, I vvil giue to eate of the tree of life, vvhich is in the Paradise of my God.

∷ By this vve see is plainely refuted that vvhich some Heretikes hold, that a man once in grace or charitie can neuer fall from it.

† And to the Angel of the Church of Smyrna vvrite, 8 Thus saith * the first and the last, vvho vvas dead, and liueth, † I knovv thy tribulation and thy ∷ pouertie, but thou art 9 riche: and thou art blasphemed of them that say them selues to be Ievves and are not, but are the synagogue of Satan. † Feare none of these thinges vvhich thou shalt suffer. 10 Behold the Deuil vvil send some of you into prison that you may be tried: and you shal haue tribulation ten daies. Be thou faithful vntil death: and I vvil giue thee ∷ the crovvne of life. † He that hath an eare, let him heare vvhat the Spirit saith 11 to the Churches, He that shal ouercome, shal not be hurt of the ∷ second death.

* Apoc. 1, 17.

∷ This Church representeth the state of them that are spoiled of their goodes, emprisoned, & manifoldly afflicted for the catholike faith.

∷ The singular revvard of Martyrdom.

∷ The death of the body is the first death: the death of the soule, the secōd. vvhich Martyrs are surest to escape of al men.

† And to the Angel of the Church of Pergamus vvrite, 12 Thus saith he that hath the sharpe tvvo edged svvord, † I 13 knovv vvhere thou dvvellest, vvhere the seate of Satan is: and thou holdest my name, and hast not denied my faith. And in those daies Antipas my faithful vvitnesse, vvho vvas slaine among you, ∷ vvhere Satan dvvelleth. † But I haue 14 against thee a fevv thinges: because thou hast there, them that hold the doctrine of Balaam, vvho taught Balac " to cast a scandal before the children of Israel, to eate and commit fornication: † so hast thou also them that hold the 15 doctrine of the Nicolaïtes. † In like maner doe penance. if 16 not: I vvil come to thee quickly, and vvil fight against them vvith the svvord of my mouth. † He that hath an eare, let 17 him heare vvhat the Spirit saith to the Churches, To him that ouercōmeth I vvil giue the hidden manna, and vvil giue him a vvhite [c] counter: and in the counter, a nevv name vvritten, vvhich no man knovveth, but he that receiueth it.

∷ The special residence of Satan is vvhere the faithful are persecuted for Christes truth. vvhere not to deny the Cath. faith for feare, is much here commended.

Nu. 24, 14. 25, 2.

c ψῆφον. calculū

† And to the Angel of the Church of Thyatira vvrite, 18 Thus saith the Sonne of God, vvhich hath eies as a flame of fire,

19 fire, and his feete like to latten. † I knovv thy :: vvorkes, and faith, and thy charitie, and ministerie, and thy patience
20 and thy last vvorkes moe then the former. † But I haue against thee a fevv thinges: because thou permittest "the vvoman *Iezabel, vvho calleth her self a propheteſſe, to teache, and to seduce my seruantes, to fornicate, and to eate
21 of thinges sacrificed to idols. † And I gaue her a time that she might do penance: and " she vvil not repent from her
22 fornication. † Behold I vvil cast her into a bedde: and "they that commit aduoutrie vvith her, shal be in very great tri-
23 bulation, vnleſſe they do penance from their vvorkes: † and her children I vvil kil vnto death, and al the Churches shal knovv *that I am he that searcheth the reines and hartes, and I vvil giue to euery one of you :: according to his
24 vvorkes. † But I say to you the rest vvhich are at Thyatira, vvhosoeuer haue not this doctrine, vvhich haue not knowen the ˋ depth ˊ of Satan, as they say, I vvil not cast vpon you an
25 other vveight. † Yet that vvhich you haue, hold til I come.
26 † And he that shal ouercome and keepe my vvorkes vnto
27 the end: "I vvil giue him povver ouer the nations, † and *he shal rule them vvith a rod of yron, and as the veſſel of a
28 potter shal they be broken, † :: as I also haue receiued of
29 my father: and I vvil giue him the morning starre. † He that hath an eare, let him heare vvhat the Spirit saith to the Churches.

3 Reg. 18.

1 Reg. 16. Ps. 7, 10 Ier. 11, 20.

ˋdepthes

Ps. 2, 9.

:: None of these are any thing vvorth vvithout the other.

:: Vvho seeth not here that good vvorkes deserue al so saluatiõ, as il workes damnation: and that it is not faith alone that God revvardeth but that faith vvhich vvorketh by charitie?

:: This great priuilege of Saincts riseth of the povver and preeminence of Christ, vvhich his father gaue him according to his humanitie, and therfore to deny it to Saincts, is to deny it to Christ him self.

ANNOTATIONS
CHAP. II.

1. *Holdeth the seuen.*] Much to be obserued, that Christ hath such care ouer the Church and the Bishops thereof, that he is said here to beare them vp in his right hand, and to vvalke in the middes of them: no doubt to vphold and preserue them and to guide them in al truth.

Christs care of his Church.

2. *Thy vvorkes, labour, patience &c.*] Things required in a Bishop. first, good vvorkes, and great patience in tribulation. next, zeale and sharpe discipline tovvard offenders is here cõmended in them. thirdly, vvisedom & diligence in trial of false Apostles and preachers comming in sheepeskinnes: vvhere is signified the vvatchful prouidence that ought to be in them, that Heretikes enter not into their flockes.

Special vertues required in a Bishop.

5. *Vvil moue.*] Note that the cause vvhy God taketh the truth from certaine countries, and remoueth their Bishops or Churches into captiuitie or desolation, is the sinne of the Prelates and people. And that is the cause (no doubt) that Christ hath taken avvay our golden candlesticke, that is, our Church in England. God graunt vs to remember our fall, to doe penance and the former vvorkes of charitie vvhich our first Bishops and Church vvere notable and renovvmed for.

Sinne is the cause that God taketh the Cath. faith from cõtries.

6. *Because thou hatest.*] Vve see here that of al things, Christian people (specially Bishops) should haue great zeale against Heretikes and hate them, that is, their vvicked doctrine and conditions, euen as God hateth them. for vvhich onely zeale, our Lord saith here that he beareth vvith some Churches and Prelates, and saueth them from perishing.

Zeale against Heretikes.

Of

Nicolaites the first Heretikes so called, as a paterne of Arians, Lutherans, and the like peculiar callings.

6. *Of the Nicolaites.*] Heretikes haue their callings of certaine persons, as is noted at large *Act.* 11, 26. These had their name of Nicolas, one of the 7 first Deacons that vvere chosen *Act.* 6. Vvho is thought to haue taught communitie of vvomen or vviues, and that it vvas lavvful to eate of meates offered to idols. Vvhich later point is such a thing, as if one should hold it lavvful to receiue the bread or vvine of the nevv Communion, vvhich is a kinde of *Idolothyta*, that is, *idolatrous meates*. for though such creatures be good by creation, yet they be made execrable by profane blessings of Heretikes or Idolaters. And concerning the name of Nicolaites giuen here by our Lord him self to those Heretikes, it is a very paterne and marke vnto the faithful for euer, vvhat kinde of men they should be, that should be called after the like sort, Arians, Macedonians, Nestorians, Lutherans, Zuinglians, &c. See S. Hierom *cont. Lucifer. in fine.*

Balaam ouercomming Gods people by persuasion of lecherie and belicheere, vvas a type of Heretikes.

14. *To cast a scandal.*] Iosephus vvriteth that vvhen Balaam could not curse Gods people, nor othervvise anoy them, he taught Balac a vvay hovv to ouerthrovv them: to vvit, by presenting vnto them their Heathen vvomen very beautiful, and delicate dishes of meate offered to Bel-phegor: that so being tempted they might fall to heathenish maners and displease God. To vvhich craftie counsel of Balaam the Apostle resembleth Heretikes fraude, vvho by offering of libertie of meate, vvomen, Church goodes, breache of vovves, and such other licentious allurements, cause many moe to fall, then by their preaching.

li. 4. Antiq. c. 6.

2 Pet. 2, 15
Iuda v. 11.

Zeale against Heretikes.

20. *The vvoman Iezabel.*] He vvarneth Bishops to be zelous and stout against false Prophets and Heretikes of vvhat sort soeuer, by alluding couertly to the example of holy Elias that in zeale killed 450 false prophets of Iezabel, and spared not Achab nor Iezabel them selues, but told them to their faces that they troubled Israel, that is, the faithful people of God. And vvhether there vvere any such great vvoman then, a furtherer and promotour of the Nicolaites, vvhom the Prophete should here meane, it is hard to say.

3 Reg. 18.

Achab and Iezabel.

Free vvil.
God is not author of euil.

21. *She vvil not repent.*] See free vvil here most plainely, and that God is not the proper cause of obduration or impenitence, but man him self onely. Our Lord giueth sinners so long life, specially to expect their amendment: but Iezabel (to vvhom the Apostle here alludeth) vvould neuer repent.

They that communicate vvith Heretikes, shal be dãned vvith them

22. *They that cõmit aduoutrie vvith her.*] Such as communicate vvith Heretikes, shal be damned (alas) vvith them. for, not onely such as vvere in their hartes, of Iezabels religion, or invvardly beleeued in Baal, but such as externally for feare vvorshipped him (vvhich the Scriptures call, bovving of their knees to Baal) are culpable. as novv many bovv their knees to the Communion, that bovv not their hartes.

3 Reg. 19. v. 18. Ro. 11.

Saincts also are Patrones, not only Angels.

26. *I vvil giue him povver.*] Obserue that not onely Angels haue povver and regiment ouer Countries vnder God, but novv for the honour of Christs humane nature, and for his ministerie in the vvorld, the Saincts deceased also, being in heauen, haue gouernement ouer men and Prouinces, and therfore haue to doe vvith our affaires in the vvorld. Vvhich is against the Heretikes of these daies, that to take avvay our praiers to Saincts, vvould spoile them of many soueraine dignities, vvherein the Scriptures make them equal vvith Angels.

CHAP. III.

He is commaunded to vvrite to the Churches of Sardis, Philadelphia, and Laodicia: recalling them that erre to penance by threatening, but praising the rest, and promising revvard to him that ouercommeth: 15 detesting also the cold indifferent Christian. 20 He saith that God knocketh at the doore of mens hartes by offering his grace, for to enter in to him that vvil open vnto him by consent of free vvil.

Nd to the Angel of the Church of Sardis, 1 write, Thus saith he that hath the seuẽ Spirites of God, and the seuen starres, I know thy vvorkes, that thou hast the name that thou liuest, and thou art dead. † Be vigilant, 2 and confirme the rest of the things vvhich vvere to die. For I finde not thy vvorkes ful before my God. † Haue in 3 minde therfore in vvhat maner thou hast receiued and heard: and

and keepe, and doe penance. If therfore thou vvatch not,* I vvil come to thee as a theefe, & thou shalt not knovv vvhat houre I vvil come to thee. 4 † But thou hast a fevv names in Sardis, [c] vvhich haue not defiled their garments: and they shal vvalke vvith me in vvhites, because they ∷ are vvorthy. 5 † "He that shal ouercome, shal thus be vested in vvhite garmentes, and I vvil not put his name out of the booke of life, and I vvil confesse his name before my father, and before his Angels. 6 † He that hath an eare, let him heare vvhat the Spirit saieth to the Churches.

7 † And to the Angel of the Church of Philadelphia vvrite, Thus saith the Holy one and the True one, he that hath the* key of Dauid: he that openeth, and no man shutteth: shutteth, and no man openeth. 8 † I know thy vvorkes. Behold I haue giuen before thee a doore opened vvhich no man can shut: because thou hast a litle povver, and hast kept my vvord, and hast not denied my name. 9 † Behold I vvil giue of the synagogue of Satan, vvhich say they be Ievves, and are not, but doe lie. Behold I vvil make them come and "adore before thy feete. and they shal knovv that I haue loued thee. 10 † because thou hast kept the vvord of my patience, and I vvil keepe thee from the houre of tentation, vvhich shal come vpon the vvhole vvorld to tempt the inhabitants on the earth. 11 † Behold I come quickely: hold that vvhich thou hast, "that no man take thy crovvne. 12 † He that shal ouercome, I vvil make him a piller in the temple of my God: and he shal goe out no more: and I vvil vvrite vpon him the name of my God, and the name of the citie of my God, nevv Hierusalem vvhich descendeth out of heauen from my God, and my nevv name. 13 † He that hath an eare, let him heare vvhat the Spirit saith to the Churches.

14 † And to the Angel of the Church of Laodicia vvrite, Thus saith [c] Amen, the faithful and true vvitnesse,* vvhich is the beginning of the creature of God. 15 † I knovv thy vvorkes, that thou art neither colde, nor hote. I vvould thou vvere colde, or hote. 16 † But because thou art "lukevvarme, and neither cold nor hote, I vvil begin to vomite thee out of my mouth. 17 † Because thou saiest, That I am riche, and enriched, and lacke nothing: and knovvest not that thou art a miser, and miserable, and poore, and blinde, and naked. 18 † I counsel thee to bye of me gold fire-tried, that thou maiest

Marginal references: *1 Thes. 5, 2. 2 Pet. 3, 10. Apo. 16, 15.* — *Esa. 22, 22.* — c ὁ ἀμὴν — *Ecclesiastici 24, 9. 14. Col. 1, 15.*

c Such as haue not cōmitted deadly sinne after baptisme.

∷ Note that there is in mā a vvorthinesse of the ioyes of heauen, by holy life. & this is a cōmō speache in holy Scripture, that man is worthy of God, of heauē, of saluatiō.

be made riche: and maiest be clothed in vvhite garmentes, that the confusion of thy nakednes appeare not: and vvith eie-salue anoint thine eies, that thou maiest see. † I, * vvhom 19 I loue, do rebuke and chastise. Be zelous therfore and doe penance. † Behold I stand at the doore and ∴ knocke. if 20 any man shal heare my voice, and open the gate, I vvil enter in to him, and vvil suppe vvith him, and he vvith me. † He 21 that shal ouercome, I vvil giue vnto him to sitte vvith me in my throne: as I also haue ouercome, and haue sitten vvith my father in his throne. † He that hath an eare, let him heare 22 vvhat the Spirit saith to the Churches.

Prou. 3, 12. Heb. 12, 6.

∴ God first calleth vpō man and knocketh at the doore of his hart: that is to say, offereth his grace. and it lieth in man to giue cōsent by free wil holpen also by his grace.

ANNOTATIONS
CHAP. III.

Doing vvel in respect of revvard.

5. *He that shal ouercome.*] In al these speaches to diuers Bishops and their Churches, he continually encourageth them to constancie in faith and good life, by setting before their eies the revvard of the next life. And yet the Caluinists vvould haue no man do good in respect of such revvard.

Adoration of creatures, called Dulia.

9. *Adore before thy feete.*] You see this vvord of adoration is in Scriptures vsed for vvorship of creatures also, and that to fall before the feete of holy men or Angels for duety and reuerence, is not idolatrie, except the proper honour due to God, be giuen vnto them. See the Annotations vpō the 19 & 22 Chapter concerning the Apostles prostration before the Angel. And the Aduersaries euasion, saying that the adoration vvas of God onely: and that, *before the feete* of the partie, signifieth nothing els but, *in his presence*, is false and against the phrase of Scriptures. as 4 *Reg.* 4. vvhere the Sunamite adored Elisæus, falling dovvne before his feete. and 4 *Reg.* 2. the sonnes of the Prophets adored him in the same sort. and here this adoration can not be meant but of the Bishop or Angel of Philadelphia, because he promiseth this honour as a revvard, and as an effecte of his loue tovvardes him, saying, *And they shal knovv that I haue loued thee.* And that vvhich he saith in the 22 Chapter, *I fel dovvne to adore before the feete of the Angel*: the very same he expresseth thus in the 19 Chapter, *I fel before his feete to adore him*: making it al one, to adore before his feete, and to adore him.

Perseuērance in good & continuing to the end.

11. *That no man take thy crovvne.*] That is, his crovvne of euerlasting life and glorie, if he perseuēre not to the end in faith & good vvorkes: othervvise an other shal enter into his place, as Mathias did both to the dignitie of the Apostleship, & to the heauenly crovvne due for the vvel vsing and executing of the same function: vvhich Iudas might and should haue had, if he had perseuēred to the end. and as the Gentiles came into the grace and place of the Ievves. Other difficulties concerning this kinde of speache are resolued in Schoolemen, and are not here to be stoode vpon.

Neuters or indifferents in religion.

16. *Lukevvarme.*] Zeale and feruour is commendable, specially in Gods cause: and the Neuters that be neither hote nor cold, are to Christ and his Church burdenous and lothsome, as lukevvarme vvater is to a mans stomake, prouoking him to vomite. and therfore he threateneth to void vp such Neuters out of his mouth.

CHAP. IIII.

The 2 part. first, the booke with 7 seales: secōdly, 7 Angels with trumpets.

1. *A doore being open in heauen, he savv one sitting in a throne, 4 and round about him foure and tvventie seniors sitting, 6 and the foure beastes here described, 9 vvhich vvith the 24 seniors continually glorified him that sate in the throne.*

AFTER

1 AFTER these thinges I looked, and behold a doore open in heauen, and the first voice which I heard, vvas as it vvere of a trompet speaking vvith me, saying, Come vp hither, and I vvil shevv thee the thinges vvhich must be done quickly after these. 2 † Immediatly I vvas in spirit: and behold there vvas a seate sette in heauen, and vpon the seate one sitting. 3 † And he that sate, vvas like in sight, to the Iasper stone, and the Sardine: and there vvas a raine-bovv round about the seate, like to the sight of an Emeraud. 4 † And round about the seate, foure and tvventie seates: and vpon the thrones, foure and twentie seniors sitting, clothed about in vvhite garmentes, and on their heades crovvnes of gold. 5 † And from the throne proceeded lightenings, and voices, and thunders: and seuen lampes burning before the throne, 6 vvhich are the seuen Spirites of God. † And in the sight of the seate, as it vvere a sea of glasse like to crystall: and in the middes of the seate and round about the seate :: foure beastes 7 ful of eies before and behind. † And the first beast, like to a lion: and the second beast, like to a calfe: and the third beast, hauing the face as it vvere of a man: and the fourth beast, like 8 to an egle flying. † And the foure beastes, euery one of them had sixe vvinges round about: and vvithin they are ful of eies. and they had no rest day and night, saying, "*Holy, Holy, Holy, Lord God omnipotent*, vvhich vvas, and vvhich is, and vvhich 9 shal come. † And vvhen those beastes gaue glorie and honour and benediction to him that sitteth vpon the throne, 10 that liueth for euer and euer: † the foure and tvventie seniors fel dovvne before him that sitteth in the throne, and adored him that liueth for euer and euer, and cast their 11 crownes before the throne, saying, † Thou art vvorthie O Lord our God to receiue glorie and honour and povver: because thou hast created al thinges, and for thy vvil they vvere and haue been created.

Es. 6, 3.

THE 2 VISION. In vvhich is represented vnto vs the glorie and maiestie of God in heauen, and the incessant honour & praises of al Angels and Saincts assisting him. Vvhich is resembled in the daily honour done to him by al orders and sortes of holy men in the Church militant also.

:: These foure beastes, and the like described *Ezech. 1.* by the iudgement of the holy Doctors signifie the 4 Euangelistes, and in them al true preachers. the man, Mathevv: the liō, Marke: the calfe, Luke: the egle, Iohn: See the causes hereof in the Summe of the 4 Euangelist. *pag. 1. S. Grego. in 1 Ezech.*

ANNOTATIONS
CHAP. IIII.

8. *Holy, holy, holy.*] This vvord is thrise repeated here, and *Esa. 6:* and to the imitation therof, in the seruice of the holy Church, at *Te Deum*, and at Masse, specially in the Preface next before the great mysteries, for the honour of the three persons in the B. Trinitie, and that the Church militant may ioyne vvith the triumphant, and vvith al the orders of Angels, vvho also are present at

The *Sanctus* thrise repeated.

at the consecration, and doe seruice there to our common Lord and Maister. as S. Chrysostom vvriteth *li. 6 de Sacerdotio.* and *ho. 1. de verb. Esa. to. 1.* The Greekes call it, the hymne *Trisagios*, that is, *Thrise holy*.

CHAP. V.

4 S. Iohn vveeping, because no man could open the booke sealed vvith seuen seales: 6 the Lambe that vvas slaine, opened it: vvhich being done, 8 the foure beastes and foure and tvventie seniors, vvith an innumerable multitude of Angels & al creatures, did glorifie him excedingly.

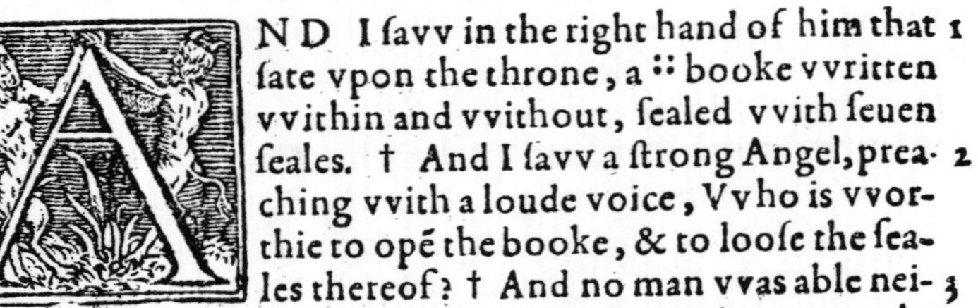

THE 5 VISION. :: S. Gregorie taketh it to be the booke of holy Scripture. *li. 4. Dialog. c. 42.*

:: He speaketh not of the damned in Hel, of vvhom there could be no question: but of the faithful in Abrahams bosome, & in Purgatorie.

c So did Iacob (*Gen. 49*) call Christ, for his kingly fortitude in subduing the vvorld vnto him.

b The Epistle vpon al-Hallovves eue.

:: So Christ is called for that he is the immaculate host or sacrifice for our sinnes.

:: This maketh against the Caluinistes vvho are not cōtent to say that vve merite not, but that Christ merited not for him self. Calu. *Philip. 2. v. 9.*

The Epistle in a votiue Masse of the holy Angels.

AND I savv in the right hand of him that sate vpon the throne, a :: booke vvritten vvithin and vvithout, sealed vvith seuen seales. 2 † And I savv a strong Angel, preaching vvith a loude voice, Vvho is vvorthie to opē the booke, & to loose the seales thereof? 3 † And no man vvas able neither in heauen nor in earth, nor :: vnder the earth, to open the booke, nor looke on it. 4 † And I vvept much because no man vvas found vvorthie to open the booke, nor to see it. 5 † And one of the seniors said to me, Vveepe not: behold c the * lion of the tribe of Iuda, the roote of Dauid, hath vvonne, to open the booke, and to loose the seuen seales thereof.

Gen. 49, 9.

6 †b And I savv, and behold in the middes of the throne and of the foure beastes and in the middes of the seniors, :: a Lambe standing as it were slaine, hauing seuen hornes & seuen eies: vvhich are the seuen spirites of God, sent into al the earth. 7 † And he came, and receiued the booke out of the right hand of him that sate in the throne. 8 † And vvhen he had opened the booke, the foure beastes and the foure and tvventie seniors fel before the Lambe, hauing euery one harpes, and golden vials ful of odours, which are" the praiers of sainctes: 9 † and they sang a nevv canticle, saying, Thou art vvorthie o Lord to take the booke, and to open the seales thereof: :: because thou vvast slaine, and hast redeemed vs to God in thy bloud out of euery tribe and tonge and people and nation, 10 † and * hast made vs to our God" ` a kingdom' and priestes, and vve shal reigne vpon the earth.

1 Pet. 2. `*kinges*

11 † And I looked, and heard the voice of many Angels round about the throne, and of the beastes & of the seniors: and the number of them vvas * thousandes of thousandes, † saying

Dan. 7. 10.

12 † saying vvith a loud voice, The Lambe that vvas slaine, is vvorthie to receiue povver, and 'diuinitie', and vvisedom, & strength, and honour, and glorie, and benediction. ⊣ † And 13 "euery creature that is in heauen, and vpon the earth, and vnder the earth, and that are in the sea, and that are therein: al did I heare saying, * To him that sitteth in the throne, & :: to the Lambe, benediction and honour and glorie and povver for euer and euer. † And the foure beastes said, Amen. And 14 the foure and tvventie seniors fel on their faces: and adored him that liueth for euer and euer. ⊣

'riches

Apoc. 4, 11.

:: Al the said creatures are bound to giue honour, not onely to God, but to Christ as man, and our redeemer: & so they here doe.

ANNOTATIONS
CHAP. V.

8. *The praiers of Saincts.*] Hereby it is plaine that the Saincts in heauen offer vp the praiers of faithful and holy persons in earth (called here saincts, and in Scripture often) vnto Christ. And among so many diuine & vnsearcheable mysteries set dovvne vvithout exposition, it pleased God yet, that the Apostle him self should open this one point vnto vs, that these odours be the laudes and praiers of the faithful, ascending and offered vp to God as incense, by the Saincts in heauen. that so the Protestants may haue no excuse of their errour, That the Saincts haue no knovvledge of our affaires or desires.

The Saincts in heauen offer our praiers to God.

10. *A kingdom and priests.*] To serue God and subdue vices and sinnes, is to reigne or to be a king spiritually. likevvise to offer vnto him the sacrifices of good vvorkes, is to be a priest after a sort: though neither the one nor the other in proper speache. See the Annotation before Chap. 1. v. 6.

Spiritual kings and Priests.

13. *Euery creature.*] He meaneth the creatures in heauen, as Angels and Saincts. the holy persons in earth, and those that vvere in Limbo, or be in Purgatorie (for of the damned in hel he can not speake in this case:) lastly, of the peoples in Ilands (here called the sea) vvhich the Prophets vse often to name seuerally, vvhen they foretel the spreading of Christs glorie through the vvorld. as Esa. c. 49. *Heare ye Ilandes and you people a far of. &c.*

Limbus Patrum and Purgatorie.

CHAP. VI.

1 Foure seales of the seuen being opened, there folovv diuerse effectes against the earth. 9 vvhen the fifth seale vvas opened, the soules of martyrs desire that the iudgement may be hastened: 12 and at the opening of the sixt, there are signes shevved of the iudgement to come.

1 AND I savv that the Lambe had opened one of the seuen seales, and I heard one of the foure beastes, saying, as it vvere the voice of thunder, Come, and see. † And 2 I savv: And behold a vvhite horse, and he that sate vpon him had a bovv, and there vvas a crovvne giuen him, and he vvent forth conquering that he might conquer.

† And vvhen he had opened the ſecond ſeale, I heard the 3 ſecond beaſt, ſaying, Come, & ſee. † And there vvent forth an 4 other horſe, redde: and he that ſate thereon, to him it vvas giuen that he ſhould take peace from the earth, and that they ſhould kil one an other, and a great ſvvord vvas giuen to him.

† And vvhen he had opened the third ſeale, I heard the 5 third beaſt, ſaying, Come, and ſee. And behold a blacke horſe, and he that ſate vpon him, had a balance in his hand. † And 6 I heard as it vvere a voice in the middes of the foure beaſtes ſaying: Tvvo poundes of vvheate for a penie, and thriſe tvvo poundes of barley for a penie, and vvine and oile hurt thou not.

† And vvhen he had opened the fourth ſeale, I heard a 7 voice of the fourth beaſt, ſaying, Come, & ſee. † And behold 8 a pale horſe: and he that ſate vpon him, his name vvas death, and hel folovved him. and povver vvas giuen to him ouer the foure partes of the earth, to kil vvith ſvvord, vvith famine, and vvith death, and vvith beaſtes of the earth.

† And vvhen he had opened the fifth ſeale: I ſavv " vnder 9 the altar the ſoules of them that vvere ſlaine for the vvord of God, and for the teſtimonie vvhich they had. † " and they 10 cried vvith a loude voice, ſaying, Hovv long Lord, holy & true, iudgeſt thou not and " reuengeſt thou not our bloud of them that dvvel on the earth? † And vvhite ſtoles vvere 11 giuen, to euery one of them :: one: and it vvas ſaid to them, that they ſhould reſt yet a litle time, "til their fellovv-ſeruātes be complete, and their brethren, that are to be ſlaine euen as they.

:: This one ſtole ſignifieth the glorie or bliſſe of the ſoule onely, but at the day of iudgement they ſhal haue it doubled by adding the glorie of their body alſo.

† And I ſavv, vvhen he had opened the ſixt ſeale, and [c] be- 12 hold there vvas made a great earth-quake, and the ſunne became blacke as it vvere ſacke cloth of heare: and the vvhole moone became as bloud: † and the ſtarres from heauen fel 13 vpō the earth, as the figge tree caſteth her greene figges when it is ſhaken of a great vvinde: † and heauen departed as a 14 booke folded together: and euery hil, and ilandes vvere moued out of their places. † And the kinges of the earth, & 15 princes, and tribunes, and the riche, and the ſtrong, and euery bond-man, and free-man * hid them ſelues in the dennes and the rockes of mountaines. † And they ſay to the moun- 16 taines

c The tribulation that ſhal fall in the time of Antichriſt.

Osee.10. Lu. 23, 30. taines and the rockes: * Fall vpon vs, and hide vs from the face of him that sitteth vpon the throne, and from the wrath
17 of the Lambe: † because the great day of their wrath is come, and vvho shal be able to stand?

ANNOTATIONS
CHAP. VI.

9. *Vnder the altar.*] Christ as man (no doubt) is this altar, vnder vvhich the soules of al Martyrs liue in heauen, expecting their bodies, as Christ their head hath his body there already. And for correspondence to their place or state in heauen, the Church laieth commonly their bodies also or relikes neere or vnder the altars, vvhere our Sauiours body is offered in the holy Masse: and hath a special prouiso that no altars be erected or consecrated vvithout some part of a Saincts body or relikes. *Conc. African. can. 50. Carthag. 5. can. 14.* See S. Hierom *cont. vigilant c. 3.* S. Augustine *de ciuit. li. 8. c. 27.* S. Gregorie *li. 5. ep. 50. li. 1. ep. 52. li. 2. ep. 58.* Vvhervnto the Prophet seemeth here to allude, making their soules also to haue their being in heauen, as it vvere vnder the altar. But for this purpose note vvel the vvordes of S. Augustine (or vvhat other auncient Writer soeuer vvas the author thereof) *Ser. 11 de Sanctis. Vnder the altar (saith he) of God I savv the soules of the slaine. What is more reuerent or honorable, then to rest vnder that altar on vvhich sacrifice is done to God, and in vvhich our Lord is the Priest: as it is vvritten, Thou art a Priest according to the order of Melchisedec? Rightly do the soules of the iust rest vnder the altar, because vpon the altar our Lordes body is offered. neither vvithout cause do the iust there call for reuenge of their bloud, vvhere also the bloud of Christ is shed for sinners.* and many other goodly vvordes to that purpose.

Consecration of altars vvith Saincts relikes.

This place also the vvicked heretike Vigilantius (as S. Hierom vvriting against him vvitnesseth c. 2) abused to proue, that the soules of Martyrs and other Saincts vvere included in some certaine place, that they could not be present at their bodies and monuments (vvhere Christian people vsed in the primitiue Church to pray vnto them, as Catholike men doe yet) nor be vvhere they list, or vvhere men pray vnto them. To vvhich the holy doctor ansvvereth at large, that they be vvheresoeuer Christ is according to his humanitie: for vnder that altar they be. Part of his vvordes be these, that you may see hovv this blessed father refuted in that Heretike the Caluinistes so long before they vvere borne. *Doest thou (saith he) prescribe lavves to God? Doest thou fetter the Apostles, that they may be kept in prison til the day of iudgement, and be kept from their Lord, of vvhom it is vvritten, They folovv the Lambe vvhithersoeuer he goeth. If the Lambe be in euery place, then they that be vvith the Lambe, must be euery vvhere. And if the diuel and vvicked spirites gadding abrode in the vvorld vvith passing celeritie, be present euery vvhere: shal holy Martyrs after the sheading of their bloud, be kept close vnder an altar, that they can not sturre out from thence?* So ansvvereth this learned doctor.

Saincts be present at their tombes and relikes.

The Caluinistes heresie concerning the Saincts confuted by S. Hierom long agoe.

Apoc. 14.

Vvhich misliketh our Caluinistes so much, that they charge him of great errour, in that he saith, Christ according to his humanitie is euery vvhere, as though he vvere an Vbiquetarie Protestant. Vvhere, if they had any iudgement, they might perceiue that he meaneth not, that Christ or his Saincts should be personally present at once in euery place alike, as God is: but that their motion, speede, and agilitie to be vvhere they list, is incomparable, and that their povver and operation is accordingly. vvhich they may learne to be the holy doctors meaning, by the vvordes that folovv of the Diuel and his ministers: vvhō he affirmeth to be euery vvhere no othervvise but by their exceding celeritie of being and vvorking mischeefe novv in one place, novv in an other, and that in a moment. For though they be spirites, yet are they not euery vvhere at once according to their essence. And for our nevv Diuines it vvere a hard thing to determine, hovv long Satan (that told our Lord he had circuited the earth) vvas in his iourney, and in the particular consideration and tentation of Iob: and hovv many men he assaulted in that his one circuite. No, no. such curious companions knovv nothing, nor beleeue nothing, but that they see vvith corporal eies, and teach nothing but the vvay to infidelitie.

They vnlearnedly accuse S. Hierom as an Vbiquiste.

Hovv S. Hierō saith, Christ & his Saincts are euery vvhere.

Iob. 1.

10. *And they cried.*] S. Hierom also against the said Vigilantius reporteth, that he vsed an argument against the praiers of Saincts out of this place, for that these Martyrs cried for reuenge, and could not obtaine. But vve vvil report his vvordes, that you may see how like one heretike is to an other, these of our daies to those of old. *Thou saiest in thy booke (saith S. Hierom c. 3.) that vvhiles vve be aliue, one of vs may pray for an other: but after vve be dead, no mans praier shal be heard for an other: specially seing the Martyrs asking reuenge of their bloud, could not obtaine.* So said the Heretike. Against vvhich the holy Doctor maketh a long refutation, prouing that they pray much more after they be in heauen, then they did here in earth:

That Saincts pray for vs, S. Hierom proueth against the Heretike Vigilantius.

earth: and that they shal be much sooner heard of God, then vvhen they vvere in the vvorld.

But for the Heretikes argument framed out of these vvordes of the Apocalypse thus, *These Martyrs did not obtaine, ergo Saincts do not pray for vs*: it vvas so friuolous, and the antecedent so manifestly false, that he vouchsaued not to stand about it. For it is plaine that the Martyrs here vvere heard, and that their petition should be fulfilled in time appointed by God (vvhereunto they did and do alvvaies conforme them selues:) for it vvas said vnto them, *That they should rest yet a litle time, til &c.* And that Martyrs praiers be heard in this case, our Sauiour testifieth Luc 18 saying, *And vvil not God reuenge his elect that crie to him day and night? I say to you, he vvil quickly reuenge them.* And if God do not heare the Saincts sometime nor graunt their requestes, is it therfore consequent that they do not or may not pray? Then Christ him self should not haue praied his father to remoue the bitter cuppe of death from him, because that petition vvas not graunted.

Hovv Martyrs crie for reuenge.

10. *Reuengest thou not?*] They do not desire reuenge vpon their enemies for hatred, but of charitie and zeale of Gods honour, praying that his enemies and the persecutors of his Church and Saincts, that vvil not repent, may be confounded: and that our Lord would accelerate his general iudgement, that so they might attaine the perfect crowne of glorie promised vnto them, both in body and soule: vvhich is to desire the resurrection of their bodies, vvhich then shal triumph perfectly and fully ouer the persecutors that so cruelly handled the bodies of the elect, vvhich shal then appeare glorious to the enemies cōfusion.

11. *Til their fellovv seruantes be complete.*] There is a certaine number that God hath ordained to die for the testimonie of truth and the Catholike faith, for conformitie of the members to the head CHRIST our cheefe Martyr. and til that number be accomplished, the general condemnation of the vvicked persecutors shal not come, nor the general reward of the elect.

CHAP. VII.

The earth being to be punished, 3 they are commaunded to saue them that are signed in their foreheads: 4 vvhich are described and numbered both of the Ievves and Gentiles, blessing God. 13 Of them that vvere clothed in vvhite stoles or long robes.

AFTER these things I savv foure Angels stāding 1 vpon the foure corners of the earth, holding the foure vvindes of the earth that they should not blovv vpon the land, nor vpon the sea, nor on any tree. † [b] And I savv an other Angel ascending from the 2 rising of the sunne, hauing the signe of the liuing God: & he cried vvith a loud voice to the foure Angels, to vvhom it vvas giuen to hurt the earth and the sea, † saying, Hurt not 3 the earth and the sea, nor the trees, til ⁘ vve signe the seruants of our God in their foreheades.

b The Epistle vpon Al hallovves day.

⁘ It is an allusion to the signe of the Crosse vvhich the faithful beare in their foreheads, to shevv they be not ashamed of Christ. *S. August. tract. 43. in Io.*

† And I heard the number of them that vvere signed, an 4 hundred fourtie foure thousand vvere signed, [c] of euery tribe of the children of Israël. † Of the tribe of Iuda, tvvelue 5 thousand signed. Of the tribe of Ruben, tvvelue thousand signed. Of the tribe of Gad, tvvelue thousand signed. † Of the 6 tribe of Aser, tvvelue thousand signed. Of the tribe of Nephthali, tvvelue thousand signed. Of the tribe of Manasses,

c Of al the tribes put together, so many, 144000.

He signifieth by these thousands and the multitude folowing,

tvvelue

7 tvvelue thouſand ſigned. † Of the tribe of Simeon, tvvelue thouſand ſigned. Of the tribe of Leui, tvvelue thouſand ſig-
8 ned. Of the tribe of Iſſachar, tvvelue thouſand ſigned. † Of the tribe of Zabulon, tvvelue thouſand ſigned. Of the tribe of Ioſeph, tvvelue thouſand ſigned. Of the tribe of Beniamin, tvvelue thouſand ſigned.

al the elect: but the elect of the Ievves, to be in a certaine number: the elect of the Gentiles to be innumerable.

9 † After theſe things I ſavv c a great multitude vvhich no man could number, of al nations, and tribes, and peoples, & tonges: ſtanding before the throne, and in the ſight of the Lambe, clothed in vvhite robes, and ∷ palmes in their hands:
10 † And they cried vvith a lovvd voice, ſaying, Saluation to our God vvhich ſitteth vpon the throne, and to the Lambe.
11 † and al the Angels ſtoode in the circuite of the throne and of the ſeniors and of the foure beaſtes: and they fel in the
12 ſight of the throne vpon their faces, and adored God, † ſaying, Amen. Benediction, and glorie, and vviſedom, & thãkeſgiuing, honour and povver, and ſtrength to our God for euer and euer. Amen. ⊣

c The elect of the Gentiles.

∷ Boughes of the palme tree be tokens of triumph and victorie.

13 † And one of the ſeniors anſvvered, & ſaid to me, Theſe that are clothed in the vvhite robes, vvho be they? & whence
14 came they? † And I ſaid to him, My Lord thou knovveſt. And he ſaid to me, Theſe are they vvhich are come out of great tribulation, and haue vvaſhed their robes, and made
15 them vvhite in the bloud of the Lambe. † therfore they are before the throne of God, and they ſerue him day and night in his temple: and he that ſitteth in the throne, ſhal dvvel
16 ouer them. † * they ſhal no more hunger nor thirſt, nei-
17 ther ſhal the ſunne fall vpon them, nor any heate. † becauſe the Lambe vvhich is in the middes of the throne, ſhal rule them, and ſhal conduct them to the liuing fountaines of vvaters, and * God vvil vvipe avvay al teares from their eies. ⊣

The Epiſtle for many Martyrs.

The glorie of Martyrs.

Eſa. 49, 10.

Eſ. 25, 8. Apo. 21, 4.

CHAP. VIII.

1 The ſeuenth ſeale being opened, there appeare Angels vvith trompets: 5 and vvhen an other Angel povvred out fire taken from the altar, vpon the earth, there folovv diuers tempeſtes. 7 In like maner, vvhiles foure Angels of the ſeuen ſound their trompets, there fall ſundrie plagues.

THE 4 VISION.

ND vvhen he had opened the ſeuenth 1 ſeale, there vvas made ſilence in heauen, as it vvere halfe an houre. † And I ſavv 2 ſeuen Angels ſtanding in the ſight of God: and there vvere giuen to them ſeuen trompets. † And an other Angel 3 came, and ſtoode ∷ before the altar, hauing a golden cenſar: and there vvere giuen to him many incenſes, that he ſhould giue of the praiers of al ſainctes vpon the altar of gold, vvhich is before the throne of God. † And 4 the ſmoke of the incẽſes [c] of the praiers of the ſainctes aſcended from the hand of the Angel before God. † And the An- 5 gel tooke the cenſar, and filled it of the fire of the altar, and caſt it on the earth, and there vvere made thunders & voices and lightenings, and a great earthquake. † And the ſeuẽ An- 6 gels vvhich had the ſeuen trompets, prepared them ſelues to ſound vvith the trompet.

† And the firſt Angel ſounded vvith the trompet, and 7 there vvas made haile and fire, mingled in bloud, and it vvas caſt on the earth, & the third part of the earth was burnt, & the third part of trees vvas burnt, and al greene graſſe vvas burnt.

† And the ſecond Angel ſounded vvith the trompet: and 8 as it vvere a great mountaine burning vvith fire, vvas caſt into the ſea, and the third part of the ſea vvas made bloud: † and the third part of thoſe creatures died, vvhich had liues 9 in the ſea, and the third part of the ſhippes periſhed.

† And the third Angel ſounded vvith the trompet, and a 10 great ſtarre fel from heauen, burning as it vvere a torche, and it fel on the third part of the floudes, and on the fountaines of vvaters: † and the name of the ſtarre is called vvormevvod. 11 and the third part of the vvaters was made into Worme Wod: and many men died of the vvaters, becauſe they vvere made bitter.

† And the fourth Angel ſounded vvith the trompet, and 12 the third part of the ſunne vvas ſmitten, and the third part of the moone, and the third part of the ſtarres, ſo that the third part of them vvas darkened, and of the day there ſhined not the third part, and of the night in like maner. † And I looked, 13 and heard the voice of one egle flying through the middes of heauen, ſaying vvith a loud voice, Vvo, vvo, vvo to the inhabiters

∷ The Prieſt ſtanding at the altar praying & offering for the people in the time of the high myſteries, Chriſt him ſelf alſo being preſent vpon the altar, is a figure of this thing, & therevnto he alludeth.

c If this be S. Michael or any Angel, and not Chriſt him ſelf, as ſome take it, Angels offer vp the praiers of the faithful, as the 24 Elders did chap. 5. for this vvord, *Sainctes*, is taken here for the holy perſons on earth, as often in the Scripture: though it be not againſt the Scriptures, that the inferior Sainct or Angel in heauẽ ſhould offer their praiers to God by their ſuperiors there. But hereby vve cõclude againſt the Proteſtants, that it derogateth not from Chriſt, that Angels or Sainctes offer our praiers to God. as alſo it is plaine of Raphael *Tob.* 12, 12.

habiters on the earth: becauſe of the reſt of the voices of the three Angels vvhich vvere to ſound vvith the trompet.

CHAP. IX.

The fifth Angel ſounding the trompet, a ſtarre falleth. 3 The iſſuing forth of locuſtes from the ſmoke of the deepe pitte to vexe men, 7 and the deſcription of them. 13 The ſixt Angel ſounding, foure Angels are let looſe, 18 vvhich vvith a great troupe of horſemen do murder the third part of men.

1 AND the fifth Angel ſounded vvith the trompet, and I ſavv :: a ſtarre to haue fallen from heauen vpon the earth, and there vvas giuen to him the key of the pitte of bottomles depth. 2 † And he opened the pitte of the bottomles depth: and the ſmoke of the pitte aſcended, as the ſmoke of a great fornace: and the ſunne vvas darkened & the aier vvith the ſmoke of the pitte. 3 † And from the ſmoke of the pitte there iſſued forth [c] locuſtes into the earth. and povver vvas giuen to them, as the ſcorpions of the earth haue povver: 4 † and it vvas commaunded them that they ſhould not hurt the graſſe of the earth " nor any greene thing, nor any tree: but onely men vvhich haue not the ſigne of God in their foreheads. 5 † and it vvas giuen vnto them that they ſhould not kil them: but that they ſhould be tormented fiue monethes: and their tormentes as the tormentes of a ſcorpion vvhen he ſtriketh a man. 6 † And * in thoſe daies men ſhal ſeeke for death, and ſhal not finde it: and they ſhal deſire to die, & death ſhal flee from them.

Moſt vnderſtand al this of Heretikes.

:: The fall of an Arch heretike, as Arius, Luther, Caluin, out of the Church of God. Which haue the key of Hel to open & bring forth al the old condemned hereſies buried before in the depth.

c Innumerable pety heretikes folowing their Maiſters after the opening & the ſmoke of the bottomleſſe pit.

*Apoc. 6, 16.

7 † And the ſimilitudes of the locuſtes, like to horſes " prepared into battel: and vpō their heades as it vvere crovvnes like to gold: & their faces as the faces of men. 8 † And they had heare as the heare of vvomen: & their teeth vvere as of lions. 9 † And they had habbergions as habbergions of yron, and the voice of their vvinges as the voice of the chariotes of many horſes running into battel. 10 † and they had tailes like to ſcorpions, and ſtinges vvere in their tailes: and their povver vvas to hurt men fiue monethes. 11 † and they had ouer them a king, the Angel of the bottomles depth, vvhoſe name in Hebrevv is *Abaddon,* and in Greeke *Apollyon:* in Latin hauing the name *Exterminans.* 12 † One vvoe is gone, & behold two vvoes come yet after theſe.

The cheefe Maiſter of heretikes.

אבדון 'Απολλύων, In English, *Deſtroier.*

13 † And the ſixt Angel ſounded vvith the trompet: and I

heard one voice from the foure hornes of the golden altar, vvhich is before the eies of God, † ſaying to the ſixt Angel 14 which had the trõpet, Looſe the foure Angels which are bouñd in the great riuer Euphrates. † And the foure Angels vvere 15 looſed, vvho vvere prepared for an houre, and a day and a moneth and a yere: that they might kil the third part of men. † And the number of the armie of horſemen vvas tvventie 16 thouſand times ten thouſand. And I heard the nũber of them. † And ſo I ſavv the horſes in the viſion: & they that ſate vpõ 17 them, had habbergiõs of fire and of hyacinth and brimſtone. & the heades of the horſes were as it were the heads of lions: & from their mouth procedeth fire, & ſmoke, and brimſtone.

† And by theſe three plagues vvas ſlaine the third part of 18 men, , of the fire and of the ſmoke and of the brimſtone, vvhich proceded from their mouth. † For the povver of the 19 horſes is in their mouth, and in their tailes. for, their tailes be like to ſerpents, hauing heads: and in theſe they hurt.

† [c] And the reſt of men vvhich vvere not ſlaine vvith 20 theſe plagues, neither ∷ haue done penance from the vvorkes of their hands, not to adore Deuils and [r] Idols of gold and ſiluer and braſſe and ſtone and vvood, vvhich neither can ſee, nor heare, nor vvalke, † & haue not done penãce 21 from their murders, nor from their ſorceries, nor from their fornication, nor from their theftes.

c Pagans, Infidels, and ſinful impenitent Catholikes muſt be condemned alſo.

r

∷ This phraſe being the like both in greeke and latin, ſignifieth ſuch ſorowful & penal repentance as cauſeth a man to forſake his former ſinnes and depart from them. ου μετινόησαν ἐκ τῶν ἔργων. See the ſame phraſe. *c.* 2, 21, 22. & *Act.* 8. *v.* 22.

ANNOTATIONS
CHAP. IX.

Vvho are ſeduced by Heretikes.

4. *Nor any greene thing.*] The Heretikes neuer hurt or ſeduce the greene tree, that is, ſuch as haue a liuing faith vvorking by charitie. but commonly they corrupt him in faith vvho ſhould othervviſe haue periſhed for il life, and him that is reprobate, that hath neither the ſigne of the Croſſe (vvhich is Gods marke) in the forehead of his body, nor the note of election in his ſoule.

The manifold hypocriſie of Heretikes.

7. *Prepared into battel.*] Heretikes being euer ready to contend, do pretend victorie, and counterfeit gold: in ſhape as men, as ſmothe and delicate as vvomen, their tongues and pennes ful of gall and venim: their hartes obdurate: ful of noiſe and ſhuffling: their doctrine as peſtiferous and ful of poiſon, as the taile and ſting of a ſcorpion. but they endure for a litle ſeaſon.

Heret. tranſlation.

20. *Idols of gold.*] Here againe the nevv Tranſlatours abuſe the peeple, for *idols* ſaying *images*: the place being plainely againſt the pourtraites of the Heathen Gods, vvhich are here and in the Pſalme 95 called, *dæmonia, Diuels.*

CHAP. X.

An other ſtrong Angel crying out, 3 ſeuen thunders do ſpeake. 6 The Angel ſvveareth that there ſhal be time no more, but at the voice of the ſeuenth Angel the myſterie ſhal be fully accompliſhed. 9 He giueth Iohn a booke to deuoure. 1

AND

1 AND I savv an other Angel, strong, descending from heauen, clothed vvith a cloude, and a raine-bovv on his head, and his face vvas as the sunne, and his feete as `a piller' of fire. 2 † and he had in his hand a litle booke opened: and he put his right foote vpon the sea, and his left vpon the land. 3 † and he cried vvith a loude voice, as vvhen a lion roareth. And vvhen he had cried, the seuen thunders spake their voices. 4 † And vvhen the seuen thunders had spoken their voices, I vvas about to vvrite: and I heard a voice from heauen saying to me: Signe the things vvhich the seuen thunders haue spoken: and :: vvrite them not.

5 † And * the Angel vvhich I savv standing vpon the sea and vpon the land, [c] lifted vp his hand to heauen, 6 † and he svvare by him that liueth for euer and euer, that created heauen and those things vvhich are in it: and the earth, and those things vvhich are in it: and the sea, and those things vvhich are in it: That there shal be time no more: 7 † but in the daies of the voice of the seuenth Angel, vvhen the trompet shal beginne to sound, the mysterie of God shal be consummate, as he hath euangelized by his seruantes the Prophetes.

8 † And I heard a voice from heauen againe speaking with me, and saying: Goe, and take the booke that is opened, of the hand of the Angel standing vpon the sea and vpon the land. 9 † And I vvent to the Angel, saying vnto him, that he should giue me the booke. And he said to me, * Take the booke, and [c] deuoure it: and it shal make thy belly to be bitter, but in thy mouth it shal be :: svveete as it vvere honie. 10 † And I tooke the booke of the hand of the Angel, and deuoured it: & it vvas in my mouth as it vvere honie, svveete. and vvhen I had deuoured it, my bellie vvas made bitter, 11 † and he said to me, Thou must againe prophecie to Nations, and peoples, and tonges, and many kinges.

Marginal notes:

`` pillers

CHRIST the valiant Angel is here described.

:: Many great mysteries and truthes are to be preserued in the Church, vvhich for causes knovven to Gods prouidence are not to be vvritten in the booke of holy Scripture.

Dan. 12, 7.

c This vvas the maner of taking an othe by the true God. *as Deut. 32.*

Ezec. 3, 1

c By earnest studie and meditation.

:: Svveete in the reading, but in fulfilling, somevvhat bitter, because it cõmaũdeth workes of penance and suffering of tribulatiõs.

CHAP. XI.

S. Iohn measuring the Temple, 3 heareth of tvvo vvitnesses that shal preache: 7 vvhom the beast coming vp from the sea shal kil. 11 but they rising againe ascend into heauen, 13 and seuen thousand persons are slaine vvith an earthquake: 15 and at the sound of the seuenth Angel, the foure and tvventie seniors giue praise and thankes to God.

ND there vvas giuen me a reede like vnto a rodde: and it vvas said to me, Arise, and measure the temple of God, and the altar, and them that adore in it. † but the court vvhich is vvithout the temple, cast forth, & measure not that: because it is giuen to the Gentiles, & they shal treade vnder foote the holy citie :: two and fourtie monethes: † and I vvil giue to" my tvvo vvitnesses, and they shal prophecie a thousand tvvo hundred sixtie daies, clothed vvith sacke-clothes. † These are the two oliue trees and the tvvo candlestickes that stand in the sight of the Lord of the earth. † And if any man vvil hurt them, fire shal come forth out of their mouthes, and shal deuoure their enemies. and if any man vvil hurt them: so must he be slaine. † These haue power to shut heauen, that it raine not in the daies of their prophecie: and they haue povver ouer the vvaters to turne them into bloud, and to strike the earth vvith al plague as often as they vvil.

:: Three yeres and a halfe. vvhich is the time of Antichrists reigne and persecution.

† And vvhen they shal haue finished their testimonie: the :: beast vvhich ascended from the depth, shal make vvarre against them, and shal ouercome them, and kil them. † And their bodies shal lie in the streates of the [c] great citie, vvhich is called spiritually Sodom and Ægypt, vvhere their Lord also vvas crucified. † And there shal of tribes, and peoples, and tonges, and Gentiles, see their bodies for three daies and a halfe: and they shal not suffer their bodies to be laid in monuments. † and the inhabitants of the earth :: shal be glad vpon them, and make merie: and shal send giftes one to an other, because these tvvo prophets tormented them that dvvelt vpon the earth. † And after three daies and a halfe, the spirit of life from God entred into them. And they stoode vpon their feete, and great feare fel vpon them that savv them. † And they heard a loud voice from heauen saying to them, Come vp hither. And they vvent vp into heauen in a cloude: and their enemies savv them. † And in that houre there vvas made a great earthquake: and the tenth part of the citie fel: and there vvere slaine in the earthquake names of men seuen thousand: and the rest vvere cast into a feare, and gaue glorie to the God of heauen.

:: The great Antichrist.

c He meaneth Hierusalem, named Sodom and Ægypt for the imitatiō of thē in wickednes. So that we see his cheefe reigne shal be there, though his tyrannie may extend to al places of the vvorld.

:: The wicked reioyce, vvhen holy men are executed by the tyrants of the vvorld, because their life and doctrine are burdenous vnto them.

† The second vvoe is gone: and behold the third vvoe vvil come quickly. † And the seuenth Angel sounded with a trompet

a trompet: and there vvere made loude voices in heauen saying, ∴ The kingdom of this vvorld is made our Lords & his Christs, and he shal reigne for euer and euer. Amen.

16 † And the foure and tvventie seniours vvhich sitte on their seates in the sight of God, fel on their faces, and adored God, 17 † saying: Vve thanke thee Lord God omnipotent, vvhich art, and vvhich vvast, and vvhich shalt come: because thou hast receiued thy great povver, and hast reigned.

18 † And the Gentiles vvere angrie, and thy vvrath is come, and the time of the dead, to be iudged, and ∴ to render revvard to thy seruants the prophets and sainctes, and to them that feare thy name, "litle and great, and to destroy them that haue corrupted the earth.

19 † And the temple of God vvas opened in heauen: and the arke of his testament vvas seen in his temple, and there vvere made lightenings, and voices, and an earthquake and greate haile.

∴ The kingdō of this world vsurped before by Satan & Antichrist, shal aftervvard be Christes for euer.

∴ To repay the hire or wages (for so both the Greeke vvord and the latin signifie) due to holy men, proueth against the protestāts, that they did truely merite the same in this life.

ANNOTATIONS
CHAP. XI.

3. *My tvvo vvitnesses*] Enoch and Elias, as it is commonly expounded. For, that Elias shal come againe before the later day, *it is a most notorious knovven thing* (to vse S. Augustines vvordes) *in the mouthes and hartes of faithful men.* See *li.* 20 *de Ciuit. Dei c.* 29. *Tract.* 4 *in Ioan.* and both of Enoch and Elias, *Lib.* 1 *de pec. merit. c.* 3. So the rest of the Latin Doctors. as, S. Hierom *ad Pāmach. ep.* 61 *c.* 11. *&* *in Psal.* 20. S. Ambrose *in Psal.* 45. S. Hilarie 20 *can. in Mat.* Prosper *li. vltimo de Promissionibus c.* 13. S Gregorie *li.* 14 *Moral. c.* 11. *&* *ho.* 12 *in Ezech.* Beda *in* 9 *Marci.* The Greeke fathers also, as S. Chrysostom *ho.* 58 *in Mat. &* *ho.* 4 *in* 2 *Thessal. &* *ho.* 21 *in Genes. &* *ho.* 22 *in ep. ad Hebr.* Theophylacte and Oecumenius *in* 17 *Matthæi.* S. Damascene *li.* 4 *de Orthodoxa fide c.* 27.

Enoch & Elias yet aliue, shal preach in the time of Antichrist.

Furthermore, that they liue also in Paradise, it is partly gathered out of the Scripture Eccli 44, 16. vvhere it is plainely said of Enoch, that *he is translated into Paradise,* as al our Latin exemplars do reade. and of Elias, that he vvas taken vp aliue, it is euident 4 *Reg.* 2. And S. Irenæus saith, it is the tradition of the Apostles, that they be both there. *li.* 5 *in initio. Dicunt Presbyteri* (saith he) *qui sunt Apostolorum Discipuli. So say the Priests or Auncients that are the scholers of the Apostles.* See S. Iustine *q.* 85 *ad orthodoxos.* Finally, that they shal returne into the companie of men in the end of the vvorld, to preache against Antichrist, and to inuite both Ievves and Gentiles to penance, and so be martyred, as this place of the Apocalypse seemeth plaine, so vve haue in part other testimonies hereof. *Malac.* 4. *Eccli* 44, 16. 48, 10. *Mat.* 17, 11. See also Hyppolytus booke *of Antichrist and the end of the vvorld.* Al vvhich being vvel considered, the Heretikes are to contentious and incredulous, to discredite the same, as they commonly doe.

CHAP. XII.

4 The great dragon (the Diuel) vvatching the vvoman that brought forth a man childe, to deuoure it, God tooke avvay the childe to him self, and fed the vvoman in the desert. 7 Michael fighting vvith the dragon ouercometh him. 13 Vvho being threvven dovvne to the earth, persecuteth the vvomā & her seede.

And

The Dragons incredulous & persecuting multitude, and Antichrist the cheefe head thereof.

AND a great signe appeared in heauen: ∷ a vvoman clothed vvith the sunne, and the moone vnder her feete, & on her head a crovvne of tvvelue starres: † & being with childe, she cried also traueling, and is in anguish to be deliuered. † And there vvas seen an other signe in heauen, and behold c a great red dragon hauing seuẽ heades, & ten hornes: and on his heades seuen diademes, † & his taile drevv ∷ the third part of the starres of heauen, and cast them to the earth, and the dragon stoode before the vvoman which vvas ready to be deliuered: that vvhen she should be deliuered, he might c deuoure her sonne. † And she brought forth a man childe, vvho vvas *to gouerne al nations in an yron rodde: & her sonne vvas taken vp to God and to his throne, † & " the vvoman fled into the vvildernesse where she had a place prepared of God, that there they might feede her a thousand tvvo hundred sixtie daies.

† And there vvas made " a great battel in heauen, Michael and his Angels fought vvith the dragon, and the dragon fought and his Angels: † and they preuailed not, neither vvas their place found any more in heauen. † And that great dragon vvas cast forth, the old serpent, vvhich is called the Deuil and Satan, vvhich seduceth the vvhole vvorld: and he vvas cast into the earth, & his Angels vvere throvven downe vvith him. † And I heard a great voice in heauen saying: Novv is there made saluation and force, and the kingdom of our God, and the povver of his Christ: because the accuser of our brethren is cast forth, vvho accused them before the sight of our God day and night. † And ∷ they ouercame him by the bloud of the Lambe, and by the vvord of their testimonie, and they loued not their liues euen vnto death. † Therfore reioyce ô heauens, and you that dvvel therein. Vvo to the earth and to the sea, because the Diuel is descẽded to you, hauing great vvrath, knovving that he hath a litle time.

† And after the dragon savv that he vvas throvven into the earth, he persecuted the vvomã vvhich brought forth the man-childe: † and there vvere giuen to the vvoman tvvo vvinges of a great egle, that shee might flie into the desert

vnto

Verse numbers in margin: 1, 2, 3, 4, 5, 6, 7, 8, 9, 10, 11, 12, 13, 14

Marginal notes:

∷ This is properly & principally spoken of the Church: and by allusion, of our B. Lady also.

∷ The spirites that fall from their first state into Apostasie vvith him and by his meanes.

c The Diuels endeuour agaist the Churches children, and specially our B. Ladies onely sonne the head of the rest.

∷ Vvhen the Angels or vve haue the victorie, vve must knovv it is by the bloud of Christ, and so al is referred alvvaies to him.

c The great Diuel Lucifer.

Ps. 2, 9. Apoc. 2, 27.

vnto her place, vvhere ſhe is nouriſhed for ∴ a time & times, 15 & halfe a time, from the face of the ſerpent. † And the ſerpent caſt out of his mouth after the vvoman, vvater as it vvere a floud: that he might make her " to be caried avvay vvith the 16 floud. † And the earth holpe the vvoman, and the earth opened her mouth, and ſvvallovved vp the floud vvhich the 17 dragon caſt out of his mouth. † And the dragon vvas angrie againſt the vvoman: and vvent to make battel vvith the reſt of her ſeede, vvhich keepe the commaundements of God, 18 and haue the teſtimonie of IESVS Chriſt. † And he ſtood vpon the ſand of the ſea.

∴ This often inſinuatiō that Antichriſts reigne ſhal be but three yeres & a halfe (Dan. 7, 25. Apoc. 11, 2. 3. & in this chap. v. 6. c. 13, 5.) proueth that the heretikes be exceedingly blinded vvith malice, that hold the Pope to be Antichriſt, who hath ruled ſo many ages.

ANNOTATIONS CHAP. XII.

6. *The vvoman fled.*] This great perſecution that the Church ſhal flee from, is in the time of Antichriſt, and ſhal endure but three yeres and a halfe, as is noted v. 14 in the margent. In vvhich time for al that, ſhe ſhal not vvant our Lordes protection, nor true Paſtors, nor be ſo ſecrete, but al faithful men ſhal knovv and folovv her: much leſſe ſhal ſhe decay, erre in faith, or degenerate and folovv Antichriſt, as Heretikes do vvickedly feine. As the Church Catholike novv in England in this time of perſecution, becauſe it hath no publike ſtate of regiment nor open free exerciſe of holy functions, may be ſaid to be fled into the deſert, yet it is neither vnknovven to the faithful that folovv it, nor the enemies that perſecute it: as the hidde company that the proteſtants talke of, vvas for ſome vvorldes together, neither knovven to their frendes nor foes, becauſe there vvas in deede none ſuch for many ages together. And this is true, if vve take this flight for a very corporal retiring into vvildernes. Vvhere in deede it may be, and is of moſt expounded, to be a ſpiritual flight, by forſaking the ioyes and ſolaces of the vvorld, and giuing her ſelf to contemplation and penance, during the time of perſecution vnder Antichriſt. And by enlarging the ſenſe, it may alſo very vvel ſignifie the deſolation and affliction that the Church ſuffereth and hath ſuffered from time to time in this vvildernes of the vvorld, by al the forerunners and miniſters of Antichriſt, Tyrants and Heretikes.

The Church ſhal flee as to a deſert in Antichriſts time, but not decay or be vnknovven, no not for ſo ſhort a time.

7. *A great battel.*] In the Church there is a perpetual combat betvvixt S. Michael (protector of the Church militant as he vvas ſometime of the Ievves Synagogue *Dan.* 10, 21) and his Angels, and the Deuil and his miniſters. The perfect victorie ouer vvhom, ſhal be at the iudgement. Marke here alſo the cauſe vvhy S. Michael is commonly painted fighting vvith a dragon.

S. Michael fighting vvith the dragon.

15. *To be caried avvay.*] By great perſecution he vvould dravv her, that is, her children from the true faith: but euery one of the faithful elect, gladly bearing their part thereof, ouercome his tyrannie. At vvhoſe conſtancie he being the more offended, vvorketh malicious attempts in aſſaulting the frailer ſort, vvho are here ſignified by *the reſt of her ſeede that keepe the commaundements*, but are not ſo perfect as the former.

Antichriſts attēpts to dravv from the true faith.

CHAP. XIII.

1 A beaſt riſing vp out of the ſea, hauing ſeuen heades and ten hornes & ten diademes. 5 blaſphemeth God, 7 and vvarreth againſt the Saincts & deſtroieth them. 11 And an other beaſt riſing out of the earth vvith tvvo hornes, vvas altogether for the foreſaid beaſt, conſtraining men to make and adore the image thereof, and to haue the character of his name.

ND I savv " a beast comming vp from the sea, hauing seuen heades, and ten hornes, & vpon his hornes ten diademes, and vpon his heades names of blasphemie. † And the beast vvhich I savv, vvas like to a libarde, and his feete as of a beare, and his mouth, as the mouth of a lion. And the dragon gaue him his ovvne force and great povver. † And I savv one of his heades as it vvere slaine to death: and the vvound of his death vvas cured. And al the earth vvas ∷ in admiration after the beast. † And they adored the dragon vvhich gaue povver to the beast: and they adored the beast, saying, Vvho is like to the beast? and vvho shal be able to fight vvith it? † And there was giuen to it a mouth speaking great things and blasphemies: and povver vvas giuen to it to vvorke tvvo and fourtie monethes. † And he opened his mouth vnto blasphemies tovvard God, ∷ to blaspheme his name, and his tabernacle, and those that dvvel in heauen. † And it vvas giuē vnto him " to make battail vvith the sainctes, & to ouercome them. And povver vvas giuen him vpon euery tribe and people, and tongue, and nation, † and al that inhabite the earth, adored it, * vvhose names be not written in the booke of life of the Lambe, vvhich vvas slaine from the beginning of the vvorld.

∷ They that now folow the simplest & grossest heretikes that euer were without seeing miracles, vvould then much more folow this great seducer working miracles.

∷ No heretikes euer liker Antichrist, thē these in our daies, specially in blasphemies against Gods Church, Sacraments, Saincts, ministers, and al sacred thinges.

Apoc. 3, 5

† If any man haue an eare, let him heare. † He that shal leade into captiuitie, goeth into captiuitie: * he that shal kil in the svvord, he must be killed vvith the svvord. here is the patience and the faith of saínctes.

Gen. 9, 6
Mt. 26, 52.

† And I savv ∷ an other beast cōming vp from the earth: and he had tvvo hornes, like to a lambe, & he spake as a dragon. † And al the povver of the former beast he did in his sight: and he made the earth and the inhabitants therein, to adore the first beast, vvhose vvound of death vvas cured. † And he did many signes, so that he made also fire to come dovvne from heauen vnto the earth in the sight of men. † And he seduceth the inhabitants on the earth through the signes vvhich vvere giuē him to doe in the sight of the beast, saying to them that dwel on the earth, that they should make " the image of the beast vvhich hath the stroke of the sWord, and liued. † And it vvas giuen him to giue spirit to the image of the beast, and that the image of the beast should speake: and

∷ An other false prophet inferior to Antichrist, shal vvorke vvonders also, but al referred to the honour of his maister Antichrist. So doth Caluin & other Arch-heretikes peruert the world to the honour of Antichrist, and so do their scholers also for the honour of them.

and ſhould make, that vvhoſoeuer ſhal not adore the image
16 of the beaſt, be ſlaine. † And he ſhal make al, litle & great,
and rich, and poore, and free-men, and bond-men, to haue a
17 character in their right hand, or in their foreheads. † and
that no man may bie or ſel, but he that hath" the character, or
18 the name of the beaſt, or the number of his name. † Here
is vviſdom. He that hath vnderſtanding," let him count the
number of the beaſt. For" it is the number of a man: &" the
number of him is ſixe hundred ſixtie ſixe.

ANNOTATIONS
CHAP. XIII.

1. *A beaſt comming vp.*] This beaſt is the vniuerſal companie of the vvicked, vvhoſe head is Antichriſt: & the ſame is called (*Apoc.* 17) the vvhoore of Babylon. The 7 heades be expounded (*Apoc.* 17) ſeuen kings: fiue before Chriſt, one preſent, and one to come. The 10 hornes be alſo there expounded to be 10 kings that ſhal reigne a ſhort vvhile after Antichriſt. This dragon is the Diuel, by vvhoſe povver the vvhoore or beaſt or Antichriſt vvorketh. for in the vvordes folovving (v. 3 & 4) Antichriſt is called the beaſt, to vvhom the dragon, that is, the Deuil giueth that povver of feined miracles. and as vve adore God for giuing povver to Chriſt and his folovvers, ſo they ſhal adore the Deuil for aſſiſting Antichriſt and giuing him povver.

Many myſteries expounded.

7. *To make battel vvith the ſaincts.*] He ſhal kil the ſaincts then liuing, Elias and Enoch, and infinite moe that profeſſe Chriſt. vvhereby vve muſt learne, not to maruel vvhen vve ſee the vvicked perſecute and preuaile againſt the iuſt, in this life. Then ſhal his great perſecution and crueltie trie the ſaincts patience, as his vvonderful meanes to ſeduce ſhal trie the ſtedfaſtnes of their faith, vvhich is ſignified by theſe vvordes folovving, *Here is the patience and the faith of ſaincts.* And vvhen it is ſaid, *They adored the beaſt, vvhoſe names are not vvritten in the booke of life of the Lambe,* it giueth great ſolace and hope to al them that ſhal not yeld to ſuch perſecutions, that they are of Gods elect, and their names vvritten in the booke of life.

Great perſecution by Antichriſt and his miniſters.

Their bleſſednes that continue cõſtant.

14. *The image of the beaſt.*] They that novv refuſe to vvorſhip Chriſts image, vvould then vvorſhip Antichriſts. And vve may note here, that as the making or honouring of this image vvas not againſt the honour of Antichriſt, but vvholy for it, as alſo the image erected of Nabuchodonoſor, and the vvorſhip thereof vvas altogether for the honour of him, ſo is the vvorſhip of Chriſts image, the honour of Chriſt him ſelf, and not againſt him, as Proteſtants madly imagin.

The honour of Chriſts image is for the honour of Chriſt.

17. *The character or the name.*] As belike for the peruerſe imitation of Chriſt, vvhoſe image (ſpecially as on the Roode or crucifixe) he ſeeth honoured and exalted in euery Church, he vvil haue his image adored (for that is Antichriſt, in emulation of like honour, aduerſarie to Chriſt) ſo for that he ſeeth al true Chriſtian men to beare the badge of his Croſſe in their foreheads, he likevviſe vvil force al his to haue an other marke, to aboliſh the ſigne of Chriſt. By the like emulation alſo and vvicked oppoſition he vvil haue his name and the letters thereof to be ſacred, and to be vvorne in mens cappes, or vvritten in ſolemne places, and to be vvorſhipped, as the name of IESVS is and ought to be among Chriſtian men. And as the ineffable name of God vvas among the Ievves expreſſed by a certaine number of 4 characters (therfore called *Tetragrámmaton*) ſo it ſeemeth the Apoſtle alludeth here to the number of Antichriſts name.

Antichriſts triple honour againſt the honour of Chriſt.

יהוה

And here it is much to be noted, that the Proteſtants plucking dovvne the image of Chriſt out of al Churches, & his ſigne of the croſſe from mens foreheads, and taking avvay the honour and reuerence of the name IESVS, doe make roome for Antichriſts image, & marke, and name. And vvhen Chriſts images and enſignes or armes ſhal be aboliſhed, and the Idol of Antichriſt ſet vp in ſteede thereof, as it is already begonne: then is the abomination of deſolation vvhich vvas foretold by Daniel and our Sauiour.

The Proteſtãts by aboliſhing of Chriſtes image, & croſſe and irreuerẽce to the name IESVS, make a ready vvay to the honour of Antichriſt.

18. *Let him count.*] Though God vvould not haue it manifeſt before hand to the vvorld, vvho in particular this Antichriſt ſhould be: yet it pleaſed him to giue ſuch tokens of him, that vvhen he commeth, the faithful may eaſily take notice of him, according as it is vvritten of the euent of other prophecies concerning our Sauiour, *That vvhen it is come to paſſe, you may beleeue.* In the meane time vve muſt take heede that vve iudge not ouer raſhly of Gods ſecretes, the holy vvriter

Io. 14, 29.

Antichriſts name ſecrete.

here signifying, that it is a point of high vnderstanding, illuminated extraordinarily by Gods spirit, to recken right and discipher truely before hand, Antichrists name and person.

18. *It is the number of a man.*] A man he must be, and not a Diuel or spirit, as here it is cleere, and by S. Paul 2 *Thessal.* 2. vvhere he is called, *the man of sinne.* Againe, he must be one particular person, & not a nũber, a succession, or vvhole order of any degree of men: because his proper name, and the particular number, and the characters thereof be (though obscurely) insinuated. Vvhich reproueth the vvicked vanitie of Heretikes, that vvould haue Christs ovvne Vicars, the successors of his cheefe Apostle, yea the vvhole order of them for many ages together, to be this Antichrist. Vvho by his decription here and in the said Epistle to the Thessalonians, must be one special man, and of a particular proper name, as our Lord IESVS is. And vvhosoeuer he be, these Protestants vndoubtedly are his precursors. for as they make his vvay by ridding avvay Christs images, crosse, and name, so they excedingly promote the matter by taking avvay Christs cheefe minister, that al may be plaine for Antichrist.

Antichrist shal be one special man, and of a peculiar name.

If the Pope had been Antichrist, and had been reuealed novv a good many yeres sithence, as these fellovves say he is to them, then the number of this name vvould agree to him, and the prophecie being novv fulfilled, it vvould euidently appeare that he bare the name and number here noted. for (no doubt) vvhen he commeth, this count of the letters or number of his name vvhich before is so hard to knovv, wil be easie. for he will set vp his name in euery place, euẽ as we faithful men do novv aduance IESVS. And vvhat name proper or appellatiue of al or any of the Popes do they finde to agree vvith this number, notvvithstanding they boast that they haue found the vvhole order and euery of them these thousand yeres to be Antichrist, and the rest before euen from S. Peter, forevvorkers tovvard his kingdom?

The Pope can not be Antichrist.

18. *The number 666.*] Forasmuch as the auncient expositors and other do thinke (for certaine knowledge thereof no mortal mã can haue vvithout an expresse reuelatiõ) that his name cõsisteth of so many, & such letters in Greeke, as according to their maner of numbering by the Alphabete make *666*, and forasmuch as the letters making that number, may be found in diuers names both proper & common: (as S. Irenæus findeth them in *Latinos* and *Teitan*, Hippolytus in ἀρνοῦμαι, Aretas in *Lampetis*, & some of this age in *Ludérus*, vvhich vvas Luthers name in the Alman tõgue:) therfore vve see there can be no certaintie, and euery one frameth and applieth the letters to his ovvne purpose. and most absurd folly it is of the Heretikes, to applie the vvord, *Latinos*, to the Pope: neither the vvhole order in common, nor euer any particular Pope being so called. and S. Irenæus the first that obserued it in that vvord, applied it to the Empire and state of the Romane Emperour, vvhich then vvas Heathen, and not to the Pope of his daies or after him: and yet preferred the vvord, *Teitan*, as more agreeable, vvith this admonition, that it vvere a very perilous and presumptuous thing to define any certaintie before hand, of that number and name. And truely vvhatsoeuer the Protestants presume herein of the Pope, vve may boldly discharge Luther of that dignitie. He is vndoubtedly one of Antichrists precursors, but not Antichrist him self.

Al framing of letters to expresse Antichrists name, is vncertaine.

Iren. li. 5 in fine.

CHAP. XIIII.

1 Virgins follovv the Lambe vvhithersoeuer, singing a nevv canticle. 6 One Angel Euangelizeth the Gospel: 8 an other Angel telleth the fall of Babylon: 9 the third declareth their torments that haue adored the beast. Moreouer tvvo hauing fickles, 15 one of them is commaunded to reape dovvne the corne, 18 the other to gather the grapes as in vintage, vvhich are troden in the lake of Gods vvrath.

The Epistle vpõ S. Innocents day in Christmas.

AND I looked, & behold ⁚⁚ a Lãbe stoode vpon mount Sion, and vvith him an hundred fourtie foure thousand hauing his name, and the name of his Father vvritten in their foreheads. 1

⁚⁚ Christ, and the same number of elect that were signed chap. 7.

† And I heard a voice from heauen, as the voice of many vvaters, and as the voice of great thunder: and the voice vvhich I heard, as of harpers harping on their harpes. 2 † And they sang as it vvere a nevv song before the seate and before the foure beastes, and the seniors, and no 3

man

learne μαθεῖν,

man could say 'the song, but those hundred fourtie foure thousand, that vvere bought from the earth. † These are they vvhich were not defiled vvith vvomen. For they are :: virgins. These folovv the Lambe vvhithersoeuer he shal goe. These vvere bought from among men,[c] the first fruites to God and the Lambe: † and in their mouth there vvas found no lie. for they are vvithout spot before the throne of God. ¶

:: One state of life more excellét then an other. and virgins for their puritie passing the rest, & alwaies accompanying Christ according to the Churches hymne out of this place, *Quocunque pergis, virgines sequuntur &c.*

c This the Church applieth to the holy Innocents that died first for Christ.

† And I savv an other Angel flying through the middes of heauen, hauing the eternal Gospel, to euãgelize vnto them that sit vpon the earth, and vpon euery nation, and tribe, & tõge, & people: † saying vvith a loud voice, Feare our Lord, and giue him honour, because the houre of his iudgement is come: and adore ye him * that made heauen and earth, the sea and al things that are in them, and the fountaines of vvaters.

Ps. 145. Act. 14.

† And an other Angel folovved, saying, * Fallen fallen is that great :: Babylon, vvhich of the vvine of the vvrath of her fornication made al nations to drinke.

Esa. 21. Ier. 51. Apo. 18.

:: The citie of the diuel, which is the vniuersal societie of the wicked misbeleuers & il liuers in the vvorld.

† And the third Angel folovved them, saying vvith a loud voice, If any man adore the beast and his image, and receiue the character in his forehead, or in his hand: † :: he also shal drinke of the vvine of the vvrath of God, vvhich is mingled vvith pure vvine in the cuppe of his vvrath, and shal be tormented vvith fire & brimstone in the sight of the holy Angels and before the sight of the Lambe. † and the smoke of their tormentes shal ascend for euer & euer: neither haue they rest day and night, vvhich haue adored the beast, and his image, and if any man take the character of his name.

:: The great damnatiõ that shal folovv them that forsake Christ & the Church, & worship Antichrist or his image.

† Here is the patience of sainctes, vvhich :: keepe the commaundementes of God and the faith of IESVS.

:: Faith is not ynough to saluatiõ, without fulfilling of Gods cõmaũdements.

†[b] And I heard a voice from heauen, saying to me, Vvrite, Blessed are the dead which die in our Lord." from hence forth novv, saith the Spirit, that they rest from their labours. for their vvorkes folow them.

b The Epistle in a daily Masse for the dead.

† And I savv, and behold a vvhite cloude: and vpon the cloude one sitting like to the Sonne of man, hauing on his head a crovvne of gold, and in his hand a sharpe sickle.

† And an other Angel came forth from the temple, crying vvith a loud voice to him that sate vpon the cloude, * Thrust in thy sickle, and reape, because the houre is come to reape,

Ioel 3. Mat. 13.

for the haruest of the earth is drie. † And he that sate vpon 16 the cloude, thrust his sickle into the earth, and the earth vvas reaped. † And an other Angel came forth from the temple 17 vvhich is in heauẽ, him self also hauing a sharpe sickle. † And 18 an other Angel came forth from the altar, vvhich had povver ouer the fire: and he cried vvith a loud voice to him that had the sharpe sickle, saying, Thrust in thy sharpe sickle, and gather the clusters of the vineyard of the earth: because the grapes thereof be ripe. † And the Angel thrust his sharpe 19 sickle into the earth, and gathered the vineyard of the earth, & cast it into the great [c] presse of the vvrath of God: † and 20 the presse vvas troden vvithout the citie, and bloud came forth out of the presse, vp to the horse bridles, for a thousand sixe hundred furlongs.

[c] *ληνὸν lacũ. fat, trough, lake.*

ANNOTATIONS
CHAP. XIIII.

13. ***From hence forth novv.***] This being specially spoken of Martyrs (as not onely S. Augustine seemeth to take it, but the Caluinists them selues, translating, *in domino, for our Lords cause*) the Protestants haue no reason to vse the place against Purgatorie or praier for the departed, seeing the Catholike Church and al her children confesse, that al Martyrs are straight after their death, in blisse, and neede no praiers. Vvhereof this is S. Augustines knovven sentence, *He doeth iniurie to the Martyr, that praieth for the Martyr. Ser. 17 de verb. Apost. c. 1.* and againe to this purpose he vvriteth thus most excellently tract. 84. in Ioan. *We keepe not a memorie of Martyrs at our Lords table, as vve doe of other that rest in peace, that is, for the intent to pray for them, but rather that they may pray for vs &c.*

Beza.

Praying for the dead, and vnto Saincts, at the altar.

But if vve take the vvordes generally for al deceased in state of grace, as it may be also, then vve say that euen such, though they be in Purgatorie and Gods chastisement in the next life, and neede our praiers, yet (according to the foresaid vvordes of S. Augustine) *do rest in peace,* being discharged from the labours, afflictions, and persecutions of this vvorld, and (vvhich is more) from the daily dangers of sinne and damnation, and put into infallible securitie of eternal ioy vvith vnspeakable comfort of conscience. and such in deede are more happie and blessed then any liuing, vvho yet are vsually in the Scriptures called blessed, euen in the middes of the tribulations of this life. Vvhereby vve see that these vvordes, *from hence forth they shal rest from their labours,* may truely agree to them also that are in Purgatorie, and so here is nothing proued against Purgatorie. Lastly, this aduerbe, *á modo*, in Latin, as in the Greeke ἀπάρτι, doth not properly signifie, from this present time forvvard, as though the Apostle had said, that after their death and so forvvard they are happie: but it noteth and ioyneth the time past together vvith the time present, in this sense, that such as haue died since Christs Ascension, vvhen he first entring into heauen opened it for others, goe not to *Limbus Patrum*, as they vvere vvont before Christs time, but are in case to goe straight to blisse, except the impediment be in them selues. Therfore they are here called blessed, that die novv in this state of grace & of the nevv Testament, in comparison of the old faithful and good persons.

The place abused against Purgatorie, ansvvered.

ámodo ἀπάρτι Photius in Lexico.

CHAP. XV.

THE 4 PART Of the 7 last plagues & final damnatiõ of the vvicked.

2 They that had novv ouercome the beast and his image and the number of his name, do glorifie God. 6 To seuen Angels hauing the seuen last plagues, are giuen seuen cuppes full of the vvrath of God.

AND

1 AND I savv an other signe in heauen great and maruelous: seuen Angels hauing the seuen last plagues. Because in them the wrath of God is con-2 summate. † And I savv as it vvere [c] a sea of glasse mingled vvith fire, and them that ouercame the beast and his image and the number of his name, standing vpon the sea of 3 glasse, hauing the harpes of God: † and singing ∵ the song of Moyses the seruant of God, and the song of the Lambe, saying, Great and maruelous are thy vvorkes Lord God omnipotent: iust and true are thy vvaies King of the ˋvvorldesˊ.
4 † Vvho shal not feare thee o Lord, and magnifie thy name? because thou only art holy, because al nations shal come, & adore in thy sight, because thy iudgements be manifest.

5 † And after these things I looked, and behold the temple 6 of the tabernacle of testimonie was opened in heauen: † and there issued forth the seuen Angels, hauing the seuen plagues, from the temple: reuested vvith cleane and vvhite ˋstoneˊ, & 7 girded about the breastes vvith girdles of gold. † And one of the foure beastes, gaue to the seuen Angels seuen vials of gold ful of the vvrath of the God that liueth for euer and euer.
8 † And the temple vvas filled vvith smoke at the maiestie of God, and at his povver: and no man could enter into the temple, til the seuen plagues of the seuen Angels vvere consummate.

The tribulations about the day of iudgement.

c Baptisme.

∵ The song of Moyses and Christ, is the new Testamēt and the old.

ˋ Saincts

THE FIFTH VISION.

ˋ linen λίνον λίθον.

CHAP. XVI.

Vpon the pouring out of the seuen cuppes of Gods vvrath, on the land, the sea, the fountaines, the seat of the beast, Euphrâtes and the aire: there arise sundrie plagues in the vvorld.

1 AND I heard a great voice out of the temple, saying to the seuen Angels: Goe, and poure out the seuen vials of the vvrath 2 of God vpon the earth. † And the first vvent, and poured out his vial vpon the earth, and there vvas made a cruel and very sore vvound vpon men that had the character of the beast: and vpon them that adored the image thereof.

3 † And the second Angel poured out his vial vpon the sea, and there vvas made bloud as it vvere of one dead: and

euery

euery liuing soul died in the sea.

4 † And the third poured out his vial vpon the riuers & the fountaines of vvaters: and there vvas made bloud. 5 † And I heard the Angel of the vvaters, saying: Thou art iust ô Lord, vvhich art, and vvhich vvast, the holy one, because thou hast iudged these things: 6 † :: because they haue shed the bloud of the Saincts and Prophets, & thou hast giuen them bloud to drinke. for they are vvorthie. 7 † And I heard an other, saying: Yea Lord God omnipotent, true and iust are thy iudgements.

:: The great reuenge that God vvil doe at the later day vpon the persecutors of his Saincts.

8 † And the fourth Angel poured out his vial vpon the sunne, and it vvas giuen vnto him to afflict men vvith heate and fire: 9 † and men boiled vvith great heate, and :: blasphemed the name of God hauing povver ouer these plagues, neither did they penance to giue him glorie.

:: The desperate and damned persons shal blaspheme God perpetually. vvhich shal be such onely as do not repent in this life.

10 † And the fift Angel poured out his vial vpon the seate of the beast: and his kingdom vvas made darke, and they together did eate their tonges for paine: 11 † & they blasphemed the God of heauen because of their paines and vvoundes, & [c] did not penance from their vvorkes.

c See chap. 9. v. 20 in the margent.

12 † And the sixt Angel poured out his vial vpon that great riuer Euphrátes: and dried vp the vvater thereof that a vvay might be prepared to the kings from the rising of the sunne.

13 † And I savv from the mouth :: of the dragon, and from the mouth of the beast, and from the mouth of the false-prophet ˋ three' vncleane spirites in maner of frogges. 14 † For they are the spirites of Deuils vvorking signes, and they goe forth to the kings of the vvhole earth to gather them into battel at the great day of the omnipotent God. 15 † Behold * I come as a theefe: Blessed is he that vvatcheth, & keepeth his garments, that he* vvalke not naked, and they see his turpitude. 16 † And he shal gather them into a place vvhich in Hebrevv is called [c] *Armagedon*.

:: The dragon, is the Diuel: the beast, Antichrist, or the societie wherof he is head: the false-prophet, either Antichrist him self, or the companie of Heretikes and seducers that folovv him.

c *The hil of theeues*, by S. Hieroms interpretation.

ˋ *issue forth three*

Apoc. 3. *2 Cor.* 5, 3.

17 † And the seuenth Angel poured out his vial vpon the aire, and there came forth a loud voice out of the temple from the throne, saying: It is done. 18 † And there vvere made lighteninges, and voices, and thunders, and a great earthquake vvas made, such an one as neuer hath been since men vvere vpon the earth, such an earthquake, so great. 19 † And :: the great citie vvas made into three partes: and the cities of the

:: The citie or cõmonvvealth of the vvicked deuided into three partes: into infidels, Heretikes, and euil Catho-

Gentiles

Gentiles fel. And Babylon the great came into memorie before God,* to giue her the cuppe of vvine of the indignation of his vvrath. † And euery Iland fled, and mountaines vvere not found. † And great haile like a talent came downe from heauen vpon men: and men blasphemed God for the plague of the haile: because it vvas made exceding great.

Ier. 25, 15.

likes. This citie is here called Babylō, vvhereof see the Annotat. vpon the next chapter v. 5.

CHAP. XVII.

The harlot Babylon clothed vvith diuers ornaments, 6 and drunken of the bloud of Martyrs, sitteth vpon a beast that hath seuen heades and ten hornes: 7 al which things the Angel expoundeth.

1 AND there came one of the seuen Angels vvhich had the seuen vials, & spake vvith me, saying, Come, I vvil shevv thee ∷ the damnation of the great harlot, vvhich 2 sitteth vpon c many vvaters, † vvith vvhom the kings of the earth haue fornicated, and they vvhich inhabite the earth 3 haue been drunke of the vvine of her vvhoredom. † And he tooke me avvay in spirit into the desert. And I savv a womā sitting vpon a scarlet coloured beast, ful of names of blasphemie, hauing seuen heades, and ten hornes. 4 † And the vvoman vvas clothed round about vvith purple and scarlet, and gilted vvith gold, and pretious stone, and pearles, hauing a golden cup in her hand, ful of the abomination & filthines 5 of her fornication. † And in her forehead a name vvritten, " *Mysterie:* " Babylon the great, mother of the fornications and 6 the abominations of the earth. † And I savv the vvoman " drunken of the bloud of the Saincʈes, and of the bloud of the martyrs of IESVS. And I marueled vvhen I had seen her, 7 vvith great admiration. † And the Angel said to me, Vvhy doest thou maruel? I vvil tel thee the mysterie of the woman, and of the beast that carieth her, which hath the seuen heades and the ten hornes.

∷ The final damnation of the vvhole companie of the reprobate, called here the great vvhoore.

c These many vvaters are many peoples. v. 15.

8 † The beast vvhich thou savvest, ∷ vvas, and is not, and shal come vp out of the bottomeles depth, and goe into destruction: and the inhabitants on the earth (vvhose names are not vvritten in the booke of life from the making of the vvorld) shal maruel, seeing the beast that vvas, and is not.

∷ It signifieth the short reigne of Antichrist, vvho is the cheefe horne or head of the beast.

not. † And here is vnderſtanding, that hath vviſedom. 9 The ſeuen heades: are ″ ſeuen hilles, vpon vvhich the vvoman ſitteth, and they are ſeuen kings. † Fiue are fallen, 10 one is, and an other is not yet come: & vvhen he ſhal come, he muſt tarie a ſhort time. † And the beaſt vvhich vvas, & 11 is not: ″ the ſame alſo is the eight, and is of the ſeuen, & goeth into deſtruction. † And the ten hornes vvhich thou ſaweſt: 12 are ∷ ten kings, vvhich haue not yet receiued kingdom, but ‛ſhal' receiue povver as kings one houre after the beaſt. † Theſe haue one counſel and force: and their povver they 13 ſhal deliuer to the beaſt. † Theſe ſhal fight vvith the Lambe, 14 and the Lambe ſhal ouercome them, becauſe * he is Lord of lordes, and King of kinges, & they that are vvith him, called, and elect, and faithful. † And he ſaid to me, The vvaters 15 vvhich thou ſavveſt vvhere the harlot ſitteth: are peoples, and nations, and tonges. † And the ten hornes vvhich thou 16 ſavveſt in the beaſt: theſe ſhal hate the harlot, and ſhal make her deſolate and naked, and ſhal eate her fleſh, and her they ſhal burne vvith fire. † for ∷ God hath giuen into their 17 hartes, to doe that vvhich pleaſeth him: that they giue their kingdom to the beaſt, til the vvordes of God be cōſummate. † And the vvoman vvhich thou ſavveſt: is ″ the great citie, 18 vvhich hath kingdom ouer the kinges of the earth.

∷ Some expound it of ten ſmal kingdoms, into which the Romane Empire ſhal be deuided, vvhich ſhal al ſerue Antichriſt both in his life and a litle after.

doe

1 Tim. 6, 15. Apo. 19, 16.

∷ Not forcing or mouing any to folow Antichriſt, but by his iuſt iudgement, & for puniſhment of their ſinnes, permitting thé to beleeue and cōſent to him.

ANNOTATIONS
CHAP. XVII.

The Proteſtāts here vvil needs haue Babylō to be Rome, but not in S. Peters epiſtle.

5. *Babylon.*] In the end of S. Peters firſt Epiſtle, vvhere the Apoſtle dateth it at Babylon, vvhich the auncient vvriters (as vve there noted) affirme to be meant of Rome: the Proteſtants vvil not in any vviſe haue it ſo, becauſe they vvould not be driuen to confeſſe that Peter euer vvas at Rome. but here for that they thinke it maketh for their opinion, that the Pope is Antichriſt, and Rome the ſeate and citie of Antichriſt, they vvil needes haue Rome to be this Babylon, this great vvhore, and this purple harlot. for ſuch fellovves, in the expoſition of holy Scripture, be ledde onely by their preiudicate opinions and hereſies, to vvhich they dravv al things vvithout al indifferencie and ſinceritie.

By Babylon (according to al the fathers) is ſignified, partly the vvhole ſocietie of the wicked, partly the citie of Rome, only in reſpect of the terrene &

But S. Auguſtine, Aretas, and other vvriters, moſt commonly expound it, neither of Babylon it ſelf a citie of Chaldæa or Ægypt, nor of Rome, or any one citie, vvhich may be ſo called ſpiritually, as Hieruſalem before chap. 11 is named ſpiritual Sodom and Ægypt: but of the general ſocietie of the impious, & of thoſe that preferre the terrene kingdō and cōmoditie of the vvorld, before God & eternal felicitie. The author of the Commentaries vpon the Apocalypſe ſet forth in S. Ambroſe name, vvriteth thus: *This great vvhoore ſometime ſignifieth Rome, ſpecially vvhich at that time vvhen the Apoſtle vvrote this, did perſecute the Church of God. but othervviſe it ſignifieth the vvhole citie of the Diuel, that is, the vniuerſal corps of the reprobate.* Tertullian alſo taketh it for Rome, thus. *Babylon* (ſaith he) *in S. Iohn is a figure of the citie of Rome, being ſo great, ſo proud of the Empire, and the deſtroier of the ſainčts.* Vvhich is plainely ſpoken of that citie, vvhen it vvas heathen, the head of the terrene dominion of the vvorld, the perſecutor of the Apoſtles and their ſucceſſors, the ſeate of Nero, Domitian, and the like, Chriſts ſpecial enemies, the ſinke of idolatrie, ſinne, and

li. aduerſ. Iudaeos.

falſe

false vvorship of the Pagan gods. Then vvas it Babylon, vvhen S. Iohn vvrote this, and then vvas Nero and the rest figures of Antichrist, and that citie the resemblance of the principal place (vvheresoeuer it be) that Antichrist shal reigne in, about the later end of the vvorld.

heathenish state of them that persecuted the Church

Novv to apply that to the Romane Church and Apostolike See, either novv or then, vvhich vvas spoken onely of the terrene state of that citie, as it vvas the seate of the Emperour, and not of Peter, vvhen it did slea aboue 30 Popes Christs Vicars, one after an other, & endeuoured to destroy the vvhole Church: that is most blasphemous and foolish.

The Church in Rome vvas one thing, & Babylon in Rome an other thing. Peter sate in Rome, and Nero sate in Rome. but Peter, as in the Church of Rome: Nero, as in the Babylon of Rome. Vvhich distinction the Heretikes might haue learned by S. Peter him self *ep. 1. chap. 5.* vvriting thus, *The Church saluteth you, that is in Babylon, coelect.* So that the Church and the very chosen Church vvas in Rome, vvhen Rome vvas Babylon. vvhereby it is plaine that, vvhether Babylon or the great vvhoore do here signifie Rome or no, yet it can not signifie the Church of Rome: vvhich is novv, and euer vvas, differing from the terrene Empire of the same. And if, as in the beginning of the Church, Nero and the rest of the persecuting Emperours (vvhich vvere figures of Antichrist) did principally sit in Rome, so also the great Antichrist shal haue his seate there, as it may vvel be (though others thinke that Hierusalem rather shal be his principal citie:) yet euen then shal neither the Church of Rome, nor the Pope of Rome be Antichrist, but shal be persecuted by Antichrist, and driuen out of Rome, if it be possible. for, to Christs Vicar and the Romane Church he vvil beare as much good vvil as the Protestants novv doe, and he shal haue more povver to persecute him and the Church, then they haue.

The Church of Rome is neuer called Babylon.

S. Hierom *epist. 17. c. 7.* to Marcella, to dravv her out of the citie of Rome to the holy land, vvarning her of the manifold allurements to sinne and il life, that be in so great and populous a citie, alludeth at length to these vvordes of the Apocalypse, and maketh it to be Babylon, and the purple vvhoore. but straight vvay, lest some naughtie person might thinke he meant that of the Church of Rome, vvhich he spake of the societie of the vvicked only, he addeth: *There is there in deede the holy Church, there are the triumphant monuments of the Apostles and Martyrs, there is the true confession of Christ, there is the faith praised* * *of the Apostle, and Gentilitie troden vnder foote, the name of Christian daily aduancing it self on high.* Vvhereby you see that vvhatsoeuer may be spoken or interpreted of Rome, out of this vvord Babylō, it is not meant of the Church of Rome, but of the terrene state, in so much that the said holy Doctor (*li. 2 aduers. Iouinian. c. 19.*) signifieth, that the holines of the Church there, hath vviped avvay the blasphemie vvritten in the forehead of her former iniquitie. But of the difference of the old state and dominion of the Heathen there, for vvhich it is resembled to Antichrist, and the Priestly state vvhich novv it hath, reade a notable place in S. Leo *serm. 1 in natali Petri & Pauli.*

Ro. 1.

5. *Mysterie.*] S. Paul calleth this secrete and close vvorking of abomination, the mysterie of iniquitie. 2. *Thessal. 2.* and it is called a litle after in this chapter vers. 7. *the Sacrament* (or mysterie) of the vvoman, and it is also the marke of reprobation and damnation.

Mysterie.

6. *Drunken of the bloud.*] It is plaine that this vvoman signifieth the vvhole corps of al the persecutors that haue and shal shede so much bloud of the iust: of the Prophets, Apostles, and other Martyrs from the beginning of the vvorld to the end. The Protestants folishly expound it of Rome, for that there they put Heretikes to death, and allovv of their punishment in other countries: but their bloud is not called the bloud of saincts, no more then the bloud of theeues, mankillers, and other malefactors: for the sheding of vvhich by order of iustice, no Commonvvealth shal ansvver.

This woman signifieth al persecutors of saincts.

Putting heretikes to death, is not to shede the bloud of saincts.

9. *Seuen hilles.*] The Angel him self here expoundeth these 7 hilles to be al one vvith the 7 heads and the 7 kings: & yet the Heretikes blinded excedingly vvith malice against the Church of Rome, are so madde to take them for the seuen hilles literally, vpon vvhich in old time Rome did stand: that so they might make the vnlearned beleeue that Rome is the seate of Antichrist. But if they had any consideration, they might marke that the Prophets visions here are most of them by Seuens, vvhether he talke of heads, hornes, candlestickes, Churches, kings, hilles, or other thinges: and that he alluded not to the hilles, because they vvere iust seuen, but that *Seuen* is a mystical number, as sometime *Ten* is, signifying vniuersally al of that sort whereof he speaketh. as, that the seuen heads, hilles, or kingdoms (which are here al one) should be al the kingdoms of the world that persecute the Christians: being heads and mountaines for their height in dignitie aboue others. And some take it, that there were seuen special Empires, kingdoms, or States, that vvere or shal be the greatest persecutors of Gods people. as of Ægypt, Chanaan, Babylon, the Persians, and Greekes, which be fiue. sixtly of the Romane Empire which once persecuted most of al other, and which (as the Apostle here saith) *yet is*, or standeth. but the seuenth, then vvhen S. Iohn vvrote this, vvas not come, neither is yet come in our daies: vvhich is Antichrists state, vvhich shal not come so long as the Empire of Rome standeth, as S. Paul did Prophecie. 2 *Thessal. 2.*

The Protestants madnes in expounding the 7 hilles, of Rome: the Angel himself expounding it otherwise.

11. *The same is the eight.*] The beast it self being the congregation of al these vvicked persecutors, though it consist of the foresaid seuen, yet for that the malice of al is complete in it, may be called

Vvhat is the eight beast.

called the eight. Or, Antichrist him self, though he be one of the seuen, yet for his extraordinarie vvickednes shal be counted the odde persecutor, or the accomplishment of al other, & therfore is named the eight. Some take this beast called the eight, to be the Diuel.

18. *The great citie.*] If it be meant of any one citie, and not of the vniuersal societie of the reprobate (vvhich is the citie of the Diuel, as the Church & the vniuersal fellovvship of the faithful is called the citie of God) it is most like to be old Rome, as some of the Greekes expound it, from the time of the first Emperours, til Constantines daies, vvho made an end of the persecution. for by the authoritie of the old Romane Empire, Christ vvas put to death first, and aftervvard the tvvo cheefe Apostles, & the Popes their successors, and infinite Catholike men through out the vvorld, by lesser kings vvhich then vvere subiect to Rome. Al vvhich Antichristian persecutions ceased, vvhen Constantine reigned, and yelded vp the citie to the Pope, vvho holdeth not the kingdom or Empire ouer the vvorld, as the Heathen did, but the fatherhod and spiritual rule of the Church. Hovvbeit the more probable sense is the other, of the citie of the Diuel, as the author of the homilies vpon the Apocalypse in S. Augustine, declareth.

The double interpretation of Babylon.

CHAP. XVIII.

The fall of Babylon, her iudgement, plagues and reuenges: for the vvhich, 9 the kings, 16 and marchants of the earth that sometime did cleaue vnto her, shal mourne bitterly: 20 but heauen, and the Apostles and Prophets shal reioyce.

1 AND after these things I savv an other Angel coming dovvne from heauen, hauing great povver: & the earth vvas illuminated of his glorie. 2 † And he cried out in force, saying, * Fallen fallen is Babylon the great: and it is become the habitation of Deuils, and [c] the custodie of euery vncleane spirit, and the custodie of euery vncleane and hateful bird: 3 † because al nations haue drunke of the vvine of the vvrath of her fornication: and the kings of the earth haue fornicated vvith her: and the marchantes of the earth vvere made riche by the vertue of her delicacies.

Apo. 14, 8.

c φυλακὴ

4 † And I heard an other voice from heauen, saying, Goe out from her my people: that you be not partakers of her sinnes, and receiue not of her plagues. 5 † Because her sinnes are come euen to heauen, and God hath remembred her iniquities. 6 † Render to her as she also hath rendred to you: & double ye double according to her vvorkes: In the cuppe vvherin she hath mingled, mingle ye double vnto her. 7 † As much as she hath glorified her self, & hath been in delicacies, :: so much giue her torment and mourning: because she saith in her hart, * I sit a queene, & Widow I am not, and mourning I shal not see. 8 † Therfore in one day shal her plagues come, death, and mourning, and famine, and vvith fire she shal be burnt: because God is strong that shal iudge her.

:: The measure of paines & damnation, according to the wicked pleasures or vnlawful delites of this life. Which is a sore sentence for such people as turne their whole life to iust and riot.

Es. 47, 8

† And

9 † And :: the kings of the earth, vvhich haue fornicated vvith her, & haue liued in delicacies, ſhal vveepe, & bevvaile them ſelues vpon her, vvhen they ſhal ſee the ſmoke of her

10 burning: † ſtanding farre of for the feare of her tormentes, ſaying, Vvo, vvo, that great citie Babylon, that ſtrong citie: becauſe in one houre is thy iudgement come.

11 † And the marchãtes of the earth ſhall vveepe, & mourne vpon her: becauſe no man ſhal bye their merchandiſe any

12 more, † merchandiſe of gold and ſiluer and precious ſtone, and of pearle, and fine linnen, and purple, and ſilke, & ſcarlet, and al Thyne vvood, and al veſſels of yuorie, and al veſſels of

13 precious ſtone and of braſſe and yron and marble, † and cynamon, and of odours, and ointement, and frankeincenſe, and vvine, and oile, and floure, & vvheate, and beaſtes, & ſheepe,

14 and horſes, and chariotes, & ſlaues, and ſoules of men. † And the apples of the deſire of thy ſoul are departed from thee, & al fat and goodly thinges are periſhed from thee, and they

15 ſhal no more finde them. † The marchantes of theſe things vvhich are made riche, ſhal ſtand farre from her for feare of

16 her tormẽtes, vveeping and mourning, † & ſaying, Vvo, wo, that great citie, vvhich vvas clothed vvith ſilke, and purple, and ſcarlet, and vvas gilted vvith gold, and pretious ſtone, &

17 pearles: † becauſe in one houre are ſo great riches made deſolate: and euery gouernour, and euery one that saileth into the lake, and the ſhipmen, and they that vvorke in the ſea,

18 ſtoode a farre of, † and cried ſeeing the place of her bur-

19 ning, ſaying, Vvhat other is like to this great citie? † And they threvv duſt vpon their heades, and cried vveeping and mourning, ſaying: Vvo, vvo, that great citie, in the vvhich al vvere made riche that had ſhippes in the ſea, of her prices: becauſe in one houre ſhe is deſolate.

20 † c Reioyce ouer her, heauen, and ye holy Apoſtles and Prophetes: becauſe God hath iudged your iudgement of her.

21 † And one ſtrong Angel tooke vp as it vvere a great milſtone, and threvv it into the ſea, ſaying, * Vvith this violence ſhal :: Babylon that great citie be throwen, and ſhal novv be

22 found no more. † And the voice of harpers, & of Muſicians, and of them that ſing on ſhalme and trompet, ſhal no more be heard in thee, & euery artificer of euery art ſhal be found no more in thee, and the noiſe of the mill ſhal no more be

23 heard in thee, † and the light of the lampe ſhal no more

Ier. 51. 63.

:: Kings and Marchants are moſt encombered, dangered and drovvned in the pleaſures of this vvorld: vvhoſe vvhole life & traficke is (if they be not exceding vertuous) to finde varietie of earthly pleaſures. Vvho ſeing once the extreme end of their ioyes and of al that made their heauen here, to be turned into paines & damnation eternal, then ſhal houle & vveepe to late.

c The Angels and al Saincts ſhal reioyce and laude God to ſee the wicked confounded, and Gods iuſtice executed vpon their oppreſſors & perſecutors. and this is that vvhich the Martyrs praied for, chap. 6.

:: By this it ſeemeth cleere that the Apoſtle meaneth not any one citie, but the vniuerſal companie of the reprobate, vvhich ſhal periſh in the day of iudgement: the old prophets alſo naming the vvhole nũber of Gods enemies myſtically, Babylon, as *Ierem. c. 51.*

ſhine in thee, and the voice of the bridegrome and the bride ſhal no more be heard in thee: becauſe thy marchantes were the princes of the earth, becauſe al nations haue erred in thine inchauntments. † And in her is found the bloud of the Prophets and Saincтes, and of al that vvere ſlaine in the earth. 24

CHAP. XIX.

The Saincts glorifying God for the iudgement pronounced vpon the harlot, 7 the mariage of the Lambe is prepared. 10 The Angel refuſeth to be adored of S. Iohn. 11 There appeareth one (vvho is the Word of God, and the King of kings and Lord of lords) ſitting on a horſe, vvith a great armie, and fighting againſt the beaſt and the kings of the earth and their armies: 17 the birdes of the aire being in the meane time called to deuoure their fleſh.

The Epiſtle for many martyrs.

ALLELVIA

AFTER theſes things I heard as it vvere the 1 voice of many multitudes in heauen ſaying, *Allelu-ia.* Praiſe, and glorie, and povver is to our God: † becauſe true & iuſt are his iudge- 2 mentes which hath iudged of the great harlot, that hath corrupted the earth in her vvhoredom, and hath reuenged the bloud of his ſeruants, of her handes. † And ∷ a- 3 gaine they ſaid, *Allelu-ia.* And her ſmoke aſcendeth for euer and euer. † And the foure and tvventie ſeniors fel 4 downe, and the foure beaſtes, & adored God ſitting vpon the throne, ſaying: " *Amen, Allelu-ia.* † And a voice came out from 5 the throne, ſaying: Say praiſe to our God al ye his ſeruantes: and you that feare him, litle and great. † And I heard as it 6 vvere the voice of a great multitude, and as the voice of many vvaters, & as the voice of great thunders, ſaying, *Allelu-ia:* becauſe our Lord God the omnipotent hath reigned. † Let 7 vs be glad and reioyce, and giue glorie to him: becauſe ∷ the mariage of the Lambe is come, and his vvife hath prepared her ſelf. † And it vvas giuen to her that ſhe clothe her 8 ſelf vvith ſilke glittering and vvhite. For the ſilke are " the iuſtifications of Saincтes.

∷ This often repeating of *Allelu ia* in times of reioycing, the Church doth folow in her Seruice.

∷ At this day ſhal the whole Church of the elect be finally & perfectly for euer ioyned vnto Chriſt in mariage inſeparable.

† And he ſaid to me, Vvrite, * Bleſſed be they that are 9 called to the ∷ ſupper of the mariage of the Lambe. † And he ſaid to me, Theſe vvordes of God, be true. † " And * I fel 10 before his feete, to adore him. And he ſaith to me, See thou doe not: I am thy fellovv-ſeruant, and of thy brethren that haue

Mat. 22. Lu. 14.

Apoc. 22. 9.

∷ That is the feaſt of eternal life prepared for his ſpouſe the Church.

haue the testimonie of IESVS. Adore God. For the testimonie of IESVS, is the spirit of prophecie.

11 † And I savv heauen opened, and behold a vvhite horse: and he that sate vpon him, vvas called Faithful and True, and
12 vvith iustice he iudgeth & fighteth. † And his eies as a flame of fire, and on his head many diademes. hauing a name writ-
13 ten, vvhich no man knovveth but him self. † *And he vvas clothed vvith a garment sprinkled vvith bloud: & his name
14 is called,[c] THE VVORD OF GOD. † And the hostes that are in heauen folovved him on vvhite horses clothed in
15 vvhite and pure silke. † And out of his mouth procedeth a sharpe svvord: that in it he may strike the Gentiles. And *he shal rule them in a rod of yron: and he treadeth the vvine
16 presse of the furie of the vvrath of God omnipotent. † And he hath in his garment and in his thigh vvritten, * :: KING OF KINGES AND LORD OF LORDES.

17 † And I savv one Angel standing in the sunne, & he cried vvith a loud voice saying to al the birdes that did flie by the middes of heauen, Come and assemble together to the
18 great supper of God: † that you may eate the flesh of kings, and the flesh of tribunes, and the flesh of valiants, and the flesh of horses & of them that sit on them, & the flesh of al freemen and bondmen, and of litle and great.

19 † And I savv the beast and the kings of the earth, & their armies gathered to make vvarre vvith him that sate vpon the
20 horse and vvith his armie. † And the beast vvas apprehẽded, and vvith him the false-prophet: vvhich vvrought signes before him, vvherevvith he seduced them that tooke the character of the beast, and that adored his image. These tvvo were cast aliue into the poole of fire burning also with brimstone.
21 † And the rest vvere slaine by the svvord of him that sitteth vpon the horse, vvhich procedeth out of his mouth: and al the birdes vvere filled vvith their flesh.

Es. 63, 1.

Apoc. 2, 27.

Apo. 17, 14.

[c] The second person in Trinitie, the Sonne or the Vvord of God, vvhich vvas made flesh. Io. 1.

:: Euen according to his humanitie also.

ANNOTATIONS
CHAP. XIX.

אָמֵן הַלְלוּיָה

4. *Amen, Alleluia.*] These tvvo Hebrue vvordes (as other els vvhere) both in the Greeke & Latin text are kept religiously, & not translated, vnles it be once or tvvise in the Psalmes. Yea and the Protestants them selues keepe them in the text of their English Testaments in many places. and maruel it is vvhy they vse them not in al places, but sometimes turne, *Amen*, into, *verily*, vvhereof see the Annotation *Ioan. 8. v. 34*: and in their Seruice booke they translate, *Alleluia*,

Amen, Alleluia, not translated.

into,

into, *Praise ye the Lord*, as though *Alleluia* had not as good a grace in the acte of seruing God, (vvhere it is in deede properly vsed) as it hath in the text of the Scripture.

Alleluia often vsed in the Church, specially in Easter time.

The Church Catholike doth often and specially vse this sacred vvord, to ioyne vvith the Church triumphant, consisting of Angels and Saincts, vvho here are said to laude and praise God vvith great reioycing, by this vvord *Alleluia*, and by often repetition thereof: as the Catholike Church also vseth, namely in Easter time euen til Vvhit-sontide, for the ioy of Christs resurrection, vvhich (as S. Augustine declareth *ep. ad Ianuarium*) vvas the general vse of the Primitiue Church, making a greater mysterie and matter of it, then our Protestants novv do. At other times of the yere also he saith it vvas sung in some Churches, but not in al. and S. Hierom numbereth it among the heresies of Vigilantius, That *Alleluia* could not be sung but at Easter. *Aduers. Vigilant. c.* 1.

Epist. ad Ian. c. 17. & *c.* 15.

It signifieth more then (as the Protestants traslate it) *praise ye the Lord*.

The truth is, by the vse of the Scriptures it hath more in it then, *Praise ye the Lord*, signifying vvith laude, glorifying, and praising of God, a great reioycing vvithal, mirth, and exultation of hart in the singers thereof. and that is the cause vvhy the holy Church saith, *Laus tibi Domine*, *Praise be to thee ô Lord*, in Lent and times of penance and mourning, but not *Alleluia*. vvhich (as S. Augustine also declareth) is a terme of signification and mysterie, ioyned vvith that time, and then vsed specially in the Church of God, vvhen she representeth to vs in her Seruice, the ioyes and beatitude of the next life: vvhich is done specially at Easter, by the ioyful celebrating of Christs glorious Resurrection and Ascension, after the penal time of Lent vvhich representeth the miserie of this life. See S. Augustine *Ser.* 1. & 5. *c.* 9. & 6. *c.* 9 *de Diuersis to.* 10. and his enarration vpon the 148 Psalme. for in the titles and endes of diuerse holy Psalmes this *Alleluia* is ful of mysterie & sacred signification. Vvhere vve must aske the Protestants, vvhy they haue left it out altogether, being in the Hebrue, saying neither *Alleluia*, nor, *Praise ye the Lord*, in the Bible 1577: & that nine times in the sixe last Psalmes.

False translation.

Amen and *Alleluia* should not be translated into vulgar tongues.

Moreouer the said holy Doctor (*li.* 2 *de doct. Christ. c.* 11) affirmeth that *Amen* & *Alleluia* be not translated into any other language, *propter sanctiorem authoritatem*, for the more sacred authoritie of the vvordes so remaining. and *ep.* 178. he saith that it is not lavvful to translate them. *Nam sciendum est &c. for it is to be knovven* (saith he) *that al nations do sing* Amen and *Alleluia in the Hebrue vvordes, vvhich neither the Latine man nor the Barbarous may translate into his ovvne language.* See S. Hierom also *epist.* 137. And namely for our Nation, S. Gregorie vvil beare vs vvitnes that our countrie receiued the vvord *Alleluia* vvith their Christianitie, saying thus *li.* 27 *Moral. c.* 6. *Lingua Britanniæ quæ nihil aliud nouerat quàm barbarum frendere, iamdudum in Diuinis laudibus Hebræum cœpit resonare Alleluia.* that is, *The Britan tongue, vvhich knevv nothing els but to mutter barbarously, hath begone of late in Gods diuine laudes and praises to sound the Hebrue Alleluia.* And for Iurie, S. Hierom *ep.* 17. *c.* 7 vvriteth, that the husbandmen at the plough sang *Alleluia*, vvhich vvas not then their vulgar speache. Yea he saith that in Monasteries the singing of *Alleluia* vvas in steede of a bel to call them together *ad Collectam. in Epitaph. Paulæ c.* 10.

Al nations in the Primitiue Church sang *Amen* and *Alleluia*.

The Protestats profane this vvord by translating it, and diminish the signification thereof.

This vvord is a sacred, Christian, mystical, and Angelical song. and yet in the nevv seruice booke it is turned into, *Praise ye the Lord*, and *Alleluia* is quite gone, because they list neither to agree vvith the Church of God, nor vvith the vse of holy Scriptures, no nor vvith their ovvne translations. but no maruel, that they can not sing *the song of our Lord* and of Angels *in a strange countrie*, that is, out of the Catholike Church, in the captiuitie of schisme & heresie. Lastly, vve might aske them vvhether it be al one to say *Mat.* 21, *Hosanna*, &, *Saue vs vve beseeche thee?* vvhereas Hosanna is vvithal a vvord of exceding congratulation and ioy vvhich they expressed tovvard our Sauiour. euen so *Alleluia* hath an other maner of sense and signification in it, then can be expressed by, *Praise ye the Lord*.

Psal. 136.

Iustificatiōs are good vvorkes, not as the effectes of faith iustifying, but because them selues also vvith faith iustifie a man.

8. *Iustifications of Saincts.* Here the Heretikes in their translations could not alter the vvord *iustifications* into *ordinances*, or *constitutions*, as they did falsely in the first of S. Luke, vvhereof see the Annotatiō there vers. 6. but they are forced to say in Latin, *iustificationes*, as Beza: and in English, *righteousnes*, (for *iustifications* they vvil not say in any case for feare of inconuenience.) yea and they can not deny but these iustifications be the good vvorkes of saincts. but vvhere * they make this glose, that they be so called, because they are the fruites or effect of faith and of the iustice vvhich vve haue by onely faith, it is most euidently false, & against the very text, and nature of the Word. for there is no cause vvhy any thing should be called a mans iustification, but for that it maketh him iust. so that, *iustifications*, be the vertues of faith, hope, charitie, and good deedes, iustifying or making a man iust, and not effectes of iustification. neither faith onely, but they al together be the very ornaments and invvard garments, beauty, and iustice of the soule, as here it is euident.

Beza.

S. Iohns adoring of the Angel, explicated against the Protestats abusing the same.

10. *And I fel.*] The Protestants abuse this place, and the example of the Angels forbidding Iohn to adore him being but his fellovv seruant, and appointing him to adore God, against al honour, reuerence, and adoration of Angels, Saincts, or other sanctified creatures, teaching that no religious vvorship ought to be done vnto them. But in truth it maketh for no such purpose, but only vvarneth vs that Diuine honour and the adoration due to God alone, may not be giuen to any Angel or other creature. *S. August. de vera relig. cap. vltimo.* And vvhen the Aduersaries replie that so great an Apostle, as Iohn vvas, could not be ignorant of that point, nor vvould haue giuen diuine honour vnto an Angel (for so he had been an Idolater) and therfore that he vvas not

repre-

reprehended for that, but for doing any religious reuerence or other honour vvhatsoeuer to his fellovv-seruant: vve ansvver that by the like reason, S. John being so great an Apostle, if this later kinde of reuerence had been vnlavvful and to be reprehended, as the Protestants hold it is no lesse then the other, could not haue been ignorant thereof, nor vvould haue done it.

The Protestats are refelled by their ovvne reason.

Therfore they might much better haue learned of S. Augustine (*q. 61 in Genes.*) hovv this facte of S. Iohn vvas corrected by the Angel, and vvherein the errour vvas. In effect it is thus, That the Angel being so glorious and ful of maiestie, presenting Christs person, and in his name vsing diuers vvordes proper to God, as, *I am the first and the last, and aliue and vvas dead,* and such like, might vvel be taken of S. Iohn, by errour of his person, to be Christ him self, and that the Apostle presuming him to be so in deede, adored him vvith Diuine honour: vvhich the Angel correcting, told him he vvas not God, but one of his fellovves, and therfore that he should not so adore him, but God. Thus then vve see, Iohn vvas neither so ignorant, to thinke that any vndue honour might be giuen to any creature: nor so il, to commit idolatrie by doing vndue vvorship to any Angel in heauen: and therfore vvas not culpable at al in his facte, but onely erred materially (as the Scholemen call it) that is, by mistaking one for an other, thinking that vvhich vvas an Angel, to haue been our Lord: because he knevve that our Lord him self is also * called an Angel, and hath often appeared in the visions of the faithful.

Apoc. c. 1.

S. Iohn erred only in the person, mistaking the Angel to be Christ him self, and so adoring him as God.

Esa. 9 in Græco. Malac. 3.

And the like is to be thought of the Angel appearing in the 22 of the Apocalypse, vvhether it vvere the same or an other. for that also did so appeare, that Iohn could not tell vvhether it vvere Christ him self or no, til the Angel told him. Once this is certaine, that Iohn did not formally (as they say) commit idolatrie, nor sinne at al herein, knovving al dueties of a Christian man, no lesse then an Angel of heauen, being also in as great honour vvith God, yea and in more then many Angels. Vvhich perhaps may be the cause (and consequently an other explication of this place) that the Angel knovving his great graces and merites before God, vvould not accept any vvorship or submission at his handes, though Iohn againe of like humilitie did it, as also immediatly aftervvard chap. 22. vvhich belike he vvould not haue done, if he had been precisely aduised by the Angel but a moment before, of errour & vnduetifulnes in the facte. Hovvsoeuer that be, this is euident, that this the Angels refusing of adoration, taketh not avvay the due reuerence and respect vve ought to haue to Angels or other sanctified persons and creatures. and so these vvordes, *See thou doe it not*, signifie rather an earnest refusal, then any signification of crime to be committed thereby.

S. Iohn sinned not in this adoration.

An other explication of this place.

And maruel it is that the Protestants making them selues so sure of the true sense of euery doubtful place by conference of other Scriptures, folow not here the conference and comparing of Scriptures that them selues so much or onely require. Vve vvil giue them occasion and a methode so to doe, thus. He that doubteth of this place, findeth out three things of question, vvhich must be tried by other Scriptures. The first, vvhether there ought to be or may be any religious reuerence or honour done to any creatures. taking the vvord religion or religious vvorship not for that special honour vvhich is properly and onely due to God, as S. Augustine sometimes vseth it, but for reuerence due to any thing that is holy by sanctification or application to the seruice of God. The second thing is, vvhether by vse of Scriptures, that honour be called *adoration* in latin, or by a vvord equiualent in other languages, Hebrue, Greeke, or English. Lastly, vvhether vve may by the Scriptures fall dovvne prostrate before the things, or at the feete of the persons that vve so adore. For of ciuil duetie done to our Superiors by capping, kneeling, or other courtesie, I thinke the Protestants vvil not stand vvith vs: though in deede, their arguments make as much against the one as the other.

The Protestāts by conference of Scriptures might finde religious adoratiō of creatures.

Aug. de vera relig. c. 55.

Three points herein examined and proued by Scriptures.

השתחוה

προσκυνεῖν.

But for religious vvorship of creatures (vvhich vve speake of) let them see in the Scriptures both old and nevv: first, vvhether the Temple, the tabernacle, the Arke, the propitiatorie, the Cherubins, the altar, the bread of proposition, the Sabboth, and al their holies, vvere not reuerenced by al signes of deuotion and religion: vvhether the Sacraments of Christ, the Priests of our Lord, the Prophets of God, the Gospel, Scriptures, the name of IESVS, such like (vvhich be by vse, signification, or sanctification made holy) are not novv to be reuerenced: and they shal finde al these things to haue been reuerenced of al the faithful, vvithout any dishonour of God, and much to his honour. Secondly, that this reuerence is named *adoration* in the Scriptures, these speaches do proue *Ps. 98. Adore ye his footestoole, because it is holy.* and *Hebr. 11. He adored the toppe of his rod.* Thirdly, that the Scriptures also vvarrant vs (as the nature of the vvord adoratiō giueth in al three tonges) to bowe downe our bodies, to fall flat on the ground at the presence of such things, and at the feete of holy persons, specially Angels, as Iohn doth here, these examples proue. Abraham adored the Angels that appeared to him, Moyses also the Angel that shevved him self out of the bush, vvho vvere creatures, though they represented Gods person, as this Angel here did, that spake to S. Iohn. Balaam adored the Angel that stoode before him vvith a svvord drawen. Num. 22. Iosuë adored falling flat downe before

Ps. 5. 137. Dan. 6. 3 Reg. 8. Ios. 7. Ps. 98. 131.

1 Religious vvorship of creatures.

2 The same is called adoration.

3 Falling prostrat before the persons or things adored.

Gen. 18. Exod. 3. Iosue 5.

Adoring of Angels.

before the feete of the Angel, calling him his Lord, knowing by the Angels owne testimonie, that it vvas but an Angel. Vvho refused it not, but required yet more reuerence, commaunding him to plucke of his shoes, because the ground vvas holy, no doubt so made by the presence onely of the Angel.

Adoring of Prophets and holy persons.

Yea not onely to Angels, but euen to great Prophets this deuotion vvas done, as to Daniel by Nabuchodonosor, vvho fell flat vpon his face before him, and did other great offices of religion, vvhich the Prophet refused not, because they vvere done to God rather then to him, as S. Hierom defendeth the same against Porphyrie, vvho charged Daniel vvith intolerable pride therein, and the said holy doctor alleageth the fact of Alexander the great, that did the like to * Ioiadas the high priest of the Ievves. Hovvsoeuer that be (for of the sacrifice there mentioned there may be some doubt, vvhich the Church doth alvvaies immediatly to God, and to no creature) the fact of the prophets (4 Reg. 2) to Elizeus, is plaine: vvhere they perceiuing that the double grace and spirit of Elias vvas giuen to him, fel flat dovvne at his feete and adored. So did* the Sunamite. to omit that Achior adored Iudith, falling at her feete, as a vvoman blessed of God, and infinite other places.

Dan. 2.

** or, Iaddus.*

4 Reg. 4.
Iudith. 13.

Al vvhich thinges, by comparing the Scriptures, our Aduersaries should haue found to be lavvfully done to men, and Angels, and soueraine holy creatures. Vvhereby they might conuince them selues, & perceiue, that that thing could not be forbidden S. Iohn to doe to the Angel, which they pretend: though the Angel for causes might refuse euen that vvhich S. Iohn did lawfully vnto him, as S. Peter did refuse the honour giuen him by Cornelius, according to S. Chrysostoms opinion. *ho. 23 in c* 10 *Act.* yea euen in the third chapter of this booke (if our Aduersaries vvould looke no further) they might see where this Angel prophecieth & promiseth that the Ievves should fall dovvne before the feete of the Angel of Philadelphia and adore. See the Annot. there.

CHAP. XX.

An Angel casteth the dragon (or diuel) bound, into the depth for a thousand yeres, in vvhich the soules of martyrs in the first resurrection shal reigne vvith Christ. 7 After vvhich yeres, Satan being let loose, shal raise Gog and Magog, an innumerable armie, against the beloued citie: 9 but a fire from heauen shal destroy them. 12 Then bookes are opened, and he that sitteth vpon the throne, iudgeth al the dead according to their vvorkes.

See in S. Augustine (*li. 20. de Ciuit. c. 7. 8. & seq.*) the exposition of this chapter.

1 AND I savv an Angel descending from heauen, hauing the key of the bottomles depth, and a great chaine in his hand. † 2 And he apprehended the dragon the old serpent, vvhich is the Deuil and Satan, and "bound him for a thousand yeres. † 3 and he threvv him into the depth, and shut him vp, and sealed ouer him, that he seduce no more the nations, til the thousand yeres be consummate. and after these thinges he must be loosed a litle time.

4 † And" I savv seates: and they sate vpon them, & iudgement vvas giuen them, "and the soules of the beheaded for the testimonie of IESVS, and for the vvord of God, and that adored not the beast, nor his image, nor receiued his character in their foreheads or in their handes, and haue liued, and reigned vvith Christ :: a thousand yeres. † 5 "The rest of the dead liued not, til the thousand yeres be consummate. "This is the

:: *Quid in millenario numero nisi ad proferendam nouam sobolem perfecta vniuersitas præscita generationis exprimitur? hinc per Ioannem dicitur, Et regnabunt cũ illo mille annis, quia regnum sanctæ Ecclesiæ, vniuersitatis perfectione solidatur. D. Gregor. li. 9. Moral. c. 1.*

6 the first resurrection. † Blessed and holy is he that hath part in the first resurrection. in these the second death hath not povver: but " they shal be priestes of God and of Christ: and shal reigne vvith him a thousand yeres.

7 † And vvhen the thousand yeres shal be consummate, " Satan shal be loosed out of his prison, and shal goe forth, and seduce ∷ the nations that are vpon the foure corners of the earth, * Gog, and Magog, and shal gather them into bat-8 tel, the number of vvhom is as the sand of the sea. † And they ascended vpon the bredth of the earth, and compassed 9 " the campe of the Sainctes, and the beloued citie. † And " there came dovvne fire from God out of heauen, and de-10 uoured them: † and the Deuil vvhich seduced them, vvas cast into the poole of fire and brimstone, vvhere both the beast and the false-prophet shal be tormented day and night for euer and euer.

Ezec. 38, 14. 39, 2.

∷ S. Augustine thinketh that these do not signifie any certaine natiōs but al that shal then be ioyned vvith the Diuel and Antichrist against the Church. *li. 20. de Ciuit. c. 11.* See S. Hierom *in Ezech. li. 11.*

THE 6 VISION.

11 † And I savv a great vvhite throne, and one sitting vpon it, from vvhose sight ∷ earth and heauen fled, and there vvas 12 no place found for them. † And I savv the dead, great and litle, standing in the sight of the throne, and [c] bookes vvere opened: and * " an other booke vvas opened, vvhich is of life: and the dead vvere iudged of those thinges vvhich were 13 vvritten in the bookes according to their vvorkes. † and the sea gaue the dead that vvere in it, and death and hel gaue their dead that vvere in them, and it vvas iudged of euery one ac-14 cording to their vvorkes. † And hel and death vvere cast 15 into the poole of fire. This is the second death. † And ∷ he that vvas not found vvritten in the booke of life, vvas cast into the poole of fire.

Apoc. 3, 5. 21, 27.

∷ They shal then be nevv, not the substāce, but the shape chāged. *2 Pet. 3.* See S. Augustine. *li. 20. de Ciuit. c. 14.*

c The bookes of mens consciēces, where it shal plainely be read vvhat euery mans life hath been.

∷ Such as doe no good workes, if they haue age and time to doe them, are not found in the booke of life.

ANNOTATIONS
CHAP. XX.

2. *Bound him.*] Christ by his Passion hath abridged the povver of the Deuil for a thousand yeres, that is, the vvhole time of the nevv Testament, vntil Antichrists time, vvhen he shal be loosed againe, that is, be permitted to deceiue the vvorld, but for a short time only, to vvit, three yeres and a halfe.

4. *I savv seates.*] S. Augustine (*li. 20 de Ciuit. Dei c. 9*) taketh this to be spoken, *not of the last iudgement, but of the Sees or Consistories of Bishops and Prelates, and of the Prelates them selues, by vvhom the Church is novv gouerned. As the iudgement here giuen, can be taken no othervvise better, then of that vvhich vvas said by our Sauiour* Mat. 18. *Whatsoeuer you binde in earth, shal be bound in heauen. and therfore the Apostle saith, What haue I to doe to iudge of them that are vvithout?*

1. Cor. 5.

Bishops consistories & iudicial power.

4. *And the soules.*] *He meaneth* (saith S. Augustine in the place alleaged) *the soules of Martyrs, that they shal in the meane time, during these thousand yeres, vvhich is the time of the Church militant, be in heauen vvithout their bodies, and reigne vvith Christ. for, the soules* (saith he) *of the godly departed, are*

During a thousand yeres (that is the time of

this militant Church) saints reigne vvith Christ in soule only.

not separated from the Church, vvhich is euen novv the kingdom of Christ. for els there should be kept no memorie of them at the altar of God in the communicating of the body of Christ: neither should it auaile to hasten to Baptisme in the perils of death, for feare of ending our life vvithout it: nor to hasten to be reconciled, if vve fortune for penance or of il conscience to be separated from the same body. And vvhy are al these things done, but for that the faithful departed also be members of the Church? And though for an example the Martyrs be onely named here, yet it is meant of others also that die in the state of grace.

The rest are dead and damned in soule, during the same time.

5. *The rest liued not.*] The rest vvhich are not of the happie number aforesaid, but liued and died in sinne, reigne not vvith Christ in their soules during this time of the nevv Testament, but are dead in soule spiritually, and in body naturally, til the day of iudgement. *S. August. ibidem.*

The first resurrection, of the soule only.

3. *This is the first resurrection.*] As there be tvvo regenerations, one by faith, vvhich is novv in Baptisme: and an other according to the flesh, vvhen at the later day the body shal be made immortal and incorruptible: so there are tvvo resurrections, the one novv of the soules to saluation vvhen they die in grace. vvhich is called the first, the other of the bodies at the later day. S. August. *li. 20 de Ciuit. c. 6.*

Priests, some proprely so called, some vnproprely.

6. *They shal be Priests.*] *It is not spoken* (saith S. Augustine li. 20 de Ciuit. c. 10) *of Bishops and Priests onely, vvhich are properly novv in the Church called Priests: but as vve call al, Christians, for the mystical Chrisme or ointment, so al, Priests, because they are the members of one Priest. of vvhom the Apostle Peter saith, A holy people, a kingly Priesthod.* Vvhich vvordes be notable for their learning that thinke there be none properly called Priests novv in the nevv Testament, no othervvise then al Christian men and vvomen, and a confusion to them that therfore haue turned the name Priests into Ministers.

1 Pet. 2.

The binding and loosing of Satan, expliceated by S. Augustine.

7. *Satan shal be loosed.*] In the vvhole 8 chapter of the said 20 booke *de Ciuitate Dei* in S. Augustine, is a notable commentarie of these vvordes. Vvhere first he declareth, that neither this binding nor loosing of Satan is in respect of seducing or not seducing the Church of God: prouing that vvhether he be bound or loose, he can neuer seduce the same. *The same*, saith he, *shal be the state of the Church at that time vvhen the Diuel is to be loosed, euen as since it vvas instituted. the same hath it been & shal be at al time in her children that succede eche other by birth & death.* And a litle after. *This I thought vvas therfore to be mentioned, lest any man should thinke, that during the litle time Wherein the Diuel shal be loosed, the Church shal not be vpon the earth, he either not finding it here vvhen he shal be let loose, or consuming it vvhen he shal by al meanes persecute the same.* Secondly he declareth, that the Diuel to be bound, is nothing els but not to be permitted by God to exercise al his force or fraude in tentations: as to be loosed, is to be suffered by God for a small time, that is, for three yeres and a halfe, to practise and proue al his povver and artes of tentations against the Church and her children, and yet not to preuaile against them. Thirdly this Doctor shevveth by vvhat great mercie our Lord hath tied Satan and abridged his povver during the vvhole millenarie or thousand yeres, vvhich is al the time of the nevv Testament vntil then: & vvith vvhat vvisedom he permitteth him to breake loose that litle time of three yeres and sixe moneths, tovvard the later day, vvhich shal be the reigne of Antichrist. Lastly he shevveth vvhat kinde of men shal be most subiect to the Diuels seductiō, (euen such as novv by tentation of Heretikes goe out of the Church) and vvho shal auoid it.

The short reigne of Antichrist.

Millenarij or Chiliasta.

By al vvhich vve may confute diuers false expositiōs of old & late Heretikes. first, the aūcient sect of the Millenaries, that grounded vpon these thousand yeres named by the Prophet, this heresie, that there should be so many yeres after the resurrectiō of our bodies, in vvhich vve should reigne vvith Christ in this vvorld, in our bodies, in al delites and pleasures corporal, of meates, drinkes, and such like, vvhich they called the first resurrection. of vvhich heresie Cerinthus vvas the author. *Epiph. hær. 77 in fine. Hiero. Comment. in c. 19 Mat. August. hær. 8 ad Quodvult Deum.* Eusebius also (*li. 3 historiæ c. 33*) shevveth that some principal men vvere in part (though after a more honest maner cōcerning those corporal delicacies) of the same opinion, by misconstruction of these vvordes of S. Iohn. Vvhereby vve learne and al the vvorld may perceiue, the holy Scriptures to be hard, vvhen so great clerkes did erre, and that there is no securitie but in that sense vvhich the Church allovveth of.

The Scriptures hard.

By S. Augustines foresaid explication, is euidently deduced against the Protestāts, that the Church can not erre, and that the Pope can not possibly be Antichrist.

The late Heretikes also by the said S. Augustines vvordes are fully refuted, affirming not only that the Church may be seduced in that great persecution of the Diuels loosing, but that it hath been seduced euen a great peece of this time vvhen the Diuel is bound: holding that the very true Church may erre or fall from truth to errour and idolatrie, yea (vvhich is more blasphemie) that the cheefe gouernour of the Church is Antichrist him self, and the very Church vnder him, the vvhoore of Babylon: and that this Antichrist, (vvhich the Scriptures in so many places, and here plainely by S. Augustines exposition, testifie, shal reigne but a small time, and that tovvard the last iudgement,) hath been reuealed long sithence, to be the Pope him self, Christs ovvne Vicar, and that he hath persecuted the Saincts of their secte for these thousand yeres at the least. Vvhich is no more but to make the Diuel to be loose, and Antichrist to reigne the vvhole thousand yeres, or the most part thereof, that is, almost the vvhole time of the Churches state in the nevv Testamēt: (vvhich is against this and other Scriptures euidently appointing that, to be the time of the Diuels binding:) Yea it is to make Antichrist and the Diuel vveaker tovvard the day of iudgement then before

before, and the truth better to be knovven, and the faith more common, the neerer vve come to the same iudgement: vvhich is expresly * against the Gospel. and this prophecie of S. John.

An inuincible demōstration.

Mat. 24. Lu. 18, 8.

Vve see that the sectes of Luther, Caluin, and other, be more spred through the vvorld then they vvere euer before, and consequently the Pope and his religion lessened, and his povver of punishing (or, as they call it) persecuting the said Sectaries, through the multitude of his aduersaries, diminished. How then is the Pope Antichrist, whose force shal be greater at the later end of the vvorld, then before? or how can it be othervvise, but these Sect-Maisters should be Antichrists neere precursors, that make Christs cheefe Ministers & the Churches cheefe gouernours that haue been these thousand yeres and more, to be Antichristes: and them selues and their sectes to be true, that come so neere the time of the Diuels loosing and seduction & of the personal reigne of Antichrist?

8. *The campe of the Saincts.*] S. Augustine in the said 20 booke de Ciuit. Dei cap. 11. *It is not*, saith he, *to be taken that the persecutors shal gather to any place, as though the campe of the saincts or the beloued citie should be but in one place, vvhich in deede are no other thing but the Church of Christ spred through the vvhole vvorld. And therfore vvheresoeuer the Church shal then be (vvhich shal be in al Nations euen then, for so much is insinuated by this latitude of the earth here specified) there shal the tents of saincts be, and the beloued citie of God, and there shal she be besieged by al her enemies, vvhich shal be in euery countrie vvhere she is, in most cruel and forcible sort.* So vvriteth this profound holy Doctor. Vvhereby vve see, that, as novv the particular Churches of England, Scotland, Flanders, and such like, be persecuted by their enemies in those countries, so in the time of Antichrist, the Churches of al Nations, as of Italie, Spaine, France, and al other vvhich novv be quiet, shal be assaulted as novv the foresaid are, and much more, for that the general persecution of the vvhole, shal be greater then the particular persecution of any Churches in the vvorld.

The campe of Saincts is the Catho. Church through the vvorld.

As novv Heretikes in particular countries, so Antichrist shal persecute the Churches of al nations.

9. *There came dovvne a fire.*] It is not meant of the fire of Hel (saith S. Augustine *ib. c.* 12) into which the vvicked shal be cast after the resurrection of their bodies, but of an extraordinarie helpe that God vvil send from heauen, to giue succourse to the Saincts of the Church that then shal fight against the vvicked: or, the very feruent and burning zeale of religion and Gods honour, vvhich God vvil kindle in the hartes of the faithful, to be constant against al the forces of that great persecution.

Vvhat is meant by fire from heauen.

12. *An other booke.*] This is the booke of Gods knovvledge or predestination, vvherein that vvhich before vvas hid to the vvorld, shal be opened, and vvherein the true record of euery mans vvorkes shal be conteined, and they haue their iudgemēt diuersly according to their vvorkes, and not according to faith only, or lacke of faith only. for, al infidels (as Turkes, obstinate Ievves, and Heretikes) shal neuer come to that examination, being othervvise condemned.

The booke of euery mans Workes, opened in the day of iudgement.

CHAP. XXI.

THE 5 PART. The final glorificatiō of the Church.

Heauen and earth being made nevv, S. Iohn seeth the nevv citie Hierusalem prepared and adorned for the spouse of the Lambe. 6 The iust are glorified, 7 and the vvicked thrust into the poole of fire. 12 The vvall and gates and foundations of the citie are described and measured: 18 al vvhich are gold and crystal, pretious stones and pearles.

Esa. 65, 17. 66, 22. 2 Pet. 3, 13.

The Epistle vpon the dedication of a Church.

1 AND I savv a nevv heauen and a nevv earth. for * the first heauen, and the first earth vvas gone, & the sea novv is not. † 2 And I Iohn savv [c] the holy citie Hierusalem nevv descending from heauen, prepared of God, as a bride adorned for her husband. † 3 And I heard a loud voice from the throne saying: Behold ∷ the tabernacle of God vvith men, and he vvil dvvel vvith them. And they shal be his people: and he God vvith them shal be their God. † 4 and * God shal [c] vvipe avvay al teares from their eies: and death shal be no more. nor mourning, nor crying, neither shal there be sorovv any more, ` vvhich' first thinges are gone.

c The Church triumphant.

∷ This tabernacle is Christ according to his humanitie.

Es. 25, 8. Apoc. 7, 17.

c This happie day shal make an end of al the miseries of this mortalitie.

' because the

† And he that sate in the throne, said: * Behold I make al thinges nevv. † And he said to me: Vvrite, because these vvordes be most faithful and true. † And he said to me: It is done, * I am Alpha and Omega: the beginning and the end. To him that thirsteth I vvil giue of the fountaine of the vvater of life, gratis. † He that shal ouercome, :: shal possesse these thinges, and I vvil be his God: and he shal be my sonne. † But c to the feareful, and incredulous, and execrable, and murderers, and fornicators, and sorcerers, and Idolaters, and al liers, their part shal be in the poole burning vvith fire and brimstone, vvhich is the second death.

† And there came one of the seuen Angels that had the vials ful of the seuen last plagues, and spake vvith me, saying: Come, & I vvil shevv thee the bride, the vvife of the Lambe. † And he tooke me vp in spirit vnto a mountaine great and high: and he shevved me the holy citie Hierusalem descending out of heauen from God, † :: hauing the glorie of God. and the light thereof like to a pretious stone, as it vvere to the iasper stone, euen as crystal. † And it had a vvall great and high, hauing tvvelue gates, and in the gates tvvelue Angels, & names vvritten thereon, vvhich are c the names of the tvvelue tribes of the children of Israël. † On the East, three gates: and on the North, three gates: and on the South, three gates: and on the Vvest, three gates. † And the vvall of the citie hauing tvvelue foundations: and in them, tvvelue names, of the tvvelue Apostles of the Lambe.

† And he that spake vvith me, had a measure of a reede, of gold, to measure the citie and the gates thereof, and the vvall. † And :: the citie is situated quadrangle-vvise, and the length thereof is as great as also the bredth: and he measured the citie vvith the reede for tvvelue thousand furlonges, & the length and height and bredth thereof be equal. † And he measured the vvall thereof of an hundred fourtie foure cubites, the measure of a man vvhich is of an Angel. † And the building of the vvall therof vvas of iasper stone: but the citie it self pure gold, like to pure glasse. † And the foundations of the vvall of the citie, vvere adorned vvith al pretious stone. The first foundation, the iasper: the second, the saphire: the third, the calcedónius: the fourth, the emerauld: † the fifth, the sardonix: the sixt, the sardius: the seuenth, the chrysolithus: the eight, the beryllus: the ninthe, the topázius: the tenth, the chryso-

(Verse numbers in margin: 5, 6, 7, 8, 9, 10, 11, 12, 13, 14, 15, 16, 17, 18, 19, 20)

Marginal references: Esa. 43, 19. — Apoc. 1, 8. 22, 13.

Marginal notes:

:: He that hath the victorie against sinne in the Church militant, shal haue his revvard in the triumphant.

c Al that commit mortal sinnes and repent not, shal be damned.

THE 7 AND LAST VISION.

:: The glorie of the Church triumphant.

c The names of the Patriarches and Apostles honorable and glorious in the triumphant Church.

:: See S. Hierom ep. 17. touching this description of the heauenly Hierusalem, vvhich is the Church triũphãt, teaching that these things must be taken spiritually, not carnally.

chrysóprasus: the eleuenth, the hyacinthe: the tvvelfth, the
21 amethyste. † And the twelue gates: there are twelue pearles, one to euery one: & euery gate vvas of one seueral pearle. & the streate of the citie pure gold, as it vvere trăspárent glasse.
22 † And :: temple I savv not therein. for our Lord the God omnipotent is the temple thereof, and the Lambe.
23 † And * the citie needeth not sunne nor moone, to shine in it. for the glorie of God hath illuminated it, and the Lambe is the lampe thereof.
24 † And * the Gentiles shal vvalke in the light of it: and the kinges of the earth shal bring their glorie and honour into it.
25 † And * the gates thereof shal not be shut by day: for there shal be no night there.
26 † And they shal bring the glorie and honour of nations into it.
27 † There shal :: not enter into it any polluted thing, nor that doeth abomination and maketh lie, but * they that are vvritten in the booke of life of the Lambe.

Esa. 60, 19, *Es. 60, 3.* *Esa. 60, 11,* *Apo. 20, 12.*

:: Al external sacrifice which now is necessarie dutie of the faithful, shal then cease and therfore there shal neede no material temple.

:: None not perfectly cleãsed of their sinnes, can enter into this heauenly Hierusalem.

ANNOTATION
CHAP. XXI.

18. *Pure gold.*] S. Gregorie (*li. 18. Moral. c. 28*) saith, the heauenly state is resembled to gold, pretious stone, crystal, glasse, and the like, for the puritie, claritie, glittering of the glorious bodies: vvhere one mans body, conscience, and cogitations are represented to an other, as corporal things in this life are seen through crystal or glasse.

The state of glorified bodies.

CHAP. XXII.

The tree of life being vvatered vvith liuing vvater, yeldeth fruictes euery moneth. 3 There is neither curse nor night in the citie. 6 The Angel that shevved Iohn al these things, refuseth to be adored of him. 14 He telleth him that the iust shal enter into the citie, but the rest shal be cast forth. 18 Lastly, he protesteth and threateneth against them that shal presume to adde to this prophecie, or take avvay from the same.

1 AND he shevved me a riuer of ' liuing water', cleere as crystal, proceding from the seate of God and of the Lambe.
2 † In the middes of the streate thereof, and on both sides of the riuer, :: the tree of life, yelding tvvelue fruites, rendring his fruite euery moneth, and the leaues of the tree for the curing of the Gentiles.
3 † And no curse shal be any more: and the seate of God and of the Lambe shal be in it, and his seruantes shal serue him.
4 † And they shal see his face: and his name in their foreheads.
5 † And * night shal be no

vvater of life. *Apo. 21. Esa. 60.*

:: Christ is our tree of life: in the Church, by the B. Sacramẽt: & in heauen, by his visible presence and influence of life euerlasting both to our bodies and soules: of vvhõ Salomon saith, *The tree of life to al that apprehẽd him. Prou. 3.*

no more: and they ſhal not neede the light of lampe, nor the light of the ſunne, becauſe our Lord God doth illuminate them, and they ſhal reigne for euer and euer. † And he ſaid 6 to me, Theſe vvordes are moſt faithful and true. And our Lord the God of the ſpirites of the prophetes, ſent his Angel to ſhevv his ſeruantes thoſe thinges vvhich muſt be done quickly. † And behold I come quickly. Bleſſed is he that 7 keepeth the vvordes of the prophecie of this booke.

THE CONCLVSION.

† And I Iohn vvhich haue heard, and ſeen theſe thinges. 8 And * after I had heard and ſeen, I fel dovvne :: to adore before the feete of the Angel vvhich ſhevved me theſe thinges: † and he ſaid to me, See thou doe not, for I am thy fellow-ſer- 9 uant, and of thy brethren the prophetes, and of them that keepe the vvordes of this booke. Adore God. † And he ſaith 10 to me, Seale not the vvordes of the prophecie of this booke. for the time is neere. † " He that hurteth, let him hurt yet: 11 and he that is in filth, let him be filthie yet: and he that is iuſt, [c] let him be iuſtified yet: and let the holy be ſanctified yet. † Behold I come quickly. and my revvard is vvith me, 12 * to render to euery man :: according to his vvorkes, † I am 13 * Alpha and Omega, the firſt and the laſt, the beginning and the end. † Bleſſed are they that vvaſh their ſtoles: that their 14 povver may be in the tree of life, and they may enter by the gates into the citie. † Vvithout are dogges and ſorcerers, and 15 the vnchaſt, and murderers, and ſeruers of Idols, & euery one that loueth and maketh a lie.

:: You ſee it is al one to adore before the feete of the angel, & to adore the Angel: though, to adore him, be not expreſſed as in the 19 chap. *See the anotatiō there v. 10.*

[c] Man by Gods grace & doing good workes, doth increaſe his iuſtice.

:: Heauen is the reward, hire, & repaiment for good workes, in al the Scriptures. yet the aduerſaries wil not ſee it.

Apo. 19, 10.

Ro. 2, 6.

Apo. 21, 6. 1, 8.

† I IESVS haue ſent mine Angel, to teſtifie to you theſe 16 thinges in the Churches. I am the roote and ſtocke of Dauid, the bright and morning ſtarre. † And the Spirit & the bride 17 ſay, Come. And he that heareth, let him ſay, Come. And * he that thirſteth, let him come: and he that vvil, let him take the vvater of life gratis.

Eſ. 55, 1.

† For I teſtifie to euery one hearing the vvordes of the 18 prophecie of this booke, " If any mā ſhal adde to theſe things, God ſhal adde vpon him the plagues vvritten in this booke. † And if any man ſhal diminiſh of the wordes of the booke 19 of this prophecie: God ſhal take avvay his part out of the booke of life, and out of the holy citie, and of theſe thinges that be vvritten in this booke. † ſaith he that giueth teſti- 20 monie of theſe things. Yea I come quickely: Amen. " Come

Lord

21 Lord IESVS. † The grace of our Lord IESVS Christ be vvith you al. Amen.

ANNOTATIONS
CHAP. XXII.

11. *He that hurteth.*] It is not an exhortation, but a commination or threatening, that hovv far soeuer the vvicked increase in naughtines, God hath prouided ansvverable punishment for them.

18. *If any man shal adde.*] The author of the commentaries vpon this booke, bearing the name of S. Ambrose, saith thus of this point. *He maketh not this protestation against the expositours of his prophecie, but against Heretikes. for the expositour doth adde or diminish nothing, but openeth the obscuritie of the narration, or shevveth the moral or spiritual sense. He curseth therfore Heretikes, that vsed to adde somevvhat of their ovvne that vvas false, and to take avvay other things that vvere contrarie to their heresies.* So saith this auncient vvriter. And this vvas the propertie of them in al ages, and so is it of ours novv, as vve haue noted through the vvhole Bible, and as vve haue in sundrie places set forth to the sight of al indifferent readers, in the nevv Testament. that al the vvorld may see that the Apostles curse is fallen vpon them, and may bevvare of them.

The curse agaist adding or dimishing, is against Heretikes, not Catholike expositours.

20. *Come Lord Iesu.*] And novv ô Lord Christ, most iust and merciful, vve thy poore creatures that are so afflicted for confession and defense of the holy, Catholike, and Apostolike truth, conteined in this thy sacred booke, and in the infallible doctrine of thy deere spouse our mother the Church, vve crie also vnto thy Maiestie vvith tendernesse of our hartes vnspeakable, COME LORD IESVS QVICKLY, and iudge betvvixt vs and our Aduersaries, and in the meane time giue patience, comfort, and constancie to al that suffer for thy name, and trust in thee. ô Lord God our onely helper and protector, tarie not long. AMEN.

A breefe petitiō vnto IESVS Christ, to come quickly, as S. Iohn here speaketh, and to iudge the cause of Catholikes & Protestants.

A TABLE OF THE EPISTLES AND GOSPELS, AFTER THE ROMANE VSE, VPON SVNDAIES, HOLIDAIES, and other principal daies of the yere, for ſuch as are deſirous to knovv and reade them according to this tranſlation. And therfore the Epiſtles taken out of the old Teſtament are omitted, till the edition thereof.

Vpon Sundaies, Imber Daies, and other Feries.

HE I. SVNDAY in Aduent, Epiſtle pag. 415. Goſpel pag. 199.

The 2. Sunday in Aduent, Ep. 419. Goſp. 28.

The 3 Sunday in Aduēt, Ep. 533, Goſ. 217.

Vvenesday Imber in Aduent, *Goſp. 135.

Friday Imber in Aduent, Goſp. 136.

Saturday Imber in Aduent, Ep. 554. Goſ. 143.

The 4 Sunday in Aduent, Ep. 432. Goſp. 143.

The Epiſtles omitted are taken out of the Old Teſtamēt.

Chriſtmas eue, Ep. 382. Goſp. 4.

CHRISTMAS *day at the*
- first maſſe, Ep. 597. Goſp. 139.
- ſecond Maſſe, Epiſt. 598. Goſp. 140.
- third Maſſe, Ep. 603. Goſ. 216.

S. Steuen, Ep. 305. Goſp, 66.

S. Iohn. the Euang. Goſp, 279.

Childermas day, Ep. 714, Goſp. 5.

S. Thomas of Canterburie, Ep. 608. Goſ. 248.

The Sūday within the Octaue of Chriſtmas, Ep. 504. as on Twelfth eue. Goſp. 14'. verſe 33 vnto 41.

The CIRCVMCISION of our Lord, Ep. 597. Goſp. 140.

Tvvelfth Eue, Ep. 504. Goſp. 6.

The EPIPHANIE of our Lord called Tvvelfth day, Goſp. 5.

The 1 Sunday after the Epiphanie, Ep. 412. Goſp. 141.

The 2 Sunday after the Epiphanie, Ep. 413. Goſp. 220.

The 3 Sunday after the Epiphanie, Epiſ. 413. Goſp. 19.

The 4 Sunday after the Epiph. Ep. 414. Goſp. 20.

The 5 Sunday after the Epiph. Ep. 542. Goſp. 35.

The 6 Sunday after the Epiph. Ep. 546. Goſp. 36,

The Sunday of Septuageſme, Ep 443. Goſp. 56.

The Sunday of Sexageſme. Ep. 489. Goſp. 159.

The ſunday of Quinquageſme, Epiſt. 456. Goſp. 191.

Vpon Aſhweneſday, Goſp. 15.

Thurſday after Aſhweneſday, Goſp. 20.

Friday

For Saincts and Festiual daies, peculiar and proper.

For Saincts generally and in common.

IN *votiue Masses, that is, such as are said according to mens deuotion for diuers peculiar causes.*

In Masses of Requiem.

AN AMPLE AND PARTICVLAR TABLE DIRECTING THE READER TO AL CATHOLIKE truthes, deduced out of the holy Scriptures, and impugned by the Aduersaries.

A

D

Deuotion

I

N

O

P

 men

T

V

W

THE EXPLICATION OF CERTAINE VVORDES

IN THIS TRANSLATION, NOT FAMILIAR to the vulgar reader, vvhich might not conueniently be vttered otherwise.

A

Abstracted, Dravven avvay. pag.642.
Acquisition, Getting, purchasing. pag 514.
Aduent, The comming. pag 69.
Adulterating, Corrupting. See pag.475.478.
Agnition, knovvledge or acknovvledging.p.600.
Allegorie, a Mystical speache, more then the bare letter. pag.505. See the Annot. p.508.
Amen, expounded pag.244.
Anathema, expounded p.405.
Archisynagogue, expounded pag.99.
Assist. pag.135, signifieth the Angels standing and attēding, alvvaies readie to doe their ministerie.
Assumption, p.165, Christs departure out of this vvorld by his death and Ascension.
Azymes, Vnleauened bread. p.75

C

Calumniate, By this vvord is signified violent oppression by vvord or deede. pag.143.
Catechizeth, and, *Catechized*. p.510. He catechizeth that teacheth the principles of the Christian faith: and they that heare and learne, are catechized, and are therfore called often in the Annotations, *Catechumens*.
Character, a marke or stampe. pag.723.
Commessations, Immoderate bankets, and belly cheere, vvith vvanton riotousnes. p.509.
Condigne, comparable. p.400.
Contristate, This vvord signifieth to make heauie and sad. pag 519.
Cooperate, signifieth vvorking vvith others, p. 401. likevvise *Cooperation, Cooperateurs*.
Corbana, expounded pag.80.

D

Depositum. p. 582. See the Annot.pag.584. It may signifie also, Gods graces giuen vs to keepe, pa. 587.v.14. Also v.12 ibid. See the Annot.
Didrachme, expounded pag.49.

Domi-

Dominical day, Sunday. See Annot. p. 701. 702.
Donaries, giftes offered to God for his Temple, &c. 199.

E

Euacuated from Christ, that is, Made voide and hauing no part vvith him. p. 503.
The scandal of the crosse *euacuated*, that is, made voide, cleane taken avvay. ibidem.
Euangelize, signifieth such preaching of good tidinges, as cōcerneth the Gospel. *See the preface*,
Eunuches, gelded men
Euro-aquilo, A north-eastvvinde. p. 368.
Exinanited, abased excedingly. p. 528.

G

Gratis, an vsual vvord to signifie, for nothing, freely, for Godamercie, vvithout desert.

H

Holocauste, a kinde of sacrifice vvhere *al vvas burnt* in the honour of God. p. 625.
Hostes, sacrifices. p. 445.

I

Inuocated, called vpon, praied vnto. p. 316. Hereof vve say, *Inuocation of Saincts*, and to inuocate.
Issue, good euent. pag 445.
Iustice, taken in the nevv Testament, not as it is cōtrarie to vvrong or iniurie, but for that qualitie vvhereof a man is iust and iustified. p. 391.

N

Neophyte, expounded p. 569.

P

Paraclete, expounded pag. 260.
Parasceue, the Ievves Sabboth-eue, Good friday, p. 130. v. 43. *See the Preface.*
Pasche, Easter, and the Paschal lambe. p. 201.
Pentecost, vvhitsuntide, &c. the space of fiftie daies.
Prefinition, A determination before. p. 517.
Prepuce, expounded pag. 387.
Prescience, foreknovvledge. p. 294.
Preuaricatour, transgressor: and *preuarication*, trāsgression. p. 336. 337.
Loaues of *Proposition*, so called, because they vvere proposed and set vpon the table in the Temple, before God. pag. 31.

R

Repropitiate the sinnes. pag. 605. that is, make a reconciliation for them.
Resolution, the separation of the body and the soule, the departing out of this life. p. 592.
Resuscitate the grace, that is, Raise, quicken, renew and reviue the grace vvhich othervvise languisheth and decaieth. pag. 586.

S

Sabbatisme, A time of resting and ceasing from labours. pag. 607.
Sacrament, for mysterie. p. 513.
Sancta Sanctorum, The holies of holies, that is, the inmost and holiest place of the Ievves Temple, as it vvere the Chauncel. pag. 621.
Superedified, Builded vpon Christ the principal stone pag. 657.

T

Tetrarch, Gouernour or Prince of the 4 part of a countrie. p. 38.
Thrones, an higher order of Angels. p. 537.

V

Victims, Sacrifices. p. 308.

The faultes correcte thus.

Pag.			
8	*1 Cor. 7.*		*2 Cor. 7.*
38	Tetrach,		Tetrarch.
42	fifth vveeke,		first vveeke.
78	If the Sacrament,		In the Sacrament.
148	*Matth. 9,*		*Matth. 19.*
188	Scandale,		Scandals.
204	*Ignat. ep. 5.*	Reade	*ep. 7.* Ibid. in 3 copies the Greeke set amis.
213	*li. 39 de consens.*		*li. 3.*
215	Eighteth yere,		Eighth.
238	Transubstantion,		Transubstantiation.
409	Cathec, 17.		Catech. 18.
440	Continencie,		Incontinencie.
446	ἃ ἰυλογοῦμιν		ὃ ἰυλογιῦμιν.
449	Is it not novv,		It is not novv.
552	Beguile v,		Beguile vs.
576	*Eusebius li. 5. c. 2,*		*Theodorete.*

LAVS DEO.